# THE
# ADOPTION
# DIRECTORY

# THE
# ADOPTION
# DIRECTORY

## 2nd Edition

The Most Comprehensive Guide to Family-Building Options Including
State Statutes on Adoption, Public and Private Adoption Agencies,
Adoption Exchanges, Foreign Requirements and Adoption Agencies,
Independent Adoption Services, Foster Parenting, and Support Groups

## *Ellen Paul, Editor*

 **Gale Research Inc.**

*An International Thomson Publishing Company*

 I(T)P

NEW YORK • LONDON • BONN • BOSTON • DETROIT • MADRID
MELBOURNE • MEXICO CITY • PARIS • SINGAPORE • TOKYO
TORONTO • WASHINGTON • ALBANY NY • BELMONT CA • CINCINNATI OH

Ellen Paul, *Editor*

Gale Research Inc. Staff

Monica M. Hubbard, *Coordinating Editor*
Laurel Sprague, *Assistant Editor*

Benita L. Spight, *Data Entry Services Manager*
Gwendolyn S. Tucker, *Data Entry Coordinator*
Rhonda Willis, *Data Entry Supervisor*
Kenneth Benson, *Data Entry Associate*

Theresa Rocklin, *Technical Support Services Manager*
Charles Beaumont, *Programmer*

Mary Beth Trimper, *Production Director*
Shanna Heilveil, *Production Assistant*

Cynthia D. Baldwin, *Art Director*
C.J. Jonik, *Desktop Publisher/Typesetter*

♾️™ This book is printed on acid-free paper that meets the minimum requirements of American National Standard for Information Sciences-Permanence Paper for Printed Library Materials, ANSI Z39.48-1984.

*If your plan is for one year, plant rice;*
*For ten years, plant trees;*
*For a hundred years, nurture children.*

*Kwan-tz*

# Contents

# Preface

The need to parent is, perhaps, the highest of our human drives. Parenting is the most significant way many of us will affect the future. Certainly it is the most rewarding way. As human beings we want to pass on what we've learned and to smooth the way for those who will come after us.

To be thwarted in that pursuit is a hard thing, indeed. In 1979, my husband and I opted to have our third child by adoption. As parents I know that makes us especially fortunate in that we do have children both by birth and adoption. But the most important thing I learned is that one method is not better than the other, just different. Parenthood is the end: adoption or birth are just means. It really is just as exciting to wait at the airport for your child to be delivered by Korean Air as it is to wait in the delivery room for your child to be delivered by the obstetrician. Considering international airline schedules, they take about the same amount of time, too.

*The Adoption Directory* is about options in parenthood. It is not an adoption handbook or manual, of which there are many providing invaluable how-to information, nor is it meant to take their place. Rather *The Adoption Directory* supplements them by providing a source of specific information about adoption agencies, private facilitators, support groups and laws on adoption in all fifty states, the District of Columbia, and seven foreign countries.

I don't pretend to know what is the best option for anyone else--a private or public agency, foster parenting, or private, open, or foreign adoption--but options for parenthood exist. I've included information on as many organizations within each option as would respond to my questionnaires.

## How *The Adoption Directory* Was Compiled

In early 1994, when we began exploring the advisability of publishing a second edition of *The Adoption Directory*, I made a few telephone calls just to see if everyone was in the same place in which I found them for the first edition. I discovered to my chagrin that there was at least a 60% change in just addresses and telephone numbers. The information in this second edition is, therefore, completely new.

In March, 1994, I began mailing questionnaires to public and private agencies, support groups, independent facilitators, exchanges, foreign embassies or consulates and foster placement agencies throughout the U.S. and Canada. In some cases, if the entry appeared in the first edition of *The Adoption Directory*, a copy of their first listing appeared with a request to update the information. The questionnaires were designed to elicit the information that would help a reader decide if that source were the right agency, support group or individual to help in the quest for parenthood: Was the wait too long? Did it cost too much? Were the requirements too stringent? The new questionnaires were a refinement on those for the first edition in that they attempted to define waiting times more specifically.

My original mailing numbered close to 7000 pieces, culled from the lists of agencies sent to me by each state's or province's mandated licensing agency, national support groups, legal directories, and the referrals of respondents.

The questionnaire stated that there was no charge for being included in *The Adoption Directory*, and non-respondents were sent questionnaires again in August. In many cases, to clarify information or to elicit a response from a non-respondent, I telephoned.

The information found in each entry is in response to this formal questionnaire, sometimes enriched with material from the respondent's printed brochures or telephone conversations, but always adhering as closely as possible to the respondent's own words. In no instance was material from the first edition included in the second edition without the review of the respondent.

My intention is to provide a sense of each respondent's individuality and uniqueness to enable readers to make an intelligent selection about the option and specific agency/exchange/support group/independent facilitator that will best meet their needs. A consistent format allows readers to compare respondents on an equal footing.

Inclusion in *The Adoption Directory* is not an endorsement nor recommendation. The information is provided so that each reader will exercise his or her own judgment in electing or declining to work with any given listee.

## Who Can Benefit from Using *The Adoption Directory*?

In the course of compiling data for *The Adoption Directory* many people shared with me the reasons they believed a comprehensive directory of all sources in and around adoption would be worthwhile. Among those who could benefit most are:

### Prospective Adoptive or Foster Parents:
Applying for adoption or foster parenting can be complex, even mysterious. Regulations vary radically from state to state and agency to agency. *The Adoption Directory* attempts to resolve some of the complexities by providing a one-stop source of available options, presenting the criteria of who may apply, providing a contact person and clearing some of the mystery by outlining the process as well as providing the names of organizations whose membership, goals, and activities can provide support.

### Adoption Professionals:
*The Adoption Directory* should provide networking options for professionals in the field and up-to-date information on other regions and states' procedures that will allow new avenues of service to prospective adoptive parents and children.

### Pregnancy Counselors and Birthparents Considering an Adoption Decision:
For those experiencing a crisis pregnancy or those who counsel them, *The Adoption Directory* provides information on the options for infant placement either through agencies or independently as well as support groups of other parents who have made adoption decisions for their children.

### Attorneys and Independent Facilitators:
In response to my questionnaire many professionals in the area of independent adoption expressed a need for a one-stop information source of other professionals with whom they could network under the Interstate Compact on the Placement of Children as well as a concise reference for other states' statutes on adoption.

### Physicians:
Very often physicians are placed in the position of frontline counselors when patients begin to deal with infertility. As a reference source for caring professionals, *The Adoption Directory* would be a valuable resource that presents other avenues to parenthood as well.

### Support Groups:
*The Adoption Directory* is the only source of national, regional, and local adoption-related organizations. Since by their very nature support groups know the value of strength in numbers, *The Adoption Directory* should prove a valuable tool by linking groups pursuing similar goals-- whether these goals are advocacy, infertility peer counseling, adoptive and/or foster family support or adoptee search--and preventing duplication of effort.

## Acknowledgments

I would like to extend my thanks and acknowledge the contributions of all the respondents to this directory, especially Wanda Scott, Nevada's Adoption Specialist, who was always accessible and knowledgeable and Rubin Orenstein, Program Coordinator for Children and Residential Services in New Brunswick who on two separate occasions discussed foster care within the province with me. I would also be remiss if I did not acknowledge the contribution of Josephine Redding, Executive Assistant, International Thomson Publishing, who used her considerable translation skills to turn my English questionnaires into French and to Jonna DeSimone who translated the Spanish material into English.

I particularly wish to acknowledge the contributions of my editor, Monica M. Hubbard, who coordinated Gale Research Inc.'s word processing program with mine and who spoke with me endlessly on how to make the second edition even better and more informative than the first.

Lastly, but most especially, I again want to thank my family. My son, Greg, who got me thinking about this project to begin with, is now a teenager. My two oldest children have fledged the nest, but that meant that my husband and the remaining two had to listen to twice as much complaining. Thanks, guys. I love you all.

## A Last Word

With each edition I hope *The Adoption Directory* will grow to provide more and more options in parenthood.

If you would like to be included in the next edition of *The Adoption Directory*, please direct your inquiries to:

*The Adoption Directory*
Gale Research Inc.
835 Penobscot Bldg.
Detroit, MI 48226-4094

# How to Use *The Adoption Directory*

*The Adoption Directory* is about options, and there are many described in the publication: public and private agencies, adoption exchanges, foreign adoption agencies, independent adoption services, foster care and support groups and organizations available to assist parents and children.

The specific information provided varies with each section, but generally entries contain the following types of data:

**Sequential entry number**--Entries are numbered sequentially throughout *The Adoption Directory*. Citations in the index refer to these entry numbers.

**Name** of the agency, organization, facilitator, etc.

**Address** and telephone information, branch office locations are also provided when available.

**Basic data** about the agency or organization, ranging from descriptions of the children generally placed by an agency to parental requirements to the home study process.

---

**\*124\***
**Lutheran Social Services**
4406 Georgia Ave., N.W.
Washington, DC 20011
Phone: (202) 723-3000
Fax: (202) 723-3303

**Branch address:**
7401 Leesburg Pike, P.O. Box 3363, Falls Church, VA 22403
Phone: (703) 698-5026
7410 New Hampshire, Takoma Park, MD 20912
Phone: (301) 434-0080

**Contact:** Roselyn Williams, Director of Adoption Services.
**Date Established:** 1917; Adoption Department: 1956.
**Description:** Non-profit, private multi-service agency.
**Area served:** Residents within a 50 mi. radius of Washington, DC, including Maryland and Virginia.
**Requirements:** Applicants should be age appropriate to the child placed; can be single or married; if married, marriage should be of at least 2 yrs. duration.
**Fees:** Application: $100; home study: $1050; post-placement fee: $600.
**Number of children placed last year:** 101.
**Description of children:** U.S. infants and older children, some with special needs. Home studies for international and interstate adoptions.
**Adoption procedure:** 1) File application; 2) attend orientation meeting; 3) complete materials in application packet; 4) undergo home study process; 5) placement; 6) post-placement services; 7) finalization.
**Average length of time to complete home study:** 6-8 wks.
**Number of interviews:** 4.
**Home study description:** Assessment of background information, health and finances, religion, hobbies, marital relationship and any previous marriages, police and Child Abuse Registry clearances, parenting capability, home visit and interviews with others in the home, recommendation of references, motivation to adopt and type of child requested, guardianship plan in event of parents' untimely death, understanding of adoption, feelings toward birthparents who choose adoptive placements for their children, daily routine of family, worker's evaluation and agency's recommendation.
**Average wait for a child after approval of a home study:** 6-12 mos.
**Foster care:** Temporary.

# State or Province Statutes on Adoption

The first section is divided by state or province. Each listing begins with the legislative policy in regard to specific adoption issues. The information found in these sections was solicited from the adoption specialist, coordinator or program director in the state or province's licensing agency.

State/province data should be the first place to check when exploring the adoption process in order to discover the following type of information:

**Independent placement by an intermediary?** May someone other than a licensed agency or the birth parent(s) place a child in an adoptive home?

**Independent placement?** May the birth parents place their child directly in an adoptive home?

**Subsidies provided?** What kind of adoption subsidies does the state provide? For example: If the child has a chronic medical condition, will the state provide a financial payment even after the adoption is finalized?

**Costs defined by law?** Are the costs or fees associated with independent adoption defined or controlled by law?

**Infertility coverage?** Does the state require insurance companies to cover medical treatments associated with infertility?

**Home study required?** Is a home study required in the case of independent adoption and must it be conducted before or after placement?

**Prospective adoptive parents advertise for a child?** Is it lawful for prospective adoptive parents to place media advertisements for an adoptable child or a birth mother considering adoptive placement for her unborn child? In some states such advertising is a misdemeanor since the media is considered an intermediary in those instances.

**Surrogacy laws?** Are contracts for the services of surrogate mothers recognized before the law?

**Access to agencies in other jurisdictions?** May residents of one state or province access the adoption services in another state/province or foreign country?

**Judicial termination of birth parent(s)' rights?** Can only a judge decide if the birth parent(s)' rights should be terminated or does the state recognize voluntary relinquishments? Must both parents either relinquish their rights or have them terminated or is the relinquishment by one birth parent sufficient to allow the adoption to proceed?

**Time given a birth mother to revoke her consent?** What is the time period allowed biological parents after which they have no legal claim to their child?

**Court handling adoptions?** In which court are adoption hearings heard?

**Who controls the adoption of native/aboriginal children?** Is the primary agent in the adoption of native/aboriginal children the state/province or the tribe/band?

**Adoption records sealed?** Is all the information pertaining to an adoption, including the adoptee's original birth certificate, unavailable even to the parties to the adoption? Under what circumstances can adoption information be accessed?

**Photo-listing book available?** Does the state provide a photo-listing book of children waiting for adoptive placement in that state?

## Public Adoption Agencies

Following the state's statutes on adoption in Section I are public agencies in that state. *The Adoption Directory* includes agencies, both public and private, that provide direct service. Although a central licensing agency exists for each state, that agency is not always the provider of direct service.

Consequently in some states, like Connecticut, there is one address for the public agency because it provides direct home study and placement services to all state residents (and sometimes to non-state residents, as well); in other states, like Indiana, there is a central address with the addresses of county or regional offices throughout the state. These are state-regulated and county or regionally-administered agencies: the central office sets policy and procedures, but applicants must contact the office nearest to them.

In still other states, such as Illinois, a half dozen or more regional offices are the direct providers of service and set their own procedures. And finally in other states, such as New York, many more county offices are listed since these states are county-regulated wherein the counties themselves set policy, perform home studies and place children. Not all counties may be represented in these states although all were sent questionnaires.

Public agency entries contain such data as a description of the agency, the area served, requirements for prospective parents, explanation of fees, description of the children placed by that agency, an overview of the application process, and an explanation of the home study process including the number of interviews required.

## Private Adoption Agencies

The private agencies located in each state follow the public agencies in Section I. Users should be aware that private agencies may serve residents of neighboring or all states as well. In general, public agencies have fewer requirements and no fees; whereas private agencies may be profit based. Private agency entries provide the same types of data as public adoption agencies.

## Foster Care

While foster parenting provides another option for parenthood, it differs significantly from adoption. Ideally foster care offers a temporary substitute family for a child whose own family is helped to prepare for his/her return. Whereas adoption is forever, foster care is not. Unfortunately, some temporary placements become long-term or even permanent, but the relationship between foster parent and child does not have the legal permanence of an adoption.

Children are placed in foster care for a myriad of reasons, and various kinds of foster care placement categories have resulted. (Complete definitions of these categories can be found in the Glossary.)

Emergency placements usually last for no more than 30 days and are the result of some sudden and traumatic incident, such as abuse, which necessitates the child's immediate removal.

Temporary placements are the most common and have the child's successful reunion with his/her birth family as an immediate goal.

Pre-adoptive foster placements precede almost all adoptions and cover the period from placement to court finalization while the child lives with his/her adoptive family. The placement is supervised by the agency placing the child.

Therapeutic foster care may be indicated for a juvenile offender, an emotionally handicapped or developmentally delayed child, an adolescent mother and her infant or a youngster recently released from a substance abuse rehabilitation program. Specially trained foster parents help these children and adolescents learn new living and coping skills and provide an environment which discourages recidivism.

Permanent foster care may not be ideal but it may be the best situation for a child for whom adoption is not possible because of age or special needs. In the case of some groups, such as Native Americans, foster care provides permanency for the child while preserving a threatened heritage.

Of course, foster care categories are not fixed and very often emergency foster care will become a temporary placement or a therapeutic placement will become pre-adoptive.

The agencies whose entries appear in *The Adoption Directory* are licensed by their states to evaluate and authorize prospective foster homes. Sometimes they are public state or county agencies and sometimes they are private agencies, health care facilities or schools which, as a service to the children in their care, reach out to and prepare foster parents to receive children who would profit from foster placement.

This section lists agencies alphabetically by state and includes descriptions of the agency, requirements, licensing procedures, inspections, the types of children available, stipends, and additional financial assistance.

## Independent Adoption Services

Independent facilitators are not child-placing agencies but may provide professional intermediary services, such as assisting in locating an adoptable child, performing home studies, and/or providing legal services to finalize the adoption of an identified child. Independent adoption services are listed alphabetically by state and include such information as the name and address(es) of the service and descriptions of the services provided, parental requirements, fees, licensing, etc.

## Support Groups and Organizations

Support groups exist for adoptive families, prospective adoptive parents, foster parents, families of foreign-born children, families of children with special needs, couples dealing with infertility, adoptees-in-search and birthparents who have relinquished their children for adoption. They provide a wonderful source of fellowship, advice and very often have contacts and referrals not available elsewhere. At one time or another adoptive families will probably be touched by the aims of all of these groups.

In alphabetical order by state, support group entries offer complete contact information, as well as data on membership size, budget, staffing, local or regional branches, services offered, publications and meetings.

## Adoption Exchanges

Adoption exchanges do not usually place children directly but provide exposure for waiting children over large geographic areas and may provide matching services between families looking for a particular type of child and a child waiting adoptive placement. Most of the children listed on exchanges are older, members of sibling groups who cannot be separated, minorities or have mental, physical and/or emotional handicaps or chronic medical problems.

The exchanges regularly publish lists and pictures of children along with information on how to contact the agencies handling them. Some exchanges also list families who are willing to accept children with special needs, so that agencies over a wide geographic area may contact them.

Entries in this section provide contact information for the exchanges and list procedures, fees, frequency of list updates, requirements for using the service, and descriptions of the types of children listed.

## Foreign Adoption

Many U.S.-based agencies provide intercountry adoption programs; these agencies can be found in Section I and are identified under the descriptions of children placed. A listing of U.S. agencies placing foreign-born children can be accessed through the Subject Index under the subject heading Intercountry.

Those agencies that appear in the chapter on foreign adoption are actually located in foreign countries and will place children directly with U.S. families who apply.

This country-by-country listing identifies the documents required for foreign nationals seeking to adopt native children and provides descriptions of the children available and legal procedures. The listings for both public and private foreign agencies, where available, follow the national requirements and include address and telephone information, contact, requirements, fees and descriptions of the process involved.

## Glossary and Additional Titles in Adoption

Included in the Glossary are the many legal and specialized reference terms found in the entries. Additional Titles in Adoption provides sources that may assist readers in exploring adoption options.

## Appendices Provide Valuable Supplemental Information

**Appendix 1** is a state-by-state listing of the repositories of vital records where individuals can write for certified copies of birth, marriage and divorce records. **Appendix 2** contains an alphabetical list of the Immigration and Naturalization Service offices in the United States as well as methodology for filing the I-600 Petition and the I-600A Petition necessary to bring orphan children into the United States.

## Indexes Provide Additional Access to Entries

*The Adoption Directory* provides three access points to the material in the main sections: the **Subject Index,** the **Geographic Index,** and the **Alphabetical Index.** All citations in the indexes refer back to the entry numbers that run sequentially throughout the text.

For the **Subject Index,** subject categories emphasize topics of special interest. U.S. agencies that place foreign-born children, for example, are indexed under the subject heading Intercountry.

The **Geographic Index** lists all entries by geographic location of main offices and branches. Organizations are listed alphabetically by city within each state or province.

The **Alphabetical Index** lists, in a single alphabetic sequence, all agencies, organizations, and firms listed in *The Adoption Directory*.

# THE
# ADOPTION
# DIRECTORY

# List of Abbreviations

The abbreviations below are used throughout the directory:

| | |
|---|---|
| Assn. | Association |
| Assoc. | Associates |
| Ave. | Avenue |
| Bldg. | Building |
| Blvd. | Boulevard |
| Cir. | Circle |
| Co. | County |
| Corp. | Corporation |
| Ct. | Court |
| Ctr. | Center |
| Dept. | Department |
| Div. | Division |
| Dr. | Drive |
| E. | East |
| Expy. | Expressway |
| Ext. | Extension |
| Fl. | Floor |
| Fwy. | Freeway |
| Hwy. | Highway |
| Inc. | Incorporated |
| Ln. | Lane |
| mo. | month |
| Mt. | Mount |
| N. | North |
| N.E. | Northeast |
| N.W. | Northwest |
| pg. | page |
| Pk. | Park |
| Pl. | Place |
| R.D. | Rural Delivery |
| Rd. | Road |
| Rm. | Room |
| R.R. | Rural Route |
| Rte. | Route |
| S. | South |
| S.E. | Southeast |
| Sq. | Square |
| Sr. | Sister |
| St. | Street |
| Ste. | Suite |
| S.W. | Southwest |
| Terr. | Terrace |
| Tpke. | Turnpike |
| W. | West |
| wk. | week |
| yr. | year |

# State Statutes and Adoption Agencies

## ALABAMA

## STATUTES

★1★

**Independent placement by intermediary?** Only the parent of birth parent or a specified relation.

**Independent placement by birth parents?** Yes.

**Subsidies provided?** Special needs, time-limited, long-term and non-recurring.

**Adoption cost defined by law?** All costs must have prior court approval.

**Insurance for infertility?:** No.

**Home study required by state?** Required before placement unless waived by the court for good and sufficient reason.

**Prospective adoptive parent advertise for a child?** No.

**Surrogacy laws?** No law forbids it.

**Residents access agencies of other states or countries?** Permitted.

**Requires judicial termination of birth parents' rights?** One or both birth parents may consent to the adoption of a minor child by individuals. Parental rights are terminated by the court of jurisdiction.

**Time given to a birthmother to revoke her consent:** 5 or 14 days, if the court finds the withdrawal is reasonable and in the best interests of the child.

**Court handling adoptions?** Probate.

**Adoption of Native Children:** Tribe.

**Adoption records sealed?** Yes, but at age 19 an adoptee may access non-identifying information.

**Photo-listing book available?** *Waiting Children*.

## PUBLIC AGENCIES

★2★

**Alabama Department of Human Resources**
Office of Adoptions
50 N. Ripley St.
Montgomery, AL 36130
Phone: (205) 242-9500
Fax: (205) 242-0939

**Contact:** Shirley Scanlan.

**Date established:** 1935.

**Description:** Non-profit, public welfare agency.

**Area served:** Residents of the State of Alabama.

**Requirements:** Adults, 19 yrs. and older, single or married at least 3 yrs.

**Fees:** No agency fees. Criminal records clearance: $49 per person.

**Number of children placed last year:** 133.

**Description of children:** 94 children with special needs.

**Adoption procedure:**
1) Submit application;
2) complete home study;
3) participate in group preparation;
4) if approved, wait for placement;
5) placement;.

**Average length of time between application and start of home study:** Varies.

**Average length of time to complete home study:** 3-4 mos.

**Number of interviews:** 4-5.

**Home study description:** Combination of group training and individual interviews which includes both educational and evaluatory components.

**Average wait for a child after approval of a home study:** Varies.

**Foster care:** Emergency, short and long-term and permanent.

## PRIVATE AGENCIES

★3★

**AGAPE of Central Alabama, Inc.**
P.O. Box 230472
Montgomery, AL 36123
Phone: (205) 272-9466
(800) 239-1020

**Branch address:**
P.O. Box 26575, Birmingham, AL 35126
Phone: (205) 733-9755

P.O. Box 1541, Enterprise, AL 36331
Phone: (205) 393-1990

**Contact:** Carol Esco.

**Date established:** 1979.

**Description:** Non-profit private agency licensed by the State of Alabama.

**Area served:** Residents of central Alabama.

**Requirements:** Applicants must be affiliated with the Church of Christ, in good health and with a maximum of 1 child in the home, if applying for white infant.

**Fees:** Sliding scale based on 12% of gross annual income.

**Number of children placed last year:** 7.

**Description of children:** White, black and biracial infants.

**Adoption procedure:**
1) File application;
2) complete home study;
3) if approved, wait for placement;
4) placement;
5) post-placement supervision;
6) finalization.

**Average length of time between application and start of home study:** 1 mo. or less.

**Average length of time to complete home study:** 2 mos.

**Number of interviews:** 5.

**Home study description:** Evaluation of personal information, family background, current family relationships, and motivation to adopt.

**Average wait for a child after approval of a home study:** 24 or more mos.

**Foster care:** Temporary, long-term and permanent.

★ 4 ★
**AGAPE of North Alabama, Inc.**
2733 Mastin Lake Rd.
Huntsville, AL 35810
Phone: (205) 859-4481
Fax: (205) 859-4483

**Mailing address:**
P.O. Box 3887, Huntsville, AL 35810

**Branch address:**
2002 Darby Dr., Florence, AL 35630
Phone: (205) 767-1084

**Contact:** Polly Huber.

**Date established:** 1969.

**Description:** Non-profit licensed child-placing agency.

**Area served:** Residents of the northern third of Alabama.

**Requirements:** Couples married at least 3.5 yrs., one person in couple must be member of Church of Christ, who are physically and financially able to care for a child. Will place with single parent.

**Fees:** Adoptive placement fee based on 10% of gross annual income; home study fee: $600.

**Number of children placed last year:** 12.

**Description of children:** Infants and older children.

**Adoption procedure:** Follows state-set procedures.

**Average length of time between application and start of home study:** 1-6 mos.

**Average length of time to complete home study:** Minimum 8 wks.

**Number of interviews:** 10 group education, 2 home visits.

**Home study description:** Strengths/needs assessment, stability of individual and marriage, educational and employment history, recommendation of references and criminal records check, reconciliation of childlessness and knowledge of adoption.

**Average wait for a child after approval of a home study:** 24 or more mos.

**Foster care:** Temporary and long-term.

★ 5 ★
**Family Adoption Services, Inc.**
631 Beacon Pkwy. W., Ste. 102
Birmingham, AL 35209
Phone: (205) 290-0077

**Contact:** Maryon A. Allen.

**Date established:** 1991.

**Description:** Private agency licensed by the State of Alabama.

**Area served:** Primarily residents of the State of Alabama.

**Requirements:** Couples married at least 3 yrs. who are between the ages of 25 and 45 yrs., in good health and who can document infertility and who have sufficient income and health insurance.

**Fees:** Application fee: $450; home study fee: $1,000; agency fee: $5750 domestic, $6750 non-domestic.

**Number of children placed last year:** 12.

**Description of children:** Infants.

**Adoption procedure:** Complies with Alabama state law.

**Average length of time between application and start of home study:** 1-6 mos.

**Average length of time to complete home study:** 3-4 mos.

**Number of interviews:** 4.

**Home study description:** Investigation of applicants to ascertain their fitness to parent which includes, but is not limited to, moral, emotional, physical and financial soundness, stability of their marriage, and desire to parent.

**Average wait for a child after approval of a home study:** 12-24 mos.

**Foster care:** Rare.

★ 6 ★
**Lifeline Children's Services, Inc.**
2908 Pump House Rd.
Birmingham, AL 35243
Phone: (205) 967-0811

**Contact:** John H. Carr, Director or Chuck Johnson, L.B.S.W.

**Date established:** 1981.

**Description:** Private, non-profit agency.

**Area served:** Residents of Alabama.

**Requirements:** Committed Christian married couples who are childless and infertile and financially secure. At time of placement at least one parent must take a 3 mos. leave from full-time employment.

**Fees:** $600 non-refundable application fee; remaining fees are based on actual adoption-related expenses.

**Number of children placed last year:** 39.

**Description of children:** Healthy infants, special needs, and biracial children.

**Adoption procedure:**
1) File initial application;
2) attend individual interview;
3) return completed questionnaire to determine Christian commitment;
4) submit autobiography for each spouse;
5) complete fingerprint checks;
6) home visit by caseworker;
7) forward medical reports and personal references;
8) approval process;
9) wait for placement; and
10) placement.

**Average length of time between application and start of home study:** 12-24 mos.

**Average length of time to complete home study:** Varies with applicants' location in state.

**Number of interviews:** At least 3.

**Home study description:** Home study process encompasses but is not limited to an evaluation of stability of marriage and finances, Christian faith and involvement in church, recommendation of references, ability to parent and motivation to adopt.

**Average wait for a child after approval of a home study:** 12-24 mos.

**Foster care:** Temporary.

★7★
**Villa Hope**
4 Office Park Circle, Ste. 303
Birmingham, AL 35223
Phone: (205) 870-7359
Fax: (205) 871-6629

**Contact:** Patricia Baldwin.

**Date established:** 1988.

**Description:** Non-profit, tax exempt child placing agency licensed by the Alabama State Department of Human Resources.

**Area served:** Residents of Alabama, for social services; placements throughout U.S.

**Requirements:** Varies by child's country of origin.

**Fees:**
Application fee: $100;
home study: $825;
post-placement: $200-$550.

**Number of children placed last year:** 41.

**Description of children:** Latin American children and children with special needs of all ages.

**Adoption procedure:**
1) File preliminary application;
2) attend informational meeting (Alabama families only for step #2);
3) file formal application;
4) complete home study;
5) if approved, placement;
6) finalization in foreign country or U.S. depending upon child's country of origin;
7) if former, finalization in U.S.;
8) naturalization.

**Average length of time between application and start of home study:** 1 mo. or less.

**Average length of time to complete home study:** 2 wks.

**Number of interviews:** 4.

**Home study description:** Call or write for outline.

**Average wait for a child after approval of a home study:** Varies by country of origin.

**Foster care:** For children in the U.S. on medical visas.

# ALASKA

## STATUTES

★8★

**Independent placement by intermediary?** Intermediaries may place 2 or fewer children a year.

**Independent placement by birth parents?** Yes, by birth parents.

**Subsidies provided?** Title IV-E funded, non-recurring costs which may include medical, legal, special needs and basic maintenance.

**Adoption cost defined by law?** No.

**Insurance for infertility?:** No.

**Home study required by state?** Required except in the case of stepparent or close relative adoption. The law does not specify before or after placement.

**Prospective adoptive parent advertise for a child?** No law forbids it.

**Surrogacy laws?** No law forbids it.

**Residents access agencies of other states or countries?** Permitted.

**Requires judicial termination of birth parents' rights?** Voluntary relinquishments are recognized.

**Time given to a birthmother to revoke her consent:** 10 days.

**Court handling adoptions?** Superior.

**Adoption of Native Children:** Tribe has the authority to complete *tribal adoptions* which the court recognizes.

**Adoption records sealed?** Sealed unless both parties to the adoption agree to an open adoption. At age 18 yrs. an adoptee has access to non-identifying information even if the records have been sealed.

**Photo-listing book available?** Alaska participates in the *Northwest Adoption Exchange*.

## PUBLIC AGENCIES

★9★
**Division of Family and Youth Services of Alaska**
P.O. Box 110630
Juneau, AK 99811-0630
Phone: (907) 465-3170
Fax: (907) 465-3397

**Contact:** Nina Kinney.

**Date established:** 1959.

**Description:** Public, state agency.

**Area served:** Residents of Alaska.

**Requirements:** Adults.

**Fees:** None.

**Number of children placed last year:** 91.

**Description of children:** Children of all ages, most with special needs.

**Adoption procedure:**
1) File application;
2) complete home study with reference reports and medicals;
3) if approved, placement;
4) post-placement supervision;
5) file petition to adopt;
6) Division of Family and Youth Services consent;
7) finalization.

**Average length of time between application and start of home study:** Varies.

**Average length of time to complete home study:** Varies.

**Number of interviews:** Individual interviews with each family member, at least 2 more visits, and at least 4 interviews total.

**Home study description:** Assessment of applicant(s)' personality, emotional maturity, background, marital relationship (if applicable), feelings about children, resolution of infertility and readiness to adopt, motivation to adopt, health, home and neighborhood, feelings and attitudes about biological parents, any children in the family, employment and finances, religion, and type of child requested.

**Average wait for a child after approval of a home study:** Varies.

**Foster care:** Temporary, long-term and permanent.

# PRIVATE AGENCIES

## ★ 10 ★
**Association of Village Council Presidents, Inc.**
Pouch 219
Bethel, AK 99559
Phone: (907) 543-3521

**Contact:** Patrick Samson, Director.

**Date established:** 1964.

**Description:** Private, non-profit child placing agency.

**Area served:** Residents of southwest Alaska.

**Requirements:** Applicants are considered on a case by case review.

**Fees:** $20 for issuance of child's new birth certificate.

**Number of children placed last year:** 10.

**Description of children:** Children from infancy to 18 yrs., some with special needs.

**Adoption procedure:** Conducts both traditional and state adoptions.

**Average length of time between application and start of home study:** Varies.

**Average length of time to complete home study:** Varies.

**Number of interviews:** Varies.

**Home study description:** Follows home study requirements set by the State of Alaska.

**Average wait for a child after approval of a home study:** Varies.

**Foster care:** Emergency, long-term and therapeutic.

## ★ 11 ★
**Catholic Social Services**
3710 E. 20th, Ste. 1
Anchorage, AK 99508
Phone: (907) 258-2673

**Contact:** Elaine Stoneburner, Adoption Supervisor.

**Description:** Non-profit private agency.

**Area served:** Residents of Alaska.

**Requirements:** Couples married 4 yrs. with no more than 1 child, who have adequate financial resources to care for a child; and in good physical and emotional health. At time of placement one parent must take an 8 wk. parental leave from full-time employment. Diagnosed infertile couples are shown preference. Applicants must remain in Alaska for 2 yrs. from time of application.

**Fees:** Vary.

**Number of children placed last year:** 20.

**Description of children:** Primarily infants.

**Adoption procedure:**
1) Complete a 5-week educational series;
2) complete home study;
3) if accepted and references are favorable, family name is placed on waiting list for placement;
4) placement;
5) 6 mos. post-placement supervisory; and
6) finalization.

**Average length of time between application and start of home study:** Varies.

**Average length of time to complete home study:** 2-4 mos.

**Number of interviews:** 4.

**Home study description:** Evaluation of background, family information, marriage and courtship, issues surrounding infertility, motivation to adopt, finances, criminal/police checks and references.

**Average wait for a child after approval of a home study:** 12-24 mos.

**Foster care:** Temporary.

## ★ 12 ★
**Fairbanks Counseling and Adoption**
P.O. Box 71544
Fairbanks, AK 99707
Phone: (907) 456-4729
Fax: (907) 456-4623

**Contact:** Melody Jamieson.

**Date established:** 1978.

**Description:** Non-profit private agency licensed with the State of Alaska.

**Area served:** Residents of Alaska.

**Requirements:** Couples married at least 2 yrs. who are between the ages of 23 and 45 yrs., who are in good health, who have sufficient income to insure financial stability and who have no more than one child and a significant fertility problem.

**Fees:** U.S. infant: $5000; special needs: variable.
Intercountry: $1925-$2475 includes home study, facilitation and post placement; foreign fees extra. Home study for independent adoption: $975.

**Number of children placed last year:** 8.

**Description of children:** Primarily infants, some special needs infants. In addition to domestic adoptions, helps facilitates overseas adoptions.

**Adoption procedure:**
1) Attend intake interview;
2) file application;
3) complete home study;
4) if approved, wait for birthparent selection for placement;
5) termination of birthparents' rights and relinquishment;
6) placement;
7) post-placement supervision;
8) finalization.

**Average length of time between application and start of home study:** 1-6 mos.

**Average length of time to complete home study:** 20 hrs.

**Number of interviews:** 10 hrs. of individual, group, and in-home interviews.

**Home study description:** Evaluation of general biographical information, applicants' upbringing, parenting styles and methods of discipline, methods of resolving arguments and stress, education on adoption issues, etc.

**Average wait for a child after approval of a home study:** 24 or more mos.

**Foster care:** Temporary.

# ARIZONA

## STATUTES

★ 13 ★

**Independent placement by intermediary?** Not permitted.

**Independent placement by birth parents?** By birth parents.

**Subsidies provided?** Non-recurring adoption expenses, maintenance and special services.

**Adoption cost defined by law?** Yes.

**Insurance for infertility?:** Unknown.

**Home study required by state?** Required before placement.

**Prospective adoptive parent advertise for a child?** Not permitted.

**Surrogacy laws?** Not addressed in law.

**Residents access agencies of other states or countries?** Permitted.

**Requires judicial termination of birth parents' rights?** Voluntary consents by both birth parents when the child is no younger than 72 hrs. are recognized.

**Time given to a birthmother to revoke her consent:** None.

**Court handling adoptions?** Superior/Juvenile Court.

**Adoption of Native Children:** Tribe.

**Adoption records sealed?** Sealed, but at age 21 yrs. adoptees may access the records through an intermediary program.

**Photo-listing book available?** Participant in the *Arizona Adoption Exchange.*

## PUBLIC AGENCIES

★ 14 ★

**Arizona Department of Economic Security**
1789 W. Jefferson
Phoenix, AZ 85007
Phone: (602) 542-2362

**Branch address:**
395 S. Washington St., St. Johns, AZ 85936
Phone: (602) 337-4359

549 E. 4th St., Benson, AZ 85602
Phone: (602) 586-3671

204 Bisbee Rd., Bisbee, AZ 85603
Phone: (602) 432-5337

1205 F Ave., Douglas, AZ 85607
Phone: (602) 364-2465

2981 E. Tacoma St., Sierra Vista, AZ 85635
Phone: (602)458-4003

256 S. Curtis, Wilcox, AZ 85643
Phone: (602) 384-4616

397 Malpais, Ste. 11, Flagstaff, AZ 86001
Phone: (602) 779-3681

630 N. Navajo, Ste. 3, Page, AZ 86040

Phone: (602) 645-8103

2066 W. Apache Tr., Ste. 101, Apache Junction, AZ 85220
Phone: (602) 983-0320

122 E. Highway 260, Ste. 1100, Payson, AZ 85541
Phone: (602) 425-4521

938 Thacher Blvd., Safford, AZ 85546
Phone: (602) 428-2711

300 N. Coronado Blvd., Clifton, AZ 85533
Phone: (602) 865-4131

1032 Hopi Ave., Parker, AZ 85344
Phone: (602) 669-9293

3001 W. Indian School, Ste. 201, Phoenix, AZ 85017
Phone: (602) 277-3564

4020 N. 20th St., Phoenix, AZ 85016
Phone: (602) 265-0612

519 E. Beale, Ste. 130, Kingman, AZ 86401
Phone: (602) 753-5056

232 London Bridge Rd., Lake Havasu, AZ 86403
Phone: (602) 680-6001

3090 Hwy. 95, Stes. 8-10, Riviera, AZ 86442
Phone: (602) 763-2828

Wagon Wheel Plaza, Ste. 7, Rt. 2, Box 1740, Lakeside, AZ 85929
Phone: (602) 537-2979

401 N. Marshall, Casa Grande, AZ 85222
Phone: (602) 426-3529

319 E. Third St., Winslow, AZ 86047
Phone: (602) 289-3312

Catholic Social Services, 899 N. Wilmont, Ste. C-4, Tucson, AZ 85711
Phone: (602) 745-8791

1155 N. Arizona Blvd., Coolidge, AZ 85228
Phone: (602) 723-5351

480 Grand Ave., Nogales, AZ 85621
Phone: (602) 287-4126

1509A W. Gurley, Prescott, AZ 86301
Phone: (602) 445-1860

1645 Cottonwood St., Ste. A, Cottonwood, AZ 86326
Phone: (602) 634-7561

3780 S. 4th Ave., Ste. 2A-B, Yuma, AZ 85365
Phone: (602) 341-1159

**Contact:** Carol Rourke.

**Description:** Administrative offices and adoption exchange for the State of Arizona.

**Area served:** Residents of the State of Arizona.

**Requirements:** Adults 21 yrs. and older.

**Fees:** None.

**Number of children placed last year:** 250.

**Description of children:** Primarily children with special needs.

**Adoption procedure:**
1) Attend informational meeting;
2) submit application;
3) complete home study;
4) attend training classes;
5) if approved by court, placement;
6) file Petition to Adopt;
7) 6 mos. post-placement supervision;
8) finalization.

**Average length of time between application and start of home study:** By state law, the time from application to the completion of home study must be less than 90 days.

**Average length of time to complete home study:** Within 90 days.

**Number of interviews:** 6 classes and 2-3 interviews.

**Home study description:** Evaluation of background, experiences with children, lifestyle, resources in applicant's area, support network, and expectations of adoption and adopted child.

**Average wait for a child after approval of a home study:** Minimum of 1 yr.

**Foster care:** Emergency, temporary, long-term, therapeutic, and pre-adoptive.

# PRIVATE AGENCIES

★ 15 ★

**Adoption Care Center, Inc.**
1845 S. Dobson, Ste. 202
Mesa, AZ 85202
Phone: (602) 820-1121

**Contact:** Rick DiMaggio, Administrator.

**Date established:** 1989.

**Description:** Private, non-profit child placing agency licensed by the State of Arizona.

**Area served:** U.S. residents.

**Requirements:** Birth parents select adoptive parents.

**Fees:** Home study: $850; placement fee $0 - $1800.

**Number of children placed last year:** 27.

**Description of children:** Primarily newborn infants.

**Adoption procedure:** 1) Inquiry; 2) home study; 3) portfolio development; 4) birth parent selection; 5) placement.

**Average length of time between application and start of home study:** Less than 1 mo.

**Average length of time to complete home study:** Unavailable.

**Number of interviews:** Unavailable.

**Average wait for a child after approval of a home study:** 12 mos.

**Foster care:** None.

★ 16 ★

**Aid to Adoption of Special Kids - Arizona**
234 N. Central, No. 127
Phoenix, AZ 85004
Phone: (602) 254-2275
Fax: (602) 254-0302

**Contact:** Rachel Oesterle, Executive Director.

**Date established:** 1984.

**Description:** Non-profit private agency licensed in the State of Arizona.

**Area served:** Residents of the State of Arizona.

**Requirements:** Adults, 25 yrs. or older.

**Fees:** $2500.

**Number of children placed last year:** 30.

**Description of children:** Older; minority; physically, mentally and/or emotionally handicapped.

**Adoption procedure:**
1) Attend information meeting;
2) complete pre-certification classes;
3) complete Taylor Johnson Temperment Analysis;
4) home study;
5) child search;
6) placement;
7) post-placement services;
8) finalization;
9) post-placement services.

**Average length of time between application and start of home study:** 1-6 mos.

**Average length of time to complete home study:** 3 mos.

**Number of interviews:** 6.

**Home study description:** Evaluation of motivation; skills to parent special needs children; background, marital and family relationships; support systems and resources; financial and medical reports and references.

**Average wait for a child after approval of a home study:** 1-6 mos.

**Foster care:** Specialized medical foster care for dependent children.

★ 17 ★

**Arizona Children's Home Association**
2700 S. 8th Ave.
Tucson, AZ 85713
Phone: (602) 622-7611
(800) 947-7611
Fax: (602) 624-7042

**Mailing address:**
P.O. Box 7277, Tucson, AZ 85713

**Branch address:**
1550 E. Meadowbrook Ave., Ste. 100, Phoenix, AZ 85014
Phone: (800) 944-7611

**Contact:** Marcie Velen, Director of Permanency Planning.

**Date established:** 1912.

**Description:** Non-profit private agency licensed by the Arizona Dept. of Economic Security.

**Area served:** Residents of the State of Arizona. Partial services available to out-of-state parties.

**Requirements:** Couples married at least 2 yrs., one of whom must be younger than 50 yrs. All requirements may be waived for special needs placement.

**Fees:** Sliding scale up to $11,500. Partial services available.

**Number of children placed last year:** 30.

**Description of children:** Primarily infants with some older children.

**Adoption procedure:**
1) Telephone screening for basic requirements and attend orientation;
2) submit preliminary information form;
3) office interview;
4) return completed application;

5) complete home study;
6) if approved, placement;
7) file petition 1 mo. from date of placement;
8) post-placement supervision;
9) finalization.

**Average length of time between application and start of home study:** 1-6 mos.

**Average length of time to complete home study:** 60 days.

**Number of interviews:** 5-7.

**Home study description:** Evaluation of financial, emotional, marital and physical (health) stability.

**Average wait for a child after approval of a home study:** 12-24 mos.

**Foster care:** Temporary and fost-adopt.

### ★ 18 ★
**Black Family And Child Services**
2323 N. 3rd St., Ste. 202
Phoenix, AZ 85004
Phone: (602) 256-2948

**Contact:** Darryl Brisco.

**Date established:** 1984.

**Description:** Non-profit, community-based and community-operated organization providing services to children and families.

**Area served:** Residents of the Greater Phoenix metropolitan area.

**Requirements:** Applicants must be 21 yrs. and older have an independent source of income and a private telephone.

**Fees:** Application: $50; home study: $500.

**Number of children placed last year:** 170.

**Description of children:** African-American children between the ages of birth and 18 yrs. who have problems from emotional and physical abuse.

**Adoption procedure:** 1) Attend 7 wk. pre-adoption training; 2)complete autobiography and other materials; 3) certification process; 4) pre-placement meetings with child; 5) placement.

**Average length of time between application and start of home study:** 1-6 mos.

**Average length of time to complete home study:** 1 mo.

**Number of interviews:** 3-4.

**Home study description:** Assessment of home, neighborhood, religion, childhood, employment history, hobbies, child rearing philosophy, civic and professional memberships, marital history and social life.

**Average wait for a child after approval of a home study:** 2 yrs. for infants and toddlers.

**Foster care:** Short and long-term.

### ★ 19 ★
**Catholic Community Services of South Arizona, Inc.**
P.O. Box 5746
Tucson, AZ 85703-0746
Phone: (602) 623-0344
Fax: (602) 624-0381

**Branch address:**
Catholic Community Services of Western Arizona, 1700 S. 1st., Ste. 100, Yuma, AZ 85364
Phone: (602) 783-3308

Catholic Community Services of Cochise, 101 First St., Sierra Vista, AZ 85635
Phone: (602) 458-3640

**Contact:** Lexann Downey-Lewis or Lynn Schubert.

**Date established:** 1933.

**Description:** Non-profit private agency licensed in Arizona.

**Area served:** Residents of Pima, Pinal, Yuma, Cochise, Santa Cruz, Grahm, Greenlee and La Paz counties.

**Requirements:** Flexible. Age should be appropriate for child placed.

**Fees:** Sliding scale. Formula depends on adoption program followed: domestic, foreign or medical.

**Number of children placed last year:** 34.

**Description of children:** Infants, special needs infants and foreign-born children from 0-17 yrs.

**Adoption procedure:**
1) Telephone inquiry to have name added to application waiting list;
2) applicants periodically contact agency to keep their name on the list of interested pre-applicants;
3) complete series of group meetings and interviews;
4) if approved, names placed in selection pool for placement;
5) placement;
6) post-placement services for 8-10 mos.; and
7) finalization.

**Average length of time between application and start of home study:** 1-6 mos.

**Average length of time to complete home study:** 3 mos.

**Number of interviews:** 10.

**Home study description:** Evaluation of stability of applicants' and their marriage; finances; motivation to parent; emotions surrounding adoption and birthparents.

**Average wait for a child after approval of a home study:** 12-24 mos.

**Foster care:** Temporary.

### ★ 20 ★
**Christian Family Care Agency**
3603 N. 7th Ave.
Phoenix, AZ 85013
Phone: (602) 234-1935
Fax: (602) 234-0022

**Contact:** Christine Gray, M.A., Director of Social Services.

**Date established:** 1982.

**Description:** Private non-profit agency licensed by the State of Arizona.

**Area served:** Primarily residents of Maricopa County, AZ with limited service to residents of the other counties of Arizona and the U.S.

**Requirements:** Couples married at least 3 yrs., who have a medical diagnosis of infertilityand no more than 2 children, who are at least 25 yrs. old and whose combined ages when divided by 2 is no more than 43 yrs., who subscribe to CFCA Statement of Faith, and must be in agreement with the agency's philosophy regarding open adoption. The primary childcare giver must not be employed outside the home for the first 6 mos. after placement.

**Fees:** Agency placement inclusive fee of $9500. Designated adoption fees: homestudy - $1200; RCPC - $600; final report - $400. Other services are provided at an hourly fee of $75.

**Number of children placed last year:** 34.

**Description of children:** Infants, 30% of whom had special needs because of race or age.

**Adoption procedure:**
1) Complete and return preliminary sheets;
2) complete home study process;
3) participate in adoption education classes;
4) home study certified by Juvenile Court;
5) birthparents participate in adoptive family selection by means of non-identifying information.

**Average length of time between application and start of home study:** 1-6 mos.

**Average length of time to complete home study:** 90 days.

**Number of interviews:** 5-7.

**Home study description:** Evaluation of biographical background information, status of current marriage and any previous marriages, children of applicants, motivation to adopt, home and neighborhood, medical reports, religious background, attitudes toward children and birthparents and child desired.

**Average wait for a child after approval of a home study:** 12-24 mos.

**Foster care:** Short-term.

★ 21 ★

**Commonwealth Adoptions International, Inc.**
201 N. Jessica
Tucson, AZ 85710
Phone: (602) 886-1396
Fax: (602) 885-6396

**Contact:** Sara Eutsey, Director of Social Service or Jim Mayhew, Executive Director.

**Date established:** 1993.

**Description:** Private, non-profit child placing agency licensed by the State of Arizona.

**Area served:** No geographic restrictions.

**Requirements:** Couples married at least 1 yr. Prospective adoptive mother may be no more than 45 yrs. older than her adopted child.

**Fees:** Home study: $900; adoption finalization: $600. Estimated international adoption fees and costs (for one adult): $17,010 - $18,525.

**Number of children placed last year:** Newly licensed agency.

**Description of children:** Foreign-born children between the ages of 5 mos. and 6 yrs., some with special needs.

**Adoption procedure:** Unavailable.

**Average length of time between application and start of home study:** Unavailable.

**Average length of time to complete home study:** Less than 1 mo.

**Number of interviews:** 2 - 3.

**Home study description:** Assessment of child desired, marital relationship, childhood and parenting style.

**Average wait for a child after approval of a home study:** 1- 6 mos.

**Foster care:** Only in the event of a disrupted placement.

★ 22 ★

**Dillon Southwest**
3014 N. Hayden Rd., Ste. 101
Scottsdale, AZ 85251
Phone: (602) 945-2221

**Contact:** Emilie Sundie.

**Date established:** 1983.

**Description:** Non-profit adoption and child placing agency.

**Area served:** Residents of Arizona.

**Requirements:** Couples married at least 3 yrs. who are between the ages of 25 and 43 yrs. who are in good health and who avail themselves of conventional medical care.

**Fees:** $9400 includes application, home study, parent education, post-placement services and child's transportation to U.S.

**Number of children placed last year:** 40.

**Description of children:** South Korean infants.

**Adoption procedure:**
1) Attend orientation;
2) file pre-application;
3) attend group workshop;
4) file formal application;
5) complete home study and state adoption certification;
6) presentation of child;
7) child's arrival;
8) post-placement follow-up;
9) finalization; and
10) child's naturalization.

**Average length of time between application and start of home study:** 1 mo. or less.

**Average length of time to complete home study:** 2-3 mos.

**Number of interviews:** 4-5.

**Home study description:** Guidelines established by the Maricopa County Juvenile Court.

**Average wait for a child after approval of a home study:** 1-6 mos.

**Foster care:** Temporary.

★ 23 ★

**Family Service Agency**
1530 E. Flower St.
Phoenix, AZ 85014
Phone: (602) 264-9891
Fax: (602) 234-2639

**Contact:** Shirley Pusey, Adoption and Pregnancy Counselor.

**Date established:** 1902.

**Description:** Non-profit private agency licensed by the Arizona Dept. of Economic Security.

**Area served:** Adoptive home study: primarily Maricopa Co. residents.

**Requirements:** Couples who are married 3 or more yrs., who are in good health but apparently infertile and who manage their income well.

**Fees:**
Application interview: $250;
home study: $1900;
placement: sliding fee scale of 20% of gross annual income with a minimum of $4500 and a maximum of $11,500.

**Number of children placed last year:** 25.

**Description of children:** Infants and occasionally, toddlers of all races.

**Adoption procedure:**
1) File initial application;
2) attend orientation;
3) complete home study;
4) if approved, placement;
5) post-placement services; and
6) finalization.

**Average length of time between application and start of home study:** 1-6 mos.

**Average length of time to complete home study:** 3 mos.

**Home study description:** Evaluation of personal and marital history; previous marriages (if any); children (if any); home finances; health; child raising attitudes; long-range plans; degree of openness about adoption; and plans for future contact with birth family.

**Average wait for a child after approval of a home study:** 6-12 mos.

**Foster care:** Temporary.

★ 24 ★
**House of Samuel, Inc.**
2430 N. Sycamore
Tucson, AZ 85712
Phone: (602) 325-2662
Fax: (602) 322-6908

**Contact:** Adoption intake worker.

**Date established:** 1974.

**Description:** Non-profit private agency licensed in the State of Arizona.

**Area served:** Domestic adoptions: residents of Arizona. Intercountry adoptions: residents of U.S.

**Requirements:** Christian married couples for infant adoption.

**Fees:** $6000 includes home study.

**Number of children placed last year:** 15.

**Description of children:** U.S. infants, foreign-born, special needs, and older children.

**Adoption procedure:** Call or write for outline.

**Average length of time between application and start of home study:** 1-6 mos.

**Average length of time to complete home study:** 6 wks.

**Number of interviews:** 3.

**Home study description:** Call or write for outline.

**Average wait for a child after approval of a home study:** 6-12 mos.

**Foster care:** Temporary, long-term and permanent.

# ARKANSAS

## STATUTES

★ 25 ★

**Independent placement by intermediary?** Permitted.

**Independent placement by birth parents?** Permitted.

**Subsidies provided?** Maintenance, legal and special.

**Adoption cost defined by law?** Reasonable fees.

**Insurance for infertility?:** Yes.

**Home study required by state?** Required after placement.

**Prospective adoptive parent advertise for a child?** Restrictions on advertising exist.

**Surrogacy laws?** Permitted.

**Residents access agencies of other states or countries?** Permitted.

**Requires judicial termination of birth parents' rights?** Voluntary relinquishment consents by both legal parents are recognized.

**Time given to a birthmother to revoke her consent:** 10 days.

**Court handling adoptions?** Juvenile Division of the Chancery Court.

**Adoption of Native Children:** Tribe.

**Adoption records sealed?** Sealed, but at age 18 yrs. adoptees may access non-identifying information and at age 21 yrs. adoptees may access identifying information if all parties are registered.

**Photo-listing book available?** Division of Children and Family Services Adoption Portfolio.

## PUBLIC AGENCIES

★ 26 ★
**Department of Human Services**
**Division of Family and Human Services**
Adoption Services
P.O. Box 1437 Slot 808
Little Rock, AR 72203-1437
Phone: (501) 682-8462
Fax: (501) 682-8991

**Mailing address:**
   P.O. Box 1437, Little Rock, AR 72203-1437

**Contact:** Gloria Aboagye, Manager Adoptions.

**Description:** Public state agency, licensed as child placement agency by the State of Arkansas.

**Area served:** Residents of the State of Arkansas and individuals and agencies from other states who are eligible for services via the Interstate Compact on the Placement of Children.

**Requirements:** Single adults or legally married couples between the ages of 23 and 55 yrs. who are in good physical and mental health and who have sufficient income and resources to provide stability and security.

**Fees:** None.

**Number of children placed last year:** 119.

**Description of children:** Children of all ages, some with special needs.

**Adoption procedure:**
   1) File application;
   2) attend initial interview;
   3) return completed forms;
   4) complete home study which may include Team Training;
   5) if approved, child match;
   6) placement;
   7) post-placement services;
   8) finalization.

**Average length of time between application and start of home study:** Varies.

**Average length of time to complete home study:** 3-6 mos.

**Number of interviews:** 3 or more.

**Home study description:** Assessment of entire applicant family, background, relationships, health, education, attitudes, motivation to adopt, finances, employment, stability, resources, preferences, recommendation of references, etc.

**Average wait for a child after approval of a home study:** Varies.

**Foster care:** Short and long-term and permanent.

# PRIVATE AGENCIES

**★ 27 ★**
**Bethany Christian Services of Little Rock**
1100 N. University Ave., Ste. 66
Little Rock, AR 72207
Phone: (501) 664-5729
Fax: (501) 664-5740

**Contact:** Rhonda Love, Director.
**Date established:** 1985.
**Description:** Private, non-profit agency.
**Area served:** Residents of Arkansas.
**Requirements:** Couples married for at least 3 yrs. who are between the ages of 25 and 38 yrs., who are infertile and have no more than 1 child and who are both members of the same pro-life, evangelical church.
**Fees:** $7500 plus any unpaid medical bills of birthmother.
**Number of children placed last year:** 13.
**Description of children:** Black, white, and biracial infants, special needs, international.
**Adoption procedure:**
1) File preliminary application;
2) submit formal application;
3) complete family assessment and interview process;
4) reference and law enforcement checks;
5) if approved, wait for placement;
6) placement.
**Average length of time between application and start of home study:** 1-6 mos.
**Average length of time to complete home study:** Approx. 3 mos.
**Number of interviews:** 4.
**Home study description:** Complete social, spiritual, marital, financial, psychological and educational history and assessment.
**Average wait for a child after approval of a home study:** 12-24 mos.
**Foster care:** Temporary.

# CALIFORNIA

# STATUTES

**★ 28 ★**

**Independent placement by intermediary?** Not permitted.
**Independent placement by birth parents?** Permitted.
**Subsidies provided?** Maintenance, medical and psychological.
**Adoption cost defined by law?** Cost elements are defined by law, amounts are not.
**Insurance for infertility?:** Unknown.
**Home study required by state?** Required after placement.
**Prospective adoptive parent advertise for a child?** Illegal to advertise in California.
**Surrogacy laws?** Not addresses in law.
**Residents access agencies of other states or countries?** Permitted.
**Requires judicial termination of birth parents' rights?** Voluntary relinquishments by both birth parents are recognized.

**Time given to a birthmother to revoke her consent:** In the case of an independent adoption, up until finalization but withdrawal is subject to court approval.
**Court handling adoptions?** Superior or Juvenile at county's option.
**Adoption of Native Children:** Per the Indian Child Welfare Act as required and applicable in individual cases.
**Adoption records sealed?** Sealed, at age 18 or 21 yrs., depending upon the date of the adoption, adoptees may access non-identifying information.
**Photo-listing book available?** *California's Waiting Children.*

# PUBLIC AGENCIES

**★ 29 ★**
**Alameda County Social Services Dept.**
**Adoption Services (I)**
330 Franklin St.
Oakland, CA 94607
Phone: (510) 268-2422

**Mailing address:**
   P.O. Box 12677, Oakland, CA 94607
**Contact:** Social worker.
**Date established:** 1949.
**Description:** Public, county agency mandated to place children by the California Dept. of Social Services.
**Area served:** Residents of Alameda County.
**Requirements:** Adults, 21 yrs. or older, in good health, who have sufficient income to meet a child's need and the capacity to parent.
**Fees:** Home study: $500, which can be waivered.
**Number of children placed last year:** 100.
**Description of children:** Primarily infants and toddlers between birth-4 yrs., most with special needs.
**Adoption procedure:** 1) Inquiry and telephone screening; 2) orientation; 3) MAPP and home study; 4) if approved, wait for placement.
**Average length of time between application and start of home study:** 1-6 mos.
**Average length of time to complete home study:** 4 mos. maximum.
**Number of interviews:** 2.
**Home study description:** Educational and assessment process which includes MAPP training, verifications, references, fingerprint checks, family history, and family's ability and willingness to work with the agency.
**Average wait for a child after approval of a home study:** Maximum of 24 mos. Not every family studied receives a child.
**Foster care:** Temporary and long-term.

**★ 30 ★**
**Department of Children's Services**
**Adoptions Division**
695 S. Vermont Ave.
Los Angeles, CA 90005
Phone: (213) 738-3264
Fax: (213) 383-1502

**Branch address:**
   Independent Adoptions Unit, Metro North Office, 3160 W. 6th St., 2nd Fl., Los Angeles, CA 90020

Lancaster Adoptions Unit, Antelope Valley Office, 251-H Ave., K-6, Lancaster, CA 93535

Covina Adoptions Unit, Covina Office, 800 S. Barranca Ave., 4th Fl., Covina, CA 91723

Lakewood Adoptions Unit, Lakewood Office, 4060 Watson Plaza Dr., Lakewood, CA 90712

**Contact:** Amy Wong-Martinez, MAPP Coordinator, (213) 738-3221.
**Date established:** 1949.
**Description:** Non-profit, public agency.
**Area served:** Residents of Los Angeles County.
**Requirements:** Flexible.
**Fees:** $500 adoption fee which may be reduced or waived.
**Number of children placed last year:** 1152.
**Description of children:** Minority children, older children, children with special needs.
**Adoption procedure:**
1) Attend group meeting;
2) complete adoptive home study;
3) home study approval;
4) child search;
5) wait for placement;
6) placement;
7) post-placement supervision;
8) finalization;
9) post-adoption services, as required.
**Average length of time between application and start of home study:** Variable.
**Number of interviews:** Minimum of 2.
**Home study description:** The adoption home study process for all applicants who wish to adopt a child through Los Angeles County is called the Model Approach to Partnership in Parenting (MAPP) program. This is a group process which helps prepare adoptive applicants for children who are available for adoption. The MAPP program requires a ten meeting comitment. The meetings are held ten consecutive weeks, one day per week. Each meeting is three hours long and is led by a social worker and adoptive parent. The social worker will also meet separately with the applicant in the applicant's home to have individual interviews and gather needed documents.
**Average wait for a child after approval of a home study:** Variable.
**Foster care:** A fost/adopt is a special situation where approved adoptive families take children into their homes pending the termination of the birth parents rights to the child. Once these rights are ended, adoptive placement can take place.

★ 31 ★
**El Dorado County Dept. of Social Services**
**Adoption Services**
7553 Green Valley Rd.
Placerville, CA 95667
Phone: (916) 621-7444
Fax: (916) 621-0935

**Contact:** Alice Henry.
**Date established:** 1966.
**Description:** Non-profit, public county agency.
**Area served:** Residents of Alpine and El Dorado counties.
**Requirements:** Single applicants or couples married at least 3 yrs.

**Fees:** $500 can be reduced or waived.
**Number of children placed last year:** 15.
**Description of children:** Primarily children with special needs.
**Adoption procedure:**
1) Submit preliminary application;
2) attend intake interview;
3) file application with supporting documentation;
4) complete home study;
5) if approved, placement;
6) post-placement supervision;
7) finalization.
**Average length of time between application and start of home study:** 1-6 mos.
**Average length of time to complete home study:** 6 mos.
**Number of interviews:** 4 or more.
**Home study description:** Assessment which includes but is not limited to medical and employment reports, information on children in the home, marital history, recommendation of references, and criminal record check.
**Average wait for a child after approval of a home study:** 6-12 mos.
**Foster care:** Temporary, long-term and permanent.

★ 32 ★
**Fresno County Department of Social Services**
1404 L St.
Fresno, CA 93721
Phone: (209) 453-6402

**Mailing address:**
P.O. Box 1912, Fresno, CA 93721

**Contact:** Mindy Vertiz.
**Description:** Public, county agency.
**Area served:** Residents of Fresno County.
**Requirements:** Adults, 18 yrs. and older, who are married at least 1 yr. or single, and who are at least 10 yrs. older than the child placed.
**Fees:** $500 maximum which may be reduced or waived.
**Number of children placed last year:** 73.
**Description of children:** 95% children with special needs.
**Adoption procedure:**
1) Attend informational meeting;
2) return completed questionnaire;
3) attend screening interview;
4) complete group adoptive study;
5) if approved, wait for placement;
6) placement;
7) post-placement supervision;
8) finalization.
**Average length of time between application and start of home study:** 1-6 mos.
**Average length of time to complete home study:** 1 yr.
**Number of interviews:** 12 group and 2 individual.
**Home study description:** Group process which involves assessment, education and guest speakers and covers such topics as child behavior, behaviors related to abuse and neglect, separation, loss and transition, the long-range impact of adoption, openness and others.
**Average wait for a child after approval of a home study:** 1-6 mos.
**Foster care:** Fost-adopt.

## ★ 33 ★
**Marin County Department of Health and Human Services Adoptions**
10 N. San Pedro Rd.
San Rafael, CA 94913
Phone: (415) 499-7118

**Contact:** Ione Bezenek.

**Date established:** 1965.

**Description:** Non-profit, public county full service agency.

**Area served:** Residents of Marin County.

**Requirements:** Flexible.

**Fees:** $500 which may be reduced or waived.

**Number of children placed last year:** 13.

**Description of children:** Children with special needs from 18 mos. to 11 yrs.

**Adoption procedure:**
1) Attend orientation;
2) file application;
3) complete home study with supporting documentation;
4) if approved, placement;
5) post-placement supervision;
6) finalization.

**Average length of time between application and start of home study:** 1-6 mos.

**Average length of time to complete home study:** Unavailable.

**Number of interviews:** Unavailable.

**Home study description:** Assessment of applicant(s)' awareness of the needs of children with special needs, the special care involved, and the applicant(s)' willingness and ability to meet those needs.

**Average wait for a child after approval of a home study:** 12-24 mos.

**Foster care:** Temporary and long-term.

## ★ 34 ★
**Merced County Human Services Agency**
P.O. Box 112
Merced, CA 95341-0112
Phone: (209) 385-3000

**Contact:** Rich Brown.

**Date established:** Unavailable.

**Description:** Full service public adoption agency licensed by the State of California.

**Area served:** Residents of Merced County.

**Requirements:** Open.

**Fees:** Placement: $500 (Fee can be waived or reduced).

**Number of children placed last year:** Unavailable.

**Description of children:** Boys and girls from birth to 18 yrs. of all races many with emotional, medical or behavioral special needs.

**Adoption procedure:** 1) Initial orientation group meeting: 2) application; 3) home study and interviews; 4) 6 adoption education classes.

**Average length of time between application and start of home study:** 24 mos. or longer.

**Average length of time to complete home study:** 3 mos.

**Number of interviews:** 4.

**Home study description:** Assessment of social family history, current lifestyle and functioning, relationship with children and family resources.

**Average wait for a child after approval of a home study:** 6 mos. to 5 yrs. depending upon the type of child desired.

**Foster care:** Emergency, short- and long-term.

## ★ 35 ★
**County of Orange Social Service Agency Adoptions Program**
1920 E. 17th St., Ste. 126
Santa Ana, CA 92702
Phone: (714) 568-4636
Fax: (714) 704-8200

**Contact:** "On duty" person.

**Date established:** 1966.

**Description:** Non-profit, public, county agency.

**Area served:** Residents of Orange County.

**Requirements:** Flexible.

**Fees:** Home study: maximum of $500.

**Number of children placed last year:** 158.

**Description of children:** Children with a wide range of special needs who are dependents of the juvenile court.

**Adoption procedure:**
1) Attend orientation;
2) file application;
3) complete home study with supporting checks and clearances;
4) if approved, placement;
5) supervision of placement;
6) finalization.

**Average length of time between application and start of home study:** 1 mo. or less.

**Average length of time to complete home study:** 6 mos.

**Number of interviews:** 4.

**Home study description:** Assessment of ability to parent, social background, financial stability, work and life adjustment.

**Average wait for a child after approval of a home study:** 24 or more mos.

**Foster care:** Temporary.

## ★ 36 ★
**Riverside County Department of Social Services**
10281 Kidd
Riverside, CA 92503
Phone: (909) 358-3555

**Contact:** Adoption receptionist.

**Area served:** Residents of Riverside County.

**Requirements:** Adults over the age of 21 yrs. either single or married 18 mos. who have adequate health to parent and sufficient income to support another family member.

**Fees:** $500 maximum which can be reduced or waived.

**Number of children placed last year:** 116.

**Description of children:** Primarily children between infancy and 7 yrs. who have adverse parental backgrounds.

**Adoption procedure:**
1) Telephone intake;
2) attend informational meeting;
3) submit application;
4) admission to waiting list for study;
5) participate in group study;
6) if approved, wait for placement;
7) post-placement supervision;
8) finalization.

**Average length of time between application and start of home study:** 0-4 yrs.

**Average length of time to complete home study:** 3-6 mos.

**Number of interviews:** 4.

**Home study description:** Educational and evaluatory process which includes motivation to adopt, stability of applicants in all phases of their lives, lifestyle, background and childhood, parenting styles and methods of discipline.

**Average wait for a child after approval of a home study:** 0-3 yrs. There is no waiting for African-American applicants or for foster parents who which to adopt the child they are fostering.

**Foster care:** None.

★ 37 ★
**Sacramento County Department of Health and Human Services**
3701 Branch Center Rd.
Sacramento, CA 95827
Phone: (916) 366-2467
Fax: (916) 366-2419

**Contact:** Adoption intake worker.

**Description:** Public, county agency.

**Area served:** Primarily residents of Sacramento County.

**Requirements:** None.

**Fees:** $500 fee for home study completion, which may be reduced or waived.

**Number of children placed last year:** 60-80.

**Description of children:** Primarily children with special needs.

**Adoption procedure:**
1) Attend orientation meeting;
2) submit application;
3) participate in group training and individual interviews;
4) if approved, placement;
5) post-placement supervision;
6) finalization.

**Average length of time between application and start of home study:** 6-12 mos.

**Average length of time to complete home study:** 6 mos.

**Number of interviews:** 7 group and 4 interviews.

**Home study description:** Educational and evaluatory process which examines background, medical and financial information, employment history, verifications of vital records and type of child desired. Process involves paperwork to be submitted by adoptive applicant within 90 days.

**Average wait for a child after approval of a home study:** 1-6 mos.

**Foster care:** Adoptive placements and some low risk adoptive placements.

★ 38 ★
**San Bernardino Adoption Service**
494 N. "E" St.
San Bernardino, CA 92415-0080
Phone: (714) 387-5220
Fax: (909) 387-5353

**Branch address:**
 9638 7th St., Rancho Cucamonga, CA 91730
 Phone: (909) 945-3800

**Contact:** Tom Sansone, LCSW, Regional Manager.

**Date established:** 1951.

**Description:** Non-profit, state-licensed, public agency.

**Area served:** Residents of San Bernardino County.

**Requirements:** Open.

**Fees:** Maximum of $500.

**Number of children placed last year:** 342.

**Description of children:** Infants and children, some with special needs.

**Adoption procedure:**
 1) Attend parenting orientation meeting;
 2) submit application;
 3) attend screening interview;
 4) attend intake interview;
 5) participate in 6 group home study meetings;
 6) attend wrap-up interview;
 7) case disposition;
 8) yearly update until placement;
 9) placement;
10) supervision of placement;
11) finalization.

**Average length of time between application and start of home study:** 1-6 mos.

**Average length of time to complete home study:** 3 mos.

**Number of interviews:** 6 group and 3 individual.

**Home study description:** A total and in-depth assessment of parenting ability.

**Average wait for a child after approval of a home study:** Varies.

**Foster care:** Temporary.

★ 39 ★
**San Diego County Adoption**
5454 Ruffin Rd.
San Diego, CA 92123-1313
Phone: (619) 495-5426
Fax: (619) 495-5454

**Branch address:**
 TAYARI, 995 Gateway Ctr. Way, Ste. 303, San Diego, CA 92102
 Phone: (619) 266-6060

 NUESTRO NINOS, 1261 Third Ave., Chula Vista, CA 91911
 Phone: (619) 476-6259

 1320 Union Plaza Ct., Oceanside, CA 92054
 Phone: (619) 754-3431

**Contact:** Sharon Harrington, Adoption Manager.

**Date established:** 1948.

**Description:** Non-profit agency licensed to place children and conduct home studies.

**Area served:** Residents of San Diego County; out-of-county/ICPC inquiries.

**Requirements:** Adults who are at least 10 yrs. older than the adoptive child; if married, at least 2 yrs. unless it is a subsequent marriage, in which case couple must be married 3 or more yrs.; who have recent physical examinations for each family member including a TB test and blood serulogy for each family member over 18 yrs. of age.

**Fees:** $500 plus finger print and child abuse index processing. Fees can be waived or on sliding scale. AAP may be available.

**Number of children placed last year:** 448.

**Description of children:** Infants and special needs.

**Adoption procedure:**
 1) Complete applicant inquiry form during initial telephone inquiry;

2) attend orientation;
3) file pre-application;
4) if applying for child with special needs, complete group home study;
4) if applying for infant, complete individual home study;
5) if approved, wait for placement;
6) placement;
7) 6 mos. post-placement supervision;
8) finalization.

**Average length of time between application and start of home study:** 1-6 mos.

**Average length of time to complete home study:** Infant adoption: 6-8 mos.; special needs adoption: 2-4 mos.

**Number of interviews:** Varies; 3-5.

**Home study description:** Evaluation of family background, current family's needs, priorities and interests and the type of child desired.

**Average wait for a child after approval of a home study:** 12-24 mos.

**Foster care:** Temporary, long-term and permanent.

**★ 40 ★**
**San Francisco Department of Social Services**
**Adoption Services**
1440 Harrison St.
San Francisco, CA 94120
Phone: (415) 558-2338
Fax: (415) 558-2632

**Mailing address:**
 P.O. Box 7988, San Francisco, CA 94120
**Contact:** Adoptions/homefinding.
**Description:** Public, county agency.
**Area served:** Primarily residents of San Francisco County but will work with others interested in the county's "waiting children".
**Requirements:** Adults, 21 yrs. and older.
**Fees:** $500 maximum which may be reduced or waived.
**Number of children placed last year:** 200 or more.
**Description of children:** Children with special needs.
**Adoption procedure:**
 1) Telephone intake;
 2) participate in in-depth interview;
 3) attend 10 wk. MAPP program;
 4) complete home study;
 5) if approved, wait for placement;
 6) placement;
 7) post-placement supervision;
 8) finalization.

**Average length of time between application and start of home study:** 6-12 mos.

**Average length of time to complete home study:** 10 or more mos.

**Number of interviews:** 7 group and 4 home visits.

**Home study description:** Process involves training and assessment of stability, background, recommendation of references, health, home and environment and motivation to adopt.

**Average wait for a child after approval of a home study:** 6-12 mos.

**Foster care:** Emergency, temporary, fost-adopt, therapeutic, permanent and "Baby Moms," a program for medically fragile infants.

**★ 41 ★**
**San Luis Obispo County Department of Social Services**
P.O. Box 8119
San Luis Obispo, CA 93403-8119
Phone: (805) 781-1705

**Mailing address:**
 P.O. Box 8119, San Luis Obispo, CA 93403-8119
**Contact:** Miki Gillman, Supervisor; Sharon Murray, Legal Clerk.
**Date established:** 1952.
**Description:** Non-profit, full service, public agency licensed by the State of California.
**Area served:** Residents of San Luis Obispo County.
**Requirements:** Applicants must be in good physical and mental health and able to support themselves.
**Fees:** Home Study: $500. Finger printing, medical exam and filing fee additional.
**Number of children placed last year:** 59.
**Description of children:** Children with special needs.
**Adoption procedure:** 1) Applicant questionnaire; 2) orientation; 3) pre-application interview; 4) application process which includes interviews, verifications of health, employment, income, marital status, military service, etc.; 5) placement; 6) minimum of 6 mos. post-placement supervision.

**Average length of time between application and start of home study:** 1-6 mos.

**Average length of time to complete home study:** 6 mos.

**Number of interviews:** Minimum of 4.

**Home study description:** Assessment which covers such issues as conflict resolution, interpersonal relations, child rearing practices including discipline; support systems, role of religion in family life, family health, types of losses experienced and how resolved.

**Average wait for a child after approval of a home study:** 6-12 mos.

**Foster care:** Emergency, temporary, long-term, specialized and fost-adopt.

**★ 42 ★**
**Santa Barbara County Department of Social Services**
234 Camino del Remedio
Santa Barbara, CA 93110
Phone: (805) 681-4571
Fax: (805) 681-4402

**Branch address:**
 2125 S. Centerpointe Pkwy., Santa Maria, CA 93455
 Phone: (805) 346-7114
**Contact:** Monica Bradley, Supervisor (Santa Barbara); Sandra Thomas, Supervisor (Santa Maria).
**Date established:** 1954.
**Description:** Public, county agency licensed by the California Department of Social Services.
**Area served:** Residents of Santa Barbara County.
**Requirements:** Very flexible.
**Fees:** Maximum of $500.
**Description of children:** Infants and children with special needs.
**Adoption procedure:**
 1) Initial inquiry;
 2) attend interview;
 3) complete application process;
 4) if approved, placement;
 5) post-placement supervision;

6) finalization.

**Average length of time between application and start of home study:** Varies.

**Average length of time to complete home study:** 3-5 mos.

**Number of interviews:** 4 or more.

**Home study description:** Assessment of stability of lifestyle and applicant(s)' desire to rear children to reach their potential.

**Average wait for a child after approval of a home study:** Varies.

**Foster care:** Temporary.

**★ 43 ★**

**Santa Clara County Social Services Agency - Adoptions**
1725 Technology Dr.
San Jose, CA 95110-1360
Phone: (408) 441-5116

**Contact:** Joan Anderson, Home Studies SW Supervisor (408) 441-5211; Gwen Westphal, Relinquishments SW Supervisor (408) 441-5269; Sharon Gilson, Manager (408) 441-5457.

**Date established:** 1959.

**Description:** Public child placing agency licensed by the State of California to provide full adoption services.

**Area served:** Residents of Santa Clara County.

**Requirements:** Open.

**Fees:** Home study: $500 maximum.

**Number of children placed last year:** 87.

**Description of children:** Primarily dependent children of Hispanic or African-American heritage with special needs who come through the Juvenile Court system.

**Adoption procedure:** 1) Telephone inquiry; 2) application; 3) home study; 4) matching process; 5) placement; 6) post-placement supervision; 7) finalization.

**Average length of time between application and start of home study:** Less than 1 mo.

**Average length of time to complete home study:** 6 mos.

**Number of interviews:** Minimum of 4.

**Home study description:** Assessment which includes background and reference checks and includes such issues as type of child requested, child care plan, motivation to adopt, adoption issues, parenting philosophies and practices, applicant(s)' childhood(s), marital relationship (if applicable), ethnicity, description of children in the home and of the home and neighborhood.

**Average wait for a child after approval of a home study:** 42% are fost-adopt conversions; remainder: 8- 18 mos.

**Foster care:** Temporary and fost-adopt.

**★ 44 ★**

**Santa Cruz County Department of Human Resources Adoptions**
1040 Emeline Ave.
Santa Cruz, CA 95060
Phone: (408) 454-4044
Fax: (408) 454-4651

**Contact:** Valerie Sudduth.

**Date established:** 1970.

**Description:** State licensed public adoption agency.

**Area served:** Residents of Santa Cruz County.

**Requirements:** Adoptive parent applicants must be 10 yrs. older than adoptees.

**Fees:** Maximum of $500.

**Number of children placed last year:** 24.

**Description of children:** Primarily children between the ages of 1 and 8 yrs. and a few infants.

**Adoption procedure:**
1) Attend orientation;
2) file application;
3) complete home study;
4) if approved, placement;
5) finalization.

**Average length of time between application and start of home study:** 1-6 mos.

**Average length of time to complete home study:** 2-3 mos.

**Number of interviews:** 4.

**Home study description:** Assessment of childhood, marriage (if applicable), experience with children, financial ability and criminal record clearance.

**Average wait for a child after approval of a home study:** 6-24 mos.

**Foster care:** Temporary, long-term, fost-adopt and permanent.

**★ 45 ★**

**Shasta County Adoptions**
1615 Continental St.
Redding, CA 96001
Phone: (916) 225-5791

**Contact:** Carol C. Minard, L.C.S.W.

**Date established:** 1950.

**Description:** Non-profit, public child placing agency licensed by the State of California.

**Area served:** Residents of Shasta County.

**Requirements:** Open.

**Fees:** Home study: $500.

**Number of children placed last year:** 28.

**Description of children:** Children between the ages of birth and 10 yrs. who have special needs and who have been abused and/or neglected or who have been substance exposed.

**Adoption procedure:** 1) Inquiry meeting; 2) intake interview; 3) application; 4) licensure; 5) adoptive home study; 6) placement; 7) post-placement supervision; 8) finalization.

**Average length of time between application and start of home study:** 1 - 6 mos.

**Average length of time to complete home study:** 4 mos.

**Number of interviews:** 6.

**Home study description:** Assessment which includes such issues as stability and flexibility, family support system, length of marriage (if applicable), parenting experience, experience with grief and loss and capability of dealing with sexually molested children.

**Average wait for a child after approval of a home study:** 1 - 6 mos.

**Foster care:** Temporary.

**★ 46 ★**

**State Department of Social Services**
**Chico District Office**
520 Cohasset Rd., No. 11
Chico, CA 95926
Phone: (916) 891-1986
Fax: (916) 895-6148

**Contact:** Bill Jemison.

**Date established:** 1977.

**Description:** Public child-placing agency.

**Area served:** Residents of Butte, Colusa, Glenn, Lassen, Modoc, Plumas, Sierra, Siskiyou, Tehama and Trinity counties.

**Requirements:** None.

**Fees:** Home study: $500.

**Number of children placed last year:** 70.

**Description of children:** Primarily school aged children, some with special needs.

**Adoption procedure:**
1) Submit preliminary application;
2) attend intake interview;
3) file application with supporting documentation;
4) complete home study;
5) if approved, placement;
6) post-placement supervision;
7) finalization.

**Average length of time between application and start of home study:** 1 mo. or less.

**Average length of time to complete home study:** 6 mos.

**Number of interviews:** 4.

**Home study description:** Comprehensive and child-centered assessment.

**Average wait for a child after approval of a home study:** 6-12 mos.

**Foster care:** None.

★ 47 ★

**Tulare County Adoptions**
3340 W. Mineral King
Visalia, CA 93277
Phone: (209) 733-6180

**Contact:** Pao-Lin Hurley, Adoption Supervisor.

**Date established:** 1949.

**Description:** Public child placing agency licensed by the State of California.

**Area served:** Residents of Kings and Tulare counties.

**Requirements:** Follows state guidelines.

**Fees:** None.

**Number of children placed last year:** 112.

**Description of children:** Children with special needs.

**Adoption procedure:** 1) Inquiry; 2) application; 3) home study; 4) family recruitment/child match; 5) placement; 6) post-placement supervision; 7) finalization.

**Average length of time between application and start of home study:** 6-12 mos.

**Average length of time to complete home study:** 6-12 mos.

**Number of interviews:** 3.

**Home study description:** Assessment process which addresses such issues as motivation to adopt and infertility, child desired, marriage, if applicable, discipline methods, children in the home, family history, home and neighborhood, employment and health.

**Average wait for a child after approval of a home study:** 1-6 mos.

**Foster care:** Temporary and long-term.

★ 48 ★

**Ventura County Public Social Services Agency**
4651 Telephone Rd., Ste. 205
Ventura, CA 93003
Phone: (805) 654-3454
(800) 660-5474
Fax: (805) 658-4190

**Contact:** Sydne Hampton.

**Date established:** 1959.

**Description:** Public, county agency licensed by the California Dept. of Social Services.

**Area served:** Residents of Ventura County.

**Requirements:** Flexible.

**Fees:** Maximum of $500.

**Number of children placed last year:** 85.

**Description of children:** Primarily children age 1 to 7 and up, many with special needs.

**Adoption procedure:**
1) Attend orientation;
2) file application;
3) complete home study;
4) if approved, placement;
5) post-placement supervision;
6) finalization.

**Average length of time between application and start of home study:** 1-6 mos.

**Average length of time to complete home study:** 3 mos.

**Number of interviews:** 4 or more.

**Home study description:** Assessment of background, personality, experience with children, attitudes, life experiences and motivation to adopt.

**Average wait for a child after approval of a home study:** Varies greatly depending on family's openness to special needs.

**Foster care:** Temporary, long-term and permanent.

# PRIVATE AGENCIES

★ 49 ★

**AASK America**
**Aid to Adoption of Special Kids**
2201 Broadway, Ste. 702
Oakland, CA 94612
Phone: (415) 434-2275
Fax: (510) 451-2023

**Contact:** Bob Diamond, Executive Director.

**Date established:** 1973.

**Description:** Non-profit adoption agency for special children licensed in the State of California.

**Area served:** Residents of the U.S.

**Requirements:** Adults, 21 yrs. and older, who are at least 10 yrs. older than the child placed.

**Fees:** Sliding scale.

**Number of children placed last year:** 40.

**Description of children:** Physically, cognitively and/or emotionally handicapped children, many of whom are minorities, school age and/or in sibling groups.

**Adoption procedure:**
1) Attend informational meeting;
2) participate in Prospective Parent Seminar;
3) attend individual interview;

4) complete home study;
5) matching;
6) placement process;
7) post-placement supervision and parent support;
8) finalization.

**Average length of time between application and start of home study:** Varies.

**Average length of time to complete home study:** Varies.

**Number of interviews:** 3-4.

**Home study description:** An educational process through which families learn of the types of children needing adoptive homes and learn what is involved in providing loving, adoptive homes for them. It is also a preparation period which allows the caseworker to discover ways in which the adoptive family can be assisted once the child is placed.

**Average wait for a child after approval of a home study:** Varies.

**Foster care:** Pre-adoptive and Legal Risk adoption.

★ 50 ★
**Adopt International**
121 Springdale Way
Redwood City, CA 94062
Phone: (415) 369-7300
Fax: (415) 369-7400

**Contact:** Lynne Jacobs.

**Date established:** 1983.

**Description:** Non-profit child placing agency open to all U.S. families with CIS, Belarus, China, and Peru programs.

**Area served:** Marin, San Francisco, San Mateo, Santa Clara, Alameda, Sonoma, Napa, Santa Cruz, Solano, and Contra Costa counties.

**Requirements:** Requirements vary by country of adoptive child.

**Fees:** Application fee: $150; home study: $2400.

**Number of children placed last year:** 120.

**Description of children:** Infants and toddlers, older children, and special needs children.

**Adoption procedure:**
1) Submit application;
2) file with INS;
3) complete home study;
4) compile and have approved supporting documents;
5) wait for placement. If working with cooperating agency, submit home study, foreign program application, and other documents and wait for placement.

**Average length of time between application and start of home study:** 1 mo. or less.

**Average length of time to complete home study:** 6-8 wks.

**Number of interviews:** 4 or more.

**Home study description:** Compilation and assessment of personal, family, educational and career histories, medical and financial reports, references and fingerprints; and discussion of marital and child rearing issues.

**Average wait for a child after approval of a home study:** 1-6 mos.

**Foster care:** Pre-adoptive.

★ 51 ★
**Adoption Connection of Jewish Family and Children's Services**
1600 Scott St.
San Francisco, CA 94115
Phone: (415) 561-1252

**Branch address:**
490 El Camino Real, Belmont, CA 94002

1330 Lincoln Ave., San Rafael, CA 94901

320 College Ave., No. 205, Santa Rosa, CA 95401

**Contact:** Laura Chasko.

**Date established:** 1984.

**Description:** Private, non-profit child placing agency licensed by the State of California.

**Area served:** Residents of the San Francisco Bay area.

**Requirements:** Applicants must be in reasonably good health and should demonstrate financial stability.

**Fees:** Application: $50; home study: $750 - $2000 sliding scale. Total adoption fees including application and home study range from $2150 to $5400 depending on income.

**Number of children placed last year:** Unavailable.

**Description of children:** Primarily healthy Caucasian infants.

**Adoption procedure:** 1) Orientation meeting; 2) application; 3) home study; 4) pre-adoption workshop; 5) counseling; 6) placement; 7) post-placement supervision; 8) finalization.

**Average length of time between application and start of home study:** Less than 1 mo.

**Average length of time to complete home study:** 2 mos.

**Number of interviews:** 3.

**Home study description:** Educational and assessment process which covers such topics as employment, housing, finances, autobiographical information and references and which is designed to help applicants become parents.

**Average wait for a child after approval of a home study:** 6 - 24 mos.

**Foster care:** Temporary.

★ 52 ★
**Adoption Horizons, Inc.**
**The Birth Parent Center**
630 "J" St.
Eureka, CA 95501
Phone: (707) 444-9909
Fax: (707) 443-9580

**Contact:** Jay Rezzonico, Executive Director.

**Date established:** 1982.

**Description:** Adoption Horizons is a non-profit, private adoption agency licensed by the State of California. The Birth Parent Center provides counseling and support services to enrolled birth parents and does adoption facilitation.

**Area served:** Residents of Del Norte, Humboldt, Mendocino and Trinity counties.

**Requirements:** Applicants must be at least 21 yrs. old, single or married at least 2 yrs.

**Fees:** Application: $75; home study: $3500; required Adoption Study Classes: $50/person.

**Number of children placed last year:** 15.

**Description of children:** Healthy U.S. newborns, children with special needs and foreign born children.

**Adoption procedure:** 1) Introductory meeting; 2) Adoption Study Classes; 3) application/review/contract; 4) home study; 5) child search; 6) placement; 7) finalization.

**Average length of time between application and start of home study:** 1-6 mos.

**Average length of time to complete home study:** 3 mos.

**Number of interviews:** Minimum of 4.

**Home study description:** Assessment which covers such topics as motivation to adopt, the type of child desired, applicant(s)' history and description, finances, community of residence, health, religion, references and recommendations.

**Average wait for a child after approval of a home study:** Infants placed through The Birth Parent Center: 1-6 mos.; children placed through Adoption Horizons: 6 - 12 mos.

**Foster care:** None.

★ 53 ★
**Adoption Services International**
2021 Sperry Ave., Ste. 41
Ventura, CA 93003
Phone: (805) 644-3067
Fax: (805) 644-9270

**Contact:** Sandra Browne, Executive Director.

**Date established:** 1984.

**Description:** Non-profit private agency licensed by the State of California.

**Area served:** Residents of California.

**Requirements:** Couples married for at least 2 yrs. who are 25 yrs. or older. Other requirements depend upon the adopted child's country of origin.

**Fees:**
Preapplication fee: $75;
application fee: $165;
home study fee: $1500;
post-placement fees: $1000.
Overseas fees are additional.

**Number of children placed last year:** 70.

**Description of children:** Foreign-born children from 0-16 yrs.

**Adoption procedure:**
 1) Attend pre-application interview;
 2) complete home study;
 3) if approved, placement;
 4) 4 post-placement visits; and
 5) finalization.

**Average length of time between application and start of home study:** 1 mo. or less.

**Average length of time to complete home study:** 2-3 mos.

**Number of interviews:** 4.

**Home study description:** Evaluation of background; current lifestyle; marital relationship; any children in the home; and motivation to adopt.

**Average wait for a child after approval of a home study:** 1-6 mos.

**Foster care:** None.

★ 54 ★
**Adoptions Unlimited**
11800 Central Ave., Ste. 110
Chino, CA 91710
Phone: (909) 902-1412
Fax: (909) 624-4591

**Mailing address:**
 P.O. Box 462, Chino, CA 91710

**Contact:** Maria Ramirez, Program Coordinator.

**Date established:** 1982.

**Description:** Non-profit private agency licensed in southern California.

**Area served:** Residents of Imperial, Kern, Los Angeles, Orange, Riverside, San Bernardino, San Diego, San Luis Obispo, Santa Barbara, and Ventura counties.

**Requirements:** Couples married 2 or more yrs. Other requirements vary by child's country of origin.

**Fees:**
Home study: $1,400;
post-placement services: $1,400.
All other fees vary by program.

**Number of children placed last year:** 50.

**Description of children:** U.S. special needs, U.S. infants and foreign-born children of all ages.

**Adoption procedure:**
 1) Registration;
 2) home study;
 3) complete dossier;
 4) search;
 5) placement;
 6) post-placement supervision;
 7) finalization.

**Average length of time between application and start of home study:** 1 mo. or less.

**Average length of time to complete home study:** 6 wks.

**Number of interviews:** 4.

**Home study description:** Evaluation of background, family stability, motivation to adopt, type of child desired, etc.

**Average wait for a child after approval of a home study:** Depends on program.

**Foster care:** Temporary.

★ 55 ★
**Bal Jagat**
**Children's World, Inc.**
9311 Farralone Ave.
Chatsworth, CA 91311
Phone: (818) 709-4737
Fax: (818) 709-4737

**Contact:** Hemlata Momaya, MSW.

**Date established:** 1983.

**Description:** Non-profit intercountry adoption agency, recognized by the governments of India and China and licensed with the State of California.

**Area served:** Bal Jagat is licensed to do home studies in Los Angeles, Orange San Bernardino, Santa Barbara, San Diego, and Ventura counties.

**Requirements:** Adults over the age of 25 yrs. who are in good health and financially able to care for a child.

**Fees:**
Orientation: $60;
application: $300;
home study: $1500;
post-placement services: $850.

**Number of children placed last year:** 50.

**Description of children:** Infants, toddlers and pre-teens from around the world.

**Adoption procedure:**
1) Attend orientation;
2) complete home study;
3) prepare and send dossier;
4) information on and pictures of child are presented to applicant(s);
5) paperworks and documentation to INS;
6) child arrives in U.S. or prospective parents travel to foreign countries.

**Average length of time between application and start of home study:** 1 mo. or less.

**Average length of time to complete home study:** 6-8 wks.

**Number of interviews:** 4.

**Home study description:** Evaluation which includes but is not limited to applicant(s)' childhood, finances, health, religion, education, occupation and interest in adopted child's country of origin.

**Average wait for a child after approval of a home study:** 1-12 mos.

**Foster care:** None.


★ 56 ★
**Bay Area Adoption Services**
465 Fairchild Dr., Ste. 215
Mountain View, CA 94043
Phone: (415) 964-3800
Fax: (415) 964-6467

**Contact:** Andrea Stawitcke, Executive Director.

**Date established:** 1984.

**Description:** International non-profit adoption agency licensed in the San Francisco Bay area and placing children from 37 countries.

**Area served:** Residents of Alameda, Contra Costa, Marin, San Benito, San Francisco, San Mateo, Santa Clara, Santa Cruz, Napa, Solano, Sonoma, and San Joaquin counties.

**Requirements:** Applicants must be 10 yrs. older than child placed. If married, at least 1 yr. duration. Since B.A.A.S. does not have custody of adoptable children, other requirements may be imposed by the child's agency or birth country.

**Fees:** $2600-$3400.

**Number of children placed last year:** Unavailable.

**Description of children:** Foreign-born children ranging in age from infancy to 16 yrs. from 37 different countries.

**Adoption procedure:**
1) Attend general orientation;
2) attend pre-adoption classes;
3) complete home study;
4) forward paperwork and documentation to INS;
5) assistance with sources;
6) travel to child's birth country or child arrives in U.S.
7) post-placement supervision.

**Average length of time between application and start of home study:** 1-6 mos.

**Average length of time to complete home study:** 6-8 wks.

**Number of interviews:** 4.

**Home study description:** Evaluation of family history, medical information, finances, relationships, employment, education and others.

**Average wait for a child after approval of a home study:** 6-12 mos.

**Foster care:** None.

★ 57 ★
**Bethany Christian Services, North Region**
2937 Veneman Ave., No. 265-C
Modesto, CA 95356
Phone: (209) 522-5121
Fax: (209) 522-1499

**Contact:** Lynette Stime, Director.

**Date established:** 1981.

**Description:** Non-profit, licensed adoption agency.

**Area served:** Adoptive applicants in 35 northern California counties and pregnant women in northern California.

**Requirements:** Couples married 3 or more yrs., who are members of a Christian church and have a recognized fertility problem. Requirements vary for children with special needs.

**Fees:** $6750 plus reasonable pregnancy-related expenses.

**Number of children placed last year:** 20.

**Description of children:** All races; some children with special needs.

**Adoption procedure:**
1) Submit pre-application;
2) attend orientation and educational seminar;
3) submit formal application;
4) complete home study;
5) if approved, wait for placement;
6) placement;
7) post-placement supervision;
8) court finalization.

**Average length of time between application and start of home study:** 1-6 mos.

**Average length of time to complete home study:** 3-5 mos.

**Number of interviews:** 3-4.

**Home study description:** Educational and evaluatory process which verifies employment, checks law enforcement conviction records; and includes parent preparation and time for the agency to become familiar with the family.

**Average wait for a child after approval of a home study:** 12-24 mos.

**Foster care:** Temporary.


★ 58 ★
**Bethany Christian Services, South Region**
9928 Flower St., Ste. 202
Bellflower, CA 90706-5453
Phone: (310) 804-3448
Fax: (310) 804-6460

**Contact:** Bonnie Adkins-DeJong.

**Date established:** 1985.

**Description:** Non-profit, private agency.

**Area served:** Residents of Los Angeles, Orange, Riverside, San Bernardino, and San Diego counties.

**Requirements:** Couples married at least 3 yrs. who are between the ages of 25 and 39 yrs., who are infertile and have no more than 1 child and who are members of an Evangelical Christian church.

**Fees:** Sliding scale based on combined income between $5500-$9800.

**Number of children placed last year:** 50.

**Description of children:** White and biracial infants.

**Adoption procedure:**
1) File preliminary application;
2) attend orientation meeting;
3) submit formal application;

4) complete home study;
5) if approved, placement;
6) post-placement supervision;
7) finalization.

**Average length of time between application and start of home study:** 6-12 mos.

**Average length of time to complete home study:** 3-4 wks.

**Number of interviews:** 4.

**Home study description:** Assessment of motivation to adopt, applicants' social backgrounds, marriage and family life, religious commitment, employment and finances, home and community life.

**Average wait for a child after approval of a home study:** 12-24 mos.

**Foster care:** Temporary.

## ★ 59 ★
**Catholic Charities Adoption Agency of San Diego**
349 Cedar St.
San Diego, CA 92101
Phone: (619) 231-2828
(800) CARE-002
Fax: (619) 234-2272

**Contact:** Delia K. Sables or Rosemary Smith.

**Date established:** 1984.

**Description:** Non-profit adoption agency licensed in San Diego utilizing an open adoption process.

**Area served:** Residents of Imperial and San Diego counties.

**Requirements:** Requirements reflect birthparent(s)' preferences. Usually married couples who are practicing some religion and who have no children.

**Fees:** 10% of gross income which includes home study, 8-week preparation seminar, and post-placement supervision.

**Number of children placed last year:** 15.

**Description of children:** Infants, several of whom were of mixed ethnicity; some with special needs.

**Adoption procedure:**
1) Telephone intake;
2) attend orientation;
3) attend seminars and submit formal application;
4) complete home study process;
5) if approved,placement;
6) 6 mos. post-placement supervisory which includes 4 home visits;and
7) finalization.

**Average length of time between application and start of home study:** 1-6 mos.

**Average length of time to complete home study:** 3-4 mos.

**Number of interviews:** 8 three hr. group seminars;
1 home visit;
8 hrs. of interviews in 4 sessions.

**Home study description:** Evaluation which includes but is not limited to personal references, medicals, employment verification and credit references, range of acceptance in an adopted child.

**Average wait for a child after approval of a home study:** 12-24 mos.

**Foster care:** Temporary.

## ★ 60 ★
**Catholic Charities of San Francisco**
2045 Lawton St.
San Francisco, CA 94122
Phone: (415) 665-5100
Fax: (415) 665-8586

**Contact:** Adoption Unit.

**Date established:** 1953.

**Description:** Non-profit, licensed private agency.

**Area served:** Residents of San Francisco, San Mateo and Marin counties with services available throughout the Greater Bay Area for special needs and inter-country adoption.

**Requirements:** Flexible and based on needs of children.

**Fees:** Sliding scale. Usually no fees for special needs adoption.

**Number of children placed last year:** 30.

**Description of children:** Infants, foreign-born and special needs.

**Adoption procedure:**
1) Complete full home study;
2) attend preparation;
3) if approved, placement (birth parents may participate fully in selection of their child's adoptive home);
4) post-placement supervision;
5) legal finalization.

**Average length of time between application and start of home study:** 1-6 mos.

**Average length of time to complete home study:** 2-6 mos.

**Number of interviews:** Minimum of 4.

**Home study description:** The primary purpose of adoption is to provide homes for children who need them. Since children have many different needs, the agency looks for a wide variety of adoptive parents as potential resources for these children.

**Average wait for a child after approval of a home study:** Varies by needs of child.

**Foster care:** Pre-adoptive.

## ★ 61 ★
**Children's Home Society of California**
1300 W. 4th St.
Los Angeles, CA 90017-1475
Phone: (213) 389-6750

**Branch address:**
3200 Telegraph Ave., Oakland, CA 94609-3077
Phone: (510) 655-7408

550 Bercut Dr., Ste. G, Sacramento, CA 95814-0105
Phone: (916) 658-0100

7695 Cardinal Ct., San Diego, CA 92123-3399
Phone: (619) 278-7800

2400 Moorpark, Ste. 312, San Jose, CA 95128-2625
Phone: (408) 293-8940

300 S. Sycamore St., Santa Ana, CA 92701-5792
Phone: (714) 835-8252

6851 Lennox Ave., Van Nuys, CA 91405
Phone: (818) 908-5055

**Contact:** Maureen Hughes, Program Manager.

**Date established:** 1891.

**Description:** Non-profit, private children's services agency accredited by the Council on Accreditation of Services for Families and Children and a member of the Child Welfare League of America and the California Association of Services for Children.

**Area served:** Residents of the State of California. Limited areas and services.

**Requirements:** Vary with program.

**Fees:** Depends on service.

**Number of children placed last year:** Approx. 100.

**Description of children:** Infants.

**Adoption procedure:** Assisted designated adoptions and post adoption services.

**Average length of time to complete home study:** 2-6 mos.

**Number of interviews:** 4 plus educational seminar.

**Home study description:** Evaluatory and educational process.

**Foster care:** Treatment, respite care, emergency, pre-adoptive and fost-adopt.

**★ 62 ★**
**Christian Adoption and Family Services**
P.O. Box 891561
Temecula, CA 92589
Phone: (909) 676-9486

**Contact:** Supervisor or office manager.

**Date established:** 1959.

**Description:** Non-profit private agency licensed in 5 counties of southern California.

**Area served:** Residents of Los Angeles, Orange, Riverside, San Bernardino and San Diego counties.

**Requirements:** Couples married at least 3 yrs. who are evangelical Protestants and who are under the age of 40 yrs.

**Fees:** Sliding scale based on income: $3500-$9000.

**Number of children placed last year:** 0.

**Description of children:** Infants, many biracial.

**Adoption procedure:**
1) Attend orientation;
2) complete home study;
3) if approved, placement;
4) 6 mos. post-placement supervision;
5) finalization.

**Average length of time between application and start of home study:** Varies.

**Average length of time to complete home study:** 3 mos.

**Number of interviews:** 4.

**Home study description:** Evaluation of marital stability, resolution of infertility (if applicable), readiness for adoption, and acceptance of open adoption.

**Average wait for a child after approval of a home study:** 12-24 mos.

**Foster care:** Temporary.

**★ 63 ★**
**Chrysalis House**
2134 W. Alluvial
Fresno, CA 93711
Phone: (209) 432-7170
Fax: (209) 432-6196

**Contact:** Josie-Lee Kuhlman, Executive Director.

**Date established:** 1985.

**Description:** Non-profit private agency licensed in 16 counties in central California for domestic and inter-country adoption and home finding.

**Area served:** Residents of Fresno, Kern, Madera, Mariposa, Merced, Kings, Los Angeles, Ventura, Tulare, Santa Barbara, and San Joaquin counties.

**Requirements:** Flexible.

**Fees:**
Registration: $50;
home study: $2000;
placement: $2000.

**Number of children placed last year:** 30.

**Description of children:** U.S., foreign-born infants and infants with special needs.

**Adoption procedure:**
1) Complete registration;
2) complete home study;
3) if approved, search for child through pregnancy counseling, adoption exchanges, waiting Children's Library;
4) relinquishment, if necessary;
5) fost-adopt placement;
6) post-placement supervision.

**Average length of time between application and start of home study:** 0-6 mos.

**Average length of time to complete home study:** 2 mos.

**Number of interviews:** 5.

**Home study description:** Evaluation of application, autobiography, supplement to application, employment and medical reports, references, finger print and Child Abuse Registry checks, birth, marriage and divorce (if applicable) records, 2 photographs of applicants, etc.

**Average wait for a child after approval of a home study:** 12-24 mos.

**Foster care:** Pre-adoptive and therapeutic.

**★ 64 ★**
**Families for Children**
3650 Auburn Blvd., Ste. A-200
Sacramento, CA 95821
Phone: (916) 974-8744
Fax: (916) 487-1494

**Contact:** Ursula De Vere, Executive Director.

**Date established:** January 1, 1989.

**Description:** Non-profit Public Benefit Corporation and private child placing agency licensed by the State of California and member of California Association of Services for Children.

**Area served:** No residency restrictions.

**Requirements:** Applicants must be at least 21 yrs. old, be in good health and have a stable income.

**Fees:** Application: $50; home study: $5000; placement fee: $3000. No fees for fost/adopt or special needs placement.

**Number of children placed last year:** 6.

**Description of children:** Infants and children with special needs.

**Adoption procedure:** Follow guidelines set by the State of California.

**Average length of time between application and start of home study:** 1 - 6 mos.

**Average length of time to complete home study:** 3 wks.

**Number of interviews:** 6 - 8.

**Home study description:** Assessment which covers such topics as motivation to adopt, background and description of personality, childhood, quality of marital (if applicable) and family relationships, general lifestyle, philosophy of parenting, perceptions of adoption triangle, type of child requested and includes caseworker's evaluation, interviews with other children already in the home and documentation.

**Average wait for a child after approval of a home study:** Within 12 mos.

**Foster care:** Long-term, therapeutic and permanent.

★ 65 ★
**Family Connections Adoption Agency**
1528 Oakdale Rd.
Modesto, CA 95355
Phone: (209) 524-8844
Fax: (209) 524-2139

**Mailing address:**
  P.O. Box 576035, Modesto, CA 95355

**Contact:** Audrey Foster, Director.

**Date established:** 1983.

**Description:** Private, non-profit Christian agency.

**Area served:** Residents of California.

**Requirements:** Single or married; if married, marriage must be of at least 2 yr. duration.

**Fees:** $1000 includes application, home study, and post-placement supervision for U.S.; $1500 for intercountry.

**Number of children placed last year:** 100.

**Description of children:** Waiting U.S. and foreign-born children of all ages.

**Adoption procedure:**
 1) Attend orientation;
 2) complete Pre-Adopts;
 3) participate in intake interview;
 4) attend home study group sessions;
 5) participate in individual interviews;
 6) have buddy family visit;
 7) home visit.

**Average length of time between application and start of home study:** 0-1 mos.

**Average length of time to complete home study:** 2-3 mos.

**Number of interviews:** 7 group and 4 individual.

**Home study description:** A combination of group and individual meetings with some peer counseling to evaluate a family's warmth, stability and desire to nurture.

**Average wait for a child after approval of a home study:** 6-12 mos.

**Foster care:** None.

★ 66 ★
**The Family Network, Inc.**
284 Foam St., No. 103
Monterey, CA 93940
Phone: (408) 655-5077
(800) 888-0242
Fax: (408) 655-3811

**Branch address:**
  Premier Bldg., Ste. 320, 9378 Olive St., St. Louis, MO 63132
  Phone: (314) 567-0707

**Contact:** Luke W. Leonard, MSW.

**Date established:** 1979.

**Description:** Not-for-profit, tax deductible, Missouri licensed child placing agency. Also licensed in California.

**Area served:** U.S. residents.

**Requirements:** Adults between the ages of 25-50 yrs. who are in good health and have adequate income.

**Fees:** Approx. $10,000-$20,000 includes social services, attorney fees, foster care, medical costs, travel, etc.

**Number of children placed last year:** Approx. 75.

**Description of children:** U.S. infants and special needs, foreign (China, Guatemala, Colombia, India, and Russia).

**Adoption procedure:**
 1) Telephone inquiry;
 2) write letter of intent;
 3) attend personal interviews (if possible);
 4) complete home study;
 5) if approved, placement;
 6) post-placement reports.

**Average length of time between application and start of home study:** 0-1 mos.

**Average length of time to complete home study:** 4-6 wks.

**Number of interviews:** 3.

**Home study description:** Comprehensive evaluation of applicant(s)' family life.

**Average wait for a child after approval of a home study:** 1-24 mos.

**Foster care:** Temporary.

★ 67 ★
**Future Families, Inc.**
3233 Valencia Ave.
Aptos, CA 95003
Phone: (408) 662-0202
Fax: (408) 662-3321

**Branch address:**
  1671 The Alameda, Ste. 201, San Jose, CA 95126
  Phone: (408) 298-8789

**Contact:** Adoption intake worker.

**Date established:** 1984.

**Description:** Non-profit private agency licensed in the South San Francisco and Monterey Bay areas.

**Area served:** Residents of Alameda, Monterey, San Benito, San Mateo, Santa Clara and Santa Cruz counties.

**Requirements:** Flexible.

**Fees:**
Application: $35;
if gross income exceeds $65,000, fee: $800 (negotiable).

**Number of children placed last year:** 15.

**Description of children:** Special needs, emotionally/behaviorally disordered.

**Adoption procedure:**
 1) Application;
 2) home study;
 3) 25 hrs. of training;
 4) if approved, placement;
 5) post-placement services and participation in support group.

**Average length of time between application and start of home study:** 1-6 mos.

**Average length of time to complete home study:** 1 mo.

**Number of interviews:** 5.

**Home study description:** Full and comprehensive study, which among others, evaluates emotional stability. Families are required to attend 25 hrs. of training and monthly support groups following placement.

**Average wait for a child after approval of a home study:** 1-6 mos.

**Foster care:** Temporary, long-term and therapeutic.

### ★68★
### Hand In Hand Foundation
187 Helen Ct.
Santa Cruz, CA 95065
Phone: (408) 476-1866

**Contact:** Fred Barnes, Director.

**Date established:** 1972.

**Description:** Private child placement agency specializing adoption of children with special needs and permanent treatment foster homes.

**Area served:** Residents of California.

**Requirements:** None.

**Fees:** Home Study: $500.

**Number of children placed last year:** 8.

**Description of children:** Children with special needs many of whom come from a history of abuse.

**Adoption procedure:** 1) Application; 2) training; 3) placement; 4) on-going follow-up.

**Average length of time between application and start of home study:** Less than 1 mo.

**Average length of time to complete home study:** 4 mos.

**Number of interviews:** Unavailable.

**Home study description:** Follows guidelines set by the State of California.

**Average wait for a child after approval of a home study:** 1 - 6 mos.

**Foster care:** Long-term and permanent.

### ★69★
### Help The Children, Inc.
41 W. Yokuts Ave., Ste. 107
Stockton, CA 95207-5722
Phone: (209) 478-5585
Fax: (209) 478-5586

**Contact:** Lois Paul, Executive Director.

**Date established:** 1987.

**Description:** Private, not-for-profit, adoptive-parent-led child placing agency licensed by the State of California.

**Area served:** Residents of the US and Canada.

**Requirements:** Varies with program.

**Fees:** Application: $400-600; home study: $1000; foreign program: $1500; domestic: sliding scale.

**Number of children placed last year:** 25.

**Description of children:** Primarily foreign-born children.

**Adoption procedure:** Unavailable.

**Average length of time between application and start of home study:** Less than 1 mo.

**Average length of time to complete home study:** 2-3 mos.

**Number of interviews:** Minimum of 4.

**Home study description:** Follows guidelines set by the California Department of Human Services and the Immigration and Naturalization Service.

**Average wait for a child after approval of a home study:** 6 - 24 mos.

**Foster care:** None.

### ★70★
### Holy Family Services, Counseling and Adoption
155 N. Occidental Blvd.
Los Angeles, CA 90026
Phone: (213) 387-1600
(800) 464-2367
Fax: (213) 381-7804

**Branch address:**
1403 S. Main St., Santa Ana, CA 92707
Phone: (714) 835-5551

**Contact:** David Ballard, LCSW, Executive Director.

**Date established:** 1949.

**Description:** Non-profit, non-sectarian private agency licensed by the California Dept. of Health.

**Area served:** Residents of Los Angeles, Orange, Ventura, San Bernardino, and Riverside Counties.

**Requirements:** Couples married at least 2 yrs. who are practicing some religion. Singles are considered on an individual basis.

**Fees:** 11% of family's gross income at time of application up to a maximum of $9000. Fees may be reduced or waived under special circumstances.

**Number of children placed last year:** 60.

**Description of children:** Infants and toddlers, some who were of mixed race or who had physical handicaps.

**Adoption procedure:**
1) Register;
2) attend orientation meeting;
3) participate in 2-session workshop;
4) submit application;
5) complete home study;
6) if approved, placement;
7) 6 mos. post-placement supervision with 4 visits;
8) finalization.

**Average length of time between application and start of home study:** 1 mo. or less.

**Average length of time to complete home study:** 3-6 mos.

**Number of interviews:** 4.

**Home study description:** An evaluation to determine if an applicant couple is stable enough to provide a loving home for a child.

**Average wait for a child after approval of a home study:** 6-12 mos.

**Foster care:** Temporary.

### ★71★
### Indian Child And Family Services
41811 Johnston
Hemet, CA 92544
Phone: (909) 671-8832

**Contact:** Ron Woods.

**Date established:** 1980.

**Description:** Full service, private child placing agency licensed by the State of California.

**Area served:** Residents of southern California.

**Requirements:** Applicants must be enrolled members of federally recognized tribes.

**Fees:** None except for infant adoption where fees are based on a sliding scale.

**Number of children placed last year:** 15.

**Description of children:** Native American children from infancy to 12 yrs.

**Adoption procedure:** 1) Pre-application; 2) home study; 3) pre-placement visits; 4) placement; 5) 1 yr. post-placement supervision; 6) finalization.

**Average length of time between application and start of home study:** Less than 1 mo.

**Average length of time to complete home study:** 3 mos.

**Number of interviews:** 4.

**Home study description:** Follow guidelines set by the California Department of Human Services with the addition of tribal verification.

**Average wait for a child after approval of a home study:** 12-24 mos.

**Foster care:** Temporary.

★ 72 ★
**Infant of Prague Adoption Service**
6059 N. Palm Ave.
Fresno, CA 93704
Phone: (209) 447-3333
Fax: (209) 447-3322

**Contact:** Judith A. Casson, MSW, Director.

**Date established:** 1953.

**Description:** Non-profit, private agency licensed in the State of California.

**Area served:** Residents of 11 central valley counties of California: Fresno, Inyo, Kern, Kings, Madera, Mariposa, Merced, Sacramento, San Joaquin, Stanislaus, and Tulare.

**Requirements:** Couples married at least 3 yrs. who are age appropriate to the child placed.

**Fees:** $5500 flat fee for home study and placement services, plus 3% of gross income up to a maximum of $3000.

**Number of children placed last year:** 27.

**Description of children:** 21 Infants and 6 children from 18 mos. to 9 yrs., including 1 sibling set of 3, 20 Anglo, 5 Hispanic, 1 Black-Hispanic, and 1 Black-Anglo.

**Adoption procedure:**
 1) Attend general information group;
 2) submit preliminary application;
 3) attend 5 sessions of educational group;
 4) home visit;
 5) if approved, placement;
 6) 4 supervisory visits;
 7) finalization.

**Average length of time between application and start of home study:** 1-6 mos.

**Average length of time to complete home study:** 3-4 mos.

**Number of interviews:** 4.

**Home study description:** Process which requires fingerprint clearances, medical reports and references among others but which emphasizes informing the adoptive couple about family building through adoption.

**Average wait for a child after approval of a home study:** 6-12 mos.

**Foster care:** Pre-adoptive.

★ 73 ★
**International Christian Adoptions**
41475 Rider Way, No.2
Temecula, CA 92590
Phone: (909) 695-3336

**Contact:** Janice Moore.

**Date established:** 1990.

**Description:** Non-profit, private child placing agency licensed by the State of California.

**Area served:** Residents of the U.S.

**Requirements:** Varies by program.

**Fees:** Application: $500; home study, relinquishment and post-placement supervision: $2500.

**Number of children placed last year:** 70.

**Description of children:** Foreign-born and U.S. children, some of whom had special needs.

**Adoption procedure:** 1) Inquiry; 2) orientation at which time the remainder of the program is outlined.

**Average length of time between application and start of home study:** Less than 1 mo.

**Average length of time to complete home study:** 4-6 mos.

**Number of interviews:** 4.

**Home study description:** Information given at the time of orientation.

**Average wait for a child after approval of a home study:** Varies with program selected.

**Foster care:** None.

★ 74 ★
**Kinship Center**
30 Ragsdale Dr., Ste. 210
Monterey, CA 93940-5758
Phone: (408) 649-3033
Fax: (408) 649-4843

**Contact:** J. Carol Biddle, MSW, Executive Director.

**Date established:** 1984.

**Description:** Non-profit private child-placing agency licensed in the State of California. Also hosts monthly support groups for adoptive parents, birth parents, and foster parents.

**Area served:** Residents of Monterey and San Benito counties.

**Requirements:** Flexible.

**Fees:** $0-$5000.

**Number of children placed last year:** 35.

**Description of children:** U.S. and foreign-born infants, prescoolers, school age and special needs children.

**Adoption procedure:**
 1) Telephone inquiry;
 2) attend informational meeting;
 3) file application;
 4) participate in interview with agency staff;
 5) complete home study;
 6) if approved, placement;
 7) post-placement contact (individual and support group);
 8) finalization.

**Average length of time between application and start of home study:** 1 mo. - 1 yr. Special needs adoptions have priority.

**Average length of time to complete home study:** 2-4 mos.

**Number of interviews:** 4-5 individual and 5 educational groups.

**Home study description:** Follows guidelines set by the State of California.

**Average wait for a child after approval of a home study:** Varies by program.

**Foster care:** Pre-adoptive, therapeutic and respite care.

### ★ 75 ★
**Life Adoption Services**
440 W. Main St.
Tustin, CA 92680
Phone: (714) 838-5433
Fax: (714) 838-1160

**Contact:** Joan LeJeune.

**Date established:** 1985.

**Description:** Non-profit private agency licensed in California.

**Area served:** Residents of California.

**Requirements:** Flexible.

**Fees:**
Registration fee: $100;
home study: $1600;
post-placement services: $1000.

**Number of children placed last year:** Apprx. 80.

**Description of children:** Domestic and foreign-born children.

**Adoption procedure:**
1) Telephone inquiry for registration packet and application;
2) submit application;
3) complete home study;
4) if approved, study sent overseas;
5) foreign agency sends child referral;
6) if family is agreeable, immigration and travel arrangements are made;
7) placement;
8) 6 mos. post-placement services;
9) finalization.

**Average length of time between application and start of home study:** 1 mo. or less.

**Average length of time to complete home study:** 2 mos.

**Number of interviews:** 4.

**Home study description:** Call or write for outline.

**Average wait for a child after approval of a home study:** 6-12 mos.

**Foster care:** None.

### ★ 76 ★
**North Bay Adoptions**
Lakewood Village Shopping Center
9068 Brooks Road S.
Windsor, CA 95492
Phone: (707) 837-0277
Fax: (707) 837-0280

**Contact:** Blaine Goodwin or Sidne Goodwin, Adoption Coordinators.

**Date established:** 1991.

**Description:** Non-profit, international corporation licensed by the State of California as a child placing agency.

**Area served:** Residents of Alameda, Colusa, Contra Costa, Lake, Marin, Mendocino, Napa, San Francisco, Solano, Sonoma and Yolo counties.

**Requirements:** Applicants must be at least 25 yrs. old and a U.S. citizen, single or if married, at least 1 yr.

**Fees:** Application: $150; home study: $2400; pre-adoption education classes: $450. Financial assistance is available in the form of low interest loans to qualified applicants through a special lending program with a local bank.

**Number of children placed last year:** 6.

**Description of children:** Foreign-born children between the ages of 4 mos. and 14 yrs.

**Adoption procedure:** 1) Application; 2) pre-adoption classes; 3) compile dossier; 4) home study and country selection; 5) dossiers sent to foreign country; 6) child referral; 7) placement; 8) post- placement supervision; 9) finalization.

**Average length of time between application and start of home study:** 1-6 mos.

**Average length of time to complete home study:** 2 days to 1 yr. depending upon family's needs. The average is 3 mos.

**Number of interviews:** 3 for single applicants; 4 for married applicants.

**Home study description:** Assessment which covers such topics as background information, type of child desired, marriage, if applicable, religion, adoption and fertility issues, parenting abilities, home and community, finances and employment history, physical, mental and emotional health and includes summary of references and social worker's recommendation.

**Average wait for a child after approval of a home study:** 6-12 mos.

**Foster care:** None.

### ★ 77 ★
**Partners for Adoption**
4527 Montgomery Dr., Suite A
Santa Rosa, CA 95405
Phone: (707) 539-9068
(800) 956-0212
Fax: (707) 539-9466

**Mailing address:**
P.O. Box 2791, Santa Rosa, CA 95405

**Contact:** Rose Marie Nielsen.

**Date established:** 1983.

**Description:** Non-profit agency licensed in 10 counties in northern California.

**Area served:** Residents of Alameda, Contra Costa, Lake, Marin, Mendocino, Napa, San Francisco, San Mateo, Solano, and Sonoma counties.

**Requirements:** Applicants must possess the desire and ability to parent.

**Fees:** $6500.

**Number of children placed last year:** 40.

**Description of children:** All types and ages: newborns, special needs, i.e. over age 3, sibling groups, minority, physical or emotionally handicapped; and foreign-born.

**Adoption procedure:**
1) File application;
2) attend 6 pre-adoptive sessions;
3) complete individual home study;
4) child match;
5) meet INS requirements, if intercountry adoption;
6) placement;
7) post-placement services;
8) finalization.

**Average length of time between application and start of home study:** 1-6 mos.

**Average length of time to complete home study:** 2 mos.

**Number of interviews:** 4.

**Home study description:** Home study is a description of the existing family and physical home setting and an evaluation of background, marriage (if applicable), medical and financial status, police clearance and fingerprinting.

**Average wait for a child after approval of a home study:** 12-24 mos.

**Foster care:** Fost-Adopt; certify families for foster care.

★ 78 ★

**Sierra Adoption Services**
123 Nevada St.
Nevada City, CA 95959
Phone: (916) 265-6959
Fax: (916) 265-9223

**Mailing address:**
P.O. Box 361, Nevada City, CA 95959

**Branch address:**
8928 Volunteer Ln., Ste. 240, Sacramento, CA 95826
Phone: (916) 368-5114

**Date established:** 1983.

**Description:** Private, non-profit adoption agency.

**Area served:** Residents of Sacramento, Solano, Yolo, Yuba, Sutter, Butte, San Joaquin, Amador, El Dorado, Placer, Nevada and Sierra.

**Requirements:** Applicants should be at least 21 yrs. old. Single applicants are welcome. Couples should be married at least 1 yr. at the time of application. Income requirements are minimal.

**Fees:** There are no fees to adopt most children. Intercountry and fee based adoptions: $2200 or more.

**Number of children placed last year:** 15.

**Description of children:** Children with special needs.

**Adoption procedure:** 1) Telephone or visit; 2) attend free Exploring Adoption meetings scheduled monthly; 3) begin home study which includes 6 wks. of Exploring Adoption 2; 4) make formal application; 5) complete intake interview; 6) home visits; 7) upon approval of home study, begin child search and matching: 9) pre-placement visitation: 10 ) placement; 11)finalization.

**Average length of time between application and start of home study:** Formal application occurs as part of the home study process.

**Average length of time to complete home study:** 4-6 mos.

**Number of interviews:** Approx. 4.

**Home study description:** Families participate in an in-depth exploration of adoption issues and how to be a successful parent of a child who has suffered traumatic losses.

**Average wait for a child after approval of a home study:** After successful completion of home study, up to one year.

**Foster care:** Fost-adopt and temporary.

# COLORADO

## STATUTES

★ 79 ★

**Independent placement by intermediary?** No.
**Independent placement by birth parents?** Permitted.
**Subsidies provided?** Medical, maintenance and some non-recurring legal.

**Adoption cost defined by law?** No.
**Insurance for infertility?:** Unknown.
**Home study required by state?** Required before placement.
**Prospective adoptive parent advertise for a child?** Permitted.
**Surrogacy laws?** Not addressed in law.
**Residents access agencies of other states or countries?** Yes, but the home study must be conducted by a licensed Colorado agency.
**Requires judicial termination of birth parents' rights?** Required by both parents, if known.
**Time given to a birthmother to revoke her consent:** None unless fraud or duress can be proved in which case there is a 70 day redress period.
**Court handling adoptions?** District Court.
**Adoption of Native Children:** Tribe has primary agency.
**Adoption records sealed?** Sealed, but at age 21 yrs. adoptees may access non-identifying information or petition the court to appoint an intermediary who searches the records and seeks the consent of the individual named in the petition to reveal identifying information or arrange contact.
**Photo-listing book available?** Participant in the
**Rocky Mountain Adoption Exchange** photo listing.

## PUBLIC AGENCIES

★ 80 ★

**Colorado State Department of Social Services**
1575 Sherman St.
Denver, CO 80203-1714
Phone: (303) 866-3209
Fax: (303) 866-2214

**Branch address:**
Adams County, 7190 Colorado Blvd., Commerce City, CO 80022
Phone: (303) 287-8831

Alamosa County, P.O. Box 1310, Alamosa, CO 81101
Phone: (719) 589-2581

Arapahoe County, 1400 W. Littleton Blvd., Littleton, CO 80120
Phone: (303) 795-4850

Archuleta County, P.O. Box 240, Pagosa Springs, CO 81147
Phone: (303) 264-2182

Baca County, 772 Colorado St., Springfield, CO 81073
Phone: (719) 523-4131

Bent County, Box 326, Las Animas, CO 81054
Phone: (719) 456-2620

Boulder County, 3400 Broadway, Boulder, CO 80304
Phone: (303) 441-1000

Chaffee County, P.O. Box 1007, Salida, CO 81201
Phone: (719) 539-6627

Cheyenne County, P.O. Box 146, Cheyenne Wells, CO 80810
Phone: (719) 767-5629

Clear Creek County, Box 2000, Georgetown, CO 80444

Phone: (303) 569-3251

Conejos County, P.O. Box 68, Conejo, CO 81129
Phone: (719) 376-5455

Costilla County, Box 249, San Luis, CO 81152
Phone: (719) 672-4131

Crowley County, Courthouse Annex, P.O. Box 186, Ordway, CO 81063
Phone: (719) 267-3546

Custer County, Courthouse, Westcliffe, CO 81252
Phone: (719) 783-2371

Delta County, Courthouse Annex, 560 Dodge St., Delta, CO 81416
Phone: (303) 874-2030

Denver County, 2200 W. Alameda, Denver, CO 80223
Phone: (303) 727-3666

Dolores County, Courthouse, P.O. Box 485, Dove Creek, CO 81324
Phone: (303) 677-2250

Douglas County, 401 S. Wilcox, Castle Rock, CO 80104
Phone: (303) 688-4825

Eagle County, P.O. Box 660, Eagle, CO 81631
Phone: (303) 328-8840

Elbert County, P.O. Box 6, Simla, CO 80835
Phone: (719) 541-2369

El Paso County, P.O. Box 2692, Colorado Springs, CO 80901
Phone: (719) 444-5530

Fremont County, Box 631, Canon City, CO 81212
Phone: (719) 275-2318

Garfield County, 109 8th St., No. 306, Glenwood Springs, CO 81602
Phone: (303) 945-9191

Gilpin County, 280 Jankowski Dr., Black Hawk, CO 80422
Phone: (303) 582-5444

Grand County, Box 204, Hot Sulphur Spring, CO 80451
Phone: (303) 725-3331

Gunnison County and Hinsdale County, 200 E. Virginia, Gunnison, CO 81230
Phone: (303) 641-3244

Huerfano County, 121 W. 6th St., Walsenburg, CO 81089
Phone: (719) 738-2810

Jackson County, P.O. Box 338, Walden, CO 80480
Phone: (303) 723-4750

Jefferson County, 900 Jefferson County Pkwy., Golden, CO 80401-6010
Phone: (303) 277-1388

Kiowa County, Box 187, Eads, CO 81036
Phone: (719) 438-5541

Kit Carson County, 251 16th St., Ste. 101, Burlington, CO 80807
Phone: (719) 346-8732

Lake County, P.O. Box 884, Leadville, CO 80461
Phone: (719) 486-0772

La Plata County, 1060 E. 2nd Ave., Durango, CO 81301
Phone: (303) 382-6150

Larimer County, 1501 Blue Spruce Dr., Ft. Collins, CO 80524-2000
Phone: (303) 498-6300

Las Animas County, 204 S. Chestnut St., Trinidad, CO 81082
Phone: (719) 846-2276

Lincoln County, P.O. Box 37, Hugo, CO 80821
Phone: (719) 743-2404

Logan County, Box 1746, Sterling, CO 80751
Phone: (303) 522-2194

Mesa County, P.O. Box 20000-5035, Grand Junction, CO 81502
Phone: (303) 241-8480

Mineral County, P.O. Box B, Del Norte, CO 81132
Phone: (719) 657-3381

Moffat County, 595 Breeze St., Craig, CO 81625
Phone: (303) 824-8282

Montezum County, 109 W. Main, Rm. 203, Cortez, CO 81321
Phone: (303) 565-3769

Montrose County, P.O. Box 216, Montrose, CO 81402
Phone: (303) 249-3401

Morgan County, P.O. Box 220, Ft. Morgan, CO 80701
Phone: (303) 867-8291

Otero County, Box 494, La Junta, CO 81050
Phone: (719) 384-2280

Ouray County, P.O. Box M, Ouray, CO 81427
Phone: (303) 325-4437

Park County, P.O. Box 156, Fairplay, CO 80440
Phone: (719) 836-2771

Phillips County, 246 S. Interocean, Holyoke, CO 80734
Phone: (303) 854-2280

Pitkin County, 0405 Castle Creek Rd., No. 8, Aspen, CO 81611
Phone: (303) 920-5350

Prowers County, P.O. Box 1157, Lamar, CO 81052
Phone: (719) 336-7486

Pueblo County, 212 W. 12th St., Pueblo, CO 81003
Phone: (719) 583-6160

Rio Blanco County, Box 688, Meeker, CO 81641
Phone: (303) 787-5011

Rio Grande County, P.O. Box B, Del Norte, CO 81132

Phone: (719) 657-3381

Routt County, P.O. Box 772790, Steamboat Springs, CO 80477
Phone: (303) 879-1540

Saguache County, P.O. Box 215, Saguache, CO 81149
Phone: (719) 655-2537

San Juan County, 1060 E. 2nd Ave., Durango, CO 81301
Phone: (303) 387-5631

San Miguel County, P.O. Box 96, Telluride, CO 81435
Phone: (303) 728-4411

Sedgwick County, 106 W. 1st, P.O. Box 27, Juleburg, CO 80737
Phone: (303) 474-3397

Summit County, Courthouse, Box 326, Breckenridge, CO 80424
Phone: (303) 453-2561

Teller County, P.O. Box 9033, Woodland Park, CO 80866-9033
Phone: (719) 687-6268

Washington County, Courthouse, Akron, CO 80720
Phone: (303) 345-2238

Weld County, P.O. Box A, Greely, CO 80631
Phone: (303) 352-1551

Yuma County, 310 Ash, Wray, CO 80758
Phone: (303) 332-4877

**Contact:** Barbara Killmore.

**Date established:** C. 1935.

**Description:** Public supervising agency. Counties provide direct service.

**Area served:** Residents of the State of Colorado.

**Requirements:** Adults, 21 yrs. and older.

**Fees:** $500 maximum.

**Number of children placed last year:** Approx. 348.

**Description of children:** 90% were children with special needs.

**Adoption procedure:** Procedures vary from county to county. Colorado law stipulates that applicants file petition within 30 days after adoptive placement and that the placement be supervised for a minimum of 6 mos. before finalization. In the case of adoption of children with special needs supervision of placement usually extends for 1 yr.

**Average length of time between application and start of home study:** Varies.

**Average length of time to complete home study:** 2-3 mos.

**Number of interviews:** 4.

**Home study description:** Assessment of applicant(s)' childhood and background, health, financial capability to meet present needs, home and environment and capacity to parent.

**Average wait for a child after approval of a home study:** Varies.

**Foster care:** Temporary, short and long-term and permanent.

## PRIVATE AGENCIES

★81★
**Adoption Alliance**
3090 S. Jamaica Ct., No. 106
Aurora, CO 80014
Phone: (303) 337-1731

**Contact:** Virginia Appel, Executive Director.

**Date established:** 1989.

**Description:** Private, non-profit child placing agency licensed by the State of Colorado.

**Area served:** Residents of Colorado for domestic adoptions and U.S. residents for international adoptions.

**Requirements:** Flexible.

**Fees:** Pre-Application: $50; formal application: $100; home study: $1000. Processing fees vary by program. Post-placement and court fees for domestic adoptions. International agency/attorney fees for international adoptions.

**Number of children placed last year:** 92.

**Description of children:** Infants, children with special needs and foreign-born children.

**Adoption procedure:** 1) Preliminary application; 2) formal application; 3) home study; 4) processing; 5) placement; 6) post-placement supervision; 7) finalization.

**Average length of time between application and start of home study:** Less than 1 mo.

**Average length of time to complete home study:** 4 - 6 wks.

**Number of interviews:** 4-6.

**Home study description:** Follows Child Welfare League of America standards and addresses such issues as family's emotional stability, marital stability, experience with children, parenting goals and techniques.

**Average wait for a child after approval of a home study:** 6-12 mos.

**Foster care:** Temporary, long-term and permanent.

★82★
**Adoption Choice Center**
1119 N. Wahsatch Ave., Ste. 2
Colorado Springs, CO 80903
Phone: (719) 444-0198

**Contact:** Ellen Levy, MSSW, LCSW, Director.

**Date established:** 1990.

**Description:** Private, for-profit child placement agency licensed by the State of Colorado.

**Area served:** Residents of the US.

**Requirements:** Open.

**Fees:** Application: $500; home study: $1250; total fees: $10,000 approx.

**Number of children placed last year:** 25.

**Description of children:** Healthy newborn infants.

**Adoption procedure:** 1) Inquiry; 2) aaplication; 3) home study. Small agency which conducts semi-open, designated and interstate adoptions.

**Average length of time between application and start of home study:** Less than 1 yr.

**Average length of time to complete home study:** 1 mo.

**Number of interviews:** 3-5.

**Home study description:** Assessment which addresses such issues as motivation for adoption, personal history, marital relationship, experience and philosophy of child rearing, home and community.

**Average wait for a child after approval of a home study:** 6-12 mos.

**Foster care:** Temporary.

### ★ 83 ★
**The Adoption Option, Inc.**
2600 S. Parker Rd., Ste. 2-320
Aurora, CO 80014
Phone: (303) 695-1601
(800) 878-1601
Fax: (303) 695-1626

**Branch address:**
7625 W. 5th Ave., Lakewood, CO 80226

**Contact:** Carol Holliday.

**Date established:** 1981.

**Description:** Private, nonprofit agency licensed by the Colorado Dept. of Social Services.

**Area served:** Residents of Colorado.

**Requirements:** Couples married at least 1.5 yrs. at the beginning of the home study and are at least 25 yrs. old at the beginning of home study.

**Fees:**
Application fee: $100;
home study fee: $1800 (sliding scale for minority program);
post-placement fee: $1000;
birthparent counseling: $3000;
crisis intervention: $4700.

**Number of children placed last year:** 49.

**Description of children:** Primarily white and minority infants; some older children and children with special needs.

**Adoption procedure:**
1) Telephone inquiry;
2) attend informational meeting: 4 possible (non-mandatory);
3) complete home study;
4) if approved, non-identifying profile of adoptive family presented to birthparents for family selection for their child;
5) placement.

**Average length of time between application and start of home study:** 1 mo. or less.

**Average length of time to complete home study:** 2 mos.

**Number of interviews:** Usually 4 including 1 home visit.

**Home study description:** An assessment and educational process which looks at personal history, financial and emotional ability to support a child, health, views on parenting, comfort level with adoption as a means of family building and teaches prospective adoptive parents about adoption issues.

**Average wait for a child after approval of a home study:** 12-24 mos. for Anglo child; children of color wait usually much shorter.

**Foster care:** Temporary.

### ★ 84 ★
**Adoptions: Advocacy and Alternatives**
2500 S. College
Ft. Collins, CO 80525
Phone: (303) 493-5868

**Branch address:**
1115 Seventh St., Greeley, CO 80525

**Contact:** Joanne F. Gallagher, L.C.S.W., Placement Supervisor.

**Date established:** 1992.

**Description:** Private, non-profit, non-sectarian child placing agency licensed in the State of Colorado.

**Area served:** Residents of Colorado; Designated adoption: U.S.

**Requirements:** Married couples must be younger than 45 yrs,. in good health and have sufficient income to support a child.

**Fees:** Application: $500; home study: $3500; birth parent counseling: $3500; birth parent support: $2500 or more.

**Number of children placed last year:** 17.

**Description of children:** Primarily infants and a few children with special needs.

**Adoption procedure:** Client directed adoptions: 1) placement agreement; 2) placement; 3) file for adoption; 4) post-placement services; 5) adoption finalization.

**Average length of time between application and start of home study:** 1 - 6 mos.

**Average length of time to complete home study:** 2 mos.

**Number of interviews:** 4 - 6.

**Home study description:** Assessment and educational process which includes 2 day-long workshops, interviews and home visit, foster care certification, parent and child care training.

**Average wait for a child after approval of a home study:** 12 - 24 mos.

**Foster care:** Temporary and pre-adoptive.

### ★ 85 ★
**Bethany Christian Services of Colorado**
2140 S. Ivanhoe St., Ste. 106
Denver, CO 80222
Phone: (303) 758-4484

**Contact:** Deborah Jost, Director.

**Date established:** 1977.

**Description:** Non-profit, private agency licensed by the Colorado Dept. of Social Services.

**Area served:** Residents of Colorado and Wyoming.

**Requirements:** Vary by program.

**Fees:** Vary by program.

**Number of children placed last year:** 27.

**Description of children:** U.S. infants, some with special needs.

**Adoption procedure:**
1) Initial inquiry;
2) submit preliminary application;
3) admission to waiting list;
4) file formal application;
5) complete assessment and education;
6) if approved, placement;
7) post-placement supervision;
8) finalization.

**Average length of time between application and start of home study:** 1-6 mos.

**Average length of time to complete home study:** 1 mo.

**Number of interviews:** 4-6.

**Home study description:** Complete family assessment which includes recommendation of references, medical and financial reports. Education is an integral part of the process.

**Average wait for a child after approval of a home study:** 12-24 mos.

**Foster care:** Agency provides licensed foster care through county Dept. of Social Service.

★ 86 ★

**Catholic Community Services of Colorado Springs**
29 W. Kiowa St.
Colorado Springs, CO 80903
Phone: (719) 636-2345
Fax: (719) 636-1216

**Contact:** Susan Massa, MSW.

**Date established:** 1987.

**Description:** Non-profit private agency.

**Area served:** Residents of the Diocese of Colorado Springs.

**Requirements:**
1) Traditional program:
Must be at least 21 yrs. of age and married at least 2 yrs.;
2) Designated program:
No specific requirements.

**Fees:** Sliding fee scale available for low-income families.

**Number of children placed last year:** 10.

**Description of children:** Caucasian and minority infants, older/waiting children.

**Adoption procedure:**
1) File application;
2) complete home study;
3) if approved, placement;
4) supervisory period; and
5) finalization.

**Average length of time between application and start of home study:** 1-6 mos.

**Average length of time to complete home study:** 2 mos.

**Number of interviews:** 4-6.

**Home study description:** Evaluation of health, background and family attitudes, psychological and marital stability and attitudes toward adoption.

**Average wait for a child after approval of a home study:** 12-24 mos.

**Foster care:** Temporary.

★ 87 ★

**Chinese Children Adoption International**
1100 W. Littleton Blvd.
Littleton, CO 80120
Phone: (303) 347-2224

**Date established:** 1992.

**Description:** Private, non-profit child placing agency licensed by the State of Colorado.

**Area served:** Residents of the U.S. Home study and post-placement services: Colorado residents only.

**Requirements:** Applicants must be between the ages of 35 and 50 yrs.

**Fees:** Preliminary Application: $50; formal application: $100; home study: $850 (Colorado residents only); orientation and training: $450 (Colorado residents only); post-placement supervision/legal: $500 (Colorado residents only); translation: $650; Chinese representative service: $800; international postage: $200; international telephone calls and FAX: $350; administration: $450; international travel and miscellaneous expenses extra. Chinese Government and Orphanage: adoptee rearing fee: $3000 (approx.); child placement: $1000.

**Number of children placed last year:** 11.

**Description of children:** Chinese children from 3 - 20 mos.

**Adoption procedure:** 1) Pre-application; 2) formal application; 3) orientation; 4) FBI/INS filing; 5) home study and dossier authentication; 6) translation; 7) dossier sent to China; 8) dossier approval; 9) child match; 10) travel to China; 11) visit child; 12) sign agreement; 12) registration and notarization; 13) adoption finalized; 14) child's passport; 15) travel to Guangzhou; 16) visa and physical exam for child; 17) return to U.S.; 18) translation; 19) post-placement supervision; 20) adoption validation; 21) naturalization.

**Average length of time between application and start of home study:** Less than 1 mo.

**Average length of time to complete home study:** 1-2 mos.

**Number of interviews:** 5.

**Home study description:** Assessment which includes references, interviews and home visit and addresses such topics as social history, children already in the family, marriage and family life, health, finances and employment history, home and community, adoption issues, child rearing and discipline and cross-cultural issues.

**Average wait for a child after approval of a home study:** 1 - 6 mos.

**Foster care:** None.

★ 88 ★

**Christian Family Services of Colorado, Inc.**
1399 So. Havanna St., Ste. 204
Aurora, CO 80012
Phone: (303) 337-6747

**Contact:** Pamela A. Fincher.

**Date established:** 1985.

**Description:** Private, non-profit child placing agency licensed by the State of Colorado.

**Area served:** Residents of the U.S.

**Requirements:** Christian, married couples.

**Fees:** Application: $75. Total fees: $6000, but can be reduced depending upon income.

**Number of children placed last year:** 10-15.

**Description of children:** Primarily infants.

**Adoption procedure:** Unavailable.

**Average length of time between application and start of home study:** Less than 1 mo.

**Average length of time to complete home study:** 1 mo.

**Number of interviews:** 4-6.

**Home study description:** Unavailable.

**Average wait for a child after approval of a home study:** 12-24 mos.

**Foster care:** Temporary.

★ 89 ★

**Colorado Adoption Center**
2801 S. Remington, Ste. 2040
Ft. Collins, CO 80525
Phone: (303) 223-8409

**Branch address:**
4175 Harlan, Ste. 101, Wheat Ridge, CO 80033
Phone: (303) 467-3128

**Contact:** Julie Haralson.

**Date established:** 1985.

**Description:** Non-profit, private agency licensed in the State of Colorado.

**Area served:** Residents of Colorado.

**Requirements:** Requirements vary with program selected.

**Fees:** Vary with program selected.

**Number of children placed last year:** Unavailable.

**Description of children:** Primarily infants of all races, in domestic and foreign programs.

**Adoption procedure:** Call or write for outline.

**Average length of time between application and start of home study:** 1 mo. or less.

**Average length of time to complete home study:** Varies.

**Number of interviews:** Varies with program.

**Home study description:** Educational and evaluatory process which assesses the quality of the applicant's relationships.

**Average wait for a child after approval of a home study:** Varies.

**Foster care:** Temporary.


★90★

**Colorado Christian Services**

4796 S. Broadway
Englewood, CO 80110
Phone: (303) 761-7236

**Branch address:**

Colorado Christian Services - Oklahoma P.O. Box 3600, Oklahoma City, OK 73136-2000

**Contact:** Devonne Carter, Placement Supervisor.

**Date established:** 1963.

**Description:** Private, non-profit agency licensed both in Colorado and Oklahoma.

**Area served:** Residents of the U.S. and Canada and U.S. citizens worldwide.

**Requirements:** Applicants must be members of the Church of Christ.

**Fees:** Application: $150; home study: $1050; placement: $5600; education: $300; post-placement: $700.

**Number of children placed last year:** 23.

**Description of children:** Infants.

**Adoption procedure:** 1) Preliminary application; 2) Church Elder reference; 3) formal application; 4) work and personal references; 5) autobiographies; 6) medical history and examination; 7) 2 day educational group; 6) Profile book and home study; 7) placement documents; 8) post-placement supervision; 9) finalization.

**Average length of time between application and start of home study:** 1-6 mos.

**Average length of time to complete home study:** 14- 22 hrs.

**Number of interviews:** 3-4.

**Home study description:** Assessment of family background, religion, marriage, health, communication skills, conflict resolution skills, feelings surrounding infertility, children in the home, education, employment history, preferences in an adoptive child and the child's background.

**Average wait for a child after approval of a home study:** 6 - 24 mos.

**Foster care:** Temporary prior to child's relinquishment.


★91★

**Designated Adoption Services of Colorado, Inc.**

1420 Vance St., Ste. 202
Lakewood, CO 80215
Phone: (303) 232-0234
Fax: (303) 232-0517

**Contact:** Judy O'Connor, MSW or Toni Magle, MSW.

**Date established:** 1988.

**Description:** Non-profit private agency licensed in the State of Colorado.

**Area served:** Residents of U.S. but based in Colorado.

**Requirements:** Couples married at least 2 yrs. who are in good health and who have adequate income to raise a child.

**Fees:** Traditional program: $7000; designated program: $5000.

**Number of children placed last year:** 20.

**Description of children:** Caucasian infants. Sometimes toddlers and special needs children.

**Adoption procedure:**

1) Complete home study;
2) relinquishment counseling for birthparents;
3) placement;
4) post-placement services for 6 mos. - 1 yr.

**Average length of time between application and start of home study:** 1 mo. or less.

**Average length of time to complete home study:** 2 mos.

**Number of interviews:** Approx. 4-5.

**Home study description:** An evaluation of the relationship between husband and wife to determine if adoptive home will be a secure and nurturing environment in which a child should be placed. We discuss many adoption issues, especially open adoption.

**Average wait for a child after approval of a home study:** 12-24 mos.

**Foster care:** Temporary.


★92★

**Friends of Children of Various Nations, Inc.**

1756 High St.
Denver, CO 80218
Phone: (303) 321-8251
Fax: (303) 322-3153

**Contact:** Cheryl L. Markson, Executive Director or Connie Higgins, Administrative Assistant.

**Date established:** 1967.

**Description:** Non-profit private aid and adoption agency licensed for child placement in the State of Colorado. F.C.V.N. also offers relinquishment counseling, post adoption counseling, older child support group, parent support group, and culture camp information for children from India and Korea.

**Area served:** Current programs in India, Vietnam, Columbia, and Costa Rica and waiting children from the U.S. F.C.V.N networks with many agencies for placement of children from a variety of countries. Residents of Colorado processed for all programs. Residents outside of Colorado can be processed for India or Vietnam.

**Requirements:** Adult married or single applicants accepted. All requirements are imposed by child's country of origin.

**Fees:** Preliminary application fee: $50; formal application fee: $150; home study fee is 4% of gross annual income, with upper limit of $3600.

**Number of children placed last year:** Unavailable.

**Description of children:** Children from India, Vietnam, Columbia, Costa Rica, and the U.S. between the ages of 0 and 16 yrs. some of whom have special needs.

**Adoption procedure:**

1) Submit pre-application;
2) attend orientation meeting;
3) file formal application;

4) complete home study;
5) if approved, child offer and assignment;
6) pre-arrival services;
7) arrival;
8) post-placement supervision;
9) finalization.

**Average length of time between application and start of home study:** 1-6 mos.

**Average length of time to complete home study:** 9 wks. plus individual work.

**Number of interviews:** Unavailable.

**Home study description:** Group and individual process.

**Average wait for a child after approval of a home study:** 6-24 mos.

**Foster care:** Temporary.

## ★ 93 ★

**Hand In Hand International Adoptions**
1617 W. Colorado Ave.
Colorado Springs, CO 80904
Phone: (719) 473-8844
Fax: (719) 632-8428

**Branch address:**
   3102 N. Country Club, Tucson, AZ 85716
   Phone: (602) 327-5550

**Contact:** Sharon D'Giallonardo, Programs Coordinator; MaryLee Schupp, Executive Director.

**Date established:** 1977.

**Description:** Private, non-profit child placing agency licensed in the State of Colorado.

**Area served:** Residents of Colorado and networking agency for out-of-state families.

**Requirements:** Haiti: Applicants must be between the ages of 21 and 45 yrs. old. The younger parent may be no less than 18 yrs. older than the adopted child. Single applicants are considered and couples must be married a minimum of 2 yrs. Commonwealth of Independent States (formerly USSR): Applicants must be at least 21 yrs. old.
Thailand: Married couples both of whom are at least 25 yrs. old with a minimum age difference of 15 yrs. between adopted child and the younger parent. No more than 3 children already in the home.
Philippines: Couples married at least 3 yrs. who are between the ages of 25 and 40. The younger parent may be no less than 15 yrs. older than the adopted child. Christian families are preferred.
Chile: Couples married at least 3 yrs. who are between the ages of 30 and 55. The younger parent may be no less than 18 yrs. older than the adopted child. Preference given to childless couples.
Paraguay: Singles older than 35 are accepted. Couples must be married at least 3 yrs. if they are older than 35, 5 yrs. if they are younger than 35 and have a history of infertility problems. Applicants must be between the ages of 30 and 55 yrs.
Costa Rica: Couples married at least 3 yrs. who are between the ages of 25 and 60.
China: Single applicants are accepted. Couples must be married at least 1 yr. Childless couples preferred. Applicants should be 35 yrs. and older. If under 35, infants available with minor medically correctable handicaps.

Guatemala: Singles accepted. Couples must be married at least 2 yrs. Applicants must be between the ages of 21 and 55 with a minimum age difference of 18 yrs. between the younger adoptive parent and the adopted child.

**Fees:** Haiti: $7300-7800. Commonwealth of Independent States: $12,600 (siblings: $17,000). Thailand: $6150. Philippines: $7200. Chile: $16,800-$17,400. Paraguay: $16,800-$17,400. Costa Rica: $9200-$9700. China: $12,100. Guatemala: $14,400.

**Number of children placed last year:** 65.

**Description of children:** Varies with program selected. Some sibling groups, some children with medically correctable special needs.

**Adoption procedure:** 1) Submit application; 2) complete home study; 3) prepare dossier; 4) submit to foreign government for approval; 5) child match and acceptance by adoptive family; 6) travel to child's country of birth may be required; 7) placement; 8) post-placement supervision; 9) finalization; 10) naturalization.

**Average length of time between application and start of home study:** Less than 1 mo.

**Average length of time to complete home study:** 1 mo.

**Number of interviews:** Unavailable.

**Home study description:** Evaluation of background information, medical reports, employment history and references, parenting skills, motivation to adopt and type of child desired.

**Average wait for a child after approval of a home study:** 1 - 24 mos.

**Foster care:** Temporary.

## ★ 94 ★

**Hope's Promise**
309 Jerry St., Ste. 202
Castle Rock, CO 80104
Phone: (303) 660-0277

**Contact:** Paula Freeman, MSW, Executive Director.

**Date established:** May, 1990.

**Description:** Private, non-profit child placing agency licensed by the State of Colorado.

**Area served:** Residents of the U.S.

**Requirements:** Accepts singles. Couples must be married a minimum of 2 yrs. Applicants should be between the ages of 21 and 50 yrs. and have proof of medical insurance. Preference is given to Evangelical Christian applicants.

**Fees:** Application: $75; home study: $1000; Nepal: $5700 - $6500 (Colorado residents); domestic infant: $7300 plus medical and legal; designated: $3400 plus medical and legal; relinquishment counseling for out-of-state placement: $3000; older/special needs: $1000; post-placement: 6 mos.: $950 and 12 mos.: $1200; ICPC Administration: $250.

**Number of children placed last year:** 43.

**Description of children:** Children between the ages of infancy and 15 yrs. most of whom were U.S. born.

**Adoption procedure:** 1) Application; 2) home study; 3) adoption education classes; 4) child referral; 5) placement; 6) post-placement supervision; 7) finalization.

**Average length of time between application and start of home study:** Less than 1 mo.

**Average length of time to complete home study:** 1-3 mos.

**Number of interviews:** Minimum of 5.

**Home study description:** Assessment which addresses such issues as family of origin and background checks, medical background, finances and employment history, education, marriage and family, home and community, motivation to adopt and issues surrounding adoption, type of child desired and philosophy of child rearing.

**Average wait for a child after approval of a home study:** Usually within 1 yr.

**Foster care:** Temporary infant care.

★ 95 ★

**Innovative Adoptions, Inc.**
1850 Race St.
Denver, CO 80206
Phone: (303) 355-2107

**Branch address:**
   Adopt!, Inc.- Montana, Missoula, MT

**Contact:** Wendy Somers.

**Date established:** 1987.

**Description:** Private, non-traditional adoption agency licensed in Colorado and Montana offering programs in traditional/semi-open adoption, designated/parent initiated adoption, foreign adoption and private/independent adoption. "Creating Families" a center for surrogacy provides services in traditional surrogacy, in vitro fertilization, donor surrogacy, and egg donor programs.

**Area served:** Residents of the U.S. for placement. Residents of Colorado and Montana for home studies and post-placement services.

**Requirements:** Open.

**Fees:** Application: $175; home study: $1000. Other fees range from $4500 - $15,000 depending upon program chosen.

**Number of children placed last year:** 33.

**Description of children:** Infants of all ethnicities, some with limited special needs.

**Adoption procedure:** 1) Application; 2) orientation by telephone; 3) home study; 4) selection of profile by birth parent(s); 5) match; 6) birth; 7) relinquishment; 8) placement.

**Average length of time between application and start of home study:** Less than 1 mo.

**Average length of time to complete home study:** 60 days.

**Number of interviews:** 4-6.

**Home study description:** Process of education and assessment combined with support which addresses such issues as home environment, marital stability, resolution of infertility, motivation to adopt, adoption challenges, parenting values and skills and social history.

**Average wait for a child after approval of a home study:** 6-12 mos.

**Foster care:** Temporary.

★ 96 ★

**Lutheran Family Services of Colorado**
363 S. Harlan St.
Denver, CO 80226
Phone: (303) 922-3433
Fax: (303) 922-7335

**Branch address:**
   3707 Parkmoor Village Dr., Colorado Springs, CO 80917
   Phone: (719) 597-0700

   503 Remington, Fort Collins, CO 80524

Phone: (303) 484-5955

**Contact:** Chet Evenson.

**Date established:** 1948.

**Description:** Non-profit private child placing agency licensed in Colorado.

**Area served:** Residents of Colorado.

**Requirements:** Varies depending on program.

**Fees:** Varies by program but averages $6000-$10,000.

**Number of children placed last year:** 60.

**Description of children:** U.S. infants only.

**Adoption procedure:**
   1) Initial interviews;
   2) assessment process;
   3) attend group education series.

**Average length of time between application and start of home study:** 1-6 mos.

**Average length of time to complete home study:** 4 mos.

**Home study description:** Follows Child Welfare League of America guidelines.

**Average wait for a child after approval of a home study:** 6-12 mos.

**Foster care:** Temporary and long-term.

★ 97 ★

**Small Miracles Foundation of the Rockies**
6160 S. Syracuse Way, Ste. 310
Englewood, CO 80111
Phone: (303) 220-7611

**Contact:** Brenda Retrum.

**Date established:** 1992.

**Description:** Private, non-profit child placing agency licensed by the State of Colorado.

**Area served:** Residents of the U.S.

**Requirements:** Married couples who have a documented history of infertility.

**Fees:** Application: $315; home study: $2010; birth mother outreach, birth parent services, adoptive parent services, placement and post-placement services; $9555.

**Number of children placed last year:** 15.

**Description of children:** Infants.

**Adoption procedure:** 1) Application; 2) home study; 3) birth parent/adoptive parent match; 4) birth; 5) placement; 6) post-placement supervision.

**Average length of time between application and start of home study:** 1-6 mos.

**Average length of time to complete home study:** 1 mo.

**Number of interviews:** 3.

**Home study description:** Assessment of medical history, substance abuse, finances, premises inspection, infertility status, finger print and child abuse registry search, autobiographical information, attitudes towards parenting and adoption.

**Average wait for a child after approval of a home study:** 6-12 mos.

**Foster care:** Temporary.

# CONNECTICUT

## STATUTES

★ 98 ★

**Independent placement by intermediary?** Not permitted.

**Independent placement by birth parents?** Not permitted.

**Subsidies provided?** Medical and financial.

**Adoption cost defined by law?** N/A.

**Insurance for infertility?:** No.

**Home study required by state?** N/A.

**Prospective adoptive parent advertise for a child?** Permitted.

**Surrogacy laws?** Unknown.

**Residents access agencies of other states or countries?** Permitted.

**Requires judicial termination of birth parents' rights?** Voluntary relinquishments through the Probate Court, wherein every effort to locate and notify both parents, are recognized.

**Time given to a birthmother to revoke her consent:** 20 days.

**Court handling adoptions?** Probate Court.

**Adoption of Native Children:** Indian Child Welfare Act of 1978 is a federal law.

**Adoption records sealed?** Sealed until an adoptee reaches the age of 18 yrs.

**Photo-listing book available?** *Connecticut Adoption Resource Exchange* Book.

## PUBLIC AGENCIES

★ 99 ★

**Department of Children and Youth Services, CT**
White Hall, Bldg. 2
Undercliff Rd.
Meriden, CT 06450
Phone: (203) 238-6640
(800) 842-6347
Fax: (203) 238-6287

**Contact:** Jean B. Watson, Adoption Services Coordinator.

**Description:** Public, state agency.

**Area served:** Residents of the State of Connecticut.

**Requirements:** Adults, 21 yrs. and older whose health is adequate to parent.

**Fees:** None.

**Number of children placed last year:** 219.

**Description of children:** Children with special needs.

**Adoption procedure:**
1) Applicants for children with special needs participate in group series;
2) applicant for non-special needs children are admitted to waiting list;
3) complete 2 in-home interviews with caseworker;
4) if approved, wait for placement;
5) placement;
6) post-placement supervision;
7) finalization.

**Average length of time between application and start of home study:** 1-6 mos.

**Average length of time to complete home study:** 3-4 mos.

**Number of interviews:** 7 group and 2 individual.

**Home study description:** Educational and evaluative process in which adoptive applicants assist in the writing of their own home studies. Topics covered: parenting skills, birthparents, legal aspects of adoption, stability, applicants' childhoods, background checks, home and community and recommendation of references.

**Average wait for a child after approval of a home study:** 1-6 mos.

**Foster care:** Temporary.

## PRIVATE AGENCIES

★ 100 ★

**Catholic Charities of Hartford**
**Catholic Family Services**
896 Asylum Ave.
Hartford, CT 06105
Phone: (203) 522-8241
Fax: (203) 527-1919

**Branch address:**
220 Colony St., Meriden, CT 06450
Phone: (203) 235-2507

56 Church St., Waterbury, CT 06702
Phone: (203) 755-1196

478 Orange St., New Haven, CT 06511
Phone: (203) 787-2207

**Contact:** Elizabeth A. Went, CISW, Director of Administrative Services.

**Date established:** 1919.

**Description:** Non-profit private agency licensed by the State of Connecticut Dept. of Children and Families and accredited by Council on Accreditation of Services for Families and Children.

**Area served:** Residents of, or employed in, Hartford, Litchfield and New Haven counties.

**Requirements:** Flexible depending on type of adoption. Triad: Traditional, identified, foreign, special needs.

**Fees:** Sliding scale based on graduated percent of real assets with a maximum of $15,000. Triad fees vary for identified and foreign adoptions.

**Number of children placed last year:** 35 (excluding foreign adoptions).

**Description of children:** 32 healthy infants and 3 special needs.

**Adoption procedure:**
1) Register with agency;
2) attend group or individual orientation;
3) return completed primary application;
4) home study;
5) if approved, placement;
6) post-adoption review;
7) finalization. There may be some variation in procedure among the various branches.

**Average length of time between application and start of home study:** 6-12 mos.

**Average length of time to complete home study:** 3-4 mos.

**Number of interviews:** 8.

**Home study description:** Evaluation of social history, finances, police checks, references, autobiographies, medical reports, home check, parental expectations, etc.

**Average wait for a child after approval of a home study:** 12-24 mos.

**Foster care:** Temporary.

**★ 101 ★**
**Catholic Charities of Norwich**
**Catholic Family Services**
11 Bath St.
Norwich, CT 06360
Phone: (203) 889-8346
Fax: (203) 889-2658

**Branch address:**
33 St. John Sq., Middletown, CT 06457

**Contact:** John Smey.

**Date established:** 1928.

**Description:** Non-profit private agency licensed in the State of Connecticut.

**Area served:** Residents of Middlesex, New London, Tolland and Windham counties in Connecticut and a portion of Suffolk County-Fishers Island, NY.

**Requirements:** Couples married 3 or more yrs. who are childless and have a medical diagnosis of infertility and a letter of reference from pastor/minister.

**Fees:** $75 application fee; sliding scale based on 10-15% of total family income.

**Number of children placed last year:** 3.

**Description of children:** Infants.

**Adoption procedure:**
1) Initial inquiry;
2) names added to waiting list;
3) Attend 7 joint interviews;
4) attend 2 individual interviews;
5) submit letters of reference;
6) home visit; and
7) approval process.

**Average length of time between application and start of home study:** 24 or more mos.

**Average length of time to complete home study:** 3 mos.

**Number of interviews:** 8.

**Home study description:** Evaluation of family background; health; employment and finances; religion; home setting and neighborhood; childrearing philosophy and methods of discipline; issues surrounding adoption and birthparents; and expectations for a child.

**Average wait for a child after approval of a home study:** 12-24 mos.

**Foster care:** Temporary.

**★ 102 ★**
**A Child Among Us - The Center for Adoption, Inc.**
2410 New London Tpk.
South Glastonbury, CT 06073
Phone: (203) 657-2467

**Contact:** Lil Flint, Executive Director.

**Date established:** 1993.

**Description:** Non-profit, non-sectarian child placing agency licensed by the State of Connecticut.

**Area served:** Residents of Connecticut.

**Requirements:** Applicants must be at least 23 yrs. old. and willing to meet biological parents.

**Fees:** Application: $150; home study: $1500; placement fees: sliding scale.

**Number of children placed last year:** 11.

**Description of children:** Infants.

**Adoption procedure:** 1) Meet with director; 2) application; 3) home study; 4) birth parent selection; 5) placement; 6) post-placement supervision; 7) finalization.

**Average length of time between application and start of home study:** Less than 1 mo.

**Average length of time to complete home study:** 4-6 wks.

**Number of interviews:** 4.

**Home study description:** Assessment which follows state requirements and addresses such issues as family history, drug and alcohol use, marital history, if applicable, motivation to adopt among others.

**Average wait for a child after approval of a home study:** 6 - 12 mos.

**Foster care:** Temporary.

**★ 103 ★**
**Family And Children's Aid of Mid-Fairfield, Inc.**
9 Mott Ave.
Norwalk, CT 06840
Phone: (203) 972-0093

**Contact:** Anne Facto, C.I.S.W., Manager of Adoption Services.

**Date established:** 1942.

**Description:** Private, non-profit family service agency licensed by the State of Connecticut to place children.

**Area served:** Residents of Connecticut and Massachusetts and Vermont for Korean placements.

**Requirements:** Applicants should be in general good health and of approximately child bearing age.

**Fees:** Application: $100; home study: $1250; placement for U.S. newborns: $20,000; identified program: 7 1/2% of income and range from $3750 - $10,000; out-of-state placements: $1500; Korean program: 10% of income and range from $3750 - $7000 plus Korean fee ($6863) plus airfare.

**Number of children placed last year:** 80.

**Description of children:** Foreign and U.S. born infants.

**Adoption procedure:** 1) Initial interview; 2) adoption group classes; 3) home visit; 4) wait for placement; 5) placement; 6) post-placement supervision; 7) finalization.

**Average length of time between application and start of home study:** Less than 1 mo.

**Average length of time to complete home study:** 2 mos.

**Number of interviews:** 4-6.

**Home study description:** Assessment which addresses issues of background, education, income, employment, child care plans, life style, family relationships, motivation to adopt, philosophy of child rearing and issues surrounding adoption.

**Average wait for a child after approval of a home study:** Foreign placements: 1-6 mos. Domestic placement: 12-24 mos. depending upon birth parents selection.

**Foster care:** Temporary.

**★ 104 ★**
**Franciscan Family Care Center, Inc.**
267 Finch Ave.
Meriden, CT 06451
Phone: (203) 237-8084
Fax: (203) 630-1776

**Mailing address:**
P.O. Box 417, Meriden, CT 06451

**Contact:** Sr. Shaun Vergauwen, F.S.E.

**Date established:** 1978.

**Description:** Non-profit private agency.

**Area served:** Residents of Connecticut.

**Requirements:** Applicants must be Roman Catholic for domestic adoptions.

**Fees:** $950 home study plus post-placement services.

**Number of children placed last year:** Unavailable.

**Description of children:** Infants. Home studies also done for foreign adoptions.

**Adoption procedure:**
1) Attend joint interview;
2) attend individual interviews;
3) home visit.

**Average length of time between application and start of home study:** 1 mo. or less.

**Average length of time to complete home study:** 2 mos.

**Number of interviews:** 4.

**Home study description:** Evaluation of family background, health, education, marital relationship, employment history, attitudes toward parenting and adoption related issues, e.g. birthparents and adoptee search.

**Average wait for a child after approval of a home study:** Varies.

**Foster care:** Temporary.

## ★ 105 ★
**Hall Neighborhood House, Inc.**
**Adoption Services**
52 Green St.
Bridgeport, CT 06608
Phone: (203) 334-3900

**Contact:** Dorothy Jeffries-Anderson, Ed.D, NCC, Director.

**Date established:** 1984.

**Description:** Non-profit private agency licensed in the State of Connecticut.

**Area served:** Residents of the Greater Bridgeport area.

**Requirements:** Applicants must have sufficient income to meet their own needs and have generally good health.

**Fees:** Donations.

**Number of children placed last year:** 2.

**Description of children:** Children from 0-18 yrs. some of whom have special needs, are members of minority groups or siblings.

**Adoption procedure:**
1) Submit application;
2) participate in 8 wk. group study course;
3) complete home study;
4) licensure;
5) child match;
6) pre-placement visits;
7) placement;
8) finalization.

**Average length of time between application and start of home study:** 1-6 mos.

**Average length of time to complete home study:** 4 mos.

**Number of interviews:** 6.

**Home study description:** Evaluation of background, marital relationship and fertility status, parenting skills and motivation to adopt, health, children (if any), and parenting skills.

**Average wait for a child after approval of a home study:** 12-24 mos.

**Foster care:** Temporary and long-term.

## ★ 106 ★
**International Alliance For Children, Inc. (IAC)**
23 S. Main St.
New Milford, CT 06776
Phone: (203) 354-3417

**Date established:** 1975.

**Description:** Non-profit, private child placing agency licensed by the State of Connecticut, Department of Children and Youth Services.

**Area served:** Residents of Connecticut and New York.

**Requirements:** Couples married at least 3 yrs. who are between the ages of 25 and 45 yrs. who are in general good health and who have the minimum of a high school education. Only one previous divorce per spouse is allowable and one spouse must be a U.S. citizen.

**Fees:** Application: $100; home study: $1250; placement: $8500.

**Number of children placed last year:** 13.

**Description of children:** Infants and toddlers.

**Adoption procedure:** 1) Preliminary application; 2) Parent Orientation meeting; 3) intake interview; 4) home study; 5) wait for child match; 6) assignment and acceptance of child; 7) placement; 8) post-placement supervision; 9) finalization; 10) naturalization.

**Average length of time between application and start of home study:** 1-6 mos.

**Average length of time to complete home study:** 4-6 wks.

**Number of interviews:** 5.

**Home study description:** Learning process for both the adoptive applicants and IAC which includes reference interviews, a home visit and addresses such issues as personal history, motivation and preparation for adoption, child rearing ideas and practices, religious practices, financial security, health, special interests, hobbies and talents, issues of adoption and heritage, involvement with the extended family and their reaction to cross-cultural adoption, future plans for the adopted child.

**Average wait for a child after approval of a home study:** 1-6 mos.

**Foster care:** None.

## ★ 107 ★
**Jewish Family Service of Bridgeport**
2370 Park Ave.
Bridgeport, CT 06604
Phone: (203) 366-5438
Fax: (203) 366-1580

**Contact:** Kenneth Hessin, Adoption Coordinator.

**Date established:** 1929.

**Description:** Non-profit private agency licensed in the State of Connecticut.

**Area served:** Residents of Bridgeport, Monroe, Stratford, Easton, Trumbull and some outlying areas.

**Requirements:** Flexible.

**Fees:** Home study: $800. Home study updated: $250.

**Number of children placed last year:** 0.

**Description of children:** N/A.

**Adoption procedure:** Jewish Family Service only does home studies for out-of-state and foreign adoption.

**Average length of time between application and start of home study:** 1 mo. or less.

**Average length of time to complete home study:** 1 mo.

**Number of interviews:** 4.

**Home study description:** Evaluation of background, marital and social history, finances, religion, motivation to adopt, and issues related to childrearing.

**Average wait for a child after approval of a home study:** Varies.

**Foster care:** None.

### ★ 108 ★
**Jewish Family Service of Greater Hartford**
740 N. Main St.
West Hartford, CT 06117
Phone: (203) 236-1927
Fax: (203) 236-6483

**Contact:** Phillip Wiener, Executive Director or Maci Wiener, Supervisor, Adoption Dept.

**Date established:** 1913.

**Description:** Non-profit, private full-service social service agency licensed by the Connecticut Dept. of Children and Youth Services.

**Area served:** Primarily residents of Connecticut; out-of-state if family is willing to travel at least one time to Connecticut.

**Requirements:** Flexible by program. For agency placements, prefer Jewish married couples.

**Fees:** Sliding scale based on family's gross income with a minimum of $5000 and a maximum of $15,000. Fees also vary by type of placement. Average is between $8000 and $12000.

**Number of children placed last year:** 3 direct; about 40 through various sources.

**Description of children:** Latin and Caucasian infants.

**Adoption procedure:**
1) Initial inquiry;
2) file application;
3) complete home study;
4) identify child (if identified adoption) or referral to foreign agency;
5) placement;
6) post-placement supervision;
7) finalization.

**Average length of time between application and start of home study:** 1 mo. or less.

**Average length of time to complete home study:** Approx. 2 mos.

**Number of interviews:** 8.

**Home study description:** In-depth psychological evaluation reviewing personal history, marital issues, parenting experience in own family and expectations and extensive discussion of adoption-related issues, e.g., genetic vs. environmental factors, feelings of birthparents and adoptees, biological heritage and search, intercultural aspects, if applicable, and family's readiness to adopt and comfort with adoption as a means of family building.

**Average wait for a child after approval of a home study:** Depends on program.

**Foster care:** Rarely, temporary.

### ★ 109 ★
**Jewish Family Service of New Haven**
1440 Whalley Ave.
New Haven, CT 06515
Phone: (203) 389-5599
Fax: (203) 389-5904

**Contact:** Intake worker.

**Description:** Non-profit private family service agency.

**Area served:** State of Connecticut.

**Requirements:** Flexible.

**Fees:**
Home study: $1200;
total agency fees average $7000 when JFS provides all services.

**Number of children placed last year:** 20.

**Description of children:** Children of all ages, domestic and foreign born.

**Adoption procedure:** Call and request information. We will see people to get started as soon as they feel ready to a start a home study.

**Average length of time between application and start of home study:** 1 mo. or less.

**Average length of time to complete home study:** Usually 2-4 mos.

**Number of interviews:** Dependent on group or individual study.

**Home study description:** Mix of group and individual sessions, with an educational focus.

**Average wait for a child after approval of a home study:** 6-12 mos.

**Foster care:** Short-term infant if direct placement is not indicated.

### ★ 110 ★
**Lutheran Social Services of New England, Inc. Connecticut**
2139 Silas Pease Hwy., Ste. 201
Rocky Hill, CT 06067
Phone: (203) 257-9899
(800) 286-9889
Fax: (203) 257-0340

**Contact:** Annette Ballou.

**Date established:** 1871.

**Description:** Non-profit, private agency licensed in Connecticut.

**Area served:** Residents of Connecticut.

**Requirements:** Couples married at least 2 yrs. who are at least 25 yrs. old and in good health. Singles accepted for some programs. Other requirements may be imposed by child's country of origin.

**Fees:** International: $1500-$3500 plus additional fees to source. Identified: $7,000-$10,000 plus all allowable expenses.

**Number of children placed last year:** 27.

**Description of children:** Healthy caucasian infants in identified adoptions; children of all ages, some with special needs, from many countries in the international program.

**Adoption procedure:**
1) Initial inquiry;
2) file application;
3) attend 1 group session;
4) complete individual interview process;
5) if approved, child referral.

**Average length of time between application and start of home study:** Less than 1 mo.

**Average length of time to complete home study:** 3 mos.

**Number of interviews:** 1 group and 4-5 individual.

**Home study description:** Assessment of family's ability to parent a foreign-born child and deal with cultural issues.

**Average wait for a child after approval of a home study:** 6-12 mos.

**Foster care:** Short-term for infants going into adoption.

★ 111 ★
**New Haven Family Alliance**
5 Science Park S.
New Haven, CT 06511
Phone: (203) 786-5970

**Contact:** Ray Hall, Supervisor; Abby Savin, Coordinator.

**Date established:** 1993.

**Description:** Private, non-profit social service agency licensed by the Department of Children and Youth Services.

**Area served:** Residents of the Greater New Haven area.

**Requirements:** Follows guidelines set by the State of Connecticut.

**Fees:** None.

**Number of children placed last year:** 5.

**Description of children:** Children with special needs.

**Adoption procedure:** 1) Inquiry; 2) 8-9 wks. training program; 3) paper work, finger printing and protective services check; 4) home study; 5) child match; 6) placement.

**Average length of time between application and start of home study:** 1 - 6 mos.

**Average length of time to complete home study:** Minimum of 1 mo.

**Number of interviews:** 3-4.

**Home study description:** Included in 8-9 wk. training program which addresses parenting issues around discipline, effective child guidance, impact of placement on the family and the child.

**Average wait for a child after approval of a home study:** 6-12 mos.

**Foster care:** Temporary and long-term.

★ 112 ★
**Thursday's Child, Inc.**
227 Tunxis Ave.
Bloomfield, CT 06002
Phone: (203) 242-5941

**Contact:** Iris Arenson Abbot, Executive Director.

**Date established:** 1981.

**Description:** Small personalized non-profit agency licensed by the State of Connecticut.

**Area served:** Residents of Connecticut and out of staters for specific final decree programs.

**Requirements:** Agency's requirements are very flexible but complies with any requirements imposed by cooperating foreign or domestic agencies.

**Fees:**
Application fee: $200;
home study fees are based on a sliding scale;
additional fees for foreign agencies.

**Number of children placed last year:** 25.

**Description of children:** Primarily foreign-born infants, some healthy U.S. infants, and sometimes older children and children with special needs. Licensed and registered in Honduras, China, and Vietnam; placement from other countries available.

**Adoption procedure:**
1) File application;
2) complete home study;
3) wait for placement;
4) placement;
5) post-placement supervision;
6) finalization. As part of its very personalized service, Thursady's Child, Inc. encourages and expects adoptive applicants to participate with other adoptive families as part of the adoption procedure.

**Average length of time between application and start of home study:** 2 mos. or less.

**Average length of time to complete home study:** Few mos.

**Number of interviews:** 3-8.

**Home study description:** Traditional evaluation which in addition to the usual information looks at the applicants' level of commitment through their participation in the adoptive parent network.

**Average wait for a child after approval of a home study:** Varies according to program.

**Foster care:** Rarely.

★ 113 ★
**The Village for Families and Children**
1680 Albany Ave.
Hartford, CT 06105
Phone: (203) 236-4511
Fax: (203) 231-8449

**Branch address:**
110 Main St., Manchester, CT 06040

**Contact:** Janet L. Jackson.

**Date established:** 1809.

**Description:** Non-profit, voluntary, multi-service agency.

**Area served:** Residents of the upper two-thirds of Connecticut.

**Requirements:** Very flexible for special needs placement; more rigid for infant adoption.

**Fees:** Sliding scale.

**Number of children placed last year:** 16.

**Description of children:** 13 older or special needs children and 3 infants.

**Adoption procedure:**
1) Request for service;
2) attend orientation;
3) participate in educational series;
4) intake interview;
5) complete home study;
6) pre-placement visits;
7) placement;
8) post-placement supervision;
9) finalization.

**Average length of time between application and start of home study:** 1-6 mos.

**Average length of time to complete home study:** 3 mos.

**Number of interviews:** 7-10.

**Home study description:** Evaluation of background, marriage, law enforcement and reference checks, health and crisis management, experiences with and expectations of a child in order to determine the family's capacity to parent.

**Average wait for a child after approval of a home study:** 12-24 mos.

**Foster care:** Pre-adoptive.

# DELAWARE

## STATUTES
★ 114 ★

**Independent placement by intermediary?** Not permitted.

**Independent placement by birth parents?** Not permitted.

**Subsidies provided?** Medical/psychological and maintenance.

**Adoption cost defined by law?** N/A.

**Insurance for infertility?:** Yes.

**Home study required by state?** N/A.

**Prospective adoptive parent advertise for a child?** Not permitted.

**Surrogacy laws?** Not addresses in law.

**Residents access agencies of other states or countries?** Yes, but the home study must be conducted by an agency licensed by the Delaware Division of Child Protective Services.

**Requires judicial termination of birth parents' rights?** Voluntary relinquishments to a licensed agency by both parents are recognized.

**Time given to a birthmother to revoke her consent:** 30 day period to revoke parental relinquishment.

**Court handling adoptions?** Family Court.

**Adoption of Native Children:** Delaware has no recognized tribes.

**Adoption records sealed?** Sealed.

**Photo-listing book available?** *DELADOPT* is a monthly listing of children who need or may need adoptive families. There are no photos and not all children are legally free.

## PUBLIC AGENCIES

★ 115 ★
**Division of Family Services**
**Delaware Youth and Family Center**
1825 Faulkland Rd.
Wilmington, DE 19805
Phone: (302) 633-2650
Fax: (302) 633-2652

**Branch address:**
Children's Service Center, 62 Rockford Rd., Wilmington, DE 19806
Phone: (302) 577-3824

Williams Service Center, 805 River Rd., Dover, DE 19901
Phone: (302) 739-4800

Georgetown Service Center, 546 S. Bedford St., Georgetown, DE 19947
Phone: (302) 856-5460

**Contact:** Carol King.

**Description:** Public agency. Division of Family Services welcomes inquiries concerning adoption. In the State of Delaware, however, the state agency is involved only with adoptions of children in DFS foster homes. Others will be advised and referred to the private licensed agencies within the State.

**Area served:** State of Delaware.

**Requirements:** Adults 21 yrs. or older with adequate income to meet the family's needs.

**Fees:** None.

**Number of children placed last year:** 45.

**Description of children:** Children in the custody of the State of Delaware, most of whom have special needs.

**Adoption procedure:** Division of Family Services refers interested prospective adoptive families to private Delaware licensed agencies for home study but does place children with families who have approved home studies.

**Average length of time between application and start of home study:** N/A.

**Average length of time to complete home study:** N/A.

**Number of interviews:** N/A.

**Home study description:** Home studies are conducted by private Delaware licensed agencies.

**Average wait for a child after approval of a home study:** Depends on child's legal status: 1) legally free; 2) petition for termination of parental rights has been filed; or 3) permanency plan has been changed from reunion with birth family to adoption. Children in the first category are placed first while children in the third category may be introduced and begin visitation with a prospective adoptive family, but must wait for placement.

**Foster care:** Emergency shelter, temporary, therapeutic, and long-term.

## PRIVATE AGENCIES

★ 116 ★
**Catholic Charities of Wilmington, Delaware**
4th St. and Greenhill Ave.
Wilmington, DE 19805
Phone: (302) 655-9624

**Mailing address:**
P.O. Box 2610, Wilmington, DE 19805

**Branch address:**
442 S. New St., Dover, DE 19901

21 Chestnut St., Georgetown, DE 19947

1405 Wesley Dr., Ste. 36, Salisbury, MD 21801

**Contact:** Neomi Litonjua, Social Worker.

**Date established:** 1931.

**Description:** Non-profit private agency licensed by the State of Delaware.

**Area served:** Residents of the Delaware counties of Kent, New Castle and Sussex and the Maryland counties of Caroline, Cecil, Dorchester, Kent, Queen Anne, Somerset, Talbot, Wicomico and Worcester.

**Requirements:** Couples married at least 2 yrs. who are no older than 40 yrs. and who are childless. Some requirements may be waived for special needs adoption.

**Fees:**
Application fee: $35;
sliding scale for home study, placement, supervision and finalization services with a range from $2700-$8000.

**Number of children placed last year:** 15.

**Description of children:** Infants, sibling groups and older children of all races. Home studies and supervision conducted for foreign adoptions but no placement.

**Adoption procedure:**
1) Initial inquiry with Director of Children's Services;
2) attend information meeting;
3) complete application materials;
4) complete home study;
5) if approved, placement;
6) supervision; and
7) finalization.

**Average length of time between application and start of home study:** 1-6 mos. for special needs and African-Americans; 24 or more for white infants.

**Average length of time to complete home study:** 2.5 mos.

**Number of interviews:** 6.

**Home study description:** Evaluation of family background, marital relationship, personal and financial stability, emotions surrounding childlessness and motivation to adopt; feeling toward birthparents and adoptees.

**Average wait for a child after approval of a home study:** 24 or more mos.

**Foster care:** Primarily temporary, some long-term.

---

# DISTRICT OF COLUMBIA

## STATUTES

★ 117 ★

**Independent placement by intermediary?** No.

**Independent placement by birth parents?** Permitted to the 3rd degree of consanguity.

**Subsidies provided?** Maintenance, medical and non-recurring legal.

**Adoption cost defined by law?** No.

**Insurance for infertility?:** Unknown.

**Home study required by state?** Required before placement if child is born out of D.C. and after placement if the child is born in DC.

**Prospective adoptive parent advertise for a child?** No law addresses it.

**Surrogacy laws?** No law addresses it.

**Residents access agencies of other states or countries?** Permitted provided home study is conducted by a licensed D.C. agency.

**Requires judicial termination of birth parents' rights?** Voluntary consents by both birth parents which are notarized are recognized.

**Time given to a birthmother to revoke her consent:** Only set aside for good cause under the *Best Intention of the Child* statute.

**Court handling adoptions?** Superior Court.

**Adoption of Native Children:** In compliance with the ICWA.

**Adoption records sealed?** Sealed.

**Photo-listing book available?** In progress.

## PUBLIC AGENCIES

★ 118 ★
**Child and Family Services Division**
**Adoption Resources Branch**
609 "H" St., N.E., 3rd Fl.
Washington, DC 20002
Phone: (202) 724-8602
Fax: (202) 724-4782

**Contact:** Wilfred Hamm.

**Date established:** 1892.

**Description:** Non-profit, public agency.

**Area served:** Residents of Washington, D.C. and those within a 25 mi. radius of Washington in Maryland and Virginia.

**Requirements:** Adults over the age of 21 at the time of application, who are in good health, who have sufficient income to meet the needs of their own family, who have adequate living space for an adopted child and who are either single or married; if married, the marriage must be of at least 1 yr. duration.

**Fees:** None.

**Number of children placed last year:** 163.

**Description of children:** Primarily black infants, toddlers and children with special needs.

**Adoption procedure:**
1) Intake;
2) attend orientation;
3) complete pre-service training;
4) submit completed application;
5) undergo home study;
6) placement;
7) post-placement supervision;
8) finalization.

**Average length of time between application and start of home study:** 1 mo. or less.

**Average length of time to complete home study:** 5 mos.

**Number of interviews:** 2 or more.

**Home study description:** Assessment of parenting capabilities, autobiographical data, finances and health, personal and school references, police and child abuse/neglect clearances; home and environment.

**Average wait for a child after approval of a home study:** 1-6 mos.

**Foster care:** Emergency, short-term, long-term and on-going.

## PRIVATE AGENCIES

★ 119 ★
**Adoption Center of Washington**
1900 M St., N.W.
Washington, DC 20036
Phone: (202) 452-8278

**Contact:** Marlene Drucker, L.C.S.W., Director of Social Services.

**Date established:** 1992.

**Description:** Private, non-profit child placing agency licensed by the District of Columbia's Department of Human Services.

**Area served:** No geographic restrictions.

**Requirements:** Applicants must have health and income adequate to child rearing. Applicants for infants must be younger than 50 yrs.

**Fees:** Application: $500. Home study: $1200. Agency fee: $4500. Foreign fee: $9500 - $13,500.

**Number of children placed last year:** 42.

**Description of children:** Children from Central America, China, Republic of Georgia and Russia from 2 mos. to school age.

**Adoption procedure:** 1) File application; 2) attend meeting, if local resident; 3) submit home study; 4) receive agency acceptance; 5) compile dossier; 6) travel to child's country of origin for placement.

**Average length of time between application and start of home study:** Less than 1 mo.

**Average length of time to complete home study:** 6 wks.

**Number of interviews:** 3.

**Home study description:** Home studies are conducted for residents of the District of Columbia and conform to the standards set by the Department of Human Services.

**Average wait for a child after approval of a home study:** 1 - 6 mos. if documents are already in order at time of application; 6 - 12 mos. otherwise.

**Foster care:** None.

### ★ 120 ★

**Adoption Service Information Agency, Inc. (ASIA)**
7720 Alaska Ave., N.W.
Washington, DC 20012
Phone: (202) 726-7193

**Branch address:**
8555 - 16th St., Ste. 603, Silver Spring, MD 20910

7659 Leesburg Pike, Falls Church, VA 22043

**Contact:** Mary S. Durr, Director of Professional Services.

**Date established:** 1982.

**Description:** Private, non-profit child placing agency licensed by Department of Human Services of the District of Columbia, the Maryland Department of Human Resources and the Virginia Department of Social Services.

**Area served:** Residents of DC, Maryland, North Carolina, Virginia and West Virginia.

**Requirements:** Vary by child's country of origin.

**Fees:** Application: $100; agency fee: $5000 includes home study and post-placement services. Program fees vary by child's country of origin.

**Number of children placed last year:** 101.

**Description of children:** Infants and children from India, Korea, Sri Lanka, Thailand and Uzbekistan.

**Adoption procedure:** 1) Application; 2) group in-take; 3) individual interview; 4) home study; 5) childselection/acceptance; 6) arrival and placement; 7) post-placement supervision; 8) finalization; 9) naturalization.

**Average length of time between application and start of home study:** 1 - 6 mos.

**Average length of time to complete home study:** 3 - 6 mos.

**Number of interviews:** Minimum of 4.

**Home study description:** Assessment of emotional health, finances, community status and stability of marriage, if applicable.

**Average wait for a child after approval of a home study:** Varies by child's country of origin.

**Foster care:** Pre-adoptive.

### ★ 121 ★

**Associated Catholic Charities**
1438 Rhode Island Ave., NE
Washington, DC 20018
Phone: (202) 526-4100
Fax: (202) 526-1829

**Branch address:**
Montgomery County Regional Office, 1504 St. Camillus Dr., Silver Springs, MD
Phone: (301) 434-2550

**Contact:** Any staff in Pregnancy and Adoption Services.

**Date established:** 1922.

**Description:** Non-profit, multi-service, child-placing agency licensed in the District of Columbia.

**Area served:** The Archdiocese of Washington, DC which includes Washington, DC, Calvert, Charles, Montgomery, Prince Georges and St. Mary's counties in Maryland.

**Requirements:**
1) Age: varies with age of child.
2) Marital status: married 3 years; accepts singles.
3) Religion: does not have to be Catholic but must be spiritually-based.

**Fees:** Based on sliding scale: average: $3500.

**Number of children placed last year:** 17.

**Description of children:** Domestic, minority children, some special needs.

**Adoption procedure:**
1) File application;
2) attend intake meeting;
3) complete home study;
4) if approved, placement;
5) post-placement supervision.

**Average length of time between application and start of home study:** 1 mo. or less.

**Average length of time to complete home study:** 6-8 wks.

**Number of interviews:** Minimum of 3.

**Home study description:** Evaluation of individual stability and stability as a couple; motivation to adopt; and their ability to meet the needs of an adopted child.

**Average wait for a child after approval of a home study:** 1-6 mos.

**Foster care:** Temporary for children awaiting permanent placement.

### ★ 122 ★

**Cradle of Hope Adoption Center, Inc.**
1815 B St., NW, Ste. 1050
Washington, DC 20006
Phone: (202) 296-4700

**Contact:** Mary Essley, Director of Social Services.

**Date established:** 1991.

**Description:** Private, non-profit international adoption agency licensed by the District of Columbia.

**Area served:** Residents of the U.S., Canada and Europe.

**Requirements:** Applicants must be between the ages of 30 and 55 yrs. who have adequate income to support a child.

**Fees:** Application: $500; home study: $1500; foreign program fees additional.

**Number of children placed last year:** Unavailable.

**Description of children:** Foreign born children between the ages of 6 mos. and 10 yrs. some with minor special needs or medical issues.

**Adoption procedure:** 1) Application; 2) home study and approval; 3) submission of dossier; 4) child referral and acceptance; 5) travel and placement.

**Average length of time between application and start of home study:** Less than 1 mo.

**Average length of time to complete home study:** 2 mos.

**Number of interviews:** 4.

**Home study description:** Assessment of family background, health, education, employment, description of home and neighborhood, motivation to adopt, attitudes toward birth parents, fiances, experiences with children, child care plans.

**Average wait for a child after approval of a home study:** 1 - 6 mos.

**Foster care:** None.

★ 123 ★
**Family And Child Services of Washington, DC**
929 L St., N.W.
Washington, DC 20001
Phone: (202) 289-1510 x179

**Contact:** Deanna Phelps, L.I.C.S.W., Program Director, Adoption Services.

**Date established:** 1947.

**Description:** Non-profit, private child placing agency licensed in the states of DC, Maryland and Virginia.

**Area served:** Residents within a 50 mi. radius of Washington, DC.

**Requirements:** Flexible.

**Fees:** Home study for healthy infants: 5% of gross annual income not to exceed $2500. Legal fees and police check extra.

**Number of children placed last year:** 30.

**Description of children:** African-American infants, 50% of whom have special needs.

**Adoption procedure:** 1) Application; 2) join waiting list for infants 10-12 mos.; 3) home study; 4) selection of child; 5) pre-placement visits; 6) placement; 7) post-placement supervision; 8) finalization.

**Average length of time between application and start of home study:** Less than 1 mo.

**Average length of time to complete home study:** 3-5 mos.

**Number of interviews:** 3-4.

**Home study description:** Assessment which includes references, medical checks, police and protective services checks, income and expenses.

**Average wait for a child after approval of a home study:** 1-6 mos.

**Foster care:** Temporary.

★ 124 ★
**Lutheran Social Services**
4406 Georgia Ave., N.W.
Washington, DC 20011
Phone: (202) 723-3000
Fax: (202) 723-3303

**Branch address:**
7401 Leesburg Pike, P.O. Box 3363, Falls Church, VA 22403
Phone: (703) 698-5026

7410 New Hampshire, Takoma Park, MD 20912
Phone: (301) 434-0080

**Contact:** Roselyn Williams, Director of Adoption Services.

**Date established:** 1917; Adoption Department: 1956.

**Description:** Non-profit, private multi-service agency.

**Area served:** Residents within a 50 mi. radius of Washington, DC, including Maryland and Virginia.

**Requirements:** Applicants should be age appropriate to the child placed; can be single or married, if married, marriage should be of at least 2 yrs. duration.

**Fees:**
Application: $100;
home study: $1050;
post-placement fee: $600.

**Number of children placed last year:** 101.

**Description of children:** U.S. infants and older children, some with special needs. Home studies for international and interstate adoptions.

**Adoption procedure:**
1) File application;
2) attend orientation meeting;
3) complete materials in application packet;
4) undergo home study process;
5) placement;
6) post-placement services;
7) finalization.

**Average length of time between application and start of home study:** 1 mo. or less.

**Average length of time to complete home study:** 6-8 wks.

**Number of interviews:** 4.

**Home study description:** Assessment of background information, health and finances, religion, hobbies, marital relationship and any previous marriages, police and Child Abuse Registry clearances, parenting capability, home visit and interviews with others in the home, recommendation of references, motivation to adopt and type of child requested, guardianship plan in event of parents' untimely death, understanding of adoption, feelings toward birthparents who choose adoptive placements for their children, daily routine of family, worker's evaluation and agency's recommendation.

**Average wait for a child after approval of a home study:** 6-12 mos.

**Foster care:** Temporary.

★ 125 ★
**World Child, Inc.**
4300 Sixteenth St., N.W.
Washington, DC 20011
Phone: (202) 829-5244

**Branch address:**
1400 Spring St., Ste. 410, Silver Spring, MD 20910

**Date established:** 1983.

**Description:** Private, non-profit child placing agency licensed by the District of Columbia.

**Area served:** Citizens of the U.S. both in the U.S. and abroad.

**Requirements:** Open.

**Fees:** Application: $100; home study: $1000; referral fee: $3500 - $5000; foreign fee: $8000 -$13,000.

**Number of children placed last year:** 174.

**Description of children:** Foreign born infants and children some in sibling groups and some with special needs.

**Adoption procedure:** 1) Application; 2) home study; 3) program referral; 4) child search and dossierpreparation; 5) child referral; 6) travel and placement.

**Average length of time between application and start of home study:** Less than 1 mo.
**Average length of time to complete home study:** 3 mos.
**Number of interviews:** 5.
**Home study description:** Home studies conducted for residents of DC only.
**Average wait for a child after approval of a home study:** 1 - 6 mos.
**Foster care:** None.

# FLORIDA

## STATUTES

★ 126 ★

**Independent placement by intermediary?** Permitted.
**Independent placement by birth parents?** Permitted but intermediary services are required.
**Subsidies provided?** Non-recurring costs of adoption reimbursement, medical and maintenance.
**Adoption cost defined by law?** Yes.
**Insurance for infertility?:** No.
**Home study required by state?** A preliminary study is required before placement and a full study before finalization.
**Prospective adoptive parent advertise for a child?** Unknown.
**Surrogacy laws?** Yes.
**Residents access agencies of other states or countries?** Permitted, but must comply with the ICPC and have a licensed child placing agency for reception of child.
**Requires judicial termination of birth parents' rights?** Voluntary consents by both birth parents are recognized.
**Time given to a birthmother to revoke her consent:** Until Juvenile Court termination hearing.
**Court handling adoptions?** Civil Court.
**Adoption of Native Children:** Tribe.
**Adoption records sealed?** Sealed but adoptees, 21 yrs. and older may access non-identifying information.
**Photo-listing book available?** *Florida Waiting Children.*

## PUBLIC AGENCIES

★ 127 ★
**Florida Department of Health and Rehabilitative Services**
2811 Industrial Plaza Dr.
Tallahassee, FL 32308
Phone: (904) 487-2383
**Branch address:**
3300 N. Pace Blvd., P.O. Box 8420, Pensacola, FL 32505
Phone: (904) 444-8685

Ambassador Bldg., 2005 Apalachee Pkwy., Tallahassee, FL 32301
Phone: (904) 488-0506

1001 Madison Ave., Madison, FL 32340
Phone: (904) 488-5072

450 Jenks Ave., Panama City, FL 32401

Phone: (904) 872-7640

6 S. Key St., Quincy, FL 32351
Phone: (904) 627-9531

1000 N.E. 16th Ave., Box 33, Gainesville, FL 32609
Phone: (904) 336-5244

3001 W. Silver Springs Blvd., Ocala, FL 32675
Phone: (904) 620-3257

P.O. Box 52239, Jacksonville, FL 32231
Phone: (904) 359-6169

210 N. Palmetto Ave., Daytona Beach, FL 32114
Phone: (904) 238-4880

11351 Ulmerton Rd., Largo, FL 34648-1630
Phone: (813) 588-3628

7625 Little Rd., New Port Richey, FL 34654
Phone: (813) 841-4146

1425 S.R. 52, Dade City, FL 33525
Phone: (813) 521-1265

1313 Tampa St., Tampa, FL 33602
Phone: (813) 272-3627

200 N. Kentucky, Lakeland, FL 33801
Phone: (813) 680-5550

303 13th Ave. E., Bradenton, FL 33508
Phone: (813) 746-4999

115 U.S. 27 N., Sebring, FL 33870
Phone: (813) 382-2141

1000 Woodcock Rd., Orlando, FL 32805
Phone: (407) 897-4130

705 Avocado Ave., Cocoa, FL 32922
Phone: (407) 690-3765

P.O. Box 60085, Ft. Meyers, FL 33906
Phone: (813) 338-1207

1864 17th St., Sarasota, FL 33577
Phone: (813) 361-6081

1436C Old Dixie Hwy., Vero Beach, FL 32960
Phone: (407) 770-6722

111 Georgia Ave., West Palm Beach, FL 33401
Phone: (407) 837-5446

821 Martin Luther King, Jr. Blvd., Stuart, FL 33494
Phone: (407) 283-3136

1102 S. U.S. 1, Ft. Pierce, FL 34950
Phone: (407) 467-3025

1403 N.W. 40th Ave., Lauderhill, FL 33313
Phone: (305) 797-8384

1150 S.W. 1st St., Miami, FL 33130
Phone: (305) 325-2654

1111 12th St., Key West, FL 33040
Phone: (305) 292-6728

**Contact:** Adoption supervisor or worker.

**Description:** Public, state agency.

**Area served:** Residents of the State of Florida.

**Requirements:** Flexible.

**Fees:** None.

**Number of children placed last year:** Approx. 1200.

**Description of children:** Children with special needs.

**Adoption procedure:** Procedures may vary by district, but follow this general pattern:
1) Attend orientation meeting;
2) submit application;
3) participate in training;
4) undergo individual home study;
5) if approved, wait for placement;
6) placement;
7) post-placement supervision;
8) finalization.

**Average length of time between application and start of home study:** Varies.

**Average length of time to complete home study:** 2.5 - 3 mos.

**Number of interviews:** 6-10 wks. of group and individual training.

**Home study description:** Assessment of applicant(s)' ability to accept and deal with the special needs of the type of child requested.

**Average wait for a child after approval of a home study:** Varies.

**Foster care:** Emergency, short and long-term, pre-adoptive, therapeutic and permanent.


# PRIVATE AGENCIES

## ★ 128 ★
**Adoption By Choice**
4102 W. Linebaugh Ave., Ste. 200
Tampa, FL 33624
Phone: (813) 960-2229

**Contact:** Debra West, Executive Director.

**Date established:** 1989.

**Description:** Non-profit, private child placing agency licensed by the State of Florida.

**Area served:** Residents of the territorial United States.

**Requirements:** Married couples are preferred.

**Fees:** Pre-application: $75; application: $1000; advocating fees: $2000. Placement and birth mother fees additional.

**Number of children placed last year:** 110.

**Description of children:** Infants and toddlers, some with special needs.

**Adoption procedure:** Unavailable.

**Average length of time between application and start of home study:** Less than 1 mo.

**Average length of time to complete home study:** 2 hrs.

**Number of interviews:** 2.

**Home study description:** Assessment which addresses such issues as childhood, financial status, courtship and marriage, church and community involvement, family and relatives, references and law enforcement clearances, personal strengths and weaknesses and attitudes towards adoption.

**Average wait for a child after approval of a home study:** 12 - 24 mos.

**Foster care:** None.


## ★ 129 ★
**Adoption Connection, Inc.**
327 Plaza Real, Ste. 313
Boca Raton, FL 33432
Phone: (407) 367-7429
(800) 892-7429

**Contact:** Judith M. Bailey, Executive Director.

**Date established:** Unavailable.

**Description:** Private, non-profit child placing agency licensed by the State of Florida.

**Area served:** Residents of all U.S. states except Connecticut, Massachusetts and Michigan.

**Requirements:** Open.

**Fees:** Application: $150; home study: $2000. Total costs: $25,000.

**Number of children placed last year:** Unavailable.

**Description of children:** Infants.

**Adoption procedure:** 1) Application request; 2) application process; 3) home study; 4) birth mother match; 5) birth and surrender; 6) post-placement supervision; 7) finalization.

**Average length of time between application and start of home study:** 1-6 mos.

**Average length of time to complete home study:** 1 mo.

**Number of interviews:** 4.

**Home study description:** Assessment of family and home, ability to parent, references, finances and medical reports.

**Average wait for a child after approval of a home study:** 6-12 mos.

**Foster care:** None.


## ★ 130 ★
**A Bond of Love Adoption Agency**
2520 Tamiami Tr.
Sarasota, FL 34239
Phone: (813) 957-0064
(800) ABL-4-LIFE

**Contact:** Suzanne Martin, Executive Director.

**Date established:** 1992.

**Description:** Private, non-profit child placing agency licensed by the State of Florida.

**Area served:** Residents of the U.S.

**Requirements:** Married couples must be at least 25 yrs. old.

**Fees:** Application: $50; home study: $1500; Agency service fee: $15,000.

**Number of children placed last year:** 34.

**Description of children:** Infants.

**Adoption procedure:** 1) Adoptive couple send ABL *Dear Birth Mother* letter; 2) birth mother chooses adoptive family; 3) living and medical expenses agreement; 4) birth and placement; 5) post-placement supervision; 6) finalization.

**Average length of time between application and start of home study:** Less than 1 mo.

**Average length of time to complete home study:** 2-3 wks.

**Number of interviews:** 3-4.

**Home study description:** Assessment which includes criminal and abuse clearances, references from friends and employers, credit check, driving record and interviews with caseworker.

**Average wait for a child after approval of a home study:** 6-12 mos.

**Foster care:** Temporary.

---

★ 131 ★
**Catholic Charities Bureau, Inc.**
P.O. Box 543
St. Augustine, FL 32085
Phone: (904) 829-6300

**Contact:** Rebecca Stringer.

**Date established:** 1975.

**Description:** Non-profit private child-placing agency licensed by the State of Florida that provides home study services for foreign adoptions and independent adoptions.

**Area served:** Residents of Flagler, Putnam and St. Johns counties.

**Requirements:** Adults no older than 65 yrs. who are in good physical and psychological health, who can provide 5 references, and who can provide financial support and adequate living space for a child. Additional requirements for healthy, white infants: couples married at least 2 yrs. who are between the ages of 21 and 42 yrs., who are infertile and have no more than 1 child.

**Fees:** Based on scale.

**Adoption procedure:**
1) File preliminary application;
2) file formal application;
3) complete home study;
4) if approved, placement;
5) post-placement supervision;
6) finalization.

**Average length of time between application and start of home study:** Varies.

**Average length of time to complete home study:** 3 mos.

**Number of interviews:** 4-6.

**Home study description:** Evaluation of autobiographical material, references, financial and medical reports.

**Average wait for a child after approval of a home study:** 24 or more mos.

**Foster care:** Temporary.

---

★ 132 ★
**Catholic Charities: Counseling Services of Collier County**
2210 Santa Barbara Blvd.
Naples, FL 33923
Phone: (813) 455-2655

**Contact:** Edward J. Ullmann, Jr., ACSW, LCSW, Diplomate.

**Date established:** 1976.

**Description:** Private, non-profit child placing agency licensed by the State of Florida and an agency of the Diocese of Venice.

**Area served:** Residents of Collier, Lee and Hendry counties.

**Requirements:** Couples married at least 3 yrs. who are between the ages of 25 and 49 yrs. who have had a recent physical examination, whose income can support another person and who practice a religion.

**Fees:** Application: $500 proposed; home study: $7000 proposed.

**Number of children placed last year:** 5.

**Description of children:** Infants, some with special needs.

**Adoption procedure:** 1) Attend *Facts & Procedures* meeting; 2) application; 3) home study; 4) approval and profile work-up; 5) out-reach training meeting with birth parents; 6) placement; 7) post-placement supervision; 8) finalization.

**Average length of time between application and start of home study:** 6 mos.

**Average length of time to complete home study:** 4 mos.

**Number of interviews:** 10.

**Home study description:** Assessment which addresses such issues as infertility, adoption, openness, birth parents, religion, parenting, finances and adjustment.

**Average wait for a child after approval of a home study:** 12 - 24 or more mos.

**Foster care:** Temporary infant care.

---

★ 133 ★
**Catholic Charities, Diocese of St. Petersburg, Inc.**
6533 9th Ave. N., Ste. 1E
St. Petersburg, FL 33710
Phone: (813) 345-9126
Fax: (813) 347-8140

**Contact:** Charles Beracqua, Director.

**Date established:** 1968.

**Description:** Non-profit child placing agency licensed by the Florida Dept. of Health and Rehabilitative Services.

**Area served:** Residents of Pinellas, Hillsborough, Pasco, Hernando, and Citrus counties.

**Requirements:** Couples married at least 3 yrs. who are between the ages of 25 and 39, in good health, with less than 2 children and medical documentation of fertility problem. If re-applying for a second child, first child must be at least 15 mos. old. Special needs adoption: flexible on some criteria.

**Fees:** $9000. Special needs adoption: fees negotiable.

**Number of children placed last year:** 10.

**Description of children:** Infants with special needs.

**Adoption procedure:**
1) Provide intake information;
2) attend initial interview;
3) file application;
4) complete adoption study;
5) if approved, placement;
6) post-placement supervision; and
7) finalization.

**Average length of time between application and start of home study:** 12-24 mos.

**Average length of time to complete home study:** 3-6 mos.

**Number of interviews:** 6-8.

**Home study description:** Evaluation of emotional stability of applicants and marital stability; acceptance of adopted child and comfort with adoption; and financial stability.

**Average wait for a child after approval of a home study:** 12-24 mos.

**Foster care:** Temporary.

★ 134 ★
## Catholic Community Services
### Archdiocese of Miami - Broward Region
1300 S. Andrews Ave.
Ft. Lauderdale, FL 33316
Phone: (305) 522-2513
Fax: (305) 522-7153

**Contact:** Lee Smith, LCSW, Adoption Services Specialist.
**Date established:** 1957.
**Description:** Non-profit Catholic family service agency.
**Area served:** Residents of Broward County.
**Requirements:** Couples married at least 2 yrs. at time of placement, neither of whom is over 40 yrs. of age at time of application, who practice some religious faith and who have no more than 1 child.
**Fees:** 10% of adjusted gross income with a maximum of $9500.
**Number of children placed last year:** 2.
**Description of children:** Infants.
**Adoption procedure:**
1) File preliminary application;
2) name added to waiting list;
3) complete home study;
4) if approved, placement;
5) 6 mos. post-placement supervision;
6) finalization.
**Average length of time between application and start of home study:** 1-6 mos. for black or biracial infants; 24 or more mos. for healthy white infants.
**Average length of time to complete home study:** 3-4 mos.
**Number of interviews:** 1 home visit and 2 individual.
**Home study description:** In-depth psychological assessment of couple to determine their ability to meet with agency's criteria for eligibility; police and abuse registry checks.
**Average wait for a child after approval of a home study:** 1-6 mos. for black or biracial; 12-24 mos. for white.
**Foster care:** Pre-adoptive.

★ 135 ★
## Catholic Social Services (of Orlando)
1771 N. Semoran Blvd.
Orlando, FL 32807
Phone: (407) 658-1818

**Branch address:**
319 Riveredge Blvd., Ste. 109, Cocoa, FL 32922
Phone: (407) 636-6144

**Contact:** Allan Rettig, Adoption Counselor.
**Date established:** 1962.
**Description:** Private, non-profit child placing agency licensed by the Florida Department of Health and Rehabilitative Services.
**Area served:** Residents of Brevard, Lake, Marion, Orange, Osceola, Polk, Seminole, Sumpter and Volusia counties.
**Requirements:** Couples married at least 5 yrs. who are between the ages of 25 and 40 yrs. and who are active in the church of their choice.
**Fees:** Application: $200; home study: $7000.
**Number of children placed last year:** 24.
**Description of children:** Healthy infants and children with special needs.
**Adoption procedure:** 1) Intake & preliminary application; 2) review; 3) application; 4) home study; 5)placement; 6) post-placement supervision; 7) finalization and Agreed Openness Contracts.

**Average length of time between application and start of home study:** 12 - 24 mos.
**Average length of time to complete home study:** 3 mos.
**Number of interviews:** 4.
**Home study description:** Assessment which addresses such issues as family of origin, marital and family history, finances, criminal/abuse registry checks; employment history, religion, ability to parent, home, attitudes toward adoptive parenting and openness.
**Average wait for a child after approval of a home study:** 12 - 24 mos.
**Foster care:** Temporary.

★ 136 ★
## Catholic Social Services (of Tallahassee)
855 W. Carolina St.
Tallahassee, FL 32309
Phone: (904) 222-2180

**Mailing address:**
P.O. Box 20165, Tallahassee, FL 32309

**Contact:** Mrs. Janet K. Berry, MSW.
**Date established:** 1965.
**Description:** Private, non-profit child placing agency licensed by the Florida Department of Health and Rehabilitative Services.
**Area served:** Residents of Franklin, Gadsden, Jefferson, Leon, Liberty, Madison, Taylor and Wakulla counties.
**Requirements:** Applicants must be at least 25 yrs. old, have sufficient income to meet a child's needs and be in general good health. Other criteria may apply to specific adoption programs.
**Fees:** Application: $0 - $700; home study: $0 - $7800; post-placement supervision: $75/hr.
**Number of children placed last year:** 24.
**Description of children:** U.S. and foreign-born infants.
**Adoption procedure:** 1) Interview with social worker; 2) background and reference checks; 3) counseling for type of child sought; 4) placement; 5) post-placement supervision; 6) finalization.
**Average length of time between application and start of home study:** Less than 1 mo.
**Average length of time to complete home study:** 1 - 6 mos.
**Number of interviews:** 6.
**Home study description:** Process of assessment and self-reflection which addresses such issues as adoptive parent(s)' childhood, interactions, career, marriage (if applicable), child rearing philosophies, attitudes toward adoption and birth parents, suitability to adopt.
**Average wait for a child after approval of a home study:** 12 - 24 mos.
**Foster care:** Temporary.

★ 137 ★
## The Children's Home Society of Florida
3027 San Diego Rd.
Jacksonville, FL 32207
Phone: (904) 396-4084
Fax: (904) 398-6318

**Mailing address:**
P.O. Box 10097, Jacksonville, FL 32207

**Branch address:**
P.O. Box 5616, Jacksonville, FL 32247-5616
Phone: (904) 396-2641

212 Pasadena Pl., Orlando, FL 32803-3828
Phone: (407) 422-4441

5700 - 54th Ave. N., St. Petersburg, FL 33709-2095
Phone: (813) 546-4626

105 N.E. 3rd St., Ft. Lauderdale, FL 33301-1094
Phone: (305) 763-6573

1524 Carson St., Ft. Myers, FL 33901-2598
Phone: (813) 334-2008

401 S.E. 19th Ave., Ocala, FL 34471-2554
Phone: (904) 629-7597

2274 N. U.S. Hwy. 1, Ft. Pierce, FL 34946-8914
Phone: (407) 489-5601

820 E. Park Ave., Bldg. E, Ste. 100, Tallahassee, FL 32301
Phone: (904) 921-0772

201 Osceola Ave., Daytona Beach, FL 32114-6185
Phone: (904) 255-7407

218 Hardee Ln., Rockledge, FL 32955
Phone: (407) 636-0126

842 S. Missouri Ave., Lakeland, FL 33801-4740
Phone: (813) 688-7968

3600 Broadway, West Palm Beach, FL 33407-4889
Phone: (407) 844-9785

800 N.W. 15th St., Miami, FL 33136-1495
Phone: (305) 324-1262

875 Royce St., Pensacola, FL 32503
Phone: (904) 494-5990

**Contact:** Jean S. Price, Vice President of Social Services.

**Date established:** 1902.

**Description:** Non-profit private agency licensed by the Florida Dept. of Health & Rehabilitative Services.

**Area served:** Residents of the State of Florida.

**Requirements:** Adults, 23 yrs. and older who are in reasonably good health.

**Fees:** Fees are based on cost of providing services and can be reduced or waived depending upon the need.

**Number of children placed last year:** 280.

**Description of children:** Healthy and special needs children from 0 to 18 yrs. of white, black, Hispanic and mixed racial backgrounds.

**Adoption procedure:**
1) Attend orientation meeting;
2) file application;
3) complete assessment and preparation for adoption;
4) placement;
5) post-placement supervision.

**Average length of time between application and start of home study:** Varies.

**Average length of time to complete home study:** Approx. 2 mos.

**Number of interviews:** 2 or more.

**Home study description:** A thorough review and understanding of applicants in order to ascertain their ability to parent a child not born to them and the kind of child they can best parent.

**Average wait for a child after approval of a home study:** Depends upon kind of child adoptive parents request.

**Foster care:** Temporary.

★ 138 ★
**Christian Family Services**
2720 S.W. 2nd Ave.
Gainesville, FL 32607
Phone: (904) 378-6202
Fax: (904) 378-6205

**Contact:** Adoption intake.

**Date established:** 1978.

**Description:** Non-profit, private child placing agency licensed by the Florida Dept. of Health and Rehabilitative Services.

**Area served:** U.S. residents.

**Requirements:** Married couples between the ages of 25 and 45 yrs. who are active members of independent Churches of Christ or Christian churches.

**Fees:** Adoption fees vary with an average of $9000.

**Number of children placed last year:** 5.

**Description of children:** Infants.

**Adoption procedure:**
1) Submit application;
2) home study completed by approved agency in applicants' state of residence;
3) attend interview at Christian Family Services;
4) if approved, wait for placement.

**Average length of time between application and start of home study:** 1-6 mos.

**Average length of time to complete home study:** 2-3 mos.

**Number of interviews:** Varies.

**Home study description:** Assessment of each family member's background, psychological/personality testing, financial and medical reports, marital relationship, spiritual life, and childrearing philosophy.

**Average wait for a child after approval of a home study:** 12-24 mos.

**Foster care:** Temporary.

★ 139 ★
**Christian Home and Bible School**
P.O. Box 1017
Mt. Dora, FL 32757
Phone: (904) 383-2155
Fax: (904) 383-3112

**Contact:** Charles W. Shepherd, Director of Social Services.

**Date established:** 1945.

**Description:** Non-profit Florida corporation.

**Area served:** Residents of Florida.

**Requirements:** Christian couples married at least 3 yrs., who are not more than 40 yrs. older than the child they wish to adopt, who are in good physical and mental health, who are financially secure, who are either infertile or who have been advised by a physician not to have children, or who have 3 or more children of one sex and wish to adopt a child of the opposite sex.

**Fees:** 12% combined gross annual income ($3000-$8000 range) which includes $50 initial processing fee and $500 home study fee.

**Number of children placed last year:** 1.

**Description of children:** 1 white.

**Adoption procedure:**
1) File completed application and financial statement;
2) arrange forwarding of 3 references, physician's report, and resumes;
3) complete Child Abuse Registry clearance;
4) complete adoptive study;
5) if approved, placement.

**Average length of time between application and start of home study:** 24 or more mos.

**Number of interviews:** 3.

**Home study description:** The adoptive study will include but not be limited to assessments of both spouses' personal and family histories, life as a couple, spiritual life and child-rearing philosophy.

**Average wait for a child after approval of a home study:** 24 or more mos.

**Foster care:** Temporary and long-term.

★ 140 ★
**Gift of Life, Inc. Adoption Services**
136 Fourth St. N.
St. Petersburg, FL 33704
Phone: (813) 822-5433
(800) 216-LIFE

**Contact:** Lisa Davis, Executive Director.

**Date established:** 1993.

**Description:** Private, non-profit, interdenominational child placing agency licensed by the Pinellas County Department of Health and Rehabilitative Services.

**Area served:** Residents of the State of Florida.

**Requirements:** For Caucasian infant program: Couples married at least 2 yrs. with no more than 2 previous divorces who are between the ages of 23 and 45 yrs.

**Fees:** Caucasian infant program: Pre-Application: $50 (in-state), $50 (out-of-state); application: $750 (in- and out-of-state); home study: $2200 (in-state); home study review: $2200 (out-of-state); placement: $12,000 (in-state), $14,000 (out-of-state); total: $15,000 (in-state), $17000 (out-of-state).

**Number of children placed last year:** 9 (new agency).

**Description of children:** Infants, 3 with special needs.

**Adoption procedure:** 1) Pre-application; 2) formal application and release of information forms; 3) home study; 4) approval of home study and wait for placement; 5) placement; 6) post-placement supervision; 7) finalization.

**Average length of time between application and start of home study:** 1 - 6 mos.

**Average length of time to complete home study:** 3 mos.

**Number of interviews:** 1 - 4.

**Home study description:** The home study is designed to evaluate the suitability of the applicants as adoptive parents, to provide information about the adoption process and adoptive parenting and to answer any questions for the prospective adoptive parents. The process addresses such issues as adoption motivation, family support, health, finances, references, personal, marital and social information and philosophy of parenting. The social worker who conducts the home visit will counsel with the applicants and compile all information which is then presented at a professional staff meeting. All applicants are notified in writing whether or not they have been approved.

**Average wait for a child after approval of a home study:** 12 - 24 mos.

**Foster care:** Temporary and therapeutic.

★ 141 ★
**Hearts & Homes For Children**
858 N. Xavier Ave.
Fort Myers, FL 33919
Phone: (813) 481-4548

**Mailing address:**
P.O. Box 07342, Fort Myers, FL 33919

**Contact:** Beverly McGurk, Executive Director.

**Date established:** 1988.

**Description:** Private, non-profit child placing agency licensed by the Florida Department of Health and Rehabilitative Services.

**Area served:** Residents of Florida.

**Requirements:** Applicants must be either married or single.

**Fees:** Application: $200; home study: based on income. Country fees additional.

**Number of children placed last year:** 14.

**Description of children:** Infants, foreign-born children and children with special needs.

**Adoption procedure:** 1) Application; 2) initial interview; 3) home study; 4) placement; 5) post-placement supervision; 6) finalization.

**Average length of time between application and start of home study:** Less than 1 mo.

**Average length of time to complete home study:** 3 mos.

**Number of interviews:** 3.

**Home study description:** Assessment which covers all areas of functioning: historical, physical, emotional, health finances, communication and others.

**Average wait for a child after approval of a home study:** 6 - 12 mos.

**Foster care:** Rarely.

★ 142 ★
**Jewish Family and Community Services**
3601 Cardinal Point Dr.
Jacksonville, FL 32257
Phone: (904) 448-1933
Fax: (904) 448-0349

**Contact:** Doug Shine, LCSW, Director of Family Services.

**Description:** Non-profit social service agency.

**Area served:** Residents of the local community and by extension some parts of Florida and some sections of the U.S.

**Requirements:** Flexible except for those imposed by the State of Florida and/or a child's country of origin.

**Fees:** Variable based on type of adoption.

**Number of children placed last year:** Agency, independent, and interstate: 43.

**Description of children:** Infants, foreign-born children and children with special needs.

**Adoption procedure:** No children are currently available. Agency will refer to other sources.

**Average length of time between application and start of home study:** 1 mo. or less.

**Average length of time to complete home study:** Always within 2-4 wks.

**Number of interviews:** 1-2.

**Home study description:** Call or write for outline.

**Average wait for a child after approval of a home study:** Variable based on location of child(ren).

**Foster care:** Temporary.

### ★ 143 ★
**Jewish Family Service of Broward County**
6100 Hollywood Blvd.
Hollywood, FL 33024
Phone: (305) 966-0956
Fax: (305) 966-1022

**Branch address:**
8358 W. Oakland Park Blvd., Ste 304, Ft. Lauderdale, FL 33351
Phone: (305) 749-1505

**Contact:** Rosemar Marsten, Supervisor.

**Date established:** 1962.

**Description:** Non-profit private agency licensed by the State of Florida.

**Area served:** Residents of Broward County.

**Requirements:** Jewish married couples who are in good health and who are no more than 40 yrs. older than child placed.

**Fees:** Home study fee: $1000; adoption fee: 10% of income.

**Number of children placed last year:** 1.

**Description of children:** N/A.

**Adoption procedure:** Call or write for outline.

**Average length of time between application and start of home study:** 1-6 mos.

**Average length of time to complete home study:** 1 mo.

**Number of interviews:** 4 including 1 in-home.

**Home study description:** Evaluation of family background, relationships, problem solving ability, health and finances.

**Average wait for a child after approval of a home study:** 12-24 mos.

**Foster care:** Yes.

### ★ 144 ★
**St. Vincent Adoption Services**
18601 S.W. 97th Ave.
Miami, FL 33157
Phone: (305) 255-3978
Fax: (305) 232-3542

**Contact:** Nicole C. Clark, B.A.

**Description:** Non-profit private agency licensed by the Florida Dept. of Health and Rehabilitative Services, accredited by the Council of Services for Families and Children and a member of the Child Welfare League of America and Catholic Charities, USA.

**Area served:** Residents of Dade County.

**Requirements:** Married couples who are at least 25 yrs. old at time of application and no more than 40 yrs. old at time of finalization, who have no more than 2 children, who are in reasonably good health, financially stable and practicing members of the faith of their choice. Requirements for age, marital status and number of children may be waived for special need adoption.

**Fees:** Based on a sliding scale; approx. 10% of gross income.

**Number of children placed last year:** 1.

**Description of children:** U.S. children from 0 to 18 yrs., some with special needs.

**Adoption procedure:**
1) File application;
2) attend orientation meeting;
3) complete home study;
4) participate in individual counseling sessions;
5) referral;
6) placement;
7) post-placement supervision;
8) finalization.

**Average length of time between application and start of home study:** 6-12 mos.

**Average length of time to complete home study:** 6-12 wks.

**Number of interviews:** 4 or more.

**Home study description:** Call or write for outline.

**Average wait for a child after approval of a home study:** 24 or more mos.

**Foster care:** Through Catholic Foster Services.

### ★ 145 ★
**Suncoast International Adoptions, Inc.**
14277 Walsingham Rd.
Largo, FL 34644
Phone: (813) 596-3135
Fax: (813) 593-0106

**Contact:** Jane A. Pearce, Executive Director.

**Date established:** 1981.

**Description:** Non-profit private agency licensed by the Florida Dept. of Health and Rehabilitative Services.

**Area served:** Residents of many areas of Florida.

**Requirements:** Singles or couples married at least 2 yrs., if remarried, at least 5 yrs., who are at least 25 yrs. old, in good health, and at least one of whom is a U.S. citizen.

**Fees:**
Application fee: $75;
home study and post-placement reports: $900;
additional fees to foreign agencies.

**Number of children placed last year:** 30.

**Description of children:** Foreign-born infants and toddlers, some of whom had minor correctable special needs.

**Adoption procedure:**
1) Submit application;
2) attend 3 interviews;
3) law enforcement clearance and Child Abuse Registry check;
4) forward medical reports and references;
5) finger printing and FBI check;
6) prepare dossier and send to INS;
7) referral of child;
8) placement;
9) post-placement supervision;
10) finalization.

**Average length of time between application and start of home study:** 1 mo. or less.

**Average length of time to complete home study:** 45-90 days.

**Number of interviews:** 3.

**Home study description:** Evaluation of description of family, marriage (if applicable), education and occupation, finances and medical information, living arrangements, religion, interests, activities and recommendation of references.

**Average wait for a child after approval of a home study:** 6-12 mos.

**Foster care:** Short-term.

# GEORGIA

## STATUTES

★ 146 ★

**Independent placement by intermediary?** Not permitted.

**Independent placement by birth parents?** Permitted.

**Subsidies provided?** Medical, legal, maintenance and special services.

**Adoption cost defined by law?** Medical and legal costs are defined.

**Insurance for infertility?:** No.

**Home study required by state?** Evaluation required after placement for court report.

**Prospective adoptive parent advertise for a child?** Not permitted.

**Surrogacy laws?** No law addresses it.

**Residents access agencies of other states or countries?** Permitted if in compliance with the ICPC.

**Requires judicial termination of birth parents' rights?** Voluntary surrenders by both birth parents are recognized.

**Time given to a birthmother to revoke her consent:** 10 days.

**Court handling adoptions?** County Superior Court.

**Adoption of Native Children:** Georgia has no recognized tribes.

**Adoption records sealed?** Sealed, but at age 21 yrs. adoptees may access non-identifying information or get permission and request agency to search for identifying information.

**Photo-listing book available?** *My Turn Now.*

## PUBLIC AGENCIES

★ 147 ★
**Division of Family and Children's Services (Georgia)**
**State Adoption Unit**
2 Peachtree St., S.W., Ste. 13-400
Atlanta, GA 30303
Phone: (404) 657-3550
Fax: (404) 657-3624

**Contact:** Anne Jewett, Chief, State Adoption Unit.

**Description:** Public state agency.

**Area served:** Residents of the State of Georgia.

**Requirements:** Applicants must be age appropriate to the child placed, in general good health and have sufficient income to meet their own needs.

**Fees:** None.

**Number of children placed last year:** 582.

**Description of children:** Primarily special needs.

**Adoption procedure:**
1) Initial inquiry to county department in county of applicant's residence;
2) name added to inquiry list for home study;
3) complete home study;
4) if approved, study circulated for child match;
5) once child is identified, placement;
6) post-placement supervision;
7) request releases;
8) obtain Affidavit of Release;
9) file petition in Superior Court;
10) finalization.

**Average length of time between application and start of home study:** 1-6 mos.

**Average length of time to complete home study:** Varies with county office.

**Number of interviews:** Varies with county office; 10 wks. of MAPP plus at least 2 interviews.

**Home study description:** Evaluation of background information and current situation, motivation to adopt and parenting experience and skills; Model Approach to Partnership in Parenting (MAPP) class required.

**Average wait for a child after approval of a home study:** 1-6 mos.

**Foster care:** Temporary and long-term.

## PRIVATE AGENCIES

★ 148 ★
**Adoption Planning, Inc.**
17 Executive Park Dr., Ste. 480
Atlanta, GA 30329
Phone: (404) 248-9105

**Contact:** Rhonda Fishbein, Executive Director.

**Date established:** 1990.

**Description:** Private, non-profit child placing agency licensed by the State of Georgia.

**Area served:** Residents of the U.S. with the exception of New York State.

**Requirements:** Open.

**Fees:** Application: $350; home study: $1200; placement and services fee: $19,800.

**Number of children placed last year:** 27.

**Description of children:** Infants.

**Adoption procedure:** 1) Preliminary application; 2) formal application; 3) home study; 4) wait for selection by birth mother; 5) birth and placement; 6) post-placement supervision; 7) finalization.

**Average length of time between application and start of home study:** 6 - 12 mos.

**Average length of time to complete home study:** 2 mos.

**Number of interviews:** 3.

**Home study description:** Assessment process which includes the compilation of birth and marriage certificates, divorce decrees, if applicable, references, medical reports, financial data, and police clearances and addresses such issues as attitudes toward adoption and parenting issues.

**Average wait for a child after approval of a home study:** 12 - 24 mos.

**Foster care:** Temporary.

★ 149 ★
**Adoption Services, Inc.**
205 W. McDonald St
Pavo, GA 31778
Phone: (912) 859-2654
Fax: (912) 859-2412
**Mailing address:**
P.O. Box 155, Pavo, GA 31778
**Contact:** Roxanne Walker, Administrative Assistant; Janice M. Finch, Executive Director.
**Date established:** 1989.
**Description:** Private, non-profit child placing agency licensed by the State of Georgia.
**Area served:** Residents of Georgia.
**Requirements:** Flexible.
**Fees:** Application: $25; home study: $1000; post-placement: $150; report to court: $250.
**Number of children placed last year:** 46.
**Description of children:** Children with special needs.
**Adoption procedure:** 1) Inquiry; 2) application; 3) caseworker assignment; 4) home study; 5) home study approval and circulation of study; 6) child match; 7) placement; 8) post-placement supervision; 9) finalization.
**Average length of time between application and start of home study:** Less than 1 mo.
**Average length of time to complete home study:** 60 - 120 days.
**Number of interviews:** 3 - 5.
**Home study description:** Assessment which includes description of applicant(s) and marriage (if applicable), criminal clearances, references; and addresses such issues as motivation and readiness to adopt and acceptance of infertility; attitudes of extended family; type of child desired; parenting experience and attitudes about parenting a non-biological child; methods of discipline; finances, home, health and support systems.
**Average wait for a child after approval of a home study:** 1 - 24 mos. depending upon type of child sought.
**Foster care:** None.

★ 150 ★
**Catholic Social Services, Inc. of Atlanta**
680 W. Peachtree St., NW
Atlanta, GA 30308-1984
Phone: (404) 881-6571
Fax: (404) 888-7816
**Contact:** Jean Reiss.
**Date established:** 1973.
**Description:** Non-profit private agency licensed by the State of Georgia.
**Area served:** Residents of the metropolitan Atlanta area.
**Requirements:** Couples one of whom must be 37 yrs. or younger at time of application, who are in good health with a normal life expectancy and who have adequate income to support themselves and an adopted child.
**Fees:** $13,400. Negotiable for special needs placement.
**Number of children placed last year:** Approx. 7.
**Description of children:** Primarily newborn infants.

**Adoption procedure:**
1) File application;
2) participate in group preparation sessions;
3) complete home study;
4) placement.
**Average length of time between application and start of home study:** 1-6 mos.
**Average length of time to complete home study:** 6-8 wks.
**Number of interviews:** At least 2 joint interviews and 1 individual for each family member.
**Home study description:** Assessment of individual, marital, social, financial and medical factors of the prospective adoptive family.
**Average wait for a child after approval of a home study:** 12-24 mos.
**Foster care:** Temporary.

★ 151 ★
**Covenant Care Services**
363 Pierce Ave., Ste. 202
Macon, GA 31204
Phone: (912) 741-9829
(800) 226-5683
**Contact:** Iris Archer, Executive Director.
**Date established:** 1989.
**Description:** Private, non-profit, Christian child placing agency licensed by the State of Georgia.
**Area served:** Residents of the State of Georgia.
**Requirements:** Couples married at least 3 yrs., if married only once, 5 yrs. if in a subsequent marriage, who are between the ages of 25 and 45 yrs. and who are members of the same Christian church.
**Fees:** Pre-application: $25; home study: $500; minority placement: $2000 - $3500; Caucasian placement: $4000 - $6000.
**Number of children placed last year:** 12.
**Description of children:** 51% Caucasian infants; 35% African American infants; 14% biracial infants.
**Adoption procedure:** 1) Pre-application; 2) application; 3) home study; 4) placement; 5) post-placement supervision; 6) petition and consent; 7) finalization.
**Average length of time between application and start of home study:** Between pre-application and home study: 24 or more mos.
**Average length of time to complete home study:** 6 wks. to 3 mos.
**Number of interviews:** 3 - 4.
**Home study description:** Assessment which includes autobiographical and health information, a criminal records check, references and evaluation of home and community; and addresses such issues as spiritual well-being; issues related to infertility, stability of marriage and motivation to adopt.
**Average wait for a child after approval of a home study:** 12 - 24 mos.
**Foster care:** Pre-adoptive and specialized.

★ 152 ★
**Family Partners Worldwide, Inc.**
1776 Peachtree St., NW, Ste. 210 North
Atlanta, GA 30309
Phone: (404) 872-6787

**Contact:** Cathy M. Tench, Director of Clinical Services.

**Date established:** 1982.

**Description:** Private, non-profit agency licensed to place children by the Georgia Department of Human Resources.

**Area served:** No geographical restrictions.

**Requirements:** No agency requirements, but applicants must meet the standards by their state or country of residence as well as the child's custodial state or country.

**Fees:** Application: $500; home study: $2000. Referral, foreign adoption processing, and escort fees (if applicable) are extra.

**Number of children placed last year:** 76.

**Description of children:** Foreign and U.S. born infants and children, some with special needs.

**Adoption procedure:** 1) Successfully complete a home study in state or country of residence; 2) application with all supporting documentation; 3) child referral and acceptance; 4) placement or travel; 5) post-placement supervision; 6) finalization.

**Average length of time between application and start of home study:** Less than 1 mo. (if agency conducts home study).

**Average length of time to complete home study:** 2-4 mos. (if agency conducts home study).

**Number of interviews:** Minimum of 3.

**Home study description:** Assessment which includes description of applicants, family background, home and community, finances and references and addresses such issues as motivation to adopt, experiences with children, parenting skills, family interaction, expectations of child and religion.

**Average wait for a child after approval of a home study:** 6-12 mos.

**Foster care:** Pre-adoptive.

★ 153 ★
**Heart to Heart Adoption Service**
**Lutheran Ministries of Georgia, Inc.**
756 W. Peachtree St. N.E.
Atlanta, GA 30308
Phone: (404) 607-7126
Fax: (404) 875-9258

**Branch address:**
    P.O. Box 318, Gainesville, GA 30503

    Ascension Lutheran Church, Old Canton Rd. and County Line Rd., P.O. Box 12246, Jackson, MS 39211
    Phone: (601) 977-9948

**Contact:** Joyce Hayes, MSW, Program Manager/Adoptions.

**Date established:** 1983.

**Description:** Non-profit, private agency licensed by the Georgia Dept. of Human Resources.

**Area served:** Domestic adoptions: residents of Georgia; international adoptions: primarily Georgia and Mississippi residents but some other out-of-state residents.

**Requirements:** Religious affiliation and active membership required. Child's country of origin may also impose additional requirements.

**Fees:**
Application fee: $100.
Home study: $1,500.
Program fees vary.

**Number of children placed last year:** 59.

**Description of children:** U.S. infants, foreign-born infants and children and children with special needs.

**Adoption procedure:**
1) Attend orientation;
2) file application;
3) complete home study process which may include group and individual sessions;
4) if approved, placement;
5) post-placement supervision;
6) finalization.

**Average length of time between application and start of home study:** 0-1 mos.

**Average length of time to complete home study:** 3-4 mos.

**Number of interviews:** 5-6.

**Home study description:** Assessment of family history, current lifestyle, attitudes, relationships, security, health and home.

**Average wait for a child after approval of a home study:** Varies, depending on country and program.

**Foster care:** Temporary.

★ 154 ★
**HOPE for Children, Inc.**
1511 Johnson Ferry Rd., Ste. 100
Marietta, GA 30062
Phone: (404) 977-0813

**Contact:** David Malutinok, Executive Director; Kent Brand, Director of Social Services.

**Date established:** 1991.

**Description:** Private, incorporated child placing agency licensed by the Georgia Department of Human Resources.

**Area served:** Primarily residents of the State of Georgia.

**Requirements:** Married couples who are active members of a Christian church, in good health with adequate income and one of whom is no older than 45 yrs.

**Fees:** Application: $250; home study: $2500; update fee for out-of-state residents: $500.

**Number of children placed last year:** 7.

**Description of children:** U.S. born infants. International program expanding.

**Adoption procedure:** 1) Telephone orientation session; 2) application; 3) home study; 4) placement; 5) post- placement supervision; 6) finalization.

**Average length of time between application and start of home study:** Less than 1 mo.

**Average length of time to complete home study:** 4 - 6 wks.

**Number of interviews:** 3 - 5.

**Home study description:** Assessment which includes information about marriage, child-rearing and adoption concepts.

**Average wait for a child after approval of a home study:** 12 - 24 mos.

**Foster care:** Temporary.

★ 155 ★
**The Open Door Adoption Agency, Inc.**
116 E. Monroe St.
Thomasville, GA 31792
Phone: (912) 228-6339
(800) 868-6339
Fax: (912) 228-4726

**Mailing address:**
    P.O. Box 4, Thomasville, GA 31792

**Contact:** Mary H. Malone, Executive Director.

**Date established:** 1987.

**Description:** Non-profit private agency licensed by the State of Georgia.

**Area served:** Residents of Georgia for full adoption services and placement of healthy white infants; residents of the U.S. for placement of special needs children.

**Requirements:** Couples married at least 3 yrs., who are at least 25 yrs. old, have no more than 1 child, must demonstrate a personal concern for the spiritual growth of their children in a Judeo-Christian faith and who are willing to house a birthmother. Singles and families with more than one child may apply for special needs children.

**Fees:**
Application fee: $100.
Commitment fee: $2000
Direct Service fee: $16,000 (healthy white infants) or $8000 (special needs).

**Number of children placed last year:** 59.

**Description of children:** Infants and children.

**Adoption procedure:**
1) Participate in 3 required training sessions;
2) complete home study;
3) placement;
4) post-placement supervision.

**Average length of time between application and start of home study:** 1-6 mos.

**Average length of time to complete home study:** 6 wks. - 3 mos.

**Number of interviews:** 3-4.

**Home study description:** An exhaustive evaluation of marriage questionnaires, law enforcement checks, autobiographies, references, adoption related issues and others.

**Average wait for a child after approval of a home study:** 6-24 mos.

**Foster care:** Interim care while waiting placement.

★ 156 ★
**Parent And Child Development Services**
21 E. Broad St.
Savannah, GA 31401
Phone: (912) 238-2777

**Contact:** Patricia Barrett, Director, Adoptions.

**Date established:** Agency: 1801; adoption services: 1947.

**Description:** Private, non-profit adoption service licensed by the Georgia Department of Human Services.

**Area served:** Residents of Bryan, Bulloch, Candler, Chatham, Effingham, Evans, Glynn, Liberty, Long, McIntosh, Screvan, Tattnall and Wayne counties of southeast Georgia for Caucasian infant program; statewide for minority placements.

**Requirements:** Applicants may be single or married and less than 45 yrs. Single applicants must be at least 25 yrs. old.

**Fees:** Application: $200; group training: $300; home study for Caucasian infant program: $1500. Total fees for Caucasian infant program: $11,000.

**Number of children placed last year:** 8.

**Description of children:** 5 Caucasian infants and 3 African American infants.

**Adoption procedure:** 1) Initial inquiry; 2) information meeting; 3) application; 4) 6 wks. group training; 5) home study; 6) placement; 7) 2 mos. post-placement supervision; 8) finalization.

**Average length of time between application and start of home study:** 12 - 24 mos.

**Average length of time to complete home study:** 2 mos.

**Number of interviews:** 3.

**Home study description:** Assessment which includes Child Abuse and Criminal Records checks, references and medical reports and addresses such issues as personal background, previous relationships, financial stability, occupation and education.

**Average wait for a child after approval of a home study:** 6 - 12 mos. for minority placements, 24 or more mos. for Caucasian infant placements.

**Foster care:** Pre-adoptive.

★ 157 ★
**ROOTS, Planting Seeds to Secure Our Future, Inc.**
6600 Old National Hwy.
College Park, GA 30349
Phone: (404) 907-0615

**Contact:** Ms. Toni Oliver, Executive Director.

**Date established:** 1992.

**Description:** Non-profit private child placing agency licensed by the Georgia Department of Human Resources.

**Area served:** Residents of Greater Atlanta.

**Requirements:** Single or legally married adults 25 yrs. or older who are in good health and free of communicable diseases.

**Fees:** None.

**Number of children placed last year:** 11.

**Description of children:** Primarily African American sibling groups of 3 or more who are between the ages of 3 and 16 yrs.

**Adoption procedure:** 1) Inquiry; 2) attend orientation session; 3) MAPP sessions; 4) home visits; 5) pre-placement visitation; 6) placement; 7) post-placement supervision; 8) finalization.

**Average length of time between application and start of home study:** 6 - 12 mos.

**Average length of time to complete home study:** Unavailable.

**Number of interviews:** Minimum of 3.

**Home study description:** Process of education and assessment which includes the family's motivation to adopt, strengths and needs and a mutual determination by the applicant(s) and caseworker of the family's ability to meet the specific needs of a child.

**Average wait for a child after approval of a home study:** 6 - 12 mos.

**Foster care:** None.

# HAWAII

## STATUTES

★ 158 ★

**Independent placement by intermediary?** No.

**Independent placement by birth parents?** Permitted, if the prospective adoptive parent(s) are known to the birth parents.

**Subsidies provided?** Maintenance and medical.

**Adoption cost defined by law?** No.

**Insurance for infertility?** Unknown.

**Home study required by state?** Required only if the court so orders.

**Prospective adoptive parent advertise for a child?** Illegal.

**Surrogacy laws?** Unavailable.

**Residents access agencies of other states or countries?** Permitted.

**Requires judicial termination of birth parents' rights?** Voluntary relinquishment by both birth parents are recognized.

**Time given to a birthmother to revoke her consent:** Until placement. Court approval is required after placement.

**Court handling adoptions?** Family Court.

**Adoption of Native Children:** In compliance with ICWA.

**Adoption records sealed?** Sealed until the adoptee reaches the age of 18 yrs.

**Photo-listing book available?** None.

# PUBLIC AGENCIES

★ 159 ★
**Department of Human Services**
**Family & Adult Services Division**
P.O. Box 339
Honolulu, HI 96809-0339
Phone: (808) 832-5105
Fax: (808) 586-5700

**Branch address:**
East Hawaii Social Services, P.O. Box 1562, Hilo, HI 96721-1562
Phone: (808) 933-4420

Kauai Social Services, P.O. Box 1707, Lihue, HI 96766
Phone: (808) 241-3350

Maui Social Services, 35 Lunalilo St., Wailuku, HI 96793
Phone: (808) 243-5467

West Hawaii Social Services, P.O. Box 230, Captain Cook, Kona, HI 96704
Phone: (808) 323-2022

**Contact:** Intake worker.

**Date established:** 1937.

**Description:** State agency.

**Area served:** Residents of the State of Hawaii.

**Requirements:** Adults.

**Fees:** None.

**Number of children placed last year:** 38-40.

**Description of children:** Mostly children with special needs: older children, drug exposed infants, children who have been abused and/or neglected or who have behavior problems.

**Adoption procedure:** 1) Orientation meeting; 2) application; 3) home study; 4) child referral; 5) placement; 6) post-placement supervision; 7) finalization.

**Average length of time between application and start of home study:** 1-6 mos.

**Average length of time to complete home study:** 2-3 mos.

**Number of interviews:** Minimum of 3-4 with each applicant, couple, and family.

**Home study description:** Assessment which includes family history and stability; health information with physician's report; description of home and environment; finances; reference reports; marital relationship, if applicable; description of all household members including any children; motivation to adopt; childrearing methods and plans to tell adoptee of his/her own adoption.

**Average wait for a child after approval of a home study:** 1-2 mos. depending upon applicant(s)' request and the children available.

**Foster care:** Emergency, short and long-term and permanent.

# PRIVATE AGENCIES

★ 160 ★
**Catholic Services to Families**
200 N. Vineyard Blvd., Ste. 200
Honolulu, HI 96817
Phone: (808) 536-1794

**Date established:** 1947.

**Description:** Private child placing agency licensed by the Hawaii Department of Human Services and accredited by the Council on Accreditation of Service for Families and Children.

**Area served:** Residents of Hawaii.

**Requirements:** Applicants must be in good health and financially able to support a child. Age requirements may be enforced by the child's country of origin.

**Fees:** Application: $85; home study: $800. Other fees are based on a sliding scale.

**Number of children placed last year:** 5.

**Description of children:** Infants and relative placements from the Philippines.

**Adoption procedure:** Varies with adoption program.

**Average length of time between application and start of home study:** 1 - 6 mos.

**Average length of time to complete home study:** 6 wks.

**Number of interviews:** 5.

**Home study description:** Assessment which includes autobiographical information, references and financial information and addresses such issues as marital history, philosophy of childrearing, motivation to adopt, and other issues surrounding adoption.

**Average wait for a child after approval of a home study:** Domestic: 24 or more mos.; international: 6 - 12 mos.

**Foster care:** Temporary and pre-adoptive.

★ 161 ★
**Hawaii International Child**
P.O. Box 240486
Honolulu, HI 96824
Phone: (808) 377-0881
Fax: (808) 373-5095

**Contact:** Intake worker.

**Date established:** 1975.

**Description:** Non-profit private agency licensed by the Hawaii Dept. of Human Services.

**Area served:** U.S.

**Requirements:** Flexible.

**Fees:** Varies. Home study: $950; application: $100.

**Number of children placed last year:** 25.

**Description of children:** U.S. and foreign-born children from infancy to 17 yrs.

**Adoption procedure:**
1) Initial inquiry;
2) submit application;
3) reference and background checks;
4) complete home study;
5) child assignment;
6) post-placement supervision;
7) finalization.

**Average length of time between application and start of home study:** 2 wks.

**Average length of time to complete home study:** 1 wk.

**Number of interviews:** 2.

**Home study description:** Evaluation includes but is not limited to background information, law enforcement clearances, recommendation of references and motivation to adopt.

**Average wait for a child after approval of a home study:** 6-12 mos.

**Foster care:** Emergency.

# IDAHO

## STATUTES

★ 162 ★

**Independent placement by intermediary?** Permitted.

**Independent placement by birth parents?** Permitted.

**Subsidies provided?** Non-recurring, medical and financial.

**Adoption cost defined by law?** Only medical and legal expenses are allowed.

**Insurance for infertility?:** Unknown.

**Home study required by state?** Pre-placement and post-placement studies required.

**Prospective adoptive parent advertise for a child?** Not permitted.

**Surrogacy laws?** Not addressed in law.

**Residents access agencies of other states or countries?** Permitted.

**Requires judicial termination of birth parents' rights?** The written consent in the presence of a judge by both birth parents is recognized.

**Time given to a birthmother to revoke her consent:** None.

**Court handling adoptions?** Magistrate Court.

**Adoption of Native Children:** Compliance with ICWA.

**Adoption records sealed?** Sealed but may remain open at the request of the adoptive parents at the time of the adoption hearing.

**Photo-listing book available?** Participant in the *Northwest Adoption Exchange.*

## PUBLIC AGENCIES

★ 163 ★
**Department of Health and Welfare of Idaho**
**Division of Family and Community Services**
450 W. State St., 3rd Fl.
Boise, ID 83720
Phone: (208) 334-5697

**Branch address:**
Region I, 1250 Ironwood Dr., Ste. 204, Coeur d'Alene, ID 83814
Phone: (208) 769-1515

Region II, 1118 "F" St., Lewiston, ID
Phone: (208) 799-4400

Region III, 111 Poplar, Caldwell, ID 83605
Phone: (208) 459-7456

Region IV, 4355 Emerald St., Boise, ID 83706-2038
Phone: (208) 334-6700

Region V, 601 Poleline Rd., Ste. 1, Twin Falls, ID 83301
Phone: (208) 736-3020

Region VI, 1070 Hiline, Box 4166, Pocatello, ID 83201
Phone: (208) 235-2949

Region VII, 150 Shoup Ave., Ste. 19, Idaho Falls, ID 83402
Phone: (208) 528-5790

**Contact:** Adoption worker.

**Description:** Non-profit, public, state agency.

**Area served:** Residents of the State of Idaho.

**Requirements:** Applicants should be of typical child rearing age, in good health and have sufficient income to support a child.

**Fees:**
Application: $50;
home study: $450 (normal, healthy child through age 3 yrs.);
supervision: $300;
medical cost: $1750;
court report to finalize adoption: $200.
Applicants for older children or children with special needs are eligible for non-recurring adoption reimbursement of up to $2000.

**Number of children placed last year:** 50.

**Description of children:** 1 infant, 15 pre-schoolers, and 34 older children.

**Adoption procedure:**
1) Submit application;
2) complete home study;
3) if approved, child match coordinated at central office;
4) supervision of placement and filing of petition to adopt;
5) finalization.

**Average length of time between application and start of home study:** 1-6 mos.

**Average length of time to complete home study:** Within 3 mos.

**Number of interviews:** Varies.

**Home study description:** Assessment of family background of applicants, biographical information, personality and physical description of applicants, physical aspects of home, education and work history, religion, marital history, motivation to adopt, parenting skills, other household members, health and finances and recommendation of references.

**Average wait for a child after approval of a home study:** Varies.

**Foster care:** Emergency, short and long-term and permanent.

## PRIVATE AGENCIES

**★ 164 ★**
**Children's Aid of Idaho**
2308 N. Cole Rd., Ste. E
Boise, ID 83704
Phone: (208) 376-0558

**Branch address:**
Patty Fonnesback, Counselor, P.O. Box 51, Arimo, ID 83214
Phone: (208) 254-9328

Corie Poulsen, Counselor, 845 Mae Dr., Twin Falls, ID 83301
Phone: (208) 733-7233

Jan Palmer, Counselor, Lewiston, ID
Phone: (208) 743-7653

Krista James, Counselor, Idaho Falls, ID
Phone: (208) 522-9667

**Contact:** Helen Fairbourn, Counselor or Bonnie Capell, Counselor.

**Date established:** 1992.

**Description:** Private, non-profit, non-denominational agency licensed to place children in adoptive homes and to conduct home studies for prospective adoptive parents by the Idaho Department of Health and Welfare.

**Area served:** Residents of Idaho.

**Requirements:** Open.

**Fees:** Application: $100; home study: $600; court report: $200; post-placement services: $100.

**Number of children placed last year:** 2.

**Description of children:** Infants.

**Adoption procedure:** 1) Pre-application report: 2) present adoption petition; 3) adoption petition signed before the court; 4) presentation of court report.

**Average length of time between application and start of home study:** Less than 1 mo.

**Average length of time to complete home study:** Unavailable.

**Number of interviews:** 1 -2.

**Home study description:** Assessment which includes review of applicants birth and marriage certificates, criminal history checks and autobiographies and addresses such issues as applicant(s)' background, medical reports and other pertinent material.

**Average wait for a child after approval of a home study:** 1 - 6 mos.

**Foster care:** None.

**★ 165 ★**
**Christian Counseling Services**
1920 E. 17th St., Ste. 109
Idaho Falls, ID 83404
Phone: (208) 529-4673

**Contact:** Carol Henrie.

**Date established:** 1982.

**Description:** Non-profit counseling and adoption agency licensed by the State of Idaho.

**Area served:** Primarily residents of the State of Idaho, however, applicants whose home studies were completed while they were state residents can still be served if they move.

**Requirements:** The youngest prospective adoptive parent, in any couple, should be no more than 40 yrs. old at time of application and should have no more than 1 child.

**Fees:**
Application: $100.
Home study: $600.
Home study up-date: $200.
Placement fee: $1000 actual legal, medical and foster care costs.

**Number of children placed last year:** 0.

**Description of children:** Primarily U.S. infants.

**Adoption procedure:**
1) Attend explanatory meeting;
2) submit application with references;
3) waiting period for home study;
4) participate in workshop;
5) complete home study;
6) if approved, profiles of first 2 families on waiting list for placement who meet the preferences of the birthmother are shown to her for final selection;
7) placement;
8) 6 mos. post-placement supervision;
9) finalization.

**Average length of time between application and start of home study:** 1 mo. or less.

**Average length of time to complete home study:** 1 mo.

**Number of interviews:** 4.

**Home study description:** Evaluation of background and birth family; personal interests, educational and occupational history, marital history and relationship, religious background and present level of involvement; experience with children and adoption; flexibility and openness; what type of child and what type of background adoptive parents would accept and not accept. From the home study the adoption social worker writes a profile of the prospective adoptive parents to be shown to birthparents.

**Average wait for a child after approval of a home study:** 24 or more mos.

**Foster care:** Temporary.

**★ 166 ★**
**Community Counseling and Adoption Services of Idaho, Inc.**
6054 Emerald St.
Boise, ID 83704
Phone: (208) 322-1262

**Contact:** Carol Walker.

**Date established:** 1984.

**Description:** Non-profit adoption agency licensed to place children in the State of Idaho.

**Area served:** Residents of the State of Idaho.

**Requirements:** Couples married at least 2 yrs. who are below the age of 45 yrs., in good health, with fewer than 2 children and the ability to support another person.

**Fees:**
Application fee: $50;
home study fee: $600;
psychological evaluation fee: $500;
placement fee: $2000.
Adoptive parents also pay for the prenatal care of the birthmother, 6 mos. follow-up therapy for birthmother, if needed, hospital fees, and medical expenses of the infant.

**Number of children placed last year:** 8.

**Description of children:** Infants.

**Adoption procedure:**
1) File application;
2) attend initial interview;
3) complete psychological testing;
4) fingerprinting clearance and reference checks;
5) submit background information and medical and financial reports;
6) home visit;
7) if approved, placement;
8) post-placement supervision; and
9) finalization.

**Average length of time between application and start of home study:** 12-24 mos.

**Average length of time to complete home study:** 3 mos.

**Number of interviews:** 4.

**Home study description:** Home study assesses the suitability of adoptive home and adoptive parents.

**Average wait for a child after approval of a home study:** 6-12 mos.

**Foster care:** Use licensed foster homes, if needed.

**★ 167 ★**
**Idaho Youth Ranch Adoption Services**
7025 Emerald St.
P.O. Box 8538
Boise, ID 83707
Phone: (208) 377-2613
Fax: (208) 377-2819

**Contact:** Jeannie Swenson, LSW, or Marilyn Howard, LSW.

**Date established:** 1983.

**Description:** Non-profit private agency licensed in the State of Idaho for residents of Ada, Bannock, Canyon, Elmore, Gem, Twin Falls and Valley counties.

**Requirements:** Couples married 3 or more yrs., who have no more than 1 child and a medical diagnosis of infertility, who have no more than 3 marriages between both spouses, who are between the ages of 21 and 45 yrs. and whose medical insurance will cover the adopted child from the date of placement.

**Fees:**
Application: $75;
home study: $500;
placement: $2000 plus costs related to prenatal care, legal fees, labor, delivery and medical care for the infant.
Average total fees: $7000.

**Number of children placed last year:** 10.

**Description of children:** 7 infants, 3 foreign-born.

**Adoption procedure:**
1) Submit pre-application Summary Sheet;
2) complete application agreement;
3) undergo home study;
4) if approved, placement;
5) 6 mos. post-placement supervision;
6) finalization.

**Average length of time between application and start of home study:** 12-24 mos.

**Average length of time to complete home study:** 1 mo.

**Number of interviews:** 4.

**Home study description:** The basic information required in a home study includes: verification of age, residence, marriage, physical and mental health, financial stability, attitudes about children, religion, infertility issues, family background, plans to tell child about adoption, and open adoption education.

**Average wait for a child after approval of a home study:** 12-24 mos.

**Foster care:** Temporary; used occasionally as most placements are direct from hospitals.

**★ 168 ★**
**Lutheran Social Services of Washington and Idaho**
2201 Government Way, Ste. J
Coeur d'Alene, ID 83814
Phone: (208) 667-1898

**Contact:** Donna Euler.

**Date established:** 1956.

**Description:** Non-profit, private agency licensed in Idaho and Washington State.

**Area served:** Residents of eastern Washington and northern Idaho.

**Requirements:** Married couples who have a medical diagnosis of infertility and are childless or have only one child.

**Fees:** Fees are charged for application, home study, placement, post-placement supervision, medical and legal costs.

**Number of children placed last year:** 12.

**Description of children:** Primarily healthy infants but some special needs children are occasionally available.

**Adoption procedure:**
1) Return completed interest registration form;
2) admission to waiting list;
3) complete home study;
4) if approved, wait for placement (birthparents participate in selection);
5) placement;
6) post-placement supervision;
7) finalization.

**Average length of time between application and start of home study:** 12-24 mos.

**Average length of time to complete home study:** 1-2 mos.

**Number of interviews:** 2 group and 1-2 individual; 16 hours of group training.

**Home study description:** Group process which offers support, education, an opportunity to meet birthparents, adult adoptees and other adoptive parents. Couples assist in writing their own home studies.

**Average wait for a child after approval of a home study:** 12-24 mos.

**Foster care:** Foster/adopt program available in Washington state.

# ILLINOIS

## STATUTES

**★ 169 ★**

**Independent placement by intermediary?** Permitted.

**Independent placement by birth parents?** Permitted.

**Subsidies provided?** Medical, legal, financial and maintenance.

**Adoption cost defined by law?** Yes.

**Insurance for infertility?:** Unknown.

**Home study required by state?** The court reviews a written investigation after placement.

**Prospective adoptive parent advertise for a child?** Permitted.

**Surrogacy laws?** Not addressed in law.

**Residents access agencies of other states or countries?** Yes.

**Requires judicial termination of birth parents' rights?** Birth parents may consent to the adoption in court.

**Time given to a birthmother to revoke her consent:** None.

**Court handling adoptions?** Circuit Court.

**Adoption of Native Children:** State and tribe through the ICWA.

**Adoption records sealed?** Sealed, but at age 18 yrs.(or younger with parental consent) adoptees may access the court records concerning their own adoption with court sanction.

**Photo-listing book available?** *Adopt Me* published bi-monthly by the Adoption Information Center of Illinois.

# PUBLIC AGENCIES

★ 170 ★
**Illinois Department of Children and Family Services**
**Aurora Office**
8 E. Galena Blvd., 4th Fl.
Aurora, IL 60506
Phone: (312) 344-3237

**Contact:** Adoption Unit.

**Description:** Public agency.

**Area served:** Residents of the 8 collar counties of Cook County.

**Requirements:** Adults, 21 yrs. and older, who are married or single, and who are in good health.

**Fees:** None.

**Number of children placed last year:** 97.

**Description of children:** Children with special needs.

**Adoption procedure:**
1) Telephone intake;
2) attend orientation;
3) complete training, application and home study process;
4) if approved, wait for placement;
5) post-placement supervision;
6) finalization.

**Average length of time between application and start of home study:** Varies.

**Average length of time to complete home study:** 8 or more wks.

**Number of interviews:** 6-8 and 3 home visits.

**Home study description:** Assessment which includes but is not limited to background, motivation to adopt, recommendation of references, home and environment.

**Average wait for a child after approval of a home study:** Varies.

**Foster care:** Temporary, short and long-term, pre-adoptive and therapeutic.

★ 171 ★
**Illinois Department of Children and Family Services**
**Champaign Office**
2125 S. 1st St.
Champaign, IL 61820
Phone: (217) 333-2420

**Contact:** Karen Taylor, Adoption Coordinator.

**Description:** Public, county agency.

**Area served:** Residents of Champaign, Clark, Coles, Cumberland, DeWitt, Douglas, Edgar, Ford, Iroquois, Livingston, McLean, Macon, Moultrie, Piatt, Shelby and Vermillion counties.

**Requirements:** Adults, 21 yrs. and older, who are either single or married and who are in good health.

**Fees:** None.

**Number of children placed last year:** 116.

**Description of children:** Primarily children with special needs.

**Adoption procedure:**
1) Attend orientation meeting;
2) admission to waiting list;
3) complete training and home study;
4) if approved, wait for placement;
5) placement;
6) post-placement supervision;
7) finalization.

**Average length of time between application and start of home study:** 6-12 mos.

**Average length of time to complete home study:** 3 mos.

**Number of interviews:** 10 group and 4-5 home visits.

**Home study description:** Assessment of stability, background checks, support systems, community and/or church involvement, acceptance and openness to adoption.

**Average wait for a child after approval of a home study:** Dependent on range of special needs applicant(s) are willing to accept.

**Foster care:** Emergency, short and long-term, permanent, specialized, and treatment.

★ 172 ★
**Illinois Department of Children and Family Services**
**Fairview Heights Office**
10251 Lincoln Trail, Ste. 3
Fairview Heights, IL 62208
Phone: (618) 394-2100

**Contact:** Adoption unit.

**Description:** Area office of the public state agency.

**Area served:** Residents of Bond, Clinton, Madison, Monroe, Randolph, St. Clair and Washington counties.

**Requirements:** Adults, 21 yrs. and older who have sufficient income to provide for a child.

**Fees:** None.

**Number of children placed last year:** 101.

**Description of children:** Black children of school age and white children with handicaps.

**Adoption procedure:**
1) Initial inquiry;
2) waiting period while agency assesses the needs of the children waiting placement in order to study the most suitable homes;
3) attend meeting with master adoptive parent;
4) participate in individual orientation with caseworker;
5) complete 8 sessions of group preparation;
6) meet licensing requirements;

7) complete home study;
8) placement;
9) post-placement supervision;
10) finalization.
Steps 5, 6 and 7 very often are not sequential but happen in concord.

**Average length of time between application and start of home study:** Orientation programs are offered several times during the year.

**Average length of time to complete home study:** 12 wks. of classes.

**Home study description:** Exploration of adoptions begins with a meeting with an intake worker to discuss adoption in general and the kinds of children available. Applicants then begin 12 wks. of classroom work during which time they meet with master adoptive parents and at least 3 times individually with a resource worker to discuss issues raised and their responses. During this time the licensing process also begins which includes fingerprinting, home visits, and criminal record checks.

**Average wait for a child after approval of a home study:** Varies depending on the child sought.

**Foster care:** Legal risk.

---

**★ 173 ★**
**Illinois Department of Children and Family Services**
**Marion Office**
2309 W. Main St.
Marion, IL 62959
Phone: (618) 993-7249

**Contact:** Family Development Unit.
**Description:** Public, county agency.
**Area served:** Residents of Alexander, Clay, Crawford, Edwards, Effingham, Fayette, Franklin, Gallatin, Hamilton, Hardin, Jackson, Jasper, Jefferson, Johnson, Lawrence, Marion, Massac, Perry, Pope, Pulaski, Richland, Saline, Union, Wabash, Wayne, White and Williamson counties.
**Requirements:** Adults, 21 yrs. and older, who are either single or legally married, who have no contagious or life threatening illness and who have a stable income.
**Fees:** None.
**Number of children placed last year:** 22.
**Description of children:** Children with special needs.
**Adoption procedure:**
1) Telephone intake;
2) attend informational meeting;
3) participate in group study and home visit;
4) if approved, wait for placement;
5) placement;
6) post-placement supervision;
7) finalization.
**Average length of time between application and start of home study:** 2 1/2-3 mos.
**Average length of time to complete home study:** 4 mos.
**Number of interviews:** 13 wks. of group meetings and a minimum of 2 individual interviews.
**Home study description:** Process includes educational and evaluatory facets and covers background checks, child behavior, adoption issues, applicant(s)' personality, parenting styles, the kind of child desired and best suited to the prospective adoptive home.
**Average wait for a child after approval of a home study:** Dependent on the range of special needs applicant(s) are willing to accept. Wait for health children 5 yrs. and younger: 10 yrs.

**Foster care:** Emergency, short- and long-term, and legal-risk.

---

**★ 174 ★**
**Illinois Department of Children and Family Services**
**Peoria Office**
2301 N.E. Adams
Peoria, IL 61803
Phone: (309) 686-8700

**Contact:** Adoption intake worker.
**Description:** Public regional office.
**Area served:** Residents of Bureau, Fulton, Henderson, Henry, Knox, La Salle, McDonough, Marshall, Mercer, Peoria, Putnam, Rock Island, Stark, Tazewell, Warren, Williamson and Woodford counties.
**Requirements:** Adults, 21 yrs. and older, who are either single or married at least 1 yr., who have adequate health and sufficient income to meet the family's present needs.
**Fees:** None.
**Number of children placed last year:** 96.
**Description of children:** Children mostly between 5 and 12 yrs. old.
**Adoption procedure:**
1) Attend informational meeting;
2) attend training sessions;
3) participate in interview process;
4) if approved, child match;
5) wait for placement;
6) post-placement supervision;
7) finalization.
**Average length of time between application and start of home study:** 1-6 mos.
**Average length of time to complete home study:** 2-3 mos.
**Number of interviews:** Minimum of 3.
**Home study description:** Assessment of background, experience with children, parenting skills, recommendation of references, health and finances.
**Average wait for a child after approval of a home study:** Special needs: 3-6 mos; infant: 24 or more mos.
**Foster care:** Pre-adoptive; most adoptions are foster care conversions.

---

**★ 175 ★**
**Illinois Department of Children and Family Services**
**Rockford Office**
200 S. Wyman St., 2nd Fl.
Rockford, IL 61101-1232
Phone: (815) 987-7200

**Contact:** Adoption Workers.
**Description:** Public, county agency.
**Area served:** Residents of Boone, Carroll, DeKalb, Jo Daviess, Lee, Ogle, Stephenson, Whiteside and Winnebago counties.
**Requirements:** Adults, 21 yrs. and older, who are either single or married 1 or more yrs., whose health would allow them to care for a child and who have sufficient income to meet the family's present needs.
**Fees:** None.
**Number of children placed last year:** 80.
**Description of children:** Children with special needs.
**Adoption procedure:**
1) Attend informational meeting;
2) submit application;

3) participate in group study and individual interviews;
4) if approved, wait for placement;
5) placement;
6) post-placement supervision;
7) finalization.

**Average length of time between application and start of home study:** 1-6 mos.

**Average length of time to complete home study:** 3 mos.

**Number of interviews:** 4 group and 2-3 individual.

**Home study description:** Evaluatory and educational process which considers parenting expereince, ability to meet a child's needs, family functioning, flexibility and sense of humor.

**Average wait for a child after approval of a home study:** 6-12 mos.

**Foster care:** Emergency, short and long-term and therapeutic.

## ★ 176 ★
**Illinois Department of Children and Family Services**
**Springfield Office**
4500 S. 6th Street Rd.
Springfield, IL 62703
Phone: (217) 786-6830

**Contact:** Adoption Unit.

**Description:** Public, regional agency.

**Area served:** Residents of Adams, Brown, Calhoun, Cass, Christian, Green, Hancock, Jersey, Logan, Macoupin, Mason, Menard, Montgomery, Morgan, Pike, Sangamon, Schuyler and Scott counties.

**Requirements:** Adults, 21 yrs. and older, who are either legally married or single.

**Fees:** None.

**Number of children placed last year:** 60.

**Description of children:** Primarily children with special needs.

**Adoption procedure:**
1) Initial inquiry and intake;
2) return completed information sheet;
3) attend information night;
4) participate in 4-6 sessions of pre-service training;
5) complete home study;
6) if approved, placement;
7) post-placement supervision;
8) finalization;
9) contracted post-finalization services.

**Average length of time between application and start of home study:** Less than 1 mo.

**Average length of time to complete home study:** 3 mos.

**Number of interviews:** Minimum of 2 family assessments.

**Home study description:** Educational and evaluatory process which discusses parenting issues, separation and attachment, long-term commitment, behavior of traumatized children and ability to accept children with a "past".

**Average wait for a child after approval of a home study:** Dependent on appropriateness of child match.

**Foster care:** Legal risk.

# PRIVATE AGENCIES

## ★ 177 ★
**ABC Counseling & Family Services**
207 W. Jefferson, Ste. 100
Bloomington, IL 61701
Phone: (309) 828-3367
Fax: (309) 827-4539

**Contact:** Lynn Willard or Barb O'Neal.

**Date established:** 1990.

**Description:** Private child placing agency licensed by the Illinois Department of Children and Family Services.

**Area served:** Residents of the State of Illinois.

**Requirements:** Applicants must be at least 21 yrs. old and be either single or legally married.

**Fees:** Home study: $1000; Identified Adoption Counseling: $75/hr; Guardianship: $500; post-placement supervision: $300.

**Number of children placed last year:** 19.

**Description of children:** Infants placed through identified adoptions.

**Adoption procedure:** 1) Initial inquiry; 2) information packet sent; 3) completion of agency application andfoster care application; 4) personal interview; 5) home study which includes 10-12 wks. of classes; 6) home visit; 7) wait for approval.

**Average length of time between application and start of home study:** 1 - 3 mos.

**Average length of time to complete home study:** 3 mos.

**Number of interviews:** 1 in-home, maximum of 2.

**Home study description:** Assessment which includes references and background checks and addresses such issues as motivation to adopt, other adoption issues, social and family history, finances, home and community.

**Average wait for a child after approval of a home study:** ABC facilitates mostly identified adoptions. Wait for placement depends upon how quickly the adoptive parents identify a birth family and come to an adoption agreement.

**Foster care:** None.

## ★ 178 ★
**The Baby Fold**
108 E. Willow
Normal, IL 61761
Phone: (309) 452-1170

**Contact:** Deborah Armstrong, Associate Director of Child Welfare Services.

**Date established:** 1902.

**Description:** Private, non-profit child welfare agency licensed by the Illinois Department of Children and Family Services.

**Area served:** Residents of the 54 counties of central Illinois.

**Requirements:** Applicants must be at least 21 yrs. old and be either single or legally married.

**Fees:** None. Adoption assistance is available to help cover daily living expenses, medical needs and legal expenses related to the adoption.

**Number of children placed last year:** 15.

**Description of children:** Children with special needs who are over the age of 6 yrs. and/or who have emotional/ physical disabilities; sibling groups; African-American children.

**Adoption procedure:** 1) Application; 2) orientation meeting; 3) formal application; 4) interviews; 5) group training; 6) licensing; 7) pre-placement visits; 8) placement; 9) post-placementsupervision; 10) finalization; 11) post-legal services, as required.

**Average length of time between application and start of home study:** 1 - 6 mos.

**Average length of time to complete home study:** 3 - 6 mos.

**Number of interviews:** 4 plus group training.

**Home study description:** Educational and assessment process which includes autobiographical, employment and financial information, reference, medical and background checks and addresses such issues as parenting and discipline and type of child desired.

**Average wait for a child after approval of a home study:** 1 - 6 mos.

**Foster care:** Emergency, short and long-term, therapeutic, fost-adopt and permanent.


★ 179 ★
**Bethany Christian Services of Evergreen Park**
9730 S. Western, Ste. 203
Evergreen Park, IL 60642
Phone: (312) 422-9626
Fax: (708) 422-4649

**Contact:** Yvonne L. Tolbert.

**Date established:** 1984.

**Description:** Non-profit, private child-welfare agency licensed by the Illinois Dept. of Children and Family Services.

**Area served:** Residents of Illinois.

**Requirements:** Couples married at least 3 yrs. who are between the ages of 25 and 38 yrs., who have no more than 1 child and a diagnosis of infertility and who are active members of an evangelical Christian church. Requirements for adoption of foreign-born children may vary by child's country of origin.

**Fees:**
Application: $550;
total fees: $7500.

**Number of children placed last year:** 25.

**Description of children:** Caucasian, African-American, and foreign-born infants.

**Adoption procedure:**
1) Submit preliminary application;
2) return completed formal application;
3) complete home study;
4) if approved, placement;
5) 6 mos. post-placement supervision;
6) finalization.

**Average length of time between application and start of home study:** Varies.

**Average length of time to complete home study:** 4 mos.

**Number of interviews:** 4-6.

**Home study description:** Assessment of marriage, religious views, individual adjustment and motivation to adopt.

**Average wait for a child after approval of a home study:** Varies.

**Foster care:** Temporary.


★ 180 ★
**Catholic Charities (of Waukegan)**
1 N. Genesee, Ste. 203
Waukegan, IL 60085
Phone: (708) 249-2500
(800) 942-3930
Fax: (708) 623-6750

**Branch address:**
116 N. Lincoln, Round Lake, IL 60073
Phone: (708) 546-5733

**Contact:** Barbara Webb (Waukegan and Round Lake offices).

**Date established:** 1945.

**Description:** Non-profit private agency licensed in Illinois.

**Area served:** Lake County.

**Requirements:** Couples married at least 2 yrs. who are between the ages of 23 and 40 and who have a medical diagnosis of infertility. Black families may be over 40 and have children in the family. Special Needs Adoption Program (older children free for adoption) - no ceiling on age requirements.

**Fees:**
Special needs: fees and donations are waived or negotiable.
White infants: $750 for home study and 10% of combined gross income placement donation.

**Number of children placed last year:** 11.

**Description of children:** Special needs, infants, and older children beyond six years.

**Adoption procedure:** Applicants for white infants attend an Adoption Information Meeting. If family is assessed as appropriate, preadoptive counseling begins and they attend a Special Needs Adoption workshop.

**Average length of time between application and start of home study:** 1-6 mos.

**Average length of time to complete home study:** 6 mos.

**Number of interviews:** Approx. 8.

**Home study description:** Evaluation of family history, background, health record, including infertility; attitudes toward adoption in its many aspects.

**Average wait for a child after approval of a home study:** 6-12 mos.

**Foster care:** Temporary.


★ 181 ★
**Catholic Charities of the Archdiocese of Chicago**
126 N. Des Plaines
Chicago, IL 60661
Phone: (317) 655-7000

**Branch address:**
1 N. Genesee St., Ste. 203, Waukegan, IL 60085
Phone: (708) 249-3500

**Contact:** Mary Lou O'Brien, Program Director.

**Date established:** 1914.

**Description:** Private, not-for-profit child welfare agency licensed by the Illinois Department of Children and Family Services.

**Area served:** Residents of Cook and Lake counties.

**Requirements:** Varies with type of child requested.

**Fees:** Unavailable.

**Number of children placed last year:** Unavailable.

**Description of children:** Infants, foreign-born children and children with special needs.

**Adoption procedure:** 1) Application; 2) background clearances; 3) licensing; 4) group and individual education and preparation; 5) placement; 6) post-placement supervision; 7) finalization; 8) post-legal services, as required.

**Average length of time between application and start of home study:** Unavailable.

**Average length of time to complete home study:** Unavailable.

**Number of interviews:** Unavailable.

**Home study description:** Assessment which includes an educational component and addresses such issues as family history and relationships, lifestyle, type of child requested and attitudes toward birth parents and adoption.

**Average wait for a child after approval of a home study:** Unavailable.

**Foster care:** Temporary, long-term and medical.

★ 182 ★
**Catholic Social Service of Belleville**
617 S. Belt W.
Belleville, IL 62220
Phone: (618) 277-9200

**Branch address:**
100 S. Monroe, Marion, IL 62959-2559

361 N. Main St., Breese, IL 62230-1524

604 N. Market St., Mt. Carmel, IL 62863-0023

**Contact:** Susan Reilmann, Director of Child Welfare.

**Date established:** 1947.

**Description:** Non-profit private agency.

**Area served:** Residents of Alexander, Clay, Clinton, Edwards, Franklin, Gallatin, Hamilton, Hardin, Jackson, Jefferson, Johnson, Lawrence, Marion, Massac, Monroe, Perry, Pope, Randolph, Richland, St. Clair, Saline, Union, Washington, Wayne, White and Williamson counties.

**Requirements:** Must have a religious affiliation with some church and be willing to participate in an open adoption relationship.

**Fees:** $75 per hr.

**Number of children placed last year:** 14.

**Description of children:** Infants, foreign-born, and special needs children.

**Adoption procedure:**
1) File application;
2) begin home study and participate in Enrich Program;
3) complete joint, individual interviews and home visit;
4) adoptive home profile written and presented to birthmother.

**Average length of time between application and start of home study:** 1 mo. or less.

**Average length of time to complete home study:** 2-3 mos.

**Number of interviews:** 5-6.

**Home study description:** Evaluation of family and marital stability; attitudes of personal satisfaction and parental readiness. Adoption issue preparation for parents and child.

**Average wait for a child after approval of a home study:** Varies.

**Foster care:** Temporary and long-term.

★ 183 ★
**Catholic Social Service of Peoria**
413 N.E. Monroe
Peoria, IL 61603
Phone: (309) 671-5720
Fax: (309) 671-5270

**Branch address:**
603 N. Center, Bloomington, IL 61701
Phone: (309) 829-6307

10 Henson Pl., Ste. C, Champaign, IL 61820
Phone: (217) 352-6565

816 20th St., Rock Island, IL 61201
Phone: (309) 788-9581

3053 Grand Ave., Galesburg, IL 61401
Phone: (309) 342-1136

**Contact:** R. Joseph Knapp, Adoption/Women's Conseling & Support Services Coordinator.

**Date established:** C. 1870.

**Description:** Private non-profit agency whose emphasis is pro-life.

**Area served:** State of Illinois.

**Requirements:** Healthy Caucasian Infant Program: single or married, at least 21 yrs. of age and capable of passing a criminal background check. Four letters of unrelated reference and one reference from a priest or minister. Good physical health verified by physical exam. Proof of sufficient financial resources. Commitment to Pro-Life philosophy. Special Needs: eligibility determined on an individual basis.

**Fees:**
Special needs: no fees.
Home study fee: $1200; adoption fee for healthy infant: $4800.

**Number of children placed last year:** Healthy white infants; minority children and children with special needs.

**Description of children:** Infants, children with special needs and minority children.

**Adoption procedure:**
1) Initial inquiry and basic eligibility established;
2) attend adoption orientation meeting;
3) name added to waiting list;
4) annual up-date of waiting list and quarterly mailings;
5) attend initial interview with adoption worker;
6) complete and return formal application materials;
7) participate in home study classes/groups;
8) individual home and office interviews;
9) adoption worker writes the home study;
10) adoption worker submits foster license materials;
11) Adoption Committee reviews application and home study;
12) if approved, adoptive applicants are "Approved & Waiting";
13) Adoptive Portrait of applicants is put into circulation;
14) matched or ranked adoptive portraits are held waiting infants birth;
15) after infant's birth, Adoption Coordinator confirms match or re-matches infant and notifies prospective adoptive parents;
16) placement day at Peoria office;
17) post-placement supervision for 6 mos.;
18) finalization.

**Average length of time between application and start of home study:** 1-6 mos.

**Average length of time to complete home study:** 3-6 mos.

**Number of interviews:** Approx. 6.

**Home study description:** Evaluation of individual social history, orientation to adoption, motivation for adoption, self-assessment, marital assessment, religion and values, parenting and discipline, infertility and grief resolution, birthparent empathy, child care plan, child desired, and plans to tell child of his/her adoption and adoptee search and birthparent contact.

**Average wait for a child after approval of a home study:** 12-24 mos.

**Foster care:** Temporary, long-term and permanent.

## ★ 184 ★
**Central Baptist Family Services**
201 N. Wells, Ste. 1642
Chicago, IL 60606
Phone: (312) 782-0874

**Contact:** Eric J. Spencer, Adoption Supervisor.

**Description:** Non-profit, private child-placing agency.

**Area served:** Residents of the City of Chicago and surrounding suburbs.

**Requirements:** Singles or married couples who are free from major health, emotional and economic problems, have adequate space in their home, and are of legal age.

**Fees:** Sliding scale as follows:
Family income less than $12,000: waiver;
$12,000-$20,000: 3/4 of 1% income;
$20,100-$30,000: 1% of income;
$30,100-$40,000: 1-1 1/2% of income;
$40,100-50,000: 1-1 3/4% of income;
$50,100 or more: 2% of income.

**Number of children placed last year:** 13.

**Description of children:** Black infants and black, Hispanic and white children with special needs.

**Adoption procedure:**
1) Initial telephone inquiry;
2) submit completed "Family Information Sheet";
3) attend orientation and training sessions;
4) complete home study;
5) if approved, child match and placement;
6) post-placement supervisory;
7) finalization.

**Average length of time between application and start of home study:** 1 mo. or less.

**Average length of time to complete home study:** 1 mo.

**Number of interviews:** 2-3.

**Home study description:** Evaluation of family background, medical information, finances and family functioning.

**Average wait for a child after approval of a home study:** 1-6 mos.

**Foster care:** Emergency, long-term (regular & specialized), and professional.

## ★ 185 ★
**Children's Home and Aid Society of Illinois**
730 N. Main St.
Rockford, IL 61103
Phone: (815) 962-1043
Fax: (815) 962-1272

**Contact:** Peggy Franklin, Adoptions Coordinator.

**Date established:** 1883.

**Description:** Not-for-profit, non-sectarian United Way agency licensed by the State of Illinois.

**Area served:** Residents of Boone, Carroll, DeKalb, Jo Daviess, Lee, Ogle, Stephenson, Whiteside and Winnebago counties.

**Requirements:** Adults, 23 yrs. and older, if married, marriage must be of at least 2 yrs. duration. Other requirements vary with programs.

**Fees:**
No fees for special needs.
Application: $250;
home study: $1000;
remainder of fees vary with program but shall not exceed
  $15,000 total.

**Number of children placed last year:** 30.

**Description of children:** U.S. and foreign-born infants and children with special needs.

**Adoption procedure:**
1) Attend orientation meeting;
2) screening;
3) complete home study;
4) if approved, placement;
5) 6 mos. post-placement supervisory;
6) finalization.

**Average length of time between application and start of home study:** 1 mo. or less.

**Average length of time to complete home study:** 4-6 mos.

**Number of interviews:** Approx. 6 individual plus group.

**Home study description:** A process of individual interviews, a home visit and required group study.

**Average wait for a child after approval of a home study:** Depends on the type of child requested.

**Foster care:** Temporary.

## ★ 186 ★
**The Cradle Society**
2049 Ridge Ave.
Evanston, IL 60201
Phone: (312) 475-5800

**Contact:** Joyce Muller, ASSW.

**Date established:** 1923.

**Description:** Non-profit, privately-funded, non-sectarian agency licensed by the State of Illinois.

**Area served:** Residents of Cook, DuPage, Kane, Lake, McHenry and Will counties in Illinois, immediate Philadelphia and New York City area. Geographical area is flexible for special needs placement.

**Requirements:** Couples married at least 3 yrs. who are between the ages of 23 and 39 yrs., who are childless, in general good physical health with a medically documented infertility problem. Some requirements are flexible for special needs placement.

**Fees:** None. Donations are accepted after placement of child.

**Number of children placed last year:** Approx. 70.

**Description of children:** U.S. infants of all races, some with correctable or non-correctable medical problems.

**Adoption procedure:**
1) Telephone intake;
2) submit preliminary form;
3) complete home study;
4) if approved, wait for placement;
5) placement;
6) 6 mos. post-placement supervision;
7) finalization.

**Average length of time between application and start of home study:** 1-6 mos.

**Average length of time to complete home study:** 2-4 mos.

**Number of interviews:** 5-7.

**Home study description:** Evaluation of individual autobiographies, finances and employment, health report, references and finger print check.

**Average wait for a child after approval of a home study:** 6-12 mos.

**Foster care:** None.

★ 187 ★
**Evangelical Child and Family Agency**
1530 N. Main St.
Wheaton, IL 60187
Phone: (708) 653-6400
Fax: (708) 653-6490

**Branch address:**
4319 W. Irving Park Rd., Chicago, IL 60641
Phone: (312) 545-2248

2401 N. Mayfair Rd., Milwaukee, WI 53226
Phone: (414) 476-9550

**Contact:** Intake worker.

**Date established:** 1950.

**Description:** Non-profit child welfare agency licensed by the Illinois Dept. of Children and Family Services and by the Wisconsin Dept. of Health and Social Services.

**Area served:** Residents of Illinois and Wisconsin.

**Requirements:** Christian couples married at least 2 yrs. who are in generally good physical and emotional health and who have adequate financial resources and insurance coverage. After placement adoptive mothers may not be employed outside the home for the first 6 mos. (for infant adoption).

**Fees:** Unavailable.

**Number of children placed last year:** 52.

**Description of children:** Caucasian and minority children and children with special needs from infancy to early adolescence.

**Adoption procedure:**
1) Submit application;
2) complete home study and physical examination;
3) if approved, placement;
4) 6 mos. post-placement supervision;
5) legal finalization.

**Average length of time between application and start of home study:** 1-6 mos.

**Average length of time to complete home study:** 3 mos.

**Number of interviews:** 1-2 in home and 4-5 office visits.

**Home study description:** Evaluation of personal history, marital relationship, emotions surrounding infertility and decision to adopt.

**Average wait for a child after approval of a home study:** 12-24 mos.

**Foster care:** Temporary, long-term and therapeutic.

★ 188 ★
**Family Care Services**
234 S. Wabash
Chicago, IL 60604
Phone: (312) 427-8790
(800) 244-4416
Fax: (312) 427-8365

**Contact:** Marion J. Middleton.

**Date established:** C.1850.

**Description:** Non-profit private agency licensed by the State of Illinois.

**Area served:** Residents of Illinois within travel-distance of Chicago.

**Requirements:** Applicants must be age appropriate to the child placed and of the same faith, if specified.

**Fees:** None.

**Number of children placed last year:** 10.

**Description of children:** 0-18 yrs. old.

**Adoption procedure:**
1) File application;
2) complete home study;
3) licensing of adoptive parents;
4) selection of child;
5) placement;
6) post-placement supervision;
7) legal finalization.

**Average length of time between application and start of home study:** 1-6 mos.

**Average length of time to complete home study:** 3 mos.

**Number of interviews:** Average of 8.

**Home study description:** Evaluation which includes but is not limited to background information, current data, health and financial reports.

**Average wait for a child after approval of a home study:** 1-6 mos.

**Foster care:** Temporary, long-term and specialized.

★ 189 ★
**Family Counseling Clinic, Inc.**
19300 W. Highway 120
Grayslake, IL 60030
Phone: (708) 223-8107

**Contact:** Sandra Arbit, Adoption Supervisor.

**Date established:** 1970.

**Description:** Private, for-profit child welfare agency licensed by the Illinois Department of Children and Family Services.

**Area served:** Residents of Cook, Dupage, Kane, Lake, McHenry and parts of Will counties.

**Requirements:** Open. International program and birth parents may impose their own criteria.

**Fees:** Application: $150; home study: $1500 ($150 application fee deducted); post-placement services and reports: $600; China Program fees: $2000; Agency placement: $3000; identified adoption/birth parent counseling: $75/hr.

**Number of children placed last year:** 46.

**Description of children:** Primarily infants and toddlers, 21 foreign-born.

**Adoption procedure:** 1) Inquiry; 2) application; 3) home study which explores both identified and international adoption programs. Remainder of process varies with the program selected. In either program placement is followed by post-placement supervision which includes some group meetings and finalization.

**Average length of time between application and start of home study:** Less than 1 mo.

**Average length of time to complete home study:** 2 - 3 mos.

**Number of interviews:** 3.

**Home study description:** Educational and assessment process which addresses such issues as personal history, individual likes, strengths, difficulties, understanding of the needs of children, adoption issues and possibly trans-social or trans-cultural issues.

**Average wait for a child after approval of a home study:** China program: 1-6 mos. Domestic infants: depends on birth family search and match.

**Foster care:** None.

★ 190 ★
**Family Service Agency of Adams County**
915 Vermont St.
Quincy, IL 62301
Phone: (217) 222-8254
Fax: (217) 222-4512

**Contact:** Martha Butler, Adoption Coordinator.

**Date established:** 1947.

**Description:** Illinois non-profit, child welfare agency.

**Area served:** 120 mi. radius of Quincy, within the state borders of Illinois. We serve Illinois families only.

**Requirements:** Couples married at least 4 years who are at least high school graduates and who are no more than 40 years older than adopted child for agency adoptions. Independent and foreign adoption requirements vary.

**Fees:** Billed hourly according to current fee schedule. Clerical is 1/2 of therapist cost. Pay schedule can be arranged over a year.

**Number of children placed last year:** Not available.

**Description of children:** A few infants placed through agency. Infants/children identified by family (independent adoptions). We also work with foreign placing agencies to help families locate a foreign-born child.

**Adoption procedure:** Family Service Agency of Adams Co. assists with out-of-state, foreign and independent placement. The procedure varies accordingly.

**Average length of time between application and start of home study:** Varies, usually fairly short.

**Average length of time to complete home study:** 3-4 mos.

**Number of interviews:** 5-7.

**Home study description:** Outline sent on request.

**Average wait for a child after approval of a home study:** Depends on type of adoption.

**Foster care:** Teens In Crisis Program; relative foster homes.

★ 191 ★
**Lifelink/Bensenville Home Society**
331 S. York Rd.
Bensenville, IL 60106
Phone: (708) 766-5800
Fax: (708) 860-5130

**Branch address:**
905 S. Russell, Champaign, IL 61821
Phone: (217) 352-5283

2201 7th Ave., Moline, IL 61265
Phone: (309) 762-5645

318 N. Church, Rockford, IL 61101
Phone: (815) 965-2231

6100 Center Grove Rd., Edwardsville, IL 62025

Phone: (618) 656-8278

**Contact:** Grace Vosyka.

**Date established:** 1895.

**Description:** Non-profit, child placing agency licensed by the State of Illinois.

**Area served:** Residents of the State of Illinois.

**Requirements:** Couples married at least two years who are between the ages of 23 and 60. Additional requirements depend upon the program chosen.

**Fees:** $1800 to $13,000 depending upon program. Fees waived for special needs.

**Number of children placed last year:** 140.

**Description of children:** Infants, special needs and foreign-born children of all ages.

**Adoption procedure:**
1) Attend orientation meeting;
2) complete a formal application and self-study;
3) meet individually and jointly with a social worker;
4) have a home visit;
5) complete licensing and immigration requirements;
6) if approved, wait for placement.

**Average length of time between application and start of home study:** 1 mo. or less.

**Average length of time to complete home study:** 3-6 mos.

**Number of interviews:** At least 4.

**Home study description:** Home study assesses applicant's emotional stability, the stability of their marriage, ability to parent and to handle adoption issues with a child.

**Average wait for a child after approval of a home study:** 6-24 mos.

**Foster care:** Emergency, short and long-term.

★ 192 ★
**Lutheran Social Services of Illinois**
**Foster, Adoption and Maternity Services**
11740 S. Western Ave.
Chicago, IL 60643
Phone: (312) 239-3700
Fax: (312) 239-5296

**Branch address:**
4840 W. Byron St., Chicago, IL 60641
Phone: (312) 282-7800

**Contact:** Ezillia Bell, Program Director.

**Date established:** 1867.

**Description:** Non-profit, private child welfare agency licensed by the Illinois Dept. of Children and Family Services.

**Area served:** Residents of Cook, DuPage, Grundy, Kane, Kankakee, Kendall, and Will counties.

**Requirements:** Applicants should be no more than 40 yrs. older than the child placed, in good health, with adequate income, single or married, if married, marriage should be of at least 2 yrs. duration.

**Fees:**
Application fee: $30;
home study: $800;
maximum total fees: $6700.

**Number of children placed last year:** 60.

**Description of children:** Infants of all races; foreign-born children of all ages and children with special needs of all races and ages.

**Adoption procedure:**
1) Attend Adoption Information meeting;

2) file application;
3) complete home study;
4) attend 6 hrs. of pre-adoptive training;
5) placement;
6) attend 6 hrs. of post-placement training.

**Average length of time between application and start of home study:** 1 mo. or less.

**Average length of time to complete home study:** 2-3 mos.

**Number of interviews:** 6.

**Home study description:** Assessment of motivation to adopt, interpersonal relationships, parenting skills, infertility issues, community's and extended family's attitudes and support of adoption.

**Average wait for a child after approval of a home study:** 1-6 mos.

**Foster care:** Temporary and long-term.

## ★ 193 ★
**Maternity and Adoption Services of Baptist Children's Home**
4243 Lincolnshire Dr.
Mt. Vernon, IL 62864
Phone: (618) 242-4944
Fax: (618) 242-2568

**Contact:** Carla Monroe, ACSW.

**Date established:** 1985.

**Description:** Non-profit, private child welfare agency licensed by the Illinois Dept. of Children and Family Services.

**Area served:** Residents of Illinois.

**Requirements:** Couples married at least 3 yrs. who are no older than 40 yrs., who have no more than 1 child presently in the home, who are unable to have additional children and who are Southern Baptists. Applicants for children with special needs should be Christian married couples who have adequate financial means.

**Fees:**
Application fee: $100;
adoption fees for healthy, white infant: 12% of adjusted gross income plus $600 legal fees;
adoption fees for children with special needs are based on family's resources;
home study for private adoption: $1000 plus travel expenses;
post-placement services for private adoption: $500 plus travel expenses.

**Number of children placed last year:** 17.

**Description of children:** 13 white, 3 black, and 3 biracial.

**Adoption procedure:**
1) Initial inquiry;
2) file application;
3) complete home study;
4) meet licensure requirements;
5) placement;
6) 6 mos. post-placement supervision;
7) finalization.

**Average length of time between application and start of home study:** 24 or more mos.

**Average length of time to complete home study:** 3 mos.

**Number of interviews:** Unavailable.

**Home study description:** Assessment of background checks and fingerprinting, employment history and finances, medical reports, suitability of home and religious affiliation.

**Average wait for a child after approval of a home study:** 6-12 mos.

**Foster care:** Temporary.

## ★ 194 ★
**New Life Adoption Services**
3525 W. Peterson, Ste. 222
Chicago, IL 60659
Phone: (312) 478-4773
(312) 478-4715

**Contact:** Ciony R. Gawat, LSW, MSSW, Executive Director.

**Date established:** 1991.

**Description:** Private, Not-for-profit child placing agency licensed by the Illinois Department of Children & Family Service.

**Area served:** Residents of Illinois - full-service; residents of U.S. - placement.

**Requirements:** Applicants must be 35 yrs. or younger, single or legally married, in good health and emotionally stable with sufficient income to raise a child. Preference shown to Christian applicants.

**Fees:** Application: $150; home study and post-placement services: $2500. International fees additional.

**Number of children placed last year:** 7.

**Description of children:** Infants and toddlers from India, the Philippines and the U.S.

**Adoption procedure:** 1) Formal application; 2) home study; 3) placement; 4) post-placement supervision; 5) finalization.

**Average length of time between application and start of home study:** 12 - 24 mos.

**Average length of time to complete home study:** 2 - 3 mos.

**Number of interviews:** 4 - 5.

**Home study description:** Clinical assessment which addresses such issues as family background, the marital relationship, if applicable and parenting philosophy and skills. If the social worker is unsure of the family, a second professional opinion is sought or a psychological evaluation is requested.

**Average wait for a child after approval of a home study:** 12 - 24 mos.

**Foster care:** Specialized.

## ★ 195 ★
**St. Mary's Services**
717 W. Kerchoff Rd.
Arlington Heights, IL 60005
Phone: (708) 870-8181
(800) 252-4152
Fax: (708) 870-8325

**Branch address:**
7600 S. Wolf Rd., Burr Ridge, IL 60525
Phone: (708) 246-5012

210 McHenry Ave., Crystal Lake, IL 60014
Phone: (815) 459-9403

1133 N. LaSalle, Chicago, IL 60610
Phone: (312) 787-2591

**Contact:** Intake worker (Mondays 9 a.m.-12 noon).

**Date established:** 1894.

**Description:** Non-profit Chrisitan agency. Provides homestudy and post placement supervision for couples seeking international placements.

**Area served:** Residents of northern Illinois.

**Requirements:** Applicants must be practicing Christians. Other eligibility standards vary by type of child.

**Fees:** Based on sliding scale.

**Number of children placed last year:** 25.

**Description of children:** Infants of all races.

**Adoption procedure:**
1) Telephone inquiry and information gathering;
2) send autobiographical letter:
3) complete home study;
4) if accepted, complete licensing procedures;
5) placement.

**Average length of time between application and start of home study:** 1 mo. or less.

**Average length of time to complete home study:** 3 wks.

**Number of interviews:** Unavailable.

**Home study description:** Thorough study to assess character and maturity level.

**Average wait for a child after approval of a home study:** 6-12 mos.

**Foster care:** Temporary; brief; pending placement.

## ★ 196 ★
### Seegers Lutheran Center
### Lutheran Child and Family Services
333 W. Lake
Addison, IL 60101
Phone: (708) 628-6448

**Branch address:**
7620 Madison, Box 5078, River Forest, IL 60305
Phone: (708) 771-7180

2408 Lebanon Ave., Belleville, IL 62221
Phone: (618) 234-8904

**Contact:** LaNell Hill, Director of Adoptions (Addison); Mary Thurman, Director of Adoptions (Belleville).

**Date established:** 1873.

**Description:** Non-profit, private agency accredited by the Council of Accreditation of Services for Families and Children, member of the Child Care Association of Illinois, Family Builders Through Adoption and the Child Welfare League of America.

**Area served:** Residents of Illinois.

**Requirements:** Varies by adoption program. Applicants must be at least 21 yrs. old and meet the licensing standards for foster homes established by Illinois Department of Children & Family Services.

**Fees:** Varies with program. No fees for special needs adoption. Identified/international application, home study and post-placement supervision: $1500.

**Number of children placed last year:** 188.

**Description of children:** U.S. white, black, biracial infants and children, foreign-born children and children with special needs. Many of the children have been already identified by the prospective adoptive family.

**Adoption procedure:** Agency offers programs in international adoption, identified adoption, special needs adoption and infant adoption. Procedures vary with the program chosen. Out-of-state program available for out-of-state parents who have identified an Illinois birthmother and who are working with adoption agency/attorney in their state as required by their state. Usual procedure is telephone intake, application, home study, child or birth parent identification, placement, post-placement supervision, finalization.

**Average length of time between application and start of home study:** Less than 1 mo.

**Average length of time to complete home study:** 6-8 wks.

**Number of interviews:** Varies with program; usually 3-5.

**Home study description:** General assessment of family including medical and financial reports, marriage and ability to rear a child.

**Average wait for a child after approval of a home study:** Most applicants either are working with an international agency or have identified a birth family for placement.

**Foster care:** Temporary.

## ★ 197 ★
### Sunny Ridge Family Centers
2 S. 426 Orchard Rd.
Wheaton, IL 60187
Phone: (312) 668-5117
Fax: (708) 668-5144

**Branch address:**
Schuyler Square South, Ste. 301, 9105A Indianapolis Blvd., Highland, IN 46322

**Contact:** Arlene Betts, ACSW.

**Date established:** 1926.

**Description:** Non-profit private agency licensed in Illinois and Indiana.

**Area served:** Residents of Illinois and Indiana.

**Requirements:** Domestic adoption: parents must be infertile, have a combined age of less than 80 yrs., be in good health, of a united faith and able to support a child.

**Fees:**
International and pre-arranged adoption services: home study and post-placement services: $3500; total fees: $5700 plus medical.

**Number of children placed last year:** 125.

**Description of children:** Mostly infants, some bi-racial children and children with special needs.

**Adoption procedure:**
1) Submit application;
2) attend group meeting;
3) return completed information packet and write autobiography;
4) have individual and joint interviews;
5) home visit;
6) complete psychological profile;
7) if approved, complete court procedures and placement;
8) post-placement supervisory visits;
9) finalization.

**Average length of time between application and start of home study:** Varies.

**Average length of time to complete home study:** 1-2 mos.

**Number of interviews:** 4 interviews and 2 group appointments.

**Home study description:** Evaluation of references, psychological health, quality of marriage, physical health, personality description, infertility status, background, parenting views, financial situation, current life situation, motivation and attitude toward adoption, housing, religion and plans for the future.

**Average wait for a child after approval of a home study:** Varies.

**Foster care:** Temporary for infants waiting termination of parental rights.

# INDIANA

## STATUTES

★ 198 ★

**Independent placement by intermediary?** Permitted.

**Independent placement by birth parents?** Permitted.

**Subsidies provided?** AAP and county subsidy.

**Adoption cost defined by law?** Elements are defined but not the amounts.

**Insurance for infertility?:** No.

**Home study required by state?** No, but a report with recommendations is required by the court regarding the proposed adoption.

**Prospective adoptive parent advertise for a child?** Permitted.

**Surrogacy laws?** Surrogacy contracts are not recognized by the law.

**Residents access agencies of other states or countries?** Permitted.

**Requires judicial termination of birth parents' rights?** Voluntary relinquishments are recognized.

**Time given to a birthmother to revoke her consent:** Within 30 days.

**Court handling adoptions?** Probate Court.

**Adoption of Native Children:** No registered tribes in Indiana.

**Adoption records sealed?** Sealed, but at age 21 yrs. adoptees may access their records.

**Photo-listing book available?** *Indiana Adoption Resource Exchange* photo listing.

## PUBLIC AGENCIES

★ 199 ★

**Family and Social Services Administration of Indiana Division of Family and Children**
Bureau of Family Protection and Preservation
402 W. Washington St., Rm. W364
Indianapolis, IN 46204-2739
Phone: (317) 232-5613
Fax: (317) 232-4436

**Branch address:**
1145 Bollman St., P.O. Box 227, Decatur, IN 46733
Phone: (219) 724-9169

4820 New Haven Ave., Ft. Wayne, IN 46803
Phone: (219) 425-4100

401 W. 5th St., Ste. B, P.O. Box 226, Fowler, IN 47944
Phone: (317) 884-0120

2330 Midway, Ste. 3, P.O. Box 587, Columbus, IN 47201
Phone: (812) 376-9361

124 N. Jefferson St., P.O. Box 717, Hartford City, IN 47348
Phone: (317) 348-2902

P.O. Box 548, Lebanon, IN 46052
Phone: (317) 482-3023

121 Locust Ln., P.O. Box 325, Nashville, IN 47448

Phone: (812) 988-2239

U.S. Hwy 421 N.W., P.O. Box 276, Delphi, IN 46923
Phone: (317) 564-2409

1714 Dividend Dr., Logansport, IN 46947
Phone: (219) 722-3677

1200 Madison St., Clarksville, IN 47129
Phone: (812) 288-5400

1015 E. National Ave., P.O. Box 433, Brazil, IN 47834
Phone: (812) 448-8731

57 N. Jackson St., P.O. Box 725, Frankfort, IN 46041
Phone: (317) 654-8571

304 Indiana Ave., P.O. Box 129, English, IN 47118
Phone: (812) 338-2701

P.O. Box 618, Washington, IN 47501
Phone: (812) 254-0690

Durbin Plaza, 138 Front St., Lawrenceburg, IN 47025
Phone: (812) 537-5131

119 E. Main St., P.O. Box 484, Greensburg, IN 47240
Phone: (812) 663-6768

934 W. 15th St., P.O. Box 1528, Auburn, IN 46706
Phone: (219) 925-2810

333 S. Madison, P.O. Box 1528, Muncie, IN 47305
Phone: (317) 747-7750

611 Bartly St., P.O. Box 230, Jasper, IN 47546
Phone: (812) 482-2585

608 Oakland Ave., Elkhart, IN 46516
Phone: (219) 293-6551

1720 Western Ave., Connersville, IN 47331
Phone: (317) 825-5261

824 University Woods Dr., Ste. 9, New Albany, IN 47150

305 Union St., Covington, IN 47932
Phone: (317) 793-4821

483 Main St., Brookville, IN 47012
Phone: (317) 647-4081

1920 Rhodes St., P.O. Box 820, Rochester, IN 46975
Phone: (219) 223-3413

Franklin Bldg., 800 S. Prince St., Princeton, IN 47670
Phone: (812) 385-4727

840 N. Miller Ave., Marion, IN 46952
Phone: (317) 668-4500

Hwy. 231 South, P.O. Box 443, Bloomfield, IN 47424
Phone: (812) 384-4405

938 N. 10th St., Noblesville, IN 46060
Phone: (317) 773-2183

120 W. McKenzie, Ste. F, Greenfield, IN 46140

Phone: (317) 467-6360

2026 Highway 337, NW, P.O. Box 366, Corydon, IN 47112
Phone: (812) 738-8166

6781 E. U.S. 36, Ste. 200, Danville, IN 46122
Phone: (317) 272-4917

1416 Broad St., New Castle, IN 47362
Phone: (317) 529-3450

105 W. Sycamore St., Kokomo, IN 46901
Phone: (317) 457-9510

88 Home St., Huntington, IN 46750
Phone: (219) 356-4420

220 S. Main St., P.O. Box C, Brownstown, IN 47220
Phone: (812) 358-2421

116 N. Van Rensselaer, Ste. 16, P.O. Box 279, Rensselaer,
 IN 47978
Phone: (219) 866-4186

Hwy. 67 West, P.O. Box 1034, Portland, IN 47371
Phone: (219) 726-7933

1405 Bear St., Madison, IN 47250
Phone: (812) 265-2027

939 Veterans Dr., P.O. Box 367, Vernon, IN 47282
Phone: (812) 346-2254

80 S. Jackson St. f, Franklin, IN 46131
Phone: (317) 736-3730

1050 Washington Ave., P.O. Box 235, Vincennes, IN 47591
Phone: (812) 882-3920

205 N. Lake St., Warsaw, IN 46580
Phone: (219) 267-8108

421 S. Detroit St., LaGrange, IN 46761
Phone: (219) 463-3451

800 Massachusetts St., Gary, IN 46350
Phone: (219) 886-6000

1230 State Rd. 2, West, P.O. Box 1402, LaPorte, IN 46350
Phone: (219) 326-5870

P.O. Box 99, Bedford, IN 47421
Phone: (812) 279-9706

P.O. Box 2479, Anderson, IN 46018-2479
Phone: (317) 649-0142

145 S. Meridian St., Indianapolis, IN 46225
Phone: (317) 233-5877

1850 Walter Glaub Dr., Plymouth, IN 46563
Phone: (219) 935-4046

Elm St., P.O. Box 88, Shoals, IN 47581
Phone: (812) 247-2871

1250 W. Main St., Peru, IN 46970
Phone: (317) 473-6611

401 E. Miller Dr., Bloomington, IN 47402
Phone: (812) 336-6351

307 Binford St., Crawfordsville, IN 47933
Phone: (317) 362-5600

1250 S. Morton Ave., Martinsville, IN 46151
Phone: (317) 342-7101

250 E. State St., P.O. Box 520, Morocco, IN 47963
Phone: (219) 285-2206

107 Weber Rd., Albion, IN 46701
Phone: (219) 636-2021

125 N. Walnut St., P.O. Box 26, Rising Sun, IN 47040
Phone: (812) 438-2530

326 N. Gospel, P.O. Box 5, Paoli, IN 47454
Phone: (812) 723-3616

14 N. Washington St., Spencer, IN 47460
Phone: (812) 829-2281

116 W. Ohio, Rockville, IN 47872
Phone: (317) 569-3156

316 E. Hwy 66, Tell City, IN 47586
Phone: (812) 547-7055

RR #1, Box 41A, Petersburg, IN 47567
Phone: (812) 354-9716

152 Indiana Ave., Valparaiso, IN 46383
Phone: (219) 462-2112

1809 Main St., P.O. Box 568, Mount Vernon, IN 47620
Phone: (812) 838-4429

614 W. 11th St., P.O. Box 130, Winamac, IN 46996
Phone: (219) 946-3312

620 Tennessee St., Ste. A, Greencastle, IN 46135
Phone: (317) 653-9780

2 OMCO Sq., Ste. 200, Winchester, IN 47394
Phone: (317) 584-2811

630 S. Adams, P.O. Box 215, Versailles, IN 47042
Phone: (812) 689-6295

1340 N. Cherry, P.O. Box 397, Rushville, IN 46173
Phone: (317) 932-2392

R.R. #6, Box 137A+, Scottsburg, IN 47170
Phone: (812) 752-2503

42 E. Washington, Shelbyville, IN 46176
Phone: (317) 392-5040

900 Old Plank Rd., P.O. Box 25, Rockport, IN 47635
Phone: (812) 649-9111

318 E. Culver Rd., Knox, IN 46534
Phone: (219) 772-3411

317 S. Wayne St., Ste. 2A, Angola, IN 46703

Phone: (219) 665-3713

P.O. Box 4638, South Bend, IN 46634
Phone: (219) 236-5300

128 S. State St., P.O. Box 348, Sullivan, IN 47882
Phone: (812) 268-6326

801 E. Main St., Vevay, IN 47043
Phone: (812) 427-3232

324 South St., Lafayette, IN 47901
Phone: (317) 742-0400

Court House, P.O. Box 36, Tipton, IN 46072
Phone: (317) 675-7441

303A N. Main St., P.O. Box 344, Liberty, IN 47353
Phone: (317) 458-5121

100 E. Sycamore St., P.O. Box 154, Evansville, IN 47701-0154
Phone: (812) 421-5500

215 W. Extension St., P.O. Box 218, Newport, IN 47966
Phone: (317) 492-3305

30 N. 8th St., Terre Haute, IN 47807
Phone: (812) 234-0100

89 W. Canal St., Wabash, IN 46992
Phone: (219) 563-8471

5 Railroad St., Williamsport, IN 47993
Phone: (317) 762-6125

1302 Millis Ave., P.O. Box 412, Boonville, IN 47601
Phone: (812) 897-2270

13 Westminster Center, Salem, IN 47167
Phone: (812) 883-4305

25 S. 3rd St., Richmond, IN 47374
Phone: (317) 973-9200

114 S. Main Place, P.O. Box 332, Bluffton, IN 46714
Phone: (219) 824-3530

P.O. Box 365, Rm. G-2, Monticello, IN 47960
Phone: (219) 583-5742

115 S. Line St., Columbia City, IN 46725
Phone: (219) 244-6331

**Contact:** Norma Stewart.

**Date established:** 1936.

**Description:** Public state agency designated to place children.

**Area served:** Residents of the State of Indiana.

**Requirements:** Applicants must be at least 21 yrs. old and age appropriate to the child placed, when all other factors are equal.

**Fees:** Home study and placement fees can be charged for infant placement. The fees cannot exceed the actual cost incurred by the court office for medical expenses of mother and children and the costs for time and travel associated with the home studies and investigations.

**Number of children placed last year:** 2854.

**Description of children:** Infants, children with special needs, stepparent and relative adoptions, independent and private agency adoptions.
**Adoption procedure:**
1) Application;
2) agency's adoption priorities;
3) family preparation assessment process;
4) pre-placement visits
5) placement;
6) post-placement supervision;
7) finalization;
8) post-legal adoption services, as needed.
**Average length of time between application and start of home study:** Varies by county, usually 6 mos. or less.
**Average length of time to complete home study:** Varies by county, usually 1-4 mos.
**Number of interviews:** Varies with each county agency.
**Home study description:** Written assessment which includes identifying information, description of family structure, family history, parenting style and strengths, social supports and resources, home environment and community, issues surrounding parenting and adoption, finances, and child specific assessment.
**Average wait for a child after approval of a home study:** Special needs: Varies by county, usually less than 1 yr. Others: Varies by county, usually 0-6 yrs.
**Foster care:** Temporary, long-term and permanent.

# PRIVATE AGENCIES

★ 200 ★
**Adoption Resource Services, Inc.**
810 W. Bristol St., Ste. R
Elkhart, IN 46514
Phone: (219) 262-2499

**Branch address:**
2000 N. Wells St., YWCA Bldg. No. 1, Ft. Wayne, IN 46808-2400
Phone: (219) 422-4660
**Contact:** Ruth A. Mark, Executive Director.
**Date established:** 1986.
**Description:** Not-for profit private, non-sectarian agency licensed by the Indiana Department of Public Welfare.
**Area served:** Residents of the State of Indiana.
**Requirements:** Couples married at least 3 yrs. who are 25 to 46 yrs. old, in good health, have adequate income, are unable to have a child or have no more than 1 child, and live in the state of Indiana; if second marriage, must be married for 5 yrs. or more.
**Fees:**
Application fee: $75;
home study: $950;
placement: $15,950.
**Number of children placed last year:** 23.
**Description of children:** Healthy newborn infants and children up to 3 yrs. of age.
**Adoption procedure:**
1) Telephone pre-screening;
2) request application;
3) submit application;
4) schedule initial interview;
5) complete background material;

6) undergo home study process;
7) if approved, wait for placement.

**Average length of time between application and start of home study:** 1-2 mos.

**Average length of time to complete home study:** After home study home work packet has been completed by couple and returned to agency, 1-3 mos.

**Number of interviews:** Unavailable.

**Home study description:** Evaluation of family history, religious beliefs and practices, marital stability, quality of family's communication, financial status, approach to parenting, and status of couples grief work with their infertility.

**Average wait for a child after approval of a home study:** 12-24 mos.

**Foster care:** Rare, if so only a night. Place infant from discharge from hospital directly into the adoptive home.

## ★ 201 ★

**The Adoption Support Center, Inc.**
6331 N. Carrollton Ave.
Indianapolis, IN 46220
Phone: (317) 255-5916
(800) 274-1074

**Contact:** Julie Craft or Mary Brill, co-founders.

**Date established:** 1986.

**Description:** Profit-based Indiana licensed child placement agency.

**Area served:** Residents of Indiana and surrounding states.

**Requirements:** Non-judgmental screening: each case is considered individually.

**Fees:**
Orientations: $70;
domestic home studies: $950;
international home studies: $1000;
adoption fee: $6000.

**Number of children placed last year:** 45.

**Description of children:** Infants (some with special needs).

**Adoption procedure:**
1) Attend orientation;
2) complete home study;
3) wait for selection by birthmother.

**Average length of time between application and start of home study:** 1 mo. or less.

**Average length of time to complete home study:** 6 wks.

**Number of interviews:** 1 office visit, 1 home visit, 1 class, then 3-6 mos. of post-adoption follow up.

**Home study description:** A teaching and counseling tool which includes an adoption orientation class, psycho-social evaluation, a home visit, newborn parenting classes, autobiographies, marriage evaluation, infertility history, issues surrounding adoption, finances, parenting skills, references, support systems and environment.

**Average wait for a child after approval of a home study:** 2 mos.-2 yrs. (with an average placement of 9.4 mos.).

## ★ 202 ★

**Adoptions Alternatives**
116 S. Taylor St.
South Bend, IN 46616
Phone: (219) 232-5881

**Branch address:**
  61 N. St. Joseph St., Niles, MI 49120

Phone: (616) 3350

**Contact:** Nancy Walton, M.S., Adoption Program.

**Date established:** 1988.

**Description:** Private, not-for-profit child placing agency licensed by the Indiana Division of Family and Social Services and the Michigan Department of Social Services and offering programs in agency, attorney-assisted, international and special needs adoption.

**Area served:** Residents of Indiana and Michigan.

**Requirements:** Couples must be married at least 2 yrs. who are at least 25 yrs. old and in good health.

**Fees:** Application: $50; home study: $850; post-placement supervision: $450. International fees additional.

**Number of children placed last year:** 15.

**Description of children:** Primarily foreign-born infants and children. Countries of origin include Brazil, China, India, Korea, Romania and Russia.

**Adoption procedure:** 1) Informational meeting; 2) application; 3) home study; 4) placement; 5) post-placement supervision; 6) finalization.

**Average length of time between application and start of home study:** Less than 1 mo.

**Average length of time to complete home study:** 2 mos.

**Number of interviews:** 5.

**Home study description:** Assessment which includes family history, references and police clearances, health reports and addresses such issues as the marital relationship, finances, motivation to adopt, type of child requested and parenting skills.

**Average wait for a child after approval of a home study:** 6 -12 mos.

**Foster care:** None.

## ★ 203 ★

**Americans for African Adoptions, Inc. (AFAA)**
8910 Timberwood Dr.
Indianapolis, IN 46234-1952
Phone: (317) 271-4567
Fax: (317) 271-4567

**Contact:** Cheryl Shotts, Founder/Managing Director.

**Date established:** 1986.

**Description:** Private, non-profit, tax-exempt adoption agency licensed by the Indiana Department of Children and Social Services.

**Area served:** No geographic restrictions for placement. Home study and supervision: residents of central Indiana.

**Requirements:** Applicants must be between the ages of 23 and 60 yrs.

**Fees:** Application: $4750; home study (Indiana residents only): $750; escort expenses and child's one-way airfare average: $2100 - $2300.

**Number of children placed last year:** 8.

**Description of children:** Children from infancy to 15 yrs., some sibling groups and some children with special needs from Ethiopia, Mali, Sierra Leone and Uganda.

**Adoption procedure:** 1) Telephone inquiry; 2) application; 3) home study and dossier compilation; 4)placement.

**Average length of time between application and start of home study:** 6 - 12 mos.

**Average length of time to complete home study:** 1 mo.

**Number of interviews:** 2 - 3.

**Home study description:** Assessment which follow guidelines set by the Indian Department of Children and Social Services.

**Average wait for a child after approval of a home study:** 6 - 12 mos.

**Foster care:** None.

---

★ 204 ★

**Baptist Children's Home and Family Ministries**
354 West St.
Valparaiso, IN 46383
Phone: (219) 462-4111
Fax: (219) 464-9540

**Branch address:**

2150 S. Center Blvd., Springfield, OH 45506
Phone: (513) 322-0006

224 1/2 N.W. Abilene, Ankeny, IA 50021
Phone: (515) 964-0986

**Contact:** Intake worker.

**Date established:** 1955.

**Description:** Non-profit multi-service agency.

**Area served:** Residents of the U.S.

**Requirements:** Applicants should be members of churches which support the ministry.

**Fees:** Sliding scale based on income.

**Number of children placed last year:** 30.

**Description of children:** Primarily infants.

**Adoption procedure:**
1) Submit pre-application;
2) file application;
3) wait for home study;
4) complete home study;
5) if approved, wait for placement;
6) placement.

**Average length of time between application and start of home study:** 12-24 mos.

**Average length of time to complete home study:** 6-9 mos.

**Number of interviews:** 4.

**Home study description:** Call or write for outline.

**Average wait for a child after approval of a home study:** 12-24 mos.

**Foster care:** Temporary and long-term.

---

★ 205 ★

**Bethany Christian Services (of Indiana)**
830 Cedar Pkwy.
Schererville, IN 46375
Phone: (219) 864-0800

**Contact:** Michaelyn Sloan, Coordinator.

**Date established:** 1986.

**Description:** Private, non-profit child placing agency licensed by the Indiana Department of Children and Social Services and accredited by the Council on Accreditation of Services for Families & Children and a member of the Evangelical Council for Financial Accountability.

**Area served:** Residents of Indiana.

**Requirements:** Applicants for domestic adoption program must have a personal relationship with Jesus Christ. Additional requirements may be asked of applicants for foreign adoption program.

**Fees:** Application: $550; home study: $1250; placement & post-placement services: $5700. Medical, legal and interim care costs are additional.

**Number of children placed last year:** 22.

**Description of children:** 20 U.S. born and 2 foreign born.

**Adoption procedure:** 1) Preliminary application: 2) formal application; 3) home study; 4) wait for child match; 5) placement; 6) post-placement supervision; 7) finalization.

**Average length of time between application and start of home study:** Less than 1 mo.

**Average length of time to complete home study:** 3 mos.

**Number of interviews:** 4 - 5.

**Home study description:** Assessment which includes documentation of birth, marriage, divorce, if applicable, criminal records checks, pet immunizations, medical reports and insurance, information from employer and personal references and addresses such issues as finances and autobiographical information.

**Average wait for a child after approval of a home study:** Domestic adoption: 24 or more mos.

**Foster care:** Temporary and pre-adoptive.

---

★ 206 ★

**Bethany Christian Services of Indianapolis**
6144 Hillside Ave., Ste. 10
Indianapolis, IN 46220-2474
Phone: (317) 254-8479
Fax: (317) 254-8480

**Contact:** Linda Wrestler.

**Date established:** 1983.

**Description:** Non-profit, private child-placing agency licensed by the Indiana Dept. of Public Welfare.

**Area served:**
Domestic adoptions: residents of the southern two thirds of Indiana.
For international adoptions: residents statewide.

**Requirements:** At least one parent must be a U.S. citizen; adoptive parent must be no more than 45 yrs. older than the child placed; a minimum of 2 yr. marriage. Single parents must be at least 25 yrs. old. All applicants must demonstrate financial stability.

**Fees:**
Bethany fee for a first placement: $4000;
total cost $7000-$12,000 or more depending on child's country of origin.

**Number of children placed last year:** 34.

**Description of children:** Primarily Asian children but some children from South America and Eastern Europe.

**Adoption procedure:**
1) Initial inquiry;
2) attend preliminary information meeting;
3) complete home study;
4) meet requirements of foreign agency and immigration;
5) sharing of background information of child selected;
6) if accepted, placement;
7) post-placement supervision;
8) legal finalization;
9) naturalization.

**Average length of time between application and start of home study:** 1-6 mos.

**Average length of time to complete home study:** 3 mos.

**Number of interviews:** 4.

**Home study description:** Evaluation of parenting skills, attitudes toward adoption, acceptance of a child from another culture and others.

**Average wait for a child after approval of a home study:** 6-12 mos.

**Foster care:** Temporary.

★ 207 ★
**Catholic Charities Bureau, Evansville**
Court Bldg., Ste. 603
123 N.W. 4th St.
Evansville, IN 47708
Phone: (812) 423-5456

**Contact:** Msgr. Kenneth Knapp, Acting Director or Martha Halterman, Supervisor.

**Date established:** 1937.

**Description:** Non-profit, private agency licensed in the State of Indiana.

**Area served:** Residents of Daviess, Dubois, Gibson, Greene, Knox, Martin, Pike, Posey, Spencer, Sullivan, Vanderburgh, and Warrick counties.

**Requirements:** Couples married at least 3 yrs. at least one of whom is Roman Catholic, who are at least 24 yrs. old and who must submit the results of a medical examination with blood and lung tests.
  Age and religious requirement is waived for special needs adoption and single applicants may apply.

**Fees:** Adoptive home study and post-placement supervision: not to exceed $2700.

**Number of children placed last year:** Unavailable.

**Description of children:** Caucasian infants and children with special needs.

**Adoption procedure:**
Infant Adoption:
1) Initial inquiry;
2) return pre-application and family summary at a later date;
3) return complete application material;
4) admission to Infant Adoption List;
5) complete home study;
6) if approved, wait for placement;
7) placement;
8) 1 yr. post-placement supervision;
9) finalization.
Special Needs Adoption:
1) Submit application material including medical, etc.;
2) caseworker assigned;
3) complete home study;
4) placement;
5) 1 yr. post-placement supervision;
6) finalization.

**Average length of time between application and start of home study:** Varies.

**Average length of time to complete home study:** 3-6 mos.

**Number of interviews:** Varies.

**Home study description:** Evaluatory process which includes discussions of background, communication styles, motivation to adopt, type of child desired, any children in the home, methods of discipline, religion, finances and others.

**Average wait for a child after approval of a home study:** Varies.

**Foster care:** Temporary and long-term.

★ 208 ★
**Catholic Charities of Ft. Wayne**
315 E. Washington Blvd.
Ft. Wayne, IN 46802
Phone: (219) 422-7511
(800) 686-7459
Fax: (219) 422-4585

**Contact:** Adoption Department.

**Date established:** 1922.

**Description:** Non-profit private agency licensed by the State of Indiana. Catholic Social Services was absorbed by Catholic Charities in 1989.

**Area served:** Residents of Adams, Allen, DeKalb, Huntington, Noble, Steuben, Wabash, Wells and Whitley counties.

**Requirements:** Flexible.

**Fees:**
Application: $60;
group series: $200;
home study: $700;
placement fee: sliding scale, minimum of $2500 and maximum of $10,000;
special needs or minority: fees can be waived.

**Number of children placed last year:** 19.

**Description of children:** Healthy white infants, toddlers, minority and special needs.

**Adoption procedure:** Applicants for healthy white infants:
1) Attend general information meeting;
2) name added to waiting list for an application;
3) attend adoption group meetings;
4) complete home study;
5) if approved, placement;
6) 6 mos. post-placement supervision; and
7) finalization.

**Average length of time between application and start of home study:** 6-12 mos.

**Average length of time to complete home study:** 10-12 hrs.

**Number of interviews:** 5 plus group meetings.

**Home study description:** Evaluation of family stability, adoption as a postive means of family building, attitude towards birth parents, openness of adoption, infertility resolution, and bonding process.

**Average wait for a child after approval of a home study:** 6-12 mos.

**Foster care:** Temporary infant care.

★ 209 ★
**Catholic Social Services of South Bend**
120 S. Taylor St.
South Bend, IN 46601
Phone: (219) 234-3111
Fax: (219) 289-1034

**Contact:** Intake worker.

**Date established:** Catholic Social Services was established in 1958. Prior to that date, the agency was referred to as Catholic Charities. Records of the earliest adoption are dated 1933.

**Description:** Non-profit private agency.

**Area served:** Residents of St. Joseph, Marshall, Elkhart, Kosciusko, and La Grange counties.

**Requirements:** Applicants for healthy white infants: married couples who are younger than 47 yrs., infertile, and who have no more than 1 child. After placement, one parent must remain in the home full-time for two months.

**Fees:**
1) Healthy white infant: application fee: $60; remaining fees are 12% of applicant couple's adjusted gross combined annual income and include a home study fee of $600 and the Adoption Education fee of $200.
2) Special needs: $300 study fee. Donations are accepted to offset the cost of care.

**Number of children placed last year:** 26.

**Description of children:** Healthy infants and children with special needs.

**Adoption procedure:**
1) Telephone inquiry;
2) intake and informational interview;
3) complete and return application;
4) participate in Adoption Education Group;
5) complete home study;
6) if approved, wait for parent-infant match.

**Average length of time between application and start of home study:** 6-12 mos.

**Average length of time to complete home study:** 2-4 mos.

**Number of interviews:** 5 and 5 mandatory sessions of the Adoption Education Group.

**Home study description:** Assessment of couple's emotional maturity, marital stability, potential parenting ability, financial responsibility, medical reports, autobiographies, and current knowledge of adoption.

**Average wait for a child after approval of a home study:** 12-24 mos. for open adoption; 24 or more mos. for semi-open adoption.

**Foster care:** Pre-adoptive.

**★ 210 ★**
**Childplace**
2420 Hwy. 62
Jeffersonville, IN 47130
Phone: (812) 282-8248
Fax: (812) 282-3291

**Branch address:**
3248 Taylor Blvd., Louisville, KY 40215
Phone: (502) 363-1633

**Contact:** Peggy Harper or Jolian Drain.

**Date established:** 1979.

**Description:** Non-profit private agency licensed in Indiana, Kentucky, and West Virginia.

**Area served:** Residents of Indiana and Kentucky.

**Requirements:** Couples married at least 3 yrs. who are between the ages of 21 and 39 yrs. and who are both active members of the Church of Christ.

**Fees:**
Home study: $750;
placement fee: $6000 and up depending on cost of child care.

**Number of children placed last year:** 19.

**Description of children:** Healthy Caucasian and biracial infants.

**Adoption procedure:**
1) Submit Basic Information Form;
2) attend orientation;
3) file application;
4) complete home study;
5) if approved, placement;
6) 6 mos. post-placement supervision;
7) finalization.

**Average length of time between application and start of home study:** 1-6 mos.

**Average length of time to complete home study:** Varies.

**Number of interviews:** 3.

**Home study description:** Evaluation of family background, marital relationship, parenting philosophies and methods of discipline, plans for the future.

**Average wait for a child after approval of a home study:** 6-12 mos.

**Foster care:** Temporary.

**★ 211 ★**
**Children's Bureau of Indianapolis**
615 N. Alabama, Rm. 426
Indianapolis, IN 46204
Phone: (317) 634-6481
Fax: (317) 264-2714

**Branch address:**
Homes for Black Children, 3131 E. 38th St., Indianapolis, IN 46218
Phone: (317) 545-5281

**Contact:** Clara Anderson, Associate Director.

**Date established:** 1851.

**Description:** Private agency licensed by the State of Indiana.

**Area served:** Residents of the State of Indiana.

**Requirements:** Flexible.

**Fees:** No fees.

**Number of children placed last year:** 50.

**Description of children:** Minority infants and school age children with special needs.

**Adoption procedure:**
1) Send letter of interest or call;
2) attend group meeting;
3) file application;
4) complete home study;
5) placement;
6) finalization.

**Average length of time between application and start of home study:** 1-6 mos.

**Average length of time to complete home study:** Unavailable.

**Number of interviews:** 5-6, plus group study preparation.

**Home study description:** Evaluation which includes but is not limited to biographical information, health history and motivation to adopt. Some home studies are done as a group process.

**Average wait for a child after approval of a home study:** 6-12 mos.

**Foster care:** Temporary and long-term.

**★ 212 ★**
**Coleman Adoption Services, Inc.**
615 N. Alabama, No. 419
Indianapolis, IN 46204
Phone: (317) 638-0965

**Contact:** Jeanine Jones.

**Date established:** 1894.

**Description:** Non-profit, private agency licensed in Indiana.

**Area served:** Residents of Indiana.

**Requirements:** For healthy, Caucasian infants: couples married at least 3 years, whose average age is 43 or less, and have a diagnosed fertility problem.

**Fees:**
Healthy, Caucasian infants: $13,500 total fee.
Special needs: $2300-$5400 total fee.

**Number of children placed last year:** 37.

**Description of children:** 9 healthy, Caucasian infants; 20 black or bi-racial infants; 2 medical needs, 1 set of twins, 1 sibling group of 4.

**Adoption procedure:**
1) Initial inquiry;
2) file application;
3) complete home study;
4) if approved, placement;
5) 3 mos. post-placement supervision;
6) finalization.

**Average length of time between application and start of home study:** 1-6 mos.

**Average length of time to complete home study:** 3 mos.

**Number of interviews:** 3.

**Home study description:** Evaluation of autobiographies, personal questionnaires, medicals, financial statement and references.

**Average wait for a child after approval of a home study:** 6-12 mos.

**Foster care:** Temporary and short-term. Most adoptive placements do not include foster care but are direct from the hospital.

★ 213 ★
**Compassionate Care**
253 N. Main St.
Oakland City, IN 47660
Phone: (812) 749-4152

**Contact:** Dr. John G. Clanton, Director.

**Date established:** 1989.

**Description:** Private, non-profit child placing agency licensed by the Indiana Division of Family and Social Services and a branch of the General Baptist Family and Children's Ministries, Inc.

**Area served:** Residents of Illinois, Indiana and Michigan.

**Requirements:** Christian families.

**Fees:** Application: $300; home study: $1200. Placement fee bases on income: $3500-$7500.

**Number of children placed last year:** 0.

**Description of children:** Usually infants.

**Adoption procedure:** 1) Application; 2) submit letters of references; 3) complete spiritual life survey; 4) marriage/family report; 5) financial review; 6) criminal affidavit; 7) medical and psychological reports, if applicable; 8) home study; 9) placement; 10) 3 post-placement supervisory visits; 11) finalization.

**Average length of time between application and start of home study:** 24 or more mos.

**Average length of time to complete home study:** 3 mos.

**Number of interviews:** 1 - 3.

**Home study description:** Assessment which includes documentation of birth and marriage, physical descriptions of applicants, financial assessment and insurance and addresses such issues as applicants' upbringing, education, employment, hobbies, strengths and weaknesses, marital relationship, parenting and management skills and type of contact with biological family.

**Average wait for a child after approval of a home study:**
Varies with child availability.

**Foster care:** Temporary.

★ 214 ★
**Greater Love Adoption Decision (G.L.A.D.)**
5000 First Ave.
Evansville, IN 47724
Phone: (812) 424-4523

**Mailing address:**
P.O. Box 9105, Evansville, IN 47724

**Contact:** Shirley Pry, Adoption Caseworker.

**Date established:** 1987.

**Description:** Private child placing agency licensed by the Indiana Division of Family & Social Services.

**Area served:** Residents of Indiana for all services. Placement offered to out-of-state residents working with cooperating licensed agencies.

**Requirements:** Couples married at least 3 yrs. who are at least 20 yrs. old, in good health with the reasonable expectation to see their adoptive child grow to maturity, who have no more than 1 child are active members of a Christian church and who can demonstrate that they can manage on their income.

**Fees:** Application: $100; home study: $1100; placement fee: 10% of gross income figured on the income year prior to placement with a minimum of $5000 and a maximum of $20000. Post-placement supervision: $50/visit. Medical, legal, housing costs are extra.

**Number of children placed last year:** Unavailable.

**Description of children:** Infants.

**Adoption procedure:** 1) Application; 2) added to waiting list; 3) home study and office visit; 4) portfolio preparation; 5) birth mother review and selection; 6) parental rights terminated; 7) placement; 8) post-placement supervision; 9) finalization.

**Average length of time between application and start of home study:** 12 - 24 mos.

**Average length of time to complete home study:** 3 - 4 wks.

**Number of interviews:** 3-4.

**Home study description:** Assessment which includes description of home and family; criminal history reports, health and financial reports, references and recommendations and addresses such issues as understanding of and motivation for adoption, marital relationship, abilities and plans for childcare.

**Average wait for a child after approval of a home study:** 6 - 12 mos.

**Foster care:** Temporary.

★ 215 ★
**Jeremiah Agency, Inc.**
P.O. Box 864
Greenwood, IN 46142
Phone: (317) 887-2434

**Contact:** Diane Webster or Karen Waltz.

**Date established:** 1984.

**Description:** Private, not-for-profit agency licensed by the Indiana Division of Family and Social Services to place children.

**Area served:** No geographic boundaries.

**Requirements:** Married couples who are members in good standing of their church and who demonstrate sound financial management.

**Fees:** Home study: $500 - $1000. Medical, legal fees and agency donation are extra.

**Number of children placed last year:** 2.

**Description of children:** Infants.

**Adoption procedure:** 1) Letter of interest to be placed on waiting list; 2) addition to list with a 5 yr. minimum wait; 3) home study when placement appears imminent.

**Average length of time between application and start of home study:** 5 yr. minimum.

**Average length of time to complete home study:** Unavailable.

**Number of interviews:** Varies.

**Home study description:** Assessment which includes home visit and examination and addresses such issues as a family's background, social, emotional and financial history; attitudes about child rearing and issues surrounding adoption.

**Average wait for a child after approval of a home study:** 1 - 6 mos.

**Foster care:** None.

## ★ 216 ★
**Lutheran Child and Family Services**
1525 N. Ritter Ave.
Indianapolis, IN 46219
Phone: (317) 359-5467
Fax: (317) 375-9322

**Contact:** Max Blankenburg, ACSW, CCSW.

**Date established:** 1883.

**Description:** Non-profit, licensed child placing agency.

**Area served:** Residents of the State of Indiana.

**Requirements:** Couples married at least 2 yrs.

**Fees:**
Special needs adoption: $600 plus travel;
infant adoption: $10,000.

**Number of children placed last year:** 5.

**Description of children:** Infants and children with special needs.

**Adoption procedure:**
1) File application;
2) attend agency interviews;
3) complete 1 home visit;
4) undergo physical examination;
5) if approved, placement.

**Average length of time between application and start of home study:** 1 mo. or less.

**Average length of time to complete home study:** 3-6 mos.

**Number of interviews:** 3 or more.

**Home study description:** Evaluation and education process.

**Average wait for a child after approval of a home study:** Varies.

**Foster care:** Temporary.

## ★ 217 ★
**Lutheran Social Services of Fort Wayne**
330 Madison St.
Ft. Wayne, IN 46857-1329
Phone: (219) 426-3347
Fax: (219) 424-2248

**Mailing address:**
 P.O. Box 11329, Ft. Wayne, IN 46857-1329

**Contact:** Constance J. Loucks.

**Date established:** 1901.

**Description:** Non-profit, private agency licensed by the Indiana Dept. of Public Welfare.

**Area served:** Residents of the 12 counties of northeast Indiana.

**Requirements:** Adults between the ages of 20 and 45 yrs.

**Fees:**
12% of income with a minimum of $2500 and a maximum of $7500;
home study: $1000.

**Number of children placed last year:** 24.

**Description of children:** 7 foreign-born children, 5 children with special needs and 11 others.

**Adoption procedure:**
 1) Initial inquiry;
 2) submit application;
 3) complete home study;
 4) if approved, placement.

**Average length of time between application and start of home study:** 1 mo. or less.

**Average length of time to complete home study:** 2 mos.

**Number of interviews:** 4.

**Home study description:** Call or write for guidelines.

**Average wait for a child after approval of a home study:** 24 or more mos.

**Foster care:** Occasionally, short-term.

## ★ 218 ★
**Lutheran Social Services of Indiana**
1400 N. Broad St.
Griffith, IN 46319
Phone: (219) 838-0996
Fax: (219) 838-0999

**Contact:** Ruth Werth, Adoption Specialist.

**Date established:** Unavailable.

**Description:** Private, not-for-profit agency licensed to place children, conduct home studies and post-placement supervision by the Indiana Division of Family and Social Services.

**Area served:** Residents of Indiana.

**Requirements:** Applicants may be single or legally married, must present a doctor's health recommendation and be active in their faith.

**Fees:** Home study: $1265. Placement and legal fees are extra.

**Number of children placed last year:** 7.

**Description of children:** Primarily Caucasian infants and 2 children with special needs.

**Adoption procedure:** 1) Inquiry; 2) home study; 3) placement; 4) finalization.

**Average length of time between application and start of home study:** Varies with type of child requested.

**Average length of time to complete home study:** 12 hrs.

**Number of interviews:** 3.

**Home study description:** Assessment which addresses such issues as marriage, family of origin, self-image, education, motivation to adopt, and other adoption issues including plans to tell child of his/her own adoption, philosophy of childrearing and methods of discipline.

**Average wait for a child after approval of a home study:** Varies.

**Foster care:** Temporary.

★ 219 ★
**St. Elizabeth's Home**
2500 Churchman Ave.
Indianapolis, IN 46203
Phone: (317) 787-3412

**Contact:** Mary Rose Nevitt.

**Date established:** 1915.

**Description:** Non-profit private agency.

**Area served:** Residents of the State of Indiana.

**Requirements:** Applicants must be Indiana residents, 21 yrs. or older.

**Fees:** Sliding scale.

**Number of children placed last year:** 13.

**Description of children:** Healthy infants and children with special needs.

**Adoption procedure:**
1) Attend general informational meeting;
2) submit application;
3) forward medical reports and references;
4) waiting period for home study;
5) home study;
6) wait for placement.

**Average length of time between application and start of home study:** 24 or more mos.

**Average length of time to complete home study:** 3 mos.

**Number of interviews:** 3-4.

**Home study description:** Evaluation of family history, marital relationship, security and stability, understanding of adoption issues.

**Average wait for a child after approval of a home study:** 12-24 mos.

**Foster care:** Temporary.

★ 220 ★
**The Villages of Indiana, Inc.**
2405 N. Smith Pike
Bloomington, IN 47401
Phone: (812) 332-1245
(800) 874-6880
Fax: (317) 486-1520

**Contact:** Gina Alexander or Roberta Henry-Baker.

**Date established:** 1985.

**Description:** Non-profit group homes for special needs children.

**Area served:** Residents of Indiana.

**Requirements:** Participation in foster/adoptive parent training.

**Fees:** None.

**Number of children placed last year:** 5.

**Description of children:** Emotionally and behaviorally handicapped children.

**Adoption procedure:**
1) Complete 8 wk. foster care training;
2) 1 yr. foster care placement;
3) file petition and finalize adoption.

**Average length of time between application and start of home study:** 1-6 mos.

**Average length of time to complete home study:** 3 mos.

**Number of interviews:** Varies.

**Home study description:** Evaluation of motivation to adopt, personalities of parents and biological children (if any), family relationships, attitudes toward foster parenting and foster child, parenting styles and education.

**Average wait for a child after approval of a home study:** 1-6 mos.

**Foster care:** Long-term foster care is the first priority of The Villages of Indiana, Inc.

# IOWA

## STATUTES

★ 221 ★
**Independent placement by intermediary?** Permitted.

**Independent placement by birth parents?** Intermediary services are required.

**Subsidies provided?** Maintenance and special services which may include attorney fees, medical, medical transportation, child care, outpatient counseling and therapy, supplies and equipment.

**Adoption cost defined by law?** Adoption expenditures must be filed with the court.

**Insurance for infertility?:** Unknown.

**Home study required by state?** Required before placement except in the case of relative adoptions.

**Prospective adoptive parent advertise for a child?** Permitted.

**Surrogacy laws?** No law prohibits it.

**Residents access agencies of other states or countries?** Permitted.

**Requires judicial termination of birth parents' rights?** Valid signature of both parents on a release of custody form which may be signed no earlier than 72 hrs. after the birth of the child.

**Time given to a birthmother to revoke her consent:** Any time prior to hearing for termination of parental rights.

**Court handling adoptions?** District Juvenile Court.

**Adoption of Native Children:** Indian Child Welfare Act is a federal law.

**Adoption records sealed?** Sealed except in cases where a birth parent has filed an affidavit to reveal his/her name when the adoptee reaches the age of 18 yrs.

**Photo-listing book available?** *Iowa's Waiting Children.*

## PUBLIC AGENCIES

★ 222 ★
**Iowa Department of Human Services**
Hoover State Office Building
Des Moines, IA 50319
Phone: (515)281-5358

**Branch address:**
Iowa Bldg. 6th Fl., 221 Fourth Ave. SE, Cedar Rapids, IA 52401

417 E. Kanesville Blvd., Council Bluffs, IA 51503

428 Western Ave., 3rd Fl., Davenport, IA 52801

1200 University Ave., Davenport, IA 52801

Mohawk Sq., 22 N. Georgia Ave., Mason City, IA 50401

226 W. Main, Ottumwa, IA 52501

507 Seventh St., Sioux City, IA 51101-1009

KWWL Bldg., 3rd Fl., 500 E. 4th St., Waterloo, IA 50704

**Contact:** Charlcie Parrish, Adoption Unit Manager.

**Description:** Non-profit, public agency.

**Area served:** Residents of the State of Iowa.

**Requirements:** Applicants may be single or married, but must have adequate health to parent, sufficient income to provide for a child and be no more than 40 yrs. older than the child placed.

**Fees:** None.

**Number of children placed last year:** 200.

**Description of children:** 60% of the children placed were special needs.

**Adoption procedure:** Procedure explained at time of initial inquiry.

**Average length of time between application and start of home study:** 1-3 yrs.

**Average length of time to complete home study:** 20 or more hrs.

**Number of interviews:** 2-3.

**Home study description:** An evaluation of applicant(s)' health, marital history, community involvement, income, motivation to adopt and child rearing methods.

**Average wait for a child after approval of a home study:** Varies with kind of child desired.

**Foster care:** Temporary and long-term.

# PRIVATE AGENCIES

## ★ 223 ★
### Bethany Christian Services (of Des Moines)
6000 Douglas, Ste. 230
Des Moines, IA 50322-3300
Phone: (515) 270-0824

**Contact:** Marlae Lee, MSW.

**Date established:** 1984.

**Description:** Private, non-profit child placement agency licensed by the Iowa Department of Human Services.

**Area served:** Primarily residents of central and south central Iowa.

**Requirements:** Professed Christian couples married at least 3 yrs. who believe that life begins at conception and who have fewer than 2 children to participate in the Caucasian infant program. The number of children already in the home varies somewhat for participants in the biracial program.

**Fees:** Total fees: 23% of adjusted gross income for 1 yr.

**Number of children placed last year:** 9.

**Description of children:** Caucasian and biracial infants, some with special needs.

**Adoption procedure:** 1) Application; 2) attend informational meeting; 3) assessment with interviews; 4)adoptive parenting classes; 5) documentation; 6) approval process; 7) placement; 8)post-placement supervision; 9) finalization.

**Average length of time between application and start of home study:** 6-12 mos.

**Average length of time to complete home study:** 1 - 2 mos.

**Number of interviews:** 3-4.

**Home study description:** Preparatory and educational process which includes a series of parenting classes, completion of necessary paperwork such as statements of income, reference letters, copies of vital records and insurance policies and addresses such issues as emotional, physical and spiritual health, family stability, readiness for parenthood and applicants' relationship with Jesus Christ.

**Average wait for a child after approval of a home study:** 6 mos. to 2 yrs. The wait for families approved for biracial program is much briefer.

**Foster care:** Temporary.

## ★ 224 ★
### Bethany Christian Services of Northwest Iowa
123 Albany St., S.E.
Orange City, IA 51041
Phone: (712) 737-4831
(800) BETHANY
Fax: (712) 737-3238

**Mailing address:**
P.O. Box 143, Orange City, IA 51041

**Contact:** Adri M. Ruisch, Branch Supervisor.

**Date established:** 1974.

**Description:** Non-profit, private agency licensed in South Dakota, Minnesota and Iowa.

**Area served:** Residents of Minnesota, Nebraska, North Dakota, South Dakota and Iowa.

**Requirements:** Couples married at least 3 yrs. who are between the ages of 25 and 38 yrs. who have less than 2 children and a diagnosed fertility problem and who are both active members of an evangelical, Bible-teaching church.

**Fees:** Sliding scale.

**Number of children placed last year:** 30.

**Description of children:** Caucasian and biracial infants, children with disabilities, international.

**Adoption procedure:** Agency informs applicants of the steps in the adoption process upon the submission of the preliminary application.

**Average length of time between application and start of home study:** 12-24 mos.

**Average length of time to complete home study:** 6 mos.

**Number of interviews:** 4 or more.

**Home study description:** Family assessment includes feelings about adoption, effective parenting and what type of child would best fit into applicants' family.

**Average wait for a child after approval of a home study:** 12-24 mos.

**Foster care:** Temporary.

## ★ 225 ★
### Catholic Charities, Inc., Des Moines
1601 Grand Ave.
Des Moines, IA 50303
Phone: (515) 244-3761
(800) 669-3761
Fax: (515) 237-5070

**Mailing address:**
 P.O. Box 723, Des Moines, IA 50303

**Branch address:**
 315 W. Pierce St., Council Bluffs, IA 51503

**Contact:** Duane Weiland, Jeri Liston.

**Date established:** 1924.

**Description:** Non-profit private agency licensed in the State of Iowa and accredited through the Council on Accreditation.

**Area served:** Residents of 23 southwestern counties of Iowa.

**Requirements:** Married couples who are married at least 2 yrs. at the time home study is begun; who are no more than 40 yrs. old when their name is added to the adoption waiting list and no more than 40 yrs. old at the time of placement. Couple must have some faith commitment. Applications are accepted from both Catholic and non-Catholic families.

**Fees:** Sliding scale based on family income. Fee includes service and a medical fee.

**Number of children placed last year:** 11.

**Description of children:** Infants.

**Adoption procedure:**
 1) Attend initial inquiry interview;
 2) participate in 4 educational workshops;
 3) psychological test administered;
 4) placement;
 5) post-placement period which includes 1 home visit and 2 office visits.

**Average length of time between application and start of home study:** 1-6 mos.

**Average length of time to complete home study:** 6 mos.

**Number of interviews:** 5.

**Home study description:** Evaluation which includes but is not limited to identifying information about applicant couple; family background; marital relationship; education and employment; religion; finances; home and family; special interests; general health and fertility; motivation for parenthood and adoption; attitudes toward adoption and birthparents; child rearing practices; experiences with children; expectations of a child; and references.

**Average wait for a child after approval of a home study:** 24 or more mos.

**Foster care:** Temporary.

★ 226 ★
**Catholic Charities of the Archdiocese of Dubuque**
P.O. Box 1309
Dubuque, IA 52001
Phone: (319) 588-0558

**Branch address:**
 1430 2nd Ave., S.E., Cedar Rapids, IA 52403

 208 5th St., Ames, IA 50010

 First National Bldg., Ste. 402, Waterloo, IA 50703

 600 1st St. N.W., Mason City, IA 50401

**Contact:** Nancy K. Kinley, Adoption Coordinator.

**Date established:** 1931.

**Description:** Private non-profit child placing agency licensed by the State of Iowa.

**Area served:** Residents of the counties of the Archdiocese of Dubuque.

**Requirements:** Couples married at least 3 yrs. who have at least a high school diploma or equivalent, whose minimal annual income is $20,000, who have completed psychological testing, who are childless and have a medical diagnosis of infertility, who have an active faith life, and who are not older than 40 yrs. at the time of application.

**Fees:**
Fees are subject to change.
Application: $375;
home study: $900-$2100;
placement & post-placement services: $2100;
medical costs for birthmother and infant: $3000.

**Number of children placed last year:** 16.

**Description of children:** Primarily caucasian U.S. infants; some mixed race infants.

**Adoption procedure:** The Adoption List is open to residents of the Archdiocese of Dubuque only and opens every 18 mos.
 1) Complete pre-screening;
 2) attend education day;
 3) complete pre-placement investigation and interview process.

**Average length of time between application and start of home study:** 1-6 mos.

**Average length of time to complete home study:** 1-2 mos.

**Number of interviews:** 2-3.

**Home study description:** Evaluation of individual and marital stability; education and employment history; family of origin history; religious and financial information; parenting skills and motivation to adopt.

**Average wait for a child after approval of a home study:** 6-12 mos.

**Foster care:** Temporary.

★ 227 ★
**Catholic Charities of the Diocese of Sioux City, Iowa, Inc.**
1601 Military Rd.
Sioux City, IA 51103
Phone: (712) 252-4547
Fax: (712) 252-3785

**Branch address:**
 409 1/2 W. 7th St., Carroll, IA 51401
 Phone: (712) 792-9597

 3 N. 16th St., Ft. Dodge, IA 50501
 Phone: (515) 576-4156

**Contact:** Audra L. Cole, ACSA, LSW, or Molly Twohig, MSW.

**Date established:** 1942.

**Description:** Not-for-profit child placing agency licensed by the State of Iowa.

**Area served:** Residents of 24 counties of northwest Iowa and Dakota County in Nebraska.

**Requirements:** Couples married at least 2 yrs., who are no older than 45 yrs., have a religious faith, sufficient income to support a family, have adequate health to fulfill parental responsibilities, are childless, and have a medical diagnosis of infertility.

**Fees:** Sliding scale with a maximum of $9000.

**Number of children placed last year:** 6.

**Description of children:** Infants and special needs.

**Adoption procedure:**
 1) Attend individual intake screening;
 2) waiting list for study;
 3) file complete application;

4) attend individual interview;
5) request 4 references and send letters of recommendation (1 of which must be from a clergyman);
6) submit medical examinations for all family members;
7) participate in 3 group meetings;
8) home visit;
9) if approved, placement on waiting list;
10) placement;
11) supervisory/post-placement study; and
12) finalization.

**Average length of time between application and start of home study:** 6-12 mos.

**Average length of time to complete home study:** 2-3 mos.

**Number of interviews:** 3 full day group sessions, 1 home visit, and 1 office visit.

**Home study description:** Evaluatory and preparatory process wherein the following are discussed: agency policy and procedures; infertility and the grief process; birth parents; child and adolescent development; marriage and family roles; baby care; special issues and trends in adoption.

**Average wait for a child after approval of a home study:** 1-6 mos.

**Foster care:** Temporary (infants waiting for placement).

## ★ 228 ★
**The Crittenton Center**
1105 - 28th St.
Sioux City, IA 51104
Phone: (712) 255-4321

**Contact:** Lupe Hittle, Executive Director.

**Date established:** 1894.

**Description:** Private, non-profit social welfare agency licensed to place children by the Iowa Department of Human Services.

**Area served:** Residents of western and northwestern Iowa.

**Requirements:** In the process of review.

**Fees:** Total program fee: $5000.

**Number of children placed last year:** 0, usually several a year.

**Description of children:** Infants.

**Adoption procedure:** 1) Submission of introductory letter ; 2) application; 3) home study; 4) wait for placement; 5) placement; 6) post-placement supervision; 7) finalization.

**Average length of time between application and start of home study:** 12 - 24 mos.

**Average length of time to complete home study:** 6 - 9 mos.

**Number of interviews:** 2 - 4.

**Home study description:** Assessment which includes reference checks, criminal records and child abuse registry checks and addresses such issues as social and medical history and home environment.

**Average wait for a child after approval of a home study:** 24 or more mos.

**Foster care:** Temporary.

## ★ 229 ★
**Hillcrest Family Services**
205 12th St. S.E.
Cedar Rapids, IA 52403
Phone: (319) 362-3149
Fax: (319) 362-8923

**Contact:** Nancy Lee Ziese, MSW, Adoption Coordinator.

**Date established:** 1918.

**Description:** Non-profit child placing agency licensed in the State of Iowa.

**Area served:** All of Iowa excluding the southwest quadrant.

**Requirements:** Couples married at least 3 yrs. who have adequate income to provide for a child, are in good health but have medical documentation of fertility study. Parental age depends on program.

**Fees:** Sliding scale based on income.

**Number of children placed last year:** 23.

**Description of children:** Infants, foreign-born children and children with special needs.

**Adoption procedure:**
1) Criminal record and child abuse registry clearances;
2) file application;
3) attend individual and joint interviews;
4) undergo psychological and physical examinations;
5) submit references; and
6) home visit.

**Average length of time between application and start of home study:** 1-6 mos.

**Average length of time to complete home study:** 2-6 months.

**Number of interviews:** 5.

**Home study description:** Evaluation of motivation to adopt, type of child desired; personal history of each applicant; physical/psychological reports; economic stability and good use of resources; safe and adequate home environment; and good standing in community.

**Average wait for a child after approval of a home study:** 12-24 mos.

**Foster care:** Temporary.

## ★ 230 ★
**Lutheran Social Services of Iowa**
3116 University Ave.
Des Moines, IA 50311
Phone: (515) 277-4476
Fax: (515) 277-0206

**Branch address:**
1323 Northwestern, Ames, IA 50010
Phone: (515) 232-7262

3125 Cottage Grove Ave., Des Moines, IA 50310
Phone: (515) 274-4946

1500 Sycamore, Iowa City, IA 52240
Phone: (319) 351-4880

1327 6th St., SW, Mason City, IA 50401
Phone: (515) 423-6313

4240 Hickory Ln., Ste. 100, Sioux City, IA 51106
Phone: (712) 276-1073

1510 Logan, Waterloo, IA 50703
Phone: (319) 233-3579

**Contact:** Lyn Lienhard, Executive Vice-President.

**Date established:** 1939.

**Description:** Non-profit, private family service agency licensed by the Iowa Dept. of Human Services and accredited by the Council on Accreditation of Services for Families and Children.

**Area served:** Residents of Iowa.

**Requirements:** Give evidence of a Christian faith, be free of chronic medical problems, be childless, have a medical opinion stating the unlikelihood of bearing children, have an income of at least $11,000 and be within the maximum age of 34. No age limitation for special needs adoption.

**Fees:**
Application fee: $75 (non-refundable);
adoption fee: sliding fee based on couple's adjusted gross income from $1000 to $9874;
special needs adoption: no application fee and adoption fee adjusted per case situation.

**Number of children placed last year:** 9.

**Description of children:** Infants.

**Adoption procedure:**
1) Submit letter of intent;
2) attend group orientation meeting;
3) file application;
4) complete family study and group education;
5) if approved, placement;
6) post-placement supervision;
7) finalization.

**Average length of time between application and start of home study:** 12-24 mos.

**Average length of time to complete home study:** Approx. 24 hrs.

**Number of interviews:** Unavailable.

**Home study description:** Assessment of identifying information, finances and employment, living arrangements, medical reports and past and present family interaction.

**Average wait for a child after approval of a home study:** 12-24 mos.

**Foster care:** Temporary and therapeutic.

# KANSAS

## STATUTES

★ 231 ★

**Independent placement by intermediary?** Permitted.

**Independent placement by birth parents?** No.

**Subsidies provided?** Medical, maintenance, non-recurring legal and special services.

**Adoption cost defined by law?** No.

**Insurance for infertility?:** Unknown.

**Home study required by state?** Required before placement.

**Prospective adoptive parent advertise for a child?** Illegal.

**Surrogacy laws?** Permitted.

**Residents access agencies of other states or countries?** Permitted.

**Requires judicial termination of birth parents' rights?** Voluntary relinquishments secured no earlier than 48 hrs. after birth are recognized.

**Time given to a birthmother to revoke her consent:** None.

**Court handling adoptions?** Probate Court.

**Adoption of Native Children:** Tribe.

**Adoption records sealed?** Sealed until adoptees become 18 yrs. old.

**Photo-listing book available?** *Family Focus.*

## PUBLIC AGENCIES

★ 232 ★
**Department of Social and Rehabilitative Services**
**Youth & Adult Services**
West Hall Bldg.
300 S.W. Oakley
Topeka, KS 66606
Phone: (913) 296-8138
Fax: (913) 296-4649

**Contact:** Patricia Long.

**Date established:** 1934.

**Description:** Public welfare agency.

**Area served:** State of Kansas.

**Requirements:** Flexible.

**Fees:** None.

**Number of children placed last year:** 220.

**Description of children:** Special needs older children who may have a medical condition or a physical, mental, or emotional disability, sibling groups, and children of color.

**Adoption procedure:** Call or write for local Social and Rehabilitative Services office.

**Average length of time between application and start of home study:** Begin training process within 2-3 mos.

**Average length of time to complete home study:** 3-6 mos.

**Number of interviews:** 4-5.

**Home study description:** Evaluation of ability to parent special needs children and law enforcement and child abuse registry checks.

**Average wait for a child after approval of a home study:** 6-12 mos.

**Foster care:** Temporary.

## PRIVATE AGENCIES

★ 233 ★
**Adoption by Gentle Shepherd, Inc.**
6310 Lamar Ave., Ste. 140
Overland Park, KS 66202
Phone: (913) 432-1353

**Branch address:**
501 Lindbergh, St. Louis, MO 63141

**Contact:** Sue Jensen, Administrative Assistant.

**Date established:** 1983.

**Description:** Private, non-profit child placing agency licensed by the Kansas Department of Social and Rehabilitative Services and the Missouri Department of Social Services.

**Area served:** Residents of the U.S. and some foreign countries.

**Requirements:** Singles are accepted, but couples must be married at least 2 yrs. Applicants should be in the 21-50 yr. age range, be non-smokers, indicate a religious faith, be certified in infant CPR and show proof of health insurance. Birth parents participate in the selection process.

**Fees:** Pre-application: $75; application, group and assessment meeting: $1350; home study/home study review: $1000; approval and advocation: $250; placement and post placement (in state): $7700; placement and post placement (out-of-state): $8300. Birth mother expenses and legal fees are extra.

**Number of children placed last year:** 48.

**Description of children:** Infants and children, both U.S. and foreign born, some with special needs.

**Adoption procedure:** 1) Pre-application; 2) application; 3) group and assessment meeting; 4) home study; 5) approval and birth parent selection; 6) placement; 7) post-placement supervision; 8) finalization.

**Average length of time between application and start of home study:** 1 - 6 mos.

**Average length of time to complete home study:** 2 wks.

**Number of interviews:** 3.

**Home study description:** Assessment which includes a description of home and community child abuse registry checks and addresses such issues as personal history, marriage, religion, issues surrounding infertility and adoption, thoughts on birth parents, finances and health.

**Average wait for a child after approval of a home study:** 1-12 mos.

**Foster care:** None.

★ 234 ★
**Adoption Centre Inc. of Kansas**
622 N. Saint Francis
Wichita, KS 67214
Phone: (316) 265-5289
(800) 804-3632
Fax: (316) 265-3953

**Contact:** Jane Goseland.

**Date established:** 1993.

**Description:** Private, for profit agency licensed by the State of Kansas.

**Area served:** All U.S.

**Requirements:** Vary and are determined by the birth parents. Up-to-date home study (not more than one yr. old) and clearance with child abuse registry necessary. Applicants must be at least 25 yrs. of age and married at least three yrs.

**Fees:** $250 application fee; $7500 agency fee; $1500 attorney fee plus any medical or living expenses incurred by the birth mother.

**Number of children placed last year:** 43.

**Description of children:** Mostly healthy Caucasian infants; some minority infants and older children.

**Adoption procedure:** 1) Telephone inquiry; 2) information packet; 3) application, composition of "Dear Birth Mother" letter and family photo album; 4) home study privately contracted by licensed social worker; 5) wait for birth parent selection; 6) birth and placement; 7) post-placement supervision completed by privately contracted licensed social worker; 8) finalization.

**Average length of time between application and start of home study:** At this time Adoption Centre Inc. is not conducting home studies, but anticipates offering this service in the near future. Prospective adoptive parents are responsible for undergoing a home study with a worker or agency licensed by the state of residence.

**Average length of time to complete home study:** Varies with privately contracted worker or agency.

**Number of interviews:** Varies with each privately contracted worker or agency.

**Home study description:** Must comply with applicants' state requirements.

**Average wait for a child after approval of a home study:** Placement is totally dependent on birth parent selection. Birth parents read "Dear Birth Mother" letters and family photo albums and make their selection accordingly. There may be direct contact between the birth and adoptive parents before, at the time of, or after birth, but always under the supervision of the agency.

**Foster care:** Pre-adoptive.

★ 235 ★
**Adoption Option**
12754 Goddard
Overland Park, KS 66213
Phone: (816) 224-1525

**Branch address:**
200 S.E. Douglas, Lee's Summit, MO 64063

**Contact:** Hillary Merryfield.

**Date established:** 1986.

**Description:** Private child placing agency licensed by the Missouri Department of Social Services.

**Area served:** Residents of Kansas and Missouri.

**Requirements:** U.S. infants: Couples married at least 3 yrs. who are in the mid-20 to mid-40 yr. age range, who are in good health and who are financially capable of caring for a child. International: Applicants need not be married for all programs and may be older.

**Fees:** Home study: $1000; post-placement services: $75/hr.; Birth Parent Home Study: $400; counseling: $60/hr.

**Number of children placed last year:** 40.

**Description of children:** U.S. Infants and foreign born infants and children.

**Adoption procedure:** After completion of home study, pictures and letters are presented to birth parents seeking adoptive placements for their children. Prospective adoptive families are also instructed in networking techniques to locate a birth family. Home studies are also conducted for prospective adoptive parents pursuing international adoptions.

**Average length of time between application and start of home study:** 1 - 6 mos.

**Average length of time to complete home study:** 8 hrs.

**Number of interviews:** 2.

**Home study description:** Assessment which addresses such issues family and marital relationship, values and attitudes toward child rearing, motivation to adopt and other issues surrounding adoption.

**Average wait for a child after approval of a home study:** 12 - 24 mos.

**Foster care:** Temporary.

★ 236 ★
**American Adoptions**
11560 W. 95th St., Ste. 143
Overland Park, KS 66214
Phone: (913) 492-2229

**Branch address:**
11011 Antioch, Overland Park, KS 66212

**Contact:** Susan.

**Date established:** 1991.

**Description:** Private, not-for-profit, child placing agency licensed by the Kansas Department of Social and Rehabilitative Services and the Missouri Department of Social Services.

**Area served:** Residents of the U.S.

**Requirements:** Applicants must be 21 yrs. or older and married at least 2 yrs.

**Fees:** Application: $75; home study: $750. Total fees: $7000 (approx.).

**Number of children placed last year:** 12.

**Description of children:** Infants.

**Adoption procedure:** 1) Pre-application; 2) home study; 3) activation; 4) dissemination of profiles and advertising; 5) placement; 6) post-placement supervision; 7) finalization.

**Average length of time between application and start of home study:** Less than 1 mo.

**Average length of time to complete home study:** 2 wks.

**Number of interviews:** 2-3.

**Home study description:** Organized and comprehensive assessment which addresses such issues as background, personality, family history and medical checks.

**Average wait for a child after approval of a home study:** 12 - 24 mos. Adoptive applicants influence their waiting time directly by their diligence in their child search.

**Foster care:** Temporary.

**★ 237 ★**
**Catholic Charities of Salina, Inc.**
425 W. Iron Ave.
P.O. Box 1366
Salina, KS 67402-1366
Phone: (913) 825-0208
Fax: (913) 826-9708

**Branch address:**
2707 Vine, Ste. 17, Hays, KS 67601
Phone: (913) 625-2644

**Contact:** Myra L. Frey, LSCSW, Adoptions.

**Date established:** 1958.

**Description:** Non-profit private agency.

**Area served:** Residents of the Diocese of Salina.

**Requirements:** Couples married at least 3 yrs. who are no older than 40 yrs. in good health with some proof of infertility and who have some church affiliation. Preference is shown to applicants under 38 yrs.

**Fees:**
Home study/application fee: $500;
  regular placement: $3500-$5000, less if special needs child (usually means black/white infant).

**Number of children placed last year:** 12.

**Description of children:** 11 white infants and 1 biracial infant.

**Adoption procedure:**
1) Attend information session in office;
2) waiting period;
3) complete home study and adoption workshop;
4) waiting period;
5) placement.

**Average length of time between application and start of home study:** 1-6 mos.

**Average length of time to complete home study:** 2-4 mos.

**Number of interviews:** Approx. 5.

**Home study description:** Evaluation which includes but is not limited to: background; infertility issues; marital history; adoption issues; and miscellaneous issues, e.g. finances, housing, etc.

**Average wait for a child after approval of a home study:** 6-24 mos.

**Foster care:** Temporary infant.

**★ 238 ★**
**Catholic Social Service of Great Bend**
2546 20th St.
Great Bend, KS 67530
Phone: (316) 792-1393
(800) 794-9756
Fax: (316) 792-1393

**Branch address:**
Dodge City Office, 910 Central, P.O. Box 137, Dodge City, KS 67801
Phone: (316) 227-1500

Garden City Office, 118 1/2 Grant, No. 3, Garden City, KS 67846
Phone: (316) 272-0010

**Contact:** Deborah J. Snapp, Program Director.

**Date established:** 1965.

**Description:** Non-profit private agency licensed by the State of Kansas.

**Area served:** Residents of the Diocese of Dodge City, an area bounded by the north county line of Barton County, west to the Colorado State line, south to the Oklahoma State line, and east to the eastern border of Barton County.

**Requirements:** Couples married at least 3 yrs., in good health as attested to by a physician, and with the recommendation of their pastor or minister.

**Fees:**
Independent home study: $500;
adoption fees: $4800;
adoptive couple is additionally responsible for medical, living, and foster care expenses for birthmother and child. Insurance generally covers medical.

**Number of children placed last year:** 7.

**Description of children:** Infants.

**Adoption procedure:** If a family falls within the requirements, they are invited to submit a preliminary application. If the application is favorably reviewed, the family's name is placed on a waiting list. After the home study is completed, there is a secondary review process. If approved, birthmother may select family for placement. After placement, there is a 6 mos. post-placement supervisory before legal finalization.

**Average length of time between application and start of home study:** 1-6 mos.

**Average length of time to complete home study:** Up to 6 mos.

**Number of interviews:** 2 group meetings and 4 to 6 individual interviews.

**Home study description:** Evaluation of parental skills and readiness; motivation; marital stability in all facets of its functioning; social and spiritual philisophies.

**Average wait for a child after approval of a home study:** 12-24 or more mos.

**Foster care:** Temporary.

**★ 239 ★**
**Catholic Social Services, Inc. of Wichita**
425 N. Topeka
Wichita, KS 67202
Phone: (316) 263-0507
Fax: (316) 263-5259

**Contact:** Loreen Olson, LMSW.

**Date established:** 1950.

**Description:** Profit-based private agency.

**Area served:** Residents of the Diocese of Wichita and southeast Kansas.

**Requirements:** Couples married 3 yrs. who are in good health, but suffer from infertility and who hold a religious faith.

**Fees:** Fees subject to change.

**Number of children placed last year:** 8.

**Description of children:** Newborn infants of all races.

**Adoption procedure:**
1) Telephone inquiry;
2) complete home study;
3) if approved, wait for placement;
4) placement;
5) post-placement services; and
6) finalization.

**Average length of time between application and start of home study:** 1 mo. or less.

**Average length of time to complete home study:** 4 wks.

**Number of interviews:** 7-10.

**Home study description:** Evaluation which includes but is not limited to biographical information, health and financial reports, and stability of applicants and marriage.

**Average wait for a child after approval of a home study:** 6-12 mos.

**Foster care:** Temporary.

★ 240 ★

**Children's Foundation - Adoption and Counseling**
602 W. Amity
Louisburg, KS 66053
Phone: (913) 837-4303

**Mailing address:**
P.O. Box 1133, Louisburg, KS 66053

**Branch address:**
St. Joseph Hospital 930 Carondelet Dr., Ste. 300, Kansas City, MO 64114
Phone: (816) 822-8383

**Contact:** Melissa Hann, Director.

**Date established:** 1990.

**Description:** Private, non-profit foundation licensed to place children by the Kansas Department of Social and Rehabilitative Services and the Missouri Dept. of Social Services.

**Area served:** Residents of the U.S. and Canada as well as U.S. citizens living abroad.

**Requirements:** Open.

**Fees:** Application: $100; formal application, home study and placement: $3500.

**Number of children placed last year:** 60.

**Description of children:** Children of all ages and nationalities, some with special needs.

**Adoption procedure:** 1) Pre-application; 2) background checks and clearances; 3) formal application and home study; 4) Immigration and Naturalization documentation; 5) child match; 6) travel; 7) placement; 8) post-placement supervision; 9) finalization.

**Average length of time between application and start of home study:** Less than 1 mo.

**Average length of time to complete home study:** 2 - 4 wks.

**Number of interviews:** 3 - 4.

**Home study description:** Assessment process which includes general description of applicant(s), home and community, references, recommendations and verifications, employment and finances and addresses such issues as background, health, religion, courtship, marriage and/or previous marriages, if applicable, attitudes toward parenting and adoption and type of child desired.

**Average wait for a child after approval of a home study:** 1 - 12 mos. depending upon child's country of origin.

**Foster care:** Temporary in specific countries.

★ 241 ★

**Family Life Services**
305 S. Summit St.
Arkansas City, KS 67005
Phone: (316) 442-1688
(800) 922-7874

**Contact:** Tim Durham.

**Date established:** 1986.

**Description:** Non-profit, private agency licensed by the Kansas Dept. of Social and Rehabilitative Services.

**Area served:** Primarily residents of Kansas.

**Requirements:** Active Christian married couples who are no older than 43 yrs.

**Fees:** $1200 for all pre-adoption stages. Adoption fee is 10% of adjusted gross income.

**Number of children placed last year:** 2.

**Description of children:** Infants from birth to 6 mos.

**Adoption procedure:**
1) Submit application;
2) participate in psychological evaluation, family composite and parent study;
3) reference checks;
4) complete home study;
5) if approved, wait for placement.

**Average length of time between application and start of home study:** 1 mo. or less.

**Average length of time to complete home study:** 2-4 mos.

**Number of interviews:** 2-4.

**Home study description:** General review of home, relationships, stability and adjustments.

**Average wait for a child after approval of a home study:** 12-24 mos.

**Foster care:** Temporary.

★ 242 ★

**Four Tribes Social Services Program**
Box 206
Horton, KS 66439
Phone: (913) 486-2837
Fax: (913) 486-2949

**Branch address:**
P.O. Box 142, Mayetta, KS 66509
Phone: (913) 966-2141

**Contact:** Zoe Ann Amey, Executive Director.

**Date established:** 1979.

**Description:** Semi-private, semi-tribal child placing agency licensed in the State of Kansas.

**Area served:** Native American residents of 5 counties in northeastern Kansas.

**Requirements:** Strong preference shown to Native American applicants.

**Fees:** None.

**Number of children placed last year:** 2.

**Description of children:** Native American children.

**Adoption procedure:** Contact agency.

**Average length of time between application and start of home study:** 24 or more mos.

**Average length of time to complete home study:** 90 days.

**Number of interviews:** 2.

**Home study description:** Evaluation which includes but is not limited to health, autobiographies and child rearing philosophies.

**Average wait for a child after approval of a home study:** 24 or more mos.

**Foster care:** Temporary, long-term, permanent (if relative placement).

★ 243 ★
**Gentle Shepherd Child Placement Services**
304 S. Clairborne, Ste. 201
Olathe, KS 66062
Phone: (913) 764-3811

**Branch address:**
1200 E. 104th St., Ste. 202, Kansas City, MO 64131

**Contact:** Gayle Rundberg, Executive Director.

**Date established:** 1983.

**Description:** Non-profit private agency licensed in State of Kansas and Missouri, member of the National Committee for Adoption and Alternatives to Abortion International.

**Area served:** Residents of the U.S., excluding Connecticut and Wisconsin.

**Requirements:** Couples married at least 1.5 yrs. at time of pre-application, between the ages of 21 and 45 yrs. Marital and age requirement is flexible for Black Infant program. Thai Program: Applicants between the ages of 30 and 45 yrs., with no less than 15 yrs. between the adoptive parent and child. One parent must travel to Thailand to escort child home.

**Fees:** Varies with program.
1)U.S. white infant program:
Pre-application: $50.
Application (scaled on income): $500-$2000.
Home study: $600.
Placement plus medical expenses: $7000-$8000
2)Biracial infant program:
Pre-application: $50.
Application: $300.
Home study: $600.
Placement: $2000 plus medical costs
3)Black infant program:
Pre-application: $25.
Application: $25.
Home study: $600.
Placement: $1000 plus medical costs
4)All programs: Interstate Compact Fee (for all non-Kansas residents): $150.
5)Home study update or review: $300.

**Number of children placed last year:** 35.

**Description of children:** Primarily infants, 1 toddler and 1 school age child.

**Adoption procedure:**
1) File pre-application when the list for the desired program is open;
2) participate in 2-day group assessment;

3) attend application meeting;
4) complete home study;
5) if domestic infant adoption, non-identifying profile shown to birthparents for selection; if foreign-born, dossier and home study sent to foreign agency;
6) placement.

**Average length of time between application and start of home study:** 1 mo. - 1 yr., average is 3-4 mos.

**Average length of time to complete home study:** 1 mo.

**Number of interviews:** 3 or more.

**Home study description:** Educational and evaluatory process which looks at background, employment history and income, insurance coverage, issues surrounding infertility and parenting philosophies.

**Average wait for a child after approval of a home study:**
Domestic newborns: 3 mos. - 2yrs.
Biracial: 6-12 mos.
Thailand: 1 yr.
Black infant: 1-8 mos.

**Foster care:** Temporary.

★ 244 ★
**Inserco**
5120 E. Central, Ste. A
Wichita, KS 67208
Phone: (316) 681-3840

**Contact:** Irvin R. Penner, LSCSW.

**Date established:** 1986.

**Description:** Private, profit-based agency.

**Area served:** U.S. residents.

**Requirements:** Married couples who are younger than 45 yrs., in good health, and who are active members of their faith.

**Fees:**
Home study: $500-$650;
post-placement: $200.
other fees on a cost basis.

**Number of children placed last year:** 8.

**Description of children:** White U.S. infants and 5 Latin American children.

**Adoption procedure:**
1) Initial inquiry;
2) file application;
3) complete home study;
4) wait for birthparent selection or foreign placement;
5) placement;
6) post-placement supervision.

**Average length of time between application and start of home study:** 1-6 mos.

**Average length of time to complete home study:** 2 mos.

**Number of interviews:** 3 or more.

**Home study description:** Evaluation of background, financial status, parenting skills, recommendation of references and motivation to adopt.

**Average wait for a child after approval of a home study:** Varies.

**Foster care:** None.

## ★ 245 ★
**Kansas Children's Service League**
Gateway Center, Tower 2, Ste. 212
4th and State Ave.
Kansas City, KS 66101
Phone: (913) 621-2016
Fax: (913) 371-0509

**Mailing address:**
P.O. Box 17-1273, Kansas City, KS 66101

**Contact:** Rosemary Alexander.

**Date established:** 1894.

**Description:** Private, non-profit child placing agency licensed by the Kansas Department of Social and Rehabilitative Services and the Missouri Department of Social services and accredited through the Council on Accreditation for Families and Children, Inc. and a member of the Child Welfare League of America.

**Area served:** Residents within a 6 mile radius of the agency's office.

**Requirements:** Each applicant is evaluated individually.

**Fees:** Home study: sliding scale from $300 - $1000. Attorney and court costs are additional.

**Number of children placed last year:** 13.

**Description of children:** Black and biracial children between the ages of birth and 3 yrs.

**Adoption procedure:** 1) Application; 2) home study; 3) pre-placement visits; 4) placement; 5) post-placement supervision; 6) finalization.

**Average length of time between application and start of home study:** Less than 1 mo.

**Average length of time to complete home study:** 3 - 6 mos.

**Number of interviews:** 5 or more.

**Home study description:** Assessment which includes documentation of marriage and divorce, if applicable, criminal history clearances and medical examinations and addresses financial and social issues.

**Average wait for a child after approval of a home study:** 1 - 6 mos. Wait is longer for single parents.

**Foster care:** Emergency and short-term.

## ★ 246 ★
**Kansas Children's Service League**
**Black Adoption Program**
630B Minnesota Ave., Ste. 310
Kansas City, KS 66101
Phone: (913) 621-2016
Fax: (913) 371-0509

**Mailing address:**
P.O. Box 17-1273, Kansas City, KS 66101

**Branch address:**
Linwood Center, Rm. W-104, 3200 Wayne, Kansas City, MO 64109
Phone: (816) 921-0654

**Contact:** Rosemary Alexander, District Director.

**Date established:** KCSL-1893; Black Adoption Program: 1973.

**Description:** Not-for-profit, private agency licensed in Kansas and Missouri.

**Area served:** Residents of the State of Kansas and metropolitan Kansas City, MO.

**Requirements:** Adults, 21 yrs. or older, who are single or in a stable marriage, who have a stable income. At least 1 spouse must be black.

**Fees:** Sliding scale based on adjusted gross income from $300 to $1000.

**Number of children placed last year:** 25.

**Description of children:** Black and biracial children between the ages of 0 and 16 yrs.

**Adoption procedure:**
1) Submit application;
2) attend introductory session;
3) complete home study process;
4) participate in support groups;
5) if approved, placement;
6) post-placement supervision;
7) finalization.

**Average length of time between application and start of home study:** 1-6 mos.

**Average length of time to complete home study:** 6-12 wks.

**Number of interviews:** 5-6.

**Home study description:** Assessment of identifying information, family background, description of family, home and community, health and finances, marital relationship (if applicable), parenting methods, motivation to adopt, child care plans and child desired.

**Average wait for a child after approval of a home study:** 6-12 mos.

**Foster care:** Temporary.

## ★ 247 ★
**Lutheran Social Service of Kansas and Oklahoma**
1855 N. Hillside
Wichita, KS 67214
Phone: (316) 686-6645
Fax: (316) 686-0453

**Branch address:**
2901 N. Classen Blvd., Oklahoma City, OK 73106
Phone: (405) 528-3124

**Contact:** Virginia Rodman, Director of Children's Services.

**Date established:** 1879.

**Description:** Non-profit, private agency licensed in the State of Kansas and Oklahoma.

**Area served:** Residents of Kansas and Oklahoma.

**Requirements:** Active members of a Christian congregation who have a stable income. Age requirement is flexible but agency prefers that child reach majority before the oldest parent reaches retirement age. Single applicants may apply for minority and special needs programs.

**Fees:**
No fees for children with special needs;
minority infant: cost-share agreement;
Caucasian infant: $7100.

**Number of children placed last year:** 34.

**Description of children:** 50% infants and 50% children with special needs.

**Adoption procedure:**
1) File application with supporting paperwork;
2) attend educational workshop;
3) complete home study;
4) if approved, placement;
5) post-placement supervision;
6) legalization.

**Average length of time between application and start of home study:** Varies by program.

**Average length of time to complete home study:** Varies by program.

**Number of interviews:** 3.

**Home study description:** Study emphasizes education and preparation for adoption and includes a standard evaluation of family's functioning and ability to successfully parent an adopted child.

**Average wait for a child after approval of a home study:** Varies by program.

**Foster care:** Specialized.

★ 248 ★
**The James A. Roberts Agency**
5300 College Blvd., Ste. B
Overland Park, KS 66211-1609
Phone: (913) 469-9680
Fax: (913) 469-8324

**Branch address:**
   8301 State Line Rd., Ste. 216, Kansas City, MO 64114-2019
   Phone: (816) 523-4440

**Contact:** James Roberts, ACSW, Director.

**Date established:** 1991.

**Description:** Private child placing agency licensed by the Missouri Department of Social Services. James A. Roberts has attained the designation of Social Work Diplomate which has international recognition and works primarily with families who have found an adoptive match or are seeking an available child.

**Description of services:** 1) Adoptive home study for domestic, international or special needs placements; 2) birth parent study preparation; 3) adoption-related counseling; 4) adoptive placement adjustment counseling.

**Area served:** None specified.

**Requirements:** Applicants must be married for one year prior to commencing the home study.

**Fees:** Home study: $700 - $900; consultation: $75/hr.

**Number of children placed last year:** 10.

**Description of children:** Assists families in conducting in formulating a child search strategy, but has no pool of available children awaiting placement.

**Average length of time between application and start of home study:** Less than 1 mo.

**Average length of time to complete home study:** 2 - 4 wks.

**Number of interviews:** 2 - 4.

**Home study description:** Assessment which includes police background and child abuse registry checks, finances, and addresses such issues as the marital relationship, extended family relationships, parenting appropriateness and personal adjustments.

**Average wait for a child after approval of a home study:** Dependent on prospective adoptive family's search diligence.

**Foster care:** Pre-adoptive.

# KENTUCKY

## STATUTES

★ 249 ★
**Independent placement by intermediary?** Illegal.
**Independent placement by birth parents?** Permitted.
**Subsidies provided?** Medical, non-recurring legal, maintenance and specialized.

**Adoption cost defined by law?** No, but costs must be approved by the judge in every termination and adoption hearing.

**Insurance for infertility?:** Unknown.

**Home study required by state?** Required before placement.

**Prospective adoptive parent advertise for a child?** Prohibited.

**Surrogacy laws?** Prohibited.

**Residents access agencies of other states or countries?** Permitted if in compliance with the ICPC.

**Requires judicial termination of birth parents' rights?** Voluntary and informed consents by both parents are recognized when taken no sooner than 72 hrs. after the child's birth.

**Time given to a birthmother to revoke her consent:** If the investigative report is approved prior to the consent, 20 days from the consent. If the investigative report is approved after the consent, then 20 days from the approval of the investigative report.

**Court handling adoptions?** Circuit Court except in Jefferson County, where adoption proceeding are heard in Family Court.

**Adoption of Native Children:** Bureau of Indian Affairs is first consulted.

**Adoption records sealed?** Sealed, but at age 18 yrs. adoptees may access non-identifying information. At age 21 yrs. adoptees may solicit the court where the adoption was finalized for a search.

**Photo-listing book available?**

**SNAP Book.**

## PUBLIC AGENCIES

★ 250 ★
**Department for Social Services**
**State of Kentucky**
275 E. Main St.
Frankfort, KY 40621
Phone: (502) 564-2147

**Contact:** Adoptions Unit.

**Date established:** 1895.

**Description:** Public agency which licenses other agencies in the State of Kentucky and primary child placing agency.

**Area served:** Residents of the State of Kentucky.

**Requirements:** Applicants must be in good health, married or single (not cohabiting), between 21-65 yrs. old with age appropriate to the child, and who have sufficient income to care for their existing family.

**Fees:** None.

**Number of children placed last year:** 1198.

**Description of children:** Minority and biracial children from 0-18 yrs., mentally, physically and emotionally handicapped children, large sibling groups of 3 or more.

**Adoption procedure:**
1) Contact local Recruitment and Certification Staff;
2) attend informational meeting;
3) complete MAPP training;
4) participate in individual and in-home interviews with caseworker;
5) forward references, medical reports, marriage and divorce records and child abuse registry clearances.

**Average length of time between application and start of home study:** Varies with rotation of MAPP training.

**Average length of time to complete home study:** 6 mos.

**Number of interviews:** Minimum of 2 plus 30 hrs. of group preparation.

**Home study description:** Evaluation of background, personalities, health and finances, home and community standing; knowledge of children, methods of discipline, understanding and acceptance of the problems of a special needs child; MAPP self-assessment in 12 areas.

**Average wait for a child after approval of a home study:** Dependent on range of special needs applicant(s) are willing to accept.

**Foster care:** Emergency, temporary, long-term, permanent, and therapeutic.

# PRIVATE AGENCIES

★ 251 ★
**Bluegrass Christian Adoption Services, Inc.**
1910 Harrodsburg Rd., Ste. 202
Lexington, KY 40503
Phone: (606) 276-2222
Fax: (606) 277-7999

**Contact:** Jerry Sweers, Executive Director.

**Date established:** 1987.

**Description:** Private, non-profit, non-denominational child placing facility licensed by the Commonwealth of Kentucky.

**Area served:** Residents of the state of Kentucky.

**Requirements:** Couples married at least 3 yrs., who are between the ages of 25-45 yrs., who are residents of Kentucky for at least 1 yr. prior to application, and who can show evidence of good health. Priority emphasis placed on spiritual maturity of couple. Applicants must be comfortable with agency Statement of Faith.

**Fees:** Sliding scale based on 10% of gross yearly earnings which includes $300 application fee and $600 home study fee.

**Number of children placed last year:** 10.

**Description of children:** Black, Caucasian and biracial infants under the age of 1 yr.

**Adoption procedure:**
1) File preliminary application;
2) receive information packet;
3) attend group session;
4) file formal application;
5) complete home study;
6) if approved and once parental rights are terminated, placement;
7) post-placement supervisory visits; and
8) finalization in court.

**Average length of time between application and start of home study:** 1-6 mos.

**Average length of time to complete home study:** 3 hrs.

**Number of interviews:** 2.

**Home study description:** Evaluation of statistical information; type of child desired; motivation to adopt; marital and family issues; childrearing philosophy; Christian history; spiritual evaluations; and physical surroundings.

**Average wait for a child after approval of a home study:** 1-3 yrs.

**Foster care:** Temporary.

★ 252 ★
**Catholic Social Services (of Lexington)**
1310 Leestown Rd.
Lexington, KY 40508
Phone: (606) 253-1993

**Contact:** Jennie Howard, Adoption Specialist.

**Description:** Non-profit child placement agency licensed through the Kentucky Cabinet for Human Resources.

**Area served:** Residents of the Diocese of Lexington.

**Requirements:** Couples married at least 3 yrs., neither of whom is older than 43 yrs., who are childless and unable to conceive a biological child. Applicants may have been divorced but only once.

**Fees:** $5000-$10,000 based on income.

**Number of children placed last year:** 20.

**Description of children:** White, black, biracial infants; some special needs infants.

**Adoption procedure:**
1) Application process wherein applicant's name is added to waiting list. Applicants contact agency every 6 mos. to advise them of their continued interest;
2) attend group orientation meeting;
3) attend individual interview;
4) complete group screening;
5) file formal application;
6) complete home study;
7) if approved, names added to placement waiting list;
8) placement;
9) 6 mos. post-placement supervisory; and
10) finalization.

**Average length of time between application and start of home study:** 12-24 mos.

**Average length of time to complete home study:** 3 mos.

**Number of interviews:** 7 group sessions plus 5 individual, including 3 couple, 1 individuals, and 1 home visit.

**Home study description:** A partial list of topics for discussion include: child rearing, infertility, marriage and family, plans to tell adoptee about his/her adoption, openness, and feelings about birthparents.

**Average wait for a child after approval of a home study:** 6-12 mos.

**Foster care:** Temporary.

★ 253 ★
**Children's Home of Northern Kentucky**
200 Home Rd.
Covington, KY 41011
Phone: (606) 261-8768
Fax: (606) 291-2431

**Contact:** Sandy Hamilton, Adoption Coordinator.

**Date established:** 1989.

**Description:** Private, non-profit child placing agency licensed by the Kentucky Department for Social Services.

**Area served:** Residents of Kentucky.

**Requirements:** Single or legally married applicants must be between the ages of 21 and 60 yrs. and in good health.

**Fees:** Application: $25; home study: $1750; home study update: $1000; post-placement supervision: $300; finalization: $100.

**Number of children placed last year:** 40.

**Description of children:** Primarily Korean infants.

**Adoption procedure:** 1) Inquiry; 2) application; 3) home study; 4) child match; 5) placement; 6) post-placement supervision; 7) finalization.

**Average length of time between application and start of home study:** Less than 1 mo.

**Average length of time to complete home study:** 4 - 6 wks.

**Number of interviews:** 3 - 4.

**Home study description:** Assessment which includes dossier compilation, background and reference checks and addresses such issues as family of origin, education and employment history, parenting skills and philosophy and motivation to adopt.

**Average wait for a child after approval of a home study:** Less than 1 mo.

**Foster care:** None.

### ★ 254 ★
**Jewish Family and Vocational Service**
3640 Dutchman Ln.
Louisville, KY 40205
Phone: (502) 452-6341

**Contact:** Judy Freundlich Tiell, L.C.S.W.

**Date established:** 1908.

**Description:** Private, non-profit human services agency licensed by the Kentucky Department for Social Services.

**Area served:** Residents of Kentucky.

**Requirements:** None.

**Fees:** Home study: $1500.

**Number of children placed last year:** 0.

**Description of children:** Agency conducts home studies, but does not place children.

**Average length of time between application and start of home study:** Less than 1 mo.

**Average length of time to complete home study:** 2 - 4 mos.

**Number of interviews:** 4 - 5.

**Home study description:** Assessment which includes autobiographical information, medicals and health history, financial information, references, child abuse and police records checks, personality and character and addresses such issues as the marital relationship, if applicable and attitudes about parenting.

**Average wait for a child after approval of a home study:** Child placement is not under the auspices of the agency.

**Foster care:** None.

### ★ 255 ★
**Kentucky One Church One Child Program**
**Louisville Urban League**
1535 W. Broadway
Louisville, KY 40203
Phone: (502) 581-6827
Fax: (502) 585-2335

**Contact:** Judy A. Jones, Director.

**Date established:** 1982.

**Description:** Non-profit social service agency.

**Area served:** Primarily residents of the State of Kentucky.

**Requirements:** Adults, 21 yrs. and older, who are in general good health.

**Fees:** None.

**Number of children placed last year:** 10.

**Description of children:** Black and biracial children from 0-10 yrs., some with special needs and 4 sibling groups.

**Adoption procedure:** The Kentucky One Church One Child Program has gone to total recruitment statewide. Once a family is identified, they are referred to their local child welfare agency for adoption services.

**Average length of time between application and start of home study:** 1-6 mos.

**Average length of time to complete home study:** 2-3 mos.

**Number of interviews:** 3-4.

**Home study description:** Assessment of family strengths, ideas about parenting, expectations of children, flexibility and level of commitment to a child with special needs. Child Welfare Agency uses MAPP curriculum.

**Average wait for a child after approval of a home study:** 6-12 mos.

**Foster care:** Inquiry for foster care is accepted.

### ★ 256 ★
**Methodist Home of Kentucky**
**Mary Kendall Adoptions**
193 Phillips Ct.
Owensboro, KY 42303
Phone: (502) 683-3723

**Contact:** Leslie Armstrong, Adoption Coordinator.

**Date established:** 1989.

**Description:** Private, non-profit home study agency licensed by the Kentucky Department for Social Services to provide home investigations for families pursuing private adoption.

**Area served:** Residents of Kentucky.

**Requirements:** Applicants for domestic placements must be at least 21 yrs. old, at least 25 yrs. old for foreign placements, single or legally married at least 2 yrs.

**Fees:** Preliminary application: $25; formal application: $150; home study: sliding scale from $1000 to $2500.

**Number of children placed last year:** 25.

**Description of children:** Home studies conducted for primarily U.S. and foreign born infants.

**Adoption procedure:** 1) Preliminary application; 2) formal application; 3) home study and applications submitted to placing agency; 4) child referral received from placing agency; 5) placement; 6) post-placement supervision; 7) finalization.

**Average length of time between application and start of home study:** Less than 1 mo.

**Average length of time to complete home study:** 2 mos.

**Number of interviews:** 4.

**Home study description:** Assessment which includes office and home visits and follow the requirements of the Kentucky Department for Social Services.

**Average wait for a child after approval of a home study:** Placement is not under the auspices of the agency.

**Foster care:** None.

# LOUISIANA

## STATUTES
### ★ 257 ★
**Independent placement by intermediary?** Permitted.
**Independent placement by birth parents?** Permitted.

**Subsidies provided?** Maintenance, legal-non-recurring and special services.

**Adoption cost defined by law?** No.

**Insurance for infertility?:** No.

**Home study required by state?** Required before placement and before finalization.

**Prospective adoptive parent advertise for a child?** Permitted.

**Surrogacy laws?** Illegal.

**Residents access agencies of other states or countries?** Yes in accordance with the ICPC.

**Requires judicial termination of birth parents' rights?** Voluntary surrenders by both birth parents are recognized.

**Time given to a birthmother to revoke her consent:** 5 days after a voluntary surrender by birth parents. If the surrender is by only one parent, relinquishment is irrevocable upon execution.

**Court handling adoptions?** Family or Juvenile Court.

**Adoption of Native Children:** Tribe.

**Adoption records sealed?** Sealed.

**Photo-listing book available?** *LARE*, the Louisiana Adoption Resource Exchange.

# PUBLIC AGENCIES

★ 258 ★
**Department of Social Services**
Commerce Bldg., 6th Fl.
333 Laurel
Baton Rouge, LA 70821
Phone: (504) 342-4041
(800) 259-2456
Fax: (504) 342-9087

**Mailing address:**
   P.O. Box 3318, Baton Rouge, LA 70821

**Contact:** Ada K. White, Adoption Program Manager.

**Description:** Public adoption agency.

**Area served:** Residents of the State of Louisiana.

**Requirements:** Adults, 18 yrs. or older, single or married, if married, marriage must be of at least 2 yrs. duration, who are in good physical and emotional health, have adequate space for another family member and who meet minimum income requirements.

**Fees:** No agency fees.

**Number of children placed last year:** 296.

**Description of children:** Infants, older children, sibling groups, and children with special needs.

**Adoption procedure:**
   1) Initial inquiry;
   2) attend orientation meeting;
   3) participate in Model Approach to Partnership in Parenting training;
   4) complete home visits;
   5) forward medical reports and have criminal clearance checks;
   6) if approved, placement.

**Average length of time between application and start of home study:** 1 mo. or less.

**Average length of time to complete home study:** 10 wks.

**Number of interviews:** 2-3.

**Home study description:** A learning process in which the agency provides information about the children available and about adoption/foster care issues and the applicants provide information about themselves. The training aspect of the study focuses on motivation, commitment, parenting skills, discipline, birth family issues, understanding the impact of foster care on a child(ren), separation and attachment and adoption related issues.

**Average wait for a child after approval of a home study:** Varies.

**Foster care:** Temporary and long-term.

★ 259 ★
**Department of Social Services (of Baton Rouge)**
**Office of Community Services**
P.O. Box 66789
Baton Rouge, LA 70896
Phone: (504) 342-0494
Fax: (504) 342-0418

**Branch address:**
   P.O. Box 1778, Covington, LA 70434
   Phone: (504) 893-6225

**Contact:** Susan Bueche.

**Date established:** C. 1952.

**Description:** Non-profit, public adoption program.

**Area served:** Residents of the Baton Rouge region.

**Requirements:** Adults between the ages of 21 and 65 yrs. who are not more than 50 yrs. older than the child placed, who are in good physical and emotional health and who are either single or legally married.

**Fees:** None.

**Number of children placed last year:** 70-80.

**Description of children:** School age children, children with educational needs, emotional problems and physical handicaps and black infants.

**Adoption procedure:**
   1) Intake;
   2) attend orientation;
   3) participate in 30 hrs. of pre-service training;
   4) complete home study;
   5) if approved, child match and placement.

**Average length of time between application and start of home study:** Varies.

**Average length of time to complete home study:** 3-4 mos.

**Number of interviews:** Group and 2 or more home visits.

**Home study description:** Assessment of family history and composition, parenting styles and discipline practices, money management and physical examination, activities, social contacts, criminal records check and recommendation of references.

**Average wait for a child after approval of a home study:** Varies.

**Foster care:** Temporary and long-term.

## ★ 260 ★
**Department of Social Services of Louisiana**
**Division of Children, Youth & Family Services**
122 St. John St.
State Office Bldg. Rm. 423
Monroe, LA 71201
Phone: (318) 362-3362
(800) 256-8654
Fax: (318) 362-3013

**Mailing address:**
  P.O. Box 3047, Monroe, LA 71201

**Contact:** Adoption Unit.

**Description:** Public social service agency.

**Area served:** Residents of the 12 civil parishes of the Monroe Region.

**Requirements:** Adults, 18 yrs. or older who are no more than 50 yrs. older than the child placed, who are in good physical and mental health, who have adequate income to support a child and adequate living space for a child. Applicants can be single or married, if married, marriage must be of at least 2 yr. duration.

**Fees:** No agency costs.

**Number of children placed last year:** 82.

**Description of children:** African-American infants, children with special needs, sibling groups, and older children.

**Adoption procedure:**
  1) Initial inquiry;
  2) attend Orientation and GPS Training;
  3) file application;
  4) complete criminal records check and individual and family interviews;
  5) if approved, family selected for child;
  6) pre-placement visits;
  7) placement;
  8) 6 mos. post-placement supervision;
  9) finalization.

**Average length of time between application and start of home study:** 2 wks.

**Average length of time to complete home study:** 6 wks.

**Number of interviews:** Minimum of 2.

**Home study description:** Home study consists of GPS training, individual and family interviews to obtain information on the family's functioning and lifestyle, parenting abilities, motivation and attitudes for adoption, individualization of adoptive parents marital relationship and extended family.

**Average wait for a child after approval of a home study:** Placements are based on each child's needs rather than an applicant's certification.

**Foster care:** Emergency, temporary, long-term, and alternative family care program.

## ★ 261 ★
**Lafayette Regional Office of Community Services**
1353 Surrey St.
Lafayette, LA 70501
Phone: (318) 262-5970
(800) 256-8611

**Contact:** Foster/Adoptive Homefinding Worker.

**Description:** Public, state agency.

**Area served:** Residents of Acadia, Evangeline, Iberia, Lafayette, St. Landry, St. Martin, St. Mary and Vermilion Parishes.

**Requirements:** Single applicants or couples married at least 2 yrs. who are between the ages of 21 and 65 yrs. and not more than 50 yrs. older than the child placed, who are in good physical and emotional health and whose income will support another family member.

**Fees:** None.

**Number of children placed last year:** 42.

**Description of children:** Older children and children with special needs.

**Adoption procedure:**
  1) Initial inquiry;
  2) attend 3 wks. of pre-service training;
  3) open application file;
  4) complete 10 wks. of GPS training;
  5) meet certification requirements;
  6) placement;
  7) 6 mos. post-placement supervision;
  8) finalization.

**Average length of time between application and start of home study:** 4 mos.

**Average length of time to complete home study:** 3-4 mos.

**Number of interviews:** Approx. 3.

**Home study description:** Process of self-assessment which includes evaluation and 10 wks. of GPS training.

**Average wait for a child after approval of a home study:** Dependent on range of special needs an applicant is willing to accept.

**Foster care:** Emergency, temporary, long-term, and therapeutic.

## ★ 262 ★
**Office of Community Service (of Alexandria, LA)**
900 Murray St.
Alexandria, LA 71301
Phone: (318) 487-5212
(318) 487-5146
Fax: (318) 484-2178

**Mailing address:**
  P.O. Box 832, Alexandria, LA 71301

**Contact:** Sara J. Alford.

**Date established:** 1940.

**Description:** Public child welfare service agency.

**Area served:** Residents of Avoyelles, Catahoula, Concordia, Grant, Lasalle, Rapides, Vernon and Winn Parishes.

**Requirements:** Flexible.

**Fees:** $150-$250 for adoption reports and home studies in civil cases.

**Number of children placed last year:** 50.

**Description of children:** Infants and children with special needs.

**Adoption procedure:**
  1) Attend orientation;
  2) submit application;
  3) complete training;
  4) submit medical and legal documentation;
  5) complete home visits and individual interviews;
  6) if approved, placement.

**Average length of time between application and start of home study:** 1-6 mos.

**Average length of time to complete home study:** 9 mos.

**Number of interviews:** Unavailable.

**Home study description:** Evaluation of motivation to adopt, parenting skills, child care experiences, health and legal status.

**Average wait for a child after approval of a home study:** 6-12 mos.

**Foster care:** Temporary and long-term.

★ 263 ★
**Office of Community Services**
**Lake Charles Region**
P.O. Box 16865
Lake Charles, LA 70616
Phone: (318) 491-2189
Fax: (318) 491-2059

**Contact:** Katherine Mouton, Richard Ott, or Donna Fertitta.

**Date established:** C. 1935.

**Description:** Public, state agency.

**Area served:** Residents of Allen, Beauregard, Calcasieu, Cameron, and Jefferson Davis parishes.

**Requirements:** Applicants can be married or single. Other requirements vary with age and type of child requested.

**Fees:** None.

**Number of children placed last year:** Unavailable.

**Description of children:** Infants and children with special needs.

**Adoption procedure:**
 1) Attend 10 wk. training;
 2) participate in 3 home visits;
 3) complete self-assessment and submit references;
 4) if approved, placement;
 5) 6 mos. post-placement supervision;
 6) finalization.

**Average length of time between application and start of home study:** 1-6 mos.

**Average length of time to complete home study:** 3.5 mos.

**Number of interviews:** 3.

**Home study description:** Assessment of family background, value system, parenting models or experience.

**Average wait for a child after approval of a home study:** Varies; infant adoption requires a much longer wait than an older special needs child.

**Foster care:** Temporary, long-term and permanent.

★ 264 ★
**State of Louisiana**
**Department of Social Services**
**Office of Community Services**
Division of Children, Youth and Family Services
1525 Fairfield Ave., Rm. 850
Shreveport, LA 71101-4388
Phone: (318) 676-7100

**Contact:** Adoption Homefinding Unit.

**Description:** Non-profit, state agency.

**Area served:** Homestudies done for Louisiana residents; children in the custody of the State of Louisiana are placed in adoptive homes both inside and outside Louisiana.

**Requirements:** Adults between the ages of 21 and 65 yrs. at the time of certification who are no more than 50 yrs. older than the child placed, free of communicable diseases, physically and mentally able to parent a child; and whose income is sufficient to incorporate another family member. Applicants may be single, married at least two yrs., divorced, or widowed.

**Fees:** None for children in the state's custody.

**Number of children placed last year:** Approx. 22.

**Description of children:** Primarily children with special needs: older, sibling groups, minority, physically, mentally and emotionally handicapped.

**Adoption procedure:**
 1) Submit application;
 2) attend 10 wks. of GPS training;
 3) complete home study;
 4) if approved, child search and match;
 5) pre-placement visitation process;
 6) placement;
 7) 6-18 mos. post-placement supervision;
 8) finalization;
 9) post-adoption services, as needed.

**Average length of time between application and start of home study:** GPS training sessions are an integral part of the home study and are scheduled every 4-6 wks.

**Average length of time to complete home study:** Minimum of 90 days.

**Number of interviews:** 2-3 home consultations.

**Home study description:** Evaluation of parenting ability, family functioning, motivation for adoption, social history, home capacity, and acceptance of adoption by all family members. Prospective adoptive homes must meet the minimum licensing standards for health and safety.

**Average wait for a child after approval of a home study:** Dependent on the range of special needs applicants are willing to accept.

**Foster care:** Emergency, short- and long-term, and alternate family care.

# PRIVATE AGENCIES

★ 265 ★
**Bethany Christian Services (of Baton Rouge)**
4854 Constitution Ave., Ste. 1-D
Baton Rouge, LA 70809
Phone: (504) 927-3235

**Contact:** Ann Droy, Director.

**Date established:** 1989.

**Description:** Private, non-profit child placing agency licensed by the Louisiana Department of Health and Human Resources.

**Area served:** Residents of Louisiana.

**Requirements:** Committed Christians who must sign a statement of faith.

**Fees:** Application: $550; home study: $1000. Medical, legal, interim and placement fees are extra.

**Number of children placed last year:** 10.

**Description of children:** Caucasian, biracial and minority infants.

**Adoption procedure:** 1) Pre-application; 2) formal application; 3) reference checks and home study; 4) approval and birth parent surrender; 5) placement ceremony; 6) post-placement supervision; 7) finalization.

**Average length of time between application and start of home study:** Less than 1 mo.

**Average length of time to complete home study:** 3 mos.

**Number of interviews:** 3 includes 2 home visits.

**Home study description:** Assessment which addresses such issues as family background, martial stability and compatibility, motivation to adopt, child rearing and understanding of adoption.

**Average wait for a child after approval of a home study:** Up to 12 mos. depending upon the type of child requested.

**Foster care:** Temporary.

★ 266 ★
**Caring Alternatives**
**Volunteers of America**
3900 N. Causeway Blvd., Ste. 700
Metairie, LA 70002
Phone: 1 (800) 535-9646
(504) 836-5225

**Contact:** Adoption worker.

**Date established:** 1939.

**Description:** Private, non-proft agency licensed in the State of Louisiana.

**Area served:** Preference shown to residents of Louisiana but out-of-state placements are possible.

**Requirements:** Couples married between 3 and 5 yrs. who are not older than 43 yrs. who are financially self-sustaining.

**Fees:**
Application fee: $500;
home study: $1500;
adoption fee based on 20% of couple's adjusted gross income.

**Number of children placed last year:** 15.

**Description of children:** Black, white, biracial newborn infants, some with special needs.

**Adoption procedure:**
1) Submit application;
2) complete home study;
3) if approved, placement;
4) 6 mos. post-placement supervision;
5) finalization.

**Average length of time between application and start of home study:** 1-6 mos.

**Average length of time to complete home study:** 3-6 mos.

**Number of interviews:** 4.

**Home study description:** Evaluation of adoptive parents' background, education and employment history, finances, housing, marital history and religion.

**Average wait for a child after approval of a home study:** 12-24 mos.

**Foster care:** Temporary.

★ 267 ★
**Catholic Community Services of Baton Rouge**
**Counseling, Maternity and Adoption Department**
**Diocese of Baton Rouge**
4884 Constitution Ave., Ste. 1-B
Baton Rouge, LA 70808
Phone: (504) 927-4930
Fax: (504) 927-9246

**Contact:** Janice D. Sapp, BCSW, Dept. Director and Caseworker Supervisor.

**Date established:** 1964 under the name of Catholic Social Services.

**Description:** "A" Louisiana State License for Adoption placement and temporary foster care of clients' infants.

**Area served:** Diocesan area of Baton Rouge - 12 surrounding civil parishes (Ascension, Assumption, East Baton Rouge, East Feliciana, West Feliciana, Iberville, Livingston, Pointe Coupee, St. Helena, St. James and Tangipahoa parishes).

**Requirements:** Couples married at least 3 yrs. neither of whom is older than 43 yrs., who have stable employment and not more than 1 child already in the home.

**Fees:**
Black adoptive couples: $50;
white adoptive couples: $500 (applied to home study fee which is based on income);
interstate/intercountry adoptive home studies: $700 plus expenses.

**Number of children placed last year:** 14.

**Description of children:** Infants.

**Adoption procedure:**
1) File pre-application;
2) attend 5 group meetings;
3) submit completed 8 pg. application;
4) submit supporting documentation (birth and marriage certificates, medicals, etc.);
5) participate in individual and home interviews;
6) compose autobiographies;
7) if approved, placement;
8) 2 supervisory home visits;
9) agency files for revised birth certificate;
10) agency attorney petitions court for hearing date;
11) attend court hearing and finalization.

**Average length of time between application and start of home study:** 6-12 mos.

**Average length of time to complete home study:** 3 mos.

**Number of interviews:** 3 or more.

**Home study description:** Evaluation of medical and family background, courtship, present family life, personal autobiographies, type of child desired, financial status, stability of marriage and check of Louisiana Criminal Identification Bureau.

**Average wait for a child after approval of a home study:** 12-24 mos.

**Foster care:** Temporary (at least 2 wks.) to allow the birthmother time to decide to surrender her infant or assume parenting responsibilities.

★ 268 ★
**Catholic Social Services of Lafayette**
1408 Carmel Ave.
Lafayette, LA 70506
Phone: (318) 261-5654

**Contact:** Paula Milner, Director.

**Description:** Private, non-profit child placing agency licensed by the Louisiana Department of Health and Human Resources.

**Area served:** Residents of the Diocese of Lafayette and Lake Charles.

**Requirements:** Open.

**Fees:** Application: $100; home study: $1000; placement: $6000.

**Number of children placed last year:** 15.

**Description of children:** Infants.

**Adoption procedure:** 1) Apply to waiting list; 2) autobiography; 3) group study; 4) home study; 5) approval placement; 6) post-placement supervision; 7) finalization.

**Average length of time between application and start of home study:** 12-24 mos.

**Average length of time to complete home study:** 3 mos.

**Number of interviews:** 5.

**Home study description:** Assessment which includes the composition of an autobiography, the compilation of marriage record, police clearances, physicals and group interaction and addresses such issues as those surrounding infertility and adoption, placement planning and others.

**Average wait for a child after approval of a home study:** 12 - 24 mos.

**Foster care:** None.

## ★ 269 ★
**Christian Homes**
**A Program of Louisiana Child Care and Placement Services, Inc.**
9080 Southwood Dr.
Shreveport, LA 71118
Phone: (318) 686-2243

**Contact:** Charles Hampton, MSW.

**Date established:** 1967.

**Description:** Non-profit private agency licensed in the State of Louisiana.

**Area served:** Residents of Louisiana.

**Requirements:** Adults between the ages of 21 and 45 yrs. of age, who are in good health and members of the Church of Christ. Applicants may be older than 45 yrs. if adopting older children.

**Fees:**
Application fee: $50;
home study: $650;
adoption fee: $7500 for newborn (vaginal delivery);
minimal to no fees for older or special needs placements.

**Number of children placed last year:** 0.

**Adoption procedure:**
1) Submit application;
2) complete home study;
3) participate in training;
4) placement;
5) 6 or more mos. post-placement supervision;
6) finalization. Also provides home studies and supervision for private (attorney) adoptions, international adoptions, and interstate adoptions.

**Average length of time between application and start of home study:** 1-6 mos.

**Average length of time to complete home study:** 3 mos.

**Number of interviews:** 3.

**Home study description:** Evaluation of family history, views on parenting and adoption and stability of marriage (if applicable).

**Average wait for a child after approval of a home study:** 24 or more mos.

**Foster care:** Temporary or long-term state and voluntary placements.

## ★ 270 ★
**Gail House**
8676 Goodwood Blvd., Ste. 105
Baton Rouge, LA 70808-7714
Phone: (504) 926-0070
(800) 259-BABY
Fax: (504) 926-4010

**Contact:** Debbie Crochet, Director.

**Date established:** 1985.

**Description:** Non-profit, private maternity home and child-placing agency licensed by the State of Louisiana.

**Area served:** Residents of Louisiana.

**Requirements:** Married couples who have had no more than one previous marriage, who are between the ages of 24 and 45 yrs., who are members of some church and who are financially stable.

**Fees:** Based on sliding scale, with income.

**Number of children placed last year:** 6.

**Description of children:** White, black and biracial infants.

**Adoption procedure:**
1) Submit inquiry;
2) attend orientation;
3) return completed application;
4) complete home study;
5) if approved, wait for placement.

**Average length of time between application and start of home study:** 1-6 mos.

**Average length of time to complete home study:** 3-5 mos.

**Number of interviews:** 4.

**Home study description:** Assessment of background information, lifestyle, religious beliefs, social life, adoption related issues, e.g. feelings about birthparents, etc.

**Average wait for a child after approval of a home study:** Varies: 2-4 mos. to 2-4 yrs.

**Foster care:** Temporary.

## ★ 271 ★
**Holy Cross Child Placement Agency, Inc.**
929 Olive St.
Shreveport, LA 71104
Phone: (318) 222-7892
Fax: (318) 222-7647

**Contact:** Rev. Donald D. Heacock, DCSW.

**Date established:** 1984.

**Description:** Non-profit child-placing agency.

**Area served:** Residents of the United States.

**Requirements:** None.

**Fees:** $200.

**Number of children placed last year:** 15.

**Description of children:** Newborn infants.

**Adoption procedure:** Call or write for outline.

**Average length of time between application and start of home study:** Varies.

**Average length of time to complete home study:** 2-3 hrs.

**Number of interviews:** 3-4.

**Home study description:** A process which involves individual interviews and a physical visit to the home.

**Average wait for a child after approval of a home study:** Varies.

**Foster care:** None.

## ★ 272 ★
**The Jewish Children's Regional Service**
5342 St. Charles Ave.
New Orleans, LA 70175
Phone: (504) 899-1595
(800) 729-5277

**Mailing address:**
    P.O. Box 15225, New Orleans, LA 70175

**Contact:** Esther R. Garbus, MSW, BCSW.

**Date established:** 1967.

**Description:** Non-profit agency licensed by the State of Louisiana as a child-serving and child-placing agency.

**Area served:** Residents of Alabama, Arkansas, Louisiana, Mississippi, Oklahoma, Tennessee and Texas.

**Requirements:** Married Jewish couples.

**Fees:** Sliding scale.

**Number of children placed last year:** 0.

**Description of children:** Healthy white infants.

**Adoption procedure:** Once the home study is complete and approved, JCRS notifies agencies who accept surrenders that an approved family is waiting and, with the family's consent, sends a copy of the home study to the agency which expressed interest. If the local agency has a child suitable for the family, the family is informed and they make the arrangements, including payment of the agency's fee, to pick up the child. JCRS then provides post-placement services and assists the family's lawyer in preparing materials for the court hearing.

**Average length of time between application and start of home study:** 1-6 mos.

**Average length of time to complete home study:** 6-8 mos.

**Number of interviews:** 4.

**Home study description:** Evaluation of current family relationships, health, finances, lifestyle, child rearing philosophy and practices.

**Average wait for a child after approval of a home study:** 24 or more mos.

**Foster care:** None.

★ 273 ★
**Jewish Family Service (of New Orleans)**
2026 St. Charles Ave.
New Orleans, LA 70130
Phone: (504) 524-8475

**Contact:** Roberta Hirsu.

**Date established:** 1948.

**Description:** Private, non-profit agency licensed to place children by the Louisiana Department of Health and Human Resources.

**Area served:** Residents of Jefferson, Orleans, Plaquemines, St. Bernard, St. Charles and St. Tammany parishes.

**Requirements:** Jewish married couples.

**Fees:** Home Study: $500. Other fees are on a sliding scale based on income.

**Number of children placed last year:** 3.

**Description of children:** Infants.

**Adoption procedure:** Contact agency.

**Average length of time between application and start of home study:** Less than 1 mo.

**Average length of time to complete home study:** 2 - 3 mos.

**Number of interviews:** 6 - 12.

**Home study description:** Assessment which includes autobiographical information and which gauges a family's suitability for adoption.

**Average wait for a child after approval of a home study:** 6 -12 mos.

**Foster care:** None.

★ 274 ★
**St. Elizabeth Foundation**
8054 Summa Ave., Ste. A
Baton Rouge, LA 70809
Phone: (504) 769-8888

**Contact:** Lillie Gallagher, Director.

**Date established:** May, 1988.

**Description:** Private, non-profit, non-denominational Christian agency licensed to place children by the Louisiana Department of Health and Human Services.

**Area served:** Residents of southeast and southwest Louisiana.

**Requirements:** Couples married at least 3 yrs. who are at least 24 yrs. old, in good health with a physician's verification of infertility and no more than 1 child in the home who is at least 2 yrs. old. The wife may be no older than 43 yrs. and the husband may be no older than 45 yrs. old.

**Fees:** Application: $500; home study: $1500; remainder of fees: $9000 - $18,000 based on previous yr.'s income tax return.

**Number of children placed last year:** 28.

**Description of children:** Caucasian and biracial newborns, toddlers, some with special needs.

**Adoption procedure:** 1) Preliminary application; 2) informational meeting; 3) formal application; 4) home study meeting; 5) home study; 6) placement on waiting list.

**Average length of time between application and start of home study:** 1 - 6 mos.

**Average length of time to complete home study:** 3 - 4 mos.

**Number of interviews:** 4.

**Home study description:** Assessment which includes physical description of applicants and addresses such topics as marital relationship, parenthood, infertility, adoption issues, religion, finances and employment, family background, health and home environment.

**Average wait for a child after approval of a home study:** 12 - 24 mos.

**Foster care:** None.

★ 275 ★
**St. Gerard's Adoption Network, Inc.**
P.O. Box 769
Eunice, LA 70535
Phone: (318) 457-1111
Fax: (318) 457-9052

**Contact:** Adoption intake.

**Date established:** 1988.

**Description:** Private child placing agency licensed by the State of Louisiana.

**Area served:** Open.

**Requirements:** Call or write for guidelines.

**Fees:** Application fee: $100; fee for birthmother obtained through advertising: $8000; Fee for referrals: $4075; agency fees do not include any legal, medical, or living expenses for the birthmother.

**Number of children placed last year:** 4.

**Description of children:** Infants.

**Adoption procedure:** Procedures conform to the laws of the State of Lousiana and will be explained upon inquiry. Birthparents participate in the selection of adoptive parents.

**Average length of time between application and start of home study:** 12-24 mos.

**Average length of time to complete home study:** Unavailable.

**Number of interviews:** 5.

**Home study description:** Call or write for guidelines.

**Average wait for a child after approval of a home study:** 24 or more mos.

**Foster care:** Available for infants if Interstate Compact on the Placement of Children approval is required.

★ 276 ★
**St. Vincent's Infant and Maternity Program**
**Associated Catholic Charities**
1000 Howard Ave., Ste. 1200
New Orleans, LA 70113
Phone: (504) 596-3224

**Contact:** Administrator.

**Date established:** 1924.

**Description:** Non-profit private agency licensed by the Louisiana Department of Health and Human Resources.

**Area served:** Archdiocese of New Orleans. Area may expand for homes for minority and/or special needs children.

**Requirements:** Couples married at least 2 yrs. who are between the ages of 25 and 40 yrs. and are in good health. Exceptions are made for minority and/or special needs children. If applicants are Catholic, the marriage should be valid in the church; if non-Catholic, the child is to be reared in the faith of the couple. Priority is given to childless couples; couples with other children are considered for minority and/or special needs children.

**Fees:** $50 fee is required with all formal applications. Legal fees and court costs are the responsibility of the applicants (about $850). Caucasian home study and placement: $7,000-$10,000. Minority home study and placement: $1,200-$1,800. International, private, and interstate compact home studies: $1,200-$1,500. All fees are income based. Fees for special needs and/or older children are negotiable.

**Number of children placed last year:** 44.

**Description of children:** Newborn infants; older children/special needs children placed when available; networking with international agencies for children of all ages.

**Adoption procedure:** A couple may call or write for a questionnaire, which is placed in a waiting file for formal application to adopt. Couples adopting Caucasian infants can expect to wait up to five years for an application. Couples adopting minority and/or special needs children receive an application within two months. Couples requesting a home study for international, private, or interstate compact placements are served on an as-needed basis.

**Average length of time between application and start of home study:** Varies.

**Average length of time to complete home study:** 4-6 wks.

**Number of interviews:** 4-6.

**Home study description:** Evaluation of motivation to adopt, family relationships, feeling about infertility, parenting methods including discipline, attitudes toward birthparents and different cultures, and plans to share adoption information with child.

**Average wait for a child after approval of a home study:** Varies.

**Foster care:** Temporary.

★ 277 ★
**Special Delivery Adoption Services, Inc.**
3141 Moss Point
Baton Rouge, LA 70808
Phone: (504) 924-2507
Fax: (504) 927-0614

**Contact:** Nina S. Broyles, Executive Director, Attorney and Social Worker.

**Date established:** 1987.

**Description:** Non-profit, private licensed agency.

**Area served:** United States.

**Requirements:** Flexible.

**Fees:** Application fee: $100 (non-refundable); agency fee: $0-$15,000.

**Number of children placed last year:** 35.

**Description of children:** Infants to 4 years of age.

**Adoption procedure:**
1) Initial inquiry;
2) submit application;
3) complete home study;
4) if approved, placement;
5) 6 mos. post-placement supervision;
6) finalization at 6 mos.

**Average length of time between application and start of home study:** 1 mo. or less.

**Average length of time to complete home study:** 2 mos.

**Number of interviews:** 4-6.

**Home study description:** Evaluation of applicants' socio-economic history, relationships and marital history, health and income, and home and surroundings.

**Average wait for a child after approval of a home study:** 6-12 mos.

**Foster care:** Provided by agency.

★ 278 ★
**Volunteers of America**
360 Jordan St.
Shreveport, LA 71101
Phone: (318) 221-5000

**Branch address:**
1756 Elliott St., Alexandria, LA 71301
Phone: (318) 442-8026

**Contact:** Richard T. Caffarel or Carolyn Wells.

**Date established:** 1935.

**Description:** Non-profit, private agency licensed in Louisiana and Arkansas (with license recognition in Connecticut).

**Area served:** Residents of north, central, and southwest Louisiana (the 318 area code) and the southern third of Arkansas.

**Requirements:** Couples married at least 3 yrs. who are between the ages of 25 and no more than 50 yrs. older than the child. Some requirements may be flexible for minority children or children with special needs.

**Fees:** Sliding scale based on family income: one-sixth paid at application, one-sixth paid at home study completion, two-thirds paid at placement.

**Number of children placed last year:** 13.

**Description of children:** Infants.

**Adoption procedure:**
1) Initial inquiry;
2) attend preliminary interview with completed Letter of Information;

3) admission to waiting list;
4) semi-annual review of prospective applicants to begin home study;
5) attend Orientation Meeting;
6) submit application;
7) complete self-study assignments, individual interviews and home visit;
8) attend Evaluation Conference;
9) if approved, receive Letter of Approval and wait for placement;
10) placement;
11) 6 or more mos. supervision of placement;
12) attorney files Adoption Petition in Caddo Parish Juvenile Court;
13) adoptive parents and child attend court hearing;
14) revised birth certificate mailed to family several mos. following Final Decree of Adoption.

**Average length of time between application and start of home study:** The application is the first step of the home study.

**Average length of time to complete home study:** Varies depending on family's readiness.

**Number of interviews:** 4.

**Home study description:** Assessment which includes but is not limited to family background, individual life experiences, other family members, family activities, beliefs and practices, home and environment, strengths and limitations and discussion of the child placement process.

**Average wait for a child after approval of a home study:** Varies depending on type of child to be considered.

**Foster care:** Short-term family care available for infants between release from hospital and adoptive placement.

---

# MAINE

## STATUTES

★ 279 ★

**Independent placement by intermediary?** Prohibited.

**Independent placement by birth parents?** Permitted.

**Subsidies provided?** Medical, maintenance, non-recurring legal and retroactive.

**Adoption cost defined by law?** Court requires a full disclosure of costs.

**Insurance for infertility?:** Unknown.

**Home study required by state?** If child is not a Maine resident, required before placement; if child is a resident of Maine, may be done after placement.

**Prospective adoptive parent advertise for a child?** Prohibited.

**Surrogacy laws?** Not addressed in law.

**Residents access agencies of other states or countries?** Permitted.

**Requires judicial termination of birth parents' rights?** Both legal parents must appear before the court, first, to be advised of their rights and the gravity of their decision, and second, not less than 3 days later, to consent to the adoption.

**Time given to a birthmother to revoke her consent:** None.

**Court handling adoptions?** Probate Court.

**Adoption of Native Children:** In compliance with ICWA.

**Adoption records sealed?** Sealed, except for cases prior to 1953. Non-identifying information is available to adoptees 18 yrs. and older and court records can be opened with the consent of the judge.

**Photo-listing book available?** *Northern New England Adoption Exchange* Photo-listing Book.

## PUBLIC AGENCIES

★ 280 ★
**Maine Department of Human Services**
**Child and Family Services**
2 Anthony Ave., Sta. 11
Augusta, ME 04333
Phone: (207) 624-2971
(800) 452-1926
Fax: (207) 624-5864

**Branch address:**
Dept. of Human Services, Rockland, ME 04841
Phone: (207) 596-4262

Dept. of Human Services, Skowhegan, ME 04976
Phone: (207) 474-4800

**Contact:** Ellen Beerits and Stephanie Merrill, Adoption Supervisors.

**Description:** Public, state agency.

**Area served:** Residents of the six counties of central Maine.

**Requirements:** Adults, 23 yrs. and older, who have a stable income and whose health is adequate to parent. Applicants for children under the age of 5 yrs. should be no more than 45 yrs. older than the child placed.

**Fees:** None.

**Number of children placed last year:** 100.

**Description of children:** Primarily special needs children who have been severly abused and neglected and who have been legally freed for adoption.

**Adoption procedure:**
1) Telephone intake;
2) attend general information group;
3) application;
4) participate in group education series;
5) complete home study with assigned caseworker;
6) criminal, Child Protective Services, and Motor Vehicle clearances;
7) if approved, wait for placement;
8) post-placement supervision;
9) finalization.

**Average length of time between application and start of home study:** Varies.

**Average length of time to complete home study:** 8 mos.

**Number of interviews:** 7 group and 3 or more individual.

**Home study description:** Assessment includes but is not limited to autobiographies, background, criminal record checks, recommendation of references and type of child best suited to the adoptive home.

**Average wait for a child after approval of a home study:** Varies with type of child requested.

**Foster care:** Emergency, short and long-term, therapeutic and permanent.

# PRIVATE AGENCIES

### ★ 281 ★
**Good Samaritan Agency**
450 Essex St.
Bangor, ME 04401
Phone: (207) 942-7211
(800) 249-1811

**Contact:** Debbie Giguere, Casework Supervisor.

**Date established:** 1902.

**Description:** Private, non-profit social services agency licensed to place children by the Maine Department of Human Services.

**Area served:** Residents of Maine.

**Requirements:** Applicants must have been in current living status for at least 2 yrs.

**Fees:** Application: $250; home study: $1800; placement and supervision: $1800 plus travel expenses in state.

**Number of children placed last year:** 11.

**Description of children:** Caucasian and minority infants.

**Adoption procedure:** 1) Application; 2) application review and background clearances; 3) home study visits; 4) home peer review; 5) birth family search; 6) placement; 7) post-placement supervision; 8) finalization.

**Average length of time between application and start of home study:** Less than 1 mo.

**Average length of time to complete home study:** 3 mos.

**Number of interviews:** 4 - 5.

**Home study description:** In depth examination of life style, motivation to adopt, communication and problem-solving skills, general health, stability of relationships and family dynamics.

**Average wait for a child after approval of a home study:** Caucasian infant program: 24 or more mos.; all other programs: 6 - 12 mos.

**Foster care:** Temporary.

### ★ 282 ★
**The Maine Children's Home for Little Wanderers**
34 Gilman St.
Waterville, ME 04901
Phone: (207) 873-4253
Fax: (207) 872-7548

**Branch address:**
11 Mulliken Ct., Augusta, ME 04330
Phone: (207) 622-1552

**Contact:** Sharon Abrams, Executive Director.

**Date established:** 1899.

**Description:** Private, non-profit child placing agency licensed by the Maine Department of Human Services.

**Area served:** Residents of Maine.

**Requirements:** Requirements vary with the program selected.

**Fees:** $1500 - $6000.

**Number of children placed last year:** Approx. 8.

**Description of children:** Caucasian and African American infants and foreign born children.

**Adoption procedure:** 1) Interview; 2) application; 3) background checks; 4) educational classes; 5) office interviews and home visit; 6) acceptance; 7) placement; 8) post-placement supervision; 9) finalization.

**Average length of time between application and start of home study:** Varies with program selected.

**Average length of time to complete home study:** 4 mos.

**Number of interviews:** 7.

**Home study description:** Assessment which includes the compilation of vital records, biographies, description of the applicant(s) and their home and community, photos, reference letters, Child Protective Screening and Criminal History Record checks and addresses such issues as marital history, other children in the home, health, finances, religion, feelings about infertility (if applicable), adoption, birth parents and adoption, parenting experience and discipline philosophy.

**Average wait for a child after approval of a home study:** 1 mo. - 5 yrs.

**Foster care:** Temporary.

### ★ 283 ★
**St. Andre Home, Inc.**
283 Elm St.
Biddeford, ME 04005
Phone: (207) 282-3351

**Contact:** Sr. Theresa Therrien, LCSW.

**Date established:** 1954.

**Description:** Non-profit private agency.

**Area served:** Residents of the State of Maine.

**Requirements:** Couples married at least 3 yrs. who are between the ages of 22 and 38 yrs., who are childless and who are practicing members of a major recognized religious group.

**Fees:**
Application: $300;
home study: $2325;
placement: $2625;
supervision: $750;
total: $6000.

**Number of children placed last year:** 3.

**Description of children:** Infants.

**Adoption procedure:**
1) Initial inquiry;
2) submit application;
3) complete home study;
4) wait for placement;
5) if approved, placement;
6) post-placement supervision;
7) finalization.

**Average length of time between application and start of home study:** 1-6 mos.

**Average length of time to complete home study:** 30 hrs.

**Number of interviews:** 5 or more.

**Home study description:** The agency explores the couple's personality functioning, emotional maturity, marital relationship, feelings about children and childlessness, motivation to adopt and their responsibility to help their child know, understand and accept his/her adoption. During this phase, the agency contacts references both in person and through written correspondence and obtains medical information.

**Average wait for a child after approval of a home study:** 12-24 mos.

**Foster care:** Temporary.

### ★ 284 ★
**Sharing In Adoption**
2 Springbrook
Gorham, ME 04038
Phone: (207) 839-2934

**Contact:** Karen Z. Atkinson, Executive Director.

**Date established:** 1988.

**Description:** Private child placing agency licensed by the Maine Department of Human Services.

**Area served:** Residents of Maine from Kittery to Bangor.

**Requirements:** Applicants must be between the ages of 25 and 52 yrs., single or legally married at least 2 yrs.

**Fees:** Domestic adoption: $11,000 - $16,000. International adoption: $10,000 - $20,000.

**Number of children placed last year:** 52.

**Description of children:** Caucasian and Hispanic U.S. infants and foreign born infants and toddlers.

**Adoption procedure:** 1) Interview; 2) application packet; 3) home study and dossier or birth parent resume; 4) locate birth family (U.S. adoptions); 5) placement; 6) post-placement services.

**Average length of time between application and start of home study:** Less than 1 mo.

**Average length of time to complete home study:** 4 wks.

**Number of interviews:** 6 -7.

**Home study description:** Assessment which follows guidelines established by the Maine Department of Human Services and which addresses motivation to adopt, marital stability, if applicable, philosophy of adoption and discipline practices, attitudes about birth parents and child's background, communication and expectations of child.

**Average wait for a child after approval of a home study:** 6 - 12 mos.

**Foster care:** None.

# MARYLAND

## STATUTES

★ 285 ★

**Independent placement by intermediary?** Illegal.

**Independent placement by birth parents?** Permitted.

**Subsidies provided?** Financial, medical and service.

**Adoption cost defined by law?** No.

**Insurance for infertility?:** Unknown.

**Home study required by state?** Not required, but most courts demand an evaluation of the adoptive home before finalization.

**Prospective adoptive parent advertise for a child?** Illegal.

**Surrogacy laws?** Illegal.

**Residents access agencies of other states or countries?** In accordance with the ICPC.

**Requires judicial termination of birth parents' rights?** Both birth parents relinquish their parental rights through a court process.

**Time given to a birthmother to revoke her consent:** 30 days.

**Court handling adoptions?** Circuit Court.

**Adoption of Native Children:** ICWA is a federal law.

**Adoption records sealed?** Sealed, but adult adoptees may access non-identifying information.

**Photo-listing book available?** Maryland Adoption Resource Exchange Book.

## PUBLIC AGENCIES

★ 286 ★
**Allegany County Department of Social Services**
P.O. Box 1420
Cumberland, MD 21502
Phone: (301) 777-2053
Fax: (301) 777-5527

**Contact:** Karen Crosby; Charlene Platter.

**Date established:** 1988.

**Description:** Non-profit public agency.

**Area served:** Residents of Allegany County.

**Requirements:** Adults, 18 yrs. and older, who are financially self-sufficient, and have normal life expectancies; resident in Allegany Co., MD.

**Fees:** None.

**Number of children placed last year:** 6.

**Description of children:** Special needs.

**Adoption procedure:**
1) File application;
2) complete home study;
3) if approved, placement process;
4) post-placement supervision; and
5) finalization.

**Average length of time between application and start of home study:** 12-24 mos.

**Average length of time to complete home study:** 60-90 days.

**Number of interviews:** 7.

**Home study description:** Assessment of family life, references, attitudes toward adoption, adoptee search, etc.

**Average wait for a child after approval of a home study:** 12-24 mos.

**Foster care:** Primarily temporary.

★ 287 ★
**Anne Arundel County Department of Social Services**
80 West St.
Annapolis, MD 21404-1787
Phone: (410) 974-8637

**Mailing address:**
P.O. Box 1787, Annapolis, MD 21404-1787

**Contact:** Mrs. Ann Dorsey.

**Description:** Public, county agency.

**Area served:** Residents of Anne Arundel County.

**Requirements:** Couples married at least 1 yr. who are 18 yrs. and older.

**Fees:** None.

**Number of children placed last year:** 20.

**Description of children:** Children with special needs, especially African-American males.

**Adoption procedure:**
1) Telephone inquiry;
2) attend orientation;
3) applicants for special needs adoption attend training;
4) special needs applicants submit application;
5) complete home study;
6) if approved, wait for placement;
7) post-placement supervision;
8) finalization.

**Average length of time between application and start of home study:** 1-6 mos.

**Average length of time to complete home study:** 90-180 days.

**Number of interviews:** 3 or more.

**Home study description:** Assessment which includes but is not limited to recommendation of references, marital relationship, home and community, religion and other family members.

**Average wait for a child after approval of a home study:** Varies.

**Foster care:** Emergency, short and long-term, pre-adoptive and legal risk.

★ 288 ★
**Baltimore City Department of Human Resources**
3007 E. Biddle St.
East Baltimore, MD 21213
Phone: (410) 361-5508/9

**Mailing address:**
   1510 Guilford Ave., East Baltimore, MD 21213

**Contact:** Adoption Unit.

**Date established:** 1950.

**Description:** Public non-profit agency licensed by the State of Maryland.

**Area served:** Residents of the City of Baltimore.

**Requirements:** Adults between the ages of 21 and 55 yrs. who have reasonably good health and income sufficient to meet their own needs.

**Fees:** None.

**Number of children placed last year:** 107.

**Description of children:** Children from 0 to 17 yrs., primarily with special needs.

**Adoption procedure:**
   1) Attend informational meeting;
   2) file application;
   3) complete home study;
   4) presentation of possible child match and observation;
   5) placement;
   6) post-placement supervision;
   7) finalization.

**Average length of time between application and start of home study:** 6-12 wks.

**Average length of time to complete home study:** 60-90 days.

**Number of interviews:** Minimum of 4.

**Home study description:** Evaluation of personality, family relationships, emotional maturity and stability, quality of marriage (if applicable), feelings about education, health, income, housing, feelings about and experiences with children, attitudes about, understanding of and motivation to adopt.

**Average wait for a child after approval of a home study:** Dependent on range of special needs the applicant(s) are willing to accept.

**Foster care:** Temporary, emergency, fost-adopt, and therapeutic.

★ 289 ★
**Baltimore County Department of Social Services**
Investment Bldg. 3rd Fl.
620 York Rd.
Towson, MD 21204-4125
Phone: (410) 887-2106

**Contact:** Adoption Unit.

**Description:** Public, county agency mandated to place children by the Maryland Dept. of Social Services.

**Area served:** Residents of Baltimore County excluding the City of Baltimore.

**Requirements:** Adults 21 yrs. and older who have a normal life expectancy and who are living within their means.

**Fees:** None.

**Number of children placed last year:** 25.

**Description of children:** Children with special needs.

**Adoption procedure:**
   1) Attend informational meeting;
   2) return completed registration form;
   3) wait for home study while agency assesses the needs of the children awaiting placement in order to study the most promising homes;
   4) undergo home study and complete group training;
   5) if approved, placement;
   6) supervision of placement;
   7) finalization.

**Average length of time between application and start of home study:** 1-6 mos.

**Average length of time to complete home study:** 90 days.

**Number of interviews:** 4.

**Home study description:** Assessment of background, stability of relationship, flexibility, coping mechanisms, experience with children, value system and ability to commit to a relationship.

**Average wait for a child after approval of a home study:** 8 mos.

**Foster care:** Emergency, short and long-term, permanent, and therapeutic.

★ 290 ★
**Calvert County Department of Social Services**
200 Duke St.
Prince Frederick, MD 20678
Phone: (410) 535-8700

**Contact:** Rebecca Watson, Licensing Worker; Deborah Guled, Supervisor; Minnie Owens.

**Description:** County public agency.

**Area served:** Residents of Calvert County, Maryland.

**Requirements:** Minimal restrictions.

**Fees:** No agency fees, but charges for water analysis, fingerprinting and adoption finalization.

**Number of children placed last year:** Approx. 20.

**Description of children:** Children between the ages of birth and 18 yrs.

**Adoption procedure:** 1) Initial screening; 2) admission to waiting list; 3) undergo training; 4) home study; 5) registration with Maryland Adoption Resource Exchange; 6) identification of child for family; 7) transitional visitation; 8) placement; 9) 6 mos. post-placement supervision; 10) finalization.

**Average length of time between application and start of home study:** Homes are prioritized for study with applicants interested in children between the ages of 6 and 18 yrs., sibling groups, children with mental or physical handicaps or African-American homes seeking African-American children receiving earlier study.

**Average length of time to complete home study:** 40 days.

**Number of interviews:** 3.

**Home study description:** Home study includes but is not limited to social, medical and employment histories, parenting experience, finances and issues surrounding child acceptance such as special needs, age and race.

**Average wait for a child after approval of a home study:** Varies with kind of child applicant will accept.

**Foster care:** Mostly temporary, but some long-term.

**★ 291 ★**
**Carroll County Department of Social Services**
10 Distillery Dr.
Westminster, MD 21157
Phone: (410) 848-8880
(410) 876-2190

**Contact:** Helga Anderson, Adoption Worker.

**Description:** Public agency licensed to place children by the Maryland Department of Social Services.

**Area served:** Residents of Carroll County.

**Requirements:** Placements will be age appropriate.

**Fees:** Court and attorney fees.

**Number of children placed last year:** 9.

**Description of children:** Sibling groups and children with special needs.

**Adoption procedure:** 1) Adoption informational meeting; 2) 7 wks. of foster/adoptive parent training; 3) inspections and home study; 4) placement; 5) post-placement supervision; 6)finalization.

**Average length of time between application and start of home study:** Special needs: 6 - 12 mos.; children from 0 - 5 yrs.: 24 or more mos.

**Average length of time to complete home study:** 6 - 12 mos.

**Number of interviews:** 3.

**Home study description:** Assessment of background information, vital records, education, medical reports, fire inspections, references, fingerprint, protective services and police clearances, employment and financial information, present family situation, marital stability, if applicable, and child rearing experiences.

**Average wait for a child after approval of a home study:** Special needs: 6 - 12 mos.; children from 0 - 5 yrs.: 24 or more mos.

**Foster care:** Temporary and long-term.

**★ 292 ★**
**Cecil County Department of Social Services**
170 E. Main St.
Elkton, MD 21911
Phone: (410) 996-0500
Fax: (410) 996-0605

**Contact:** Catherine M. Lane.

**Description:** Public adoption agency.

**Area served:** Residents of Cecil, Kent, Queen Anne, Caroline, and Talbot counties.

**Requirements:** None.

**Fees:** None.

**Number of children placed last year:** 24.

**Description of children:** Special needs and infant.

**Adoption procedure:**
1) File application;
2) complete group study process;
3) forward medical reports;

4) pass sanitary survey and police clearances;
5) if approved, placement;
6) 6 mos. supervision; and
7) finalization.

**Average length of time between application and start of home study:** 1-6 mos.

**Average length of time to complete home study:** 90 days.

**Number of interviews:** 7 group sessions and 2 individual.

**Home study description:** Call or write for outline.

**Average wait for a child after approval of a home study:** 12-24 mos.

**Foster care:** Temporary.

**★ 293 ★**
**Frederick County Department of Social Services**
118 N. Market St.
Frederick, MD 21705
Phone: (301) 694-2458
Fax: (301) 694-4550

**Mailing address:**
 P.O. Box 237, Frederick, MD 21705

**Contact:** Kathy Conaway, Child Welfare Supervisor.

**Description:** Public agency.

**Area served:** Residents of Frederick County.

**Requirements:** Adults, 18 yrs. or older.

**Fees:** None.

**Number of children placed last year:** 6.

**Description of children:** Primarily special needs.

**Adoption procedure:**
1) Return Interest Registration Form;
2) name placed on waiting list (list reviewed 3 times a year);
3) attend orientation sessions;
4) return medical reports and have sanitary survey;
5) if approved, placement;
6) 6 mos. supervision;
7) placement.

**Average length of time between application and start of home study:** Varies.

**Average length of time to complete home study:** 6 wks. - 3 mos.

**Number of interviews:** 6-7.

**Home study description:** A joint effort by the adoptive family and the social worker to determine if adoption is right for the applicant family. Applicants will be asked to attend meetings with the caseworker and with other prospective adoptive families. Applicants will be given information about children, parenting skills and adoption issues. Applicants will be asked to consider their expectations for a child, their reasons for wishing to adopt, their financial situation, the reaction of friends and family to adoption and many other factors.

**Average wait for a child after approval of a home study:** Varies.

**Foster care:** Temporary, long-term and permanent.

**★ 294 ★**
**Montgomery County Department of Social Services**
401 Hungerford Dr.
Rockville, MD 20850
Phone: (301) 217-3618

**Contact:** Adoption Unit.

**Description:** Public, county agency mandated to place children by the Maryland Dept. of Social Services.

**Area served:** Residents of Montgomery County.

**Requirements:** Applicants must be in good health and have a normal life expectancy.

**Fees:** None.

**Number of children placed last year:** 40.

**Description of children:** Older and/or minority children and sibling groups.

**Adoption procedure:**
1) Telephone or write Adoption Unit;
2) attend information meeting;
3) call for appointment;
4) complete individualized home study;
5) if applying for special needs child, attend series of group meetings;
6) wait for placement.

Agency conducts primarily fost-adopt conversions but finds homes for children with exceptional special needs.

**Average length of time between application and start of home study:** Varies.

**Average length of time to complete home study:** 2-6 mos.

**Number of interviews:** Minimum of 3.

**Home study description:** Assessment of lifestyle, relationships, coping skills, motivation to adopt, parenting abilities, and the ability to work through difficult situations and learn from them.

**Average wait for a child after approval of a home study:** Most children are already being fostered in the prospective adoptive home.

**Foster care:** Legal risk, emergency, short and long-term.


★ 295 ★
**Prince George's County Department of Social Services**
6111 Ager Rd.
Hyattsville, MD 20782-2799
Phone: (301) 808-5561
Fax: (301) 808-5506

**Contact:** Gail Johnson or Ellen Baron.

**Description:** Public, state agency.

**Area served:** Residents of Prince George's County.

**Requirements:** Adults, 21 yrs. and older, who have a normal life expectancy, are financially stable, have appropriate room for child; married or single.

**Fees:** None.

**Number of children placed last year:** Approx. 40-50.

**Description of children:** Children with special needs; black infants; sibling groups.

**Adoption procedure:**
1) Attend intake meeting;
2) submit an application with supplementary forms;
3) participate in training;
4) complete home study;
5) if approved, wait for placement;
6) placement;
7) post-placement supervision;
8) finalization.

**Average length of time between application and start of home study:** 1-6 mos.

**Average length of time to complete home study:** 90 days.

**Number of interviews:** 3-4.

**Home study description:** Assessment which includes but is not limited to background information and police clearances, finances, stability and type of child requested.

**Average wait for a child after approval of a home study:** 6-12 mos.

**Foster care:** Emergency, short and long-term.


★ 296 ★
**Somerset County Department of Social Services**
Mt. Vernon Rd.
Princess Anne, MD 21853-0369
Phone: (410) 651-5350

**Mailing address:**
P.O. Box 369, Princess Anne, MD 21853-0369

**Contact:** Lexine Lowe, MSW, LCSW, Regional Adoption Worker.

**Date established:** 1985.

**Description:** Public regional child placement agency.

**Area served:** Residents of Somerset, Wicomico and Worcester counties.

**Requirements:** Flexible.

**Fees:** None.

**Number of children placed last year:** 13.

**Description of children:** Older, minority and sibling groups.

**Adoption procedure:**
1) Attend group meeting;
2) return questionnaire, sanitary survey and medical report(s);
3) police clearances and references checked;
4) home visit;
5) home study written;
6) applicant family registered with Maryland Adoption Resource Exchange;
7) referral and matching;
8) placement;
9) 6 mos. supervision;
10) finalization.

**Average length of time between application and start of home study:** 1-6 mos.

**Number of interviews:** 3 group meetings and 2-3 home visits.

**Home study description:** Garnering of basic demographic information and an effort to establish a partnership with applicant family to evaluate their strengths and weaknesses.

**Average wait for a child after approval of a home study:** Depends on type of child, age/race, the family hopes to adopt; no wait for older black children.

**Foster care:** Temporary and pre-adoptive primarily.


★ 297 ★
**Washington County Department of Social Services**
122 N. Potomac St.
Hagerstown, MD 21741
Phone: (301) 791-4067
Fax: (301) 791-5994

**Mailing address:**
P.O. Box 1419, Hagerstown, MD 21741

**Contact:** Ann Pittman or Dick Snyder.

**Date established:** 1936.

**Description:** State agency.

**Area served:** Residents of Washington County.

**Requirements:** Applicants should be no more than 40 yrs. older than child placed.

**Fees:** None.

**Number of children placed last year:** 20.

**Description of children:** Older, special needs children.

**Adoption procedure:**
1) Written or telephone inquiry;
2) complete individual home study;
3) submit necessary paperwork;
4) caseworker gives verbal presentation of child;
5) if older child, visitation process;
6) placement;
7) 6 mos. supervision;
8) finalization.

**Average length of time between application and start of home study:** 1-6 mos.

**Average length of time to complete home study:** 90 days.

**Number of interviews:** 5-6.

**Home study description:** Assessment of background, marriage (if applicable), childrearing philosophy, issues surrounding adoption, difficulties and adjustment of children, and recommendation of references.

**Average wait for a child after approval of a home study:** Depends on the willingness of the family to accept a special needs child.

**Foster care:** Temporary, long-term and permanent.

### ★ 298 ★
**Wicomico County Department of Social Services**
201 Baptist St.
Salisbury, MD 21801
Phone: (301) 543-6900
Fax: (410) 543-6682

**Mailing address:**
   P.O. Box 2298, Salisbury, MD 21801

**Contact:** Paula M. Erdie.

**Description:** Public agency.

**Area served:** Residents of Wicomico County.

**Requirements:** Non-discriminatory.

**Fees:** None.

**Number of children placed last year:** 3.

**Description of children:** Infants and children with special needs.

**Adoption procedure:**
1) Written or telephone inquiry;
2) complete home study;
3) submit necessary clearances.

**Average length of time between application and start of home study:** 6-12 mos.

**Average length of time to complete home study:** 1 yr.

**Number of interviews:** 4.

**Home study description:** Assessment of demographic information, issues surrounding parenthood and adoption and others according to Maryland law.

**Average wait for a child after approval of a home study:** 24 or more mos.

**Foster care:** Short-term.

# PRIVATE AGENCIES

### ★ 299 ★
**Adoption Alliances**
**Jewish Family Services**
5750 Park Heights Ave.
Baltimore, MD 21215
Phone: (301) 466-9200
(800) 803-0170
Fax: (410) 664-0551

**Contact:** Louise Schnaier or Myra Hettleman.

**Date established:** 1856.

**Description:** Non-profit agency of the Associated Jewish Charties and Welfare Fund, licensed by the State of Maryland Department of Human Resources, accredited by the Council of Accreditation of Services for Families and Children and a member of the Association of Jewish Family & Children's Services and Family Service of America.

**Area served:** Residents of the City of Baltimore and the surrounding counties of Baltimore, Howard, Harford, Carroll, Anne Arundel, and Montgomery. Other Maryland counties served on an as needed basis.

**Requirements:** Varies according to program. Please inquire.

**Fees:** $1100 for home study; $7500 for traditional placement.

**Number of children placed last year:** 15 placements facilitated.

**Description of children:** Infant, children with special needs, foreign-born children and an identified program.

**Adoption procedure:**
1) Complete home study;
2) if approved, client may locate an identified placement, pursue an inter-country adoption, or wait for a traditional or special needs placement;
3) placement; and
4) post-placement services.

**Average length of time between application and start of home study:** 1 mo. or less.

**Average length of time to complete home study:** 2-3 mos.

**Number of interviews:** 4-5.

**Home study description:** Educational and evaluatory experience wherein the prospective adoptive parents consider adoption-related issues and how they can provide a loving and growth-providing environment for a child.

**Average wait for a child after approval of a home study:** Varies depending upon program pursued.

**Foster care:** Temporary, long-term and permanent.

### ★ 300 ★
**The Adoption Resource Center, Inc.**
6630 Baltimore National Pike, 100-B
Baltimore, MD 21228
Phone: (410) 744-6393

**Contact:** Fran Aherns or Diana Adams.

**Date established:** 1991.

**Description:** Private, non-profit child placing agency licensed by the Maryland Department of Social Services.

**Area served:** Comprehensive services for residents of the State of Maryland. No geographic restrictions for international program.

**Requirements:** No agency requirements, but individual programs may exact their own requirements.

**Fees:** Application: $200 ($400 out-of-state); home study: $1200; post-placement: $525; agency fee for international program: $3500.

**Number of children placed last year:** 75.

**Description of children:** U.S. infants adopted privately and foreign born infants and children of all ages, some with special needs.

**Adoption procedure:** 1) Application; 2) home study: 3) referral for placement agency or application to agency's placement program; 4) child match; 5) placement; 6) post-placement supervision; 7) finalization.

**Average length of time between application and start of home study:** Less than 1 mo.

**Average length of time to complete home study:** 1 - 3 mos.

**Number of interviews:** 5.

**Home study description:** Assessments which explores the needs and priorities of prospective adoptive parents and the type of child which would be the best match; individual/marital strengths, support system and parenting skills.

**Average wait for a child after approval of a home study:** 1 - 6 mos.

**Foster care:** None.

★ 301 ★

**Adoptions Forever, Inc.**
5830 Hubbard Dr.
Rockville, MD 20852
Phone: (301) 468-1818

**Contact:** Jeffrey Berman, Associate Director.

**Date established:** 1993.

**Description:** Private, not-for-profit child placing agency licensed by the Maryland Department of Social Services.

**Area served:** Residents of the U.S.

**Requirements:** Applicants must be 45 yrs. or younger. In the case of married couples, only one spouse must be younger than 45 yrs.

**Fees:** Application: $300; home study: $1100. Total fees: $5500 - $7500 and do not include medical and other expenses.

**Number of children placed last year:** New agency.

**Description of children:** Infants. International program in development.

**Adoption procedure:** 1) Birth parents relinquish parental rights to agency; 2) agency petitions court for guardianship; 3) birth and placement; 4) post-placement services: 5) finalization.

**Average length of time between application and start of home study:** Less than 1 mo.

**Average length of time to complete home study:** 3 - 4 wks.

**Number of interviews:** 3 - 4.

**Home study description:** Comprehensive examination of adoptive applicants which includes proof of employment and fiscal viability, health reports, criminal records clearances and resolution of infertility issues.

**Average wait for a child after approval of a home study:** 6 - 12 mos.

**Foster care:** Temporary.

★ 302 ★

**The Barker Foundation**
7945 MacArthur Blvd., Ste. 206
Cabin John, MD 20818
Phone: (301) 229-8300
(800) 673-8489
Fax: (301) 229-0074

**Branch address:**
   c/o McLean Professional Park Family Counseling Center, 1495 Chainbridge Rd., McLean, VA 22101

**Contact:** Mrs. Robin Allen, Executive Director.

**Date established:** 1945.

**Description:** Non-profit private agency licensed in the District of Columbia, Virginia, and Maryland.

**Area served:** Residents within 30 mi. radius of Washington, DC for domestic adoptions and within 50 mi. radius for international.

**Requirements:** For U.S. born infants, couples married at least 2 yrs. who are between the ages of 25 and 42 yrs. who are in good health with a medical diagnosis of infertility. International adoptions and agency assisted placements have varying requirements.

**Fees:**
Registration fee: $50;
domestic fee range: $0-$12,000;
international: $3000 for home study.

**Number of children placed last year:** 44.

**Description of children:** 28 U.S. infants, white, black and biracial; and 16 foreign-born, infants and older.

**Adoption procedure:**
1) Attend informational meeting;
2) complete registration form;
3) participate in small groups and individual meetings;
4) file full application with financial, health forms, references, law enforcement and Child Abuse Registry checks;
5) home visit;
6) if approved, placement;
7) 1 yr. post-placement supervision.

**Average length of time between application and start of home study:** 1-6 mos.

**Average length of time to complete home study:** 6 mos.

**Number of interviews:** 6.

**Home study description:** Evaluation which includes but is not limited to acceptance of adoption as a means of family building, parenting skills and flexibility. Caseworker also shares information on adoption procedures with applicant couple.

**Average wait for a child after approval of a home study:** 1-6 mos. for international; 12-24 mos. for domestic.

**Foster care:** Pre-adoptive.

★ 303 ★

**Bethany Christian Services of Maryland**
1641 Rte. 3 N., Ste. 205
Crofton, MD 21114-2466
Phone: (410) 721-2835
Fax: (410) 721-5523

**Contact:** Phyllis A. Lee.

**Date established:** 1981.

**Description:** Private counseling and child-placement agency.

**Area served:** Residents of the State of Maryland.

**Requirements:** Couples married at least 2 yrs., who have fewer than 2 children and a diagnosis of infertility, who are active members of an evangelical, Bible-teaching church and who believe in the sanctity of human life beginning atconception.

**Fees:** Sliding scale with a maximum of $7500.

**Number of children placed last year:** 46.

**Description of children:** Healthy white, black and biracial infants under 1 yr. of age.

**Adoption procedure:**
1) Initial inquiry;
2) file preliminary application;
3) attend group educational meeting;
4) participate in assessment interview;
5) if accepted, submit formal application;
6) attend joint and individual interviews;
7) home visit;
8) if approved, placement.

**Average length of time between application and start of home study:** 1-6 mos.

**Average length of time to complete home study:** 6-8 wks.

**Number of interviews:** 5.

**Home study description:** Assessment of social information, health and finances, family life, home and community, adoption attitudes and recommendation of references.

**Average wait for a child after approval of a home study:** 6-12 mos.

**Foster care:** Temporary.

★ 304 ★
**Catholic Charities of Baltimore**
19 W. Franklin St.
Baltimore, MD 21201
Phone: (410) 659-4050
(800) CARE-002
Fax: (410) 659-4060

**Contact:** Ellen Warnock-Eckhart or Mary Ellen Bean.

**Date established:** 1980.

**Description:** Non-profit, private agency licensed in the State of Maryland.

**Area served:** Residents of Maryland, Louisiana through Associated Catholic Charities of New Orleans and Missouri through Catholic Services for Children & Youth in St. Louis (Louisiana and Missouri for Philippine placements only).

**Requirements:** Guatemala: Couples married at least 3 yrs. between the ages of 25 and 45 yrs. old who must take a leave of absence of between 3 and 6 mos. after placement. Single female applicants will be considered and applicants older than 45 yrs. may be considered for older children. Korea: Couples married at least 3 yrs., between the ages of 25 and 40 yrs. for a healthy infant and no older than 44 yrs. for a child with special needs; who have no more than 3 other children and who must take a leave of at least 3 mos. after placement. Philippines: Couples married at least 3 yrs. who must take a leave of absence of between 3 and 6 mos. after placement. Husband must be between 25 and 45 yrs. old and wife, between 25 and 40 yrs. old. Russia & the Newly Independent States: Couples married at least 3 yrs. who will be no more than 45 yrs. older than an adopted child who must take a 3-6 mos. leave of absence after child is placed. Single applicants considered on a case-by-case basis. Viet Nam: Couples married at least 3 yrs., but single and older applicants accepted. Prospective adoptive parents must take a 3-6 mos. leave of absence after placement.

**Fees:** Application: $100; family assessment: $2000; facilitation and processing fee: $1000; post-placement fee: $500. Country fees: Korea: cooperating agency, transportation and Associated Catholic Charities Program fees: $7095; Philippines: placement, orphanage donation, transportation, Associated Catholic Charities Program, processing and referral fees: $5500; Guatemala: cooperating agency, attorney fee, transportation, accommodations and US visa application: $11,050; Viet Nam: cooperating agency, transportation and Associated Catholic Charities Placement fees: $11,000 -$11,600; Russia and the Newly Independent States: cooperating agency application, acceptance and placement fees, transportation for adoptive parent and child, accommodations, visa and physical exam: $15,375.

**Number of children placed last year:** 80.

**Description of children:** Korea: infant boys and girls, some with special needs. Philippines: boys and girls 6 mos. and older with the potential for good health; some children with special needs. Guatemala: Boys and girls 6 mos. to 4 yrs. with little known medical and social background; some children with special needs. Viet Nam: Infants and toddlers, some with special needs, some sibling groups. Russia & Newly Independent States: Some infant and many toddlers, pre-schoolers and school-age children with the potential for good health; some sibling groups and children with special needs.

**Adoption procedure:** 1) File application; 2) attend interview; 3) complete group study process; 4) completehome visit and individual interviews; 5) documents written and sent abroad; 6) child referral;7) child arrival or parent travel; 8) post-placement supervision; 9) finalization in US.

**Average length of time between application and start of home study:** 6 mos. or less.

**Average length of time to complete home study:** 6 wks.

**Number of interviews:** 4-8.

**Home study description:** Evaluation of personal maturity, stability of marriage (if applicable); parenting philosophy and/or experience, acceptance of differences, willingness to learn, flexibility and sense of humor.

**Average wait for a child after approval of a home study:** Korea: 9-12 mos.; Philippines: 12-15 mos.; Guatemala: 12-18 mos. from dossier completion; Viet Nam: 9-12 mos. from dossier completion; Russia and the Newly Independent States: 6-12 mos. from dossier completion.

**Foster care:** None.

★ 305 ★
**Children's Choice**
213 - 219 W. Main St.
Salisbury, MD 21801
Phone: (410) 546-6106

**Branch address:**
Scott Plaza II, Philadelphia, PA 19113
Phone: (215) 521-6270

728 Blackhorse Pike, Ste.D, Turnersville, NJ 08012
Phone: (609) 228-5223

**Contact:** Cindy Ruby, L.C.S.W.-C., Adoption Worker.

**Date established:** 1992.

**Description:** Private, non-profit child placing agency with a Christian base licensed by the Maryland Department of Social Services.

**Area served:** Residents of Maryland.

**Requirements:** Flexible.

**Fees:** Home study: $1000.

**Number of children placed last year:** Unavailable.

**Description of children:** Children with special needs.

**Adoption procedure:** 1) Application; 2) compilation of documents; 3) home visit and 2 interviews; 4) homestudy approved; 5) registration with adoption exchanges; 6) child match; 7) pre-placement visits; 8 ) placement; 9) post-placement; 10) supervision.

**Average length of time between application and start of home study:** Less than 1 mo.

**Average length of time to complete home study:** 3 mos.

**Number of interviews:** 3.

**Home study description:** Assessment which addresses such issues as motivation to adopt, attitudes toward adoption, type of child desired, emotional and physical strengths and weaknesses, employment and financial status, background and education, discipline techniques and spiritual beliefs.

**Average wait for a child after approval of a home study:** Varies with type of child desired.

**Foster care:** Specialized.

★ 306 ★
**Family & Children's Services of Central Maryland**
204 W. Lanvale St.
Baltimore, MD 21217
Phone: (410) 744-8863
(410) 669-9000

**Contact:** Ellen A. Sheps.

**Date established:** 1900.

**Description:** Private, non-profit, United Way agency licensed to place children by the Maryland Department of Human Resources, accredited by the Council on Accreditation of Services for Families and Children and a member of the Child Welfare League of America, Family Service America, National Association for HomeCare and the United Way of Central Maryland.

**Area served:** Primarily residents of Maryland.

**Requirements:** Applicants must be between the ages of 21 and 45 yrs., either single or legally married with an income above the poverty level.

**Fees:** Application: $50; home study: $2000. Other fees on a sliding scale based on income.

**Number of children placed last year:** 39.

**Description of children:** Primarily African American infants.

**Adoption procedure:** 1) Telephone inquiry; 2) personal interview; 3) group discussion series; 4) home study; 5) pre-placement visits; 6) placement; 7) post-placement supervision; 8) finalization.

**Average length of time between application and start of home study:** 1 - 6 mos.

**Average length of time to complete home study:** 1 - 2 mos.

**Number of interviews:** 4.

**Home study description:** Educational and assessment process of autobiographical information and which includes individual and group discussions with adoptive parents, birth parents, and adoptees.

**Average wait for a child after approval of a home study:** Less than 1 mo.

**Foster care:** Specialized and long-term.

★ 307 ★
**Jewish Social Service Agency**
**Adoption Options**
6123 Mantras Rd.
Rockville, MD 20852
Phone: (301) 881-2229

**Branch address:**
7345 McWhorter Pl., Ste. 100, Annandale, VA 22003
Phone: (703) 750-5400

**Contact:** Felicia Kraft, Adoptions Supervisor.

**Date established:** 1893.

**Description:** Private, non-profit, full service family agency licensed as a child placing agency by the DC Department of Human Services, the Maryland Department of Social Services and the Virginia Department of Social Services.

**Area served:** Residents of the metropolitan Washington, DC area.

**Requirements:** Jewish couples married at least 1 yr. who are no older than 42 yrs. in good health and with adequate income to provide for a family.

**Fees:** Application: $2500; home study: $1100. Placement fee is based on a sliding scale.

**Number of children placed last year:** 30 or more.

**Description of children:** U.S. infants and foreign born infants and children. Also facilitates identified adoptions.

**Adoption procedure:** 1) Inquiry; 2) home study; 3) prepare birth parent letters and begin advertising; 4) meet birth parent(s); 5) birth and placement; 6) post-placement supervision; 7) finalization.

**Average length of time between application and start of home study:** Less than 1 mo.

**Average length of time to complete home study:** 2 mos.

**Number of interviews:** 5.

**Home study description:** Assessment which addresses such issues as marriage, family, children, employment and philosophy of discipline.

**Average wait for a child after approval of a home study:** Wait for U.S. infants is dependent upon birth parent selection and for international placements upon child match made by the placing agency.

**Foster care:** Pre-adoptive.

# MASSACHUSETTS

## STATUTES
★ 308 ★

**Independent placement by intermediary?** Illegal.

**Independent placement by birth parents?** Permitted.

**Subsidies provided?** Medical and maintenance.

**Adoption cost defined by law?** Unknown.

**Insurance for infertility?:** No.

**Home study required by state?** Required before placement.

**Prospective adoptive parent advertise for a child?** Not addressed in law.

**Surrogacy laws?** Not addressed in law.

**Residents access agencies of other states or countries?** Permitted.

**Requires judicial termination of birth parents' rights?** Voluntary surrenders by both birth parents are recognized.

**Time given to a birthmother to revoke her consent:** None.

**Court handling adoptions?** Probate or District Court.

**Adoption of Native Children:** ICWA is a federal law.

**Adoption records sealed?** Sealed, but adoptees aged 18 yrs. and older may access their records.

**Photo-listing book available?** Massachusetts Adoption Resource Exchange Book.

# PUBLIC AGENCIES

★309★

**Department of Social Services of Massachusetts**
24 Farnsworth St.
Boston, MA 02210
Phone: (617) 727-0900
Fax: (617) 261-7435

**Branch address:**
90 North St., Dunham Mall, Pittsfield, MA 02101
Phone: (413) 499-7370

1 Arch Pl., 3rd Fl., Greenfield, MA 01301
Phone: (413) 774-5546

240 Main St., Memorial Hall, Northampton, MA 01060
Phone: (413) 586-8480

113-127 Hampden St., Holyoke, MA 01040
Phone: (413) 536-4762

1694 Main St., 3rd Fl., Springfield, MA 01103

125 N. Elm St., 4th Fl., Westfield, MA 01085
Phone: (413) 784-1686

76 Summer St., Rm. 210, Fitchburg, MA 01420
Phone: (508) 345-2101

185 Church St., Whitinsville, MA 01588
Phone: (508) 234-6213

72 Cambridge St., Smokestack Pl., Rm. 300, Worcester, MA 01603
Phone: (508) 791-1200

33 E. Merrimack, Lowell, MA 01852
Phone: (508) 452-8970

11 Lawrence St., 4th Fl., Lawrence, MA 01840
Phone: (508) 685-8384

200 Main St., Haverhill, MA 01830
Phone: (508) 373-3913

3 Broadway, Beverly, MA 01915

20 Wheeler St., Lynn, MA 01902
Phone: (617) 596-0200

151 Everett Ave., 3rd Fl., Chelsea, MA 02150
Phone: (617) 889-3820

22 Pleasant St., Malden, MA 02148
Phone: (617) 321-0130

411 Waverly Oaks Rd., Waltham, MA 02154
Phone: (617) 894-8770

810 Memorial Dr., Cambridge, MA 02139
Phone: (617) 868-1400

63 Fountain St., Framingham, MA 01701
Phone: (508) 872-8122

541 Main St., South Weymouth, MA 01701
Phone: (617) 331-6600

67 Mechanic St., Attleboro, MA 02703
Phone: (508) 226-4553

143 Main St., Brockton, MA 02401
Phone: (508) 584-6980

61 Industrial Park Rd., Plymouth, MA 02360
Phone: (617) 585-6533

21 Spring St., Taunton, MA 02780
Phone: (508) 822-7761

240 Elm St., Fall River, MA 02720
Phone: (508) 675-1145

800 Purchase St., New Bedford, MA 02740
Phone: (508) 997-3361

32 Commercial St., South Yarmouth, MA 02664
Phone: (508) 394-1325

123 Morton St., Jamaica Plain, MA 02130
Phone: (617) 524-5474

85 E. Newton St., 2nd Fl., Boston, MA 02118
Phone: (617) 266-9298

55 Dimock St., Roxbury, MA 02119
Phone: (617) 445-5485

1448-1452 Dorchester Ave., One Fields Corner, Dorchester, MA 02122
Phone: (617) 288-0300

**Contact:** Terrence Flynn, Adoption Program Manager.

**Date established:** 1980.

**Description:** Non-profit, public agency.

**Area served:** Residents of Massachusetts.

**Requirements:** Adults, 21 yrs. and older who have good parenting skills and can provide adequate food and shelter, and physical and emotional stability.

**Fees:** None.

**Number of children placed last year:** 441.

**Description of children:** Children between the ages of 0 and 18 yrs. some of whom had special needs and some of whom were members of sibling groups.

**Adoption procedure:**
1) Submit application;
2) initial review of application and written notification of eligibility or ineligibility;
3) complete training and home study;
4) notification of Dept. decision on home study;
5) placement;
6) 6 mos. post-placement supervision;
7) finalization.

**Average length of time between application and start of home study:** 1-6 mos.

**Average length of time to complete home study:** 3 mos.

**Number of interviews:** 10 group plus individual and home visit.

**Home study description:** Educational and evaluatory process which includes background checks, recommendation of references, medical reports, ability to meet children's needs and group training classes.

**Average wait for a child after approval of a home study:** 6-12 mos.

**Foster care:** Emergency, temporary, long-term and specialized.

# PRIVATE AGENCIES

★ 310 ★
**Adoption Center, Inc.**
55 Wheeler St.
Cambridge, MA 02138
Phone: (617) 864-5437

**Contact:** Judith M. Bailey, Executive Director.

**Date established:** 1986.

**Description:** Private, non-profit child placing agency licensed by the Massachusetts Department of Social Services.

**Area served:** Residents of Connecticut, Massachusetts and Michigan.

**Requirements:** Flexible.

**Fees:** Application: $150; home study: $2000. Total costs: $25,000.

**Number of children placed last year:** 120.

**Description of children:** Infants.

**Adoption procedure:** 1) Application request; 2) application process; 3) home study; 4) approval and childmatch; 5) birth, surrender and placement; 6) post-placement supervision; 7) finalization.

**Average length of time between application and start of home study:** 1 - 6 mos.

**Average length of time to complete home study:** 1 mo.

**Number of interviews:** 4.

**Home study description:** Assessment which includes references, financial statements and medical reports and gauges prospective adoptive parents' readiness to receive a child in an adoptive placement.

**Average wait for a child after approval of a home study:** 6 -12 mos.

**Foster care:** Temporary.

★ 311 ★
**Adoption Resource of Jewish Family and Children's Services, Boston**
31 New Chardon St.
Boston, MA 02114
Phone: (617) 227-5587
(800) 533-4346
Fax: (617) 227-3220

**Branch address:**
   637 Washington St., Brookline, MA 02146

   6 Pleasant St., Malden, MA 02148

   1017 Turnpike St., Ste. 33, Canton, MA 02021

**Contact:** Adoption intake.

**Date established:** 1944.

**Description:** Non-profit licensed agency.

**Area served:** Residents of Massachusetts.

**Fees:**
Application fee: $125;
home study: $1500;
post-placement services: $1200.
Program/placement fees are a separate expense.

**Number of children placed last year:** 15.

**Description of children:** Infants.

**Adoption procedure:**
  1) Attend informational meeting;
  2) file application;
  3) complete home study;
  4) if approved, placement;
  5) post-placement supervision;
  6) documents prepared for finalization.

**Average length of time between application and start of home study:** 1 mo. or less.

**Average length of time to complete home study:** 8 wks.

**Number of interviews:** 4.

**Home study description:** An educational and evaluative process to assess applicant(s)' readiness and capacity for adoptive parenting and to help them prepare for adoptive parenthood.

**Average wait for a child after approval of a home study:** 12-24 mos.

**Foster care:** Temporary.

★ 312 ★
**Alliance for Children, Inc.**
40 William St., Ste. G80
Wellesley, MA 02181
Phone: (617) 431-7148
(800) 782-2250
Fax: (617) 431-7474

**Branch address:**
   500 Prospect St., Pawtucket, RI 02860
   Phone: (401) 725-9555

**Contact:** Ruth Rich, Communications Coordinator.

**Date established:** 1974.

**Description:** Private, non-profit agency licensed in the Commonwealth of Massachusetts.

**Area served:** Residents of the State of Massachusetts.

**Requirements:** Requirements vary with child's country of origin. Generally, however, to adopt internationally, applicants must be in good physical and mental health, at least one parent must be 25 yrs. or older and a citizen of the U.S.

**Fees:**
Home study fee which includes pre-placement services, post-placement supervision and finalization in MA: sliding scale from $700-$3500;
administrative fee (intercountry adoptions): $750;
resource fee: $7000-$16,000.

**Number of children placed last year:** 160.

**Description of children:** U.S. and foreign-born children from 2 wks. - 10 yrs., some with special needs.

**Adoption procedure:**
  1) Submit preliminary form;
  2) attend orientation meeting;
  3) participate in 2 two-hr. pre-screening meetings;

4) complete home study and dossier (for inter-country adoptions);
5) if approved, referral and networking for placement;
6) placement;
7) post-placement supervision.

**Average length of time between application and start of home study:** 6-12 mos.

**Average length of time to complete home study:** 2-3 mos.

**Number of interviews:** 5-7.

**Home study description:** The purpose of the study is to explore the prospective parents' feelings about parenthood, their motivation for adoption, their marital relationship, their backgrounds, the type of child they are able to accept, their ability to provide for the proper financial and emotional support of the children, etc.

**Average wait for a child after approval of a home study:** 1-6 mos.

**Foster care:** Temporary.

### ★ 313 ★
**Beacon Adoption Center, Inc.**
66 Lake Buel Rd.
Great Barrington, MA 01230
Phone: (413) 528-2749
(413) 528-5036

**Contact:** Deborah McCurdy, LICSW, Adoption Supervisor.

**Date established:** 1990.

**Description:** Private, non-profit child placing agency licensed by the Massachusetts Department of Social Services.

**Area served:** Residents of Berkshire, Franklin, Hampden and Hampshire counties of western Massachusetts.

**Requirements:** Applicants must be between 21 and 59 yrs., single or if married, marriage should be of at least 1 yr.'s duration.

**Fees:** Application: $75; home study: $1500 (includes updates, if needed); post-placement services: $900. Placement fees from cooperating agencies are additional.

**Number of children placed last year:** 19.

**Description of children:** Asian, Eastern European and Latin American infants and toddlers.

**Adoption procedure:** 1) Telephone inquiry; 2) exploratory interview or evening group meeting; 3) application; 4)) home study: 5) applicants select a placing agency; 6) child match; 7) placement; 8) post-placement supervision; 9) finalization; 10) naturalization.

**Average length of time between application and start of home study:** Less than 1 mo.

**Average length of time to complete home study:** 3 - 4 mos.

**Number of interviews:** 4 - 5.

**Home study description:** Non-intensive, facilitating process which educates prospective adoptive parents and prepares them for an intercountry placement. It offers step-by-step practical assistance with procedures.

**Average wait for a child after approval of a home study:** 12 - 15 mos.

**Foster care:** None.

### ★ 314 ★
**Berkshire Center for Families and Children**
480 West St.
Pittsfield, MA 01201
Phone: (413) 448-8281
Fax: (413) 448-6051

**Contact:** Claudia Finck, ACSW, LICSW.

**Date established:** 1887.

**Description:** Private, non-profit social service agency licensed by the Office for Children of the Commonwealth of Massachusetts.

**Area served:** Residents of Massachusetts.

**Requirements:** Persons with stable and adequate income to cover the needs of an additional family member and who are in good health who have the ability to parent a child who joins the family through adoption, have stable relationships, and criminal record clearance.

**Fees:** Home study fee: $2000; post-placement fee: $700; finalization fee: $550.

**Number of children placed last year:** 9.

**Description of children:** Infants, older children, foreign-born children, and children with special needs.

**Adoption procedure:**
1) Initial inquiry;
2) complete home study;
3) if approved, wait for placement;
4) placement;
5) post-placement supervision;
6) finalization;
7) post-finalization services.

**Average length of time between application and start of home study:** 1 mo. or less.

**Average length of time to complete home study:** 1-3 mos.

**Number of interviews:** Approx. 8.

**Home study description:** Examination of family of origin, relationships, health history, ability to parent a child who is adopted, financial status, autobiographies, law enforcement clearances, attitudes toward birthparents, education, and preparation regarding adoption issues.

**Average wait for a child after approval of a home study:** 24 or more mos.

**Foster care:** Temporary.

### ★ 315 ★
**The Brightside for Families and Children**
2112 Riverdale St.
West Springfield, MA 01090
Phone: (413) 788-7366
(800) 333-3424
Fax: (413) 747-0182

**Contact:** Adoption Resource Center.

**Date established:** 1881.

**Description:** Private, non-profit agency. Licensed and accredited locally, nationally, and internationally.

**Area served:** U.S.

**Requirements:** Many factors are considered in evaluating the individual's or couple's ability to successfully parent.

**Fees:** Charged per service.

**Number of children placed last year:** 25.

**Description of children:** U.S. and foreign-born infants and children, some with special needs.

**Adoption procedure:**
1) Information meeting available and initial consultation available;
2) home study;
3) placement;
4) post-placement supervision;
5) finalization.

**Average length of time between application and start of home study:** 1 mo. or less.

**Average length of time to complete home study:** 8-10 wks.

**Number of interviews:** 5-7.

**Home study description:** Assessment of a couple's/individual's ability to parent.

**Average wait for a child after approval of a home study:** 12-24 mos.

**Foster care:** Temporary, long-term and guardianship for infants and toddlers.

★ 316 ★
**Cambridge Adoption and Counseling Associates, Inc.**
111 Mt. Auburn St.
Watertown, MA 02172
Phone: (617) 923-0370
Fax: (617) 923-1499

**Mailing address:**
  P.O. Box 190, Watertown, MA 02172

**Contact:** Madeline Daniels, MSW, ACSW, LICSW, Executive Director.

**Date established:** 1980.

**Description:** Non-profit corporation licensed by the Commonwealth of Massachusetts Office for Children and a member of the Massachusetts Council of Human Service Providers.

**Area served:** Residents of the Commonwealth of Massachusetts.

**Requirements:** Applicants must be between the ages of 25 and 55 yrs., in reasonably good health and who can demonstrate financial stability. In inter-country placement child's country of origin may impose additional requirements.

**Fees:** Application fee: $100; all other fees are on a sliding scale basis.

**Number of children placed last year:** Under 100.

**Description of children:** Healthy infants and toddlers from Brazil, Chile, China, India, Kazakhstan, India, Moldova, Paraguay, Peru, Republic of Al Tai, Romania, Russia, Ukraine, and the U.S.

**Adoption procedure:**
1) Attend orientation meeting;
2) submit application;
3) participate in individual or group counseling sessions;
4) complete home study;
5) compile dossier and comply with immigration/naturalization requirements for foreign adoptions.

**Average length of time between application and start of home study:** 1 mo. or less.

**Average length of time to complete home study:** 1 mo.

**Number of interviews:** 6.

**Home study description:** Each case is handled on an individual basis.

**Average wait for a child after approval of a home study:** 1-6 mos.

**Foster care:** Temporary.

★ 317 ★
**Cambridge Family and Children's Service**
929 Massachusetts Ave.
Cambridge, MA 02139
Phone: (617) 876-4210

**Contact:** Audrey Banks, Director of Adoptions.

**Date established:** 1873.

**Description:** Private, non-profit child placing agency licensed by the Office for Children.

**Area served:** Residents of the U.S.

**Requirements:** Applicants must be at least 21 yrs. old.

**Fees:** None.

**Number of children placed last year:** 15.

**Description of children:** African American infants and children aged 5 and older of European American and African American ethnicity.

**Adoption procedure:** 1) Initial inquiry; 2) application; 3) 10 wks of MAPP training; 4) home study; 5)placement; 6) post-placement supervision; 7) finalization.

**Average length of time between application and start of home study:** 1 - 6 mos.

**Average length of time to complete home study:** 10 wks.

**Number of interviews:** 3.

**Home study description:** Assessment which includes a general sharing of information and includes background, marital status, sibling relationships, home environment, health, criminal records checks, references and methods of discipline.

**Average wait for a child after approval of a home study:** 1 - 12 mos.

**Foster care:** Short-term and specialized.

★ 318 ★
**Catholic Charities of Worcester**
15 Ripley St.
Worcester, MA 01610
Phone: (508) 798-0191

**Branch address:**
  79 Elm St., Southbridge, MA 01550

  53 Highland Ave., Fitchburg, MA 01420

**Contact:** Sara Snow Glenn, LICSW.

**Date established:** 1951.

**Description:** Non-profit private agency licensed by the Massachusetts Office for Children and accredited by the National Council on Accreditation.

**Area served:** Residents of central Massachusetts.

**Requirements:** Call or write for guidelines.

**Fees:** Sliding scale based on income.

**Number of children placed last year:** 16.

**Description of children:** Infants and children with special needs.

**Adoption procedure:** Call or write for outline.

**Average length of time between application and start of home study:** 1-6 mos.

**Average length of time to complete home study:** Unavailable.

**Number of interviews:** 10-12.

**Home study description:** Unavailable.

**Average wait for a child after approval of a home study:** Varies depending on applicant(s) specifications.

**Foster care:** Temporary.

★ 319 ★
**Concord Family Service**
Community Agencies Bldg.
Concord, MA 01742
Phone: (508) 369-4909
Fax: (508) 371-1463

**Contact:** Nancy H. Clayman, Coordinator of Adoption Services.

**Date established:** 1814 (1980 for adoption program).

**Description:** Non-profit family service agency licensed by the Massachusetts Office for Children and accredited by Council for Accreditation.

**Area served:** Eastern Massachusetts.

**Requirements:** Varies.

**Fees:** Varies.

**Number of children placed last year:** Less than 10.

**Description of children:** Birth to adolescence.

**Adoption procedure:**
1) File pre-application;
2) agency invites applicants to submit complete application and written materials;
3) participate in pre-adoptive counseling;
4) placement;
5) post-placement support;
6) legal finalization.

**Average length of time between application and start of home study:** Varies.

**Average length of time to complete home study:** 3 mos.

**Number of interviews:** 6-8 and possibly group.

**Home study description:** Exploration of individual background, couple's relationship, philosophy of parenting, adoption related issues, emotions surrounding infertility and its resolution; attitudes toward differences and expectations of a child.

**Average wait for a child after approval of a home study:** Varies.

**Foster care:** Temporary.

★ 320 ★
**Florence Crittenton League**
119 Hall St.
Lowell, MA 01854
Phone: (508) 452-9671
Fax: (508) 970-0070

**Contact:** Mrs. I. Keegan, Executive Director.

**Date established:** 1907.

**Description:** Private, non-profit agency licensed by the Massachusetts Office for Children.

**Area served:** Residents of the eastern part of Massachusetts.

**Requirements:** Couples married 3 or more yrs. who are younger than 40 yrs.

**Fees:**
$3500 out-of-state placement
$3500 for overseas adoption
Total cost for overseas $15,000 - $20,000.

**Number of children placed last year:** 60.

**Description of children:** Children from the U.S., Colombia, Russia, and China.

**Adoption procedure:**
1) File application;
2) complete home study;

3) if approved, placement;
4) post-placement supervision;
5) finalization.

**Average length of time between application and start of home study:** 0-1 mos.

**Average length of time to complete home study:** 1-2 mos.

**Number of interviews:** 4.

**Home study description:** Evaluation of health and financial reports, marital relationship, recommendation of references, home and environment.

**Average wait for a child after approval of a home study:** 6-12 mos.

**Foster care:** Temporary.

★ 321 ★
**Greater Boston Catholic Charities**
270 Washington St.
Somerville, MA 02143
Phone: (617) 625-1920

**Contact:** Shirley A. Conway.

**Date established:** 1904.

**Description:** Non-profit, private agency licensed in the State of Massachusetts.

**Area served:** Residents of Boston and 50 surrounding towns.

**Requirements:** None.

**Fees:** Sliding scale.

**Number of children placed last year:** 52.

**Description of children:** 24 healthy, white infants; 5 healthy children of color; 23 special needs (DSS contracts).

**Adoption procedure:** Call or write for details.

**Average length of time between application and start of home study:** Varies.

**Average length of time to complete home study:** Varies.

**Number of interviews:** Varies.

**Home study description:** Call or write for description.

**Average wait for a child after approval of a home study:** Varies.

**Foster care:** Primarily temporary.

★ 322 ★
**Hope Adoptions, Inc.**
9 Brookline St.
Townsend, MA 01469
Phone: (508) 597-5969

**Contact:** Andy, John or Mary.

**Date established:** 1992.

**Description:** Private, non-profit child placing agency licensed by the Massachusetts Department of Social Services.

**Area served:** Residents of Massachusetts.

**Requirements:** Open.

**Fees:** Application: $500. Full program fee (including home study, costs and expenses): $11,000.

**Number of children placed last year:** 12.

**Description of children:** Infants.

**Adoption procedure:** 1) Application; 2) home study group weekend; 3) home study completion; 4) birth family outreach and support group participation; 5) birth and placement; 6) post-placement supervision; 7) finalization.

**Average length of time between application and start of home study:** Less than 1 mo.

**Average length of time to complete home study:** 2 mos.

**Number of interviews:** 3.

**Home study description:** Assessment which includes a criminal records check, 3 personal and a medical reference, financial statement and addresses the motivation to adopt and the family's attitude toward adoption.

**Average wait for a child after approval of a home study:** 12 - 24 mos.

**Foster care:** Temporary.

★ 323 ★
**Jewish Family Service of Greater Springfield, Inc.**
15 Lenox St.
Springfield, MA 01108
Phone: (413) 737-2601
Fax: (413) 737-0323

**Contact:** Lisa Burch, LIC. SW.

**Description:** Non-profit, non-sectarian private agency licensed by the Commonwealth of Massachusetts offering programs in traditional adoption and designated intrastate and interstate adoption.

**Area served:** Residents of Massachusetts.

**Requirements:** No religious requirement. Traditional adoption closed to new applicants.

**Fees:** Sliding scale.

**Number of children placed last year:** 5.

**Description of children:** Infants.

**Adoption procedure:** Procedures differ depending upon applicant's choice of traditional or designated adoption.

**Average length of time between application and start of home study:** 24 or more mos.

**Average length of time to complete home study:** 8-10 interview hrs.

**Home study description:** Evaluation of social and marital history, current lifestyle, and prospective parenting style.

**Average wait for a child after approval of a home study:** 6-12 mos.

**Foster care:** Short-term.

★ 324 ★
**Jewish Family Service of Metrowest**
14 Vernon St.
Framingham, MA 01701
Phone: (508) 875-3100

**Contact:** Dale Eldridge, Coordinator, Adopters' Services.

**Date established:** 1981.

**Description:** Private, non-profit, non-sectarian agency licensed by the Office for Children and accredited by the Council on Accreditation on Services for Families and Children.

**Area served:** Residents of Massachusetts.

**Requirements:** Each applicant is considered individually. Chronic health problems require documentation of treatment and prognosis. No income, marital status, nor religious requirements.

**Fees:** Application fee: $175.; Home study fee: $1750. Agency fees range up to $9000. Other fees vary and are dependent on the kind of adoption, i.e. interstate, identified, agency to agency. A sliding scale is available.

**Number of children placed last year:** 21.

**Description of children:** Mostly Caucasian infants, several infants of mixed racial heritage and one Afro-American infant.

**Adoption procedure:** 1) Attend optional free informational meeting which are held monthly; 2) Make application; 3) home study; 4) connect with birthmother or placing agency; 5) placement;6) post-placement supervision; 7) finalization.

**Average length of time between application and start of home study:** Less than 1 month.

**Average length of time to complete home study:** 2 mos.

**Number of interviews:** 5.

**Home study description:** The home study is a descriptive profile of the individual and the couple, if relevant, including background, family relationships, values, priorities, health, finances, present lifestyle and interests. It includes checks of references and Criminal Records. A 9 session support and information workshop is part of the home study.

**Average wait for a child after approval of a home study:** 6-24 mos.

**Foster care:** Temporary infant care.

★ 325 ★
**Lutheran Social Services of New England, Inc., MA**
416 Belmont St.
Worcester, MA 01604
Phone: (508) 791-4488
(800) 890-4488
Fax: (508) 753-7472

**Contact:** Paula Wisnewski.

**Date established:** 1988.

**Description:** Non-profit, full-service private agency of the Evangelical Lutheran Church in America and the Lutheran Church, Missouri Synod. Licensed in Massachusetts.

**Area served:** Residents of Massachusetts.

**Requirements:** Couples married at least 2 yrs. who are at least 25 yrs. and in good health. Singles accepted for some programs. Other requirements may be imposed by child's country of origin.

**Fees:** Agency fees: $3600; aditional fees paid to foreign agency for international adoptions. Special needs: $250. Identified adoptions: $7,000-$10,000 plus allowable expenses.

**Number of children placed last year:** 15.

**Description of children:** International children of all ages, some with special needs; healthy caucasian infants, and special needs children in the care of DSS.

**Adoption procedure:**
1) Initial inquiry;
2) file application;
3) attend 1-8 group sessions;
4) complete individual interview process;
5) if approved, child referral.

**Average length of time between application and start of home study:** 1 mo. or less.

**Average length of time to complete home study:** 3 mos.

**Number of interviews:** 1-10 group and 2-4 individual.

**Home study description:** Assessment of family's ability to parent a child not born to them and to deal with the adoption issues usually faced by the type of child they're seeking to adopt.

**Average wait for a child after approval of a home study:** 12-24 mos.

**Foster care:** Short-term, infants going into adoption.

**★ 326 ★**
**New England Home for Little Wanderers**
20 Linden St., 3rd Fl.
Boston, MA 02134
Phone: (617) 232-8610
Fax: (617) 783-2220
**Branch address:**
161 S. Huntington Ave., Boston, MA 02130
Phone: (617) 232-8610
**Contact:** Marilyn Sneden, Adoption Program Director.
**Date established:** 1865.
**Description:** Private, non-profit agency licensed by the Massachusetts Office for Children and a member of the Child Welfare League of America.
**Area served:** Residents of the Greater Boston area and all of Massachusetts.
**Requirements:** Each applicant is examined on his/her own merits.
**Fees:** Home study: $2500; update: $1000; post-placement supervision: $1500.
**Number of children placed last year:** 10.
**Description of children:** Infants, special needs, and foreign-born.
**Adoption procedure:**
1) Participate in Pre-Service Training Series;
2) complete home study;
3) reference and law enforcement checks;
4) forward medical reports;
5) wait for placement.
**Average length of time between application and start of home study:** 1 mo. or less.
**Average length of time to complete home study:** 3-4 mos.
**Number of interviews:** 6.
**Home study description:** Evaluation of individual and marital history; individual strengths and needs; experience with children and motivation to adopt.
**Average wait for a child after approval of a home study:** 6-12 mos.
**Foster care:** Temporary and long-term.

**★ 327 ★**
**Project Impact**
25 West St.
Boston, MA 02111
Phone: (617) 451-1472
Fax: (617) 338-5514
**Contact:** Robert E. Lewis, Executive Director.
**Date established:** 1976.
**Description:** Non-profit adoption and foster care agency for special needs children only.
**Area served:** Residents of the State of Massachusetts.
**Requirements:** None.
**Fees:** None.
**Number of children placed last year:** 25.
**Description of children:** Children and adolescents with special needs.
**Adoption procedure:** Applicants must attend a group training process and have a child-specific home study.
**Average length of time between application and start of home study:** Varies.
**Average length of time to complete home study:** 3-4 months.

**Number of interviews:** Varies.
**Home study description:** Home study is tailored to the child for whom the applicants are applying.
**Average wait for a child after approval of a home study:** Varies.
**Foster care:** Long-term special needs.

**★ 328 ★**
**Protestant Social Service Bureau**
776 Hancock St.
Quincy, MA 02170
Phone: (617) 773-6203
**Contact:** Heather L.M. Rodiger.
**Date established:** 1947.
**Description:** Private agency licensed to place children by the Massachusetts Office for Children.
**Area served:** Residents of south east Massachusetts.
**Requirements:** Open.
**Fees:** First interview: $60. Total fees through finalization: 10% of gross income with a maximum of $8000. No fees for children in the custody of the Department of Social Services.
**Number of children placed last year:** 32.
**Description of children:** Children with special needs, foreign born children and a few U.S. infants.
**Adoption procedure:** 1) Initial interview; 2) series of educational group meetings; 3) home study; 4) childmatch; 5) placement; 6) post-placement supervision; 7) finalization.
**Average length of time between application and start of home study:** 1 - 6 mos.
**Average length of time to complete home study:** 3 - 4 mos.
**Number of interviews:** Unavailable.
**Home study description:** Assessment which addresses such issues as relationship between parents, with extended family and the community; motivation to adopt, parenting skills and ability to deal with frustration.
**Average wait for a child after approval of a home study:** Varies with type of child requested: special needs placements may be immediate; foreign placements may take from 1 - 2 yrs.
**Foster care:** Temporary.

**★ 329 ★**
**Southeastern Adoption Services, Inc.**
P.O. Box 356
Marion, MA 02738
Phone: (508) 996-6683
Fax: (508) 996-6683
**Contact:** Beverly Baccelli.
**Date established:** 1982.
**Description:** Non-profit private agency licensed by the Massachusetts Office for Children.
**Area served:** Residents of Boston, west of Boston, southeastern Massachusetts, Cape Cod, Nantucket and Martha's Vineyard.
**Requirements:** Flexible.
**Fees:** Home study: $1200-$1400; post-placement services: $600.
**Number of children placed last year:** 25.
**Description of children:** Identified U.S. children, Asian, East European, and Latin American.

**Adoption procedure:** Agency provides home study services, assistance with INS procedures for inter-country adoptions, liaison work with placement agency selected by client and post-placement supervision.

**Average length of time between application and start of home study:** 1 mo. or less.

**Average length of time to complete home study:** 6-8 wks.

**Number of interviews:** 3 or more.

**Home study description:** Exploration of attitudes toward adoption and understanding of cross-cultural issues.

**Average wait for a child after approval of a home study:** 6-12 mos.

**Foster care:** None.

**★ 330 ★**
**Wide Horizons For Children, Inc.**
282 Moody St.
Waltham, MA 02154
Phone: (617) 894-5330
(617) 734-4828
Fax: (617) 899-2769

**Branch address:**

34 Connecticut Blvd., East Hartford, CT 06108
Phone: (203) 291-8610

430 Main St., Agawam, MA 01001
Phone: (413) 789-3557

5 State St., Concord, NH 03301
Phone: (603) 224-5174

22 Yerk Ave., Ronkonkoma, NY 11779
Phone: (516) 585-1008

116 Andre Ave., Wakefield, RI 02879
Phone: (401) 783-4537

P.O. Box 53, Monkton, VT 05469
Phone: (802) 658-2070

**Contact:** Intake worker.

**Date established:** 1974.

**Description:** Private, non-profit child welfare agency licensed to place children in Connecticut, Massachusetts, New Hampshire, New York, Rhode Island and Vermont.

**Area served:** Residents of Connecticut, Massachusetts, New Hampshire, New York, Rhode Island and Vermont.

**Requirements:** Single applicants must be at least 25 yrs. old. Couples should be married a minimum of 2 yrs. One parent must remain home during the first 3 mos. after placement. Additional requirements may be made by specific countries and/or agencies.

**Fees:** Application: $200; home study: 2/3 of 6% of income. Program fees vary by country.

**Number of children placed last year:** 286.

**Description of children:** Infants and children from the following countries: Chile, China, Colombia, Costa Rica, El Salvador, Guatemala, India, Korea, Lithuania, Moldavia, Nepal, Paraguay, Peru, The Philippines, Russia, Taiwan, U.S. and Viet Nam. Some in sibling groups and some with special needs.

**Adoption procedure:** 1) General information meeting; 2) application; 3) medical reports; 4) letters of reference; 5) interviews; 6) pre-adoptive parent groups; 7) home study; 8) child referral; 9)placement; 10 ) post-placement supervision; 11) finalization; 12) naturalization.

**Average length of time between application and start of home study:** Less than 1 mo.

**Average length of time to complete home study:** 3 mos.

**Number of interviews:** 3.

**Home study description:** Assessment which includes financial and medical reports, proof of insurance coverage and checks that the home is clean, safe and equipped with smoke detectors and covers personal and biographical information.

**Average wait for a child after approval of a home study:** 6 - 12 mos.

**Foster care:** Temporary.

# MICHIGAN

## STATUTES

**★ 331 ★**

**Independent placement by intermediary?** Illegal.

**Independent placement by birth parents?** Permitted.

**Subsidies provided?** Support and medical subsidies.

**Adoption cost defined by law?** While cost elements are defined, amounts are not, but amounts must be deemed reasonable by the court at the time of the hearing.

**Insurance for infertility?:** Unknown.

**Home study required by state?** Required before placement and must be conducted by an agency licensed by the Michigan Department of Social Services.

**Prospective adoptive parent advertise for a child?** Not addressed in law.

**Surrogacy laws?** Permitted.

**Residents access agencies of other states or countries?** Permitted, but adoptions finalized in Michigan must involved an agency licensed by the Michigan Department of Social Services.

**Requires judicial termination of birth parents' rights?** Yes, in County Probate Court.

**Time given to a birthmother to revoke her consent:** None.

**Court handling adoptions?** County Probate Court.

**Adoption of Native Children:** Tribe, if the child is a ward of the tribe; state, if the child is a ward of the state.

**Adoption records sealed?** Yes, the release of identifying and non-identifying information to adoptees, 18 yrs. and older, is governed by law.

**Photo-listing book available?** Michigan Adoption Resource Exchange Book.

## PUBLIC AGENCIES

**★ 332 ★**
**Berrien County Department of Social Services**
401 Eighth St.
Benton Harbor, MI 49022
Phone: (616) 934-2096

**Contact:** Ann C. Cuhran, Adoption Specialist.

**Description:** County social service agency licensed to place children through the Michigan Department of Social Services.

**Area served:** Residents of Berrien County.

**Requirements:** Open.

**Fees:** No agency fee. Probate Court filing fee: $70.

**Number of children placed last year:** 60.

**Description of children:** Children with special needs, primarily over the age of 5 yrs., in sibling groups and minorities.

**Adoption procedure:** 1) Application; 2) home study; 3) child match; 4) pre-placement visitation; 5) placement; 6) post-placement supervision; 7) finalization.

**Average length of time between application and start of home study:** Less than 1 mo.

**Average length of time to complete home study:** 1 - 3 mos.

**Number of interviews:** 3 - 4.

**Home study description:** Assessment which includes general character, description of home and community, physical exams, personal and professional references, background checks, family and employment history and addresses such issues as child rearing practices and motivation to adopt.

**Average wait for a child after approval of a home study:** 1 - 6 mos.

**Foster care:** Emergency, short- and long-term, therapeutic and permanent.

## ★ 333 ★
### Calhoun County Department of Social Services
190 E. Michigan
Battle Creek, MI 49017
Phone: (616) 966-1350
Fax: (616) 966-2835

**Contact:** Nancy French, Supervisor; Cindy Thielen, Deb Falconer, Dave Stevens, Adoption Workers.

**Description:** Public agency.

**Area served:** Residents of Calhoun and Eaton counties.

**Requirements:** Married couples, 21 years of age and older and singles, 21 years and older.

**Fees:** Court fees: approx. $65; amended birth certificate: $26.

**Number of children placed last year:** 52.

**Description of children:** Children between the ages of 6 mos. and 18 yrs., most of whom were adopted by their foster parents and relatives.

**Adoption procedure:**
1) Complete adoptive home study;
2) obtain necessary consents;
3) petition for subsidies and contracts;
4) file Petition to Adopt.

**Average length of time between application and start of home study:** 1-6 mos.

**Average length of time to complete home study:** 3-6 months.

**Number of interviews:** 4-6.

**Home study description:** Assessment of medical evaluations and references; social and emotional histories; type of child(ren) desired; and recommendations.

**Average wait for a child after approval of a home study:** 1-6 mos.

**Foster care:** Temporary, long-term and permanent.

## ★ 334 ★
### Genesee County Department of Social Services
125 E. Union
Flint, MI 48502
Phone: (313) 768-2218

**Contact:** Margaret Vaughter.

**Description:** Non-profit, public agency.

**Area served:** Residents of Genesee County.

**Requirements:** Adults in good physical health.

**Fees:** None.

**Number of children placed last year:** 63.

**Description of children:** Children with special needs.

**Adoption procedure:**
1) File application;
2) complete home study;
3) if approved, child/family match;
4) placement;
5) post-placement supervisory;
6) finalization.

**Average length of time between application and start of home study:** Varies.

**Average length of time to complete home study:** 2 mos.

**Number of interviews:** 4.

**Home study description:** Assessment of background information; ability to meet the needs of a child; stability of family life; and medical evaluation.

**Average wait for a child after approval of a home study:** Varies.

**Foster care:** Temporary, long-term and permanent.

## ★ 335 ★
### Hillsdale County Department of Social Services
15 Care Dr.
Hillsdale, MI 49242
Phone: (517) 439-2280

**Mailing address:**
P.O. Box 705, Hillsdale, MI 49242

**Contact:** Laura Nye, Adoption Worker.

**Description:** Public county-based multi-service agency licensed by the Michigan Department of Social Services.

**Area served:** Residents of Branch and Hillsdale counties.

**Requirements:** Open.

**Fees:** None.

**Number of children placed last year:** 18.

**Description of children:** Children with special needs from 2 to 16 yrs.

**Adoption procedure:** Foster care to adoption conversions are immediate provided the child has been in thehome for a year or more. Other adoptions require home study and 1 yr. of post-placementsupervision.

**Average length of time between application and start of home study:** Less than 1 mo.

**Average length of time to complete home study:** 2 mos.

**Number of interviews:** 4.

**Home study description:** Assessment which includes background information, family's support system and the type of child desired.

**Average wait for a child after approval of a home study:** 24 or more mos.

**Foster care:** Emergency, short and long-term and permanent.

## ★ 336 ★
### Ingham County Dept. of Social Services
5303 S. Cedar
Lansing, MI 48909
Phone: (517) 887-9670
Fax: (517) 887-9500

**Mailing address:**
P.O. Box 30088, Lansing, MI 48909

**Contact:** Adoption worker.

**Description:** Non-profit public agency.

**Area served:** Residents of Ingham, Clinton and Shiawassee counties.

**Requirements:** Departmental policy establishes criteria.

**Fees:** None.

**Number of children placed last year:** 14.

**Description of children:** Special needs primarily, but place all types of children.

**Adoption procedure:** Call or write for details.

**Average length of time between application and start of home study:** 1-6 mos.

**Average length of time to complete home study:** Varies.

**Number of interviews:** Varies.

**Home study description:** Call or write for outline.

**Average wait for a child after approval of a home study:** 6-12 mos.

**Foster care:** Temporary, permanent and long-term.


★ 337 ★
**Kalamazoo County Department of Social Services**
322 Stockbridge
Kalamazoo, MI 49001
Phone: (616) 337-4993

**Contact:** Lyn James, Services Supervisor.

**Description:** Public agency.

**Area served:** Residents of Kalamazoo County.

**Requirements:** None.

**Fees:** Minimal: court filing fee and amended birth certificate fee.

**Number of children placed last year:** 26.

**Description of children:** Primarily children with special needs and groups of older siblings.

**Adoption procedure:**
1) Initial inquiry;
2) complete adoptive family study;
3) file petition and order to terminate State of Michigan's custody;
4) if study is approved, placement;
5) 1 yr. supervisory period;
6) finalization.

**Average length of time between application and start of home study:** 1-6 mos.

**Average length of time to complete home study:** 1 yr.

**Number of interviews:** 5 in-home.

**Home study description:** Assessment of family background, child rearing practices and family strengths and weakness.

**Average wait for a child after approval of a home study:** 1-6 mos.

**Foster care:** Temporary, long-term and permanent.


★ 338 ★
**Kent County Department of Social Services**
415 Franklin, S.E.
Grand Rapids, MI 49507
Phone: (616) 247-6003
Fax: (616) 247-6058

**Contact:** Roger Vander Woude, MSW, Adoption Services.

**Date established:** 1939.

**Description:** Public, county agency.

**Area served:** Residents of Kent, Ionia, Mecosta, and Montcalm counties.

**Requirements:** None.

**Fees:** None.

**Number of children placed last year:** 18.

**Description of children:** Children with special needs.

**Adoption procedure:**
1) Initial inquiry;
2) submit application;
3) complete home study;
4) if approved, wait for placement;
5) placement;
6) post-placement supervision;
7) finalization.

**Average length of time between application and start of home study:** 1 mo. or less.

**Average length of time to complete home study:** 2 mos.

**Number of interviews:** 4.

**Home study description:** Traditional study which includes but is not limited to background, parenting ability, current lifestyle, motivation to adopt and type of child applicant(s) can best parent.

**Average wait for a child after approval of a home study:** 1-6 mos.

**Foster care:** Long-term, when necessary.


★ 339 ★
**Lenawee County Department of Social Services**
1040 S. Winter St., Ste. 3013
Adrian, MI 49221
Phone: (517) 264-6300
(517) 264-6427

**Contact:** David Fisher or Scott Virgo.

**Description:** Public county child placing agency licensed by the Michigan Department of Social Services.

**Area served:** Residents of Lenawee County.

**Requirements:** Applicants must be at least 18 yrs. old.

**Fees:** No agency fees. Court filing fees and birth certificate application.

**Number of children placed last year:** 12.

**Description of children:** Primarily older children who became wards of the Department of Social Services due to abuse and/or neglect.

**Adoption procedure:** 1) Inquiry; 2) application; 3) home study; 4) 18 hrs. of orientation; 5) pre-placement visitation; 6) placement; 7) post-placement supervision; 8) finalization.

**Average length of time between application and start of home study:** 1 - 6 mos.

**Average length of time to complete home study:** 4 mos.

**Number of interviews:** 4.

**Home study description:** Assessment which includes individual and joint interviews, review of family histories, references and medical reports, community involvement and current parenting beliefs.

**Average wait for a child after approval of a home study:** 1 - 24 mos. depending upon the type of child requested.

**Foster care:** Temporary, long term and permanent.

## ★ 340 ★
**Macomb County Department of Social Services**
21885 Dunham Rd.
Mt. Clemens, MI 48043
Phone: (313) 469-6759

**Contact:** Janice Giulioli, Foster Care/Adoption Supervisor.

**Description:** Non-profit state agency.

**Area served:** Residents of Lapeer and Macomb counties.

**Requirements:** Adult applicants who can provide the following:
3 letters of recommendation,
birth certificate(s),
marriage certificate (if applicable),
letter from employer,
divorce decree(s) if applicable,
income tax statement,
medical history and a recent physical examination, including a TB test.

**Fees:** None.

**Number of children placed last year:** 41.

**Description of children:** Children who are older, in large sibling groups or emotionally impaired. All children placed have been abused or neglected, including drug exposed.

**Adoption procedure:**
1) Complete Adoption Inquiry Form;
2) meet with adoption worker;
3) submit formal application and autobiography;
4) complete family evaluation;
5) if approved, waiting period of up to 12 mos. with a possible 6 mos. extension for placement;
6) placement or removal to inactive list.

**Average length of time between application and start of home study:** 6-12 mos.

**Average length of time to complete home study:** Varies.

**Number of interviews:** Varies.

**Home study description:** Evaluation will include contact with each member of the family and a home visit wherein the following are assessed: motivation to adopt; emotional stability; compatibilty of the adoptive parent(s); adjustment of children currently in the home; parenting ability; family's acceptance of an adopted child; family's appreciation of another race or culture; type of child desired; and record of convictions (if any).

**Average wait for a child after approval of a home study:** Varies according to adoptive family's willingness to adopt difficult and/or special needs children or sibling groups.

**Foster care:** Temporary, long-term and permanent.

## ★ 341 ★
**Michigan Department of Social Services**
P.O. Box 30037
Lansing, MI 48909
Phone: (517) 373-3513

**Contact:** Social worker.

**Date established:** C.1900.

**Description:** Public agency.

**Area served:** Residents of the State of Michigan.

**Requirements:** Adults who are physically capable of caring for a child.

**Fees:** None.

**Number of children placed last year:** 800.

**Description of children:** Sibling groups, older, minority and handicapped children.

**Adoption procedure:**
1) Attend group orientation session;
2) file application;
3) complete family evaluation;
4) if approved, child/family match;
5) placement;
6) 1 yr. supervisory period;
7) finalization.

**Average length of time between application and start of home study:** 1-6 mos.

**Average length of time to complete home study:** 3 mos.

**Number of interviews:** 4.

**Home study description:** Assessment of motivation to adopt, emotional stability, family attitude toward adoption, parenting ability, type of child(ren) desired; conviction record and references.

**Average wait for a child after approval of a home study:** 1-6 mos.

**Foster care:** Emergency, temporary, long-term and permanent.

## ★ 342 ★
**Michigan Department of Social Services**
**Northern Michigan Adoption Program**
701 S. Elmwood, Ste. 20
Traverse City, MI 49684
Phone: (616) 922-5377
Fax: (616) 922-5249

**Contact:** Roger E. Quinn, Chief Administrator.

**Date established:** 1982.

**Description:** Public child welfare agency for special needs adoption.

**Area served:** 29 counties of northern Michigan.

**Requirements:** Adults, 21 years and older, who have the ability to parent children with special needs.

**Fees:** No home study fee.

**Number of children placed last year:** 65.

**Description of children:** Only children with special needs, school aged and older; some sibling groups, most children being state of court wards.

**Adoption procedure:**
1) File application;
2) complete family evaluation;
3) if approved, child/family match;
4) placement;
5) post-placement supervision;
6) finalization.

**Average length of time between application and start of home study:** 1-6 mos.

**Average length of time to complete home study:** 6 mos.

**Number of interviews:** 3-5.

**Home study description:** During a family evaluation every member of the family is contacted. It includes but is not limited to a home visit, an assessment of the motivation to adopt; emotional stability and compatibility of the adoptive parent(s); adjustment of any children in the home; family's attitude toward adoption and their plans to discuss adoption with the adopted child; parenting ability; family's attitude and appreciation of a child of a different race or ethnic group (if applicable); type of child(ren) desired; caseworker's recommendation of child best served by the family; and the recommendation of 3 references.

**Average wait for a child after approval of a home study:** 1-12 mos.

**Foster care:** Temporary.

**★ 343 ★**
**Monroe County Department of Social Services**
1051 S. Telegraph Rd.
Monroe, MI 48161
Phone: (313) 243-7452

**Contact:** Joyce Ballard Davis.

**Date established:** 1929.

**Description:** Non-profit public agency licensed through the State of Michigan.

**Area served:** Residents of Monroe County.

**Requirements:** Adults between the ages of 18 and 65 yrs.

**Fees:** None.

**Number of children placed last year:** 2.

**Description of children:** Special needs.

**Adoption procedure:**
  1) Submit completed application with references;
  2) undergo law enforcement check and medical examination;
  3) attend training;
  4) complete home study;
  5) if approved, child search and match;
  6) pre-placement visitation process;
  7) placement;
  8) 1 yr. post-placement supervision;
  9) finalization.

**Average length of time between application and start of home study:** Varies.

**Average length of time to complete home study:** 3 mos.

**Number of interviews:** 2-3.

**Home study description:** Evaluation of family history, employment, education, child rearing techniques, structure of home and references.

**Average wait for a child after approval of a home study:** Varies.

**Foster care:** Temporary, long-term and permanent.

**★ 344 ★**
**Oakland County Department of Social Services**
196 Oakland Ave.
Pontiac, MI 48053
Phone: (810) 858-1560

**Contact:** Adoption supervisor.

**Description:** Public, county agency.

**Area served:** Primarily residents of Oakland County for complete adoption services.

**Requirements:** Applicants are reviewed on a case by case basis.

**Fees:** None.

**Number of children placed last year:** Approx. 33.

**Description of children:** Primarily large sibling groups and older children; special needs children.

**Adoption procedure:**
  1) Submit application;
  2) complete home study;
  3) if approved, pre-placement visitation;
  4) placement;
  5) post-placement supervision;
  6) finalization.

**Average length of time between application and start of home study:** Varies.

**Average length of time to complete home study:** Varies.

**Number of interviews:** Varies.

**Home study description:** Assessments are child-specific and cover home and environment, motivation to adopt, childhood of applicant(s), parenting ability and experience and methods of discipline.

**Average wait for a child after approval of a home study:** Varies.

**Foster care:** Emergency, short and long-term, pre-adoptive.

**★ 345 ★**
**Tuscola County Department of Social Services**
1365 Cleaver Rd.
Caro, MI 48723
Phone: (517) 673-9100
Fax: (517) 673-9209

**Contact:** Suzanne Reed, Supervisor.

**Description:** Public, state agency.

**Area served:** Residents of Huron, Sanilac and Tuscola counties.

**Requirements:** Call or write for guidelines.

**Fees:** None.

**Description of children:** Tuscola Dept. of Social Services provides adoptive services to children in Huron, Sanilac and Tuscola counties. Most of the children have special needs because of abuse and neglect.

**Adoption procedure:** The majority of adoptions handled by the Department are for foster children already living in the adoptive applicants' home.

**Average length of time between application and start of home study:** 1-6 mos.

**Average length of time to complete home study:** 2 mos.

**Number of interviews:** Unavailable.

**Home study description:** Assessment of family, social, medical, financial and employment histories and parenting practices.

**Average wait for a child after approval of a home study:** 1-6 mos.

**Foster care:** Temporary, long-term and permanent.

**★ 346 ★**
**Upper Michigan Adoption Program**
2940 College Ave.
Escanaba, MI 49829
Phone: (906) 786-5394

**Branch address:**
  Chippewa County Department of Social Services, 208 Bingham, P.O. Box 809, Sault Ste. Marie, MI 49783
  Phone: (906) 999-9999

**Contact:** Richard F. Miketinac, Adoption Supervisor.

**Date established:** 1988.

**Description:** Public regional agency licensed to place children by the Michigan Department of Social Services.

**Area served:** Residents of Michigan's Upper Peninsula.

**Requirements:** Open.

**Fees:** No agency fees. Court filing fee: $65; birth certificate: $26.

**Number of children placed last year:** Unavailable.

**Description of children:** Children with special needs.

**Adoption procedure:** 1) Child match; 2) application; 3) home study; 4) videos of prospective adoptive family and identified child exchanged; 5) pre-placement visitation; 6) file adoption petition; 7) placement; 8) post-placement supervision; 9) finalization.

**Average length of time between application and start of home study:** Immediate because family has already expressed interest in a particular child.

**Average length of time to complete home study:** 6 - 12 wks.

**Number of interviews:** 3.

**Home study description:** Exploratory and preparatory process which covers information on special needs adoption in general as well as specific information about the identified child, police and protective services records checks, medical reports and references and addresses such issues as motivation to adopt, family history, marital compatibility, adjustment of children in the home, financial resources and the family's attitude toward accepting an adopted child.

**Average wait for a child after approval of a home study:** None.

**Foster care:** None.


★ 347 ★
**Van Buren County Department of Social Services**
P.O. Box 7
Hartford, MI 49057
Phone: (616) 621-2869

**Contact:** Chris Wirick.

**Description:** County department of social services.

**Area served:** Residents of Van Buren County.

**Requirements:** Ability to parent special needs child(ren) and a stable income/financial resources.

**Fees:** Court costs: approx. $70.

**Number of children placed last year:** 13.

**Description of children:** Primarily older children with emotional problems.

**Adoption procedure:**
1) File application with references;
2) complete home study and criminal records check;
3) home visit(s).

**Average length of time between application and start of home study:** 1-6 mos.

**Average length of time to complete home study:** 2-4 mos.

**Number of interviews:** 2-4.

**Home study description:** Thorough assessment which includes but is not limited to housing, income, parenting ability and stability of marriage (if applicable).

**Average wait for a child after approval of a home study:** Varies.

**Foster care:** Temporary and pre-adoptive.


★ 348 ★
**Wayne County Child and Family Services**
2929 Russell
Detroit, MI 48207
Phone: (313) 396-0357
Fax: (313) 396-0232

**Contact:** Judith Arey or Rita McLenaghan.

**Description:** Division of county department of social services.

**Area served:** Residents of Wayne County.

**Requirements:** Capability to parent adopted children with special needs.

**Fees:** Court and petition fees.

**Number of children placed last year:** 122.

**Description of children:** Black children 5 yrs. and older, white children 10 yrs. and older, handicapped children.

**Adoption procedure:**
1) Attend Adoptive Parent Preparation group;
2) participate in in-home interviews;
3) placement;
4) 1 yr. post-placement service.

**Average length of time between application and start of home study:** 1-6 mos.

**Average length of time to complete home study:** 4 mos.

**Number of interviews:** 6-10.

**Home study description:** Assessment of personal and marital (if applicable) history; parenting experience; expectations of adopted child; and exploration of adoption issues.

**Average wait for a child after approval of a home study:** Varies.

**Foster care:** Temporary and occasionally permanent.


# PRIVATE AGENCIES

★ 349 ★
**Adoption Associates, Inc.**
6491 San Ru
Jenison, MI 49428
Phone: (616) 669-9696

**Branch address:**
3609 Country Club Dr., St. Clair Shores, MI 48082

**Date established:** 1989.

**Description:** Private, non-profit child placing agency licensed by the Michigan Department of Social Services and specializing in privately-released infants and international adoptions.

**Area served:** Residents of Michigan.

**Requirements:** Applicants musts be between the ages of 21 and 45 yrs.

**Fees:** Application: $60; home study: $750 (U.S.) and $850 (international). Additional fees based on time and expenses.

**Number of children placed last year:** 78 U.S. and 35 international.

**Description of children:** Healthy U.S. newborns and foreign born infants and children, some with special needs.

**Adoption procedure:** 1) Home study; 2) formulation of networking system to reach birthparents; 3) agency facilitation with placement.

**Average length of time between application and start of home study:** Less than 1 mo.

**Average length of time to complete home study:** 2 mos.

**Number of interviews:** 6.

**Home study description:** Assessment which addresses such issues as health, employment, social and marital history; culture and child rearing.

**Average wait for a child after approval of a home study:** 6-12 mos. for U.S. newborns.

**Foster care:** Temporary.


★ 350 ★
**The Adoption Cradle, Inc.**
554 Capital Ave. SW
Battle Creek, MI 49015
Phone: (616) 963-0794
Fax: (616) 963-7140

**Contact:** Anne J. Hacker, Executive Director.

**Date established:** 1984.

**Description:** Non-profit, private agency licensed by the State of Michigan.

**Area served:** Birthparents in the State of Michigan; adoptive families: United States; special needs adoptions: United States.

**Requirements:** Couples married at least 2 yrs. who are between the ages of 21 and 50 yrs. who are childless due to medically diagnosed infertility, who have a clear police record and are financially self-supporting.

**Fees:**
Application: $600;
placement and home study: 10% of annual income with a minimum of $2000 and a maximum of $6400.

**Number of children placed last year:** 42.

**Description of children:** White, black and biracial children 0-18 yrs. of age; special needs children.

**Adoption procedure:**
1) Complete and return application;
2) home study is prepared;
3) adoptive couple prepares autobiographical profile for birthparents' consideration;
4) birthparents select adoptive family;
5) direct placement of child considered;
6) upon termination of biological parents' rights, court petition is filed;
7) placement;
8) 4 post-placement supervisory visits in adoptive home; and
9) finalization in 6 mos.

**Average length of time between application and start of home study:** Varies with type of adoption.

**Average length of time to complete home study:** 2 mos.

**Number of interviews:** Approx. 3-4.

**Home study description:** Evaluation of autobiographies; local and state police clearances; physicians' reports including infertility work-up; 3 letters of reference; interviews and in-home visits; marriage and divorce (if applicable) records; and a copy of the previous year's IRS 1040 form.

**Average wait for a child after approval of a home study:** Varies.

**Foster care:** Pre-adoptive/direct placement allowed with birthparent and adoptive parent consent. Agency uses licensed homes as well when appropriate.

**★ 351 ★**
**Americans for International Aid and Adoption**
877 S. Adams
Birmingham, MI 48009
Phone: (810) 645-2211
Fax: (810) 645-2288

**Branch address:**
P.O. Box 6051, Spokane, WA 99207-0901
Phone: (509) 487-8921

8199 Wheaton Rd., Baldwinsville, NY 13027
Phone: (315) 638-9449

**Date established:** 1975.

**Description:** Non-profit licensed child placement agency.

**Area served:** Direct adoption services to residents of Michigan, New York and Washington State. Adoptive placement services to all U.S. residents.

**Requirements:** Varies according to program. Korean infant program: Applicants must be married 3 yrs., be a minimum of 25 yrs. old and a maximum of 44; have $20,000 minimum annual income; no more than 4 children already at home; and a minimum of high school education. China infant girls program: Childless couples married a minimum of 2 yrs. and at least 35 yrs. old preferred. Exceptions for special needs children. Travel required for both parents. Indian program: Couples under 45 yrs. old, married a minimum of 2 yrs., with not more than one divorce and 2 children already in the home. Children are also available from Vietnam and Russia. Please inquire.

**Fees:**
Application fee: $100;
homestudy/supervision: $1400-$1800 sliding scale based on income;
overseas program fee: varies by country, please inquire.

**Number of children placed last year:** 120.

**Description of children:** Indian, Korean, Russian, and Vietnamese children from infancy to 16 yrs., some sibling groups, some with medical conditions; Chinese infant girls.

**Adoption procedure:**
1) File questionnaire;
2) submit formal application;
3) complete home study;
4) child referral;
5) meet legal and immigration requirements;
6) child's transportation;
7) 6 or more mos. post-placement supervision;
8) finalization;
9) naturalization.

**Average length of time between application and start of home study:** Under 3 mos.

**Average length of time to complete home study:** 1-2 mos.

**Number of interviews:** 3-4.

**Home study description:** Evaluation of biographical information, health and financial reports, lifestyle, qualifications and qualities for parenting, especially for a transracial and cross cultural child.

**Average wait for a child after approval of a home study:** 1-6 mos.

**Foster care:** Rarely.

**★ 352 ★**
**Bethany Christian Services (of Eastern Michigan)**
32500 Concord, Ste. 250
Madison Heights, MI 48071
Phone: (810) 588-9400

**Contact:** Cheryl A. Morian, Branch Supervisor.

**Date established:** 1944.

**Description:** Private, non-profit human services agency licensed to place children by the Michigan Department of Social Services.

**Area served:** Residents of eastern Michigan.

**Requirements:** Singles may apply for international program. U.S. Program: Committed Christian couples married at least 3 yrs. who are between the ages of 25 and 45 yrs. and in reasonably good health.

**Fees:** Application: $50; home study: $1500. Post-placement, liaison, program and legal fees are additional.

**Number of children placed last year:** 85.

**Description of children:** U.S. infants, foreign born children and children with special needs.

**Adoption procedure:** 1) Preliminary application; 2) Orientation Meeting; 3) home study process; 4) childreferral; 5) placement and filing of petition; 6) 1 yr. post-placement supervision; 7) finalization.

**Average length of time between application and start of home study:** Less than 1 mo.

**Average length of time to complete home study:** 1 - 2 mos.

**Number of interviews:** 4 - 6.

**Home study description:** Assessment which includes family background including health, marital and financial stability, compatibility, motivation to adopt and resolution of infertility, child rearing and understanding of adoption.

**Average wait for a child after approval of a home study:** Dependent on program selected.

**Foster care:** Cradle care.


★ 353 ★
**Bethany Christian Services (of Grand Rapids)**
901 Eastern Ave., N.E.
Grand Rapids, MI 49506
Phone: (616) 459-6273

**Branch address:**
135 N. State St., Holland, MI 49423
Phone: (616) 396-0623

6995 W. 48th St., P.O. Box 173, Fremont, MI 49412
Phone: (616)924-3390

**Contact:** Harold Wiersma.

**Date established:** 1944.

**Description:** Private, non-profit multi-service agency licensed to place children in Arkansas, California, Colorado, Delaware, Georgia, Illinois, Indiana, Iowa, Louisiana, Maryland, Massachusetts, Michigan, Minnesota, Mississippi, Missouri, New Hampshire, New Jersey, New York, North Carolina, Pennsylvania, Rhode Island, South Carolina, South Dakota, Tennessee, Vermont, Virginia, Washington, Wisconsin and Wyoming and accredited by the Council on Accreditation of Services for Families & Children and a member of the Evangelical Council for Financial Accountability.

**Area served:** Residents of Arkansas, California, Colorado, Delaware, Georgia, Illinois, Indiana, Iowa, Louisiana, Maryland, Massachusetts, Michigan, Minnesota, Mississippi, Missouri, New Hampshire, New Jersey, New York, North Carolina, Pennsylvania, Rhode Island, South Carolina, South Dakota, Tennessee, Vermont, Virginia, Washington, Wisconsin and Wyoming.

**Requirements:** Applicants must be committed Christians and active members of a Christian church.

**Fees:** Unavailable.

**Number of children placed last year:** 767.

**Description of children:** U.S. and foreign born children, some minorities, some sibling groups and some with special needs.

**Adoption procedure:** 1) Informational meeting/adoption education seminar; 2) interview process; 3) adoptive parenting classes; 4) documentation and background checks; 5)approval process; 6) profile dissemination or other child match process; 7) placement; 8) post-placement supervision; 9) finalization.

**Average length of time between application and start of home study:** Unavailable.

**Average length of time to complete home study:** Unavailable.

**Number of interviews:** Unavailable.

**Home study description:** Assessment which includes a review of income and residence, references, copies of wills, police record and child protective services checks and insurance verification and addresses a family's emotional, spiritual and physical health, stability and readiness for parenthood, relationship with Jesus Christ and the completion of a family profile.

**Average wait for a child after approval of a home study:** Depends on program selected.


★ 354 ★
**Bethany Christian Services (of Van Buren County)**
919 E. Michigan Ave.
Paw Paw, MI 49079
Phone: (616) 657-7096

**Contact:** Melissa Peterson Foster Care Licensing/Adoptions.

**Date established:** 1988.

**Description:** Private, non-profit child placing agency licensed by the Michigan Department of Social Services.

**Area served:** Residents of Van Buren County.

**Requirements:** Open.

**Fees:** Application: $70.

**Number of children placed last year:** 7.

**Description of children:** Children with special needs.

**Adoption procedure:** 1) Application; 2) home study; 3) approval; 4) placement; 5) post-placement supervision; 6) finalization.

**Average length of time between application and start of home study:** Less than 1 mo.

**Average length of time to complete home study:** 1 mo.

**Number of interviews:** 3.

**Home study description:** Assessment which includes personal information, marital history, financial stability, community resources and children already in the home.

**Average wait for a child after approval of a home study:** 1 - 6 mos.

**Foster care:** Emergency, short- and long-term and specialized.


★ 355 ★
**D.A. Blodgett Services for Children and Families**
805 Leonard St., N.E.
Grand Rapids, MI 49503
Phone: (616) 451-2021
(800) 968-2021
Fax: (616) 451-8936

**Contact:** Jill Tyler-Skinner, Coordinator, Permanency Planning and Support Services.

**Date established:** 1887.

**Description:** Non-profit, non-sectarian child welfare agency licensed by the Michigan Dept. of Social Services.

**Area served:** Residents of Kent County and surrounding western Michigan counties.

**Requirements:** Flexible.

**Fees:**
Infant adoption: $2000-$8000;
no fees for the adoption of children who are permanent wards of the state.

**Number of children placed last year:** 100.

**Description of children:** 91 children with special needs and 9 infants.

**Adoption procedure:**
1) Attend 2 informational meetings;
2) complete 3 training sessions;
3) join and attend the monthly meetings of the adoptive parent support group;
4) file application;
5) complete home study;
6) undergo physical examination and forward results and health history;
7) if approved, wait for placement.

**Average length of time between application and start of home study:** 1-6 mos.

**Average length of time to complete home study:** 3-4 mos.

**Number of interviews:** 6-8.

**Home study description:** A very thorough, multi-generational family assessment and social history.

**Average wait for a child after approval of a home study:** 12-24 mos. for special needs; 24 or more mos. for infants.

**Foster care:** Temporary, long-term, permanent and specialized.

★ 356 ★
**Catholic Family Services of Kalamazoo**
1819 Gull Rd.
Kalamazoo, MI 49001
Phone: (616) 381-9800
Fax: (616) 381-2932

**Contact:** Adoption specialist.

**Description:** Non-profit private agency.

**Area served:** Residents of Allegan, Barry, Berrien, Branch, Calhoun, Cass, Kalamazoo, St. Joseph, and Van Buren counties.

**Requirements:** Couples of all faiths married 2 or more years who are infertile unless adopting special needs children.

**Fees:**
Application fee: $200;
home study fee is based on a percentage of total adoption fee with a maximum of approx. $3500.

**Number of children placed last year:** 8.

**Description of children:** 4 infants, 4 special needs children one of which was African-American.

**Adoption procedure:**
1) Telephone inquiry;
2) written request for appointment;
3) attend intake interview;
4) name added to waiting list;
5) complete home study;
6) wait for placement;
7) placement.

**Average length of time between application and start of home study:** Varies.

**Average length of time to complete home study:** Unavailable.

**Number of interviews:** 3-4 individual plus 6 adoption education classes.

**Home study description:** An educational and evaluatory process in which applicants' childhoods, marriage and parenting styles, attitudes on adoption and birthparents are discussed. During the group series prospective adoptive parents meet with birthparents who have placed their children for adoption, adult adoptees, a foster mother who discusses infant care and another adoptive couple who discuss bridging.

**Average wait for a child after approval of a home study:** Varies.

**Foster care:** Temporary.

★ 357 ★
**Catholic Human Services, Inc.**
111 S. Michigan
Gaylord, MI 49735
Phone: (517) 732-6761
Fax: (517) 732-6763

**Contact:** John Feys.

**Date established:** 1972.

**Description:** Private social service agency.

**Area served:** Only residents of the 21 counties of northern Michigan.

**Requirements:** Couples married at least 3 yrs., who are in good health, have some recognized religious faith and who are not yet 43 yrs. old.

**Fees:** Call for schedule of fees.

**Number of children placed last year:** Unavailable.

**Description of children:** Infants.

**Adoption procedure:**
1) Attend orientation and educational meeting;
2) undergo adoption counseling;
3) wait for selection by birthmother;
4) placement;
5) post-placement supervision;
6) finalization.

**Average length of time between application and start of home study:** Varies.

**Average length of time to complete home study:** Varies.

**Number of interviews:** Varies.

**Home study description:** An assessment to determine the openness, flexibility and stability of prospective adoptive home.

**Average wait for a child after approval of a home study:** Varies.

**Foster care:** Pre-adoptive.

★ 358 ★
**Catholic Services of Macomb**
235 S. Gratiot Ave.
Mount Clemens, MI 48043
Phone: (810) 468-2616

**Branch address:**
12434 Twelve Mile Rd., Ste. 201, Warren, MI 48093
Phone: (810) 558-7551

45100 Sterritt, Ste. 103, Utica, MI 48317
Phone: (810) 254-2900

**Contact:** Joanne Ales, Director of Child Welfare.

**Date established:** 1958.

**Description:** Private, non-profit multi-service agency licensed through the State of Michigan as a child placement agency.

**Area served:** Residents of Michigan.

**Requirements:** Applicants must be in good physical and emotional health, age appropriate to the child requested and have sufficient income to support a family.

**Fees:** Application: $100; home study: $6300.

**Number of children placed last year:** 15.

**Description of children:** Infants.

**Adoption procedure:** 1) Initial inquiry; 2) orientation meeting; 3) application and placement on waiting list; 4) interview; 5) group education; 6) home study; 7) Adoptive Parent Outreach Program (optional); 8) matching/placement process; 9) supervision of placement; 10) finalization.

**Average length of time between application and start of home study:** 2 yrs. or more.

**Average length of time to complete home study:** Unavailable.

**Number of interviews:** Unavailable.

**Home study description:** Assessment which includes physical examinations, criminal and protective services records checks, references and addresses such topics as motivation for adoption, attitude toward adoption and plan for discussing adoption with adopted child, personal and family history, emotional stability, compatibility and parenting ability and the preparation of a family profile.

**Average wait for a child after approval of a home study:** 6 - 12 mos.

**Foster care:** Temporary.


★ 359 ★
**Catholic Social Service**
**St. Vincent Home**
2800 W. Willow
Lansing, MI 48917
Phone: (517) 323-4734

**Contact:** Kathleen N. Giddings, Adoption Specialist.

**Date established:** 1948.

**Description:** Private, non-profit agency licensed to place children by the Michigan Department of Social Services.

**Area served:** Residents of Clinton, Eaton, Jackson, Ingham and Shiowassee counties.

**Requirements:** Caucasian Infants: Married couples who are no older than 40 yrs. at the time of application. Requirements for other programs are flexible.

**Fees:** Caucasian infants: application: $300; caucasian infants total fees: $7000. ourt filing fees range from $60 - $75 depending on county.

**Number of children placed last year:** 22.

**Description of children:** Children with special needs and 4 infants.

**Adoption procedure:** 1) Application; 2) home study; 3) parenting class; 4) other agency functions; 5)placement; 6) post-placement supervision; 7) finalization. Special needs placements require anadditional educational component.

**Average length of time between application and start of home study:** Caucasian infants: 24or more mos.; special needs: less than 1 mo.

**Average length of time to complete home study:** 2 - 3 mos.

**Number of interviews:** Minimum of 6.

**Home study description:** Assessment which includes social and genetic history, religious affiliation, health, references, residence and community and addresses such topics as relationships with family and friends, marital status and other children, ideas on child rearing, infertility issues and motivation to adopt, experiences and feeling on adoption.

**Average wait for a child after approval of a home study:** Special needs: 6 - 12 mos.; caucasian infant: dependent on birth parent selection.

**Foster care:** Emergency, short and long-term, and permanent.

★ 360 ★
**Catholic Social Services/Oakland County**
50 Wayne St.
Pontiac, MI 48342
Phone: (810) 548-4044
Fax: (810) 333-3718

**Branch address:**
26105 Orchard Lake Rd., Farmington Hills, MI 48018
Phone: (810) 471-4140

**Contact:** Margaret Huggard, Executive Director.

**Date established:** 1947.

**Description:** Private child placing agency for adoption and foster care licensed by the Michigan Department of Social Services, Bureau of Registration.

**Area served:** Infant program: residents of Lapeer and Oakland counties; special needs: statewide.

**Requirements:**
Infant program: couples married at least 2 yrs. who are younger than 40 yrs., economically stable, and in good health.
Special needs: no requirements.
Requirements for open adoption/cooperative adoption set by birthparents.

**Fees:** Infants program: court set fee of 8% of primary age earner's gross annual income.

**Number of children placed last year:** 30.

**Description of children:** 14 infants and 16 State Wards which included sibling groups, minority and special needs children.

**Adoption procedure:**
1) Attend orientation;
2) file application;
3) complete assessment and/or preparation groups;
4) complete home study;
5) if approved, court petition and introduction;
6) file petition and placement;
7) quarterly supervisory visits;
8) recommendation for completion and court ceremony for finalization.

**Average length of time between application and start of home study:** Varies because of open adoption - adoption outreach practice.

**Average length of time to complete home study:** 18 hrs.

**Number of interviews:** 3-4 or more.

**Home study description:** Assessment of social history, motivation to adopt, empathy with birthparents, birthparent selection and parental abilities.

**Average wait for a child after approval of a home study:** Varies.

**Foster care:** Temporary.


★ 361 ★
**Catholic Social Services of Flint**
202 E. Boulevard Dr., #210
Flint, MI 48503
Phone: (810) 232-9950
Fax: (810) 232-7599

**Contact:** Betty Rathfon, Child Welfare Coordinator.

**Date established:** 1941.

**Description:** Private, non-profit agency licensed by the State of Michigan.

**Area served:** Residents of Genesee County.

**Requirements:** Couples married at least 3 yrs. or single individuals who are stable and in reasonably good health.

**Fees:**
Application fee: $125. Other fees vary dependent on income.

**Number of children placed last year:** 20.

**Description of children:** Children from 0-10 yrs., some with special needs.

**Adoption procedure:**
1) Telephone screening;
2) attend group inquiry meeting;
3) participate in initial office interview;
4) complete home study group meeting;
5) home visit;
6) if approved, placement.

**Average length of time between application and start of home study:** Varies.

**Average length of time to complete home study:** 4-6 mos.

**Number of interviews:** 6 group and 2 or more individual.

**Home study description:** Evaluation of family background, marriage, finances, personal values, interests and activities.

**Average wait for a child after approval of a home study:** Varies.

**Foster care:** Primarily pre-adoptive.

★ 362 ★
**Catholic Social Services of Kent County**
1152 Scribner, NW
Grand Rapids, MI 49504
Phone: (616) 456-1443
Fax: (616) 732-6391

**Contact:** Arlene Chettleburgh or Joe Carmody.

**Date established:** 1942.

**Description:** Non-profit multi-service agency licensed by the State of Michigan as a child placing agency and accredited by the Council on Accreditation.

**Area served:** Residents of Ionia, Kent, Mecosta, Montcalm and Osceola counties.

**Requirements:**
Infant adoption: no health problems that would interfere with parenting and the financial ability to care for a child. Special needs: applicants assessed on an individual basis for commitment, ability to work with children, and ability to provide emotionally and financially.

**Fees:** Sliding fee scale based on income or $85 an hour.

**Number of children placed last year:** 50.

**Description of children:** Infants, older and special needs children.

**Adoption procedure:**
1) Telephone inquiry;
2) attend orientation meeting;
3) return completed application;
4) complete group and individual studies, including home visit;
5) if approved, participate in support/training groups until placement;
6) placement;
7) 1 yr. post-placement supervision;
8) finalization.

**Average length of time between application and start of home study:** Varies.

**Average length of time to complete home study:** 3-4 wks.

**Number of interviews:** 2-3.

**Home study description:** Evaluation of family and individual history; medical and financial reports; education and employment; marriage and infertility issues; previous parenting experience; religion, home environment and structure; support systems and community resources; and mental health/substance abuse (if applicable).

**Average wait for a child after approval of a home study:** Varies.

**Foster care:** Temporary, long-term and permanent.

★ 363 ★
**Catholic Social Services of Lansing**
**St. Vincent Home for Children**
2800 W. Willow
Lansing, MI 48917
Phone: (517) 323-4734
Fax: (517) 323-0257

**Contact:** Donald Ballentine, Executive Director.

**Description:** Non-profit private agency.

**Area served:** Residents of Clinton, Eaton, Ingham, Jackson and Shiawassee counties.

**Requirements:** Married couples who are not older than 40 yrs. at time of application and who are infertile, for infants; greater flexibility for special needs.

**Fees:**
$300 application fee;
$7000 total, for infants; no fee for special needs.

**Number of children placed last year:** 22.

**Description of children:** Infants, older children, and children with special needs.

**Adoption procedure:**
1) Participate in group intake;
2) file application;
3) waiting list period;
4) complete home study;
5) if approved, placement;
6) supervisory period; and
7) finalization.

**Average length of time between application and start of home study:** 1-6 mos. for special needs; 3 yrs. for infants.

**Average length of time to complete home study:** 2-3 mos.

**Number of interviews:** 6 or more.

**Home study description:** Evaluation of life experiences and emotional adjustment; family information and marital stability; religion; health; finances; references; description of home and neighborhood; other children in home (if applicable); emotions surrounding infertility; motivation for adoption and attitude toward adoption; plans for discipline.

**Average wait for a child after approval of a home study:** Varies widely.

**Foster care:** Temporary, specialized, long-term and permanent.

★ 364 ★
**Catholic Social Services of Monroe County**
16 E. 5th St.
Monroe, MI 48161
Phone: (313) 242-3800
Fax: (313) 242-6203

**Branch address:**
8330 Lewis Ave., Temperance, MI 48182
Phone: (313) 847-1523

**Contact:** Audrey Majauskas, MA/CSW.

**Date established:** 1952.

**Description:** Not-for-profit private agency licensed in the State of Michigan.

**Area served:** Residents of Monroe County.

**Requirements:** Couples married at least 3 yrs. who have no biological children and who are U.S. citizens. Adoptive mother cannot be more than 38 yrs. old to apply for adoption of child between the ages of 0 and 5 yrs.

**Fees:** Sliding fee scale from $3500-$6000.

**Number of children placed last year:** 3 infants and 1 child with special needs.

**Description of children:** Infants and children with special needs.

**Adoption procedure:**
1) Complete application;
2) have home study;
3) if approved, wait for appropriate child to become available;
4) placement;
5) file petition;
6) 1 yr. post-placement supervisory; and
7) finalization.

**Average length of time between application and start of home study:** 24 or more mos.

**Average length of time to complete home study:** 6 mos.

**Number of interviews:** 8-12.

**Home study description:** Evaluation of personal histories; courtship and marriage; child rearing philosophies; motivation to adopt and attitude toward adoption; employment history and finances; health; home and environment; religion; references and recommendations.

**Average wait for a child after approval of a home study:** 12-24 mos.

**Foster care:** Temporary.

★ 365 ★
**Catholic Social Services of St. Clair County**
2601 13th St.
Port Huron, MI 48060
Phone: (810) 987-9100
Fax: (810) 987-9105

**Contact:** Sandy Burns or Cynthia L. Willey-King.

**Date established:** 1947.

**Description:** Non-profit United Way agency accredited by Child Welfare League of America, Federation of Michigan Private Child & Family Agencies and certified by COA.

**Area served:** Only residents of St. Clair County.

**Requirements:** Christian couples married at least 3 yrs., who are younger than 38 yrs. at time of application and younger than 40 yrs. at time of placement; who have normal health and a maximum of 2 children and no divorces.

**Fees:** $4500.

**Number of children placed last year:** 4.

**Description of children:** Normal healthy infants.

**Adoption procedure:**
1) Telephone inquiry;
2) initial assessment by adoption worker;
3) participate in orientation meeting;
4) complete and return application;
5) complete individual and joint interviews;
6) complete group study;
7) home visits;
8) if approved, waiting period;

9) placement;
10) 1 yr. post-placement supervision;
11) finalization.

**Average length of time between application and start of home study:** 1 mo. or less.

**Average length of time to complete home study:** 2 mos.

**Number of interviews:** 6-8.

**Home study description:** Evaluation of couple's ability to accept infertility, to relate to the adoptive status of child, to appreciate the changes in adoption law and the role of birthparents; and to handle adoption information with their child. Recommendation of type of child to place with them based on their desires, strengths, and abilities.

**Average wait for a child after approval of a home study:** 12-24 mos.

**Foster care:** Temporary and pre-adoptive.

★ 366 ★
**Catholic Social Services of the Upper Peninsula**
347 Rock St.
Marquette, MI 49855
Phone: (906) 228-8630

**Branch address:**
1103 Ludington St., Escanaba, MI 49829
Phone: (906) 786-7212

616 Shelden, Ste. 211, Houghton, MI 49931
Phone: (906) 482-1624

500 S. Stephenson, Ste. 400, Iron Mountain, MI 49801
Phone: (906) 774-3323

105 Mansfield, Ironwood, MI 49938
Phone: (906) 932-0138

409 Ashmun St., Ste. 204, Sault Ste. Marie, MI 49783
Phone: (906) 635-1508

**Contact:** Linda Kearney, M.A., C.S.W., Child Welfare Supervisor.

**Description:** Private, non-profit agency licensed to place children by the Michigan Department of Social Services.

**Area served:** None.

**Requirements:** Couples married at least 3 yrs. who are between the ages of 25 and 45 yrs. and who are infertile.

**Fees:** Application: $100; home study: $3000; orientation: $200; training: $1600; licensing, change of placement and billing: $900; supervisories (4): $1000. Total fees: $6800.

**Number of children placed last year:** 10.

**Description of children:** Infants.

**Adoption procedure:** 1) Application; 2) orientation; 3) training; 4) interview with child welfare supervisor; 5) licensing; 6) home study; 7) wait for placement; 8) placement.

**Average length of time between application and start of home study:** 1 - 6 mos.

**Average length of time to complete home study:** 36 hrs.

**Number of interviews:** 11.

**Home study description:** Assessment which includes home environment, medical and financial reports, references, criminal background checks, social worker's recommendation and addresses such topics as personality, education and occupation, hobbies, family background, religion, attitudes toward adoption, parenthood and type of child desired.

**Average wait for a child after approval of a home study:** 12 - 24 mos.

**Foster care:** Pre-adoptive.

★ 367 ★
**Catholic Social Services of Washtenaw County**
117 N. Division
Ann Arbor, MI 48104-1590
Phone: (313) 662-4534

Fax: (313) 662-7580

**Branch address:**
101 S. Huron St., Ypsilanti, MI 48197
Phone: (313) 484-1260

**Contact:** Lois Plantefaber.

**Date established:** 1959.

**Description:** Non-profit family service and child placing agency licensed by the State of Michigan.

**Area served:** Individuals who live or work in Washtenaw County.

**Requirements:** Must live or work in Washtenaw County. No age or marriage limitations.

**Fees:** Sliding scale with a maximum of $9000.

**Number of children placed last year:** 15.

**Description of children:** Infants.

**Adoption procedure:**
1) Attend informational meeting;
2) submit request for service;
3) complete pre-placement counseling;
4) participate in education groups;
5) complete family assessment;
6) selected for placement;
7) placement;
8) 1 yr. post-placement supervision;
9) finalization.

**Average length of time between application and start of home study:** 1-6 mos.

**Average length of time to complete home study:** Approx. 4 mos.

**Number of interviews:** 5 education groups and 4-6 individual.

**Home study description:** Evaluation of family history and relationships, marriage history and relationship, motivation to adopt and how adoption decision was made; parenting an adopted child and childrearing values; and desired contact with birth family.

**Average wait for a child after approval of a home study:** 12-24 mos.

**Foster care:** Regular and pre-adoptive.

★ 368 ★
**Child and Family Service of Holt**
4801 Willoughby, Ste. 1
Holt, MI 48842
Phone: (517) 699-1600
Fax: (517) 699-2749

**Contact:** Dr. John Hemmer.

**Date established:** 1911.

**Description:** Non-profit private agency licensed for child placement by the State of Michigan, Department of Social Services; accredited by the Council on Accreditation of Services for Families and Children, Inc. and a member of the Michigan Federation of Private Child and Family Agencies.

**Area served:** Residents of Clinton, Eaton, Ingham and Shiawassee counties.

**Requirements:** Each case is evaluated on an individual basis.

**Fees:** 10% of income for voluntarily released infants.

**Number of children placed last year:** 25.

**Description of children:** All special needs.

**Adoption procedure:**
1) Attend initial interview and group training;
2) complete adoption study;
3) if approved, identify adoptive child;
4) placement;
5) 1 yr. post-placement supervision;
6) finalization.

**Average length of time between application and start of home study:** Depends on type of child.

**Average length of time to complete home study:** Varies.

**Number of interviews:** Varies.

**Home study description:** A series of evaluative interviews to determine whether or not adoption is a good plan for applicant family.

**Average wait for a child after approval of a home study:** Varies depending on type of child desired.

**Foster care:** Temporary.

★ 369 ★
**Child and Family Services of Holland**
412 Century Ln.
Holland, MI 49423
Phone: (616) 396-2301

**Branch address:**
321 S. Beechtree, Grand Haven, MI 49417

1342 Baldwin, S.W., Jenison, MI 49417

**Contact:** Wendy Ward.

**Date established:** 1957.

**Description:** Non-profit private agency.

**Area served:** Residents of Allegan, Kent, Muskegon, Newaygo, Oceana, and Ottawa counties.

**Requirements:** Infant placement: couples married at least 2 yrs. who are between the ages of 21 and 35 yrs.

**Fees:**
Application fee: $50;
home study fee is a sliding scale based on income.

**Number of children placed last year:** 21.

**Description of children:** Infants and special needs children.

**Adoption procedure:**
1) Submit application;
2) attend group orientation;
3) screening interview;
4) complete home study;
5) placement process;
6) 1 yr. post-placement supervision;
7) finalization.

**Average length of time between application and start of home study:** Varies.

**Average length of time to complete home study:** 4 mos.

**Number of interviews:** 6.

**Home study description:** Evaluation of references, finances, family history, personal assessment and home's physical setting.

**Average wait for a child after approval of a home study:** Varies.

**Foster care:** Temporary, long-term and intensive treatment.

## ★ 370 ★
**Child and Family Services of Michigan, Inc. (Howell)**
3075 E. Grand River
Howell, MI 48843
Phone: (517) 546-7530
Fax: (517) 546-0050

**Contact:** Jeri McKeon Anderson, ACSW, Executive Director.

**Date established:** 1973.

**Description:** Non-profit, private, non-sectarian family service agency licensed by the Michigan Dept. of Social Services.

**Area served:** Residents of Livingston County.

**Requirements:** Couples married at least 2 yrs. who are in good physical and emotional health, who have adequate income to meet their needs, sufficient insurance and show sound financial management. One spouse must be age 40 or less for infant placement.

**Fees:** Application fee: $100 (non-refundable but applicable toward total fees).

**Number of children placed last year:** 5.

**Description of children:** Infants and special needs.

**Adoption procedure:**
1) Initial inquiry;
2) attend adoption group meeting;
3) screening process;
4) complete home study;
5) if approved, wait for placement;
6) placement;
7) 6 mo. post-placement supervision;
8) finalization.

**Average length of time between application and start of home study:** 6-12 mos.

**Average length of time to complete home study:** 6 mos.

**Number of interviews:** Approx. 6.

**Home study description:** Evaluation of health and financial reports, references, law enforcement checks, family and marital history, parenting styles and abilities, infertility resolution and support systems. Adoption instruction is also included.

**Average wait for a child after approval of a home study:** 24 or more mos.

**Foster care:** Pre-adoptive, respite care, short-term, and intensive.

## ★ 371 ★
**Child and Family Services of Saginaw County**
2806 Davenport
Saginaw, MI 48602
Phone: (517) 790-7500

**Contact:** Mari Sargent, Adoption Specialist.

**Date established:** 1870.

**Description:** Private, non-profit agency licensed to place children by the Michigan Department of Social Services.

**Area served:** Residents of Bay, Gratiot, Midland, Saginaw and Tuscola counties.

**Requirements:** Open.

**Fees:** Application: $750; home study: $750; placement, supervision and finalization: $2500; court fees: $80; birth certificate: $26.

**Number of children placed last year:** 19.

**Description of children:** U.S. infants, children with special needs and foreign-born infants and children.

**Adoption procedure:** 1) Preliminary application; 2) home study; 3) child match; 4) court processing and supervision; 5) finalization; 6) post-adoption services, as needed.

**Average length of time between application and start of home study:** Special needs: Less than 1 mo.;U.S. Infant: 24 or more mos.

**Average length of time to complete home study:** 3 mos.

**Number of interviews:** 15 - 20 hrs.

**Home study description:** Assessment and preparatory process which includes biographical, psychological, medical economic and employment information and education in child development, adoption and parenting approaches.

**Average wait for a child after approval of a home study:** Special needs: 6 - 12 mos.; healthy U.S. infant: 2 yrs. or more.

**Foster care:** Pre-adoptive.

## ★ 372 ★
**Child and Family Services of Southwestern Michigan, Inc.**
2000 S. State St.
St. Joseph, MI 49085
Phone: (616) 983-5545
(800) 562-4270
Fax: (616) 983-4920

**Contact:** Adoption intake worker.

**Date established:** 1891.

**Description:** Non-profit private agency licensed by the Michigan Dept. of Social Services.

**Area served:** Residents of Berrien, Cass and Van Buren counties.

**Requirements:** Couples married at least 2 yrs. who are at least 21 yrs. old, who have less than 2 children and who have a medical diagnosis of infertility. Marital and infertility requirement waived for special needs placements.

**Fees:** $4000 or less;
no fees for special needs placements.

**Number of children placed last year:** 0.

**Description of children:** Infants of all races and children with special needs.

**Adoption procedure:**
1) Submit application with $150 fee;
2) name added to waiting list;
3) complete home study;
4) if approved, placement;
5) 1 yr. post-placement supervision;
6) finalization.

**Average length of time between application and start of home study:** 6-12 mos.

**Average length of time to complete home study:** 2-3 mos.

**Number of interviews:** 6.

**Home study description:** Evaluation of individual social history, marital relationship, parenting theories, motivation to adopt, finances, home environment, law enforcement clearances, medical and financial reports and issues surrounding biological family.

**Average wait for a child after approval of a home study:** 24 or more mos.

**Foster care:** Temporary and long-term.

## ★ 373 ★
**Child and Parent Services**
30600 Telegraph Rd., No. 3360
Bingham Farms, MI 48025
Phone: (810) 646-7790
Fax: (810) 646-4544

**Contact:** Judy Etkin or Cathy Eisenberg.

**Date established:** 1987.

**Description:** Privately funded, non-traditional adoption agency licensed by the Michigan Dept. of Social Services.

**Area served:** Residents of southeast Michigan and applicants of other areas if they refer a birthmother who releases a child for adoptive placement.

**Requirements:** Couples married at least 2 yrs. at placement who are between the ages of 25 and 45 yrs. who have a medical diagnosis of infertility and less than 2 children from current spouse and who are financially self-supporting.

**Fees:**
Application fee: $500;
home study fee: $1000;
placement fees are $7040 in most counties, $7040 maximum in Oakland County.

**Number of children placed last year:** 30.

**Description of children:** Primarily infants.

**Adoption procedure:**
1) Intake appointment;
2) file preliminary application;
3) return completed application;
4) attend orientation;
5) complete home study;
6) if approved, placement;
7) file petition;
8) post-placement supervision;
9) finalization.

**Average length of time between application and start of home study:** 24 or more mos.

**Average length of time to complete home study:** Unavailable.

**Number of interviews:** Unavailable.

**Home study description:** Evaluation of background material on both adoptive parents, recommendation of references, any children in the home, marriage, financial status, parental ability, motivation to adopt including infertility work-up and placement requested.

**Average wait for a child after approval of a home study:** 6-12 mos.

**Foster care:** Short-term and legal risk adoption.

## ★ 374 ★
**Christian Care/Baptist Childrens Home and Family Ministry**
214 N. Mill St.
St. Louis, MI 48880
Phone: (517) 681-2171
(800) 292-3678
Fax: (517) 681-3601

**Contact:** Bill McCurdy.

**Date established:** 1953.

**Description:** Non-profit private agency licensed in the State of Michigan.

**Area served:** Residents of the State of Michigan.

**Requirements:** Adoptive parents must be of like doctrine in their faith.

**Fees:**
Home study: $1000;
placement fee: $4000 minimum or 20% of annual income up to $7000.

**Number of children placed last year:** 6.

**Description of children:** Infants.

**Adoption procedure:**
1) Submit pre-application;
2) file application;
3) waiting period;
4) complete home study;
5) if approved, wait for placement;
6) placement.

**Average length of time between application and start of home study:** 24 or more mos.

**Average length of time to complete home study:** Unavailable.

**Number of interviews:** 3.

**Home study description:** Evaluation of family's spiritual life; 5 questionnaires among them a marriage survey; financial stability and planning; medical reports and the Taylor/Johnson test.

**Average wait for a child after approval of a home study:** 6-12 mos.

**Foster care:** Temporary, long-term and permanent.

## ★ 375 ★
**Christian Cradle, Inc.**
416 Frandor, Ste. 205
Lansing, MI 48912
Phone: (517) 351-7500
Fax: (517) 351-4810

**Contact:** C. Fran Card, Director.

**Date established:** 1985.

**Description:** Non-profit private agency licensed by the Michigan Dept. of Social Services.

**Area served:** Residents of the State of Michigan.

**Requirements:** Applicants must be members of an Evangelical church.

**Fees:** $3000-$6000.

**Number of children placed last year:** 27.

**Description of children:** Primarily newborn infants.

**Adoption procedure:**
1) Initial inquiry;
2) file application;
3) complete home study;
4) wait for selection by birthmother;
5) placement;
6) post-placement supervision;
7) finalization.

**Average length of time between application and start of home study:** 1-6 mos.

**Average length of time to complete home study:** 3 mos.

**Number of interviews:** 6.

**Home study description:** A thorough assessment of applicant couple's life and all else which will help the agency determine if they will be good parents.

**Average wait for a child after approval of a home study:** 6-24 mos.

**Foster care:** Pre-adoptive and short-term.

★ 376 ★
**Christian Family Services**
17105 W. 12 Mile Rd.
Southfield, MI 48076
Phone: (313) 557-8390

**Contact:** M. Lee Gardner, MA, Executive Director.

**Date established:** 1948.

**Description:** Non-profit private agency licensed in the State of Michigan.

**Area served:** Residents of Macomb, Oakland, and Wayne counties.

**Requirements:** Couples who attend fundamental, evangelical churches which contribute to Christian Family Services support.

**Fees:** Application fee: $200. Adoption fees are set by counties and are based on family income.

**Number of children placed last year:** Approx. 10-15 per year.

**Description of children:** Primarily infants, a few toddlers.

**Adoption procedure:**
1) File preliminary application;
2) complete application and home study;
3) if approved, placement;
4) 1 yr. post-placement supervisory; and
5) finalization.

**Average length of time between application and start of home study:** 6-12 mos.

**Average length of time to complete home study:** 3-4 mos.

**Number of interviews:** 3 plus 1 home visit.

**Home study description:** Evaluation which includes but is not limited to: family background; marital and financial stability; and attitude toward adoption.

**Average wait for a child after approval of a home study:** 6-12 mos.

**Foster care:** Temporary.


★ 377 ★
**Community, Family and Children's Services**
228 S. 3rd
Alpena, MI 49707
Phone: (517) 356-6385
Fax: (517) 356-4909

**Branch address:**
1000 Hastings, Traverse City, MI 49684
Phone: (616) 947-8110

**Contact:** John Feys.

**Date established:** 1947.

**Description:** Non-profit private agency.

**Area served:** Residents of the 11 counties surrounding Alpena.

**Requirements:** Couples married at least 3 yrs., who are younger than 40 yrs. All applicants must have a medical examination.

**Fees:** $4700.

**Number of children placed last year:** 17.

**Description of children:** Infants.

**Adoption procedure:**
1) Initial inquiry;
2) submit application during period when applications are open;
3) complete home study;
4) if approved, wait for selection by birthparent;
5) placement;
6) post-placement supervision;
7) finalization.

**Average length of time between application and start of home study:** 6-12 mos.

**Average length of time to complete home study:** 6 mos.

**Number of interviews:** 15 hrs.

**Home study description:** Evaluation of motivation to adopt, issues surrounding infertility, marital relationship, family background, parenting philosophies and issues surrounding adoption, e.g. birthparents.

**Average wait for a child after approval of a home study:** 12-24 mos.

**Foster care:** Pre-adoptive.


★ 378 ★
**Evergreen Children's Services**
21590 Greenfield, Ste. 204
Oak Park, MI 48237
Phone: (313) 862-1000
Fax: (313) 862-6464

**Contact:** Dana J. Marra.

**Date established:** 1986.

**Description:** Non-profit private agency.

**Area served:** Residents of Genesee, Huron, Livingston, Macomb, Monroe, Oakland, St. Clair, Washtenaw and Wayne counties.

**Requirements:** Adults between the ages of 21 and 65 yrs. who are in good health and have adequate income to support themselves and an adopted child.

**Fees:** None.

**Number of children placed last year:** 59.

**Description of children:** Children with special needs.

**Adoption procedure:**
1) Attend 18 hrs. of training;
2) file application;
3) series of visits with selected child;
4) file petition;
5) placement;
6) supervisory period; and
7) finalization.

**Average length of time between application and start of home study:** 1-6 mos.

**Average length of time to complete home study:** 1 mo.

**Number of interviews:** 4.

**Home study description:** Evaluation of social and marital history, lifestyle, values and experience, emotional stability and parenting ability.

**Average wait for a child after approval of a home study:** 6-12 mos.

**Foster care:** Temporary and long-term.


★ 379 ★
**Family Adoption Consultants**
421 W. Crosstown Pkwy.
Kalamazoo, MI 49005
Phone: (616) 343-3316

**Mailing address:**
P.O. Box 50489, Kalamazoo, MI 49005

**Branch address:**
310 University Dr., Rochester, MI 48063

8536 Crow Dr., Ste. 218, Macedonia, OH 44056

**Contact:** Lorene Cook, Tina Jackson, Michele Para, Kathy Luz or Barb Irvin.

**Date established:** 1982.

**Description:** Private, non-profit child placing agency licensed by the Ohio Department of Human Services and the Michigan Department of Social Services.

**Area served:** Residents of Michigan and Ohio and will network with the residents of other states.

**Requirements:** Variable by program selected.

**Fees:** Preliminary application: $100; home study: sliding scale based on income. ravel, birth parent services, dossier and supervision are additional.

**Number of children placed last year:** 161.

**Description of children:** U.S. and foreign-born infants, toddlers and older children and children with special needs.

**Average length of time between application and start of home study:** Less than 1 mo.

**Average length of time to complete home study:** Unavailable.

**Number of interviews:** 3 -5.

**Home study description:** Assessment which addresses such topics as family background, marital relationship, if applicable, child rearing practices, ideals, adoption preparation and planning, exploration of family's needs, hopes and desires and how adoption can meet those needs.

**Average wait for a child after approval of a home study:** Special needs: Less than 1 mo. Intercountry: 1- 6 mos. U.S. Infant: 6 - 12 mos.

**Foster care:** Pre-adoptive.

★ 380 ★

**Family and Children's Services of Calhoun County**
182 W. Van Buren
Battle Creek, MI 49015
Phone: (616) 965-3247
Fax: (616) 966-4135

**Contact:** Rick Pahl, Interim Director.

**Date established:** 1917.

**Description:** Non-profit private agency.

**Area served:** Residents of Barry and Calhoun counties.

**Requirements:** Varied.

**Fees:** Sliding scale.

**Number of children placed last year:** N/A.

**Description of children:** Children of all ages.

**Adoption procedure:**
1) File application;
2) wait for adoptive study;
3) complete home study;
4) if approved, wait for placement;
5) placement;
6) post-placement supervision;
7) finalization.

**Average length of time between application and start of home study:** 12-24 mos.

**Average length of time to complete home study:** 1 yr.

**Number of interviews:** 15.

**Home study description:** Extensive and intensive evaluation which is child specific.

**Average wait for a child after approval of a home study:** 12-24 mos.

**Foster care:** Regular and specialized.

★ 381 ★

**Family Service And Children's Aid**
115 W. Michigan
Jackson, MI 49204
Phone: (517) 787-7920
(517) 787-2738

**Mailing address:**
P.O. Box 6128, Jackson, MI 49204

**Contact:** Cheri De Haan.

**Date established:** 1943.

**Description:** Private, non-profit child placing agency licensed by the Michigan Department of Social Services.

**Area served:** Residents of Jackson County and area immediately surrounding it.

**Requirements:** Varies with program selected. Applicants for infant adoption can be no more than 40 yrs. older than the adoptive child.

**Fees:** Application: $100; home study: Based on sliding scale for infant adoption.

**Number of children placed last year:** 4.

**Description of children:** Infants and children with special needs.

**Adoption procedure:** 1) Contact agency; 2) complete preliminary paperwork; 3) attend informational meeting; 4) complete adoption training; 5) complete application; 6) home study; 7) child match; 8) placement; 9)file adoption petition; 10) post-placement supervision; 11) finalization.

**Average length of time between application and start of home study:** Varies with program selected.

**Average length of time to complete home study:** 3 mos.

**Number of interviews:** 6 - 10.

**Home study description:** Assessment which includes family history, education and employment history, marital relationship and which covers such topics as motivation to adopt, resolution of infertility, parenting beliefs and practices, type of child desired and capacity to parent a child with special needs, if applicable.

**Average wait for a child after approval of a home study:** Infant: 1 - 2 yrs.; special needs: 1-12 mos.

**Foster care:** Temporary, long-term, pre-adoptive and specialized.

★ 382 ★

**Golden Cradle International**
1660 Cliffs Landing, No.3
Ypsilanti, MI 48198
Phone: (313) 485-4533

**Contact:** Sunie Stockler, Director.

**Date established:** 1990.

**Description:** Private, non-profit child placing agency licensed by the Michigan Department of Social Services and specializing in placing children from Brazil.

**Area served:** No geographic restrictions.

**Requirements:** Applicants must be at least 21 yrs. old.

**Fees:** Application: $3500; home study and post-placement services: $1350.

**Number of children placed last year:** Unavailable.

**Description of children:** Caucasian infants and some older children.

**Adoption procedure:** 1) Inquiry; 2) compilation of dossier and translation into Portuguese; 3) approval of documents in Brazil; 4) child referral; 5) placement; 6) post-placement supervision.

**Average length of time between application and start of home study:** Less than 6 mos.

**Average length of time to complete home study:** 1 mo.

**Number of interviews:** 3.

**Home study description:** Unavailable.

**Average wait for a child after approval of a home study:** 1 - 6 mos.

**Foster care:** None.

★ 383 ★

**Huron Services for Youth, Inc.**
27676 Cherry Hill Rd.
Garden City, MI 48135
Phone: (313) 422-5401
Fax: (313) 994-5440

**Branch address:**
 1952 S. Industrial Hwy., Ann Arbor, MI 48104-4614
 Phone: (313) 994-4224

**Contact:** Sheryl Dex.

**Date established:** 1975.

**Description:** Private, non-profit child placing agency licensed by the Michigan Department of Social Services and certified by The Council on Accreditation of Services for Families and Children and affiliated with The Michigan Federation of Private Child and Family Agencies, The Michigan Association of Children's Alliances, The Child Welfare League of America, the Foster Family-based Treatment Association and the Washtenaw United Way.

**Area served:** Residents within one hr.'s drive of either branch location.

**Requirements:** Applicants must be at least 18 yrs, old, single or legally married at least 2 yrs. and have sufficient income to meet their family's needs.

**Fees:** None.

**Number of children placed last year:** Unavailable.

**Description of children:** Children between the ages of birth and 14 yrs. who are characterized by some or all of the following: emotionally impaired and in need of intensive support system; background of both physical/emotional abuse and neglect; background of minor delinquency; need for permanency to deal with special needs and behavioral problems; sibling groups. A large percentage are 5 yrs. and older, part of large sibling groups and minorities.

**Adoption procedure:** 1) Inquiry; 2) 14 hrs. pre-service training; 3) home study and licensing; 3) pre-placement visits; 4) placement; 5) post-placement supervision; 6) finalization; 7) post-legal services,as needed.

**Average length of time between application and start of home study:** 1 - 12 mos.

**Average length of time to complete home study:** 10 hrs.

**Number of interviews:** 4.

**Home study description:** Assessment which covers motivation to adopt, home and community, physical descriptions of adoptive applicants, personality traits, personal history, school and employment history, experience with children, support systems, feelings about adoption, birth parents and children with special needs.

**Average wait for a child after approval of a home study:** Unavailable.

**Foster care:** Temporary, long-term, permanent and specialized.

★ 384 ★

**International Adoption Consultants**
40 64 Seventh St.
Wyandotte, MI 48192
Phone: (313) 281-4488
Fax: (313) 281-2914

**Contact:** Francine Verduce.

**Date established:** 1993.

**Description:** Private, non-profit child placing agency licensed by the Michigan Department of Social Services.

**Area served:** Residents of the U.S. and Canada.

**Requirements:** One spouse or single applicant must be at least 25 yrs. old and younger than 50 yrs. and have a minimum annual income of $24,000. Couples must be married at least 2 yrs.

**Fees:** Application: $100. Home study (includes 1 post-adoption visit): $1000. Agency fee: $2000. Facilitators fee: $15,000.

**Number of children placed last year:** 30.

**Description of children:** Infants and children to 10 yrs. of age, some with minor correctable medical problems.

**Adoption procedure:** 1) Inquiry; 2) application; 3) orientation meeting. Additional assistance and information are available to applicants once they are accepted into the program.

**Average length of time between application and start of home study:** 1 - 6 mos.

**Average length of time to complete home study:** 6 wks.

**Number of interviews:** 3.

**Home study description:** Home study are conducted by International Adoption Consultants, Inc. which comply with the standards set by the Michigan Department of Social Services, but the agency will also accept home studies conducted by other licensed agencies which they review and approve.

**Average wait for a child after approval of a home study:** 6 - 9 mos.

**Foster care:** None.

★ 385 ★

**Jewish Family Service of Southfield, Michigan**
24123 Greenfield Rd.
Southfield, MI 48075
Phone: (810) 559-1500
Fax: (810) 559-9858

**Contact:** Mrs. Esther Krystal, MSW.

**Date established:** 1925.

**Description:** Non-profit private agency licensed by the Michigan Dept. of Social Services.

**Area served:** Residents of Macomb, Oakland and Wayne counties.

**Requirements:** Married Jewish couples who are in good health and infertile.

**Fees:** Determined by the Probate Court.

**Number of children placed last year:** 3.

**Description of children:** Infants and school age children.

**Adoption procedure:**
 1) Telephone inquiry;
 2) name added to waiting list;
 3) begin home study. Referred and designated adoption available.

**Average length of time between application and start of home study:** 24 or more mos.

**Average length of time to complete home study:** 2 mos.

**Number of interviews:** 6.

**Home study description:** Evaluation of background information, stability of marriage, parenting skills, and emotions surrounding adoption.

**Average wait for a child after approval of a home study:** 24 or more mos.

**Foster care:** Temporary and long-term.

### ★ 386 ★
**Judson Center**
23077 Greenfield, Ste. 107
Southfield, MI 48075
Phone: (810) 443-5000

**Branch address:**
    4410 W. 13 Mile Rd., Royal Oak, MI 48073
    Phone: (313) 549-4339

**Contact:** Anne Carpenter, Adoption Supervisor.

**Date established:** 1924.

**Description:** Private, non-profit agency licensed to place children by the Michigan Department of Social Services.

**Area served:** Residents of the Tri-County area and neighboring counties.

**Requirements:** Applicants must have medical clearances.

**Fees:** Court fees only which vary by county.

**Number of children placed last year:** 38.

**Description of children:** Children with special needs.

**Adoption procedure:** 1) Inquiry; 2) home study including record clearances and references; 3) Michigan Stateconsent; 4) pre-placement visitation; 5) placement; 6) adoption petition filed; 7) post-placementsupervision; 8) finalization.

**Average length of time between application and start of home study:** 1 - 6 mos.

**Average length of time to complete home study:** 4 mos.

**Number of interviews:** 3 - 4.

**Home study description:** Assessment which includes documentation of birth and marriage certificates, background information, home and community, marital relationship and parenting skills.

**Average wait for a child after approval of a home study:** 6 - 12 mos.

**Foster care:** Temporary, long-term and permanent.

### ★ 387 ★
**Keane Center for Adoption**
930 Mason
Dearborn, MI 48124
Phone: (313) 277-4664

**Contact:** Christine Brail, MSW, Director.

**Date established:** June, 1989.

**Description:** Private, non-profit child placing agency licensed by the Michigan Department of Social Services.

**Area served:** Residents of Michigan.

**Requirements:** Applicants will be preferably younger than 50 yrs.

**Fees:** Home study only: $1000; total adoption fees: $6000.

**Number of children placed last year:** 35.

**Description of children:** Infants.

**Adoption procedure:** 1) Termination of birth parent(s)' rights after child's birth; 2) placement order followsfiling of adoption petition; 3) post-placement services; 4) finalization.

**Average length of time between application and start of home study:** 1 - 6 mos.

**Average length of time to complete home study:** 1 - 2 mos.

**Number of interviews:** 5.

**Home study description:** Assessment which includes family and background information, personal histories, health reports and letters of reference, criminal records checks, worker's evaluation of personal and marital stability and parenting skills.

**Average wait for a child after approval of a home study:** Each case is individual.

**Foster care:** Pre-adoptive.

### ★ 388 ★
**LDS Social Services**
37634 Enterprise Ct.
Farmington Hills, MI 48331
Phone: (313) 553-0902

**Contact:** Leland R. Hardy, Agency Director.

**Description:** Non-profit private agency.

**Area served:** Residents of Michigan.

**Requirements:** Members of the Church of Jesus Christ of Latter Day Saints who were married in the temple and who are preferably no more than 40 yrs. old, with a medical study of infertility problem.

**Fees:**
$400 study fee;
$4000 adoptive fee.

**Number of children placed last year:** Unavailable.

**Description of children:** Primarily newborns.

**Adoption procedure:**
1) Initial agency inquiry;
2) complete interview process;
3) documentation and verification of references, Criminal Record Check, financial report, sanitary survey, etc.
4) 1 yr. waiting period from completion of study;
5) placement.

**Average length of time between application and start of home study:** 12-24 mos.

**Average length of time to complete home study:** 13 or more mos.

**Number of interviews:** 4.

**Home study description:** Evaluation of stability of marriage and relationships with extended family, peers, co-workers, health reports and other information which meets the statutes of the licensing state.

**Average wait for a child after approval of a home study:** 24 or more mos.

**Foster care:** Temporary infant boarding and birthmother pre-delivery.

### ★ 389 ★
**Lutheran Adoption Service**
21700 Northwestern Hwy., Ste. 1490
Southfield, MI 48075
Phone: (810) 423-2770

**Branch address:**
    801 Waverly Rd., Ste. 202, Lansing, MI 48917
    Phone: (517) 321-7663

    6019 W.S. Saginaw Rd., Bay City, MI 48707
    Phone: (517) 686-7650

**Contact:** Jim Lewis, Director.

**Date established:** 1977.

**Description:** Private child placing agency licensed by the Michigan Department of Social Services.

**Area served:** Residents of the Lower Peninsula of Michigan.

**Requirements:** Applicants must manifest good health and mental stability.

**Fees:** Variable.

**Number of children placed last year:** 195.

**Description of children:** 10 infants, 10 pre-schoolers, 175 children with special needs.

**Adoption procedure:** 1) Application; 2) orientation; 3) educational groups; 4) home study; 5) child match.

**Average length of time between application and start of home study:** Less than 1 mo.

**Average length of time to complete home study:** 3 mos.

**Number of interviews:** 4 - 5.

**Home study description:** Assessment which includes a criminal background check and addresses such topics as family background, ability to parent and experience with children.

**Average wait for a child after approval of a home study:** 6 - 12 mos.

**Foster care:** Temporary.

★ 390 ★
**Lutheran Social Services**
135 W. Washington St.
Marquette, MI 49855
Phone: (906) 226-7410

**Contact:** Ruth A. Almen, MSW, Supervisor.

**Date established:** 1990.

**Description:** Private, non-profit agency licensed to place children by the Michigan Department of Social Services.

**Area served:** Residents of Upper Michigan.

**Requirements:** Couples must be younger than 46 yrs. and be married a minimum of 2 yrs.

**Fees:** Application: $1350; home study: $1700; birth parent counseling: $3300; post-placement supervision: $850.

**Number of children placed last year:** 9.

**Description of children:** Healthy infants and toddlers.

**Adoption procedure:** Unavailable. Call for Information Packet.

**Average length of time between application and start of home study:** 1 - 6 mos.

**Average length of time to complete home study:** 3 mos.

**Number of interviews:** 3 - 6.

**Home study description:** Assessment which includes individual and group meetings, home and office visits, family and character references, police records' checks and physician's approval and which addresses such topics as personal and family background, infertility and open adoption, employment history.

**Average wait for a child after approval of a home study:** 6 - 12 mos.

**Foster care:** Temporary.

★ 391 ★
**Methodist Children's Home Society**
26645 W. 6 Mile Rd.
Detroit, MI 48240
Phone: (313) 531-4060
Fax: (313) 531-1040

**Contact:** John R. Schmidt.

**Date established:** 1917.

**Description:** Non-profit private agency licensed by the State of Michigan and accredited by the Council on Accreditation.

**Area served:** Residents of the State of Michigan.

**Requirements:** Age of adoptive parents depends upon the age of the child to be placed. Individual consideration is given to marital status, health and racial/cultural origin.

**Fees:** None.

**Number of children placed last year:** 29.

**Description of children:** Infants, older, emotionally impaired children and children with special needs.

**Adoption procedure:** Application and home study proceed promptly for minority and special needs children.

**Average length of time between application and start of home study:** 1 mo. or less.

**Average length of time to complete home study:** 3-4 mos.

**Number of interviews:** 5-6.

**Home study description:** Evaluation of personal and marital history, parenting experience and type of child desired.

**Average wait for a child after approval of a home study:** 1-6 mos.

**Foster care:** Temporary, long-term, permanent.

★ 392 ★
**Morning Star Adoption Resource Services, Inc.**
2300 N. Woodward, Ste. 9
Royal Oak, MI 48073
Phone: (810) 399-2740

**Contact:** Patricia Hannah, ACSW, Executive Director, or Marilyn Ruedisueli, Adoption Coordinator.

**Date established:** 1987.

**Description:** Non-profit private child welfare agency licensed by the Michigan Dept. of Social Services.

**Area served:** Residents of the State of Michigan.

**Requirements:** Flexible depending upon program.

**Fees:**
Pre-application fee: $50;
formal application; $150;
home study: $950;
supervision; $700;
foreign agency fees additional.

**Number of children placed last year:** 73.

**Description of children:** U.S. infants: 40; and foreign born children: 33.

**Adoption procedure:**
1) Initial inquiry;
2) submit preliminary application;
3) return completed formal application packet;
4) complete home study;
5) wait for child referral;
6) complete legal and immigration requirements;
7) travel to escort child home (not applicable in domestic adoptions);
8) placement;
9) post-placement supervision;
10) finalization.

**Average length of time between application and start of home study:** 1 mo. or less.

**Average length of time to complete home study:** 2 mos.

**Number of interviews:** 3-6.

**Home study description:** Evaluatory and educational process which looks at psycho-social history, attitudes on marriage, infertility (if applicable); spouse and children (if any); income; and dynamics of adoption, especially international adoption.

**Average wait for a child after approval of a home study:** Depends on program and country family is working with.

**Foster care:** Pre-adoptive.

★ 393 ★
**Oakland Family Services**
114 Orchard Lake Rd.
Pontiac, MI 48341
Phone: (810) 858-7766
**Branch address:**
2351 W. 12 Mile Rd., Berkeley, MI 48072

2045 E. West Maple, Ste. 405D, Walled Lake, MI 48088

5886 Dixie Hwy., Waterford, MI 48095

50 Wayne St., Pontiac, MI 48058

**Contact:** Nancy Rebar, ACSW, Children's Services Supervisor.
**Date established:** 1923.
**Description:** Private multi-service agency.
**Area served:** Residents of Oakland County and residents of other counties for special needs placements.
**Requirements:** Couples married at least 2 yrs. who are younger than 43 yrs. and who have a medical diagnosis of infertility. Requirements are flexible for special needs placements.
**Fees:**
8% of primary wage earner's income with a maximum of $7000; fees waived for special needs placements.
**Number of children placed last year:** 20.
**Description of children:** Black and white U.S. children of varying ages.
**Adoption procedure:**
1) Initial inquiry;
2) attend orientation meeting;
3) wait for adoptive study;
4) complete home study;
5) wait for placement;
6) placement;
7) post-placement supervision;
8) finalization.
**Average length of time between application and start of home study:** 1-6 mos.
**Average length of time to complete home study:** 3 mos.
**Number of interviews:** Unavailable.
**Home study description:** Evaluation of motivation to adopt, issues surrounding adoption, e.g. birthparents; childrearing philosophies; and family and marital history. If family is applying for a special needs child, the study also addresses separation and attachment and behaviors common in such placements.
**Average wait for a child after approval of a home study:** 1-6 mos.
**Foster care:** Short and long-term.

★ 394 ★
**Orchards Children's Services**
30233 Southfield Rd., Ste. 118
Southfield, MI 48076
Phone: (810) 433-8653

**Contact:** Miriam Berentstein.
**Date established:** 1963.
**Description:** Non-profit child welfare agency.
**Area served:** Primarily Wayne, Macomb and Oakland counties and other accessible counties.
**Requirements:** Applicants' health and age should not prevent adequate parenting of adopted child and their income should be stable.
**Fees:** Court fees only, approximately $90.
**Number of children placed last year:** 160.
**Description of children:** Both black and white children of both sexes between the ages of 3 and 15 yrs.
**Adoption procedure:**
1) File court petition;
2) placement with court approval;
3) 1 yr. supervisory visits;
4) finalization;
5) independent adoption services.
**Average length of time between application and start of home study:** Depends on match.
**Average length of time to complete home study:** 3-4 mos.
**Number of interviews:** 5-6.
**Home study description:** Mutual assessment of family's social history, strengths and ability to parent a child.
**Average wait for a child after approval of a home study:** Depends on child.
**Foster care:** Temporary, long-term and permanent.

★ 395 ★
**St. Vincent and Sarah Fisher Center**
27400 W. 12 Mile Rd.
Farmington Hills, MI 48334-4200
Phone: (810) 626-8932
(313) 626-7527

**Contact:** Linda Brook, MSW, CSW, Adoption Coordinator.
**Date established:** February, 1992.
**Description:** Private, non-profit multi-service agency licensed by the Michigan Department of Social Services to place children and affiliated with the Michigan Association of Children's Alliances, Michigan Federation of Private Child and Family Agencies, the National Conference of Catholic Charities and accredited by The Council on Accreditation of Services for Families and Children, Inc.
**Area served:** Residents of Macomb, Oakland, Washtenaw and Wayne counties.
**Requirements:** U.S. citizens who are no younger than 23 yrs. old who are either single or in a stable marriage and who have sufficient income to meet the family's needs.
**Fees:** No agency fees. Court filing and birth certificate costs vary by county.
**Number of children placed last year:** 16.
**Description of children:** Children with special needs.
**Adoption procedure:** 1) Inquiry; 2) orientation; 3) pre-service training; 4) home study; 5) compilation of child's history, physical, emotional and educational functioning; 6) child match; 7) filing of adoption petition; 8) placement; 9) post-placement supervision; 10) finalization; 11) post- legal services, as needed.
**Average length of time between application and start of home study:** 1 - 6 mos.
**Average length of time to complete home study:** 2 mos.
**Number of interviews:** 3.

**Home study description:** Exploratory and educational process which includes the compilation of vital records, health reports, employment verifications, references and criminal records clearances and addresses such issues as motivation to adopt, emotional stability, social history, children in the home, immediate and extended family's attitude toward adoption, parenting ability, home and community, type of child desired and ability to meet that child's special needs.

**Average wait for a child after approval of a home study:** Waiting period is longer for younger children or if the prospective adoptive family has narrow parameters for the type of child they will accept.

**Foster care:** Short and long-term, permanent and specialized.

**★396★**
**Sault Tribe Binogii Placement Agency**
1529 Marquette Ave.
Sault Ste. Marie, MI 49783
Phone: (906) 635-6538
Fax: (906) 635-4842

**Branch address:**
3035 Mackinac Tr., St. Ignace, MI 49781

P.O. Box 248, Manistique, MI 49854

**Contact:** Binogii Supervisor.

**Date established:** 1985.

**Description:** Non-profit private child placement agency licensed by the Michigan Dept. of Social Services.

**Area served:** Residents of Alger, Chippewa, Delta, Luce, Mackinac, Schoolcraft and part of Marquette counties.

**Requirements:** Applicants must have valid proof of membership in a federally recognized Indian tribe and meet the agencies requirements cited in their Adoption Needs Statement.

**Fees:** None.

**Number of children placed last year:** Approx. 14.

**Description of children:** 1 infant, 5 sibling groups, and 2 pre-schoolers.

**Adoption procedure:**
1) Complete paperwork;
2) background and law enforcement clearances;
3) complete home study and submit medical reports;
4) wait for placement.

**Average length of time between application and start of home study:** 1 mo. or less.

**Average length of time to complete home study:** 3 mos.

**Number of interviews:** 4-6.

**Home study description:** Complete and thorough evaluation of background and current situation.

**Average wait for a child after approval of a home study:** Varies.

**Foster care:** Temporary.

**★397★**
**Teen Ranch, Inc.**
2861 Main St.
Marlette, MI 48453
Phone: (517) 635-7511

**Branch address:**
15565 Northland Dr., Ste. 300E, Southfield, MI 48075
Phone: (313) 443-2900

**Contact:** Jodi Shinn - Marlette; Mike Lynch - Southfield.

**Date established:** 1985.

**Description:** Private, non-profit social service agency licensed to place children by the Michigan Department of Social Services.

**Area served:** Residents of southeastern Michigan and north to the "thumb" area.

**Requirements:** Applicants must be at least 21 yrs. old and meet the standards for foster home licensing.

**Fees:** Home study: $1800.

**Number of children placed last year:** 27.

**Description of children:** Children from birth to 17 yrs. most of whom were fost-adopt conversions.

**Adoption procedure:** 1) Inquiry; 2) orientation; 3) application; 4) home study; 5) licensure; 6) child match; 7) pre-placement visitation; 8) placement; 9) filing of adoption petition; 10) 1 yr. post- placement supervision; 11) finalization.

**Average length of time between application and start of home study:** 1 - 6 mos.

**Average length of time to complete home study:** 2 mos.

**Number of interviews:** 4 - 6.

**Home study description:** Assessment which includes such topics as applicant(s)' social history, quality and stability of relationships, financial security, parenting skills, home environmental factors, motivation to adopt and type of child desired.

**Average wait for a child after approval of a home study:** Varies with type of child requested.

**Foster care:** Temporary, long-term and permanent.

**★398★**
**Touch of Hope Adoption Center**
12 S. Center
Hartford, MI 49057
Phone: (616) 621-2411
(800) 358-4438
Fax: (616) 621-2735

**Contact:** Laura Dyas.

**Date established:** 1988.

**Description:** Private non-profit agency licensed through the State of Michigan.

**Area served:** Residents of Michigan.

**Requirements:** Adults up to age of 50 yrs. who belong to some organized Christian faith. All couples must have a clergy reference.

**Fees:** Sliding scale: $5750-$7000.

**Description of children:** Infants and older children.

**Adoption procedure:**
1) Name added to waiting list;
2) complete home study;
3) if approved, waiting list for placement;
4) placement.

**Average length of time between application and start of home study:** 6-12 mos.

**Average length of time to complete home study:** 2-4 wks.

**Number of interviews:** Orientation and home study process.

**Home study description:** Evaluation of lifestyle, religion, background and family life; individuality, parenting philosophy and disciplinary styles.

**Average wait for a child after approval of a home study:** 6-12 mos.

**Foster care:** Temporary.

# MINNESOTA

## STATUTES

★ 399 ★

**Independent placement by intermediary?** Illegal.

**Independent placement by birth parents?** Permitted.

**Subsidies provided?** Comprehensive assistance program which includes medical, monthly assistance and reimbursement for other expenses as well.

**Adoption cost defined by law?** Yes.

**Insurance for infertility?:** Unknown.

**Home study required by state?** Required before placement.

**Prospective adoptive parent advertise for a child?** Permitted.

**Surrogacy laws?** Not addressed in law.

**Residents access agencies of other states or countries?** In compliance with the ICPC.

**Requires judicial termination of birth parents' rights?** Direct consents for the adoption of the child by specific persons are recognized.

**Time given to a birthmother to revoke her consent:** 60 days after placement.

**Court handling adoptions?** Juvenile Division of the District Court.

**Adoption of Native Children:** ICWA is a federal law.

**Adoption records sealed?** Yes, but under certain conditions adoptees, 18 yrs. and older, may access their adoption records.

**Photo-listing book available?** *Minnesota's Waiting Children.*

## PUBLIC AGENCIES

★ 400 ★
**Carver County Community Social Services**
Courthouse, Box 7
Chaska, MN 55318
Phone: (612) 361-1600
Fax: (612) 361-1660

**Contact:** Becky Varone.

**Description:** Non-profit, public agency.

**Area served:** Residents of Carver County.

**Requirements:** Each case is reviewed on an individual basis.

**Fees:** None.

**Number of children placed last year:** Unavailable.

**Description of children:** Special needs, waiting children.

**Adoption procedure:**
  1) Submit application and accompanying forms;
  2) attend home and office visits;
  3) meet with the adoptive family of a waiting child;
  4) complete reading assignment on adopting the older child.
Remainder of process varies with each applicant family.

**Average length of time between application and start of home study:** 1-6 mos.

**Average length of time to complete home study:** 1.5 mos.

**Number of interviews:** At least 3.

**Home study description:** Evaluatory and educational process.

**Average wait for a child after approval of a home study:** 24 or more mos.

**Foster care:** Primarily temporary.

★ 401 ★
**St. Louis County Social Services
Adoption Unit-5th Floor**
Government Services Unit
320 W. 2nd St.
Duluth, MN 55802
Phone: (208) 726-2000

**Contact:** Intake worker.

**Description:** Non-profit, public county agency.

**Area served:** Residents of St. Louis County, MN, only.

**Requirements:** Open.

**Fees:** Sliding fee.

**Number of children placed last year:** 19.

**Description of children:** Infants, sibling groups, children with special needs and foreign-born children.

**Adoption procedure:**
  1) Initial inquiry;
  2) admission to waiting list;
  3) submit application;
  4) complete home study;
  5) if approved, wait for placement.

**Average length of time between application and start of home study:** 1-6 mos.

**Average length of time to complete home study:** 2 mos.

**Number of interviews:** 3-4.

**Home study description:** Call or write for outline.

**Average wait for a child after approval of a home study:** 6-12 mos.

**Foster care:** Temporary, long-term and permanent.

★ 402 ★
**Washington County Social Services**
P.O. Box 30
Stillwater, MN 55082
Phone: (612) 430-6571

**Contact:** Candace Tollefson.

**Description:** County social service agency.

**Area served:** Residents of Washington County.

**Requirements:** Flexible. Applicants should be no more than 40 yrs. older than adopted child, be physically and emotionally stable, and have the necessary financial resources to care for a child.

**Fees:** None for special needs. 2% of total gross income for healthy white infant to age 4, maximum $1000.

**Number of children placed last year:** 5-15.

**Description of children:** Infants and toddlers; older and/or special needs children from throughout Minnesota.

**Adoption procedure:**
  1) Initial inquiry;
  2) attend a series of adoption classes;
  3) submit application;
  4) complete home study;
  5) registration on state adoption exchange;
  6) wait for placement.

**Average length of time between application and start of home study:** 1-6 mos.

**Average length of time to complete home study:** 6 wks.

**Number of interviews:** At least 3.

**Home study description:** Home study is an evaluation of applicant's background, current relationships and lifestyle, and parenting philosophy. Applicants must write autobiographies, have police background checks and reference checks.

**Average wait for a child after approval of a home study:** 12-24 mos.

**Foster care:** Temporary, long-term, permanent, residential treatment and group home.

# PRIVATE AGENCIES

★ 403 ★
**Caritas Family Services**
305 7th Ave., N.
St. Cloud, MN 56303
Phone: (612) 252-4121
Fax: (612) 259-8761

**Contact:** Jim Wagner.

**Date established:** 1910.

**Description:** Non-profit private Catholic agency licensed in the State of Minnesota.

**Area served:** Residents of the Minnesota counties which make up the Diocese of St. Cloud and the Diocese of New Ulm.

**Requirements:** Catholic couples married at least 3 yrs. who are not older than 35 yrs., who have a normal life expectancy and a minimum income of $20,000. Applicants for Korean adoptions may be 40 yrs. older than the child placed.

**Fees:**
Registration: $50;
fees for home study, placement and supervision are a sliding scale based on 7% of annual income with a minimum of $2000 and a maximum of $5000.

**Number of children placed last year:** 21.

**Description of children:** 11 infants, 2 children with special needs, and 8 bi-racial children.

**Adoption procedure:**
1) Initial inquiry;
2) attend orientation;
3) file application;
4) complete adoption education;
5) undergo home study;
6) if approved, placement;
7) 3 mos. post-placement supervision;
8) finalization.

**Average length of time between application and start of home study:** 1-6 mos.

**Average length of time to complete home study:** 6 mos.

**Number of interviews:** 3.

**Home study description:** An assessment which looks for applicants who have a positive marriage relationship, a happy childhood (or understanding through therapy) and positive experiences with children.

**Average wait for a child after approval of a home study:** 12-24 mos.

**Foster care:** Temporary and pre-adoptive.

★ 404 ★
**Catholic Charities, Inc.**
**Diocese of Crookston**
1200 Memorial Dr.
Crookston, MN 56716
Phone: (218) 281-4224

**Mailing address:**
P.O. Box 610, Crookston, MN 56716

**Contact:** Karen Myszkowski, Pregnancy/Adoption Counselor.

**Description:** Non-profit, private agency licensed through the Minnesota Dept. of Human Services.

**Area served:** Residents of Becker, Beltrami, Clay, Clearwater, Hubbard, Kittson, Lake of the Woods, Mahnomen, Marshall, Pennington, Polk, Red Lake, and Roseau counties.

**Requirements:** Couples married at least 3 yrs. who are no older than 45 yrs., who are in good health and members of a Christian church.

**Fees:** Sliding scale based on income from $1500 to $6000.

**Number of children placed last year:** 4.

**Description of children:** Infants from birth to 1 yr.

**Adoption procedure:** Call or write for outline.

**Average length of time between application and start of home study:** 2-3 yrs.

**Average length of time to complete home study:** Several mos.

**Number of interviews:** Unavailable.

**Home study description:** Assessment of background, marriage, education and employment, parenting ability and motivation to adopt.

**Average wait for a child after approval of a home study:** 2-3 yrs.

**Foster care:** Temporary.

★ 405 ★
**Catholic Charities of the Archdiocese of St. Paul/Minneapolis**
1600 University Ave. W., Ste. 400
St. Paul, MN 55104
Phone: (612) 641-1180
Fax: (612) 641-1005

**Contact:** Mary Ann Sullivan, MSW, LISW.

**Date established:** 1859.

**Description:** Non-profit private agency licensed in the State of Minnesota.

**Area served:** Residents of the 12 counties of the Archdiocese of St. Paul/Minneapolis.

**Requirements:** Varies by program.

**Fees:** Domestic program: $4000 - $8000 depending on service contracted to defray foster care costs for a total of $4000.

**Number of children placed last year:** 37.

**Description of children:** Domestic program: infants, special needs, few toddlers.

**Adoption procedure:** Covered in orientation program.

**Average length of time between application and start of home study:** 24 or more mos.

**Average length of time to complete home study:** 2-5 mos.

**Number of interviews:** 4-5 and other program events.

**Home study description:** Covered in orientation program.

**Average wait for a child after approval of a home study:** 12-24 mos.

**Foster care:** Short-term.

## ★ 406 ★
**Catholic Charities of the Diocese of Winona**
55 W. Sanborn St.
Winona, MN 55987
Phone: (507) 454-4643
(800) CARE-002
Fax: (507) 454-8106

**Mailing address:**
  P.O. Box 588, Winona, MN 55987
**Branch address:**
  111 Riverfront, Winona, MN 55987
  Phone: (507) 454-2270

  903 W. Center St., Rochester, MN 55902
  Phone: (507) 287-2047

  423 W. 7th St., Mankato, MN 56001
  Phone: (507) 387-5586

  1118 Oxford St., Worthington, MN 56187
  Phone: (507) 376-9757

**Contact:** Lloyd W. Lenarz.
**Date established:** 1947.
**Description:** Non-profit, private agency licensed by the Minnesota Dept. of Human Services.
**Area served:** Residents of the 20 counties on the southern border of Minnesota.
**Requirements:** Married couples between the ages of 23 and 38 yrs. who are in good health.
**Fees:** Sliding scale based on income and family size.
**Number of children placed last year:** 14.
**Description of children:** Caucasian infants, some with special needs.
**Adoption procedure:** Call or write for outline.
**Average length of time between application and start of home study:** 1 mo. or less.
**Average length of time to complete home study:** 3-4 mos.
**Number of interviews:** 10-15.
**Home study description:** Assessment of background information and current functioning in all areas.
**Average wait for a child after approval of a home study:** 12-24 mos.
**Foster care:** Temporary.

## ★ 407 ★
**Children's Home Society of Minnesota**
2230 Como Ave.
St. Paul, MN 55108
Phone: (612) 646-6393

**Contact:** Diane Daehlin, Adoption Division Director.
**Date established:** 1889.
**Description:** Private, non-profit, non-sectarian child welfare agency licensed to place children by the Minnesota Department of Social Services.
**Area served:** Residents of the U.S.
**Requirements:** Vary by program selected.
**Fees:** Application: $45; home study and other fees vary by program selected.
**Number of children placed last year:** 405.
**Description of children:** U.S. and foreign born infants and children with special needs.

**Adoption procedure:** 1) Orientation; 2) application/registration; 3) pre-adoptive counseling; 4) home study; 5) child match; 6) placement; 7) post-placement supervision; 8) finalization.
**Average length of time between application and start of home study:** 1 - 6 mos.
**Average length of time to complete home study:** 1 - 4 mos.
**Number of interviews:** Variable.
**Home study description:** Assessment which addresses such topics as marital relationship, health and emotional status, financial resources, goals and issues relating to adoption.
**Average wait for a child after approval of a home study:** Dependent on program selected.
**Foster care:** Cradle care.

## ★ 408 ★
**Crossroads, Inc.**
4620 W. 77th St., Ste. 105
Minneapolis, MN 55435
Phone: (612) 831-5707
Fax: (612) 831-5129

**Contact:** Myrna H. Otte or Ann M. Sinnott.
**Date established:** 1976.
**Description:** Non-profit, non-sectarian, non-public adoption agency licensed by the State of Minnesota.
**Area served:** Residents of Minnesota and very limited services to out-of-state families for specific programs.
**Requirements:** Applicants are evaluated on an individual basis although the requirements of foreign governments are honored.
**Fees:**
Comprehensive fee: $2700;
referring agency fee: $800.
**Number of children placed last year:** 107.
**Description of children:** 50% U.S. children, some with special needs, some infants, and some special needs infants; 50% foreign-born, some with special needs, some infants, and some special needs infants.
**Adoption procedure:**
 1) File application;
 2) attend 2 educational sessions;
 3) participate in at least 2 interviews;
 4) child search;
 5) placement;
 6) post-placement supervision;
 7) support group participation (on-going);
 8) finalization.
**Average length of time between application and start of home study:** 1-6 mos.
**Average length of time to complete home study:** 2-6 mos.
**Number of interviews:** 2 group and 2 or more individual.
**Home study description:** Evaluation of biographical information, social history, marriage (if applicable) and lifestyle, home, neighborhood, schools and community, health, religion, employment and finances, parenting philosophy, children in the home, child preference, attitude toward adoption and the attitudes of friends and family, law enforcement checks and vital records documentation.
**Average wait for a child after approval of a home study:** 1-18 mos., depending on child source.
**Foster care:** Temporary.

## ★409★
**HOPE Adoption and Family Services International, Inc.**
421 S. Main St.
Stillwater, MN 55082
Phone: (612) 439-2446
Fax: (612) 439-2071

**Contact:** Anne McManus, Executive Director; Coleen Gregor, Social Services Supervisor.

**Date established:** 1978.

**Description:** Non-profit child placing agency licensed in Minnesota and Wisconsin.

**Area served:** Residents of Minnesota and northwest Wisconsin living within 150 mile radius of Stillwater, MN: about 14 counties in regular service and another 10 or 11 by special arrangement.

**Requirements:** Adults over the age of 21. All other requirements are very flexible. Seeking minority parents.

**Fees:**
$2700 includes family preparation and post-placement supervision including recommendation to court for legal finalization.

**Number of children placed last year:** Average 60-70 children per year.

**Description of children:** Infants to teenagers from the US and other countries. About 1/3 are children with special needs.

**Adoption procedure:**
1) Attend informational meeting;
2) complete adoption study;
3) apply to child-finding source or agency
4) placement;
5) post-placement supervision (3 mos. in MN; 6 mos. in WI);
6) finalization.

**Average length of time between application and start of home study:** 0-1 mos.

**Average length of time to complete home study:** 3-6 mos.

**Number of interviews:** 3-5, at least one meeting in the home and 3 office visits.

**Home study description:** Evaluation of motivation to adopt, upbringing, relationships, receipt and verification of birth, marriage and divorce (if applicable) certificates, medical reports, references from non-relatives, and letters of clearance from the local police or sheriff's departments in all areas the applicants have lived during the previous 5 yrs.

**Average wait for a child after approval of a home study:** 6-12 mos.

**Foster care:** HOPE employs 3 foster families who care for local infants while their birthparents are completing the termination of parental rights and adoptive parents selected are preparing to receive the child.

## ★410★
**The Lutheran Home**
611 W. Main St.
Belle Plaine, MN 56011
Phone: (612) 873-2215
(800) 852-9672

**Branch address:**
9350 Portland Ave. S., Bloomington, MN 55420

1460 Almond Ave., St. Paul, MN 55108

**Contact:** Rebecca Staab.

**Date established:** 1982.

**Description:** Private, non-profit child placing agency licensed by the Minnesota Department of Social Services.

**Area served:** Residents of Minnesota.

**Requirements:** Agency placements: Members of the Wisconsin Evangelical Lutheran Synod. Designated adoptions: Birth parents select adoptive family.

**Fees:** Application: $100; home study: $1000; placement fee: $4000. Travel expenses and partial adoption services: $40/hr.

**Number of children placed last year:** 2.

**Description of children:** 1 foreign born and 1 mixed race infant.

**Adoption procedure:** 1) Application; 2) home visit; 3) home study; 4) placement on waiting list; 5) birth parent review and selection; 6) placement; 7) post-placement supervision; 8) finalization.

**Average length of time between application and start of home study:** Less than 1 mo.

**Average length of time to complete home study:** 3 mos.

**Number of interviews:** 2.

**Home study description:** Assessment which includes review of health records, background, references and home inspection.

**Average wait for a child after approval of a home study:** Mixed race infants: 6 - 12 mos.

**Foster care:** Cradle care.

## ★411★
**Lutheran Social Service of Minnesota**
2414 Park Ave.
Minneapolis, MN 55435
Phone: (612) 871-0221
(800) 261-6482
Fax: (612) 871-0354

**Contact:** Adoption intake.

**Date established:** 1865.

**Description:** Non-profit, private agency.

**Area served:** Residents of Minnesota.

**Requirements:** Vary with program selected.

**Fees:** Vary with different programs.

**Number of children placed last year:** 80.

**Description of children:** Minnesota infants, children with special needs, and foreign-born children from Colombia, Latin America, Russia, China, and Vietnam.

**Adoption procedure:** Call for agency procedures.

**Average length of time between application and start of home study:** 1 mo. or less.

**Average length of time to complete home study:** 2 wks.-3 mos.

**Number of interviews:** Varies.

**Home study description:** Call or write for outline.

**Average wait for a child after approval of a home study:** Depends on program.

**Foster care:** Temporary.

## ★412★
**New Horizons Adoption Agency, Inc.**
Frost-Benco Bldg.
Hwy. 254
Frost, MN 56033
Phone: (507) 878-3200

**Mailing address:**
P.O. Box 623, Frost, MN 56033

**Contact:** Maryls Ubben, Executive Director.

**Date established:** 1987.

**Description:** Private, non-profit child placing agency licensed by the Iowa Department of Human Services, the Minnesota Department of Social Services and the South Dakota Department of Social Services.

**Area served:** Residents of Iowa, Minnesota and South Dakota.

**Requirements:** Applicants must be active members of a Christian Church.

**Fees:** Application: $55; home study: $1800 (approx.). Program fees, transportation and escort fees are additional.

**Number of children placed last year:** 53.

**Description of children:** Black, Caucasian and biracial U.S. children and foreign born children from Guatemala, Haiti, India, Paraguay, Russia, Ukraine and Vietnam.

**Adoption procedure:** 1) Information request; 2) pre-application; 3) application; 4) orientation/educational meeting; 5) home study; 6) child referral; 7) placement; 8) post-placement supervision; 9) finalization.

**Average length of time between application and start of home study:** 1 - 6 mos.

**Average length of time to complete home study:** Unavailable.

**Number of interviews:** 3 or more.

**Home study description:** Assessment which includes descriptions of the prospective adoptive couple, any children in the home, health, attitude toward adoption and motivation to adopt, relationships, spiritual life, income, criminal/child abuse records checks, home description and the type of child desired.

**Average wait for a child after approval of a home study:** Varies.

**Foster care:** Cradle care.

★ 413 ★
**New Life Family Services**
1515 E. 66th St.
Minneapolis, MN 55423
Phone: (612) 866-7643

**Branch address:**
745 White Bear Ave., St. Paul, MN 55106
Phone: (612) 776-8121

9920 Zilla St., Ste.100, Coon Rapids, MN 55433
Phone: (612) 755-3035

814 N. Broadway, Rochester, MN 55906
Phone: (507) 282-3377

**Date established:** 1973.

**Description:** Private, non-profit, Christian social service agency licensed to place children by the Minnesota Department of Social Services and member of the Evangelical Council for Financial Accountability (EFCA).

**Area served:** Residents within a 25 mile radius of an agency office.

**Requirements:** At the time of application applicants must be between the ages of 21 and 39 yrs., residents of Minnesota for at least 1 yr., married at least 2 yrs. with no more than 1 child, in good health and financially stable.

**Fees:** Application: $35; home study: $4000; full service adoption: $7000; limited service: $4000.

**Number of children placed last year:** 18.

**Description of children:** 10 Caucasian infants, 7 infants with special needs and 1 foreign born infant.

**Adoption procedure:** 1) Preliminary application; 2) placement on waiting list; 3) informational meeting; 4)application process; 5) home study; 6) child referral; 7) placement; 8) post-placementsupervision; 10) finalization.

**Average length of time between application and start of home study:** 2 yrs. or more.

**Average length of time to complete home study:** 5 mos.

**Number of interviews:** 4.

**Home study description:** Assessment which includes biographical and identifying information on all household members, marriage relationship, support systems, parenting philosophy and skills, experience with and attitudes toward adoption, cross-cultural attitudes, ethical and religious values and beliefs, health, income and financial management, home neighborhood and verifications.

**Average wait for a child after approval of a home study:** 2 yrs. or more.

**Foster care:** Temporary.

★ 414 ★
**Wellspring Adoption Agency, Inc.**
1219 University Ave., S.E.
Minneapolis, MN 55414
Phone: (612) 379-0980

**Branch address:**
111 Third Ave. S., Ste. 240, Minneapolis, MN 55401

**Contact:** Lara Martinson, Administrative Assistant.

**Date established:** 1989.

**Description:** Private, non-profit corporation licensed to place children by the Minnesota Department of Social Services and offering facilitation of identified adoption services.

**Area served:** Residents of the U.S.

**Requirements:** Open.

**Fees:** Application: $150; home study: $3500; Domestic Infant Program: $4000.

**Number of children placed last year:** 88.

**Description of children:** Primarily Caucasian infants and toddlers.

**Adoption procedure:** 1)Orientation meeting; 2) intake meeting; 3) home study in state of residence; 4) training and counseling program; 5) placement; 6) post-placement visits and reports; 7) finalization.

**Average length of time between application and start of home study:** Less than 1 mo.

**Average length of time to complete home study:** 2 mos.

**Number of interviews:** 3.

**Home study description:** Assessment which includes criminal, child protective services and domestic abuse records checks, medical examinations, financial statement including a copy of the previous year's tax return and written responses to a variety of questions.

**Average wait for a child after approval of a home study:** 6-12 mos.

**Foster care:** None.

# MISSISSIPPI

## STATUTES

★ 415 ★

**Independent placement by intermediary?** Permitted.

**Independent placement by birth parents?** Permitted.

**Subsidies provided?** Finalization fees, Medicaid and monetary payment.

**Adoption cost defined by law?** In general terms.

**Insurance for infertility?:** Unknown.

**Home study required by state?** No.

**Prospective adoptive parent advertise for a child?** Permitted.

**Surrogacy laws?** Permitted.

**Residents access agencies of other states or countries?** Permitted.

**Requires judicial termination of birth parents' rights?** Voluntary relinquishments by both birth parents are recognized.

**Time given to a birthmother to revoke her consent:** None.

**Court handling adoptions?** Chancery Court.

**Adoption of Native Children:** Tribe.

**Adoption records sealed?** Yes.

**Photo-listing book available?** Mississippi Adoption Resource Exchange Book.

# PUBLIC AGENCIES

★ 416 ★
**Mississippi Department of Human Services**
P.O. Box 352
Jackson, MS 39205
Phone: (601) 359-4980
(800) 821-9157
Fax: (601) 359-4978

**Contact:** Adoption intake worker.

**Date established:** 1936.

**Description:** State human service.

**Area served:** Residents of the State of Mississippi.

**Requirements:** Couples married at least 3 yrs. who are at least 23 yrs. old but no more than 37 yrs. older than the child placed, and who are financially able to provide for their own needs and the needs of their adopted child.

**Fees:** None.

**Number of children placed last year:** 103.

**Description of children:** Special needs.

**Adoption procedure:** Contact Department of Human Services, Adoption Unit.

**Average length of time between application and start of home study:** Varies.

**Average length of time to complete home study:** 4 mos.

**Number of interviews:** 4 or more.

**Home study description:** Group educational process.

**Average wait for a child after approval of a home study:** Varies.

**Foster care:** Temporary, long-term and permanent.

# PRIVATE AGENCIES

★ 417 ★
**Bethany Christian Services of Mississippi**
2618 Southerland Dr.
Jackson, MS 39216
Phone: (601) 366-4282

**Branch address:**
100 N. 33rd Ave., Hattiesburg, MS 39401

116 Lawrence Dr., Ste.3, Columbus, MS 39702

**Date established:** 1984.

**Description:** Private, non-profit child placement agency licensed by the Mississippi.

**Area served:** Residents of Mississippi.

**Requirements:** Applicants must be committed Christians and active members of a Christian church.

**Fees:** Unavailable.

**Number of children placed last year:** 20.

**Description of children:** Infants.

**Adoption procedure:** 1) Preliminary application; 2) formal application; 3) group meeting; 4) individual interviews; 5) home visit; 6) reference checks and physicals; 7) wait for placement; 8) placement; 9) post-placement supervision; 10) finalization.

**Average length of time between application and start of home study:** 6 - 12 mos.

**Average length of time to complete home study:** 6 mos.

**Number of interviews:** 4.

**Home study description:** Assessment which addresses such issues as marital relationship, emotional, spiritual and physical stability.

**Average wait for a child after approval of a home study:** 12 - 24 mos. Briefer for children with special needs.

**Foster care:** Temporary.

★ 418 ★
**Catholic Social and Community Services, Inc.**
**Diocese of Biloxi**
P.O. Box 1457
Biloxi, MS 39533
Phone: (601) 374-8316
(601) 374-8317
Fax: (601) 435-7949

**Contact:** Beth Riley.

**Date established:** 1977.

**Description:** Non-profit private agency licensed by the State of Mississippi.

**Area served:** Residents of the Diocese of Biloxi including the counties of Hancock, Harrison, Jackson, George, Stone, Pearl River, Walthall, Marion, Lamar, Forrest, Perry, Greene, Wayne, Jones and Covington.

**Requirements:** Adults between the ages of 25 and 40 yrs. (exceptions can be made for waiting children), able to provide financially for a child. A stable marriage of 5 yrs. is preferred but not required.

**Fees:**
Full service adoption: sliding scale based on income;
home study & write-up: $500;
home study, follow-up and finalization: $1000.

**Number of children placed last year:** 9.

**Description of children:** Infants.

**Adoption procedure:**
1) Applicant inquiry;
2) complete and return preliminary form;
3) file formal application;
4) attend group meeting for new applicants;
5) reference checks and interview process;
6) if approved, placement;
7) supervisory period;
8) finalization in Harrison County Chancery Court.

**Average length of time between application and start of home study:** 1-6 mos for African-American infants; 24 or more mos. for caucasian infants.

**Average length of time to complete home study:** 4-6 mos.

**Number of interviews:** 3 or more.

**Home study description:** Evaluation of the prospective adoptive parents' attitudes, values, stability and lifestyle and preparation for the special challenges adoption brings.

**Average wait for a child after approval of a home study:** 12-24 mos.

**Foster care:** Temporary.

★ 419 ★
**Mississippi Children's Home Society and Family Service Association**
P.O. Box 1078
Jackson, MS 39215-1078
Phone: (601) 352-7784
Fax: (601) 968-0021

**Contact:** Linda West.

**Date established:** 1912.

**Description:** Non-profit, non-sectarian private agency licensed by the Mississippi Dept. of Human Services and a member of the Child Welfare League of America. Handles open, closed, identified, and foreign adoptions.

**Area served:** Residents of the State of Mississippi.

**Requirements:** Couples married at least 3 yrs. who are no more than 40 yrs. older than child placed, who are in good physical and mental health, who have sufficient income, insurance and living space to provide for an additional family member.

**Fees:** Sliding scale based on income from $0 - $10,000.

**Number of children placed last year:** 42.

**Description of children:** U.S. and foreign-born children from infancy to adolescence, some with special needs.

**Adoption procedure:**
1) Initial inquiry;
2) attend informational meeting;
3) file application;
4) complete home study;
5) matching process;
6) placement;
7) post-placement supervision;
8) finalization.

**Average length of time between application and start of home study:** Varies.

**Average length of time to complete home study:** 2-3 mos.

**Number of interviews:** 3-4.

**Home study description:** Educational and evaluatory process of home, finances, childrearing philosophies, attitudes toward adoption and birthparents.

**Average wait for a child after approval of a home study:** Varies.

**Foster care:** None.

# MISSOURI

## STATUTES

★ 420 ★

**Independent placement by intermediary?** Permitted.

**Independent placement by birth parents?** Permitted as well as relatives of the third degree.

**Subsidies provided?** Maintenance, legal, Medicaid and some special services.

**Adoption cost defined by law?** Yes.

**Insurance for infertility?:** Unknown.

**Home study required by state?** Pre- and post-placement reports are required.

**Prospective adoptive parent advertise for a child?** Not addressed in law.

**Surrogacy laws?** Illegal.

**Residents access agencies of other states or countries?** Permitted.

**Requires judicial termination of birth parents' rights?** Voluntary relinquishments are valid.

**Time given to a birthmother to revoke her consent:** 45 day appeal period in which to show fraud or coercion.

**Court handling adoptions?** Circuit Court except in St. Louis City, Jackson and St. Louis Counties where adoption proceedings are heard in Family Court.

**Adoption of Native Children:** Tribal court has primary jurisdiction.

**Adoption records sealed?** Yes, but at age 21 yrs. or older, adoptees may access their adoption records via a prescribed protocol.

**Photo-listing book available?** Missouri Adoption Photolisting Service.

## PUBLIC AGENCIES

★ 421 ★
**Greene County Division of Family Services**
101 Park Central Square
Springfield, MO 65806
Phone: (417) 895-6000
Fax: (417) 895-6080

**Contact:** Adoption Unit.

**Description:** Public county agency mandated to place children by the Maryland Department of Social Services.

**Area served:** Residents of Greene County.

**Requirements:** Adults, 21 yrs. and older, single or married at least 2 yrs., who are financially stable.

**Fees:** None.

**Number of children placed last year:** 80.

**Description of children:** Primarily sibling groups and children with special needs.

**Adoption procedure:**
1) Attend orientation session;
2) return completed application;
3) complete home study;
4) if approved, wait for placement;
5) placement;
6) post-placement supervision;

7) finalization.

**Average length of time between application and start of home study:** 1 yr.

**Average length of time to complete home study:** 3-4 mos.

**Number of interviews:** 4.

**Home study description:** Evaluation which includes parent education training and study of background information, flexibility, parenting models or experience and methods of discipline. The entire process is designed to be a self-assessment to help the adoptive applicants explore their parenting skills in relation to children with special needs.

**Average wait for a child after approval of a home study:** In most cases the prospective adoptive parents are already fostering the child they are seeking to adopt. The wait for other adoptive applicants is dependent upon the range of special needs they are willing to accept.

**Foster care:** Emergency, temporary, long-term, pre-adoptive, and career parenting.

★ 422 ★
**Henry County Family Services**
P.O. Box 626
Clinton, MO 64734
Phone: (816) 885-5531

**Contact:** Sheryl Stone, Social Service Supervisor I.

**Description:** Public social service agency mandated by the State of Missouri to offer child placement services.

**Area served:** Residents of Bates, Henry and St. Clair Counties.

**Requirements:** Open.

**Fees:** None.

**Number of children placed last year:** 10.

**Description of children:** 2 infants, children with special needs and sibling groups.

**Adoption procedure:** 1) Application; 2) screening; 3) pre-service training; 4) home study; 5) wait for placement/child match; 6) placement; 7) post-placement supervision; 8) finalization.

**Average length of time between application and start of home study:** 1 - 6 mos.

**Average length of time to complete home study:** 6 mos.

**Number of interviews:** 4.

**Home study description:** Assessment which includes family history, lifestyle, parenting practices and ability to parent a child with special needs, motivation to adopt and others.

**Average wait for a child after approval of a home study:** 12 - 24 mos.

**Foster care:** Emergency, short and long-term, permanent and specialized.

★ 423 ★
**Missouri Department of Social Services**
P.O. Box 88
Jefferson City, MO 65103
Phone: (314) 751-2502
(800) 554-2222
Fax: (314) 526-3971

**Contact:** County office.

**Description:** Non-profit, public, social services agency. Toll free number is only within state.

**Area served:** Residents of the State of Missouri.

**Requirements:** Adults, 21 yrs. and older, who are married or single.

**Fees:** None.

**Number of children placed last year:** 567.

**Description of children:** Children with special needs.

**Adoption procedure:** Application procedures may vary from county to county. Applicants must apply in their county of residence.
  1) Submit application;
  2) attend orientation and/or education meeting(s);
  3) complete adoptive family assessment;
  4) wait for placement;
  5) placement;
  6) 9 mos. post-placement supervision;
  7) finalization. In some counties, applicants are asked to attend special training focused on introduction to the skills needed to parent special needs children.

**Average length of time between application and start of home study:** Varies.

**Average length of time to complete home study:** Approx. 3 mos.

**Number of interviews:** 4 or more.

**Home study description:** Assessment of family's motivation to adopt, life history and personality description(s), current relationship, parenting style and methods of discipline, health, employment and money management ability, home and community, and recommendation of references.

**Average wait for a child after approval of a home study:** Varies.

**Foster care:** Temporary and long-term.

# PRIVATE AGENCIES

★ 424 ★
**Adoption by Gentle Shepherd**
501 N. Lindbergh
St. Louis, MO 63141
Phone: (314) 993-1600

**Contact:** Mary Ann Crutchfield.

**Date established:** 1994.

**Description:** Private, non-profit child placement agency licensed by the Missouri Department of Social Services.

**Area served:** Residents of the U.S.

**Requirements:** Applicants should be between 21 to 50 yrs., single, or if married, at least 2 yrs., have health insurance, be certified in infant CPR and non-smokers.

**Fees:** Pre-application: $75; application and group and assessment meeting: $1350; home study/home study review: $1000; approval and advocation: $250; placement and post-placement services: $7700 and $8300 (out of state).

**Number of children placed last year:** New agency.

**Description of children:** Newborns, children with special needs and foreign-born children.

**Adoption procedure:** 1) Pre-application; 2) application; 3) home study; 4) placement; 5) post-placement supervision; 6) finalization.

**Average length of time between application and start of home study:** 1 - 6 mos.

**Average length of time to complete home study:** 2 wks.

**Number of interviews:** 3.

**Home study description:** Assessment which includes personal history, marital information, child abuse records checks, description of home and community, religion, infertility overview, adoption parameters, finances, thoughts on adoption and birth parents among others.

**Average wait for a child after approval of a home study:** 1 - 12 mos.

**Foster care:** None.

★ 425 ★
**Bethany Christian Services of St. Louis**
7700 Clayton Rd., Ste. 205E
St. Louis, MO 63117
Phone: (314) 644-3535
(800) 238-4269

**Contact:** Adoption intake worker.

**Date established:** 1979.

**Description:** Non-profit, private agency.

**Area served:** Residents of the State of Missouri.

**Requirements:** Couples married at least 3 yrs., with fewer than 2 children and a diagnosis of infertility who are active members of an evangelical, Bible-teaching church and who believe in the sanctity of human life beginning at conception.

**Fees:** Sliding scale.

**Number of children placed last year:** 4.

**Description of children:** White, black and biracial infants.

**Adoption procedure:**
1) Submit preliminary application;
2) attend informational meeting;
3) file formal application;
4) complete home study process;
5) if approved, placement;
6) 9 mos. post-placement supervision;
7) finalization.

**Average length of time between application and start of home study:** 1-6 mos.

**Average length of time to complete home study:** 2-3 mos.

**Number of interviews:** 4 and home visit.

**Home study description:** Assessment of 3 personal references and recommendations from pastor and employer, family makeup, infertility history, marriage, parenting philosphies and methods of discipline and attitude toward adoption.

**Average wait for a child after approval of a home study:** 12-24 mos.

**Foster care:** Temporary.

★ 426 ★
**Catholic Charities of Kansas City-St. Joseph, Inc.**
1112 Broadway
Kansas City, MO 64105
Phone: (816) 221-4377
(800) 875-4377
Fax: (816) 221-9116

**Branch address:**
123 Ming, Warrensburg, MO 64093
Phone: (816) 747-2241

1302 Faroan St., St. Joseph, MO 64501
Phone: (816) 232-2885

**Contact:** Adoption, Unwed Parents Division.

**Date established:** 1900.

**Description:** Non-profit, church sponsored licensed child placing agency.

**Area served:** Residents of Missouri except residents of St. Louis City and St. Louis County.

**Requirements:** Catholic or Protestant couples married at least 4 yrs. who have a high school diploma/GED, are in good health and have a pastor's reference. If Catholic, applicants must have a valid Catholic marriage recognized by the Church.

**Fees:**
Healthy white infant: $11,700;
biracial child: $5000;
black infant: $1000. International, home study, post-placement and special needs children fees vary with program.

**Number of children placed last year:** 30.

**Description of children:** U.S. white, black and biracial infants, older children, international children.

**Adoption procedure:**
1) Name added to Adoption List;
2) file pre-application;
3) return complete application;
4) attend group meeting;
5) complete adoption study;
6) if approved, selection of couple for placement;
7) temporary custody awarded in court hearing;
8) 9 mos. post-placement supervision;
9) final adoption hearing.

**Average length of time between application and start of home study:** 6-12 mos.

**Average length of time to complete home study:** 2-3 or more mos.

**Number of interviews:** 4 interviews.

**Home study description:** Evaluation of information on each spouse's birth, nationality, education, occupation, interests, health, and religion; assessment of marital relationship, home, neighborhood, attitudes toward home and family life, childrearing practices, birthparents and relinquishment, telling child about adoption and search.

**Average wait for a child after approval of a home study:** Dependent on program.

**Foster care:** Temporary.

★ 427 ★
**The Children's Home Society of Missouri**
9445 Litzsinger Rd.
St. Louis, MO 63144
Phone: (314) 968-2350

**Contact:** Robert R. Sheahan, President or Karen Nolte, Vice-President.

**Date established:** 1891.

**Description:** Non-profit, private, non-sectarian statewide social agency licensed in the State of Missouri.

**Area served:** Residents of Missouri, primarily those in the St. Louis area.

**Requirements:** Couples married 5 yrs. at completion of home study who are in the childbearing age range and who have medically established infertility, who have no major health problems, some religious affiliation and sufficient income to support a child.

**Fees:**
Home study fee: $800;
placement fee: minimum of $6000; if income exceeds $50,000/yr., placement fee is 12% of annual income. Fees vary for special needs placements.

**Number of children placed last year:** 18.

**Description of children:** Primarily infants.

**Adoption procedure:**
1) Preliminary registration;
2) attend group meeting;
3) attend screening interview;
4) complete home study;
5) if approved, placement;
6) 12 mos. post-placement supervision;
7) finalization.

**Average length of time between application and start of home study:** Varies.

**Average length of time to complete home study:** Unavailable.

**Number of interviews:** 4 or more.

**Home study description:** Assessment of applicants' ability to parent an adopted child.

**Average wait for a child after approval of a home study:** Varies.

**Foster care:** Temporary.

★ 428 ★
**Christian Family Services, Inc.**
8039 Watson Rd., Ste. 120
St. Louis, MO 63119
Phone: (314) 960-2216

**Branch address:**
9955 Binkum Rd., Fairview Heights, IL 62208
Phone: (618) 397-7678

**Contact:** Ginny Lester, Adoption Social Worker.

**Date established:** 1973.

**Description:** Private, non-profit child placing agency licensed by the Missouri Department of Social Services.

**Area served:** Residents of Illinois and Missouri.

**Requirements:** Applicants must be members of the Church of Christ and no more than 45 yrs. older than the child placed.

**Fees:** Application: $50; home study: $650; placement fee: sliding scale based on income, between $5,000-$8,000; follow-up: $100; finalization and travel: $150.

**Number of children placed last year:** 5.

**Description of children:** Infants and children with special needs.

**Adoption procedure:**
1) Initial inquiry;
2) file application;
3) complete home study;
4) if approved, wait for placement;
5) placement.

**Average length of time between application and start of home study:** 1 - 6 mos.

**Average length of time to complete home study:** 3 - 5 mos.

**Number of interviews:** 3 - 4.

**Home study description:** Process which assesses a family's readiness to adopt and which explores a variety of issues including background checks, stability of marital relationship, infertility and adoption issues and the mechanism used to cope with them.

**Average wait for a child after approval of a home study:** 2 yrs. or more.

**Foster care:** Temporary.

★ 429 ★
**Family Therapy of the Ozarks**
1345 E. Sunshire, Ste. 108
Springfield, MO 65804
Phone: (417) 882-7700

**Contact:** Susie Wampler, MSW.

**Date established:** 1987.

**Description:** Private, profit-based agency licensed in the State of Missouri to conduct home studies.

**Area served:** Residents of Barry, Cedar, Christian, Dade, Greene, Jasper, Lawrence, Polk, Stone, Taney, and Webster counties.

**Requirements:** N/A.

**Fees:** Home study; $800 plus mileage.

**Number of children placed last year:** 2.

**Description of children:** Infants.

**Adoption procedure:** Please inquire.

**Average length of time between application and start of home study:** 1 mo. or less.

**Average length of time to complete home study:** 4-6 wks.

**Number of interviews:** 3-4.

**Home study description:** An in-depth study which assesess the applicant's appropriateness to be adoptive parents.

**Foster care:** None.

★ 430 ★
**Highlands Child Placement Services**
5506 Cambridge Ave.
Kansas City, MO 64129
Phone: (816) 924-6565
(800) 235-0652
Fax: (816) 924-3409

**Contact:** Rev. Robert J. Michels, Administrator.

**Date established:** 1966.

**Description:** Not-for-profit private agency licensed in Arkansas, Kansas, Missouri, and Connecticut.

**Area served:** Residents of the U.S.

**Requirements:** Couples married at least 3 yrs. who are between the ages of 21 and 40 yrs. Preference shown to members of the Assemblies of God. Primary preference also shown to childless couples and secondary preference shown to couples with only 1 child with the inability to have more.

**Fees:**
Adoption fee: $4000;
waiver of consent fee: $200;
court fee: $124;
attorney's fee: $450.

**Number of children placed last year:** 16.

**Description of children:** Primarily infants, some of whom are biracial.

**Adoption procedure:**
1) File preliminary application form;
2) submit secondary application with financial statement, autobiography and references;
3) complete home study;
4) if approved, admission to waiting list;
5) placement.

**Average length of time between application and start of home study:** 24 or more mos.

**Average length of time to complete home study:** 3-4 mos.

**Number of interviews:** 3.

**Home study description:** Evaluation of background, employment, religion, marriage, parenting skills and classes, methods of discipline, references, and home visit.

**Average wait for a child after approval of a home study:** 6-12 mos.

**Foster care:** Pre-adoptive.

## ★ 431 ★
**Jewish Family and Children's Services**
655 Craig Rd., Ste. 150
St. Louis, MO 63141
Phone: (314) 993-8018

**Branch address:**
9385 Olive, St. Louis, MO 63132
Phone: (314) 993-1000

**Contact:** Peter Walker, Coordinator, Services to Children and Adoption.

**Date established:** 1863.

**Description:** Private, non-profit agency licensed to place children by the Missouri Department of Social Services.

**Area served:** Great Metropolitan area of St. Louis.

**Requirements:** Jewish married couples who have no more than 1 child and have a medical documentation of infertility.

**Fees:** Application: $100; home study: $880; birth parent counseling: $80/hr.; post-placement supervision: $1040.

**Number of children placed last year:** 1.

**Description of children:** Infant.

**Adoption procedure:** 1) Inquiry; 2) application; 3) placement on waiting list; 4) home study; 5) wait for placement; 6) placement; 7) post-placement supervision; 8) finalization. Agency will also facilitate independent adoptions.

**Average length of time between application and start of home study:** 2 yrs. or more.

**Average length of time to complete home study:** 3 - 4 mos.

**Number of interviews:** 4 - 5.

**Home study description:** Assessment which meets the requirements of the Missouri Department of Social Services.

**Average wait for a child after approval of a home study:** 12 - 24 mos.

**Foster care:** None.

## ★ 432 ★
**LIGHT House Adoption Agency**
1409 E. Meyer Blvd.
Kansas City, MO 64131
Phone: (816) 361-2233

**Contact:** Shirley Gibson.

**Date established:** 1985.

**Description:** Non-profit, state licensed child placing and foster care agency.

**Area served:** Area of service unlimited.

**Requirements:** Couples who are between the ages of 25 and 40, married at least 3 yrs., not have more than 1 child, and committed Christians active in the same Pro-Life, Bible teaching church.

**Fees:** Pre-application fee: $25. Total average fees are based on adjusted gross income and range between $7500 and $12,000.

**Number of children placed last year:** 21.

**Description of children:** 99% infants.

**Adoption procedure:**
1) File application and screening by committee;
2) attend information meeting;
3) file formal application and second review;
4) home study and final approval. Birthmothers choose through non-identifying profiles and so choices are not based on a chronological order.

**Average length of time between application and start of home study:** 6-12 mos.

**Average length of time to complete home study:** 2 mos.

**Number of interviews:** 3-4.

**Home study description:** Basic information pertaining to background, marital situation, finances, adoption issues, motivation to adopt, and religion.

**Average wait for a child after approval of a home study:** 24 or more mos.

**Foster care:** Temporary infant care.

## ★ 433 ★
**Love Basket, Inc.**
4472 Goldman Rd.
Hillsboro, MO 63050
Phone: (314) 797-4100
Fax: (314) 789-4978

**Contact:** Frank R. Block, ACSW, LCSW.

**Date established:** 1982.

**Description:** Non-profit private agency licensed in Minnesota, Missouri, Connecticut, and Illinois.

**Area served:** Residents of U.S. states and territories. Missouri residents given preference for Caucasian infants.

**Requirements:** Single applicants must be 26 yrs. or older. Married couples may be 23 yrs. or older and married at least 3 yrs. Previous divorce is acceptable.

**Fees:** Domestic adoption fees are on a sliding scale based on income.
Foreign adoption fees: $8000-$14,000 depending upon country (India or El Salvador).

**Number of children placed last year:** 50.

**Description of children:** 15 U.S. children who were either white, mixed-race, or black and 35 Indian children.

**Adoption procedure:** Call or write for outline.

**Average length of time between application and start of home study:** 1-6 mos.

**Average length of time to complete home study:** 4-6 wks.

**Number of interviews:** 2-3.

**Home study description:** Evaluation of background, marriage, if applicable, finances, motivation to adopt, and others.

**Average wait for a child after approval of a home study:** 6-12 mos. for children from India; 24 or more mos. for caucasian infants.

**Foster care:** Temporary.

## ★ 434 ★
**Lutheran Family and Children's Services of Missouri**
4625 Lindell, Ste. 501
St. Louis, MO 63108
Phone: (314) 361-2121
Fax: (314) 361-2835

**Branch address:**
833 Broadway, Cape Girardeau, MO 63701
Phone: (314) 334-5866

**Contact:** Paulette Foerster, Coordinator, Child Welfare.

**Date established:** 1883.

**Description:** Non-profit, private agency licensed by the Missouri Dept. of Social Services and accredited by the Council on Accreditation of Services for Families and Children.

**Area served:** Residents of Missouri.

**Requirements:** Protestant Christian couples married 3 yrs. who are between the ages of 23 and 40 yrs., who have no more than 1 child and a diagnosis of infertility, who are in reasonably good health and have adequate income to provide for an additional family member. Age, religious, marital status and family size requirements are flexible for special needs, minority and international programs.

**Fees:**
Domestic program: fee is 20% of combined adjusted gross income with a minimum of $6000 and a maximum of $15,000.
Special needs program: 5% of combined adjusted gross income, not to exceed $4500.
Foreign program: homestudy - $1200; post-placement visits are $250/visit; travel or escort expenses and related costs.

**Number of children placed last year:** 55.

**Description of children:** 28 infants and 27 foreign-born.

**Adoption procedure:**
1) Attend orientation meeting;
2) file application;
3) complete home study;
4) participate in individual counseling session;
5) attend group workshop;
6) comply with immigration/naturalization requirements for international adoption;
7) placement;
8) post-placement supervision.

**Average length of time between application and start of home study:** 1 mo. or less.

**Average length of time to complete home study:** 3 mos.

**Number of interviews:** Several group and individual.

**Home study description:** Educational and evaluatory process.

**Average wait for a child after approval of a home study:** 24 or more mos.

**Foster care:** Temporary.

★ 435 ★

**Missouri Baptist Children's Home**
11300 St. Charles Rock Rd.
Bridgeton, MO 63044
Phone: (314) 739-6811
(800) 264-6224
Fax: (314) 739-6325

**Contact:** Paul McFerron.

**Date established:** 1886.

**Description:** Non-profit private agency licensed by the State of Missouri.

**Area served:** Residents of the State of Missouri.

**Requirements:** Applicants must be Baptists.

**Fees:**
Home study: $1000;
adoption fee: $10% of gross income plus a percentage of hospital bill if over $3000.

**Number of children placed last year:** 9.

**Description of children:** 7 infants and 2 adolescents.

**Adoption procedure:** Follows procedures set by Missouri State statutes.

**Average length of time between application and start of home study:** 1-6 mos.

**Average length of time to complete home study:** 3-6 mos.

**Number of interviews:** 3 or more.

**Home study description:** An assessment of the stability of the prospective adoptive home.

**Average wait for a child after approval of a home study:** 24 or more mos.

**Foster care:** Long-term.

★ 436 ★

**Worldwide Love for Children, Inc.**
1601-L W. Sunshine
Springfield, MO 65807
Phone: (417) 869-3151

**Contact:** Barbara Barksdale Jones, Administrator; Ann Bluehdorn, Placement Director; Marjory Ray, Director, Esther's Maternity Haven.

**Date established:** 1981.

**Description:** Non-profit adoption and pregnancy counseling agency and home for 14-21 year olds with crisis pregnancies.

**Area served:** Residents of the State of Missouri.

**Requirements:** Couples married at least 3 yrs. who are no older than 43 yrs. of age, have a stable income and are of some Christian faith. Exceptions to good health are reviewed individually.

**Fees:**
Registration fee: $100;
home study process: $1500;
placement: $3000-$6000 plus medical expenses of birthmother and child, if not covered by Medicaid or insurance.

**Number of children placed last year:** Average one per month over last three years.

**Description of children:** Infants, foreign and special needs.

**Adoption procedure:**
1) Complete registration;
2) attend orientation sessions;
3) file formal application with home study fee;
4) if approved, family put in pool from which birthmothers can select adoptive family for their infants;
5) infant placed in foster care and birthmother meets adoptive family in closed session on first name basis;
6) placement;
7) post-placement supervisory.

**Average length of time between application and start of home study:** 1-6 mos.

**Average length of time to complete home study:** 30 days.

**Number of interviews:** 2 joint interviews and 1 individual for each family member.

**Home study description:** Evaluation of adoptive parents' background, stability of marriage and finances; children in home (if any); motivation to adopt and adoption issues; child desired; parenting skills; religion; health and resolution of infertility; and home atmosphere.

**Average wait for a child after approval of a home study:** Varies.

**Foster care:** Temporary.

# MONTANA

## STATUTES

★ 437 ★

**Independent placement by intermediary?** Illegal.

**Independent placement by birth parents?** Permitted.

**Subsidies provided?** Medical, maintenance and non-recurring costs associated with the adoption.

**Adoption cost defined by law?** Elements are defined.

**Insurance for infertility?:** No.

**Home study required by state?** Required before placement.

**Prospective adoptive parent advertise for a child?** Illegal.

**Surrogacy laws?** Not addressed in law.

**Residents access agencies of other states or countries?** Permitted with an approved adoption study from a Montana-licensed agency.

**Requires judicial termination of birth parents' rights?** Voluntary relinquishments by both birth parents are recognized.

**Time given to a birthmother to revoke her consent:** Until the court hearing on the adoption, but the birth parent must demonstrate that it is in the best interests of the child.

**Court handling adoptions?** District Court.

**Adoption of Native Children:** Tribe.

**Adoption records sealed?** Sealed.

**Photo-listing book available?** None.


## PUBLIC AGENCIES

★ 438 ★

**Department of Family Services of Montana**
Box 8005
Helena, MT 59604
Phone: (406) 444-5900
Fax: (406) 444-5956

**Branch address:**
1211 Grand Ave., Billings, MT 59101
Phone: (406) 252-5601

202 S. Black, Bozeman, MT 59715
Phone: (406) 585-9984

700 Casey, Ste. A, Butte, MT 59701
Phone: (406) 496-4950

501 Court Square, Box 9, Glasgow, MT 59230
Phone: (406) 228-8221

2300 12th Ave. S., Ste. 106, Great Falls, MT 59405
Phone: (406) 727-7746

610 Woody, Missoula, MT 59802
Phone: (406) 523-4100

Box 216, Kalispell, MT 59901
Phone: (406) 755-5950

Box 880, Miles City, MT 59301
Phone: (406) 232-1385

PO Box 817, Helena, MT 59624

Phone: (406) 444-2030

221 5th St., SW, Sidney, MT 59270
Phone: (406) 482-1903

1210 E. Main, Courthouse Annex, Cut Bank, MT 59427
Phone: (406) 873-5534

314 4th Ave., Haure, MT 59501
Phone: (406) 265-1233

210 N. 2nd St., Hamilton, MT 59840
Phone: (406) 363-1961

300 First Ave., N, Ste. 201, Lewistown, MT 59457
Phone: (406) 538-7731

**Contact:** Betsy Stimetz, Adoption Consultant.

**Description:** Public agency of the State of Montana.

**Area served:** Residents of Montana.

**Requirements:** Adoptive parent training.

**Fees:** None.

**Number of children placed last year:** 100.

**Description of children:** Special needs.

**Adoption procedure:**
1) Initial inquiry;
2) participate in adoptive parent training;
3) complete home study;
4) if approved, placement;
5) post-placement services to adoptive parents and child;
6) finalization.

**Average length of time between application and start of home study:** Varies.

**Average length of time to complete home study:** 3-6 mos.

**Number of interviews:** 3-5 and training.

**Home study description:** Call or write for outline.

**Average wait for a child after approval of a home study:** Varies.

**Foster care:** Temporary and long-term.


# NEBRASKA

## STATUTES

★ 439 ★

**Independent placement by intermediary?** No.

**Independent placement by birth parents?** Permitted.

**Subsidies provided?** Medical, legal and maintenance.

**Adoption cost defined by law?** No.

**Insurance for infertility?:** Unknown.

**Home study required by state?** Required before placement.

**Prospective adoptive parent advertise for a child?** Permitted.

**Surrogacy laws?** Surrogacy contracts are not enforcable.

**Residents access agencies of other states or countries?** In consort with a Nebraska agency under the ICPC.

**Requires judicial termination of birth parents' rights?** Voluntary relinquishments are recognized.

**Time given to a birthmother to revoke her consent:** None.

**Court handling adoptions?** County Court.

**Adoption of Native Children:** Tribal Court.

**Adoption records sealed?** Sealed but at age 25 yr. adoptees may have access to their adoption records.

**Photo-listing book available?** Provided and kept in the central office of the Department of Social Services.

# PUBLIC AGENCIES

## ★440★
**Nebraska Department of Social Services**
P.O. Box 95026
Lincoln, NE 68509
Phone: (402) 471-9331

**Mailing address:**
P.O. Box 95026, Lincoln, NE 68509

**Branch address:**
1313 Farnam-on-the-Mall, Omaha, NE 68102
Phone: (402) 595-2904

1001 "O" St., Lincoln, NE
Phone: (402) 471-5188

Courthouse, 612 Grant, Beatrice, NE 68310
Phone: (402) 223-6000

205 1/2 W. 1st St., P.O. Box 2121, Grand Island, NE 68802
Phone: (308) 385-6100

1030 S. "D" St., P.O. Box 508, Broken Bow, NE
Phone: (308) 872-2491

Craft State Office Bldg., 200 S. Silber, North Platte, NE 69101
Phone: (308) 535-8200

1030 "N" St., Gering, NE
Phone: (308) 436-6500

Stone Bldg., P.O. Box 339, Norfolk, NE 68701
Phone: (402) 370-3132

**Contact:** Mary Dyer, Adoption Specialist.

**Description:** Public, state agency.

**Area served:** Residents of the State of Nebraska.

**Requirements:** Adults, 19 yrs. and older. Each applicant is evaluated individually.

**Fees:** None, although home study fees can be charged for private adoptions.

**Number of children placed last year:** 131.

**Description of children:** Primarily children with special needs.

**Adoption procedure:**
1) Attend informational meeting;
2) participate in preparation classes;
3) complete self-study packet;
4) undergo home study;
5) if approved, wait for placement;
6) placement;
7) post-placement supervision;
8) finalization.

**Average length of time between application and start of home study:** Varies with each branch.

**Average length of time to complete home study:** Approx. 2-3 mos.

**Number of interviews:** Minimum of 3.

**Home study description:** Assessment which includes but is not limited to background checks, motivation to adopt and readiness to incorporate an adopted child into the family, home and environment, recommendation of 3 references, Child Protective Services and police clearances and children in the family (if any).

**Average wait for a child after approval of a home study:** Varies with matching procedure and needs of children.

**Foster care:** Short and long-term, emergency, legal-risk, therapeutic and subsidized.

# PRIVATE AGENCIES

## ★441★
**Adoption Links Worldwide**
3528 Dodge St., No. 26
Omaha, NE 68131
Phone: (402) 342-1234
(800) 66-CHILD
Fax: (402) 342-3074

**Contact:** Diane K. Baumgartner, Executive Director.

**Date established:** 1987, re-incorporated 1993.

**Description:** Licensed, non-profit, international child placing agency.

**Area served:** All states for child placement. Home studies for Nebraska.

**Requirements:** Singles, couples 25-50 years old. Additional requirements depend on foreign country regulations.

**Fees:** Vary with country and services provided.

**Number of children placed last year:** 55.

**Description of children:** Children from Colombia, Guatemala, Honduras, Vietnam, Bulgaria, Peru, and Ecuador. Networking for Russia, China, etc.

**Adoption procedure:** Call for information and interview. Application packet follows.

**Average length of time between application and start of home study:** 1 mo. or less.

**Average length of time to complete home study:** 6 wks.

**Number of interviews:** 3.

**Home study description:** Compilation of standard dossier requirements.

**Average wait for a child after approval of a home study:** Varies depending on type of child and country requested.

**Foster care:** None.

## ★442★
**Black Homes for Black Children Program**
**Child Saving Institute**
115 S. 46th St.
Omaha, NE 68132
Phone: (402) 553-6000

**Contact:** Tisa Hardin-Partridge, Adoption Specialist.

**Date established:** 1893.

**Description:** Private, non-profit child placing agency licensed by the Nebraska Department of Social Services.

**Area served:** Residents of Nebraska.

**Requirements:** Black or biracial couples who are between the ages of 20 and 50 yrs. old, who have been married at least 2 yrs. and who have a stable income.

**Fees:** Finalization fee is variable.

**Number of children placed last year:** 13.

**Description of children:** Black and biracial infants.

**Adoption procedure:** 1) Application; 2) home study; 3) placement; 4) post-placement supervision; 5)finalization.

**Average length of time between application and start of home study:** Less than 1 mo.

**Average length of time to complete home study:** 1 - 2 mos.

**Number of interviews:** 4 - 6.

**Home study description:** Thorough assessment which includes home visits and addresses such areas as health, income, personal issues, children, the extended family and others.

**Average wait for a child after approval of a home study:** 1 - 12 mos.

**Foster care:** Temporary.

## ★ 443 ★
**Catholic Social Services of Lincoln**
237 S. 70th St., Ste. 220
Lincoln, NE 68510
Phone: (402) 489-1834
Fax: (402) 489-2046

**Branch address:**
Catholic Social Service, 235 N. St. Joseph Ave., Hastings, NE 68901

**Contact:** Beverly Macek.

**Description:** Non-profit private agency.

**Area served:** Residents of southern and western Nebraska.

**Requirements:** Actively practicing Christian couples who are married at least 3 yrs., who are no older than 38 yrs. and who have adequate income to support themselves and a child.

**Fees:** $7,500.

**Number of children placed last year:** 12.

**Description of children:** Infants.

**Adoption procedure:**
1) File preliminary application;
2) arrange forwarding of pastoral and 5 personal references;
3) attend group orientation;
4) file application;
5) complete home study;
6) if approved, placement;
7) post-placement home study;
8) file reports and finalization.

**Average length of time between application and start of home study:** 12-24 mos.

**Average length of time to complete home study:** 6 wks.

**Number of interviews:** 5.

**Home study description:** Home study falls into two parts, pre-placement which evaluates emotions surrounding infertility, birthparents and preferences in an adopted child; and post-placement which evaluates the physical and emotional development of the child placed, the home, and the developing relationship between the parents and child.

**Average wait for a child after approval of a home study:** 6-12 mos.

**Foster care:** Temporary for infants and birthmothers.

## ★ 444 ★
**Child Saving Institute**
115 S. 46th St.
Omaha, NE 68132
Phone: (402) 553-6000
Fax: (402) 553-2428

**Contact:** Marcia A. Blum, MSW, Supervisor, Family Service Program.

**Date established:** 1892.

**Description:** Non-profit private agency.

**Area served:** Residents of Nebraska.

**Requirements:** Married couples between the ages of 21 and 43 yrs. who have sufficient income to provide for another family member, and who can provide physical examinations demonstrating good health. Marital and age requirements flexible for special needs adoption.

**Fees:** Application fee: $100; adoption home study group meeting: $300; adoption home study individual meetings: $850; birthparent counseling and support fee: $1000; matching and mediation fee: $50/hr.; relinquishment services: $500; post placement supervision: $350; interstate compact fee: $250. In addition, miscellaneous fees, extra legal fees, and travel expenses are billed to the adoptive couple. No fee for families working through Black Homes for Black Children.

**Number of children placed last year:** 26.

**Description of children:** White, Asian, black, and biracial infants.

**Adoption procedure:**
1) Telephone inquiry;
2) return completed application;
3) attend pre-adoption meeting with program supervisor;
4) placement on waiting list;
5) attend 2 day adoptive group meeting;
6) complete home study;
7) if approved, placement;
8) post-placement service period; and
9) finalization.

**Average length of time between application and start of home study:** 6-12 mos.

**Average length of time to complete home study:** 2 mos.

**Number of interviews:** 2 day group meeting plus 3 visits.

**Home study description:** Evaluation of applicant(s)' background; family and parenting skills; marriage and family communication; flexibility; and type of child applicant(s)' will consider.

**Average wait for a child after approval of a home study:** 6-12 months.

**Foster care:** Temporary.

## ★ 445 ★
**Jewish Family Service of Omaha**
333 S. 132nd St.
Omaha, NE 68154
Phone: (402) 330-2024

**Contact:** Cindy Ridgeway, C.M.S.W,.

**Description:** Non-profit agency of the Jewish Federation of Omaha.

**Area served:** Residents of Nebraska.

**Requirements:** Couples married 2.5 or more yrs. at time of application, 3 or more yrs. at time of placement, both of whom are Jewish, members of a local congregation and in agreement that their child will be raised Jewish, who are no older than 45 yrs. at time of placement of a first child and who have a medical diagnosis of infertility.

**Fees:** $5000 plus medical expenses in excess of $3000.

**Number of children placed last year:** 1.

**Description of children:** Infant.

**Adoption procedure:**
1) Attend initial interview;
2) file application;
3) submit fertility work-up;
4) arrange for character references from non-family members to be sent to agency;
5) attend individual interviews;
6) home visit;
7) if approved, name added to waiting list for placement;
8) placement;
9) 6 mos. post-placement supervision.

**Average length of time between application and start of home study:** 1-6 mos.

**Average length of time to complete home study:** 12-16 wks.

**Number of interviews:** 4.

**Home study description:** Assessment of applicants' childhood; educational and professional background; marriage and relationships; present situation; infertility related issues; childrearing philosophy and experiences; and attitudes on adoption.

**Average wait for a child after approval of a home study:** 24 or more mos.

**Foster care:** None.


★ 446 ★
**Lutheran Family Services**
120 S. 24th St.
Omaha, NE 68102
Phone: (402) 342-7007
Fax: (402) 342-6408

**Contact:** Robert Campbell.

**Date established:** 1892.

**Description:** Non-profit, private agency licensed in the State of Nebraska.

**Area served:** Residents of the State of Nebraska only.

**Requirements:** Active members of the same Christian church in the community of family residence who have adequate medical insurance and no more than one child and combined age is no more than 85. If married, applicants must be married at least 2 yrs. at time of formal application. Agency prefers that an age difference of no more than 45 yrs. exist between parent and child in all adoptive placements. Family size requirement flexible for special needs placements.

**Fees:** Contract home study: $1200.

**Number of children placed last year:** 29.

**Description of children:** 19 healthy white infants, 4 foreign-born children, 4 biracial, 1 older child and 1 identified adoption.

**Adoption procedure:**
1) Initial inquiry;
2) attend Pre-Adoption Group interview;
3) applicants for infants register and join waiting pool;
4) applicants for other placements file formal application;
5) attend individual office interviews with supporting documentation;

6) participate in group seminar;
7) home visit;
8) placement;
9) 6 or more mos. post-placement supervision;
10) finalization.

**Average length of time between application and start of home study:** Random selection drawing to start home study process held once a year in January.

**Average length of time to complete home study:** 3-5 mos.

**Number of interviews:** 3 plus group.

**Home study description:** Educational and evaluatory process which includes background material, marital relationship, issues surrounding infertility, parenting preparation for adoption, legal issues surrounding adoption, birthparents and adult adoptees, recommendation of references, finances and employment record and medical reports.

**Average wait for a child after approval of a home study:** Birthparents do the choosing of adoptive family they want to parent their child thus there is no waiting period average.

**Foster care:** Temporary.


★ 447 ★
**Nebraska Children's Home Society**
3549 Fontenelle Blvd.
Omaha, NE 68104
Phone: (402) 451-0787
Fax: (402) 451-0360

**Branch address:**
Offices are located in Kearney, Fremont, Grand Island,, Lincoln, Norfolk, North Platte and Scottsbluff, but all, inquiries are handled through the Omaha office.,

**Date established:** 1893.

**Description:** Non-profit, nonsectarian child placement and child caring agency licenced by the State of Nebraska Dept. of Social Services.

**Area served:** Residents of Nebraska.

**Requirements:** Couples married for at least 2 yrs. who are financially responsible. The age difference between parent and child should be no more than 40 yrs. Preference is shown to those couples who share a common faith which they practice regularly together.

**Fees:** No fees. It is the philosophy of the Nebraska Children's Home Society that adoptive parents will want to voluntarily contribute to the support of the agency.

**Number of children placed last year:** 120.

**Description of children:** Primarily infants, some pre-schoolers, school-age children, sibling groups and children with special needs.

**Adoption procedure:**
1) Write introductory letter which includes biographical information, medical treatment for infertility, and the age and sex of the child they would like to adopt;
2) attend group information sharing;
3) forward information on infertility workup from their doctor;
4) attend interview at the Omaha office;
5) attend additional group meetings and individual interviews;
6) if approved, wait while the Nebraska Children's Home Society attempts to find the home that is most suitable for a particular child, or selection by birth parents;
7) placement;
8) 6 mos. supervisory period;
9) legal finalization.

**Average length of time between application and start of home study:** 1-6 mos.

**Average length of time to complete home study:** 1 yr.

**Number of interviews:** 6 individual and 2 group.

**Home study description:** The home study focuses on parent preparation and helping the couple understand the difference between biological parenthood and adoptive parenthood and the feelings of birthparents.

**Average wait for a child after approval of a home study:** Varies.

**Foster care:** Temporary.

# NEVADA

## STATUTES

★ 448 ★

**Independent placement by intermediary?** Illegal.

**Independent placement by birth parents?** Permitted.

**Subsidies provided?** Medical, maintenance and legal.

**Adoption cost defined by law?** N/A.

**Insurance for infertility?:** No.

**Home study required by state?** Required before placement.

**Prospective adoptive parent advertise for a child?** Illegal.

**Surrogacy laws?** Surrogacy contracts are recognized.

**Residents access agencies of other states or countries?** Permitted.

**Requires judicial termination of birth parents' rights?** Voluntary relinquishments in the presence of a licensed social worker are valid.

**Time given to a birthmother to revoke her consent:** None.

**Court handling adoptions?** Family Court.

**Adoption of Native Children:** Tribe.

**Adoption records sealed?** Yes.

**Photo-listing book available?** Nevada Adoption Exchange Book.

## PUBLIC AGENCIES

★ 449 ★
**State of Nevada**
**Division of Child and Family Services**
6171 W. Charleston Blvd., Bldg. 15
Las Vegas, NV 89158
Phone: (702) 486-7650

**Branch address:**
410 E. John St., Carson City, NV 89710
Phone: (702) 687-4943

850 Elm St., Elko, NV 89801
Phone: (702) 738-2534

725 Avenue K, P.O. Box 506, Ely, NV 89301
Phone: (702) 289-1640

1735 Kaiser St., Fallon, NV 89406
Phone: (702) 423-8566

1000 "C" St., P.O. Box 1508, Hawthorne, NV 89415
Phone: (702) 945-3602

535 Western St., P.O. Box 776, Lovelock, NV 89419
Phone: (702) 273-7157

610 Belrose St., Las Vegas, NV 89158
Phone: (702) 486-7800

565 N. Main St., P.O. Box 1491, Tonopah, NV 89049
Phone: (702) 482-6626

560 Mill St., Ste. 350, Reno, NV 89502
Phone: (702) 688-2600

501 Bridge St., Rm. 5, P.O. Box 1590, Winnemucca, NV 89446
Phone: (702) 623-6555

14 Pacific St., Yearington, NV 89447
Phone: (702) 463-3151

**Contact:** Wanda Scott.

**Description:** State social welfare agency.

**Area served:** Residents of the State of Nevada.

**Requirements:** Applicants must be at least 21 yrs. old and 10 yrs. older than the adopted child.

**Fees:** No charge for special needs. Non-special needs: $0-$2500 (Nevada residents); $0-$1000 (out-of-state).

**Number of children placed last year:** 160.

**Description of children:** Infants, children and infants with special needs.

**Adoption procedure:** Special needs adoption:
1) File application;
2) pre-service training;
3) complete home study;
4) reference, law enforcement and child abuse registry checks;
5) if approved, placement;
6) post-placement supervision;
7) finalization.
Non-special needs:
1) Inquiry; 2) placement on waiting list; 3) application; 4) home study; 5) reference, law enforcement and child abuse registry checks; 6) if approved, placement; 7) post-placement supervision; 8) finalization.

**Average length of time between application and start of home study:** Applicants for non-special needs adoption spend 3 1/2-4 yrs. on the waiting list before filing an application. Applicants for special needs adoption may apply and be studied almost immediately depending upon the range of special needs they are willing to accept and the type of children awaiting adoptive homes.

**Average length of time to complete home study:** 90 days.

**Number of interviews:** Minimum of 4-5.

**Home study description:** Educational and assessment process which includes applicant(s)'s background, education, finances, housing, marital history, health and fertility, motivation to adopt, type of child desired, and parental ability and/or experience.

**Average wait for a child after approval of a home study:** Varies according to availability and range of special needs that the family is willing to accept.

**Foster care:** Temporary, long-term and permanent.

# PRIVATE AGENCIES

### ★ 450 ★
**Catholic Community Services of Nevada (Las Vegas)**
808 S. Main
Las Vegas, NV 89101
Phone: (702) 385-3351

**Branch address:**
275 E. 4th St., P.O. Box 5415, Reno, NV 89503
Phone: (702) 322-7073

**Contact:** Patricia Gutierrez or Jani Novotny.

**Description:** Private, non-profit community service agency licensed to place children by the Nevada Division of Child and Family Services.

**Area served:** Residents of Nevada.

**Requirements:** Couples married at least 3 yrs. with no more than 2 divorces, the wife being no older than 40 yrs. and the husband being no older than 45 yrs. who have been residents of Nevada for at least 6 mos, in good health, who have no more than 1 child and documentation of infertility.

**Fees:** Maximum fees: $7500.

**Number of children placed last year:** 20.

**Description of children:** Infants, some mixed race, minorities and drug exposed.

**Adoption procedure:** 1) Orientation; 2) 4 preparation classes; 3) home visit and personal interviews; 4) police checks and background clearances; 5) profile preparation; 6) wait for birth parent selection.

**Average length of time between application and start of home study:** 6 - 12 mos.

**Average length of time to complete home study:** 6 mos.

**Number of interviews:** 2.

**Home study description:** Exploratory and preparatory process which includes preparatory session for semi-open adoption, the writing of autobiographies, finger printing, police and child abuse registry checks and addresses such issues as type of child desired, goals and discipline for the child, adoption issues and how the applicants would respond to meeting the birth parents.

**Average wait for a child after approval of a home study:** 12 - 24 mos.

**Foster care:** Cradle care.

### ★ 451 ★
**Catholic Community Services of Nevada (Reno)**
P.O. Box 5415
Reno, NV 89513
Phone: (702) 322-7073

**Branch address:**
P.O. Box 1926, Las Vegas, NV 89125
Phone: (702) 385-2662

**Contact:** Meta-Marie Lorigan.

**Date established:** 1940.

**Description:** Non-profit private agency licensed in the State of Nevada.

**Area served:** Residents of Nevada.

**Requirements:** Applicants must be in good health and have sufficient income to care for themselves and an adopted child.

**Fees:** Placement: sliding scale with a limit of $7500.

**Number of children placed last year:** 13.

**Description of children:** Primarily infants.

**Adoption procedure:**
1) Name placed on waiting list;
2) file application;
3) check for police, sheriff, and child abuse clearances;
4) check references;
5) physicals;
6) complete home study;
7) if approved, wait for appropriate placement.

**Average length of time between application and start of home study:** 1-6 mos.

**Average length of time to complete home study:** 120 days maximum.

**Number of interviews:** 4 or more.

**Home study description:** Evaluation of social history, references, law enforcement and child abuse registry checks, maritial relationship, family functioning, community relationships, home and neighborhood, income and finances, and ability to parent an adopted child.

**Average wait for a child after approval of a home study:** 12-24 mos.

**Foster care:** Temporary.

### ★ 452 ★
**Jewish Family Service Agency**
3909 S. Maryland Pkwy., Ste. 205
Las Vegas, NV 89119
Phone: (702) 732-0304
Fax: (702) 794-2033

**Contact:** Rose Gordon.

**Date established:** 1987.

**Description:** Non-profit private agency.

**Area served:** Residents of Clark County, NV. In special circumstances, residents from other parts of Nevada.

**Requirements:** Jewish couples married 2 or more yrs. who are at least 21 yrs. of age.

**Fees:**
Application fee: $25;
home study: $400;
total placement fee: Sliding scale with a maximum of $7500.

**Number of children placed last year:** 1.

**Description of children:** Infant.

**Adoption procedure:**
1) File application;
2) attend joint office interview and individual interviews;
3) home visit;
4) if approved, placement;
5) post-placement supervisory visits; and
6) finalization.

**Average length of time between application and start of home study:** 1-6 mos.

**Average length of time to complete home study:** 2 mos.

**Number of interviews:** 4.

**Home study description:** Evaluation of background information; medical and financial references; and ability to parent an adopted child.

**Average wait for a child after approval of a home study:** Varies.

**Foster care:** None.

**★ 453 ★**
**Latter Day Saints Social Services**
**LDS Social Services**
513 S. 9th St.
Las Vegas, NV 89101
Phone: (702) 385-1072
Fax: (702) 385-3053

**Contact:** Intake worker.
**Date established:** 1965.
**Description:** Non-profit private agency licensed in Nevada.
**Area served:** Residents of Nevada.
**Requirements:** Married couples who are members of the Church of Jesus Christ of Latter Day Saints and who are referred by their bishop.
**Fees:** Sliding scale.
**Number of children placed last year:** Unavailable.
**Description of children:** Infants.
**Adoption procedure:**
1) Initial agency inquiry;
2) complete investigatory study;
3) wait for placement; and
4) placement.

**Average length of time between application and start of home study:** 1-6 mos.
**Average length of time to complete home study:** 1 or more yrs.
**Number of interviews:** 4.
**Home study description:** Evaluation of family's lifestyle, physical description of home and neigborhood, quality of homemaking and living quarters provided for child.
**Average wait for a child after approval of a home study:** 12-24 mos.
**Foster care:** Temporary on rare occasion.

# NEW HAMPSHIRE

## STATUTES

**★ 454 ★**

**Independent placement by intermediary?** Illegal.
**Independent placement by birth parents?** Permitted.
**Subsidies provided?** Financial and medical.
**Adoption cost defined by law?** No.
**Insurance for infertility?:** No.
**Home study required by state?** Required and must be initiated at least 30 days prior to the placement of an unrelated child.
**Prospective adoptive parent advertise for a child?** Permitted.
**Surrogacy laws?** Permitted if the surrogacy arrangement has been judicially preauthorized pursuant to RSA 168-B:23 and all parties are eligible under the law.
**Residents access agencies of other states or countries?** Permitted, but home study must be conducted by an agency licensed by the New Hampshire Division for Children and Youth Services.
**Requires judicial termination of birth parents' rights?** Relinquishments must take place before a judge.
**Time given to a birthmother to revoke her consent:** None without a court hearing which determines if the withdrawal is in the best interests of the child.

**Court handling adoptions?** County Probate Courts.
**Adoption of Native Children:** Case by case basis.
**Adoption records sealed?** Yes, but non-identifying information is available to adoptees aged 21 yrs. and older and to adoptive parents. Birth parents may sign a release of information which is filed with the licensed child-placing agency which would release identifying information to an adoptee, 21 yrs. or older.
**Photo-listing book available?** Participates in the Maine-New Hampshire-Vermont Exchange.

## PUBLIC AGENCIES

**★ 455 ★**
**Division for Children, Youth and Families, New Hampshire**
6 Hazen Dr.
Concord, NH 03301
Phone: (603) 271-4455
(800) 852-3310
Fax: (603) 271-4726

**Contact:** Cathy Atkins.
**Description:** Public agency.
**Area served:** Residents of New Hampshire.
**Requirements:** Flexible.
**Fees:** None.
**Number of children placed last year:** 75.
**Description of children:** Older children with special needs.
**Adoption procedure:**
1) Attend inquiry meeting;
2) complete training;
3) undergo home study;
4) if approved, placement.

**Average length of time between application and start of home study:** 6-12 mos.
**Average length of time to complete home study:** Varies.
**Number of interviews:** Varies.
**Home study description:** Assessment of background, family style, parenting philosophy, medical reports, recommendation of references and abuse/neglect and law enforcement clearances.
**Average wait for a child after approval of a home study:** Varies.
**Foster care:** Temporary and long-term.

## PRIVATE AGENCIES

**★ 456 ★**
**Child and Family Services of New Hampshire**
99 Hanover St.
P.O. Box 448
Manchester, NH 03105
Phone: (603) 668-1920
(800) 640-6486
Fax: (603) 668-6260

**Contact:** Intake worker.
**Date established:** 1850.
**Description:** Non-profit, private multi-service agency licensed in the State of New Hampshire. Agency adoption program as well as private adoption programs.

**Area served:** Residents of New Hampshire.

**Requirements:** For agency placements preference shown to childless couples under the age of 40 yrs.

**Fees:** Sliding scale.

**Number of children placed last year:** 12.

**Description of children:** Infants.

**Adoption procedure:**
1) File application;
2) admission to waiting list for home study;
3) complete home study;
4) if approved, wait for placement (for private adoption home studies, there is no wait).

**Average length of time between application and start of home study:** 24 or more mos.

**Average length of time to complete home study:** 3-6 mos.

**Number of interviews:** 3-4.

**Home study description:** Educational process which includes some group activity and emphasizes preparing family for adoption.

**Average wait for a child after approval of a home study:** 6-12 mos.

**Foster care:** Pre-adoptive.


★ 457 ★
**Lutheran Social Services of New England, Inc.**
85 Manchster St.
Concord, NH 03301-5140
Phone: (603) 224-8111
(800) 244-8119
Fax: (603) 224-8111

**Contact:** Robert Kay, MSW.

**Date established:** 1985.

**Description:** Non-profit, private agency licensed in the State of New Hampshire for international adoption.

**Area served:** Residents of New Hampshire.

**Requirements:** Vary by child's country of origin.

**Fees:**
Application: $100;
agency fee: $1800;
foreign program costs and travel additional.
Total fees are estimated at $12,000 to $14,000 or more.

**Number of children placed last year:** 4.

**Description of children:** Foreign-born children from infancy to adolescence, some sibling groups and some with special needs.

**Adoption procedure:**
1) Submit interest questionnaire;
2) attend informational meeting;
3) file application;
4) complete home study;
5) country and child assignment;
6) travel to child's country of origin (if necessary);
7) post-placement supervision;
8) finalization.

**Average length of time between application and start of home study:** 1 mo. or less.

**Average length of time to complete home study:** 2-3 mos.

**Number of interviews:** 3-5.

**Home study description:** Assessment of autobiographies, motivation to adopt, health, plans for family, understanding of foreign/multicultural adoption, etc.

**Average wait for a child after approval of a home study:** 12-24 mos.

★ 458 ★
**New Hampshire Catholic Charities, Inc.**
215 Myrtle St.
Manchester, NH 03104
Phone: (603) 669-3030
(800) 562-5249
Fax: (603) 626-1252

**Contact:** Elaine C. Langton; Robert P. Clohosey.

**Date established:** 1945.

**Description:** Non-profit private agency licensed by the State of New Hampshire.

**Area served:** Residents of New Hampshire.

**Requirements:** Catholic couples married at least 3 yrs. who are childless.

**Fees:** Sliding scale with a maximum of $4000.

**Number of children placed last year:** 5.

**Description of children:** All races and ages.

**Adoption procedure:** Call or write for outline.

**Average length of time between application and start of home study:** 24 or more mos.

**Average length of time to complete home study:** 3 mos.

**Number of interviews:** 3-8.

**Home study description:** A complete and in-depth evaluation of the applicants.

**Average wait for a child after approval of a home study:** 12-24 mos.

**Foster care:** Short-term.


# NEW JERSEY

## STATUTES
★ 459 ★

**Independent placement by intermediary?** Permitted.

**Independent placement by birth parents?** Permitted.

**Subsidies provided?** Medical, legal and maintenance.

**Adoption cost defined by law?** No.

**Insurance for infertility?:** No.

**Home study required by state?** Before placement if an intermediary is involved and after placement, if placed without an intermediary's services.

**Prospective adoptive parent advertise for a child?** Permitted.

**Surrogacy laws?** Not addressed in law.

**Residents access agencies of other states or countries?** Yes, if licensed.

**Requires judicial termination of birth parents' rights?** Required before a judge.

**Time given to a birthmother to revoke her consent:** None.

**Court handling adoptions?** Superior Court.

**Adoption of Native Children:** ICWA is a federal law.

**Adoption records sealed?** Yes, but adult adoptees may access non-identify information.

**Photo-listing book available?** *Profiles of Waiting Children.*

# PUBLIC AGENCIES

## ★ 460 ★
**New Jersey Division of Youth and Family Services Adoption Unit**
50 E. State St., CN 717
Trenton, NJ 08625
Phone: (609) 633-6906

**Branch address:**
650 Bloomfield Ave., Bloomfield, NJ 07003
Phone: (201) 680-3530

34 Lexington Ave., Trenton, NJ 08625
Phone: (609) 530-4500

2 Sidoni Ln., Hammonton, NJ 08037
Phone: (609) 567-1515

22 Mill St., Paterson, NJ 07501
Phone: (201) 742-0063

100 Metroplex Dr., Ste. 106, Edison, NJ 08817
Phone: (908) 819-7272

**Contact:** JoAnne Kleinert.
**Date established:** 1899.
**Description:** Non-profit public agency licensed by the State of New Jersey, Bureau of Licensing and New Jersey Exchange.
**Area served:** Residents of the State of New Jersey.
**Requirements:** Couples in a stable marriage who have relatively good health and the youngest of whom will be 65 yrs. or younger when the child placed reaches the age of 18 yrs.
**Fees:** None.
**Number of children placed last year:** 655.
**Description of children:** Children from birth to 18 yrs., most of whom have special needs.
**Adoption procedure:**
1) File application;
2) complete group process for home study;
3) participate in individual interviews;
4) pre-placement services;
5) placement;
6) finalization.
**Average length of time between application and start of home study:** Varies, depending on family's flexibility in terms of accepting special needs children.
**Average length of time to complete home study:** Unavailable.
**Number of interviews:** 6-7.
**Home study description:** Primarily an educational process but also assessment of medical and financial reports, references and criminal records checks.
**Average wait for a child after approval of a home study:** Varies.
**Foster care:** Emergency, temporary, long-term and permanent.

## ★ 461 ★
**New Jersey Division of Youth and Family Services Adoption Unit (for mid-Jersey)**
100 Metroplex Dr., Ste. 106
Edison, NJ 08817
Phone: (908) 819-7272
(800) 543-3127
Fax: (908) 819-8445

**Contact:** Valerie Kelly, Manager.
**Description:** Non-profit state agency.
**Area served:** Residents of Union, Middlesex, and suburban Essex (excluding Newark) counties.
**Requirements:** Adults, 18 yrs. or older.
**Fees:** None.
**Number of children placed last year:** N/A.
**Description of children:** Primarily special needs children from birth to adolescence.
**Adoption procedure:**
1) Call or write for application;
2) complete home study;
3) if approved, wait for placement.
**Average length of time between application and start of home study:** 1-6 mos.
**Average length of time to complete home study:** 2 mos.
**Number of interviews:** 4 group, 2 individual/home visits.
**Home study description:** Evaluation of biographic and background information which allows the agency to determine if a family can successfully parent a special needs child. Flexibility, willingness to seek outside help and applicants' lack of need to have children live up to an image are foremost.
**Average wait for a child after approval of a home study:** Varies.
**Foster care:** Temporary.

# PRIVATE AGENCIES

## ★ 462 ★
**A.M.O.R. Adoptions, Inc.**
12 Grenoble Ct.
Matawan, NJ 07747
Phone: (908) 583-0174

**Contact:** Marian McAndrews, Administrative Director.
**Date established:** 1988.
**Description:** Private, non-profit child placing agency licensed to place children from both foreign and domestic sources by the New Jersey Department of Human Services.
**Area served:** Residents of the U.S. and Canada.
**Requirements:** All applicants must demonstrate financial ability to support a child. Applicants for inter-country adoptions should be 21 yrs. or older and married at least 2 yrs.
**Fees:** Application: $100; home study: $700; interview: $150; fingerprinting (NJ requirement): $75/person.
**Number of children placed last year:** 25.
**Description of children:** US and foreign-born children from infancy to 12 yrs.
**Adoption procedure:** 1) Inquiry; 2) program selection and application; 3) dossier compiled, notarized and certified; 4) dossier sent to child's country of origin; 5) dossier translated and filed in court; 6) home study; 7) case referred to Birth Registry, Passport and American Consulate.
**Average length of time between application and start of home study:** Less than 1 mo.
**Average length of time to complete home study:** 3 - 4 mos.
**Number of interviews:** 3.
**Home study description:** Assessment which includes documentation of birth, marriage and divorce(s), (if any), health checks, fingerprinting and criminal records checks, finances and references.

**Average wait for a child after approval of a home study:** 1 - 6 mos.

**Foster care:** None.

★ 463 ★

**Adoption And Infertility Services, Inc.**
P.O. Box 447
Lincroft, NJ 07738
Phone: (908) 946-0880

**Branch address:**
43 Main St., Holmdel, NJ 07738
Phone: (908) 946-0890

**Contact:** Diane Propert, Executive Director.

**Date established:** 1989.

**Description:** Private, non-profit child placing agency licensed by the New Jersey Department of Human Services offering identified, enhanced identified, independent, international, interstate and direct placements.

**Area served:** Residents of New Jersey.

**Requirements:** None.

**Fees:** Application: $65; adoption consultation: $150; home study: $600; CHRI fingerprint background check: $75; portfolio consultation and filing fee: $200; Enhanced Identified Service fee: $50; direct infant placement fee: $10,000; identified adoption placement fee: $2500; post-placement supervision: $200/visit; pre- and post-adoption seminars: $25/session; hourly rate: $100. Legal fees, birth and delivery expenses and other birth parent expenses are extra.

**Number of children placed last year:** 17.

**Description of children:** Primarily infants, one with special needs, one toddler and one 5 yr. old.

**Adoption procedure:** 1) Group information session; 2) private adoption consultation; 3) application; 4) home study; 5) portfolio and/or enhanced identified consultation; 6) advertising for birth family begun; 7) complete portfolio; 8) pre-adoption seminar; 9) placement; 10) post-placement supervision; 11) finalization.

**Average length of time between application and start of home study:** Less than 1 mo.

**Average length of time to complete home study:** 4 wks.

**Number of interviews:** 3.

**Home study description:** Assessment which includes documentation of birth, marriage(s) and divorce(s) (if any), Criminal Record Check form, physician's letter stating status of health, Income verification, military discharge (if applicable) and recent photos and addresses such topics as motivation for adoption and feeling about infertility, type of child requested, social history, marital relationship, religion, parenting attitudes, attitude toward adoption, finances and a description of the home.

**Average wait for a child after approval of a home study:** Varies with type of service selected.

**Foster care:** None.

★ 464 ★

**Bethany Christian Services**
1120 Goffle Rd.
Hawthorne, NJ 07506
Phone: (201) 427-2566

**Contact:** Adoption intake worker.

**Date established:** 1961.

**Description:** Non-profit, private agency.

**Area served:** Residents of northern New Jersey and parts of New York.

**Requirements:** Couples married at least 3 yrs. who are between the ages of 25 and 38 yrs. who are members of an evangelical Protestant church and who are in excellent health.

**Fees:** Sliding scale based on income with a minimum of $5000 and a maximum of $16,000.

**Number of children placed last year:** 3.

**Description of children:** Black, biracial and white children, some with special needs.

**Adoption procedure:**
1) Submit full application with 6 references;
2) complete home study and interview process;
3) if approved, placement;
4) post-placement supervision;
5) finalization.

**Average length of time between application and start of home study:** 1-6 mos.

**Average length of time to complete home study:** 6-8 mos.

**Number of interviews:** 5.

**Home study description:** Extremely thorough assessment which includes but is not limited to feelings about adoption, effective parenting and which type of child would best fit into the adoptive home.

**Average wait for a child after approval of a home study:** 24 or more mos.

**Foster care:** Temporary.

★ 465 ★

**Casa Del Mundo, Inc.**
260 Highway 202/31, Ste. 300
Flemington, NJ 08822
Phone: (908) 782-9393
Fax: (908) 782-3367

**Mailing address:**
P.O. Box 2141, Flemington, NJ 08822

**Contact:** Carol S. Perlmutter, Executive Director.

**Date established:** 1990.

**Description:** Private, not-for-profit child placing agency licensed by the New Jersey Department of Human Services.

**Area served:** Citizens of the U.S.

**Requirements:** Flexible. Some requirements will be imposed by the child's country of origin.

**Fees:** Application: $75; home study: $675. Additional fees ranging from $3000 - $4500 depending upon the child's country of origin.

**Number of children placed last year:** 30 - 40.

**Description of children:** Foreign-born children from infancy to 4 yrs.

**Adoption procedure:** 1) Preliminary application; 2) contract; 3) home study; 4) dossier compilation; 5) dossier sent to selected country; 6) child referral; 7) dossier processing; 8) placement by travel to child's country of origin or child escorted.

**Average length of time between application and start of home study:** Less than 1 mo.

**Average length of time to complete home study:** 2 - 3 mos.

**Number of interviews:** 3.

**Home study description:** Discussion of applicant's social background, motivation to adopt, employment and education, family relationships, child rearing practices and type of child sought.

**Average wait for a child after approval of a home study:** 1 - 6 mos. Wait can be longer for infants from Latin America.

**Foster care:** None.

---

**★ 466 ★**

**Catholic Charities, Diocese of Trenton**
47 N. Clinton Ave.
Trenton, NJ 08618
Phone: (609) 394-5181

**Mailing address:**
Administrative Office, 115 W. Pearl St., Trenton, NJ 08618

**Branch address:**
145 Maple Ave., Red Bank, NJ 07701

**Contact:** Edna Holland, ACSW.

**Date established:** C. 1920.

**Description:** Non-profit private agency licensed by the State of New Jersey.

**Area served:** Residents of Burlington, Mercer, Monmouth and Ocean counties.

**Requirements:** Couples married at least 3 yrs. who are younger than 39 yrs. for a first placement and younger than 41 yrs. for a second placement. All other requirements are determined on an individual basis.

**Fees:**
$50 application fee;
$800 home study.
Remainder of fees are on a sliding scale based on 12% of joint annual income.

**Number of children placed last year:** 18.

**Description of children:** Infants.

**Adoption procedure:** Call or write for outline.

**Average length of time between application and start of home study:** 12-24 mos.

**Average length of time to complete home study:** 6 mos.

**Number of interviews:** 10.

**Home study description:** Psycho-social assessment.

**Average wait for a child after approval of a home study:** Varies.

**Foster care:** Short-term.

---

**★ 467 ★**

**Catholic Charities, Metuchan Diocese**
**Department of Maternity and Adoption Services**
P.O. Box 358
Millington, NJ 07946
Phone: (908) 604-6992
Fax: (908) 604-8646

**Contact:** Sr. Patricia Kelly, MSBT, ACSW, Director of Maternity and Adoption Services.

**Date established:** 1983.

**Description:** Non-profit private agency licensed in New Jersey.

**Area served:** Residents of Hunterdon, Middlesex, Somerset and Warren counties.

**Requirements:** Couples married at least 5 yrs., at least one of whom is a practicing Catholic, who are between the ages of 25 and 39 yrs., who are childless, financially stable and in good physical and emotional health.

**Fees:**
Sliding scale based on 10% of couple's gross annual income. total includes $300 application fee and $500 non-refundable home study fee. Both fees are deducted from the total fee.

**Number of children placed last year:** 16.

**Description of children:** Primarily healthy U.S. infants.

**Adoption procedure:**
1) Attend group information meeting;
2) return completed application;
3) complete home study;
4) if approved, placement;
5) 8-10 mos. post-placement supervision;
6) finalization and issuing of amended birth certificate.

**Average length of time between application and start of home study:** 1-6 mos.

**Average length of time to complete home study:** 2 mos.

**Number of interviews:** 5.

**Home study description:** Evaluation of family background, finances, marriage and issues surrounding infertility, religious convictions, expectations for a child and attitudes surrounding adoption, i.e. search and future contact with birthparents.

**Average wait for a child after approval of a home study:** 24 or more mos.

**Foster care:** Temporary.

---

**★ 468 ★**

**Catholic Community Services of the Newark Archdiocese**
**Associated Catholic Charities**
499 Belgrove Dr.
Kearny, NJ 07032
Phone: (201) 991-3770
Fax: (201) 991-7306

**Contact:** Barbara Larson.

**Date established:** 1903.

**Description:** Non-profit private agency licensed by the State of New Jersey Bureau of Licensing.

**Area served:** Residents of Bergen, Essex, Hudson and Union counties.

**Requirements:** Couples married at least 3 yrs. who are childless, in good health, and who have sufficient income to maintain a family according to present costs.

**Fees:** 12% of combined gross income.

**Number of children placed last year:** 20.

**Description of children:** Infants from 0-1 yr. including some with special needs.

**Adoption procedure:** Processing according to N.J. State regulations. Finalization can occur 6-9 mos. after satisfactory placement.

**Average length of time between application and start of home study:** 1-6 mos.

**Average length of time to complete home study:** 3-4 mos.

**Number of interviews:** 10-12.

**Home study description:** Very complete evaluation which includes but is not limited to personal and religious history, medical reports, employment record, and police clearances.

**Average wait for a child after approval of a home study:** 12-24 mos.

**Foster care:** Temporary child care only - up to 3 mos.

---

**★ 469 ★**

**Catholic Social Services of Vineland**
810 Montrose St.
Vineland, NJ 08360
Phone: (609) 691-1841

**Contact:** Ann E. Gallagher, ACSW.

**Date established:** 1944.

**Description:** Non-profit private agency licensed in the State of New Jersey.

**Area served:** Residents of Atlantic, Camden, Cape May, Cumberland, Gloucester and Salem counties.

**Requirements:** Couples married in the Catholic Church, at least one of whom is Catholic, who are between the ages of 23 and 37 yrs. and in good health.

**Fees:** Home study fee: $800; placement fee: 10% of previous year W2 income.

**Number of children placed last year:** 12.

**Description of children:** Infants and special needs.

**Adoption procedure:**
1) File application;
2) complete home study;
3) file court papers;
4) complete home visits and interviews;
5) approval process.

**Average length of time between application and start of home study:** 1-6 mos.

**Average length of time to complete home study:** 4-6 mos.

**Number of interviews:** 6 or more.

**Home study description:** Evaluation which includes but is not limited to the following factors: personal, financial, education and professional.

**Average wait for a child after approval of a home study:** 12-24 mos.

**Foster care:** Temporary.

★ 470 ★
**Children's Home Society of New Jersey**
929 Parkside Ave.
Trenton, NJ 08618
Phone: (609) 695-6274
Fax: (609) 394-5769

**Branch address:**
19 Main St., Clinton, NJ 08809
Phone: (908) 735-9458

Cross River Mill Village, 1200 River Ave., Ste. 2C, Lakewood, NJ 08701
Phone: (908) 905-6363

**Contact:** Patricia Nardone.

**Date established:** 1894.

**Description:** Non-profit private agency licensed in the State of New Jersey and a member of the Child Welfare League of America.

**Area served:** Residents of New Jersey and Bucks County, PA.

**Requirements:** Flexible.

**Fees:** Flexible depending on services required and income. Between $350-$14,400.

**Number of children placed last year:** 29.

**Description of children:** U.S. white infants and older children, black and biracial children of all ages and children with significant physical, mental and emotional handicaps; 18 international children.

**Adoption procedure:**
1) File application;
2) complete home study;
3) placement;
4) 6 mos. post-placement supervision;
5) finalization.

**Average length of time between application and start of home study:** 1 mo. or less.

**Average length of time to complete home study:** 3-4 mos.

**Number of interviews:** 5-6.

**Home study description:** Educational and evaluative process which familiarizes the agency with the applicant family to determine which child they can parent most effectively and raises the awareness of the applicant family on issues surrounding adoption.

**Average wait for a child after approval of a home study:** 6-12 mos.

**Foster care:** Temporary infant foster care; foster care for pregnant and parenting teens.

★ 471 ★
**Christian Homes for Children**
275 State St.
Hackensack, NJ 07601
Phone: (201) 342-4235
Fax: (201) 342-0246

**Branch address:**
P.O. Box 357, Sparta, NJ 07871
Phone: (201) 579-7596

**Contact:** Adoption intake.

**Date established:** 1988.

**Description:** Non-profit, private agency licensed by the Dept. of Human Services, Division of Youth and Family Services in NJ.

**Area served:** Residents of New Jersey and New York.

**Requirements:** Christian couples married at least 2 yrs. who are in good health, who are childless or who have one child adopted through Christian Homes for Children, and who are age appropriate to the child they are requesting to adopt. Single applicants may be considered.

**Fees:**
Sliding fee scale ranging from minimum of $2000 to maximum of $8000.
First placement - 10% of family's gross annual income.
second placement - 8% of gross annual income.
intercountry Adoption Studies
home study without supervision: $750.
home study with supervision: $1500.
home study for immigration visa - $750.

**Number of children placed last year:** 5.

**Description of children:** Infants, children with special needs and older children.

**Adoption procedure:**
1) Return completed preliminary application and statement of faith;
2) attend pre-adoptive group meeting;
3) submit formal application;
4) complete home study;
5) if approved, wait for placement;
6) placement.

**Average length of time between application and start of home study:** 6-12 mos.

**Average length of time to complete home study:** 6-9 mos.

**Number of interviews:** 3 or more.

**Home study description:** Assessment of medical reports on all family members; letters of reference from employers, personal acquaintances, a neighbor, pastor; financial and education forms; copies of birth certificates, marriage license and armed forces papers (if applicable); fingerprint criminal history investigation; physical description of applicants; motivation and attitude toward adoption; interests; hobbies; strengths, weaknesses, parental models, childrearing practices and discussion of corporal punishment; marital relationship; attitude of other family members toward adoption; each applicant's family life history; description of type of child adoptive applicants are willing to accept; income and insurance coverage and child care arrangements for working parents.

**Average wait for a child after approval of a home study:** 24 or more mos.

**Foster care:** Temporary and occasionally long-term.

★ 472 ★
**Family and Children's Services**
40 North Ave.
Elizabeth, NJ 07207
Phone: (908) 352-7474

**Mailing address:**
 P.O. Box 314, Elizabeth, NJ 07207

**Contact:** Adoption Department.

**Date established:** 1893.

**Description:** Private, non-profit United Way, FSA counseling and outpatient mental health center licensed to place children by the New Jersey Division of Youth and Family Services.

**Area served:** Residents of New Jersey.

**Requirements:** Open.

**Fees:** Application: $60. Home study: $600. Agency placement: $9000. Fee for service for identified adoption: $70/session.

**Number of children placed last year:** 1 agency placement and 35 facilitations of identified adoptions.

**Description of children:** Infants.

**Adoption procedure:** 1) Telephone inquiry and intake: 2) information packet sent; 3) application; 4) interview; 5) home study; 6) source identification; 7) placement; 8) post-placement supervision.

**Average length of time between application and start of home study:** Less than 1 mo.

**Average length of time to complete home study:** 6 wks.

**Number of interviews:** Minimum of 3.

**Home study description:** Educational and assessment process which is enhanced by the Center's availability of counseling services and which meets the criteria of the New Jersey Division of Youth and Family Services.

**Average wait for a child after approval of a home study:** In most cases birth family identification is done by the adopting family.

**Foster care:** Pre-adoptive.

★ 473 ★
**Golden Cradle Adoption Services, Inc.**
1101 N. Kings Hwy., Ste. G-102
Cherry Hill, NJ 08034
Phone: (609) 667-BABY
(800) 327-2229
Fax: (609) 667-KIDS

**Contact:** MaryAnne Giello, MSS, LSW, Executive Director.
**Date established:** 1983.

**Description:** Private, non-profit, non-sectarian child welfare agency licensed by the State of New Jersey.

**Area served:** Residents of New Jersey and the mid-Atlantic region.

**Requirements:** Couples who are married at least 2 yrs. and are at least 25 yrs. old and in good physical and mental health with a normal life expectancy, with diagnosed infertility.

**Fees:** $20,500 for traditional infant adoption; sliding scale fee for medically needy and minority placement.

**Number of children placed last year:** 56.

**Description of children:** Primarily healthy, white infants; some special needs and healthy minority infants.

**Adoption procedure:**
 1) Initial inquiry and screening;
 2) submit completed application;
 3) preliminary selection of applicants;
 4) complete standardized psychological personality profile evaluation;
 5) if accepted, applicants attend 3 educational meetings;
 6) secure home study;
 7) in person meeting with social worker;
 8) Golden Cradle reviews home study;
 9) if approved, wait for placement;
10) placement;
10) 6.5 mos. post-placement supervision;
11) finalization.

**Average length of time between application and start of home study:** 1-6 mos.

**Average length of time to complete home study:** 3-6 mos.

**Number of interviews:** 3 group seminars and 1 individual.

**Home study description:** Required documents and verifications include: marriage license; divorce decree(s), if applicable; New Jersey state and Federal fingerprinting; verification of income; insurance coverage; physician's medical reports; child's medical reports, if applicable; 5-6 references, autobiographies, etc. All this documentation is also noted in the home study evaluation report. Areas of importance covered in the home study include: family background, marital relationship, employment and residence history, motivation for adoption, infertility history, plans for child care and guardianship when child arrives, type of child preferred.

**Average wait for a child after approval of a home study:** Varies, 6-24 mos.

**Foster care:** Temporary.

★ 474 ★
**Growing Families, Inc.**
178 South St.
Freehold, NJ 07728
Phone: (908) 431-4330

**Contact:** Rose M. Averbach, ACSW, Executive Director.

**Date established:** 1989.

**Description:** Private, non-profit corporation licensed to place children by the New Jersey Department of Human Services.

**Area served:** Residents of the US.

**Requirements:** Applicants must be 27 yrs. or older, financially solvent, single, or if married, at least 3 yrs.

**Fees:** Application: $150 (non-refundable); home study: $600. Domestic adoptions: identified: $2500 (within NJ); agency enhanced: $2800; portfolios: $250; traditional: $7000. International adoptions: program fee: $2000 -$4000; Brazil: $12,000; Chile: $4000; China: $10,000; Colombia: $7500; Guatemala: $13,500; Honduras: $10,000 plus foster care; Paraguay: $12,000 plus foster care.

**Number of children placed last year:** 35.

**Description of children:** U.S. infants and foreign-born children.

**Adoption procedure:** 1) Inquiry; 2) selection of program; 3) application; 4) home study; 5) dossier or profile compilation; 6) dossier referral or birth parent search; 7) child match or birth parent selection; 8) placement.

**Average length of time between application and start of home study:** Less than 1 mo.

**Average length of time to complete home study:** 8 wks.

**Number of interviews:** 3.

**Home study description:** Assessment which includes the collection of birth and marriage records, divorce decrees, if any, proof of income, photographs of adoptive applicants, employment records, police, FBI and state records checks and which addresses such topics as preparedness to adopt and the type of child desired.

**Average wait for a child after approval of a home study:** Time indicated is for child assignment: Brazil: 1 - 2 mos.; Chile: 6 mos.; China: 3 mos.; Colombia: 2 mos.; Guatemala: 1 - 2 mos.; Paraguay: 3 mos.

**Foster care:** Cradle care.


★ 475 ★
**Homestudies, Inc.**
1182 Teaneck Rd.
Teaneck, NJ 07666
Phone: (201) 833-9030

**Contact:** Marie Shukaitis, Executive Director.

**Date established:** 1982.

**Description:** Private, not-for-profit child placing agency licensed by the New Jersey Department of Human Services providing home study and post-placement services as well as placements from Romania and Russia.

**Area served:** Full service: residents of New Jersey; placements: all U.S. residents.

**Requirements:** Applicants must be age appropriate to the child requested, have medical certification of good health and demonstrate an ability to manage their own finances.

**Fees:** Home study: $700; post-placement report: $200.

**Number of children placed last year:** 23.

**Description of children:** Primarily infants, both U.S. and foreign-born.

**Adoption procedure:** 1) Application; 2) home study; 3) seminar; 4) forward dossier; 5) child assignment; 6) placement; 7) post-placement supervision; 8) finalization.

**Average length of time between application and start of home study:** 1 - 2 wks.

**Average length of time to complete home study:** 2 mos.

**Number of interviews:** Minimum of 3.

**Home study description:** Assessment which includes physical descriptions of applicants, their home and community, medical and financial summaries, social histories and which covers such topics as attitudes toward and reasons for adoption, child rearing principles and the type of child desired.

**Average wait for a child after approval of a home study:** 1 - 6 mos.

**Foster care:** None.


★ 476 ★
**Jewish Family And Children's Services**
**Jewish Family Services of Monmouth County**
705 Summerfield Ave.
Asbury Park, NJ 07712
Phone: (908) 774-6886
(908) 536-0050

**Branch address:**
23 Kilmer Dr., Bldg. 3, Morganville, NJ 07751

**Contact:** Roberta Taffer, Coordinator of Adoption Program.

**Date established:** 1993.

**Description:** Private, non-profit multi-service agency licensed by the New Jersey Department of Human Services to conduct home studies and post-placement supervisions.

**Area served:** Residents of Monmouth County, NJ.

**Requirements:** Applicants between the ages of 21 and 47 yrs. who are in good health.

**Fees:** $125/hr.

**Average length of time between application and start of home study:** Less than 1 mo.

**Average length of time to complete home study:** 2 - 3 mos.

**Number of interviews:** 5.

**Home study description:** Assessment which includes identifying information and fingerprinting and addresses such topics as family background, type of childhood, relationship with parents, siblings, education, employment history, interests and hobbies, marital and family relationships including communication and support systems, experience with children, feelings about birth parents and motivation to adopt.

**Average wait for a child after approval of a home study:** Agency does not make placements.

**Foster care:** None.


★ 477 ★
**Jewish Family And Children's Services of Southern New Jersey**
100 Park Blvd. N.
Cherry Hill, NJ 08002
Phone: (609) 662-8611

**Contact:** Marlene Winn, Adoption Specialist.

**Date established:** 1944.

**Description:** Private, non-profit agency licensed by the Department of Human Services and accredited by the Council on Accreditation for Services for Families and Children offering educational and preparatory services for prospective adoptive families, but not placements.

**Area served:** Residents of Burlington, Camden and Gloucester counties of Southern New Jersey.

**Requirements:** Couples married at least 3 yrs. who are at least 21 yrs. old and a minimum of 10 yrs. and a maximum of 47 yrs. older than the child to be adopted.

**Fees:** Application: $50; home study: $700; FBI and N.J. fingerprinting: $50/adult.

**Number of children placed last year:** Referrals only.

**Adoption procedure:** 1) Telephone inquiry; 2) 4 session support group; 3) placement agency referral; 4) home study. After a child has been placed in the adoptive home, JFS will conduct the post-placement supervision.

**Average length of time between application and start of home study:** Less than 1 mo.

**Average length of time to complete home study:** 3 mos.

**Number of interviews:** 3 -5.

**Home study description:** The goal of the assessment is to access the suitability and readiness of the applicant(s) to parent a child. Information is obtained on family background and relationships, support systems and how disagreements are handled, motivation and attitudes towards adoption, anticipated methods of discipline, the type of child desired, cross-cultural challenges, if applicable, maturity, sensitivity, emotional stability and ability to cope with problems.

**Average wait for a child after approval of a home study:** Agency does not make placements.

**Foster care:** None.

★ **478** ★

**Jewish Family Service**
**Adoption Resource Center**
517 Ryders Ln.
East Brunswick, NJ 08816
Phone: (908) 257-4100

**Branch address:**
Medical Arts Bldg., Concordia Shopping Center, Cranbury, NJ 08512
Phone: (609) 395-7979

**Contact:** Karen Rispoli, Coordinator of Adoption Services.

**Date established:** 1980.

**Description:** Private, non-profit, social service and child placement agency licensed by the New Jersey Department of Human Services.

**Area served:** Residents of southern Middlesex County.

**Requirements:** None.

**Fees:** Application: $65; home study: $600; counseling: $80/session; support groups: $15/session; preliminary ACI: $50; final ACI: $300.

**Number of children placed last year:** Agency does not make placements.

**Adoption procedure:** 1) Adoption consultation; 2) file application; 3) compilation of documents; 4) homestudy; 5) infant care classes; 6) preliminary Adoption Complaint Investigation; 7) final AdoptionComplaint Investigation; 8) adoptive parent support group; 9) placement; 0) post-placementsupervision; 11) finalization.

**Average length of time between application and start of home study:** Less than 1 mo.

**Average length of time to complete home study:** 3 - 4 wks.

**Number of interviews:** 3.

**Home study description:** Educational and preparatory process which examines applicant(s) ability to provide a loving home. Study includes medical and financial reports, child care plans and addresses such topics as social history, marital relationship, adoption expectations, role of parents and expectations of a child.

**Average wait for a child after approval of a home study:** Depends on placing agency.

**Foster care:** None.

**Jewish Family Service of Central New Jersey**
655 Westfield Ave.
Elizabeth, NJ 07208
Phone: (908) 352-8375

**Branch address:**
346 South Ave., Fanwood, NJ 07023
Phone: (908) 889-4848

**Contact:** Adoption Coordinator.

**Date established:** 1912.

**Description:** Private, non-profit beneficiary agency of the Jewish Federation of Central New Jersey and the United Ways of Eastern Union County, Cranford, Scotch Plains, Westfield, Plainfield, North Plainfield and Fanwood and licensed by the New Jersey Department of Human Services.

**Area served:** Residents of Union County and Somerset County north of Hwy. 78.

**Requirements:** Adoptive applicants shall be at least 18 yrs. old and a minimum of 10 yrs. older than the child being adopted; have income indicative of the ability to manage finances and health indicative of the ability to parent.

**Fees:** Home study: $300; post-placement services: $300.

**Number of children placed last year:** Agency does not offer placement services.

**Adoption procedure:** The Jewish Family Service adoption program offers counseling, home studies, andpost-placement supervision.

**Average length of time between application and start of home study:** Less than 1 mo.

**Average length of time to complete home study:** Approx. 3 mo.

**Number of interviews:** 4.

**Home study description:** Assessment of capacity and readiness for parenthood which consists of a series of interviews and comprises a collaborative effort to provide an accurate appraisal of the applicant(s)' parenting skills. The study includes identifying information, legal, financial, reference and health reports, fingerprint documentation and addresses such topics as marital status, emotional health and maturity, experience and plans for parenting, extended family's attitude toward adoption, proposed methods of discipline and type of child desired.

**Average wait for a child after approval of a home study:** Agency does not make placements.

**Foster care:** None.

**Lutheran Social Ministries of New Jersey**
120 Rte. 156
Yardville, NJ 08620
Phone: (609) 585-0303
(800) 458-0651
Fax: (609) 585-0511

**Contact:** Rev. Joyce A. Seip, Director, Family and Children's Services.

**Date established:** 1904.

**Description:** Non-profit, private agency licensed in the State of New Jersey.

**Area served:** Residents of New Jersey.

**Requirements:** Applicants should generally be no more than 40 yrs. older than the child placed and in reasonably good health.

**Fees:** $2000 - $12,500 depending upon type of child and income.

**Number of children placed last year:** 35.

**Description of children:** Primarily black and biracial children.

**Adoption procedure:** Call for agency procedures.

**Average length of time between application and start of home study:** 1-6 mos.

**Average length of time to complete home study:** 2 mos.

**Number of interviews:** 3.

**Home study description:** Agency follows requirements prescribed by the State of New Jersey.

**Average wait for a child after approval of a home study:** 12-24 mos.

**Foster care:** Temporary.

★ 481 ★
**Spaulding for Children**
36 Prospect St.
Westfield, NJ 07090
Phone: (908) 233-2282
Fax: (908) 233-5654

**Branch address:**
60 Evergreen Ave., East Orange, NJ 07017
Phone: (201) 678-4975

707 Market St., Camden, NJ 08102
Phone: (609) 964-3838

**Contact:** Earnestine Simpson-Stevenson, Executive Director.

**Date established:** 1971.

**Description:** Private, non-profit specialized adoption agency.

**Area served:** Residents of New Jersey.

**Requirements:** Adults of legal age who are interested in considering the adoption of a waiting child.

**Fees:** None.

**Number of children placed last year:** 22.

**Description of children:** Adolescents, sibling groups, school age black children and children of all ages and races with significant mental or medical disabilities.

**Adoption procedure:** Process includes an orientation meeting and an adoption course prior to filing an application.

**Average length of time between application and start of home study:** 1 mo. or less.

**Average length of time to complete home study:** 2 mos.

**Number of interviews:** 3 or more.

**Home study description:** Mutual collaboration between agency and family to determine if the family can meet the challenges of adopting a waiting child.

**Average wait for a child after approval of a home study:** 1 mo. or less.

**Foster care:** None.

# NEW MEXICO

## STATUTES

★ 482 ★
**Independent placement by intermediary?** Illegal.

**Independent placement by birth parents?** Permitted.

**Subsidies provided?** Medical, legal and maintenance.

**Adoption cost defined by law?** Yes.

**Insurance for infertility?:** No.

**Home study required by state?** Required before placement.

**Prospective adoptive parent advertise for a child?** Permitted.

**Surrogacy laws?** Permitted.

**Residents access agencies of other states or countries?** Permitted.

**Requires judicial termination of birth parents' rights?** Yes before a District Court judge.

**Time given to a birthmother to revoke her consent:** None.

**Court handling adoptions?** District Court.

**Adoption of Native Children:** Tribe and/or state.

**Adoption records sealed?** Yes and can only be opened with a court order by adoptees, 18 yrs. and older.

**Photo-listing book available?** Participates in the Rocky Mountain Adoption Exchange photo-listing.

## PUBLIC AGENCIES

★ 483 ★
**Children, Youth and Families Dept. (New Mexico)**
**Social Services Division**
P.O. Drawer 5160
Santa Fe, NM 87502-5160
Phone: (505) 827-8456
1-800-432-2075
Fax: (505) 827-8480

**Contact:** Jan P. Stanley, Supervisor, Central Adoptions.

**Description:** Non-profit, state agency.

**Area served:** Residents of the State of New Mexico.

**Requirements:** Applicants should be age appropriate to the child placed; should have stable employment or sufficient resources to provide for a child and provide for his/her future. Applicants may be single or married; if married, applicant couples must be legally married for at least 2 yrs. or have cohabited for at least 2 yrs. prior to the marriage.

**Fees:** Legal fees for finalization although these may be subsidized by the Human Services Department for special needs children. Fingerprinting of applicant(s): $24.

**Number of children placed last year:** 200.

**Description of children:** Children over the age of 8, members of ethnic and racial minority groups, members of sibling groups, and children with moderate to severe psychological, developmental or physical disabilities.

**Adoption procedure:**
1) Initial telephone inquiry;
2) Central Adoption Unit sends "Los Ninos," the New Mexico Adoption Exchange's brochure featuring special needs children and a list of New Mexico licensed child placement agencies;
3) adoption social worker contacts applicant(s) within 10 working days;
4) attend orientation-intake meeting in applicant(s)' area;
5) participate in group educational-training session;
6) complete application.

**Average length of time between application and start of home study:** 1-6 mos.

**Average length of time to complete home study:** 4 mos.

**Number of interviews:** 2-3 or more.

**Home study description:** An evaluation which includes but is not limited to reference questionnaire checks, FBI/police clearances, description of home and neighborhood and current family relationships.

**Average wait for a child after approval of a home study:** Varies.

**Foster care:** Emergency, temporary, special needs and pre-adoptive.

# PRIVATE AGENCIES

## ★ 484 ★
**Catholic Social Services of Santa Fe, Inc.**
138 Park Ave.
Santa Fe, NM 87501-1833
Phone: (505) 982-0441

**Contact:** Pamela Schachel, LMSW, LPCC/Supervisor or Allison Gregory, Adoption Worker, LPC.

**Date established:** 1947.

**Description:** Non-profit social service agency licensed in the State of New Mexico.

**Area served:** Residents of Albuquerque, Espanola, Gallup, Grants, Las Cruces, Las Vegas, Los Alamos, Silver City and Taos, New Mexico.

**Requirements:** Christian adults who are no older than 40 yrs., in good health, and who have sufficient income to provide for a family.

**Fees:**
$100 application fee;
$900 pre-placement study;
sliding fee scale at time of placement.

**Number of children placed last year:** 8.

**Description of children:** U.S. infants.

**Adoption procedure:**
1) Telephone for appointment;
2) initial interview;
3) couple interviews;
4) individual interview;
5) home visit;
6) if approved, placement;
7) post-placement services; and
8) finalization.

**Average length of time between application and start of home study:** 1-6 mos.

**Average length of time to complete home study:** 6 mos.

**Number of interviews:** 4 or more.

**Home study description:** Assessment of marital relationship, health and financial ability to parent.

**Average wait for a child after approval of a home study:** 24 or more mos.

**Foster care:** Temporary.

## ★ 485 ★
**Chaparral Maternity and Adoption Services**
1503 University Blvd., NE
Albuquerque, NM 87102
Phone: (505) 243-2586
Fax: (505) 243-0446

**Contact:** Rebecca L. Holland.

**Date established:** 1969.

**Description:** Private, not-for-profit maternity and adoption services agency.

**Area served:** Residents of the State of New Mexico.

**Requirements:** Couples married at least 3 yrs. who are of childbearing age, who have adequate income to support another family member and who are in good health.

**Fees:**
Application/home study: $850;
placement: $7800.

**Number of children placed last year:** 20.

**Description of children:** Infants in reasonably good health.

**Adoption procedure:**
1) Submit application;
2) if approved, complete home study;
3) if approved, admission to waiting list;
4) placement;
5) post-placement follow-up;
6) finalization.

**Average length of time between application and start of home study:** 1-6 mos.

**Average length of time to complete home study:** 3-6 mos.

**Number of interviews:** One for each spouse and one joint interview.

**Home study description:** Evaluation of autobiographies, vital records verification, income tax return, recommendation of references, FBI checks, medical reports, home visit and interviews.

**Average wait for a child after approval of a home study:** 24 or more mos.

**Foster care:** Temporary.

## ★ 486 ★
**Child-Rite, Inc.**
2008 Rosina
Santa Fe, NM 87505
Phone: (505) 988-5177

**Branch address:**
P.O. Box 1448, Taos, NM 87571

120 Madeira, N.E., Albuquerque, NM 87108

**Contact:** Nancy Abell.

**Date established:** 1989.

**Description:** Private, non-profit child placing agency licensed by the New Mexico Department of Children, Youth and Families.

**Area served:** Residents of New Mexico.

**Requirements:** Open.

**Fees:** None.

**Number of children placed last year:** 10.

**Description of children:** Children with special needs.

**Adoption procedure:** 1) Pre-service training; 2) home study; 3) child match; 4) placement; 5) post-placement supervision; 6) finalization.

**Average length of time between application and start of home study:** 1 - 6 mos.

**Average length of time to complete home study:** 2 mos.

**Number of interviews:** 4.

**Home study description:** Assessment which addresses such topics as parenting styles, strengths and needs and the type of child sought.

**Average wait for a child after approval of a home study:** 12 - 24 mos.

**Foster care:** None.

★487★
**Christian Child Placement Service**
HC 69, Box 48
Portales, NM 88130
Phone: (505) 356-4232

**Branch address:**
1441 E. Mesa, Las Cruces, NM 87801
Phone: (505) 522-8103

**Contact:** Charles Anderson.

**Date established:** 1979.

**Description:** Non-profit private agency licensed in the State of New Mexico.

**Area served:** Residents of New Mexico and west Texas.

**Requirements:** Christian couples married at least 2 yrs. who have the recommendation of their local minister. Preference shown to members of the Church of Christ.

**Fees:** Sliding scale based on income; from $6000 to $7200.

**Number of children placed last year:** 5.

**Description of children:** Infants.

**Adoption procedure:**
1) Submit application with reference and health checks;
2) attend adoptive couples' group seminar;
3) complete home study;
4) if approved, admission to waiting list for placement;
5) placement;
6) file petition;
7) finalization.

**Average length of time between application and start of home study:** 6-12 mos.

**Average length of time to complete home study:** 1-3 mos.

**Number of interviews:** Seminar and 1 home visit.

**Home study description:** Evaluation of martial history and quality of present marriage, finances and health, personal backgrounds and motivation to adopt.

**Average wait for a child after approval of a home study:** 24 or more mos.

**Foster care:** Temporary.

★488★
**Families for Children**
**A Division of New Mexico Boys Ranch**
6209 Hendrix Rd. N.E.
Albuquerque, NM 87110
Phone: (505) 881-4200
Fax: (505) 888-1595

**Contact:** Ron Gloetzner, CSW, MPA, Program Director.

**Date established:** 1982.

**Description:** Non-profit, private agency licensed by the State of New Mexico.

**Area served:** Residents of New Mexico.

**Requirements:**
Age: For infant adoption, applicants must be at least 22 and no more than 45; age requirement is flexible for older child adoption.
Health: For infant adoption, infertility is required. Applicants must be in reasonably good health. Applicants with health problems or handicaps are given individual consideration.
Religion: Applicants must be practicing members of a mainstream Protestant or Catholic Christian church.
Financial staus: Applicants must demonstrate financial stability.

Marital status: Preference is given to married couples who have been married at least 3 yrs. Single parents are considered if they have an adequate support system.

**Fees:** $5000-$5500 and includes $300 application fee (non-refundable); home study $500; placement and post-placement $4800 and up for newborns, $1000-$2500 for children over 2 yrs.

**Number of children placed last year:** 3.

**Description of children:** 3 infants.

**Adoption procedure:**
1) Applicants must attend a 3 hr. adoption and orientation seminar;
2) submit preliminary application;
3) file final application;
4) complete home study;
5) attend 16 hr. adoptive parent training seminar;
6) if approved, placement;
7) post-placement supervision; and
8) finalization.

**Average length of time between application and start of home study:** 1-6 mos.

**Average length of time to complete home study:** 3-6 mos.

**Number of interviews:** 2-6.

**Home study description:** During the process of home study the following are evaluated: applicants' temperaments, motivation to adopt, background, religious faith, marriage, crisis management styles, parenting skills, and type of child desired. References are checked and verified.

**Average wait for a child after approval of a home study:** 12-24 mos.

**Foster care:** Temporary and long-term.

★489★
**La Familia Placement Services, Inc.**
707 Broadway, NE, Ste. 103
Albuquerque, NM 87102
Phone: (505) 292-3678
Fax: (505) 766-9157

**Contact:** Beverly Nomberg, ACSW.

**Date established:** 1987.

**Description:** Non-profit, private agency licensed in the State of New Mexico.

**Area served:** Residents of the State of New Mexico and interstate adoption.

**Requirements:** Each applicant is given individual consideration.

**Fees:**
Application: $100;
all fees on a sliding scale based on income; the range is $50-$200/hr. All work is billed at an hourly rate. A home study takes approximately 15 hrs. Placement fee: $2000.

**Number of children placed last year:** 20.

**Description of children:** Infants, one child with special needs.

**Adoption procedure:**
1) File application;
2) attend intake interview;
3) complete home study;
4) child search;
5) placement;
6) post-placement;
7) investigation.

**Average length of time between application and start of home study:** 1-6 mos.

**Average length of time to complete home study:** 3 mos.

**Number of interviews:** Approx. 4 and 1 home visit.

**Home study description:** Extensive background investigation including a state and federal criminal investigation and compilation of information on marital relationship or lifestyle in order to evaluate stability.

**Average wait for a child after approval of a home study:** 6-12 mos.

**Foster care:** Infant and treatment foster care.

★ 490 ★
**Rainbow House International**
19676 Hwy. 85
Belen, NM 87002
Phone: (505) 865-5550

**Branch address:**
547 Humboldt, Denver, CO 80218
Phone: (303) 830-2108

**Contact:** Intake worker.

**Date established:** 1984.

**Description:** Private, non-profit child placing agency licensed by the Colorado Department of Social Services and the New Mexico Department of Children, Youth and Families.

**Area served:** Residents of Colorado and New Mexico for full service and will network with agencies in other states.

**Requirements:** Varies with country selected. Applicants should not be more than 45 yrs. older than child placed.

**Fees:** Application: $150; home study: $800/New Mexico and $1500/Colorado; post-placement supervision: $1000; country fees are additional.

**Number of children placed last year:** 100.

**Description of children:** Foreign born children from infancy to 11 yrs. and U.S. children with special needs.

**Adoption procedure:** 1) Pre-application; 2) formal application; 3) orientation; 4) *Adoption Issues* classes; 5) home study; 6) dossier preparation; 7) INS processing and clearance; 8) child match; 9) placement; 10 ) post-placement supervision; 11) finalization.

**Average length of time between application and start of home study:** Less than 1 mo.

**Average length of time to complete home study:** 2 mos. or less.

**Number of interviews:** Minimum of 3.

**Home study description:** Thorough assessment which conforms to the guidelines of the Colorado Department of Social Services and the New Mexico Department of Children, Youth and Families.

**Average wait for a child after approval of a home study:** 6 - 12 mos.

**Foster care:** None.

★ 491 ★
**Triad Adoption and Counseling Services, Inc.**
2811 Indian School Rd. NE
Albuquerque, NM 87106
Phone: (505) 266-0456
Fax: (505) 255-6924

**Contact:** Vonda C. Cheshire, Administrative Director.

**Date established:** 1986.

**Description:** Non-profit private agency licensed by the New Mexico Dept. of Human Services.

**Area served:** Primarily resident of New Mexico for domestic adoptions.

**Requirements:** Applicants should be in the childbearing age range and have adequate health and life expectancy to see a child to maturity.

**Fees:**
Orientation: $65;
home study: $950;
placement fee: $7500.

**Number of children placed last year:** 30.

**Description of children:** Primarily Hispanic and Anglo infants, some Hispanic/Anglo and Anglo or Hispanic/black, and some black.

**Adoption procedure:**
1) Attend orientation/educational meeting;
2) file application;
3) complete home study;
4) applicants prepare autobiographical album using only first names;
5) albums presented to birthparents;
6) child match and birthparents relinquish parental rights;
7) placement;
8) post-placement supervision;
9) adoption decree finalizes adoption.

**Average length of time between application and start of home study:** Varies depending on orientation class availability.

**Average length of time to complete home study:** 4 wks.

**Number of interviews:** 4-6. If out-of-state, adoptive family must provide home study and Triad will prepare New Mexico addendum (1-2 interviews).

**Home study description:** Assessment of readiness to parent, health, financial and marital stability, attitudes toward open adoption and knowledge of child development.

**Average wait for a child after approval of a home study:** 1-24 mos. (birthparents do the matching; to date no families have waited too far past 24 mos.).

**Foster care:** Temporary.

# NEW YORK

## STATUTES

★ 492 ★

**Independent placement by intermediary?** Illegal.

**Independent placement by birth parents?** Permitted.

**Subsidies provided?** Maintenance, medical and non-recurring adoption expenses.

**Adoption cost defined by law?** Specific dollar amounts are not set forth, but costs must be reasonable and actual.

**Insurance for infertility?:** Unknown.

**Home study required by state?** Required before placement and a pre-finalization study is required before finalization.

**Prospective adoptive parent advertise for a child?** Not addressed in law.

**Surrogacy laws?** Surrogate motherhood is legal as long as no fee for being a surrogate is charged or paid. Surrogacy contracts are void and unenforceable.

**Residents access agencies of other states or countries?** Permitted.

**Requires judicial termination of birth parents' rights?** Birth parents may sign a *consent to adopt*.

**Time given to a birthmother to revoke her consent:** 45 days after execution unless signed in the presence of the court when they are irrevocable.

**Court handling adoptions?** Family Court or Surrogate's Court.

**Adoption of Native Children:** ICWA is federal law. State law standards which do not conflict apply otherwise.

**Adoption records sealed?** Yes, but adoptees over the age of 18 yrs. may access non-identifying information through the State Adoption Information Exchange and may access identifying information if both the birth parent and the adoptee are registered.

**Photo-listing book available?** *Blue Book* and *Family Album*.


# PUBLIC AGENCIES

### ★ 493 ★
**Albany County Department of Social Services**
40 Howard St.
Albany, NY 12207
Phone: (518) 447-7515

**Contact:** Social worker.

**Description:** Public, county agency mandated to place children by the New York State Department of Social Services.

**Area served:** Residents of Albany County.

**Requirements:** Adults, 18 yrs. and older.

**Fees:** None.

**Number of children placed last year:** 48.

**Description of children:** School age children, children with special needs, sibling groups.

**Adoption procedure:**
 1) Telephone intake;
 2) return completed application;
 3) attend orientation meeting;
 4) MAPP training;
 5) complete home study;
 6) if approved, wait for placement;
 7) pre-placement visitation process;
 8) placement;
 9) 6 or more mos. post-placement supervision;
10) finalization.

**Average length of time between application and start of home study:** MAPP sessions are scheduled semi-annually.

**Average length of time to complete home study:** 6 mos.

**Number of interviews:** Minimum of 2 self-assessments.

**Home study description:** The home study includes medical and financial reports, auotbiographies, any children in the home, description of home, community resources, flexibility, tenacity and commitment to a child with a "past," recommendation of references, and child abuse registry clearances. MAPP Training is an integral part of the process and places more responsibility for decision making on the applicant(s).

**Average wait for a child after approval of a home study:** Dependent upon the range of special needs the applicants are willing to accept.

**Foster care:** Legal risk, short and long-term.


### ★ 494 ★
**Chautauqua County Department of Social Services**
Hall R. Clothier Bldg.
Mayville, NY 14757
Phone: (716) 661-8040

**Branch address:**
 South County Office Bldg., 110 E. 4th St., Jamestown, NY 14701

 Liberty Square Office Bldg., 335 Central Ave., Dunkirk, NY 14048
 Phone: (716) 366-8800

**Contact:** Charlotte Johnson, Supervisor B.

**Description:** County, public agency licensed through the New York State Department of Social Services.

**Area served:** Residents of Chautauqua County.

**Requirements:** Open.

**Fees:** None.

**Number of children placed last year:** 4.

**Description of children:** Children with special needs - fost-adopt conversions.

**Adoption procedure:** 1) Child match through Blue Book, Cap Book, etc.; 2) initial interview; 3) ResourceFamily Training; 4) application; 5) background checks; 6)home study; 7) pre-placementvisitation; 8) placement; 9) post-placement supervision; 10) finalization.

**Average length of time between application and start of home study:** 12 - 24 mos.

**Average length of time to complete home study:** 6 mos.

**Number of interviews:** 2.

**Home study description:** Assessment which includes State Central Registry, Criminal and Family Court clearances, reference reports, verification of income, documentation of birth and marriage (if applicable) and which covers such topics as individual's history, physical and mental health, losses and separation, discipline, stability of marriage and relationships, type of child desired, proposed methods of parenting a handicapped or hard-to-place child.

**Average wait for a child after approval of a home study:** Special needs: 12 - 24 mos.; infants: 2 yrs. or more.

**Foster care:** Temporary, long-term, therapeutic, and permanent.


### ★ 495 ★
**Chemung County Department of Social Services**
425-447 Pennsylvania Ave.
Elmira, NY 14904
Phone: (607) 737-5410

**Contact:** Leone Burnham.

**Date established:** 1967.

**Description:** Non-profit public agency.

**Area served:** Residents of Chemung County.

**Requirements:** Pregnant or parenting persons and those wishing to adopt.

**Fees:** None.

**Number of children placed last year:** 28.

**Description of children:** All ages and levels of ability. No foreign adoptions.

**Adoption procedure:**
 1) Submit application;
 2) participate in adoptive parent training;
 3) complete adoption study;
 4) if approved, placement;
 5) trial period;
 6) finalization.

**Average length of time between application and start of home study:** Varies.

**Average length of time to complete home study:** 4 mos. to 1 yr.

**Number of interviews:** Minimum of 3.

**Home study description:** Wide-range evaluation which includes but is not limited to: background, references, autobiographies and police/child abuse registry reports.

**Average wait for a child after approval of a home study:** 24 or more mos.

**Foster care:** Temporary, long-term and permanent.

**★ 496 ★**
**Delaware County Department of Social Services**
111 Main St.
Delaware, NY 13753
Phone: (607) 746-2325

**Contact:** Deb Mueller or Jill Goodspeed.

**Description:** Public county agency.

**Area served:** Residents of Delaware County.

**Requirements:** Single or applicants married at least 1 yr. who are in good health and who have a stable income.

**Fees:** None.

**Number of children placed last year:** 12.

**Description of children:** Primarily special needs.

**Adoption procedure:** Call or write for details.

**Average length of time between application and start of home study:** 6-12 mos.

**Average length of time to complete home study:** 6 mos.

**Number of interviews:** 2 or more.

**Home study description:** Assessment of family's understanding of children, particularly those who have gone through a family disruption; desire to adopt; finances; and housing.

**Average wait for a child after approval of a home study:** 24 or more mos.

**Foster care:** Temporary and long-term.

**★ 497 ★**
**Dutchess County Department of Social Services**
60 Market St.
Poughkeepsie, NY 13601
Phone: (914) 431-5343
Fax: (914) 431-5400

**Contact:** Theresa Rosencrans, Adoption Supervisor.

**Description:** Non-profit, public agency.

**Area served:** Residents of Dutchess County.

**Requirements:** Applicants must demonstrate the ability to parent.

**Fees:** None.

**Number of children placed last year:** 34.

**Description of children:** Handicapped and waiting children.

**Adoption procedure:**
1) Make written or telephone inquiry;
2) submit application;
3) complete home study;
4) if approved, selection and meeting with child;
5) placement;
6) post-placement supervision;
7) finalization.

**Average length of time between application and start of home study:** 1-6 mos.

**Average length of time to complete home study:** 3-6 mos.

**Number of interviews:** Depends on the family.

**Home study description:** Group home studies consist of an orientation, home visit, assessment of health report(s), references and character.

**Average wait for a child after approval of a home study:** Varies.

**Foster care:** Emergency, temporary, long-term and permanent.

**★ 498 ★**
**Erie County Department of Social Services**
95 Franklin St.
Buffalo, NY 14202
Phone: (716) 858-8778

**Contact:** Adoption Unit.

**Description:** Public, county agency mandated to place children by the New York State Dept. of Social Services.

**Area served:** Residents of Erie County.

**Requirements:** Adults, 18 yrs. or older; if married, at least one year.

**Fees:** None.

**Number of children placed last year:** 100.

**Description of children:** Primarily children with special needs.

**Adoption procedure:**
1) Initial inquiry;
2) MAPP training;
3) submit application;
4) complete home study;
5) if approved, placement;
6) supervision of placement;
7) legal finalization.

**Average length of time between application and start of home study:** MAPP sessions are usually scheduled at least quarterly.

**Average length of time to complete home study:** 2-3 months.

**Number of interviews:** Minimum of 4.

**Home study description:** After completing MAPP training, adoptive applicants will be trained in the following 12 skills:
1) Knowledge of their own family;
2) effective communication;
3) knowledge of children:
4) building on strengths to meed family needs;
5) working in partnership;
6) becoming loss and attachment experts;
7) behavior management;
8) building connections and self-esteem;
9) building self-esteem;
10) assessing impact of adoption on own family;
11) insuring home health and safety;
12) making an informed decision.

**Average wait for a child after approval of a home study:** Depends on range of special needs family is willing to accept.

**Foster care:** Temporary and long-term.

**★ 499 ★**
**Essex County Department of Social Services**
Court St.
Elizabethtown, NY 12932
Phone: (518) 873-3424

**Contact:** Linda Jackson, Homefinder/Adoption Caseworker.

**Description:** County, public social service agency licensed to place children through the New York State Department of Social Services.

**Area served:** Residents of Essex County.

**Requirements:** Applicants must be at least 18 yrs. old, single, or if married, at least 1 yr.

**Fees:** None.

**Number of children placed last year:** 1.

**Description of children:** Child with special needs.

**Adoption procedure:** 1) Orientation; 2) pre-certification training; 3) individual interview; 4) application; 5)background checks; 6) home study; 7) Blue Book search and child match; 8) placement; 9) post-placement supervision; 10) finalization.

**Average length of time between application and start of home study:** 1 - 6 mos.

**Average length of time to complete home study:** 6 mos.

**Number of interviews:** 3.

**Home study description:** Assessment which covers child care experience, finances, education and training, health, references, employment history, family background, motivation to adopt and thoughts on methods of discipline, stability and capability.

**Average wait for a child after approval of a home study:** 6 - 24 mos.

**Foster care:** Emergency, short and long-term.

★ 500 ★

**Fulton County Department of Social Services**
4 Daisy Ln.
Box 549
Johnstown, NY 12095
Phone: (518) 762-0615
Fax: (518) 762-0080

**Contact:** Judy Van Heusen.

**Description:** Public agency.

**Area served:** Residents of Fulton County.

**Requirements:** Applicants must be 21 yrs. or older.

**Fees:** None.

**Number of children placed last year:** 5.

**Description of children:** Abused and/or neglected preschoolers who were placed in foster care and subsequently surrendered for adoption.

**Adoption procedure:**
1) Submit application;
2) participate in adoptive applicant orientation and training;
3) complete home study, reference, police and child abuse registry checks;
4) if approved, placement;
5) post-placement supervision;
6) finalization.

**Average length of time between application and start of home study:** 1-6 mos.

**Average length of time to complete home study:** Up to 3 mos.

**Number of interviews:** 4 home visits, 2 in-person interviews.

**Home study description:** Home study includes an evaluation of the home itself, autobiographies of applicants, applicants' child care experiences, employment history, finances, education, detailed references which describe applicant(s) as parents or parent substitutes, and the type of child with whom the applicant(s) would be most and least comfortable.

**Average wait for a child after approval of a home study:** 1-6 mos.

**Foster care:** Emergency and short-term. State of New York mandates that foster care shall not exceed 2 years. Foster placement is reviewed by Family Court after 12 months although a child may be reunited with his birth family much sooner.

★ 501 ★

**Hamilton County Department of Social Services**
725 White Birch Ln.
Indian Lake, NY 12842-0725
Phone: (518) 648-6131

**Mailing address:**
   P.O. Box 725, Indian Lake, NY 12842-0725

**Contact:** Arthur D. Haynes, Jr., Commissioner.

**Description:** County public agency mandated to place children by the New York State Department of Social Services.

**Area served:** Residents of Hamilton County.

**Requirements:** Applicants must be at least 18 yrs. old.

**Fees:** None.

**Number of children placed last year:** 0.

**Description of children:** N/A.

**Adoption procedure:** 1) Application; 2) home study; 3) background clearances; 4) child match; 5) pre-placement visitation; 6) placement; 7) post-placement supervision; 8) finalization.

**Average length of time between application and start of home study:** Unavailable.

**Average length of time to complete home study:** Less than 6 mos.

**Number of interviews:** 6.

**Home study description:** Assessment which includes background information, criminal and abuse registry clearances, motivation to adopt as well as any children in the home and follow the regulations proscribed by the New York State Department of Social Services.

**Average wait for a child after approval of a home study:** 2 yrs. or more.

**Foster care:** Emergency, short and long-term.

★ 502 ★

**Jefferson County Department of Social Services**
250 Arsenal St.
Watertown, NY 13601
Phone: (315) 782-9030

**Contact:** Adoption Caseworker.

**Description:** County, public agency mandated to place children by the New York State Department of Social Services.

**Area served:** Residents of Jefferson County.

**Requirements:** Applicants must be at least 21 yrs. old with sufficient income to support themselves.

**Fees:** None.

**Number of children placed last year:** 28.

**Description of children:** Unavailable.

**Adoption procedure:** 1) Application; 2) home study; 3) medicals and background clearances; 4) preparatory classes; 5) licensure; 6) child match; 7) placement; 8) post-placement supervision; 9) finalization.

**Average length of time between application and start of home study:** Less than 1 mo.

**Average length of time to complete home study:** 4 - 6 mos.

**Number of interviews:** Unavailable.

**Home study description:** Assessment which includes background information, condition and safety of the home, extended family and community, personal interests, children already in the home, childrearing style and motivation to adopt.

**Average wait for a child after approval of a home study:** African American placements: 1 - 7 mos.; Caucasian placements: 2 yrs. or more.

**Foster care:** Temporary, long-term and permanent.

## ★ 503 ★
**New York City Department of Social Services**
**Division of Adoption/Foster Care Services/Home Assessment Services/Centralized Services**
2 Lafayette St., 11th Fl.
New York, NY 10007
Phone: (212) 433-7000
Fax: (212) 385-5555

**Contact:** Intake worker.

**Description:** Public, county agency.

**Area served:** Residents of the 5 boroughs of New York City and those within a 50 mile radius of New York City.

**Requirements:** Adults, 18 yrs. or older, who are either legally single, legally married, or legally separated and who are in good health with no communicable diseases.

**Fees:** Adoptive parent is responsible for own attorney's fee for finalization.

**Number of children placed last year:** Unavailable.

**Description of children:** Children with special needs, older children, and sibling groups.

**Adoption procedure:**
1) Submit application;
2) attend orientation meeting;
3) applicants for healthy, white infants admitted to waiting list; applicants for waiting children undergo home study;
4) if approved, wait for placement, child search and match;
5) placement;
6) post-placement supervision;
7) finalization.

**Average length of time between application and start of home study:** 1-6 mos.

**Average length of time to complete home study:** 4 mos.

**Number of interviews:** Minimum of 4.

**Home study description:** Assessment which includes but is not limited to parenting skills, socialization, fertility problems, if any, financial stability, marital history and family background.

**Average wait for a child after approval of a home study:** 12-24 mos.

**Foster care:** Emergency, short and long-term, therapeutic and pre-adoptive.

## ★ 504 ★
**Niagara County Department of Social Services**
100 Davison St.
Lockport, NY 14094
Phone: (716) 439-7707

**Mailing address:**
P.O. Box 506, Lockport, NY 14094

**Branch address:**
301 Tenth St., Niagara Falls, NY 14302

**Contact:** Beverly Ziemendorf.

**Description:** County, public agency mandated to place children by the New York Department of Social Services.

**Area served:** Residents of Niagara County.

**Requirements:** None.

**Fees:** None.

**Number of children placed last year:** 39.

**Description of children:** Infants, toddlers and youths, some minorities and some with special needs.

**Adoption procedure:** 1) Initial intake; 2) interview; 3) background checks and clearances; 4) home study including medicals and references; 5) pre-service training; 6) review of home study; 7) placement.

**Average length of time between application and start of home study:** 6 - 12 mos.

**Average length of time to complete home study:** 6 mos.

**Number of interviews:** Unavailable.

**Home study description:** Assessment which includes background of prospective adoptive parent(s), any children in the home, interests, employment, religion, medical and psychological information.

**Average wait for a child after approval of a home study:** 2 yrs. or more.

**Foster care:** Temporary and long-term.

## ★ 505 ★
**Onondaga County Department of Social Services**
421 Montgomery St.
Syracuse, NY 13202
Phone: (315) 435-2850
Fax: (315) 435-3590

**Contact:** Denise Larmondra or Dorothy McPherson.

**Description:** Public child welfare agency.

**Area served:** Residents of the city of Syracuse and Onondaga County.

**Requirements:** None.

**Fees:** None.

**Number of children placed last year:** 87.

**Description of children:** Waiting children and foster children freed for adoption.

**Adoption procedure:**
1) File application;
2) complete home study;
3) if approved, selection and placement of child;
4) 6 mos. supervisory;
5) finalization.

**Average length of time between application and start of home study:** 1-6 mos. for older children; 24 or more months for infants.

**Average length of time to complete home study:** 3 mos.

**Number of interviews:** Up to 7.

**Home study description:** Social study of applicants and immediate family members, parenting skills, life style, expectations, degree of adaptability and commitment.

**Average wait for a child after approval of a home study:** Varies.

**Foster care:** Emergency, temporary and long-term.

## ★ 506 ★
**Orange County Department of Social Services**
Box Z
Goshen, NY 10924
Phone: (914) 294-5788
Fax: (914) 294-3688

**Contact:** Mary Anne Bensen.

**Description:** Public child welfare agency.

**Area served:** Residents of Orange County.

**Requirements:** Adults, age 18 or older.

**Fees:** None.

**Number of children placed last year:** 49.

**Description of children:** Primarily children with special needs.

**Adoption procedure:**
1) Attend orientation meeting;
2) file application;
3) complete group study process;
4) if approved, placement;
5) post-placement supervision;
6) finalization.

**Average length of time between application and start of home study:** Varies.

**Average length of time to complete home study:** 4 or more mos.

**Number of interviews:** 1 or more.

**Home study description:** Assessment of autobiographical information, family functioning and lifestyle through group and individual meetings and a home visit.

**Average wait for a child after approval of a home study:** Varies.

**Foster care:** Emergency, short-term, long-term and fost-adopt.

## ★ 507 ★
**Otsego County Department of Social Services**
County Office Bldg.
197 Main St.
Cooperstown, NY 13326
Phone: (607) 547-4355
Fax: (607) 547-6437

**Contact:** Janice L. Brenner.

**Description:** Non-profit, public agency.

**Area served:** Residents of Otsego County.

**Requirements:** Applicants who are in good health, have a stable income, and who, if married, have a marriage of 1 yr. or more.

**Fees:** None.

**Number of children placed last year:** 8.

**Description of children:** Infants to teens, some special needs.

**Adoption procedure:**
1) Submit preliminary application;
2) file application;
3) complete home study;
4) if approved, placement;
5) 6 mos. post-placement supervision;
6) finalization.

**Average length of time between application and start of home study:** Varies.

**Average length of time to complete home study:** 10 hrs.

**Number of interviews:** 4.

**Home study description:** Evaluation of autobiographies; references; background, criminal and probation checks; home safety; experience with children; marital history; medical reports; goals and strengths.

**Average wait for a child after approval of a home study:** Varies.

**Foster care:** Temporary and long-term.

## ★ 508 ★
**Putnam County Department of Social Services**
110 Old Rt. 6
Carmel, NY 10512
Phone: (914) 225-7040
Fax: (914) 225-8635

**Contact:** Adoption intake worker.

**Description:** Public, county agency.

**Area served:** Residents of Putnam County.

**Requirements:** Adults, 18 and older, who are either married or single and whose health is adequate to parent.

**Fees:** None.

**Number of children placed last year:** 1.

**Description of children:** N/A.

**Adoption procedure:**
1) Submit application;
2) attend interview;
3) complete home study;
4) if approved, waiting period for child match (support group services available);
5) pre-placement visitation;
6) placement;
7) post-placement supervision;
8) finalization.

**Average length of time between application and start of home study:** Varies.

**Average length of time to complete home study:** 6 mos.

**Number of interviews:** 3-4.

**Home study description:** Assessment which includes but is not limited to children in the home, health and motivation to adopt.

**Average wait for a child after approval of a home study:** Varies.

**Foster care:** Emergency, short and long-term, fost-adopt and therapeutic.

## ★ 509 ★
**Rensselaer County Department of Social Services**
133 Bloomingrove Dr.
Troy, NY 12181
Phone: (518) 283-2000
Fax: (518) 283-7884

**Contact:** Adoption Unit.

**Description:** Public, county agency.

**Area served:** Residents of Rensselaer County.

**Requirements:** Adults, 18 yrs. or older, who are either legally married or legally single, and who are in good health.

**Fees:** None.

**Number of children placed last year:** 8.

**Description of children:** Primarily children with special needs and some non-special needs toddlers.

**Adoption procedure:**
1) Attend orientation;

2) submit application;
3) complete home study;
4) if approved, wait for placement;
5) placement;
6) supervision of placement;
7) finalization.

**Average length of time between application and start of home study:** 6-12 mos.

**Average length of time to complete home study:** 2-3 mos.

**Number of interviews:** Approx. 8.

**Home study description:** Assessment which includes but is not limited to applicant(s)' background, medical and financial information, stability, parenting ability and experience and attitudes toward discipline.

**Average wait for a child after approval of a home study:** 24 or more mos.

**Foster care:** Emergency, short and long-term.

### ★ 510 ★
**St. Lawrence County Department of Social Services**
6 Judson St.
Canton, NY 13617
Phone: (315) 379-2348

**Contact:** Mrs. Linda Covey.

**Description:** Public county agency mandated to place children by the New York State Department of Social Services.

**Area served:** Residents of St. Lawrence County.

**Requirements:** Applicants must be at least 21 yrs. old and have some source of income.

**Fees:** No agency fees.

**Number of children placed last year:** 5.

**Description of children:** Children with special needs.

**Adoption procedure:** 1) Information meeting; 2) 5 sessions of training; 3) home study; 4) wait for placement; 5) placement; 6) post-placement supervision; 7) finalization.

**Average length of time between application and start of home study:** 1 - 6 mos.

**Average length of time to complete home study:** 6 mos. or more.

**Number of interviews:** 3 or more.

**Home study description:** Assessment which includes applicant(s)' background, ability to parent, financial stability, Criminal Record and Child Abuse Registry clearance and sense of humor.

**Average wait for a child after approval of a home study:** 2 yrs. or more.

**Foster care:** Temporary.

### ★ 511 ★
**Schenectady County Department of Social Services**
620 State St., 4th Fl.
Schenectady, NY 12305
Phone: (518) 388-4456
Fax: (518) 382-1256

**Contact:** Carolyn Williams, Supervisor of Adoption/Foster Home Finding.

**Description:** Public, county agency.

**Area served:** Residents of Schenectady County.

**Requirements:** Adults, 18 yrs. and older, who are in good health, financially stable and who are single or married at least 1 yr.

**Fees:** None.

**Number of children placed last year:** 10-15.

**Description of children:** Children with special needs.

**Adoption procedure:**
1) Send letter of inquiry;
2) complete training;
3) undergo home study;
4) if approved, wait for placement;
5) placement;
6) supervision of placement;
7) finalization.

**Average length of time between application and start of home study:** Varies.

**Average length of time to complete home study:** 2-3 mos.

**Number of interviews:** 3 or more.

**Home study description:** Evaluatory and educational process which discusses child behavior, particularly those behaviors associated with loss and separation; the possibility of continued contact with the birth family; adoption subsidies; discipline; background of applicant(s); and type of child requested.

**Average wait for a child after approval of a home study:** Varies.

**Foster care:** Emergency, short and long-term.

### ★ 512 ★
**Schoharie County Department of Social Services**
Schoharie County Office Bldg.
Schoharie, NY 12157
Phone: (518) 295-8319

**Contact:** Adoption Unit.

**Description:** Non-profit public agency.

**Area served:** Residents of Schoharie County.

**Requirements:** Adults over 18 years of age who are self-supporting and who have the physical and emotional capability to care for a child.

**Fees:** None.

**Number of children placed last year:** Approx. 6.

**Description of children:** Children from pre-school age to 18 yrs., some with special needs.

**Adoption procedure:**
1) Telephone inquiry;
2) file initial application;
3) attend orientation;
4) participate in 5 wk. training session;
5) home visit(s);
6) if approved, selection and placement of child;
7) supervisory period;
8) finalization.

**Average length of time between application and start of home study:** 1 mo. or less.

**Average length of time to complete home study:** 5 or more wks.

**Number of interviews:** 1-3 home visits.

**Home study description:** Educational and self-evaluatory process which assesses the needs of the applicant family and adoptive child.

**Average wait for a child after approval of a home study:** 12-24 mos.

**Foster care:** Emergency, short and long-term.

**★ 513 ★**
**Suffolk County Department of Social Services**
P.O. Box 2000
Hauppauge, NY 11787
Phone: (516) 854-9484

**Contact:** Adoption unit.

**Description:** Public, county agency.

**Area served:** Residents of Suffolk County.

**Requirements:** Adults, 18 yrs. and older.

**Fees:** None.

**Number of children placed last year:** 55.

**Description of children:** Children from 0-13 yrs., most with special needs.

**Adoption procedure:**
1) Telephone intake and screening;
2) attend group meeting or admission to waiting list;
3) file application;
4) complete home study;
5) if approved, wait for placement;
6) placement;
7) post-placement supervision;
8) finalization.

**Average length of time between application and start of home study:** 1-6 mos.

**Average length of time to complete home study:** 4 mos.

**Number of interviews:** 30 hour pre-certification training (MAPP/GPS); 10 sessions, 3 hours each plus 2-4 home consultations.

**Home study description:** MAPP/GPS model. Assessment of family profile and functioning, stability, lifestyle, motivation to adopt and extended family's attitude toward adoption, parenting skills and the kind of child requested.

**Average wait for a child after approval of a home study:** Varies.

**Foster care:** Emergency, short and long-term and therapeutic.

**★ 514 ★**
**Tioga County Department of Social Services**
P.O. Box 240
Owego, NY 13827
Phone: (607) 687-5000

**Contact:** Gail Simpson, Director of Services or Darlene Weidman, Supervisor, Foster Care.

**Description:** Public county agency mandated to place children by the New York State Department of Social Services.

**Area served:** Residents of Tioga County.

**Requirements:** None.

**Fees:** None.

**Number of children placed last year:** 3.

**Description of children:** Children in the custody of the Department of Social Services.

**Adoption procedure:** 1) Inquiry; 2) application; 3) 4 orientation classes; 4) home study; 5) placement; 6) petition court for decree of adoption; 7) post-placement supervision; 6) finalization.

**Average length of time between application and start of home study:** 1 - 6 mos.

**Average length of time to complete home study:** 4 mos.

**Number of interviews:** Minimum of 2.

**Home study description:** Assessment which conforms with the guidelines set by the New York State Department of Social Services and includes Child Abuse Registry and Criminal Records clearances, questionnaires, financial statement and medical reports, autobiographies and references.

**Average wait for a child after approval of a home study:** 2 yrs. or more.

**Foster care:** Temporary and long-term.

**★ 515 ★**
**Tompkins County Department of Social Services**
301 Harris B. Dates Dr.
Ithaca, NY 14850
Phone: (607) 274-5285
Fax: (607) 274-5619

**Contact:** Senior adoption worker.

**Description:** Non-profit county department of social services.

**Area served:** Residents of Tompkins County.

**Requirements:** Completed home study by New York State Dept. of Social Services.

**Fees:** Expenses for applicant(s)' physical exam(s).

**Number of children placed last year:** Not available.

**Description of children:** Children who are older, handicapped or who have other special needs.

**Adoption procedure:** Call or write for details.

**Average length of time between application and start of home study:** 6-12 mos.

**Average length of time to complete home study:** 6 months.

**Number of interviews:** Unavailable.

**Home study description:** Call or write for criteria.

**Average wait for a child after approval of a home study:** 6-24 mos.

**Foster care:** Emergency, short and long-term.

**★ 516 ★**
**Warren County Department of Social Services**
Municipal Center Annex
Lake George, NY 12845
Phone: (518) 761-6315

**Contact:** Nancy Manning, Adoption Caseworker.

**Description:** Public county agency mandated to place children by the New York State Department of Social Services.

**Area served:** Residents of Warren County.

**Requirements:** Applicants must be at least 21 yrs. old and in good health.

**Fees:** None.

**Number of children placed last year:** 6.

**Description of children:** Children between the ages of 8 and 12 yrs. with special needs.

**Adoption procedure:** 1) Inquiry; 2) application; 3) interviews; 4) references and background checks; 5) auto- biography and self-study packet; 6) medical statement; 7) attitude survey; 8) subsidy summary; 9) attorney's packet; 10) 13 hrs. of training; 11) placement.

**Average length of time between application and start of home study:** Less than 1 mo.

**Average length of time to complete home study:** 6 mos.

**Number of interviews:** 6.

**Home study description:** Assessment which includes identifying information, background information, birth certificates, physical and personality descriptions, education and employment, ethnic origin and religion, marital and interpersonal relationships, health, home and finances, and experience with children.

**Average wait for a child after approval of a home study:** Fost-adopt conversions: 6 - 12 mos.; others: 2 yrs. or more.

**Foster care:** Temporary.

★ 517 ★
**Westchester County Department of Social Services**
112 E. Post Rd., 4th Fl.
White Plains, NY 10601
Phone: (914) 285-KIDS
Fax: (914) 285-6021

**Contact:** Mrs. Phyllis Farber.

**Description:** Non-profit, public, county agency.

**Area served:** Residents of Westchester County.

**Requirements:** Adults, 21 yrs. and older who are in good health.

**Fees:** None.

**Number of children placed last year:** 25.

**Description of children:** Children from infancy to age 15 yrs., many with special needs.

**Adoption procedure:**
 1) Initial inquiry;
 2) participate in group orientation;
 3) complete home study;
 4) if approved, wait for placement;
 5) placement;
 6) post-placement supervision;
 7) finalization.

**Average length of time between application and start of home study:** 1-6 mos.

**Average length of time to complete home study:** 6-8 wks.

**Number of interviews:** 2.

**Home study description:** Assessment of applicant(s)' childhood, health, income, attitudes of other family members concerning adoption, type of child desired and methods of discipline.

**Average wait for a child after approval of a home study:** 6-12 mos.

**Foster care:** Emergency, short and long-term, therapeutic, pre-adoptive and permanent.

★ 518 ★
**Wyoming County Department of Social Services**
466 N. Main
Warsaw, NY 14569
Phone: (716) 786-8900

**Contact:** Janet E. Sternberg, Case Supervisor.

**Description:** Non-profit, public agency.

**Area served:** Residents of Wyoming County.

**Requirements:** Applicants must demonstrate parental ability.

**Fees:** None.

**Number of children placed last year:** 1.

**Description of children:** Infants and children with special needs.

**Adoption procedure:**
 1) Attend intake appointment;
 2) file application;

 3) complete group and/or individual home study;
 4) if approved, selection and placement of child;
 5) supervisory period;
 6) finalization.

**Average length of time between application and start of home study:** 1-6 mos.

**Average length of time to complete home study:** 3 mos.

**Number of interviews:** 3-4.

**Home study description:** Assessment of emotional climate of home, parental commitment and motivation to adopt.

**Average wait for a child after approval of a home study:** 6-12 mos.

**Foster care:** Temporary and long-term.

# PRIVATE AGENCIES

★ 519 ★
**The Angel Guardian Home**
6301 12th Ave.
Brooklyn, NY 11219
Phone: (718) 232-1500
Fax: (718) 837-9543

**Contact:** Kathleen Negri.

**Date established:** 1899.

**Description:** Voluntary, not-for-profit agency subject to the regulations of the New York City and New York State Depts. of Social Service.

**Area served:** Residents of the 5 boroughs of New York City.

**Requirements:** Adults over the age of 18 yrs. who are in general good health and who have a regular source of adequate income.

**Fees:** None.

**Number of children placed last year:** 97.

**Description of children:** Minority children with special needs, white children over the age of 7 yrs., sibling groups, and children with special needs.

**Adoption procedure:**
 1) Attend orientation meeting;
 2) submit application packet with all requested documentation;
 3) participate in group training;
 4) participate in home visits;
 5) if approved, wait for placement.

**Average length of time between application and start of home study:** Varies.

**Average length of time to complete home study:** 3-6 mos.

**Number of interviews:** 3 or more.

**Home study description:** Evaluation of family composition and functioning; community resources; family finances; health; personal history; living and sleeping arrangements; previous child care experiences; motivation to adopt; parenting philosophies and methods of discipline.

**Average wait for a child after approval of a home study:** Varies.

**Foster care:** Emergency, temporary, long-term and kinship foster care.

★ 520 ★
**Bethany Christian Services (of Burnt Hills)**
105 Lakehill Rd.
Burnt Hills, NY 12027-9507
Phone: (518) 384-1851

**Contact:** Cathy Dressler, M.S.W., Branch Supervisor.

**Date established:** 1991.

**Description:** Private, non-profit child placing agency licensed by the New York Department of Social Services and accredited by the Council on Accreditation of Services for Families and Children.

**Area served:** Residents within a 100 mi. radius of Burnt Hills in the counties of Albany, Saratoga and Schenectady.

**Requirements:** Applicants must be committed Christian and active in a Christian Church.

**Fees:** Unavailable.

**Number of children placed last year:** 4.

**Description of children:** Infants.

**Adoption procedure:** 1) Inquiry; 2) placement on waiting list; 3) application; 4) preparation; 5) approval; 6) placement; 7) post-placement; 8) finalization.

**Average length of time between application and start of home study:** Prospective applicants must telephone to ascertain if the agency has openings for adoptive couples.

**Average length of time to complete home study:** 3 mos.

**Number of interviews:** 3.

**Home study description:** Bethany typically prepares its prospective adoptive families by having them attend an informational meeting or adoption education seminar; attend a series of adoptive parenting classes; complete necessary paperwork; evaluate their relationship with Jesus Christ and undergo an interview process which covers such topics as emotional, spiritual and physical health as well as family stability and readiness for parenthood.

**Average wait for a child after approval of a home study:** 2 yrs. or more.

**Foster care:** Cradle care.

## ★ 521 ★
**Catholic Charities of Ogdensburg**
716 Caroline St.
P.O. Box 296
Ogdensburg, NY 13669
Phone: (315) 393-2255

**Branch address:**
63 E. Main St., P.O. Box 896, Malone, NY 12953
Phone: (518) 483-1460

4914 S. Catherine St., Plattsburgh, NY 12901
Phone: (518) 561-0470

812 State St., Watertown, NY 13601
Phone: (315) 788-4330

**Contact:** Winny Burns.

**Date established:** 1917.

**Description:** Non-profit private agency.

**Area served:** Residents of Clinton, Essex, Franklin, Hamilton, Herkimer, Jefferson, Lewis and St. Lawrence counties.

**Requirements:** Couples married at least 2 yrs. who have no felony record nor current abuse of alcohol/drugs.

**Fees:** Sliding fee scale based on income beginning at $550.

**Number of children placed last year:** 1.

**Description of children:** Infants.

**Adoption procedure:**
1) Application phase;
2) complete individual interviews;
3) attend group interview;

4) complete home study;
5) if approved, placement.

**Average length of time between application and start of home study:** 1-6 mos.

**Average length of time to complete home study:** 4-6 mos.

**Number of interviews:** 4.

**Home study description:** Home visit is an overall description of home and premises, level of housekeeping, the infant's room, and compliance with DSS regulations.

**Average wait for a child after approval of a home study:** 24 or more mos.

**Foster care:** Temporary.

## ★ 522 ★
**Catholic Charities of Utica**
1408 Genesee St.
Utica, NY 13502
Phone: (315) 724-3167

**Branch address:**
119 E. Walnut St., Oneida, NY 13421

212 W. Liberty, Rome, NY 13440
Phone: (315) 337-8600

**Contact:** Shari Kimball, Coordinator, Child and Family Development.

**Description:** Private, non-profit agency licensed to place children by the New York State Department of Social Services.

**Area served:** Residents of Madison and Oneida counties.

**Requirements:** Applicants must be at least 18 yrs. old.

**Fees:** No fees for special needs placements. Application: $50; home study: $750; placement: sliding scale.

**Number of children placed last year:** Unavailable.

**Description of children:** Infants.

**Adoption procedure:** 1) Orientation; 2) application; 3) home study; 4) placement on waiting list; 5) placement; 6) post-placement supervision; 7) finalization.

**Average length of time between application and start of home study:** 1 - 6 mos.

**Average length of time to complete home study:** 3 - 6 mos.

**Number of interviews:** Varies.

**Home study description:** Assessment which includes references, family background, marital history, criminal and child abuse records checks, finances and employment, medical history and education and which covers such issues as interpersonal relationships, discipline and attitudes toward birth parents.

**Average wait for a child after approval of a home study:** Varies with the type of child requested.

**Foster care:** Cradle care.

## ★ 523 ★
**Catholic Family Center of the Diocese of Rochester**
Sibley Tower Bldg., 7th Fl.
25 Franklin St.
Rochester, NY 14604-1007
Phone: (716) 546-7220
Fax: (716) 325-3867

**Contact:** Adoption intake worker.

**Description:** Private agency.

**Area served:** Residents of the Diocese of Rochester which includes the City of Rochester and 11 surrounding counties.

**Requirements:** Varies by type of child requested.

**Fees:**
$100 application fee (non-refundable);
$1000 home study fee.

**Number of children placed last year:** 66.

**Description of children:** Infants, foreign-born, children with special needs and minority children.

**Adoption procedure:**
1) Initial inquiry;
2) if applying for adoption of white infant, waiting period;
3) complete home study;
4) search for child;
5) placement;
6) 6 mos. post-placement supervision; and
7) finalization.

**Average length of time between application and start of home study:** Varies depending on child requested.

**Average length of time to complete home study:** 2-6 mos.

**Number of interviews:** 4 or more.

**Home study description:** Group process and individual interviews.

**Average wait for a child after approval of a home study:** Varies depending on child requested.

**Foster care:** Temporary and long-term.


★ 524 ★
**Children's Aid Society of New York**
150 E. 45th St.
New York, NY 10017
Phone: (212) 949-4800

**Branch address:**
105 E. 22nd St., New York, NY 10010

**Contact:** Cynthia Y. Terrell.

**Date established:** 1853.

**Description:** Voluntary, non-sectarian agency licensed in New York State.

**Area served:** Residents of New York State and others within commuting distance.

**Requirements:** Adults, 18 yrs. and older.

**Fees:** None.

**Number of children placed last year:** 58.

**Description of children:** Primarily special needs.

**Adoption procedure:**
1) Attend orientation meeting;
2) return completed application;
3) undergo home study;
4) if approved, wait for placement.

**Average length of time between application and start of home study:** 1 mo. or less.

**Average length of time to complete home study:** 3-6 mos.

**Number of interviews:** Individual interviews with every household member, 1 home visit and 2 joint interviews (if applicable).

**Home study description:** Overall assessment of family's stability, motivation to adopt, ability to accept non-biological child, flexibility regarding child desired, child abuse clearance, verification of income, current physical examination, marriage and birth certificates.

**Average wait for a child after approval of a home study:** Varies.

**Foster care:** Temporary.


★ 525 ★
**Community Maternity Services**
27 N. Main Ave.
Albany, NY 12203
Phone: (518) 482-8836
Fax: (518) 482-5805

**Branch address:**
41 W. Main Ave., Cobleskill, NY 12043
Phone: (518) 234-3541

39 Walnut St., Oneonta, NY 13820
Phone: (607) 432-9314

61 West St., Ilion, NY 13357
Phone: (315) 894-9941

Lower Amherst St., Lake George, NY 12845
Phone: (518) 668-316

19 Bulkey St., Granville, NY 12832
Phone: (518) 642-1471

23 Fremont St., Gloversville, NY 12078
Phone: (518) 725-6016

240 Second St., Troy, NY 12180
Phone: (518) 274-9245

**Contact:** Mary G. Creighton, Associate Executive Director.

**Date established:** 1971.

**Description:** Private, non-profit agency of the Catholic Charities of the Diocese of Albany and licensed to place children by the New York State Department of Social Services.

**Area served:** Residents of the 14 counties of the Albany Roman Catholic Diocese.

**Requirements:** Open.

**Fees:** Application: $250; home study: 12% of the total gross family income. Attorney fees for adoption finalization are not included.

**Number of children placed last year:** 40.

**Description of children:** U.S. infants, children with special needs and foreign-born children.

**Adoption procedure:** 1) Telephone inquiry; 2) exploratory interview; 3) orientation meeting; 4) selection of program; 5) placement on waiting list of that program; 6) adoption preparation; 7) placement; 8) post-placement supervision; 9) finalization.

**Average length of time between application and start of home study:** Infant: 4 - 5 yrs.; other: 3 - 12 mos.

**Average length of time to complete home study:** 2 mos.

**Number of interviews:** 8 - 10.

**Home study description:** Exploratory and preparatory process in which documents pertaining to finances, health, references, employment, education as well as an autobiography are collected and which familiarizes the applicants with parenting through adoption and which covers such areas of discussion as acceptance of adoption in relation to birth parents and adoptees and may include cross-cultural and the parenting of minority or special needs children. It is designed to be a positive experience which helps applicants integrate the adoption experience to this time and learn more about themselves as individuals and parents.

**Average wait for a child after approval of a home study:** 6 - 12 mos.

**Foster care:** Temporary.

## ★ 526 ★
**Downey Side...Families for Youth**
401 E. 34th St., Ste. 85
New York, NY 10001-3984
Phone: (212) 629-8599

**Branch address:**
999 Liberty St., Springfield, MA 01104
Phone: (413) 781-2123

**Contact:** Terence J. Taffe, OFM, CP, Director, New York Region; Peter Power, Director, Massachusetts Region.

**Date established:** 1968.

**Description:** Private agency licensed in Connecticut, Massachusetts, New Jersey, New York and Vermont.

**Area served:** Residents of New England, New Jersey and New York.

**Requirements:** Adheres to state's requirements.

**Fees:** None
Adoption course: $50/person or $75/couple.

**Number of children placed last year:** Approx. 65.

**Description of children:** U.S. children, 8 yrs. and older, many of whom have special needs.

**Adoption procedure:**
1) Participate in 8 wk. adoption course;
2) complete self-assessment;
3) placement;
4) post-placement support.

**Average length of time between application and start of home study:** Varies.

**Average length of time to complete home study:** Approx. 8 wks.

**Number of interviews:** 8 group and 1 home visit.

**Home study description:** A self-assessment and preparation process.

**Average wait for a child after approval of a home study:** Varies.

**Foster care:** Permanent.

## ★ 527 ★
**Family Focus Adoption Services**
54-40 Little Neck Pkwy., Ste. 3
Little Neck, NY 11362
Phone: (718) 224-1919
Fax: (718) 225-8360

**Contact:** Maris H. Blechner, Executive Director.

**Date established:** 1987.

**Description:** Non-profit, private adoption agency founded and staffed by adoptive parents and child advocates.

**Area served:** Residents of New York City, Long Island, New York State as far north as Albany, and New Jersey.

**Requirements:** Adults, 18 yrs. and older.

**Fees:**
No fees for waiting children.
Fees for private adoption: home study: $750; update home study: $375; post-placement services: $280.

**Number of children placed last year:** 55.

**Description of children:** Primarily children with special needs.

**Adoption procedure:**
1) Attend Adoption Information Meeting;
2) submit application and necessary paperwork;
3) attend 6 parenting sessions;
4) complete family study;
5) child search;

6) placement;
7) post-placement supervision;
8) finalization.

**Average length of time between application and start of home study:** 1 mo. or less.

**Average length of time to complete home study:** 8-12 wks.

**Number of interviews:** 3 or more home visits.

**Home study description:** Call or write for outline.

**Average wait for a child after approval of a home study:** Varies.

**Foster care:** None.

## ★ 528 ★
**Family Service of Westchester**
1 Summit Ave.
White Plains, NY 10606
Phone: (914) 948-8004

**Contact:** Linda D. Durrani, Director, Adoption and Children's Services, or Barbara Melamed.

**Date established:** 1953.

**Description:** Non-profit, non-sectarian private agency licensed in Connecticut, New Jersey and New York.

**Area served:** The tri-state area of New York, New Jersey, and Connecticut.

**Requirements:** Adults over the age of 18 yrs. who are single or if married, marriage must be of 1 yr. duration.

**Fees:**
Application fee: $150;
complete adoption service: $3000-$15,000;
home study as a separate service: domestic, $750;
    international, $1200;
post-placement supervision only: $85/hr.

**Number of children placed last year:** 17.

**Description of children:** U.S. infants, foreign-born children and children with special needs.

**Adoption procedure:**
1) File application;
2) complete home study;
3) if approved, placement;
4) post-placement supervision;
5) finalization.

**Average length of time between application and start of home study:** 1 mo. or less.

**Average length of time to complete home study:** 6 wks.

**Number of interviews:** 2-4.

**Home study description:** Evaluation of biographical information, education, finances, physical and mental health, marital relationship (if applicable), adjustment to infertility, childrearing philosophies and methods of discipline and understanding of adoption-related issues.

**Average wait for a child after approval of a home study:** 6-12 mos.

**Foster care:** Temporary.

## ★ 529 ★
**The Family Tree Adoption Agency, Inc.**
1743 Route 9
Clifton Park, NY 12065
Phone: (518) 371-1336

**Contact:** Cindi Frank or Dianna McGreevy, Directors.

**Date established:** 1991.

**Description:** Private, non-profit child placing agency licensed by the New York State Department of Social Services.

**Area served:** Residents within a 50 mi. radius of the agency.

**Requirements:** Applicants must be at least 18 yrs. old. They may be single or, if married, at least 1 yr.

**Fees:** Unavailable.

**Number of children placed last year:** Unavailable.

**Description of children:** U.S. infants and toddlers and children with special needs.

**Adoption procedure:** 1) Orientation; 2) formulation of family biography and strategies to contact birth parents; 3) birth family identification; 4) home study; 5) placement; 6) post-placement supervision; 7) finalization.

**Average length of time between application and start of home study:** Dependent on birth parent identification.

**Average length of time to complete home study:** Unavailable.

**Number of interviews:** 3.

**Home study description:** Learning experience which will expand prospective adoptive parents' understanding of adoption which includes participation in group adoption seminars as well as individual home visits.

**Average wait for a child after approval of a home study:** Home studies do not usually begin until a birth family has been identified.

**Foster care:** Cradle care.


## ★ 530 ★
### Edwin Gould Services for Children
41 E. 11th St.
New York, NY 10003
Phone: (212) 598-0050
(800) 564-2217
Fax: (212) 598-0796

**Contact:** Suzy Sanford, Adoption Coordinator, FBH.

**Date established:** 1939.

**Description:** Non-profit private child care agency.

**Area served:** Residents of New York City.

**Requirements:** Call or write for list.

**Fees:** None.

**Number of children placed last year:** 30.

**Description of children:** Children from infancy to adolescence, some with special needs.

**Adoption procedure:**
1) Initial inquiry;
2) complete home study;
3) child and family match;
4) placement;
5) 6 mos. post-placement supervision;
6) finalization.

**Average length of time between application and start of home study:** Varies.

**Average length of time to complete home study:** 6-8 wks.

**Number of interviews:** Unavailable.

**Home study description:** Evaluation of medical and financial reports, religion, living conditions, relationships and social history, child care experiences, New York State child abuse registry clearance, criminal/psychiatric history, recommendation of references and vital records documentation.

**Average wait for a child after approval of a home study:** Varies.

**Foster care:** Temporary and long-term.

## ★ 531 ★
### Harlem-Dowling West Side Center for Children and Family Services
2090 Adam Clayton Powell, Jr. Blvd., 3rd Fl.
New York, NY 10027
Phone: (212) 749-3656
Fax: (212) 678-1094

**Contact:** Rubye M. Bulluck.

**Date established:** 1836.

**Description:** Non-profit private agency licensed in New York City and State and New Jersey.

**Area served:** Residents of the metropolitan New York City area and New Jersey.

**Requirements:** Adults over the age of 21 yrs. who have adequate income for their own needs and those of an additional family member and who are in good health.

**Fees:**
No fee for children under Harlem-Dowling's care;
fee is charged for Private Adoption Infant Program (black infants).

**Number of children placed last year:** 57.

**Description of children:** Primarily healthy black and Hispanic children from newborn to 12 yrs., some with varying degrees of emotional problems.

**Adoption procedure:**
1) Initial agency inquiry;
2) attend adoption information/orientation meeting;
3) complete home study;
4) home study reviewed by agency's Review Committee;
5) if accepted, applicants attend adoption preparation meetings;
6) assignment to caseworker;
7) child search;
8) placement;
9) post-placement supervision;
10) preparation for finalization and finalization.

**Average length of time between application and start of home study:** 1-6 mos.

**Average length of time to complete home study:** 1 mo.

**Number of interviews:** 2.

**Home study description:** Evaluation of general background information, family size and description, home, employment, interests, health, methods of discipline, child requested, motivation to adopt and adoption rationale.

**Average wait for a child after approval of a home study:** 6-12 mos.

**Foster care:** Temporary, emergency foster boarding, and Boarder Baby programs.
A special unit responds to foster children with a history of sexual abuse and a program assists foster parents who care for children with the AIDS virus.


## ★ 532 ★
### Lutheran Community Services, Inc.
27 Park Pl.
New York, NY 10007
Phone: (212) 406-9110
Fax: (212) 406-9130

**Contact:** John LaPallo.

**Date established:** 1888.

**Description:** Non-profit, private agency licensed by the State of New York.

**Area served:** Residents of New York State.

**Requirements:** Adults, 18 yrs. and older, who are financially able to meet the needs of present family, who have no record of child abuse or neglect, who are emotionally fit to parent a child and who have an average life expectancy.

**Fees:**
No fee for waiting children;
home study for international or private adoptions: $600.

**Number of children placed last year:** 63.

**Description of children:** 63 under 12 yrs. (7 newborn infants), 12 over age 12 yrs., some with emotional and/or physical handicaps. All children were initially foster children who became eligible for adoption.

**Adoption procedure:**
1) Attend adoption orientation;
2) submit application with required documentation;
3) complete home study;
4) child search;
5) placement;
6) 6 mos. post-placement supervision;
7) finalization.

**Average length of time between application and start of home study:** 1-6 mos.

**Average length of time to complete home study:** 6-8 wks.

**Number of interviews:** 2.

**Home study description:** Assessment of family background, education and employment history, financial status, religion, home setting, hobbies and interests, childrearing methods and discipline, child care arrangements and type of child desired.

**Average wait for a child after approval of a home study:** Varies.

**Foster care:** Emergency, short and long-term and fost-adopt.

★ 533 ★
**Mission of the Immaculate Virgin - Mount Loretto**
6581 Hylan Blvd.
Staten Island, NY 10307
Phone: (718) 317-2602

**Contact:** Mary Lynn Hagedorn, Program Director; Kerry Cain, Adoption Supervisor.

**Date established:** 1985.

**Description:** Private, non-profit agency licensed to place children by the New Jersey Department of Human Services and the New York State Department of Social Services.

**Area served:** Residents of the 5 boroughs of New York City and residents of New Jersey within a 50 mile radius of the agency.

**Requirements:** Applicants must be at least 18 yrs. old, either married or single, have a source of income and be in good health.

**Fees:** No agency fees. Attorney fees for finalization.

**Number of children placed last year:** 31.

**Description of children:** Children with special needs, most of whom have been fostered in the prospective adoptive home.

**Adoption procedure:** 1) Attorney files adoption application; 2) agency prepares legal documents; 3) attorney files documents; 4) adoption supervision; 5) finalization.

**Average length of time between application and start of home study:** Less than 1 mo.

**Average length of time to complete home study:** 12 hrs.

**Number of interviews:** 4.

**Home study description:** Study which compiles with the New York and New Jersey state regulations.

**Average wait for a child after approval of a home study:** None, since most are fost-adopt conversions.

**Foster care:** Temporary and long-term.

★ 534 ★
**New Beginnings Family and Children's Services, Inc.**
141 Willis Ave.
Mineola, NY 11501
Phone: (516) 747-2204
Fax: (516) 747-2505

**Branch address:**
8 Pennsylvania Ave., Matamoras, PA 18336
Phone: (717) 491-2366

**Contact:** Chong H. Park, Executive Director.

**Date established:** 1985.

**Description:** Non-profit private agency licensed in Connecticut, New Jersey, New York, and Pennsylvania.

**Area served:** New York State, New Jersey, Pennsylvania, and Connecticut.

**Requirements:** Requirements differ by child's country of origin. For New York State special needs children, the only requirement is that the applicant be an adult, 21 years or older.

**Fees:** Vary according to individual program.

**Number of children placed last year:** Approx. 220.

**Description of children:** New York State special needs children and children from Colombia, Korea, Paraguay, Vietnam, Thailand, China, Hong Kong, and Peru.

**Adoption procedure:**
1) Telephone inquiry for intake and information;
2) pre-applications are mailed if the applicant meets the requirements of the country or program.

**Average length of time between application and start of home study:** 1 mo. or less.

**Average length of time to complete home study:** 1 mo. or less.

**Number of interviews:** 1-3.

**Home study description:** Encourages prospective parents to attend Parent Training and Preparation Workshops for 2 consecutive days and complete home visits.

**Average wait for a child after approval of a home study:** Varies depending on program.

**Foster care:** None.

★ 535 ★
**New Hope Family Services, Inc.**
3519 James St.
Syracuse, NY 13206
Phone: (315) 437-8300
Fax: (315) 437-9107

**Branch address:**
8 Laurel Ave., East Islip, NY 11730
Phone: (516) 581-3092

**Contact:** Larry D. Taylor, LSW, Executive Director; Joan G. Meier, Director of Client Services.

**Date established:** 1965.

**Description:** Voluntary, non-profit family service agency authorized by the New York State Dept. of Social Services.

**Area served:** Residents of New York State.

**Requirements:** Flexible, but honors requirements of foreign agencies and placing birthparents.

**Fees:**
Application: $200;
Home study: $900;
Other fees with type of service.

**Number of children placed last year:** Average of 20 per year.

**Description of children:** U.S. and foreign-born infants, some special needs.

**Adoption procedure:**
1) Initial inquiry;
2) attend informational meeting held at various locations state-wide;
3) submit application;
4) complete home study;
5) if approved, referral to foreign agency or selection by birthparents;
6) placement;
7) 6-12 mos. post-placement supervision;
8) finalization.

**Average length of time between application and start of home study:** 9-15 mos.

**Average length of time to complete home study:** 2-4 mos.

**Number of interviews:** 2 or more.

**Home study description:** Follows requirements set by the New York State Department of Social Services.

**Average wait for a child after approval of a home study:** 24 or more mos.

**Foster care:** Temporary and respite care.

## ★ 536 ★
**New Life Adoption Agency, Inc.**
117 S. State St.
Syracuse, NY 13202-1103
Phone: (315) 422-7300
Fax: (315) 475-7727

**Contact:** Maura McLean.

**Date established:** Unavailable.

**Description:** Private, not-for-profit adoption agency licensed by the New York State Department of Social Services.

**Area served:** Residents of the U.S.

**Requirements:** None, but child's country of origin may impose its own requirements.

**Fees:** Preliminary application: $100; domestic home study: $1200, international home study: $1500; application: $500. Placement fees, post-placement fees and intercountry fees vary.

**Number of children placed last year:** Unavailable.

**Description of children:** Children from the U.S., China, Russia and the Ukraine who are primarily younger than 4 yrs. Some sibling groups and some children minor special needs.

**Adoption procedure:** 1) Preliminary application; 2) full application; 3) home study; 4) dossier and immigration approval (if international adoption); 5) placement (travel involved to China); 6) post- placement services.

**Average length of time between application and start of home study:** Less than 1 mo.

**Average length of time to complete home study:** 1 - 2 mos.

**Number of interviews:** 3 - 4.

**Home study description:** Process designed to match the right children with the right homes. Agency works with the applicants to prepare a comprehensive home study which takes into account all their hopes, wants and needs and which conforms to the requirements set by the State of New York and the child's country of origin.

**Average wait for a child after approval of a home study:** China: 1 - 6 mos.; Russia and the Ukraine: 6- 12 mos.; U.S.: varies.

**Foster care:** Pre-adoptive.

## ★ 537 ★
**Our Lady of Victory Infant Home**
790 Ridge Rd.
Lackawanna, NY 14218
Phone: (716) 828-9500
Fax: (716) 828-9526

**Contact:** Julie Skura.

**Date established:** 1907.

**Description:** Non-profit, private agency licensed by the New York State Dept. of Social Services.

**Area served:** Residents within a 100 mi. radius of the agency.

**Requirements:** Each case is considered on its own merits.

**Fees:** 5% of annual income.

**Number of children placed last year:** 12.

**Description of children:** Infants.

**Adoption procedure:**
1) Initial inquiry;
2) submit application;
3) admission to waiting list;
4) complete home study;
5) if approved, wait for placement;
6) placement.

**Average length of time between application and start of home study:** 24 or more mos.

**Average length of time to complete home study:** Approx. 4-6 mos.

**Number of interviews:** 3-4.

**Home study description:** Evaluation of prospective adoptive parents' background, marital history, finances, home and surroundings, type of child desired and attitudes toward adoption-related issues.

**Average wait for a child after approval of a home study:** 6-12 mos.

**Foster care:** Temporary.

## ★ 538 ★
**St. Joseph's Services for Children and Families**
540 Atlantic Ave.
Brooklyn, NY 11217
Phone: (718) 858-8700

**Contact:** Debra Fishkin, Director of Adoption.

**Date established:** 1826.

**Description:** Non-profit, private agency licensed by the State of New York.

**Area served:** Primarily residents of Brooklyn and Queens but will serve residents of other New York City boroughs.

**Requirements:** Flexible.

**Fees:** None.

**Number of children placed last year:** 105.

**Description of children:** New York City foster children, mostly black and Hispanic, of all ages with special needs.

**Adoption procedure:**
1) Attend orientation;
2) submit application;
3) undergo home study;
4) complete training;
5) obtain state Central Registry clearance;
6) if approved, placement.

**Average length of time between application and start of home study:** 1-6 mos.

**Average length of time to complete home study:** 4 mos.

**Number of interviews:** 3.

**Home study description:** Evaluation of background information; interviews with adoptive parents and other members of the household; childhood and education of applicants; quality of health; quality of adoptive parents' relationship; physical features of adoptive home and neighborhood.

**Average wait for a child after approval of a home study:** Depends on type of child desired.

**Foster care:** Emergency, temporary, long-term and therapeutic.

★ 539 ★
**Spence-Chapin Services to Families and Children**
6 E. 94th St.
New York, NY 10128
Phone: (212) 369-0300
(800) 321-5683
Fax: (212) 369-8589

**Contact:** Adoption Inquiry.

**Date established:** 1916.

**Description:** Voluntary, non-sectarian child welfare and adoption agency.

**Area served:** Residents of the Greater New York area; those within a 100 mile radius.

**Requirements:** Vary depending on program/county. Call for further information.

**Fees:** Sliding scale based on income.

**Number of children placed last year:** 162.

**Description of children:** Infants of all races form the U.S., Asia, Latin America, and Eastern Europe.

**Adoption procedure:**
1) Initial inquiry;
2) attend orientation meeting;
3) participate in intake screening interview;
4) if approved, file formal application;
5) complete home study;
6) placement;
7) post-placement supervision;
8) finalization.

**Average length of time between application and start of home study:** 1-6 mos.

**Average length of time to complete home study:** 2-3 mos.

**Number of interviews:** 3-4.

**Home study description:** Educational process which prepares applicant family for adoptive placement.

**Average wait for a child after approval of a home study:** 6-12 mos.

**Foster care:** Temporary.

★ 540 ★
**Talbot Perkins Children's Services**
116 W. 32nd St., 12th Fl.
New York, NY 10001
Phone: (212) 736-2510
(800) 981-TPCS
Fax: (212) 268-5159

**Contact:** Bob Sloan, Director of Foster Care and Adoption.

**Date established:** 1927.

**Description:** Voluntary, non-profit multi-service child welfare agency licensed in the New York metropolitan area.

**Area served:** Residents of New York City and the New York metropolitan area.

**Requirements:** Adults over the age of 18 yrs. who have a source of income and sufficient health to care for a child.

**Fees:**
None for families adopting children in the foster care system.
Home study for families adopting privately: $600.
Post-placement visit after private placement: $150/per visit.

**Number of children placed last year:** 45.

**Description of children:** Minority, older and handicapped children from New York City's foster care system.

**Adoption procedure:**
1) Submit application;
2) attend foster care orientation meeting;
3) complete home study;
4) if approved, search for child;
5) child selection and acceptance by applicant family;
6) pre-placement visits;
7) placement;
8) 6 mos. post-placement supervision;
9) finalization.

**Average length of time between application and start of home study:** Varies.

**Average length of time to complete home study:** 1-4 mos.

**Number of interviews:** 3-5 including a home visit.

**Home study description:** Evaluation of motivation to adopt and understanding of adoption, detailed personal history, family of origin, health, religion, employment, financial resources, experiences with children, lifestyle, home, marital relationship (if applicable), methods of discipline, attitudes toward adoption related issues and Child Abuse Registry clearance.

**Average wait for a child after approval of a home study:** Varies.

**Foster care:** Temporary, long-term and fost-adopt.

★ 541 ★
**V.I.D.A., Inc.**
**Voices for International Development and Adoption, Inc.**
354 Allen St.
Hudson, NY 12534
Phone: (518) 828-4527
Fax: (518) 828-0688

**Mailing address:**
P.O. Box 833, Hudson, NY 12534

**Contact:** D.A. Blackburn, Ph.D., A.C.S.W.; Dr. DeGuerre A. Blackburn, Ph.D., A.C.S.W.,Executive Director.

**Date established:** 1986.

**Description:** Private, not-for-profit corporation licensed to place children by the Connecticut Department of Children and Youth Services, the Florida Department of Health and Rehabilitative Services, the Indiana Division of Families and Children, the New Jersey Department of Human Services, New York State Department of Social Services and the West Virginia Department of Health and Human Resources.

**Area served:** Residents of the U.S. and U.S. citizens living abroad as well as Canadian and European families.

**Requirements:** Applicants must be at least 21 yrs. old with a stable income. Agency will work with single or married applicants; if married, marriage must be of at least 1 yr. duration with 3 or more years preferred.

**Fees:** Application: $250; home study: $1750; Agency administration fees: $3750.

**Number of children placed last year:** 40.

**Description of children:** Primarily infants and toddlers from Central and South America, Bulgaria, Japan and the Philippines.

**Adoption procedure:** 1) Inquiry; 2) program selection; 3) application; 4) home study; 5) dossier preparation and referral; 6) child match; 7) placement; 8) post-placement supervision; 9) finalization.

**Average length of time between application and start of home study:** Less than 1 mo.

**Average length of time to complete home study:** 2 - 3 wks.

**Number of interviews:** 3.

**Home study description:** Assessment which includes health and age of adoptive applicant(s); information about the home, length of marriage and other children in the home, if applicable, income and individual psychological examinations.

**Average wait for a child after approval of a home study:** 6 - 12 mos.

**Foster care:** None.

---

# NORTH CAROLINA

## STATUTES

★ 542 ★

**Independent placement by intermediary?** Illegal.

**Independent placement by birth parents?** Permitted.

**Subsidies provided?** Title IV-E and Title IV-B provide medical, remedial and psychological services.

**Adoption cost defined by law?** Only medical expenses of the birth mother and child attendant to the child's birth may be paid by the adopting parents.

**Insurance for infertility?:** No.

**Home study required by state?** Prospective adoptive parents must notify the director of social services no less than 72 hrs. before any child younger than 12 yrs. is placed in anticipation of adoption.

**Prospective adoptive parent advertise for a child?** Illegal.

**Surrogacy laws?** Not addressed in law.

**Residents access agencies of other states or countries?** Permitted.

**Requires judicial termination of birth parents' rights?** Birth parents may sign a "Consent to Adoption by Parent, Guardian Ad Litem, Guardian of the Person of the Child.".

**Time given to a birthmother to revoke her consent:** 30 days.

**Court handling adoptions?** Superior Court.

**Adoption of Native Children:** ICWA is federal law.

**Adoption records sealed?** Yes, only non-identifying information can be released without Court sanction.

**Photo-listing book available?**

**PALS** Book.

## PUBLIC AGENCIES

★ 543 ★
**Alamance County Department of Social Services**
1950 Martin St.
Burlington, NC 27215
Phone: (910) 228-6441

**Mailing address:**
P.O. Box 3406, Burlington, NC 27215

**Contact:** Mrs. Carole Matthews, Supervisor.

**Description:** Public agency.

**Area served:** Residents of Alamance County.

**Requirements:** Adults, 21 yrs. and older, who have an income that can accommodate a child and his/her needs and sufficient life expectancy to rear a child to adulthood.

**Fees:** None.

**Number of children placed last year:** 15.

**Description of children:** Primarily African-American school age sibling groups.

**Adoption procedure:**
1) Submit application;
2) attend MAPP training;
3) participate in individual interviews;
4) if approved, placement;
5) post-placement supervision;
6) finalization.

**Average length of time between application and start of home study:** 1-6 mos.

**Average length of time to complete home study:** Depends upon scheduling of MAPP training.

**Number of interviews:** 4-6.

**Home study description:** Evaluation of family history, health and fertility, employment and marital stability, motivation to adopt and parenting skills. Study also seeks to identify the type of child the applicant can successfully parent.

**Average wait for a child after approval of a home study:** Depends on range of special needs family is willing to accept and the number of children awaiting adoptive placement.

**Foster care:** Temporary and long-term.

★ 544 ★
**Cleveland County Department of Social Services**
130 S. Post Rd.
P.O. Drawer 900
Shelby, NC 28150
Phone: (704) 487-0661

**Contact:** Rebecca Williams.

**Date established:** 1937.

**Description:** Public county agency.

**Area served:** Residents of Cleveland County.

**Requirements:** Adults, 21 yrs. and older, who are financially stable, whose present health is good, and who have medical documentation of infertility.

**Fees:** None.

**Number of children placed last year:** 10.

**Description of children:** Black and white infants, older children, sibling groups and children with special needs.

**Adoption procedure:**
1) Initial inquiry;
2) admission to waiting list for orientation meeting;
3) attend parenting class;
4) complete home study;
5) if approved, child search;
6) placement;
7) 1 yr. post-placement supervision;
8) finalization.

**Average length of time between application and start of home study:** 1-6 mos.

**Average length of time to complete home study:** 3-6 mos.

**Number of interviews:** Unavailable.

**Home study description:** Joint and individual process which assesses strengths and weaknesses, health and personal adjustment; capacity to parent an adopted child, readiness to parent and to adopt; and the type of child who would benefit from being placed in their home. The study provides experience for growth and change in the applicants' attitudes and expectations as they begin to have a better understanding of what is involved in adoption.

**Average wait for a child after approval of a home study:** 12-24 mos.

**Foster care:** Temporary.


★545★
**Craven County Department of Social Services**
P.O. Box 12039
New Bern, NC 28561
Phone: (919) 636-4900
Fax: (919) 636-4946

**Contact:** Adoption intake worker.

**Description:** Public agency.

**Area served:** Residents of Craven County.

**Requirements:** Flexible.

**Fees:** None.

**Number of children placed last year:** 15-20.

**Description of children:** Black and biracial infants, sibling groups, physically, mentally, emotionally and behaviorally handicapped children; older children.

**Adoption procedure:**
1) Initial inquiry;
2) file application;
3) home study;
4) if approved, placement;
5) file adoption petition;
6) 1 yr. post-placement supervision;
7) finalization.

**Average length of time between application and start of home study:** Varies.

**Average length of time to complete home study:** 4 mos.

**Number of interviews:** Unavailable.

**Home study description:** Evaluation of biographical and background information, openness and acceptance of adoption, methods of discipline and willingness to share affection, response to crises and support systems.

**Average wait for a child after approval of a home study:** Varies.

**Foster care:** Temporary and occasionally long-term.


★546★
**Cumberland County Department of Social Services**
421 Maiden Ln.
Fayetteville, NC 28302
Phone: (910) 323-1540
Fax: (910) 323-1509

**Mailing address:**
P.O. Box 2429, Fayetteville, NC 28302

**Contact:** Lee Roberts or Rosemary Zimmerman.

**Date established:** C. 1935.

**Description:** Public, county agency.

**Area served:** Residents of Cumberland County.

**Requirements:** Adults between the ages of 25 and 40 yrs., who are able to manage their income appropriately, who can present medical documentation of fertility studies, and who are either single, divorced, widowed or married; if married, marriage should be of at least 2 yrs. duration at the time of application. Age, length of marriage and fertility studies requirements waived for placement of black and older children and children with special needs.

**Fees:** None.

**Number of children placed last year:** 23.

**Description of children:** Children of all ages, races and nationalities, some with special needs.

**Adoption procedure:**
1) Submit application;
2) complete home study;
3) if approved, placement;
4) 1 yr. post-placement supervision;
5) finalization.

**Average length of time between application and start of home study:** 1-6 mos.

**Average length of time to complete home study:** 6 mos.

**Number of interviews:** 4 group and 4 or more individual.

**Home study description:** Assessment of motivation to adopt, parenting experiences, family history, human sexuality, feelings surrounding and resolution of infertility, marital and family strengths and needs. Agency uses the Model Approach to Partnership in Parenting (MAPP) as study model.

**Average wait for a child after approval of a home study:** 12-24 mos.

**Foster care:** Temporary, some long-term and fost-adopt.


★547★
**Davidson County Department of Social Services**
P.O. Box 788
Lexington, NC 27292
Phone: (704) 242-2500
Fax: (704) 249-7588

**Contact:** The Jackson or Paula Sink.

**Description:** Public, county agency.

**Area served:** Residents of Davidson County.

**Requirements:** Adults, 21 yrs. and older who are age appropriate to the type of child requested, whose health and income are adequate to provide for a child and who have no adoption application pending with another agency.

**Fees:** None.

**Number of children placed last year:** 9.

**Description of children:** Primarily children with special needs.

**Adoption procedure:**
1) Submit application;
2) attend parent preparation classes;

3) complete home study;
4) if approved, child search;
5) placement;
6) 1 yr. post-placement supervision during which time both the Petition to Adopt and the Interlocutory Decree are filed;
7) file Final Order and issue amended birth certificate.

**Average length of time between application and start of home study:** 1-6 mos.

**Average length of time to complete home study:** 2-3 mos.

**Number of interviews:** 8 classes and 3-5 individual.

**Home study description:** Assessment of life and marital history, family adjustment, flexibility, stability, home and environment, religion, recommendation of references, parenting skills, plans for child care, health and finances.

**Average wait for a child after approval of a home study:** Varies.

**Foster care:** Temporary.

### ★548★
**Forsyth County Department of Social Services**
P.O. Box 999
Winston-Salem, NC 27102
Phone: (919) 727-2023

**Contact:** Mary Lou Rix.

**Description:** Non-profit, public, county agency.

**Area served:** Residents of Forsyth County.

**Requirements:** Adults over the age of 21 yrs. who are either single or married; if married, evidence of stable union.

**Fees:** None.

**Number of children placed last year:** Unavailable.

**Description of children:** Infants, children with special needs and older children; mostly black children of all ages.

**Adoption procedure:**
1) File application;
2) submit references, medical reports, financial statement and law enforcement checks;
3) complete home study and training;
4) if approved, child search and placement;
5) 1 yr. post-placement supervision;
6) finalization.

**Average length of time between application and start of home study:** 6-12 mos.

**Average length of time to complete home study:** 3 mos.

**Number of interviews:** 5 plus training.

**Home study description:** Assessment of family stability, background, strengths, needs, acceptance of adoption and type of child desired.

**Average wait for a child after approval of a home study:** Varies with child desired.

**Foster care:** Temporary, short and long-term.

### ★549★
**Guilford County Department of Social Services**
**Adoption Unit**
301 N. Eugene St.
Greensboro, NC 27402
Phone: (919) 373-3834
Fax: (910) 333-6868

**Mailing address:**
  P.O. Box 3388, Greensboro, NC 27402

**Contact:** Helen D. Ahspaugh, Supervisor Adoption Services.

**Date established:** C. 1930.

**Description:** Non-profit public agency.

**Area served:** Residents of Guilford County.

**Requirements:** Applicants may be married or single, if married, applicants must be married at least 3 yrs. before placement.

**Fees:** None.

**Number of children placed last year:** 35.

**Description of children:** Children from infancy to 17 yrs., primarily minority, or over 10 yrs. old, or with an uncorrectable mental, physical or emotional handicap, or members of a sibling group of 3 or more.

**Adoption procedure:**
1) Attend individual interview or general orientation meeting;
2) submit formal application;
3) complete adoption study and training;
4) if approved, placement;
5) 1 yr. post-placement supervision.

**Average length of time between application and start of home study:** 1-6 mos. for special needs child; 24 or more mos. for white healthy children under 10 yrs. old.

**Average length of time to complete home study:** 3-6 mos.

**Number of interviews:** 8 group and 3-6 individual.

**Home study description:** Agency focuses on training potential adoptive parents in adoption issues so that they can make an informed decision on their ability to parent the type of child needing placement.

**Average wait for a child after approval of a home study:** 1-6 mos. for special needs child.

**Foster care:** Temporary, long-term and permanent.

### ★550★
**Harnett County Department of Social Services**
P.O. Box 669
Lillington, NC 27546
Phone: (910) 893-7500
Fax: (910) 893-6604

**Contact:** Cynthia T. Milton, Adoption Supervisor.

**Description:** Public, county agency.

**Area served:** Residents of Harnett County.

**Requirements:** Applicants must be married 3 yrs.

**Fees:** None.

**Number of children placed last year:** 12.

**Description of children:** Infants and children with special needs.

**Adoption procedure:**
1) File application;
2) attend adoption education classes;
3) complete home study;
4) if approved, placement;
5) supervision of placement;
6) finalization.

**Average length of time between application and start of home study:** 24 or more mos.

**Average length of time to complete home study:** 6-8 wks.

**Number of interviews:** Unavailable.

**Home study description:** Assessment of parents' ability to meet the needs of adopted children and the type of child they can parent.

**Average wait for a child after approval of a home study:** Varies.

**Foster care:** Temporary and long-term.

★551★
**Lenoir County Department of Social Services**
P.O. Box 6
Kinston, NC 28501
Phone: (919) 559-6211
Fax: (919) 559-6380

**Contact:** Deloris Bunch.

**Description:** Government mandated, state agency.

**Area served:** Residents of Lenoir County.

**Requirements:** Couples, 21 yrs. and older, who are married at least 3 yrs.

**Fees:** None.

**Number of children placed last year:** 6.

**Description of children:** Children of all ages and races.

**Adoption procedure:**
1) Initial inquiry;
2) file application;
3) complete home study;
4) if approved, child search and placement;
5) 1 yr. post-placement supervision;
6) finalization.

**Average length of time between application and start of home study:** 1-6 mos.

**Average length of time to complete home study:** 2-3 mos.

**Number of interviews:** 3.

**Home study description:** Assessment of support systems, marital stability, problem-solving ability and stress levels.

**Average wait for a child after approval of a home study:** 6-12 mos.

**Foster care:** Temporary and some long-term.


★552★
**Nash County Department of Social Services**
P.O. Drawer 819
Nashville, NC 27856
Phone: (919) 459-9818
Fax: (919) 459-9833

**Contact:** Carl M. Daughtry, Director.

**Date established:** 1939.

**Description:** Public welfare agency.

**Area served:** Residents of Nash County.

**Requirements:** Adults, 21 yrs. and older, single or married at least 2 yrs., who have sufficient income to support another family member and whose health is adequate to parent.

**Fees:** None.

**Number of children placed last year:** 10.

**Description of children:** Infants and children with special needs.

**Adoption procedure:**
1) Attend Adoption Orientation Meeting;
2) submit application and acceptance sheet;
3) admission to waiting list;
4) Model Approach to Partnerships in Parenting Class (MAPP)
5) complete home study;
6) if approved, child search and match;
7) placement;
8) 1 yr. post-placement supervision;
9) finalization.

**Average length of time between application and start of home study:** 6-12 mos.

**Average length of time to complete home study:** 4-6 mos.

**Number of interviews:** 6 or more.

**Home study description:** Evaluation which includes but is not limited to a description of the applicant(s), their home and community, background information, courtship, marriage and family, health and fertility, education, employment and finances, recommendation of references, attitudes toward adoption and type of child requested.

**Average wait for a child after approval of a home study:** 6-12 mos.

**Foster care:** Temporary and long-term.


★553★
**New Hanover County Department of Social Services**
P.O. Drawer 1559
Wilmington, NC 28402
Phone: (910) 341-4798
Fax: (910) 341-4360

**Contact:** Barbara B. Brown, Supervisor.

**Description:** Public, county agency.

**Area served:** Residents of New Hanover County.

**Requirements:** Adults over the age of 18 yrs. single or married; if married both spouses must be interested in adopting.

**Fees:** None.

**Number of children placed last year:** 1.

**Description of children:** Black and white children, some sibling groups and some with special needs.

**Adoption procedure:**
1) Attend information meeting;
2) submit initial application;
3) participate in 10 sessions of training;
4) complete interview process, questionnaire and autobiography;
5) if approved, child search and placement;
6) 1 yr. supervision of placement;
7) finalization.

**Average length of time between application and start of home study:** Varies.

**Average length of time to complete home study:** 2 mos.

**Number of interviews:** 5.

**Home study description:** Overall assessment of family's strength, need, background including court check, acceptance of adoption and preferences.

**Average wait for a child after approval of a home study:** Depends on child requested.

**Foster care:** Temporary, long-term and permanent.


★554★
**Orange County Department of Social Services**
300 W. Tryon St.
Hillsborough, NC 27278
Phone: (919) 732-8181
Fax: (919) 644-3005

**Contact:** Jenifer Montsinger, Adoption Supervisor.

**Description:** Non-profit public agency.

**Area served:** Residents of Orange County.

**Requirements:** Flexible.

**Fees:** None.

**Number of children placed last year:** 27.

**Description of children:** 8 infants (black, foreign-born and white) and 19 children between the ages of 2 and 10 yrs. (black and white).

**Adoption procedure:**
1) Initial inquiry;
2) complete home study;
3) if approved, placement;
4) post-placement supervision for 1 yr. during which time family files petition to adopt, order-of-reference and interlocutory decree and agency files 2 court reports;
5) finalization.

**Average length of time between application and start of home study:** 1-6 mos. for black infants/older children; 12-24 mos. for white, healthy infants.

**Average length of time to complete home study:** 1-3 mos.

**Number of interviews:** 6.

**Home study description:** Detailed study of adoptive applicants' family background and current situation.

**Average wait for a child after approval of a home study:** Varies greatly.

**Foster care:** Temporary, long-term and permanent.

★ 555 ★
**Pitt County Department of Social Services**
1717 W. 5th St.
Greenville, NC 27858
Phone: (919) 413-1101
Fax: (919) 413-1252

**Contact:** Paula Tyson, Adoption Social Worker or Melissa Hatcher, Adoption Supervisor.

**Date established:** C. 1921.

**Description:** County-operated public agency.

**Area served:** Residents of Pitt County.

**Requirements:** Adults 18 yrs. and older who are sufficiently healthy to parent a child.

**Fees:** None.

**Number of children placed last year:** 8.

**Description of children:** 5 black and 3 white, ages 4 to 15 yrs.

**Adoption procedure:**
1) Submit application;
2) complete home study;
3) if approved, placement;
4) post-placement supervision period and filing of petition and reports;
5) interlocutory decree issued;
6) final order and amended birth certificate issued.

**Average length of time between application and start of home study:** 12-24 mos.

**Average length of time to complete home study:** 8-12 wks.

**Number of interviews:** 5.

**Home study description:** Evaluation of family background; health history, including fertility; employment and financial information; attitudes toward adoption and childrearing; motivation to adopt and type of child requested.

**Average wait for a child after approval of a home study:** 12-24 mos.

**Foster care:** Temporary and long-term.

★ 556 ★
**Randolph County Department of Social Services**
P.O. Box 3239
Asheboro, NC 27204
Phone: (910) 318-6400
Fax: (910) 318-6853

**Contact:** Mrs. Susan French, Adoptions Social Worker.

**Date established:** 1937.

**Description:** County-operated public social services agency.

**Area served:** Residents of Randolph County.

**Requirements:** Applicants should have sufficient life expectancy to parent a child to adulthood. Applicants for infants must be childless.

**Fees:** None.

**Number of children placed last year:** 7.

**Description of children:** 6 children with special needs, 1 white male infant.

**Adoption procedure:**
1) File application;
2) complete home study and MAPP classes;
3) if approved, wait for placement and/or register on state adoption exchange;
4) placement;
5) 1 yr. post-placement supervision;
6) finalization.

**Average length of time between application and start of home study:** 1-6 mos.

**Average length of time to complete home study:** 6 mos.

**Number of interviews:** 6 or more, at least 2 of which are in-home.

**Home study description:** Evaluation of biographical information on all family members; issues surrounding infertility and its resolution, if applicable; type of child applicant(s)' believe they can best parent.

**Average wait for a child after approval of a home study:** Varies.

**Foster care:** Temporary, long-term, pre-adoptive and permanent.

★ 557 ★
**Rowan County Department of Social Services**
105 Corriher Ave.
Salisbury, NC 28144
Phone: (704) 638-3189
Fax: (704) 638-3134

**Contact:** Clayton Jones or Cindy Reaves.

**Description:** Non-profit, public, county agency.

**Area served:** Residents of Rowan County.

**Requirements:** Adults, 18 yrs. and older, single or married; if married, marriage must be of at least 1 yr. duration.

**Fees:** None.

**Number of children placed last year:** 6.

**Description of children:** Black infants and white school-age children.

**Adoption procedure:**
1) Submit formal application with references, medical and financial reports;
2) complete adoption study;
3) if approved, child search and placement;
4) 1 yr. post-placement supervision;
5) finalization.

**Average length of time between application and start of home study:** 24 or more mos.

**Average length of time to complete home study:** 90 days.

**Number of interviews:** 7.

**Home study description:** Evaluation of personality, background, marital stability, medical and employment reports, social data and attitudes surrounding adoption-related issues.

Average wait for a child after approval of a home study: 12-24 mos.

Foster care: Temporary, long-term and permanent.

★ 558 ★
**Union County Department of Social Services**
P.O. Box 489
Monroe, NC 28111
Phone: (704) 289-6581
Fax: (704) 282-6200

Contact: Sandi Summerlin.

Description: Public, county agency.

Area served: Residents of Union County.

Requirements: Adults, 21 yrs. and older, who are residents of the county for at least 6 mos., single or married; if married, marriage must be of at least 3 yrs. duration.

Fees: None.

Number of children placed last year: 12.

Description of children: Infants, older children and children with special needs, some inter-country placements.

Adoption procedure:
1) Submit application;
2) attend adoption classes and office interviews;
3) reference and court records checks;
4) home conferences;
5) submit autobiographies and financial statement;
6) if approved, state-wide search for child and placement;
7) 1-3 yrs. post-placement supervision;
8) finalization.

Average length of time between application and start of home study: 6-12 mos.

Average length of time to complete home study: 6 mos.

Number of interviews: 9.

Home study description: Assessment of family history, relationships, stability and functioning; degree of acceptance of different types of children; and type of child that could best be placed with adoptive applicants.

Average wait for a child after approval of a home study: Varies.

Foster care: Temporary, long-term, pre-adoptive and permanent.

★ 559 ★
**Wake County Department of Social Services**
220 Swinburne St.
Raleigh, NC 27610
Phone: (919) 212-7000

Mailing address:
P.O. Box 46833, Raleigh, NC 27610

Contact: Adoption Unit.

Date established: 1932.

Description: County-operated public agency.

Area served: Residents of Wake County.

Requirements: Adults, 21 yrs. and older.

Fees: None.

Number of children placed last year: 20.

Description of children: Minority children with special needs.

Adoption procedure: Applicant is assigned to a Parent Preparation Group. Upon completion of the 8 wk. course, agency and applicant complete individual assessment.

Average length of time between application and start of home study: Parent preparation classes are scheduled every 2 mos.

Average length of time to complete home study: 4-6 mos.

Number of interviews: 3-6.

Home study description: Joint decision making process by the agency and the applicant(s) which includes family evaluative materials, self-assessment, and a combination of group and individual study.

Average wait for a child after approval of a home study: Dependent upon age of the child requested and the children awaiting adoptive placement.

Foster care: Emergency, temporary, long-term, and therapeutic.

## PRIVATE AGENCIES

★ 560 ★
**Bethany Christian Services of Asheville**
25 Reed St.
Asheville, NC 28813
Phone: (704) 274-7146
1-800-BETHANY

Mailing address:
P.O. Box 15569, Asheville, NC 28813

Branch address:
P.O. Box 470036, Charlotte, NC 28247
Phone: (704) 541-1833

P.O. Box 12094, Raleigh, NC 27605
Phone: (919) 828-6281

Contact: Dahlene S. Morse, Branch Supervisor.

Date established: 1984.

Description: Private, not-for-profit child-placing and caring agency licensed by the North Carolina Dept. of Human Resources.

Area served: Residents within a 150 mi. radius of either the Asheville or Raleigh offices.

Requirements: Vary by program.

Fees: Professional and medical service fees.

Number of children placed last year: 28.

Description of children: Domestic white, black, and biracial infants, some with special needs and foreign-born children from different countries.

Adoption procedure:
1) Submit letter of inquiry;
2) file preliminary application;
3) if accepted, file formal application;
4) attend informational meeting;
5) complete home study;
6) if approved, placement;
7) 1 yr. post-placement supervision;
8) finalization and naturalization (if foreign-born).

Average length of time between application and start of home study: 1-6 mos.

Average length of time to complete home study: 3 mos.

Number of interviews: 4.

Home study description: Assessment of motivation to adopt, child-rearing patterns, background information, medical and financial reports, recommendation of references, etc.

**Average wait for a child after approval of a home study:** 1-6 mos.

**Foster care:** Temporary.

★ **561** ★
**Carolina Adoption Services, Inc.**
2708 N. Church St.
Greensboro, NC 27405
Phone: (910) 275-9660

**Contact:** Rosemary Martin, C.C.S.W., Director.

**Date established:** December, 1993.

**Description:** Private, non-profit child placement agency licensed by the North Carolina Department of Social Services.

**Area served:** Full service for North Carolina residents; placements for cooperating U.S. agencies.

**Requirements:** Applicants must be 25 yrs. and older with average health and income.

**Fees:** Application: $150; home study: $1500; placement: $2500. International adoption fees including agency and legal fees, travel and documentation range from $8,000 - $14,000.

**Number of children placed last year:** New agency.

**Description of children:** Infants and children from Latin America and Eastern Europe; U.S. children with special needs.

**Adoption procedure:** 1) Inquiry; 2) application; 3) home study; 4) adoption committee decision; 5) dossier preparation; 6) dossier referred to placing country; 7) child assignment; 8) child acceptance; 9) travel for placement; 10) post-placement services.

**Average length of time between application and start of home study:** Less than 1 mo.

**Average length of time to complete home study:** 1 mo.

**Number of interviews:** 5 - 6.

**Home study description:** Educational and supportive process wherein the agency learns about the applicant(s) as individuals, and a couple, if applicable; their motivation to adopt, readiness for parenting and parenting style, their value system and child care plans.

**Average wait for a child after approval of a home study:** 1 - 12 mos.

**Foster care:** Pre-adoptive.

★ **562** ★
**Catholic Social Ministries of the Diocese of Raleigh, Inc.**
400 Oberlin Rd., Ste. 350
Raleigh, NC 27605
Phone: (919) 832-0225

**Branch address:**
111 Boone Tr., Fayetteville, NC 28306
Phone: (910) 424-2020

P.O. Box 8241, Greenville, NC 27835-8241

**Contact:** Roderick B. O'Connor, ACSW, Regional Director (Raleigh); Sr. Dorothy Ann Pyle, MSW, Director (Fayetteville); Elaine Franzetti, MSW (Greenville).

**Date established:** 1972.

**Description:** Licensed non-profit private agency. The information given below describes the international/interstate adoption in which CSM is not the placing agency but does home studies and post-placement supervision. CSM's traditional adoption placement program has seen a decline in the number of babies placed while the waiting list has remained long. Potential adoptive parents are urged to apply for the international/interstate program.

**Area served:** Residents of the Diocese of Raleigh (eastern half of North Carolina, within 150 mile radius of Raleigh).

**Requirements:** Couples married at least 3 yrs., at least one of whom must be a practicing Catholic, who are financially stable and in reasonably good health.

**Fees:** $100 application fee; $990 home study fee; $775 post-placement supervision fee. Mileage supplement where applicable.

**Description of children:** Children of various ages and racial/ethnic backgrounds from different countries.

**Adoption procedure:** 1)Receive and review information packet; 2)complete and return application; 3)home study, including group sessions; 4)acceptance by international placing agency; 5)completion of immigration forms; 6)placement (often in country of origin); 7)post-placement supervision; 8)finalization.

**Average length of time between application and start of home study:** 2-3 wks.

**Average length of time to complete home study:** 3-4 mos.

**Number of interviews:** 5-7.

**Home study description:** Evaluation which includes but is not limited to applicants' readiness for adoptive parenthood and the lifestyle and environment in which the child will be raised.

**Average wait for a child after approval of a home study:** 24 or more mos.

**Foster care:** Temporary.

★ **563** ★
**Catholic Social Services of Charlotte**
116 E. 1st St.
Charlotte, NC 28202
Phone: (704) 343-9954
Fax: (704) 333-3943

**Branch address:**
75 Blue Ridge Ave., Asheville, NC 28806
Phone: (904) 255-0146

621 W. Second St., Winston-Salem, NC 27101
Phone: (910) 727-0705

**Contact:** Mrs. Elizabeth K. Thurbee, ACSW, Executive Director and Diocesan Director ofAdoption Services.

**Date established:** 1948.

**Description:** Private non-profit agency licensed by the State of North Carolina.

**Area served:** Residents of the 46 counties of the Diocese of Charlotte.

**Requirements:** Couples married at least 3 yrs., who are active in the Christian denomination of their choice, who have no more than 1 child and who have completed fertility testing and treatment.

**Fees:** $200 application fee; $1500 home study fee; $150 education fee; $150 approval fee; placement and supervision fee is 10% of gross income.

**Number of children placed last year:** 15.

**Description of children:** Primarily healthy white infants and a few black and biracial infants. Agency has also started a program for placement of Russian children.

**Adoption procedure:**
1) Attend intake interview;
2) submit application;
3) review of application by Approval Committee;
4) if accepted, complete home study;
5) review of home study by Approval Committee;
6) if approved, placement;
7) 12 mos. post-placement supervision;
8) file petition within 2 mos. of placement;
9) finalization.

**Average length of time between application and start of home study:** 1-6 mos.

**Average length of time to complete home study:** 6 mos.

**Number of interviews:** Normally 7-8 interviews are the minimum; additional interviews if needed.

**Home study description:** Evaluation of personal data; feelings about self, marriage and parenting; issues surrounding fertility and the grief process; motivation to adopt and issues surrounding adoption; attitudes toward birthparents; degrees of openness.

**Average wait for a child after approval of a home study:** 12-24 mos.

**Foster care:** Temporary.


★ 564 ★
**The Children's Home Society of North Carolina**
740 Chestnut St.
Greensboro, NC 27415
Phone: (910) 274-1538
(800) 632-1400
Fax: (910) 274-7347

**Mailing address:**
P.O. Box 14608, Greensboro, NC 27415

**Branch address:**
Wilcar Executive Bldg., 223 Tenth St., Greenville, NC 27834

4904 Professional Court, Ste. 203, Raleigh, NC 27609

**Contact:** Sandy Cook, Executive Director.

**Date established:** 1902.

**Description:** Private, non-profit, non-sectarian adoption and foster care services agency licensed by the North Carolina State Dept. of Human Resources, accredited by the Council on Accreditation of Services for Families and Children and a member of the Child Welfare League of America.

**Area served:** Residents of the State of North Carolina.

**Requirements:** Couples whose health indicates a normal life expectancy, who have a physician's statement of infertility, who have adequate financial resources for another family member and can provide a loving, safe home. Requirements are flexible for special needs placements.

**Fees:** Fees are charged on a sliding scale basis. Fees are payable as services are provided.

**Number of children placed last year:** 184.

**Description of children:** Infants and children with special needs.

**Adoption procedure:**
1) Initial telephone inquiry;
2) attend orientation meeting;
3) submit application;
4) attend primary screening interview;

5) if accepted, complete home study;
6) placement;
7) 1 yr. post-placement supervision;
8) final order.

**Average length of time between application and start of home study:** 1-6 mos.

**Average length of time to complete home study:** 3-6 mos.

**Number of interviews:** 5-8.

**Home study description:** A complete assessment of family background, physical description of applicant couple, educational and occupational history, interests, health and finances, references, strengths and weaknesses, lifestyle, ability and readiness to parent, expectations of a child in order to understand the individual character and uniqueness of each family unit and its total offering to a child.

**Average wait for a child after approval of a home study:** 12-24 mos.

**Foster care:** Temporary.


★ 565 ★
**Christian Adoption Services, Inc.**
624 Matthew-Mint Hill Rd., Ste. 134
Matthews, NC 28105
Phone: (704) 847-0038
Fax: (704) 841-1538

**Contact:** James Woodward.

**Date established:** 1979.

**Description:** Private, non-profit organization which holds 501 (c) (3) tax exemption under the IRS and which is licensed to place children by the Oklahoma Department of Human Services.

**Area served:** Direct services to residents within a 100 mi. radius of Asheville, Charlotte, Durham, Fayettesville and Greensboro, NC. Placement throughout the U.S.

**Requirements:** Practicing Christian singles or couples married for 2 -5 yrs. who are no older than 45 yrs. old, and in good health, physically and emotionally.

**Fees:** Application: $100; home study: $1500. Foreign program fees and post-placement supervision fees are additional. Adoption fees for domestic infants: $10,000 plus personal expenses for child and birth mother. Fees sometimes waived for waiting children.

**Number of children placed last year:** 24.

**Description of children:** Primarily infants and toddlers from Asia and Latin America; sibling groups and children with special needs upon request. A small domestic program is in the formative stages.

**Adoption procedure:** 1) Pre-adoption process including application, snapshot and statements of faith; 2) dossier development; 3) dossier sent abroad; 4) placement via travel or child escort: 5) post-placement services; 6) finalization; 7) naturalization.

**Average length of time between application and start of home study:** 1 - 6 mos.

**Average length of time to complete home study:** 2 mos.

**Number of interviews:** 4.

**Home study description:** Assessment which includes health reports and clearances, personal descriptions, family background, childhood, education and occupation, marital relationship and children already in the family, adoptive experiences and attitudes, parenting assessment, religion, cross cultural attitudes, lifestyle, finances and money management, home and community, references and a description of the child recommended for placement.

**Average wait for a child after approval of a home study:** 6 - 12 mos.

**Foster care:** Cradle care.

**★ 566 ★**
**Family Services, Inc.**
610 Coliseum Dr.
Winston-Salem, NC 27106
Phone: (919) 722-8173
Fax: (910) 724-6491

**Contact:** Rebecca L. Nagaishi, ACSW.

**Date established:** C. 1900.

**Description:** Non-profit private agency licensed for child placing by the North Carolina Dept. of Human Resources.

**Area served:** Residents of Davie, Forsyth, Stokes and Yadkin counties.

**Requirements:** Caucasian infant: couples married at least 3 yrs. who are over 25 yrs. of age and under 40 yrs. of age.

**Fees:** 7% of family income.

**Number of children placed last year:** 8.

**Description of children:** Infants.

**Adoption procedure:**
1) File application;
2) undergo home assessment;
3) committee decision process;
4) if approved, placement;
5) 1 yr. post-placement supervision.

**Average length of time between application and start of home study:** Varies.

**Average length of time to complete home study:** 4-6 mos.

**Number of interviews:** 6-8.

**Home study description:** Assessment of family and marital history, individual personalities, maturity and financial stability, positive interpretation of adoption and openness to needs of birthparents.

**Average wait for a child after approval of a home study:** Varies.

**Foster care:** Temporary.

**★ 567 ★**
**Lutheran Family Services in the Carolinas**
P.O. Box 12287
Raleigh, NC 27605
Phone: (919) 832-2620
Fax: (919) 832-0591

**Contact:** Joyce Gourley, Director of Adoptions.

**Date established:** Adoption program: 1986.

**Description:** Non-profit, private agency licensed by the North Carolina Dept. of Human Resources and South Carolina Dept. of Social Services.

**Area served:** Residents of North Carolina and South Carolina.

**Requirements:** Varies with child's country of origin.

**Fees:** Application fee: $150;
home study: $950;
post-placement supervision for North Carolina adoption: $650; for South Carolina per visit and report: $130.

**Number of children placed last year:** 65.

**Description of children:** International children.

**Adoption procedure:**
1) Call for application;
2) return completed application;

3) complete home study;
4) referral to international placing agency;
5) compile dossier;
6) travel to escort child;
7) post-placement supervision;
8) finalization.

**Average length of time between application and start of home study:** 1 mo. or less.

**Average length of time to complete home study:** 3 mos.

**Number of interviews:** 4-6.

**Home study description:** Assessment of the family's readiness to adopt which looks at adoption and international issues and helps prepare them for adoptive parenthood.

**Average wait for a child after approval of a home study:** Dependent on placing agency.

**Foster care:** Emergency, short and long-term.

# NORTH DAKOTA

## STATUTES

**★ 568 ★**

**Subsidies provided?** Non-recurring medical and maintenance.

**Adoption cost defined by law?** All costs are reviewed by the court and may include expenses related to the child's birth including medical, legal and placement.

**Insurance for infertility?:** Unknown.

**Home study required by state?** Required before placement.

**Prospective adoptive parent advertise for a child?** Permitted.

**Surrogacy laws?** Surrogate agreements are void.

**Residents access agencies of other states or countries?** Permitted adopting parents have the permission of the state.

**Requires judicial termination of birth parents' rights?** By both birth parents in the presence of court personnel in writing.

**Time given to a birthmother to revoke her consent:** 10 days.

**Court handling adoptions?** District Court.

**Adoption of Native Children:** On reservation: tribal agency and court; off reservation: Tribal or District court.

**Adoption records sealed?** Yes, but at age 18 yrs. adoptees can initiate an agency search.

**Photo-listing book available?** Yes.

## PUBLIC AGENCIES

**★ 569 ★**
**North Dakota Department of Human Services**
**Division of Children and Family Services**
600 East Blvd.
Bismarck, ND 58505
Phone: (701) 224-2316
(800) 755-2730
Fax: (701) 224-2359

**Contact:** Adoption unit.

**Description:** Public, state agency.

**Area served:** Residents of North Dakota.

**Requirements:** Vary with child-placing agency.

**Fees:** Established by costs justification.

**Number of children placed last year:** 406.

**Description of children:** Infants, foreign-born children, children with special needs and step-parent and relative adoptions.

**Adoption procedure:**
1) Initial inquiry;
2) file application;
3) studied by non-profit licensed child placing agency;
4) placement approved by central office;
5) post-placement supervision by child-placing agency;
6) finalization including consent of custodian of child.

**Average length of time between application and start of home study:** Varies by agency and type of adoption. Special needs: 1-6 mos.

**Average length of time to complete home study:** 6 mos.

**Number of interviews:** Varies by agency and type of adoption. Some agencies require group participation.

**Home study description:** Assessment of all aspects of family life. Standard Home Study Assessment Format required across all agencies.

**Average wait for a child after approval of a home study:** Varies by type of child and their needs.

**Foster care:** Temporary, long-term and permanent.

# PRIVATE AGENCIES

★570★
**Catholic Family Service (of Fargo)**
2537 S. University
Fargo, ND 58103
Phone: (701) 235-4457
Fax: (701) 239-8266

**Branch address:**
1223 12th St. S., Bismarck, ND 58504
Phone: (701) 255-1793

505 University Ave., Ste. 1, Grand Forks, ND 58201
Phone: (701) 775-4196

**Contact:** Adoption intake worker.

**Date established:** 1926.

**Description:** Non-profit private agency licensed in North Dakota.

**Area served:** Residents of North Dakota.

**Requirements:** Couples in a valid Catholic marriage who are no older than 40 yrs. than child placed, who are infertile and who have no more than 1 child. Requirements are flexible for special needs adoption.

**Fees:**
$100 pre-application fee;
$350 application fee;
$2910 home study fee;
$1940 post-placement services;
$5300 total.

**Number of children placed last year:** 14.

**Description of children:** Infants, foreign-born and special needs.

**Adoption procedure:**
1) Attend inquiry meeting;
2) file pre-application;
3) file application and fee agreement;
4) complete adoption study;
5) if approved, placement;
6) post-placement services;

7) legal adjudication.

**Average length of time between application and start of home study:** 24 or more mos.

**Average length of time to complete home study:** 2-3 mos.

**Number of interviews:** 4-6.

**Home study description:** Call or write for outline.

**Average wait for a child after approval of a home study:** 12-24 mos.

**Foster care:** Temporary.

★571★
**Christian Family Life Services, Inc.**
1201 12th Ave. N.
Fargo, ND 58102
Phone: (701) 237-4473
(800) 747-2304
Fax: (701) 280-9062

**Contact:** Ann Dahl, LSW, MSC or Rita Kolle, LSW.

**Date established:** 1985.

**Description:** Non-profit private agency licensed in Minnesota and North Dakota.

**Area served:** Residents of Minnesota and North Dakota.

**Requirements:** Couples of the Christian faith married at least 3 yrs. who are between the ages of 21 and 40 yrs., in general good health, who have adequate income, and who are living a Christ-centered life.

**Fees:** $6500 plus termination fee and possible foster care. Home study comprises approx. $2000 of the total fee. Occasionaly may be asked to help with medical bills.

**Number of children placed last year:** 11.

**Description of children:** Primarily healthy white infants, occasionally biracial infants.

**Adoption procedure:**
1) File application;
2) waiting period of up to 2 yrs.;
3) complete home study;
4) if approved, admission to waiting list for placement;
5) notification;
6) placement;
7) 6 mos. post-placement supervisory and
8) finalization.

**Average length of time between application and start of home study:** 1-6 mos.

**Average length of time to complete home study:** 1-2 mos.

**Number of interviews:** 4.

**Home study description:** Evaluation of health, lifestyle, marriage relationship, values, character, employment history and stability, reason(s) for and acceptance of infertility, and child rearing philosophy.

**Average wait for a child after approval of a home study:** 6-12 mos.

**Foster care:** Temporary.

★572★
**Lutheran Social Services of North Dakota**
1325 11 St., S.
Fargo, ND 58107
Phone: (701) 235-7341
Fax: (701) 235-7359

**Mailing address:**
P.O. Box 389, Fargo, ND 58107

**Branch address:**
721 Memorial Hwy., Bismarck, ND 58504
Phone: (701) 223-1510

**Contact:** Adoption coordinator.

**Description:** Non-profit, private agency.

**Area served:** Residents of North Dakota only.

**Requirements:** Couples married at least 2 yrs. who are no older than 44 yrs., who have no more than 1 child and a diagnosis of infertility and who are members of a Christian church.

**Fees:**
Healthy, Caucasian infant: $7200;
$200 fee for in-state children with special needs;
$1600-$2600 for identified, relative, foreign adoption home studies and post-placement supervision.

**Number of children placed last year:** N/A.

**Description of children:** Caucasian infants, through infant program and identified adoption. Beginning international adoption.

**Adoption procedure:** Open inquiry for healthy Caucasian infants. Agency will do pre-adoption counseling for international, out-of-state or identified adoptions as needed.

**Average length of time between application and start of home study:** 1 mo. or less for identified and international; otherwise dependent on program needs and birthparent trends for infant program.

**Average length of time to complete home study:** 3 mos.

**Number of interviews:** Minimum of 1 day group study and 1 home visit.

**Home study description:** Call or write for outline.

**Average wait for a child after approval of a home study:** Dependent upon couple's flexibility.

**Foster care:** Pre-adoptive.

★ 573 ★
**New Horizons Adoptions**
2823 Woodland Dr.
Bismarck, ND 58504
Phone: (701) 258-8650
(800) 358-8150

**Contact:** Nancy Kleingartner.

**Date established:** 1983.

**Description:** Private agency.

**Area served:** Residents of North Dakota.

**Requirements:** Varies with program requested.

**Fees:**
Application: $150;
Home study: $1400;
Post-placement services: $600.

**Number of children placed last year:** 38.

**Description of children:** U.S. and foreign-born children from 0-15 yrs., some with special needs.

**Adoption procedure:**
1) Register;
2) return completed application;
3) complete home study and compile supporting documentation for foreign source;
4) child referral;
5) compile additional documentation for immigration;
6) placement;
7) 6 or more mos. post-placement supervision;
8) finalization;
9) naturalization.

**Average length of time between application and start of home study:** 0-1 months.

**Average length of time to complete home study:** 1 month.

**Number of interviews:** 12-14 hrs.

**Home study description:** Evaluation of health, relationships, economics, values, leisure activities, occupation, housing and parenting skills.

**Average wait for a child after approval of a home study:** 12-24 months.

**Foster care:** Temporary.

★ 574 ★
**The Village Family Service Center**
1201 25th St. S.
Fargo, ND 58106-9859
Phone: (701) 235-6433
(800) 627-8220

**Mailing address:**
P.O. Box 9859, Fargo, ND 58106-9859

**Branch address:**
415 E. Ave. A, Bismarck, ND 58501
Phone: (701) 255-1165

215 N. 3rd St., Grand Forks, ND 58201
Phone: (701) 746-4584

308 2nd Ave. S.W., Minot, ND 58701
Phone: (701) 852-3328

**Contact:** Sharon Maier.

**Date established:** 1891.

**Description:** Non-profit private agency licensed through the North Dakota Dept. of Human Services.

**Area served:** Residents of North Dakota.

**Requirements:** Married couples who are preferably no more than 40 yrs. older than the child placed with them, who have fewer than 2 children, are financially stable, and, in cases where an applicant has been in treatment for drug or alcohol abuse, he/she must present a summation of treatment and have maintained sobriety for 3 yrs. Marital status requirement and requirement for number of children in applicant's home does not apply for special needs adoption.

**Fees:** Call or write for fee schedule.

**Number of children placed last year:** 29.

**Description of children:** Healthy white infants between the ages of 0-4 yrs.; special needs children; and foreign-born children.

**Adoption procedure:**
1) Written or telephone inquiry;
2) complete and return application form during office interview;
3) applicants' name added to waiting list;
4) attend 3 educational/informational group meetings;
5) complete home study;
6) if approved, placement;
7) 6 mos. post-placement supervisory;
8) finalization.

**Average length of time between application and start of home study:** 12-24 mos.

**Average length of time to complete home study:** 3-6 mos.

**Number of interviews:** 3 group and 3-4 individual.

**Home study description:** Educational and evaluatory process.

**Average wait for a child after approval of a home study:** 12-24 mos.

Foster care: Temporary.

# OHIO

## STATUTES

★ 575 ★

**Independent placement by intermediary?** Permitted.

**Independent placement by birth parents?** Illegal.

**Subsidies provided?** Title IV-E Adoption Assistance, maintenance and post-finalization special services.

**Adoption cost defined by law?** No.

**Insurance for infertility?:** No.

**Home study required by state?** Required before placement.

**Prospective adoptive parent advertise for a child?** Illegal.

**Surrogacy laws?** Permitted.

**Residents access agencies of other states or countries?** Permitted.

**Requires judicial termination of birth parents' rights?** Required by both parents before the court or a licensed agency.

**Time given to a birthmother to revoke her consent:** 6 mos.

**Court handling adoptions?** Probate.

**Adoption of Native Children:** Tribe.

**Adoption records sealed?** Yes.

**Photo-listing book available?** The Ohio Adoption Photo Listing.

## PUBLIC AGENCIES

★ 576 ★
**Ashtabula County Children Services Board**
P.O. Box 458
Ashtabula, OH 44004
Phone: (216) 998-1811

**Contact:** Mark Dougherty, Supervisor or Denise Smith, Adoption Worker.

**Description:** Public agency.

**Area served:** Residents of Ashtabula County.

**Requirements:** Open.

**Fees:** None.

**Number of children placed last year:** 11.

**Description of children:** Special needs.

**Adoption procedure:**
1) Intake
2) attend educational group meetings;
3) file formal application and complete home study;
4) if approved, placement;
5) post-placement supervision;
6) finalization.

**Average length of time between application and start of home study:** 1-6 mos.

**Average length of time to complete home study:** 4-5 wks.

**Number of interviews:** 2 in home, plus individual interview with each family member.

**Home study description:** Self-study process which compiles information and identifies the most appropriate type of child for the applicant family.

**Average wait for a child after approval of a home study:** Varies.

**Foster care:** Temporary and long-term.

★ 577 ★
**Belmont County Children Services Board**
410 Fox Shannon Pl.
St. Clairsville, OH 43950
Phone: (614) 695-3813

**Contact:** Judith G. Eilert, Adoption Specialist.

**Description:** Non-proft public agency licensed by the State of Ohio.

**Area served:** Primarily residents of Belmont County.

**Requirements:** In compliance with the State of Ohio's adoption rules as set forth in the revised Child Welfare Manual.

**Fees:** None.

**Number of children placed last year:** 9.

**Description of children:** Special needs and infant.

**Adoption procedure:**
1) Initial inquiry;
2) complete questionnaire and application;
3) attend classes;
4) complete home visit and interviews;
5) submit supporting paperwork;
6) home study written and submitted for approval.

**Average length of time between application and start of home study:** 1-6 mos.

**Average length of time to complete home study:** 1 yr.

**Number of interviews:** 3 or more.

**Home study description:** Study follows guidelines set forth in the Ohio Child Welfare Manual.

**Average wait for a child after approval of a home study:** 24 or more mos.

**Foster care:** Temporary, long-term and will soon have permanent.

★ 578 ★
**Brown County Department of Human Services**
775 Mt. Orab Pike
Georgetown, OH 45121
Phone: (513) 378-6104

**Contact:** Geri Cahall, Adoption Worker.

**Description:** Public county agency mandated to place children by the Ohio Department of Human Services.

**Area served:** Residents of Brown County.

**Requirements:** Single applicants must be at least 21 yrs. old. Couples must be married at least 1 yr. and one spouse must be 21 yrs, or older.

**Fees:** No agency fees.

**Number of children placed last year:** 2.

**Description of children:** Healthy children.

**Adoption procedure:** 1) Application; 2) reference and records checks; 3) financial, medical and vital records verification; 4) home study; 5) wait for placement; 6) placement; 7) post-placement supervision; 8) finalization.

**Average length of time between application and start of home study:** 1 - 6 mos.

**Average length of time to complete home study:** 150 days.

**Number of interviews:** 6.

**Home study description:** Assessment which includes marital and family stability, description of home, parenting ability and experience with children.

**Average wait for a child after approval of a home study:** 2 yrs. or more.

**Foster care:** Temporary and long-term.

---

★ 579 ★

**Butler County Children's Services Board**
300 N. Fair Ave.
Hamilton, OH 45011
Phone: (513) 887-4055
(800) 325-2685

**Contact:** Darlene Campbell, Adoption Supervisor.

**Description:** Public county agency mandated to place children by the Ohio Department of Human Services.

**Area served:** Residents of Butler County or families fostering children in the custody of Butler County.

**Requirements:** Single applicants must be at least 21 yrs. old. Couples must be married at least 1 yr. and one spouse must be at least 21 yrs. All applicant must have demonstrate the ability to manage financially and health adequate to the task of parenthood.

**Fees:** None.

**Number of children placed last year:** 38.

**Description of children:** Children with special needs.

**Adoption procedure:** 1) 12 hrs. of orientation; 2) home study; 3) placement; 4) post-placement supervision; 5)finalization.

**Average length of time between application and start of home study:** 1 - 6 mos.

**Average length of time to complete home study:** 3 - 4 mos.

**Number of interviews:** 4.

**Home study description:** Assessment which includes a brief history of each household member as well as the applicants' relationship, exploration of past stresses and mean of coping with same, exploration of the positive and negative aspects of parenting, support systems and applicant(s)' expectations of an adopted child.

**Average wait for a child after approval of a home study:** 1 - 6 mos. for a child younger than 8 yrs. with minimal problems.

**Foster care:** Temporary and long-term.

---

★ 580 ★

**Carroll County Department of Human Services**
95 E. Main St.
Carrollton, OH 44615
Phone: (216) 627-2571

**Mailing address:**
   P.O. Box 216, Carrollton, OH 44615

**Contact:** Jon D. Smith, Social Service Worker III.

**Description:** Non-profit public agency.

**Area served:** Residents of Carroll County.

**Requirements:** Adults, 21 yrs. or older.

**Fees:** None.

**Number of children placed last year:** 2.

**Description of children:** Special needs.

**Adoption procedure:**
 1) Agency sends preliminary information upon request;
 2) file application;
 3) agency verifies references
 4) complete home study and home visits

5) networking and matching through Adoption Listing Service of Ohio.

**Average length of time between application and start of home study:** Varies.

**Average length of time to complete home study:** 30 days.

**Number of interviews:** 4.

**Home study description:** Evaluation which includes but is not limited to type of home and environment; applicants understanding of agency's and client's role; and applicant's ability to parent.

**Average wait for a child after approval of a home study:** Varies.

**Foster care:** Temporary and long-term.

---

★ 581 ★

**Champaign County Department of Human Services**
2380 S. Route 68
Urbana, OH 43078-0353
Phone: (513) 652-1346

**Mailing address:**
   P.O. Box 353, Urbana, OH 43078-0353

**Contact:** Kathy M. Bailey, Social Worker.

**Description:** Public county agency mandated to place children by the Ohio Department of Human Services.

**Area served:** Residents of Champaign County.

**Requirements:** Applicants must be at least 22 yrs. old, married or single.

**Fees:** No agency fees.

**Number of children placed last year:** 2.

**Description of children:** Children with special needs.

**Adoption procedure:** 1) Application; 2) home study; 3) workshop; 4) up-dates; 5) placement; 6) post-placement supervision.

**Average length of time between application and start of home study:** Less than 1 mo.

**Average length of time to complete home study:** 3 mos.

**Number of interviews:** 4 - 6.

**Home study description:** Assessment which includes an a description of the family, applicant(s)' childhood, health, finances, extended family relationships, motivation to adopt, feeling toward birth families, marital relationships, family life activities and leisure time.

**Average wait for a child after approval of a home study:** 12 - 24 mos.

**Foster care:** Temporary, long-term and permanent.

---

★ 582 ★

**Clark County Department of Human Services**
1345 Lagonda Ave.
Springfield, OH 45503
Phone: (513) 327-1811
Fax: (513) 323-3885

**Contact:** Lynn House.

**Description:** Non-profit public children's services agency.

**Area served:** Residents of Clark County.

**Requirements:** Flexible.

**Fees:** None.

**Number of children placed last year:** 24.

**Description of children:** Primarily children with special needs.

**Adoption procedure:**
1) File application;
2) complete home study.

**Average length of time between application and start of home study:** 1-6 mos.

**Average length of time to complete home study:** 6 wks.

**Number of interviews:** Group meetings plus 4-5 individual.

**Home study description:** Evaluation of family background, current lifestyle, medical report(s), references and social information, applicant's ability to parent, etc.

**Average wait for a child after approval of a home study:** 12-24 mos.

**Foster care:** Temporary, long-term and permanent.

★ 583 ★
**Coshocton County Children Services Board**
318 Chestnut St.
Coshocton, OH 43812
Phone: (614) 622-2292

**Contact:** Alberta K. German, Executive Director.

**Description:** Non-profit public agency.

**Area served:** Residents of Coshocton County.

**Requirements:** Adults who are 21 yrs. or older, married at least 1 yr. or single, who are in good physical health and have adequate income.

**Fees:** $100.

**Number of children placed last year:** 2.

**Description of children:** N/A.

**Adoption procedure:**
1) Complete group home study process;
2) if approved, placement;
3) 6 mos. supervisory;
4) finalization.

**Average length of time between application and start of home study:** 1-6 mos.

**Average length of time to complete home study:** 8 wks.

**Number of interviews:** 2.

**Home study description:** Evaluation of personal and background information; medical report(s); criminal records clearances; and references.

**Average wait for a child after approval of a home study:** 12-24 mos.

**Foster care:** Temporary and occasionally long-term.

★ 584 ★
**Cuyohoga County Department of Children and Family Services**
3955 Euclid Ave.
Cleveland, OH 44115
Phone: (216) 431-4500

**Contact:** Adoption Unit.

**Description:** Public, county agency.

**Area served:** Primarily residents of Cuyahoga County for full adoption services.

**Requirements:** Adults, 18 yrs. and older, who are in reasonably good health, who are age appropriate to the child placed and whose current marital status (single, married, divorced or widowed) has been stable for at least 1 yr.

**Fees:** None.

**Number of children placed last year:** 175.

**Description of children:** Children with special needs.

**Adoption procedure:**
1) Attend preservice training;
2) submit application;
3) complete home study;
4) if approved, wait for placement;
5) placement;
6) post-placement supervision;
7) finalization.

**Average length of time between application and start of home study:** 1-6 mos.

**Average length of time to complete home study:** 3-6 mos.

**Number of interviews:** 6.

**Home study description:** Assessment of stability, family values, criminal background checks, ability to parent a child not born to applicant(s), support systems, problem solving techniques, methods of discipline and a discussion of the type of child applicant(s) is best suited to parent.

**Average wait for a child after approval of a home study:** 1-24 mos.

**Foster care:** Emergency, short and long-term and fost-adopt.

★ 585 ★
**Erie County Department of Human Services**
221 W. Parish St.
Sandusky, OH 44870
Phone: (419) 626-6781
Fax: (419) 626-5854

**Contact:** Cindy Christian, Laura Miller.

**Description:** Public, county agency.

**Area served:** Residents of Erie and surrounding counties.

**Requirements:** Adults, 18 yrs. and older, who are in good health and stable financial situation, and if married, at least 1 yr.

**Fees:** None.

**Number of children placed last year:** 8.

**Description of children:** Primarily black and biracial children from 0 to 18 yrs.

**Adoption procedure:**
1) Initial inquiry;
2) attend introductory meeting;
3) submit application;
4) participate in educational class;
5) complete home study;
6) if approved, wait for placement;
7) placement;
8) post-placement supervision;
9) finalization.

**Average length of time between application and start of home study:** 1-6 mos.

**Average length of time to complete home study:** 2 mos.

**Number of interviews:** 3 or more.

**Home study description:** Assessment which includes but is not limited to background, recommendation of references, stability in all aspect of applicant(s)' life, ability to accept a child with special needs and support systems.

**Average wait for a child after approval of a home study:** 12-24 mos.

**Foster care:** Emergency, short and long-term.

★ 586 ★
**Fairfield County Children's Services**
1587 Granville Pike
Lancaster, OH 43130
Phone: (614) 653-4060

**Contact:** Adoption intake worker.

**Description:** Non-profit public agency.

**Area served:** Residents of Fairfield County or non-county residents who have completed home studies.

**Requirements:** Flexible.

**Fees:** None.

**Number of children placed last year:** Approx. 15.

**Description of children:** No infants.

**Adoption procedure:** Call or write for outline.

**Average length of time between application and start of home study:** 1-6 mos.

**Average length of time to complete home study:** 2-3 mos.

**Number of interviews:** 3 or more.

**Home study description:** Call or write for guidelines.

**Average wait for a child after approval of a home study:** 6-12 mos.

**Foster care:** Emergency, long-term and permanent.


★ 587 ★
**Franklin County Department of Children's Services**
525 E. Mound St.
Columbus, OH 43201
Phone: (614) 341-6060

**Contact:** Adoption Recruitment.

**Description:** Public county agency mandated by the Ohio Dept. of Human Services. A program called Black Family Connections can be reached at (614) 341-6000.

**Area served:** Residents of Franklin County.

**Requirements:** Adults, 21 yrs. and older, who are in good health and stable financial situation, and who are single, divorced or married 1 yr. or more.

**Fees:** None.

**Number of children placed last year:** 149.

**Description of children:** Children with special needs.

**Adoption procedure:**
1) Attend orientation meeting;
2) participate in 8 educational meetings;
3) submit application with autobiography;
4) complete home study with homework assignments, health, finger printing, law enforcement and credit checks;
5) if approved, wait for placement;
6) placement;
7) post-placement supervision;
8) finalization.

**Average length of time between application and start of home study:** Training classes are scheduled monthly.

**Average length of time to complete home study:** 12 wks.

**Number of interviews:** 8 groups and minimum of 2 home consultations.

**Home study description:** Assessment which includes but is not limited to applicant(s)' stability in all phases of life, commitment to and empathy with a child with special needs, willingness to risk and support systems.

**Average wait for a child after approval of a home study:** 90 days, or applicant(s) are listed with the Adoption Listing Service of Ohio.

**Foster care:** Emergency, short and long-term and therapeutic.


★ 588 ★
**Guernsey County Childrens Services Board**
274 Highland Ave.
Cambridge, OH 43725
Phone: (614) 439-5555
(800) 296-3511

**Contact:** Connie McVey, Adoption Program Coordinator.

**Description:** Public county agency mandated to place children by the Ohio Department of Human Services.

**Area served:** Residents of Guernsey County for at least 1 yr.

**Requirements:** Applicants must demonstrate an ability to cover their own financial needs and have an unchanged marital status for the previous 2 yrs.

**Fees:** None.

**Number of children placed last year:** 8.

**Description of children:** Children from birth to 13 yrs. who were members of sibling groups or who had behavioral and emotional problems.

**Adoption procedure:** 1) Application; 2) Adoptive Orientation classes; 3) autobiographies and compilation of other documents; 4) home study; 5) child search; 6) placement; 7) post-placement supervision; 8) finalization.

**Average length of time between application and start of home study:** 1 - 6 mos.

**Average length of time to complete home study:** 6 mos.

**Number of interviews:** 3.

**Home study description:** A compilation of extensive childhood and adult life experiences, parenting abilities, motivation, expectations and personal characteristics. The type of child or children to be parented is discussed in detail.

**Average wait for a child after approval of a home study:** 6 -12 mos.

**Foster care:** Temporary.


★ 589 ★
**Hamilton County Department of Human Services**
628 Sycamore St.
Cincinnati, OH 45202
Phone: (513) 632-6366
Fax: (513) 632-6816

**Contact:** Adoption intake worker.

**Date established:** 1949.

**Description:** Non-profit public agency licensed in Ohio.

**Area served:** Residents of Hamilton County. Home studies accepted from other agencies for children with special needs.

**Requirements:** Adults, 21 yrs. or older, who have adequate financial resources. Maximum age is determined by the age of the child placed. Physical examination are also required.

**Fees:** None.

**Number of children placed last year:** 97.

**Description of children:** Primarily children with special needs and minority children. Very few white infants.

**Adoption procedure:**
1) Attend orientation meeting;
2) participate in preparation classes;
3) complete questionnaire and autobiographical material;
4) have caseworker interviews.

**Average length of time between application and start of home study:** 1-6 mos.

**Average length of time to complete home study:** 4 mos. or 120 days.

**Number of interviews:** Varies with applicant family size and composition.

**Home study description:** Evaluation of family history, current adjustment, problem solving methods, family relationships, and ability to incorporate special needs child into family.

**Average wait for a child after approval of a home study:** 6-12 mos.

**Foster care:** Temporary, long-term and permanent.

### ★ 590 ★
**Hancock County Department of Human Services**
**Children's Protective Services**
7814 County Rd. 140
Findlay, OH 45840
Phone: (419) 424-7022

**Contact:** Cyndi Scanland, Adoption Specialist.

**Description:** Public county agency mandated to place children by the Ohio Department of Human Services.

**Area served:** Residents of Hancock County.

**Requirements:** Applicants must be at least 21 yrs. old with an unchanged marital status for the previous 12 mos. and must demonstrate both the financial capability and the mental and physical health to adopt a child.

**Fees:** None for children with special needs. Private adoptions: home study: $250; updates: $100; post-placement visitation: $100; court report: $50.

**Number of children placed last year:** 4.

**Description of children:** Children with special needs.

**Adoption procedure:** 1) Application; 2) documentation; 3) home study; 4) approval and wait for placement; 5) placement; 6) post-placement supervision; 7) finalization.

**Average length of time between application and start of home study:** 1 - 6 mos.

**Average length of time to complete home study:** 160 days.

**Number of interviews:** 4.

**Home study description:** Assessment which addresses such topics as family history, education, employment, marriage, religion, interests and activities, health, fertility issues, home environment, parenting and coping skills and problem solving.

**Average wait for a child after approval of a home study:** Varies.

**Foster care:** Temporary, long-term and permanent.

### ★ 591 ★
**Knox County Children's Services/Department of Human Services**
117 E. High St.
Mt. Vernon, OH 43050
Phone: (614) 397-7177

**Contact:** Tim Crouse or Janet Graddick.

**Description:** Non-profit public agency.

**Area served:** Residents of Knox County.

**Requirements:** None.

**Fees:** None.

**Number of children placed last year:** 12.

**Description of children:** Primarily special needs.

**Adoption procedure:**
1) Attend 14 hrs. orientation training;
2) file application and autobiography;

3) pass police clearances;
4) if approved, placement;
5) 6 mos. supervision; and
6) finalization.

**Average length of time between application and start of home study:** 1-6 mos.

**Average length of time to complete home study:** 3 mos.

**Number of interviews:** 3.

**Home study description:** Evaluation of applicant(s)' strengths, marriage relationship (if applicable), parenting ability and type of child desired.

**Average wait for a child after approval of a home study:** 24 or more mos.

**Foster care:** Temporary, long-term and permanent.

### ★ 592 ★
**Lawrence County Department Of Human Services**
1100 S. 7th St.
Ironton, OH 45638
Phone: (614) 532-3324
Fax: (514) 532-9490

**Mailing address:**
P.O. Box 539, Ironton, OH 45638

**Contact:** Allen Caldwell.

**Description:** Non-profit public agency.

**Area served:** Residents of Lawrence County.

**Requirements:** As prescribed by Ohio Revised Code and Ohio Administrative Code Rules and Laws.

**Fees:** None.

**Number of children placed last year:** 4.

**Description of children:** Children with special needs and adolescents (13-17 yrs.).

**Adoption procedure:** Complete application and home study process.

**Average length of time between application and start of home study:** 1 mo. or less.

**Average length of time to complete home study:** 2 mos.

**Number of interviews:** 4.

**Home study description:** Evaluation of medical, marital and income verifications, references and law enforcement checks.

**Average wait for a child after approval of a home study:** 12-24 mos.

**Foster care:** Temporary and permanent.

### ★ 593 ★
**Licking County Department of Human Services**
74 S. 2nd St.
Newark, OH 43055
Phone: (614) 349-6225

**Contact:** Bruce Anderson, Adoption Supervisor.

**Description:** Public, county agency mandated to place children by the Ohio Department of Human Services.

**Area served:** Residents of Licking County.

**Requirements:** Applicants must be at least 21 yrs. of age.

**Fees:** None.

**Number of children placed last year:** 20 - 25.

**Description of children:** Children with special needs.

**Adoption procedure:** 1) Application; 2) documentation; 3) home study; 4) approval and child match; 5) placement; 6) post-placement supervision; 7) finalization.

**Average length of time between application and start of home study:** Special needs: 6 -12 mos.; others: 2 yrs. or more.

**Average length of time to complete home study:** 2 - 3 mos.

**Number of interviews:** 5 -6.

**Home study description:** Comprehensive assessment which follows the directives set forth by the Ohio Department of Human Services.

**Average wait for a child after approval of a home study:** Special needs: 6 - 24 mos.

**Foster care:** Emergency, temporary, long-term and treatment.

★ 594 ★
**Logan County Children's Services Board**
1855 Rte. 47 W.
Bellafontaine, OH 43311
Phone: (513) 599-7290
Fax: (513) 599-7296

**Contact:** Rachel Gillespie, Adoption Supervisor; Linda Gerber, Adoption Caseworker.

**Date established:** 1897.

**Description:** Non-profit public agency licensed by the Ohio Dept. of Human Services to provide services to abused, neglected and dependent child.

**Area served:** Residents of Logan County.

**Requirements:** Adults, 21 yrs. or older, who are in stable health and financial situation. Maximum of 40 yrs. between adoptive mother and child. If married, at least 2 yrs.

**Fees:** None.

**Number of children placed last year:** 0.

**Adoption procedure:**
1) Applicants screened for basic eligibility;
2) attend orientation and information meeting;
3) complete necessary paperwork;
4) complete home study;
5) if approved, placement;
6) post-placement supervision.

**Average length of time between application and start of home study:** 1-6 mos.

**Average length of time to complete home study:** 2-3 mos.

**Number of interviews:** Approx. 4.

**Home study description:** Evaluation of background, marital relationship(s), health, finances, religion, hobbies, home and neighborhood, references and criminal records check, ability to cope with stress, and attitudes about and experiences with children.

**Average wait for a child after approval of a home study:** 24 or more mos.

**Foster care:** Emergency, temporary, long-term, and treatment.

★ 595 ★
**Lucas County Children's Service Board**
705 Adams St.
Toledo, OH 43624
Phone: (419) 327-3627
Fax: (419) 327-3249

**Contact:** Adoption Unit.

**Description:** Public, county agency.

**Area served:** Residents of Lucas County and occasionally residents of neighboring counties when seeking to adopt children in the custody of Lucas County.

**Requirements:** Adults, 21 yrs. and older whose health is adequate to parent.

**Fees:** None.

**Number of children placed last year:** 135.

**Description of children:** Children with special needs.

**Adoption procedure:**
1) Request information;
2) participate in 16 hrs. of orientation;
3) complete home study;
4) if approved, wait for placement;
5) placement;
6) supervision of placement;
7) finalization.

**Average length of time between application and start of home study:** 1-6 mos.

**Average length of time to complete home study:** 150-180 days.

**Number of interviews:** 3.

**Home study description:** Assessment which includes but is not limited to parenting models and experience, current family functioning and ability to risk. The study also covers the kinds of behavior children may exhibit because of separation and loss and allows the applicant to self-assess if they can parent a child with special needs and what kinds of special needs they would consider.

**Average wait for a child after approval of a home study:** Dependent on the range of special needs the applicants are willing to accept.

**Foster care:** Emergency, short and long-term and fost-adopt.

★ 596 ★
**Madison County Department of Human Services**
249 W. High St.
London, OH 43140
Phone: (614) 852-4770

**Contact:** Carol Ansel.

**Description:** Non-profit public children's services agency.

**Area served:** Residents of Madison County.

**Requirements:** Legally married or single persons.

**Fees:** None.

**Number of children placed last year:** 2.

**Description of children:** Not available.

**Adoption procedure:**
1) Check references
2) child abuse and police clearances;
3) complete home study;
4) if approved, placement;
5) post-placement services; and
6) finalization.

**Average length of time between application and start of home study:** Varies.

**Average length of time to complete home study:** 4-6 hrs.

**Number of interviews:** 2.

**Home study description:** Evaluation of family background, religious beliefs, strengths and weaknesses, childrearing philosophy and description of child desired.

**Average wait for a child after approval of a home study:** Varies.

**Foster care:** Temporary.

## ★ 597 ★
**Mahoning County Children Services**
2801 Market St.
Youngstown, OH 44507
Phone: (216) 783-0411
Fax: (216) 783-5342

**Contact:** Carolyn Taylor, Adoption Supervisor.

**Description:** Public children's service agency.

**Area served:** Residents of Mahoning County and will accept applications for children with special needs from applicants within a 75 mi. radius of Mahoning Co.

**Requirements:** Adults, 21 yrs. and older; if applicants are married, marriage must be of a one yr. duration or greater. Requirements may be waived for special needs adoption.

**Fees:** None.

**Number of children placed last year:** 24 placements, 32 finlizations.

**Description of children:** U.S. children of all ages, races and special needs.

**Adoption procedure:**
1) Submit interest form;
2) attend educative group series;
3) file application and related forms;
4) attend interviews;
5) if approved, placement;
6) post-placement services;
7) finalization; and
8) post-finalization services, if required.

**Average length of time between application and start of home study:** 1-6 mos.

**Average length of time to complete home study:** 1-6 mos.

**Number of interviews:** 3 or more.

**Home study description:** Evaluation of background, marital history; self-awareness and ability to handle stress; ability to individualize; interest in adoption and child-rearing experiences; and type of child best suited to applicant(s).

**Average wait for a child after approval of a home study:** Identified adoption: 1 mo. or less.

**Foster care:** Temporary.

## ★ 598 ★
**Marion County Children Service Board**
1680 Marion-Waldo Rd.
Marion, OH 43302
Phone: (614) 389-2317
Fax: (614) 389-3499

**Contact:** Leslie Carney-McGee, Placement Services Supervisor.

**Date established:** 1902.

**Description:** County children's services board.

**Area served:** Residents of Marion County and out-of-country residents who are requesting a child in the custody of Marion County.

**Requirements:** Single or married; if married, at least 1 yr. Adoptive parents should be no more than 45 yrs. older than child placed if adopting non-special needs.

**Fees:** None.

**Number of children placed last year:** 5.

**Description of children:** Older children, sibling groups and abused, neglected and/or dependent children.

**Adoption procedure:**
1) Complete Personal History Data Sheet;

2) attend orientation meeting;
3) complete home and office caseworker visits;
4) submit medical report(s) and references;
5) police and Child Abuse Registry checks;
6) if approved, name added to placement waiting list;
7) placement conference;
8) placement;
9) post-placement supervision; and
10) finalization.

**Average length of time between application and start of home study:** 1-6 mos.

**Average length of time to complete home study:** 3 mos.

**Number of interviews:** 3 or more.

**Home study description:** Evaluation of personality, background, life experiences, education and financial status, religion, home, support network and expectations for a child.

**Average wait for a child after approval of a home study:** 24 or more mos.

**Foster care:** Temporary, long-term, and therapeutic.

## ★ 599 ★
**Mercer County Department of Human Services**
311 S. Main St.
Celina, OH 45822
Phone: (419) 586-5106

**Contact:** Adoption worker.

**Description:** Public, county agency mandated to place children by the Ohio Department of Human Services.

**Area served:** Residents of Mercer County.

**Requirements:** Applicants must be at least 21 yrs. old.

**Fees:** None unless home study is sent to another agency whereby the charge is $90.

**Number of children placed last year:** 2.

**Description of children:** Pre-school and school age children.

**Adoption procedure:** 1) Inquiry 2) child match; 3) home study; 4) pre-placement visitation; 5) placement; 6) post-placement services; 7) finalization.

**Average length of time between application and start of home study:** Less than 1 mo.

**Average length of time to complete home study:** 120 - 150 days.

**Number of interviews:** 2 - 4.

**Home study description:** Assessment which includes applicants' childhood, personal information, home, finances, child development and methods of discipline and issues surrounding adoption.

**Average wait for a child after approval of a home study:** 12 - 24 mos.

**Foster care:** Temporary, long-term and permanent.

## ★ 600 ★
**Monroe County Department of Human Services**
100 Home Ave.
Woodsfield, OH 43793-0638
Phone: (614) 472-1602

**Mailing address:**
P.O. Box 638, Woodsfield, OH 43793-0638

**Contact:** Gary W. Truax, Social Services Supervisor.

**Description:** Public county agency mandated to place children by the Ohio Department of Human Services.

**Area served:** Residents of Monroe County.

**Requirements:** None other than residency.

**Fees:** Mailing and reproduction costs.

**Number of children placed last year:** 0.

**Description of children:** N/A.

**Adoption procedure:** 1) Inquiry; 2) application; 3) home study; 4) child match; 5) pre-placement visitation, if applicable; 6) placement; 7) post-placement supervision; 8) finalization.

**Average length of time between application and start of home study:** 1 -6 mos.

**Average length of time to complete home study:** 6 mos.

**Number of interviews:** 4.

**Home study description:** Assessment which includes all information mandated by Ohio State law.

**Average wait for a child after approval of a home study:** 2 yrs. or more.

**Foster care:** Emergency, short and long-term and permanent.

★ 601 ★
**Montgomery County Children Services**
3501 Merrimac Ave.
Dayton, OH 45405
Phone: (513) 276-6121
Fax: (513) 277-1127

**Contact:** Yvonne C. Marvin or Donna Kay.

**Description:** Non-profit county children's services board.

**Area served:** Residents of Montgomery County.

**Requirements:** Adults, 21 yrs. or older, who are financially able to meet existing family needs, and who are in stable physical and mental health.

**Fees:** None.

**Number of children placed last year:** 70.

**Description of children:** School age and minority children, sibling groups, children with special needs.

**Adoption procedure:**
1) Attend information session;
2) complete 4 interviews;
3) participate in 4-session pre-adoption education group series;
4) if approved, placement;
5) 6 or more mos. post-placement supervision;
6) finalization.

**Average length of time between application and start of home study:** 1 mo. or less.

**Average length of time to complete home study:** 6-8 wks.

**Number of interviews:** 4 individual and 4 group.

**Home study description:** Evaluation of background and social history; finances; parenting philiosophy and experiences; and family's image of desired child.

**Average wait for a child after approval of a home study:** Varies.

**Foster care:** Temporary and long-term.

★ 602 ★
**Noble County Department of Human Services**
38 Olive St.
Caldwell, OH 43724
Phone: (614) 732-2392
Fax: (614) 732-4108

**Mailing address:**
   P.O. Box 250, Caldwell, OH 43724

**Contact:** Konny Bates.

**Description:** Public agency.

**Area served:** Residents of Noble County.

**Requirements:** Adults between the ages of 21 and 55 yrs., who are in good health and who have sufficient income to support another family member.

**Fees:** None.

**Number of children placed last year:** 1.

**Description of children:** Children under the age of 18 yrs.

**Adoption procedure:**
1) Attend in-take interview;
2) submit application;
3) complete home study;
4) if approved, wait for placement;
5) placement;
6) post-placement supervision;
7) finalization.

**Average length of time between application and start of home study:** 1 mo. or less.

**Average length of time to complete home study:** 30 days.

**Number of interviews:** 2-3.

**Home study description:** An assessment which includes but is not limited to parenting experiences and models, health and financial reports, home and environment, recommendation of references and motivation to adopt.

**Average wait for a child after approval of a home study:** 6-12 mos.

**Foster care:** Emergency, short and long-term.

★ 603 ★
**Ottawa County Department of Human Services**
8444 W. State Rte. 163
Oak Harbor, OH 43449
Phone: (419) 898-3688
Fax: (419) 898-2436

**Contact:** Janice Nietfeld-Briggs.

**Description:** Public county agency.

**Area served:** Residents of Ottawa County.

**Requirements:** Couples married at least 3 yrs., neither of whom has been divorced more than once, who are 21 yrs. old or more, have no past or present records of violating the law, are physically and emotionally healthy, residents of the county for at least one year, high school graduates and financially capable of providing for a child.

**Fees:** None.

**Number of children placed last year:** 1.

**Description of children:** 1 child between 13-17 yrs.

**Adoption procedure:**
1) Initial inquiry;
2) submit references and undergo criminal records check;
3) if approved, admission to waiting list for home study;
4) complete home study;
5) if approved, wait for placement;
6) placement;
7) 6 mos. post-placement supervision;
8) finalization.

**Average length of time between application and start of home study:** 1 mo. or less.

**Average length of time to complete home study:** 2-3 mos.

**Number of interviews:** 4.

**Home study description:** A home study is an accumulation and evaluation of the following information: family background, marital and divorce (if applicable) history, education, work record, home fire inspection and well test (if applicable), reasons for adopting, and experiences with and expectations of children.

**Average wait for a child after approval of a home study:** 24 or more mos.

**Foster care:** Temporary, long-term and permanent.

★ 604 ★

**Perry County Children's Services**
526 Mill St.
New Lexington, OH 43764
Phone: (614) 342-3836

**Contact:** Judith A. Nash, Adoption Caseworker.

**Description:** Public county agency mandated by the Ohio Department of Human Services.

**Area served:** Residents of Perry County.

**Requirements:** Open.

**Fees:** None.

**Number of children placed last year:** 1.

**Description of children:** Child under 6 yrs.

**Adoption procedure:** 1) Application; 2) home study; 3) child match; 4) pre-placement visitation; 5) placement; 6) post-placement supervision; 7) finalization.

**Average length of time between application and start of home study:** 1 - 6 mos.

**Average length of time to complete home study:** 3 mos.

**Number of interviews:** 5.

**Home study description:** Process which includes Criminal Records and reference checks, personal assessment and assessment of the home.

**Average wait for a child after approval of a home study:** 12 - 24 mos.

**Foster care:** Temporary, long-term and therapeutic.

★ 605 ★

**Putnam County Department of Human Services**
1225 E. 3rd St.
Ottawa, OH 45875
Phone: (419) 523-4580
Fax: (419) 523-6130

**Contact:** Traci Kohls.

**Description:** Non-profit state agency.

**Area served:** Residents of Putnam County.

**Requirements:** No criminal record and financially able to support child.

**Fees:** $150 for initial home study; $50 home study update; $75 for report on proposed adoption; $60 for post-placement visitation.

**Number of children placed last year:** 5.

**Description of children:** N/A.

**Adoption procedure:** Call or write for packet.

**Average length of time between application and start of home study:** 1-6 mos.

**Average length of time to complete home study:** 2 mos.

**Number of interviews:** 3.

**Home study description:** Evaluation of applicants' personal histories; personalities; marital relationship (if applicable); health; family life; finances; religion; criminal record check, including fingerprinting. References required.

**Average wait for a child after approval of a home study:** 12-24 mos.

**Foster care:** Temporary, long-term and permanent.

★ 606 ★

**Scioto County Children Services**
3940 Gallia St.
New Boston, OH 45662
Phone: (614) 456-4164
Fax: (614) 456-6728

**Contact:** Resource supervisor.

**Description:** County agency.

**Area served:** Residents of Scioto County.

**Requirements:** Flexible.

**Fees:** None.

**Number of children placed last year:** 0.

**Description of children:** Primarily children with special needs.

**Adoption procedure:**
1) File application;
2) complete home study;
3) specific children presented during interview process;
4) placement;
5) post-placement supervision; and
6) finalization.

**Average length of time between application and start of home study:** 1-6 mos.

**Average length of time to complete home study:** 2 mos.

**Number of interviews:** 4-6.

**Home study description:** Evaluation of home, family relationships, income and finances, any children in the home, medical/psychological health and drug/alcohol history (if any); police and law enforcement clearances.

**Average wait for a child after approval of a home study:** 24 or more mos.

**Foster care:** Temporary, long-term and permanent.

★ 607 ★

**Seneca County Department of Human Services**
3362 S. Township Rd. 151
Tiffin, OH 44883
Phone: (419) 447-5011
(800) 825-5011
Fax: (419) 447-5345

**Contact:** Karen Y. Sherer or Kathy Smith.

**Description:** Public social services agency.

**Area served:** Home studies completed for residents of Seneca Co. only. Placement services extended to residents of other counties as well.

**Requirements:** Call or write for guidelines.

**Fees:** None.

**Number of children placed last year:** 11.

**Description of children:** Children with special needs; older children; a few pre-schoolers.

**Adoption procedure:** Residents of Seneca County may call or write for an application.

**Average length of time between application and start of home study:** 1-6 mos.

**Average length of time to complete home study:** 1-2 mos.

**Number of interviews:** Minimum of 4 with each member of the household.

**Home study description:** An evaluation to determine the stability of the applicant(s)' and their home.

**Average wait for a child after approval of a home study:** Varies.

**Foster care:** Temporary and permanent.

★ 608 ★
**Shelby County Children Services Board**
401 E. Court St.
Sidney, OH 45365
Phone: (513) 498-7213
Fax: (513) 498-7216

**Contact:** Michael Lieber.

**Description:** State-mandated child protective services agency.

**Area served:** Residents of Shelby County.

**Requirements:** Adults, between the ages of 21 and 60 yrs., single or, if married, at least 2 yrs., who are high school graduates or equivalent, who have been divorced not more than once and who have no criminal record.

**Fees:** $15 fee for criminal check.

**Number of children placed last year:** 5.

**Description of children:** 3 special needs; 2 healthy, white.

**Adoption procedure:**
1) File preliminary application;
2) record and reference checks;
3) complete home study;
4) if approved, wait for placement.

**Average length of time between application and start of home study:** Less than 1 mo.

**Average length of time to complete home study:** 2-4 mos.

**Number of interviews:** At least 4.

**Home study description:** Evaluation of autobiographies, personal references, financial and medical reports, thoughts on adoption, etc.

**Average wait for a child after approval of a home study:** 24 or more mos.

**Foster care:** Emergency and short-term.

★ 609 ★
**Stark County Department of Human Services**
220 E. Tuscarawas St.
Canton, OH 44702
Phone: (216) 438-8789
Fax: (216) 438-8706

**Contact:** Adoption recruiters.

**Description:** Public, county agency.

**Area served:** Residents of Stark County only for infants; residents from other areas interested in special needs children.

**Requirements:** Adults, 21 yrs. and older, who are single or married 2 or more yrs., who are in good health and financially able to meet their own family's needs.

**Fees:** None.

**Number of children placed last year:** 54.

**Description of children:** Primarily children with special needs.

**Adoption procedure:**
1) Attend informational meeting;
2) submit completed interest form;
3) participate in group training;

4) complete individual interview process;
5) if approved, wait for placement;
6) placement;
7) post-placment supervision;
8) finalization.

**Average length of time between application and start of home study:** 6-12 mos.; highly dependent upon kind of child desired.

**Average length of time to complete home study:** 3-4 mos.

**Number of interviews:** 6 group and 3-4 individual.

**Home study description:** Educational and evaluatory process which discusses separation issues and emotional problems of children placed, coping strategies, health, finances and background of applicant(s) and recommendation of references.

**Average wait for a child after approval of a home study:** 6-12 mos.; highly dependent upon kind of child desired.

**Foster care:** Emergency, temporary and long-term.

★ 610 ★
**Summit County Children Services Board**
264 S. Arlington St.
Akron, OH 44306-1399
Phone: (216) 379-1992
(216) 379-1990

**Contact:** Linda Loveland, Supervisor.

**Description:** Non-profit, licensed by the State of Ohio.

**Area served:** Residents of Summit County and surrounding area for children with special needs.

**Requirements:** Adults, 21 yrs. and older who are in good health and who have adequate income to support a child. Both singles and married couples are desirable applicants.

**Fees:** None.

**Number of children placed last year:** 94.

**Description of children:** Preschoolers to adolescents, most with special needs.

**Adoption procedure:**
1) Submit application;
2) complete home study;
3) if approved, child match;
4) placement;
5) post-placement supervision;
6) finalization.

**Average length of time between application and start of home study:** 1-6 mos.

**Average length of time to complete home study:** 2-3 mos.

**Number of interviews:** 3-4.

**Home study description:** Evaluation of present family composition, school and employer references, law enforcement clearances, church affiliation, finances, and the type of child requested.

**Average wait for a child after approval of a home study:** 1-6 mos.

**Foster care:** Mostly temporary, some long-term.

★ 611 ★
**Tuscarawas County Department of Human Services**
247 Stonecreek Rd., N.W.
New Philadelphia, OH 44663
Phone: (216) 339-7791

**Contact:** Alona Reichman, Supervisor.

**Description:** Public county agency mandated to place children by the Ohio Department of Human Services.

**Area served:** Residents of Tuscarawas County.

**Requirements:** Applicants must be at least 21 yrs. old.

**Fees:** None.

**Number of children placed last year:** 10.

**Description of children:** Infants and older children, some with special needs.

**Adoption procedure:** 1) Inquiry; 2) application; 3) home study; 4) child match; 5) pre-placement visitation, if applicable; 6) placement; 7) post-placement supervision; 8) finalization.

**Average length of time between application and start of home study:** 1 - 6 mos.

**Average length of time to complete home study:** 3 mos.

**Number of interviews:** 2.

**Home study description:** Assessment which includes reference checks and all state clearances proscribed by the Ohio Department of Human Services.

**Average wait for a child after approval of a home study:** Varies with the type of child sought.

**Foster care:** Temporary, long-term and therapeutic.


★612★
**Warren County Children Services**
416 S. East St.
Lebanon, OH 45036
Phone: (513) 933-1331
Fax: (513) 933-2957

**Contact:** Adoption coordinator.

**Description:** State mandated child protective services agency.

**Area served:** Residents of Warren County.

**Requirements:** In compliance with Ohio Department of Human Services.

**Fees:** None.

**Number of children placed last year:** 7.

**Description of children:** Special needs.

**Adoption procedure:**
1) File application;
2) attend interview in which applicant families are screened in relation to the children who are available;
3) complete home study and training;
4) begin networking with exchanges for child match;
5) placement;
6) post-placement supervision;
7) finalization; and
8) post-finalization services, if required.

**Average length of time between application and start of home study:** 1-6 mos.

**Average length of time to complete home study:** 2-3 mos.

**Number of interviews:** 6 or more.

**Home study description:** Evaluation of applicant(s)' background and family lifestyle; description of home; marital and family relationships; financial and health reports; references; childrearing experiences; motivation to adopt and attitudes on adoption-related issues.

**Average wait for a child after approval of a home study:** 1-6 mos.

**Foster care:** Temporary and long-term.

★613★
**Wood County Department of Human Services**
1928 E. Gypsy Lane Rd.
Bowling Green, OH 43402
Phone: (419) 352-7566
Fax: (419) 353-6091

**Mailing address:**
P.O. Box 679, Bowling Green, OH 43402

**Contact:** Susan M. Shanks, LSW, Permanency/Adoption Specialist.

**Description:** Non-profit county agency.

**Area served:** Residents of Wood County.

**Requirements:** Adults, 21 yrs. or older.

**Fees:** None.

**Number of children placed last year:** 11.

**Description of children:** Children with special needs.

**Adoption procedure:**
1) Adoption inquiry;
2) orientation/training/information meetings;
3) application;
4) approval/denial of application;
5) applicants complete documents;
6) approval/denial of documents;
7) 2-4 home visits;
8) approval/denial of home study;
9) wait for placement;
10) placement;
11) post-placement supervision;
12) finalization.

**Average length of time between application and start of home study:** 1-6 mos.; depends on the applicants.

**Average length of time to complete home study:** Depends on the applicants.

**Number of interviews:** 8-10, includes orientation and training and home study interviews.

**Home study description:** Evaluatuion of background, relationships, abilities and other undefinables depending upon the type of child desired.

**Average wait for a child after approval of a home study:** Depends on type of child wanted.

**Foster care:** Temporary and occasionally long-term.


# PRIVATE AGENCIES

★614★
**Adoption by Gentle Care**
17 Brickel
Columbus, OH 43215-1501
Phone: (614) 469-0007
(800) 824-9633
Fax: (614) 621-2229

**Contact:** Nappy M. Hetzler.

**Date established:** 1985.

**Description:** Non-profit, private, interdenominational child placement agency licensed by the State of Ohio.

**Area served:** Residents of Ohio.

**Requirements:** Couples married at least 3 yrs. who are at least 21 yrs. old who have no more than 1 child or if childless, must attend a parenting class, must be non-smokers and intend to rear their child with religious and moral values. Applicants must allow at least 18 mos. from the birth or placement of a first child to the placement of a second child.

**Fees:**
Pre-application fee: $150 (non-refundable). All programs:
Application fee: $2000;
home study within Ohio: $1200;
home study review out-of-state: $400;
placement within Ohio: $6150;
placement out of state: $7350;
foreign placement: $10,000;
special programs in-state: $1050, out-of-state: $1250;
home study only: $1200-$1700 depending upon location and time frame.
Gentle Care also provides services to applicants pursuing independent adoption; pre-arranged/targeted placement: $2650. Fee schedule is available.

**Number of children placed last year:** N/A.

**Description of children:** Newborn black, white, biracial and foreign infants; older and special needs children; and Questionable Health Program which consists of children whose parents have a questionable genetic problem which the children might inherit, e.g. Muscular Dystrophy or Cystic Fibrosis.

**Adoption procedure:** Pre-application for black, biracial, older and special needs children are accepted and reviewed all through the year. Pre-applications for healthy, white infants are reviewed only during the months of January and July no matter when they are received. Applicants are notified of acceptance or lack of acceptance onto waiting list.
Once a couple reaches the top portion of the list, they attend a mandatory Group and Assessment meeting. Upon completion, they attend an Individual Assessment meeting wherein the couple and agency decide if they should continue in the adoption process.
If accepted, applicants' application forms are accepted.
Agency and couple prepare home study.
Adoptive family accepts placement.

**Average length of time between application and start of home study:** 6-12 mos.

**Average length of time to complete home study:** Varies.

**Number of interviews:** 2 home visits and 2 office visits.

**Home study description:** Evaluation which includes but is not limited to background, marital history, religion, issues surround infertility, health and the type of child couple wishes to adopt.

**Average wait for a child after approval of a home study:** 6-12 mos.

**Foster care:** In some circumstances.

★ 615 ★
**Beech Brook**
**Spaulding Adoption Program**
3737 Lander Rd.
Cleveland, OH 44124
Phone: (216) 831-2255

**Contact:** John C. Cowles.

**Date established:** 1976.

**Description:** Private, non-profit multi-service mental health agency licensed to place children by the Ohio Department of Human Services.

**Area served:** Residents of the Greater Cleveland area.

**Requirements:** Applicants must demonstrate the financial capability to support a child.

**Fees:** None.

**Number of children placed last year:** 15.

**Description of children:** School age children with a history of multiple placements and/or abuse and neglect.

**Adoption procedure:** 1) Introductory meeting; 2) 8 hrs. of classes; 3) home study; 4) pre-placement visitation; 5) placement; 6) post-placement supervision; 7) adoption decree filed; 8) finalization.

**Average length of time between application and start of home study:** Less than 1 mo.

**Average length of time to complete home study:** 2 mos.

**Number of interviews:** 6.

**Home study description:** Assessment which includes the state requirements of finger printing, criminal records checks, medical exams and references and which addresses such issues as family background, upbringing, current functioning, relationships and ability to understand and deal with emotionally disturbed children.

**Average wait for a child after approval of a home study:** Less than 1 mo. since the child to be placed is identified before the home study is begun.

**Foster care:** Specialized.

★ 616 ★
**Catholic Community Services, Inc. of Trumbull County**
2932 Youngstown Rd., SE
Warren, OH 44484
Phone: (216) 369-4254
Fax: (216) 369-4525

**Contact:** Kathleen McCulloh, MA, Executive Director.

**Date established:** 1939.

**Description:** Non-profit charitable and social service organization.

**Area served:** Residents of Trumbull County.

**Requirements:** Married couples who have a stable relationship and fertility problems.

**Fees:** Fees for home study dependent on necessary paperwork. Flat rate for agency completed home study to finalization.

**Number of children placed last year:** 4.

**Description of children:** Newborn infants.

**Adoption procedure:**
1) File preliminary form;
2) have initial interview;
3) complete application;
4) undergo home study;
5) if appproved, placement;
6) 6 mos. post-placement supervisory;
7) finalization.

**Average length of time between application and start of home study:** 1-6 mos.

**Average length of time to complete home study:** Approx. 4 mos.

**Number of interviews:** 6-8.

**Home study description:** Evaluation which includes but is not limited to, background information; marital and economic stability; and motivation to adopt.

**Average wait for a child after approval of a home study:** 12-24 or more mos.

**Foster care:** Temporary for infants surrendered to agency.

★617★
**Catholic Service League, Inc.**
4495 Market St.
Youngstown, OH 44512
Phone: (216) 788-8726

**Contact:** Elaine Martin, LISW, ACSW, Adoption Coordinator.

**Date established:** 1935.

**Description:** Private, non-profit multi-service agency licensed to place children by the Ohio Department of Human Services and accredited by the Council on Accreditation of Services for Families and Children, Inc.

**Area served:** Residents of Columbiana and Mahoning counties in Ohio.

**Requirements:** Open.

**Fees:** Home study: sliding scale.

**Number of children placed last year:** 11.

**Description of children:** Caucasian and biracial infants and children and 1 child from Korea.

**Adoption procedure:** 1) Telephone inquiry; 2) placement on interest list; 3) information meeting; 4) training groups; 5) home study; 6) placement; 7) post-placement supervision; 8) finalization.

**Average length of time between application and start of home study:** Healthy Caucasian infants: 2 yrs. or more.
Special needs: Less than 1 mo.

**Average length of time to complete home study:** 3 mos.

**Number of interviews:** 4.

**Home study description:** Assessment which complies with all requirements mandated by the Ohio Department of Human Services including references and medicals and which focuses on applicants' motivation, flexibility, readiness for parenting and acceptance in community.

**Average wait for a child after approval of a home study:**
Special needs and International: 1 - 6 mos.
Caucasian Infants: 12 - 24 mos.

**Foster care:** Cradle Care.

★618★
**Catholic Social Service of Columbus**
197 E. Gay St.
Columbus, OH 43215
Phone: (614) 221-5891
Fax: (614) 228-1125

**Branch address:**
417 W. Church St., Newark, OH 43055

45 N. 4th St., Zanesville, OH 43701

524 Sixth St., Portsmouth, OH 45662

**Contact:** Mary Evelyn Ruetty, MSW, LISW, Associate Director.

**Date established:** 1948.

**Description:** Non-profit private agency.

**Area served:** Residents of 23 Ohio counties within the Diocese of Columbus.

**Requirements:**
Newborn white infant adoption: Married couples who have no more than one child and who are practicing members of an organized religion.
Special needs adoption: All requirements are flexible except for religious observance.

**Fees:**
Newborn white infant: $6000.

Special needs: variable.

**Number of children placed last year:** 12.

**Description of children:** 6 white infants; 6 black infants.

**Adoption procedure:**
1) Telephone request to be placed on pre-waiting list;
2) attend intake interview;
3) file application;
4) name added to waiting list for home study;
5) home study.

**Average length of time between application and start of home study:** 0-1 mos.

**Average length of time to complete home study:** 3 mos.

**Number of interviews:** Varies.

**Home study description:** Discussion of both spouses' background; marital relationship; relationship of any child in the home or other member of the household; finances and employment history; religion; activities and interests; home environment and references; motivation to adopt and expectations for a child; finger printing.

**Average wait for a child after approval of a home study:** 6-12 mos.

**Foster care:** Temporary.

★619★
**Catholic Social Services of Lake County**
8 N. State St., Ste. 455
Painesville, OH 44077
Phone: (216) 352-6191

**Branch address:**
28706 Euclid Ave., Wickliffe, OH 44092

**Contact:** Karen Anderson, Supervisor, Adoption Services.

**Date established:** 1947.

**Description:** Private, sectarian agency offering a variety of adoption services including open, independent and special needs as well as home studies and post-placement services for international adoption and licensed by the Ohio Department of Human Services.

**Area served:** Primarily residents of Cuyahoga, Geauga and Lake counties.

**Requirements:** Applicants must be younger than 47 yrs. and be married at least 1 yr.

**Fees:** Application: $500; home study: sliding scale; placement fee: $3420.

**Number of children placed last year:** 27.

**Description of children:** Caucasian and minority infants, medically fragile infants and foreign born infants and toddlers.

**Adoption procedure:** 1) Interest registration form; 2) compilation of profile; 3) home study; 4) 6 group sessions; 5) meet with birth family; 6) placement; 7) post-placement supervision; 8) finalization.

**Average length of time between application and start of home study:** Unavailable.

**Average length of time to complete home study:** 1 mo.

**Number of interviews:** 4.

**Home study description:** Assessment which includes personal interviews with each member of the household and 6 group sessions in which the issues of infertility, birth family needs, attachment and life long adoption issues are raised.

**Average wait for a child after approval of a home study:** 6 - 12 mos.

**Foster care:** Temporary.

## ★ 620 ★
**Catholic Social Services of Southwestern Ohio**
100 E. 8th St.
Cincinnati, OH 45202
Phone: (513) 241-7745
Fax: (513) 241-4333

**Branch address:**
   140 N. 5th St., Hamilton, OH 45011
   Phone: (513) 863-6129

**Contact:** Jan Schaefer.

**Date established:** 1914.

**Description:** Non-profit private agency licensed by the State of Ohio.

**Area served:** Residents of Adams, Brown, Clermont, Clinton, Highland, Hamilton, Butler and Warren counties.

**Requirements:** Couples married at least 1 yr. at time of application who are no older than 36 yrs. at time of application, who are in good physical and emotional health, and at least one of whom is a practicing Catholic.

**Fees:**
Healthy, white infant: $4550;
special needs adoption fees on an individual basis.

**Number of children placed last year:** 7.

**Description of children:** Infants.

**Adoption procedure:**
1) Send letter requesting to adopt;
2) attend screening interview;
3) attend 4 education and support sessions;
4) complete home study;
5) placement;
6) post-placement supervisory; and
7) finalization.

**Average length of time between application and start of home study:** 24 or more mos.

**Average length of time to complete home study:** 6-8 wks.

**Number of interviews:** Approx. 5.

**Home study description:** Educational, supportive and evaluatory process wherein the following are considered: background information, physical and financial reports, marital history, motivation and desire to adopt, parenting skills and love of child for child's sake.

**Average wait for a child after approval of a home study:** 12-24 mos.

**Foster care:** Temporary.

## ★ 621 ★
**Children's Home of Cincinnati, Inc.**
5050 Madison Rd.
Cincinnati, OH 45227
Phone: (513) 272-2800
Fax: (513) 272-2807

**Contact:** Intake worker.

**Description:** Non-profit child welfare league and adoption agency.

**Area served:** Residents of Hamilton and Clermont counties.

**Requirements:** Couples married at least 3 yrs. who are between the ages of 25 and 37 yrs. and who have no more than one child.

**Fees:** Sliding scale which includes a $300 home study fee.

**Number of children placed last year:** 24.

**Description of children:** 13 black infants, 9 white, and 2 biracial.

**Adoption procedure:**
1) Attend orientation;
2) complete 4 group education sessions;
3) attend individual interview;
4) have home visit;
5) if approved, placement.

**Average length of time between application and start of home study:** 6-12 mos.

**Average length of time to complete home study:** Call or write for time frame.

**Number of interviews:** Varies.

**Home study description:** Call or write for details.

**Average wait for a child after approval of a home study:** 24 or more mos.

**Foster care:** Temporary.

## ★ 622 ★
**Crittendon Family Services**
1229 Sunbury Rd.
Columbus, OH 43219
Phone: (614) 252-5229

**Branch address:**
   1414 E. Broad St., Columbus, OH 43205

**Contact:** Kimberly Shaw, Placement Coordinator.

**Date established:** 1920.

**Description:** Private, non-profit United Way agency licensed to place children by the Ohio Department of Human Services.

**Area served:** Residents or employees in Franklin County.

**Requirements:** Applicants must be at least 21 yrs. old, in good health, preferably married at least 1 yr., 2 yrs. for infants in demand, and have no more than 1 child and demonstrate an ability to meet their own financial demands.

**Fees:** Application: $80; home study: $900; post-placement supervision: $120/visit; birth parent service fee: $1000.

**Number of children placed last year:** 18.

**Description of children:** U.S. infants and foreign-born infants and children.

**Adoption procedure:** 1) Application packet; 2) home study; 3) approval and wait for placement; 4) placement; 5) post-placement supervision; 6) finalization.

**Average length of time between application and start of home study:** 1 - 6 mos.

**Average length of time to complete home study:** 1 - 3 mos.

**Number of interviews:** 5.

**Home study description:** Assessment which includes but is not limited to interest and motivation to adopt, psych-social history of applicants, history of marital relationship(s), exploration of applicants' extended families' views of adoption, expectations of parenthood and of the child the family is interested in adopting and a discussion of child-centered adoption issues.

**Average wait for a child after approval of a home study:** 12 - 24 mos.

**Foster care:** Pre-adoptive.

## ★ 623 ★
**European Adoption Consultants**
9800 Boston Rd.
North Royalton, OH 44133
Phone: (216) 237-3554
(216) 237-9423

**Contact:** Margaret Cole, Executive Director.

**Date established:** 1991.

**Description:** Not-for-profit corporation licensed by the State of Ohio for child placement.

**Area served:** Residents of US.

**Requirements:** No agency requirements but foreign programs have their own requirements.

**Fees:** Pre-application: $100; registration: $500; home study: $950-$1750; dossier fee: $1150-$1650; international program processing: $3500. These fees do not cover transportation, emigration of the child to the U.S., immigration fees, visas, passports, or post-placement supervision and legal fees, if necessary. Foreign Program fees paid directly to the agency/office in the foreign country range from $7000 to $11,000.

**Number of children placed last year:** 84.

**Description of children:** Children from Russia, Belarus, the Ukraine, Kazakhstan, Latvia, Uzbekistan, China, Guatemala, Paraguay, Brazil, Peru, Lithuania, Moldavia and Romania from infancy to 5 yrs., some with minimal special needs.

**Adoption procedure:** 1) Telephone for information packet; 2) complete preliminary application; 3) file registration packet and begin home study; 4) compile dossier and Immigration & Naturalization requirements; 5) sign International contract and remit International Program Processing fee; 6) attend seminars and support groups; 7) child match; 8) travel to child's birth country and finalize adoption; 9) file post-placement supervision reports with EAC; 10) US finalization.

**Average length of time between application and start of home study:** Several weeks.

**Average length of time to complete home study:** 1 mos.

**Number of interviews:** 4.

**Home study description:** Includes background, reference and criminal records checks; explores adoption issues and cultural differences as well as parenting skills.

**Average wait for a child after approval of a home study:** Varies with age of child and country, but usually from 2-12 mos.

**Foster care:** None.

★624★
**Family Service Association**
248 N. Fifth St.
Steubenville, OH 43952
Phone: (614) 283-4763
Fax: (614) 283-2929

**Contact:** Susan Coxen, LSW, Adoption Specialist.

**Date established:** 1930.

**Description:** Private, non-profit United Way sponsored agency licensed by the Ohio Department of Human Services and the West Virginia Department of Human Services.

**Area served:** Residents of Belmont and Jefferson counties in Ohio and Brook, Hancock and Ohio counties in West Virginia.

**Requirements:** None.

**Fees:** Home study fee: $65/hr.

**Number of children placed last year:** Agency conducts home studies only.

**Description of children:** N/A.

**Adoption procedure:** 1) Inquiry; 2) initial interview; 3) joint interview; 4) home visit with all family members present.

**Average length of time between application and start of home study:** Less than 1 mo.

**Average length of time to complete home study:** 3 - 4 mos.

**Number of interviews:** Minimum of 4.

**Home study description:** Assessment which seeks to determine a family's ability to parent an adopted child by collecting financial, emotional, physical and social information on the individuals involved.

**Average wait for a child after approval of a home study:** Agency does not place children.

**Foster care:** None.

★625★
**Family Service of Summit County**
212 E. Exchange St.
Akron, OH 44304
Phone: (216) 376-9494
Fax: (216) 376-4525

**Branch address:**
480 W. Tuscarawas, No. 101, Barberton, OH 44203
Phone: (216) 753-3064

**Contact:** Patricia Giannos, LISW.

**Date established:** C. 1928.

**Description:** Not-for-profit private agency accredited by the Council on Accreditation of Services for Families and Children and Family Service America.

**Area served:** White infants: residents or employees in Summit County; minority infants: residents of the State of Ohio and sometimes out-of-state residents.

**Requirements:** Couples married at least 3 yrs. who are between the ages of 25 and 38 yrs. and who are in good health. Single applicants are considered in specific cases and minority applicants may have 2 or more children before adoptive placement.

**Fees:**
Application: $100;
other fees are on a sliding scale based on income from $1500 to $3700.

**Number of children placed last year:** 8.

**Description of children:** Black, white and biracial children under the age of 6 mos.

**Adoption procedure:**
1) Telephone intake;
2) attend group meeting;
3) submit application with references;
4) complete home study;
5) if approved, family admitted to waiting list;
6) placement.

**Average length of time between application and start of home study:** 1-6 mos.

**Average length of time to complete home study:** 6-10 wks.

**Number of interviews:** Approx. 6.

**Home study description:** Intense assessment of how family functions as a unit and individually.

**Average wait for a child after approval of a home study:** 24 or more mos.

**Foster care:** Temporary.

★626★
**HARAMBEE: Services to Black Families**
1468 E. 55th St.
Cleveland, OH 44103
Phone: (216) 391-7044
Fax: (216) 391-7131

**Contact:** Mary E. Pope, Director of Social Services.

**Date established:** 1981.

**Description:** Non-profit, private agency licensed by the Ohio Dept. of Human Services.

**Area served:** Adoptive families residing in Ohio; will do interstate placements for children coming into Ohio.

**Requirements:** Black, biracial or inter-racial individuals or couples who are at least 23 yrs. old and in good physical, emotional and mental health.

**Fees:** Sliding scale.

**Number of children placed last year:** 25.

**Description of children:** Black and biracial children between the ages of birth to 12 yrs.

**Adoption procedure:**
1) Submit application;
2) complete home study;
3) attend training program;
4) participate in support group for adoptive parents program;
5) pre-placement;
6) placement;
7) post-placement supervision;
8) legal finalization.

**Average length of time between application and start of home study:** 1 mo. or less.

**Average length of time to complete home study:** 1-3 mos.

**Number of interviews:** 5-6.

**Home study description:** Assessment of background, parenting experience, motivation to adopt, character, finances and relationships.

**Average wait for a child after approval of a home study:** 1-6 mos.

**Foster care:** None.

★ 627 ★
**Jewish Family Service of Sylvania**
6525 Sylvania Ave.
Sylvania, OH 43560
Phone: (419) 885-2561
(800) 484-7877
Fax: (419) 885-7427

**Contact:** Kathryn B. Linver, B.S., C.S.W., Adoption Social Worker.

**Date established:** 1970.

**Description:** Private, non-profit agency licensed to place children by the Ohio Department of Human Services.

**Area served:** Residents of Lucas county and those within a 2 hr. radius of the agency.

**Requirements:** Couples must be married at least 2 yrs. and at least 1 spouse must be Jewish.

**Fees:** Application: $150; home study: sliding scale based on gross annual income from $325 -$900; post-placement services: sliding scale from $740 - $6000.

**Number of children placed last year:** 3.

**Description of children:** Caucasian and multi-racial infants.

**Adoption procedure:** 1) Application; 2) medicals and background checks; 3) home study; 4) wait for placement; 5) placement; 6) post-placement supervision; 7) finalization.

**Average length of time between application and start of home study:** Less than 1 mo.

**Average length of time to complete home study:** 6 - 8 wks.

**Number of interviews:** 4.

**Home study description:** Assessment which includes references, fingerprinting and police checks, documentation of births and marriages and which addresses such issues as physical, mental, moral and financial capacities, ability to rear and educate, home and community, motivation to adopt and the type of child desired, personality and background, family relationships, health, religion, interests, attitudes and experiences with children.

**Average wait for a child after approval of a home study:** 12 - 24 mos.

**Foster care:** Pre-adoptive.

★ 628 ★
**Jewish Family Services of Akron**
83 N. Miller Rd., Ste. 202
Akron, OH 44333
Phone: (216) 867-3388

**Contact:** Mimi Surloff, LISW, Adoption Coordinator.

**Description:** Private, non-profit family service agency licensed to place children by the Ohio Department of Human Services.

**Area served:** Residents of Summit County, United Way and Akron Jewish Community Federation Catchment areas.

**Requirements:** Applicants for healthy, Caucasian infants in the custody of Jewish Family Services must be Jewish. Applicants for all other programs must follow the guidelines set by the Ohio Department of Human Services.

**Fees:** Application: $150; home study: $750 (application fee is applied to home study fee).

**Number of children placed last year:** 2.

**Description of children:** 1 child with special needs and 1 foreign-born child.

**Adoption procedure:** 1) Application; 2) initial screening interview; 3) home study; 4) 4 -6 hrs. Adoptive Parent Education; 5) approval; 6) placement; 7) post-placement supervision; 8) finalization.

**Average length of time between application and start of home study:** Less than 1 mo.

**Average length of time to complete home study:** 2 - 3 mos.

**Number of interviews:** 6 - 8.

**Home study description:** Assessment which includes pertinent family history, background of each applicant, motivation to adopt, issues surrounding adoption and infertility, marital history and adjustments, parenting attitudes and experiences, health status and financial stability, home and community appropriateness and reasons for type of child sought.

**Average wait for a child after approval of a home study:** Dependent on type of child requested.

**Foster care:** None.

★ 629 ★
**Jewish Family Services of Dayton**
4501 Denlinger Rd.
Dayton, OH 45426
Phone: (513) 854-2944
Fax: (513) 854-2850

**Contact:** Marilyn Lustig.

**Description:** Non-profit child placing agency licensed by the State of Ohio, Department of Human Services.

**Area served:** Residents of Greene, Montgomery and Preble counties, Ohio.

**Requirements:** Must meet state guidelines regarding age, income and health. Marital status will be considered for each situation. Family must be Jewish to have a child placed with them by Jewish Family Service. Families of other religious affiliations may receive all other services.

**Fees:** Home study: $900. Supervisory followup visits are charged on an hourly rate of $60/hr.

**Number of children placed last year:** 0.

**Adoption procedure:**
1) Return complete adoption application;
2) attend home and office visits;
3) provide references and other forms;
4) read at least two books on adoption. Remaining procedure varies according to circumstances.

**Average length of time between application and start of home study:** 1 mo. or less.

**Average length of time to complete home study:** 6 wks.

**Number of interviews:** 4-5.

**Home study description:** The following information is collected and evaluated: background information regarding parents, siblings, school, and employment; current information regarding family, employment, income, housing, criminal involvement (if any), and health; letters of reference.

**Average wait for a child after approval of a home study:** By networking with other agencies, most families we serve find a child within 12 to 18 mos., but this agency rarely has custody of a child requiring placement.

**Foster care:** Temporary.

★630★
**LIMIAR: U.S.A., Inc.**
2373 Brunswick Ln.
Hudson, OH 44236
Phone: (216) 653-8129
Fax: (216) 653-8129

**Contact:** Nancy Cameron.

**Date established:** 1984.

**Description:** Non-profit information and coordination center for Brazilian organization LIMIAR, Associacao de Apoio a Crianca e Familia Substituta located in Sao Paulo, S.P., Brazil.

**Area served:** Families throughout the U.S., Canada, and Europe.

**Requirements:** Applicants must be at least 16 yrs. older than adopted child. Both parents must travel. No length of marriage requirements. Applicants must be at least 21 yrs. of age.

**Fees:** None, but a donation is requested.

**Number of children placed last year:** Approx. 100.

**Description of children:** Brazilian children of all ages; many sibling groups; and some with special needs.

**Adoption procedure:**
1) File preliminary application;
2) submit home study and supporting documentation;
3) have documents translated;
4) child match;
5) submit translated documents to Brazilian court;
6) travel to Brazil;
7) return home with adopted child.

**Average length of time between application and start of home study:** N/A.

**Average length of time to complete home study:** See above.

**Number of interviews:** See above.

**Home study description:** Traditional, non-country specific home study is preferred.

**Average wait for a child after approval of a home study:** 1-6 mos.

**Foster care:** None.

★631★
**Lutheran Social Services of Central Ohio**
57 E. Main St.
Columbus, OH 43215
Phone: (614) 228-5209
Fax: (614) 228-1471

**Contact:** Mr. Gayle Hahn, MSW, LISW.

**Date established:** Adoption program: 1969.

**Description:** Non-profit, private family service agency.

**Area served:** Residents of Adams, Athens, Belmont, Coshocton, Delaware, Fairfield, Fayette, Franklin, Gallia, Guernsey, Highland, Hocking, Jackson, Knox, Lawrence, Licking, Madison, Marion, Meigs, Monroe, Morgan, Morrow, Muskingum, Noble, Perry, Pickaway, Pike, Ross, Scioto, Union, Vinton and Washington counties.

**Requirements:** Couples married a minimum of 1 yr. for some programs, 2 yrs. for others and who are in stable or reasonably good health. Applicants for healthy, white infants must be married at least 2 yrs. and childless. Age requirement for all programs is to be at least 21 years old.

**Fees:**
Application fee: $50 (non-refundable);
White infant program: $4529;
Foreign Adoption Program: $1652;
Special Needs Adoption Program: sliding scale based on income and family size from $210 to $2478; fees may be waived;
Black Adoption Service Fee: sliding scale based on income and family size from $210 to $2478.

**Number of children placed last year:** 50.

**Description of children:** White, black and biracial infants, school age children and children with special needs; foreign-born children.

**Adoption procedure:**
1) Submit application;
2) complete home study, receive adoption education;
3) if approved, placement;
4) 6 mos. post-placement supervision;
5) finalization.

**Average length of time between application and start of home study:** 1-6 mos.

**Average length of time to complete home study:** 6 wks.

**Number of interviews:** 4.

**Home study description:** Assessment of identifying information, home, finances, education and employment, marriage and marital adjustment, family background, personality, stability, site and safety check, employment verification and recommendation of references and police clearances.

**Average wait for a child after approval of a home study:** 1-6 mos.

**Foster care:** Temporary.

**★ 632 ★**
**Lutheran Social Services of the Miami Valley**
P.O. Box 292680
Dayton, OH 45429
Phone: (513) 643-0020
Fax: (513) 643-9970

**Branch address:**
    233A Northland Blvd., Cincinnati, OH 45246
    Phone: (513) 326-5430

**Contact:** Ed Petry.

**Date established:** Adoption program: 1967.

**Description:** Non-profit, private agency licensed by the Ohio Dept. of Human Services.

**Area served:** Residents of Brown, Butler, Champaign, Clark, Clermont, Clinton, Darke, Greene, Hamilton, Logan, Mercer, Miami, Montgomery, Preble, Shelby and Warren counties.

**Requirements:** Childless couples married at least 2 yrs. who are members of a local Protestant congregation, who are between the ages of 25 and 40 yrs., who have a record of fertility studies or a doctor's recommendation to adopt. Requirements may be flexible for minority and foreign-born placements.

**Fees:** Varies with program. $700-$1000 for home study for international adoption.

**Number of children placed last year:** 45.

**Description of children:** 9 white infants, 10 black children aged 2 yrs. and younger, 19 foreign-born children.

**Adoption procedure:**
1) File Interest Registration form;
2) attend information meeting;
3) submit formal application;
4) participate in group sessions which focus on birthparents, adoptive parents and adoptees;
5) home visit;
6) if approved, placement.

**Average length of time between application and start of home study:** 1-6 mos.

**Average length of time to complete home study:** 3-6 wks. after group sessions.

**Number of interviews:** 3 group, individual, and home visit.

**Home study description:** Evaluation of description of family members, education and employment, marital adjustment, health, description of home, finances, motivation to adopt, etc.

**Average wait for a child after approval of a home study:** Varies with type of adoption.

**Foster care:** Temporary.

**★ 633 ★**
**Lutheran Social Services of Toledo**
2149 Collingwood Blvd.
Toledo, OH 43620
Phone: (419) 243-9178

**Branch address:**
    1604 E. Perkins, Ste. 202, Sandusky, OH 44870
    Phone: (419) 625-3291

    1110 E. State St., Fremont, OH 43420
    Phone: (419) 334-3431

    1931 E. 2nd St., Defiance, OH 43512
    Phone: (419) 782-7800

    1011 Sandusky, Ste. I, Perrysburg, OH 43551
    Phone: (419) 872-9111

    113 W. Rensselaer, P.O. Box 868, Bucyrus, OH 44820
    Phone: (419) 562-6070

    158 E. Maumee Ave., Napoleon, OH 43545
    Phone: (419) 592-2445

    509 Center St., P.O. Box 727, Bryan, OH 43506
    Phone: (419) 636-3387

    115 E. Lima St., Findlay, OH 45840
    Phone: (419) 422-7917

**Contact:** Joyce E. Willier, Administrative Assistant.

**Date established:** 1911.

**Description:** Non-profit private agency that also provides home studies and post-placement supervision.

**Area served:** Northwestern Ohio.

**Requirements:** For healthy caucasian infants, must be N.W. Ohio residents, between the ages of 21 and 40 years of age, active members of the Lutheran Church, and have no more than one child born to either spouse.

**Fees:** Sliding fee schedule based on gross annual income and the number of dependents.

**Number of children placed last year:** 6.

**Description of children:** Infants, both caucasian and black, healthy, and with special needs.

**Adoption procedure:**
1) File application;
2) complete home study;
3) selection of child;
4) placement;
5) finalization.

**Average length of time between application and start of home study:** 24 or more mos.

**Average length of time to complete home study:** 3 mos.

**Number of interviews:** 6-8.

**Home study description:** Evaluation which includes but is not limited to family and social history.

**Average wait for a child after approval of a home study:** 24 or more mos.

**Foster care:** Temporary infant only.

**★ 634 ★**
**Mid-Western Children's Home**
Box 48
Pleasant Plain, OH 45162
Phone: (515) 877-2141
(800) 644-2141
Fax: (515) 877-2145

**Contact:** Chris Jones.

**Date established:** 1967.

**Description:** Non-profit private agency licensed by the Ohio Dept. of Human Services.

**Area served:** Residents of Ohio, West Virginia, Michigan, Kentucky, Pennsylvania and Indiana.

**Requirements:** Couples married at least 1 yr. who are 21 yrs. or older, but not 40 yrs. older than the adopted child, and who are members of the Church of Christ.

**Fees:** $2000-$6000 sliding scale based on income. Fee includes $500 home study fee.

**Number of children placed last year:** Approx. 2.

**Description of children:** Infants to 18 yrs., all races, some special needs.

**Adoption procedure:**
1) File preliminary application;
2) name added to waiting list;
3) complete home study and orientation;
4) if approved, placement;
5) 6 mos. post-placement supervisory period; and
6) finalization.

**Average length of time between application and start of home study:** 24 or more mos.

**Average length of time to complete home study:** Approx. 2 mos.

**Number of interviews:** 3-5.

**Home study description:** Evaluation of stability of home life and marriage, health, personality, finances and social history.

**Average wait for a child after approval of a home study:** 6-12 mos.

**Foster care:** Temporary, long-term and permanent.

★635★
**Northeast Ohio Adoption Services**
8029 E. Market St.
Warren, OH 44484
Phone: (216) 856-5582
(216) 539-4828
Fax: (216) 856-5586

**Contact:** Barbara L. Roberts, Executive Director.

**Date established:** 1978.

**Description:** Non-profit, private agency licensed by the Ohio Dept. of Human Services.

**Area served:** Primarily residents of northeast Ohio.

**Requirements:** Flexible.

**Fees:** None.

**Number of children placed last year:** 37.

**Description of children:** Children with special needs: older children, teens, and sibling groups.

**Adoption procedure:**
1) Initial inquiry;
2) attend orientation meeting;
3) participate in educational group series;
4) submit application;
5) complete family assessment;
6) placement;
7) post-placement services;
8) legalization;
9) post-legalization services.

**Average length of time between application and start of home study:** 1-6 mos.

**Average length of time to complete home study:** 2-6 mos.

**Number of interviews:** 4-6.

**Home study description:** Assessment of background information; type and degree of special needs child family can consider and accept; and ability to work with and commit to children with special needs.

**Average wait for a child after approval of a home study:** Depends on family's ability to consider waiting children.

**Foster care:** Temporary and treatment foster care.

★636★
**United Methodist Children's Home**
1045 N. High St.
Worthington, OH 43085
Phone: (614) 885-5020
Fax: (614) 885-4058

**Description:** Non-profit, private agency licensed by the State of Ohio.

**Area served:** Residents of Ohio.

**Requirements:** Adults 21 yrs. of age and older who are in good physical and mental health and have adequate financial resources and the ability to manage them.

**Fees:** $3000 covers home study and post-placement supervision; $1000 for foreign adoption home study.

**Number of children placed last year:** 4.

**Description of children:** U.S. and foreign infants and older children.

**Adoption procedure:**
1) Attend group meeting;
2) file application;
3) complete home study;
4) if approved, placement;
5) post-placement supervisory;
6) finalization.

**Average length of time between application and start of home study:** 1-6 mos.

**Average length of time to complete home study:** 2 mos.

**Number of interviews:** 3.

**Home study description:** Evaluation of marital and family relationships, home life, interests, activities and attitudes.

**Average wait for a child after approval of a home study:** 6-12 mos.; depends on resources and type of child desired.

**Foster care:** None.

# OKLAHOMA

## STATUTES

★637★

**Independent placement by intermediary?** Permitted.

**Independent placement by birth parents?** Permitted.

**Subsidies provided?** Medical, maintenance and non-recurring legal.

**Adoption cost defined by law?** No.

**Insurance for infertility?:** No.

**Home study required by state?** Required before placement.

**Prospective adoptive parent advertise for a child?** Permitted.

**Surrogacy laws?** Not addressed in law.

**Residents access agencies of other states or countries?** Permitted.

**Requires judicial termination of birth parents' rights?** Voluntary relinquishments are recognized.

**Time given to a birthmother to revoke her consent:** 30 days.

**Court handling adoptions?** Juvenile Court.

**Adoption of Native Children:** Tribe or state depending upon which has custody.

**Adoption records sealed?** Sealed.

**Photo-listing book available?** None.

# PUBLIC AGENCIES

**★ 638 ★**
**Oklahoma Department of Human Services**
P.O. Box 25352
Oklahoma City, OK 73125
Phone: (405) 521-2475
Fax: (405) 521-4373

**Contact:** Jane Morgan or county Department of Human Services.

**Description:** Non-profit, public agency.

**Area served:** Residents of the State of Oklahoma.

**Requirements:** Parent(s)' age should be appropriate to the age of the child; family must live in a locality which provides protection from identification and interference from biological parent(s); medical evaluation to ensure parent(s) are physically capable of caring for a child; verification of all marriages and divorces; positive recommendations from references; recent photos of all family members; and criminal and child abuse background check.

**Fees:** None.

**Number of children placed last year:** 330.

**Description of children:** Children with special needs.

**Adoption procedure:** Adoption program is state administered; procedures are consistent statewide.

**Average length of time between application and start of home study:** 1-6 mos.

**Average length of time to complete home study:** 4 mos.

**Number of interviews:** 4 or more.

**Home study description:** Educational and evaluatory process which includes 30 hr. training program and discussion of background, lifestyle, personality, medical and financial reports and the recommendation of references.

**Average wait for a child after approval of a home study:** 12-24 mos.

**Foster care:** Temporary and long-term therapeutic.

# PRIVATE AGENCIES

**★ 639 ★**
**Adoption Affiliates**
6136 E. 32nd Pl.
Tulsa, OK 74135
Phone: (918) 664-2275
(800) 256-4679

**Branch address:**
215 W. Olmos Dr., San Antonio, TX 78212
Phone: (512) 824-9977

**Contact:** Sherri Fink or Kristi Newell.

**Description:** Private, non-profit child placing agency licensed by the Oklahoma New Mexico and Texas.

**Area served:** Residents of Oklahoma, New Mexico and Texas.

**Requirements:** Open.

**Fees:** Comprehensive Fee: $17,000; special needs: $8000.

**Number of children placed last year:** 42.

**Description of children:** Infants.

**Adoption procedure:** 1) Inquiry; 2) waiting list; 3) informational meeting; 4) formal application; 5) home study; 6) placement; 7) post-placement services; 8) finalization.

**Average length of time between application and start of home study:** Less than 1 mo.

**Average length of time to complete home study:** 3 - 4 wks.

**Number of interviews:** 2 - 3.

**Home study description:** A thorough assessment which includes the state requirements set by both Oklahoma and Texas and which includes an educational seminar.

**Average wait for a child after approval of a home study:** Less than 1 yr.

**Foster care:** Temporary.

**★ 640 ★**
**The Adoption Center**
P.O. Box 52460
Tulsa, OK 74152
Phone: (918) 582-5467

**Contact:** Suzanne Joyce.

**Date established:** 1986.

**Description:** Non-profit child placing agency licensed by the State of Oklahoma.

**Area served:** Residents of 22 counties in northeastern Oklahoma.

**Requirements:** Anglo infant program: couples between the ages of 25 and 35 years who are married at least 3 yrs. and infertile. Foreign-born program: At least 25 yrs. old. Other requirements vary with child's country of origin. Waiting American child program: requirements vary by child's agency.

**Fees:**
Application fee: $150.
Home study fee: $500.
No fees for special needs adoptions of state custody children.

**Number of children placed last year:** 55.

**Description of children:** Anglo infants, waiting American children of all ages and foreign-born children of all ages.

**Adoption procedure:** Call or write for details.

**Average length of time between application and start of home study:** Varies.

**Average length of time to complete home study:** 1-3 mos.

**Number of interviews:** 2 office visits and 1 home visit.

**Home study description:** Evaluatory and educational process which includes a 16 hr. workshop.

**Average wait for a child after approval of a home study:** Varies.

**Foster care:** Temporary Anglo infant program places child in foster care for 30 days pending relinquishment.

**★ 641 ★**
**Appletree Adoptions, Inc.**
P.O Box 52697
Tulsa, OK 74152
Phone: (918) 747-9998

**Contact:** Suzanne Ash, Executive Director.

**Date established:** 1993.

**Description:** Private child placing agency specializing in semi-open adoptions and licensed by the Oklahoma Department of Human Services.

**Area served:** Residents of the U.S.

**Requirements:** Couples must be married at least 2 yrs., own a home suitable for raising a family and demonstrate the ability to provide a college education for the adopted child.

**Fees:** Application: $600; home study and placement: $17,000.

**Number of children placed last year:** 7.

**Description of children:** 6 Caucasian infants and 1 biracial infant.

**Adoption procedure:** Applications are taken twice yearly in January and June. 1) Prospective applicantinterview for one of a few available positions; 2) compilation of blind profile for birth motherreview; 3) upon selection, home study conducted; 4) birth and placement.

**Average length of time between application and start of home study:** N/A.

**Average length of time to complete home study:** Unavailable.

**Number of interviews:** 4.

**Home study description:** Detailed assessment which requires criminal background checks and other approvals, description of home and 4 home visit, preparation of blind profile and financial statements.

**Average wait for a child after approval of a home study:** Home study is conducted during birth mother's 8th month of pregnancy.

**Foster care:** Cradle care.

### ★642★
**Associated Catholic Charities of Oklahoma City**
425 N.W. 7
Oklahoma City, OK 73101
Phone: (405) 232-8514
Fax: (405) 232-1435

**Mailing address:**
    P.O. Box 1516, Oklahoma City, OK 73101

**Contact:** Mia Mbroh, Adoption Specialist.

**Date established:** 1910.

**Description:** Non-profit social service agency licensed for child placement.

**Area served:** Residents of western Oklahoma.

**Requirements:** Infant adoption program: couples married 3 or more yrs., who are no older than 43 yrs. of age, infertile, with no more than one child, and who attend some church regularly. Special needs adoption program: flexible.

**Fees:**
Fees for special needs adoption: negotiable.
For infant adoption: home study - $400; placement - $5300 plus 5% of gross annual salary.

**Number of children placed last year:** 6.

**Description of children:** Newborn infants of all races.

**Adoption procedure:**
1) File pre-application;
2) complete formal application;
3) home study;
4) if approved, pre-placement preparation;
5) placement;
6) 6 mos. supervisory; and
7) finalization.

**Average length of time between application and start of home study:** 12-24 mos.

**Average length of time to complete home study:** 1-3 mos.

**Number of interviews:** Unavailable.

**Home study description:** Evaluation of marriage and the stability of the relationship; religion; attitudes about adoption and birthparents; motivation to adopt and feeling about infertility; parenting skills including discipline methods; health; finances; and references.

**Average wait for a child after approval of a home study:** 24 or more mos.

**Foster care:** Temporary.

### ★643★
**Bethany Adoption Service, Inc. of Oklahoma**
3940 N. College
Bethany, OK 73008-0531
Phone: (405) 789-5423

**Mailing address:**
    P.O. Box 531, Bethany, OK 73008-0531

**Contact:** Jack H. Petty, Executive Director.

**Date established:** 1989.

**Description:** Private, non-profit child placing agency licensed by the Oklahoma Department of Human Services.

**Area served:** Residents of Oklahoma.

**Requirements:** Flexible.

**Fees:** Application: $25; home study: $500; placement fee: $8000 average.

**Number of children placed last year:** 20.

**Description of children:** Infants and children with special needs.

**Adoption procedure:** Unavailable.

**Average length of time between application and start of home study:** 1 - 6 mos.

**Average length of time to complete home study:** 20 days.

**Number of interviews:** 2.

**Home study description:** Assessment which includes but is not limited to background, Criminal Records checks, financial statement, family make-up and health history.

**Average wait for a child after approval of a home study:** 12 - 24 mos.

**Foster care:** Temporary.

### ★644★
**Catholic Charities of Tulsa**
739 N. Denver
Tulsa, OK 74106
Phone: (918) 585-8167

**Contact:** Rita E. Wilson, Adoption Supervisor.

**Date established:** 1951.

**Description:** Non-profit private agency.

**Area served:** Residents of the Diocese of Tulsa.

**Requirements:** Couples married at least 5 yrs., at least one of whom is a Catholic, who are in good health and who are not older than 40 yrs. at the time of application.

**Fees:** $500 home study fee plus medical costs which average about $5800.

**Number of children placed last year:** 5.

**Description of children:** Infants.

**Adoption procedure:**
1) File petition for adoption;
2) investigation;
3) if approved, placement;
4) post-placement supervision and filing of reports;
5) finalization.

**Average length of time between application and start of home study:** 12-24 mos.

**Average length of time to complete home study:** 2 mos.

**Number of interviews:** 4.

**Home study description:** Evaluation of individual and marital stability; family background; health and financial reports; personality and emotional health; education; any history of drug or alcohol abuse; motivation to adopt and experience with children; methods of discipline; etc.

**Average wait for a child after approval of a home study:** 12-24 mos.

**Foster care:** Temporary.

## ★ 645 ★
**Cradle of Lawton, Inc.**
902 N.W. Kingswood Rd.
Lawton, OK 73505
Phone: (405) 536-2478

**Contact:** Jan Howenstine, President.

**Date established:** 1990.

**Description:** Private, incorporated, non-profit, Christian child placing agency licensed by the Oklahoma Department of Human Services.

**Area served:** Residents of Lawton, OK and the surrounding areas.

**Requirements:** Applicants must provide a pastoral reference and attend monthly support group meetings throughout the application process.

**Fees:** Membership Fee: $200; home study: varies according to distance. Medical and legal costs are additional.

**Number of children placed last year:** 3.

**Description of children:** Newborn infants.

**Adoption procedure:** 1) Support group meeting; 2) pre-application; 3) individual interview; 4) formal application; 5) home study; 6) wait for placement; 7) placement; 8) post-placement supervision; 9) finalization.

**Average length of time between application and start of home study:** Less than 1 mo.

**Average length of time to complete home study:** 2 - 3 mos.

**Number of interviews:** 2.

**Home study description:** Assessment which conforms with the requirements set by the Oklahoma Department of Human Services.

**Average wait for a child after approval of a home study:** 12 - 24 mos.

**Foster care:** None.

## ★ 646 ★
**Crisis Pregnancy Outreach**
11604 E. 58th St.
Tulsa, OK 74146
Phone: (918) 254-1875
(918) 254-9897

**Mailing address:**
   P.O. Box 470583, Tulsa, OK 74146

**Contact:** Cheryl Bauman, Director.

**Date established:** 1983.

**Description:** Private, non-profit home mission of Christian Chapel and licensed to place children by the Oklahoma Department of Human Services.

**Area served:** Residents of the U.S.

**Requirements:** Christian couples who agree that the adoptive mother will not work outside the home until the adopted child is in 1st Grade.

**Fees:** Application: $35; home study: $350; adoption fee: $1750. Medical and legal expenses are additional and usually range between $6000 and $8000.

**Number of children placed last year:** 11.

**Description of children:** Newborn infants.

**Adoption procedure:** 1) Pre-application; 2) application; 3) Lifebook preparation; 4) personal interview; 5)profile compiled; 6) birth mother selection; 7) home study; 8) birth and placement; 9) post- placement supervision; 10) finalization.

**Average length of time between application and start of home study:** 6 - 12 mos.

**Average length of time to complete home study:** 1 mo.

**Number of interviews:** 2.

**Home study description:** Assessment which conforms with all regulations set by the Oklahoma Department of Human Services.

**Average wait for a child after approval of a home study:** 1 - 6 mos.

**Foster care:** None.

## ★ 647 ★
**Deaconess Home: Pregnancy and Adoption Services**
5300 N. Grand Blvd., Ste. 210
Oklahoma City, OK 73112-5517
Phone: (405) 949-4200

**Contact:** Janice Reimers, Director of Home Services.

**Date established:** December 31, 1900.

**Description:** Non-profit private agency licensed by the Oklahoma Department of Human Services.

**Area served:** Residents of U.S.

**Requirements:** Call or write for guidelines.

**Fees:** Initial adoption interview: $350; adoption fee will vary from $5,000-$10,000.

**Description of children:** Infants.

**Adoption procedure:**
   1) Send letter of request;
   2) preliminary information form; QQ3) initial interview and testing;
   4) file application;
   5) submit letters of reference;
   6) complete home study in state of residence.

**Average length of time between application and start of home study:** Varies.

**Average length of time to complete home study:** Varies.

**Number of interviews:** Unavailable.

**Home study description:** Evaluation of background, parenting philosophy including methods of discipline; home setting; motivation to adopt; and family relationships.

**Average wait for a child after approval of a home study:** 24 or more mos.

**Foster care:** Temporary.

## ★ 648 ★
**Dillon International, Inc.**
7615 E. 63rd Pl., Ste. 100
Tulsa, OK 74133
Phone: (918) 250-1561
Fax: (918) 250-5624

**Contact:** Carol Webb.

**Date established:** 1973.

**Description:** Private child-placing agency for international children licensed in Oklahoma.

**Area served:** Residents of Oklahoma and Texas for Korean placement; residents of all states for Indian placements.

**Requirements:** Couples married at least 3 yrs. who are between the ages of 25 and 45 yrs. Preference shown to members of a Christian faith.

**Fees:**
Pre-application: $50;
formal application: $200;
placement fees: $500. Country fees are also applicable and vary greatly.

**Number of children placed last year:** 66.

**Description of children:** Foreign-born infants.

**Adoption procedure:**
1) File pre-application;
2) submit application;
3) complete home study or forward home study done by a local agency;
4) if approved, child assignment;
5) meet requirements of Immigration and Naturalization Service;
6) placement;
7) 6-9 mos. post-placement supervision;
8) finalization.

**Average length of time between application and start of home study:** 1-6 mos.

**Average length of time to complete home study:** 30-45 days.

**Number of interviews:** 3-4.

**Home study description:** Dillon follows guidelines set by the country with which the applicant family chooses to work.

**Average wait for a child after approval of a home study:** Varies by child's country of origin.

**Foster care:** Temporary.

### ★649★
**The Family Tree Adoption and Counseling Center**
448 Claremont Ave.
Norman, OK 73069
Phone: (405) 360-8134

**Contact:** L. Anne Babb, Ph.D., Executive Director.

**Date established:** 1993.

**Description:** Private, non-profit child placing agency licensed by the Oklahoma Department of Human Services.

**Area served:** Residents of Oklahoma.

**Requirements:** Flexible.

**Fees:** Application: $25 - $110; home study: $500 - $850; placement fees: $0 - $4000.

**Number of children placed last year:** 5.

**Description of children:** Infants through open adoption, children with special needs and foreign-born children.

**Adoption procedure:** 1) Pre-application; 2) application; 3) home study; 4) placement; 5) 6 - 12 mos. post- placement supervision; 6) finalization.

**Average length of time between application and start of home study:** 1 - 6 mos.

**Average length of time to complete home study:** 3 - 6 mos.

**Number of interviews:** 3 - 5.

**Home study description:** Assessment which includes health, financial and criminal background checks; references, and psychological tests, if requested by birth parents.

**Average wait for a child after approval of a home study:** Usually within 12 mos.

**Foster care:** Emergency, fost-adopt and therapeutic.

### ★650★
**MetroCenter for Family Ministries, Inc.**
P.O. Box 2380
Edmond, OK 73083
Phone: (405) 359-1400

**Contact:** Dr. Ken Pearce, Executive Director.

**Date established:** 1984.

**Description:** Non-profit private child placing agency licensed by the State of Oklahoma.

**Area served:** Residents of the State of Oklahoma and surrounding states through the Interstate Compact on the Placement of Children.

**Requirements:** Couples married at least 3 yrs. who are at least 24 yrs. old and whose median age is not older than 40 yrs., who have no more than 2 children and who are active members in the same local Christian church.

**Fees:**
Application fee: $100 (non-refundable);
home study: $500;
administrative fee: $4000.

**Number of children placed last year:** Unavailable.

**Description of children:** Infants.

**Adoption procedure:**
1) Submit completed application;
2) return completed questionnaire with financial statement, 8 letters of reference and medical reports on both spouses;
3) screening by Committee;
4) complete home study with Adoption Workshop;
5) if approved, admission to waiting list;
6) placement (if possible).

**Average length of time between application and start of home study:** Varies.

**Average length of time to complete home study:** Unavailable.

**Number of interviews:** 2.

**Home study description:** Assessment of family and individual background, marital history and current marriage, description of home and neighborhood, reference summary and type of child desired.

**Average wait for a child after approval of a home study:** Varies.

**Foster care:** Temporary.

### ★651★
**NSO-Project Adopt**
**Project Adopt Neighborhood Services Organization, Inc.**
2915 N. Classen Blvd., Ste. 215
Oklahoma City, OK 73106
Phone: (405) 525-3072

**Contact:** Tonya Walker or Carole Patten.

**Date established:** 1982.

**Description:** Private, non-profit organization of the United Way and the United Methodist Church, licensed to place children by the Oklahoma Department of Human Services.

**Area served:** Residents of Oklahoma.

**Requirements:** Couples must be married at least 2 yrs. and be at least 23 yrs. old.

**Fees:** Application: $7100; home study: $500.

**Number of children placed last year:** 14.

**Description of children:** Caucasian and minority infants and foreign-born children.

**Adoption procedure:** 1) Application; 2) home study; 3) wait for placement; 4) placement; 5) supervision; 6) finalization.

**Average length of time between application and start of home study:** 1 - 6 mos.

**Average length of time to complete home study:** 3 - 6 mos.

**Number of interviews:** 4 - 6.

**Home study description:** Assessment which includes social history, medicals, work experience, autobiographies, references and background checks.

**Average wait for a child after approval of a home study:** 1 - 3 yrs.

**Foster care:** Pre-adoptive.

★ 652 ★
**Small Miracles International**
7430 S.E. 15th, Ste. 204
Midwest City, OK 73110
Phone: (405) 732-7295
Fax: (405) 732-7297

**Branch address:**
568B S. Oliver, Wichita, KS 67218
Phone: (316) 686-4000

**Contact:** Margaret Orr, Director.

**Date established:** 1985.

**Description:** Private, non-profit agency which holds 501(c)(3) tax exemption under the IRS and which is licensed by the Arkansas Department of Human Services, the Kansas Department of Social and Rehabilitative Services and the Oklahoma Department of Human Services.

**Area served:** No geographic restrictions.

**Requirements:** Applicants should be between the ages of 25 and 55 yrs. have a high school diploma or equivalency and medical insurance.

**Fees:** Application: $150; home study: $800. Program fees vary and are additional.

**Number of children placed last year:** 40.

**Description of children:** Infants, toddlers and school age children of all races, some with special needs.

**Adoption procedure:** 1) Registration; 2) formal application; 3) home study; 4) home study review; 5) child referral; 6) placement; 7) post-placement supervision; 8) finalization.

**Average length of time between application and start of home study:** Less than 1 mo.

**Average length of time to complete home study:** 4 wks.

**Number of interviews:** 3.

**Home study description:** Assessment which includes motivation to adopt and ability to parent children with no physical resemblance, an unknown history and little medical information.

**Average wait for a child after approval of a home study:** 1 - 6 mos.

**Foster care:** Temporary.

★ 653 ★
**Small Miracles International**
7430 S.E. 15th St., Ste. 204
Midwest City, OK 73110
Phone: (405) 732-7295
Fax: (405) 732-7297

**Contact:** Margaret Orr or Debra Lawson.

**Date established:** 1985.

**Description:** Non-profit child placement agency licensed by the states of Oklahoma, Arkansas, and Kansas.

**Area served:** Residents of Oklahoma, Arkansas, and Kansas and all U.S. for some services.

**Requirements:** Adults between the ages of 25 and 55 yrs. who have a high school diploma or equivalent and health insurance. If married, at least 2 yr. duration. Child's country of origin may impose additional requirements.

**Fees:** $40 pre-application fee; $150 formal application fee; $800 home study (Oklahoma residents only); $800 post-placement services (Oklahoma residents only).

**Number of children placed last year:** 25.

**Description of children:** Infants, foreign, minority and special needs.

**Adoption procedure:**
1) File pre-application;
2) file formal application;
3) attend informational meeting;
4) complete home study or submit homestudy for approval;
5) if accepted, prepare dossier for some programs;
6) child search and referral;
7) placement.

**Average length of time between application and start of home study:** 1 mo. or less.

**Average length of time to complete home study:** 6 wks.-3 mos.

**Number of interviews:** Varies.

**Home study description:** Evaluation of applicant(s)' stability, ability to parent, and suitability of home.

**Average wait for a child after approval of a home study:** 6-12 mos.

**Foster care:** Temporary.

# OREGON

## STATUTES
★ 654 ★

**Independent placement by intermediary?** No.

**Independent placement by birth parents?** Permitted.

**Subsidies provided?** Medical and special needs.

**Adoption cost defined by law?** No, but the law requires that a sworn expense disclosure statement be filed and reviewed by the court.

**Insurance for infertility?:** Unknown.

**Home study required by state?** Required prior to filing adoption petition.

**Prospective adoptive parent advertise for a child?** Permitted.

**Surrogacy laws?** Not addressed in law.

**Residents access agencies of other states or countries?** Permitted.

**Requires judicial termination of birth parents' rights?** Notarized voluntary relinquishments are valid. Oregon's birth father registry requires an affidavit of the birth mother that the birth father has not 1) registered with the state; 2) been married to her; 3) supported or lived with her or the child in the 60 days prior to birth.

**Time given to a birthmother to revoke her consent:** None.

**Court handling adoptions?** Circuit.

**Adoption of Native Children:** Tribe.

**Adoption records sealed?** Sealed, but non-identifying information is available to adoptees 18 yrs. and older.

**Photo-listing book available?** Oregon participates in the photo-listing of

**The Northwest Adoption Exchange.**

# PUBLIC AGENCIES

## ★655★
**Oregon Childrens Services Division**
500 Summer St.
Salem, OR 97310-1017
Phone: (503) 378-4452

**Contact:** Diana Roberts, Permanency and Adoptions Manager.

**Description:** State agency.

**Area served:** Residents of the State of Oregon.

**Requirements:** Requirements are based on the needs of the child to be placed.

**Fees:** None.

**Number of children placed last year:** 468.

**Description of children:** 40% over the age of 8 yrs. Primarily special needs children.

**Adoption procedure:**
1) Initial inquiry, either written or telephoned;
2) complete home study;
3) if approved, placement;
4) up to 1 yr. post-placement supervision; and
5) finalization.

**Average length of time between application and start of home study:** Varies.

**Average length of time to complete home study:** 90-120 days.

**Number of interviews:** Unavailable.

**Home study description:** Evaluation of family history, medical reports, financial/employment background and references.

**Average wait for a child after approval of a home study:** Varies.

**Foster care:** Temporary and long-term.

# PRIVATE AGENCIES

## ★656★
**Adventist Adoption and Family Services**
6040 S.E. Belmont St.
Portland, OR 97215
Phone: (503) 232-1211

**Branch address:**
P.O. Box C, 8903 U.S. 31-33, Berrien Springs, MI 49103

P.O. Box 3828, Vancouver, WA 98662

**Contact:** Fern Ringering (Oregon Office); Wilma Darby or Lynda Bell (Michigan branch).

**Date established:** 1950.

**Description:** Non-profit, private agency.

**Area served:** Residents of the U.S. and Canada.

**Requirements:** Couples married at least 2 yrs. who are not older than 40 yrs., who have no more than 1 child living in their home, who are in good health but have a fertility problem and who share the same religious belief. Requirements are more flexible for placement of a biracial child.

**Fees:**
Application: $125.
Home study: $700.
Adoption fees: $11,400.
Post-placement: $250.

**Number of children placed last year:** 30.

**Description of children:** Primarily infants, some foreign-born.

**Adoption procedure:**
1) Submit pre-application;
2) screening;
3) application;
4) if approved, complete home study;
5) if approved, admission to waiting list;
6) placement;
7) post-placement supervision;
8) finalization.

**Average length of time between application and start of home study:** 1 mo. or less.

**Average length of time to complete home study:** 2-3 mos.

**Number of interviews:** 4.

**Home study description:** Assessment of background, religion, recommendation of references, home, childrearing attitudes and experiences, financial stability and motivation to adopt. Includes criminal checks, physical and emotional stability, expectations, flexibility, nurturing capacity and stbility of marriage.

**Average wait for a child after approval of a home study:** 1-5 yrs.

**Foster care:** Temporary, long-term and permanent.

## ★657★
**Albertina Kerr Center for Children**
424 N.E. 22nd
Portland, OR 97232
Phone: (503) 239-8101

**Branch address:**
722 N.E. 162nd Ave., Portland, OR 97230
Phone: (503) 255-4205

**Contact:** Adoption Unit Secretary.

**Date established:** 1900 - 1910.

**Description:** Private, non-profit child placing agency licensed by the Oregon Children's Services Division.

**Area served:** Residents of Oregon.

**Requirements:** Unavailable.

**Fees:** Unavailable.

**Number of children placed last year:** Unavailable.

**Description of children:** Children with special needs.

**Adoption procedure:** 1) Application packet; 2) educational classes; 3) home visitation; 4) child match; 5) committee meets on application; 6) approval ; 7) placement; 8) post-placement supervision; 9) finalization.

**Average length of time between application and start of home study:** Less than 1 mo.

**Average length of time to complete home study:** 3 mos.

**Number of interviews:** 2 - 6.

**Home study description:** Unavailable.

**Average wait for a child after approval of a home study:** 12 - 24 mos.

**Foster care:** Long-term, permanent and therapeutic.

★ **658** ★

**Heritage Adoption Services**
516 S.E. Morrison St., Ste. 714
Portland, OR 97212
Phone: (503) 233-1099

**Date established:** 1991.

**Description:** Private, non-profit, non-sectarian child placing agency licensed by the Oregon Department of Human Resources.

**Area served:** Residents of Australia, Canada, England and the U.S.

**Requirements:** Applicants should be younger than 60 yrs.

**Fees:** Application: $250; home study: $1040. Fees for individual programs vary.

**Number of children placed last year:** 75.

**Description of children:** Infants from China, Guatemala, Russia and the U.S. and older children from Russia.

**Adoption procedure:** 1) Inquiry; 2) application; 3) home study; 4) dossier preparation and referral, ifinternational program; 5) placement which may include travel; 6) post-placement supervision; 7) finalization.

**Average length of time between application and start of home study:** Less than 1 mo.

**Average length of time to complete home study:** 1 mo.

**Number of interviews:** 2.

**Home study description:** Assessment which includes autobiography, parenting motivation, health, finances and lifestyle.

**Average wait for a child after approval of a home study:** 1 - 6 mos.

**Foster care:** None.

★ **659** ★

**Holt International Children's Services**
1195 City View
Eugene, OR 97402
Phone: (503) 687-2202

**Branch address:**
3807 Pasadena Ave., Ste. 170, Sacramento, CA 95821

2200 Abbott Dr., Ste. 203, Carter Lake, IA 51510

340 Scotch Rd., 2nd Fl., Trenton, NJ 08628

**Contact:** Adoption intake worker.

**Date established:** 1956.

**Description:** Non-profit corporation.

**Area served:** All of the U.S. when adopting from all countries except Korea. For healthy Korean children, Holt places in Oregon, New Jersey, Iowa, Nebraska, eastern South Dakota, and select counties of California near Los Angeles and Sacramento. Special needs Korean children can be placed in other states. Please inquire.

**Requirements:** Adults between the ages of 21 and 45 yrs. who are in good health and whose minimum income is $20,000 (Thai placements require a minimum income of $30,000). Most programs require applicants be married a minimum of 2 yrs., some programs will accept single applicants.

**Fees:** $5900-$7900; home study and travel (if required) additional.

**Number of children placed last year:** 599.

**Description of children:** Children of all ages, some with special needs.

**Adoption procedure:**
1) File application;
2) complete home study;
3) selection and acceptance of child;
4) legal processing and arrangement of transportation;
5) child's arrival;
6) post-placement services;
7) finalization;
8) naturalization.

**Average length of time between application and start of home study:** 1-6 mos.

**Average length of time to complete home study:** Varies.

**Number of interviews:** Varies.

**Home study description:** Evaluation of self, background, strengths and weaknesses, current lifestyle and values and the suitability of the foregoing to inter-country adoption. The following areas are considered: personal history, parenting issues, any children in the home, motivation to adopt, home, community, finances, health, references and family values.

**Average wait for a child after approval of a home study:** 24 or more months.

**Foster care:** None.

★ **660** ★

**Journeys of the Heart Adoption Services**
905 E. Main St.
Hillsboro, OR 97123
Phone: (503) 681-3075

**Mailing address:**
P.O. Box 482, Hillsboro, OR 97123

**Contact:** Susan Tompkins, Director.

**Date established:** 1993.

**Description:** Private, non-profit child placing agency licensed by the Oregon Department of Human Resources.

**Area served:** Residents of the U.S.

**Requirements:** Flexible, but agencies and governments may impose their own criteria.

**Fees:** Education Seminar: $35; application: $100.
Local Birth Mother Program: Flat fee: $12,000 - $13,000.
Other domestic programs: Minority Infants from other agencies, sliding scale: $1000 - $1600.
International Program: sliding scale: $1000 - $1600. Program fees: China: $14,000; Romania: $14,000-$15,000; Vietnam: $10,000-$11,000; Guatemala: $14,300 - $15,300; Africa: $3650 - $6500; India: $11,000 - $12,000; Colombia: $12,000; Bulgaria: $12,000; Siberia: $7500; Korea: $6000 - $7000 plus travel; Russia: $3000 -$16,000.

**Number of children placed last year:** 5 - 10 Caucasian infants, minority infants and foreign born children.

**Description of children:** Caucasian infants, minority infants and foreign born children.

**Adoption procedure:** 1) Inquiry; 2) 1 day seminar or equivalent; 3) application; 4)home study and dossier preparation, if applicable; 5) child match; 6) placement (may include travel or escort service); 7) post-placement supervision; 8) finalization.

**Average length of time between application and start of home study:** Upon completion of application and contract for services.

**Average length of time to complete home study:** 2 - 4 wks.

**Number of interviews:** Unavailable.

**Home study description:** Assessment which includes education and parent preparation.

**Average wait for a child after approval of a home study:** Varies with program selected.

**Foster care:** Pre-adoptive.

★ 661 ★
**Open Adoption and Family Services, Inc.**
440 Charnelton St.
Eugene, OR 97401
Phone: (503) 343-4825
**Branch address:**

2950 S.E. Stark St., Ste. 230, Portland, OR 97214
Phone: (503) 233-9660

440 Charnelton St., Eugene, OR 97401
Phone: (503) 343-4825

**Contact:** Corinne Lane.

**Date established:** 1985.

**Description:** Private, non-profit agency licensed by the Oregon Department of Human Resources and the Washington Department of Health and Social Services.

**Area served:** Residents of Oregon and Washington.

**Requirements:** Besides being able to provide a stable and loving home, birth parents set all other requirements.

**Fees:** Home study: $1500 - $2100; seminar: $$250; intake fee: $250 - $385; pool entry fee: $1000; mediation: $2100 - $4700; placement fee: $1450 - $1815.

**Number of children placed last year:** 58.

**Description of children:** Primarily infants and some children 1 yr. and older.

**Adoption procedure:** 1) Seminar; 2) application and intake interview; 3) family preparation; 4) pool entry; 5)mediation; 6) placement; 7) post-placement supervision; 8) court report; 9) finalization.

**Average length of time between application and start of home study:** 1 - 6 mos.

**Average length of time to complete home study:** 8 wks.

**Number of interviews:** 3.

**Home study description:** A written description of the prospective adoptive home which includes an introduction, a description of the home and neighborhood, the family's lifestyle, values and religion, parenting attitudes and philosophies, preparation for adoption, descriptions of the prospective adoptive mother and father, their marital relationship, financial information, the reports of references, the social worker's summary and recommendations.

**Average wait for a child after approval of a home study:** 6 -12 mos.

**Foster care:** None.

★ 662 ★
**Open Adoption & Family Services, Inc.**
2950 S.E. Stark St., Ste. 230
Portland, OR 97214
Phone: (503) 233-9660
Fax: (503) 233-5929
**Branch address:**

440 Charnelton St., Eugene, OR 97401
Phone: (503) 343-4825

1402 3rd Ave., Ste. 818, Seattle, WA 98101
Phone: (206) 682-9770

**Contact:** Director.

**Date established:** 1985.

**Description:** Non-profit private adoption agency licensed by the State of Oregon and the State of Washington.

**Area served:** Residents of Oregon and Washington.

**Requirements:** Besides being able to provide a stable and loving home, birth parents set all other requirements.

**Fees:** Range from $7800-$10,500.

**Number of children placed last year:** 58.

**Description of children:** 90% white infants and toddlers; 10% minorities.

**Adoption procedure:**
1) Attend informational meeting;
2) attend pre-adoption seminar;
3) file application;
4) begin home study;
5) complete home study;
6) enter pool;
7) selection by birth parents;
8) begin mediation;
9) birth and adoptive parents plan birthing and adoption together;
10) infant's birth;
11) adoptive parents take infant home;
12) 6 mos. post-placement supervisory;
13) finalization and on-going relationship with birthparents.

**Average length of time between application and start of home study:** 1 mo. or less.

**Average length of time to complete home study:** 2-3 mos.

**Number of interviews:** 3.

**Home study description:** Agency prepares a picture of the adoptive family's special qualities without using identifying information so that birth parents can make an informed decision on their child's placement.

**Average wait for a child after approval of a home study:** 6-12 mos.

**Foster care:** None.

★ 663 ★
**PLAN International Adoption Service**
P.O. Box 667
McMinnville, OR 97128
Phone: (503) 472-8452
Fax: (503) 472-1831

**Contact:** Ann Scott, Director; Judy Elkins and Sandy Temple, Foreign Directors.

**Date established:** 1975.

**Description:** Private, non-profit agency licensed in the State of Oregon and various foreign countries.

**Area served:** All areas served.

**Requirements:** Flexible.

**Fees:** Application fee: $150 (non-refundable). Foreign costs vary.

**Number of children placed last year:** 133.

**Description of children:** Infants, older children and sibling groups from China, India, Vietnam, Colombia, Russia, Guatemala, Peru; African-American babies.

**Adoption procedure:**
1) Initial inquiry;
2) file application;
3) complete home study;
4) make immigration and travel arrangements (foreign adoption);
5) wait for match;
6) placement.

**Average length of time between application and start of home study:** Varies.

**Average length of time to complete home study:** Varies.

**Number of interviews:** Varies.

**Home study description:** Call or write for guidelines.

**Average wait for a child after approval of a home study:** Depends on program.

# PENNSYLVANIA

## STATUTES

★ 664 ★

**Independent placement by intermediary?** Permitted.

**Independent placement by birth parents?** Permitted.

**Subsidies provided?** Medical, legal and maintenance.

**Adoption cost defined by law?** Yes.

**Insurance for infertility?:** No.

**Home study required by state?** Required before placement.

**Prospective adoptive parent advertise for a child?** Permitted.

**Surrogacy laws?** Not addressed in law.

**Residents access agencies of other states or countries?** Permitted.

**Requires judicial termination of birth parents' rights?** Voluntary relinquishments by both birth parents are valid.

**Time given to a birthmother to revoke her consent:** Until the court decrees termination.

**Court handling adoptions?** Court of Common Pleas.

**Adoption of Native Children:** Tribe.

**Adoption records sealed?** Yes, but adoptees, aged 18 yrs. and older, may access their adoption records under prescribed conditions prescribed by law.

**Photo-listing book available?** Pennsylvania Adoption Exchange (PAE) Photo Listing Book.

## PUBLIC AGENCIES

★ 665 ★
**Beaver County Children and Youth Agency**
500 Market St.
Beaver, PA 15009
Phone: (412) 775-4510
Fax: (412) 775-3316

**Contact:** Adoption Unit.

**Description:** Public, county agency mandated to place children by the Pennsylvania Dept. of Public Welfare.

**Area served:** Residents of Beaver County.

**Requirements:** Couples married at least 2 yrs. who are 21 yrs. and older, whose health is adequate to parent and who are financially stable. Singles are also accepted.

**Fees:**
Application: $50.
Home study: $300.
Supervision of placement: $300.
Fees may be reduced or waived.

**Number of children placed last year:** 7.

**Description of children:** Children with special needs.

**Adoption procedure:**
1) Intake;
2) admission to waiting list;
3) submit application;
4) complete home study;
5) if approved, wait for placement;
6) placement;
7) supervision of placement;
8) finalization.

**Average length of time between application and start of home study:** 1-6 mos.

**Average length of time to complete home study:** 3 mos.

**Number of interviews:** 1-4.

**Home study description:** Assessment of psychological and medical reports, child abuse and criminal clearances, recommendation of references, finances and insurance coverage, background and motivation to adopt.

**Average wait for a child after approval of a home study:** Varies widely.

**Foster care:** Fost-adopt, emergency, short- and long-term.

★ 666 ★
**Berks County Children and Youth Agency**
**County Services Center**
633 Court St.
Reading, PA 19601
Phone: (610) 478-6700
Fax: (610) 478-6799

**Contact:** Adoption unit.

**Description:** Public, county agency.

**Area served:** Residents of Berks County.

**Requirements:** Requirements are flexible for special needs adoption.

**Fees:** None.

**Number of children placed last year:** 45.

**Description of children:** Children with special needs.

**Adoption procedure:** Berks County seeks adoptive placements for children within its custody through private agencies in the county. The agency does perform home studies for foster parents who wish to adopt the child they are fostering.

**Number of interviews:** Ongoing.

**Foster care:** Emergency, short and long-term, fost-adopt and therapeutic.

★667★

**Bucks County Children and Youth Agency**
Bucks County Bank Center, Ste. 200
4259 W. Swamp Rd.
Doylestown, PA 18901
Phone: (215) 348-6900
(800) 922-5783
Fax: (215) 348-6989

**Contact:** Intake Unit.

**Description:** Public, county agency.

**Area served:** Residents of Bucks County.

**Requirements:** Adults, 21 yrs. and older, who are financially able to support a child.

**Fees:** None.

**Number of children placed last year:** 5.

**Description of children:** Children with special needs.

**Adoption procedure:** Children in the custody of Bucks County who are freed for adoption are most often placed through private adoption agencies in Bucks County. Bucks County Children and Youth Agency will perform home studies for foster to adoption conversions for foster parents who are already fostering the child they plan to adopt.

**Average length of time between application and start of home study:** Varies.

**Average length of time to complete home study:** 1-2 mos.

**Number of interviews:** 3.

**Home study description:** A second home study in addition to the home study for foster placement is performed and covers, among other subjects, background checks, insurance coverage, health, verification of all marriages and divorces and motivation to adopt.

**Average wait for a child after approval of a home study:** Varies.

**Foster care:** Emergency, short and long-term and therapeutic.

★668★

**Dauphin County Children and Youth Agency**
25 S. Front St.
Harrisburg, PA 17101-2025
Phone: (717) 255-2870
Fax: (717) 257-1584

**Contact:** Resource Unit.

**Description:** Public, county agency.

**Area served:** Residents of Dauphin County.

**Requirements:** Adults, 21 yrs. and older, whose health is adequate to parent.

**Fees:** None.

**Number of children placed last year:** 5-8.

**Description of children:** Primarily children with special needs who were adopted by their foster parents.

**Adoption procedure:**
1) Submit application;
2) admission to waiting list;
3) attend intake meeting;
4) complete home study;
5) if approved, wait for placement;
6) placement;

7) post-placement supervision;
8) finalization.

**Average length of time between application and start of home study:** 1-6 mos.

**Average length of time to complete home study:** 3-6 mos.

**Number of interviews:** 1 group and 4 individual.

**Home study description:** Assessment of background checks, child abuse registry clearance, recommendation of references, health and finances, childrearing practices and motivation to adopt.

**Average wait for a child after approval of a home study:** 24 or more mos.

**Foster care:** Short and long-term, permanent and fost-adopt.

★669★

**Delaware County Children and Youth**
5th and Penn Sts.
Chester, PA 19013
Phone: (215) 891-4800
Fax: (215) 891-0538

**Contact:** Adoption coordinator.

**Date established:** 1950.

**Description:** Public, county agency mandated to place children by the Pennsylvania Dept. of Public Welfare.

**Area served:** Residents of Delaware County.

**Requirements:** Adults over the age of 25 yrs. who have adequate income to meet their family's needs, who have completed a medical examination and have a physician's statement concerning their fertility and who are either single or married.

**Fees:** None.

**Number of children placed last year:** 25.

**Description of children:** Primarily children from birth to 12 yrs. with special needs.

**Adoption procedure:**
1) Telephone intake;
2) attend orientation meeting;
3) file application;
4) undergo home assessment;
5) attend pre-service training meetings;
6) if approved, wait for placement.

**Average length of time between application and start of home study:** Pre-service Training, an integral part of the home study process, is scheduled at least semi-annually.

**Average length of time to complete home study:** 2 mos.

**Number of interviews:** 2-3.

**Home study description:** Assessment of individual and family history, understanding of child development, issues relating to parenthood and adoption, and parental experience.

**Average wait for a child after approval of a home study:** Brief wait for applicants willing to take legal risk placements.

**Foster care:** Emergency, short- and long-term.

★670★

**Erie County Children and Youth Agency**
606 W. 2nd St.
Erie, PA 16507
Phone: (814) 451-6600

**Contact:** Adoption Unit.

**Description:** Public, county agency mandated to place children by the Pennsylvania Dept. of Public Welfare.

**Area served:** Residents of Erie County.

**Requirements:** Adults, 21 yrs. and older, who are either legally married or legally single, and whose health is adequate to parent.

**Fees:** None.

**Number of children placed last year:** 50.

**Description of children:** Primarily children with special needs who are presently being fostered by the family that wishes to adopt them.

**Adoption procedure:** Applicants for adoption in Erie County are referred to private agencies in the county for adoption services. Updating of home studies for foster parents who apply to adopt their foster children is also done by referral to private adoption agencies.

**Home study description:** Required information includes background checks, Childline and state police clearances, health and finances and the recommendation of 6 references.

**Average wait for a child after approval of a home study:** Most prospective adoptive parents are already fostering the child they are seeking to adopt.

**Foster care:** Emergency, short and long-term, and therapeutic.

★ 671 ★

**Lancaster County Children and Youth Social Service Agency**
900 E. King St.
Lancaster, PA 17602
Phone: (717) 299-7925
Fax: (717) 299-7929

**Contact:** Adoption Unit.

**Date established:** 1956.

**Description:** Public, county child welfare agency mandated to place children by the Pennsylvania Dept. of Public Welfare.

**Area served:** Residents of Lancaster County.

**Requirements:** Adults 21 yrs. and older.

**Fees:** None.

**Number of children placed last year:** 20.

**Description of children:** Children with special needs.

**Adoption procedure:**
1) Submit application;
2) criminal & child abuse clearances, medical reference;
3) Adoption Agreement form;
4) file Intent to Adopt with court;
5) home visits;
6) file intermediary report;
7) finalization, preparation and execution.

**Average length of time between application and start of home study:** 1 mo.

**Average length of time to complete home study:** 1 mo.

**Number of interviews:** 3-4.

**Home study description:** Agency performs home studies for approved foster parents who wish to adopt their foster children, not for the general public. In those cases the evaluation consists of law enforcement clearances, family functioning, marital relationship (if applicable), extended family support, commitment to child and ability to handle problems.

**Average wait for a child after approval of a home study:** Within 1 yr. Agency does mostly fost-adopt conversions which are usually completed within 6 mos.

**Foster care:** Emergency, long and short-term.

★ 672 ★

**Montgomery County Office of Children and Youth**
Logan Square
1800 Markley St.
Norristown, PA 19401
Phone: (215) 278-5800

**Contact:** Adoption Unit.

**Description:** Public, county children and youth agency.

**Area served:** Residents of Montgomery County.

**Requirements:** Adults, 21 yrs. and over.

**Fees:** None.

**Number of children placed last year:** 35.

**Description of children:** Children with special needs. Most adoptions handled are fost-adopt conversions.

**Adoption procedure:**
1) Initial inquiry;
2) submit application;
3) attend group training;
4) complete home study;
5) placement;
6) post-placement supervision;
7) finalization.

**Average length of time between application and start of home study:** 1-3 mos.

**Average length of time to complete home study:** 3 mos.

**Number of interviews:** Minimum of 2.

**Home study description:** A combination of 3 group and individual sessions which address adoption-specific issues such as separation and loss.

**Average wait for a child after approval of a home study:** Most children are already being fostered in the adoptive home.

**Foster care:** Fost-adopt, emergency, short- and long-term.

★ 673 ★

**Philadelphia County Children and Youth Agency**
UGI Bldg., 3rd Fl.
1401 Arch St.
Philadelphia, PA 19102
Phone: (215) 686-7007

**Contact:** Adoption Unit.

**Description:** Public, county agency.

**Area served:** Residents of Philadelphia County.

**Requirements:** Adults, 21 yrs. and older whose health is adequate to parent.

**Fees:** None.

**Number of children placed last year:** 150.

**Description of children:** Children with special needs.

**Adoption procedure:**
1) Initial inquiry and telephone screening;
2) return completed 1 pg. Interest Form;
3) referral through state-wide Adoption Network for agency to conduct home study;
4) during home study process, applicant(s) receive information on children listed on the Pennsylvania Adoption Exchange and other exchanges for a match.

**Average length of time between application and start of home study:** County does not conduct home studies.

**Average wait for a child after approval of a home study:** Family recieves information on children waiting adoptive placement during the home study process. If a child match is achieved, placement can be almost immediate.

**Foster care:** Emergency, short and long-term, fost-adopt, and therapeutic.

★674★

**Schuylkill County Children and Youth Agency**
410 N. Centre St.
Pottsville, PA 17901
Phone: (717) 628-1050
(800) 722-8341
Fax: (717) 628-1012

**Contact:** George Williams.

**Date established:** C. 1967.

**Description:** Non-profit public county children and youth agency.

**Area served:** Residents of Schuylkill County.

**Requirements:** Singles or married couples who are in basic good health and whose income could support an additional family member.

**Fees:** Home study: $750.

**Number of children placed last year:** 5.

**Description of children:** Infants, preschoolers, and school age children.

**Adoption procedure:**
1) Submit application with autobiography;
2) admission to waiting list;
3) attend orientation;
4) complete adoption study;
5) if approved, wait for placement;
6) placement.

**Average length of time between application and start of home study:** 12-24 mos.

**Average length of time to complete home study:** 2-3 mos.

**Number of interviews:** 4-5.

**Home study description:** Assessment of applicant's childhood, family, education, health history, religious history, marriage and family functioning, finances, home and community, issues surrounding infertility, motivation and attitudes toward adoption, description of child desired and expectations of that child, experiences with children, recommendation of references, criminal history and child line registry report.

**Average wait for a child after approval of a home study:** 12-24 mos.

**Foster care:** Temporary, long-term and permanent.

★675★

**Washington County Children and Youth Agency**
502 Court House Sq.
Washington, PA 15301
Phone: (412) 228-6884

**Contact:** Adoption Unit.

**Description:** Public, county agency mandated to place children by the Pennsylvania Department of Public Welfare.

**Area served:** Residents of Washington County.

**Requirements:** Adults, 21 yrs. and older, but preferably no more than 35 yrs. older than the child placed, who are financially stable, whose health is adequate to parent, who may be single or married, if married, marriage should be of at least 3 yrs. duration. Some requirements may be flexible.

**Fees:**
Home study and education classes: $250.

**Adoption investigation:** $300 which may be waived if Washington County Children & Youth Agency performed the home study.

**Number of children placed last year:** 15.

**Description of children:** Children with special needs.

**Adoption procedure:**
1) Telephone intake;
2) admission to waiting list;
3) attend informational meeting;
4) return completed Interest Registration Form;
5) participate in educational classes;
6) complete home study;
7) if approved, wait for placement;
8) placement;
9) post-placement supervision;
10) finalization.

**Average length of time between application and start of home study:** 1-6 mos.

**Average length of time to complete home study:** 6 wks.

**Number of interviews:** 3.

**Home study description:** Assessment of background, parenting ability, type of child desired, health and finances, home and neighborhood.

**Average wait for a child after approval of a home study:** 12-24 mos.

**Foster care:** Emergency, short and long-term and therapeutic.

★676★

**York County Children and Youth Services**
100 W. Market St.
York, PA 17401
Phone: (717) 846-8496
Fax: (717) 771-9884

**Contact:** Connie Stern.

**Description:** Public, county child welfare agency mandated to place children by the Pennsylvania Department of Public Welfare.

**Area served:** Residents of York County.

**Requirements:** Couples married at least 1 yr. who are generally between the ages of 21 and 50 yrs., who have no life threatening illness or communicable disease and who are not on public assistance. Singles are considered on a case by case basis.

**Fees:**
Application fee: $25.
Home study: $400.
Supervision and court reports: $400.

**Number of children placed last year:** Unavailable.

**Description of children:** Children with special needs, fost-adopt conversions, foreign born children and a few infants.

**Adoption procedure:**
1) File preliminary application;
2) attend 3-4 educational classes;
3) have individual interviews and home visit;
4) complete supporting documentation and paperwork;
5) placement;
6) supervision;
7) finalization.

**Average length of time between application and start of home study:** Special needs: 1 mo. or less. Infants: indefinite.

**Average length of time to complete home study:** 2 mos.

**Number of interviews:** 3-4 group and 3 individual.

**Home study description:** Evaluation of motivation to adopt, background, emotional and marital stability, health and finances, home, experiences with children and adoption, recommendation of references and readiness to adopt.

**Average wait for a child after approval of a home study:** Special needs: depends on the range of special needs that applicants are willing to accept. Infants: indefinite.

**Foster care:** Temporary, long-term and emergency.

# PRIVATE AGENCIES

★ 677 ★
**Adoptions From The Heart**
76 Rittenhouse Pl.
Ardmore, PA 19003
Phone: (610) 642-7200

**Branch address:**
 18-20 Washington Ave., Haddonfield, NJ 08033
 Phone: (609) 795-5400

 18 A Trolley Sq., Wilmington, DE 19806
 Phone: (302) 658-8883

 1224 W. Hamilton St., Allentown, PA 18102
 Phone: (610) 740-0200

 1525 Oregon Commons, Lancaster, PA 19601
 Phone: (717) 399-7766

**Contact:** Maxine G. Chalker, Executive Director.

**Date established:** 1985.

**Description:** Private, non-profit, non-sectarian child placing agency licensed by the Delaware Services for Children, Youth and Their Families, the New Jersey Department of Human Services and the Pennsylvania Department of Public Welfare and specializing in open adoptions.

**Area served:** U.S. minority placements: residents of the U.S. Caucasian infants and girls from China: residents of Delaware, New Jersey, New York and Pennsylvania.

**Requirements:** Minority placements: open. Chinese program: couples married at least 2 yrs. who have no children and who are 35 yrs. or older.

**Fees:** Application: $100 or $400; home study: $750. Placement fees: Minority: $4500; Caucasian infant: $9000. Legal fees are extra.

**Number of children placed last year:** 105.

**Description of children:** Primarily Caucasian infants by open adoption and Chinese baby girls.

**Adoption procedure:** 1) Informational meeting; 2) educational course; 3) home study; 4) dossier preparation, if applicable; 5) wait for selection by birth parents, if applicable; 6) placement; 7) post- placement supervision; 8) finalization.

**Average length of time between application and start of home study:** Less than 1 mo.

**Average length of time to complete home study:** 2 - 4 mos.

**Number of interviews:** 2 - 3.

**Home study description:** Assessment which includes group meeting and an in-home visit, autobiographies, 3 - 5 references, medicals, police and child abuse registry clearances.

**Average wait for a child after approval of a home study:** 4 mos. - 2 yrs.

**Foster care:** None.

★ 678 ★
**Bethanna**
1030 Second St. Pike
Southampton, PA 18966
Phone: (215) 355-6500

**Branch address:**
 605 E. Mt. Pleasant Ave., Philadelphia, PA 19119

**Contact:** Tina Burkholder, Supervisor.

**Date established:** 1990.

**Description:** Private, non-profit child placing agency licensed by the Pennsylvania Department of Public Welfare.

**Area served:** Residents of Bucks, Chester, Delaware, Montgomery and Philadelphia counties.

**Requirements:** Open.

**Fees:** None.

**Number of children placed last year:** 15.

**Description of children:** Children with special needs.

**Adoption procedure:** 1) Orientation; 2) application; 3) home study; 4) child match; 5) pre-placement visitation; 6) placement; 7) *intent to adopt* filed; 8) consent from county; 9) finalization.

**Average length of time between application and start of home study:** Less than 1 mo.

**Average length of time to complete home study:** 3 - 4 wks.

**Number of interviews:** 2.

**Home study description:** Assessment which includes autobiographical information, medical and financial statements, and which addresses such issues as infertility, if applicable, discipline practices, extended family and community's response to adoption, trans-racial issues, child care plan, marital relationship, if applicable, and other children in the home.

**Average wait for a child after approval of a home study:** Unavailable.

**Foster care:** Temporary.

★ 679 ★
**Bethany Christian Services of Ft. Washington**
550 Pinetown Rd., No. 205
Ft. Washington, PA 19034
Phone: (215) 628-0202
(800) BETHANY

**Contact:** Trish Small, Director.

**Date established:** 1980.

**Description:** Non-profit, private agency licensed by the Pennsylvania Dept. of Public Welfare.

**Area served:** Eastern Pennsylvania, Delaware, and South Jersey.

**Requirements:** Christian couples married at least 3 yrs. who have no more than 1 child and a diagnosis of infertility.

**Fees:** Preliminary application fee: $50; formal application fee: $300; home study: $1150. The foregoing fees are included in the total fee of $8000.

**Number of children placed last year:** 27.

**Description of children:** Primarily infants; a few older children under 4 yrs.

**Adoption procedure:** 1) Submit preliminary application; 2) attend group meeting; 3) file formal application; 4) complete home study; 5) if approved, placement; 6) 6-12 mos. post-placement services.

**Average length of time between application and start of home study:** 6-12 mos.

**Average length of time to complete home study:** 3-6 mos.

**Number of interviews:** 2-3.

**Home study description:** Evaluation of individual and couple stability; finances and insurance; personal and employment history; criminal and Child Abuse Registry clearances; written autobiographies, and required pastoral reference.

**Average wait for a child after approval of a home study:** 24 or more mos.

**Foster care:** Temporary.


★ 680 ★
**Bethany Christian Services of Lancaster**
113 N. Lime St.
Lancaster, PA 17602-2922
Phone: (717) 472-4898
Fax: (717) 399-3543

**Contact:** Miriam Carter, Interim Director.

**Date established:** 1984.

**Description:** Non-profit, private agency licensed by the Pennsylvania Dept. of Public Welfare.

**Area served:** Eastern Pennsylvania, Delaware, and South Jersey.

**Requirements:** Christian couples married at least 3 yrs. who have no more than 1 child and a diagnosis of infertility.

**Fees:**
Preliminary application fee: $25;
formal application fee: $800;
home study: $1500;
foregoing fees are included in the total fee of $7225.

**Number of children placed last year:** 15.

**Description of children:** Primarily infants.

**Adoption procedure:**
1) Submit preliminary application;
2) attend group meeting;
3) file formal application;
4) complete home study;
5) if approved, placement;
6) 6-12 mos. post-placement services.

**Average length of time between application and start of home study:** 1-6 mos.

**Average length of time to complete home study:** 3-6 mos.

**Number of interviews:** At least 3.

**Home study description:** Evaluation of individual and couple stability, finances and insurance, personal and employment history, criminal and Child Abuse Registry clearances, required pastoral reference, and written autobiographies.

**Average wait for a child after approval of a home study:** 12-24 mos.

**Foster care:** Many placements are directly into the adoptive family (risk). Foster care is available for situations that warrant it.


★ 681 ★
**Welcome House Special Services of the Pearl S. Buck Foundation**
P.O. Box 181
Green Hills Farm
Perkasie, PA 18944-0181
Phone: (215) 249-1516
(800) 220-BUCK
Fax: (215) 249-9657

**Branch address:**
   P.O. Box 505, Shippensburg, PA 17257

120 Spring Ln., Delmont, PA 15626

P.O. Box 1079, Hockessin, DE 19707

5905 W. Broad St., Ste. 300, Richmond, VA 23230
Phone: (804) 288-3920

P.O. Box 596, Christiansburg, VA 24073

**Contact:** Marie Mercer, Director of Social Services, or Ken Keuffel, Public Relations.

**Date established:** 1949.

**Description:** Non-profit, private agency licensed in Delaware, Maryland, New Jersey, Pennsylvania and Virginia.

**Area served:** Residents of Delaware, Maryland, New Jersey, Pennsylvania and Virginia.

**Requirements:** Varies according to program.

**Fees:**
Application: $150;
welcome house fee: varies according to program.

**Number of children placed last year:** N/A.

**Description of children:** U.S. children with special needs and foreign-born children, some with special needs. Ages range from 0 to 16 yrs.

**Adoption procedure:**
   1) Attend information meeting;
   2) submit application;
   3) attend preparational classes;
   4) individual in-home interview with social worker;
   5) child referral;
   6) placement;
   7) post-placement supervision;
   8) support provided through workshops and parent support groups;
   9) finalization.

**Average length of time between application and start of home study:** 1-6 mos.

**Average length of time to complete home study:** 2 mos.

**Number of interviews:** 1-4.

**Home study description:** Group preparation which examines applicant's understanding of children's needs, family stability, availability of support systems, flexibility, ability to express emotion and financial stability.

**Average wait for a child after approval of a home study:** Varies.

**Foster care:** None.


★ 682 ★
**Catholic Charities Counseling and Adoption Services of Erie**
329 W. 10th St.
Erie, PA 16502
Phone: (814) 456-2091
(800) 673-2535

**Branch address:**
   786 E. State St., Sharon, PA 16146
   Phone: (412) 346-4142

   Deposit Bank Bldg., DuBois, PA 15801
   Phone: (814) 571-4717

**Contact:** Mrs. Nancy Monicatti, Director (Erie).

**Date established:** 1953.

**Description:** Non-profit private agency licensed by the Pennsylvania Department of Public Welfare.

**Area served:** Residents of the 13 counties of the Diocese of Erie.

**Requirements:** Requirements vary according to the various programs: domestic, Korean, Latin American or special needs.

**Fees:**
$150 application fee;
$1,000 home study fee applied to total fee at time of finalization.
Total fees vary according to the various programs cited above.

**Number of children placed last year:** Unavailable.

**Description of children:** Infants, older children and children with special needs from the U.S. and Korea.

**Adoption procedure:**
1) Attend preliminary interview;
2) if eligible, file application;
3) placement on appropriate waiting list;
4) complete home study;
5) if approved, wait for placement;
6) placement;
7) post-placement supervision;
8) finalization.

**Average length of time between application and start of home study:** Varies.

**Average length of time to complete home study:** 2-3 mos.

**Number of interviews:** 4 interviews and home visits.

**Home study description:** Evaluation of background information and autobiographies, physicals with laboratory tests, financial statements, Act 33 clearances and references.

**Average wait for a child after approval of a home study:** 1-6 mos.

**Foster care:** Temporary.


**★ 683 ★**
**Catholic Charities of Greensburg**
115 Vannear Ave.
Greensburg, PA 15601
Phone: (412) 837-1840

**Contact:** Cheryl Giesey.

**Date established:** 1958.

**Description:** Non-profit private agency.

**Area served:** Residents of the Diocese of Greensburg including the counties of Armstron, Fayette, Indiana and Westmoreland.

**Requirements:**
Infant adoption: married couples, 35 yrs. and younger, who are in good health. Preference is shown to infertile, childless couples.
Singles, older applicants and families with children are eligible for Waiting Child Program.

**Fees:**
$100/hr.; average process is 10-20 hrs.
Applicants for Waiting Child Program may participate in a reduced cost program.

**Number of children placed last year:** Unavailable.

**Description of children:** White, biracial, and foreign infants.

**Adoption procedure:**
1) Attend orientation;
2) file application;
3) attend individual and group sessions;
4) complete home study;
5) matching process;
6) placement;
7) post-placement supervision;
8) finalization.

**Average length of time between application and start of home study:** 24 or more mos.

**Average length of time to complete home study:** 12 mos.

**Number of interviews:** Varies.

**Home study description:** Evaluation of family, marital and educational background; health and employment history; references; strengths and weaknesses; religious affiliation and practices; parenting experiences and/or experiences with children.

**Average wait for a child after approval of a home study:** 24 or more mos.

**Foster care:** Temporary.


**★ 684 ★**
**Catholic Charities of the Diocese of Harrisburg, PA., Inc.**
4800 Union Deposit Rd.
Harrisburg, PA 17105
Phone: (717) 657-4804
Fax: (717) 657-8683

**Mailing address:**
P.O. Box 3551, Harrisburg, PA 17105

**Contact:** Kay S. Eisenhour, MSW, LSW.

**Date established:** 1938.

**Description:** Non-profit private agency licensed by the Commonwealth of Pennsylvania, Department of Public Welfare.

**Area served:** Residents of 15 counties within the Roman Catholic Diocese of Harrisburg.

**Requirements:** Married couples who are no more than 40 yrs. old, have satisfactory health, sufficient income and who practice some religious faith.

**Fees:** $25 application fee; additional costs incurred by agency and home study.

**Number of children placed last year:** 14.

**Description of children:** Healthy white and minority infants and children with special needs, international children, and older children through Adoption Exchange.

**Adoption procedure:**
1) File application;
2) participate in group meetings;
3) interviews and home visit;
4) if approved, placement;
5) post-placement supervisory visits; and
6) finalization.

**Average length of time between application and start of home study:** Varies according to type of child requested.

**Average length of time to complete home study:** 6 mos.

**Number of interviews:** 3.

**Home study description:** Evaluation of home environment, family life, parenting skills, facilities and resources of adoptive family, and ability to manage their resources.

**Average wait for a child after approval of a home study:** Varies according to type of child requested.

**Foster care:** Pre-adoptive infant only, as needed; direct placement also available.

**★685★**
**Catholic Charities of the Diocese of Pittsburgh, Inc.**
212 9th St.
Pittsburgh, PA 15222
Phone: (412) 456-6960
Fax: (412) 456-6990

**Contact:** Martha Beamer, Adoption Services Director.

**Date established:** 1950.

**Description:** Non-profit private agency licensed in State of Pennsylvania.

**Area served:** Residents of the Diocese of Pittsburgh.

**Requirements:** Flexible.

**Fees:** Sliding scale.

**Number of children placed last year:** Unavailable.

**Description of children:** U.S. infants and special needs children.

**Adoption procedure:**
 1) Contact agency;
 2) name added to waiting list.
Inquire for other details.

**Average length of time between application and start of home study:** Varies.

**Average length of time to complete home study:** 6 mos.

**Number of interviews:** Varies.

**Home study description:** Evaluation of character, stability and parenting potential.

**Average wait for a child after approval of a home study:** Varies.

**Foster care:** Temporary.


**★686★**
**Catholic Social Agency (of Allentown)**
928 Union Blvd.
Allentown, PA 18103
Phone: (610) 435-1541
Fax: (610) 435-4367

**Contact:** Lynne Shampain, Supervisor Adoption Department.

**Date established:** 1954.

**Description:** Non-profit agency annually approved by the Pennsylvania Dept. of Public Welfare.

**Area served:** Residents of Berks, Carbon, Lehigh, Northampton and Schuylkill counties.

**Requirements:** Couples married at least 2 yrs., who are affiliated with a church or religious institution.

**Fees:**
Fees subject to change;
current application fee: $200; current home study fee: $800; current total fees: $8450.

**Number of children placed last year:** 12.

**Description of children:** Healthy white infants and infants with special needs. Statewide adoption network of special needs children.

**Adoption procedure:**
 1) File pre-application;
 2) return completed application;
 3) waiting period for home study;
 4) complete home study;
 5) if approved, waiting period for placement;
 6) placement;
 7) 6 mos. post-placement supervision;
 8) court finalization;
 9) post adoption services.

**Average length of time between application and start of home study:** 1-6 mos.

**Average length of time to complete home study:** 6 mos.

**Number of interviews:** 4.

**Home study description:** Comprehensive evaluation which includes but is not limited to social and health histories; current relationships; values and knowledge of adoption; preparation regarding adoption issues.

**Average wait for a child after approval of a home study:** 12-24 mos.

**Foster care:** Short and long-term.


**★687★**
**Catholic Social Services**
**Archdiocese of Philadelphia**
222 North 17th St.
Philadelphia, PA 19103
Phone: (215) 587-3900

**Contact:** Helen L. Prim, Administrator, Pregnancy and Adoption Services.

**Date established:** 1912.

**Description:** Non-profit, multi-purpose social services agency licensed in Pennsylvania and by the State of New Jersey as a child-placement agency.

**Area served:** Residents of Bucks, Chester, Delaware, Montgomery and Philadelphia counties. Residents of New Jersey and New York for hard-to-place children.

**Requirements:** Couples who are no more than 40 yrs. older than the adopted child, at least one of whom is a practicing Catholic. Religious requirement is flexible for intercountry adoption and singles are considered for minority, special needs and Indian children.

**Fees:** Varies with particular program.

**Number of children placed last year:** 24.

**Description of children:** Infants, children with special needs, Korean, black and biracial children.

**Adoption procedure:** Varies with particular program.

**Average length of time between application and start of home study:** Varies with program.

**Average length of time to complete home study:** 3-4 mos.

**Number of interviews:** 3 office and a home study.

**Home study description:** Agency follows state prescribed procedures.

**Average wait for a child after approval of a home study:** Varies with program.

**Foster care:** Temporary.


**★688★**
**Catholic Social Services of Lackawanna County**
400 Wyoming Ave.
Scranton, PA 18503-1272
Phone: (717) 346-8936
(800) 982-4310
Fax: (717) 341-1293

**Contact:** Edward Casey.

**Date established:** 1939.

**Description:** Non-profit private agency licensed in Pennsylvania.

**Area served:** Residents of Lackawanna, Susquehanna, Wayne, Pike, Monroe, Lycoming, Tioga, and Bradford counties.

**Requirements:** Married couples who are 25 yrs. to 40 yrs old, who are in good health and who practice some form of organized religion.

**Fees:** $1500 home study; $1500 placement, supervision, and legal assistance.

**Adoption procedure:**
1) Attend screening interview;
2) attend individual interviews;
3) home visit;
4) if approved, placement;
5) 3 post-placement supervisory visits.

**Average length of time between application and start of home study:** 12-24 mos.

**Average length of time to complete home study:** 3 mos.

**Number of interviews:** 4.

**Home study description:** Evaluation of family background, marital stability, experience with children, child rearing philosophy and motivation to adopt.

**Average wait for a child after approval of a home study:** 24 or more mos.

**Foster care:** None.

---

★ 689 ★

**Children's Aid Home and Society of Somerset County**
P.O. Box 1195
Somerset, PA 15501
Phone: (814) 443-1637
Fax: (814) 445-8481

**Contact:** Patricia B. Stone.

**Date established:** 1889.

**Description:** Non-profit agency licensed by the Pennsylvania Dept. of Welfare, Office of Children & Youth.

**Area served:** Residents of Somerset County and within 100 mile radius of Somerset County.

**Requirements:** No specific requirements.

**Fees:** Fees vary: special needs, domestic, foreign.

**Number of children placed last year:** 5.

**Description of children:** Foreign-born children with special needs.

**Adoption procedure:** Call or write for details.

**Average length of time between application and start of home study:** 1 mo. or less.

**Average length of time to complete home study:** Varies.

**Number of interviews:** Varies.

**Home study description:** Evaluation of demographic information, health, motivation to adopt, dynamics of family unit, acceptance of adoption, and others.

**Average wait for a child after approval of a home study:** 6-12 mos.

**Foster care:** Temporary, long-term, and specialized (MH diagnosed).

---

★ 690 ★

**The Children's Aid Society of Clearfield, PA**
1004 S. Second St.
Clearfield, PA 16830
Phone: (814) 765-2685

**Contact:** Joyce Graham, Adoption Assistant.

**Date established:** Agency established in 1890; adoption program in 1986.

**Description:** Private, non-profit agency licensed in the State of Pennsylvania.

**Area served:** Residents of the counties of central Pennsylvania.

**Fees:**
Home study fee: $1500;
placement fee: $2500.

**Number of children placed last year:** 10.

**Description of children:** Children with special needs.

**Adoption procedure:**
1) File application;
2) participate in group home study sessions;
3) undergo individual and in-home interviews;
4) wait for placement;
5) placement;
6) 6 or more mos. post-placement supervision;
7) finalization.

**Average length of time between application and start of home study:** 6-12 mos.

**Average length of time to complete home study:** 10 wks.

**Number of interviews:** 7 group, 2 in-home and individual interviews.

**Home study description:** Assessment of biographical information, health and finances, education, parenting experiences, values and motivation to adopt.

**Average wait for a child after approval of a home study:** 12-24 mos.

**Foster care:** None.

---

★ 691 ★

**The Children's Aid Society of Franklin County**
255 Miller St.
Chambersburg, PA 17201
Phone: (717) 263-4159

**Mailing address:**
P.O. Box 353, Chambersburg, PA 17201

**Contact:** Jane Englerth, Caseworker.

**Date established:** 1884.

**Description:** Non-profit, private agency licensed by the Pennsylvania Dept. of Public Welfare.

**Area served:** Residents of Franklin and nearby counties.

**Requirements:** Flexible but generally no more than a 40-45 yr. age difference between prospective adoptive parent(s) and child and evidence of financial responsibility. Fertility studies required of applicants seeking to adopt healthy infants.

**Fees:**
Application: $50;
study fee: $600;
placement and supervision: $800.

**Number of children placed last year:** 6.

**Description of children:** U.S. children up to age 10; some with special needs. Will provide adoptive studies and supervision services for American and foreign children from other agencies.

**Adoption procedure:**
1) Attend in-person intake interview;
2) complete adoptive study;
3) selection of child;
4) placement;
5) 6 mos. supervisory period;
6) finalization.

**Average length of time between application and start of home study:** 6-12 mos.

**Average length of time to complete home study:** 6-10 wks.

**Number of interviews:** 4-6.

**Home study description:** Assessment of health and finances, state police and Dept. of Public Welfare clearances, recommendation of references, home and environment, personal life history and attitudes and experiences surrounding adoption, biological family, cultural issues, childrearing and infertility (if applicable).

**Average wait for a child after approval of a home study:** 6-12 mos.

**Foster care:** Temporary and occasionally long-term.

★692★
**Children's Aid Society of Mercer County**
350 W. Market St.
Mercer, PA 16137
Phone: (412) 662-4730
Fax: (412) 662-4295

**Mailing address:**
P.O. Box 167, Mercer, PA 16137

**Contact:** Deborah Judy, Adoption Supervisor.

**Date established:** 1889.

**Description:** Non-profit, private agency licensed by the Pennsylvania Dept. of Public Welfare.

**Area served:** Residents of Mercer County and surrounding areas.

**Requirements:** Adults, 21 yrs. and older, who are in reasonably good health and who are financially capable of providing for another family member. Applicants may be single or married but not in the process of divorce.

**Fees:**
Application: $200;
family summary: $870;
placement services: $1210;
child search: $612;
infant services: $2475;
administration: $150.

**Number of children placed last year:** 20.

**Description of children:** 8 white and biracial children and 12 children from Latin America and Korea.

**Adoption procedure:**
1) Initial registration;
2) return completed application;
3) complete family summary;
4) child search;
5) placement;
6) 6 mos. post-placement supervision;
7) finalization.

**Average length of time between application and start of home study:** 1-6 mos.

**Average length of time to complete home study:** 6-10 wks.

**Number of interviews:** 2-3.

**Home study description:** Group or individual process which examines autobiographies, financial status, law enforcement clearances, employment and medical history, physical location and condition of residence.

**Average wait for a child after approval of a home study:** 12-24 mos.

**Foster care:** Temporary.

★693★
**Family Adoption Center**
1201 Allegheny Tower
625 Stanwix St.
Pittsburgh, PA 15222
Phone: (418) 288-2138
(800) 422-2971
Fax: (418) 288-9036

**Contact:** Roberta Miller.

**Date established:** 1983.

**Description:** Non-profit, private, non-sectarian infant adoption agency licensed in the State of Pennsylvania.

**Area served:** Residents of western Pennsylvania.

**Requirements:** Married couples who are childless and infertile.

**Fees:** $9675.

**Number of children placed last year:** Approx. 15.

**Description of children:** Healthy, white newborn infants.

**Adoption procedure:**
1) Telephone request for information sheet;
2) submit application;
3) if approved, complete interview and pre-adoption screening series;
4) wait for placement;
5) placement.

**Average length of time between application and start of home study:** 12-24 mos.

**Average length of time to complete home study:** 8 or more wks.

**Number of interviews:** 1.

**Home study description:** An 8-wk. group series completed with a counselor and 6 couples followed by a home visit.

**Average wait for a child after approval of a home study:** 6-12 mos.

**Foster care:** None.

★694★
**Family Service**
630 Janet Ave.
Lancaster, PA 17601
Phone: (717) 397-5241
Fax: (717) 397-2530

**Contact:** Adoption staff.

**Date established:** 1904.

**Description:** Private, multi-service agency.

**Area served:** Residents of Lancaster County only. Special needs program extends beyond Lancaster County.

**Requirements:** Couples married at least 2 yrs. who are no older than 40 yrs. at time of intake call, who are in good health but who have some infertility problem, and who have no more than 1 child in the home. Requirements vary for special needs program and foreign program.

**Fees:** Total agency fee for foreign program: $5000 plus travel and cooperating agency fees. Total agency fee for infant program: $5000.

**Number of children placed last year:** 28.

**Description of children:** Primarily Caucasian infants but some foreign-born and older children and children with special needs.

**Adoption procedure:**
1) Intake call:
2) admission to waiting list;
3) attend application interview;
4) complete home study;

5) if approved, placement;
6) post-placement supervision;
7) finalization.

**Average length of time between application and start of home study:** 1-6 mos.

**Average length of time to complete home study:** 3 mos.

**Number of interviews:** 3-4 individual and 6-8 group sessions.

**Home study description:** Evaluation of marital stability, family history, parenting styles, criminal and child abuse clearances, health and financial stability and readiness to adopt.

**Average wait for a child after approval of a home study:** 6-12 mos.

**Foster care:** Temporary.

★ 695 ★
**Family Service and Children's Aid Society of Venango County**
716 E. Second St.
Oil City, PA 16301
Phone: (814) 677-4005
Fax: (814) 677-6159

**Contact:** Janet Schwabenbauer.

**Date established:** 1887.

**Description:** Non-profit, private agency licensed by the Pennsylvania Dept. of Public Welfare.

**Area served:** Residents within a 2 hr. drive of Oil City.

**Requirements:** Couples married at least 3 yrs. who are in good physical and mental health.

**Fees:**
Home study: $900; supervisory fee: $750; legal and medical costs additional.

**Number of children placed last year:** 6.

**Description of children:** U.S. and foreign-born infants; children with special needs.

**Adoption procedure:**
1) Attend application interview;
2) complete individual home study;
3) if approved, placement;
4) adoption supervision;
5) finalization.

**Average length of time between application and start of home study:** 1-6 mos.

**Average length of time to complete home study:** 6 wks.

**Number of interviews:** 4.

**Home study description:** Call or write for guidelines.

**Average wait for a child after approval of a home study:** 6-12 mos.

**Foster care:** Temporary.

★ 696 ★
**Jewish Family and Children's Services**
1610 Spruce St.
Philadelphia, PA
Phone: (215) 545-3290
Fax: (215) 750-0368

**Branch address:**
10125 Verree Rd., Philadelphia, PA 19116
Phone: (215) 698-9950

**Contact:** Susan Jolles, Adoption Supervisor.

**Date established:** 1880's.

**Description:** Non-profit private agency licensed in Pennsylvania and New Jersey.

**Area served:** Residents of Philadelphia and surrounding counties.

**Requirements:** Healthy infant: Jewish couples married 2 or more yrs., who are no older than 40 yrs., have a stable work history and sufficient income to support a child; are in good health with a normal life expectancy. All criteria are flexible for special needs adoption.

**Fees:**
Application fee: $50;
home study: $700;
placement: $3500.

**Number of children placed last year:** 0.

**Description of children:** Infants and older children.

**Adoption procedure:**
1) File application;
2) complete home study;
3) if approved, placement;
4) post-placement supervision;
5) finalization;
6) post-placement services, i.e. workshops and parents' group.

**Average length of time between application and start of home study:** 1 mo. or less.

**Average length of time to complete home study:** 3-4 wks.

**Number of interviews:** 4.

**Home study description:** Evaluation of applicant(s)' coping skills, sensitivity to others and acceptance of differences, emotions surrounding infertility, marital relationship, support systems and maturity level.

**Average wait for a child after approval of a home study:** Varies.

**Foster care:** Temporary, long-term and permanent.

★ 697 ★
**Love the Children**
221 W. Broad St.
Quakertown, PA 18951
Phone: (215) 536-4180
Fax: (215) 536-2582

**Branch address:**
Love the Children of Massachusetts, P.O. Box 334, Cambridge, MA 02238
Phone: (617) 576-2115

**Contact:** Intake worker.

**Date established:** 1978.

**Description:** Non-profit, private agency licensed in Massachusetts, New Jersey, New York and Pennsylvania.

**Area served:** Residents of Massachusetts, New Jersey, New York and Pennsylvania.

**Requirements:** Couples married at least 3 yrs., who have no more than 2 divorces between them, who are under the age of 40 yrs., who have no life threatening conditions including obesity and who have no more than 1 child.

**Fees:** Call or write for fee schedule.

**Number of children placed last year:** Unavailable.

**Description of children:** Korean children.

**Adoption procedure:** Applications open in June.

**Average length of time between application and start of home study:** 1-6 mos.

**Average length of time to complete home study:** Varies.

**Number of interviews:** Varies.

**Home study description:** Write for guidelines.

**Average wait for a child after approval of a home study:** Usually within 1 yr.

**Foster care:** None.

★ 698 ★
**Lutheran Children & Family Service**
2278 Mt. Carmel Ave.
Glenside, PA 19038-4620
Phone: (215) 881-6800
Fax: (215) 884-3110

**Contact:** Richard Gitlen, MSW, LSW, Regional Director.

**Date established:** 1925.

**Description:** Non-profit, private adoption agency licensed by the Pennsylvania Dept. of Public Welfare.

**Area served:** Residents of Philadelphia, Bucks, Chester, Delaware and Montgomery counties and others on a case by case basis.

**Requirements:** None except for those imposed by foreign programs.

**Fees:**
Application: $100;
home study: $1225;
intermediary/child search: $600-$6700;
supervision: $600.

**Number of children placed last year:** 40.

**Description of children:** U.S. and foreign-born infants and children with special needs from U.S., Latin America and Asia.

**Adoption procedure:**
1) Inquiry;
2) attend informational meeting;
3) participate in adoption groups;
4) complete home study;
5) placement;
6) post-placement supervision;
7) finalization.

**Average length of time between application and start of home study:** 1-6 mos.

**Average length of time to complete home study:** 3-4 mos.

**Number of interviews:** 2 group meetings and 1-2 home visits.

**Home study description:** Evaluation of autobiographies, income verification, employment, child raising experience, motivation to adopt, flexibility, internal, social and community resources and understanding of adoption.

**Average wait for a child after approval of a home study:** Varies.

**Foster care:** Short and long-term.

★ 699 ★
**Lutheran Service Society of Western Pennsylvania**
1011 Old Salem Rd., Ste. 107
Greensburg, PA 15601
Phone: (412) 837-9385

**Contact:** Kirsti L. Adkins, Program Director, Adoptions.

**Date established:** 1978.

**Description:** Not-for-profit, private agency licensed by the Pennsylvania Dept. of Public Welfare.

**Area served:** Residents of nine southwestern counties of Pennsylvania.

**Requirements:** Very flexible: applicants should be between the ages of 25 and 60 yrs. and have adequate health to parent and sufficient income to meet their needs. Foreign agencies or identified adoptions may impose additional requirements.

**Fees:** Vary by program. Fees for placement of older children may be offset by financial incentives.

**Number of children placed last year:** 51.

**Description of children:** 27 foreign-born children, mostly infants; 16 U.S. infants and 8 U.S. older children.

**Adoption procedure:** Older children:
1) Interest registration;
2) attend group training;
3) complete home study;
4) child search and match;
5) placement;
6) post-placement supervision;
7) finalization.
International/private:
1) File application;
2) complete home study;
3) child match;
4) placement;
5) post-placement supervision;
6) finalization.

**Average length of time between application and start of home study:** 1 mo. or less.

**Average length of time to complete home study:** 1 mo.

**Number of interviews:** 2 home visits.

**Home study description:** Assessment of lifestyle, marital history, parenting style, motivation to adopt, etc.

**Average wait for a child after approval of a home study:** 6-12 mos.; varies with type of adoption.

**Foster care:** None.

★ 700 ★
**Project STAR**
6301 Northumberland St.
Pittsburgh, PA 15217
Phone: (412) 244-3066

**Contact:** Mary Pat Zebroski, Program Manager.

**Date established:** 1985.

**Description:** Private, non-profit child placement program licensed by the Pennsylvania Department of Public Welfare.

**Area served:** Residents within 1 hr. travel time of Pittsburgh.

**Requirements:** Flexible.

**Fees:** None.

**Number of children placed last year:** 20.

**Description of children:** Children with special needs of all ages.

**Adoption procedure:** 1) Inquiry; 2) 8 wk. preparation; 3) child match; 4) placement; 5) post-placement supervision; 6) finalization.

**Average length of time between application and start of home study:** 1 - 6 mos.

**Average length of time to complete home study:** 6 - 8 mos.

**Number of interviews:** 3 or more.

**Home study description:** Assessment which includes childhood experiences, parenting skills and potential, relationship with extended family, available support systems and personal references.

**Average wait for a child after approval of a home study:** 1 -12 mos.

**Foster care:** Fost-adopt.

**★ 701 ★**
**Today's Adoption Agency, Ltd.**
P.O. Box G
Hawley, PA 18428
Phone: (717) 226-0808
Fax: (717) 226-3760

**Contact:** Denise Zuvic, Director.

**Date established:** 1988.

**Description:** Non-profit, private international adoption agency.

**Area served:** Residents of the U.S.

**Requirements:** Couples married at least 1 yr. (singles are accepted) who are between the ages of 27 and 60 yrs. (approximate), who meet the INS requirements for health and income and who have no more than 2 divorces between them.

**Fees:**
Application: $150;
seminar: $50 (not required);
agency fee: $3000-$4500 depending on program.
Foreign fees set by country.

**Number of children placed last year:** 50.

**Description of children:** Foreign-born children from infancy to 5 yrs.

**Adoption procedure:**
1) Submit application with photograph of applicant(s);
2) send documents for foreign adoption to agency;
3) secure home study from separate agency;
4) if approved, admission to waiting list;
5) file I-600A form with INS;
6) legal work processed in child's birth country;
7) once visa is approved, child can travel to U.S. or adoptive parents can travel to escort child;
8) post-placement supervision;
9) finalization.

**Average length of time between application and start of home study:** 1 mo. or less.

**Average length of time to complete home study:** 1 mo.

**Number of interviews:** 3.

**Home study description:** Agency writing study determines guidelines.

**Average wait for a child after approval of a home study:** 1-6 mos.

**Foster care:** None.

**★ 702 ★**
**Tressler Lutheran Services**
836 S. George St.
York, PA 17403-2298
Phone: (717) 845-9113
Fax: (717) 852-8439

**Branch address:**
1139 Chester St., Williamsport, PA 17701
Phone: (717) 327-9333

**Contact:** Barbara Holtan, Director.

**Date established:** 1971.

**Description:** Private, non-profit social service agency licensed to place children by the Pennsylvania Department of Public Welfare.

**Area served:** Residents of the following 26 counties of Central Pennsylvania: Adams, Bedford, Blair, Cambria, Centre, Clearfield, Clinton, Columbia, Cumberland, Dauphin, Franklin, Fulton, Huntingdon, Juniata, Lancaster, Lebanon, Lycoming, Mifflin, Montour, Northumberland, Perry, Snyder, Somerset, Tioga, Union and York.

**Requirements:** Flexible.

**Fees:** Application and Home Study: $1025. Fees for international adoption are additional.

**Number of children placed last year:** 40.

**Description of children:** Children with special needs and foreign born children.

**Adoption procedure:** 1) Initial inquiry; 2) Interest Registration Form: 3) selection of applicants for home study based on their interests outlined in the Interest Registration Form; 4) informal meeting; 5) group adoptive parent training meetings; 6) individual in-home meeting; 7) required paperwork; 8) completion of study and registration with appropriate adoption exchanges; 9) placement; 10) post-placement supervision; 11) finalization.

**Average length of time between application and start of home study:** 1 - 6 mos.

**Average length of time to complete home study:** 3 mos.

**Number of interviews:** 9 group and 1 individual.

**Home study description:** Group Family Preparation in which 10 to 15 couples or single parents meet and share feelings, experiences, expectations and fears. Information about children available for adoption is shared.

**Average wait for a child after approval of a home study:** 6 - 12 mos.

**Foster care:** None.

# RHODE ISLAND

## STATUTES

**★ 703 ★**

**Independent placement by intermediary?** Prohibited.

**Independent placement by birth parents?** Permitted.

**Subsidies provided?** Medical, non-recurring legal, maintenance and day care.

**Adoption cost defined by law?** Not addressed in law.

**Insurance for infertility?:** No.

**Home study required by state?** Required after placement.

**Prospective adoptive parent advertise for a child?** Prohibited.

**Surrogacy laws?** Not recognized.

**Residents access agencies of other states or countries?** Permitted provided a licensed Rhode Island agency conducts the home study.

**Requires judicial termination of birth parents' rights?** Voluntary relinquishments by both birth parents are recognized.

**Time given to a birthmother to revoke her consent:** Until the court finalizes the adoption.

**Court handling adoptions?** Family Court.

**Adoption of Native Children:** Tribe.

**Adoption records sealed?** Sealed, but adoptees 21 yrs. and older may access medical information.

**Photo-listing book available?** Ocean State Adoption Resource Exchange publishes a photo-listing of Rhode Island's waiting children.

# PUBLIC AGENCIES

★ 704 ★
**Rhode Island Department for Children, Youth & Families**
610 Mt. Pleasant Ave.
Providence, RI 02908-1935
Phone: (401) 457-4654
Fax: (401) 457-4541

**Contact:** Richard Prescott or Patricia A. Keogh.

**Date established:** 1980.

**Description:** Public child welfare agency.

**Area served:** Residents of Rhode Island.

**Requirements:** Open. Each applicant is considered in light of the child requested.

**Fees:** None.

**Number of children placed last year:** 35-40.

**Description of children:** Primarily children between the ages of 5 and 17 yrs., some of whom were members of sibling groups, some minorities and some with handicapping conditions.

**Adoption procedure:**
1) Initial inquiry;
2) submit application;
3) criminal and Child Abuse Registry clearances;
4) complete 10 session assessment and group training process;
5) if approved, placement;
6) 6 or more mos. post-placement supervision;
7) finalization.

**Average length of time between application and start of home study:** 1-6 mos.

**Average length of time to complete home study:** 3 mos.

**Number of interviews:** 10 group and 2-3 individual.

**Home study description:** Assessment of emotional strengths and limitations; experience with children; openness and ability to commit to an older/special needs child; lifestyle, supportive network, etc.

**Average wait for a child after approval of a home study:** 6-12 mos.

**Foster care:** Temporary and some long-term.

# PRIVATE AGENCIES

★ 705 ★
**Catholic Social Services**
433 Elmwood Ave.
Providence, RI 02907
Phone: (401) 467-7200

**Contact:** Christine Chester, CISW; Lynda Notte, BA.

**Date established:** 1926.

**Description:** Non-profit sectarian counseling agency licensed in Rhode Island and Connecticut, member of National Committee for Adoption, Catholic Charities, U.S.A., and accredited by the Council on Accreditation of Services for Families and Children.

**Area served:** Residents of the State of Rhode Island.

**Requirements:** Healthy infant adoption program: Couples married in the Roman Catholic Church at least 3 yrs. who are between the ages of 25 and 39 yrs. with a maximum average of 35 yrs., who are in good physical, mental and emotional health; who are childless and have a medical diagnosis of infertility. The principal wage earner must have a minimum gross income of $15,000/yr. and one adoptive parent must not be employed for a minimum period of 6 mos. after placement.
Requirements pertaining to maximum age, number of children, religion and employment outside the home after placement may not apply in some special needs adoptions.

**Fees:** Application: $300. Sliding fee scale based on 10% of combined annual income. Fee reduction possible based upon child's individual special needs.

**Number of children placed last year:** 17.

**Description of children:** Infants, biracial children and children with special needs.

**Adoption procedure:**
1) Telephone inquiry;
2) attend 2 group informational meetings;
3) complete and return formal application, medical and financial reports, birth and marriage certificates, references, etc.;
4) complete home study;
5) if approved, wait for placement;
6) placement;
7) 6 or more mos. post-placement supervision;
8) legal finalization.

**Average length of time between application and start of home study:** 1-6 mos.

**Average length of time to complete home study:** 6-8 wks.

**Number of interviews:** 6-8.

**Home study description:** Evaluation of family background, education and work history, marriage, health and infertility, motivation to adopt, perception of birthparents, plans to share adoption information with child, parenting methods and discipline, expectations of child and attitudes toward search.

**Average wait for a child after approval of a home study:** 12-24 mos.

**Foster care:** Temporary.

★ 706 ★
**Children's Friend and Service**
153 Summer St.
Providence, RI 02903
Phone: (401) 331-2900
Fax: (401) 331-3285

**Contact:** Lenette Azzi-Lessing, ACSW, Executive Director.

**Date established:** 1834.

**Description:** Non-profit, private agency licensed by the Rhode Island Dept. for Children and Their Families.

**Area served:** Residents of Rhode Island.

**Requirements:** Flexible.

**Fees:** Sliding scale based on income.

**Number of children placed last year:** 24.

**Description of children:** Infants and special needs.

**Adoption procedure:**
1) Preliminary registration;
2) submit application;
3) complete evaluation/education process;
4) placement;
5) post-placement supervision;
6) finalization.

**Average length of time between application and start of home study:** 1-6 mos.

**Average length of time to complete home study:** 3 mos.

**Number of interviews:** 6-7.

**Home study description:** Assessment of capacity to accept a child with his/her needs and background who is born to another; capacity to parent; ability to provide positive experience for child and meet a child's special needs.

**Average wait for a child after approval of a home study:** Varies.

**Foster care:** Temporary.

★ 707 ★
**Gift of Life Adoption Services, Inc.**
P.O. Box 40864
Providence, RI 02940
Phone: (401) 826-8470
Fax: (401) 826-1919

**Contact:** Donna Ricci, Director.

**Date established:** 1992.

**Description:** Private, non-profit child placing agency licensed by the Rhode Island Department for Children and Their Families.

**Area served:** Residents of the U.S. Full service for residents of Rhode Island.

**Requirements:** Child's country of origin determines requirements.

**Fees:** Application: $50. Home Study and Program Fees are additional.

**Number of children placed last year:** 25.

**Description of children:** Infants and toddlers from Eastern Europe.

**Adoption procedure:** 1) Preliminary application; 2) filing with INS; 3) dossier preparation; 4) home study; 5) dossier referral; 6) child match; 7) placement; 8) post-placement supervision; 9) finalization.

**Average length of time between application and start of home study:** Less than 1 mo.

**Average length of time to complete home study:** 3 - 4 wks.

**Number of interviews:** 3 - 4.

**Home study description:** Assessment which includes but is not limited to extended family, childhood, marital relationship, medical information and police clearances.

**Average wait for a child after approval of a home study:** 2 - 12 mos.

**Foster care:** None.

# SOUTH CAROLINA

## STATUTES

★ 708 ★

**Independent placement by intermediary?** Permitted.

**Independent placement by birth parents?** Permitted.

**Subsidies provided?** Medical, supplemental benefits and Title IV-E.

**Adoption cost defined by law?** No.

**Insurance for infertility?:** No.

**Home study required by state?** Required before placement.

**Prospective adoptive parent advertise for a child?** Permitted.

**Surrogacy laws?** Unknown.

**Residents access agencies of other states or countries?** Permitted.

**Requires judicial termination of birth parents' rights?** Voluntary relinquishments by both birth parents are recognized.

**Time given to a birthmother to revoke her consent:** None.

**Court handling adoptions?** Family Court.

**Adoption of Native Children:** Indian Council.

**Adoption records sealed?** Sealed but at age 18 yrs. adopted may access their adoption records.

**Photo-listing book available?** *South Carolina Seedlings.*

## PUBLIC AGENCIES

★ 709 ★
**South Carolina Department of Social Services**
**Children, Family and Adult Services**
1535 Confederate Ave. Extension
Columbia, SC 29202
Phone: (803) 734-6095
(800) 922-2504

**Mailing address:**
P.O. Box 1520, Columbia, SC 29202

**Branch address:**
Area I- Beaufort, Berkeley, Charleston, Colleton, Dorchester, Hampton, and Jasper counties, Park 3300, Ste. 310, 3300 W. Montague Ave., North Charleston, SC 29418
Phone: (800) 922-1518

Area II-Aiken, Allendale, Bamberg, Barnwell, Calhoun, Edgefield, Lexington, Orangeburg, and Saluda counties, Koger Center, Santee Bldg., Ste. 103, Columbia, SC 29210
Phone: (800) 922-9583

Area III-Anderson, Greenville, Laurens, Oconee, Greenwood, A bbeville, McCormick, and Pickens counties, 211 Century Dr., Greenville, SC 29607
Phone: (800) 868-6595

Area IV-Darlington, Dillon, Florence, Georgetown, Horry, Marion, Marlboro and Williamsburg counties, Florence Business and Technology Center, 181 E. Evans St., Ste. 112, Florence, SC 29506
Phone: (800) 763-6637

Area V-Clarendon, Fairfield, Kershaw, Lee, Richland, Newberr y, and Sumter counties, Market Place Office Mall, 1001 Harden St., Ste. 225, Columbia, SC 29205
Phone: (803) 253-6294

Area VI-Cherokee, Chester, Lancaster, Spartanburg, Union, Ch esterfield, and York counties, Control Data Business and Technology Center, 454 S. Anderson Rd., Rock Hill, SC 29730
Phone: (800) 922-1537

**Contact:** Central Intake Office: (800) 922-2504.

**Description:** Non-profit, public, state agency.

**Area served:** Residents of South Carolina and out-of-state applicants with approved homestudy for current year.

**Requirements:** Applicants must be of legal age. For infant adoptions preference is shown to applicants no older than 40 yrs. who are childless and unable to have biological children.

**Fees:**
Applicants for infants and pre-schoolers: $25;
applicants for interstate services: $50;
applicants for intercountry services: $75;
home study: Group preparation: $175; individual preparation: $300.
Post-placement services for infants and pre-schoolers: $200-$1750.
No fees on special needs, black, or biracial children.

**Number of children placed last year:** 350.

**Description of children:** Large sibling groups, children older than 8 yrs. and black boys older than 6 yrs., and children with physical, emotional and mental handicaps; children placed are between 0 and 17 yrs. old.

**Adoption procedure:**
 1) Inquiry;
 2) application;
 3) assessment;
 4) preparation workshops;
 5) home visit;
 6) pre-placement investigation;
 7) if approved, pre-placement visitation in the case of older children or placement;
 8) supervisory assistance;
 9) finalization.

**Average length of time between application and start of home study:** Varies.

**Average length of time to complete home study:** 3-6 mos.

**Number of interviews:** 6.

**Home study description:** Assessment of identity information, motivation to adopt, ability to parent, financial status, law enforcement clearances, applicant(s)' background, problem solving, preference in a child, attitude toward child's background and adoption and interaction with group or caseworker.

**Foster care:** Emergency, short and long-term and pre-adoptive.


# PRIVATE AGENCIES

★710★
**Catholic Charities Adoption Services**
**Diocese of Charleston, South Carolina**
1662 Ingram Rd.
Charleston, SC 29407
Phone: (800) 222-7333
Fax: (803) 769-2179

**Contact:** Maria Lescord, Adoption Coordinator.

**Date established:** 1940.

**Description:** Non-profit private agency licensed by the Dept. of Social Services of South Carolina.

**Area served:** Residents of the State of South Carolina.

**Requirements:** Christian couples married at least 3 years, who are in good physical and psychological health, and who are financially stable. Husband must not be older than 45 yrs., wife no older than 40 yrs. Wife is asked not to work outside the home after adoptive placement for the period of supervision.

**Fees:** $100 application fee. Minimum donation is requested after placement (tax deductible).

**Number of children placed last year:** N/A.

**Description of children:** Primarily newborn infants.

**Adoption procedure:**
 1) File application;
 2) attend office interviews;
 3) home study;
 4) home visit;
 5) if approved, wait for placement;
 6) placement;
 7) 6 mos. post-placement supervision;
 8) finalization.

**Average length of time between application and start of home study:** Varies.

**Average length of time to complete home study:** 1-2 mos.

**Number of interviews:** Varies.

**Home study description:** Evaluation of personal, pastor, physician and employer references, family life, employment history, moral standards, ability to parent, attitude toward and experiences with children.

**Average wait for a child after approval of a home study:** 12-24 mos.

**Foster care:** Temporary.


★711★
**Children Unlimited, Inc.**
P.O. Box 11463
Columbia, SC 29211
Phone: (803) 799-8311
(800) 822-0877
Fax: (803) 765-0284

**Contact:** Yolanda Fields.

**Date established:** 1977.

**Description:** Non-profit private agency for school age and handicapped children licensed by the State of South Carolina.

**Area served:** Residents of South Carolina.

**Requirements:** Adults age 21 yrs. and older who have adequate health and life expectancy to care for an adopted child.

**Fees:** None. There are legal fees for finalization but these can be provided for by state subsidies.

**Number of children placed last year:** 20-25.

**Description of children:** Children 10-16 yrs., some younger children have permanent physical or mental handicaps. Some sibling groups.

**Adoption procedure:**
 1) Telephone intake;
 2) attend interview (at the Columbia office or in home);
 3) complete study process;
 4) if approved, placement;
 5) 1 yr. post-placement supervisory; and
 6) finalization. Full array of post-adopt services available.

**Average length of time between application and start of home study:** 1-6 mos.

**Average length of time to complete home study:** Varies with family situation and prospective child's needs.

**Number of interviews:** Varies with family situation and prospective child's needs.

**Home study description:** Evaluatory and self-study process in which the following are discussed: parenting skills and philosophy; children's behavior; adoption adjustment; the types of children applicant will consider; preparation specific to identified child.

**Average wait for a child after approval of a home study:** Varies.

**Foster care:** None.

★ 712 ★
**Christian Family Services**
5072 Tara Tea Dr.
Fort Mill, SC 29715
Phone: (803) 548-6030
Fax: (803) 548-5896

**Contact:** Any staff member.

**Date established:** 1990.

**Description:** Private, non-profit nondenominational Christian agency licensed to place children by the South Carolina Department of Social Services.

**Area served:** Full service: residents of South Carolina. Identified adoption and special needs adoption: U.S. residents.

**Requirements:** Practicing and professing Christians singles or couples married at least 2 yrs. who belong to the same Christian Church.

**Fees:** Child Placement Fee: $4500; identified placement: $3500. Home Study: $800 (couples); $600 for singles. International: $1000 plus mileage. Attorney fees, birth mother medical and living expenses are additional.

**Number of children placed last year:** 38.

**Description of children:** Caucasian, African American, biracial and Hispanic infants.

**Adoption procedure:** 1) Preliminary application: 2) agency orientation; 3) home study; 4) placement; 5) post-placement; 6) finalization.

**Average length of time between application and start of home study:** 1 - 6 mos.

**Average length of time to complete home study:** 15 - 25 hrs.

**Number of interviews:** 2 - 4.

**Home study description:** An evaluation of the prospective adoptive family to determine if adoption is appropriate for them and the prospective adoptive child. It includes reference letters, medical reports, Child Abuse and Neglect investigation, copies of vital records.

**Average wait for a child after approval of a home study:** 12 - 18 mos.

**Foster care:** Temporary.

★ 713 ★
**Southeastern Children's Home**
155 Children's Way
Duncan, SC 29334
Phone: (803) 439-0259

**Contact:** Robert C. Kimberly, Executive Director.

**Date established:** 1968.

**Description:** Non-profit, private child-placing agency licensed in the State of South Carolina.

**Area served:** Residents of South Carolina.

**Requirements:** Couples married at least 3 yrs. who are over the age of 21 yrs., in good physical health and members of the Church of Christ.

**Fees:**
Application fee: $25;
home study: $1000;
adoption fee: 12% of gross income.

**Number of children placed last year:** 3.

**Description of children:** Infants and children with special needs.

**Adoption procedure:**
1) File application;

2) forward references and secure child protective services and criminal records clearances;
3) attend 2-3 interviews;
4) complete home study;
5) forward physician's statement;
6) if approved, wait for placement;
7) placement.

**Average length of time between application and start of home study:** Varies.

**Average length of time to complete home study:** 3 mos.

**Number of interviews:** 2-4.

**Home study description:** Description of family, marriage, community, finances, philosophy of childrearing and motivation to adopt.

**Average wait for a child after approval of a home study:** 12-24 mos.

**Foster care:** Temporary, long-term and permanent.

# SOUTH DAKOTA

## STATUTES

★ 714 ★

**Independent placement by intermediary?** Illegal.

**Independent placement by birth parents?** Permitted.

**Subsidies provided?** Medical, maintenance and non-recurring adoption expenses.

**Adoption cost defined by law?** No.

**Insurance for infertility?:** Not addressed in law.

**Home study required by state?** Required before placement.

**Prospective adoptive parent advertise for a child?** Not addressed in law.

**Surrogacy laws?** Not addressed in law.

**Residents access agencies of other states or countries?** Permitted.

**Requires judicial termination of birth parents' rights?** Birth mother must appear in court no earlier than 5 days after the birth of her child; birth father, if known, may use power of attorney.

**Time given to a birthmother to revoke her consent:** 30 day appeal period.

**Court handling adoptions?** Circuit Court.

**Adoption of Native Children:** Tribe - state.

**Adoption records sealed?** Yes, but at age 18 yrs. adoptees may access their records.

**Photo-listing book available?** None.

## PUBLIC AGENCIES

★ 715 ★
**South Dakota Department of Social Services**
**Child Protective Services**
700 Governors Dr.
Pierre, SD 57501
Phone: (605) 773-3227
Fax: (605) 773-4855

**Branch address:**
P.O. Box 2440, Rapid City, SD 57701
Phone: (605) 394-2434

912 E. Sioux, Pierre, SD 57501
Phone: (605) 773-3521

P.O. Box 670, Watertown, SD 57201
Phone: (605) 882-5050

P.O. Box 708, Brookings, SD 57006
Phone: (605) 688-4330

602 Jennings Ave, Box 830, SDSDSDUS4 570, 490, 57745
Phone: (605) 745-5100

300 E. 6th St., Sioux Falls, SD 57102-0490
Phone: (605) 339-6477

**Contact:** DiAnn Kleinsasser, Program Specialist.

**Date established:** 1939.

**Description:** Public child welfare agency.

**Area served:** Residents of the State of South Dakota.

**Requirements:** Applicants must be U.S. citizens, at least 21 years old; must have sufficient income to care for a child; and sanitary and sufficient living space equipped with working smoke detectors outside of sleeping areas. Preference shown to married couples who have no more than one child.

**Fees:** None for special needs adoption.

**Number of children placed last year:** 63.

**Description of children:** All special needs.

**Adoption procedure:**
1) Initial inquiry;
2) submit application;
3) complete home study;
4) if approved, wait for placement;
5) placement;
6) 6 mos. post-placement supervision;
7) finalization.
Applications are currently closed for infant adoption.

**Average length of time between application and start of home study:** 1-6 mos.

**Average length of time to complete home study:** 3-6 mos.

**Number of interviews:** At least 2 with one home visit.

**Home study description:** A complete adoptive study including 30 hrs. of group preparation and select process (MAPP).

**Average wait for a child after approval of a home study:** 12-24 mos.

**Foster care:** Temporary, long-term and permanent.

# PRIVATE AGENCIES

★716★
**Catholic Family Services**
3100 W. 41st St.
Sioux Falls, SD 57105
Phone: (605) 333-3375
Fax: (605) 333-3346

**Branch address:**
310 15th SE, Aberdeen, SD 57401
Phone: (605) 226-1304

**Contact:** Shannon Miles (Sioux Falls); Mary Pardew (Aberdeen).

**Date established:** 1961.

**Description:** Non-profit private agency.

**Area served:** Residents of South Dakota.

**Requirements:** Couples married at least 3 yrs. at time of application, who are between the ages of 21 and 42 yrs., at least one of whom is Catholic. Home studies also completed for special needs and foreign-born children whose requirements vary by the placing agency.

**Fees:** Infants: $1800-$6100; home study alone: $650.

**Number of children placed last year:** 5.

**Description of children:** Primarily Caucasian infants; occasionally biracial or special needs infants.

**Adoption procedure:**
1) Attend informational group meeting;
2) file application;
3) complete home study;
4) if approved, wait for placement;
5) placement;
6) 6 mos. post-placement supervision;
7) finalization.

**Average length of time between application and start of home study:** 6-12 mos.

**Average length of time to complete home study:** 3-5 mos.

**Number of interviews:** 5-6.

**Home study description:** Evaluation of family or origin, marital relationship, health, finances and housing, discipline styles, expectations of children, attitudes toward birthparents and adoptees' desire to search, in order to determine couple's ability to provide a stable, nurturing environment for a child.

**Average wait for a child after approval of a home study:** 24 or more mos.

**Foster care:** Temporary.

★717★
**Christian Counseling Services**
231 S. Phillips, Ste. 255
Sioux Falls, SD 57102
Phone: (605) 336-6999

**Contact:** Vinette Bomhoff, Director.

**Date established:** 1984.

**Description:** Private, non-profit agency licensed to place children by the South Dakota Department of Social Services.

**Area served:** Residents of South Dakota.

**Requirements:** Committed married Christian must be no older than 40 yrs., be in good health but have proof of infertility and have a stable income.

**Fees:** Application: $150; home study: $750 - $1000; adoption fee: $6000 - $8000. Medical fees may be additional.

**Number of children placed last year:** 12.

**Description of children:** Infants.

**Adoption procedure:** 1) Inquiry; 2) profile preparation including letters and pictures; 3) birth parent selection (birth parents may wish to meet prospective adoptive parents); 4) birth parents' rights terminated; 5) placement; 6) post-placement supervision; 7) finalization.

**Average length of time between application and start of home study:** 1 - 6 mos.

**Average length of time to complete home study:** 3 mos.

**Number of interviews:** 8 hrs.

**Home study description:** Assessment which includes marriage and family commitment, Abuse/Neglect and Criminal Background checks, attitude toward birth parents, openness and ability to share.

**Average wait for a child after approval of a home study:** 2 yrs. or more.

**Foster care:** Temporary.

**★718★**
**LDS Social Services**
2525 W. Main, No. 309
Rapid City, SD 57702
Phone: (605) 342-3500
Fax: (605) 342-3501

**Contact:** Adoption intake worker.

**Description:** Non-profit private agency.

**Area served:** Residents of northwest Minnesota, South Dakota, North Dakota, and northeast Wyoming.

**Requirements:** Married couples who are members of the Church of Jesus Christ of Latter Day Saints.

**Fees:** $400 application fee; $3600 additional fees.

**Number of children placed last year:** 3.

**Description of children:** Infants.

**Adoption procedure:**
 1) referral by local bishop;
 2) file application and related forms;
 3) complete home study;
 4) placement.

**Average length of time between application and start of home study:** 1-6 mos.

**Number of interviews:** 4.

**Home study description:** Evaluation of background, health, quality of marriage, infertility, employment history and financial management, home and quality of homemaking.

**Average wait for a child after approval of a home study:** 12-24 mos.

**Foster care:** Temporary.

**★719★**
**Lutheran Social Services of South Dakota**
600 W. 12th St.
Sioux Falls, SD 57104
Phone: (605) 336-3347
Fax: (605) 336-9141

**Contact:** Julie Klinger, Social Worker.

**Date established:** 1920.

**Description:** Non-profit, private agency licensed by the South Dakota Dept. of Social Services.

**Area served:** Residents of the State of South Dakota.

**Requirements:** Couples in a stable married union for at least 2 yrs. who are under the age of 42 yrs., who have a medical fertility work-up and who are affiliated with a Christian church.

**Fees:** Vary with adoption service provided.

**Number of children placed last year:** 12.

**Description of children:** Primarily newborn U.S. infants, some foreign-born children and children with special needs.

**Adoption procedure:**
 1) Attend orientation meeting;
 2) file application;
 3) participate in group counseling;
 4) home visit;
 5) referral of child;
 6) placement;
 7) post-placement supervision;
 8) finalization;
 9) post-legal adoption services.

**Average length of time between application and start of home study:** 1-6 mos.
**Average length of time to complete home study:** 2-4 mos.
**Number of interviews:** Varies.

**Home study description:** Evaluation of personal and interpersonal relationship, communication, parenting skills and techniques, use and management of financial resources, understanding of birthparents and others that comply with the requirements of the State of South Dakota.

**Average wait for a child after approval of a home study:** 6-24 mos.

**Foster care:** Short-term and long-term for multi-handicapped children.

# TENNESSEE

## STATUTES

**★720★**

**Independent placement by intermediary?** Illegal.

**Independent placement by birth parents?** Permitted.

**Subsidies provided?** Non-recurring, maintenance, medical and psychological, psychiatric treatment, hospitalization, residential, etc.

**Adoption cost defined by law?** Yes, only medical costs of mother and child attendant to the birth and legal costs of the adoption may be paid.

**Insurance for infertility?:** Unknown.

**Home study required by state?** Required before placement if child is born in Tennessee and after under the ICPC.

**Prospective adoptive parent advertise for a child?** Permitted.

**Surrogacy laws?** Permitted.

**Residents access agencies of other states or countries?** Yes, in compliance with the ICPC.

**Requires judicial termination of birth parents' rights?** Required by the birth mother before a judge.

**Time given to a birthmother to revoke her consent:** 15 days.

**Court handling adoptions?** Chancery or Circuit Court.

**Adoption of Native Children:** Under advice of the Bureau of Indian Affairs.

**Adoption records sealed?** Yes, adoptive parents and adoptees, age 18 yrs. or older, may access non-identifying information. Identifying information is available to adoptees, 21 yrs. and older, with a court order.

**Photo-listing book available?** *Tennessee Adoption Profiles.*

## PUBLIC AGENCIES

**★721★**
**Tennessee Department of Human Services**
400 Deaderick St.
Nashville, TN 37248-9000
Phone: (615) 741-5935

**Contact:** Jane Chittuck, Program Manager.

**Date established:** 1937.

**Description:** Non-profit state human services agency.

**Area served:** Residents of the State of Tennessee.

**Requirements:** Adults, 21 yrs. and older.

**Fees:** None.

**Number of children placed last year:** 336.

**Description of children:** Healthy white children from 0- 8 yrs., minority, sibling groups and white children 9 yrs. and over.

**Adoption procedure:**
1) Submit application;
2) complete home study process;
3) if approved, placement;
4) 6 mos. post-placement supervision;
5) file petition to adopt;
6) 6 mos. post-petition supervision;
7) finalization.

**Average length of time between application and start of home study:** 1-6 mos.

**Average length of time to complete home study:** 2-6 mos.

**Number of interviews:** 10 group, 2 home consultations.

**Home study description:** Evaluation of parenting potential for older child, commitment to adoption, flexibility, support systems and type of child desired.

**Average wait for a child after approval of a home study:** 12-24 mos.

**Foster care:** Temporary, long-term and permanent.

# PRIVATE AGENCIES

★722★
**Associated Catholic Charities of East Tennessee**
119 Dameron Ave.
Knoxville, TN 37917
Phone: (615) 524-9896
(800) 227-3002

**Branch address:**
125 N. Market St., 120 1/2 Boone St., Chattanooga, TN 37405
Phone: (615) 267-6767

**Contact:** Emily B. Auten, MSW, Director (615) 267-1297.

**Description:** Private, non-profit adoption agency licensed by the Tennessee Department of Human Services.

**Area served:** Residents of Tennessee.

**Requirements:** Age: Combined ages divided by 2 must be no more than 42 yrs.
Income: Sufficient income and management skills to provide for a child.
Health: Reasonably good with infertility documentation.
Marital status: Married at least 3 yrs. *waived for special needs placements*
Religion: Catholic and other Christian faiths.

**Fees:** Home Study: $800. International home study: $1000; independent home study: $800-$1000. Legal fees are not included.

**Number of children placed last year:** 6.

**Description of children:** 3 U.S. and 3 foreign born infants and toddlers.

**Adoption procedure:** 1) Orientation meeting; 2) application; 3) group home study; 4) compliance with INS (for international adoptions); 4) out-reach training (for independent adoptions); 5) child referral; 6) placement; 7) post-placement supervision; 8) finalization.

**Average length of time between application and start of home study:** 1 - 6 mos.

**Average length of time to complete home study:** 4 mos.

**Number of interviews:** 5.

**Home study description:** Groups discussion on motivation to adopt, parenting skills and idea, attitudes toward birth parents, strength of marriage relationship, extended family support system and system of family values.

**Average wait for a child after approval of a home study:** 2 yrs. or more.

**Foster care:** Temporary.

★723★
**Bethany Christian Services of Chattenooga**
4719 Brainerd Rd., Ste. D
Chattanooga, TN 37411
Phone: (615) 622-7360

**Contact:** Robert Gerow.

**Date established:** 1982.

**Description:** Non-profit, private agency licensed by the Tennessee Dept. of Human Services.

**Area served:** Residents of the 615 area code of Tennessee.

**Requirements:** Married couples who have no more than 1 child, who are active members of an evangelical, Bible-teaching Christian church, and who believe in the sanctity of human life beginning at conception.

**Fees:** Sliding scale with a maximum of $14,000.

**Number of children placed last year:** 21.

**Description of children:** White, black, and biracial infants.

**Adoption procedure:**
1) Submit preliminary application;
2) return completed formal application;
3) complete home study;
4) if approved, admission to waiting list;
5) placement;
6) post-placement supervision;
7) finalization and naturalization (if international adoption).

**Average length of time between application and start of home study:** 6-12 mos.

**Average length of time to complete home study:** 2-3 mos.

**Number of interviews:** Minimum of 4.

**Home study description:** A family assessment is conducted by a Bethany social worker, who explores with the applicants their feelings about adoption, discusses effective parenting and considers which child might best fit into their family.

**Average wait for a child after approval of a home study:** 12-24 mos.

**Foster care:** Temporary.

★724★
**Catholic Charities of Tennessee, Inc.**
30 White Bridge Rd.
Nashville, TN 37205
Phone: (615) 352-3089
(800) CARE-002
Fax: (615) 352-8591

**Contact:** Donna T. Taylor, Department Director.

**Date established:** 1962.

**Description:** Non-profit private agency licensed by the State of Tennessee.

**Area served:** Residents of the State of Tennessee middle region.

**Requirements:** Couples in a valid marriage for at least 3 yrs., who are financially sound and in good health, and whose average age is not more than 45 yrs. older than the child they are adopting.

**Fees:** Placement fee is a sliding scale based on 15% of gross income with a minimum of $4000 and a maximum of $12,000.

**Number of children placed last year:** 15.

**Description of children:** Primarily white infants but also black, biracial, and foreign-born infants.

**Adoption procedure:**
1) Attend orientation meeting;
2) complete home study and required forms;
3) if approved, placement;
4) 1 yr. post-placement supervision.

**Average length of time between application and start of home study:** 1-6 mos.

**Average length of time to complete home study:** 2 - 2.5 mos.

**Number of interviews:** 6 group sessions, individual interviews, and a home visit.

**Home study description:** Evaluation of autobiographies, social histories, marriage, personal achievements, motivation to adopt, issues surrounding infertility, parenting, stresses from children, support systems, birthparents, and child desired.

**Average wait for a child after approval of a home study:** Varies depending on type of adoption.

**Foster care:** Temporary.

**★ 725 ★**
**Child and Family Services**
114 Dameron Ave.
Knoxville, TN 37917
Phone: (615) 524-7483
Fax: (615) 524-4790

**Contact:** Charles Gentry, Executive Director or Barbara S. Collins, Adoptions Counselor.

**Date established:** 1929.

**Description:** Private, non-profit agency licensed by the State of Tennessee, accredited by Family Service of America and a member of the Child Welfare League of America.

**Area served:** Residents within a 100 mi. radius of Knoxville.

**Requirements:**
Special needs adoption: flexible.
Infant adoption: Couples married at least 3 yrs. who are between the ages of 21 and 42 yrs., who are childless and who have a medical diagnosis of infertility.

**Fees:**
Home study: $500;
service fee based on income.

**Number of children placed last year:** 4.

**Description of children:** One child with special needs and 3 infants.

**Adoption procedure:**
1) Attend screening interview;
2) submit application;
3) participate in 6 wk. group preparation and complete home study;
4) 2-3 home visits;
5) if approved, pre-placement planning and visits;
6) placement;
7) 1 yr. post-placement supervision;
8) finalization.

**Average length of time between application and start of home study:** 24 or more mos.

**Average length of time to complete home study:** Approx. 3 mos.

**Number of interviews:** 6 wk. group and 4-5 individual.

**Home study description:** Assessment of background and autobiographies; employment history, marital relationship and family functioning; parenting abilities and expectations; medical and financial reports and recommendation of references.

**Average wait for a child after approval of a home study:** 24 or more mos.

**Foster care:** Temporary.

**★ 726 ★**
**Christian Counseling Services**
515 Woodland St.
Nashville, TN 37206
Phone: (615) 254-8341
Fax: (615) 254-8336

**Mailing address:**
P.O. Box 60383, Nashville, TN 37206

**Contact:** Pam Page or Jan Harvey.

**Date established:** 1972.

**Description:** Licensed private child-placing agency serving Christian families.

**Area served:** Residents of Tennessee.

**Requirements:** Protestant couples who attend the same church, who are married at least 4 yrs. when home study begins, who are at least 21 yrs. old and no more than 42 at the time of home study, who have no more than 1 child and a medical diagnosis of infertility, who abstain from alcoholic beverage and tobacco, who are in good health and who show evidence of sound financial practices and are able to support an adoptive child. After placement the adoptive mother must not work for at least 3 mos.

**Fees:** 14% of combined incomes at time of application with a minimum of $5000 and a maximum of $12,000.

**Number of children placed last year:** 11.

**Description of children:** Black, biracial and white infants.

**Adoption procedure:**
1) File application;
2) attend orientation meeting;
3) participate in individual counseling sessions;
4) complete home study;
5) if approved, wait for selection by birthmother;
6) 1 yr. post-placement supervision;
7) finalization hearing in court.

**Average length of time between application and start of home study:** 12-24 mos.

**Average length of time to complete home study:** Varies.

**Number of interviews:** Varies.

**Home study description:** Compilation of any information necessary to ascertain that adoptive applicants meet the agency's requirements and possess the characteristics necessary to be good parents.

**Average wait for a child after approval of a home study:** Varies.

**Foster care:** Temporary.

**★ 727 ★**
**Church of God Home for Children**
P.O. Box 4391, S.
Sevierville, TN 37864
Phone: (615) 453-4644

**Contact:** Edna Shults.

**Date established:** 1920.

**Description:** Non-profit, private Christian agency licensed by the Tennessee Dept. of Human Services.

**Area served:** Full adoption service to the residents of Tennessee; placement service to all U.S. residents.

**Requirements:** Preference shown to childless couples between the ages of 25 and 40 yrs. who are active Christians.

**Fees:** Home study: $750.

**Number of children placed last year:** 10.

**Description of children:** Infants and children over 8 yrs. of age.

**Adoption procedure:**
1) Submit preliminary application;
2) attend interviews;
3) reference checks;
4) child match;
5) placement;
6) post-placement supervision;
7) filing of petition;
8) finalization.

**Average length of time between application and start of home study:** 0-1 mos.

**Average length of time to complete home study:** 2 mos.

**Number of interviews:** 4.

**Home study description:** A thorough study which follows the guidelines of the Child Welfare League of America.

**Average wait for a child after approval of a home study:** Varies.

**Foster care:** Temporary.


★728★
**Family and Children's Service**
201 23rd Ave. N.
Nashville, TN 37203
Phone: (615) 320-0591
Fax: (615) 321-3813

**Contact:** Kathy Rogers, Adoption Director.

**Date established:** 1950.

**Description:** Private agency.

**Area served:** Residents of the State of Tennessee.

**Requirements:** Open.

**Fees:** None.

**Number of children placed last year:** 20.

**Description of children:** Children with special needs.

**Adoption procedure:**
1) Initial inquiry;
2) submit application;
3) complete home study and group sessions;
4) wait for placement;
5) placement;
6) post-placement supervision;
7) finalization.

**Average length of time between application and start of home study:** 1 mo. or less.

**Average length of time to complete home study:** 6 mos.

**Number of interviews:** 5 individual and 7 group.

**Home study description:** Educational and self-assessment models which cover an evaluation of family strengths and assisting the family to define realistic limits.

**Average wait for a child after approval of a home study:** Varies.

**Foster care:** None.


★729★
**Jewish Family Service**
6560 Poplar
Memphis, TN 38138
Phone: (901) 767-8511

**Contact:** Penny Glatstein, Adoption Supervisor.

**Date established:** 1950.

**Description:** Private, non-profit social service agency licensed to place children by the Tennessee Department of Human Services.

**Area served:** Residents of the Memphis area in both Tennessee and Mississippi.

**Requirements:** Priority is given to Jewish applicants.

**Fees:** Application: $100. Home Study: $500. Placement Fee: sliding scale. Post-placement supervision: $500.

**Number of children placed last year:** 9.

**Description of children:** Infants and children with special needs.

**Adoption procedure:** 1) Inquiry; 2) application; 3) home study: 4) wait for placement (agency will also work with applicants searching for birth parents who will place their child); 5) placement; 6) post-placement supervision; 7) finalization.

**Average length of time between application and start of home study:** Less than 1 mo.

**Average length of time to complete home study:** Varies.

**Number of interviews:** 2 joint and 2 individual.

**Home study description:** Assessment which includes background and family information, documentation and which covers all adoption related issues.

**Average wait for a child after approval of a home study:** Birth parents select adoptive home.

**Foster care:** Temporary.


★730★
**Porter-Leath Children's Center**
868 N. Manassas
Memphis, TN 38107
Phone: (901) 577-2500

**Contact:** Jane Watkins, Director of Program Services.

**Date established:** 1856.

**Description:** Non-profit, private agency licensed by the Tennessee Dept. of Human Services, supported by the United Way and a member of the Child Welfare League of America.

**Area served:** Residents of Tennessee and extension services to out-of-state residents.

**Requirements:** Adults between the ages of 24 and 42 yrs. who have average health.

**Fees:**
Application fee: $250;
placement fee is a sliding scale from $1500 to $8000.

**Number of children placed last year:** 12.

**Description of children:** Black and biracial children.

**Adoption procedure:**
1) Submit application;
2) complete home study;
3) if approved, placement;
4) post-placement supervision;
5) finalization.

**Average length of time between application and start of home study:** 1-6 mos.

**Average length of time to complete home study:** 4-6 wks.

**Number of interviews:** 4-6.

**Home study description:** Follows guidelines of the Child Welfare League of America.

**Average wait for a child after approval of a home study:** 6-12 mos.

**Foster care:** Temporary, long-term, permanent, and emergency foster care.

---

★731★
**St. Peters Home for Children**
**Maternity and Adoptive Services**
1805 Poplar Ave.
Memphis, TN 38104
Phone: (901) 725-8240
Fax: (901) 725-8243

**Contact:** Debra Dunn, LCSW, Director.

**Date established:** 1852.

**Description:** Non-profit private agency licensed by the Tennessee Department of Human Services.

**Area served:** Residents of western Tennessee for white, black, and biracial placements; only Catholic families outside of Shelby County.

**Requirements:** Couples married at least 3 yrs. who are between the ages of 25 and 45 yrs., who have no children in the home, who are in good health and members of some church and who have no record of felony convictions. Some requirements are flexible for black and biracial placements.

**Fees:**
Placement for white children: $10,000;
placement for black or biracial: $3000. Application: $25.

**Number of children placed last year:** 13.

**Description of children:** White, black, and biracial infants.

**Adoption procedure:**
1) Register when lists are open;
2) admission to waiting list (wait measured by time);
3) complete home study classes and interviews;
4) wait for placement;
5) placement.

**Average length of time between application and start of home study:** 12-24 mos.

**Average length of time to complete home study:** 6-7 wks.

**Number of interviews:** 6-7.

**Home study description:** Assessment of the strength of the marriage relationship, resolution of infertility, parenting styles and willingness to accept an adopted child.

**Average wait for a child after approval of a home study:** 24 or more mos.

**Foster care:** Cradle care.

---

★732★
**Small World Ministries**
401 Bonnaspring Dr.
Hermitage, TN 37076
Phone: (615) 883-4372
Fax: (615) 885-7582

**Contact:** Write or call for information.

**Date established:** 1986.

**Description:** Non-profit, private agency licensed in New Jersey and Tennessee for domestic and international adoptions.

**Area served:** U.S.

**Requirements:** Christian couples married at least 3 yrs. who are between the ages of 25 and 45 yrs. of age and who have a combined annual income of at least $30,000.

**Fees:**
Application fee: $250;
adoption fee is a sliding scale from $5450 to $13,250.

**Number of children placed last year:** Unreleased.

**Description of children:** Infants.

**Adoption procedure:**
1) Submit preliminary application;
2) attend interview;
3) if approved, complete home study;
4) if approved, attend preparation classes;
5) placement;
6) post-placement supervision;
7) file petition to adopt;
8) finalization.

**Average length of time between application and start of home study:** 1 mo. or less.

**Average length of time to complete home study:** 30 days.

**Number of interviews:** 2.

**Home study description:** Assessment of character, values and ethical standards, physical and mental health, cause of infertility (if applicable), financial security, health and fire safety conditions within the home and motivation to adopt.

**Average wait for a child after approval of a home study:** 6-12 mos. for international; 24 or more mos. for domestic adoptions.

**Foster care:** Temporary.

---

★733★
**Tennessee Baptist Children's Home, Inc.**
5001 Maryland Way
Brentwood, TN 37027
Phone: (615) 371-2000
Fax: (615) 371-2069

**Contact:** Dr. Gerald L. Stow, President/Treasurer.

**Date established:** 1891.

**Description:** Non-profit, private religiously-affiliated agency licensed by the Tennessee Dept. of Human Services.

**Area served:** Residents of the State of Tennessee.

**Requirements:** Married couples with no divorces between them, who are residents of Tennessee for at least 1 yr., who are in good physical and mental health with an established reason for infertility and who are members of a Tennessee Baptist church. Prospective adoptive mother must be no older than 40 yrs. at time of placement and must remain in the home full-time for 6 mos. after placement; prospective adoptive father may be no older than 45 yrs. at time of placement.

**Fees:** Healthy, white infant: $4000.

**Number of children placed last year:** 7.

**Description of children:** Older children, biracial children and infants.

**Adoption procedure:**
1) Initial inquiry;
2) submit application;
3) wait for home study;
4) complete home study;
5) if approved, wait for placement;
6) placement;

7) post-placement supervision;
8) adoptive family files petition to adopt 6 mos. after placement;
9) agency presents confidential court report within 60 days;
10) agency presents final report;
11) finalization 1 yr. after placement.

**Average length of time between application and start of home study:** 24 or more mos.

**Average length of time to complete home study:** 2-3 mos.

**Number of interviews:** 3.

**Home study description:** Assessment of family and personal history, family systems, marital relationship, personality traits, spiritual commitment, health and medical information, financial information, recommendation of references, autobiographical information, employment history and other activities.

**Average wait for a child after approval of a home study:** 12-24 mos.

**Foster care:** Temporary and long-term.

★734★
**Tennessee Conference Adoption Service**
900 Glendale Ln.
Nashville, TN 37204
Phone: (615) 292-3500
(800) 320-1506
Fax: (615) 292-0368

**Contact:** Mrs. Debbie Robinson, Director.

**Date established:** 1984.

**Description:** Non-profit adoptive and birthmother services licensed by the State of Tennessee.

**Area served:** Residents of middle Tennessee.

**Requirements:** Couples married at least 3 yrs. who are between the ages of 25 and 45 and in good health.

**Fees:** Sliding scale from $5000-$10,000.

**Number of children placed last year:** 20.

**Description of children:** Infants, foreign-born children and children with special needs of all races.

**Adoption procedure:**
1) File application;
2) waiting period;
3) complete home study;
4) placement;
5) post-placement supervisory;
6) finalization.

**Average length of time between application and start of home study:** 1-6 mos.

**Average length of time to complete home study:** 1 mo.

**Number of interviews:** 3 or more.

**Home study description:** Documentation and verification of all items pertaining to the home study.

**Average wait for a child after approval of a home study:** 6-24 mos.

**Foster care:** Temporary.

★735★
**West Tennessee Baptist Children's Home**
6896 Highway 70
Memphis, TN 38134
Phone: (901) 386-3961
(901) 386-3971
Fax: (901) 382-9754

**Contact:** Kelly D. May.

**Date established:** 1950.

**Description:** Non-profit, private agency licensed with the Tennessee Dept. of Human Services.

**Area served:** Residents of west Tennessee.

**Requirements:** Married couples, the husband of whom is no older than 44 yrs. and the wife no older than 42 yrs., who have adequate income to support a child, who are in good health as determined by a physician and who are active members of a Tennessee Baptist church. Age requirement may be flexible for non-infant placements.

**Fees:** Infant adoption: $4000.

**Number of children placed last year:** 3.

**Description of children:** Infants, older children and children with special needs.

**Adoption procedure:**
1) Submit letter of inquiry;
2) if eligibility requirements are met, admission to waiting list;
3) complete home study;
4) if approved, placement;
5) 1 yr. post-placement supervision;
6) finalization.

**Average length of time between application and start of home study:** 24 or more mos.

**Average length of time to complete home study:** 1 mo.

**Number of interviews:** 1-3.

**Home study description:** Evaluation of recommendation of references, financial status, medical information, stability of applicants and their marriage.

**Average wait for a child after approval of a home study:** 6-12 mos.

**Foster care:** Temporary, long-term and permanent.

# TEXAS

## STATUTES

★736★

**Independent placement by intermediary?** Illegal.

**Independent placement by birth parents?** Permitted.

**Subsidies provided?** Federal and state subsidies as well as non-recurring adoption expenses.

**Adoption cost defined by law?** No.

**Insurance for infertility?:** No.

**Home study required by state?** An adoptive social study is required before the adoption may be consummated.

**Prospective adoptive parent advertise for a child?** Permitted.

**Surrogacy laws?** Not addressed in law.

**Residents access agencies of other states or countries?** Permitted.

**Requires judicial termination of birth parents' rights?** Voluntary relinquishments are recognized. Citations by publication on missing parent are issued if both parents are not present to relinquish.

**Time given to a birthmother to revoke her consent:** 60 days.

**Court handling adoptions?** District State Court.

**Adoption of Native Children:** Tribe.

**Adoption records sealed?** Sealed, but at age 21 yrs. adoptees may access non-identifying information.

**Photo-listing book available?** *Texas Adoption Resource Exchange.*

# PUBLIC AGENCIES

## ★ 737 ★
**Child Protective Services**
**Texas Department of Protective and Regulatory Services**
Region 10
P.O. Box 99002
El Paso, TX 79999
Phone: (915) 542-4535

**Contact:** Adoption Unit.

**Description:** Public, regional agency.

**Area served:** Residents of El Paso and surrounding counties. Accept out-of-area home studies if they comply with Texas minimum standards for child placing agencies.

**Requirements:** Adults, 21 yrs. and older who are single or married at least 2 yrs.

**Fees:** None.

**Number of children placed last year:** 48.

**Description of children:** Children with special needs.

**Adoption procedure:**
1) Attend information meeting;
2) file application;
3) home screening visit;
4) participate in 10 wks. of pre-adoption training;
5) complete home study;
6) if approved, wait for placement;
7) placement;
8) post-placement supervision;
9) finalization.

**Average length of time between application and start of home study:** 1-6 mos.

**Average length of time to complete home study:** Varies.

**Number of interviews:** 1 individual, 1 joint, 1 with others in the home, and contact with adult children.

**Home study description:** Assessment which includes but is not limited to applicant(s)' childhood, education, employment history, marital history, methods of resolving differences, expectations of children, income, and management ability.

**Average wait for a child after approval of a home study:** Varies.

**Foster care:** Short and long-term and permanent.

## ★ 738 ★
**Department of Protective and Regulatory Services**
Region 8
P.O. Box 23990
San Antonio, TX 78223-0990
Phone: (210) 337-3601

**Contact:** Adoption Unit.

**Description:** Public, regional agency of the Texas Dept. of Protective and Regulatory Services.

**Area served:** Residents of Atascosa, Bandera, Bexar, Calhoun, Comal, DeWitt, Dimmit, Edwards, Frio, Gillespie, Gollad, Gonzales, Guadalupe, Jackson, Karnes, Kendall, Kerr, Kinney, LaSalle, Layaca, Medina, Real, Uvalde, Valverde, Victoria, and Wilson counties.

**Requirements:** Single adults or couples married at least 2 yrs., who are 21 yrs. and older and who are age appropriate to the child requested. If a prior marriage exists for either partner, the current marriage must be of at least 3 yrs. duration.

**Fees:** None.

**Number of children placed last year:** 49.

**Description of children:** Primarily children with special needs.

**Adoption procedure:**
1) Submit application;
2) attend intake interview;
3) parenting classes;
4) home study;
5) if home study is approved, wait for placement;
6) placement;
7) post-placement supervision;
8) finalization.

**Average length of time between application and start of home study:** Varies. Those studies that are child-specific are prioritized.

**Average length of time to complete home study:** 3 mos.

**Number of interviews:** 1 interview per family member and 1 joint interview with all family members present.

**Home study description:** Process which includes MAPP training and applicant(s)' motivation to adopt, ability to meet the needs of a child with special needs and parenting experience or experience with children.

**Average wait for a child after approval of a home study:** 6-12 mos.

**Foster care:** Emergency, short and long-term, therapeutic, pre-adoptive and permanent.

## ★ 739 ★
**Texas Department of Human Services**
Region 1
P.O. Box 3700
Amarillo, TX 79116-3700
Phone: (806) 358-6211

**Contact:** Debbie Boeka.

**Date established:** 1936.

**Description:** Public, regional office licensed by the State of Texas for child placement.

**Area served:** Residents of the 24 counties of the Texas Panhandle.

**Requirements:** Flexible.

**Fees:** None.

**Number of children placed last year:** 48.

**Description of children:** Children with special needs.

**Adoption procedure:**
1) Submit application;
2) if accepted, attend group preparation;
3) complete home study;
4) if approved, placement;
5) 6 or more mos. post-placement supervision;
6) finalization.

**Average length of time between application and start of home study:** 1-6 mos.

**Average length of time to complete home study:** 3 mos.

**Number of interviews:** Minimum of 1 home visit and 1 individual.

**Home study description:** Assessment of applicant(s)' tolerance to frustration, acceptance of behaviors of special needs children, ability to cherish and insight into children's needs.

**Average wait for a child after approval of a home study:** 1-6 mos.

**Foster care:** Temporary, long-term and permanent.

### ★ 740 ★
**Texas Department of Human Services**
**Region 7**
7901 Cameron Rd.
Austin, TX 78761
Phone: (512) 834-3279

**Mailing address:**
P.O. 15995, Austin, TX 78761

**Branch address:**
108-110 N. Main, Belton, TX 76513
Phone: (817) 939-4272

302 E. 24th, Bryan, TX 77801

504 W. 6th, Waco, TX 76703

**Contact:** Sylvia Tarver.

**Description:** Regional office of the public state agency.

**Area served:** Counties in Austin, Bryan, Belton and Waco areas.

**Requirements:** Applicants must be age appropriate to the child placed, single or married at least 2 yrs. and have stable employment.

**Fees:** None.

**Number of children placed last year:** Unavailable.

**Description of children:** Sibling groups and children with special needs.

**Adoption procedure:**
1) Submit preliminary form;
2) if approved, attend 8 sessions of training;
3) complete home study;
4) if approved, child match;
5) pre-placement visitation process;
6) placement;
7) 6 mos. post-placement supervision;
8) finalization.

**Average length of time between application and start of home study:** 1-6 mos.

**Average length of time to complete home study:** 4-12 wks.

**Number of interviews:** 8 group and 3 or more individual.

**Home study description:** Assessment of childhood, marital history, background checks, financial and medical reports, etc.

**Average wait for a child after approval of a home study:** 1-6 mos.

**Foster care:** Temporary.

### ★ 741 ★
**Texas Department of Protection and Regulatory Services**
4635 Scott
Houston, TX 77027
Phone: (713) 696-7379

**Contact:** Sandra Besig, Supervisor.

**Date established:** 1969.

**Description:** Non-profit, public agency.

**Area served:** Residents of Harris County.

**Requirements:** Adults, 25 yrs. and older who are in good health.

**Fees:** None.

**Number of children placed last year:** Approx. 100.

**Description of children:** Black and Hispanic children of all ages, Anglo children over 6, children with special needs: abused, abandoned and neglected.

**Adoption procedure:** Telephone for preliminary screening.

**Average length of time between application and start of home study:** Varies.

**Average length of time to complete home study:** 2-3 mos.

**Number of interviews:** 4.

**Home study description:** Educational and evaluatory process in which applicants attend 6-session preparation group and assess family history, references and verifications.

**Average wait for a child after approval of a home study:** Varies.

**Foster care:** Temporary and protective.

### ★ 742 ★
**Texas Department of Protective and Regulatory Services**
901 W. Wall
Midland, TX 79701
Phone: (915) 686-2273
Fax: (915) 686-2272

**Contact:** Nancy Miller.

**Description:** Non-profit regional office of the state Department of Protective and Regulatory Services.

**Area served:** Residents of 17 counties in the Permian Basin.

**Requirements:** Flexible.

**Fees:** None.

**Number of children placed last year:** Approx. 20.

**Description of children:** Children with special needs.

**Adoption procedure:**
1) Intake screening;
2) complete group study;
3) file application and submit autobiographies;
4) complete interviews;
5) if approved, placement;
6) post-placement supervision;
7) finalization.

**Average length of time between application and start of home study:** 12-24 mos.

**Average length of time to complete home study:** 1-6 mos.

**Number of interviews:** 4-5.

**Home study description:** Evaluation which includes but is not limited to applicant(s)' flexibility and ability to handle a child who may occasionally display severe behavior problems.

**Average wait for a child after approval of a home study:** 12-24 mos.

**Foster care:** Temporary and long-term.

### ★ 743 ★
**Texas Department of Protective and Regulatory Services**
1112 E. Copeland Rd., Ste. 400
Arlington, TX
Phone: (800) 228-8226
Fax: (817) 856-4211

**Contact:** Helen Grape, Program Director; Harlan Thatcher, Supervisor; Michele Bland, P.D.; Rose Benham, P.D.

**Date established:** 1939.

**Description:** Non-profit regional office of Texas Department of Protective and Regulatory Services.

**Area served:** Residents of Tarrant, Dallas, Denton, Hunt, Hood, Parker, Erath, Ellis, Kaufman, Collin, Grayson, Fannin, Cooke, Wise, Palo Pinto, Johnson, Sommervell, Rockwall and Navarro counties.

**Requirements:** None.

**Fees:** $100 per applicant per medical examination; $150 filing fee (court costs). Costs are approximate.

**Number of children placed last year:** 200.

**Description of children:** Minority, older, sibling groups, physically, mentally and/or emotionally handicapped.

**Adoption procedure:**
1) Attend 10 wk. Model Approach to Parents in Partnership class;
2) complete home study;
3) complete criminal clearances and medical examinations;
4) attend individual interviews.

**Average length of time between application and start of home study:** 1-6 mos.

**Average length of time to complete home study:** 3 mos. (after MAPP training).

**Number of interviews:** 4.

**Home study description:** Motivation, skills, and committment to adopt a special needs child.

**Average wait for a child after approval of a home study:** 1-6 mos.

**Foster care:** Temporary and long-term.

★ 744 ★
**Texas Department of Protective and Regulatory Services**
701 W. 51st St.
P.O. Box 149030, E-559
Austin, TX 78714-9030
Phone: (512) 450-3298
(800) 233-3405
Fax: (512) 450-3782

**Contact:** Ella Zamora, Program Specialist.

**Description:** Texas Department of Protective and Regulatory Services is divided in 11 regions located throughout the state.

**Area served:** Residents of the State of Texas and private adoption agencies.

**Requirements:** Adults, 21 yrs. or older, single or married, if married, at least 2 yrs., with the ability to meet a child's needs.

**Fees:** None.

**Number of children placed last year:** 634.

**Description of children:** Usually older, minority, sibling groups, or children with handicapping conditions.

**Adoption procedure:**
1) File application;
2) complete home study process;
3) reference checks and police clearances;
4) search for appropriate child;
5) placement;
6) 6 mos. post-placement supervision.

**Average length of time between application and start of home study:** Varies.

**Average length of time to complete home study:** Unavailable.

**Number of interviews:** Unavailable.

**Home study description:** Evaluation of family's background, lifestyle, medical report(s), recommendation of references, police background check, and applicant(s)' ability to provide for a child's needs.

**Average wait for a child after approval of a home study:** Varies.

**Foster care:** Temporary which on occasion becomes long-term.

★ 745 ★
**Texas Department of Protective and Regulatory Services**
901 S. 4th St.
Abilene, TX 79602
Phone: (915) 672-6814

**Contact:** Judith K. Phaneuf.

**Description:** Non-profit regional office of the Texas Dept. of Protective and Regulatory Services.

**Area served:** Residents of 44 counties of north central Texas.

**Requirements:** Applicants must have adequate health and life expectancy to parent a child into adulthood and be financially stable.

**Fees:** None.

**Number of children placed last year:** 60.

**Description of children:** Sibling groups, minority and older children to age 18 yrs.

**Adoption procedure:**
1) File preliminary application;
2) complete 10 sessions of Model Approach to Parents in Partnership training;
3) attend individual interviews;
4) complete formal application.

**Average length of time between application and start of home study:** 1-6 mos.

**Average length of time to complete home study:** 9 mos.

**Number of interviews:** 4 or more.

**Home study description:** Evaluation of social and family history; applicant(s)' ability and desire to parent special needs child(ren).

**Average wait for a child after approval of a home study:** Varies.

**Foster care:** Temporary and long-term.

★ 746 ★
**Texas Department of Protective and Regulatory Services Region 11**
4410 Dillon, Ste. 36
Corpus Christi, TX 78415
Phone: (512) 878-7771

**Mailing address:**
P.O. Box 7622, Corpus Christi, TX 78415

**Branch address:**
1413 E. Corral, P.O. Box 831, Kingsville, TX 78363
Phone: (512) 592-9351

2501 Maple St., McAllen, TX 78501
Phone: (210) 682-1301

**Contact:** Adoption Supervisor or Worker.

**Description:** Public regional office of the Texas Dept. of Protective and Regulatory Services.

**Area served:** Residents of Aransas, Bee, Brooks, Cameron, Duval, Hidalgo, Jimm Hogg, Kenedy, Klegerb, Live Oak, McMullen, Nueces, Refugio, San Patricio, Starr, Webb, Willacy, and Zapata counties.

**Requirements:** Singles and couples married 2 yrs. who are at least 21 yrs. old, who are in good health with no criminal record.

**Fees:** None.

**Number of children placed last year:** 39.

**Description of children:** Sibling groups, Hispanic children, school age children and children with special needs.

**Adoption procedure:**
1) Submit application;
2) attend 10 wks. of MAPP;
3) home consultation;
4) if approved, child match;
5) placement;
6) supervision of placement;
7) finalization.

**Average length of time between application and start of home study:** MAPP training is scheduled quarterly.

**Average length of time to complete home study:** 4-6 mos.

**Number of interviews:** 2 in-home.

**Home study description:** Assessment of motivation to adopt, quality of marriage (if applicable), flexibility, support systems and ability to use agency resources to assist placement.

**Average wait for a child after approval of a home study:** Within 1 yr.

**Foster care:** Emergency, temporary, long-term, and therapeutic.

★ 747 ★
**Texas Department of Protective and Regulatory Services Region 5**
P.O. Box 630050
Nacogdoches, TX 75963
Phone: (409) 569-7931

**Contact:** Judy Bowman.

**Description:** Non-profit regional office of the state Department of Human Services.

**Area served:** Residents of Nacogdoches, San Augustine, Sabine, Shelby and Polk counties.

**Requirements:** Flexible.

**Fees:** None.

**Number of children placed last year:** 28.

**Description of children:** Special needs.

**Adoption procedure:**
1) Inquiry;
2) attend training group;
3) file application;
4) complete home study;
5) matching of applicant family with particular child;
6) pre-placement visitation;
7) placement;
8) post-placement supervision;
9) finalization;
10) post-finalization support, if required.

**Average length of time between application and start of home study:** 6-12 mos.

**Average length of time to complete home study:** 1-3 mos.

**Number of interviews:** Several, at least 1 in-home.

**Home study description:** Educational and evaluatory process wherein the applicants learn about adoption and the children who need adoptive families and assess themselves to decide if adoption is right for them.

**Average wait for a child after approval of a home study:** 1-6 mos.

**Foster care:** Temporary, long-term and permanent.

★ 748 ★
**Texas Department of Protective and Regulatory Services Region 6**
4635 Southwest Freeway
Houston, TX 77027
Phone: (713) 940-5165

**Contact:** Sandra Besig.

**Date established:** 1969.

**Description:** Non-profit regional office of the State Department of Human Services.

**Area served:** Residents of Harris County.

**Requirements:** Adults, 25 yrs. or older, who have adequate income to meet family's needs; if married, at least 2 yrs. duration, if remarried, at least 3 yrs. duration.

**Fees:** None.

**Number of children placed last year:** Approx. 100.

**Description of children:** Children who have been abused and/or neglected: white children over 8 yrs., minority children over 2 yrs.

**Adoption procedure:**
1) Attend adoption preparation group;
2) complete home study;
3) pre-placement visitation process;
4) placement;
5) 6 mos. post-placement supervision;
6) finalization.

**Average length of time between application and start of home study:** Depends on availability of children desired; if family wants waiting child, no wait.

**Average length of time to complete home study:** 6-8 wks.

**Number of interviews:** 4.

**Home study description:** Verification of health, employment, police and protective services checks, marriage(s) and divorce(s) (if applicable), references, and evaluation of applicant(s)' autobiographies, family-marital functioning and motivation to adopt.

**Average wait for a child after approval of a home study:** Varies.

**Foster care:** Temporary.

# PRIVATE AGENCIES

★ 749 ★
**Abrazo Adoption Associates**
10010 San Pedro, Ste. 540
San Antonio, TX 78216
Phone: (210) 342-5683

**Contact:** Placement coordinator.

**Date established:** 1994.

**Description:** Private, non-profit child placement agency licensed by the Texas Department of Protective and Regulatory Services.

**Area served:** U.S. citizens except residents of New York and Connecticut.

**Requirements:** Applicants must be at least 25 yrs. old, either single or married at least 2 yrs., emotionally stable, financially sound and have medical documentation of infertility.

**Fees:** Pre-Application: $25; application: $125; orientation: $150; agency fee: $4500 - $5500. Case-specific fees may be additional.

**Number of children placed last year:** New agency.

**Description of children:** Caucasian and Hispanic newborns; some toddlers and sibling groups.

**Adoption procedure:** 1) Pre-application; 2) application; 3) orientation; 4) agency acceptance; 5) child match; 6) placement; 7) post-placement supervision; 8) finalization.

**Average length of time between application and start of home study:** At the discretion of prospective adoptive parents.

**Average length of time to complete home study:** 2 - 4 wks.

**Number of interviews:** Minimum of 5.

**Home study description:** Assessment which must meet the requirements of the Texas Department of Human Services as well as those of the applicant(s)' own state, if not a Texas resident.

**Average wait for a child after approval of a home study:** 6 -12 mos. but may vary with racial or sex preference.

**Foster care:** Pre-adoptive.

★ 750 ★

**Adopt A Special Kid/Texas, Inc.**
**AASK/Texas, Inc.**
1060 W. Pipeline Rd., Ste. 106
Hurst, TX 76053
Phone: (817) 595-0497
(817) 589-2592 metro

**Contact:** Director of Social Services.

**Date established:** 1992.

**Description:** Private, non-profit adoption agency licensed by the Texas Department of Protective and Regulatory Services and affiliated with AASK AMERICA.

**Area served:** Residents of the U.S.

**Requirements:** Open.

**Fees:** No agency fees. Court costs and attorney fees are the responsibility of the applicant.

**Number of children placed last year:** 27.

**Description of children:** Children with special needs.

**Adoption procedure:** 1) Informational meeting; 2) application process; 3) adoptive parent training; 4) home study; 5) approval; 6) child match; 7) placement; 8) post-placement supervision; 10) finalization.

**Average length of time between application and start of home study:** 2-3 mos.

**Average length of time to complete home study:** 1 mo.

**Number of interviews:** Individual plus family.

**Home study description:** Assessment which meets all the requirements determined by the Texas Department of Protective and Regulatory Services.

**Average wait for a child after approval of a home study:** Within 6 mos. If a placement is not made within 6 mos., the home study must be updated.

**Foster care:** Pre-adoptive and fost-adopt.

★ 751 ★

**Adoption Access, Inc.**
8340 Meadow Rd., No. 231
Dallas, TX 75231
Phone: (214) 750-4847
(800) 373-3484

**Branch address:**
1025 S. Jennings, No. 401, Ft. Worth, TX 76104-3262

**Contact:** Deborah D. Hug, Director; Kimberly Cole, Assistant Director.

**Date established:** 1993.

**Description:** Private child placing agency licensed by the Texas Department of Protective and Regulatory Services.

**Area served:** Residents of the U.S.

**Requirements:** Married couples, one spouse of which must be younger than 50 yrs.

**Fees:** Application and Home Study: $500. Placement: $19,300 for Texas residents, $20,300 for out-of-state. All fees are guaranteed. Applicants are not liable for breaches.

**Number of children placed last year:** 26.

**Description of children:** Caucasian children and children of mixed ethnicity from infancy to age 2 yrs.

**Adoption procedure:** 1) Inquiry; 2) application; 3) home study; 4) child match; 5) placement; 6) post-placement supervision; 7) finalization.

**Average length of time between application and start of home study:** Less than 1 mo.

**Average length of time to complete home study:** 1 mo.

**Number of interviews:** 2.

**Home study description:** Assessment which includes medical, financial and insurance statements, documentation of marriage and divorce, if any, and which addresses such issues as applicants' childhood, marital relationship, feeling about birth parents and issues surrounding adoption, extended family's feelings, expectations for the adopted child, thoughts on child rearing and discipline, motivation and readiness to adopt.

**Average wait for a child after approval of a home study:** 3 - 8 mos.

**Foster care:** Cradle care.

★ 752 ★

**Adoption Advisory, Inc.**
3607 Fairmount
Dallas, TX 75219
Phone: (214) 520-0004
Fax: (214) 522-3502

**Contact:** Mark J. Siegel.

**Date established:** 1985.

**Description:** Non-profit, private agency.

**Area served:** Residents of Texas.

**Requirements:** Each applicant is considered individually but may be no older than 55 yrs. and physically, emotionally and financially capable of caring for a newborn infant.

**Fees:**
Home study: $1650;
adoption fee: $18,300.

**Number of children placed last year:** 46.

**Description of children:** Newborn infants.

**Adoption procedure:**
1) Submit application;
2) if approved, child match;
3) adoption contract signed and fees paid;
4) child placed from hospital with adoptive parents;
5) termination of parental rights filed and hearing held;
6) post-placement supervision;
7) adoption petition filed and hearing held;
8) finalization.

**Average length of time between application and start of home study:** 1 mo. or less.

**Average length of time to complete home study:** 1 mo.

**Number of interviews:** 3.

**Home study description:** Assessment of financial, emotional, and physical capability to care for an infant; attitude toward birthparents; parenting philosophy and methods of discipline; marital stability (if applicable) and goals for a child.

**Average wait for a child after approval of a home study:** 6-12 mos.

**Foster care:** Only in unusual circumstances.

★ 753 ★
**Adoption Advocates**
800 N.W. Loop 410, Ste. 355
San Antonio, TX 78216
Phone: (210) 344-4838

**Contact:** Jane Hall, Executive Director.

**Date established:** 1991.

**Description:** Private, non-profit organization which holds 501(c)(3) tax exemption under the IRS and which is licensed to place children by the Texas Department of Protective and Regulatory Services.

**Area served:** Residents of the U.S.

**Requirements:** Singles or couples married at least 2 yrs. with no more than 2 previous marriages for either spouse. One prospective applicant must be between the ages of 21 and 50 yrs.

**Fees:** Inquiry Application: $25. Adoption Application: $125. Home Study: Contract basis. Agency fee: $7000.

**Number of children placed last year:** 71.

**Description of children:** Primarily newborns, some toddlers and children with special needs.

**Adoption procedure:** 1) Inquiry Application; 2) Adoption Application; 3) acceptance to program; 4) match with birth parent; 5) placement; 6) post-placement supervision; 7) finalization.

**Average length of time between application and start of home study:** Unavailable.

**Average length of time to complete home study:** Unspecified.

**Number of interviews:** Minimum of 3.

**Home study description:** Assessment which includes motivation for adoption, physical, mental and emotional health status of all persons living in the home, quality of marital and family relationships, applicants' feeling about their parents and childhood, values and practices in regard to child care and discipline, feelings about adoption and birth parents, attitude of extended family regarding adoption, expectations and plans for adopted child, documentation of marriage and divorce, if any, police/abuse checks and 3 personal references.

**Average wait for a child after approval of a home study:** 1 - 12 mos.

**Foster care:** Temporary.

★ 754 ★
**Adoption Affiliates, Inc.**
215 W. Olmos Dr.
San Antonio, TX 78212
Phone: (210) 824-9977

**Contact:** Executive Director.

**Date established:** 1987.

**Description:** Non-profit, private agency.

**Area served:** Residents of Oklahoma and Texas.

**Requirements:** Couples must be married and have a relationship of at least two years.

**Fees:** $17,000 inclusive. $8000 for harder to place children.

**Number of children placed last year:** 42.

**Description of children:** Infants.

**Adoption procedure:**
1) Return completed questionnaire;
2) attend information meeting and seminar;
3) complete adoption study;
4) placement;
5) post-placement supervision;
6) finalization.

**Average length of time between application and start of home study:** 6-12 mos.

**Average length of time to complete home study:** 3 mos.

**Number of interviews:** 5 hrs.

**Home study description:** Evaluation of background information, education and employment, personality, marital stability, motivation to adopt, and ability to provide security and stability for for an adopted child.

**Average wait for a child after approval of a home study:** 6-12 mos.

**Foster care:** Temporary.

★ 755 ★
**Adoption Services Associates**
8703 Wurzbach Rd.
San Antonio, TX 78240
Phone: (512) 699-6088
(800) 648-1807
Fax: (210) 691-8836

**Contact:** Linda Zuflacht or Jim Timmens.

**Date established:** 1984.

**Description:** Private, non-sectarian adoption agency licensed by the Texas Dept. of Human Services.

**Area served:** Primarily residents of New Jersey, New York and Texas but work with other U.S. residents.

**Requirements:** U.S. residents who have no more than 2 children in the home and who are in good health. At least one adoptive parent must be younger than 45 yrs.

**Fees:**
Application fee: $225;
adoption fee: $6500 but may vary depending on actual costs.

**Number of children placed last year:** Approx. 150.

**Description of children:** Newborn Anglo and Hispanic infants.

**Adoption procedure:**
1) Initial inquiry;
2) submit application;
3) attend interview;
4) complete home study;
5) if accepted, wait for placement;
6) placement;
7) 6 mos. post-placement supervision;
8) finalization.

**Average length of time between application and start of home study:** Varies.

**Average length of time to complete home study:** Varies.

**Number of interviews:** Varies.

**Home study description:** Assessment of emotions and attitudes surrounding self, marriage, birthparents, adoption, discipline and the attitudes of the extended family on the foregoing.

**Average wait for a child after approval of a home study:** 12-24 mos.

**Foster care:** Temporary.


★ 756 ★

**Adoption Services, Inc.**
3500 Overton Park W.
Fort Worth, TX 76109
Phone: (817) 921-0718

**Contact:** Eileen Anderson Stancukas.

**Date established:** 1987.

**Description:** Private child-placing agency licensed by the Texas Dept. of Human Services.

**Area served:** Residents of north Texas.

**Requirements:** Variable.

**Fees:**
Home study for U.S. child: $950.
Home study for foreign-born child: $950.
Rates for other services vary.

**Number of children placed last year:** Agency does not place children.

**Description of children:** Agency specializes in writing studies for international placements, but will work with applicants who are working with out-of-state or independent placements or toward the adoption of any child. Also works with families adopting from state agencies.

**Adoption procedure:** Adoption Services, Inc. will make referrals to placing agencies or perform home studies for prospective adoptive parents who are currently working with a placing agency of their own choosing. Adoption Services, Inc. will also provide assistance in working with U.S. Immigration and Naturalization for foreign placements and provide post-placement supervision after child has been placed in the adoptive home.

**Average length of time between application and start of home study:** 1 mo. or less.

**Average length of time to complete home study:** 2 mos.

**Number of interviews:** 3.

**Home study description:** Thorough and sensitive evaluations which are adapted to the needs of the placing agency and recognize the needs of the child as the first and highest goal.

**Foster care:** None.


★ 757 ★

**Alternatives in Motion, Inc.**
20619 Aldine-Westfield
Humble, TX 77338
Phone: (713) 776-6508
Fax: (713) 821-0356

**Contact:** Jan Deets or Anne Landry.

**Date established:** 1984.

**Description:** Non-profit, private agency licensed by the Texas Dept. of Human Services.

**Area served:** Non-specific. Agency can operate internationally.

**Requirements:** Each applicant is considered on his/her own merits.

**Fees:**
Orientation: $50;
application: $500;
special needs placement: $3000-$7000;
Hispanic placement: $17,000;
Anglo placement: $17,000.

**Number of children placed last year:** 59.

**Description of children:** Infants and children with special needs.

**Adoption procedure:**
1) Initial inquiry;
2) attend orientation;
3) submit application;
4) complete home study;
5) if approved, wait for placement;
6) placement;
7) post-placement supervision;
8) finalization.

**Average length of time between application and start of home study:** 6-12 mos.

**Average length of time to complete home study:** 1 mo.

**Number of interviews:** 3 or more.

**Home study description:** Assessment of financial reports, verification of marriage(s) and divorce(s) (if applicable), emotions and attitudes surrounding applicant's childhood, parents, marital relationship, infertility (if applicable), expectations of a child, childrearing and methods of discipline, motivation to adopt and adoption-related issues, i.e. birthparents, plans to share adoption information with the child placed and motivation to adopt.

**Average wait for a child after approval of a home study:** 1-6 mos.

**Foster care:** Pre-adoptive.


★ 758 ★

**Andrel Adoptions, Inc.**
3908 Manchaca Rd.
Austin, TX 78704-6736
Phone: (512) 448-4605

**Contact:** Vika Andrel or Trudy McEachern.

**Description:** Private, non-profit corporation licensed to place children by the Texas Department of Protective and Regulatory Services.

**Area served:** Residents of the U.S. with the exception of New York State.

**Requirements:** Couples married for at least 1 yr. who are no older than 55 yrs.

**Fees:** Application: $250. Home study: $750. Placement fee: $4500. ICPC, if any: $350. Post-placement services: $1800. Advertising fee: $1000. Escrow and administration fee: $2500. Birth mother expenses, if applicable: $500 - $5000. Medical fee: $2000.

**Number of children placed last year:** 35.

**Description of children:** Children from birth to 3 yrs., some foreign born and some with special needs.

**Adoption procedure:** 1) Profiles of prospective adoptive applicants shown to birth parents; 2) selection; 3) termination of parental rights after child's birth; 4) placement; 5) post-placement supervision; 6) finalization.

**Average length of time between application and start of home study:** Less than 1 mo.

**Average length of time to complete home study:** 2 wks.

**Number of interviews:** 2.

**Home study description:** Assessment which includes autobiographies, financial reports, physician's report, record of marriage, criminal history clearances, 3 letters of reference, insurance documentation and which addresses such issues as parenting methods, stability of marriage and support from extended family.

**Average wait for a child after approval of a home study:** 6 - 12 mos.

**Foster care:** Cradle care.

★ 759 ★
**Blessed Trinity Adoptions, Inc.**
8507 Havner Ct.
Houston, TX 77037
Phone: (713) 999-7276

**Contact:** Weanell Byrd, Executive Director.

**Date established:** 1989.

**Description:** Private, non-profit child placing agency licensed by the Texas Department of Protective and Regulatory Services.

**Area served:** Residents of the U.S.

**Requirements:** Applicants must be between the ages of 25 and 55 yrs. with no health restrictions. Singles accepted on a case-by-case basis. Couples must be married at least 3 yrs.

**Fees:** Application: $50. Home study: $1000.

**Number of children placed last year:** 110.

**Description of children:** 85% infants, 15% toddlers; 80% Caucasian, 10% Hispanic and 10% African American.

**Adoption procedure:** Unavailable.

**Average length of time between application and start of home study:** Less than 1 mo.

**Average length of time to complete home study:** 3 mos.

**Number of interviews:** 3.

**Home study description:** Assessment which adheres to the requirements of the Texas Department of Protective and Regulatory Services.

**Average wait for a child after approval of a home study:** Up to 2 yrs.

**Foster care:** Temporary.

★ 760 ★
**Catholic Charities of Houston**
3520 Montrose Blvd.
Houston, TX 77006-4350
Phone: (713) 526-4611
(800) 222-9383
Fax: (713) 526-1546

**Branch address:**
18301 Egret Bay, Webster, TX 77598
Phone: (713) 333-9700

**Contact:** Mary Lou Kelly, LMSW.

**Date established:** 1943.

**Description:** Non-profit private agency licensed by the State of Texas.

**Area served:** Residents of Harris and surrounding counties.

**Requirements:** Couples married 2 or more yrs. who are between the ages of 25 and 50 yrs., who have some religious affiliation, who have no more than 1 child, who are in good health and have sufficient income to raise a child.

**Fees:**
$100 application fee
$1000 home study

$8000-$15,000 placement fee
Catholic Charities also offers an Identified Adoption Program in which birthparents come to the agency with a pre-selected family in mind for their unborn child. The Identified Adoption Program carries a separate fee schedule.

**Number of children placed last year:** 30.

**Description of children:** Primarily infants and some children with special needs.

**Adoption procedure:**
1) File application;
2) attend seminars;
3) complete home study;
4) if approved, placement;
5) post-placement supervision;
6) court finalization.

**Average length of time between application and start of home study:** 0-1 mos.

**Average length of time to complete home study:** 6 wks.

**Number of interviews:** 6.

**Home study description:** Evaluation of personal background, maritial history, acceptance of infertility and adoption, motivation to adopt and child preference.

**Average wait for a child after approval of a home study:** 12-24 mos.

**Foster care:** Temporary.

★ 761 ★
**Catholic Counseling Services of Dallas**
3725 Blackburn
Dallas, TX 75219
Phone: (214) 526-2772

**Mailing address:**
P.O. Box 190507, Dallas, TX 75219

**Branch address:**
300 N. Green St., 1216 W. Magnolia, Longview, TX 75601

**Contact:** Bill Betzen or Linda Hall.

**Date established:** 1891.

**Description:** Private, non-profit maternity counseling and adoption agency licensed by the Texas Department of Protective and Regulatory Services.

**Area served:** Residents of 70 counties of Northeast Texas.

**Requirements:** Christian couples, married at least 2 yrs. who are between 23 and 49 yrs. of age and who have completed all the infertility treatments they intend to pursue.

**Fees:** Application: $1000. Home study: $1000. Application, home study, approval and placement fee: $7000 plus 10% of annual income.

**Number of children placed last year:** 28.

**Description of children:** Caucasian, Hispanic, African American and biracial infants.

**Adoption procedure:** 1) Adoption orientation; 2) session with staff member; 3) acceptance; 4) home study; 5) seminar; 6) bi-weekly meetings; 7) placement; 8) post-placement supervision; 9) finalization.

**Average length of time between application and start of home study:** Less than 1 mo.

**Average length of time to complete home study:** 3 - 6 mos.

**Number of interviews:** 3.

**Home study description:** Educational process which complies with all requirements established by the Texas Department of Protective and Regulatory Services.

**Average wait for a child after approval of a home study:** 6 - 12 mos.

**Foster care:** Temporary.

★ 762 ★
**Catholic Family and Children's Services, Inc.**
**Archdiocese of San Antonio**
2903 W. Salinas
San Antonio, TX 78207
Phone: (210) 433-3256

**Branch address:**
  811 E. Mistletoe, San Antonio, TX 78212
  Phone: (210) 734-5054

**Contact:** Adoption coordinator (at branch phone number).

**Date established:** 1941.

**Description:** Non-profit, licensed by the State of Texas as a child-placing agency.

**Area served:** Residents of Bexar and 21 surrounding counties of the Archdiocese of San Antonio.

**Requirements:** Couples married at least 3 yrs. if in a first marriage, if divorced and re-married, at least 5 yrs., between the ages of 25 and 38 yrs., with medical diagnosis of fertility impairment or advice against pregnancy, and who are active members of a major Christian religion.

**Fees:** 20% of gross household income with a minimum of $5000 and a maximum of $15,000.

**Number of children placed last year:** 4.

**Description of children:** Infants only.

**Adoption procedure:**
  1) Attend 9 hrs. of adoptive parent seminars;
  2) complete individual and joint interviews;
  3) home visit;
  4) if approved, placement;
  5) finalization.

**Average length of time between application and start of home study:** 1-6 mos.

**Average length of time to complete home study:** 2 mos.

**Number of interviews:** 5.

**Home study description:** Evaluation of childhood experiences, marital stability and resolution of fertility impairment, health, individual emotional functioning, and attitudes toward adoption.

**Average wait for a child after approval of a home study:** 6-12 mos. for Hispanic infants; 1-2 yrs. for anglo infants.

**Foster care:** Temporary.

★ 763 ★
**Catholic Family Services, Inc.**
**Diocese of Amarillo and Lubbock**
200 S. Tyler St.
Amarillo, TX 79101
Phone: (806) 376-4571
Fax: (806) 345-7911

**Mailing address:**
  P.O. Box 15127, Amarillo, TX 79101

**Contact:** Kathy Caldwell, LSW or Pat Greenwood, LSW.

**Date established:** 1964.

**Description:** Non-profit private agency licensed with the State of Texas which also maintains a registry for adoptees and birthparents which is accessible, with mutual consent, to adoptees and birthparents when the adoptee reaches the age of 21.

**Area served:** Residents of the 46 counties which comprise the Diocese of Amarillo and Lubbock.

**Requirements:** Couples married at least 2 yrs. if in a first marriage for both, 5 yrs. if either has been divorced, who are between the ages of 21 and 45 yrs., who are healthy enough and have sufficient life expectancy to rear a child to adulthood, who have no more than one child and a medical diagnosis of infertility. Exceptions can be made to the eligibility criteria for special needs placements.

**Fees:** Sliding scale based on gross income.

**Number of children placed last year:** 11.

**Description of children:** Infants.

**Adoption procedure:**
  1) Initial inquiry;
  2) attend orientation;
  3) file application with references and medical reports;
  4) complete home study;
  5) if approved, placement;
  6) 6 mos. post-placement supervision;
  7) finalization.

**Average length of time between application and start of home study:** 1-6 mos.

**Average length of time to complete home study:** 15 hrs.

**Number of interviews:** 2-3.

**Home study description:** Evaluation of family background, courtship and integrity of marriage, health and financial reports and attitude toward adoption.

**Average wait for a child after approval of a home study:** 12-24 mos.

**Foster care:** Temporary.

★ 764 ★
**Child Placement Center/Agape Social Services**
8500 N. Stemmons Fwy., Ste. 2080
Dallas, TX 75247
Phone: (214) 631-6784

**Contact:** Suzy Lackmeyer, Executive Director; Janie Hernandez, Administrator.

**Date established:** 1981.

**Description:** Non-profit, private child-placing agency licensed by the Texas Dept. of Human Services.

**Area served:** Residents of the U.S.

**Requirements:** Adults between the ages of 21 and 45 yrs. who are in good health; single or married; if married, marriage must be of at least 3 yrs. duration. Previous marriage is not an impediment and transracial placements are considered.

**Fees:** Sliding scale placement fee, foster care, and travel for non-Texas residents.

**Number of children placed last year:** 40.

**Description of children:** Minority race domestic children and children with significant handicaps.

**Adoption procedure:**
  1) Submit application paperwork;
  2) participate in seminar;
  3) complete home study;
  4) placement;
  5) 6 mos. post-placement supervision;
  6) finalization.

**Average length of time between application and start of home study:** 1-6 mos.

**Average length of time to complete home study:** 6 wks.

**Number of interviews:** 3-4.

**Home study description:** Outlined by licensing entity in Texas.

**Average wait for a child after approval of a home study:** Varies.

**Foster care:** Temporary.

★ 765 ★
**Child Placement Center of Texas**
2212 Sunny La.
Killeen, TX 76541
Phone: (817) 690-5959

**Branch address:**
1 Liberty Pl., 100 N. 6th, Ste. 402, Metro Centre, Ste. 111, 3833 S. Texas Ave., Waco, TX 76701

**Contact:** Samantha Fisher, Director of Interstate Placements.

**Date established:** 1980.

**Description:** Private, non-profit child placing agency licensed by the Texas Department of Protective and Regulatory Services.

**Area served:** Residents of the U.S. with the exception of New York State.

**Requirements:** Singles or couples married at least 3 yrs. whose health is adequate to the task of parenting and who are financially stable. Generally prefer that applicants be between the ages of 24 and 45 yrs. and that the primary caregiver remain home to care for the child for the first 2 mos. after placement. Members of religions which prevent a child from receiving medical care are not accepted.

**Fees:** Application: $100. Placement fee: sliding scale.

**Number of children placed last year:** 40.

**Description of children:** All racial and nationality groups from infancy to early adolescence some with special needs.

**Adoption procedure:** 1) Inquiry; 2) application; 3) home study; 4) complete documentation; 5) first aid and CPR certification; 6) approval; 7) placement; 8) post-placement supervision; 9) finalization.

**Average length of time between application and start of home study:** 1 - 6 mos.

**Average length of time to complete home study:** 2 - 3 mos.

**Number of interviews:** 3 - 4.

**Home study description:** Assessment which includes medical examinations for all family members, statement of income and extent of insurance coverage, marriage and divorce documentation, if applicable, 5 references, pictures of the home and family and vaccination certificates for any household pets and which addresses such issues as applicants' childhood and parents, methods of discipline and expectations of the adopted child, feeling about birth parents, extended family's thoughts about adoption and how to tell child he/she is adopted.

**Average wait for a child after approval of a home study:** 6 - 24 mos.

**Foster care:** Temporary and long-term.

★ 766 ★
**Christian Homes of Abilene**
P.O. Box 270
Abilene, TX
Phone: (915) 677-2205

**Contact:** Margaret Ballew.

**Date established:** 1962.

**Description:** Non-profit maternity home and adoption agency.

**Area served:** Primarily residents of Texas but will occasionally consider out-of-state applicants.

**Requirements:** Preference shown to applicants over 40 yrs. of age, who are in good health, and members of the Christian faith.

**Fees:** Based on sliding scale: $12,500-$21,000.

**Number of children placed last year:** Approx. 40.

**Description of children:** Infants.

**Adoption procedure:** Telephone or write to receive pre-application.

**Average length of time between application and start of home study:** 1-6 mos.

**Average length of time to complete home study:** 2 mos.

**Number of interviews:** 3.

**Home study description:** In compliance with standard set by the Texas Dept. of Human Resources.

**Average wait for a child after approval of a home study:** 6-12 mos.

**Foster care:** No, most placements are direct from the hospital.

★ 767 ★
**Christ's Haven for Children**
P.O. Box 467
Keller, TX 76244
Phone: (817) 431-1544

**Contact:** Diane Davis, MSW, Director of Social Services.

**Date established:** 1958.

**Description:** Private, non-profit child placing agency and group home licensed by the Texas Department of Protective and Regulatory Services and supported by the Church of Christ.

**Area served:** Residents of Texas and nearby locales in Oklahoma.

**Requirements:** Married couples who are in good health and not more than 40 yrs. older than the child they plan to adopt with sufficient income to support a child. First preference is shown to members of the Church of Christ.

**Fees:** Application: $250.

**Number of children placed last year:** 7.

**Description of children:** Children between the ages of 2 and 12 yrs.

**Adoption procedure:** 1) Application; 2) reference checks; 3) home study; 4) placement; 5) post-placement supervision; 6) finalization.

**Average length of time between application and start of home study:** 1 - 6 mos.

**Average length of time to complete home study:** 1 mo.

**Number of interviews:** 4 - 6.

**Home study description:** Assessment which includes family background, medical and psychological information, education and employment, couple's courtship and marriage, views on discipline and dating, church affiliation and the type of child desired.

**Average wait for a child after approval of a home study:** Varies with type of child desired.

**Foster care:** Temporary.

★ 768 ★
**A Cradle of Hope**
**Adoption Counseling Center**
311 N. Market, Ste. 300
Dallas, TX 75202
Phone: (214) 939-3000
(214) 747-4500

**Contact:** Carla Calabrese.

**Date established:** 1991.

**Description:** Private, for profit child placing agency licensed by the Texas Department of Protective and Regulatory Services and conducting designated and international adoptions.

**Area served:** Residents of Texas.

**Requirements:** Open.

**Fees:** Home Study: $600.

**Number of children placed last year:** 18.

**Description of children:** U.S., Romanian and Russian children from infancy to 8 yrs.

**Adoption procedure:** 1) Educational seminar; 2) home study; 3) INS application, if applicable; or, outreach/networking to locate birth family; 4) documentation; 5) support group meetings; 6) child match; 7) placement; 8) post-placement supervision; 9) finalization.

**Average length of time between application and start of home study:** Less than 1 mo.

**Average length of time to complete home study:** 3 wks.

**Number of interviews:** 3.

**Home study description:** Assessment which conforms with the guidelines set by the Texas Department of Protective and Regulatory Services. Center's goal is to be flexible and to develop a personal relationship with the families with whom it works.

**Average wait for a child after approval of a home study:** 12 - 24 mos.

**Foster care:** None.


★ 769 ★
**Cradle of Life Adoption Agency, Inc.**
245 N. 4th St.
Beaumont, TX 77701
Phone: (409) 832-3000

**Contact:** Mel W. Shelander, Director.

**Date established:** 1988.

**Description:** Private child placing agency licensed by the Texas Department of Protective and Regulatory Services.

**Area served:** Residents of Texas.

**Requirements:** Applicants must be between the ages of 24 and 45 yrs., be in good health and affiliated with a main line religion. Couples must be married for at least 3 yrs. If prior marriage, they must be married for 5 yrs.

**Fees:** Application: $50. Home study: $1500. Caucasian infant placement: $14,000 - $19,500. Minority placement: $3000 and up.

**Number of children placed last year:** 13.

**Description of children:** Newborn infants.

**Adoption procedure:** 1) Inquiry form; 2) formal application; 3) references; 4) medicals and financial information; 5) home study interviews; 6) training; 7) placement; 8) post-placement supervision; 9) finalization.

**Average length of time between application and start of home study:** 6 - 12 mos.

**Average length of time to complete home study:** Varies.

**Number of interviews:** 3 - 4.

**Home study description:** Assessment which includes environment of the home, basic care and safety issues, home health, water, firearm and fire safety and in which the following topics and others may be discussed: motivation to adopt, feelings about applicant(s)' childhood, parents and themselves, feeling about children, marital relationship and infertility, helping children understand about adoption, feeling about child's biological parents, readiness of applicant(s)' to adopt, thoughts about discipline, expectations of the child, income and management abilities.

**Average wait for a child after approval of a home study:** 6 - 12 mos.

**Foster care:** Cradle Care.


★ 770 ★
**DePelchin Children's Center**
100 Sandman
Houston, TX 77007
Phone: (713) 861-8136

**Branch address:**
5307 Decker Dr., Ste. 2, Baytown, TX 77520
Phone: (713) 424-3322

18301-A Egret Bay Blvd., Houston, TX 77058
Phone: (713) 333-9700

10435 Greenbough, Stafford, TX 77477
Phone: (713) 499-5681

1520 Lake Front Circle, Ste. 200, The Woodlands, TX 77380
Phone: (713) 367-8003

505 Bains St., Brookshire, TX 77423
Phone: (713) 375-5110

**Contact:** Nelda C. Lewis, Ph.D., LMSW-AP, Adoption Program Director.

**Date established:** 1892.

**Description:** Private, non-profit multi-service agency licensed to place children by the Texas Department of Protective and Regulatory Services, accredited by the Child Welfare League of America and the Joint Commission on Accreditation of Healthcare Organizations and a member agency of the United Way of the Texas Gulf Coast.

**Area served:** Those who live or work in Ft. Bend, Harris, Montgomery or Waller counties.

**Requirements:** Applicants must be at least 21 yrs. old and no more than 40 yrs. older than the child they wish to adopt. Applicants may be single, if married, for at least 2 yrs.

**Fees:** Application: $50. Home study and other fees vary.

**Number of children placed last year:** 37.

**Description of children:** Children of all races from infancy up; some with special needs.

**Adoption procedure:** 1) Orientation meeting; 2) seminar; 3) application; 4) individual interview; 5) wait for child match; 6) placement; 7) post-placement supervision; 8) finalization.

**Average length of time between application and start of home study:** 1 - 6 mos.

**Average length of time to complete home study:** 3 - 6 mos.

**Number of interviews:** Minimum of 4.

**Home study description:** Assessment which includes health, finances, education and employment and in which such topics as applicant(s)' childhood, parenting style, marriage experience (if applicable), infertility resolution (if applicable), readiness to adopt, feelings about birth parents, openness and type of child desired are discussed.

**Average wait for a child after approval of a home study:** Varies according to availability of children and selection by birth parents.

**Foster care:** Temporary, long-term, therapeutic and habilitative.

★ 771 ★
**Gift of Love Adoption Agency**
1420 W. Mockingbird, Ste. 395
Dallas, TX 75247
Phone: (214) 819-2424
(800) 934-2367

**Contact:** Rob Smith, LMSW-ACP, Executive Director.

**Date established:** 1992.

**Description:** Private child placing agency licensed by the Texas Department of Protective and Regulatory Services and a member of the National Association of Social Workers, Academy of Certified Social Workers, Mental Health Association of Greater Dallas and the North American Council on Adoptable Children.

**Area served:** Residents of Texas with limited services to residents of other states.

**Requirements:** Applicants may be no older than 50 yrs. at the time of application with health adequate to the task of parenting. Singles or couples married at least 2 yrs.

**Fees:** Application: $1650.
Brazilian adoption: $14,500.
Minority adoption: $5000 minimum.
  U.S. adoptions: $9500 administration fee plus $10,000 deposit for birth mother expenses with any remaining monies refunded to the adoptive parents.

**Number of children placed last year:** Unavailable.

**Description of children:** Healthy newborn infants and Brazilian children.

**Adoption procedure:** 1) Application; 2) home study; 3) child match; 4) placement; 5) post-placement supervision; 6) finalization.

**Average length of time between application and start of home study:** Less than 1 mo.

**Average length of time to complete home study:** 4 - 8 wks.

**Number of interviews:** 2 - 3 per individual household member.

**Home study description:** Thorough evaluation of applicant(s)' preparedness to parent an adopted child which includes medical exams for each family member, birth and marriage certificates and divorce decrees, if applicable, tax returns, employment verification, adoption decree and copy of any past home study, pictures of family and home and complete background information.

**Average wait for a child after approval of a home study:** 6 - 12 mos.

**Foster care:** Temporary.

★ 772 ★
**The Gladney Center**
2300 Hemphill St.
Fort Worth, TX 76110
Phone: (817) 926-3304

**Contact:** Marilyn Anderson, Director of Adoption (817) 922-6017.

**Date established:** 1887.

**Description:** Private, non-profit residential and community based maternity services and infant placement agency.

**Area served:** U.S.

**Requirements:** Couples who are capable of providing emotional, financial, and marital stability and are of an appropriate age to parent an infant.

**Fees:** Vary depending on program.

**Number of children placed last year:** 250.

**Description of children:** 250 infants (caucasian and minority).

**Adoption procedure:**
  1) Address letter of inquiry to The Gladney Center;
  2) submit information sheet with family background information and photograph;
  3) attend orientation meeting;
  4) return completed formal application;
  5) applicants interviewed jointly, individually and in-home;
  6) if approved, wait for placement.

**Average length of time between application and start of home study:** 1-6 mos.

**Average length of time to complete home study:** 6 mos.

**Number of interviews:** 4.

**Home study description:** Evaluation of emotional, financial, marital and familial stability and the family's readiness to adopt.

**Average wait for a child after approval of a home study:** 6-12 mos.

**Foster care:** Temporary.

★ 773 ★
**High Plains Children's Home & Family Services, Inc.**
1501 W. 58th
Amarillo, TX 79114
Phone: (806) 355-6588

**Mailing address:**
  P.O. Box 7448, Amarillo, TX 79114

**Contact:** Lola Brownlee or Tanya Graham, Maternity-Adoption Caseworker.

**Date established:** 1967.

**Description:** Private, non-profit child placing agency licensed by the Texas Department of Protective and Regulatory Services.

**Area served:** Residents of U.S.

**Requirements:** Couples married at least 3 yrs. who are physically and mentally health and members of the Church of Christ.

**Fees:** Application and home study: $2500. Placement fees: variable.

**Number of children placed last year:** 6.

**Description of children:** Infants.

**Adoption procedure:** 1) Application; 2) references and Criminal Background checks; 3) home study; 4) waiting period; 5) placement; 6) post-placement supervision; 7) finalization.

**Average length of time between application and start of home study:** Less than 1 mo.

**Average length of time to complete home study:** 10 hrs.

**Number of interviews:** 4.

**Home study description:** Assessment which includes attitudes toward adoption, birth parents, relationship between spouses, children and extended family, feelings about childhood and expectations for children adopted and/or biological.

**Average wait for a child after approval of a home study:** 2 yrs. or more.

**Foster care:** Cradle Care.

★ 774 ★
**Homes of St. Mark**
1302 Marshall
Houston, TX 77006
Phone: (713) 522-2800
Fax: (713) 522-3769

**Contact:** Intake worker.

**Date established:** 1957.

**Description:** Non-profit, private adoption and maternity service agency licensed by the Texas Dept. of Human Resources which also provides foster care and post-adoption services.

**Area served:** Residents of Texas.

**Requirements:** Minimum standards mandated by the State of Texas are followed. No arbitrary policies related to age, length of marriage, religion, etc. Birthparents choose adoptive family.

**Fees:** $15,000-$25,000.

**Number of children placed last year:** 28.

**Description of children:** Children of all races and ages are placed.

**Adoption procedure:**
1) Adoption information meeting at which time process is outlined;
2) paper work completed;
3) home study;
4) attend seminar;
5) attend support group for networking/outreach;
6) placement;
7) 6 mos. post-placement supervision;
8) finalization.
Note: Open adoptions are facilitated according to the desires of client.

**Average length of time between application and start of home study:** 1-6 mos.

**Average length of time to complete home study:** Unavailable.

**Number of interviews:** 4 for home study.

**Home study description:** Write for evaluation guidelines.

**Average wait for a child after approval of a home study:** 12-24 months.

**Foster care:** Well established foster care program.

★ 775 ★
**Hope Cottage**
4209 McKinney, Ste. 200
Dallas, TX 75205
Phone: (214) 526-8721
Fax: (214) 528-7168

**Contact:** Doris Marshall.

**Date established:** 1918.

**Description:** Non-profit, private adoption center licensed in the State of Texas and supported by the United Way. Hope Cottage Adoption Center offers a broad range of services to anyone touched by adoption. Largest resource for adoption literature in the Southwest with publications circulating nationwide. Catalogues of publications available upon request.

**Area served:** Within a geographic area which allows for active participation in the center's program. Will facilitate the adoption of families from other states already involved with a birthmother living in Texas.

**Requirements:** Families who embrace the philosophy of openness. Physical examinations required.

**Fees:** Seminar: $150; counseling: $200; home study: $700; adoption services fee range: $4500-$12,000; plus medical and legal expenses. Agency assisted program: unbundled services as needed. Clinical time: $95/hr. plus pass through of all other expenses.

**Number of children placed last year:** 39.

**Description of children:** 67% Caucasian infants and 33% minority infants, 1 child with special needs.

**Adoption procedure:** Prospective applicants may attend a monthly orientation meeting held the 2nd Monday of each month from 6:00 to 8:00 p.m. Application information is available at that time.

**Average length of time between application and start of home study:** 1-6 mos.

**Average length of time to complete home study:** 2-3 mos.

**Number of interviews:** Unavailable.

**Home study description:** Compilation and assessment of information pertaining to the social history of each spouse, their parenting experiences, readiness to adopt, and comfort with identified adoption.

**Average wait for a child after approval of a home study:** 6-12 mos.

**Foster care:** Pre-adoptive.

★ 776 ★
**Inheritance Adoptions**
624 Indiana Ave., Ste. 310
Wichita Falls, TX 76301
Phone: (817) 322-3678

**Mailing address:**
 P.O. Box 2563, Wichita Falls, TX 76301

**Contact:** Vicky Payne, President.

**Date established:** 1993.

**Description:** Private, non-profit child placing agency licensed by the Texas Department of Protective and Regulatory Services.

**Area served:** Residents of the U.S.

**Requirements:** Christian married couples who have a pro-life stand.

**Fees:** Eligibility Requirements: $5. Application: $50 (non-refundable). Home study and legal fees are additional.

**Number of children placed last year:** 2.

**Description of children:** Infants.

**Adoption procedure:** 1) Send $5 for Eligibility Requirements; 2) letter stating reason for choosing adoption; 3) questionnaire; 4) formal application; 5) home study.

**Average length of time between application and start of home study:** 6 - 12 mos.

**Average length of time to complete home study:** Varies.

**Number of interviews:** 2.

**Home study description:** Assessment which includes such topics as the quality of the marital and family relationships, appropriateness and safety of the home for a child and readiness of the family to parent an infant.

**Average wait for a child after approval of a home study:** New agency.

**Foster care:** Temporary.

**★ 777 ★**
**Los Ninos (The Children's) International Adoption Center**
1600 Lake Front Circle, Ste. 130
The Woodlands, TX 77380
Phone: (713) 363-2892
Fax: (713) 363-2896

**Contact:** Jean Erichsen.
**Date established:** 1982.
**Description:** Non-profit, private agency licensed in the State of Texas.
**Area served:** U.S. citizens living in the U.S. or posted abroad.
**Requirements:** Adults between the age of 25 and 50 yrs., of all races and religions, with sufficient income to cover the costs of adoption and raise a child, who are single or married; if married, marriage must be of 1 yr. duration and at least one spouse must be a U.S. citizen.
**Fees:**
Application: $500;
home study (Texas residents only): $900;
international processing fee: $4,000;
foreign program fee: $2,500-$12,000 depending upon country.
**Number of children placed last year:** 98.
**Description of children:** U.S. and foreign-born infants and children of all races and ages.
**Adoption procedure:**
1) Submit application;
2) complete home study;
3) file INS petition;
4) prepare dossier for foreign country;
5) admission to waiting pool;
6) accept assignment of child;
7) travel to foreign country to acquire adoption or guardianship decree. Escort of child to U.S. possible in some countries.
**Average length of time between application and start of home study:** 1 mo. or less.
**Average length of time to complete home study:** 1-2 mos.
**Number of interviews:** 4.
**Home study description:** Assessment of biographical background on adoptive parents and any school age children, marital relationship, lifestyle, educational level, occupation, aspirations, physical description and personality, health and finances, housing, parenting skills, cross-cultural and transracial adoption issues, recommendation of references, police clearance, readiness to adopt, type of child desired and social worker's impressions and recommendations.
**Average wait for a child after approval of a home study:** 1-6 mos.
**Foster care:** None.

**★ 778 ★**
**Loving Alternative Adoption Agency**
P.O. Box 131466
Tyler, TX 75713-1466
Phone: (214) 581-7720

**Contact:** Carol Morgan, Caseworker.
**Date established:** 1987.
**Description:** Non-profit, private agency licensed by the Texas Dept. of Human Resources.
**Area served:** Residents of the State of Texas, east Texas counties specifically.

**Requirements:** Couples married at least 3 yrs. who are between the ages of 25 and 45 yrs., who are members of the same church within the limits of traditional Christianity, who are in good health, who are financially secure with a stable employment record and who believe in the pro-life cause.
**Fees:**
Application fee: $15;
fee of $10,000 due at the time a child is placed in a home.
**Number of children placed last year:** 9.
**Description of children:** Infants, 5 of whom were biracial.
**Adoption procedure:**
1) If eligibility requirements are met, submit preliminary questionnaire;
2) admission to waiting pool;
3) file formal application;
4) agency orientation;
5) complete home study process;
6) if approved, placement.
**Average length of time between application and start of home study:** 6-12 mos.
**Average length of time to complete home study:** 1 wk.-1 mo.
**Number of interviews:** 4.
**Home study description:** Assessment of family history and relationships, growth and development of spiritual life, financial stability and others.
**Average wait for a child after approval of a home study:** 6-24 mos.
**Foster care:** Temporary.

**★ 779 ★**
**Lutheran Social Service of the South (Austin)**
P.O. Box 49589
Austin, TX 78765-9589
Phone: (512) 459-1000
Fax: (512) 452-6855

**Contact:** Karalyn Heimlich.
**Date established:** 1926.
**Description:** Non-profit, private agency affiliated with two major Lutheran synods.
**Area served:** Residents of Texas and Louisiana.
**Requirements:** Couples married at least 2 yrs. who are between the ages of 21 and 45 yrs. who have no more than 1 child. Preference shown to members of Christian congregations. Requirements may be flexible for minority and special needs placements. Requirements for international adoption are dependent on the country.
**Fees:** Sliding scale based on income and the program chosen; flat fee for international adoptions.
**Number of children placed last year:** 106.
**Description of children:** Mostly children aged 0-5 yrs.; older and foreign children. Many of the infant placements were minority children or had special needs.
**Adoption procedure:**
1) Initial inquiry and screening;
2) file application;
3) complete home study with required education;
4) if approved, placement;
5) 6 mos. post-placement supervision;
6) finalization.
**Average length of time between application and start of home study:** 1-6 mos.
**Average length of time to complete home study:** Within 3 mos.

**Number of interviews:** 3 or more.

**Home study description:** Evaluation of individual and marital stability; general attitudes toward children and childrearing; ability to deal with adoption issues; and entitlement assessment.

**Average wait for a child after approval of a home study:** 12-24 mos.

**Foster care:** Temporary.

★ 780 ★
**Lutheran Social Service of the South, Inc. (Dallas)**
3001 LBJ Fwy., No. 107
Dallas, TX 75234
Phone: (214) 620-0581
(800) 622-6697
Fax: (214) 620-0603

**Contact:** Heather Sisler, Director of Children's Services.

**Date established:** 1926.

**Description:** Non-profit, private agency.

**Area served:** Residents of north Texas (part of state-wide agency).

**Requirements:** Couples married at least 2 yrs. who are between the ages of 21 and 45 yrs. who have no more than 1 child and who are members of a Christian congregation (for Anglo infants); flexible for special needs children.

**Fees:**
$13,500-$21,500 for non-black children.

**Number of children placed last year:** 136.

**Description of children:** 66% Anglo infants; 33% special needs; 1% international.

**Adoption procedure:** Intake is always open for black, black/biracial and Hispanic families or special needs. Provide agency assisted services for families who identified their own birthmother.

**Average length of time between application and start of home study:** Varies, 2 or more yrs. for Anglo infants.

**Average length of time to complete home study:** 2-3 mos.

**Number of interviews:** Varies.

**Home study description:** Assessment of applicants' ability to provide a stable home.

**Average wait for a child after approval of a home study:** Varies.

**Foster care:** Temporary.

★ 781 ★
**Marywood Children and Family Services**
510 W. 26th St.
Austin, TX 78705
Phone: (512) 472-9251
Fax: (512) 472-4829

**Contact:** Carolyn Chamberlain, Program Director.

**Date established:** 1921.

**Description:** Private, non-profit, non-sectarian, Diocesan-sponsored children and family service agency licensed by both the Texas Dept. of Health and the Texas Dept. of Human Services and partially funded by United Way.

**Area served:** Residents of Texas; occasionally work with out of state families.

**Requirements:** Serve singles and two parent families, over the age of 21.

**Fees:** Depending on program (Marywood now offers four adoption programs). Home study: $700.

**Number of children placed last year:** 60.

**Description of children:** Infants, older children, sibling groups.

**Adoption procedure:**
1) Initial telephone inquiry;
2) adoption information meeting;
3) preliminary information form approval;
4) undergo adoption study process;
5) placement;
6) 6 mos. post-placement supervision;
7) finalization (process varies according to program).

**Average length of time between application and start of home study:** 1-6 mos.

**Average length of time to complete home study:** 4-6 wks.

**Number of interviews:** 3 or more.

**Home study description:** Assessment of general background information on family, employment, health, fertility, financial budget, motivation to adopt, feelings about birthparents, flexibility in the type of child applicants think they can parent, etc. Includes training session for prospective adoptive families.

**Average wait for a child after approval of a home study:** 6-12 mos.

**Foster care:** Marywood offers temporary foster care as well as therapeutic foster care.

★ 782 ★
**Lee and Beulah Moor Children's Home**
1100 Cliff Dr.
El Paso, TX 79902
Phone: (915) 544-4114
Fax: (915) 532-1368

**Contact:** Carol Shulse, LMSW-ACP, Adoption/Foster Care Director.

**Date established:** 1958.

**Description:** Non-profit private agency licensed by the State of Texas.

**Area served:** El Paso geographical area.

**Requirements:** Couples married at least 2 yrs. who are in good emotional and physical health, who have sufficient income to care for a child and who have some religious faith.

**Fees:** 20% of annual income with a ceiling of $12,000.

**Number of children placed last year:** 13.

**Description of children:** Infants 0-6 mos. old, occasionally children 1-10 yrs. of age.

**Adoption procedure:**
1) Attend group seminar;
2) have joint interview;
3) have individual interviews;
4) home visit;
5) reference interviews;
6) complete psychological survey;
7) submit health forms;
8) placement;
9) post-placement supervisory; and
10) finalization.

**Average length of time between application and start of home study:** 6-12 mos.

**Average length of time to complete home study:** 3 mos.

**Number of interviews:** 5.

**Home study description:** Evaluation of quality of marriage; personality functioning; child rearing philosphy; etc.

**Average wait for a child after approval of a home study:** 6-12 mos.

are not escaped.

**Foster care:** Temporary, long-term and permanent.

## ★ 783 ★
**New Life Christian Services**
19911 State Hwy. 249
Houston, TX 77070
Phone: (713) 955-1001

**Contact:** Sara Black, Director.

**Date established:** 1983.

**Description:** Non-profit, private child-placing agency licensed by the Texas Dept. of Human Resources.

**Area served:** Residents of Texas.

**Requirements:** Couples married at least 3 yrs. who are between the ages of 21 and 39 yrs., who are in good health and financially stable and who are professing Christians and recognize Jesus Christ as Lord and Savior.

**Fees:** $14,000.

**Number of children placed last year:** 15.

**Description of children:** Infants.

**Adoption procedure:**
1) Initial inquiry;
2) return completed Adoption Inquiry Letter and Forms packet;
3) attend Pre-Adoption Counseling Session in the NLSC office;
4) submit a completed application;
5) participate in individual counseling conducted by NLCS social worker;
6) have home study interview in applicants' home;
7) attend an Adoptive Preparation Seminar;
8) wait for placement;
9) placement;
10) meet and share with birthparents;
11) 6 or more mos. post-placement supervision;
12) finalization.

**Average length of time between application and start of home study:** 6-12 mos.

**Average length of time to complete home study:** 1 mo.

**Number of interviews:** 3 plus seminar.

**Home study description:** Call or write for guidelines.

**Average wait for a child after approval of a home study:** 12-24 mos.

**Foster care:** Temporary.

## ★ 784 ★
**Placement Services Agency**
P.O. Box 797365
Dallas, TX 75379
Phone: (214) 387-3312

**Contact:** Barbra Silverman, MSSW, CSW-ACP.

**Date established:** 1990.

**Description:** Private, non-profit child placing agency licensed by the Texas Department of Protective and Regulatory Services, member of the Inter-Agency Council and the National Association of Social Workers (NASW).

**Area served:** Residents of the Dallas-Ft.Worth Metroplex area.

**Requirements:** Open.

**Fees:** Home Study: $500. Travel costs may be additional.

**Number of children placed last year:** Agency conducts home studies and post-placment supervision, but does not place children.

**Description of children:** N/A.

**Average length of time to complete home study:** 2 wks. - 1 mo.

**Number of interviews:** Minimum of 3.

**Home study description:** Assessment which includes background of applicant(s), education, employment, references, criminal history checks, finances, physical and mental health, residence, marital history, any children in the home, the type of child desired and which addresses such issues as child care and discipline, motivation to adopt, infertility and other adoption-related topics.

**Average wait for a child after approval of a home study:** Agency does not do placements.

**Foster care:** None.

## ★ 785 ★
**Stoker Adoption Agency**
1435 Sweetbriar Cir.
Odessa, TX 79761
Phone: (915) 362-2113
Fax: (915) 550-9944

**Contact:** Carole Stoker, Director.

**Date established:** 1986.

**Description:** Private child placement agency licensed by the Texas Department of Protective and Regulatory Services.

**Area served:** Residents of Texas.

**Requirements:** Open.

**Fees:** Home Study: $2000. Travel, counseling and extra expenses are not included.

**Number of children placed last year:** 2.

**Description of children:** Newborn infants.

**Adoption procedure:** Agency conducts primarily closed adoptions, but will facilitate open adoptions when both parties prefer.

**Average length of time between application and start of home study:** 12 - 24 mos.

**Average length of time to complete home study:** 4 hrs.

**Number of interviews:** 2 in-person and 4 contacts.

**Home study description:** Assessment which includes descriptions of applicants, home and background and which addresses such issues as marital hisotry, if applicable, lifestyle, beliefs and expectations of the adopted child.

**Average wait for a child after approval of a home study:** Home studies are not conducted until a child becomes available.

**Foster care:** None.

## ★ 786 ★
**The Texas Cradle Society**
8600 Wurzbach Rd., Ste. 1110
San Antonio, TX 78240-4334
Phone: (512) 225-5151

**Contact:** Dorothy H. Barkley, Executive Director.

**Date established:** 1936.

**Description:** Non-profit, private agency.

**Area served:** Residents of the states of New Jersey and Texas.

**Requirements:** Couples married at least 3 yrs. who are at least 25 yrs. old and no older than 39 for the placement of a first child and no older than 44 for the placement of a second child, who are both U.S. citizens and who have no more than 1 child already in the home.

**Fees:**
Inquiry fee: $25.

Application fee: $30.

Reimbursement fees range from $7000 to $10,000 and are based on family income.

**Number of children placed last year:** 29.

**Description of children:** Full Anglo, full Hispanic, Anglo/Hispanic, black/Anglo, black/Hispanic and black.

**Adoption procedure:**
1) Submit Preliminary Application (Inquiry);
2) file application;
3) complete home study;
4) if approved, placement;
5) complete adoption study during post-placement supervision;
6) finalization.

**Average length of time between application and start of home study:** 6 mos.

**Average length of time to complete home study:** 9-12 mos.

**Number of interviews:** 5.

**Home study description:** Compilation of all documents required by Texas or New Jersey or other states (under the Interstate Compact on the Placement of Children) to determine the stability of the applicant family.

**Average wait for a child after approval of a home study:** 1 yr., substantially shorter for a black or biracial child.

**Foster care:** Temporary.

★ 787 ★

**Leslie Thacker Agency, Inc.**
1760 Harold St.
Houston, TX 77098
Phone: (713) 524-5794

**Branch address:**
911 Twentieth St., Galveston, TX 77550

**Contact:** Leslie Thacker.

**Date established:** 1978.

**Description:** Private adoption agency licensed by the Texas Dept. of Human Resources.

**Area served:** Open.

**Requirements:** Varies with type of child requested.

**Fees:** Varies by program.

**Number of children placed last year:** Unavailable.

**Description of children:** Infants, older children, some with a correctable physical defect - all Texas residents.

**Adoption procedure:** Call or write for guidelines.

**Average length of time between application and start of home study:** Varies.

**Average length of time to complete home study:** Unavailable.

**Number of interviews:** 2-3.

**Home study description:** Assessment of medical and financial reports, religion, education and occupation and recommendation of references.

**Average wait for a child after approval of a home study:** Varies.

**Foster care:** Temporary.

★ 788 ★

**Trinity Adoption Services International, Inc.**
7610 Club Lake
Houston, TX 77095
Phone: (713) 855-0042

**Contact:** Ronald Byrd, President.

**Date established:** 1992.

**Description:** Private, non-profit child placing agency licensed by the Texas Department of Protective and Regulatory Services.

**Area served:** No geographic restrictions.

**Requirements:** Single or married at least 2 yrs.

**Fees:** Application: $50. Home study: varies. Other fees: $0 - $12,500.

**Number of children placed last year:** 20.

**Description of children:** Infants of all races.

**Adoption procedure:** 1) Inquiry; 2) application; 3) home study; 4) child match and wait for placement; 5) placement; 6) post-placement supervision; 7) finalization.

**Average length of time between application and start of home study:** Less than 1 mo.

**Average length of time to complete home study:** 2 mos.

**Number of interviews:** Unavailable.

**Home study description:** Assessment which meets the criteria of the Texas Department of Protective and Regulatory Services.

**Average wait for a child after approval of a home study:** 1 - 6 mos.

**Foster care:** Pre-adoptive.

# UTAH

## STATUTES

★ 789 ★

**Independent placement by intermediary?** Permitted.

**Independent placement by birth parents?** Permitted.

**Subsidies provided?** Non-recurring for legal and other reasonable expenses; on-going for medical and maintenance.

**Adoption cost defined by law?** No.

**Insurance for infertility?:** No.

**Home study required by state?** Required before placement with visits and post-placement reports required before finalization.

**Prospective adoptive parent advertise for a child?** Permitted.

**Surrogacy laws?** Permitted.

**Residents access agencies of other states or countries?** Permitted.

**Requires judicial termination of birth parents' rights?** Relinquishments at least 24 hrs. after the birth of the child are recognized if done before an officer of the court including an attorney.

**Time given to a birthmother to revoke her consent:** None.

**Court handling adoptions?** District Court although cases are sometimes heard in Juvenile Court.

**Adoption of Native Children:** Tribal courts.

**Adoption records sealed?** Yes.

**Photo-listing book available?** Participates in the photo listing of the Rocky Mountain Adoption Exchange.

# PUBLIC AGENCIES

★790★
**Utah Department of Social Services**
645 E. 4500 S.
Salt Lake City, UT 84117
Phone: (801) 468-5465

**Mailing address:**
 P.O. Box 45500, Salt Lake City, UT 84117
**Branch address:**
 522 North 100 East, Blanding, UT 84511
 Phone: (801) 678-3211

 1050 South 500 West, Brigham City, UT 84302
 Phone: (801) 723-8591

 106 North 100 East, Cedar City, UT 84720
 Phone: (801) 586-3842

 1350 East 1420 South, P.O. Box 825, Clearfield, UT 84015
 Phone: (801) 776-7300

 252 W. Main, Ste, B-1, Delta, UT 84624
 Phone: (801) 864-3869

 115 W. Center, Kanab, UT 84741
 Phone: (801) 644-5885

 95 West 1st South, Logan, UT 84321
 Phone: (801) 752-2511

 50 S. Main, Ste. 5, Manti, UT 84642
 Phone: (801) 835-2161

 267 N. Main, Moab, UT 84532
 Phone: (801) 259-6128

 Main and Courthouse, P.O. Box 112, Nephi, UT 84648
 Phone: (801) 623-1927

 2540 Washington Blvd., P.O. Box 349, Ogden, UT 84402
 Phone: (801) 626-3300

 565 N. Main, Panguitch, UT 84659
 Phone: (801) 676-8866

 90 North 1st East, Price, UT 84501
 Phone: (801) 637-6850

 150 E. Center St., Provo, UT 84601
 Phone: (801) 374-7005

 855 East 2nd North, Roosevelt, UT 84066
 Phone: (801) 722-2445

 645 East 4500 South, Salt Lake City, UT 84107
 Phone: (801) 264-7500

 168 North 100 East, St. George, UT 84770
 Phone: (801) 673-9691

 305 N. Main, Tooele, UT 84014
 Phone: (801) 833-7350

 1052 W. Market Dr., Vernal, UT 84078
 Phone: (801) 789-5946
**Contact:** Darrell E. Bingham, Adoption Supervisor.

**Description:** Public agency.
**Area served:** Resident of the State of Utah.
**Requirements:** Couples, married at least 2 yrs., who are at least 21 yrs. old and within normal parental age of the adopted child and who are in good health. Preference shown to applicants willing to consider special needs children.
**Fees:**
$500 application fee
$300 home study.
**Number of children placed last year:** 96.
**Description of children:** Special needs.
**Adoption procedure:**
 1) Attend orientation;
 2) file application;
 3) complete home study;
 4) if approved, placement;
 5) 6 or more mos. post-placement supervision;
 6) finalization.
**Average length of time between application and start of home study:** Approx. 30 days.
**Average length of time to complete home study:** 30-45 days.
**Number of interviews:** 3-4.
**Home study description:** Call or write for guidelines.
**Average wait for a child after approval of a home study:** Approx. 9 mos. Minority applicants may have shorter wait.
**Foster care:** Temporary, long-term and permanent.

# PRIVATE AGENCIES

★791★
**An Act of Love**
**Alternative Options & Services for Children**
11638 S. High Mountain Dr.
Sandy, UT 84092
Phone: (801) 266-7615

**Branch address:**
 785 W. Chesapeake Cir., Murray, UT 84123
**Contact:** Kathy Kunkel or Kathy Searle.
**Date established:** 1993.
**Description:** Private, non-profit child placing agency licensed by the Utah Department of Human Services.
**Area served:** Residents of the U.S.
**Requirements:** Very open.
**Fees:** Application: $150. Home study: $500.
Processing and placement fees vary from program to program.
**Number of children placed last year:** 12.
**Description of children:** Children from infancy to school age, some foreign-born and some with special needs.
**Adoption procedure:** 1) Application; 2) intake interview; 3) home study; 4) parenting classes; 5) placement; 6) post-placement supervision; 7) finalization.
**Average length of time between application and start of home study:** Less than 1 mo.
**Average length of time to complete home study:** 3 - 4 wks.
**Number of interviews:** 3.
**Home study description:** Educational and assessment process which meets the requirements of the Utah Department of Human Services.

**Average wait for a child after approval of a home study:** Newborn Caucasian infant: 6-12 mos. Briefer wait for toddlers and older children.

**Foster care:** None.

### ★ 792 ★
**Children's Aid Society of Utah**
652 26th St.
Ogden, UT 84401
Phone: (801) 393-8671
Fax: (801) 394-3324

**Contact:** Sharol Waddoups, Executive Director.

**Date established:** 1910.

**Description:** Non-profit, private agency licensed by the Utah Dept. of Social Services.

**Area served:** Residents of the State of Utah.

**Requirements:** Couples married at least 3 yrs. who are under the age of 45 yrs., who are financially stable, infertile, or unable to bring a pregnancy to term, and have one or no children.

**Fees:**
Application fee: $325;
home study: $800;
placement fee: 16% of gross annual income.

**Number of children placed last year:** Not for publication.

**Description of children:** U.S. infants.

**Adoption procedure:**
1) Attend orientation;
2) submit paperwork;
3) complete interview process with social worker including 1 home visit;
4) if approved, wait for placement (birthmother takes part in selection through non-identifying information).

**Average length of time between application and start of home study:** 1-6 mos.

**Average length of time to complete home study:** 2 mos.

**Number of interviews:** 4-5.

**Home study description:** Evaluation of biographical and social information, physical descriptions, education and employment history, health and finances, home and environment, attitudes toward childbearing, and criminal and child abuse background screening.

**Average wait for a child after approval of a home study:** 12-24 or more mos.

**Foster care:** None.

### ★ 793 ★
**Children's Service Society of Utah**
576 E. South Temple
Salt Lake City, UT 84102
Phone: (801) 355-7444
Fax: (801) 355-7453

**Contact:** Marty Shannon.

**Date established:** 1883.

**Description:** Non-profit child placement agency licensed by the State Department of Social Services.

**Area served:** Infant adoption: residents of the State of Utah. Special needs adoption: residents within 100 mi. radius of Salt Lake City.

**Requirements:** For healthy infant adoption, couples married 3 or more yrs., neither of whom has been divorced more than once, who are between the ages of 24 and 45 yrs., in good health, and who have no more than 1 child. For special needs adoption, applicants are assessed on a case by case basis.

**Fees:**
Infants: Application fee: $200; home study fee: $220; placement fee: 16% of gross family income, minimum $6,000, maximum $14,000.
Special needs: Applicaton fee: $220; no home study fee; placement fee: 5% of gross family income up to $3000; training class $20 per person or $40 per couple.

**Number of children placed last year:** 25.

**Description of children:** 12 healthy Caucasian and biracial infants; 13 special needs children of all ages, races; some sibling groups.

**Adoption procedure:**
Infant Adoption:
1) Attend orientation;
2) file application;
3) complete home study;
4) attend support groups/matching phase;
5) placement;
6) 6 mos. post-placement supervisory;
7) finalization.
Special Needs Adoption:
1) Attend training class;
2) file application;
3) complete home study;
4) wait for placement;
5) placement;
6) 1 yr. post-placement supervisory;
7) finalization.

**Average length of time between application and start of home study:** 1 mo. or less.

**Average length of time to complete home study:** Infant: 1 mo.

**Number of interviews:**
Infant: 1-2;
special needs: 9-10.

**Home study description:** Evaluation which includes but is not limited to family, marital stability, parenting skills, financial stability and expectations for a child.

**Average wait for a child after approval of a home study:** 6-12 mos.

**Foster care:** None.

### ★ 794 ★
**LDS Social Services of Ogden**
2515 Lincoln Ave.
Ogden, UT 84404
Phone: (801) 621-6510

**Contact:** Thomas S. Craner, LCSW.

**Date established:** 1919.

**Description:** Non-profit private agency.

**Area served:** Residents of North Davis and Weber counties.

**Requirements:** Couples married at least 3 yrs. who are active members of the Church of Jesus Christ of Latter Day Saints who were referred by their local bishop and who were married in L.D.S. temple.

**Fees:**
$400 application fee for infant;
$100 application fee for special needs;
$4000 total fees for infant adoption;

$1000 total fees for special needs.

**Number of children placed last year:** 11.

**Description of children:** Infants and special needs.

**Adoption procedure:**
1) Complete series of interviews;
2) attend group preparation class.

**Average length of time between application and start of home study:** 6-12 mos.

**Average length of time to complete home study:** 6 mos.

**Number of interviews:** 6 group classes and 3 other interviews.

**Home study description:** Evaluation of such information which allows the agency to assure the child is placed in a safe and secure home.

**Average wait for a child after approval of a home study:** 12-24 mos.

**Foster care:** Short-term voluntary.

★ 795 ★
**Wasatch Adoptions and Children's Services**
290 W. 200 N
Kaysville, UT 84037
Phone: (801) 825-4440

**Branch address:**
1491 W. 2700 S., Syracuse, UT 84075

**Contact:** Fred or Charlene Carlson.

**Date established:** 1991.

**Description:** Private, non-profit charitable agency licensed to place children by the Utah Department of Human Services.

**Area served:** Residents of Utah.

**Requirements:** Applicants should be younger than 55 yrs., at least 10 yrs. older than the child to be adopted and in good health.

**Fees:** Application: $400 - $800. Home study: $300. Identified Adoption/International Adoption Fees: $7000 - $8500.

**Number of children placed last year:** 8.

**Description of children:** Primarily infants. International program recently added.

**Adoption procedure:** 1) Contact; 2) home study; 3) if approved, application; 4) wait for placement and child match; 5) placement; 6) post-placement supervision; 7) finalization.

**Average length of time between application and start of home study:** 6 - 12 mos.

**Average length of time to complete home study:** 1.5 mos.

**Number of interviews:** 2 - 3.

**Home study description:** Assessment which meets the requirements of the Utah Department of Human Services and includes as much background information as possible including Criminal Records and Child Abuse Registry checks.

**Average wait for a child after approval of a home study:** 6 - 12 mos.

**Foster care:** Short term.

★ 796 ★
**West Sands Adoptions**
461 East 2780 N.
Provo, UT 84604
Phone: (801) 377-4379
Fax: (801) 377-8627

**Contact:** Weston E. Whatcott, Executive Director.

**Date established:** 1993.

**Description:** Private, non-profit child placing agency which holds 501(c)(3) tax exemption under the IRS and licensed by the Utah Department of Human Services.

**Area served:** Primarily residents of Utah.

**Requirements:** Applicants must be at least 21 yrs. old, in good health, and have a stable income which they manage prudently.

**Fees:** Application: $50. Home study: $350. Post-placement services: $150. Transportation, legal costs, boarding and other fees: $4500 - $8000.

**Number of children placed last year:** 2.

**Description of children:** Taiwanese and Indian toddlers, some with special needs.

**Adoption procedure:** 1) Inquiry; 2) application; 3) home study; 4) acceptance by screening committee; 5) INS documentation; 6) child assignment; 7) placement by child escort; 8) post-placement supervision; 9) finalization; 10) naturalization.

**Average length of time between application and start of home study:** Less than 1 mo.

**Average length of time to complete home study:** 1 - 2 mos.

**Number of interviews:** 4 - 6.

**Home study description:** Assessment which meets the requirements of the Utah Department of Human Services and which also addresses the ability of the applicant(s)' to meet the needs of a foreign-born child and to parent a child of a different race.

**Average wait for a child after approval of a home study:** 6 - 12 mos.

**Foster care:** None.

# VERMONT

## STATUTES
★ 797 ★

**Independent placement by intermediary?** Permitted.

**Independent placement by birth parents?** Permitted.

**Subsidies provided?** Medical, legal and maintenance.

**Adoption cost defined by law?** No.

**Insurance for infertility?:** Legislation pending.

**Home study required by state?** Required after placement.

**Prospective adoptive parent advertise for a child?** Permitted.

**Surrogacy laws?** Permitted.

**Residents access agencies of other states or countries?** Permitted.

**Requires judicial termination of birth parents' rights?** Execution of an affidavit by both birth parents.

**Time given to a birthmother to revoke her consent:** 10 days.

**Court handling adoptions?** Probate.

**Adoption of Native Children:** Tribe.

**Adoption records sealed?** Yes, but at age 21 yrs. or older adoptees may access non-identifying information, unless consents for disclosure are on file with the Probate Court to release identifying information.

**Photo-listing book available?** Participates in the photo listing of the Northern New England Adoption Exchange.

# PUBLIC AGENCIES

**★ 798 ★**
**Social and Rehabilitative Services of Vermont**
103 S. Main St.
Waterbury, VT 05671
Phone: (802) 241-2131
Fax: (802) 241-2980

**Branch address:**

255 N. Main St., Barre, VT 05641
Phone: (802) 479-4260

1193 North Ave., Burlington, VT 05401
Phone: (802) 863-7370

Rte. 1, Box 929, Morrisville, VT 05661-9724
Phone: (802) 888-4576

173 West St., Rutland, VT 05701
Phone: (802) 773-5817

262 River St., Springfield, VT 05156-2306
Phone: (802) 885-4501

42 Eastern Ave., St. Johnsbury, VT 05819
Phone: (802) 748-8374

**Contact:** Diane Dexter, Adoption Coordinator.

**Description:** Public state agency for Vermont.

**Area served:** Residents of Vermont.

**Requirements:** Each family is evaluated individually.

**Fees:** Sliding scale.

**Number of children placed last year:** 50.

**Description of children:** Children with special needs.

**Adoption procedure:**
1) Submit application;
2) participate in Parent Preparation Groups;
3) complete home study;
4) if approved, wait for placement;
5) placement;
6) 6 mos. post-placement supervision;
7) finalization.

**Average length of time between application and start of home study:** Varies.

**Average length of time to complete home study:** 3 mos.

**Number of interviews:** 2-3.

**Home study description:** Self-study process wherein the following information is considered: childhood, marriage, infertility (if applicable), lifestyle, interests, communication methods, parenting skills and attitudes, type of child desired, etc.

**Average wait for a child after approval of a home study:** Varies.

**Foster care:** Emergency, short and long-term and legal risk.

# PRIVATE AGENCIES

**★ 799 ★**
**The Adoption Centre**
278 Pearl St.
Burlington, VT 05401
Phone: (802) 862-5855

**Contact:** Coizie Bettinger, Director.

**Date established:** 1990.

**Description:** Private, non-profit child placing agency licensed by the New York Department of Social Services and the Vermont Department of Social and Rehabilitative Services.

**Area served:** Residents of Vermont and neighboring areas of New York State.

**Requirements:** Open.

**Fees:** Application: $100. Home study and post-placement services: $1500 - $2500.

**Number of children placed last year:** 35.

**Description of children:** US infants and toddlers, both Caucasian and minority and foreign born children.

**Adoption procedure:** 1) Inquiry; 2) application; 3) home study process; 4) adoption preparation group; 5) international agency referral; 6) child referral; 7) placement; 8) post-placement supervision; 9) finalization.

**Average length of time between application and start of home study:** Less than 1 mo.

**Average length of time to complete home study:** 3 mos.

**Number of interviews:** 3 - 6.

**Home study description:** Assessment which includes preparation for adoption and which covers such topics as family background, relationship with spouse, children and extended family, home and job, motivation to adopt, experience with and attitudes toward children.

**Average wait for a child after approval of a home study:** 1 - 24 mos. depending upon program selected.

**Foster care:** None.

**★ 800 ★**
**Adoption Resource Service, Inc.**
1904 North Ave.
Burlington, VT 05401
Phone: (802) 863-5368

**Contact:** Shirley Hammond.

**Date established:** 1988.

**Description:** Non-profit, private agency licensed in the State of Vermont.

**Area served:** Residents of Vermont only.

**Requirements:** Open.

**Fees:**
Intake interview: $25;
home study (domestic): $1300 includes post-placement services;
home study (inter-country): $1600 includes post-placement services.

**Number of children placed last year:** 20.

**Description of children:** Black or bi-racial.

**Adoption procedure:**
1) Attend intake meeting;
2) sign agreement;
3) complete home study;
4) referral to placement agency.

**Average length of time between application and start of home study:** 1 mo. or less.

**Average length of time to complete home study:** 6 wks.

**Number of interviews:** 3-6.

**Home study description:** Evaluation of family and social history, medical and financial reports, education and attitudes pertinent to parenting and adoption.

**Average wait for a child after approval of a home study:** 6-12 mos.

**Foster care:** None.

**★801★**
**Vermont Catholic Charities, Inc.**
351 North Ave.
Burlington, VT 05401
Phone: (802) 658-6110
Fax: (802) 860-4511

**Branch address:**
24 1/2 Center St., Rutland, VT 05701
Phone: (802) 773-3379

**Contact:** Mary M. McNamara, Supervisor of Professional Services.

**Date established:** 1939.

**Description:** Private agency licensed by the State of Vermont.

**Area served:** Residents of the State of Vermont.

**Requirements:** Couples in a valid Catholic marriage for at least 3 yrs. who are no older than 35 yrs. at time of application and no older than 38 yrs. at time of placement, at least one of whom must be a practicing Catholic. Priority is given to childless couples. Age and marital requirement may be waived for special needs.

**Fees:** 9% of annual income.

**Number of children placed last year:** Unavailable.

**Description of children:** Infants, foreign-born and children with special needs.

**Adoption procedure:**
1) Return completed adoption questionnaire with a signed physician's statement regarding fertility problem;
2) placement on inquiry list;
3) complete home study;
4) if approved, names added to waiting list for placement;
5) placement;
6) supervisory period;
7) finalization.

**Average length of time between application and start of home study:** Varies.

**Average length of time to complete home study:** 4 mos.

**Number of interviews:** 3 or more office and 1 or more home visits.

**Home study description:** Evaluation of birth and marriage certificates, medical forms, financial statement, and formal application including references.

**Average wait for a child after approval of a home study:** Varies.

**Foster care:** Temporary.

**★802★**
**Vermont Children's Aid Society, Inc.**
79 Weaver St.
Winooski, VT 05404
Phone: (802) 655-0006
Fax: (802) 655-0073

**Mailing address:**
P.O. Box 127, Winooski, VT 05404

**Branch address:**
56 1/2 Merchants Row, Rutland, VT 05701
Phone: (802) 773-8555

32 Pleasant St., Woodstock, VT 05091

Phone: (802) 457-3084

**Contact:** Alice Siegriest, Executive Director.

**Date established:** 1919.

**Description:** Non-profit private agency licensed in Vermont and western New Hampshire.

**Area served:** Residents of the State of Vermont and Western New Hampshire.

**Requirements:** Eligibility of applicants depends upon available children and prospective adoptive family's ability to cope with their existing situation.

**Fees:** Sliding scale.

**Number of children placed last year:** 61.

**Description of children:** 10 white infants; 8 black infants; 22 foreign-born; 3 Hispanic infants; 15 biracial infants; 3 children with special needs; mostly infants but some older.

**Adoption procedure:**
1) Attend informational meeting;
2) file application;
3) complete home study;
4) if approved, placement;
5) post-placement supervision; and
6) finalization.

**Average length of time between application and start of home study:** 0-1 mos.

**Average length of time to complete home study:** 2-4 mos.

**Number of interviews:** 5-8.

**Home study description:** Evaluation which centers on family's ability to understand and cope with adoption and the particular issues surrounding the child they adopt.

**Average wait for a child after approval of a home study:** Depends on which program family chooses.

**Foster care:** Short-term pre-adoptive for infants only.

# VIRGINIA

## STATUTES

★803★

**Independent placement by intermediary?** Illegal.

**Independent placement by birth parents?** Permitted.

**Subsidies provided?** Medical, legal, maintenance and funds for any service the child would have received had he/she remained in foster care.

**Adoption cost defined by law?** No.

**Insurance for infertility?:** No.

**Home study required by state?** Required.

**Prospective adoptive parent advertise for a child?** Permitted.

**Surrogacy laws?** Permitted.

**Residents access agencies of other states or countries?** Permitted.

**Requires judicial termination of birth parents' rights?** Voluntary relinquishments by both birth parents are recognized.

**Time given to a birthmother to revoke her consent:** Until the child is 25 days old and 15 days have elapsed from the signing of the voluntary relinquishment.

**Court handling adoptions?** Circuit Court.

**Adoption of Native Children:** Local jurisdiction working through the ICWA.

**Adoption records sealed?** Yes, but at age 18 yrs. and older adoptees may access non-identifying information and identifying information with the consent of the birth parent(s).

**Photo-listing book available?** Adoption Resource Exchange of Virginia (AREVA) Photo Listing Book.


## PUBLIC AGENCIES

### ★ 804 ★
**Albermarle Department of Social Services**
401 McIntyre Rd.
Charlottesville, VA 22902
Phone: (804) 972-4010

**Mailing address:**
P.O. Box 297, Charlottesville, VA 22902

**Contact:** Carolyn Pettit.

**Description:** Public county agency mandated to place children by the Virginia Department of Social Services.

**Area served:** Residents of Albermarle County.

**Requirements:** Open.

**Fees:** Home study: $540 average.

**Number of children placed last year:** 15.

**Description of children:** Children with special needs and infants.

**Adoption procedure:** 1) Application; 2) home study; 3) placement; 4) post-placement supervision; 5) finalization.

**Average length of time between application and start of home study:** 1 - 6 mos.

**Average length of time to complete home study:** 2 mos.

**Number of interviews:** 3 - 4.

**Home study description:** Albermarle County conducts home studies for stepparent, grandparent and parental placements. All others are referred to other state agencies contracted by the State of Virginia.

**Average wait for a child after approval of a home study:** Dependent on the type of child requested.

**Foster care:** Temporary, long-term and permanent.


### ★ 805 ★
**Bristol Department of Social Services**
621 Washington St.
Bristol, VA 24201
Phone: (703) 645-7450
Fax: (703) 645-7475

**Contact:** Kay Kovacs or Robert Gose.

**Date established:** 1938.

**Description:** Public welfare agency mandated to place children by the Virginia Department of Social Services.

**Area served:** Residents of Bristol City.

**Requirements:** Open.

**Fees:** None.

**Number of children placed last year:** 5.

**Description of children:** Caucasian and African American children from infancy to 10 yrs., most with special needs.

**Adoption procedure:** 1) Application; 2) home study; 3) placement; 4) post-placement supervision; 5) finalization.

**Average length of time between application and start of home study:** 1 - 6 mos.

**Average length of time to complete home study:** 60 - 90 days.

**Number of interviews:** 6.

**Home study description:** Assessment which includes Criminal History and Child Abuse Record checks, physical examinations including a TB test, home health and safety inspections including family's fire escape plan, background information, early history, current lifestyle, experience with children, motivation to adopt and understanding of adopted children's needs.

**Average wait for a child after approval of a home study:** 2 yrs. or more.

**Foster care:** Temporary, long-term and permanent.


### ★ 806 ★
**Brunswick Department of Social Services**
228 Main St.
Lawrenceville, VA 23868
Phone: (804) 848-2142

**Mailing address:**
P.O. Box 89, Lawrenceville, VA 23868

**Contact:** Maureen J. Harris, Director.

**Date established:** 1938.

**Description:** Public county welfare agency mandated to place children by the Virginia Department of Social Services.

**Area served:** Residents of Brunswick County, Virginia.

**Requirements:** Open.

**Fees:** Home study: Sliding scale.

**Number of children placed last year:** 4.

**Description of children:** Children with special needs and infants.

**Adoption procedure:** 1) Application; 2) home study; 3) child search through other state welfare agencies and AREVA; 4) placement; 5) post-placement supervision; 6) finalization.

**Average length of time between application and start of home study:** 1 - 6 mos.

**Average length of time to complete home study:** 1 mo.

**Number of interviews:** 1 - 3.

**Home study description:** Assessment which includes educational and medical history, financial and reference reports, verification of marriage and other children's births, if applicable.

**Average wait for a child after approval of a home study:** 12 - 24 mos.

**Foster care:** Short and long-term and therapeutic.


### ★ 807 ★
**Caroline Department of Social Services**
P.O. Box 430
Bowling Green, VA 22427-0430
Phone: (804) 633-5071

**Contact:** Teresa A. Bettino, Senior Social Worker.

**Description:** Public welfare agency mandated to place children by the Virginia Department of Social Services.

**Area served:** Residents of Caroline County.

**Requirements:** Applicants must be at least 18 yrs. old.

**Fees:** Home Study: Sliding scale.

**Number of children placed last year:** 0.

**Adoption procedure:** Follows regimen set by the Virginia Department of Social Services.

Average length of time between application and start of home study: Unavailable.

Average length of time to complete home study: Unavailable.

Number of interviews: Unavailable.

Home study description: Home studies are child specific. No home study will be conducted until a child has been matched with a prospective adoptive home.

Average wait for a child after approval of a home study: Immediate.

Foster care: Temporary, long-term and permanent.

★808★

**Clarke County Department of Social Services**
32 E. Main St.
Berryville, VA 22611-1338
Phone: (703) 955-3700
Fax: (703) 955-3958

Contact: Mrs. Angie Jones, Director.

Description: Public welfare agency mandated to place children by the Virginia Department of Social Services.

Area served: Residents of Clarke County.

Requirements: Open.

Fees: Home Study: Sliding scale.

Number of children placed last year: 4.

Description of children: Children with special needs.

Adoption procedure: Follows regimen set by the Virginia Department of Social Services.

Average length of time between application and start of home study: 1 - 6 mos.

Average length of time to complete home study: Unavailable.

Number of interviews: Unavailable.

Home study description: Assessment which includes financial and medical reports, home and community and which addresses such topics as religion, thoughts on discipline and child rearing.

Average wait for a child after approval of a home study: 2 yrs. or more.

Foster care: Temporary, long-term and permanent.

★809★

**Danville Division of Social Services**
510 Patton St.
Danville, VA 24543
Phone: (804) 799-6552
(804) 799-6543
Fax: (804) 799-5102

Mailing address:
  P.O. Box 3300, Danville, VA 24543

Contact: Deborah A. Mahan, Child Welfare Supervisor.

Description: Public welfare agency mandated to place children by the Virginia Department of Social Services.

Area served: Residents of the City of Danville.

Requirements: Applicants must be at least 18 yrs. old.

Fees: Home study: Sliding scale.

Number of children placed last year: 6.

Description of children: Infants and sibling groups.

Adoption procedure: Follows regimen set by the Virginia Department of Social Services.

Average length of time between application and start of home study: 6 - 12 mos.

Average length of time to complete home study: 3 mos.

Number of interviews: 6.

Home study description: Assessment which meets all the requirements of the Virginia Department of Social Services and includes a criminal background check.

Average wait for a child after approval of a home study: 2 yrs. or more, but is dependent on the type of child requested.

Foster care: Temporary, long-term and permanent.

★810★

**Hampton Department of Social Services**
1320 LaSalle Ave.
Hampton, VA 23669
Phone: (804) 727-1947
(804) 727-1800
Fax: (804) 727-1835

Contact: Jane D. Gleason, MSW, Adoption Worker.

Date established: 1940's.

Description: Public welfare agency mandated to place children by the Virginia Department of Social Services.

Area served: Residents of Hampton, VA.

Requirements: Flexible.

Fees: None.

Number of children placed last year: Less than 10.

Description of children: Children of all ages with special needs and African American infants.

Adoption procedure: 1) Inquiry; 2) application; 3) office visit; 4) adoption group training; 5) documentation; 6) home visit; 7) approval; 8) placement; 9) post-placement supervision; 10) finalization.

Average length of time between application and start of home study: 2 mos.

Average length of time to complete home study: 3 - 6 mos.

Number of interviews: 5 - 6.

Home study description: Assessment and preparation which includes adoption training classes, Child Protective Services and police checks, the reports of references, medical and financial reports, autobiographies and background information and in which motivation to adopt and the type of child desired are discussed.

Average wait for a child after approval of a home study: Children younger than 5 yrs.: 1 - 2 yrs. Children older than 6 yrs.: 1 - 12 mos.

Foster care: Temporary, long-term and permanent.

★811★

**Henry County Department of Social Services**
P.O. Box 788
Collinsville, VA 24078-0788
Phone: (703) 634-4750
(800) 476-6535
Fax: (703) 632-0542

Contact: Debbie St. John or Alice T. Price.

Description: Public welfare agency mandated to place children by the Virginia Department of Social Services.

Area served: Residents of Henry County.

Requirements: Applicants must be at least 18 yrs. old and have sufficient income to meet their own needs.

Fees: Fees based on income for home studies.

**Number of children placed last year:** 5.

**Description of children:** Infants, one placed independently.

**Adoption procedure:** 1) Application; 2) home study; 3) placement; 4) post-placement supervision; 5) finalization.

**Average length of time between application and start of home study:** Less than 1 mo.

**Average length of time to complete home study:** 6 mos.

**Number of interviews:** Minimum of 5.

**Home study description:** Assessment which includes the status of the applicant(s)' physical, emotional and mental health, financial stability, marital relationship and which addresses such topics as applicant(s)' knowledge of child development, expectations of adoption, ability to parent a non-related child and the suitability of the home to the placement.

**Average wait for a child after approval of a home study:** 12 - 24 mos.

**Foster care:** Temporary and permanent.

★ 812 ★
**Hopewell Department of Social Services**
256 E. Cawson St.
Hopewell, VA 23860-2804
Phone: (804) 541-2330
(804) 748-0151

**Contact:** Peggy Trickler, Senior Social Worker.

**Description:** Public welfare agency mandated to place children by the Virginia Department of Social Services.

**Area served:** Primarily residents of Hopewell, VA.

**Requirements:** None.

**Fees:** None.

**Number of children placed last year:** 2.

**Description of children:** Infant and child, both with special needs.

**Adoption procedure:** Follows regimen set by the Virginia Department of Social Services.

**Average length of time between application and start of home study:** 30 -60 days.

**Average length of time to complete home study:** 2 - 4 mos.

**Number of interviews:** 3.

**Home study description:** Assessment which includes background and family history, Child Protective Services and criminal history searches, medicals, personal and employment references and the family's current situation.

**Average wait for a child after approval of a home study:** 2 yrs. or more.

**Foster care:** Temporary, long-term and permanent.

★ 813 ★
**Isle of Wight Department of Social Services**
17100 Monument Cir., Ste. A
Isle of Wight, VA 23397-0110
Phone: (804) 365-0880
Fax: (804) 365-0886

**Contact:** Ruth Butler.

**Description:** Public welfare agency mandated to place children by the Virginia Department of Social Services.

**Area served:** Residents of Isle of Wight County, VA.

**Requirements:** Open.

**Fees:** Home Study: Based on household size and income. Additional fees charged for Criminal Record check and Child Protective Services check.

**Number of children placed last year:** 4.

**Description of children:** 1 child with special needs and 3 African American boys younger than 5 yrs.

**Adoption procedure:** 1) Inquiry; 2) application; 3) home study; 4) placement; 5) sign adoptive placement agreement; 6) post-placement supervision; 7) finalization.

**Average length of time between application and start of home study:** 1 - 6 mos.

**Average length of time to complete home study:** 3 - 6 mos.

**Number of interviews:** Minimum of 3.

**Home study description:** Assessment which includes Criminal Record and Child Protective Services searches, reference reports and medicals, employment and income verification, marriage and divorce, if applicable, documentation, education, home and community and in which adoption and its lifelong ramifications are discussed.

**Average wait for a child after approval of a home study:** 6 - 12 mos.

**Foster care:** Temporary, long-term and permanent.

★ 814 ★
**James City Department of Social Services**
5249 Olde Town Rd.
Williamsburg, VA 23188
Phone: (804) 565-6855

**Contact:** Carolyn Stout, Social Worker.

**Description:** Public welfare agency mandated to place children by the Virginia Department of Social Services.

**Area served:** Residents of James City County, VA.

**Requirements:** Open.

**Fees:** Unavailable.

**Number of children placed last year:** 0.

**Description of children:** N/A.

**Adoption procedure:** Agency conducts only court ordered adoptions.

**Average length of time between application and start of home study:** 1 - 6 mos.

**Average length of time to complete home study:** 90 days.

**Number of interviews:** 3.

**Home study description:** Assessment which follows the requirements found in the service manual of the Virginia Department of Social Services.

**Average wait for a child after approval of a home study:** Agency does not make placements.

**Foster care:** Short and long-term.

★ 815 ★
**Nelson Department of Social Services**
P.O. Box 357
Lovington, VA 22949
Phone: (804) 263-8334
Fax: (804) 263-8605

**Contact:** Thomas Conner.

**Description:** Public welfare agency mandated to place children by the Virginia Department of Social Services.

**Area served:** Residents of Nelson County.

**Requirements:** Open.

**Fees:** Home Study: Sliding scale.

**Number of children placed last year:** Unavailable.

**Description of children:** Unavailable.

**Adoption procedure:** Follows regimen authorized by the Virginia Department of Social Services.

**Average length of time between application and start of home study:** Unavailable.

**Average length of time to complete home study:** Unavailable.

**Number of interviews:** Unavailable.

**Home study description:** Assessment which includes a Criminal History and Child Protective Services searches and which meets the requirements of the Virginia Department of Social Services.

**Average wait for a child after approval of a home study:** 2 yrs. or more.

**Foster care:** Temporary, long-term and permanent.

---

★816★

**Newport News Department of Social Services**
Rouse Tower
6060 Jefferson Ave.
Newport News, VA 23605
Phone: (804) 247-2300

**Contact:** Mary Hutchens, Senior Social Worker.

**Date established:** 1935.

**Description:** Public welfare agency mandated to place children by the Virginia Department of Social Services.

**Area served:** Residents of Newport News, VA.

**Requirements:** Open.

**Fees:** Home study: sliding scale.

**Number of children placed last year:** Unavailable.

**Description of children:** Unavailable.

**Adoption procedure:** Follows regimen determined by the Virginia Department of Social Services. Agency will also facilitate independent and stepparent adoptive placements.

**Average length of time between application and start of home study:** Unavailable.

**Average length of time to complete home study:** Unavailable.

**Number of interviews:** Unavailable.

**Home study description:** Assessment which includes searches of Criminal History and Child Protective Services' records and which seeks to place each child in the home best suited to his/her particular needs.

**Average wait for a child after approval of a home study:** Unavailable.

**Foster care:** Temporary, long-term and permanent.

---

★817★

**Nottoway Department of Social Services**
Business US 460 and VA Rt. 625
Nottoway, VA 23955
Phone: (804) 645-8494

**Mailing address:**
   P.O. Box 26, Nottoway, VA 23955

**Contact:** Bernetta Watkins, Social Worker Supervisor.

**Date established:** 1930's.

**Description:** Public welfare agency mandated to place children by the Virginia Department of Social Services.

**Area served:** Residents of Nottoway County, VA.

**Requirements:** Flexible.

**Fees:** Home study: varies.

**Number of children placed last year:** 2.

**Description of children:** Toddlers.

**Adoption procedure:** Agency follows regimen set by the Virginia Department of Social Services.

**Average length of time between application and start of home study:** Determined by child availability.

**Average length of time to complete home study:** Wide variation.

**Number of interviews:** 5 - 15.

**Home study description:** Assessment which seeks to gauge the stability and nurturing ability of the prospective adoptive family as well as their potential for bonding with the adopted child.

**Average wait for a child after approval of a home study:** Determined by child availability.

**Foster care:** Temporary, long-term and permanent.

---

★818★

**Portsmouth Department of Social Services**
1701 High St.
Portsmouth, VA 23704-2417
Phone: (804) 398-3600

**Contact:** Amelia R. Thompson, Senior Social Worker.

**Description:** Public welfare agency mandated to place children by the Virginia Department of Social Services.

**Area served:** Residents of Portsmouth, VA.

**Requirements:** Applicants must be older than 21 yrs. and be financially self-sufficient.

**Fees:** Home Study: Based on income and family size.
Attorney fees for private adoptions and criminal history
   searches are extra.

**Number of children placed last year:** 13.

**Description of children:** Fost-adopt conversions.

**Adoption procedure:** 1) Application; 2) home study; 3) placement (if child not already being fostered in the prospective adoptive home); 4) post-placement supervision; 5) finalization.

**Average length of time between application and start of home study:** 1 - 6 mos.

**Average length of time to complete home study:** 90 days.

**Number of interviews:** 3.

**Home study description:** Assessment which includes education and employment history, character references, criminal history and child abuse/neglect registry search, medical reports, home environment and neighborhood/community involvement and the extended family.

**Average wait for a child after approval of a home study:** 12 - 24 mos.

**Foster care:** Short-term.

---

★819★

**Pulaski Department of Social Services**
143 Third St., N.W.
Pulaski, VA 24301
Phone: (703) 980-7995

**Mailing address:**
   P.O. Box 110, Pulaski, VA 24301

**Contact:** Annette Jenkins, Social Worker.

**Description:** Public welfare agency mandated to place children by the Virginia Department of Social Services.

**Area served:** Residents of Pulaski County, VA.

**Requirements:** Applicants must be older than 18 yrs. and physically and financially capable of caring for a child.

**Fees:** Adoption search: Based on income.

**Number of children placed last year:** 1.

**Description of children:** Pre-schooler.

**Adoption procedure:** 1) Application; 2) home study; 3) child search through state adoption exchange; 4) pre-placement visitation; 5) placement; 6) post-placement supervision; 7) file adoption petition; 8) adoption report filed in circuit court; 9) finalization; 10) child evaluated for subsidies.

**Average length of time between application and start of home study:** 1 - 6 mos.

**Average length of time to complete home study:** 3 mos.

**Number of interviews:** 3.

**Home study description:** Assessment which includes personal background, references, medical reports including TB tests, criminal history and Child Protective Services searches, education and employment history, verifications of birth and marriage and the physical environment of the home.

**Average wait for a child after approval of a home study:** School age: 1 - 2 yrs. Infants: 2 yrs. or more.

**Foster care:** Temporary, long-term and permanent.

★ 820 ★
**Radford Department of Welfare and Social Services**
208 Third Ave.
Radford, VA 24141-4706
Phone: (703) 731-3658
(703) 731-3663

**Contact:** Suzanne G. Glass, Supervisor or Mary Lou Lamb, Senior Social Worker.

**Date established:** 1935.

**Description:** Public welfare agency mandated to place children by the Virginia Department of Social Services.

**Area served:** Residents of the City of Radford.

**Requirements:** Open.

**Fees:** None.

**Number of children placed last year:** 0.

**Description of children:** N/A.

**Adoption procedure:** 1) Application; 2) home study; 3) placement; 4) post-placement supervision; 5) finalization.

**Average length of time between application and start of home study:** 1 - 6 mos.

**Average length of time to complete home study:** 6 mos.

**Number of interviews:** 4 - 6.

**Home study description:** Assessment which includes, personal, medical and financial information.

**Average wait for a child after approval of a home study:** 2 yrs. or more.

**Foster care:** Temporary, long-term and permanent.

★ 821 ★
**City of Richmond Department of Social Services**
900 E. Marshall St.
Richmond, VA 23219-1538
Phone: (804) 780-7428
(804) 780-7430
Fax: (804) 780-7018

**Contact:** Jane Talley, Program Administrator.

**Date established:** Earlier than 1930.

**Description:** Public welfare agency mandated to place children by the Virginia Department of Social Services.

**Area served:** Residents of the City of Richmond and nearby.

**Requirements:** Open.

**Fees:** Criminal background check: $15. Adoption Petition filing: $20.

**Number of children placed last year:** 47.

**Description of children:** African American children between the ages of 5 and 12 yrs. with special needs.

**Adoption procedure:** Follows regimen set by the Virginia Department of Social Services and is the responsibility of the caseworker to facilitate.

**Average length of time between application and start of home study:** 1 - 6 mos.

**Average length of time to complete home study:** 4 - 6 mos.

**Number of interviews:** Varies.

**Home study description:** Assessment which includes a criminal background check, current medical information and reference reports and in which the topics of the applicant(s)' ability to raise a child not born to them and the significance of the marital relationship, if applicable, are discussed.

**Average wait for a child after approval of a home study:** African American children 5 yrs. and older: Less than 1 mo. Caucasian infant: 2 yrs. or more.

**Foster care:** Short and long-term, permanent.

★ 822 ★
**Russell County Department of Social Services**
P.O. Box 1207
Lebanon, VA 24266-1207
Phone: (703) 889-3031
(703) 889-2679
Fax: (703) 889-2662

**Contact:** Catherine L. Sandefur, Adoption Supervisor.

**Description:** Public welfare agency mandated to place children by the Virginia Department of Social Services.

**Area served:** Residents of Russell County, VA.

**Requirements:** Open.

**Fees:** Home study: sliding scale.

**Number of children placed last year:** Unavailable.

**Description of children:** Unavailable.

**Adoption procedure:** 1) Inquiry; 2) application; 3) home study; 4) placement; 5) post-placement supervision; 6) finalization.

**Average length of time between application and start of home study:** 1 - 6 mos.

**Average length of time to complete home study:** Unavailable.

**Number of interviews:** Unavailable.

**Home study description:** Written assessment comprising approximately 15 pages which describes the prospective adoptive applicant(s) from birth to the present.

**Average wait for a child after approval of a home study:** Unavailable.

**Foster care:** Short and long-term and permanent.

**★ 823 ★**
**Virginia Department of Social Services**
**Bureau of Child Welfare Services**
Theatre Row Bldg.
730 E. Broad St.
Richmond, VA 23219
Phone: (800) DO-ADOPT
Fax: (804) 692-1284

**Contact:** Adoption worker.

**Description:** Public, state agency.

**Area served:** Residents of the State of Virginia.

**Requirements:** Flexible.

**Fees:** None.

**Number of children placed last year:** 350.

**Description of children:** Primarily children with special needs.

**Adoption procedure:** Procedures vary county by county and agency by agency. The 800-DO-ADOPT number will direct an applicant to the most appropriate agency.

**Average length of time between application and start of home study:** 1-6 mos.

**Average length of time to complete home study:** 6 wks. - 3 mos.

**Number of interviews:** Unavailable.

**Home study description:** Assessment includes but is not limited to criminal records and child abuse registry checks, health, finances and moral suitability, ability to parent a child not born to the applicant, family history and education and the suitability of the child to be placed.

**Average wait for a child after approval of a home study:** 6-12 mos.

**Foster care:** Emergency, short and long-term, pre-adoptive, therapeutic and Independent Living Program.

**★ 824 ★**
**York/Poquoson Department of Social Service**
301 Goodwin Neck Rd.
Yorktown, VA 23692
Phone: (804) 890-3959
(804) 890-3930
Fax: (804) 890-3934

**Mailing address:**
P.O. Drawer 917, Yorktown, VA 23692

**Contact:** Carolyn Dodd, Supervisor, Child & Family Services.

**Description:** Public welfare agency mandated to place children by the Virginia Department of Social Services and conducting fost-adopt conversions and parental placement adoptions.

**Area served:** Residents of the City of Poquoson and York County, VA.

**Requirements:** Open.

**Fees:** Home Study: Sliding scale.

**Number of children placed last year:** 9.

**Description of children:** 8 infants placed through parental placements and 1 agency placement.

**Adoption procedure:** 1) Inquiry; 2) training and educational classes; 3) individual assessment; 4) wait for placement; 5) placement; 6) post-placement supervision; 7) finalization.

**Average length of time between application and start of home study:** 1 - 6 mos.

**Average length of time to complete home study:** Unavailable.

**Number of interviews:** 4 - 6.

**Home study description:** Process with an educational component which seeks to determine the applicant(s) stability and ability to parent a child not born to them. During the study which includes a home visit a variety of issues surrounding adoption are investigated.

**Average wait for a child after approval of a home study:** Unavailable.

**Foster care:** Temporary, long-term and permanent.

## PRIVATE AGENCIES

**★ 825 ★**
**Catholic Charities of Richmond, Inc.**
1512 Willow Lawn Dr.
Richmond, VA 23230-0565
Phone: (804) 285-5900
Fax: (804) 285-9130

**Mailing address:**
P.O. Box 6565, Richmond, VA 23230-0565

**Contact:** Barbara Smith, Adoption Coordinator.

**Date established:** 1923.

**Description:** Non-profit private agency licensed in the State of Virginia.

**Area served:** Residents of Virginia.

**Requirements:** Couples married at least 3 yrs., who are between the ages of 25 and 45 yrs.

**Fees:**
Domestic: $6,500 plus medical fees;
intercountry: $2,370 home study fee plus foreign fees.

**Number of children placed last year:** 54.

**Description of children:** U.S. and foreign children between the ages of 0 and 15 yrs.; some with special needs.

**Adoption procedure:**
1) Register;
2) file application;
3) complete home study;
4) if approved, placement;
5) post-placement supervisory; and
6) finalization.

**Average length of time between application and start of home study:** 1-6 mos.

**Average length of time to complete home study:** 3 mos.

**Number of interviews:** 8.

**Home study description:** Evaluation of social history, educational and occupational background; marital history; finances; criminal clearances; and expectations of parenthood.

**Average wait for a child after approval of a home study:** 12-24 mos.

**Foster care:** Temporary/short-term.

★ 826 ★
**Catholic Charities of Southwestern Virginia, Inc.**
820 Campbell Ave., S.W.
Roanoke, VA 24016-3536
Phone: (703) 344-5107
(800) 296-2367
Fax: (703) 344-2748

**Contact:** Adoption intake worker. Steve Ankiel , Executive Director.

**Description:** Non-profit, private child-placing agency licensed by the Virginia Dept. of Social Services.

**Area served:** Residents of the area from Harrisonburg to Bristol and from Appomattox to Grundy.

**Requirements:** Vary according to the type of child requested. No religious affiliation.

**Fees:**
Application fee: $75;
home study: $1,000;
placement fee: 10% of gross income;
intrastate processing fee (if applicable): $150.

**Number of children placed last year:** 30.

**Description of children:** U.S. and foreign-born infants.

**Adoption procedure:** Follows state procedures.

**Average length of time between application and start of home study:** 1-6 mos.

**Average length of time to complete home study:** Varies according to arrival of documentation.

**Home study description:** Assessment which includes but is not limited to recommendation of references, employment verification, autobiographies, criminal and CPS reviews, and MMPI assessments.

**Average wait for a child after approval of a home study:** 6-12 mos.

**Foster care:** Temporary.

★ 827 ★
**Catholic Charities of the Diocese of Arlington, Inc.**
3838 Cathedral Ln.
Arlington, VA 22203
Phone: (703) 841-2531
(800) 227-3002
Fax: (703) 425-2886

**Branch address:**
5294 Lyngate Ct., Burke, VA 22015
Phone: (703) 425-0100

1011 Berryville Ave., No. 1, Winchester, VA 22601
Phone: (703) 667-7940

13 S. West St., Alexandria, VA 22314
Phone: (703) 548-4227

612 Lafayette Blvd., No. 50, Fredericksburg, VA 22401

**Contact:** Helen Patricia Mudd, Director of Children's Service or intake worker (703) 425-0100.

**Date established:** 1947.

**Description:** Non-profit voluntary agency licensed in the State of Virginia.

**Area served:** Residents of the Diocese of Arlington.

**Requirements:** Couples in a valid Catholic marriage for at least 3 yrs., at least one of whom is a practicing Catholic, who are no older than 37 yrs. at time of application for a 1st placement and no older than 39 yrs. for a 2nd placement, who are in good health with a normal life expectancy; and who have completed a fertility work-up. Some requirements may be waived for minority, special needs or foreign adoption.

**Fees:** Sliding scale based on income with a minimum of $3600 and a maximum of $14,900. Home study only: $1350.

**Number of children placed last year:** 51; 21 placed by agency; balance provided by social services.

**Description of children:** Healthy white infants, special needs, minority and foreign-born children.

**Adoption procedure:**
1) Telephone inquiry and screening;
2) attend group informational meeting;
3) file application;
4) attend 4 wk. educational seminar;
5) complete individual home study.

**Average length of time between application and start of home study:** 0-1 mos.: foreign or parental placement; 12-24 mos.: Caucasian infant.

**Average length of time to complete home study:** 6-8 wks.

**Number of interviews:** 4-8.

**Home study description:** Study follows guidelines set by the State of Virginia and includes individual and marital adjustment, resolution of infertility, applicants' and extended family's attitudes and information about adoption, motivation to adopt and discussion of child desired.

**Average wait for a child after approval of a home study:** 12-24 mos.

**Foster care:** Temporary.

★ 828 ★
**Children's Home Society of Virginia**
4200 Fitzhugh Ave.
Richmond, VA 23230
Phone: (804) 353-0191

**Branch address:**
1620 5th St., S.W., Roanoke, VA 24016

**Contact:** Peter M. Pufki.

**Date established:** 1900.

**Description:** Non-profit, private, non-sectarian agency licensed by the Virginia Dept. of Social Services.

**Area served:** Residents of the Commonwealth of Virginia.

**Requirements:** Couples married at least 3 yrs. who are between the ages of 25 and 40 yrs. and have no more than 1 child. Applicants for special needs placements should be no more than 45 yrs. older than the child placed and may be single.

**Fees:** Application fee: $100. Study and supervision are on a sliding scale.

**Number of children placed last year:** 73.

**Description of children:** Infants and children with special needs.

**Adoption procedure:**
1) Initial inquiry;
2) submit application;
3) complete home study;
4) child search;
5) pre-placement visits (if older child);
6) placement;
7) 6 mos. post-placement supervision;
8) finalization.

**Average length of time between application and start of home study:** Varies depending on need for families.

**Average length of time to complete home study:** 10-12 wks.

**Number of interviews:** 5 or more.

**Home study description:** Assessment of applicants' childhood, lifestyle, relationships, parenting skills, interests and activities, employment, finances and health.

**Average wait for a child after approval of a home study:** Varies depending on child's availability and family's reach.

**Foster care:** Short-term.

★ 829 ★
**Coordinators/2, Inc.**
4206 Chamberlayne Ave.
Richmond, VA 23227
Phone: (804) 264-1026
Fax: (804) 264-1810

**Contact:** C. Lynne Edwards, Program Coordinator.

**Date established:** 1989.

**Description:** Private, non-profit child placing agency licensed by the Virginia Department of Social Services.

**Area served:** Residents of the Commonwealth of Virginia.

**Requirements:** Applicants must be at least 18 yrs. old.

**Fees:** Home Study: 2.5% of gross annual income with a maximum of $2000.
1.5% of gross annual income with a maximum of $800 for special needs placements.
Supervision: $600-$1200.
Intercountry fees for Russian program are additional.

**Number of children placed last year:** 65.

**Description of children:** Older children, sibling groups, African American children and Russian children. Infants available through parental placement.

**Adoption procedure:** 1) Application; 2) home study; 3) 2 educational workshops; 4) submission and review of written materials and exercises; 5) placement; 6) post-placement supervision; 7) finalization.

**Average length of time between application and start of home study:** Less than 1 mo.

**Average length of time to complete home study:** 2 mos.

**Number of interviews:** 3 - 4.

**Home study description:** Health, financial and social information is collected. Information about the differences between birth and adoptive parenting is shared. Worker and applicant(s) assess family's ability to respond to the differences and help adoptee cope with loss or losses and unique issues at each developmental stage.

**Average wait for a child after approval of a home study:** 6 - 12 mos.

**Foster care:** None.

★ 830 ★
**The Datz Foundation**
404 Pine St., Ste. 202
Vienna, VA 22180
Phone: (703) 242-8800
(800) 829-5683

**Branch address:**
4545 42nd St., Ste. 307, 16220 Frederick Rd., Ste. 404, Washington, DC 20016

875 Walnut St., Ste. 275-23, Gaithersburg, MD 20877

**Date established:** 1987.

**Description:** Private child placement agency non-profit and licensed by the Virginia Department of Social Services, the District of Columbia Department of Human Services and the Maryland Department of Social Services and for profit and licensed by the North Carolina Department of Social Services and providing intercountry and identified agency assisted adoption.

**Area served:** Full service for residents of D.C., Maryland, North Carolina and Virginia; placement for residents of the U.S.

**Requirements:** Flexible.

**Fees:** Application: $120; home study: $1050; placement: $5000 - $15,000; post-placement services: $300/visit.

**Number of children placed last year:** 60.

**Description of children:** U.S. infants and children; infants and children from China, Costa Rica, Guatemala, Latvia, Russia and Vietnam.

**Adoption procedure:** Out of area residents: 1) Provide agency with a home study from a licensed agency in their state of residence; 2) personal consultation is desirable, but not mandatory.
Area residents: 1) Inquiry; 2) application; 3) home study; 4) program selection.

**Average length of time between application and start of home study:** Less than 1 mo.

**Average length of time to complete home study:** 6 wks. - 2 mos.

**Number of interviews:** 3.

**Home study description:** Assessment which includes physical descriptions of all family members, home and community, family background information, criminal clearances, medical reports and salary verifications and which addresses such issues as maturity and emotional stability, compatibility and marital satisfaction, parenting abilities, feelings about children, interests, daily routine, religion, discipline practices, feelings about adoption, birth parents and motivation to adopt and the type of child desired.

**Average wait for a child after approval of a home study:** Minority domestic: Less than 1 mo. International: 6 - 12 mos.

**Foster care:** Temporary.

★ 831 ★
**Family Life Services**
1000 Villa Rd.
Lynchburg, VA 24503
Phone: (804) 847-6806
(800) LG-CHILD
Fax: (804) 384-3730

**Contact:** Ruth J. Towns, Director.

**Date established:** 1983.

**Description:** Non-profit, private agency licensed by the Virginia Dept. of Social Services.

**Area served:** U.S. residents.

**Requirements:** Evangelical Christian married couples who are between the ages of 24 and 40 yrs. who are in good health as verified by a physician and whose minimum income is $12,000/yr.

**Fees:** Sliding scale based on 15% of gross income with a minimum of $1500 and a maximum of $10,000.

**Number of children placed last year:** 30.

**Description of children:** Infants of all races.

**Adoption procedure:**
1) Submit application;
2) complete home study;
3) placement;
4) 3 post-placement supervisory visits;
5) finalization.

**Average length of time between application and start of home study:** 6-12 mos.

**Average length of time to complete home study:** 3 mos.

**Number of interviews:** 4-6.

**Home study description:** Assessment of psychological and social profile, spiritual life, finances, marriage, background, fertility work-up and parenting views and experiences.

**Average wait for a child after approval of a home study:** 12-24 mos.

**Foster care:** Temporary.

---

★ 832 ★
**Jewish Family Service of Tidewater, Inc.**
7300 Newport Ave.
P.O. Box 9503
Norfolk, VA 23505
Phone: (804) 489-3111
Fax: (804) 451-1796

**Branch address:**
2700 Spring Rd., Newport News, VA 23606
Phone: (804) 489-3111

403 Boush St., Ste. 350, Norfolk, VA 23510
Phone: (804) 622-0094

**Contact:** Harry Graber, Executive Director.

**Description:** Non-profit private agency licensed to provide adoption services in the Commonwealth of Virginia.

**Area served:** Residents of Norfolk, Virginia Beach, Suffolk, Portsmouth, Chesapeake, Hampton and Newport News.

**Requirements:** Jewish couples married for at least 3 yrs. with a valid Jewish marriage certificate, who are within 47 yrs. of age of the child being adopted, who are in good health, and able to support a child.

**Fees:**
Application and home study fee: $800;
adoption fee: 10% of couple's gross annual income to a maximum of $10,000.

**Number of children placed last year:** 1.

**Description of children:** Usually healthy, white infants.

**Adoption procedure:**
1) File application, 5 letters of recommendation, medical reports and financial statements;
2) complete home study;
3) if approved, wait for placement;
4) pre-placement training;
5) placement;
6) post-placement services;
7) finalization.

**Average length of time between application and start of home study:** 1 mo. or less.

**Average length of time to complete home study:** 3 mos.

**Number of interviews:** 5-7.

**Home study description:** Evaluation of description of applicants, family history, emotional stability and maturity, marital stability and compatibility, feelings about children and parenting abilities, financial resources, interests and activities of the family, religion and its role, individual and family attitudes toward adoption and birthparents, motivation and readiness for adoption; type of child desired and expectations of the child.

**Average wait for a child after approval of a home study:** 24 or more mos.

**Foster care:** Temporary.

---

★ 833 ★
**Jewish Family Service of Tidewater, Inc.**
403 Boush St., Ste. 350
Norfolk, VA 23510
Phone: (804) 622-0094

**Mailing address:**
P.O. Box 9503, Norfolk, VA 23505

**Branch address:**
2700 Spring Rd., Newport News, VA 23606
Phone: (804) 595-6215

7300 Newport Ave., Norfolk, VA 23505
Phone: (804) 489-3111

**Contact:** Harry Graber, Executive Director.

**Date established:** 1969.

**Description:** Private, non-profit agency licensed to place children by the Virginia Department of Social Services.

**Area served:** Residents in the Tidewater area and/or within a 50 mi. radius of the Agency's offices.

**Requirements:** No requirements for parental placements.
*Agency Placements:* Applicants must be no more than 40 yrs. older than the child placed, be in good health and have adequate income to support a child, be married a minimum of 3 yrs. with a Jewish marriage license and agree to raise the child as Jewish.

**Fees:** Home study: $800. Adoption placement fee: 10% of gross annual income up to $10,000.

**Number of children placed last year:** 1.

**Description of children:** Healthy, Caucasian infant.

**Adoption procedure:** 1) Application; 2) home study; 3) placement on waiting list; 4) placement; 5) post-placement supervision; 6) finalization.

**Average length of time between application and start of home study:** Less than 1 mo.

**Average length of time to complete home study:** 6 - 10 wks.

**Number of interviews:** 5.

**Home study description:** Assessment which includes references, criminal and child abuse history searches, physical appearance and total personality functioning, family history, emotional maturity, financial resources, interests and routines of daily living and which addresses such topics as marital satisfaction and compatibility, feelings about children, capacity to parent and discipline styles, religion and its place within the family, attitude of family members about adoption and birth parents.

**Average wait for a child after approval of a home study:** 2 yrs. or more.

**Foster care:** Pre-adoptive.

★ 834 ★
**Jewish Family Services, Inc.**
7027 Three Chopt Rd.
Richmond, VA 23226
Phone: (804) 282-5644

**Contact:** Peter Opper, Executive Director.

**Date established:** 1849.

**Description:** Non-profit, private agency licensed by the State of Virginia.

**Area served:** Residents of Virginia.

**Requirements:** Jewish couples married at least 3 yrs. who are between the ages of 21 and 45, in good health and financially stable.

**Fees:** Based on income.

**Number of children placed last year:** 0.

**Description of children:** Infants.

**Adoption procedure:**
1) Initial inquiry;
2) file application;
3) complete home study;
4) if approved, placement;
5) 6 mos. post-placement supervision;
6) finalization.

**Average length of time between application and start of home study:** 1-6 mos.

**Average length of time to complete home study:** 3 mos.

**Number of interviews:** 5 minimum.

**Home study description:** According to state guidelines.

**Average wait for a child after approval of a home study:** Varies.

**Foster care:** None.

★ 835 ★
**Shore Adoption Service**
113 Holly Crescent, Ste. 102
Virginia Beach, VA 23451
Phone: (804) 422-6361

**Contact:** Sherryl Shonyo, President or Catherine DeLapp, Executive Director.

**Date established:** Unavailable.

**Description:** Non-profit private adoption agency licensed by the Commonwealth of Virginia and specializing in parental placement adoptions.

**Area served:** Residents of Virginia.

**Requirements:** Commonwealth of Virginia mandates that applicants be at least 21 yrs. old. Any other requirements are determined by the birth parents.

**Fees:** Home study; $1900; post-placement supervision: $600; private consultation: $75/hr.

**Number of children placed last year:** 42.

**Description of children:** Primarily Caucasian infants.

**Adoption procedure:** 1) Group orientation; 2) 3 wk. educational workshop; 3) application; 4) home study. During the training workshops Shore Adoption Service helps the prospective adoptive family formulate its adoptive plan. When the home study is complete, the prospective adoptive family is ready with a photo resume to begin the search for an adoptable child. Occasionally, Shore Adoption Service is contacted directly by birth parents seeking assistance with an adoption plan for their child. Information is provided to them about prospective adoptive families whose home studies are complete. There is no additional fee for this service.

**Average length of time between application and start of home study:** 1 mo. or less.

**Average length of time to complete home study:** 2-6 mos.

**Number of interviews:** 8.

**Home study description:** Process designed to help prospective adoptive parents reach their full parenting potential.

**Average wait for a child after approval of a home study:** Adoptive parents are chosen by birth parents. Shore Adoption Services works with adoptive parents until an adoptive child is found.

**Foster care:** None.

★ 836 ★
**United Methodist Family Services of Virginia**
3900 W. Broad St.
Richmond, VA 23230
Phone: (804) 353-4461

**Branch address:**
715 Baker Rd., Ste. 201, 6335 Little River Tnpk., Virginia Beach, VA 23462
Phone: (804) 490-9791

**Contact:** Adoption Intake.

**Description:** Private, non-profit agency licensed to place children by the Virginia Department of Social Services offering programs in international, U.S. infant, and special needs adoption as well as facilitation of parental placements.

**Area served:** Residents of Virginia.

**Requirements:** Vary with program selected.

**Fees:** Application: $25. Home study: varies with program. Infant program: 4% of combined gross annual income, not to exceed $4000.

**Number of children placed last year:** More than 30.

**Description of children:** Children with special needs, foreign-born infants and children and U.S. infants.

**Adoption procedure:** 1) Inquiry; 2) application; 3) adoptive parent training; 4) home study; 5) paper work; 6) background checks; 7) placement; 8) post-placement supervision; 9) finalization.

**Average length of time between application and start of home study:** Varies with program selected.

**Average length of time to complete home study:** 6 - 8 wks.

**Number of interviews:** Minimum of 3.

**Home study description:** Process which meets the Virginia Department of Social Services requirements but which also provides training for families involved in each of the programs.

**Average wait for a child after approval of a home study:** 12 - 24 mos.

**Foster care:** Temporary, long-term and therapeutic.

★ 837 ★
**Virginia Baptist Children's Home and Family Services**
P.O. Box 849
Salem, VA 24153-0849
Phone: (703) 389-5468
Fax: (703) 389-5570

**Contact:** David Dillon.

**Date established:** 1890.

**Description:** Non-profit, private agency licensed by the Virginia Dept. of Social Services.

**Area served:** Residents of Virginia.

**Requirements:** Couples married at least 3 yrs. who are in good health, financially stable and not more than 40 yrs. old at the time of placement (age requirement may be met if the average of the spouses' ages is 40 or less or if the agency is satisfied that the child will reach his/her majority before the adoptive parents' retirement). Both spouses must be active members of a Southern Baptist Church, have a doctor's statement of infertility and be childless. Most requirements are flexible for the adoption of an older child or a child with special needs.

**Fees:**
Infant: $5000.
Negotiable for older or special needs child.

**Number of children placed last year:** 6.

**Description of children:** 1 white infant, 1 bi-racial infant, and 4 parental placements.

**Adoption procedure:**
1) Initial inquiry;
2) submit letter of interest providing biographical information in reference to agency requirements;
3) letter placed in Adoption Inquiry File by calendar year;
4) complete home study;
5) if approved, wait for placement;
6) placement.

**Average length of time between application and start of home study:** 24 or more mos.

**Average length of time to complete home study:** 1-2 mos.

**Number of interviews:** 3 or more.

**Home study description:** Follows licensing standards and includes personal and marital background, finances, home, neighborhood and others.

**Average wait for a child after approval of a home study:** 24 or more mos.

**Foster care:** Temporary and long-term (when necessary).

---

# WASHINGTON

## STATUTES

★ 838 ★

**Independent placement by intermediary?** Illegal.

**Independent placement by birth parents?** Yes.

**Subsidies provided?** Medical, legal, counseling and maintenance.

**Adoption cost defined by law?** No, although the courts do review the costs for "reasonableness".

**Insurance for infertility?:** No.

**Home study required by state?** Required before placement.

**Prospective adoptive parent advertise for a child?** Yes, with a completed favorable home study.

**Surrogacy laws?** No laws forbid it.

**Residents access agencies of other states or countries?** Not addressed in law Washington requires that only the birth mother, the child or the adoptive parents be residents or domiciled in the state for Washington courts to have jurisdiction to terminate parental rights and finalize the adoption.

**Requires judicial termination of birth parents' rights?** A duly witnessed Consent to Adoption can be signed by a birth parent before or after the child's birth, but has no legal effect until it is presented to and approved by the Court. The signed consent document cannot be presented until a minimum of 48 hours has passed since the child's birth, or since the document was signed, whichever is later. Both birth parents must relinquish their parental rights, either voluntarily or involuntarily, for an adoption to proceed.

**Time given to a birthmother to revoke her consent:** Until the Court approves the Consent to Adoption which can be no sooner than 48 hrs. after the child's birth.
Memo: Washington law also provides for enforceable adoption agreements which specify the parties' arrangements, limit the mother's expectations to those in writing and protect the validity of the adoption in the event of a dispute.

**Court handling adoptions?** County Superior Courts.

**Adoption of Native Children:** Tribe.

**Adoption records sealed?** Yes, and can be accessed only by court order when an adoptee is at least 21 yrs. old.

**Photo-listing book available?** Washington participates in the photo-listing of *The Northwest Adoption Exchange.*

## PUBLIC AGENCIES

★ 839 ★
**Washington Department of Health and Social Services**
**Children, Youth & Family Services Administration**
P.O. Box 45713
Olympia, WA 98504
Phone: (206) 753-0240
(800) 562-5682
Fax: (206) 586-1040

**Branch address:**
Region 1 Central Office, N. 1425 Washington, Spokane, WA 99220
Phone: (509) 458-2128

1100 S. Main, P.O. Box 537, Colville, WA 99114
Phone: (509) 684-7350

1620 S. Pioneer Way, P.O. Box 1399, Moses Lake, WA 98837
Phone: (509) 766-2332

P.O. Box 31, Colfax, WA 99111
Phone: (509) 397-4433

805 S. Mission St., P.O. Box 3088, Wenatchee, WA 98807
Phone: (509) 662-0561

Region 2 Central Office, 1002 N. 16th Ave., P.O. Box 12500, Yakima, WA 98909
Phone: (509) 575-2150

500 N. Morain, Ste. 2104, Kennewick, WA 99336
Phone: (509) 545-2401

521 Mountain View, P.O. Box 366, Ellensburg, WA 98926
Phone: (509) 962-7740

306 Bolin Dr., P.O. Box 470, Toppenish, WA 98948
Phone: (509) 865-4600

208 S. 8th St. (Ext N), P.O. Box 818, Sunnyside, WA 98944

Phone: (509) 839-2752

206 W. Poplar, P.O. Box 517, Walla Walla, WA 99362
Phone: (509) 527-4525

720 6th St., Clarkston, WA 99403
Phone: (509) 758-5539

Region 3 Central Office, 840 N. Boradway, Bldg. A, Everett, WA 98201
Phone: (206) 339-4768

3310 Smokey Point Dr., P.O. Box 3099, Arlington, VA 98223
Phone: (206) 653-0550

4101 Meridian, Bellingham, WA 98226
Phone: (206) 647-3100

1800 Continental Plaza, P.O. Box 310, Mount Vernon, WA 98273
Phone: (206) 428-1445

P.O. Box 1199, Oak Harbor, WA 98277
Phone: (206) 679-1002

Region 4 Central Office, 2809 26th Ave. S., Seattle, WA 98144
Phone: (206) 721-4257

15831 N.E. 8th St., Bellevue, WA 98008
Phone: (206) 649-4103

King South Office, 1313 W. Meeker, Kent, WA 98035
Phone: (206) 872-6001

Region 5 Central Office, 1949 S. State St., Tacoma, WA 98405
Phone: (206) 593-2600

3423 6th St., Ste. 217, Bremerton, WA 98312
Phone: (206) 478-4690

Region 6 Central Office, Lacey Govt. Bldg., Olympia, WA 98504-5714

5000 Capitol Blvd., P.O. Box 1908, Olympia, WA 98504
Phone: (206) 753-5156

110 W. K St., P.O. Box 1127, Shelton, WA 98584
Phone: (206) 427-2050

1016 E. 1st St., Port Angeles, WA 98362
Phone: (206) 457-2522

724 W. Robert Bush Dr., P.O. Box 87, South Bend, WA 98586
Phone: (206) 875-6501

405 W. Wishkah, P.O. Box 570, Aberdeen, WA 98520
Phone: (206) 533-1219

711 Vine St., P.O. Box 330, Kelso, WA 98626
Phone: (206) 577-2372

221 N. Main, P.O. Box 129, White Salmon, WA 98672
Phone: (509) 493-1012

907 Harney St., P.O. Box 9809, Vancouver, WA 98666
Phone: (206) 696-6771

623 Sheridan St., P.O. Box 554, Port Townsend, WA 98368
Phone: (206) 379-5020

**Contact:** Adoption Unit or worker.

**Description:** Public, state agency.

**Area served:** Residents of the State of Washington.

**Requirements:** Adults, 18 yrs. and older.

**Fees:** None.

**Number of children placed last year:** 230-250.

**Description of children:** Primarily children with special needs.

**Adoption procedure:** Procedures may vary with each regional office.
  1) Attend orientation;
  2) participate in 7 wk. training course;
  3) submit application;
  4) complete home study;
  5) if approved, wait for placement;
  6) placement;
  7) post-placement supervision;
  8) finalization.

**Average length of time between application and start of home study:** Varies.

**Average length of time to complete home study:** Varies.

**Number of interviews:** 7 group plus individual or all individual.

**Home study description:** Assessment which includes but is not limited to parenting experience or experience with children, background, lifestyle and recommendation of references.

**Average wait for a child after approval of a home study:** Varies.

**Foster care:** Emergency, short and long-term, legal-risk and permanent.

# PRIVATE AGENCIES

★ 840 ★
**Adoption Advocates International**
401 E. Front St.
Port Angeles, WA 98362
Phone: (206) 452-4777
Fax: (206) 452-1107

**Contact:** Merrily Ripley, Executive Director.

**Date established:** 1983.

**Description:** Non-profit, private agency licensed in the State of Alaska and Washington.

**Area served:** Complete adoption services provided to residents of the State of Washington; placement services provided to residents of all other states except Connecticut.

**Requirements:** Depend largely on child's country of origin but AAI requires all applicants be able to provide medical insurance from date of placement.

**Fees:**
Application fee: $75;
home study: sliding fee from $800-$1400;
processing fee: sliding scale;
foreign agency fees and transportation additional.

**Number of children placed last year:** 100.

**Description of children:** Children with special needs, aged 0-15 yrs., mostly from India, Taiwan, Bulgaria, China, Thailand, and Vietnam. Some black and biracial U.S. infants and children for Washington and Alaska only.

**Adoption procedure:**
1) Submit application;
2) return medical and financial forms, autobiography and Contract for Services rendered;
3) complete home study (and forward to AAI, if out-of-state);
4) if approved, adoption processing and child match;
5) child is escorted to U.S. or family travels to child's country;
6) 3 or more mos. post-placement supervision.

**Average length of time between application and start of home study:** 1 mo. or less.

**Average length of time to complete home study:** 1 mo.

**Number of interviews:** 3.

**Home study description:** Evaluation of applicant(s)' personal history, values and personality, commitment to adoption, marital history, others (including children) in the family, philosophy of parenting, description of home and community and description of child desired.

**Average wait for a child after approval of a home study:** 6-12 mos.

**Foster care:** Very rarely, temporary.

★841★
**Adoption Services of WACAP (Western Association of Concerned Adoptive Parents)**
315 S. 2nd
Renton, WA 98055
Phone: (206) 575-4550
Fax: (206) 575-4148

**Mailing address:**
P.O. Box 88948, Renton, WA 98055

**Contact:** Janice Nelson, Executive Director.

**Date established:** 1976.

**Description:** Non-profit, private agency licensed in Alaska and Washington.

**Area served:** Residents of the U.S.

**Requirements:** Vary with each program.

**Fees:** Vary with program: $1500-$9000.

**Number of children placed last year:** 300.

**Description of children:** Children from infancy to adolescence, some with special needs, from U.S., Colombia, Korea, India, Thailand, Philippines, Romania, Russia, and Ecuador.

**Adoption procedure:**
1) Submit application;
2) complete home study;
3) case processing and referral;
4) placement;
5) post-placement supervision;
6) finalization.

**Average length of time between application and start of home study:** 1 mo. or less.

**Average length of time to complete home study:** 3 mos.

**Number of interviews:** Approx. 3.

**Home study description:** Assessment of the applicant's background, ability to parent, recommendation of references, medical and financial information, family history and photos.

**Average wait for a child after approval of a home study:** 6-12 mos.

**Foster care:** None.

★842★
**Americans for International Aid and Adoption Washington State Branch**
P.O. Box 6051
Spokane, WA 99207-0901
Phone: (509) 484-0206
(509) 487-8921

**Contact:** Carol Ann Hollar, Branch Director.

**Date established:** 1982.

**Description:** Non-profit, private agency licensed in the State of Washington. (A branch of AIAA. National office is in Michigan).

**Area served:** Residents of Washington State.

**Requirements:** Vary by child's country of origin.

**Fees:** Sliding scale based on income.

**Number of children placed last year:** 25.

**Description of children:** U.S. and foreign-born infants and children through school age, some with special needs.

**Adoption procedure:** Varies by program chosen.

**Average length of time between application and start of home study:** 1 mo. or less.

**Average length of time to complete home study:** 2 mos.

**Number of interviews:** 3-4.

**Home study description:** Evaluation of background, marriage, health, recommendation of references, lifestyle, income, motivation to adopt, experience with children, understanding of adoption issues and cross-cultural issues (for inter-country adoption).

**Average wait for a child after approval of a home study:** 1-6 mos.

**Foster care:** Very rarely, on an emergency basis.

★843★
**Baptist Family Agency**
P.O. Box 16353
Seattle, WA 98116
Phone: (206) 938-1487
Fax: (206) 938-4067

**Contact:** Betty M. Wallin or Neal E. Gardenhire.

**Date established:** 1974.

**Description:** Non-profit, private agency licensed by the Washington Dept. of Social and Health Services.

**Area served:** Residents of the State of Washington.

**Requirements:** Christian couples who are married at least 3 yrs.

**Fees:** Sliding scale based on income.

**Number of children placed last year:** 3.

**Description of children:** 1 infant and 1 sibling pair, age 3.

**Adoption procedure:**
1) Initial inquiry;
2) submit application;
3) reference checks;
4) complete home study;
5) if approved, wait for placement;
6) placement;
7) post-placement supervision;
8) finalization.

**Average length of time between application and start of home study:** 1-6 mos.

**Average length of time to complete home study:** Unavailable.

**Number of interviews:** 3.

**Home study description:** Assessment of personality, marriage, faith, children in the home, lifestyle, interests and home.

**Average wait for a child after approval of a home study:** Varies.

**Foster care:** Temporary, long-term and permanent.

### ★844★
**Bethany Christian Services of Bellingham**
103 East Holly, No. 316
Bellingham, WA 98225
Phone: (206) 733-6042
**Branch address:**
   1213 Sixth Ave., Tacoma, WA 98405
**Contact:** Terry McNichols, Supervisor or Dawn Kroontje, Case Worker.
**Date established:** 1984.
**Description:** Non-profit, private child-placing and adoption agency licensed by the Washington Dept. of Health and Social Services.
**Area served:** Residents of Alaska, Oregon and Washington State.
**Requirements:** Couples married at least 3 yrs. who are between the ages of 25 and 38 yrs., who have no more than 1 child and a diagnosis of infertility, and who are both full members of a Christian Bible-teaching church. After placement, primary care giver is required to be at home full-time for 3 mos.
**Fees:** Sliding scale from $6500 to $9000 and includes $25 pre-application fee, $300 formal application fee and $500 home study fee.
**Number of children placed last year:** 9.
**Description of children:** Caucasian infants.
**Adoption procedure:**
 1) Submit Preliminary Application;
 2) attend initial interview;
 3) participate in individual interviews and home visit;
 4) home study prepared;
 5) profile shown to relinquishing birthmothers;
 6) placement;
 7) 6 mos. post-placement supervision;
 8) finalization.
**Average length of time between application and start of home study:** 2 mos.
**Average length of time to complete home study:** 4-5 mos.
**Number of interviews:** 3-4.
**Home study description:** Assessment of prospective adoptive parents' biographies, religion, marriage, description of home, finances, summary of references and statement of discipline.
**Average wait for a child after approval of a home study:** 1-2 yrs.
**Foster care:** Temporary.

### ★845★
**Bethany Christian Services of Bellingham**
103 E. Holly St., No. 305
Bellingham National Bank Bldg.
Bellingham, WA 98225
Phone: (800) 733-4604
Fax: (206) 367-1860
**Contact:** Dorothy Bloom.
**Date established:** 1944.
**Description:** Non-profit, private agency licensed in the states of Washington and Oregon. Merged with Hope Services.

**Area served:** Residents of the states of Washington and Oregon, primarily.
**Requirements:** Active Christian couples who are married at least 3 yrs., have no more than 2 children, and are infertile. Most requirements are flexible for the adoption of a child with special needs.
**Fees:** Sliding scale.
**Number of children placed last year:** 55 in Washington; 872 nation-wide.
**Description of children:** Infants, some children with special needs, U.S. waiting children, and some foreign programs.
**Adoption procedure:**
 1) Initial inquiry;
 2) return completed application;
 3) attend adoption orientation;
 4) complete home study;
 5) if approved, compile personal family profile for birthmothers to review;
 6) wait for selection;
 7) placement;
 8) post-placement supervision;
 9) finalization.
**Average length of time between application and start of home study:** 6-12 mos.
**Average length of time to complete home study:** 6 wks.
**Number of interviews:** 4.
**Home study description:** Evaluation of applicants' childhood, background, education, occupation, interests and values, marriage, finances, health and others.
**Average wait for a child after approval of a home study:** 6-12 for special needs; 24 or more mos. for infants.
**Foster care:** Limited.

### ★846★
**Catholic Community Service of Seattle**
100 - 23rd Ave. S.
Seattle, WA 98144
Phone: (206) 323-6336
Fax: (206) 324-4835
**Contact:** William Harris.
**Date established:** 1938.
**Description:** Non-profit private agency licensed in the State of Washington.
**Area served:**
Domestic adoptions: residents of Seattle and King County.
Foreign-born adoptions: resident of the State of Washington.
**Requirements:** Varies by program.
**Fees:** Varies by program.
**Number of children placed last year:** 50.
**Description of children:** Infants, Korean children and children with special needs.
**Adoption procedure:** Varies according to program.
**Average length of time between application and start of home study:** Varies.
**Average length of time to complete home study:** 2-4 mos.
**Number of interviews:** Unavailable.
**Home study description:** Evaluation which includes but is not limited to recommendation of references, medical reports and interviews.
**Average wait for a child after approval of a home study:** Varies.
**Foster care:** Temporary.

## ★ 847 ★

**Catholic Community Services of Tacoma**
5410 N. 44th St.
Tacoma, WA 98407
Phone: (206) 752-2455
(800) 767-2456
Fax: (206) 756-1976

**Contact:** Jan Broback.

**Date established:** 1939.

**Description:** Non-profit private agency licensed in Washington State.

**Area served:** Residents of Kitsap, Lewis, Pierce and Thurston counties.

**Requirements:** U.S. Infant program: Couples married at least 2-3 yrs. who are older than 21 yrs., are financially secure and have adequate health insurance.

**Fees:** Sliding fee scale.

**Number of children placed last year:** 17 in domestic program.

**Description of children:** White and biracial infants and toddlers.

**Adoption procedure:**
1) File pre-application;
2) return completed application;
3) complete home study;
4) placement;
5) post-placement services.

**Average length of time between application and start of home study:** 1-6 mos.

**Average length of time to complete home study:** 2 mos.

**Number of interviews:** 4 plus 6 weeks of Adoption Information classes.

**Home study description:** Evaluation of material discussed in interviews, home visit, autobiographies, physical examination and recommendation of references.

**Average wait for a child after approval of a home study:** 12-24 mos.

**Foster care:** Temporary, long-term and respite care.

## ★ 848 ★

**Catholic Community Services of Vancouver**
40 W. 12th St.
Vancouver, WA 98660
Phone: (206) 696-0379

**Contact:** Carolann Sheerin, MA, Program Director.

**Date established:** 1958.

**Description:** Non-profit private agency licensed in the State of Washington.

**Area served:** Residents of Clark, Cowlitz, Skamania and Wahkiakum counties.

**Requirements:** Couples married at least 3 yrs. who are over the age of 25 yrs., have evidence of infertility, and are in good physical and emotional health.

**Fees:** $9700 total fees for domestic adoption program; $13,000 for Korean program.

**Number of children placed last year:** 15.

**Description of children:** Foreign-born and U.S. children.

**Adoption procedure:**
1) Attend initial interview;
2) complete home study;
3) if approved, waiting period (support groups are available for waiting families);
4) arrival of child;

5) 6 mos. post-placement services;
6) finalization.

**Average length of time between application and start of home study:** 6-12 mos.

**Average length of time to complete home study:** 2-4 mos.

**Number of interviews:** 4-5.

**Home study description:** Assessment of individual interests, issues concerning family of origin, personal and marital issues, home visit and family session.

**Average wait for a child after approval of a home study:** 12-24 mos.

**Foster care:** None.

## ★ 849 ★

**The Family Foundation**
1229 Cornwall Ave., Ste. 206
Bellingham, WA 98225
Phone: (206) 676-5437
Fax: (206) 671-5744

**Contact:** Jacqueline R. Erholm, Founder and Executive Director.

**Date established:** 1985.

**Description:** Non-profit private agency licensed in Washington State and committed to placing U.S. waiting newborns and children of all races in adoptive families.

**Area served:** Residents of northwestern Washington State (Region III) and Canada within 200 miles of Bellingham.

**Requirements:** None.

**Fees:**
Application: $500;
education fee: $750;
pre-placement report: $1250;
placement: $1500.

**Number of children placed last year:** 13.

**Description of children:** 7 newborn; 2 children under the age of 6 yrs.; and 4 children ages 6-12 yrs.

**Adoption procedure:**
1) Make inquiry;
3) attend orientation interview;
4) complete Adoption Parent Preparation Training;
5) formulation of pre-placement report;
6) child search;
7) placement;
8) post-placement support; and
9) finalization.

**Average length of time between application and start of home study:** 1 mo. or less.

**Average length of time to complete home study:** Adoptive Parent Preparation Training is 24 class hrs. and approximately 12 hrs. of homework. After all paperwork is received, the home study report should be completed within 30 days.

**Number of interviews:** Adoptive Parent Preparation Training and 2 additional interviews.

**Home study description:** Evaluation of family history; suitability for adoption; skills inventory; family assessment and agency recommendations.

**Average wait for a child after approval of a home study:** 6-12 mos.

**Foster care:** Fost-adopt.

## ★ 850 ★
**Jewish Family Service**
1214 Boylston Ave.
Seattle, WA 98101
Phone: (206) 461-3240

**Branch address:**
  11101 N.E. 8th, Bellevue, WA 98004

**Contact:** Patti Gorman.

**Date established:** 1888.

**Description:** Private non-profit agency licensed in the State of Washington.

**Area served:** Residents of Greater Seattle area.

**Requirements:** Jewish couples married at least 1 yr. who are not more than 45 yrs. older than the adopted child.

**Fees:**
$25 application fee;
$650 home study;
$300 post-placement services;
$300 home study update;
$50 post-placement evaluation for legal finalization (if post-placement services not performed);
$2,000 complete package if JFS places child.

**Number of children placed last year:** 0 through agency. Some support services for private adoptions.

**Description of children:** Infants.

**Adoption procedure:** Call JFS to have name added to waiting list.

**Average length of time between application and start of home study:** Varies.

**Average length of time to complete home study:** 1 mo.

**Number of interviews:** 3-4.

**Home study description:** Evaluation of the psychological and concrete aspects of background and current lifestyle.

**Average wait for a child after approval of a home study:** Varies.

**Foster care:** Temporary, long-term and permanent for children in need of a Jewish home.

## ★ 851 ★
**Leap of Faith Adoption Services**
22601 S.E. 322nd St.
Kent, WA 98042
Phone: (206) 886-2103

**Contact:** Janice Elsemore, Director.

**Date established:** 1991.

**Description:** Private, non-profit child placing agency licensed by the Washington Department of Health and Social Services.

**Area served:** No geographic restrictions with the exception of residents of New York State.

**Requirements:** Applicants should be younger than 65 yrs.

**Fees:** Application; $300. Home study: $800. Home study updates: $50/hr. Post-Placement Services: $50/hr. Foster care (Haiti and St. Vincent): $300/mo.
*International Referral Fees*
Jamaica: $5500
St. Lucia: $5000
Haiti: $5800
St. Vincent: $5000
Escort fees are additional.

**Number of children placed last year:** 27.

**Description of children:** Toddlers and children from the Caribbean of African ancestry.

**Adoption procedure:** 1) Inquiry; 2) application; 3) home study; 4) documents submitted to child's country of origin; 5) guardianship awarded; 6) child escorted to U.S.; 7) placement; 8) post-placement supervision; 9) finalization.

**Average length of time between application and start of home study:** Less than 1 mo.

**Average length of time to complete home study:** 1 - 3 mos.

**Number of interviews:** 3.

**Home study description:** Agency will conduct home studies for those adopting independently or from another program. The fee for this service: $1000. The assessment includes transracial adoption assistance and stresses the applicant(s) ability and resources to parent a child of another race, if this is the case.

**Average wait for a child after approval of a home study:** 8 mos.

**Foster care:** None.

## ★ 852 ★
**Lutheran Social Services of Washington & Idaho**
6920 220th St. S.W., Ste. K
Mountlake Terrace, WA 98043
Phone: (206) 672-6009
Fax: (206) 670-1390

**Contact:** Intake Worker/Adoptions.

**Date established:** 1944.

**Description:** Non-profit, private agency.

**Area served:** Residents of King and Snohomish counties.

**Requirements:** Couples who are physically and emotionally healthy, financially able to assume the care a baby, and who have no criminal record.

**Fees:** $60/hr. for independent home studies; $1250 for group/individual home study;$4000 pregnancy fund; 8% of family's gross annual income for placement with LSS with $2000 maximum.

**Number of children placed last year:** Variable.

**Description of children:** Infants.

**Adoption procedure:**
  1) Initial inquiry;
  2) file application;
  3) attend 8 hrs. of preparation group;
  4) participate in individual counseling sessions;
  5) complete home study;
  6) prepare non-identifying profile for birthparents' review;
  7) wait for selection and placement;
  8) network for independent placement.

**Average length of time between application and start of home study:** Varies.

**Average length of time to complete home study:** 3-4 mos.

**Number of interviews:** Individual and group.

**Home study description:** Educational and evaluatory process which prepares the applicants for adoptive parenthood, assesses their ability to parent an adopted child, prepares them for meeting with birthparents to consider open adoption options, and to network with other agencies and independents for a matched placement.

**Average wait for a child after approval of a home study:** Varies.

**Foster care:** Permanency Planning.

**★ 853 ★**
**Medina Children's Services**
123 Sixteenth Ave.
Seattle, WA 98122
Phone: (206) 461-4520

**Mailing address:**
P.O. Box 22638, Seattle, WA 98122

**Branch address:**
4301 S. Pine St., Tacoma, WA 98408
Phone: (206) 474-3139

**Contact:** Erika R. Giles, Program Director, Adoptions & Pregnancy Counseling.

**Date established:** 1921.

**Description:** Private, non-profit, nonsectarian United Way Agency licensed to place children by the Oregon Department of Human Resources and the Washington Department of Health and Social Services.

**Area served:** Residents within a one hr.'s drive of Seattle, WA.

**Requirements:** Open.

**Fees:** Application: $50. Home study: $960. Preparation group: $300. Other fees vary with program.

**Number of children placed last year:** 31.

**Description of children:** Caucasian and minority infants, some by parental placement, children with special needs and a foreign born child.

**Adoption procedure:** 1) Series of interviews; 2) group preparation (8 - 15 hrs. depending on program); 3) child match; 4) placement; 5) post-placment supervision; 6) finalization.

**Average length of time between application and start of home study:** 1 - 6 mos.

**Average length of time to complete home study:** 2 mos.

**Number of interviews:** 4.

**Home study description:** Assessment which includes background, medical and financial information criminal history searches, life experiences to the present, marital and other relationships, experience with children, lifestyle and infertility issues, if applicable.

**Average wait for a child after approval of a home study:** Varies with type of child requested.

**Foster care:** Temporary and permanent.

**★ 854 ★**
**New Hope Child and Family Agency**
2611 N.E. 125th, Ste. 146
Seattle, WA 98125
Phone: (206) 363-1800

**Contact:** Adoption intake worker.

**Description:** Non-profit, private agency licensed in Oregon, Washington, and Idaho.

**Area served:** Residents of Oregon, Washington, and Idaho; some placements made out of the three state area, especially for international programs.

**Requirements:** Differ depending on the program.

**Fees:** Home study: $750.

**Number of children placed last year:** 80 or more.

**Description of children:** Caucasian infants, some biracial, older children, children with special needs, and children from China, Latvia, and Russia, from newborn to 8 yrs.

**Adoption procedure:**
1) Undergo screening process including interview;
2) participate in orientation series;
3) complete individual interviews and home study;

4) if approved, admission to program;
5) 4 mos. post-placement supervision;
6) finalization.

**Average length of time between application and start of home study:** 1 mo. or less.

**Average length of time to complete home study:** 4 mos.

**Number of interviews:** 4.

**Home study description:** Evaluation of recommendation of references, financial reports, questionnaires on marriage infertility and parenting, autobiographies, physical exams, and criminal check.

**Average wait for a child after approval of a home study:** 4-8 mos. international; 9-12 mos. domestic.

**Foster care:** Long-term which may become permanent.

# WEST VIRGINIA

## STATUTES

**★ 855 ★**

**Independent placement by intermediary?** Prohibited.

**Independent placement by birth parents?** Permitted.

**Subsidies provided?** Medical, maintenance and non-recurring legal.

**Adoption cost defined by law?** Fees may be reviewed.

**Insurance for infertility?:** No.

**Home study required by state?** Court may request a discreet inquiry.

**Prospective adoptive parent advertise for a child?** Not addressed in law.

**Surrogacy laws?** Not addressed in law.

**Residents access agencies of other states or countries?** Permitted.

**Requires judicial termination of birth parents' rights?** Voluntary relinquishments by both birth parents are recognized.

**Time given to a birthmother to revoke her consent:** 72 hrs.

**Court handling adoptions?** Circuit Court.

**Adoption of Native Children:** Tribe.

**Adoption records sealed?** Sealed, but at age 18 yrs. adoptees may access non-identifying information.

**Photo-listing book available?** Available.

## PUBLIC AGENCIES

**★ 856 ★**
**West Virginia Department of Human Services**
Capitol Complex, Bldg. 6
State Capitol Complex
Charleston, WV 25305
Phone: (304) 558-7980
Fax: (304) 558-8800

**Contact:** Gwen Bridges.

**Date established:** 1936.

**Description:** Public human service agency.

**Area served:** Residents of the State of West Virginia.

**Requirements:** Flexible.

**Fees:** None.

**Number of children placed last year:** 87.

**Description of children:** Children with special needs aged 0-18 yrs.

**Adoption procedure:** Call or write to the local county office of residence for intake.

**Average length of time to complete home study:** 60-90 days.

**Number of interviews:** Depends on family circumstances. Minimum of one intake and exit interview per person and two joint interviews, if couple; and interview with each child in the home.

**Home study description:** Call or write for outline.

**Average wait for a child after approval of a home study:** 6-12 mos., depending on family's acceptance level.

**Foster care:** Temporary, long-term and permanent.

# PRIVATE AGENCIES

★ 857 ★
**Burlington United Methodist Family Services, Inc.**
P.O. Box 370
Scott Depot, WV 25560
Phone: (304) 757-9127
Fax: (304) 757-9136

**Contact:** Donna McCune, Area Supervisor.

**Date established:** 1958.

**Description:** Non-profit, private agency licensed by the West Virginia Dept. of Human Services. Multi-service agency serving children, youth and families. United Methodist Child Placement Services merged with Burlington United Methodist Homes in 1989.

**Area served:** Residents of West Virginia.

**Requirements:** Adults between the ages of 23 and 40 yrs. who have adequate income to meet the needs of a child and no medical condition which would limit applicant's capacity to care for a child.

**Fees:**
Home study: $800 plus travel costs;
placement and post-placement services for child relinquished directly to agency: 8% of income;
placement by a cooperative agency: home study cost, $300 placement fee, $150 per post-placement visit plus travel cost.

**Number of children placed last year:** 27.

**Description of children:** Infants, children with special needs and foreign-born children.

**Adoption procedure:** Call agency for information.

**Average length of time between application and start of home study:** 1 mo. or less except for agency newborn.

**Average length of time to complete home study:** 3 mos.

**Number of interviews:** 3 plus group training session.

**Home study description:** Call agency for guidelines.

**Average wait for a child after approval of a home study:** 6-24 mos. for international and special needs.

**Foster care:** Temporary.

# WISCONSIN

## STATUTES

★ 858 ★
**Independent placement by intermediary?** Yes, but intermediaries may not be compensated for their services.
**Independent placement by birth parents?** Yes, with a relative.
**Subsidies provided?** Non-recurring, maintenance and Title XIX benefits.
**Adoption cost defined by law?** Yes.
**Insurance for infertility?:** Unknown.
**Home study required by state?** Required before placement.
**Prospective adoptive parent advertise for a child?** Permitted.
**Surrogacy laws?** Not addressed in law.
**Residents access agencies of other states or countries?** In compliance with ICPC.
**Requires judicial termination of birth parents' rights?** Yes.
**Time given to a birthmother to revoke her consent:** None.
**Court handling adoptions?** County Juvenile or Probate Court.
**Adoption of Native Children:** ICWA is federal law.
**Adoption records sealed?** Yes, adoptees, 18 yrs. and older, may access non-identifying information.
**Photo-listing book available?** *Adopt!*

## PUBLIC AGENCIES

★ 859 ★
**Wisconsin Department of Health and Social Services**
**Division of Community Services**
**Bureau for Children, Youth and Families**
1 W. Wilson St.
Madison, WI 53707-7851
Phone: (608) 266-0690
Fax: (608) 264-6750

**Mailing address:**
P.O. Box 7851, Madison, WI 53707-7851

**Branch address:**
Ashland District, City Hall, 601 W. 2nd St., P.O. Box 72, Ashland, WI 54806
Phone: (715) 682-7286

200 N. Jefferson, Ste. 411, Green Bay, WI 54301
Phone: (414) 448-5312

485 S. Military Rd., P.O. Box 1069, Fond du Lac, WI 54935
Phone: (414) 929-2985

3550 Mormon Coulee Rd., P.O. Box 743, La Crosse, WI 54601
Phone: (608) 785-9453

1853 N. Stevens, P.O. Box 697, Rhinelander, WI 54501
Phone: (715) 365-2516

3601 Memorial Dr., Madison, WI 53704
Phone: (608) 249-0441

141 N.W. Barstow St., Rm. 209, Waukesha, WI 53187

Phone: (414) 521-5100

718 W. Clairemont St., P.O. Box 228, Eau Claire, WI 54701
Phone: (715) 836-2174

1691 2nd Ave. S., P.O. Box 636, Wisconsin Rapids, WI 54494
Phone: (715) 422-5080

**Contact:** Karen Oghalai, Adoption Planner.
**Description:** Public, state agency.
**Area served:** Residents of Wisconsin.
**Requirements:** Applicants are evaluated on a case by case basis.
**Fees:** None.
**Number of children placed last year:** 221.
**Description of children:** Children with special needs.
**Adoption procedure:**
1) Initial inquiry;
2) attend orientation;
3) submit application;
4) complete home study;
5) if approved, placement;
6) post-placement supervision;
7) finalization.

**Average length of time between application and start of home study:** 6-12 mos.
**Average length of time to complete home study:** 3-6 mos.
**Number of interviews:** 6-8.
**Home study description:** Educational and evaluative process which examines type of child desired, experiences with children, personal experiences, strengths and weakness, education, and issues surrounding adoption.
**Average wait for a child after approval of a home study:** 1-6 mos.
**Foster care:** Temporary and pre-adoptive.

# PRIVATE AGENCIES

★ 860 ★
**Adoption Choice, Inc.**
924 E. Juneau Ave., Ste. 813
Milwaukee, WI 53202
Phone: (414) 332-7732
Fax: (414) 276-3262

**Contact:** Jill Gerlach, Director or Melinda Randa, Associate Director.
**Date established:** 1986.
**Description:** Private child welfare agency licensed by the State of Wisconsin for stepparent, foreign, independent, interstate and agency-based adoptions.
**Area served:** Complete adoption services to the residents of Wisconsin. Agency will also do interstate adoptions.
**Requirements:** Couples married at least 3 yrs., the younger spouse of which may be no older than 40 yrs. and the older spouse no older than 45 yrs.
**Fees:**
Application: $50;
home study: $1500.
**Number of children placed last year:** 45.
**Description of children:** Infants, foreign-born children and children with special needs.

**Adoption procedure:**
1) Submit application;
2) complete home study;
3) law enforcement and reference checks;
4) compile autobiographies and legal documents;
5) if approved, wait for placement;
6) placement.
**Average length of time between application and start of home study:** Varies.
**Average length of time to complete home study:** 1 mo.
**Number of interviews:** 2-3.
**Home study description:** Assessment of couples' individual backgrounds, courtship and marriage, finances, parenting experiences and philosophy, expectations of a child, etc.
**Average wait for a child after approval of a home study:** Varies.
**Foster care:** Pre-adoptive.

★ 861 ★
**The Adoption Option, Inc.**
1804 Chapman Dr.
Waukesha, WI 53186
Phone: (414) 544-4278

**Date established:** 1985.
**Description:** Non-denominational, for-profit agency licensed by the state of Wisconsin.
**Area served:** Residents of Dodge, Jefferson, Kenosha, Milwaukee, Ozaukee, Racine, Walworth, Washington and Waukesha counties.
**Requirements:** Applicants must have relatively good health, be financially responsible and have a stable family life.
**Fees:** $1800 includes home study, post-placement services and finalization. Total fees for foreign adoption: $16,000-$18,000.
**Number of children placed last year:** 25.
**Description of children:** Foreign and U.S. infants, toddlers, and adolescents.
**Adoption procedure:**
1) Intake;
2) referral;
3) home study;
4) post-placement supervision; and
5) legal finalization.
**Average length of time between application and start of home study:** 1 mo. or less.
**Average length of time to complete home study:** 2-3 wks.
**Number of interviews:** 4.
**Home study description:** Evaluation of background information; parenting skills; health; financial report; home visit; and references.
**Average wait for a child after approval of a home study:** 1-6 mos.
**Foster care:** Pre-adoptive.

★ 862 ★
**Adoption Services of Green Bay and Fox Valley, Inc.**
529 S. Jefferson St.
Green Bay, WI 54301
Phone: (414) 432-2030
(800) 310-1240

**Contact:** Judy Swalby, Adoption Coordinator.
**Date established:** 1983.

**Description:** Private fee supported child welfare agency licensed by the State of Wisconsin.

**Area served:** Families within a 200 mi. radius of Green Bay.

**Requirements:** Flexible, with applicants having good health and a good life expectancy. International agency may impose additional requirements.

**Fees:**
Initial consultation: free;
home study: $1600;
placement supervision: $500;
parent counseling: $50/hr;
step parent adoptions: $250.

**Number of children placed last year:** 40.

**Description of children:** Newborns and infants, international.

**Adoption procedure:**
1) Attend initial consultation;
2) file complete questionnaire and application;
3) complete individual adoptive home study;
4) file application for a specific child;
5) complete dossier for foreign adoption and meet immigration requirements;
6) placement;
7) post-placement supervisory; and
8) finalization.

**Average length of time between application and start of home study:** 1-6 mos.

**Average length of time to complete home study:** 1 mo.

**Number of interviews:** 3 or more.

**Home study description:** Evaluatory and learning experience wherein the following are considered: social information; motivation to adopt; attitudes about adoption; experiences with child care; and plans for the future.

**Average wait for a child after approval of a home study:** 6-12 mos.

**Foster care:** Pre-adoptive.

★ 863 ★
**Catholic Social Service of Madison**
4905 Schofield St.
Madison, WI 53716
Phone: (608) 221-2000
Fax: (608) 221-4876

**Branch address:**
25 S. Hancock St., Madison, WI 53703
Phone: (608) 256-2358

3311 Prairie Ave., Beloit, WI 53511
Phone: (608) 365-3665

2020 E. Milwaukee St., Janesville, WI 53545
Phone: (608) 752-4906

**Contact:** Grace Mrozinski.

**Date established:** 1948.

**Description:** Non-profit child-placing agency licensed by the State of Wisconsin.

**Area served:** Residents of Columbia, Dane, Grant, Green Lake, Green Sauk, Iowa, Jefferson, Lafayette, Marquette and Rock counties.

**Requirements:** Couples married 2 yrs. at least one of whom is under the age of 38 yrs. at time of placement, who are in good health with an average life expectancy and who have explored reasons for infertility, and who have sufficient income to support a child.

**Fees:**
Regular program: $7000 home study and post-placement.

**Number of children placed last year:** 16.

**Description of children:** Infants, foreign-born children, and biracial infants on a case by case basis.

**Adoption procedure:**
1) Initial inquiry;
2) attend orientation;
3) screening interview;
4) assignment to study worker;
5) complete home study;
6) home study is written and submitted to Adoption Committee;
7) if approved, appropriate child placed;
8) 6 mos. post-placement supervision;
9) finalization.

**Average length of time between application and start of home study:** 1 mo. or less.

**Average length of time to complete home study:** 6-8 wks.

**Number of interviews:** 5-6.

**Home study description:** Evaluation of social and medical history, education, religious affiliation, methods of argument resolution, expectations of a child and methods of discipline, attitudes toward birthparents, adoption, extended family's attitude toward adoption and child development.

**Average wait for a child after approval of a home study:** 1 mo. or less.

**Foster care:** Pre-adoptive.

★ 864 ★
**Catholic Social Services of Milwaukee**
2021 N. 60 St.
Milwaukee, WI 53208
Phone: (414) 771-2881
Fax: (414) 771-1674

**Branch address:**
91-A S. Main St., Fond du Lac, WI 54935

5820 Third Ave., Kenosha, WI 53140

2711 Nineteenth St., Racine, WI 53403

503 Wisconsin Ave., Sheboygan, WI 53081

840 N. Grand Ave., Waukesha, WI 53186

141 N. Main St., West Bend, WI 53095

**Contact:** Pat Wendt, MSW, Child Welfare Coordinator.

**Date established:** 1920.

**Description:** Voluntary non-profit multifunction agency licensed by the State of Wisconsin to operate as a child placement agency.

**Area served:** Residents of the ten counties of the Archdiocese of Milwaukee.

**Requirements:** Couples married at least 2 yrs. and 21 yrs. of age. No religion or family size requirements.

**Fees:**
Agency: $6,000-$10,000;
Independent: $1,500;
Special needs: 7% of income to $6,000.

**Number of children placed last year:** 34.

**Description of children:** White, black and biracial infants some of whom had major medical problems.

**Adoption procedure:**
1) Telephone intake;
2) attend information meeting;
3) prescreening with application;
4) complete home study;
5) meeting to discuss proposed child and placement planning;
6) placement;
7) 6 or more mos. post-placement supervision;
8) finalization.

**Average length of time between application and start of home study:** Agency: 1-6 mos.; independent or identified: 0-1 mo.

**Average length of time to complete home study:** 2-3 mos.

**Number of interviews:** 10-12 hrs. of interview time.

**Home study description:** Evaluation of motivation to adopt; knowledge of and comfort with adoption; issues surrounding parenthood by adoption; child rearing idea and experience; general life adjustment including interpersonal relationships; marital adjustment; financial management; religious practice; health reports and child preference.

**Average wait for a child after approval of a home study:** 12-24 mos.

**Foster care:** Short-term and therapeutic.

★ 865 ★
**Community Adoption Center, Inc.**
101 E. Milwaukee, No. 424
Janesville, WI 53545
Phone: (608) 756-0405
(800) ADOPT-ME
Fax: (608) 756-8722

**Branch address:**
   Northbrook Executive Ctr., 10701 W. North Ave., Ste. 205, Wauwatosa, WI 53226
   Phone: (414) 258-3637

   3701 Kadow St., Manitowoc, WI 54220
   Phone: (414) 682-9211

**Contact:** Anita Kropf, ACSW or Deanne Vallendorf, ACSW.

**Date established:** 1987.

**Description:** Private, profit-based corporation licensed by the State of Wisconsin.

**Area served:** Residents of the State of Wisconsin.

**Requirements:** Agency has few limitations. Other requirements may be imposed by birthparents or foreign agencies.

**Fees:**
Application: $500;
independent adoption: $1800;
foreign adoption: $2000;
healthy, white infant: $9000.

**Number of children placed last year:** C. 80.

**Description of children:** Healthy, white infants, foreign-born children, children with special needs and services for independent placements.

**Adoption procedure:**
1) Attend informational meeting;
2) submit application;
3) complete home study;
4) placement;
5) post-placement supervision;
6) finalization.

**Average length of time between application and start of home study:** 1 mo. or less.

**Average length of time to complete home study:** 30 days or less.

**Number of interviews:** 4.

**Home study description:** Assessment of individual and marital stability, financial and health reports and recommendation of references.

**Average wait for a child after approval of a home study:** Birthmother chooses from resumes.

**Foster care:** Temporary.

★ 866 ★
**Door County Counseling Services, Inc.**
345 S. 18th Ave.
Sturgeon Bay, WI 54235
Phone: (414) 743-7222
(800) 750-7222

**Contact:** Karen Ebbeson, CSW, BSSW, Adoption Social Worker.

**Date established:** 1993.

**Description:** Private, for profit corporation licensed as a child welfare placing agency by the Wisconsin Department of Health and Social Services offering agency and independent adoption.

**Area served:** Residents of northeastern Wisconsin.

**Requirements:** Flexible.

**Fees:** Orientation Fee: $100
Adoption Program Fee: $2000
Pre-Adoptive Services (includes home study): $2000
Home Study alone: $1800
Placement and Post-Placement Services: $2000
Medical, legal and foster care expenses are additional.

**Number of children placed last year:** 13.

**Description of children:** Healthy infants and children and children with special needs.

**Adoption procedure:** 1) Application; 2) physicals and background checks; 3) home study.

**Average length of time between application and start of home study:** Less than 1 mo.

**Average length of time to complete home study:** 2 - 3 mos.

**Number of interviews:** 2.

**Home study description:** Assessment which includes reference and medical reports, criminal records and Social Services searches a Driver's License check and in which the following topics and others are discussed: personal history and emotional stability, courtship and marriage, evaluation of other children, religion, home, finances and insurance evaluation, motivation to adopt, ability and desire to care for a child.,.

**Average wait for a child after approval of a home study:** New agency.

**Foster care:** Pre-adoptive.

★ 867 ★
**Evangelical Child and Family Agency**
2401 N. Mayfair Rd., Ste. 302
Milwaukee, WI 53226
Phone: (414) 476-9550
Fax: (414) 476-9501

**Contact:** Ronald E. Menningen, ACSW.

**Date established:** 1984.

**Description:** Non-profit private agency licensed in the 37 southeastern counties of Wisconsin.

**Area served:** Residents of the 37 southeastern counties of Wisconsin and others by exception granted by the State.

**Requirements:** Evangelical Christian couples married at least 2 yrs. who are no older than 35 yrs., whose health is acceptable and who have no more than 1 child. Requirements are significantly more flexible for special needs placements.

**Fees:**
Application fee: $200.
placement of healthy, white infant: $8000 (includes application fee)
placement of child with special needs: $3000.
No fees for black couples.

**Number of children placed last year:** 12.

**Description of children:** Infants, 2 of whom were biracial and 1 with special needs.

**Adoption procedure:**
1) Return preliminary questionnaire;
2) attend orientation;
3) pastoral consultation;
4) case assignment and submission of medical reports and infertility work-up;
5) complete home study;
6) if approved, presentation of child;
7) if accepted, placement;
8) 6 mos. post-placement supervision;
9) finalization.

**Average length of time between application and start of home study:** 1-6 mos.

**Average length of time to complete home study:** 4 mos.

**Number of interviews:** 5-7.

**Home study description:** Assessment which includes but is not limited to motivation to adopt, child desired, resolution of infertility, family backgrounds, marital stability, self-concept, experience with children, cultural sensitivities, and special needs opportunities.

**Average wait for a child after approval of a home study:** 12-24 mos.

**Foster care:** Temporary.


★868★
**Lutheran Counseling and Family Services, Wauwatosa**
3800 N. Mayfair Rd.
Wauwatosa, WI 53222
Phone: (414) 536-8333

**Contact:** Carol H. Bennett, Adoption Coordinator.

**Date established:** 1896.

**Description:** Private, non-profit multi-service agency licensed to place children by the Wisconsin Department of Health and Social Services.

**Area served:** Residents of Wisconsin.

**Requirements:** Members of the Lutheran Church, Missouri Synod who are younger than 39 yrs.

**Fees:** Application: $100. Home study: $6000 minimum.

**Number of children placed last year:** 13.

**Description of children:** Infants.

**Adoption procedure:** 1) Inquiry; 2) application; 3) home study; 4) wait for placement; 5) placement; 6) post-placement supervision; 7) finalization.

**Average length of time between application and start of home study:** 1 - 6 mos.

**Average length of time to complete home study:** Approx. 3 mos.

**Number of interviews:** Unavailable.

**Home study description:** Assessment which meets the requirements of the Wisconsin Department of Health and Social Services and which measures a prospective adoptive family's ability and preparedness to parent.

**Average wait for a child after approval of a home study:** 2 yrs. or more.

**Foster care:** Cradle Care.


★869★
**Lutheran Social Services of Wisconsin and Upper Michigan**
1337 N. Taylor Dr.
Sheboygan, WI 53081
Phone: (414) 458-4161

**Contact:** Rev. James K. McClurg.

**Date established:** 1960.

**Description:** Non-profit, private agency.

**Area served:** Residents of southeast Wisconsin.

**Requirements:** Married couples who have a diagnosis of infertility.

**Fees:** Write or call for fee schedule.

**Number of children placed last year:** 150.

**Description of children:** Infants, children with special needs and foreign-born children.

**Adoption procedure:**
1) Attend information meeting;
2) return completed adoption survey;
3) participate in adoption group process;
4) if approved, wait for placement.

**Average length of time between application and start of home study:** Varies.

**Average length of time to complete home study:** 2 mos.

**Number of interviews:** 8.

**Home study description:** Evaluation of family background, education, health, religion, recommendation of references, marriage, employment, description of home, any children in the home and methods of discipline.

**Average wait for a child after approval of a home study:** Varies.

**Foster care:** Temporary.


★870★
**Pauquette Children's Services**
315 W. Conant St.
Portage, WI 53901
Phone: (608) 742-8004
Fax: (608) 742-2937

**Mailing address:**
P.O. Box 162, Portage, WI 53901

**Contact:** Brian Tool.

**Date established:** 1982.

**Description:** Private, non-denominational agency licensed in the State of Wisconsin.

**Area served:** Residents of the State of Wisconsin.

**Requirements:** Adults at least 25 yrs. or older, who have sufficient income to support a child and who are in good health. Applicants may be single or married, if married, marriage must be of at least 2 yrs. duration.

**Fees:**
Foreign/domestic adoption service fee: $2600;
independent adoption service fee: $1500.

**Number of children placed last year:** 125.

**Description of children:** Primarily infants and toddlers, 75 of whom were foreign-born.

**Adoption procedure:**
1) Submit application;
2) complete home study;
3) compile documents;
4) referral;
5) completion of legal work;
6) placement;
7) post-placement services;
8) finalization.

**Average length of time to complete home study:** 10-14 hrs.

**Number of interviews:** 3-4.

**Home study description:** Evaluation of individual and marital functioning, social factors, parenting ability, health and financial information.

**Average wait for a child after approval of a home study:** 6-12 mos.

**Foster care:** Temporary.

★ 871 ★
**Special Children, Inc.**
910 N. Elm Grove Rd., No. 2
Elm Grove, WI 53122
Phone: (414) 821-2125

**Contact:** Michael Short or Beth Peters.

**Date established:** 1991.

**Description:** Private, non-profit child placing agency licensed by the Wisconsin Department of Health and Social Services.

**Area served:** Residents of Wisconsin.

**Requirements:** Open.

**Fees:** Home study: $1500. Post-placement services: $500.

**Number of children placed last year:** 28.

**Description of children:** Infants, children with special needs and foreign-born children.

**Adoption procedure:** 1) Inquiry; 2) program selection; 3) home study; 4) child match and wait for placement; 5) placement; 6) post-placement supervision; 7) finalization.

**Average length of time between application and start of home study:** Less than 1 mo.

**Average length of time to complete home study:** 1 mo.

**Number of interviews:** 2.

**Home study description:** Assessment which meets the guidelines established by the Wisconsin Department of Health and Social Services.

**Average wait for a child after approval of a home study:** Unavailable.

**Foster care:** None.

★ 872 ★
**Van Dyke, Inc.**
**Romanian Adoption Assistance**
1727 A Stahle Rd.
Sheboygan, WI 53081
Phone: (414) 452-5358

**Contact:** Mirela Van Dyke, Executive Director.

**Date established:** 1991.

**Description:** Private child placing agency licensed by the Wisconsin Department of Health and Social Services and accredited by the Romanian Committee for Adoption.

**Area served:** Residents of the U.S.

**Requirements:** Couples married at least 3 yrs. who have documentation of infertility. The prospective adoptive mother must be between 25 and 40 yrs. older than the child to be placed and the prospective adoptive father must be between 25 and 45 yrs. older.

**Fees:** Processing fee: $1950 (with home study).
$1300 (without home study).
Total cost of adoption is approximately $10,000.

**Number of children placed last year:** Agreement of cooperation in Romania: signed in June, 1994.

**Description of children:** Romanian children between the ages of 0 - 7 yrs.

**Adoption procedure:** 1) Inquiry; 2) dossier completed; 3) dossier referred to Romania; 4) Adoption Committee child referral; 5) child acceptance; 6) travel to Romania required; 7) adoption is finalized in Romania.

**Average length of time between application and start of home study:** Less than 1 mo.

**Average length of time to complete home study:** 1 - 2 mos.

**Number of interviews:** Minimum of 3.

**Home study description:** Assessment which includes history of courtship and marriage, family, personality, life philosophy, health and finances, religion, living accommodations, issues surrounding infertility and motivation to adopt among others.

**Average wait for a child after approval of a home study:** Unavailable.

**Foster care:** None.

# WYOMING

## STATUTES

★ 873 ★

**Independent placement by intermediary?** Permitted.

**Independent placement by birth parents?** Permitted.

**Subsidies provided?** Up to $399/mo. for medical costs for children with special needs.

**Adoption cost defined by law?** No.

**Insurance for infertility?:** No.

**Home study required by state?** No.

**Prospective adoptive parent advertise for a child?** Permitted.

**Surrogacy laws?** Permitted.

**Residents access agencies of other states or countries?** Permitted.

**Requires judicial termination of birth parents' rights?** Voluntary relinquishments by both parents, when possible, to the adopting parents, attorney or clergymen are recognized. An *at risk* statement must be signed by the adopting parents if relinquishment is by only one birth parent.

**Time given to a birthmother to revoke her consent:** None.

**Court handling adoptions?** District Court.

**Adoption of Native Children:** Arapahoe-Shoshone Tribes on the reservation.

**Adoption records sealed?** Yes, but adoptees, adoptive parents, birth parents and other biological relative, may petition a district court to conduct a search for biological family members through the Wyoming Confidential Intermediary Program when the adoptee reaches the age of 19 yrs.

**Photo-listing book available?** Participates in the photo listing of the Rocky Mountain Adoption Exchange.


# PUBLIC AGENCIES

★874★
**Department of Family Services of Wyoming**
Hathaway Bldg., 3rd Fl.
Cheyenne, WY 82002
Phone: (307) 777-7561
Fax: (307) 777-7747

**Branch address:**
710 Garfield, Laramie Plains Civic Center, Ste. 220, Laramie, WY 82070
Phone: (307) 745-7324

616 2nd Ave., Greybull, WY 82426
Phone: (307) 765-9453

454 Nevada (Tues. & Thurs., 9:30-12; 1:00-3:00), Lovell, WY 82431
Phone: (307) 548-6503

724 N. Commercial, Ste. 100, Gillette, WY 82716
Phone: (307) 682-7277

Box 2409, Rawlins, WY 82301
Phone: (307) 328-0612

530 Oak, Douglas, WY 82633
Phone: (307) 358-3138

Bronco Bldg. (Wed. & Thurs. 10:00-12 and 1:00-3), 506 W. Birch, Glenrock, WY 82637
Phone: (307) 436-9068

Box 57, Sundance, WY 82729
Phone: (307) 283-2014

201 N. 4th, Lander, WY 82520
Phone: (307) 332-4038

120 N. 6th E., Riverton, WY 82501
Phone: (307) 856-6521

2025 Campbell, Ste. 1, Torrington, WY 82240
Phone: (307) 532-2191

224 Springview St., Thermopolis, WY 82443
Phone: (307) 864-2158

381 N. Main, Buffalo, WY 82834
Phone: (307) 684-7281

1710 Capitol Ave., Cheyenne, WY 82001
Phone: (307) 777-7921

1100 Pine Ave., Kemmerer, WY 83101
Phone: (307) 877-6670

475 S. Spruce, Casper, WY 82601
Phone: (307) 261-2100

302 S. Main, Lusk, WY 82225
Phone: (307) 334-2153

1301 Rumsey, Cody, WY 82414
Phone: (307) 587-6246

109 W. 14th, Powell, WY 82435
Phone: (307) 754-2245

975 Gilchrist, Wheatland, WY 82201
Phone: (307) 322-3790

Box 785, Sheridan, WY 82801
Phone: (307) 672-2404

Box 1070, Pinedale, WY 82941
Phone: (307) 367-4124

1682 Sunset Dr., Rock Springs, WY 82901
Phone: (307) 382-5916

350 City View Dr., Ste. 206, Evanston, WY 82930
Phone: (307) 789-2756

801 Robertson, Worland, WY 82401
Phone: (307) 347-6181

185 Willow, Box 547, Jackson, WY 83001
Phone: (307) 733-7757

1517 W. Main, Newcastle, WY 82701
Phone: (307) 746-4657

**Contact:** George A. Lovato, Director.

**Date established:** 1948.

**Description:** State social services agency.

**Area served:** Residents of the State of Wyoming.

**Requirements:** Applicants must be adults.

**Fees:** None.

**Number of children placed last year:** 16.

**Description of children:** 5 infants and 11 special needs.

**Adoption procedure:**
1) Initial inquiry;
2) complete home study;
3) if approved, placement;
4) file Petition to Adopt;
5) 6 mos. post-placement supervision;
6) finalization.

**Average length of time between application and start of home study:** 6-12 mos.

**Average length of time to complete home study:** Varies.

**Number of interviews:** Varies.

**Home study description:** Evaulation of autobiographies of applicants, personal interests, marital history (if applicable), financial resources, health, motivation to adopt, attitudes toward adoption, living conditions and family background.

**Average wait for a child after approval of a home study:** 1-6 mos.

**Foster care:** Temporary, long-term and specialized.

## PRIVATE AGENCIES

**★ 875 ★**
**Wyoming Children's Society**
716 Randall Ave.
Cheyenne, WY 82001
Phone: (307) 632-7619

**Mailing address:**
   P.O. Box 105, Cheyenne, WY 82001

**Contact:** Carol Lindly.

**Date established:** 1911.

**Description:** Private, non-profit adoption agency.

**Area served:** Residents of the State of Wyoming.

**Requirements:** Adults 21 yrs. and older. Applicants must be married for infant adoption.

**Fees:**
Application fee: $100;
home study: $700;
infant placement fee: 15% of gross income (two-thirds due at placement, one-third at finalization).

**Number of children placed last year:** Approximately 25.

**Description of children:** Newborn infants, mixed race children, sibling groups, children who have been abused and/or neglected or who have mental or physical challenges; assist with foreign placements of children.

**Adoption procedure:**
1) Submit application;
2) reference checks;
3) complete home study;
4) if approved, birthmother chooses family from non-identifying family profile;
5) after relinquishment papers are signed, placement.

**Average length of time between application and start of home study:** 1 mo. or less.

**Average length of time to complete home study:** 2 mos.

**Number of interviews:** 3-4.

**Home study description:** Assessment of personal history, lifestyle, education and occupation, religion, recreation, health, strengths and weaknesses, parenting styles and methods of discipline, family relationships, etc.

**Average wait for a child after approval of a home study:** Varies.

**Foster care:** Very short-term.

**★ 876 ★**
**Wyoming Parenting Society**
P.O. Box 3774
Jackson, WY 83001
Phone: (307) 733-6357
Fax: (307) 733-8276

**Contact:** Marilee Enright, MSW, Director.

**Date established:** 1983.

**Description:** Private, non-profit agency licensed in the State of Wyoming.

**Area served:** Residents of Wyoming.

**Requirements:** Flexible except that infants are only placed with married couples.

**Fees:**
Placement fee: $2500;
home study fee: $750;
special needs: $750.

**Number of children placed last year:** 3.

**Description of children:** Infants and children.

**Adoption procedure:**
1) Submit application;
2) complete home study;
3) if approved, placement;
4) post-placement services;
5) finalization.

**Average length of time between application and start of home study:** Varies.

**Average length of time to complete home study:** Approx. 3 mos.

**Number of interviews:** 3.

**Home study description:** Assessment of applicants' understanding of the adoption process, capability and willingness to parent a non-biological child, maturity, flexibility and support systems among others.

**Average wait for a child after approval of a home study:** Varies.

**Foster care:** Temporary.

# ALBERTA

## STATUTES

**★ 877 ★**

**Residents access agencies of foreign countries, including U.S.?** Yes.

**Birth parents place child directly in an adoptive home?** Yes.

**Other individual place child in adoptive home?** No, third parties, other than private agencies, may no longer make adoptive placements.

**Subsidies provided?** Post-Adoption Support Program.

**Adoption records sealed?** Yes, but non-identifying information and a passive registry are provided.

**Adoption cost defined by law?** Not applicable.

**Home study required by state?** Yes, after placement.

**Provincial Exchange:** Residents of Alberta with approved home studies may view a photo-listing.

**Requires judicial termination of birth parents' rights?** Voluntary relinquishments are valid barring special circumstances.

**Time given to a birthmother to revoke her consent:** 10 days.

**Court handling adoptions?** Queen's Bench.

**Adoption of Native Children:** Placements by Alberta Family and Social Services are made in consultation with band.

## PUBLIC AGENCIES

**★ 878 ★**
**Alberta Family and Social Services**
7th St. Plaza
10030—107th St.
Edmonton, AB, Canada
Phone: (403) 422-0177
Fax: (403) 427-2048

**Branch address:**
   52 district offices.

**Contact:** Anne Scully, Program Supervisor.

**Description:** Licensed provincial agency.

**Area served:** Residents of Alberta.

**Requirements:** Applicants must be aged 18 or older.

**Fees:** None.

**Number of children placed last year:** 250 in custody.

**Description of children:** Infants and special needs children.

**Adoption procedure:** Referral to district office; initial screening; information sent to central matching; home study in response to availability of children; wait for placement.

**Average length of time between application and start of home study:** Varies.

**Average length of time to complete home study:** Varies.

**Home study description:** Assessment of background, child abuse and criminal record; training.

**Average wait for a child after approval of a home study:** Varies.

## PRIVATE AGENCIES

★879★
**Adoption By Choice**
908 Seventeenth Ave., S.W., Ste. 315
Calgary, AB, Canada T2T 0A3
Phone: (403) 245-8854

**Contact:** Carol Lamb, MSW, RSW, Program Director.

**Date established:** 1989.

**Description:** Private, non-profit adoption agency licensed by Alberta Family and Social Services.

**Area served:** Residents of Alberta, Canada.

**Requirements:** None.

**Fees:** Application: $401.25. Home study: $963. Other fees: $3500. Counseling and court/administration fees are additional.

**Number of children placed last year:** 38.

**Description of children:** Infants and toddlers.

**Adoption procedure:** Agency conducts fully open adoptions.

**Average length of time between application and start of home study:** 1 - 6 mos.

**Average length of time to complete home study:** 8 hrs.

**Number of interviews:** 2 - 3.

**Home study description:** Assessment which includes background, educational and financial information, health, religious affiliation, leisure activities, marital relationship, issues surrounding infertility, type of child desired and adoption plan.

**Average wait for a child after approval of a home study:** 12 - 24 mos.

**Foster care:** None.

★880★
**Adoption Services**
**Crossroads Counselling Centre**
542 Seventh St. S., Ste. 202
Lethbridge, AB, Canada T1J 2H1
Phone: (403) 327-7080
Fax: (403) 327-7282

**Contact:** Adoption Services Program Director.

**Date established:** 1992.

**Description:** Private, non-profit non-denominational Christian counselling centre licensed to place children by Alberta Family and Social Services and offering open adoption services.

**Area served:** Primarily residents of Southern Alberta, Canada.

**Requirements:** Couples married at least 1 yr. whose health is adequate to the task of parenthood and who have sufficient income to support a family.

**Fees:** Application: $260 (non-refundable); home assessment: $900. Total fees: $4200. Subsequent placement: $3900. Mileage costs are additional.

**Number of children placed last year:** 6.

**Description of children:** Infants.

**Adoption procedure:** 1) Preliminary application; 2) adoptive parent training; 3) home study process; 4) preparation of adoptive applicants' profile for birth parent review; 5) match meeting; 6) placement; 7) post-placement services; 8) court documentation.

**Average length of time between application and start of home study:** 1 - 2 mos.

**Average length of time to complete home study:** Within 90 days.

**Number of interviews:** 4 - 6.

**Home study description:** Assessment which meets the criteria established by Alberta Social Services and which includes demographic information and personal history, family dynamics and community relationships, home and neighborhood, income, understanding of adoption and motivation to adopt, type of child desired and the report of references.

**Average wait for a child after approval of a home study:** 6 - 30 mos.

**Foster care:** None.

★881★
**Christian Adoption Services**
276 Midpark Way, Ste. 221
Calgary, AB, Canada T2X 2B5
Phone: (403) 256-3224
Fax: (403) 256-8367

**Contact:** Wendy Robinson, BSW, Program Director.

**Date established:** 1986.

**Description:** Licensed agency.

**Area served:** Residents of Alberta.

**Requirements:** Born-again Christian couples who are active members of an Evangelical church and have documented fertility.

**Fees:** Home study assessment: $1000; $2800 to finalize; transportation and expenses extra.

**Number of children placed last year:** 12 or more annually.

**Description of children:** Primarily infants.

**Adoption procedure:** Couple requests application in writing; information packet; return application; group meeting; initial interview; home assessment; wait on approval list; birthmother selects from 3-4 profiles; placement.

**Average length of time between application and start of home study:** 1-6 mos.

**Average length of time to complete home study:** 1 mo.

**Number of interviews:** Interview, information session, home study, and workshop; support groups available.

**Home study description:** Evaluatory process which includes discussions of background, problem resolution strategies, parenting skills, adoption issues.

**Average wait for a child after approval of a home study:** 12-24 mos.

**Foster care:** None.

# BRITISH COLUMBIA

## STATUTES

★ 882 ★

**Residents access agencies of foreign countries, including U.S.?** Yes.

**Birth parents place child directly in an adoptive home?** Yes.

**Other individual place child in adoptive home?** Yes.

**Subsidies provided?** Special Services and maintenance.

**Adoption records sealed?** Yes, but non-identifying information and an active reunion registry is provided.

**Adoption cost defined by law?** The elements are defined but not the amounts.

**Home study required by state?** No, but the Ministry does conduct an inquiry after placement.

**Provincial Exchange:** Yes, the Ministry publishes and *Adoption Bulletin* every 2-3 mos.

**Requires judicial termination of birth parents' rights?** Voluntary relinquishments are valid.

**Time given to a birthmother to revoke her consent:** Anytime up to finalization when good cause is shown.

**Court handling adoptions?** Supreme Court.

**Adoption of Native Children:** Overseen by Ministry. A moratorium is currently in effect which prohibits the placement of First Nation children in non-native homes. First Nation parents, however, may still place their children in non-native homes if they so choose.

## PUBLIC AGENCIES

★ 883 ★
**Ministry of Social Services**
**Family and Child Services, Adoption Services**
Parliament Buildings
Victoria, BC, Canada V8W 3A2
Phone: (604)387-3660
Fax: (604) 356-7862

**Contact:** Supervisor.

**Description:** Public agency.

**Area served:** Residents of British Columbia.

**Requirements:** Adults 19 years or older. Preference given to married couples with health sufficient to parent. Applicants must be residents of British Columbia.

**Fees:** None.

**Number of children placed last year:** 50 infants, 114 children and special needs.

**Description of children:** Infants and children with special needs.

**Adoption procedure:** Referral to District Office; application; review; wait for home study; home study; matched.

**Average length of time between application and start of home study:** Varies from 1 mo. to 6 or more yrs.

**Average length of time to complete home study:** 6 mos. or more.

**Number of interviews:** 3 minimum.

**Home study description:** Background and criminal records checked.

**Average wait for a child after approval of a home study:** Varies.

## PRIVATE AGENCIES

★ 884 ★
**Hope Pregnancy Counseling and Adoption**
P.O. Box 8000-531
Abbotsford, BC, Canada V2S 6H1
Phone: (604)850-1002

**Contact:** Ann Welwood, Director.

**Description:** Non-denominational counseling and adoption agency.

**Area served:** Residents of British Columbia.

**Requirements:** Couples married at least two years, with one year residency in British Columbia and a current home study.

**Fees:** For application, seminars, interim care costs for infant, and birthmother's counseling.

**Number of children placed last year:** 22.

**Description of children:** Infants.

**Adoption procedure:** Letter of intent; 1-day orientation; references, medical and criminal records checked; short interview; 3 day retreat; active file; birthmother selects.

**Average length of time between application and start of home study:** Responsible for own home study.

**Number of interviews:** 1 full day.

**Home study description:** N/A.

**Average wait for a child after approval of a home study:** Varies.

# MANITOBA

## STATUTES

★ 885 ★

**Residents access agencies of foreign countries, including U.S.?** Yes, if the adoption is finalized in the child's country of origin. If a Manitoba home study is required, it must be conducted by a mandated Child and Family Services agency in Manitoba.

**Birth parents place child directly in an adoptive home?** Permitted.

**Other individual place child in adoptive home?** Illegal.

**Subsidies provided?** Start-up which covers the actual cost of transportation and related costs associated with placement requirements, equipment or structural renovations; special services which covers medical, dental or rehabilitative services; maintenance.

**Adoption records sealed?** Sealed, but non-identifying information is provided and the Post-Adoption Registry will release identifying information of registered adopted adults for birth parents or adult birth siblings not placed for adoption when both parties are registered.

**Adoption cost defined by law?** Yes, only legal fees are permissible.

**Home study required by state?** Required within the 6 mos. after placement and presented to the judge who decides whether to grant the adoption. The Department must also be notified prior to placement.

**Provincial Exchange:** Yes, Central Adoption Registry includes all applicants and available children and circulates a regular bulletin to 26 agencies.

**Requires judicial termination of birth parents' rights?** Only relinquishments to a mandated Child and Family Services agency are permitted.

**Time given to a birthmother to revoke her consent:** Until the child is placed for adoption; or within 1 yr. if there has been no adoptive placement.

**Court handling adoptions?** Queen's Bench and Family Court in more remote areas.

**Adoption of Native Children:** First nation agency on reserves; Department in all other areas.


# PUBLIC AGENCIES

★ 886 ★
**Manitoba Department of Family Services**
**Child and Family Support Branch**
2nd Floor, 114 Garry St.
Winnipeg, MB, Canada R3C 1G1
Phone: (204) 945-6964
Fax: (204) 945-6717

**Branch address:**
Winnipeg Child and Family Services - Southwest Area, 2393A Ness Ave., Winnipeg, MB R3J 1A5
Phone: (204) 944-4475

Winnipeg Child and Family Services - East Area, 123B Marion St., Winnipeg, MB R2H 0T3
Phone: (204) 233-8931

Winnipeg Child and Family Services - Northwest Area, 1386 Main St., Winnipeg, MB, Canada R2W 3V1
Phone: (204) 944-4031

Winnipeg Child and Family Services - Central Area, 2nd Fl., 831 Portage Ave., Winnipeg, MB R3G 0N6
Phone: (204) 944-4200

Interlake Region, Selkirk Mental Health Centre, 3rd Fl., Administration Bldg., 825 Manitoba Ave., Selkirk, MB R1A 2B5

Parkland Region, 27 Second Ave. S.W., Dauphin, MB R7N 3E5

Norman Region, Provincial Bldg., 79 Third St. W., The Pas, MB R9A 1M4

Eastman Region, 20 First St. S., Bausejour, MB R0E 0C0

West Region Child and Family Services, 38 First Ave. N.W., Dauphin, MB R7N 1G7
Phone: (204) 638-6941

Anishanaabe Child and Family Services, General Delivery, Fairford First Nation, Fairford, MB, Canada R0C 0X0

Intertribal Child and Family Services, Box 309, Hodgson, MB R0C 1N0

Dakota Ojibway Child and Family Services, 702 Douglas St., Brandon, MB R7A 7B2

Southeast Child and Family Services, 511 Ellice Ave., Winnipeg, MB R3B 1Y8

Child and Family Services of Western Manitoba, 340 Ninth St., Rm 100, Brandon, MB R7A 6C2
Phone: (204) 726-6030

Child and Family Services of Central Manitoba, 25 Third St., S.E., Portage la Prairie, MB R1N 1N1
Phone: (204) 857-8751

16 Churchill Health Centre, Churchill, MB R0B 0E0
**Contact:** Local office.
**Description:** Central provincial office which sets policy, monitors programs, consults on legislative changes, provides consultation and assists agencies in performing services.
**Area served:** Residents of Manitoba.
**Requirements:** Applicants must be of the age of majority.
**Fees:** None.
**Number of children placed last year:** Unavailable.
**Description of children:** Children of all ages, both Canadian and foreign-born.
**Adoption procedure:** 1) Inquiry; 2) referral to geographically mandated agency; 3) application; 4) home study; 5) approval process; 6) placement; 7) post-placement supervision; 8) finalization.
**Average length of time between application and start of home study:** Varies with office.
**Average length of time to complete home study:** 1 - 4 mos.
**Number of interviews:** Minimum of 4.
**Home study description:** Assessment which includes but is not limited to background and personal information on the applicants, home and neighborhood, motivation to adopt, the type of child desired, income and finances, health, criminal and abuse registry checks, report of references and parenting styles.
**Average wait for a child after approval of a home study:** Varies with office.
**Foster care:** Emergency, short and long-term and therapeutic.


★ 887 ★
**Thompson Region**
**Health & Family Services, Manitoba**
867 Thompson Dr. S.
Thompson, MB, Canada R8N 0C9
Phone: (204) 677-6570
**Contact:** Cheryl Martinez, Coordinator, Child & Family Services.
**Description:** Regional provincial agency mandated to place children by Manitoba Family Services.
**Area served:** Residents of the Thompson Region.
**Requirements:** Applicants must be Canadian citizens and meet the age, health and income requirements of Manitoba Family Services.
**Fees:** None.
**Number of children placed last year:** 5.
**Description of children:** Infants and pre-schoolers.
**Adoption procedure:** 1) Inquiry; 2) application; 3) home study; 4) approval/licensure; 5) placement; 6) finalization.
**Average length of time between application and start of home study:** Children with special needs: 1 - 6 mos. Healthy newborns: 24 mos. or more.
**Average length of time to complete home study:** 2 - 3 mos.

**Number of interviews:** Minimum of 4.

**Home study description:** Assessment which includes personal information, applicant(s)' childhood, marital history, children in the family, family solidarity, Criminal and Child Abuse checks, income and finances, home and neighborhood.

**Average wait for a child after approval of a home study:** Children with special needs: 12 - 24 mos. Healthy infants: 2 yrs. or more.

**Foster care:** Temporary, long-term and permanent.

### ★ 888 ★
**Winnipeg Child and Family Services (East Area)**
222 Provencher Blvd.
Winnipeg, MB, Canada R2H 0T3
Phone: (204) 944-4288

**Contact:** Robert Boulet, Supervisor.

**Date established:** 1905.

**Description:** Public provincial family service agency entrusted under the Child and Family Services Act to place children.

**Area served:** Residents of the east area of the City of Winnipeg and all municipalities east of the Red River.

**Requirements:** Flexible.

**Fees:** Post-Adoption Registry fee: $35. Search fee: $265.

**Number of children placed last year:** Unavailable.

**Description of children:** Infants, toddlers and school-age children, some with special needs and some foreign-born.

**Adoption procedure:** 1) Application; 2) group adoption meetings; 3) submission of personal information; 4) home study; 5) placement; 6) post-placement support services; 7) finalization.

**Average length of time between application and start of home study:** 1 yr. or more.

**Average length of time to complete home study:** 6 wks.

**Number of interviews:** 4 - 6.

**Home study description:** Assessment which includes physical descriptions of the applicant(s), medical, educational and financial information, information on the family of origin, criminal records and child abuse registry checks, personality and parenting styles, lifestyle, marital relationship, children in the family, motivation to adopt and openness to contact with the birth family.

**Average wait for a child after approval of a home study:** Infants: 12 - 24 mos. Pre-school children and older: 12 - 24 mos.

**Foster care:** Temporary, long-term and permanent.

## PRIVATE AGENCIES

### ★ 889 ★
**Child and Family Services of Western Manitoba**
340 Ninth St., Rm. 100
Brandon, MB, Canada R7A 6C2
Phone: (204) 726-6030
1 (800) 483-8980
Fax: (204) 726-6775

**Contact:** Kenneth G. Knight, Executive Director.

**Date established:** 1898.

**Description:** Autonomous, non-profit organization providing child and family services and financed by public and private monies.

**Area served:** Residents of southwestern Manitoba excluding First Nation Reserves.

**Requirements:** Open.

**Fees:** Registration fee for post-legal adoption services.

**Number of children placed last year:** 14.

**Description of children:** Infants, toddlers, children with special needs, foreign-born children.

**Adoption procedure:** 1) Initial inquiry; 2) initial application; 3) 8 - 9 yr. wait to begin home study for Caucasian infants; 3) Native and Metis applicants begin home study immediately.

**Average length of time between application and start of home study:** 24 or more mos.

**Average length of time to complete home study:** 10-12 hrs.

**Number of interviews:** 4-5.

**Home study description:** Educational and assessment process in which issues of health, motivation to adopt, marital and family life, parenting, finances, home and neighborhood, values and philosophy on education and religion are explored. Home study includes Criminal Records and Child Abuse Registry checks.

**Average wait for a child after approval of a home study:** 6-12 mos., but sometimes longer for female infants.

**Foster care:** Temporary, long-term, permanent and independent living.

### ★ 890 ★
**Child and Family Services of Western Manitoba**
340 Ninth St., Rm. 100
Brandon, MB, Canada R7A 6C2
Phone: (204) 726-6030
1 (800) 483-8980
Fax: (204) 726-6775

**Contact:** Kenneth G. Knight, Executive Director.

**Date established:** 1898.

**Description:** Autonomous, non-profit organization providing child and family services and financed by public and private monies.

**Area served:** Residents of southwestern Manitoba excluding First Nation Reserves.

**Requirements:** Open.

**Fees:** Registration fee for post-legal adoption services.

**Number of children placed last year:** 14.

**Description of children:** Infants, toddlers, children with special needs, foreign-born children.

**Adoption procedure:** 1) Initial inquiry; 2) initial application; 3) 8 - 9 yr. wait to begin home study for Caucasian infants; 3) Native and Metis applicants begin home study immediately.

**Average length of time between application and start of home study:** 24 or more mos.

**Average length of time to complete home study:** 10-12 hrs.

**Number of interviews:** 4-5.

**Home study description:** Educational and assessment process in which issues of health, motivation to adopt, marital and family life, parenting, finances, home and neighborhood, values and philosophy on education and religion are explored. Home study includes Criminal Records and Child Abuse Registry checks.

**Average wait for a child after approval of a home study:** 6-12 mos., but sometimes longer for female infants.

**Foster care:** Temporary, long-term, permanent and independent living.

★891★
**Cree Nation Child & Family Caring Agency**
P.O. Box 3910, Otineka Mall
The Pas, MB, Canada R9A 1S5
Phone: (204) 623-7456

**Contact:** Annette Veito, Adoption/Permanent Ward Coordinator.

**Date established:** 1993.

**Description:** Native family Service agency mandated to place children by Manitoba Family Services.

**Area served:** Residents within the Swampy Cree Tribal Council which includes Shoal River, Moose Lake and Grand Rapids.

**Requirements:** Members of the OpasKwayak Cree Nation.

**Fees:** Costs for birth, marriage and other necessary certificates.

**Number of children placed last year:** 11.

**Description of children:** Children between the ages of infancy and 12 yrs.

**Adoption procedure:** Agency follows procedures dictated in their mandate from Manitoba Family Services.

**Average length of time between application and start of home study:** 1 - 6 mos.

**Average length of time to complete home study:** 1 - 4 mos.

**Number of interviews:** 4.

**Home study description:** Assessment which includes, but is not limited to, Police and Child Abuse records checks, appearance, biographies and family of origin, personality, education and occupation, income and finances, home and neighborhood, marriage and children in the family, health including the use of drugs and alcohol, interests, hobbies and goals, attitudes and expectations as well as motivation to adopt.

**Average wait for a child after approval of a home study:** 1 - 6 mos.

**Foster care:** Temporary, long-term and specialized.

★892★
**Jewish Child and Family Service**
2055 McPhillips St.
Winnipeg, MB, Canada R2V 3C6
Phone: (204) 949-6860

**Branch address:**
   3-666 St. James St., Winnipeg, MB, Canada R3G 3J6

**Contact:** Adoption Coordinator.

**Date established:** 1952.

**Description:** Non-profit family service agency mandated to place children by Manitoba Family Services.

**Area served:** Residents of Manitoba.

**Requirements:** Applicants must be Jewish Canadian citizens and meet the requirements determined by Manitoba Family Services.

**Fees:** Counselling: Sliding scale.

**Number of children placed last year:** 5.

**Description of children:** Infants, children with special needs and foreign-born children.

**Adoption procedure:** 1) Application; 2) interview with Adoption Coordinator; 3) selection of program based on interview; 4) home study; 5) provincial registration; 6) wait for placement.

**Average length of time between application and start of home study:** 1 - 6 mos. Beginning the home study is based on the type of child the applicants' request. Home studies for applicants requesting older children with special needs are prioritized. The wait to begin a home study for applicants requesting a healthy, newborn infant through the government is 10 yrs. or more.

**Average length of time to complete home study:** 3 - 4 mos.

**Number of interviews:** Minimum of 4.

**Home study description:** Written assessment which describes the applicants in terms of their physical appearance, educational and occupational background, family of origin, race, languages spoken, religion, interests and activities, health and social history, the report of references and the worker's summary. It also addresses such topics as marital history, home and neighborhood, issues surrounding infertility and adoption, parenting style, child desired and expectations of that child.

**Average wait for a child after approval of a home study:** 2 yrs. or more.

**Foster care:** Temporary.

# NEW BRUNSWICK

## STATUTES

★893★
**Residents access agencies of foreign countries, including U.S.?** Yes via the Department of Health and Community Service.

**Birth parents place child directly in an adoptive home?** Yes.

**Other individual place child in adoptive home?** No.

**Subsidies provided?** Subsidized adoptions as per child's needs.

**Adoption records sealed?** Yes but non-identifying information and a passive post-adoption registry are provided.

**Adoption cost defined by law?** Only legal fees are permissible.

**Home study required by state?** Yes. An investigative report is required after placement.

**Provincial Exchange:** Profiles are sent to branch offices.

**Requires judicial termination of birth parents' rights?** Voluntary relinquishments are valid only in the case of newborn infants when received no earlier than 3 days after birth. All other relinquishments require judicial termination.

**Time given to a birthmother to revoke her consent:** A minimum of 6 mos. or until adoption order is signed.

**Court handling adoptions?** Family Court.

**Adoption of Native Children:** Band agencies.

## PUBLIC AGENCIES

★894★
**Department of Health and Community Service**
300 St. Mary's St.
P.O. Box 5001
Fredericton, NB, Canada E3B 5G5
Phone: (506) 453-3953
Fax: (506) 444-5178

**Branch address:**
   12 regional offices.

**Contact:** Lucy McGilligan, Adoption Supervisor.

**Description:** Public agency.

**Area served:** New Brunswick.

**Requirements:** Each case is considered individually.

**Fees:** None.

**Number of children placed last year:** 31.

**Description of children:** Infants, toddlers, and older children.

**Adoption procedure:** For infants: telephone inquiry; registration; information session; wait for home study; home study; wait for placement; placement; 6 month supervision; finalization.
For older child: telephone inquiry; information session; complete registration form; attend older child adoption seminar; home study; if approved, wait for child match; pre-placement visitation; placement; supervision for 12 or more months; finalization.

**Average length of time between application and start of home study:** Varies.

**Average length of time to complete home study:** Varies.

**Number of interviews:** 4-6.

**Home study description:** Assessment of home and finances; medical and criminal records checked; 3 references; school references for any child in the home.

**Average wait for a child after approval of a home study:** Varies.

---

# NEWFOUNDLAND

## STATUTES

★ 895 ★

**Residents access agencies of foreign countries, including U.S.?** Yes, if the adoption is finalized in another jurisdiction.

**Birth parents place child directly in an adoptive home?** Not without the permission of the Director.

**Other individual place child in adoptive home?** No.

**Subsidies provided?** Maintenance, medical and other special needs.

**Adoption records sealed?** Yes, but through the Post-Adoption Program adoptees 19 yrs. and older may access non-identifying information or request a search.

**Adoption cost defined by law?** Not addressed in law.

**Home study required by state?** Yes, before adoption can be finalized.

**Provincial Exchange:** None.

**Requires judicial termination of birth parents' rights?** Voluntary relinquishments are recognized when given no sooner than 7 days after the birth of the child.

**Time given to a birthmother to revoke her consent:** 21 days.

**Court handling adoptions?** Provincial Court or Supreme Court depending upon locale.

**Adoption of Native Children:** Provincial laws apply but the Mi'Kmaq, the only provincially recognized band, have their own agency.

# PUBLIC AGENCIES

★ 896 ★
**Department of Social Services, Newfoundland**
3rd. Fl., West Block
Confederation Bldg.
St. Johns, NF, Canada A1B 4J6
Phone: (709) 729-2668

**Mailing address:**
  P.O. Box 8700, St. Johns, NF, Canada A1B 4J6

**Contact:** Consultant for Adoption in one of the district offices.

**Description:** Provincial agency.

**Area served:** Residents of Newfoundland and Labrador.

**Requirements:** Without a letter from the Director applicants must be at least 25 yrs. old.

**Fees:** None.

**Number of children placed last year:** 18.

**Description of children:** Infants and older children.

**Adoption procedure:** 1) Inquiry and referral to district office; 2) application; 3) personal interview; 4) admission to reserve waiting list; 5) home study; 6) wait for placement; 7) placement; 8) post-placement supervision; 9) finalization.

**Average length of time between application and start of home study:** 7 yrs. for infants and 4 yrs. for older children.

**Average length of time to complete home study:** Varies by district office.

**Number of interviews:** Minimum of 4.

**Home study description:** Assessment which includes personal history from childhood to the present, education, finances, personality issues surrounding adoption and attitudes toward parenting.

**Average wait for a child after approval of a home study:** Unavailable.

**Foster care:** Emergency, short and long-term and therapeutic.

---

# NORTHWEST TERRITORIES

## STATUTES

★ 897 ★

**Residents access agencies of foreign countries, including U.S.?** Yes.

**Birth parents place child directly in an adoptive home?** Yes.

**Other individual place child in adoptive home?** No.

**Subsidies provided?** Medical, educational and maintenance.

**Adoption records sealed?** Yes, but non-identifying information is provided and Native Custom Adoptions are not sealed.

**Adoption cost defined by law?** No.

**Home study required by state?** Yes, 6 mos. after placement.

**Provincial Exchange:** Yes.

**Requires judicial termination of birth parents' rights?** Voluntary relinquishments given no sooner than 5 days after child's birth are valid.

**Time given to a birthmother to revoke her consent:** Until the order of adoption is granted.

**Court handling adoptions?** Supreme Court.

**Adoption of Native Children:** Aboriginal commissioners confirm the adoptions of aboriginal children.

## PUBLIC AGENCIES

★ 898 ★
**Department of Social Services**
**Government of the Northwest Territories**
Box 4, Precambrian Bldg.
500, 4920-52 St.
Yellowknife, NT, Canada X1A 3T1
Phone: (403)873-7943
Fax: (403) 873-0444

**Contact:** Mary Beauchamp, Coordinator, Child Protection.

**Description:** Licensed territorial agency.

**Area served:** Residents of Northwest Territories.

**Requirements:** Two years' residency.

**Fees:** None.

**Number of children placed last year:** 8-10.

**Description of children:** Varies.

**Adoption procedure:** Referral to office; appointment with intake worker; application; reference and medical check; home study; review; waiting period.

**Average length of time between application and start of home study:** 6-12 mos.

**Average length of time to complete home study:** Varies.

**Number of interviews:** Varies.

**Home study description:** Evaluatory process includes assessment of background, motivation, knowledge of mixed race children, adoption issues.

**Average wait for a child after approval of a home study:** 12-24 mos.

# NOVA SCOTIA

## STATUTES

★ 899 ★

**Residents access agencies of foreign countries, including U.S.?** Yes.

**Birth parents place child directly in an adoptive home?** Only if private and legislative requirements are met.

**Other individual place child in adoptive home?** Yes, provided legislative requirements are met.

**Subsidies provided?** Medical and maintenance.

**Adoption records sealed?** Yes, but non-identifying information and a passive adoption registry are available to adoptees 19 yrs. and older.

**Adoption cost defined by law?** Yes. No payment may be made or received in consideration of the placement or procurement of a child.

**Home study required by state?** Yes, after placement.

**Provincial Exchange:** Yes, the *Nova Scotia Adoption Exchange.*.

**Requires judicial termination of birth parents' rights?** Voluntary relinquishments are recognized if given no sooner than 15 days after the birth.

**Time given to a birthmother to revoke her consent:** Anytime prior to the filing of the notice of proposed adoption or by court order.

**Court handling adoptions?** Supreme Court.

**Adoption of Native Children:** Native agency.

## PUBLIC AGENCIES

★ 900 ★
**Department of Community Services (Nova Scotia)**
**Family and Children's Services**
P.O. Box 696
Halifax, NS, Canada B3J 2T7
Phone: (902) 424-3205

**Branch address:**

Family and Children's Services of Annapolis County, Municipal Bldg., St. George St., P.O. Box 39, Annapolis Royal, NS B0S 1A0
Phone: (902) 532-2337

Children's Aid Society of Cape Breton, Provincial Bldg., Ste.7, 360 Prince St., Sydney, NS B1P 5L1
Phone: (902) 563-3400

Children's Aid Society and Family Services of Colchester Cou nty, 58 Willow St., P.O. Box 950, Truro, NS B2N 5G7
Phone: (902) 893-5950

Family and Children's Services of Cumberland County, P.O. Box 399, Amherst, NS B4H 3Z5
Phone: (902) 667-3336

Children's Aid Society of Halifax, 5244 South St., Halifax, NS B3J 1A4
Phone: (902) 425-5420

Family and Children's Services of Harts County, 1469 King St., P.O. Box 99, Windsor, NS B0N 2T0
Phone: (902) 798-2289

Children's Aid Society of Inverness-Richmond, P.O. Box 359, Port Hawkesbury, NS B0E 2V0
Phone: (902) 625-0660

Family and Children's Services of Kings County, 76 River St., P.O. Box 188, Kentville, NS B4N 1G9
Phone: (902) 678-6176

Family and Children's Services of Lunenberg County, Provincial Bldg., 99 High St., Ste. 105, P.O. Box 170, Bridgewater, NS B4V 1V8
Phone: (902) 543-2411

Children's Aid Society of Pictou, P.O. Box 488, New Glasgow, NS, Canada B2H 5E5
Phone: (902) 755-5950

Family and Children's Services of Queen's County, 43 Carken St., P.O. Box 1360, Liverpool, NS B0T 1K0
Phone: (902) 354-2711

Children's Aid Society of Shelburne County, P.O. Box 9, Barrington, NS B0W 1E0
Phone: (902) 637-2337

Family and Children's Services of Yarmouth County, 10 Starrs Rd., Yarmouth, NS B5A 2T1
Phone: (902) 742-0700

Mi'Kmaq Family and Children's Services, P.O. Box 179, Shubenacadie, NS B0N 2H0
Phone: (902) 758-3553

Antigonish District Office, Department of Community Services, Provincial Bldg., Ste. 101, 11 James St., Antigonish, NS B2G 1R6
Phone: (902) 863-3213

Dartmouth District Office, Department of Community Services, Dartmouth Professional Centre, Ste. 100, 277 Pleasant St., Dartmouth, NS B2Y 4B7
Phone: (902) 424-3298

Digby District Office, Department of Community Services, Warwick St., P.O. Box 399, Digby, NS B0V 1A0
Phone: (902) 245-5811

Guysborough District Office, Department of Community Services, Chedabucto Mall, P.O. Box 90, Guysborough, NS B0H 1N0
Phone: (902) 533-4007

Sackville District Office, Department of Community Services, Cobequid Multi-Service Centre, 70 Memory Lane, Lower Sackville, NS B4C 2J3
Phone: (902) 865-5750

**Contact:** Adoption Unit.

**Description:** Provincial agency.

**Area served:** Residents of the Province of Nova Scotia who are either Canadian citizens or who have landed immigrant status.

**Requirements:** Applicants must be at least 19 yrs. old.

**Fees:** None.

**Number of children placed last year:** 65.

**Description of children:** Primarily older children with special needs.

**Adoption procedure:** 1) Application; 2) orientation; 3) training; 4) home study; 5) placement; 6) post-placement supervision; 7) finalization.

**Average length of time between application and start of home study:** Infants: up to 10 yrs. Children with special needs: 3 - 5 yrs.

**Average length of time to complete home study:** 6 mos.

**Number of interviews:** Minimum of 3.

**Home study description:** Assessment which includes motivation to adopt, family functioning, marriage, if applicable, interests, skills, religious and cultural issues, health including infertility, mental and physical disabilities, home health and environment, finances, references, police and child abuse records checks, child rearing practices and discipline.

**Average wait for a child after approval of a home study:** 2 yrs. or more.

**Foster care:** Temporary, long-term and permanent.

# ONTARIO

## STATUTES

★ 901 ★

**Residents access agencies of foreign countries, including U.S.?** Yes, through private licensees.

**Birth parents place child directly in an adoptive home?** No.

**Other individual place child in adoptive home?** Yes, licensees.

**Subsidies provided?** Not directly; Children's Aid Societies may use part of their Provincial funds to provide subsidies.

**Adoption records sealed?** Yes, but non-identifying information and a semi-active registry are provided.

**Adoption cost defined by law?** The elements but not the amounts.

**Home study required by state?** Yes, before placement.

**Provincial Exchange:** Semi-annual Adoption Resource Exchange Conference presents videos and slides of waiting children to approved applicants.

**Requires judicial termination of birth parents' rights?** Voluntary relinquishments before a Children's Aid Society are valid. Other voluntary relinquishments are valid when given no sooner than 8 days after the child's birth.

**Time given to a birthmother to revoke her consent:** 21 days.

**Court handling adoptions?** Family Court.

**Adoption of Native Children:** Three First Nation Children's Aid Societies operate within Ontario. If the child is a crown ward, band must be notified for placement. If the child has been voluntarily relinquished, band must be supplied with non-identifying information and given time to find a placement.

## PUBLIC AGENCIES

★ 902 ★
**Ministry of Community Social Services**
**Management and Support Branch, Adoption and Operational Services**
2 Bloor St. W., 24th Fl.
Toronto, ON, Canada M7A 1E9
Phone: (416) 327-4730
Fax: (416) 327-0573

**Contact:** Colette Kent, Registrar/Manager.

**Description:** The Adoption Unit of the Ministry of Community & Social Services reviews all proposals for private adoption and approves, does not approve, or approves with conditions the proposed placement. The Adoption Unit licenses the practitioners in private adoption. The Adoption Unit does not provide direct placement services. The Adoption Unit reviews all home studies for internationaladoption and must approve the adoption if the adoption is to be finalized in Ontario. The Ministry sets policy and supervises the programs of the 54 Children's Aid Societies in the Province.

## PRIVATE AGENCIES

★ 903 ★
**Adoption Agency & Counseling Service of Ontario**
2349 Fairview St., Ste. 107
Burlington, ON, Canada L7R 2E3
Phone: (905) 634-0009
(905) 507-4037

**Contact:** Carol Noble Lavell.

**Date established:** 1982.

**Description:** Private, non-profit agency licensed under the Ontario Child and Family Services Act.

**Area served:** Canadian provinces, especially Southern Ontario.

**Requirements:** Non-discriminatory home study.

**Fees:** Home study: $150; total cost: approx. $3,000 to $8,000. Special issues create extra cost.

**Number of children placed last year:** 397.

**Description of children:** Infants.

**Adoption procedure:** 1) Consultation; 2) homestudy; 3) group training; 4) placement; 5) supervision; 6) finalization.

**Average length of time between application and start of home study:** Varies.

**Average length of time to complete home study:** Approx. 2-3 mos.

**Number of interviews:** Approx. 3-5.

**Home study description:** Educative and evaluative process including references and medical and police record checks.

**Average wait for a child after approval of a home study:** Varies due to flexibility of applicants and birth parent choice.

**Foster care:** Available.

★904★
**Beginnings Counseling and Adoption Services of Ontario Inc.**
1 Young St., Suite 308
Hamilton, ON, Canada L8N 1T8
Phone: (905) 528-6665

**Contact:** Susan Chapman, Program Director.

**Date established:** 1984.

**Description:** Adoption agency, pregnancy counseling.

**Area served:** Province of Ontario.

**Requirements:** Please inquire.

**Fees:** For adoption placements. No fees for birthparent counseling.

**Number of children placed last year:** 7.

**Description of children:** Infants, newborns.

**Adoption procedure:** As per Ministry of Community and Social Service requirements, Province of Ontario.

**Average length of time between application and start of home study:** 24 or more mos.

**Number of interviews:** 4-6.

**Home study description:** As required.

**Average wait for a child after approval of a home study:** 24 or more mos.

**Foster care:** 2 foster homes available.

★905★
**Jewels for Jesus Adoption Agency**
6981 Millcreek Dr., Unit 22
Mississauga, ON, Canada L5N 6B8
Phone: (905) 821-7494

**Contact:** Marian Boyd, Program Coordinator or Joan Kosmachuk, Executive Director.

**Date established:** 1959.

**Description:** Charitable, not-for-profit organization.

**Area served:** Residents of the Province of Ontario.

**Requirements:** Protestant Evangelical couples, married at least 3 yrs., who are residents of Ontario, who have no more than 1 child, either biological or adopted, and who have a statement of infertility.

**Fees:** Application fee; group meeting fee; and personal interview fee.

**Number of children placed last year:** The agency seeks to keep its ratio of adoptive applicants to birth parents seeking adoptive placement for their child at 1:4.

**Description of children:** Mainly newborn infants.

**Adoption procedure:** 1) Inquiry; 2) Information packet; 3) formal application; 4) selection of adoptiveplacement by birth parent(s). Home studies and post-placement supervision are not done by the agency but by social workers licensed by the Province. Home studies may be completed either before or after formal application.

**Average length of time between application and start of home study:** N/A.

**Average length of time to complete home study:** N/A.

**Number of interviews:** N/A.

**Home study description:** N/A.

**Average wait for a child after approval of a home study:** Dependent upon birth parent selection.

**Foster care:** Short-term care of infants whose birth parents are making an adoptive decision or who are awaiting adoptive placement.

★906★
**Jewish Child and Family Services of Metro Toronto**
4600 Bathurst St.
Willowdale, ON, Canada M2R 3V3
Phone: (416)638-7800
Fax: (416) 638-7943

**Contact:** Susan Brandes.

**Description:** Children's aid society.

**Area served:** Metropolitan Toronto and certain suburbs.

**Requirements:** Both adoptive applicants must be Jewish.

**Fees:** None.

**Number of children placed last year:** 5.

**Description of children:** Primarily infants and special needs.

**Adoption procedure:** Telephone inquiry and intake; registration completed; placement on registration list depending on date of return; adoption preparation group; home study; wait for placement; placement; 6 month supervision, longer for special needs.

**Average length of time between application and start of home study:** 24 or more mos.

**Average length of time to complete home study:** 2-6 months.

**Number of interviews:** 6-7.

**Average wait for a child after approval of a home study:** 24 or more mos.

★907★
**M. M. Kelly Counseling and Adoption Agency**
115 Dunlop St., E.
Barrie, ON, Canada L4M 1A6
Phone: (705) 722-4163
Fax: (705) 722-4163

**Contact:** Marie McCallum.

**Date established:** 1985.

**Description:** Adoption agency.

**Area served:** Ontario, British Columbia, and some international countries.

**Number of children placed last year:** 7.

**Description of children:** Infants.

**Average length of time between application and start of home study:** 1-6 mos.

**Average length of time to complete home study:** 3 mos.

**Number of interviews:** 5.

Average wait for a child after approval of a home study: 24 mos. or more.

# PRINCE EDWARD ISLAND

## STATUTES

★ 908 ★

**Residents access agencies of foreign countries, including U.S.?** Occasionally.

**Birth parents place child directly in an adoptive home?** Yes.

**Other individual place child in adoptive home?** Yes.

**Subsidies provided?** No.

**Adoption records sealed?** Yes; semi-active registry.

**Adoption cost defined by law?** Guidelines in law.

**Home study required by state?** Yes.

**Provincial Exchange:** With other provinces as required.

**Requires judicial termination of birth parents' rights?** Private adoption: voluntary relinquishment permissible.
Department adoption: judicial review required unless both birth parents agree to adoption.

**Time given to a birthmother to revoke her consent:** Private: 14 days.
Departmental: 30 days.

**Court handling adoptions?** Family Court.

**Adoption of Native Children:** Placed by band or Department.

## PUBLIC AGENCIES

★ 909 ★
**Provincial Health and Community Services Agency**
P.O. Box 2000
Charlottetown, PE, Canada C1A 7N8
Phone: (902) 368-4932
Fax: (902) 368-4969

**Contact:** Virginia MacEachern, Provincial Adoption Coordinator.

**Description:** Provincial agency.

**Area served:** Residents of Prince Edward Island.

**Requirements:** Adults aged 21-40, either single or with two years of stable married life. Must own home or be in charge of who lives in residence. Must have financial stability; no alcoholics in home. Good mental health record for previous 12 months; no criminal record in last three years; no convicted child abusers. For infant adoption, must show medical evidence of infertility. No more than two children already in home.

**Fees:** None.

**Number of children placed last year:** 10-14.

**Description of children:** Infants and special needs children.

**Adoption procedure:** Written expression of interest; information packet which must be completed; referral sent to regional office; intake; adoption group and preparation; waiting period; placement.

**Average length of time between application and start of home study:** 6-12 mos.

**Average length of time to complete home study:** Varies.

**Number of interviews:** 6 group and individual.

**Home study description:** Criminal and child abuse check; background information; self study.

**Average wait for a child after approval of a home study:** 24 or more mos.

**Foster care:** None.

# QUEBEC

## STATUTES

★ 910 ★

**Residents access agencies of foreign countries, including U.S.?** Yes, in those countries approved by the Secretariat under the provisions of the Youth Assessment Act.

**Birth parents place child directly in an adoptive home?** Permitted but only to a relative by either consanguity or marriage.

**Other individual place child in adoptive home?** No.

**Subsidies provided?** For children in the custody of the Secretariat in accordance with the child's special needs.

**Adoption records sealed?** Sealed, but adoptees 14 yrs. and older may access their records if both the birth and adoptive parents have previously consented.

**Adoption cost defined by law?** N/A.

**Home study required by state?** N/A.

**Provincial Exchange:** Exchange access to National Adoption Desk.

**Requires judicial termination of birth parents' rights?** Termination by both parents is required if filiation is established. If filiation is established to only one parent, the consent of that parent is sufficient.

**Time given to a birthmother to revoke her consent:** 30 days.

**Court handling adoptions?** Tribunal Jeunesse.

**Adoption of Native Children:** Unavailable.

## PUBLIC AGENCIES

★ 911 ★
**Enfants d'Orient Adoption et Parrainage du Quebec, Inc.**
240 De Bayeux
Boucherville, PQ, Canada J4B T19
Phone: (514) 881-1514
Fax: (514) 655-8991

**Branch address:**
12 383 Fernand-Gauthier, Montreal, PQ, Canada H1E 6C4

**Contact:** Louise Kang.

**Date established:** 1983.

**Description:** Private agency recognized by the Quebec Ministry of Health and Social Services.

**Area served:** Residents of the Province of Quebec.

**Requirements:** Applicants for Taiwanese children must be married and no older than 40 yrs. Applicants for Thai children must be at least 25 yrs. old and married.

**Fees:** Application: $500. Home study, translation and legal fees are additional.

**Number of children placed last year:** 30 Taiwanese children and 10 from Thailand.

**Description of children:** Children from 3 mos. to 9 yrs.

**Adoption procedure:** 1) Evaluation of the psycho-social study and other documents; 2) dossier compilation and verification; 3) remission of dossier to child's country of origin; 4) wait for child assignment; 5) child assignment; 6) if accepted, placement.

**Average length of time between application and start of home study:** Less than 1 mo.

**Average length of time to complete home study:** N/A.

**Number of interviews:** N/A.

**Home study description:** Agency does not conduct home study.

**Average wait for a child after approval of a home study:** 1 mo.-2 yrs. or more.

**Foster care:** None.

★912★
**Les Centres jeunesse de Quebec**
**Centre de protection de l'enfance de la jeunesse**
2000 rue Mansfield, bureau 1100
Montreal, PQ, Canada H3A 2Z1
Phone: (514) 842-5181
Fax: (514) 842-4834

**Contact:** Adoption Services.

**Description:** Provincial social service agency.

**Area served:** Residents of the Province of Quebec.

**Requirements:** Applicants must be at least 18 yrs. older than the child to be adopted.

**Fees:** Unavailable.

**Number of children placed last year:** Unavailable.

**Description of children:** Children between the ages of 0 and 14 yrs. some of whom have special needs. Agency also acts in the facilitation of international adoptions.

**Adoption procedure:** 1) Inquiry; 2) application; 3) wait for home study (although home study is immediate in the cases noted); 4) if approved, wait for placement; 5) placement.

**Average length of time between application and start of home study:** Children between the ages of 0 - 6 yrs.: 24 mos. Older children and children with special needs: Immediate.

**Average length of time to complete home study:** 3 wks.

**Number of interviews:** 12 hrs.

**Home study description:** A combination of individual and group sessions which addresses many issues particular to adoption including the possibility of an *open* adoption and eventual reunion of the adoptee and the birth family.

**Average wait for a child after approval of a home study:** 18 - 24 mos.

**Foster care:** Long-term and pre-adoptive.

## PRIVATE AGENCIES

★913★
**Espoir Des Enfants En Adoption Inc.**
172, rue Riviere
Cecotomy, PQ, Canada G7G 4W4
Phone: (418) 698-2000
Fax: (418) 698-2000

**Contact:** Madame Nicole Durand, Presidente or Monsieur Michel Seguin, Vice-President.

**Date established:** 1992.

**Description:** Private, incorporated child placement agency.

**Area served:** Residents of Quebec.

**Requirements:** Couples married at least 5 yrs. who are at least 25 yrs. old who have no more than 1 child and documentation of infertility.

**Fees:** Administration Fee: $150 plus $650. Home study: $600 Approx. Program fees, travel, translation and document verification, etc.: $15,000.

**Number of children placed last year:** 4.

**Description of children:** Colombian infants.

**Adoption procedure:** 1) Placement on waiting list; 2) psycho-social evaluation; 3) dossier preparation and referral; 4) child match; 5) document forwarding; 6) travel to Colombia for placement; 7) finalization.

**Average length of time between application and start of home study:** 6 - 12 mos.

**Average length of time to complete home study:** 1 - 3 mo.

**Number of interviews:** 3 - 4.

**Home study description:** Assessment which includes identifying information on the prospective adoptive parents, the stability of the their marriage, home and community, financial, physical and psychological capacity to parent and motivation to adopt.

**Average wait for a child after approval of a home study:** 6 -12 mo.

**Foster care:** None.

★914★
**Societe D'Adoption Quebecoise Une Grande Famille**
1550 Dr. Penfield, Ste. 1808
Montreal, PQ, Canada H3G 1C2
Phone: (514) 937-9852
Fax: (514) 932-6427

**Contact:** Alexei Balakine or Victor Platonow.

**Date established:** 1992.

**Description:** Non-profit child placing agency licensed by the Government of Quebec.

**Area served:** Residents of Canada.

**Requirements:** Applicants must be between the ages of 25 and 55 yrs., in good heath and financially able to support a child.

**Fees:** Application: $50. Total fees exclusive of home study but inclusive of travel: $16,500.

**Number of children placed last year:** 45.

**Description of children:** Infants and children some with correctable medical problems.

**Adoption procedure:** 1) Dossier preparation, translation and sent to Russia; 2) once approved, child match; 3) if accepted, complete immigration proceedings in Canada; 4) travel to Russia for placement.

**Average length of time between application and start of home study:** N/A.

**Average length of time to complete home study:** N/A.

**Number of interviews:** N/A.

**Home study description:** Home studies are not conducted by the agency.

**Average wait for a child after approval of a home study:** Less than 1 yr.

**Foster care:** None.

## ★915★
**Societe Pour L'Adoption Internationale**
1383, ave. du Buisson
Sillery, PQ, Canada G1T 2C5
Phone: (418) 688-3775
Fax: (418) 688-2068

**Contact:** Jean Paul Massicote, President-Directeur general.

**Date established:** 1993.

**Description:** Not-for-profit child placing agency licensed by the Government of Quebec.

**Area served:** Residents of the Province of Quebec.

**Requirements:** Applicants must be between the ages of 30 and 50 yrs.

**Fees:** Application: $25.

**Number of children placed last year:** New agency.

**Description of children:** Unavailable.

**Adoption procedure:** 1) Dossier preparation; 2) contract signed; 3) dossier forwarded to Mexico; 4) translation and presentation of dossier by attorney to San Miguel de Allende in Mexico; 5) child match; 6) if accepted, travel to Mexico for placement.

**Average length of time between application and start of home study:** Less than 1 mo.

**Average length of time to complete home study:** 3 mos.

**Number of interviews:** Unavailable.

**Home study description:** Assessment which includes personality, ability to parent, finances, knowledge of Mexico and its culture.

**Average wait for a child after approval of a home study:** 6-12 mos.

**Foster care:** None.

## ★916★
**Soleil des Nations**
1550, Jean Nicolet
Trois-Rivieres, PQ, Canada G9A 1B5
Phone: (819) 376-5627

**Contact:** Lucie Jordan (en francais) or Christine Johnson (English).

**Date established:** 1991.

**Description:** Private, non-profit all volunteer adoption service.

**Area served:** Residents of Quebec for Colombian placements; residents of Canada for Bolivian and Haitian placements.

**Requirements:** Requirements may be determined by the child's country of origin.

**Fees:** Administration fee: $500. Orphanage donation: $250. Home study fees are the responsibility of the adoptive applicants.

**Number of children placed last year:** 47.

**Description of children:** Infants and children from Bolivia, Colombia and Haiti.

**Adoption procedure:** Unavailable.

**Average length of time between application and start of home study:** Less than 1 mo.

**Home study description:** Home studies may be conducted by a licensed social worker of the applicants' choice.

**Average wait for a child after approval of a home study:** Unavailable.

# SASKATCHEWAN

## STATUTES
★917★

**Residents access agencies of foreign countries, including U.S.?** Yes, in compliance with legislation of all jurisdictions.

**Birth parents place child directly in an adoptive home?** Yes.

**Other individual place child in adoptive home?** Yes, with permission of the Minister of Social Services.

**Subsidies provided?** Assistance may be provided in cases of a child permanently committed to the Minister because of the child's special needs where financial barriers may preclude a permanent placement. Maintenance, actual cost of service relevant to a child's special needs and health benefits may be provided.

**Adoption records sealed?** Yes, but non-identifying information and a post-adoption registry is provided.
Post Adoption Registry
2240 Albert St., 2nd Fl.
Regina, SK S4P 3V7.

**Adoption cost defined by law?** No one can agree to give or receive any payment or reward relating to an adoption except where otherwise permitted by the Adoption Act or regulations.

**Home study required by state?** Along with a social and family history applicants must present to the court evidence they are physically, psychologically and emotionally suitable to parent; that they are able to meet the needs of the child and that the proposed adoption is in the best interests of the child.

**Provincial Exchange:** Central Adoption Registry.

**Requires judicial termination of birth parents' rights?** Voluntary relinquishments are permitted.

**Time given to a birthmother to revoke her consent:** 14 days.

**Court handling adoptions?** Provincial Court.

**Adoption of Native Children:** The Department will not place First Nation children without specific written approval of the child's band.

## PUBLIC AGENCIES

★918★
**Saskatchewan Social Services**
1920 Broad St.
Regina, SK, Canada S4P 3V6
Phone: (306) 787-3653

**Contact:** Adoption Unit.

**Date established:** 1944.

**Description:** Provincial agency.

**Area served:** Residents of Saskatchewan.

**Requirements:** None.

**Fees:** None.

**Number of children placed last year:** 61.

**Description of children:** 43 older/special needs children and 18 infants.

**Adoption procedure:** 1) Referral to nearest office; 2) intake interview; 3) application; 4) central registration; 5) placement on waiting list; 6) home study; 7) central registration; 8) placement; 9) supervision of placement.

**Average length of time between application and start of home study:** 2 yrs. or more.

**Average length of time to complete home study:** 3 - 6 mos.

**Number of interviews:** Minimum of 5.

**Home study description:** Assessment which includes social and family history; emotional and physical ability to adopt; income and expenses; assets and liabilities.

**Average wait for a child after approval of a home study:** 2 yrs. or more.

**Foster care:** Emergency, short and long-term, therapeutic and permanent.

# YUKON

## STATUTES

★ 919 ★

**Residents access agencies of foreign countries, including U.S.?** Yes, through the Department of Health and Social Services.

**Birth parents place child directly in an adoptive home?** Yes.

**Other individual place child in adoptive home?** Yes.

**Subsidies provided?** Yes, for children in Department's custody.

**Adoption records sealed?** Yes; non-identifying information provided. Records may be opened with permission of adoptee and birth parents.

**Adoption cost defined by law?** No.

**Home study required by state?** Yes. May be conducted before or after placement. Written notification must be made within 30 days of placement.

**Provincial Exchange:** Access to National Adoption Desk.

**Requires judicial termination of birth parents' rights?** Voluntary relinquishment possible.

**Time given to a birthmother to revoke her consent:** 30 days if not placed. Irrevocable if child has been placed.

**Court handling adoptions?** Supreme Court.

**Adoption of Native Children:** Overseen by Department of Health and Social Services, except for Champaign Aishiahik Band.

## PUBLIC AGENCIES

★ 920 ★

**Department of Health and Social Services**
**Family and Children's Services H-10**
Box 2703
Whitehorse, YK, Canada Y1A 2C6
Phone: (403) 667-3002
(800) 661-0408
Fax: (403) 668-4613

**Contact:** Maxine Kehoe, Supervisor.

**Date established:** 1956.

**Description:** Government of Yukon agency.

**Area served:** Residents of the Yukon. No children for placement outside of Yukon.

**Requirements:** Adults 19 years or older.

**Fees:** None.

**Number of children placed last year:** 12, including step-parent and private placement.

**Description of children:** N/A.

**Adoption procedure:** Application; intake interview; home study; waiting period.

**Average length of time between application and start of home study:** 6-12 mos.

**Average length of time to complete home study:** 3 mos.

**Number of interviews:** Varies with each adoption.

**Home study description:** Child abuse and criminal records checked; 3 references; medical background and motivation to adopt assessed; full family assessment/home study.

**Average wait for a child after approval of a home study:** Varies.

**Foster care:** Provided in Yukon for children in the care of the Director of Family and Children's Services.

# Foster Care

## ALABAMA

**★921★**
**Alabama State Department of Human Resources**
50 Ripley St.
Montgomery, AL 36130
Phone: (205) 242-9500

**Contact:** Jeanette Gautney, Supervisor, Child Welfare Policy.

**Serves:** State of Alabama.

**Requirements:** Married or single applicants who have reached their majority, who have adequate income and who can provide personal references. Foster mothers may not work outside the home without the special approval of the Dept. of Human Resources.

**Description of children:** Dependent children.

**Licensing procedure:**
 1) Submit application with completed financial forms;
 2) complete examinations and inspections;
 3) attend orientation;
 4) reference checks;
 5) undergo home study.

**Average length of time for licensing:** Approx. 6 wks.

**Inspections:**
 1) Medical examinations for all household members;
 2) Criminal Records checks of all household members;
 3) finger printing of foster parents;
 4) home inspection.
Other and/or in-depth inspections as required.
After approval foster home is visited at least quarterly by social worker.

**Maximum number of children allowed in licensed foster care home:** 6, exceptions made for sibling groups.

**Interracial placement:** Permitted.

**Type of foster care and description of procedures:** Emergency, short and long-term, therapeutic and pre-adoptive.

**Per diem stipend:** Ages:
0-2 yrs. $205;
3-5 yrs. $218;
6-12 yrs. $229;
13-18 yrs. $241.

**Additional funds available:** Medical/dental and special needs.

## ALASKA

**★922★**
**Association of Village Council Presidents, Inc.**
Pouch 219
Bethel, AK 99559
Phone: (907) 543-3521

**Contact:** Patrick Samson, Social Services Director.
**Serves:** Yukon-Kuskokwim Delta of southwest Alaska.
**Requirements:** Married couples, 21 yrs. and older who have sufficient income and living space to accommodate a foster child(ren).
**Description of children:** Children of all ages, some with special needs.
**Licensing procedure:** 1) Contact Association; 2) complete background checks and submit personal references; 3) undergo inspections and home study; 4) placement.
**Average length of time for licensing:** Varies.
**Inspections:** Fire, sanitation, medical examinations for all household members.
**Maximum number of children allowed in licensed foster care home:** 5.
**Interracial placement:** Yes.
**Type of foster care and description of procedures:** Pre-adoptive, emergency, long-term and therapeutic.
**Per diem stipend:** Varies.
**Additional funds available:** Medical/dental, clothing allowance and other monies, as needed.

**★923★**
**Department of Health and Social Services, Alaska Division of Family and Youth**
P.O. Box 110630
Juneau, AK 99811-0630
Phone: (907) 465-3170
Fax: (907) 465-3397

**Contact:** Regional Office.
**Serves:** State of Alaska.
**Requirements:** Flexible but applicants must meet standards of maturity, have adequate living space for a foster child and provide 3 favorable personal references.
**Description of children:** Primarily special needs children.
**Licensing procedure:** Procedures may vary with regional office but essentially follow the following guidelines:
 1) Submit application;
 2) attend group or individual meeting;
 3) complete home study;

4) participate in training.

**Average length of time for licensing:** Varies by region.

**Inspections:**
1) Home inspection;
2) TB test for all household members over 18 yrs. (other health screening tests may be required at the discretion of the caseworker);
3) state arrest record computer check.

After placement caseworker visits at least quarterly.

**Maximum number of children allowed in licensed foster care home:** No more than 6 children, including children related to the foster parent. Of the six, no more than 2 children under 30 months of age, including those of the foster parent, are permitted; no more than 2 children with special needs, including those of the foster parent; no more than 3 children of any age who are unrelated to the foster parent are permitted. Waivers of these numbers are permitted for sibling groups.

**Interracial placement:** Permitted but not preferred.

**Type of foster care and description of procedures:** Emergency, short and long-term, pre-adoptive, permanent and some specialized.

**Per diem stipend:** Ages: 0 -30 mos.: $17.78; 31 mos. - 11 yrs.: $15.80; 12 yrs. and up: $18.76.

**Additional funds available:** Medicaid, initial clothing allowance and per diem stipend adjusted upward for geographic differential.

## ARIZONA

★924★
**Human Resource Training, Inc.**
4750 N. Black Canyon Hwy., Ste. 102
Phoenix, AZ 85017
Phone: (602) 433-1344

**Branch address:**
Parenting Skills Program, 2131 E. Broadway Rd., Ste. 15, Tempe, AZ 85282
Phone: (602) 967-6895

**Contact:** Cecilia Jones, Executive Director.

**Serves:** State of Arizona.

**Requirements:** Adults, 21 yrs. and older who meet the requirements for home size and financial eligibility and who can provide personal references.

**Description of children:** Emotionally/behaviorally disturbed children.

**Licensing procedure:**
1) Participate in 33 hrs. pre-service training class;
2) complete biography and home study;
3) reference checks, home visit and inspections.

**Average length of time for licensing:** Approx. 3 mos.

**Inspections:**
1) Fire;
2) sanitation;
3) medical examinations for all household members;
4) finger printing of foster parents.

After placement social worker visits approximately twice monthly.

**Maximum number of children allowed in licensed foster care home:** 8; 5 foster children.

**Interracial placement:** Permitted.

**Type of foster care and description of procedures:** Long-term, therapeutic and pre-adoptive.

**Per diem stipend:** $23.

**Additional funds available:** Medical/dental for court wards, clothing allowance and child's personal allowance.

★925★
**La Hacienda Foster Care Resource Center, Inc.**
5999 E. Grant Rd.
Tucson, AZ 85712
Phone: (602) 296-5551
Fax: (602) 886-3335

**Contact:** David F. Miller, Executive Director.

**Serves:** Primarily Pima County.

**Requirements:** Adults 21 yrs. and older who can provide a minimum of 4 personal references and who can meet the requirements for marital status and financial eligibility.

**Description of children:** Children who are dependent, delinquent, incorrigible, moderately emotionally disturbed or who have been abused.

**Licensing procedure:**
1) File application;
2) complete home study;
3) comply with regulatory process.

**Average length of time for licensing:** 3-4 mos.

**Inspections:**
1) Fire;
2) sanitation;
3) finger printing of foster parents;
4) medical examinations for all household members.

After placement social worker visits a minimum of 4 times a year.

**Maximum number of children allowed in licensed foster care home:** 5.

**Interracial placement:** Permitted if no racial match is available.

**Type of foster care and description of procedures:** Emergency, long-term, therapeutic and pre-adoptive.

**Per diem stipend:** $300/mo. - $1000/mo.

**Additional funds available:** Medical/dental, clothing allowance and personal child allowance.

## ARKANSAS

★926★
**Centers for Youth and Families**
6601 W. 12th St.
Little Rock, AR 72204
Phone: (501) 666-8686
Fax: (501) 664-3009

**Contact:** Kay Kimbrough.

**Serves:** 7 counties of central Arkansas.

**Requirements:** Adults between the ages of 21 and 65 yrs. who can provide personal references and who can meet the eligibility requirements of home size and financial eligibility.

**Description of children:** Physcially/sexually abused children who have varying degrees of behavioral and emotional disturbances.

**Licensing procedure:**
1) Participate in Orientation and Pre-Service Training;

2) file application with financial statement, copies of marriage and divorce records, personal references, copies of insurance policies and fire escape plan;
3) complete home study;
4) if approved, complete 50 hrs. of additional training per year.

**Average length of time for licensing:** 1-2 mos.

**Inspections:**
1) Sanitation;
2) medical examiniation of all household members with immunization records for all children;
3) law enforcement clearances and Child Abuse Registry check.

After placement social worker visits weekly because of the therapeutic approach used.

**Maximum number of children allowed in licensed foster care home:** State licensing standards allow no more than 2 children under the age of 2 yrs. nor more than 5 children in the home but Centers for Youth and Families only places a maximum of 2 children, and prefers that families have no more than 2 biological children.

**Interracial placement:** Not preferred.

**Type of foster care and description of procedures:** Therapeutic.

**Per diem stipend:** Average rate of $35/night; rates will flex depending on level of care needed for the child.

**Additional funds available:** Medical/dental and child's personal allowance.

★ 927 ★
**East Arkansas Regional Mental Health Center**
**Therapeutic Foster Care Program**
305 Valley Dr.
Helena, AR 72342
Phone: (501) 338-7321
Fax: (501) 338-6361

**Serves:** East Arkansas.

**Requirements:** Check with program for prerequisites concerning age, marital status, financial elibility and home size. Only one foster parent may work full-time outside the home.

**Description of children:** Emotionally disturbed children.

**Licensing procedure:**
1) Social worker visits prospective foster home;
2) applicants meet director;
3) complete check of criminal records, social services and references;
4) attend 25 hrs. pre-service training;
5) pre-placement visits with children; and
6) placement.

**Average length of time for licensing:** 5-6 mos.

**Inspections:**
1) Sanitation;
2) medical examinations of all members of the prospective foster home.

After placement, social worker visits the foster home at least twice monthly.

**Maximum number of children allowed in licensed foster care home:** 4.

**Interracial placement:** No.

**Type of foster care and description of procedures:** Therapeutic.

**Per diem stipend:** $12,000 annually.

**Additional funds available:** Medicaid.

★ 928 ★
**Treatment Homes, Inc.**
P.O. Box 1400
Little Rock, AR 72203
Phone: (501) 372-5039
Fax: (501) 372-5529

**Contact:** Consevella James, Executive Director.

**Serves:** State of Arkansas.

**Requirements:** Adults between the ages of 21 and 65 yrs. who can provide personal references and who meet the requirements for marital status, financial eligibility, religion and home size. If both foster parents are employed full-time outside the home, no preschool aged children can be placed with them.

**Description of children:** Children between the ages of 3 and 12 yrs. who are experiencing emotional/behavioral difficulty.

**Licensing procedure:**
1) Attend orientation meeting;
2) complete a minimum of 6 sessions of pre-service training;
3) pass required inspections;
4) criminal and child abuse background checks;
5) forward physical examination reports.

**Average length of time for licensing:** 60-90 days.

**Inspections:**
1) Sanitation;
2) medical examinations for all household members.

After placement, social worker visits weekly.

**Maximum number of children allowed in licensed foster care home:** 4.

**Interracial placement:** Not permitted.

**Type of foster care and description of procedures:** Therapeutic and pre-adoptive.

**Per diem stipend:** $700/mo. plus room and board.

**Additional funds available:** Medicaid, clothing allowance and special activities.

# CALIFORNIA

★ 929 ★
**Children's Bureau of Southern California**
3910 Oakwood Ave.
Los Angeles, CA 90004
Phone: (213) 953-7356

**Branch address:**
3030 Tyler Ave., El Monte, CA 91731
Phone: (818) 575-5897

**Contact:** Mike Foster, L.C.S.W., Director of Community Services.

**Serves:** Residents of Los Angeles, Orange and Ventura counties.

**Requirements:** Applicants must be at least 21 yrs. old and single or legally married.

**Description of children:** Latino and Caucasian infants who have been drug exposed; some sibling groups.

**Licensing procedure:** 1) Attend orientation; 2) complete application packet; 3) home study; 4) First Aid and CPR certification.

**Average length of time for licensing:** 6 - 12 mos.

**Inspections:** 1) Medical clearances for all household members; 2) 3 personal references; 3) sanitation; 4) finger printing. After placement, child's caseworker visits a minimum of 26 times a year.

**Maximum number of children allowed in licensed foster care home:** 6.

**Interracial placement:** None.

**Type of foster care and description of procedures:** Emergency, therapeutic and long-term.

**Per diem stipend:** Varies by age.

**Additional funds available:** Medical/dental; clothing as needed.

★930★
**Concept 7 Foster Family Agency**
25411 Cabot Rd., Ste. 201
Laguna Hills, CA 92653
Phone: (714) 472-0707
(800) 888-1699
Fax: (714) 472-0842

**Branch address:**
22365 Barton Rd., Ste. 310, Grand Terrace, CA 92324
Phone: (909) 783-4292

12070 E. Telegraph Rd., Ste. 207, Santa Fe Springs, CA 90670-3721
Phone: (310) 903-1957

**Contact:** Marlene Mills-Margesson.

**Serves:** Southern California.

**Requirements:** Applicants must meet the requirements of age, marital status, home size and financial eligibility and provide personal references.

**Description of children:** Children between the ages of 0 and 18 yrs. (no psychotic, assaultive or suicidal children).

**Licensing procedure:**
1) Attend orientation and trainings;
2) submit application and other required paperwork;
3) complete first aid and CPR courses;
4) home inspection and physical exam;
5) participate in 2 in-home interviews.

**Average length of time for licensing:** Approx. 6 wks.

**Inspections:**
1) Fire;
2) sanitation;
3) medical examination and TB tests for foster parents;
4) finger printing of foster parents;
after placement social worker visits weekly.

**Maximum number of children allowed in licensed foster care home:** 3.

**Interracial placement:** Permitted.

**Type of foster care and description of procedures:** Emergency and long-term.

**Per diem stipend:** $550/mo.-$650/mo. depending on age of child.

**Additional funds available:** Medi-Cal and clothing allowance.

★931★
**Mountain Circle Foster Family Agency**
P.O. Box 554
Greenville, CA 95947
Phone: (916) 284-7007
(916) 284-6609
Fax: (916) 284-7111

**Contact:** Pamela Howell Schaffer.

**Serves:** Lassen and Plumas counties.

**Requirements:** Adults, 25 yrs. and older, who can provide personal references, who are not dependent upon the foster care income for their own needs and who have adequate bedroom space.

**Description of children:** Dependent children, juvenile court wards.

**Licensing procedure:**
1) Submit application;
2) attend pre-service interviews;
3) finger print clearance;
4) complete home study;
5) participate in pre-service training.

**Average length of time for licensing:** Minimum of 12 wks.

**Inspections:**
1) Finger printing of foster parents;
2) fire;
3) sanitation;
4) medical examinations of all household members.
After placement social worker visits at least bi-weekly.

**Maximum number of children allowed in licensed foster care home:** 2 foster children.

**Interracial placement:** Permitted but so far unpracticed.

**Type of foster care and description of procedures:** Therapeutic.

**Per diem stipend:** Between $19 and $24.50 depending upon child's age and fosterparent's length of service.

**Additional funds available:** Medical/dental, clothing allowance and counseling.

★932★
**Northern Valley Catholic Social Service**
1733 Oregon St.
Redding, CA 96001
Phone: (916) 241-0552
(800) 846-1451
Fax: (916) 241-6457

**Contact:** Patricia Modrzejewski, Executive Director or Chris Moats.

**Serves:** Shasta, Tehama and Trinity counties.

**Requirements:** Adults, 21 yrs. and older, who can provide personal references and meet the requirements for home size and financial eligibility.

**Description of children:** Children from birth to 18 yrs., some sibling groups, some pregnant teens and some adolescent mothers and infants.

**Licensing procedure:**
1) Attend initial inquiry meeting;
2) submit application forms with finger prints;
3) complete home study interviews;
4) if approved, certification.

**Average length of time for licensing:** 8-12 wks.

**Inspections:**
1) Sanitation;
2) finger printing of foster parents;
3) health screening of foster parent applicants.
After placement social worker makes weekly contact.

**Maximum number of children allowed in licensed foster care home:** 6 with no more than 2 children per bedroom.

**Interracial placement:** Permitted.

**Type of foster care and description of procedures:** Emergency, long-term and therapeutic.

**Per diem stipend:** $550/mo. to $650/mo. dependant on age.

**Additional funds available:** Medical/dental, funds for training and conferences, children's special needs.

★ 933 ★
**Share Homes Foster Family Agency**
307 E. Kettleman Ln.
Lodi, CA 95240
Phone: (209) 334-6376
Fax: (209) 334-4408
**Contact:** Doug Clark, Administrator.
**Serves:** Amador, Calaveras, Sacramento, San Joaquin, and Stanislaus counties.
**Requirements:** Adults, 18 yrs. and older, who can provide personal references and meet the requirements for home size and financial eligibility.
**Description of children:** Children from infancy through age 18 yrs.
**Licensing procedure:**
  1) Participate in recruitment process;
  2) complete home evaluation;
  3) undergo home study;
  4) attend required training;
  5) certification.
**Average length of time for licensing:** 2-3 mos.
**Inspections:**
  1) Sanitation;
  2) medical examinations for all adult household members;
  3) finger printing and child abuse clearance of foster parents.
After placement social worker makes weekly contact.
**Maximum number of children allowed in licensed foster care home:** 6.
**Interracial placement:** Permitted.
**Type of foster care and description of procedures:** Emergency, long-term, pre-adoptive and therapeutic.
**Per diem stipend:** $550-$659/mo.
**Additional funds available:** Clothing allowance $30/mo. and child's personal allowance $20/mo.

★ 934 ★
**Toiyabe Indian Health Project**
**Family Services Department**
P.O. Box 1296
Bishop, CA 93515
Phone: (619) 873-6394
Fax: (619) 873-3935
**Branch address:**
  Lone Pine Satellite Clinic, P.O. Box 186, Lone Pine, CA 93545
  Phone: (619) 876-4795

  Coleville Satellite Clinic, P.O. Box 76, Coleville, CA 96107
  Phone: (916) 495-2151
**Contact:** David J. Lent, Executive Director.
**Serves:** Inyo and Mono counties.
**Requirements:** Adults, 18 yrs. and older, who can provide 3 personal references.
**Description of children:** Indian children.
**Licensing procedure:**
  1) Complete foster care application;
  2) meet agency requirements and clearances.
**Average length of time for licensing:** Approx. 6 wks.
**Inspections:**
  1) Fire;

  2) sanitation;
  3) medical examinations for all household members;
  4) finger printing of foster parents;
  5) Dept. of Motor Vehicle clearance.
After placement child's caseworker visits bi-monthly.
**Maximum number of children allowed in licensed foster care home:** 2-3.
**Interracial placement:** Permitted.
**Type of foster care and description of procedures:** Emergency, short and long-term, therapeutic and pre-adoptive.
**Per diem stipend:** N/A.
**Additional funds available:** Clothing allowance.

★ 935 ★
**Walden Environment, Inc.**
5701 Marconi Ave., Ste. A
Carmichael, CA 95608
Phone: (916) 485-1656
Fax: (916) 485-3649
**Branch address:**
  11150 Sepulveda Blvd., Ste. 204, Mission Hills, CA 91345
  Phone: (818) 365-3665

  9645 Granite Ridge Dr., Ste. 110, San Diego, CA 92123
  Phone: (619) 694-5680
**Contact:** Sue Schulte.
**Serves:** Los Angeles, Sacramento and San Diego areas.
**Requirements:** Adults, 24 yrs. and older, who are able to meet their own financial needs, who can provide room for a foster child and personal references.
**Description of children:** Children who have been physically and/or sexually abused or victims of severe neglect.
**Licensing procedure:**
  1) Attend 5 orientation sessions;
  2) finger print clearance;
  3) attend 1 interview and have 2 home inspections;
  4) present evidence of a good driving record and reference checks;
  5) forward employment record and health reports.
**Average length of time for licensing:** 2-3 mos.
**Inspections:**
  1) Finger printing of foster parents;
  2) 2 home inspections;
  3) medical examinations of foster parent applicants.
After placement social worker visits weekly.
**Maximum number of children allowed in licensed foster care home:** Open.
**Interracial placement:** Permitted.
**Type of foster care and description of procedures:** Emergency, long-term, therapeutic and pre-adoptive.
**Per diem stipend:** $20.
**Additional funds available:** Medical/dental and some incidentals.

# COLORADO

★ 936 ★
**Chaffee County Department of Social Services**
P.O. Box 1007
Salida, CO 81201
Phone: (719) 539-6627

**Contact:** Social Services Supervisor.

**Serves:** Chafee County.

**Requirements:** Applicants must provide personal references.

**Description of children:** Children of all ages and descriptions.

**Licensing procedure:**
1) Initial inquiry;
2) complete home study;
3) home inspections and reference checks.

Different types of foster care require different licensing procedures.

**Average length of time for licensing:** Within 3 mos.

**Inspections:**
1) Fire;
2) sanitation;
3) medical examinations for all household members.

**Maximum number of children allowed in licensed foster care home:** 4.

**Interracial placement:** Permitted.

**Type of foster care and description of procedures:** Emergency, long-term, therapeutic and pre-adoptive.

**Per diem stipend:** Up to $340/mo.

**Additional funds available:** Medicaid and clothing allowance.

★937★
**Denver Alternative Youth Services**
**The Family Connection**
1240 W. Bayaud
Denver, CO 80223
Phone: (303) 698-2300
Fax: (303) 698-2903

**Contact:** Bob Tiernan.

**Serves:** Denver Metropolitan area.

**Requirements:** Adults 21 yrs. and older, who can provide personal references, who meet the requirements for marital status and home size and who are financially self-sustaining. Both foster parents may be employed outside the home provided one or both has flexible job/hrs.

**Description of children:** Severely abused adolescents with emotional/behavior problems.

**Licensing procedure:**
1) Telephone screening;
2) attend 1 hr. interview;
3) complete paperwork;
4) participate in 2-hr. in-home interview on family history/background;
5) attend six 1.5-2 hr. training sessions;
6) home inspection;
7) reference, law enforcement and abuse registry checks.

**Average length of time for licensing:** 3-6 wks.

**Inspections:**
1) Fire (part of home inspection);
2) sanitation (part of home inspection);
3) medical examinations for all household members.

After approval social worker visits 6-12 times yearly.

**Maximum number of children allowed in licensed foster care home:** 4 (usually only 1 foster child).

**Interracial placement:** With young person's approval.

**Type of foster care and description of procedures:** Long-term and therapeutic.

**Per diem stipend:** $14 - $18.

**Additional funds available:** Medicaid, clothing allowance and 50% of school fees for activities.

★938★
**Denver Department of Social Services**
2200 W. Alameda Ave.
Denver, CO 80223
Phone: (303) 936-3666
Fax: (303) 727-3085

**Contact:** Doris Puga, Administrator.

**Serves:** City and County of Denver.

**Requirements:** Adults, 21 yrs. and older, who can provide 40 sq. ft. of sleeping area and personal references.

**Description of children:** Abused, neglected and abandoned children.

**Licensing procedure:**
1) Initial inquiry;
2) complete home study;
3) if approved, attend foster parent Basic Education. Different types of foster care may require different licensing procedures.

**Average length of time for licensing:** 3-6 mos.

**Inspections:**
1) Fire;
2) medical examination for all household members;
after approval social worker visits monthly.

**Maximum number of children allowed in licensed foster care home:** 4 with no more than 2 children under the age of 2 yrs.

**Interracial placement:** Permitted.

**Type of foster care and description of procedures:** Emergency, long-term, therapeutic and pre-adoptive.

**Per diem stipend:**
Ages 0-11 mos.: $200/mo;
ages 1-3 yrs.: $252/mo;
ages 4-10 yrs.: $284/mo;
ages 11-14 yrs.: $316/mo;
ages 15-21 yrs.: $338/mo.

**Additional funds available:** Medicaid, initial clothing allowance and special need.

★939★
**El Paso County Department of Social Services**
P.O. Box 2692
Colorado Springs, CO 80906
Phone: (719) 444-5901

**Contact:** Betsi Frederickson.

**Serves:** El Paso County.

**Requirements:** Couples married at least 3 yrs. who are 21 yrs. and older, who can provide 40 sq. ft. of bedroom space and 5 personal references.

**Description of children:** Abused and/or neglected children, infants and children of drug/alcohol addicted mothers, developmentally delayed children.

**Licensing procedure:**
1) Attend orientation;
2) submit application;
3) participate in two Saturday training classes;
4) reference checks and records search;
5) fingerprinting;
6) interview with licensed psychologist;
7) complete home study.

**Average length of time for licensing:** 4-6 mos.

**Inspections:**
1) Medical examinations for all household members;
2) water quality for private wells;

3) safety; fire extinguishers and smoke alarms required. After approval social worker visits monthly.

**Maximum number of children allowed in licensed foster care home:** 4 foster children.

**Interracial placement:** Permitted but not desirable.

**Type of foster care and description of procedures:** Fost-adopt and shepherding (permanent home where child maintains birth identity and may have some contact with birth family).

**Per diem stipend:** $299 per month.

**Additional funds available:** Medicaid and one $67 clothing allowance; $20 per month for respite care.

### ★ 940 ★

**The Family Extension, Inc.**
525 3rd Ave.
Longmont, CO 80502
Phone: (303) 776-1224
Fax: (303) 776-4766

**Mailing address:**
 P.O. Box 1458, Longmont, CO 80502

**Contact:** Eileen B. Bisgard, J.D.

**Serves:** State of Colorado.

**Requirements:** Adults, 21 yrs. or older, who have adequate finances and living space for a foster or adoptive child(ren), and who can provide personal references.

**Description of children:** Emotionally and/or behaviorally disordered youth with no history of severe physical aggression or active major drug abuse. Also foster-adoptive younger children and infants.

**Licensing procedure:**
 1) Complete and return application;
 2) forward medical reports and references;
 3) pass criminal and child abuse registry checks;
 4) complete training and family assessment.

**Average length of time for licensing:** 7 or more wks.

**Inspections:**
 1) Fire
 2) sanitation
 3) medical examinations on all household members.
After placement, social worker visits weekly.

**Maximum number of children allowed in licensed foster care home:** Usually 1, unless members of a sibling group.

**Interracial placement:** Permitted.

**Type of foster care and description of procedures:** Long-term, therapeutic and pre-adoptive.

**Per diem stipend:** Varies by amount of foster parent training. Fully trained 1st yr. parent with adolescent placement: $559/mo.

**Additional funds available:** Medical/dental, clothing allowance and miscellaneous, e.g. mileage.

### ★ 941 ★

**Fremont County Department of Social Services**
P.O. Box 631
Canon City, CO 81212
Phone: (719) 275-2318
Fax: (719) 275-5206

**Contact:** Foster care worker.

**Serves:** Fremont County.

**Requirements:** Adults, 21 yrs. and older, who can provide a 40 sq. ft. sleeping area, 3 personal references and who meet the financial eligibility requirements.

**Description of children:** Children who have been physically, sexually and/or emotionally abused.

**Licensing procedure:**
 1) Request for licensing rules;
 2) submit application;
 3) medical and reference checks;
 4) complete home study;
 5) attend training. Licensing procedures differ with the different types of foster care.

**Average length of time for licensing:** Approx. 1 mo.

**Inspections:** Medical examinations are required for all household members. After placement, social worker visits monthly.

**Maximum number of children allowed in licensed foster care home:** 4.

**Interracial placement:** Permitted.

**Type of foster care and description of procedures:** Emergency, long-term, therapeutic and pre-adoptive.

**Per diem stipend:** Varies with child's age.

**Additional funds available:** Medicaid, initial clothing allowance of $74.

### ★ 942 ★

**Gunnison/Hinsdale County Department of Social Services**
200 E. Virginia
Gunnison, CO 81230
Phone: (303) 641-3244

**Contact:** Anne Steinbeck, Director.

**Serves:** Gunnison and Hinsdale counties.

**Requirements:** Adults, 21 yrs. and older, who can provide personal references.

**Description of children:** Children and adolescents with some emotional problems and/or victims of abuse and/or neglect.

**Licensing procedure:**
 1) Submit application;
 2) attend orientation;
 3) complete foster home study;
 4) participate in training;
 5) reference checks, home inspections, registry checks and medicals.

**Average length of time for licensing:** 2-6 mos.

**Inspections:**
 1) Medical examinations of all household members;
 2) home inspection;
 3) Central Registry of Child Protection.

**Maximum number of children allowed in licensed foster care home:** 4 foster.

**Interracial placement:** Permitted.

**Type of foster care and description of procedures:** Emergency, short and long-term, pre-adoptive and therapeutic.

**Per diem stipend:** $299/mo.-$359/mo. depending on age of child.

**Additional funds available:** Medicaid, initial clothing allowance of $75 and respite care $20/mo.

### ★ 943 ★

**Jefferson County Department of Social Services**
8550 W. 14th Ave.
Lakewood, CO 80215
Phone: (303) 271-4043

**Contact:** Linda Zschoche.

**Serves:** Jefferson County.

**Requirements:** Adults, 21 yrs. or older, who can provide personal references and a 40 sq. ft. sleeping area per foster child.

**Description of children:** Children from birth to 21 yrs. some of whom have special needs, i.e. developmental delays, abused/neglected, delinquent behaviors and sexually abused.

**Licensing procedure:**
1) Attend pre-certification training;
2) submit required paperwork and background checks;
3) complete foster care home study;
4) submit certification requirements.

**Average length of time for licensing:** Minimum of 2 mos.

**Inspections:**
1) Well check for mountain homes;
2) central registry and criminal checks;
3) medical examination for all household members.

**Maximum number of children allowed in licensed foster care home:** 4 foster children but this number varies with situation.

**Interracial placement:** Permitted.

**Type of foster care and description of procedures:** Emergency, long-term, therapeutic and pre-adoptive.

**Per diem stipend:** Varies with age of child.

**Additional funds available:** Medicaid, one-time clothing allowance and special need.

★944★
**Mesa County Department of Social Services**
P.O. Box 20,000-5035
Grand Junction, CO 81502
Phone: (303) 241-8480

**Contact:** Ron Danekas, Joyce Seuferer, Dena Neujahr.

**Serves:** Mesa County.

**Requirements:** Adults, 21 yrs. and older, who can demonstrate financial stability, whose home is adequate for family size and foster child(ren) and who can provide personal references.

**Description of children:** Children of all ages with a wide range of problems.

**Licensing procedure:** Contact office to request information on foster care. Licensing procedure differs with the type of foster care.

**Average length of time for licensing:** Approx. 6-8 wks.

**Inspections:**
1) Finger printing of foster parent applicants;
2) medical examinations for all household members.
After approval certifying social worker visits every other month.

**Maximum number of children allowed in licensed foster care home:** 4.

**Interracial placement:** Permitted.

**Type of foster care and description of procedures:** Emergency, long and short-term, therapeutic and pre-adoptive.

**Per diem stipend:** Varies with age and kind of placement.

**Additional funds available:** Medicaid, initial clothing allowance and special needs.

# CONNECTICUT

★945★
**The Casey Family Services**
2400 Main St.
Bridgeport, CT 06606
Phone: (203) 334-6991
(800) 332-6991
Fax: (203) 330-0753

**Contact:** Mary Anne Judge, Post-Adoption Services
Casey makes a program of *Post-Adoption Services* available to families within its geographic area who have children through adoption whether adopted through the Casey Family Services or not. The service is without charge and seeks to prevent disruptions by providing medical, legal and counseling referrals.

**Serves:** Residents of Fairfield and New Haven counties.

**Requirements:** Applicants must be at least 21 yrs. old, not on public assistance and have adequate home size to provide privacy for a foster child.

**Description of children:** Children between the ages of 5 and 13 yrs. who have emotional/behavioral and/or academic problems.

**Licensing procedure:** 1) Telephone inquiry and intake; 2) attend open house or individual interview; 3) application including autobiography; 4) state and federal police searches, reference checks and medical clearances; 5) home study; 6) enrichment series.

**Average length of time for licensing:** Less than 6 mos.

**Inspections:** 1) Home health and safety; 2) medical examination for foster parents; 3) TB test and VDRL for any household members over the age of 19; 4) 3 personal references; 5) coliform test and septic inspection, if not on city water and sewer. After placement, child's caseworker contacts family 1 - 4 times monthly on as needed basis.

**Maximum number of children allowed in licensed foster care home:** Casey's policy is to place each child one at a time although sibling groups are maintained as a unit.

**Interracial placement:** Casey policy is to place each child within his/her own ethnic group although interracial placement might be permitted if it were in the best interest of the child.

**Type of foster care and description of procedures:** Long-term, therapeutic and pre-adoptive. One third of all *Casey* children are adopted by their foster parents.

**Per diem stipend:** Monthly stipend determined by child's age.

**Additional funds available:** Title XIX, clothing allowance and funds available for social and educational enhancement.

★946★
**Healing the Children Northeast, Inc.**
Old Town Farm Rd.
New Milford, CT 06776
Phone: (203) 355-1828

**Mailing address:**
P.O. Box 129, New Milford, CT 06776

**Contact:** Angie Glick.

**Serves:** Residents of Connecticut.

**Requirements:** Applicants must have an independent means of support.

**Description of children:** Medically fragile children from a variety of countries who are in the U.S. for medical or surgical treatment.

**Licensing procedure:** 1) Inquiry; 2) complete information packet; 3) pre-service training; 4) home study; 5) placement.

**Average length of time for licensing:** 3 mos.

**Inspections:** 1) Home health and safety; 2) fire inspection, if home has a woodburning stove; 3) medical clearances for all household members which must be repeated biannually; 4) 3 personal references; 5) State Police and Child Abuse Registry searches which are repeated annually. After placement, child's caseworker visits or calls a minimum of once or twice monthly.

**Maximum number of children allowed in licensed foster care home:** Usually 1 foster child.

**Interracial placement:** Permitted.

**Type of foster care and description of procedures:** Short-term, usually 3 mos. or less.

**Per diem stipend:** None.

**Additional funds available:** Medical/dental and exceptional needs.

★ 947 ★

**The Institute of Professional Practice (I.P.P.)**
P.O. Box 3887
Woodbridge, CT 06525
Phone: (203) 389-6956

**Branch address:**
118 Echo Lake Rd., Watertown, CT 06795

**Contact:** Michael Richard, Ange Steigert, Greg Murphy.

**Serves:** Residents of Connecticut.

**Requirements:** All applicants will be considered regardless of age and marital status. Applicants will be selected according to the most qualified individual for a specific child in need of placement. Income and home size should be sufficient to accommodate a child.

**Description of children:** Children and adolescents with a variety of special needs including developmental disabilities, autism, dual diagnoses, physical disabilities, sensorial impairments, severe behavior problems, and/or those who otherwise experience difficulties which impair effective community or family living.

**Licensing procedure:** 1) Application; 2) if a program need exists and there is a potential match between applicant's qualification and skills and a child's needs, complete interview process; 3) undergo Police Name Check, Fingerprint check, Protective Service check and submit 3 references; 4) sign required forms; 5) undergo home inspections and physicals; 6) complete training; 7) if child is referred by the Department of Mental Retardation, home licensure; 8) placement. Licensing procedure varies according to the needs of the child in need of placement.

**Average length of time for licensing:** 5-12 or more mos.

**Inspections:** 2-family dwellings require fire inspections. Applicants living in single family dwelling should develop a fire evacuation plan. Medical examination for all household members plus fingerprinting, police name check and protective service check. After placement caseworker visits a minimum of once every 2 mos.

**Maximum number of children allowed in licensed foster care home:** No more than 2 children under 2 yrs. of age unless a competent adult is available to care for each additional 1 or 2 children. No more than 3 non-ambulatory children who are incapable of self-preservation in the event of emergency.

**Interracial placement:** Yes.

**Type of foster care and description of procedures:** Long-term and therapeutic.

**Per diem stipend:** Depends on needs of the child and the level of parenting difficulty.

**Additional funds available:** Title 19 for medical and dental and additional monies as needed for growth and enrichment; $113.20/mo. personal allowance which covers clothing.

★ 948 ★

**Lutheran Social Services of New England, Inc.**
2139 Silas Deane Hwy. Ste. 201
Rocky Hill, CT 06067-2336
Phone: (203) 257-9899
Fax: (203) 257-0340

**Branch address:**
416 Belmont St., Worcester, MA 01604
Phone: (508) 791-3388

85 Manchester St., Concord, NH 03301
Phone: (603) 224-9346

**Contact:** Paula Wisnewski (Massachusetts); Annette Ballou (Connecticut); Bob Kay (New Hampshire).

**Date established:** 1871.

**Serves:** Full services in Massachusetts and Connecticut; partial services in New Hampshire, Maine, Vermont, and Rhode Island.

**Requirements:** Adults, age 25 yrs. and older who can provide personal references.

**Description of children:** U.S. healthy infants and international children of all ages.

**Licensing procedure:**
1) Attend general information meeting;
2) complete group training; and
3) participate in home study.

**Average length of time for licensing:** 2 mos.

**Inspections:**
1) Finger printing of applicants;
2) home checked for the presence of smoke detectors;
3) medical examinations for all household members.
After placement, social worker visits.

**Maximum number of children allowed in licensed foster care home:** Most placed shortly after birth, few foster home placements. If foster care necessary, usually short term (2 days to 2 wks.).

**Interracial placement:** Permitted.

**Type of foster care and description of procedures:** Long-term, therapeutic and pre-adoptive.

**Per diem stipend:** $15.

# DELAWARE

★ 949 ★

**CHILD, Inc.**
507 Philadelphia Pike
Wilmington, DE 19809-2177
Phone: (302) 762-8989
Fax: (302) 762-8783

**Branch address:**
Polly Drummond Office Park, Bldg. 2, Ste. 2201-A, Newark, DE 19711

**Contact:** Joseph Dell'Olio, Executive Vice-President or Patricia H. Jacobs, LCSW, Foster Care Program Director.

**Serves:** Residents of Delaware.

**Requirements:** Applicants must be between the ages of 21 and 65 yrs., have sufficient income apart from the foster care stipend to support their own household and have separate youth and adult sleeping areas.

**Description of children:** Youth adjudicated delinquent who do not require incarceration.

**Licensing procedure:** 1) Office contact; 2) meet with Counselor; 3) home study; 4) Parent Education; 5) placement.

**Average length of time for licensing:** Less than 6 mos.

**Inspections:** 1)Medical clearances; 2) 3 personal references; 3) finger printing. After placement, child's caseworker visits 2 to 4 times per month, or more frequently, if necessary.

**Maximum number of children allowed in licensed foster care home:** 6.

**Interracial placement:** Permitted.

**Type of foster care and description of procedures:** Long-term and therapeutic.

**Per diem stipend:** $32.02.

**Additional funds available:** Medical/dental and occasionally other funds for special needs.

★950★
**Children's Choice of Delaware**
910B Walker Rd.
Dover, DE 19904
Phone: (302) 678-0404
Fax: (302) 678-9080
**Branch address:**
Belvue Bldg., Ste. 102, University Office Plaza, Newark, DE 19702-5412

Scott Plaza II, Ste. 350, Philadelphia, PA 19113
Phone: (215) 521-6270
**Contact:** Cynthia Knapp.
**Serves:** State of Delaware.
**Requirements:** Adults, 21 yrs. and older, who can provide a separate bed for each foster child, adequate child care, if parents work outside the home, and 3 personal references.
**Description of children:** Children from birth to 18 yrs. who are medically needy, abused or abandoned.
**Licensing procedure:**
1) Telephone contact for application and additional information;
2) forward medical fitness report from personal physician and personal references;
3) complete home study;
4) attend evening orientation meeting.
**Average length of time for licensing:** Approx. 1 mo.
**Inspections:**
1) Fire;
2) sanitation;
3) medical examinations for all household members.
After placement, social worker visits twice monthly.
**Maximum number of children allowed in licensed foster care home:** 6.
**Interracial placement:** Permitted.
**Type of foster care and description of procedures:** Long-term, pre-adoptive and therapeutic.
**Per diem stipend:** $10-$16 depending on child's need.
**Additional funds available:** Medicaid and clothing allowance.

★951★
**Division of Family Services (Delaware)**
Administration Bldg.
Delaware Youth and Family Center
1825 Faulkland Centre Rd.
Wilmington, DE 19805
Phone: (302) 633-2655
Fax: (302) 633-2652
**Branch address:**
Children's Service Center, 62 Rockford Rd., Wilmington, DE 19806
Phone: (302) 577-3824

Williams Service Center, 805 River Rd., Dover, DE 19901
Phone: (302) 739-4800

Georgetown Service Center, 546 S. Bedford St., Georgetown, DE 19947
Phone: (302) 856-5450
**Contact:** Carol W. King.
**Serves:** State of Delaware.
**Requirements:** Applicants must meet the age requirement and supply personal references.
**Description of children:** Dependent children.
**Licensing procedure:**
1) Attend information night;
2) submit application;
3) participate in 6 wks. of training;
4) complete home study process.
**Average length of time for licensing:** Varies.
**Inspections:**
1) Home inspection;
2) medical examinations for all household members;
3) police and Child Protective Services checks.
After placement child's caseworker visits regularly.
**Maximum number of children allowed in licensed foster care home:** 6.
**Interracial placement:** Permitted but Dept. prefers same culture placements.
**Type of foster care and description of procedures:** Emergency, short and long-term and pre-adoptive.
**Per diem stipend:** Ages:
0-9 yrs.: $11.24;
10-15 yrs.: $12.79;
16 yrs. or older: $14.47.
**Additional funds available:** Supplemental payments based on level of care, medical/dental, initial clothing allowance and miscellaneous.

# DISTRICT OF COLUMBIA

★952★
**Department of Human Services**
**Commission on Social Services**
**Child and Family Services Division**
Adoption and Placement Resources Branch
609 "H" St., N.E., Rm. 313
Washington, DC 20002
Phone: (202) 724-8602
Fax: (202) 724-4782
**Contact:** Wilfred Hamm, Chief of Adoptions.

**Serves:** District of Columbia and residents in Maryland and Virginia who are within a 25 mi. radius.

**Requirements:** Adults who are at least 21 yrs. old.

**Description of children:** Unavailable.

**Licensing procedure:**
1) Attend orientation;
2) participate in 10 wks. of pre-service training;
3) complete home study and submit appropriate documentation.

**Average length of time for licensing:** 6 mos.

**Inspections:**
1) Medical examinations;
2) medical statement that any other persons in the home are free of communicable diseases;
3) sanitation (Maryland residents).
After placement social worker visits on a frequent, regular basis. Foster home is evaluated annually.

**Maximum number of children allowed in licensed foster care home:** 3 foster children.

**Interracial placement:** Permitted.

**Type of foster care and description of procedures:** Emergency, short and long-term and pre-adoptive.

**Per diem stipend:** Ages: 0-12 yrs.: $445.47/mo.; 13 yrs. and up: $536.30/mo.

**Additional funds available:** Medicaid, initial clothing allowance, and miscellaneous.

★ 953 ★
**For Love of Children**
FLOC
1711 14th St., N.W.
Washington, DC 20009
Phone: (202) 462-8686
Fax: (202) 797-2198

**Contact:** Ardrea W. Burrell, Foster Home Program Director.

**Serves:** District of Columbia.

**Requirements:** Adults 21 and over who are self-supporting.

**Description of children:** Children between the ages of 0 and 21 yrs. who have been neglected, abused or abandoned.

**Licensing procedure:**
1) File application;
2) participate in 10 wk. pre-service training;
3) have at least 3 home visits;
4) reference checks, police and protective services clearances and income verification.

**Average length of time for licensing:** 4-6 wks after completion of pre-service training.

**Inspections:**
1) Sanitation/fire inspection;
2) medical examinations for all household members;
3) finger printing of foster parents and household members;
After approval, social worker visits at least monthly.

**Maximum number of children allowed in licensed foster care home:** 6 with no more than 2 children under the age of 2 yrs.

**Interracial placement:** Permitted.

**Type of foster care and description of procedures:** Emergency, short and long-term, therapeutic and pre-adoptive.

**Per diem stipend:** $10.11 - $17.57.

**Additional funds available:** Medicaid.

# FLORIDA

★ 954 ★
**Catholic Foster Services of Miami**
18601 SW 97 Ave.
Miami, FL 33157
Phone: (305) 238-1447

**Contact:** Marianela Banet, Social Worker; Rev. Robert Tywoniak, Program Director.

**Serves:** Residents of Dade County.

**Requirements:** Applicants must be 18 yrs. and older, be financially stable and have sufficient room for a foster child, be able to provide personal references and belong to a religion recognized by the Catholic Church.

**Description of children:** Children with emotional problems.

**Licensing procedure:** 1) Contact agency; 2) complete *Initial Contact Form* 3) preliminary visit by social worker; 4) undergo screening; 4) 4 additional visits by social worker; 5) placement.

**Average length of time for licensing:** 6 mos.

**Inspections:** 1) Fingerprinting; 2) criminal background check; 3) abuse registry check: 4) home health inspection; 5) fire; 6) medical examinations of all household members. After placement, child's caseworker visits monthly.

**Maximum number of children allowed in licensed foster care home:** 5.

**Interracial placement:** Agency seeks to preserve cultural identity of each child.

**Type of foster care and description of procedures:** Long-term.

**Per diem stipend:** $200/mo. for children 0-11 yrs.; $220/mo. for children 12 and older.

**Additional funds available:** Medicaid for medical and dental; clothing allowance: $100/yr. for children 0-5 yrs., $200/yr. for children 6-18 yrs.

# GEORGIA

★ 955 ★
**ChildKind, Inc.**
3355 NE Expressway, NE, Ste. 205
Atlanta, GA 30341
Phone: (404) 936-9655

**Contact:** Michael Bailiff, Executive Director; Sheron Y. Murray, MSW, Director of Social Services.

**Serves:** Residents of the State of Georgia.

**Requirements:** Applicants must be at least 21 yrs. old, have sufficient income and adequate sleeping arrangements for a foster child.

**Description of children:** Children from birth to 17 yrs., some who are medically fragile, or HIV infected or affected, or who have other special needs. Also children who have parents in drug treatment or who have been hospitalized due to HIV/AIDS.

**Licensing procedure:** 1) Make application; 2) complete background checks; 3) home study; 4) foster parent training; 5) pass inspections; 6) placement.

**Average length of time for licensing:** 6 mos.

**Inspections:** 1) Criminal Background check for all adult household members; 2) Medical exam for all household members including TB and VDRL test; 3) sanitation, if not on county system; 4) fingerprinting 5) 3 personal references; 6) childproofing of premises.

**Maximum number of children allowed in licensed foster care home:** 3 but final number depends upon needs of children.

**Interracial placement:** Agency strives to preserve the ethnic identity of each child in need of placement.

**Type of foster care and description of procedures:** Emergency, long-term and pre-adoptive.

**Per diem stipend:** Varies by county and child's individual needs.

**Additional funds available:** Medicaid and initial clothing allowance at the beginning of each academic year.

## ★956★
**Division of Family and Children's Services**
**Agency 2 - Georgia**
2 Peachtree St., 12th Fl.
Atlanta, GA 30303
Phone: (404) 894-2891
(404) 657-3400
Fax: (404) 657-3486

**Contact:** County office.

**Serves:** State of Georgia.

**Requirements:** Adults who can provide adequate physical space for a foster child, have sufficient financial resources to meet the existing needs of their own family and who can provide 3 personal references.

**Description of children:** Children from 4 to 7 yrs., large sibling groups, behaviorally disordered and status offenders, and adolescents between the ages of 12 and 15 yrs.

**Licensing procedure:** Georgia is in the process of converting to the MAPP program for foster parent preparation. While some counties already have it in place, others may not. Program is county administered and approval process may vary but follows these guidelines:
1) Telephone inquiry and intake;
2) information packet sent to applicant;
3) attend individual or group meeting;
4) participate in MAPP training or 12 hrs. pre-service training (training may vary for specialized placements);
5) complete foster home study (study may be more in-depth for specialized placements).

**Average length of time for licensing:** 3-6 mos. depending on county.

**Inspections:**
1) Home inspection;
2) smoke detectors and fire extinguishers;
3) sanitation if own well and septic system;
4) criminal records check;
5) TB and VDRL for all household members over the age of 18 yrs.
After placement social worker contacts foster parents and child at least monthly.

**Maximum number of children allowed in licensed foster care home:** 6.

**Interracial placement:** Permitted.

**Type of foster care and description of procedures:** Emergency, short and long-term, specialized and family treatment.

**Per diem stipend:** $10.

**Additional funds available:** Medicaid, supplemental medical/dental, clothing allowance and special rate from $.50 - $1.75 depending upon the difficulty of placement.

## ★957★
**Extended Families**
P.O. Box 115435
Atlanta, GA 30303
Phone: (404) 756-0148

**Contact:** Dolores Parker, Director.

**Serves:** Residents of Metro Atlanta.

**Requirements:** Applicants must be at least 21 yrs. old, have an independent source of income and be able to provide a bedroom which cannot be shared by a child of the opposite sex or an adult for any child 5 yrs. or older.

**Description of children:** Children of school age who have been either abused and/or neglected. Some sibling groups.

**Licensing procedure:** 1) Orientation; 2) 12 hrs. of foster parent training; 3) submit application with medical report and references; 4) interviews and home visit; 5) fingerprinting and FBI clearances.

**Average length of time for licensing:** 6 mos. or less.

**Inspections:** 1) Medical clearances for all household members with TB test and VDRL screening for any household member 16 yrs. and older; 2) home health and safety; 3) 3 personal references; 4) finger printing; 5) well and coliform if not on city water and sewer. After placement, child's caseworker visits at least monthly.

**Maximum number of children allowed in licensed foster care home:** 3 foster children.

**Interracial placement:** Permitted.

**Type of foster care and description of procedures:** Long-term.

**Per diem stipend:** Monthly stipend.

**Additional funds available:** Medicaid, clothing allowance, recreational and special funds, as needed.

## ★958★
**Families First**
1105 W. Peachtree St.
Atlanta, GA 30309
Phone: (404) 853-2800

**Contact:** Foster Care Worker.

**Date established:** 1891.

**Serves:** Residents of Metro Atlanta.

**Requirements:** Applicants must be at least 21 yrs. old, have an independent source of income and be able to meet the state requirements for living space.

**Description of children:** Primarily sibling groups who have been abandoned, neglected and/or abused.

**Licensing procedure:** 1) Inquiry; 2) telephone screening; 3) application packet; 4) 5) home study.

**Average length of time for licensing:** 2 mos.

**Inspections:** 1) Medical clearances for all household members with a TB test and VDRL screen for any household member 16 yrs. and older; 2) 4 personal references; 3) home health and safety; 4) finger printing; 5) well and coliform count, if not on city water and sewer; 6) criminal records check. After placement, child's caseworker visits a minimum of monthly.

**Maximum number of children allowed in licensed foster care home:** 6.

Interracial placement: Permitted.

Type of foster care and description of procedures: Cradle care, short and long-term, therapeutic.

Per diem stipend: Average: $10/day.

Additional funds available: Medical/dental, monthly clothing, child allowance, diaper allowance and other funds as required on a case-by case basis.

★ 959 ★
**The Phoenix Institute for Adolescents, Inc.**
1395 S. Marietta Pkwy., Ste. 914
Marietta, GA 30067
Phone: (404) 514-8255

Contact: Kathleen Cone or Claudia Gunselman.

Serves: Residents of the Southeastern US.

Requirements: Follows State of Georgia's child placing regulations.

Description of children: All children are currently in treatment at the Phoenix Institute for Adolescents, Inc.

Licensing procedure: Unavailable.

Average length of time for licensing: 6 mos.

Inspections: 1) Medical examination for all household members; 2) sanitation, if home has septic tank; 3) fingerprinting; 4) personal references. After placement, child's caseworker visits annually.

Maximum number of children allowed in licensed foster care home: 6.

Interracial placement: Permitted.

Type of foster care and description of procedures: Therapeutic.

Per diem stipend: $10 per diem.

Additional funds available: Provided by each child's biological parents.

★ 960 ★
**Tender Mercy Ministries, Inc.**
P.O. Box 567524
Atlanta, GA 30356
Phone: (404) 928-3930

Contact: J. Roger Pineau.

Serves: Residents of the U.S.

Requirements: Married Protestant couples who have sufficient income for a foster child.

Description of children: Children of incarcerated parents who have no other family to assume custody.

Licensing procedure: Unavailable.

Average length of time for licensing: 6 mos.

Inspections: 1) Fingerprinting; 2) health examination for all household members; 3) personal references. After placement, child's caseworker visits monthly.

Maximum number of children allowed in licensed foster care home: 6.

Interracial placement: Permitted.

Type of foster care and description of procedures: Emergency and long-term.

Per diem stipend: None.

Additional funds available: Medical fees paid by Ministry.

★ 961 ★
**The United Methodist Children's Home**
500 S. Columbia Dr.
Decatur, GA 30030-4197
Phone: (404) 370-3100

Branch address:
736 Greene St., Augusta, GA 30903

108 1/2 Gordon St., Dalton, GA 30720

Contact: Steve Hubbard, Director of Community Services.

Serves: Residents of the North Georgia Methodist Conference area.

Requirements: Applicants must be at least 21 yrs. old and preferably not over 65 yrs. and have sufficient income to help provide for a foster child. Married applicants are preferred, but each case is considered individually. Applicants who are not Christian are considered for children of a similar faith only.

Description of children: Children of all ages and both sexes who are neglected, deprived and/or abused, some in sibling groups.

Licensing procedure: 1) Inquiry; 2) interview; 3) application process; 4) home visit; 5) pre-approval training; 6) confirmation of approval; 7) placement.

Average length of time for licensing: 6 mos.

Inspections: 1) fire; 2) sanitation; 3) finger printing; 4) medical examination for all household members; 5) 4 personal references and 1 ministerial reference. After placement child's caseworker visits monthly.

Maximum number of children allowed in licensed foster care home: 6.

Interracial placement: Permitted, if appropriate.

Type of foster care and description of procedures: Emergency, long-term and pre-adoptive.

Per diem stipend: Varies with child's age.

Additional funds available: Medicaid; monthly allowance according to the child's age; other monies available for specific needs as required.

# HAWAII

★ 962 ★
**The Casey Family Program**
1848 Nuuanu Ave.
Honolulu, HI 96817
Phone: (808) 521-9531
Fax: (808) 533-1018

Branch address:
32 Kinoole St., No. 103, Hilo, HI 96720
Phone: (808) 935-2876

Contact: Linda Santos.

Serves: Honolulu office serves residents of Oahu and Hilo office serves residents of east Hawaii.

Requirements: Applicants must be at least 21 yrs. old, have a stable income and adequate home size to provide privacy for a foster child.

Description of children: Children between the ages of 6 and 15 yrs. from difficult backgrounds.

Licensing procedure: 1) Inquiry; 2) application; 3) staff interview; 4) home study; 5) reference checks, TB test and criminal background checks; 6) interview process; 7) pre-service training; 8) placement.

**Average length of time for licensing:** 6 - 8 wks.

**Inspections:** 1) Home health and safety; 2) finger printing of all household members over the age of 18; 3) FBI and Child Protective Services searches for all household members over the age of 18; 4) 3 personal references; 5) medical examinations for foster parents.
After placement, child's caseworker visits at least monthly.

**Maximum number of children allowed in licensed foster care home:** Casey's policy is to place each child one at a time although it strives to keep sibling groups together.

**Interracial placement:** Ideally children are placed within their own ethnic group although interracial placements are permitted, if in the child's best interests.

**Type of foster care and description of procedures:** Long-term.

**Per diem stipend:** Reimbursements for food, shelter and clothing based on a child's age: $648/mo. for children under 13 yrs.; $690/mo. for children over 13 yrs.

**Additional funds available:** $100 Family Payment, Medicaid and funds available for enhancement programs.

# IDAHO

**★ 963 ★**
**The Casey Family Program**
6441 Emerald
Boise, ID 83704
Phone: (208) 377-1771

**Contact:** Division Director.

**Serves:** Residents within a 50 mile radius of Boise.

**Requirements:** Must comply with state regulations.

**Description of children:** Youth who are unlikely to be adopted or return to their birth families.

**Licensing procedure:** 1) Interview; 2) complete paperwork; 3) meet state licensing requirements.

**Average length of time for licensing:** 6 mos.

**Inspections:** 1) Finger printing; 2) medical examination; 3) sanitation; 4) personal references. After placement, child's caseworker visits annually.

**Maximum number of children allowed in licensed foster care home:** Varies.

**Interracial placement:** Permitted.

**Type of foster care and description of procedures:** Long-term.

**Per diem stipend:** Varies.

**Additional funds available:** All medical, dental, clothing and any other child-related expenses are covered by the Program.

**★ 964 ★**
**Department of Health and Welfare**
**Family and Community Services**
450 W. State
Boise, ID 83704
Phone: (208) 334-5700

**Branch address:**
Region I, 1250 Ironwood Dr., Ste. 204, Coeur d'Alene, ID 83814
Phone: (208) 769-1515

Region II, 1118 "F" St., P.O. Drawer B, Lewiston, ID

Phone: (208) 799-4400

Region III, 111 Poplar, Caldwell, ID 83605
Phone: (208) 459-7456

Region IV, 4355 Emerald, Boise, ID 83706
Phone: (208) 334-6700

Region V, 601 Poleline Rd., Ste. 1, Twin Falls, ID 83301
Phone: (208) 736-3020

Region VI, 1070 Hiline, P.O. Box 4166, Pocatello, ID 83205
Phone: (208) 235-2949

Region VII, 150 Shoup Ave., Ste. 19, Idaho Falls, ID 83402
Phone: (208) 528-5790

**Contact:** Meri Brennan, Adoption Program Specialist.

**Serves:** State of Idaho.

**Requirements:** Applicants must have sufficient income to maintain family home, have adequate living space for a foster child and provide personal references.

**Description of children:** Dependent children, some with behavioral problems.

**Licensing procedure:**
1) Submit application;
2) finger print and reference checks;
3) complete home study;
4) licensing certificate issued;
5) participate in group orientation and training.

**Average length of time for licensing:** Approx. 1 mo.

**Inspections:**
1) Home inspection;
2) finger printing of foster parents.
Additional inspections may be required depending upon circumstances.
After approval foster home is visited at least semi-annually.

**Maximum number of children allowed in licensed foster care home:** 6.

**Interracial placement:** Permitted.

**Type of foster care and description of procedures:** Emergency, short and long-term, pre-adoptive and therapeutic.

**Per diem stipend:**
1) Emergency (up to 30 days): $12.
2) Regular foster care:
Ages: 0-5 yrs. $198/mo.;
6-12 yrs. $205/mo.;
13-18 yrs. $278/mo.

**Additional funds available:** Special care allowances for children with chronic medical problems and behavioral problems in varying degrees; medical/dental, initial clothing, Christmas and birthday gift funds.

# ILLINOIS

**★ 965 ★**
**Cabrini-Green Youth and Family Services**
900 N. Franklin, Ste. 300
Chicago, IL 60610
Phone: (312) 943-8872

**Contact:** Joseph Galvin.

**Serves:** Residents within a 70 mi. radius of Chicago.

**Requirements:** Applicants must be at least 21 yrs. old have a source of income apart from the foster care stipend and have sufficient living space to meet licensing standards.

**Description of children:** Children between the ages of infancy and 18 yrs., primarily physically/sexually abused and/or neglected African American children without severe problems.

**Licensing procedure:** 1) Telephone inquiry to Licensing Representative; 2) Licensing Representative home visit; 3) sign contracts; 4) 10 wks. of orientation; 5) background checks.

**Average length of time for licensing:** 6-12 mos.

**Inspections:** 1) Home health and safety; 2) medical clearances for all household members; 3) personal references; 4) finger printing. After placement, child's caseworker visits at least monthly.

**Maximum number of children allowed in licensed foster care home:** 8.

**Interracial placement:** Permitted.

**Type of foster care and description of procedures:** Long-term and pre-adoptive.

**Per diem stipend:** $315 - $390/mo.

**Additional funds available:** Medicaid and clothing allowance on a case by case basis.

★ 966 ★
**Casa Central Foster Care Agency**
1401 N. California
Chicago, IL 60622
Phone: (312) 276-8647

**Contact:** Nilda La Luz or Illeana Gomez.

**Serves:** Residents within the city limits of Chicago.

**Requirements:** Applicants must be at least 21 yrs. old and have a stable income.

**Description of children:** Primarily Hispanic children who are wards of the Department of Children and Family Service.

**Licensing procedure:** 1) Attend Orientation meeting; 2) make application; 3) complete interview process; 4) undergo home study which includes fingerprint check; 5) placement.

**Average length of time for licensing:** 6 mos.

**Inspections:** 1) Finger printing; 2) health examinations for all household members; 3) personal references. After placement, social worker visits biannually.

**Maximum number of children allowed in licensed foster care home:** 8, provided living space allows.

**Interracial placement:** Permitted if in compliance with Burgos degree.

**Type of foster care and description of procedures:** Emergency and long-term.

**Per diem stipend:** Based on child's age.

**Additional funds available:** Medicaid and monthly clothing allowance.

★ 967 ★
**Chicago Child Care Society**
5467 South University Ave.
Chicago, IL 60615
Phone: (312) 643-0452

**Contact:** Ms. Sylvia Ragland, Director of Foster Care and Adoption Services.

**Description:** Non-profit, child welfare agency, licensed by the State of Illinois Department of Children and Family Services, providing foster care and adoption, day care, counseling for multi-problem families and services for pregnant adolescents.

**Serves:** Residents of Cook County, IL.

**Requirements:** Applicants between the ages of 21 and 65 yrs. who are self-supporting and who have sufficient living space to afford a foster child some privacy.

**Description of children:** African-American and Caucasian children between the ages of birth and 10 yrs., some in special groups and some who have special needs.

**Licensing procedure:** 1) Application; 2) Intake process; 3) assessment; 4) preparation; 5) licensing; 6) placement.

**Average length of time for licensing:** 6-12 mos.

**Inspections:** 1) Finger printing; 2) medical examination for all household members; 3) personal references.

**Maximum number of children allowed in licensed foster care home:** 8.

**Interracial placement:** Permitted.

**Type of foster care and description of procedures:** Long-term, pre-adoptive and specialized.

**Per diem stipend:** Unavailable.

**Additional funds available:** Medicaid, monthly clothing allowance and allowance for incidentals.

★ 968 ★
**Chicago Commons**
4600 S. McDowell
Chicago, IL 60609
Phone: (312) 254-2003

**Contact:** Raul Gonzalez, Juan Melendez or James Powe.

**Serves:** Residents of Cook County.

**Requirements:** Applicants must be at least 21 yrs. old who are financially stable and who can provide minimum space requirements.

**Description of children:** African American, Hispanic and Caucasian children between the ages of 1 and 18 yrs., some who have special needs.

**Licensing procedure:** 1) Telephone inquiry; 2) respond to initial questions; 3) home visits; 4) home study; 5) background inquiries; 6) licensure; 7) placement.

**Average length of time for licensing:** 6-12 mos.

**Inspections:** 1) Fire inspection; 2) sanitation; 3) medical examinations for all household members; 4) finger printing; 5) at least 3 personal references. After placement, child's caseworker visits at least monthly.

**Maximum number of children allowed in licensed foster care home:** Depends upon living space available and the needs of children.

**Interracial placement:** Permitted under specific conditions.

**Type of foster care and description of procedures:** Emergency and long-term.

**Per diem stipend:** Varies.

**Additional funds available:** Medical card is provided.

★ 969 ★
**Children's Development Center**
650 N. Main St.
Rockford, IL 61103
Phone: (815) 965-6745

**Contact:** Steve Guedet, Executive Director.

**Serves:** Residents of Boone, DeKalb, Lee, Ogle, Stephenson, Whiteside and Winnebago counties in northwest Illinois.

**Requirements:** Applicants must be at least 21 yrs. old who have sufficient funds to care for children and at least 2 bedrooms.

**Description of children:** Children who are medically fragile or developmentally delayed or disabled.

**Licensing procedure:** 1) Meet standards requirements; 2) complete training; 3) undergo home study; 4) pass screenings and inspections; 5) interview process; 6) background checks; 7) placement.

**Average length of time for licensing:** 6 mos.

**Inspections:** 1) Finger printing; 2) smoke alarms at every living level; 3) medical examinations for all household members; 4) nitrate and coliform water tests, if home well; 5) personal references. After placement, licensing worker visits a minimum of twice yearly.

**Maximum number of children allowed in licensed foster care home:** 8 with no more than 4 children under the age of 6 yrs. and no more than 2 children under the age of 2 yrs. including the foster parents' own children.

**Interracial placement:** Permitted.

**Type of foster care and description of procedures:** All.

**Per diem stipend:** $20.81 - $22.88 per diem depending upon age of child.

**Additional funds available:** Medicaid.


★ 970 ★
**Circle Family Care**
118 N. Central
Chicago, IL 60644-3199
Phone: (312) 921-1446

**Branch address:**
  4925 W. Division, Chicago, IL 60651

  4100 W. Grand, Chicago, IL 60651

**Contact:** Linda Sharber.

**Serves:** Residents of Cook County, particularly in Austin and Humboldt Park.

**Requirements:** Applicants must be 21 yrs. or older, single or married, if married, at least 1 yr.

**Description of children:** Unavailable.

**Licensing procedure:** 1) Orientation; 2) background check; 3) 8 wk. pre-service training; 4) home study; 5) upon Foster Care Review Committee's recommendation, placement.

**Average length of time for licensing:** 6 mos.

**Inspections:** 1) Site inspection; 2) finger printing check; 3) medical examination for all household members; 4) personal references. After placement, social worker visits monthly.

**Maximum number of children allowed in licensed foster care home:** 8.

**Interracial placement:** Permitted.

**Type of foster care and description of procedures:** Emergency, long-term and pre-adoptive.

**Per diem stipend:** Age 0-11 mos.: $315/mo.; 1-4 yrs.: $322/mo.; 5-8 yrs.: $337/mo.; 9-11 yrs.: $358/mo.; 12 and over: $390/mo.

**Additional funds available:** State Medical Card, clothing voucher at time of placement and additional monies per child's needs.

★ 971 ★
**The Community House**
415 W. 8th St.
Hinsdale, IL 60521
Phone: (708) 323-7500

**Contact:** Jim Gorski, Supervisor.

**Serves:** Residents of Downers Grove Township.

**Requirements:** Applicants must be at least 25 yrs. old, have an income of at least $7250 per year and have at least 2 bedrooms.

**Description of children:** Adolescents.

**Licensing procedure:** 1) Interview; 2) background check; 3) orientation.

**Average length of time for licensing:** 6-12 mos.

**Inspections:** 1) Home health and safety; 2) finger printing; 3) 3 personal references. After foster home is approved social worker visits semi-annually.

**Maximum number of children allowed in licensed foster care home:** 6.

**Interracial placement:** Permitted.

**Type of foster care and description of procedures:** Emergency.

**Per diem stipend:** $15.

**Additional funds available:** None.


★ 972 ★
**Ray Graham Association for People with Disabilities**
340 W. Butterfield Rd., Ste. 20
Elmhurst, IL 60126
Phone: (708) 530-4554

**Contact:** Laura Jett, Administrator, Foster Care.

**Serves:** Cook, DuPage, Kane, Kendall and Will counites.

**Requirements:** Applicants must provide personal references, a 40 sq. ft. sleeping area and meet the financial eligibility requirements.

**Description of children:** Individuals with developmental disabilities and high-risk infants.

**Licensing procedure:**
  1) Attend initial interview;
  2) complete 2-part application process;
  3) complete inspections and home study.

**Average length of time for licensing:** 6 mos. maximum.

**Inspections:**
  1) Fire;
  2) sanitation;
  3) medical examinations for all household members;
  4) finger printing of foster parents.
After placement social worker visits at least monthly.

**Maximum number of children allowed in licensed foster care home:** 6.

**Interracial placement:** Permitted.

**Type of foster care and description of procedures:** Emergency, long-term, pre-adoptive and therapeutic.

**Per diem stipend:** Funds provided by the Dept. of Mental Health and the Department of Children and Family Services.

**Additional funds available:** Medical/dental.


★ 973 ★
**Guardian Angel Home**
1550 Plainfield Rd.
Joliet, IL 60435
Phone: (815) 729-0930

**Contact:** Foster care worker.

**Serves:** Residents of Will County and its outlying areas.

**Requirements:** Applicants over the age of 21 yrs. who are either single or married and who have sufficient income and living space to accommodate a foster child.

**Description of children:** Children between the ages of birth and 17 yrs.

**Licensing procedure:** 1) Application; 2) initial paperwork; 3) licensure requirements; 4) interview process; 5) placement.

**Average length of time for licensing:** 6 mos.

**Inspections:** 1) Finger printing; 2) Background check; 3) medical examination for all household members; 4) 3 personal references. After placement, social worker visits monthly.

**Maximum number of children allowed in licensed foster care home:** 8.

**Interracial placement:** Permitted.

**Type of foster care and description of procedures:** Emergency and long-term.

**Per diem stipend:** Between $10 and $20 per diem.

**Additional funds available:** Medicaid, clothing voucher at time of placement and reimbursement for day care, etc.


★ 974 ★

**Hephzibah Children's Association**
946 North Blvd.
Oak Park, IL 60301
Phone: (708) 386-8417

**Branch address:**
124 S. Marion, Oak Park, IL 60301

**Contact:** Davida E. Williams, A.M., A.C.S.W., Director/Foster Care and Group Homes.

**Serves:** Residents of west and north side of Chicago and the western suburbs.

**Requirements:** Applicants over 21 yrs. who have adequate income and 40 sq. ft. of living space for 1 child and 35 additional sq. ft. for each additional child.

**Description of children:** Unavailable.

**Licensing procedure:** 1) Interview with foster care coordinator; 2) finger printing; 3) extensive home study; 4) foster parent training; 5) placement.

**Average length of time for licensing:** 6 mos.

**Inspections:** 1) Home health examination; 2) medical examinations for all household members; 3) finger printing; 4) 5 personal references. After placement, social worker visits at least twice monthly.

**Maximum number of children allowed in licensed foster care home:** 8 including adopted and biological.

**Interracial placement:** Permitted.

**Type of foster care and description of procedures:** Emergency and short-term.

**Per diem stipend:** $16.08 -$37.49 per diem.

**Additional funds available:** Medicaid and clothing vouchers.


★ 975 ★

**Jackson County Community Mental Health Center**
604 E. College St.
Carbondale, IL 62901
Phone: (618) 457-6703

**Contact:** Art Zaitz, Coordinator, Youth Service Program.

**Serves:** Residents of southern Illinois.


**Requirements:** Applicants, aged 21 yrs. and older, who have adequate space and income to provide basic necessities for themselves, their biological children and their foster children.

**Description of children:** Children seeking emergency placements are generally adolescent runaways. Children seeking therapeutic placements are between the ages of 6 and 17 yrs. and have serious behavior problems.

**Licensing procedure:** 1) Application; 2) background and reference checks; 3) medical examinations and home inspection; 4) foster parent training; 5) licensure; 6) placement.

**Average length of time for licensing:** 6 mos.

**Inspections:** 1) Finger printing; 2) medical examinations for all household members; 3) home inspection; 4) personal references. After placement social worker visits a minimum of semi-annually.

**Maximum number of children allowed in licensed foster care home:** 8.

**Interracial placement:** Permitted.

**Type of foster care and description of procedures:** Emergency and therapeutic.

**Per diem stipend:** Emergency: $19.05 per night; Therapeutic: $40 per night.

**Additional funds available:** None. Biological parents are responsible for additional expenditures.


★ 976 ★

**Kemmerer Village**
RR 1, Box 12C
Assumption, IL 62510
Phone: (217) 226-4451

**Contact:** Karen Hulner.

**Serves:** State of Illinois.

**Requirements:** Adults at least 21 yrs. old who can provide adequate living space and personal references.

**Description of children:** Abused, neglected, dependent, behavior-disordered and emotionally disturbed children.

**Licensing procedure:**
1) Complete pre-service training;
2) submit medicals;
3) complete background checks.

**Average length of time for licensing:** 3-4 mos.

**Inspections:**
1) Finger printing of foster parents;
2) medical examinations of all household members.

**Maximum number of children allowed in licensed foster care home:** 8.

**Interracial placement:** Permitted.

**Type of foster care and description of procedures:** Emergency, long-term, pre-adoptive and therapeutic.

**Per diem stipend:** Unavailable.

**Additional funds available:** Guardian provides medical/dental and clothing.


★ 977 ★

**Kendall County Human Services**
505 S. Main St.
Yorkville, IL 60560
Phone: (708) 553-4171

**Contact:** Mary Ellen Commare, MS, CADC.

**Serves:** Residents of Kendall County.

**Requirements:** Applicants must be at least 21 yrs. old, either single or a man and woman married to each other who have sufficient financial resources to provide basic necessities for themselves and their own children and the foster child(ren).

**Description of children:** Children in the custody of Kendall County Human Services.

**Licensing procedure:** Kendall County follows the Licensing Standards of the Illinois Department of Children and Family Services.

**Average length of time for licensing:** 6 mos.

**Inspections:** 1) Fire; 2) sanitation; 3) finger printing; 4) medical examination of all household members; 5) personal references. After placement, social worker visits semi-annually.

**Maximum number of children allowed in licensed foster care home:** 8.

**Interracial placement:** Permitted.

**Type of foster care and description of procedures:** Emergency.

**Per diem stipend:** $12.

**Additional funds available:** Additional expenditures are the responsibility of the biological parents.

★ 978 ★
**Lutheran Social Services of Illinois**
1001 E. Touhy
Des Plaines, IL 60018
Phone: (708) 635-4600

**Branch address:**

610 Abington St., Peoria, IL 61603
Phone: (309) 671-0300

6525 W. North Ave., Oak Park, IL 60302
Phone: (708) 445-8352

11740 S. Western Ave., Chicago, IL 60643
Phone: (312) 239-3700

555 6th St., Moline, IL 61265
Phone: (309) 797-2226

600 W. Jackson, Chicago, IL 60661
Phone: (312) 441-1040

**Contact:** Dorothy Goos.

**Serves:** Central and northern Illinois, including Metropolitan Chicago.

**Requirements:** Applicants should be no more than 40 yrs. older than the child placed, must provide personal references and meet the licensing requirements for home size.

**Description of children:** Children of all ages and races; some specialized care for medically, physically and emotionally handicapped children.

**Licensing procedure:**
1) Initial inquiry;
2) complete home study;
3) participate in pre-service and on-going training;
4) licensure.

**Average length of time for licensing:** 2-4 mos.

**Inspections:**
1) Finger printing of foster parent applicants;
2) medical examinations of all household members;
3) home inspection.

**Maximum number of children allowed in licensed foster care home:** 8.

**Interracial placement:** Permitted.

**Type of foster care and description of procedures:** Emergency, long-term, pre-adoptive and therapeutic.

**Per diem stipend:** Varies with child's age and condition.

**Additional funds available:** Medicaid and miscellaneous, if required.

★ 979 ★
**Lydia Home Association**
4300 W. Irving Park Rd.
Chicago, IL 60641-2881
Phone: (312) 736-1447

**Contact:** Doris Bauer, Executive Director.

**Serves:** Residents of Chicagoland.

**Requirements:** Applicants must be at least 21 yrs. old, be either single or legally married, have their own source of income and at least 2 bedrooms.

**Description of children:** Multi-cultural children.

**Licensing procedure:** 1) Application; 2) background checks and finger printing; 3) training; 4) home study; 5) approval and placement. Type of training will vary with the type of foster placement sought.

**Average length of time for licensing:** 3 mos.

**Inspections:** 1) Medical clearances for all household members; 2) fire; 3) personal references; 4) finger printing. After licensure, social worker visits a minimum of once a month.

**Maximum number of children allowed in licensed foster care home:** 8.

**Interracial placement:** Permitted.

**Type of foster care and description of procedures:** Emergency, short and long-term, therapeutic and specialized.

**Per diem stipend:** Varies based on age and needs of children.

**Additional funds available:** Medicaid; other monies made available as needed and as outlined in the contracts signed with the Department of Service.

★ 980 ★
**Maryville Academy**
1150 N. River Rd.
Des Plaines, IL 60016
Phone: (312) 824-6126

**Contact:** Karen Adler, Foster Care Director.

**Serves:** Chicago metropolitan area.

**Requirements:** Adults, 21 yrs. and older who can provide a 40 sq. ft. sleeping area and personal references.

**Description of children:** Sexually exploited/abused, physically abused, neglected, delinquent, emotionally disturbed children between the ages of 0 and 17 yrs.

**Licensing procedure:**
1) Attend interview;
2) return completed application and questionnaire;
3) complete state licensing procedures;
4) participate in 32 hrs. of pre-service training.

**Average length of time for licensing:** 3-6 mos.

**Inspections:**
1) Finger printing of foster parents;
2) medical examinations for all household members.
After placement social worker visits weekly.

**Maximum number of children allowed in licensed foster care home:** 5.

**Interracial placement:** Occasionally.

**Type of foster care and description of procedures:** Emergency, long-term, pre-adoptive and therapeutic.

**Per diem stipend:** $38.

**Additional funds available:** None.

★ 981 ★
**Maternity and Adoption Services of Baptist Children's Home**
4243 Lincolnshire Dr.
Mt. Vernon, IL 62864
Phone: (618) 242-4944

**Contact:** Carla Monroe, Supervisor.

**Serves:** Residents of Illinois.

**Requirements:** Southern Baptist or Evangelical married couples who are no more than 40 yrs. old and whose home size meets licensing standards of the State of Illinois.

**Description of children:** African American children who are less than 6 mos. old.

**Licensing procedure:** 1) Application; 2) home study; 3) checks and inspections.

**Average length of time for licensing:** 6 mos. or less.

**Inspections:** 1) Medical clearances for all household members; 2) personal references; 3) finger printing. After licensure social worker visits semi-annually.

**Maximum number of children allowed in licensed foster care home:** 6.

**Interracial placement:** Permitted.

**Type of foster care and description of procedures:** Emergency and pre-adoptive.

**Per diem stipend:** $250/mo.

**Additional funds available:** Clothing allowance.

★ 982 ★
**Ada S. McKinley Foster Care and Adoption Services**
2907 S. Michigan
Chicago, IL 60616
Phone: (312) 808-1080
Fax: (312) 808-6175

**Branch address:**
725 South Wells, Chicago, IL 60607
Phone: (312) 554-0600

**Contact:** Carol A. Winn, ACSW or Lisa Barkstall, LCSW.

**Serves:** Cook County.

**Requirements:** Applicants must provide personal references. Both foster parents may not be employed full-time outside the home.

**Description of children:** Unimpaired children and children who are health impaired, developmentally delayed/disabled, or have behavior disorders.

**Licensing procedure:**
1) Attend agency orientation;
2) participate in interview by orientation board;
3) complete home study and home assignments;
4) attend 10 wk. training session;
5) issuance of license.

**Average length of time for licensing:** 90 days.

**Inspections:**
1) Fire;
2) sanitation;
3) medical examinations for all household members;

4) finger printing of foster parents. After approval social worker visits semi-monthly.

**Maximum number of children allowed in licensed foster care home:** 8.

**Interracial placement:** Permitted.

**Type of foster care and description of procedures:** Emergency, therapeutic and long-term.

**Per diem stipend:** $13.00 and $20.50.

**Additional funds available:** Medical/dental, clothing allowance and miscellaneous.

★ 983 ★
**Reverend Henry Rucker Memorial Services**
8400 S. Ashland
Chicago, IL 60620
Phone: (312) 445-0222

**Branch address:**
5714 S. Calumet, Chicago, IL 60637

**Contact:** Eloise Jackson.

**Serves:** Residents of Cook County.

**Requirements:** Applicants must be at least 21 yrs. old, be self-supporting and meet the licensing standards for living space set by the Illinois Department of Children and Family Services.

**Description of children:** Children with special needs.

**Licensing procedure:** 1) Assessment; 2) finger printing; 3) licensing; 4) approval; 5) foster parent training.

**Average length of time for licensing:** Less than 6 mos.

**Inspections:** 1) Fire; 2) medical clearances for all household members; 3) personal references; 4) sanitation; 5) finger printing of adult household members. After licensing, social worker visits monthly.

**Maximum number of children allowed in licensed foster care home:** 10.

**Interracial placement:** Permitted, but same race placements are made whenever possible.

**Type of foster care and description of procedures:** Long-term, pre-adoptive and specialized.

**Per diem stipend:** Based on age of child and level of care.

**Additional funds available:** Special service fee and clothing voucher.

★ 984 ★
**Seguin Services Inc.**
3100 S. Central Ave.
Cicero, IL 60650
Phone: (708) 863-3803

**Contact:** Diane Reed, Program Director.

**Serves:** Residents of the western suburbs of Cook County.

**Requirements:** Applicants must be at least 18 yrs. old who can provide 40 sq. ft. of private sleeping space for the first foster child and 35 sq. ft. for each subsequent foster child. One foster parent must not be employed outside the home full time.

**Description of children:** Children with both intermediate and serious medical needs and children with developmental delays.

**Licensing procedure:** 1) Inquiry; 2) application; 3) home study and background checks.

**Average length of time for licensing:** Less than 6 mos.

**Inspections:** 1) Fire; 2) medical clearances for all household members; 3) personal references; 4) finger printing. After placement child's case manager visits once or twice weekly.

Maximum number of children allowed in licensed foster care home: 8 with no more than 4 children under the age of 6 yrs. and with no more than 2 children under the age of 2 yrs. Exceptions for sibling groups may be granted.

Interracial placement: Permitted.

Type of foster care and description of procedures: Emergency, long-term and pre-adoptive.

Per diem stipend: Intermediate: $41.10. Serious: $46.58.

Additional funds available: Medicaid; maximum of $500/yr, clothing allowance; child's personal allowance.

★ 985 ★
Sertoma Foster Care
4343 W. 123rd St.
Alsip, IL 60658
Phone: (312) 371-9700
Fax: (708) 371-8170

Contact: Veronica Seiber, Foster Care Coordinator.

Serves: Chicagoland area and south suburbs.

Requirements: Adults, 21 yrs. and older who can provide personal references.

Description of children: Developmentally disabled children and adults.

Licensing procedure:
1) Attend interview with Foster Care Coordinator and Social Worker;
2) complete paperwork;
3) undergo home study and inspections.

Average length of time for licensing: 2-6 mos.

Inspections:
1) Fire;
2) medical examinations for all household members;
3) finger printing of foster parents in some instances.
After approval foster home is visited 6 times annually.

Maximum number of children allowed in licensed foster care home: 7.

Interracial placement: Permitted.

Type of foster care and description of procedures: Emergency and long-term.

Per diem stipend: $23-$25.

Additional funds available: None.

★ 986 ★
Shelter, Inc.
1616 N. Arlington Heights Rd.
Arlington Heights, IL 60004
Phone: (312) 255-8060

Contact: Beth A. Hart, MSW.

Serves: Northwest suburban Chicagoland area.

Requirements: Adults, 21 yrs. and older, who can provide 5 personal references and meet the financial eligibility requirements.

Description of children: Abused, neglected and dependent children from birth to age 11 yrs.

Licensing procedure:
1) Initial inquiry;
2) complete home study and background check.

Average length of time for licensing: Approx. 3 mos.

Inspections:
1) Medical examinations for all household members;
2) finger printing of foster parents.

After placement social worker visits regularly.

Maximum number of children allowed in licensed foster care home: 8.

Interracial placement: Permitted.

Type of foster care and description of procedures: Emergency and regular.

Per diem stipend: Dependant upon age range and type of foster care services provided.

Additional funds available: Medical/dental, clothing allowance and miscellaneous.

★ 987 ★
Jayne Shover Easter Seal Rehabilitative Center, Inc.
799 S. McLean Blvd.
Elgin, IL 60123
Phone: (708) 742-3264
Fax: (708) 742-9436

Contact: Marissa Allen.

Serves: Kane, Lake and McHenry counties.

Requirements: Single or married applicants who can provide personal references and meet the requirements of age, home size and financial eligibility.

Description of children: Children with medical problems, developmental delays and other special needs.

Licensing procedure:
1) Initial inquiry;
2) submit application;
3) complete home study, inspections and clearance;
4) pass background and fingerprint checks;
5) attend ongoing training.

Average length of time for licensing: Approx. 3 mos.

Inspections:
1) Sanitation;
2) medical examinations for all household members;
3) finger printing of foster parents.
After approval social worker visits at least monthly.

Maximum number of children allowed in licensed foster care home: Depends on size of home and developmental age of child; maximum is 8.

Interracial placement: Permitted.

Type of foster care and description of procedures: Emergency and long-term.

Per diem stipend: $21.84-$24.02.

Additional funds available: Medical card.

★ 988 ★
Uhlich Children's Home
2107 W. Irving Park Rd.
Chicago, IL 60618
Phone: (312) 267-9100

Branch address:
3737 N. Mozart, Chicago, IL 60618

Contact: Maribeth Robert, Director of Foster Care.

Serves: Residents of Cook County.

Requirements: Applicants must be at least 21 yrs. old.

Description of children: Varies.

Licensing procedure: 1) Meet licensing requirements; 2) complete assessment; 3) child match.

Average length of time for licensing: Up to 12 mos.

**Inspections:** 1) Fire; 2) sanitation; 3) finger printing; medical examinations for all household members; 4) personal references. After placement agency worker visits bi-monthly.

**Maximum number of children allowed in licensed foster care home:** Dependent upon living space, abilities and scheduling of foster parents.

**Interracial placement:** Permitted.

**Type of foster care and description of procedures:** Emergency, long-term, pre-adoptive, therapeutic and medically complex.

**Per diem stipend:** $700 - $1000 per month.

**Additional funds available:** Clothing resources from the agency and some additional funds as required.

★ 989 ★
**Victor C. Neumann Association**
2354 N. Milwaukee Ave.
Chicago, IL 60647
Phone: (312) 278-1124

**Contact:** Mary R. Mucci, Director of Children's Services.

**Serves:** Residents of Greater Chicago.

**Requirements:** Applicants who are 21 yrs. old, either single or married, who have sufficient living space and income to provide for themselves and any foster children. One parent must be able to provide full-time childcare.

**Description of children:** Children who are described as abuse reactive and/or sexually aggressive.

**Licensing procedure:** The Victor C. Neumann Association follows procedures set forth by the Illinois Department of Children's and Family Services.

**Average length of time for licensing:** 6 mos.

**Inspections:** 1) Fire; 2) sanitation; 3) finger printing; 4) medical clearances for all household members; 5) personal references. After placement, social worker visits weekly.

**Maximum number of children allowed in licensed foster care home:** 1.

**Interracial placement:** Permitted.

**Type of foster care and description of procedures:** Long-term and therapeutic.

**Per diem stipend:** Foster parents are considered professionals employed by the agency.

# INDIANA

★ 990 ★
**Delaware County Office of Family and Children Services**
333 S. Madison St.
P.O. Box 1528
Muncie, IN 47308
Phone: (317) 741-0219

**Contact:** Adoptions/Foster Care Unit.

**Serves:** Delaware County.

**Requirements:** Adults who have sufficient income for their own family's needs and adequate room for a foster child(ren) and who can provide personal references.

**Description of children:** Varies.

**Licensing procedure:**
1) File application, physicals and criminal history affadavit;
2) complete home study;
3) attend foster parent training.

**Average length of time for licensing:** 60-90 days.

**Inspections:**
1) Sanitary;
2) fire (on a case by case basis);
3) medical examinations for foster parents.

**Maximum number of children allowed in licensed foster care home:** Up to 8.

**Interracial placement:** Permitted.

**Type of foster care and description of procedures:** Emergency, long-term, therapeutic and pre-adoptive.

**Per diem stipend:** $14-$18/day.

**Additional funds available:** Initial clothing allowance and medical and dental.

★ 991 ★
**Gateway Woods - Apostolic Christian Children's Home**
14505 Klopfenstein Rd.
Leo, IN 46765
Phone: (219) 627-2159

**Mailing address:**
P.O. Box 151, Leo, IN 46765

**Contact:** Tim Sauder.

**Serves:** Residents of Northeast Indiana.

**Requirements:** Christian applicants, who are at least 21 yrs. old, who either single or married, and who have adequate income and living space to provide for a foster child.

**Description of children:** Children who have been abused and/or neglected or who are delinquent.

**Licensing procedure:** Unavailable.

**Average length of time for licensing:** 6 mos.

**Inspections:** 1) Sanitation; 2) personal references; 3) medical examinations for all household members; 4) fire inspection, if number of children exceeds 5.

**Maximum number of children allowed in licensed foster care home:** 8.

**Interracial placement:** Permitted.

**Type of foster care and description of procedures:** Long-term and specialized.

**Per diem stipend:** $27.

**Additional funds available:** Medical and dental fees are paid either by the county or the biological parents.

★ 992 ★
**Indiana Youth Advocate Program, Inc.**
2511 E. 46th St., Ste. A-1
Indianapolis, IN 46205
Phone: (317) 549-1761
(800) 471-4795
Fax: (317) 546-4396

**Contact:** Dorothy Wodraska.

**Serves:** State of Indiana.

**Requirements:** Adults who are at least 22 yrs. old and in good health with a sincere interest in caring for troubled and needy youths in a stable family structure and supervised living situation.

**Description of children:** Neglected and abused children, ages 0-18 yrs.

**Licensing procedure:**
1) Make telephone inquiry;
2) receive mailed information packet;
3) attend orientation and/or personal visit;

4) file application;
5) complete criminal, civil records and reference check;
6) home study;
7) pre-service training;
8) complete first aid training;
9) licensure.

**Average length of time for licensing:** 2-3 mos.

**Inspections:**
1) Medical examinations of all members of household;
2) water/well inspection in rural area; and
3) occasionally fire inspection.

**Maximum number of children allowed in licensed foster care home:** 6.

**Interracial placement:** Permitted, but based on circumstances.

**Type of foster care and description of procedures:** Regular and therapeutic foster care, emergency and respite care, transitional independent living, and in-home advocacy service.

**Per diem stipend:** $14.00 plus additional $20-$25/day difficulty-of-care payment for special needs youth.

**Additional funds available:** Medical/dental through referring agencies; clothing allowance up to $300 per year and school expenses, if they exceed $25/yr.

★ 993 ★
**Open Arms Christian Home**
Highway 54
Switz City, IN 47465
Phone: (800) 659-2914
(812) 659-2533

**Mailing address:**
   P.O. Box 271, Switz City, IN 47465

**Contact:** Vern Reid, Executive Director.

**Serves:** Residents of the State of Indiana.

**Requirements:** Applicants must be Protestant, at least 21 yrs. old, single, married, widowed or divorced, financial solvent and have sufficient living space to meet state regulations.

**Description of children:** Children who have been abandoned and/or abused and/or neglected, or who are delinquent, or adolescent girls who are pregnant.

**Licensing procedure:** In addition to meeting the State requirements, applicants must manifest a solid Christian faith, witness to the community and complete 12 hours of training per year.

**Average length of time for licensing:** 6 mos.

**Inspections:** 1) Medical examinations for all household members; 2) at least 3 personal references; 3) home safety which may include fire and sanitation, depending upon the number of children in the home. After placement, social worker visits twice monthly and each foster child's case is reviewed quarterly.

**Maximum number of children allowed in licensed foster care home:** 8.

**Interracial placement:** Permitted.

**Type of foster care and description of procedures:** Long-term, pre-adoptive, therapeutic and independent living.

**Per diem stipend:** $25.

**Additional funds available:** Medicaid and/or county and biological parent's insurance for medical and dental fees; training stipend.

★ 994 ★
**St. Joseph County Office of Family and Social Service Administration**
**Division of Family and Children**
P.O. Box 4638
South Bend, IN 46634-4638
Phone: (219) 236-5320
(219) 236-5338
Fax: (219) 236-5400

**Contact:** Gwen Phillips, Caseworker - licensing for foster care.

**Description:** Public.

**Serves:** St. Joseph County.

**Requirements:** Applicants must provide personal references and show financial eligibility.

**Description of children:** Children surrendered for adoption; physically/sexually and/or emotionally abused children.

**Licensing procedure:**
1) Submit application with references;
2) complete 20 hrs. of foster parent training;
3) complete home study;
4) sign criminal history affadavits.
Therapeutic foster care requires different licensing procedures.

**Average length of time for licensing:** 2-6 mos.

**Inspections:**
1) Medical examination of all members of household;
2) water testing, if home is outside city limits;
3) fire inspection (if necessary).
After placement, social worker visits foster home at least bi-monthly.

**Maximum number of children allowed in licensed foster care home:** 8.

**Interracial placement:** Permitted when in the child's best interests.

**Type of foster care and description of procedures:** Emergency, long-term, pre-adoptive and therapeutic.

**Per diem stipend:**
Ages 0-4: $7.90;
ages 5-11: $9.10;
ages 12 or older: $10.95.

**Additional funds available:** Medical/dental.

★ 995 ★
**The Villages of Indiana, Inc.**
2405 N. Smith Pike
Bloomington, IN 47401
Phone: (812) 332-1245
(800) 486-1474
Fax: (317) 486-1520

**Contact:** Roberta Henry-Baker.

**Serves:** State of Indiana.

**Requirements:** Applicants must provide personal references and conform to the state's regulations regarding income eligibility and home size.

**Description of children:** School age children and adolescents with special needs, some who are emotionally/behaviorally disturbed.

**Licensing procedure:**
1) Complete 20 hrs. of pre-service training;
2) criminal affadavit and medical clearances;
3) undergo home study.

**Average length of time for licensing:** Varies.

**Inspections:** Medical examinations are required for all household members.
After placement social worker visits weekly to bi-monthly.

**Maximum number of children allowed in licensed foster care home:** 1 foster child or sibling group.

**Interracial placement:** Permitted.

**Type of foster care and description of procedures:** Long-term, therapeutic and pre-adoptive.

**Per diem stipend:** $26.75.

**Additional funds available:** Medical/dental, Medicaid; state adoption subsidy.

★ 996 ★
**Wabash County Office, Division of Family and Children**
89 W. Canal St.
Wabash, IN 46992
Phone: (219) 563-8471
Fax: (219) 563-0578

**Contact:** Connie Herman.

**Serves:** Wabash County.

**Requirements:** Applicants must provide personal references. MMPI required.

**Description of children:** Children with special needs up to age 18.

**Licensing procedure:**
1) Submit application;
2) answer questionnaire;
3) have criminal affadavit notarized;
4) complete home study and forward and have references forward required forms;
5) study and supporting documentation submitted to state for approval;
6) sign foster parent agreement;
7) placement.

**Average length of time for licensing:** Varies with response time of references, averages 2-3 mos.

**Inspections:**
1) Medical examination for all adult household members;
2) fire inspection may be required depending on number and ages of children placed.
After placement, social worker visits home regularly.

**Maximum number of children allowed in licensed foster care home:** 4 children under the age of 6 yrs. and 8 children under the age of 18 yrs., not to exceed 10 children.

**Interracial placement:** Permitted.

**Type of foster care and description of procedures:** Emergency, long-term and pre-adoptive.

**Per diem stipend:** Varies with age of child.

**Additional funds available:** Medical/dental and clothing allowance; adoption assistance for special needs children; non-recurring adoption expenses to cover attorney and court costs for adoption.

★ 997 ★
**White's Family Services**
c/o Doug Helvey
5233 S. 50 E.
Wabash, IN 46992
Phone: (219) 563-1158
Fax: (219) 563-8975

**Branch address:**
c/o Doug Selfe, 451 W. Lincolnway, Valparaiso, IN 46383

Phone: (219) 464-8020

c/o Susan Porter, 11729 Rockville Rd., Indianapolis, IN 46234
Phone: (317) 272-7221

**Contact:** David Spencer, Family Services Director.

**Serves:** Residents of Indiana and southern Michigan.

**Requirements:** Applicants must be between the ages of 21 and 65 yrs., married or single, and have sufficient income and living space to meet the licensing regulations.

**Description of children:** Children between the ages of birth and 18 yrs., who are neglected and/or abused and/or pre-delinquent and/or emotionally impaired. Some children are deaf or have medical needs. Some pregnant teens and adolescent mothers with infants and some youth in need of developing independent living skills.

**Licensing procedure:** 1) Agency orientation; 2) 20 hrs. pre-service training; 3) licensure.

**Average length of time for licensing:** 6 mos.

**Inspections:** 1) Medical examinations for all household members; and 2) personal references. After placement caseworker will visit a minimum of twice a month.

**Maximum number of children allowed in licensed foster care home:** 8.

**Interracial placement:** Permitted.

**Type of foster care and description of procedures:** Emergency, long-term, pre-adoptive, therapeutic and specialized.

**Per diem stipend:** $42 Specialized foster care. Includes replacement clothing, school fees and supplies, in home counseling, tutoring and supervised visitation, as needed. Training for all 16 yr. olds and up.

# IOWA

★ 998 ★
**Child Connect**
P.O. Box 8-C
Council Bluffs, IA 51502
Phone: (712) 325-1416
Fax: (712) 325-8488

**Contact:** Michael D. Barker, MS.

**Serves:** States of Iowa and Nebraska.

**Requirements:** Adults, 18 yrs. and older, who meet the requirements for home size and financial eligibility, and who can provide personal references. Employment outside the home on a full-time basis for both foster parents is possible but unusual.

**Description of children:** Behaviorally disordered, abused, or sibling groups, ages birth to 18.

**Licensing procedure:**
1) Submit application;
2) complete licensing process;
3) participate in pre-service training.

**Average length of time for licensing:** Approx. 30-90 days.

**Inspections:**
1) Fire;
2) sanitation;
3) Dept. of Social Services. After placement, social worker visits weekly.

**Maximum number of children allowed in licensed foster care home:** 2, but may exceed under certain circumstances.

**Interracial placement:** Permitted.

**Type of foster care and description of procedures:** Emergency, long-term, pre-adoptive but primarily therapeutic.

**Per diem stipend:** $750/mo. in Nebraska; $450 or more/mo. basic maintenance rate in Iowa.

**Additional funds available:** Medical/dental through Medicaid; $150-$250/yr. clothing allowance.

★ 999 ★
**Families of Northeast Iowa**
108 W. Maple
P.O. Box 806
Maquoketa, IA 52060
Phone: (319) 652-4958
Fax: (319) 652-2418

**Contact:** Richard E. Russman.

**Serves:** Clinton, Delaware, Dubuque and Jackson counties.

**Requirements:** Applicants must provide personal references.

**Description of children:** Children with behavior problems or children from low functioning homes.

**Licensing procedure:** Submit a complete application and complete a home study.

**Average length of time for licensing:** 60-90 days.

**Inspections:** Medical examination for all members of the household.
After placement social worker visits monthly.

**Maximum number of children allowed in licensed foster care home:** 5.

**Interracial placement:** Permitted.

**Type of foster care and description of procedures:** Emergency, long-term, pre-adoptive and therapeutic.

**Per diem stipend:** Rates established and paid by the State of Iowa.

**Additional funds available:** Medical/dental and clothing allowance.

★ 1000 ★
**Family Resources, Inc.**
115 W. 6th
Davenport, IA 52803
Phone: (319) 323-1852
Fax: (319) 359-5106

**Branch address:**
852 Middle Rd., Ste. 300, Bettendorf, IA 52722
Phone: (319) 359-8216

111 - 19th Ave., Moline, IL 61265
Phone: (309) 797-1788

**Contact:** Beth De Meyer, Foster Parent Licensing Worker or Phyllis Woodward, Adoption Specialist.

**Serves:** Scott, Muscatine, Cedar, Clinton, and Jackson counties in Iowa; Rock Island, Henry, and Mercer counties in Illinois.

**Requirements:** Adults, 18 yrs. and older who are able to meet the financial needs of their family and provide personal references.

**Description of children:** Primarily court ordered foster children by reason of neglect, physical and/or sexual abuse.

**Licensing procedure:**
1) Complete 12 hr. of preservice training (NOVA);
2) complete home study;
3) home inspected by licenser;

4) reference checks and criminal records/child abuse registry clearances;
5) physical examination.

**Average length of time for licensing:** 3 mos.

**Inspections:** Medical examinations for all household members. After placement social worker contacts home weekly.

**Maximum number of children allowed in licensed foster care home:** 5.

**Interracial placement:** Permitted.

**Type of foster care and description of procedures:** Pre-adoptive.

**Per diem stipend:** Ages:
0-5yrs.: $168/mo.;
6-11 yrs.: $213/mo.;
12-15 yrs.: $259/mo.;
16-20 yrs.: $270/mo. Amounts may vary.

**Additional funds available:** Medical/dental and $250 initial clothing allowance.

★ 1001 ★
**Forest Ridge Youth Services**
P.O. Box 515
Estherville, IA 51334
Phone: (712) 362-7026

**Contact:** Mary Hart, Director of Non-Residential Services.

**Serves:** Resident of Iowa.

**Requirements:** Applicants must be over 18 yrs. and have sufficient living space to meet state regulations.

**Description of children:** Children of all ages, some with special needs.

**Licensing procedure:** 1) Telephone or mail inquiry; 2) complete application forms; 3) undergo 12 hr. pre-service training; 4) home assessment and reference checks; 5) personal interviews.

**Average length of time for licensing:** 6 mos.

**Inspections:** 1) Medical examination of all household members; 2) personal references.

**Maximum number of children allowed in licensed foster care home:** 5.

**Interracial placement:** Permitted.

**Type of foster care and description of procedures:** Therapeutic and long-term.

**Per diem stipend:** State rate plus stipend for treatment level care.

**Additional funds available:** Title 19 for medical/dental. $250 first year clothing allowance and $100 annually thereafter. Some transportation and other, as required.

★ 1002 ★
**Quakerdale Home**
Box 8
New Providence, IA 50206
Phone: (515) 497-5294
Fax: (515) 497-5220

**Branch address:**
140 S. Barclay, Waterloo, IA 50703
Phone: (319) 233-2254

1909 Summit, Marshalltown, IA 50158
Phone: (515) 752-3912

**Contact:** Catherine Hurd (New Providence); Bill Borker (Waterloo); Jim Wieres (Marshalltown).

**Serves:** State of Iowa.

**Requirements:** Applicants must provide a bedroom per foster child and have favorable personal references.

**Description of children:** Primarily children between the ages of 11 through 18 yrs. who have completed residential treatment program and are unable to return to biological parents. Also, children 5 through 18 yrs. who need treatment services in a foster family setting.

**Licensing procedure:** 1)Contact foster care worker;
2) file application;
3) physical examination;
4) complete 12 hrs. of training.

**Average length of time for licensing:** 1-5 mos.

**Inspections:**
1) Sanitation;
2) medical clearance for foster parents.

**Maximum number of children allowed in licensed foster care home:** 5.

**Interracial placement:** Permitted.

**Type of foster care and description of procedures:** Long-term, therapeutic and preadoptive.

**Per diem stipend:** Ages 12-15 yrs.: $509-$809/mo.; ages 16-20 yrs.: $532-$832/mo.

**Additional funds available:** Medical/dental.

★ 1003 ★
**Tanager Place**
2309 C St. SW
Cedar Rapids, IA 52404
Phone: (319) 365-9164
Fax: (319) 365-6411

**Branch address:**
611 Church St., Ottumwa, IA 52501
Phone: (515) 684-5381

**Contact:** Judy Price or Ann Coe in Cedar Rapids; Vicki Donath in Ottumwa.

**Serves:** Residents of eastern and southeastern Iowa.

**Requirements:** Applicants must be at least 25 yrs. old, be sound financially and be able to provide 40 sq. ft. of bedroom space per child.

**Description of children:** Children in the custody of the Department of Human Services or who are referred by Juvenile Court officers.

**Licensing procedure:** 1) Complete 12 hrs. of pre-service training (therapeutic foster parent training requires 24 hrs. of pre-service training); 2) undergo home study with 3-4 concomitant in-home visits.

**Average length of time for licensing:** 6 mos.

**Inspections:** 1) Medical examinations for all household members; 2) personal references. After foster home is approved, social worker visits a minimum of semi-annually before placement; 3) sanitation; 4) fire check.

**Maximum number of children allowed in licensed foster care home:** 5.

**Interracial placement:** Permitted.

**Type of foster care and description of procedures:** Emergency, long-term, pre-adoptive and therapeutic.

**Per diem stipend:** $391- $423 per mo.

**Additional funds available:** Medicaid, transportation, clothing allowance and school fees.

★ 1004 ★
**Young House Family Services**
724 N. 3rd
Burlington, IA 52601
Phone: (319) 752-4000

**Mailing address:**
P.O. Box 845, Burlington, IA 52601

**Contact:** Jan Shelman, Foster Family Program.

**Serves:** Residents of southeast Iowa.

**Requirements:** Applicants must be at least 18 yrs. old, have sufficient income to meet their own needs and have at least 40 sq. ft of separate bedroom space for a foster child.

**Description of children:** Children between the ages of birth and 18 yrs., some of whom are in sibling groups and some of whom have special needs.

**Licensing procedure:** 1) 12 hrs. of pre-service training (additional hours of training are required for therapeutic placements); 2) home study and licensing procedure; 3) 2 hrs. of mandatory Child Abuse Reporting.

**Average length of time for licensing:** 6 mos.

**Inspections:** 1) Mandatory Child Abuse Reporting; 2) medical examinations for all household members; 3) personal references. After licensing, social worker visits on a bi-monthly or as needed basis.

**Maximum number of children allowed in licensed foster care home:** 5.

**Interracial placement:** Permitted.

**Type of foster care and description of procedures:** Emergency, long-term, therapeutic and pre-adoptive.

**Per diem stipend:** $308-$382 per mo.

**Additional funds available:** Title 19 for medical/dental; $250 clothing allowance; transportation fees up to $27.50/mo. and school fees: $50/yr.

# KANSAS

★ 1005 ★
**Associated Youth Services**
3111 Strong Ave.
P.O. Box 6145
Kansas City, KS 66106
Phone: (913) 831-2820
Fax: (913) 831-0262

**Contact:** Carolyn Pavelka.

**Serves:** State of Kansas.

**Requirements:** Foster parent applicants must provide personal references, have financial resources above the poverty guidelines, and be at least 5 yrs. older than foster child.

**Description of children:** Adolescent and juvenile offenders. Youths exiting state institutions.

**Licensing procedure:**
1) Contact agency;
2) complete licensing requirements;
3) attend orientation;
4) participate in on-going training.

**Average length of time for licensing:** 6-8 wks.

**Inspections:** Medical examinations for all household members. After placement, social worker contacts foster home weekly and visits at least monthly.

**Maximum number of children allowed in licensed foster care home:** Maximum of 2 foster placements.

**Interracial placement:** Permitted.

**Type of foster care and description of procedures:** Emergency, diversion, therapeutic, short- or long-term.

**Per diem stipend:** $25.96; $35 for therapeutic.

**Additional funds available:** Medicaid, clothing allowance and miscellaneous, e.g. education/job training, incentives.

---

### ★ 1006 ★
**Johnson County Mental Retardation Center**
10501 Lackman Rd.
Lenexa, KS 66219
Phone: (913) 492-6161

**Contact:** Family Support Coordinator or Children's Service Coordinator.

**Serves:** Johnson County, Kansas.

**Requirements:** Adults age 18 yrs. and older who can provide personal references and have sufficient income to provide for their own needs.

**Description of children:** Developmentally disabled (mentally and/or physically) children.

**Licensing procedure:**
1) File application and provide personal references;
2) attend personal interview;
3) licensing of home including inspections;
4) complete training.

**Average length of time for licensing:** Approx. 2 mos.

**Inspections:**
1) Fire;
2) sanitation;
3) medical examinations for all household members;
4) background criminal records check.

**Maximum number of children allowed in licensed foster care home:** 2 full-time foster children.

**Interracial placement:** Permitted but not preferred.

**Type of foster care and description of procedures:** Emergency, pre-adoptive, and respite care; also supported family living.

**Per diem stipend:** Varies according to level of care required; ranges from $30 to $57 day.

---

### ★ 1007 ★
**Wichita Child Guidance Center**
**Caring Connection**
415 N. Poplar
Wichita, KS 67214-4595
Phone: (316) 686-6671
Fax: (316) 686-1094

**Contact:** Loren Pack, ACSW.

**Description:** The Caring Connection is based on the belief that many emotionally disturbed youth can be served most effectively in a family home setting. Specially trained therapeutic foster parents work with the youth to implement a treatment plan which is monitored by a multi-disciplinary team of mental health professionals. Both the biological and the foster parents are expected to be actively involved in the team approach.

**Serves:** State of Kansas.

**Requirements:** Adults, 22 yrs. and older, who are financially self-sufficient and who can provide personal references.

**Description of children:** Children from 11 to 17 yrs. who have emotional difficulties.

**Licensing procedure:**
1) Attend orientation meeting;

2) complete and return application, Foster Family Information form, Provider Security Clearance form, foster family background information, Foster Family Home Self-Assessment, autobiography and medical history;
3) Dept. of Social and Rehabilitative Services does home environment check;
4) applicants undergo psychological testing;
5) in-home interview;
6) other evaluations completed, if necessary;
7) complete pre-service foster care training;
8) licensure.

**Average length of time for licensing:** 1-3 mos.

**Inspections:** Medical examination for all household members. After placement social worker visits 20-24 times a year.

**Maximum number of children allowed in licensed foster care home:** 1 foster child for the first year and 2 thereafter.

**Interracial placement:** Permitted.

**Type of foster care and description of procedures:** Long-term and therapeutic.

**Per diem stipend:** $31.

**Additional funds available:** Medical/dental and some miscellaneous.

---

# KENTUCKY

### ★ 1008 ★
**Bluegrass Residential and Support Services (B.R.A.S.S.)**
671 W. Hwy 80, Ste. 1
Somerset, KY 42501
Phone: (606) 678-4660

**Contact:** Joan Owens, Karen Gardner or Edie Egbert.

**Serves:** Residents of Pulaski County, KY.

**Requirements:** Applicants must be at least 21 yrs. and have a room for a foster child.

**Description of children:** Children between the ages of birth and 18 yrs. who have developmental disabilities.

**Licensing procedure:** Unavailable.

**Average length of time for licensing:** 6 mos.

**Inspections:** 1) Fire; 2) sanitation; 3) medical examinations for all adult household members; 4) fingerprinting; 5) personal references. After placement, social worker visits 2 to 3 times a month.

**Maximum number of children allowed in licensed foster care home:** 3.

**Interracial placement:** Permitted.

**Type of foster care and description of procedures:** Long-term and therapeutic.

**Per diem stipend:** $26.

**Additional funds available:** All medical and dental.

---

### ★ 1009 ★
**Mary Kendall Home**
**Methodist Home of Kentucky, Inc.**
193 Phillips Ct.
Owensboro, KY 42301
Phone: (502) 683-8545

**Contact:** Leslie Armstrong.

**Serves:** State of Kentucky.

**Requirements:** Applicants must provide personal references.

**Description of children:** Children who have been in residential child care.

**Licensing procedure:**
1) File application;
2) complete paperwork;
3) personal interviews;
4) complete home study;
5) licensing approval through the State of Kentucky.

**Average length of time for licensing:** 3 or more months.

**Inspections:**
1) Medical clearances for all household members;
2) finger printing of foster and adoptive parent(s).

**Maximum number of children allowed in licensed foster care home:** Varies with placement.

**Interracial placement:** Permitted.

**Type of foster care and description of procedures:** Emergency, long-term and pre-adoptive.

**Per diem stipend:** $9.

**Additional funds available:** Medical/dental and miscellaneous e.g. school fees, graduation expenses, etc.

### ★ 1010 ★

**Seven Counties Services, Inc.**
**Daybreak Family Treatment Homes**
1204 S. 3rd St., Ste. A
Louisville, KY 40203
Phone: (502) 589-8787

**Contact:** Jeannie Mahood.

**Serves:** Residents of Kentucky.

**Requirements:** Applicants must be at least 21 yrs. old who have income apart from foster care payments, who have adequate living and play space for a foster child and who are willing to support a foster child in their own religion.

**Description of children:** Children between the ages of 4 and 17 yrs. who are severely emotionally disturbed.

**Licensing procedure:** 1) 30 hrs. of training; 2) home study, inspections and background checks.

**Average length of time for licensing:** 6 mos.

**Inspections:** 1) Fire; 2) sanitation; 3) medical examinations for all household members; 4)finger printing; 5) personal references.

**Maximum number of children allowed in licensed foster care home:** 1 except in the case of sibling groups.

**Interracial placement:** Permitted.

**Type of foster care and description of procedures:** Therapeutic.

**Per diem stipend:** $35.

**Additional funds available:** Medical, dental and therapy as well as birthday and other individual determined needs.

### ★ 1011 ★

**Therapeutic Community Services**
**Presbyterian Foster Care Program**
One Buckhorn Ln.
Buckhorn, KY 41721
Phone: (606) 398-7245
Fax: (606) 398-7912

**Contact:** Katherine Word.

**Serves:** Children of the State of Kentucky.

**Requirements:** Adults 21 yrs. and older who can provide personal references, have sufficient time and home space and who can provide for their own financial needs. Applicants are screened with the Kentucky State Police and the State Child Abuse Registry.

**Description of children:** Majority meet criteria for emotionally disturbed children.

**Licensing procedure:**
1) Complete foster home study;
2) 24 hours of pre-certification training;
3) home studies are reviewed in a certification meeting for approval;
4) the Executive Vice-President of the agency has final approval.

**Average length of time for licensing:** 2 mos.

**Inspections:**
1) Physical examination of each household member;
2) criminal records check of applicants and all other adults living in the home;
3) preliminary safety inspection.
Once certified the home is visited weekly by a case manager and quarterly for a safety inspection.

**Maximum number of children allowed in licensed foster care home:** Depends upon the needs of the child and the availability of the foster parents. One child generally, if two children are placed in a home, the family is supported by a foster family worker.

**Interracial placement:** Permitted.

**Type of foster care and description of procedures:** The treatment program is family-based. Each child has an Individual Treatment Plan, with quarterly reviews for evaluation of progress toward completion of goals. The intent is long-term care.

**Per diem stipend:** $25 minimum.

**Additional funds available:** Medical/dental, clothing allowance and miscellaneous.

# LOUISIANA

### ★ 1012 ★

**Department of Social Services**
**Baton Rouge Region**
P.O. Box 66789
Baton Rouge, LA 70896
Phone: (504) 342-0494
Fax: (504) 342-0418

**Branch address:**
St. Tammany Office of Community Services, P.O. Box 1778, Covington, LA 70434
Phone: (504) 893-6225

**Contact:** Kay Hessick.

**Serves:** 12 parishes surrounding Baton Rouge.

**Requirements:** Adults, between the ages of 21 and 65 yrs., who can meet their own financial needs, provide adequate living space for a foster child and supply 3 personal references. Must attend 30 hours of agency provided training.

**Description of children:** Pre-schoolers through adolescents, some with behavior problems, developmental delays and learning disabilities.

**Licensing procedure:**
1) Telephone intake and screening;
2) attend orientation meeting;

3) submit application;
4) complete 30 hrs. of pre-service training;
5) undergo home study;.
**Average length of time for licensing:** 3-5 mos.
**Inspections:**
1) Fire;
2) sanitation;
3) medical examinations for all household members;
4) criminal clearance.
**Maximum number of children allowed in licensed foster care home:** 4.
**Interracial placement:** If necessary.
**Type of foster care and description of procedures:** Emergency, short and long-term and pre-adoptive.
**Per diem stipend:** Varies with age of child.
**Additional funds available:** Medical/dental; initial clothing allowance; recreation; and other, based on the individual needs of the child.

**★ 1013 ★**
**Gulf Coast Teaching Family Services**
515 South College, Ste. 100
Lafayette, LA 70501
Phone: (318) 269-1165
**Branch address:**
401 Whitney Ave. Ste 300, Gretna, LA 70053

3501 Holiday Dr., Ste. 204, New Orleans, LA 70114

154 N. Hollywood Rd., Houma, LA 70364

1012 Audry, New Iberia, LA 70560

11021 Perkins Rd., Baton Rouge, LA 70810
**Contact:** Rick Dawes, Program Director or Jada B. Alvorado, Consultant.
**Serves:** Residents of the Lafayette Region of the Office of Community Services.
**Requirements:** Applicants between the ages of 21 and 65 yrs. who are either married or single.
**Description of children:** Adolescents between the ages of 12 and 18 yrs. who are either in the custody of the Office of Youth Development because of juvenile delinquency or who are in the custody of the Office of Community Services because of abuse and/or neglect.
**Licensing procedure:** 1) Interview series consisting of 2 in-home and one office visit; 2) complete questionnaires and a facility survey; 3) documentation and finger printing; 4) in-service training.
**Average length of time for licensing:** 6 mos.
**Inspections:** 1) Fire; 2) sanitation; 3) medical examination for all household members; 4) finger printing of all household members; 5) 2 personal references. After placement, social worker visits at least monthly.
**Maximum number of children allowed in licensed foster care home:** Dependent on home size.
**Interracial placement:** Permitted, but not desirable.
**Type of foster care and description of procedures:** Emergency, pre-adoptive and therapeutic.
**Per diem stipend:** $21 to $24.57 depending upon level of care.
**Additional funds available:** Medicaid and clothing reimbursement.

**★ 1014 ★**
**Louisiana Department of Social Services**
**Office of Community Services**
P.O. Box 3318
Baton Rouge, LA 70821
Phone: (504) 342-4086

**Branch address:**
900 Murray St., P.O. Box 832, Alexandria, LA 71301
Phone: (318) 487-5054

P.O. Box 66789, Baton Rouge, LA 70896
Phone: (504) 342-0494

1353 Surrey St., Lafayette, LA 70501
Phone: (318) 265-5970

P.O. Box 16865, Lake Charles, LA 70616
Phone: (318) 491-2189

122 St. John St., State Office Building, Monroe, LA 71201-7384
Phone: (318) 362-3362

P.O. Drawer 57149, New Orleans, LA 70157
Phone: (504) 568-7413

1525 Fairfield Ave., Rm. 801, Shreveport, LA 71130
Phone: (318) 226-7100

1000 E. Plantation Rd., P.O. Box 998, Thibodaux, LA 70302
Phone: (504)447-0945

**Contact:** Regional Office.

**Serves:** Residents of the State of Louisiana.

**Requirements:** Applicants between the ages of 21 and 65 yrs. who have a stable and sufficient income to meet their own needs and who have sufficient space for a foster child.

**Description of children:** Children between the ages of birth and 18 yrs. who are in the custody of the Office of Community Services usually because of abuse and/or neglect.

**Licensing procedure:** 1) Inquiry; 2) orientation; 2) training which can vary depending upon the kinds of children to be placed; 3) home evaluation and background checks; 4) home consultation; 5) certification, if eligible.

**Average length of time for licensing:** 6-12 mos.

**Inspections:** 1) Fire; 2) finger printing; 3) personal references; medical examinations of all household members; 4) sanitation, if septic tank. After placement, child's caseworker visits at least monthly.

**Maximum number of children allowed in licensed foster care home:** 8.

**Interracial placement:** Permitted.

**Type of foster care and description of procedures:** Emergency, long-term, pre-adoptive, therapeutic.

**Per diem stipend:** $9.22 - $12.12 depending upon age.

**Additional funds available:** Medicaid, clothing allowance and some special board rates depending on child's needs.

# MAINE

★ 1015 ★
**Maine Department of Human Services**
**Social Services**
Capital Shopping Center
Augusta, ME 04333
Phone: (207) 624-8222

**Branch address:**
Dept. of Human Services, Rockland, ME 04841
Phone: (207) 596-4200

Dept. of Human Services, Skowhegan, ME 04976
Phone: (207) 474-4800

38 Pleasant St., Ft. Kent, ME 04743
Phone: (207) 834-3934

Corner Rte. 1 and Rte. 89, Caribou, ME 04736
Phone: (207) 498-8151

11 High St., Houlton, ME 04730
Phone: (207) 532-5000

100 Court St., Machias, ME 04654
Phone: (207) 255-8641

509 Forest Ave., Portland, ME 04101
Phone: (207) 774-4581

200 Main St., Lewiston, ME 04240
Phone: (207) 795-4300

208 Graham St., Biddeford, ME 04005
Phone: (207) 282-6191

Griffen Rd., Bangor, ME 04401
Phone: (207) 561-4100

125 Summer St., Dover-Foxcroft, ME 04426
Phone: (207) 564-3444

Short St., Ellsworth, ME 04605
Phone: (207) 667-5361

**Contact:** Community Care Supervisor.

**Serves:** 5 counties of Greater Central Maine.

**Requirements:** Adults, 18 yrs. and older, who have a predictable income, adequate bedroom space for a foster child and who can provide personal references.

**Description of children:** Abused and/or neglected children.

**Licensing procedure:**
1) Submit application;
2) complete home study;
3) inspection and clearances;
4) licensure.
Different types of foster care placement may require different licensing procedures.

**Average length of time for licensing:** 120 days.

**Inspections:**
1) Fire;
2) criminal clearances;
3) coliform and mineral;
4) home health and safety;
5) physical exams.

After approval social worker and licensing worker visit as needed.

**Maximum number of children allowed in licensed foster care home:** 6 children under the age of 16 yrs.

**Interracial placement:** Permitted.

**Type of foster care and description of procedures:** Emergency, long-term, pre-adoptive, and therapeutic.

**Per diem stipend:** Varies with need and age of child placed,.

**Additional funds available:** Medicaid, clothing allowance and contingency funds.

# MASSACHUSETTS

★ 1016 ★
**Massachusetts Department of Social Services**
24 Farnsworth St.
Boston, MA 02210
Phone: (617) 727-0900
Fax: (617) 261-7437

**Branch address:**
1537 Main St., Springfield, MA 01103
Phone: (413) 781-0323

20 Academy St., Arlington, MA 02174
Phone: (617) 727-1281

21 Spring St., Taunton, MA 02780
Phone: (508) 822-7761

810 Memorial Dr., Cambridge, MA 02139
Phone: (617) 868-6940

**Contact:** Catherine G. Harris, Director of Adoption Services.

**Description:** Public agency.

**Serves:** State of Massachusetts.

**Requirements:** Adults, 21 yrs. and older, who can provide personal references.

**Description of children:** Varies widely.

**Licensing procedure:**
1) File application;
2) participate in 10 three hr. sessions of pre-service training (MAPP - Massachusetts Approach to Partnership in Parenting);
3) complete home study.

**Average length of time for licensing:** 3-4 mos.

**Inspections:**
1) Medical examinations for all household members;
2) criminal records check.

**Maximum number of children allowed in licensed foster care home:** 6 foster children.

**Interracial placement:** In exceptional circumstances only.

**Type of foster care and description of procedures:** Emergency, pre-adoptive, specialized and short-term.

**Per diem stipend:**
Up to age 13 yrs.: $13.65;
13 yrs. and up: $16.20.

**Additional funds available:** Medicaid, supplemental services ($7.50/hr. as applicable) and clothing allowance: Ages 0-5 yrs.: $214/yr.; 6-12 yrs.: $362/yr.; 13 or older: $564/yr. adoption subsidy.

## ★ 1017 ★
**United Homes for Children, Inc.**
1147 Main St., Ste. 210
Tewksbury, MA 01876
Phone: (508) 640-0089

**Branch address:**
84 W. Main St., Merrimac, MA 01860

34 1/2 Beacon St., Boston, MA 02108

**Serves:** Residents of the State of Massachusetts.

**Requirements:** Applicants must be at least 25 yrs. old.

**Description of children:** Children between the ages of birth and 18 yrs. who have a variety of emotional, behavioral, psychological and/or medical difficulties.

**Licensing procedure:** 1) Complete MAPP training; 2) home study and inspections.

**Average length of time for licensing:** 6 mos.

**Inspections:** 1) Minimum of 3 personal references; 2) medical examination of all household members; 3) home safety and sanitation. After placement, social worker visits a minimum of once a month.

**Maximum number of children allowed in licensed foster care home:** 8.

**Interracial placement:** Permitted.

**Type of foster care and description of procedures:** Emergency, long-term, therapeutic, pre-adoptive and adoptive (child specific).

**Per diem stipend:** $13.20 - $40.

**Additional funds available:** Medicaid, clothing and birthday and holiday allowances.

# MICHIGAN

## ★ 1018 ★
**Area Youth for Christ - Youth Guidance - Foster Care**
157 Capital Ave. N.E.
Battle Creek, MI 49017
Phone: (616) 468-2751

**Contact:** Joel DeKoekkoek.

**Serves:** Residents of south west and south central Michigan.

**Requirements:** Christian applicants who are at least 18 yrs. old.

**Description of children:** Children between the ages of 8 and 18 yrs.

**Licensing procedure:** Guidelines set by the State of Michigan. Training will vary with the different types of foster placements.

**Average length of time for licensing:** 6 mos.

**Inspections:** 1) Personal references; 2) septic, if not on city water; 3) home safety and sanitation; 4) medical examinations of all household members.

**Maximum number of children allowed in licensed foster care home:** 4 foster children.

**Interracial placement:** Permitted, if foster parents undergo training.

**Type of foster care and description of procedures:** Emergency, long-term, pre-adoptive and independent living.

**Per diem stipend:** $13.85 - $14.50 or more depending on the level of care.

**Additional funds available:** Medicaid, biannual clothing allowance and training and support group fees.

## ★ 1019 ★
**Bay County Department of Social Services**
1230 Washington Ave.
Bay City, MI 48708
Phone: (517) 894-6200

**Contact:** Kim Bejcek, Foster Care Licensing Worker.

**Serves:** Residents of Bay County.

**Requirements:** Applicants must be at least 21 yrs. old, have sufficient fiances to meet their own needs and have adequate space for a foster child.

**Description of children:** Children in the custody of the Department of Social Services who are dependent and/or neglected; delinquent youth.

**Licensing procedure:** 1) Agency contact; 2) home visit; 3) home study; 4) orientation.

**Average length of time for licensing:** 6 mos. or less.

**Inspections:** 1) Medical clearances for all household members; 2) personal references; 3) septic and coliform, if not on city water. After foster home is approved, licensing worker visits annually and child's social worker on a regular basis.

**Maximum number of children allowed in licensed foster care home:** 8.

**Interracial placement:** Permitted.

**Type of foster care and description of procedures:** Emergency, long-term and therapeutic.

**Per diem stipend:** Children between the ages of birth and 12 yrs.: $12. Children between the ages of 13 and 18 yrs. : $14.25.

**Additional funds available:** Medicaid and semi-annual clothing allowance.

## ★ 1020 ★
**Boysville of Michigan**
8744 Clinton-Macon Rd.
Clinton, MI 49236
Phone: (517) 423-7451

**Branch address:**
925 N. River Rd., Saginaw, MI 48609

2740 W. Central, Toledo, OH 43606

19403 W. Chicago, Detroit, MI 48228

**Contact:** Brother Francis Boylan.

**Serves:** Residents of Michigan and Ohio.

**Requirements:** Applicants who are at least 21 yrs. old and who have a 40 sq, ft, room available for a foster child.

**Description of children:** Children with a wide range of behaviors.

**Licensing procedure:** 1) Agency orientation; 2) begin foster parent training; 3) meet state licensing requirements.

**Average length of time for licensing:** 6 mos.

**Inspections:** 1) Personal references; 2) medical examinations for all household members. After licensing, social worker visits weekly.

**Maximum number of children allowed in licensed foster care home:** 4.

**Interracial placement:** Permitted.

**Type of foster care and description of procedures:** Emergency, long-term and therapeutic.

**Per diem stipend:** $28.55.

**Additional funds available:** $240 annual clothing allowance.

### ★ 1021 ★
**Branch County Department of Social Sciences**
809 Marshall Rd.
Coldwater, MI 49036
Phone: (517) 279-4200

**Contact:** Laura Nye.

**Serves:** Residents of Branch and Hillsdale counties.

**Requirements:** Applicant who are between the ages of 18 and 65 yrs. who can support themselves and who have adequate living space.

**Description of children:** Children between the ages of birth and 18 yrs. who have been removed from their homes because of abuse and/or neglect.

**Licensing procedure:** 1) Complete training; 2) undergo home study.

**Average length of time for licensing:** 6 mos.

**Inspections:** 1) Sanitation; 2) medical examinations for all household members; 3) personal references. After approval social worker visits one to 12 times annually.

**Maximum number of children allowed in licensed foster care home:** 8.

**Interracial placement:** Permitted, if necessary.

**Type of foster care and description of procedures:** Emergency and long-term.

**Per diem stipend:** $24 - $14.

**Additional funds available:** Medicaid, semi-annually clothing allowance of $107.

### ★ 1022 ★
**Catholic Human Services of Alpena**
228 S. Third
Alpena, MI 49707
Phone: (517) 356-6385

**Contact:** John Feys.

**Serves:** Residents of 11 counties in northeast Michigan.

**Requirements:** Married couples who are 40 yrs. old or younger whose annual income is $150 above the poverty level and whose home meets licensing standards.

**Description of children:** Infants who will be released for adoption.

**Licensing procedure:** Follows State of Michigan's licensing standards.

**Average length of time for licensing:** 6 mos.

**Inspections:** 1) Medical examinations for all household members; 2) coliform test; 3) personal references.

**Maximum number of children allowed in licensed foster care home:** Depends upon the situation.

**Interracial placement:** Permitted.

**Type of foster care and description of procedures:** Short-term.

**Per diem stipend:** $10.85.

**Additional funds available:** None.

### ★ 1023 ★
**Chippewa County Department of Social Services**
208 Bingham Ave.
Sault Ste. Marie, MI 49783
Phone: (906) 632-3377
Fax: (906) 635-4173

**Mailing address:**
  P.O. Box 809, Sault Ste. Marie, MI 49783

**Contact:** Kathleen Langhals, Director or Christopher Stabile, Youth Services Supervisor.

**Serves:** Chippewa County.

**Requirements:** Applicants must meet the requirements for age, home size and financial eligibility and provide 3 personal references.

**Description of children:** Children from 0-18 yrs. of all races; some with special needs.

**Licensing procedure:**
  1) Initial inquiry;
  2) licensing evaluation of the home and family members;
  3) certification for licensor if requirements are met.

**Average length of time for licensing:** 1-2 mos.

**Inspections:**
  1) Medical examinations for all household members;
  2) sanitation (rural homes).
After placement social worker visits monthly.

**Maximum number of children allowed in licensed foster care home:** 8.

**Interracial placement:** Only if appropriate racial home is unavailable.

**Type of foster care and description of procedures:** Emergency and long-term.

**Per diem stipend:**
Ages: 0-12 yrs.: $12;
13-18 yrs.: $14.25.

**Additional funds available:** Medical/dental, clothing allowance and some travel.

### ★ 1024 ★
**Delta County Department of Social Services**
2940 College Ave.
Escanaba, MI 49829
Phone: (906) 786-5394

**Contact:** Richard F. Miketinac, Supervisor.

**Serves:** Residents of Delta County.

**Requirements:** Applicants must be at least 18 yrs. old, have a stable and secure income and 40 sq. ft. of separate bedroom space for a foster child.

**Description of children:** Unavailable.

**Licensing procedure:** 1) Application; 2) reference, medical clearances and background checks; 3) home study and inspections; 4) foster parent/agency agreement; 5) home inspection.

**Average length of time for licensing:** Less than 6 mos.

**Inspections:** 1) Medical clearances for all household members; 2) 3 personal references; 3) well and septic, if applicable; 4) home health and safety. After licensure, social worker visits yearly if no child is being fostered and monthly is a child is in placement.

**Maximum number of children allowed in licensed foster care home:** 8.

**Interracial placement:** Permitted.

**Type of foster care and description of procedures:** Emergency, long-term, pre-adoptive and therapeutic.

**Per diem stipend:** Children between the ages of 0 - 12 yrs.: $12. Children from 13 to 18 yrs.: $14.25.

**Additional funds available:** Medicaid and clothing allowance up to $500.

★ 1025 ★
**Gladwin County Department of Social Services**
250 N. State
Gladwin, MI 48624
Phone: (517) 426-3300

**Contact:** Mona Russell.

**Serves:** Residents of Gladwin County.

**Requirements:** Applicants must be at least 21 yrs. old, must have sufficient income to cover their own expenses and have 40 sq. ft. of separate sleeping space for a foster child.

**Description of children:** Boys and girls between the ages of birth and 17 yrs. who have been abused and/or neglected, who are delinquent youth or who have special needs including being medically fragile.

**Licensing procedure:** 1) Application; 2) background and criminal checks; 3) inspections and medical examinations; 4) fact sheet; 5) home study visit; 6) AAPI.

**Average length of time for licensing:** 6 mos.

**Inspections:** 1) Septic, if applicable; 2) 3 personal references; 3) medical clearances on all household members.

**Maximum number of children allowed in licensed foster care home:** 8.

**Interracial placement:** Permitted.

**Type of foster care and description of procedures:** Emergency, long-term and pre-adoptive.

**Per diem stipend:** Begins at $12 and is dependent upon child's age and needs.

**Additional funds available:** Medicaid and annual clothing allowance.

★ 1026 ★
**Gogebic County Department of Social Services**
100 W. Cloverland Dr.
Ironwood, MI 49938
Phone: (906) 932-3398

**Mailing address:**
P.O. Box 708, Ironwood, MI 49938

**Serves:** Residents of Gogebic County.

**Requirements:** Applicants must be at least 18 yrs. old, have an outside means of support and have a minimum of 2 bedrooms.

**Description of children:** Children who have been neglected and/or abused or who are delinquent.

**Licensing procedure:** 1) Inquiry phase; 2) application phase; 3) licensing/study phase; 4) licensing report; 5) licensing issuance phase.

**Average length of time for licensing:** 6 mos.

**Inspections:** 1) Personal references; 2) medical clearances for all household members. After licensing, social worker visits annually.

**Maximum number of children allowed in licensed foster care home:** 4.

**Interracial placement:** Permitted.

**Type of foster care and description of procedures:** Emergency and long-term.

**Per diem stipend:** Children between the ages of 0 and 12: $11.05; children from the ages of 13 to 18: $13.85.

**Additional funds available:** Medicaid and $500 initial clothing allowance.

★ 1027 ★
**Gratiot County Department of Social Services**
515 S. Pine River
Ithaca, MI 48847
Phone: (517) 875-5181

**Mailing address:**
P.O. Box 250, Ithaca, MI 48847

**Contact:** Children's Services Unit.

**Serves:** Residents of Gratiot County.

**Requirements:** Applicants must be between the ages of 21 and 65 yrs. old, have sufficient income to meet their own needs and have at least 40 sq. ft. of separate sleeping room for a foster child.

**Description of children:** Children between the ages of birth and 18 yrs. who usually are neglected and/or abused or are delinquent. They may have emotional or behavior problems and some are developmentally delayed.

**Licensing procedure:** 1) Orientation phase; 2) application phase; 3) licensing/study phase.

**Average length of time for licensing:** 2-3 mos.

**Inspections:** 1) Coliform and septic; 2) medical clearances for all household members; 3) personal references. After licensing, worker visits annually and child's caseworker visits monthly.

**Maximum number of children allowed in licensed foster care home:** 8.

**Interracial placement:** Permitted.

**Type of foster care and description of procedures:** Emergency and long-term.

**Per diem stipend:** Children 0-12 yrs. old: $12; children 13-18 yrs. old: $14.25.

**Additional funds available:** Medical/dental, clothing and extraordinary costs.

★ 1028 ★
**Huron Valley Child Guidance Clinic**
2940 Ellsworth Rd.
Ypsilanti, MI 48197
Phone: (313) 971-9605

**Contact:** Yolanda Cranford, MSW, Placement Coordinator.

**Serves:** Residents of Washtenaw County.

**Requirements:** Applicants must be younger than 65 yrs., have a specified income which covers their own family's needs and sufficient space for a foster child.

**Description of children:** Emotionally disturbed children between the ages of 8 and 17 yrs.

**Licensing procedure:** Licensing procedure mandated by the Michigan Department of Social Services.

**Average length of time for licensing:** 4 - 6 wks.

**Inspections:** 1) Medical clearances for all household members; 2) personal references; 3) sanitation, if not on city water and sewer. After placement, child's caseworker visits on a weekly basis.

**Maximum number of children allowed in licensed foster care home:** 2.

**Interracial placement:** Permitted.

**Type of foster care and description of procedures:** Therapeutic.

**Per diem stipend:** $32.

**Additional funds available:** None.

**★ 1029 ★**
**Lake County Department of Social Services**
R No. 3
Baldwin, MI 49304
Phone: (616) 745-8159

**Mailing address:**
P.O. Box 2258A, Baldwin, MI 49304

**Contact:** Service supervisor.

**Serves:** Residents of Lake County.

**Requirements:** Applicants must be 21 yrs. or older, married or single and be self-supporting.

**Description of children:** Children of all ages who are in the custody of the Dept. of Social Services because of abuse and/or neglect or delinquency.

**Licensing procedure:** Contact the Lake Co. Dept. of Social Services for an application and information packet.

**Average length of time for licensing:** 6 mos.

**Inspections:** 1) Sanitation; 2) medical clearances for all household members; 3) personal references. After a child has ben placed, the child's caseworker visits monthly.

**Maximum number of children allowed in licensed foster care home:** 8.

**Interracial placement:** Permitted.

**Type of foster care and description of procedures:** Emergency and long-term.

**Per diem stipend:** Children 0-12 yrs. old: $12; children 13-18 yrs. old: $14.25.

**Additional funds available:** Medicaid.


**★ 1030 ★**
**Lakeside Residence for Boys and Girls**
3921 Oakland Dr.
Kalamazoo, MI 49008
Phone: (616) 381-4760

**Contact:** Suzanne Friesner, Foster Care Coordinator.

**Serves:** Residents who live within a 40 mi. radius of Kalamazoo, MI.

**Requirements:** Applicants must be between the ages of 18 and 65 yrs. old, be married or single, have sufficient income to meet their own needs and have at least 40 sq. ft. of bedroom space for a foster child.

**Description of children:** Boys and girls between the ages of 10 and 17 yrs. old, of various ethnicities, with emotional, social and/or behavioral problems.

**Licensing procedure:** 1) Inquiry phase; 2) licensing/study phase; 3) 20 hrs. of initial foster parent training.

**Average length of time for licensing:** 6 mos. or less.

**Inspections:** 1) home health and safety inspection; 2) medical clearances of all household members; 3) personal references; 4) police and child abuse/neglect record check. After licensing, if no child is in placement social worker visits annually. If a child is in placement, social worker visits 1-5 times a month.

**Maximum number of children allowed in licensed foster care home:** Law 400-191 allows no more than 4 unrelated children in a licensed foster home. Total number of all children under 17 yrs. must not exceed 8 including foster children.

**Interracial placement:** Permitted.

**Type of foster care and description of procedures:** Long-term, therapeutic and Visiting Foster Family (weekends and holidays).

**Per diem stipend:** Children 0-12 yrs.: $21.05; children 13-18 yrs.: $23.30. Visiting Foster Family: children 0-12 yrs. : $12; children 13 -18 yrs.: $14.25.

**Additional funds available:** Medical/dental; residential treatment; clothing: $244/yr.; birthday: $10; Christmas: $50.


**★ 1031 ★**
**Listening Ear Crisis Center, Inc.**
107 East Illinois
Mt. Pleasant, MI 48804
Phone: (517) 772-2918

**Mailing address:**
P.O. Box 65, Mt. Pleasant, MI 48804

**Contact:** Carol Friske, Foster Care Coordinator.

**Serves:** Residents of Clare, Isabella and Montcalm counties.

**Requirements:** Applicants must be at least 25 yrs. old, have a stable income and be able to provide a 40 sq. ft. bedroom for a foster child.

**Description of children:** Runaway youth and delinquent adolescents ages 9 to 17 yrs; emotionally impaired ages 5 -17 yrs.; developmentally disabled children with medical disabilities and developmentally disabled children with behavioral challenges.

**Licensing procedure:** 1) Inquiry; 2) orientation; 3) home visit and inspection; 4) 6 hrs. pre-service training.

**Average length of time for licensing:** 6 mos. or less.

**Inspections:** 1) Fire; 2) medical clearances for all household members; 3) personal references; 4) coliform and septic, if not on city water. After foster home is approved, social worker visits monthly.

**Maximum number of children allowed in licensed foster care home:** 8 children under the age of 17 yrs.

**Interracial placement:** Permitted, if placement is in the child's and family's best interests.

**Type of foster care and description of procedures:** Emergency, long-term and therapeutic.

**Per diem stipend:** Range of $13.50 - 80.

**Additional funds available:** Medicaid and clothing allowance.


**★ 1032 ★**
**Lutheran Child and Family Service**
6019 West Side Saginaw Rd.
Bay City, MI 48707
Phone: (517) 686-7650
Fax: (517) 686-7688

**Branch address:**
20830 Rutland Dr., Southfield, MI 48075
Phone: (810) 552-1050

10811 Puritan Ave., Detroit, MI 48238
Phone: (313) 341-1121

**Contact:** Mary Lou Stewart.

**Serves:** State of Michigan.

**Requirements:** Adults between the ages of 21 and 65 who can provide 40 sq. ft. sleeping room for a foster child, who are financially capable of providing for the needs of their own family and who can provide personal references.

**Description of children:** Emotionally disturbed, mentally impaired and learning disabled children; victims of abuse, neglect and sexual abuse; and youth perpetrators.

**Licensing procedure:**
1) Initial inquiry;

2) attend orientation and a 24 hr. pre-training course;
3) home visit to meet family and check home for safety.

**Average length of time for licensing:** 3-4 mos.

**Inspections:**
1) Safety;
2) sanitation for homes with private wells and septic systems;
3) physical examinations for all household members.
After placement, social worker visits monthly for traditional foster home placements and weekly for Intensive Care foster placements.

**Maximum number of children allowed in licensed foster care home:** 8.

**Interracial placement:** Permitted.

**Type of foster care and description of procedures:** Long-term, emergency, pre-adoptive and therapeutic.

**Per diem stipend:**
Ages 0-12 $12;
ages 13-18 $14.25;
intensive foster care: $24.25.

**Additional funds available:** State provides $112 semi-annual clothing allowance; Medicaid for medical and dental care.

---

★ 1033 ★
**Macomb County Department of Social Services**
21885 Dunham Rd.
Mt. Clemens, MI 48043
Phone: (313) 469-6759

**Contact:** Janice Giulioli, Supervisor.

**Serves:** Macomb and Lapeer counties.

**Requirements:** Adults who can provide financially for existing family, 3 personal references, 40 sq. ft. sleeping room for foster child, clean police record checks, and medical clearances.

**Description of children:** Primarily older children with mental/emotional impairments and sibling groups.

**Licensing procedure:**
1) Attend orientation meeting;
2) file application;
3) submit medical and financial data;
4) home visit by licensing worker;
5) police clearance checks.

**Average length of time for licensing:** Approx. 6-9 mos.

**Inspections:**
1) Well and septic inspections (if applicable);
2) medical examinations for all household members. After placement, home is visited annually by a licensing worker and monthly by child's caseworker.

**Maximum number of children allowed in licensed foster care home:** 8.

**Interracial placement:** Permitted but not desirable.

**Type of foster care and description of procedures:** Emergency, therapeutic, pre-adoptive and occasionally long-term.

**Per diem stipend:**
Ages 0-12: $12;
ages 13-18: $14.25.

**Additional funds available:** Medicaid and semi-annual clothing allowance.

---

★ 1034 ★
**Montcalm County Department of Social Services**
P.O. Box 278
Stanton, MI 48888
Phone: (517) 831-8497

**Contact:** Dennis Major, Supervisor, Children's Services Unit.

**Serves:** Residents of Montcalm County.

**Requirements:** Applicants must be between the ages of 18 and 65 year old.

**Description of children:** Children of all ages who have either been abused and/or neglected or who are delinquent.

**Licensing procedure:** Contact the Department of Social Services for initial information and case arrangement.

**Average length of time for licensing:** 6 mos.

**Inspections:** 1) Home environmental health inspection; 2) sanitation inspection by local Health Dept; 3) personal references; 4) medical clearances of all household members by family's personal physician; 5) name clearances. When a foster child has been placed, child's caseworker visits monthly. If no child is in placement, licensing worker visits annually.

**Maximum number of children allowed in licensed foster care home:** Law 400-191 allows no more than 4 unrelated children to be in a licensed foster home. Total number of all children under 17 years must not exceed 8.

**Interracial placement:** Permitted, if the family displays a good understanding and application of cross-cultural parenting.

**Type of foster care and description of procedures:** Emergency, long-term, therapeutic and pre-adoptive.

**Per diem stipend:** Children between the ages of 0 and 12 yrs. : $12; children from 13 yrs. to 18 yrs.: $14.25.

**Additional funds available:** Medical/dental, clothing and transportation allowances.

---

★ 1035 ★
**Ogemon County Department of Social Services**
P.O. Box 307
West Branch, MI 48661
Phone: (517) 345-5135

**Contact:** James Beach.

**Serves:** Ogemon County.

**Requirements:** Adults who have adequate space for a foster child and who can provide personal references.

**Description of children:** Between the ages of 0 and 17 who have been abused, neglected or are delinquent.

**Licensing procedure:** Contact Ogemon Co. Dept. of Social Services.

**Average length of time for licensing:** 3-6 wks.

**Inspections:**
1) Fire;
2) sanitation;
3) medical examinations for all household members.
After placement, social worker visits the home at least twice yearly.

**Maximum number of children allowed in licensed foster care home:** 4-6 depending on living space.

**Interracial placement:** Permitted.

**Type of foster care and description of procedures:** Emergency, long-term, therapeutic and pre-adoptive.

**Per diem stipend:** $13.50.

**Additional funds available:** Medical/dental and clothing allowance.

**★ 1036 ★**
**Otsego County Department of Social Services**
800 Livingston Blvd.
Gaylord, MI 49735
Phone: (517) 732-1702

**Mailing address:**
P.O. Box 560, Gaylord, MI 49735

**Contact:** Cynthia G. Pushman, Services Supervisor.

**Serves:** Residents of Otsego County.

**Requirements:** Applicants must be 18 yrs. or older, have sufficient income to meet their own needs and adequate sleeping room for a foster child.

**Description of children:** Infants, children and adolescents, some of whom have been abused and/or neglected or who are delinquent.

**Licensing procedure:** Contact the Otsego County Department of Social Services.

**Average length of time for licensing:** 6 mos. or less.

**Inspections:** 1) Fire; 2) sanitation; 3) medical clearances for all household members; 4) personal references. After licensing, worker visits annually unless a child is in placement when social worker visits as often as weekly.

**Maximum number of children allowed in licensed foster care home:** Up to 4 foster children with a maximum of 8 children in total.

**Interracial placement:** Permitted.

**Type of foster care and description of procedures:** Emergency.

**Per diem stipend:** Children 0-12 yrs. :$12; children 13-18 yrs. $14.25.

**Additional funds available:** Medical/dental, clothing and other depending upon child's needs.

**★ 1037 ★**
**Ozone House**
608 N. Main
Ann Arbor, MI 48104
Phone: (313) 662-2222

**Contact:** Karyn Stone, Housing Coordinator.

**Serves:** Residents of Washtenaw County, MI.

**Requirements:** Applicants must be between the ages of 21 and 65 yrs. and be financially capable of providing for their own needs.

**Description of children:** Adolescents between the ages of 12 and 17 yrs. who are in family crisis.

**Licensing procedure:** 1) Inquiry; 2) meet with housing coordinator; 3) complete paper work; 4) personal interview.

**Average length of time for licensing:** Less than 6 mos.

**Inspections:** 1) Medical clearances for all household members; 2) personal references. After approval a social worker visits at least annually.

**Maximum number of children allowed in licensed foster care home:** No maximum.

**Interracial placement:** Permitted.

**Type of foster care and description of procedures:** Emergency short-term.

**Per diem stipend:** $15.

**Additional funds available:** Emergency clothing fund.

**★ 1038 ★**
**Rainbow Services for Youth and Families**
2373 Gordon Rd.
Alpena, MI 49707
Phone: (517) 356-3474
(800) 292-3003
Fax: (517) 354-5909

**Branch address:**
319 S. State St., Oscoda, MI 48750
Phone: (517) 739-8887

251 W. Huron, Rogers City, MI 49779
Phone: (517) 734-7342

114 N. Court, Gaylord, MI 49735
Phone: (517) 732-4861

402 Lake St., Roscommon, MI 48653
Phone: (517) 275-8948

217 Bailey St., Cheboygan, MI 49721
Phone: (616) 627-9077

221 S. Morenci, Mio, MI 48647
Phone: (517) 826-6352

**Contact:** Peggy Krajniak.

**Serves:** Northern Michigan.

**Requirements:** Applicants must provide personal references and meet the eligibility requirements for age and home size.

**Description of children:** Youths from 10 to 17 yrs.

**Licensing procedure:**
1) Initial inquiry;
2) submit application;
3) complete licensing study;
4) rules compliance;
5) contents of licensing records;
6) certification.

**Average length of time for licensing:** 2-3 mos.

**Inspections:**
1) Fire, if required;
2) medical examination of all household members;
3) sanitation, if required.

**Maximum number of children allowed in licensed foster care home:** 8.

**Interracial placement:** Permitted.

**Type of foster care and description of procedures:** Emergency, short-term and therapeutic.

**Per diem stipend:** $15.

**Additional funds available:** Responsibility of birthparents.

**★ 1039 ★**
**Roscommon County Department of Social Services**
111 Union St.
Roscommon, MI 48653
Phone: (517) 275-5107
Fax: (517) 275-5545

**Contact:** April Andrus.

**Serves:** Roscommon County.

**Requirements:** Adults under the age of 65 (unless an exception is granted), who are financially capable of accommodating their own needs, who can provide personal references, and who have adequate living space for a foster child.

**Description of children:** Neglected/abused and delinquent.

**Licensing procedure:**
1) Make inquiry;
2) file application;
3) attend training; and
4) complete home study.

**Average length of time for licensing:** 30-45 days depending on how quickly forms are returned.

**Inspections:** Sanitation.
After placement, the foster home is visited annually by a social worker.

**Maximum number of children allowed in licensed foster care home:** 8. If both parents work outside the home, placement possibilities are affected.

**Interracial placement:** Permitted but not practiced.

**Type of foster care and description of procedures:** Emergency, long-term and occasionally pre-adoptive.

**Per diem stipend:**
Ages 0-12: $12;
ages 13 and up: $14.25.

**Additional funds available:** Medical/dental, clothing allowance and other, e.g. counseling, transportation and school expenses.

★ 1040 ★
**Sanilac County Department of Social Services**
515 S. Sandusky Rd.
Sandusky, MI 48471
Phone: (810) 648-4420

**Contact:** Janies Beyer, Services Supervisor.

**Serves:** Residents of Sanilac County.

**Requirements:** Applicants must have adequate finances to meet their family's need and at least a 40 sq. ft. separate sleeping room for a foster child.

**Description of children:** Children and adolescents between the ages of birth and 5 yrs. and between the ages of 12 and 18 yrs. who may have physical and/or mental disabilities, be delinquent or who have been neglected and/or abused.

**Licensing procedure:** 1) Inquiry and information phase; 2) application phase; 3) home visitation, interviews and background checks; 4) licensure. After licensing social worker visits 2 to 12 times a year.

**Average length of time for licensing:** 6 mos. or less.

**Inspections:** Sanitation; 2) personal references; 3) child abuse and neglect record check; 4) criminal record check.

**Maximum number of children allowed in licensed foster care home:** 4.

**Interracial placement:** Permitted under the guidelines of the Michigan Department of Social Services.

**Type of foster care and description of procedures:** Emergency and long-term.

**Per diem stipend:** Children 0-12 yrs. : $12; children 13-18 yrs.: $14.25.

**Additional funds available:** Medicaid, semi-annual clothing allowance and special expenses as per individual case.

★ 1041 ★
**Spectrum Human Services**
17000 W. 8 Mile Rd.
Southfield, MI 48075
Phone: (313) 552-8020

**Branch address:**
34000 Plymouth Rd., Livonia, MI 48150

Phone: (313) 458-8736

**Contact:** Associate Director of Adoptions.

**Serves:** Macomb, Oakland, Washtenaw and Wayne counties.

**Requirements:** Adults who can provide personal references and who can meet the requirements for age, home size and financial eligibility.

**Description of children:** Children from 0 - 17 yrs. from normal to severely handicapped.

**Licensing procedure:**
1) Initial inquiry;
2) complete agency training;
3) undergo home study;
4) meet licensing requirements.

**Average length of time for licensing:** Approx. 3.5 mos.

**Inspections:** Medical examinations are required for all household members. After placement the foster care worker visits monthly and the licensing worker annually.

**Maximum number of children allowed in licensed foster care home:** 8.

**Interracial placement:** Permitted.

**Type of foster care and description of procedures:** Pre-adoptive, long-term and emergency.

**Per diem stipend:** Varies with the needs of the child.

**Additional funds available:** Clothing allowance.

★ 1042 ★
**Teaching-Family Homes of Upper Michigan**
1500 W. Washington St., Ste. 2
Marquette, MI 49855
Phone: (906) 228-7997
Fax: (906) 228-6834

**Contact:** R. Jerry Staffield, Executive Director; Rose Ann Welty or Mark Holliday, Foster Care Workers.

**Serves:** Residents of Michigan's Upper Peninsula.

**Requirements:** Applicants must be younger than 65 yrs. have sufficient income and at least a 40 sq. ft. private sleeping space per foster child,.

**Description of children:** Boys and girls between the ages of 5 and 17 yrs. who are abused and/or neglected or who are delinquent or pre-delinquent.

**Licensing procedure:** 1) Inquiry; 2) orientation of policies and procedures; 3) home study; 4) return of licensing materials; 5) reference, inspections and background checks.

**Average length of time for licensing:** Less than 6 mos.

**Inspections:** 1) Fire; 2) sanitation; 3) medical clearances for all household members; 4) personal references. After licensing, social worker visits twice monthly.

**Maximum number of children allowed in licensed foster care home:** 8.

**Interracial placement:** Permitted with a Cross Cultural Assessment.

**Type of foster care and description of procedures:** Emergency, long-term and treatment.

**Per diem stipend:** Children younger than 13 yrs.: $21.04. Children older than 13 yrs.: $23.29.

**Additional funds available:** Medicaid and clothing.

**★ 1043 ★**
**Washtenaw County O'Brien Center Foster Care Program**
2260 Platt Rd.
Ann Arbor, MI 48104
Phone: (313) 971-7870

**Contact:** Shirley Watters, Foster Care Worker.

**Serves:** Residents of Washtenaw County.

**Requirements:** Applicants must be able to support themselves financially.

**Description of children:** Children from birth to 18 yrs.

**Licensing procedure:** Complete Michigan Department of Social Services requirements for licensure.

**Average length of time for licensing:** 6 mos. or less.

**Inspections:** 1) Medical clearances for all household members; 2) coliform and septic, if not on city water; 3) 3 personal references.

**Maximum number of children allowed in licensed foster care home:** Law 400-191 allows no more than 4 unrelated children in a licensed foster home. Total number of all children under 17 yrs. must not exceed 8 including foster children.

**Interracial placement:** Permitted if applicants can pass Cross Racial Certification.

**Type of foster care and description of procedures:** Emergency and some long-term.

**Per diem stipend:** Children 0-12 yrs. : $12; children 13-18 yrs.: $14.25.

**Additional funds available:** Birth family's medical insurance or Medicaid. Clothing supplied by birth family.

**★ 1044 ★**
**Wayne Community Living Services, Inc.**
Metroplace Center
35425 Michigan Ave. W.
Wayne, MI 48184-1687
Phone: (313) 467-7600
Fax: (313) 467-7626

**Contact:** Deborah Plowden.

**Serves:** Wayne County.

**Requirements:** Adults who can provide financially for their own needs, have adequate living space for a foster child, and who can provide personal references.

**Description of children:** Children aged 0-17 yrs. with developmental disabilities.

**Licensing procedure:** Apply and complete screening process.

**Average length of time for licensing:** 3-4 mos.

**Inspections:**
1) Fire;
2) medical examinations for all members of the household;
3) if the home has a private well and septic system, sanitation inspection is also required.
After placement, social worker visits the home at least monthly.

**Maximum number of children allowed in licensed foster care home:** 3.

**Interracial placement:** Permitted.

**Type of foster care and description of procedures:** Pre-adoptive, respite and occasionally, long-term.

**Per diem stipend:** Varies according to needs of foster child.

**Additional funds available:** Medical/dental, clothing allowance and adaptive equipment, etc.

**★ 1045 ★**
**Wedgwood Christian Youth & Family Services**
3300 36th St. SE
Grand Rapids, MI 49518
Phone: (616) 942-2110

**Mailing address:**
  P.O. Box 88007, Grand Rapids, MI 49518
**Branch address:**
  2505 Ardmore SE, Grand Rapids, MI 49506

  17117 W. Nine Mile Rd., Ste. 1325, Southfield, MI 48075

  Town Hall Center, 3301 Veterans Dr., Traverse City, MI 49684

**Contact:** Mark Peterson (616) 942-7294.

**Serves:** Residents of Michigan.

**Requirements:** Applicants must be Christian, at least 21 yrs. old, have sufficient funds to cover their own needs and have adequate bedroom space for a foster child.

**Description of children:** Troubled youth from a variety of backgrounds including but not limited to abuse, neglect, delinquency and emotional instability.

**Licensing procedure:** Complete a home study and assessment and attend required training.

**Average length of time for licensing:** 6 mos. or less.

**Inspections:** 1) Medical clearances for all household members; 2) personal references; 3) septic and coliform in rural areas. After placement, child's caseworker visits weekly.

**Maximum number of children allowed in licensed foster care home:** 6, but generally 1 or 2.

**Interracial placement:** Occasionally.

**Type of foster care and description of procedures:** Emergency, long-term and therapeutic.

**Per diem stipend:** $23.92.

**Additional funds available:** Medicaid and clothing allowance.

**★ 1046 ★**
**Wolverine Human Services**
11001 Harper
Detroit, MI 48213
Phone: (313) 571-1780
Fax: (313) 571-1799

**Mailing address:**
  P.O. Box 13830, Detroit, MI 48213

**Contact:** Maureen O'Rourke, M.S.W., C.S.W., Program Director.

**Serves:** Residents of Macomb, Oakland, Warren and Washtenaw counties.

**Requirements:** Applicants must be at least 21 yrs. old, have sufficient funds to support themselves and their dependents and have a adequate and private sleeping space for a foster child.

**Description of children:** Youth between the ages of 10 and 17 yrs. who have emotional and/or psychological problems including, but not limited to, incorrigibility, behaviors resulting from physical and sexual abuse, delinquency and sexual aggression.

**Licensing procedure:** 1) Orientation; 2) 10 hrs. training; 3) interview phase; 4) family aid home inspections; 5) record clearances; 6) home study; 7) physicals and references.

**Average length of time for licensing:** 6 mos. or less.

**Inspections:** 1) Home health and safety by licensing worker; 2) septic and coliform in rural areas; 3) medical clearances for all household members; 4) 3 personal references. After placement child's caseworker visits a minimum of twice a month.

**Maximum number of children allowed in licensed foster care home:** Usually 1-2.

**Interracial placement:** Permitted.

**Type of foster care and description of procedures:** Long-term and therapeutic and occasionally emergency and pre-adoptive.

**Per diem stipend:** $28.55.

**Additional funds available:** Medicaid.

# MINNESOTA

★ 1047 ★
**Caritas Family Services**
305 7th Ave. N.
St. Cloud, MN 56303
Phone: (612) 252-4121
Fax: (612) 259-8761

**Contact:** Jim Wagner.

**Description:** Multi-service family service agency.

**Serves:** Sixteen counties within the Diocese of St. Cloud.

**Requirements:** Couples between the ages of 25 and 45 yrs. who can provide personal references and, at least, one of whom must not be employed full-time outside the home.

**Description of children:** Infants whose birth mothers are considering adoptive placement.

**Licensing procedure:**
1) File application;
2) complete home study;
3) forward references, medical reports;
4) clearance with the Bureau of Criminal Apprehension;
5) licensure.

**Average length of time for licensing:** 6 mos.

**Inspections:**
1) Fire;
2) sanitation by caseworker as part of study;
3) medical examinations for all household members.
After placement social worker visits quarterly.

**Maximum number of children allowed in licensed foster care home:** 5.

**Interracial placement:** Permitted.

**Type of foster care and description of procedures:** Temporary.

**Per diem stipend:** $13.

**Additional funds available:** Medical.

★ 1048 ★
**Crosstreets**
1619 Dayton Ave.
St. Paul, MN 55104
Phone: (612) 771-0076
Fax: (612) 771-2542

**Contact:** Pam Larson, Program Manager.

**Serves:** Ramsey County.

**Requirements:** Adults, 21 yrs. or older who can provide personal references.

**Description of children:** Runaways and adolescents in crisis.

**Licensing procedure:**
1) File application;
2) home visit by social worker;
3) reference check and submit medical reports;
4) clearance from law enforcement officials;
5) fire inspection;
6) complete 6 hrs. of training.

**Average length of time for licensing:** 1.5 mos.

**Inspections:**
1) Fire;
2) medical examinations of all household members.
After placement, social worker visits quarterly.

**Maximum number of children allowed in licensed foster care home:** 2 foster children.

**Interracial placement:** Permitted.

**Type of foster care and description of procedures:** Emergency (1-5 days).

**Per diem stipend:** Services are donated by foster parents.

**Additional funds available:** Free physical donated by local clinic.

★ 1049 ★
**Habilitative Services, Inc.**
P.O. Box 123
Windom, MN 56101
Phone: (507) 831-2050

**Contact:** Bill Olson, Director; Julianne Volk, Social Worker.

**Description:** Private.

**Serves:** Mostly southwest Minnesota but occasionally state-wide.

**Requirements:** Adults, 21 yrs. or older, who can provide personal references and who have adequate living space for a foster child.

**Description of children:** Primarily children with some physical and/or mental handicap.

**Licensing procedure:** Minnesota state law dictates licensing process.

**Average length of time for licensing:** 30-90 days.

**Inspections:**
1) Fire;
2) sanitation;
3) medical examination(s) for all household member(s);
4) complete background (criminal) check of applicant(s).
After placement, social worker visits foster home at least monthly and more often, if necessary.

**Maximum number of children allowed in licensed foster care home:** Depends on type of license.

**Interracial placement:** N/A.

**Type of foster care and description of procedures:** Emergency, long-term and therapeutic.

**Per diem stipend:** Depends on level of need of child.

**Additional funds available:** Medical/dental and clothing allowance.

★ 1050 ★
**Nekton Family Network**
One Griggs Midway Bldg.
1821 University Ave., Ste. 1
St. Paul, MN 55104-2805
Phone: (612) 644-7680

**Contact:** Joann Sorem, LIC. SW, Program Director.

**Serves:** Twin Cities metropolitan area.

**Requirements:** Adults, 21 yrs. or older, who can provide personal reference, who have adequate space for a foster child(ren), and the experience and skills necessary for specialized treatment foster care.

**Description of children:** Children with developmental and other related disabilities. Also serves adults with developmental disabilities.

**Licensing procedure:** Agency strives to find the optimum foster child/parent match before beginning home licensing.

**Average length of time for licensing:** 1-3 mos.

**Inspections:**
1) Sanitation (under some circumstances);
2) fire (under some circumstances);
3) medical examinations for all household members.
After placement social worker visits bimonthly.

**Maximum number of children allowed in licensed foster care home:** Usually 2.

**Interracial placement:** Some race placements when possible.

**Type of foster care and description of procedures:** Emergency and long-term.

**Per diem stipend:** Minimum of $40.

**Additional funds available:** Initial clothing allowance, Medical/dental through medical assistance; personal needs money for client of $57/mo.; respite care and extra staff support also available for client.

**★ 1051 ★**
**Sheriffs Youth Programs of Minnesota, Inc.**
P.O. Box 249
Austin, MN 55912
Phone: (507) 433-0100
Fax: (507) 433-6501

**Branch address:**
245 N. Prior, St. Paul, MN 55104
Phone: (612) 646-8270

**Contact:** Richard Debeau-Melting.

**Serves:** State of Minnesota.

**Requirements:** Adults, 21 yrs. and older, who can provide personal references and who meet the state's requirements for adequate living space.

**Description of children:** Older children and adolescents with behavior problems/emotionally disturbed.

**Licensing procedure:**
1) Initial inquiry;
2) criminal record check and inspections;
3) attend orientation meeting;
4) participate in interview;
5) complete 8 hrs. of training.

**Average length of time for licensing:** Approx. 6 wks.

**Inspections:**
1) Inspection by fire marshal;
2) well and water checks in rural areas;
3) medical examinations for all household members.
After placement social worker visits bi-weekly.

**Maximum number of children allowed in licensed foster care home:** 4.

**Interracial placement:** Permitted.

**Type of foster care and description of procedures:** Emergency, long-term, pre-adoptive, therapeutic and respite care.

**Per diem stipend:** $32.

**Additional funds available:** Medical/dental, clothing allowance and training.

**★ 1052 ★**
**Volunteers of America**
**Family Treatment Program**
5905 Golden Valley Rd.
Minneapolis, MN 55422
Phone: (612) 546-3242
Fax: (612) 546-2774

**Contact:** Nancy Noetzelman, Program Director.

**Description:** Licensed by the State of Minnesota as a private child-caring agency providing treatment for emotionally or behaviorally disturbed youngsters in 3 settings.

**Serves:** Metro Minneapolis-St. Paul, suburbs and some rural towns near the metro area.

**Requirements:** Adults over the age of 21 who can provide a minimum of 3 personal references and adequate living space. Preference is shown to couples.

**Description of children:** Children with emotional/behavior problems, who are mentally/physically disabled, or have medical problems.

**Licensing procedure:**
1) Telephone inquiry/assessment and screening;
2) orientation;
3) home study;
4) evaluation/feedback and recommendations;
5) training.

**Average length of time for licensing:** 2 mos. and 5-6 meetings.

**Inspections:**
1) Medical examinations for all members of household. After placement, social worker visits foster home twice a month.

**Maximum number of children allowed in licensed foster care home:** 5.

**Interracial placement:** Limited.

**Type of foster care and description of procedures:** Emergency, long-term, therapeutic and pre-adoptive.

**Per diem stipend:** $31.75.

**Additional funds available:** Medical/dental covered by Medicaid or biological parents and an initial placement fee for clothing.

# MISSISSIPPI

**★ 1053 ★**
**Alpha House**
302 Franklin St.
Tupelo, MS 38801
Phone: (601) 841-9009

**Contact:** Jerry Clayton, Director.

**Serves:** Residents of Lee County and surrounding counties of Mississippi.

**Requirements:** None.

**Description of children:** Children who are in the custody of the Department of Human Services due to neglect and/or abuse.

**Licensing procedure:** Alpha House parents are trained through the Mississippi Dept. of Human Services.

**Average length of time for licensing:** Varies.

**Inspections:** 1) Fire; 2) sanitation; 3) medical clearances; 4) personal references.

**Maximum number of children allowed in licensed foster care home:** Unavailable.

**Interracial placement:** Permitted.

**Type of foster care and description of procedures:** Long-term, therapeutic and specialized.

**Per diem stipend:** Unavailable.

**Additional funds available:** Medicaid.

★ 1054 ★
**Catholic Charities, Inc. of Jackson, MS**
P.O. Box 2248
Jackson, MS 39225-2248
Phone: (601) 355-8634
(800) 844-8655
Fax: (601) 960-8493

**Branch address:**
P.O. Box 874, Natchez, MS 39120
Phone: (601) 442-4579

**Contact:** Diocese of Jackson.

**Serves:** Northern 3/4 of Mississippi.

**Requirements:** Applicants may be married or single, must provide personal references and meet the requirements for financial eligibility and home size. Age requirements are flexible and take into account applicants' parenting experience. After placement one parent must be a "full-time parent".

**Description of children:** Infants and special needs babies.

**Licensing procedure:**
1) Submit application;
2) complete interview process;
3) participate in in-service training.

**Average length of time for licensing:** 2-3 mos.

**Inspections:**
1) Fire;
2) sanitation;
3) medical examinations for all household members.
After placement, caseworker visits monthly.

**Maximum number of children allowed in licensed foster care home:** 2.

**Interracial placement:** Permitted.

**Type of foster care and description of procedures:** Emergency and pre-adoptive.

**Per diem stipend:** $160/mo.

**Additional funds available:** Medical, clothing allowance and counseling.

★ 1055 ★
**Mississippi State Department of Human Services**
750 N. State St.
Jackson, MS 39202-3033
Phone: (601) 359-4995
(800) 948-4010
Fax: (601) 359-4978

**Mailing address:**
P.O. Box 352, Jackson, MS 39202-3033

**Branch address:**
Branch offices exist in every county.,

**Contact:** Gail Young, Program Administrator.

**Serves:** State of Mississippi.

**Requirements:** Adults must meet the requirements for age, marital status, home size, financial eligibility, and provide personal references.

**Description of children:** Neglected/abused children.

**Licensing procedure:**
1) Call local county Department of Human Services;
2) file application;
3) complete pre-service training (12 hrs. minimum);
4) complete health, law enforcement and child abuse registry checks;
5) interview process;
6) reference checks.

**Average length of time for licensing:** Up to 90 days.

**Inspections:**
1) Sanitation;
2) medical examinations for foster parent(s).
After placement, social worker visits monthly.

**Maximum number of children allowed in licensed foster care home:** 6 but may increase to 8 to accomodate sibling group.

**Interracial placement:** Permitted.

**Type of foster care and description of procedures:** Emergency, long-term, pre-adoptive and therapeutic.

**Per diem stipend:**
Ages 0-3 yrs.: $175/mo.;
4-5 yrs.: $185/mo.;
6-9 yrs.: $205/mo.;
10-12 yrs.: $225/mo.;
13-15 yrs.: $240/mo.;
16-21 yrs.: $250/mo.;
non-SSI disabled: $290/mo.
SSI: $350/mo.

**Additional funds available:** Medical/dental and miscellaneous.

# MISSOURI

★ 1056 ★
**Missouri Department of Social Services**
P.O. Box 88
Jefferson City, MO 65103
Phone: (314) 751-2502
(800) 554-2222
Fax: (314) 526-3971

**Contact:** County office.

**Description:** Toll free number only within the state of Missouri.

**Serves:** State of Missouri.

**Requirements:** Adults, 21 yrs. and older, whose home is large enough to accommodate a foster child, who can meet their own financial needs and who can provide 3 personal references.

**Description of children:** Primarily adolescents and many sibling groups.

**Licensing procedure:**
1) Initial inquiry;
2) agency sends information packet;
3) attend interview;
4) complete home study;
5) participate in required pre-service training.

**Average length of time for licensing:** Approx. 6 wks. (may vary by county).

**Inspections:**
1) Fire;

2) sanitation;
3) law enforcement and child abuse checks;
4) medical examinations and TB test for foster parents.

After placement social worker visits within the first week of placement and bi-monthly thereafter.

**Maximum number of children allowed in licensed foster care home:** 6.

**Interracial placement:** Permitted if in the best interests of the foster child.

**Type of foster care and description of procedures:** Emergency, short and long-term, pre-adoptive and therapeutic.

**Per diem stipend:** Ages:
0-5 yrs.: $212/mo.;
6-12 yrs.: $259/mo.;
13 yrs. and up: $286-$614/mo.;
therapeutic foster care: $1350/mo.

**Additional funds available:** Medicaid and special expenses.

# MONTANA

**★ 1057 ★**
**Department of Family Services, Montana**
P.O. Box 8005
Helena, MT 59604
Phone: (406) 444-5900
Fax: (406) 444-5956

**Contact:** Foster Care Program Officer.

**Description:** Public, state agency. TDD (Telephone Device for the Deaf) number: (406) 444-1697.

**Serves:** State of Montana.

**Requirements:** Applicants must provide personal references.

**Description of children:** Children of all ages and conditions.

**Licensing procedure:**
1) Initial inquiry;
2) attend training;
3) complete foster home study.

**Average length of time for licensing:** Approx. 6 mos.

**Inspections:** When a child is in placement, child's caseworker visits monthly.

**Maximum number of children allowed in licensed foster care home:** 6.

**Interracial placement:** Permitted.

**Type of foster care and description of procedures:** Emergency, long-term and pre-adoptive.

**Per diem stipend:** $10.74-$13.54.

**Additional funds available:** Medicaid and initial clothing allowance of $200 per six month period. Diaper allowance of $40/mo. Special needs allowance of $87.80/mo. Respite care allowance of $444/yr. at $4/hr. for 111 hrs. (All of these services are formulated on a per child basis).

**★ 1058 ★**
**Golden Triangle Community Mental Health Center**
P.O. Box 3089
Great Falls, MT 59403
Phone: (406) 761-0337

**Contact:** Coleen Stivers.

**Serves:** Residents of Great Falls, Browning, Havre, Chinook, Rocky Boy and Fort Belnap.

**Requirements:** Applicants must be at least 18 yrs. old and be financially stable.

**Description of children:** Children who are severely emotionally disturbed due to abuse and/or neglect.

**Licensing procedure:** 1) 14 hrs. of training; 2) interview; 3) police check; 4) psychological tests; 5) licensing; 6) reference checks.

**Average length of time for licensing:** 6 mos. or less.

**Inspections:** 1) Police background check; 2) sanitation; 3) personal references; 4) medical clearances. After placement child's caseworker visits weekly.

**Maximum number of children allowed in licensed foster care home:** 2 foster.

**Interracial placement:** Permitted.

**Type of foster care and description of procedures:** Therapeutic.

**Per diem stipend:** $22.20.

**Additional funds available:** Other funds made available on a case by case basis.

**★ 1059 ★**
**In-Care Network, Inc.**
2906 Second Ave. North, No. 316
Billings, MT 59101
Phone: (406) 259-9616

**Branch address:**
210 W. 2nd St., Hardin, MT 59034

**Contact:** William F. Snell, Jr.

**Serves:** Residents of reservations in Montana and Wyoming.

**Requirements:** Applicants between the ages of 21 and 65 yrs. who have adequate finances and living space to care for a foster child.

**Description of children:** Children of all ages, some with mild to moderate special needs.

**Licensing procedure:** 1) Preliminary application; 2) reference and background checks; 3) home study; 4) licensure.

**Average length of time for licensing:** 6 mos. or less.

**Inspections:** 1) Police background check; 2) personal references; 3) health statements: 4) home safety. After licensure, social worker visits 2 or 3 times annually when no foster child is in residence and 18 times a year or more when a child is placed.

**Maximum number of children allowed in licensed foster care home:** 1 foster child.

**Interracial placement:** Permitted.

**Type of foster care and description of procedures:** Emergency, long-term, therapeutic and transitional/independent living.

**Per diem stipend:** $600 or more.

**Additional funds available:** Medicaid, Indian Health Services; clothing allowance.

**★ 1060 ★**
**Special Training for Exceptional People (STEP)**
1501 Fourteenth St. W., No. 210
Billings, MT 59102
Phone: (406) 248-2055

**Branch address:**
511 Montana Building, Lewistown, MT 63452

17 Broadway, Red Lodge, MT 59068

**Contact:** Zara D. Frank.

**Serves:** Residents of the 11 counties in and around Yellowstone City.

**Requirements:** Applicants must be at least 21 yrs. old and have a separate bedroom for a foster child.

**Description of children:** Children from birth to 18 yrs. who have developmental disabilities.

**Licensing procedure:** Licensing procedures are completed through the Montana Department of Family Services.

**Average length of time for licensing:** 6 mos. or less.

**Inspections:** 1) Fire; 2) sanitation; 3) personal references. After licensing, social worker visits at least monthly.

**Maximum number of children allowed in licensed foster care home:** 1.

**Interracial placement:** Permitted.

**Type of foster care and description of procedures:** Emergency, long-term and therapeutic.

**Per diem stipend:** $500/mo.

**Additional funds available:** Medicaid and SSI for medical/dental and personal needs.


★ 1061 ★
**Therapeutic Foster Care Program**
**Mental Health Center**
723 Fifth Ave. East
Kalispell, MT 59901
Phone: (406) 752-6100

**Contact:** James F. Pitzen.

**Serves:** Residents of northwest Montana.

**Requirements:** Applicants must be at least 21 yrs. old and have a minimum of two bedrooms.

**Description of children:** Children who are severely emotionally disturbed.

**Licensing procedure:** 1) Enroll in program; 2) complete 24-30 hrs. training.

**Average length of time for licensing:** 6-12 mos.

**Inspections:** 1) Fire; 2) sanitation; 3) medical clearances for all household members; 4) personal references. After placement, child's worker visits from 25 to 52 times a year and foster parents must complete 24 hrs. of on-going training each year.

**Maximum number of children allowed in licensed foster care home:** 2.

**Interracial placement:** Permitted.

**Type of foster care and description of procedures:** Therapeutic.

**Per diem stipend:** $22.66.

**Additional funds available:** Medical/dental.


★ 1062 ★
**Youth Dynamics, Inc.**
2601 Virginia La.
Billings, MT 59102
Phone: (406) 245-6539

**Branch address:**
1800 Ellis St., Bozeman, MT 59715

204 N. Kendrick St., No. 2, Glendive, MT 59330

3232 S. Main, Livingston, MT 59047

11 S. 7th, Miles City, MT 59301

**Contact:** Jani Mitchell, Executive Director.

**Serves:** Residents of Montana.

**Requirements:** Applicants must be at least 21 yrs. old.

**Description of children:** Children from infancy to 18 yrs. who are emotionally disturbed.

**Licensing procedure:** 1) Application;
2) home study;
3) background checks;
4) psychological testing;
5) 12 hrs. training.

**Average length of time for licensing:** Less than 6 mos.

**Inspections:** 1) Fire; 2) sanitation; 3) statement of health; 4) personal references. After placement, child's caseworker visits weekly.

**Maximum number of children allowed in licensed foster care home:** 2-3.

**Interracial placement:** Permitted.

**Type of foster care and description of procedures:** Therapeutic.

**Per diem stipend:** $24.67.

**Additional funds available:** Medicaid and clothing allowance.


# NEBRASKA

★ 1063 ★
**Christian Heritage Children's Home**
637 Village View
Hickman, NE 68372
Phone: (402) 792-2961
Fax: (402) 792-2963

**Contact:** John C. George.

**Serves:** Southeast Nebraska.

**Requirements:** Applicants must meet the Dept. of Social Services requirements for home size and provide at least 3 personal references.

**Description of children:** Conduct-disordered children with moderate self-abusive behaviors and/or physical and developmental handicaps and or moderate mental retardation.

**Licensing procedure:**
1) Submit application;
2) attend 21 hr. training class;
3) complete home study;
4) state licensure;
5) pre-placement visits.

**Average length of time for licensing:** 1-2 mos.

**Inspections:**
1) Fire;
2) health reports.

**Maximum number of children allowed in licensed foster care home:** 2.

**Interracial placement:** Permitted.

**Type of foster care and description of procedures:** Emergency, long-term and therapeutic.

**Per diem stipend:** $500/mo. plus incentives for reports.

**Additional funds available:** Medicaid.

★ 1064 ★
**Nebraska Department of Social Services**
301 Centennial Mall S.
Lincoln, NE 68509
Phone: (402) 471-9331

**Branch address:**
1313 Farnam-on-the-Mall, Omaha, NE 68102
Phone: (402) 595-2947

1001 "O" St., Lincoln, NE
Phone: (402) 471-7000

Courthouse, 612 Grant, Beatrice, NE 68310
Phone: (402) 223-6000

205 1/2 W. 1st St., P.O. Box 2121, Grand Island, NE 68802
Phone: (308) 385-6100

1030 S. "D" St., P.O. Box 508, Broken Bow, NE
Phone: (308) 872-2491

Craft State Office Bldg., 200 S. Silber, North Platte, NE 69101
Phone: (308) 535-8200

1030 "N" St., Gering, NE
Phone: (308) 436-6500

Stone Bldg., P.O. Box 339, Norfolk, NE 68701
Phone: (402) 370-3132

Courthouse, 14th St. & 26th Ave., Columbus, NE 68601
Phone: (402) 564-1113

Courthouse, 1555 Colfax St., Blair, NE 68008
Phone: (402) 426-2329

124 E. 5th St., P.O. Box 770, Fremont, NE 68025
Phone: (402) 727-3200

Courthouse, 111 W. Court, P.O. Box 94, Pierce, NE 68767
Phone: (402) 329-4927

415 Main St., P.O. Box 340, Pender, NE 68047
Phone: (402) 385-2571

**Contact:** Adoption Supervisor.

**Serves:** State of Nebraska.

**Requirements:** Adults, 19 yrs. and older who are able to meet their own financial needs, who have sufficient living space for a foster child and who can provide 3 personal references.

**Description of children:** Abused and neglected children, dependent children, status offenders and children with behavior problems.

**Licensing procedure:**
1) Initial inquiry;
2) attend pre-service training;
3) complete home study;
4) pass licensure inspections.

**Average length of time for licensing:** Varies.

**Inspections:**
1) Central Child Abuse Registry check;
2) home inspection.
After placement social worker visits monthly.

**Maximum number of children allowed in licensed foster care home:** 6 under the age of 13 yrs. and 9 under the age of 19 yrs. (including any adults in need of care).

**Interracial placement:** Permitted.

**Type of foster care and description of procedures:** Emergency, short and long-term and pre-adoptive.

**Per diem stipend:** $22/mo.

**Additional funds available:** Medicaid, initial clothing allowance, additional monthly allowance for special needs and difficulty of placement.

# NEVADA

★ 1065 ★
**Catholic Community Services of Nevada**
808 S. Main St.
Las Vegas, NV 89125
Phone: (702) 385-3351
Fax: (702)385-0677

**Branch address:**
275 E. 4th St., Reno, NV 89513
Phone: (702) 322-7073

**Contact:** Patricia Gutuerrez, Director of Adoption Services.

**Description:** Private agency licensed by the State of Nevada.

**Serves:** Southern half of Nevada.

**Requirements:** Check with agency as to requirements for age, home size and financial eligibility. Applicants must present personal references. After foster placement, both parents may not be employed full time outside the home.

**Description of children:** Primarily newborns and toddlers who are waiting termination of parental rights before adoptive placement.

**Average length of time for licensing:** 1-6 mos.

**Inspections:**
1) Fire;
2) sanitation;
3) medical clearances for all members of the household;
4) finger printing of foster parents.
After placement, social worker visits home a minimum of twice yearly.

**Maximum number of children allowed in licensed foster care home:** 3.

**Interracial placement:** Permitted.

**Type of foster care and description of procedures:** Emergency, temporary and pre-adoptive.

**Per diem stipend:** Foster parents are reimbursed for out-of-pocket expenses only. Actual care is a donated service to the agency.

**Additional funds available:** Medical/dental and clothing allowance.

# NEW HAMPSHIRE

★ 1066 ★
**Casey Family Services**
**New Hampshire Division**
6 Chennel Dr., Ste. 100
Concord, NH 03301
Phone: (603) 224-8909
Fax: (603) 224-2584

**Contact:** Sheryl Tedford.

**Serves:** State of New Hampshire.

**Requirements:** Applicants must provide personal references and meet the New Hampshire eligibility requirements for financial eligibility and home size.

**Description of children:** Children from 5 to 13 yrs. of age.

**Licensing procedure:**
1) Initial inquiry;
2) return written information;
3) attend interview;
4) participate in pre-service training;
5) complete home study.

**Average length of time for licensing:** 3-6 mos.

**Inspections:**
1) Fire;
2) sanitation;
3) medical examinations for all household members.
After placement, social worker usually visits weekly.

**Maximum number of children allowed in licensed foster care home:** Single parent home: 4 children; two-parent home: 6 children.

**Interracial placement:** Permitted.

**Type of foster care and description of procedures:** Permanent.

**Per diem stipend:** Under age 13: $493; over age 13: $557.

**Additional funds available:** Medical/dental, clothing allowance and miscellaneous.

**★ 1067 ★**
**New Hampshire Division for Children, Youth, and Families**
6 Hazen Dr.
Concord, NH 03301
Phone: (603) 271-4711
(800) 852-3345
Fax: (603) 271-4729

**Contact:** Gail T. DeGoosh, Foster Care Specialist.

**Serves:** State of New Hampshire.

**Requirements:** Adults age 21 yrs. and older who are financially self-sufficient and who can provide 5 personal references, only one of which may be from a relative.

**Description of children:** Ages 0-18 yrs., more boys than girls, who have been abused, neglected or are in need of supervision or delinquent; some mildly to severely behaviorally disordered.

**Licensing procedure:**
1) Attend orientation;
2) complete 21 hrs. pre-service training;
3) submit application;
4) criminal records check, Child Abuse Registry check and reference checks;
5) inspections and 2 agency home visits;
6) home study.

**Average length of time for licensing:** Minimum of 2 mos.

**Inspections:**
1) Fire;
2) sanitation;
3) medical examinations for all household members.

**Maximum number of children allowed in licensed foster care home:** 6.

**Interracial placement:** Permitted.

**Type of foster care and description of procedures:** Emergency, long-term, pre-adoptive, specialized, and therapeutic.

**Per diem stipend:** General care from $10.48-$13.47; specialized care from $15.72-$20.20; emergency care: $26.93; respite: $25; therapeutic: $50.

**Additional funds available:** Medicaid and state funds for medical/dental, clothing allowance and supplemental care which ranges from $3.29 to $32.87 per day.

# NEW JERSEY

**★ 1068 ★**
**New Jersey Division of Youth and Family Services**
Capital Center
50 E. State St.
Trenton, NJ 08625
Phone: (609) 984-6080
(800) 222-0047

**Mailing address:**
CN 717, Trenton, NJ 08625

**Contact:** County offices.

**Serves:** State of New Jersey.

**Requirements:** Adults, 21 yrs. and older, in good physical and emotional health who can provide a separate bed and storage space for a foster child, and who are financially capable of meeting their own needs. Children older than 2 yrs. may not share a bedroom with an adult and children older than 5 yrs. may not share a bedroom with a child of the opposite sex.

**Description of children:** Infants and toddlers, children between the ages of 6 and 9 yrs. and adolescents many of whom have special needs, sibling groups, medically fragile infants and pre-school minority children.

**Licensing procedure:**
1) Initial inquiry;
2) submit application or attend orientation meeting followed by application;
3) complete foster home study;
4) attend 10 hrs. of pre-service training (mandatory for all applicants).

**Average length of time for licensing:** Minimum of 3 mos.

**Inspections:**
1) Home health and safety inspection;
2) state and national fingerprint clearance;
3) child abuse registry check;
4) school or day care reference for any children in the home;
5) medical examinations for all household members;
6) employment reference.
7) rabies certificate for all indoor and outdoor pets;
8) well and coliform tests if not on city water and sewer;
9) 3 personal references;
10) fire certificate if foster home is part of 3 or more family living unit.
After placement child's caseworker establishes a regular schedule of visitation based on the child's need.

**Maximum number of children allowed in licensed foster care home:** 5 foster.

**Interracial placement:** Permitted.

**Type of foster care and description of procedures:** Emergency, short and long-term, therapeutic, and pre-adoptive.

**Per diem stipend:** Ages:
0-5 yrs.: $272/mo.
6-9 yrs.: $288/mo.
10-12 yrs.: $319/mo.
13 yrs. and up: $340.

**Additional funds available:** Medicaid, monthly clothing allowance and increased board rate based on difficulty of care. Support services as necessary.

# NEW MEXICO

### ★ 1069 ★
**Healing the Children - New Mexico Chapter**
502 Georgene Dr., NE
Albuqerque, NM 87123
Phone: (505) 298-7841

**Contact:** Debbie O'Rourke, Director.

**Serves:** Residents of New Mexico.

**Requirements:** None.

**Description of children:** Children from birth to adolescence from throughout the world who have medical needs.

**Licensing procedure:** 1) Preliminary application; 2) home study; 3) 10 hrs. of training.

**Average length of time for licensing:** 6 mos. or less.

**Inspections:** 1) Medical clearances for all household members; 2) finger printing; 3) personal references. After a child is in the home, the social worker visits monthly.

**Maximum number of children allowed in licensed foster care home:** 6.

**Interracial placement:** Permitted.

**Type of foster care and description of procedures:** Specialized.

**Per diem stipend:** Voluntary program.

**Additional funds available:** All medical and dental with other needs considered on a case by case basis.

### ★ 1070 ★
**Hogares, Inc.**
1218 Griegos
Albuquerque, NM 87107
Phone: (505) 345-8471

**Contact:** Patricia Yeamans, MA, NCC.

**Serves:** Residents of New Mexico.

**Requirements:** Applicants must be 24 yrs. or older, not on public assistance and have 50 sq. ft. of space available for a foster child. Both foster parents cannot be employed outside the home.

**Description of children:** Children who are severely emotionally disturbed.

**Licensing procedure:** 1) Complete 40 hrs. of pre-service training; 2) home study.

**Average length of time for licensing:** 6 mos. or less.

**Inspections:** 1) Fire; 2) sanitation; 3) medical clearances for all household members; 4) finger printing; 5) personal references. After placement, child's caseworker visits twice weekly.

**Maximum number of children allowed in licensed foster care home:** 1.

**Interracial placement:** Permitted under special circumstances.

**Type of foster care and description of procedures:** Long-term and therapeutic.

**Per diem stipend:** $68 $13 room and board.

**Additional funds available:** Medicaid or birth parents' private insurance. Other needs considered on an individual basis.

# NEW YORK

### ★ 1071 ★
**Abbott House**
100 N. Broadway
Irvington, NY 10533
Phone: (914) 591-7300

**Contact:** Mary L. Durel, Supervisor of Adoption and Homefinding.

**Serves:** Residents of the New York City metro area.

**Requirements:** Applicants must be 21 yrs. or older and have funds separate from the foster care payments. DC Minority children from latency to adolescence, many in sibling groups.

**Licensing procedure:** 1) Inquiry; 2) application; 3) orientation; 4) home study and visit; 5) reference checks; 6) interviews; 7) State Central Registry check.

**Average length of time for licensing:** 6 mos. or less.

**Inspections:** 1) Home health and safety; 2) medical clearances for all household members; 3) 4 personal references. After licensure, foster home is visited by a social worker 4 to 12 times a year.

**Maximum number of children allowed in licensed foster care home:** 6.

**Interracial placement:** Permitted, if the community is supportive.

**Type of foster care and description of procedures:** Emergency, long-term, therapeutic, pre-adoptive and specialized.

**Per diem stipend:** Varies according to child's age and needs.

**Additional funds available:** Medical/dental and clothing.

### ★ 1072 ★
**Brookwood Child Care**
25 Washington St.
Brooklyn, NY 11201
Phone: (718) 596-5555
Fax: (718) 596-7564

**Contact:** Fatima Goldman, Executive Director.

**Serves:** Brooklyn and Queens.

**Requirements:** Adults, 21 yrs. and older, who can provide 4 personal references.

**Description of children:** Boarder babies, children with special needs, sibling groups and black and Hispanic youngsters.

**Licensing procedure:**
1) File application;
2) complete home study;
3) Child Abuse Registry clearance.

**Average length of time for licensing:** 6 or more wks.

**Inspections:**
1) Fire
2) sanitation
3) medical clearances for all members of household.
After placement, social worker visits at least monthly.

**Maximum number of children allowed in licensed foster care home:** 6 children below the age of 13. Non-foster children older than 13 yrs. are exempted.

**Interracial placement:** Permitted, following active recruitment of same race families.

**Type of foster care and description of procedures:** Emergency, long-term, therapeutic, and pre-adoptive.

**Per diem stipend:** Varies by age and child.

**Additional funds available:** Medical/dental, clothing allowance, transportation and training.

★ 1073 ★
**Catholic Family Center of the Diocese of Rochester**
Sibley Tower Bldg., 7th Fl.
25 Franklin St.
Rochester, NY 14604-1007
Phone: (716) 546-7220
Fax: (716) 325-3867

**Contact:** Catherine Brown.
**Serves:** Residents of the Diocese of Rochester.
**Requirements:** Adults, 21 yrs. and older, who can provide 4 personal references.
**Description of children:** Domestic infants, older children, special needs children, foreign-born children who are classified as orphans, and unaccompanied refugee minors.
**Licensing procedure:**
1) File a Child Abuse Clearance form with Albany;
2) submit an application;
3) complete interview process;
4) participate in foster parent training.
**Average length of time for licensing:** Within 4 mos.
**Inspections:**
1) Caseworker fire and sanitation inspections;
2) medical examination for all household members;
3) Fire Dept. approval if foster child's bedroom is on the 3rd floor or basement.
After approval, homefinder visits annually and child's caseworker on a regular basis.
**Maximum number of children allowed in licensed foster care home:** 6 under the age of 13 yrs. (unless sibling group of foster children).
**Interracial placement:** Permitted in special circumstances.
**Type of foster care and description of procedures:** Long-term, pre-adoptive, HIV positive, teen mother and baby, short-term, healthy infant.
**Per diem stipend:** Ages:
0-5 yrs.: $10.70;
6-11 yrs.: $12.85;
12-20 yrs.: $14.95 (rates increase depending on the level of are).
**Additional funds available:** Medical/dental and clothing allowance.

★ 1074 ★
**Child Development Support Corp.**
1119 Bedford Ave.
Brooklyn, NY 11216
Phone: (718) 398-2050

**Contact:** Paula Odom, Coordinator of Adoption, Homefinding and Training.
**Serves:** Residents of Brooklyn, NY.
**Requirements:** Applicants must be at least 21 yrs. or older, have sufficient income for their own needs and provide 45 sq. ft. of bedroom space for a foster child.
**Description of children:** Unavailable.
**Licensing procedure:** 1) Orientation; 2) training; 3) background checks and clearances; 4) home study; 5) certification.
**Average length of time for licensing:** 6 mos. or less.
**Inspections:** 1) Fire; 2) sanitation; 3) medical examination of all household members; 4) personal references. After certification, social worker visits monthly.

**Maximum number of children allowed in licensed foster care home:** 6.
**Interracial placement:** Not permitted.
**Type of foster care and description of procedures:** Long-term, pre-adoptive and therapeutic.
**Per diem stipend:** Varies with the level of care required.
**Additional funds available:** Medicaid and clothing allowance.

★ 1075 ★
**Children's Home of Kingston (CHK)**
26 Grove St.
Kingston, NY 12401
Phone: (914) 331-1448
Fax: (914) 331-1448

**Contact:** Coordinator of Family Foster Boarding Homes Program.
**Serves:** New York State exclusive of the 5 boroughs of New York City.
**Requirements:** Adults, 21 yrs. and older, who are financially self-sufficent, who can provide sufficient living space as determined by the Dept. of Social Services and who can provide 5 personal references.
**Description of children:** Boys age 10 yrs. or older who have emotional and behavioral problems and who may or may not have continuing involvement with birth family.
**Licensing procedure:**
1) File application;
2) return medical form and State Central Register form;
3) home study and interview to determine family appropriateness and adherence to Dept. of Social Services regulations;
4) reference checks;
5) return fire safety form.
**Average length of time for licensing:** 1-3 mos.
**Inspections:**
1) Fire;
2) medical examinations for all household members.
After placement social worker makes weekly phone contact, and visits foster home at least monthly, more often if necessary.
**Maximum number of children allowed in licensed foster care home:** Depends on home size and ability of foster parents.
**Interracial placement:** Permitted.
**Type of foster care and description of procedures:** Emergency, long-term and pre-adoptive.
**Per diem stipend:** $28.18.
**Additional funds available:** Medicaid and clothing allowance.

★ 1076 ★
**Forestdale, Inc.**
67-35 112th St.
Forest Hills, NY 11375
Phone: (718) 263-0740

**Contact:** Natalie Barnwell, Director of Permanency Planning.
**Serves:** Residents of the five boroughs of New York City.
**Requirements:** Applicants must be at least 21 yrs. old, have a means of financial support apart from foster care payments and be able to provide any foster child over the age of 2 yrs. with a bedroom shared only by another child of the same sex.

**Description of children:** Children of all ethnic groups from infancy to adolescence, some who are handicapped, some who are emotionally disturbed and some who are in large sibling groups.

**Licensing procedure:** 1) Application; 2) orientation; 3) home study; 4) child abuse and neglect record check; 5) home inspections.

**Average length of time for licensing:** 6 mos. or less.

**Inspections:** 1) Fire; 2) sanitation; 3) medical clearances for all household members; 4) personal references. After licensure, foster home is visited a minimum of 6 to 12 times annually.

**Maximum number of children allowed in licensed foster care home:** 6 unless one of the children is younger than 2 yrs., in which case 5 is the maximum.

**Interracial placement:** Permitted.

**Type of foster care and description of procedures:** Emergency, long-term and pre-adoptive.

**Per diem stipend:** Varies with child's age and level of care.

**Additional funds available:** Medical/dental and clothing.

★ 1077 ★
**Heartshare Human Services of New York**
191 Joralemon St.
Brooklyn, NY 11201
Phone: (718) 330-0600

**Branch address:**
   186 Joralemon St., Brooklyn, NY 11201

   50 Court St., Brooklyn, NY 11202

**Contact:** Concetta Gallo-Treacy.

**Serves:** Residents of the five boroughs of New York City.

**Requirements:** None.

**Description of children:** Majority are minority children.

**Licensing procedure:** 1) Inquiry; 2) home study; 3) inspections and clearances.

**Average length of time for licensing:** 6 mos. or less.

**Inspections:** 1) Medical clearances for all household members; 2) 3 personal references.

**Maximum number of children allowed in licensed foster care home:** Varies with home size.

**Interracial placement:** Permitted.

**Type of foster care and description of procedures:** Therapeutic and pre-adoptive.

**Per diem stipend:** Unavailable.

**Additional funds available:** Medical/dental, clothing and SSI.

★ 1078 ★
**Hillside Children's Center**
1183 Monroe Ave.
Rochester, NY 14610
Phone: (716) 256-7500

**Branch address:**
   1337 E. Main St., Rochester, NY 14609
   Phone: (716) 654-4524

**Contact:** Elaine Gjeltema, ACSW, Director of Adoption.

**Serves:** 90 mi. radius of Rochester, NY.

**Requirements:** Applicants who can provide adequate home size, personal references, who have sufficient income for their own needs, and meet other agency and New York State requirements.

**Description of children:** Infants, domestic and international; special needs children.

**Licensing procedure:**
  1) File application;
  2) attend interview;
  3) complete adoption preparation services;
  4) forward references and medical reports;
  5) foster care licensing for special needs (infants and international services do not require licensing).

**Average length of time for licensing:** 3 mos.

**Inspections:** Medical examinations are required for all household members. At least one home consultation prior to placement. After placement social worker visits weekly for the 1st month and 1-2 times/mo. thereafter.

**Maximum number of children allowed in licensed foster care home:** 6 under the age of 13 yrs., however, agency does not usually place more than 1 infant in a foster home.

**Interracial placement:** With interracial families or on an emergency basis.

**Type of foster care and description of procedures:** Temporary.

**Per diem stipend:** Yes.

**Additional funds available:** Medical, clothing allowance, and transportation for special needs placement.

★ 1079 ★
**Jewish Child Care Association**
575 Lexington Ave.
New York, NY 10022
Phone: (212) 371-1313

**Contact:** Mr. Ira Kayfman, CSW, Director Foster Home Division.

**Serves:** Residents of the Metropolitan New York City area including Nassau, Suffolk and Westchester County.

**Requirements:** Applicants must be 21 yrs. or older, have sufficient income to meet their own needs apart from the foster care stipend and have an adequate size bedroom for a foster child.

**Description of children:** Boarder Babies, adolescents, sibling groups and children with special and exceptional needs.

**Licensing procedure:** 1) Attend orientation; 2) submit application for a screening interview; 3) participate in pre-certification groups; 4) complete home study.

**Average length of time for licensing:** 6 mos. or less.

**Inspections:** 1) Fire; 2) sanitation; 3) medical clearances for all household members; 4) 4 personal references, including 2 in-person reference interviews. After the foster home is approved, the case assistant visits four times a year and the child's social worker visits as frequently as needed.

**Maximum number of children allowed in licensed foster care home:** Varies with home space and age of children.

**Interracial placement:** Occasionally with City approval.

**Type of foster care and description of procedures:** Emergency, long-term, pre-adoptive and therapeutic.

**Per diem stipend:** Varies with age of child and level of care.

**Additional funds available:** Medicaid, quarterly clothing allowance and other monies to cover individual needs on a case by case basis.

★ 1080 ★
**Little Flower Children's Services**
186 Joralemon St.
Brooklyn, NY 11201
Phone: (718) 875-3500

**Branch address:**
   North Wading River Rd., Wading River, NY 11792

**Contact:** Camille D. Swift, Executive Director, Adoption Department.

**Serves:** Residents of the 5 boroughs of New York City, Nassau and Suffolk counties.

**Requirements:** Applicants must be at least 21 yrs. old and have an independent source of income apart of the foster stipend.

**Description of children:** Children of all ages, most with special needs.

**Licensing procedure:** 1) Contact agency's Homefind Unit; 2) Attend orientation meeting; 3) submit application.

**Average length of time for licensing:** 12 mos. or more.

**Inspections:** 1) Fire; 2) sanitation; 3) medical clearances for all household members; 4) finger printing for Long Island applicants; 5) personal references. After approval, social worker visits monthly.

**Maximum number of children allowed in licensed foster care home:** Varies with home space available, but no more than 6 children under the age of 13 yrs.

**Interracial placement:** Placements are determined on an individual basis.

**Type of foster care and description of procedures:** Emergency, long-term, pre-adoptive, therapeutic and specialized.

**Per diem stipend:** Determined by child's age, but ranges from $401/mo. to $1332/mo.

**Additional funds available:** Medicaid and clothing allowance.

★ 1081 ★
**McMahon Services for Children**
305 Seventh Ave.
New York, NY 10001
Phone: (212) 243-7070

**Contact:** Michael Giangrasso, Adoption Supervisor.

**Serves:** Residents of New York City.

**Requirements:** Applicants who can provide a foster child bedroom space as per New York State regulations.

**Description of children:** Children who have been hard to place, some of whom have handicaps or emotional disabilities, are in sibling groups or who are older. 95% are children of racial minorities.

**Licensing procedure:** 1) Inquiry addressed to Homefinding Department; 2) orientation meeting; 3) pre-service training; 4) home study; 5) certification.

**Average length of time for licensing:** 6 mos. or less.

**Inspections:** 1) Fire; 2) sanitation; 3) medical clearances for all household members; 4) personal references. After certification, social worker visits monthly.

**Maximum number of children allowed in licensed foster care home:** No more than 6 children under the age of 12 yrs.

**Interracial placement:** Permitted under extenuating circumstances.

**Type of foster care and description of procedures:** Emergency, long-term and pre-adoptive.

**Per diem stipend:** Depending on age of child $401 to $547 per mo.

**Additional funds available:** Medicaid, monthly clothing allowance from $25 to $72 depending upon child's age, foster parent stipend exceeds standard rate for those children who have moderate to severe disabilities.

★ 1082 ★
**Ohel Children's Home and Family Services**
4510 Sixteenth Ave.
Brooklyn, NY 11204
Phone: (718) 851-6300

**Contact:** Susanne Kaplowitz, CSW, Coordinator, Homefinding and Outreach.

**Serves:** Residents of New York State.

**Requirements:** Applicants must be Jewish.

**Description of children:** Unavailable.

**Licensing procedure:** 1) Application; 2) home study.

**Average length of time for licensing:** 6 mos. or less.

**Inspections:** 1) Medical clearances for all household members; 2) 4 personal references. After approval social worker visits monthly.

**Maximum number of children allowed in licensed foster care home:** Dependent on situation.

**Interracial placement:** Permitted.

**Type of foster care and description of procedures:** Emergency, long-term and pre-adoptive.

**Per diem stipend:** Dependent on child's age.

**Additional funds available:** Medical/dental and clothing allowance.

★ 1083 ★
**Pius XII Youth and Family Services**
369 E. 149th St.
Bronx, NY 10455
Phone: (718) 993-3650

**Branch address:**
   405 Ann St., 11 King St., Newburgh, NY 12550
   Phone: (800) 562-7487

**Contact:** Homefinding Department.

**Serves:** Residents of the 5 boroughs.

**Requirements:** Applicants must be at least 21 yrs. old, able to meet their own living expenses and have bedroom space for a foster child.

**Description of children:** Sibling groups of 3 or more children, adolescents and adolescent mothers and their children.

**Licensing procedure:** 1) Orientation; 2) 14 hrs. of pre-service training; 3) completion of paperwork; 4) child abuse registry checks; 5) medical and financial forms returned; 6) home study.

**Average length of time for licensing:** Less than 6 mos.

**Inspections:** 1) Medical clearances for all household members; 2) personal references; 3) fire; 4) sanitation; 5) child abuse registry.
   After licensing, social worker visits monthly.

**Maximum number of children allowed in licensed foster care home:** 6.

**Interracial placement:** Permitted.

**Type of foster care and description of procedures:** Emergency, long-term and pre-adoptive.

**Per diem stipend:** Dependent on child's age, level of care and location of placement.

**Additional funds available:** Medicaid, monthly clothing allowance, babysitting for foster parent employed outside the home.

★ 1084 ★
**Richard Allen Center on Life**
1854 Amsterdam Ave.
New York, NY 10031
Phone: (212) 862-7160
Fax: (212) 862-4211

**Contact:** Ella S. McDonald, Executive Director or Ernest Anderson, Adoption Director.

**Serves:** Residents of New York State.

**Requirements:** Applicants must be at least 21 yrs. old and be self-supporting.

**Description of children:** Children from infancy to adolescents with infants most of whom are African American or Latino.

**Licensing procedure:** 1) Orientation; 2) training; 3) NYS Child Abuse Registry checks; 4) assessment.

**Average length of time for licensing:** 6 mos. or less.

**Inspections:** 1) Fire; 2) sanitation; 3) medical clearances for all household members; 4) personal references. After approval, foster home is visited at least once monthly by a social worker.

**Maximum number of children allowed in licensed foster care home:** 4 although some exceptions are made in the case of sibling groups.

**Interracial placement:** Permitted after every effort to find an ethnically-matched home have failed.

**Type of foster care and description of procedures:** Long-term and pre-adoptive.

**Per diem stipend:** Approximately $400 - $1300 per month depending upon child's age and special needs.

**Additional funds available:** Medical/dental, monthly clothing allowance and babysitting funds for working parents.

★ 1085 ★
**St. Augustine's Center**
**Child Welfare Services Department**
1600 Fillmore Ave.
Buffalo, NY 14211
Phone: (716) 897-4110
Fax: (716) 897-4395

**Mailing address:**
 1600 Fillmore Ave., Buffalo, NY 14211

**Contact:** Annette Peoples, Administrative Director.

**Serves:** Primarily inner city area of Buffalo.

**Requirements:** Applicants must provide personal references and are preferred to be 21 yrs. and older.

**Description of children:** Children from birth to 18 yrs. and sometimes to 21 yrs., primarily with special needs or in sibling groups.

**Licensing procedure:** For certification:
 1) attend orientation;
 2) prioritization by population in greatest need;
 3) evaluation of home, family and neighborhood;
 4) participate in training.

**Average length of time for licensing:** Approx. 1 mo. following submission of required data, clearance, etc.

**Inspections:**
 1) Medical examinations of all household members;
 2) law enforcement checks;
 3) smoke detectors.

After placement Home Find worker visits quarterly.

**Maximum number of children allowed in licensed foster care home:** 6.

**Interracial placement:** No.

**Type of foster care and description of procedures:** Emergency, long-term, therapeutic and pre-adoptive.

**Per diem stipend:** Normal, special and exception rates depending upon placement.

**Additional funds available:** Medicaid, clothing allowance and special occasions.

★ 1086 ★
**St. Dominic's Family Service Center**
343 E. 137th St.
Bronx, NY 10454
Phone: (718) 993-5765

**Contact:** Bonni Rucker, CSW, Director, FBH Program.

**Serves:** Residents of the 5 boroughs of New York City, Long Island and Rockland County.

**Requirements:** Applicants must be at least 21 yrs. old, be able to meet their own family's financial needs without foster care subsidy and have adequate living space for a foster child or children.

**Description of children:** Most children are of school age of African American or Hispanic ethnicity, have special or exceptional psychiatric, emotional, medical or educational needs. Sibling groups of 3 or more of all races and some pre-schoolers.

**Licensing procedure:** 1) 6 week Orientation program; 2) 2-3 in-home interviews; 3) 6 references including 2 in-person reference interviews; 4) NYS Child Abuse Registry Clearance.

**Average length of time for licensing:** 6-12 mos.

**Inspections:** 1) Fire; 2) sanitation; 3) medical clearances for all household members; 4) personal references.

**Maximum number of children allowed in licensed foster care home:** 6 if space permits.

**Interracial placement:** Permitted.

**Type of foster care and description of procedures:** Emergency, long-term and pre-adoptive.

**Per diem stipend:** NYS range from $300 - $500 per month.

**Additional funds available:** Medical/dental, clothing allowance and an annual reimbursement for 10 hrs. of Foster Parent Training.

★ 1087 ★
**St. Mary's Children & Family Services**
525 Convent Rd.
Syosset, NY 11791
Phone: (516) 921-0808

**Contact:** Michelle Oliveto.

**Date established:** 1894.

**Description:** Private, non-profit foster care agency licensed by the New York State Department of Social Services.

**Serves:** Residents of 5 boroughs of New York City, Nassau and Suffolk counties.

**Requirements:** None.

**Description of children:** Boys and girls between the ages of birth and 16 yrs., some with special needs and a history of multiple placements.

**Licensing procedure:** 1) Application; 2) homefinder interview; 3) references and background checks; 4) 6 orientation meetings; 5) placement.

**Average length of time for licensing:** 6 wks. - 3 mos.

**Inspections:** 1) Child Abuse Registry; 2) fingerprinting; 3) Criminal Records check; 4) motor vehicle records check; 5) home health and safety; 6) 3 references; 7) medical reports.

**Maximum number of children allowed in licensed foster care home:** 6 foster children.

**Interracial placement:** Permitted.

**Type of foster care and description of procedures:** Emergency, short and long-term.

**Per diem stipend:** Children from 0 - 5yrs.: $401 - $1332 per month. Children from 6 - 12 yrs.: $473 - $1332 per month. Children older than 13 yrs.: $547 - $1332 per month.

**Additional funds available:** Medicaid, clothing allowance and other funds available as required.

## ★ 1088 ★
**Society for Seamen's Children**
25 Hyatt St.
Staten Island, NY 10301
Phone: (718) 447-7740
Fax: (718) 720-2321

**Branch address:**
57 Willoughby St., Brooklyn, NY 11201
Phone: (718) 273-2685

**Contact:** Marcia Novey, Adoption Coordinator.

**Serves:** Boroughs of Brooklyn, Queens, and Staten Island.

**Requirements:** Adults, 21 yrs. and older.

**Description of children:** Children placed through the Commissioner of Social Services, NYC.

**Licensing procedure:**
1) Initial inquiry;
2) attend 10 orientation meetings;
3) complete home study;
4) submit legal documents and references;
5) abuse registry checks;
6) certification.

**Average length of time for licensing:** 2-3 mos.

**Inspections:** Medical examinations of all household members. After placement social worker visits at least monthly.

**Maximum number of children allowed in licensed foster care home:** 6 foster children or 6 children under age 13.

**Interracial placement:** Permitted.

**Type of foster care and description of procedures:** Emergency, long-term and pre-adoptive.

**Per diem stipend:** Scale according to child's age.

**Additional funds available:** Medical/dental, clothing allowance and special/exceptional care.

## ★ 1089 ★
**Talbot Perkins Children's Services**
116 W. 32nd St., 12th Fl.
New York, NY 10001
Phone: (212) 736-2510

**Contact:** Robert Sloan, Director of Foster Care and Adoption.

**Serves:** Residents of New York and New Jersey within a 70 mile radius of NYC.

**Requirements:** Applicants must be at least 21 yrs. old, have at least one source of income and be able to accommodate no more than 3 children in a bedroom.

**Description of children:** Minority children between the ages of birth and 18 yrs. from a multiplicity of backgrounds with a wide variety of emotional and physical needs.

**Licensing procedure:** 1) Orientation session; 2) application; 3) home study; 4) approval; and 5) placement.

**Average length of time for licensing:** 6 mos. or less.

**Inspections:** 1) Fire; 2) sanitation; 3) medical clearances for all household members; 4) personal references. After approval and before placement, social worker visits quarterly. After placement, child's caseworker visits monthly.

**Maximum number of children allowed in licensed foster care home:** 6.

**Interracial placement:** Permitted when same race placement is not available.

**Type of foster care and description of procedures:** Long-term and pre-adoptive.

**Per diem stipend:** Child Board Rate depends on child's age and level of care.

**Additional funds available:** Medicaid and agency-related transportation.

## ★ 1090 ★
**Westchester County Department of Social Services**
112 E. Post Rd.
White Plains, NY 10601
Phone: (914) 285-5321

**Contact:** Phyllis Farber or Mona Aronow.

**Serves:** Westchester County.

**Requirements:** Adults, 21 yrs. or older, who can provide personal references.

**Description of children:** School age adolescents and sibling groups.

**Licensing procedure:**
1) Participate in orientation and 5 group sessions;
2) return medicals, autobiographies and questionnaire;
3) complete home study with assigned worker.

**Average length of time for licensing:** 2-3 mos.

**Inspections:** As part of home study, social worker inspects for fire and safety hazards and for sanitation. After placement, resource worker visits foster home semi-annually.

**Maximum number of children allowed in licensed foster care home:** 6 children under the age of 12 yrs. If pre-school children are placed, one parent must provide full-time supervision.

**Interracial placement:** Permitted.

**Type of foster care and description of procedures:** Emergency and pre-adoptive.

**Per diem stipend:** $17.26.

**Additional funds available:** Medicaid, clothing allowance and mileage.

# NORTH CAROLINA

★ 1091 ★
**Professional Parenting/Adoption Plus**
204 Avery Ave.
Morganton, NC 28655
Phone: (704) 433-6812

**Branch address:**
34 Wall St., Ste. 301, Asheville, NC 28801
Phone: (704) 254-1399

3504 Vest Mill Rd., Ste. 5, Winston-Salem, NC 27103

**Contact:** Bonnie Judkins, Morganton; Kathy Nallan for Adoptions Plus.

**Description:** Adoption Plus is an auxiliary program to Professional Parent ing which seeks to place children with special needs in adoptive homes.In addition to the three steps outlines below for licensing, adoptive applicants would also complete a home study. There are no fees for adoption services.

**Serves:** Residents of North Carolina.

**Requirements:** Adults between the ages of 21 and 65 yrs. who have adequate income and sufficient living space and who can provide personal references.

**Description of children:** Emotionally disturbed, behavior disturbed and medically needy children.

**Licensing procedure:** 1) Complete training; 2) meet state licensing requirements; 3) selection.

**Average length of time for licensing:** 3 mos.

**Inspections:** 1) Fire; 2) sanitation; 3) medical examinations for all household members. After placement social worker visits a minimum of 16 times per year.

**Maximum number of children allowed in licensed foster care home:** 2.

**Interracial placement:** Permitted.

**Type of foster care and description of procedures:** Long-term and therapeutic.

**Per diem stipend:** $500/mo.

**Additional funds available:** Medicaid.

★ 1092 ★
**Youth Focus, Inc.**
211 S. Edgeworth St.
Greensboro, NC 27401
Phone: (919) 378-9109

**Contact:** David Bolton, Foster Care Coordinator.

**Serves:** Guilford County.

**Requirements:** Applicants must provide personal references and meet the agency requirements for age, marital status, home size and financial eligibility.

**Description of children:** Delinquent, pre-delinquent, neglected/abused and emotionally disturbed.

**Licensing procedure:**
1) Telephone interview;
2) office interview;
3) home visit;
4) home study;
5) 30 hrs. of training;
6) law enforcement clearances;
7) licensure.

**Average length of time for licensing:** 4-6 wks.

**Inspections:**
1) Fire;
2) sanitation;
3) medical examinations for all household members.
After placement social worker visits weekly.

**Maximum number of children allowed in licensed foster care home:** 1 foster child.

**Interracial placement:** Permitted.

**Type of foster care and description of procedures:** Emergency, long-term, pre-adoptive and specialized foster care for youths between the ages of 7-18 yrs.

**Per diem stipend:** County and state funds: $1200/mo.

**Additional funds available:** Medicaid and semi-annual clothing allowance.

# OHIO

★ 1093 ★
**Beech Brook**
3737 Lander Rd.
Cleveland, OH 44124
Phone: (216) 831-2255

**Contact:** Carla A. Johnson-Travis, LISW, Director of Treatment Foster Care.

**Serves:** Residents of the Greater Cleveland area.

**Requirements:** Applicants must be at least 21 yrs. old and evidence financial stability.

**Description of children:** Children and youth between the ages of birth and 21 yrs. with severe emotional or medical needs.

**Licensing procedure:** 1) 30 hrs. of pre-service training; 2) criminal background checks; 3) home study; 4) inspections and examinations.

**Average length of time for licensing:** 6 mos. or less.

**Inspections:** 1) Fire; 2) medical clearances for all household members; 3) finger printing; 4) personal references. After placement, social worker visits weekly.

**Maximum number of children allowed in licensed foster care home:** 2-3.

**Interracial placement:** Not permitted.

**Type of foster care and description of procedures:** Emergency, long-term, pre-adoptive and therapeutic.

**Per diem stipend:** $13.40 to $15 plus an additional $7.50 for room and board and $5 for child's personal needs.

**Additional funds available:** Medicaid and clothing by custodial agency.

★ 1094 ★
**Berea Children's home and Family Services**
434 Eastland Rd.
Berea, OH 44017-2090
Phone: (216) 234-7501
Fax: (216) 234-0787

**Contact:** Michael G. Rhoades, Director.

**Serves:** Residents of Cuyahoga, Lake, Loraine and Summit counties.

**Requirements:** Applicants must be at least 21 yrs. old, have sufficient finances to meet basic needs and adequate space for a foster child.

**Description of children:** Children with special needs, i.e. emotionally disturbed, mentally retarded/developmentally disabled, HIV positive and children affected by prenatal maternal use of crack/cocaine.

**Licensing procedure:** 1) Interview phase; 2) orientation; 3) background checks and inspections.

**Average length of time for licensing:** 6 mos. or less.

**Inspections:** 1) Fire; 2) sanitation; 3) medical clearances for all household members; 4) personal references; 5) finger printing; 6) proof of automobile insurance. After placement, child's caseworker visits a minimum of twice monthly.

**Maximum number of children allowed in licensed foster care home:** 1 therapeutic foster placement; 2 medically fragile foster placements; or 2 treatment , foster placements.

**Interracial placement:** Permitted if same race placement is unavailable.

**Type of foster care and description of procedures:** Emergency, long-term, pre-adoptive and therapeutic.

**Per diem stipend:** $11/foster child and $15/foster parent.

**Additional funds available:** Medicaid.

★ 1095 ★
**Catholic Social Services of the Miami Valley**
922 W. Riverview Ave.
Dayton, OH 45407
Phone: (513) 223-7217
(800) 300-2937

**Branch address:**
1201 Fairington Dr., Sidney, OH 45365
Phone: (800) 300-2437

**Contact:** Mary L. Clark.

**Serves:** Auglaize, Champaign, Clark, Darke, Greene, Mercer, Miami, Montgomery, Preble and Shelby counties.

**Requirements:** Adults, 21 yrs. and older who can provide 3 personal references and a reference from their priest or minister, who meet the financial eligibility requirements and have sufficient home space.

**Description of children:** Primarily infants awaiting return to birthparents or adoptive placement (foster family is usually not eligible to adopt them). All races and some have special needs.

**Licensing procedure:**
1) Telephone inquiry;
2) initial screening and explanation of program;
3) complete home study and orientation;
4) compliance with Ohio Department of Human Services requirements for substitute care.

**Average length of time for licensing:** 2 mos.

**Inspections:**
1) Finger printing of foster parents;
2) fire;
3) medical examination for all household members;
4) water/well test if home is not on city water.
After placement social worker visits at least monthly.

**Maximum number of children allowed in licensed foster care home:** 6.

**Interracial placement:** Permitted.

**Type of foster care and description of procedures:** Short-term.

**Per diem stipend:** $7.50.

**Additional funds available:** Medicaid and mileage. Special board rate for children who are approved for SSI.

★ 1096 ★
**The Child Placement Professionals, Inc.**
231 N. Main St.
Ada, OH 45810
Phone: (419) 998-1561

**Contact:** Donna Holland, Executive Director.

**Serves:** Residents of Ohio.

**Requirements:** Applicants must be at least 21 yrs. old and be financially stable.

**Description of children:** Dependent children who have been abused and/or neglected or who are delinquent.

**Licensing procedure:** Send a letter of introduction and interest.

**Average length of time for licensing:** 6 mos. or less.

**Inspections:** 1) Fire; 2) medical examinations for all household members; 3) finger printing; 4) personal references. After approval child's caseworker visits from 6 to 24 times a year.

**Maximum number of children allowed in licensed foster care home:** 10.

**Interracial placement:** Permitted.

**Type of foster care and description of procedures:** Emergency, long-term and respite.

**Per diem stipend:** $15.

**Additional funds available:** Medical/dental.

★ 1097 ★
**Compassion, Inc.**
P.O. Box 270
Hayesville, OH 44838
Phone: (419) 368-6053

**Contact:** Dr. Ken Larimore, Executive Director.

**Serves:** Residents of central and north central Ohio.

**Requirements:** Applicants must be at least 21 yrs. old and be financially self-sufficient.

**Description of children:** Children who have been physically, and/or sexually, and/or emotionally abused and/or neglected.

**Licensing procedure:** Follows procedures set forth by the Ohio Department of Human Services. Therapeutic and specialized foster parenting requires additional training.

**Average length of time for licensing:** 6 mos. or less.

**Inspections:** 1) fire; 2) medical clearances for all household members; 3) finger printing; 4) personal references. After a child is in placement, child's caseworker visits at least twice a month.

**Maximum number of children allowed in licensed foster care home:** Traditional foster placements: 3-5; specialized foster placements: 2-3; therapeutic foster placements: 1.

**Interracial placement:** Permitted.

**Type of foster care and description of procedures:** Long-term, therapeutic and specialized.

**Per diem stipend:** Traditional: $16; specialized: $18.50; therapeutic: $22.

**Additional funds available:** Medicaid; clothing allowance: $1.50 per diem; transportation: $.26 per mile; allowance: $1 per diem.

★ 1098 ★
**Family Ties Therapeutic Foster Care**
**St. Joseph Orphanage**
5400 Edalbert Dr.
Cincinnati, OH 45239
Phone: (513) 741-5683

**Contact:** Deb Robison.

**Serves:** Residents of Butler, Clermont, Hamilton and Warren counties.

**Requirements:** Applicants must be at least 21 yrs. old who are financially able to meet their own needs and who have sufficient space for a foster child.

**Description of children:** Usually children who have been abused and/or neglected who have mental health, educational or social needs and severely emotionally disturbed youth.

**Licensing procedure:** 1) Intake meeting; 2) 25 hrs. of orientation classes; 3) homestudy process and background checks; 4) interviews and inspections. After a placement, child's caseworker visits biweekly.

**Average length of time for licensing:** 6 mos. or less.

**Inspections:** Medical clearances for all household members; personal references.

**Maximum number of children allowed in licensed foster care home:** Varies.

**Interracial placement:** Permitted.

**Type of foster care and description of procedures:** Long-term, therapeutic and occasionally emergency.

**Per diem stipend:** $32.

**Additional funds available:** Medicaid.

★ 1099 ★
**Focus on Youth, Inc.**
11258 Cornell Park Dr., No.609
Cincinnati, OH 45242
Phone: (513) 489-2325

**Contact:** William E. Macke, Executive Director.

**Serves:** Residents of southwest Ohio.

**Requirements:** Applicants must be at least 21 yrs. old.

**Description of children:** Children who are either handicapped or who have been abused and/or neglected.

**Licensing procedure:** 1) 30 hrs. of pre-licensing training; 2) background checks; 30 home study.

**Average length of time for licensing:** 6 mos. or less.

**Inspections:** 1) Fire; 2) sanitation; 3) medical clearances for all household members; 4) finger printing; 5) personal references. After placement, child's caseworker visits weekly.

**Maximum number of children allowed in licensed foster care home:** Each home is evaluated individually.

**Interracial placement:** Not permitted.

**Type of foster care and description of procedures:** Emergency, long-term, pre-adoptive and therapeutic.

**Per diem stipend:** Varies with child's age and level of care.

**Additional funds available:** Medicaid.

★ 1100 ★
**Homes for Kids, Inc.**
44 S. Main St.
Niles, OH 44446
Phone: (216) 544-8005

**Mailing address:**
   P.O. Box 683, Niles, OH 44446

**Contact:** Debbie Wilson, Executive Director.

**Serves:** Residents of Ohio.

**Requirements:** Applicants must be at least 21 yrs. old and financially capable of meeting their own obligations.

**Description of children:** Dependent children who have either been abused and/or neglected or who have developmental disabilities, other special needs or who are youthful offenders.

**Licensing procedure:** 1) Inquiry; 2) application; 3) home study; 4) orientation/training.

**Average length of time for licensing:** 6 mos. or less.

**Inspections:** 1) Fire; 2) home health and safety; 3) medical clearances for all household members; 4) finger printing; 5) personal references. After placement, child's caseworker visits between 24 and 30 times a year.

**Maximum number of children allowed in licensed foster care home:** 2 foster placements.

**Interracial placement:** Unavailable.

**Type of foster care and description of procedures:** Long term and therapeutic.

**Per diem stipend:** $22.

**Additional funds available:** Medicaid or payment by custody holder; funds for day care, respite or alternative care.

★ 1101 ★
**Kids Are Really Essential, Inc. (KARE, Inc.)**
3980 Philadelphia Dr.
Dayton, OH 45405
Phone: (513) 275-5715

**Contact:** Annette Smith, Director.

**Serves:** Residents of Ohio.

**Requirements:** Applicants must be at least 21 yrs. old and have sufficient income to meet their own needs.

**Description of children:** Dependent children who are either abused and/or neglected.

**Licensing procedure:** Unavailable.

**Average length of time for licensing:** 6 mos. or less.

**Inspections:** 1) Fire; 2) medical clearances for all household members; 3) finger printing; 4) personal references. After foster home is approved, social worker visits twice monthly.

**Maximum number of children allowed in licensed foster care home:** 3 children 5 yrs. or younger.

**Interracial placement:** Permitted.

**Type of foster care and description of procedures:** Emergency, long-term, pre-adoptive and therapeutic.

**Per diem stipend:** Unavailable.

**Additional funds available:** Medicaid and $50/mo. clothing.

★ 1102 ★
**The Marsh Foundation Teaching-Family Program**
1229 E. Ridge Rd.
Van Wert, OH 45891
Phone: (419) 238-1695

**Contact:** Dan Scott, Director of Children's Programs.

**Serves:** Residents of Ohio.

**Requirements:** Applicants must be financially able to meet their own needs and have sufficient home space to meet the Stare's licensing requirements.

**Description of children:** Children between the ages of 7 and 17 yrs. who are either emotionally disturbed, or physically and sexually abused, or juvenile delinquent.

**Licensing procedure:** 1) Application; 2) interview with Foster Care Coordinator; 3) home inspections; 4) back-ground checks; 5) training.

**Average length of time for licensing:** 6 mos. or less.

**Inspections:** 1) Fire; 2) sanitation; 3) medical clearances for all household members; 4) finger printing; 5) personal references. After licensing, social worker visits weekly.

**Maximum number of children allowed in licensed foster care home:** 2 foster children.

**Interracial placement:** Permitted, but not preferable.

**Type of foster care and description of procedures:** Therapeutic and occasionally pre-adoptive.

**Per diem stipend:** $30 - $32.50.

**Additional funds available:** Medicaid and clothing provided by custodial agency.

★ 1103 ★
**Mentor Clinical Care**
175 Montrose West Ave.
Akron, OH 44321
Phone: (216) 666-2022

**Branch address:**

5755 Granger Rd., Ste. 660, Independence, OH 44131

1515 Mahoning Ave., Ste.2, Youngstown, OH 44515

2800 W. Market Ave., Ste.11, Canton, OH 44857

269 W. Main, No. 107, Norwalk, OH 44857

**Contact:** Roxana Saad, Office Manager.

**Serves:** Residents of northeast Ohio.

**Requirements:** Applicants must be at least 21 yrs. old. Preferably one adult will be able to provide full-time child care.

**Description of children:** Children with emotional or behavioral or medical problems/disabilities.

**Licensing procedure:** 1) Home study; 2) family interviews; 3) medical and background checks; 4) orientation and training.

**Average length of time for licensing:** 6 mos. or less.

**Inspections:** 1) Fire; 2) sanitation; 3) medical clearances for all household members; 4) finger-printing; 5) personal references. After placement, child's caseworker visits weekly.

**Maximum number of children allowed in licensed foster care home:** 1 client per home.

**Interracial placement:** Permitted.

**Type of foster care and description of procedures:** Emergency, long-term and therapeutic.

**Per diem stipend:** $39.

**Additional funds available:** Medicaid and $350 annual clothing allowance.

★ 1104 ★
**Options for Youth, Inc.**
398 W. Bagley Rd., Ste. 14
Berea, OH 44017
Phone: (216) 234-3147

**Branch address:**

Independence Place 4807 Rockside Rd., Rm. 400, Independence, OH 44131

**Contact:** Michael D. Rush, LISW, Executive Director.

**Serves:** Residents within a 35 mile radius of downtown Cleveland, OH.

**Requirements:** Applicants must be over 21 yrs., able to cover their own living expenses and have at least 2 bedrooms. In some circumstances both foster parents may work full-time outside the home.

**Description of children:** Children who have been severely neglected; physically, sexually and/or emotionally abused; or who are mildly to moderately emotionally disturbed.

**Licensing procedure:** 1) 6 session orientation training; 2) home study; 3) documentation; 4) show willingness to learn new discipline techniques.

**Average length of time for licensing:** 6 mos. or less.

**Inspections:** 1) Fire; 2) medical clearances for all household members; 3) finger printing; 4) personal references. After a child is in placement, caseworker visits 40 -50 times annually.

**Maximum number of children allowed in licensed foster care home:** Usually 2 - 3 foster placements. 5 children is the maximum number allowed in a licensed foster home.

**Interracial placement:** Permitted, but final decision is up to custodial county.

**Type of foster care and description of procedures:** Emergency, long-term, pre-adoptive and specialized.

**Per diem stipend:** Range of $21.75 to $23.50.

**Additional funds available:** Medicaid and one-time clothing allowance of $200 to $300.

★ 1105 ★
**Paraclete Social Outreach, Inc.**
302 1/2 Conant St.
Maumee, OH 43537
Phone: (419) 893-4187

**Contact:** Richard C. Breiner, Director.

**Serves:** Residents of Northwest Ohio.

**Requirements:** Christians applicants who are either married or single, at least 21 yrs. old, and who are financially stable.

**Description of children:** Children with special needs because of neglect and/or physical, sexual, or emotional abuse.

**Licensing procedure:** 1) Reference checks; 2) police background check; 3) medical and home inspections; 4) pre-service training; 5) interviews.

**Average length of time for licensing:** 6 mos. or less.

**Inspections:** 1) Fire; 2) sanitation; 3) medical clearances for all household members; 4) finger printing; 5) 3 personal references.

**Maximum number of children allowed in licensed foster care home:** 5.

**Interracial placement:** Permitted.

**Type of foster care and description of procedures:** Long-term, pre-adoptive and therapeutic.

**Per diem stipend:** Range of $18 to $35.

**Additional funds available:** Medical/dental, some funds available for clothing and youth enrichment on a case-by-case basis.

★ 1106 ★
**Parenthesis Family Advocates**
2275 N. High St.
Columbus, OH 43201
Phone: (614) 299-9261

**Contact:** John Shannon, Executive Director.

**Serves:** Residents of Franklin and surrounding counties.

**Requirements:** Applicants must be at least 21 yrs. old and have sufficient income to meet their own needs.

**Description of children:** Children between the ages of 9 and 18 yrs. who have been abused and/or neglected; adolescent mothers; and children whose adoptions have been disrupted.

**Licensing procedure:** 1) Inquiry; 2) interviews; 3) licensing process.

**Average length of time for licensing:** 6 mos. or less.

**Inspections:** 1) Home safety; 2) medical clearances for all household members; 3) finger printing; 4) personal references. After licensing, social worker visits monthly.

**Maximum number of children allowed in licensed foster care home:** 2-3 average.

**Interracial placement:** Permitted when absolutely necessary.

**Type of foster care and description of procedures:** Emergency, long-term, pre-adoptive, therapeutic and respite.

**Per diem stipend:** $40 - $60.

**Additional funds available:** Medical and clothing allowance provided by the placing agency.

★ 1107 ★
**Rosemont Center**
2440 Dawnlight Ave.
Columbus, OH 43211
Phone: (614) 471-2626

**Contact:** Helen M. Kuzma, MSW, LSW, Foster Care Coordinator.

**Serves:** Residents of Franklin County.

**Requirements:** Applicants must be at least 21 yrs. old and meet financial eligibility criteria.

**Description of children:** Dependent children who have been abused and/or neglected. Most will be reunited with their birth families.

**Licensing procedure:** 1) Review program information; 2) application; 3) training; 4) licensing requirements; 5) autobiographical statement and panel discussion.

**Average length of time for licensing:** 6 mos. or less.

**Inspections:** 1) Fire; 2) medical clearances for all household members; 3) coliform, if well water; 4)fingerprinting 5) 3 personal references from non-relatives. After placement, child's case worker visits weekly.

**Maximum number of children allowed in licensed foster care home:** 2 treatment foster children.

**Interracial placement:** Permitted.

**Type of foster care and description of procedures:** Long-term and therapeutic.

**Per diem stipend:** $45.

**Additional funds available:** Medical/dental and initial clothing.

★ 1108 ★
**St. Anthony Villa**
2740 W. Central Ave.
Toledo, OH 43606
Phone: (419) 473-1353

**Branch address:**
   Boysville of Michigan, 8744 Clinton Macon Rd., Clinton, MI 49236

**Contact:** Charlie Johnson or Marcia Hull.

**Serves:** Northwest Ohio.

**Requirements:** Adults, 21 yrs. and older, who can provide personal references.

**Description of children:** Boys and girls between the ages of 8 and 17 yrs. who need a structured home treatment family because of abuse/neglect and/or behavioral problems. Boys and girls 16-18 needing independent living programming.

**Licensing procedure:**
1) Attend interview with foster care therapist;
2) attend 21 hrs. of training;
3) licensing approval;
4) medical, police and reference checks;
5) fire inspection.

**Average length of time for licensing:** Approx. 3-4 wks.

**Inspections:**
1) Fire;
2) medical examination for all household members;
3) sanitation, when required.
After placement social worker visits 2 to 3 times monthly.

**Maximum number of children allowed in licensed foster care home:** 4.

**Interracial placement:** If appropriate.

**Type of foster care and description of procedures:** Long-term and therapeutic/S.I.L.

**Per diem stipend:** Above average.

**Additional funds available:** Medical/dental, clothing allowance and transportation.

★ 1109 ★
**St. Joseph Children's Treatment Center**
650 St. Paul
Dayton, OH 45410
Phone: (513) 254-3562
(800) 955-HOME
Fax: (513) 254-6777

**Contact:** Sharon Bassett.

**Serves:** State of Ohio.

**Requirements:** Adults between the ages of 22 and 60 yrs. who can provide personal references and sufficient living space for a foster child.

**Description of children:** Children with mild to moderately severe emotional, behavioral and/or mental disturbances.

**Licensing procedure:**
1) Submit application;
2) attend interview;
3) complete 14 sessions of training;
4) undergo home study;
5) licensure by the Ohio Dept. of Human Services.

**Average length of time for licensing:** Several mos.

**Inspections:**
1) Fire;
2) medical examinations for all household members;
3) finger printing of foster parents.
After licensure, foster home is visited at least every other month and foster child is seen weekly in therapy.

**Maximum number of children allowed in licensed foster care home:** 6.

**Interracial placement:** Occasionally.

**Type of foster care and description of procedures:** Therapeutic and long-term.

**Per diem stipend:** $8000/yr.

**Additional funds available:** Medical/dental, clothing allowance and funds for mileage and respite care.

★ 1110 ★
**Specialized Alternatives For Families And Youth (S.A.F.Y.)**
10100 Elida Rd.
Delphos, OH 45833
Phone: (419) 695-8010
(800) 532-7239
Fax: (419) 695-0004

**Branch address:**
102 S. Pierce St., Delphos, OH 45833
Phone: (419) 695-5011

5640 Southwyck Blvd., Ste. 2-Z, Toledo, OH 43614
Phone: (419) 865-0071

720 W. North St., Lima, OH 45801
Phone: (419) 229-6653

113 N. Ohio Ave., Sidney, OH 45365
Phone: (513) 497-7238

4977 Northcutt Pl., Ste. 143, Dayton, OH 45414
Phone: (513) 497-7238

1201 30th St., Bldg. 2, Ste. 4-B, Canton, OH 44709
Phone: (216) 492-1172

1425 E. Dublin/Granville Rd., Ste. 114, Columbus, OH 43229
Phone: (614) 846-7239

10948 Reading Rd., Ste. 313, Cincinnati, OH 45241
Phone: (513) 563-8120

24340 Miles Rd., Ste. 203, Bedford Heights, OH 44128
Phone: (216) 595-1230

SAFY of Ft. Wayne, 2000 N. Wells St., Ft. Wayne, IN 46808
Phone: (219) 422-3672

P.O. Box 536, Pittsboro, IN 46167
Phone: (317) 829-4630

SAFY of Texas, 2225 E. Randall Mill Rd., Ste. 205, Arlington, TX 76011
Phone: (817) 652-0942

SAFY of South Carolina, 1900 Broad River Rd., Columbia, SC 29210
Phone: (803) 772-6411

SAFY of Nevada, 608 S. 9th St., Las Vegas, NV 89101
Phone: (702) 385-5331

**Contact:** Divisional Director.
**Serves:** Residents of Indiana, Nevada, Ohio, South Carolina and Texas.
**Requirements:** Applicants must be 21 yrs. or older.
**Description of children:** Dependent children who are abused and/or neglected; or medically fragile; or multi-handicapped; or at-risk youth.
**Licensing procedure:** 1) 30 hrs. of orientation; 2) training; 3) application; 4) home study.
**Average length of time for licensing:** 6 mos or less.
**Inspections:** 1) Fire; 2) medical clearances for all household members; 3) personal references; 4) finger printing; 5) occasionally, sanitation. After placement, child's caseworker visits weekly.

**Maximum number of children allowed in licensed foster care home:** 1 or 2.
**Interracial placement:** Permitted but used rarely.
**Type of foster care and description of procedures:** Emergency, long-term and therapeutic.
**Per diem stipend:** Range of $13 - $60.
**Additional funds available:** Medicaid.

★ 1111 ★
**Symbiont, Inc.**
29 W. Church St.
Newark, OH 43055
Phone: (614) 345-3862
Fax: (614) 345-4812

**Contact:** Judy Vela or John Ferguson.
**Description:** Private.
**Serves:** Central Ohio.
**Requirements:** Adults, 21 yrs. or older, who can provide 5 personal references and who meet financial eligibity requirement.
**Description of children:** Abused, neglected, dependent and court ordered.
**Licensing procedure:** As outlined by the Ohio Dept. of Human Services.
**Average length of time for licensing:** 6 wks. - 3 mos.
**Inspections:**
1) Fire;
2) sanitation;
3) police check of foster parents;
4) medical examination of all household members.
After placement, social worker visits foster home weekly.
**Maximum number of children allowed in licensed foster care home:** According to State guidelines.
**Interracial placement:** Permitted.
**Type of foster care and description of procedures:** Emergency, long-term, therapeutic and pre-adoptive.
**Per diem stipend:** Depends on individual child's needs.
**Additional funds available:** Medical/dental, clothing allowance, child's allowance and miscellaneous.

★ 1112 ★
**Youth Engaged for Success, Inc.**
3560 W. Siebenthaler Ave.
Dayton, OH 45406
Phone: (513) 275-0762
Fax: (513) 275-8431

**Contact:** Barbara Mitchell Boatwright.
**Serves:** Ohio.
**Requirements:** Requirements exist for age, marital status, liability insurance, financial eligibility and living space. Applicants must also provide personal references.
**Description of children:** Dependent children between the ages of 0 and 15 yrs. who have been abused/neglected and have severe behavior, emotional, physical and/or medical problems.
**Licensing procedure:**
1) Psychological assessment;
2) home investigation;
3) orientation
4) complete on-going training.
**Average length of time for licensing:** Within 45 days.

**Inspections:**
1) Fire;
2) medical examinations for all household members;
3) fingerprinting of foster parents.
After placement, social worker visits foster home weekly.

**Maximum number of children allowed in licensed foster care home:** 5 foster, 5 biological.

**Interracial placement:** Permitted.

**Type of foster care and description of procedures:** Emergency, long-term, pre-adoptive and therapeutic.

**Per diem stipend:** $29-$56.

**Additional funds available:** Referrants provide funds for medical/dental expenses and clothing allowance.

★ 1113 ★
**Youth Services Network of S.W.O., Inc.**
4124 Linden Ave., No. 112
Dayton, OH 45432
Phone: (513) 256-9113

**Contact:** Rita M. McManus, LPC.

**Serves:** Residents of the mid- and southwest regions of Ohio.

**Requirements:** Applicants must be at least 21 yrs. old and have sound and stable finances.

**Description of children:** Children between the ages of birth and 18 yrs. some of whom have been abused and/or neglected; and some of whom have learning disabilities and some of whom are in sibling groups.

**Licensing procedure:** 1) Orientation; 2) training; 3) licensure; 4) application; 5) recommendation by agency.

**Average length of time for licensing:** 6 mos. or less.

**Inspections:** 1) Fire; 2) medical clearances for all household members; 3) personal references; 4) finger printing; 5) occasionally, sanitation. After licensure, social worker usually visits bi-weekly.

**Maximum number of children allowed in licensed foster care home:** 5.

**Interracial placement:** Permitted.

**Type of foster care and description of procedures:** Emergency, long-term, pre-adoptive, special needs, exceptional needs and respite.

**Per diem stipend:** Varies with child's age and level of care.

**Additional funds available:** Medical/dental; initial clothing voucher; educational costs and other monies sometimes made available on a case by case basis.

# OKLAHOMA

★ 1114 ★
**Genesis Project**
Rt. 2 Box 237W
Jones, OK 73049
Phone: (405) 396-2942

**Contact:** Todd Madland, Director.

**Serves:** Residents of Oklahoma.

**Requirements:** Applicants must be at least 21 yrs. old and be self-supporting.

**Description of children:** Emotionally disturbed children.

**Licensing procedure:** 1) Application; 2) background checks and inspections; 3) home study.

**Average length of time for licensing:** 6 mos. or less.

**Inspections:** 1) Fire; 2) sanitation; 3) medical clearances for all household members; 4) personal references. After placement, child's caseworker visits twice monthly.

**Maximum number of children allowed in licensed foster care home:** 2.

**Interracial placement:** Permitted.

**Type of foster care and description of procedures:** Long-term and therapeutic.

**Per diem stipend:** $30.

**Additional funds available:** None.

★ 1115 ★
**Hillcrest Health Center**
**Therapeutic Foster Care**
5514 S. Western
Oklahoma City, OK 73109
Phone: (405) 634-5848

**Contact:** Bascom Lewis, Administrator.

**Serves:** Residents of the State of Oklahoma.

**Requirements:** Couples must be married, at least 21 yrs. old and present a positive financial position.

**Description of children:** Children with a variety of presenting problems who typically are in need of therapy and support above traditional foster care.

**Licensing procedure:** 1) Preservice training; 2) health screen and background checks; 3) home study; 4) reference checks.

**Average length of time for licensing:** 6 mos. or less.

**Inspections:** 1) Home safety; 2) medical clearances for all household members; 3) personal references; 4) sanitation. After placement. child's caseworker visits at least weekly.

**Maximum number of children allowed in licensed foster care home:** 5.

**Interracial placement:** Rarely permitted.

**Type of foster care and description of procedures:** Therapeutic.

**Per diem stipend:** $35.

**Additional funds available:** Title XIX.

★ 1116 ★
**Juvenile Services, Inc.**
P.O. Box 1363
Norman, OK 73070
Phone: (405) 364-1420

**Contact:** Deanna Hendricks, Extended Families Director.

**Serves:** Cleveland Co.

**Requirements:** Applicants must provide personal references; police background check and home visit.

**Description of children:** Children from birth to 18 yrs.

**Licensing procedure:**
1) File application;
2) complete orientation;
3) attend in-depth office interview;
4) complete home study;
5) receive background and police clearances;
6) forward letters of recommendation and health report;
7) evaluation; and
8) licensure.

**Average length of time for licensing:** 60 days.

**Inspections:** Medical examinations for all household members. After placement, social worker visits 2-3 times per wk.

Maximum number of children allowed in licensed foster care home: 5.

Interracial placement: Permitted.

Type of foster care and description of procedures: Emergency, short-term only.

Per diem stipend: $10.

Additional funds available: Emergency medical and necessities, e.g. diapers.

## ★ 1117 ★
**Northern Oklahoma Youth Service Center and Shelter, Inc.**
415 W. Grand
Ponca City, OK 74601
Phone: (405) 762-8341

Contact: James Carter, Director of Services.

Serves: North central Oklahoma.

Requirements: Applicants must provide 3 personal references and meet requirements for home size and financial eligibility.

Description of children: Children from birth to 18 yrs.

Licensing procedure:
1) Submit application;
2) forward copies of insurance policies, health reports and names of references;
3) complete training.

Average length of time for licensing: 2 mos.

Inspections:
1) Sanitation;
2) medical examinations for all household members.

Maximum number of children allowed in licensed foster care home: Depends on home.

Interracial placement: Permitted.

Type of foster care and description of procedures: Emergency.

Per diem stipend: $20.

Additional funds available: None.

## ★ 1118 ★
**Payne County Youth Services**
P.O. Box 921
Stillwater, OK 74076
Phone: (405) 377-3380

Contact: Christian Winter.

Serves: Residents of Payne County.

Requirements: Applicants must be at least 21 yrs. old, be financially self-sufficient and have adequate home size for a foster child.

Description of children: Children who are in the custody of the Department of Human Services.

Licensing procedure: 1) Application; 2) training; 3) certification.

Average length of time for licensing: 6 mos. or less.

Inspections: 1) Medical clearances for all household members; 2) personal references. After placement, child's caseworker visits twice a week.

Maximum number of children allowed in licensed foster care home: 2.

Interracial placement: Permitted.

Type of foster care and description of procedures: Therapeutic.

Per diem stipend: $30.

Additional funds available: Medical/dental.

## ★ 1119 ★
**Sunbeam Family Services**
616 N.W. 21st St.
Oklahoma City, OK 73103
Phone: (405) 528-7721

Contact: Karen Hope, Therapeutic Foster Care Program Director.

Serves: Metropolitan Oklahoma City.

Requirements: Adults, at least 21 yrs. or older, who are financially self-sufficient, can provide sufficient living space for a foster child and who can provide personal references.

Description of children: Emotionally and/or behaviorally disturbed between the ages of 0 and 18 yrs. Most children are entering foster care from a more restrictive setting, e.g psychiatric residential treatment center, group home, or have failed previous foster home placement(s).

Licensing procedure:
1) File application;
2) complete home study;
3) complete 30 hours of training. Home study includes financial and medical reports, family/individual interviews, and police checks.

Average length of time for licensing: 2 mos.

Inspections:
1) Medical examinations for all household members.
Foster child and parent are seen weekly. Home is visited monthly.

Maximum number of children allowed in licensed foster care home: 5. 1 or 2 is usual.

Interracial placement: Permitted.

Type of foster care and description of procedures: Long-term and therapeutic.

Per diem stipend: $900 per month.

Additional funds available: Medical/dental.

## ★ 1120 ★
**Tulsa Boys' Home**
P.O. Box 1101
Tulsa, OK 74101
Phone: (918) 245-0231
Fax: (918) 241-5031

Contact: Gary Goodrich.

Serves: Tulsa and surrounding area.

Requirements: Applicants must provide personal references and meet the requirements of age and home size.

Description of children: Adolescents between 12 and 16 yrs. with adjustment problems.

Licensing procedure:
1) Submit application;
2) complete home study;
3) visitation process with foster child before placement.

Average length of time for licensing: 1-3 mos.

Inspections:
1) Fire;
2) medical examinations for all household members;
3) finger printing of foster parents;
4) OSBI check.
After placement social worker visits monthly.

Maximum number of children allowed in licensed foster care home: 3.

**Interracial placement:** Permitted.
**Type of foster care and description of procedures:** Long-term and therapeutic.
**Per diem stipend:** $400/mo.
**Additional funds available:** Medical/dental.

★ 1121 ★
**Youth and Family Services of North Central Oklahoma**
2925 N. Midway
Enid, OK 73701
Phone: (405) 233-7220
Fax: (405) 237-7550

**Contact:** Alan R. Anderson, Director of Placement.
**Serves:** Residents of Garfield, Grant and Major counties.
**Requirements:** Applicants must be at least 21 years old and meet financial eligibility criteria.
**Description of children:** Children in the custody of the Department of Human Services.
**Licensing procedure:** 1) Application; 2) background checks; 3) training; 4) certification.
**Average length of time for licensing:** 6 mos. or less.
**Inspections:** 1) Fire; 2) medical clearances for all household members; 3) personal references. After placement, child's caseworker visits weekly.
**Maximum number of children allowed in licensed foster care home:** 2.
**Interracial placement:** State agency prefers same race placements.
**Type of foster care and description of procedures:** Long-term and therapeutic.
**Per diem stipend:** Custody; $30; non-custody; $20.
**Additional funds available:** Medicaid and one-time clothing allocation.

★ 1122 ★
**Youth and Family Services of Washington County**
2401 SE Nowata Pl., Ste. 101
Bartlesville, OK 74006
Phone: (918) 355-1111

**Contact:** Gary Nunley, Executive Director.
**Serves:** Residents of Nowata, Orange and Washington counties.
**Requirements:** Applicants must be at least 20 yrs. old, meet licensing standards for home size and demonstrate financial stability.
**Description of children:** Children with special needs whom the Department of Human Services has determined are in need of therapeutic foster care.
**Licensing procedure:** 1) Application; 2) home study; 3) training; 4) reference checks.
**Average length of time for licensing:** 6 mos. or less.
**Inspections:** 1) Medical clearances for all household members; 2) personal references. After placement, social worker visits 26 times a year.
**Maximum number of children allowed in licensed foster care home:** 2 therapeutic foster placements.
**Interracial placement:** Permitted.
**Type of foster care and description of procedures:** Therapeutic.
**Per diem stipend:** $30.

**Additional funds available:** Medicaid and one-time Department of Human Services clothing allowance.

# OREGON

★ 1123 ★
**Children's Services Division of Oregon**
500 Summer St., N.E.
Salem, OR 97301-1017
Phone: (503) 378-4153

**Branch address:**
P.O. Box 133, Davignon Hall, Marylhurst Campus, Marylhurst, OR 97036
Phone: (503) 653-3140

815 N.E. Davis, Portland, OR 97232
Phone: (503) 731-3410

555 N.W. 5th, Corvallis, OR 97330
Phone: (503) 757-4121

P.O. Box 416 (Mailing address), 818 Commercial St., Astoria, OR 97103
Phone: (503) 325-4811

P.O. Box 807, 2534 Sykes Rd., St. Helens, OR 97051
Phone: (503) 397-3292

119 N.E. 4th Ave., Rm. 5, Newport, OR 97365
Phone: (503) 265-8213

1400 Queen St., S.E., Ste. 201, Albany, OR 97321
Phone: (503) 967-2060

680 Cottage St., N.E.,, Salem, OR 97310
Phone: (503) 378-6800

3600 E. 3rd St., Tillamook, OR 97141
Phone: (503) 842-1233

P.O. Box 198, 288 E. Ellendale, Dalls, OR 97338
Phone: (503) 623-8118

5920 N.E. Ray Circle, Ste. 200, Hillsboro, OR 97124
Phone: (503) 648-8951

2200 Country Club Ct., Woodburn, OR 97071
Phone: (503) 982-9991

P.O. Box 478, 340 Kirby St., McMinnville, OR 97128
Phone: (503) 378-8611

P.O. Box 959, 465 Elrod, Coos Bay, OR 97420
Phone: (503) 269-5961

P.O. Box 887, 480 S. Ellensburg, Gold Beach, OR 97444
Phone: (503) 247-6666

1937 W. Harvard Blvd., Roseburg, OR 97470
Phone: (503) 440-3373

P.O. Box 1549, 909 Royal Ct., Medford, OR 97504
Phone: (503) 776-6120

P.O. Box 189, 725 N.E. 6th St., Grants Pass, OR 97526

Phone: (503) 474-3120

403 Pine St., Rm. 300, Klamath Falls, OR 97601
Phone: (503) 883-5570

105 N. "G" St., Lakeview, OR
Phone: (503) 947-2273

432 W. 11th, Eugene, OR 97401
Phone: (503) 686-7555

P.O. Box 345, 2630 Frontage Rd., Reedsport, OR 97467
Phone: (503) 440-3373

P.O. Box 597, 2200 4th St., Baker, OR 97814-0597
Phone: (503) 523-6423

225 E. 4th, Prineville, OR 97754
Phone: (503) 447-6207

P.O. Box 5247, 1001 S.W. Emkay Dr., Ste. E, Bend, OR 97702
Phone: (503) 388-6161

422 W. Main, John Day, OR 97845
Phone: (503) 575-0728

113 W. Jefferson St., Burns, OR 97720
Phone: (503) 573-2086

1050 N. 1st., Ste. 115, Hermiston, OR 97838
Phone: (503) 567-7611

910 Pacific Ave., Ste. 500, Hood River, OR 97031
Phone: (503) 386-2962

925 4th St., Madras, OR 97741
Phone: (503) 475-2292

P.O. Box 927, 2449 S.W. 4th Ave., Rm. 203, Ontario, OR 97914
Phone: (503) 889-9194

P.O. Box 498, 200 N. Main St., Boardman, OR 97818
Phone: (503) 481-9482

P.O. Box 96, 425 N. Washington St., Condon, OR 97823
Phone: (503) 384-4252

State Office Bldg., 700 S.E. Emigrant St., Ste. 200, Pendleton, OR 97801
Phone: (503) 276-9220

P.O. Box 1084, 1901 Adams Ave., LaGrande, OR 97850
Phone: (503) 963-8571

P.O. Box A, 502 S. River, Enterprise, OR 97828
Phone: (503) 426-4558

700 Union St., Rm. 230, The Dalles, OR 97058
Phone: (503) 298-5136

**Contact:** Monty McLaren, Foster Care Coordinator.

**Serves:** State of Oregon.

**Requirements:** Adults, 21 yrs. and older (Native Americans may be 18 yrs. or older) who have sufficient living space for a foster child, who can show evidence that they have sufficient income to meet their own family's needs and who can provide 4 personal references.

**Description of children:** Dependent, abused, neglected, emotionally disturbed, medically fragile and mentally retarded/developmentally delayed children.

**Licensing procedure:**
1) File application in county of residence;
2) provide references, criminal clearances and financial statement;
3) complete foster home certification study;
4) participate in at least 12 hr. foster parent training course.

**Average length of time for licensing:** 90 days.

**Inspections:** Health examinations are required for foster parents.
After placement, social worker visits at least monthly and foster parents are required to complete 10 hrs. of additional training per year.

**Maximum number of children allowed in licensed foster care home:** 5. If 6 or more, foster home must meet insurance, fire and building codes.

**Interracial placement:** Permitted.

**Type of foster care and description of procedures:** Emergency, long-term, therapeutic and pre-adoptive.

**Per diem stipend:** Monthly rates as follows:
Room & Board: 0-5 yrs.: $156; 6-13 yrs.: $174; 14-18 yrs.: $226.
Clothing replacement: 0-5 yrs.: $30; 6-13 yrs.: $33; 6-13 yrs.: $49.
Personal allowance: 0-5 yrs.: $6; 6-13 yrs.: $12; 14-18 yrs.: $18.
Personal incidentals: 0-5 yrs.: $12; 6-13 yrs.: $19; 14-18 yrs.: $29.

**Additional funds available:** Medical/dental.

★ 1124 ★
**Give Us This Day, Inc.**
5806 N. Albina St.
Portland, OR 97211
Phone: (503) 288-4335

**Mailing address:**
P.O. Box 11611, Portland, OR 97211

**Branch address:**
P.O. Box 796, Portland, OR 97211

**Contact:** O. Virginia Phillips, Ph.D., Program Director.

**Serves:** Residents of the State of Oregon.

**Requirements:** Open.

**Description of children:** Children of all races with special needs, some who are older, some who are in sibling groups.

**Licensing procedure:** 1) Attend classes; 2) home certification. Certification procedures will vary with the kind of foster placement sought.

**Average length of time for licensing:** Unavailable.

**Inspections:** 1) Fire; 2) sanitation; 3) medical clearances for all household members; 4) personal references. After certification, social worker visits monthly.

**Maximum number of children allowed in licensed foster care home:** Varies.

**Interracial placement:** Permitted.

**Type of foster care and description of procedures:** Long-term and pre-adoptive.

**Per diem stipend:** $400 - $500 per mo.

**Additional funds available:** Medical/dental, food allowance and $75/mo. clothing allowance.

# PENNSYLVANIA

★ 1125 ★
**Aldersgate Youth Service Bureau**
42 N. York Rd.
Willow Grove, PA 19090
Phone: (215) 657-4545

**Contact:** Pamela Bailey, Foster Care Coordinator.

**Serves:** Residents of Philadelphia and Buck and Montgomery counties.

**Requirements:** Applicants must be at least 21 yrs. old and married couples must be married a minimum of two years.

**Description of children:** Children between the ages of birth and 18 yrs.

**Licensing procedure:** 1) Application; 2) background checks; 3) home study; 4) training; 5) certification. Some foster placements require additional training.

**Average length of time for licensing:** 6 mos. or less.

**Inspections:** 1) Home health and safety; 2) medical clearances for all household members; 3) personal references; 4) fire, if more than 3 children are placed. After placement, social worker visits twice monthly.

**Maximum number of children allowed in licensed foster care home:** 6 children under the age of 18 yrs.

**Interracial placement:** Permitted with county approval.

**Type of foster care and description of procedures:** Emergency, long-term, therapeutic and pre-adoptive.

**Per diem stipend:** $12 - $20.

**Additional funds available:** Medicaid; mileage, parking, tolls and training; $200 - $300 annual clothing allowance; occasionally day care and camp programs.

★ 1126 ★
**Alternative Program Associates**
8620 Bricelyn St. Ext.
Pittsburgh, PA 15221
Phone: (412) 371-9300

**Branch address:**
6117 Broad St., Pittsburgh, PA 15206
Phone: (412) 362-9300

**Contact:** Lori DeRoch.

**Date established:** 1979.

**Description:** APA is licensed by the Pennsylvania Department of Public Welfare and contracts with Allegheny County Children and Youth Services, Allegheny County Juvenile Court and Westmoreland County's Children's Bureau.

**Serves:** Residents of Allegheny County.

**Requirements:** Foster parents must be at least 21 yrs. old and they must have enough living space to accommodate a foster child.

**Description of children:** Children from birth to 13 years with special emotional needs.

**Licensing procedure:** 1) Application; 2) home visits; 3) home inspection, criminal records and child abuse records checks, medical exams; 4) minimum of 6 hours of training which includes CPR/first aid as well as familiarization with agency policies and procedures.

**Average length of time for licensing:** 6 mos.

**Inspections:** Fire, sanitation, criminal records, medical examinations for all household members, reference and child abuse records' checks. After placement foster homes are visited 1-4 times a month.

**Maximum number of children allowed in licensed foster care home:** 6, but number of children placed in one home is based on each child's needs and each parent's abilities.

**Interracial placement:** Only for respite care.

**Type of foster care and description of procedures:** Long-term, emergency, pre-adoptive and special needs/medically challenged.

**Per diem stipend:** Varies with child's needs and age.

**Additional funds available:** Quarterly clothing allowance of $150. APA also provides professional case management; medical/dental services; psychological services; psychiatric consultation; educational placement and advocacy services; and additional specialized services for children's needs such as speech therapy and on-going interactive treatment planning and social services.

★ 1127 ★
**Best Nest, Inc.**
1335-37 Pine St.
Philadelphia, PA 19107
Phone: (215) 546-8060

**Contact:** Fred Weaver.

**Serves:** Residents of Philadelphia and surrounding suburbs.

**Requirements:** Open.

**Description of children:** Unavailable.

**Licensing procedure:** 1) Inquiry; 2) inspections and clearances; 3) home study.

**Average length of time for licensing:** Unavailable.

**Inspections:** 1) Fire; 2) medical clearances for all household members; 3) finger printing; 4) personal references. After placement, social worker visits twice monthly.

**Maximum number of children allowed in licensed foster care home:** 6 children under the age of 18 yrs.

**Interracial placement:** Unavailable.

**Type of foster care and description of procedures:** Emergency, short-term, long-term, therapeutic, pre-adoptive and respite.

**Per diem stipend:** Varies with child and level of care.

**Additional funds available:** Medical Assistance Card and $1/day clothing allowance.

★ 1128 ★
**Catholic Social Agency of Allentown**
928 Union Blvd.
Allentown, PA 18103
Phone: (610) 435-1541
Fax: (610) 435-4367

**Contact:** Lynne Shampain, ACSW.

**Serves:** Berks, Carbon, Lehigh, Northampton and Schuylkill counties. Member of Statewide Adoption Network (SWAN).

**Requirements:** Adults, 21 yrs. and older, who are either single or married, who are not on welfare, who have some religious affiliation and who can provide personal references. For placements of children younger than school age, one parent must be at home full-time.

**Description of children:** Infants, preschool sibling groups, school age children and adolescents.

**Licensing procedure:**
1) Initial inquiry;
2) return completed application packet;
3) attend Information Night;
4) participate in interview process and a home evaluation;
5) complete training.

**Average length of time for licensing:** Approx. 6 wks. for foster parenting, 3 mos. for adoption.

**Inspections:** Medical examinations are required for all household members. After placement, social worker visits at least monthly.

**Maximum number of children allowed in licensed foster care home:** 6 under the age of 18 yrs.

**Interracial placement:** Permitted.

**Type of foster care and description of procedures:** Emergency, long-term, pre-adoptive, therapeutic and pregnant teens.

**Per diem stipend:** $9-$36.

**Additional funds available:** Medical.

★ 1129 ★
**Children and Youth Services of Delaware County**
Front and Orange Sts.
Media, PA 19063
Phone: (215) 891-4800
Fax: (610) 891-0538

**Branch address:**
Chester Regional Office, 5th & Penn Sts., Chester, PA 19013
Phone: (610) 499-5000

**Contact:** Ann Hubben, MSW.

**Serves:** Delaware County.

**Requirements:** Adults, 25 yrs. and older, whose home has at least 2 bedrooms and adequate living space, who are self-supporting and who can provide 3 personal references. Each foster child must have his/her own bed and have space for belongings. After foster placement both parents cannot be employed full-time outside the home.

**Description of children:** Children from 0-18 yrs.

**Licensing procedure:**
1) Initial inquiry;
2) particiapte in orientation visit;
3) 2 home or a combination of home and office visits by homefinder to interview all household members;
4) attend 8 group sessions for pre-service training;
5) participate in foster care/adoptive parent meeting.

**Average length of time for licensing:** 1-2 or more months.

**Inspections:** Foster homes must comply with the written safety regulations of the Department of Public Welfare.
After the foster home is approved, it is reviewed annually by homeworker and visited as often as necessary by child's caseworker.

**Maximum number of children allowed in licensed foster care home:** 6.

**Interracial placement:** Prefer to place children in homes compatible with their own culture.

**Type of foster care and description of procedures:** Emergency, short and long-term, pre-adoptive.

**Per diem stipend:**
Ages 0 - 4 yrs.: $12;
5-11 yrs.: $12.25;
12-18 yrs.: $16.25.

**Additional funds available:** Medical/dental and clothing allowance.

★ 1130 ★
**Children's Services, Inc.**
311 S. Juniper St., Ste. 409
Philadelphia, PA 19107
Phone: (215) 546-3503

**Contact:** Deborah Rogers, Director of Programs.

**Serves:** Residents of Philadelphia.

**Requirements:** Applicants must be at least 21 yrs. old, have sufficient living space to accommodate a foster child and adequate income to meet their own needs.

**Description of children:** Primarily African American children from infancy to age 14, some in sibling groups.

**Licensing procedure:** 1) Application; 2) orientation; 3) home study; 4) references and background checks; 5) 4 hrs. initial training; 6) wait for placement. Additional training may be required for elevated levels of care.

**Average length of time for licensing:** Less than 6 mos.

**Inspections:** 1) Medical clearances for all household members; 2) personal references; 3) Child Abuse and Criminal History Records; 4) home health and safety. After placement, child's caseworker visits a minimum of bi-weekly.

**Maximum number of children allowed in licensed foster care home:** 6.

**Interracial placement:** Permitted.

**Type of foster care and description of procedures:** Long-term, pre-adoptive therapeutic, adolescent mother and child and fost-adopt.

**Per diem stipend:** $10.

**Additional funds available:** Medical/dental; initial wardrobe and bi-annual supplements; child's room improvements.

★ 1131 ★
**Harborcreek Youth Services**
5712 Iroquois Ave.
Harborcreek, PA 16421
Phone: (814) 899-7664

**Contact:** Kathy Zboyovski, Supervisor Specialized Foster Care.

**Serves:** Residents of central, north- and southwestern Pennsylvania.

**Requirements:** Applicants must be at least 21 yrs. old, meet the Department of Public Works guidelines for home size and be financially self-sufficient.

**Description of children:** Children between the ages of 8 and 18 yrs. who are delinquent or dependent.

**Licensing procedure:** 1) Inquiry; 2) interviews; 3) home study; 4) criminal background checks; 5) reference checks; 6) physicals; 7) in-service training; 8) psychological assessments, if necessary.

**Average length of time for licensing:** 6 mos. or less.

**Inspections:** 1) Medical clearances for all household members; 2) home health and safety; 3) Police background check; 4) personal references. After placement, child's caseworker visits a minimum of weekly.

**Maximum number of children allowed in licensed foster care home:** 3 foster placements and a maximum of 6 children in total.

**Interracial placement:** Not usually permitted.

**Type of foster care and description of procedures:** Long-term and therapeutic.

**Per diem stipend:** $15 - $18.

**Additional funds available:** Medical/dental, psychiatric and educational; initial clothing allowance; and other allocations considered on a case by case basis.

**★ 1132 ★**
**Luzerne County Children and Youth Agency**
111 N. Pennsylvania Blvd.
Wilkes-Barre, PA 18701
Phone: (717) 826-8710

**Branch address:**
Center Plazza Rm 11, 10 W. Chestnut St., Hazelton, PA 18201

**Contact:** Judith A. Newman, Supervisor.

**Serves:** Luzerne County.

**Requirements:** Adults, 21 yrs. and older who are financially stable and who can provide 6 personal references.

**Description of children:** Children from 0-18 yrs., many of whom have special needs.

**Licensing procedure:**
1) Attend 1.5 hrs. of orientation and a minimum of 12 hrs training;
2) complete home evaluation;
3) reference checks;
4) submit financial statements and medical report(s).

**Average length of time for licensing:** Approx. 1 1/2 months.

**Inspections:** Fire.
After placement, social worker visits foster home monthly.

**Maximum number of children allowed in licensed foster care home:** 6 under the age of 18.

**Interracial placement:** Permitted.

**Type of foster care and description of procedures:** Emergency, long-term, therapeutic, pre-adoptive and specialized (MH/MR).

**Per diem stipend:** $18 except specialized which is $20.

**Additional funds available:** Medical/dental, clothing allowance and foster child's allowance.

**★ 1133 ★**
**Monroe County Children and Youth Services**
14 N. 6th St.
Stroudsburg, PA 18360
Phone: (717) 420-3590
Fax: (717) 420-3597

**Contact:** Kathleen Donson.

**Serves:** Monroe County.

**Requirements:** Adults, 21 years or older who can provide personal references and who have sufficient financial resources to meet the needs of their household.

**Description of children:** Children from 0-18 yrs., most of whom are white and have emotional problems due to abuse. Some have special needs, e.g. developmental delay.

**Licensing procedure:**
1) Attend intitial office interview;
2) return completed questionnaire form;
3) Criminal Records check and Child Abuse Registry clearance;
4) return medical statement;
5) home evaluation;
6) participate in training;
7) meet with current foster parents;
8) sign agency/foster parent agreement.

**Average length of time for licensing:** 4-8 wks.

**Inspections:**
1) Fire;
2) sanitation (at time of home evaluation);
3) finger printing of foster parents (if not state residents for at least 1 yr.);
4) medical examinations for all household members.
After placement child's caseworker visits at least monthly.

**Maximum number of children allowed in licensed foster care home:** 6.

**Interracial placement:** Permitted.

**Type of foster care and description of procedures:** Emergency, long-term, pre-adoptive and therapeutic.

**Per diem stipend:**
Ages 0-12: $13.00;
ages 13-18: $15.00.

**Additional funds available:** Medical/dental, clothing allowance ($50/mo.), child's personal allowance, mileage and personal care items which are negotiable.

**★ 1134 ★**
**Montgomery County Office of Children and Youth**
Logan Square
1880 Markley St., 2nd Fl.
Norristown, PA 19401
Phone: (610) 278-5800
Fax: (610) 278-5898

**Contact:** Kathleen Sullivan, Supervisor.

**Description:** Public, county agency.

**Serves:** Montgomery County.

**Requirements:** Adults, 21 yrs. and older, whose home is large enough to accommodate foster child(ren) and who can provide 4 personal references.

**Description of children:** Males and females from birth to 18 or more yrs. of all races, most with special needs.

**Licensing procedure:**
1) Intake call;
2) attend orientation meeting;
3) participate in 5 training sessions;
4) checks, clearances and home visit.

**Average length of time for licensing:** 60 days.

**Inspections:**
1) Fire;
2) sanitation;
3) medical examinations for all household members;
4) State Police or if recent PA resident, FBI check (finger printing required).
After placement child's caseworker visits monthly and foster home worker annually.

**Maximum number of children allowed in licensed foster care home:** 6.

**Interracial placement:** Permitted.

**Type of foster care and description of procedures:** Emergency, long-term, pre-adoptive, therapeutic and special needs.

**Per diem stipend:**
1) Regular:
Ages 0-12 yrs.: $12.25;
13 or more yrs.: $15.25.
2) Shelter care:
Ages 0-12 yrs.: $18.25;
13 or more yrs.: $18.25.
3) Special needs:
Depending on level (3 levels) can be up to double regular rate.

**Additional funds available:** Medical/dental, $400/yr. clothing allowance, long distance telephone calls, prescriptions, graduation costs, mileage, and special requests, as needed.

★ 1135 ★
**Northeast Foster Care, Inc.**
111 N. Franklin St.
Wilkes-Barre, PA 18702
Phone: (717) 826-8961

**Contact:** Lou Palmeri or Judith Krieger.

**Serves:** Residents of Lucerne and Wyoming counties.

**Requirements:** Applicants must be at least 21 yrs. old. Preferably one parent will provide full-time childcare.

**Description of children:** Children between the ages of birth and 18 yrs.

**Licensing procedure:** 1) Application; 2) office visit; 3) home study and accompanying home visit; 4) reference checks; 5) foster parents' meetings.

**Average length of time for licensing:** 6 mos. or less.

**Inspections:** 1) Medical clearances for all household members; 2) personal references. After placement, social worker visits between 26 and 52 times a year.

**Maximum number of children allowed in licensed foster care home:** 5.

**Interracial placement:** Permitted.

**Type of foster care and description of procedures:** Emergency, long-term and pre-adoptive.

**Per diem stipend:** $19.

**Additional funds available:** Medicaid; $150 quarterly clothing allowance and $10/mo. child's allowance.

★ 1136 ★
**Pinebrook Services for Children and Youth**
1033 Sumner St.
Whitehall, PA 18052
Phone: (610) 432-3919
Fax: (610) 740-9550

**Contact:** Sally Sanders.

**Serves:** Residents of eastern Pennsylvania.

**Requirements:** Applicants must be at least 21.

**Description of children:** Children between the ages of birth and 18 yrs. who are either emotionally and/or behaviorally disturbed, mildly mentally retarded; or dependent and delinquent youth.

**Licensing procedure:** 1) Informational meeting; 2) application; 3) home study; 4) safety inspections; 5) pre-service training.

**Average length of time for licensing:** 6 mos. or less.

**Inspections:** 1) Medical clearances for all household members; 2) personal references. After placement, child's social worker visits at least every other week depending on child's needs.

**Maximum number of children allowed in licensed foster care home:** 6.

**Interracial placement:** Permitted.

**Type of foster care and description of procedures:** Long-term, therapeutic, pre-adoptive and specialized.

**Per diem stipend:** Varies with program from $14 to $30.

**Additional funds available:** Medicaid, clothing allowances and other allocations made available on a case by case basis.

★ 1137 ★
**The Salvation Army**
**Children's Services**
4050 Conshohochen Ave.
Philadelphia, PA 19131
Phone: (215) 877-7720

**Contact:** Florence Rhue, Director of Foster Care.

**Serves:** Residents of Southeastern Pennsylvania, the Lehigh Valley and Berks County.

**Requirements:** Applicants must be at least 21 yrs. old, have an independent source of income and a separate bedroom for the foster child.

**Description of children:** Children between the ages of birth and 18 yrs. who have a history of physical and/or sexual abuse, neglect or who have medical, developmental or behavioral problems.

**Licensing procedure:** 1) Orientation; 2) paperwork and background clearances; 3) references and health exam; 4) home study; 5) placement.

**Average length of time for licensing:** Less than 6 mos.

**Inspections:** 1) Medical clearances for all household members; 2) personal references; 3) background clearances. After placement, child's caseworker visits a minimum of twice a month.

**Maximum number of children allowed in licensed foster care home:** 6.

**Interracial placement:** Permitted.

**Type of foster care and description of procedures:** Emergency, long-term, therapeutic and pre-adoptive.

**Per diem stipend:** Depends on level of care. Range: $30 - $63. Foster Parent stipend: $12 - $18.

**Additional funds available:** Medical/dental; clothing allowance: $50/mo.; recreation: $1/day.

★ 1138 ★
**Try Again Homes Inc.**
365 Jefferson Ave.
Washington, PA 15301-4245
Phone: (412) 228-5475
(800)245-4453(in PA)
Fax: (412) 225-7210

**Mailing address:**
 P.O. Box 1228, Washington, PA 15301-4245
**Branch address:**
 18 N. Beeson Blvd., Ste. 210, Uniontown, PA 15401

 4001 College Pkwy., Parkersburg, PA 26101

 1800 Locust Ave., Fairmont, WV 26554

 812 Quarrier St., Ste. 204, Charleston, WV 25301

**Contact:** Margaret A. Antonelli, PA Foster Care Program Director; Alison Leon, WV Foster Care Program Director.

**Serves:** Residents of West Virginia and Fayette, Greene Washington and Westmoreland counties in Pennsylvania.

**Requirements:** Applicants must be at least 21 yrs. old, if married, at least 3 yrs., have sufficient income to meet their own needs and meet state requirements for living space.

**Description of children:** Children from birth to 18 yrs.

**Licensing procedure:** 1) Application; 2) background and reference checks; 3) interview and home evaluation; 4) 2nd interview; 5) pre-service training; 6) medical examinations.

**Average length of time for licensing:** 6 mos. or less.

**Inspections:** 1) Medical clearances for all household members 18 yrs. and older; 2) 6 personal references; 3) Child Protective Services check; 4) Department of Public Works check; 5) employer or school check; 6) State Police and Child Abuse History check; 7) home health and safety; 8) WV - fingerprinting. After placement, child's caseworker visits weekly.

**Maximum number of children allowed in licensed foster care home:** 3 foster plus 3 biological/adopted.

**Interracial placement:** Permitted.

**Type of foster care and description of procedures:** Emergency, long-term, pre-adoptive, therapeutic, adolescent pregnancy and comprehensive.

**Per diem stipend:** Varies with level of care.

**Additional funds available:** Medicaid or child's family insurance and clothing allowance at the discretion of the state of county agent.

★ 1139 ★
**Washington County Children and Youth Services**
502 Court House Square
Washington, PA 15301
Phone: (412) 228-6884
(800) 248-5245
Fax: (412) 228-6939

**Contact:** Laura Borish or John Patrick.
**Description:** Public, county agency.
**Serves:** Washington County.
**Requirements:** Adults, 21 yrs. and older, who are married, single or divorced, and who can provide personal references.
**Description of children:** Children from 0-18 yrs.
**Licensing procedure:**
 1) Initial inquiry;
 2) attend orientation;
 3) participate in training;
 4) complete foster care home study with checks and clearances.
**Average length of time for licensing:** Approx. 2 mos. Currently not completing adoptive home studies.
**Inspections:**
 1) Medical examinations for all household members;
 2) home inspection for fire, safety and sanitation hazards;
 3) law enforcement and child abuse clearances.
After placement social worker visits regularly.
**Maximum number of children allowed in licensed foster care home:** 3.
**Interracial placement:** Permitted.
**Type of foster care and description of procedures:** Emergency, long and short-term and pre-adoptive.
**Per diem stipend:** Varies with age and difficulty of placement.
**Additional funds available:** Medical/dental and miscellaneous, if required.

★ 1140 ★
**Westmoreland County Children's Bureau**
303 Courthouse Square
Greensburg, PA 15601
Phone: (412) 830-3300
Fax: (412) 830-3364

**Contact:** Foster Care/Placement Resource Coordinator.
**Serves:** Westmoreland County.
**Requirements:** Adults between the age of 21 and 55 yrs. who can provide personal references.

**Description of children:** Children from 0-18 yrs. with varied degrees of behavior problems, e.g. hyperactivity, acting out, bedwetting and behaviors resulting from sexual abuse.
**Licensing procedure:**
 1) Telephone intake and screening;
 2) return completed application;
 3) attend orientation meeting;
 4) undergo foster home study and inspections;
 5) complete family background study.
**Average length of time for licensing:** Approx. 2-3 mos.
**Inspections:**
 1) Home inspection by caseworker for fire, sanitation and/or safety hazards;
 2) criminal/child abuse clearances;
 3) medical examinations for all household members.
After approval social worker visits at least quarterly.
**Maximum number of children allowed in licensed foster care home:** 6.
**Interracial placement:** Permitted.
**Type of foster care and description of procedures:** Emergency, short and long-term and therapeutic.
**Per diem stipend:**
Ages 0-5 yrs.: $13;
ages 6-11 yrs.: $14;
ages 12-18 yrs.: $15.
**Additional funds available:** Medical/dental.

★ 1141 ★
**York County Children and Youth Services**
100 W. Market St., 4th Fl.
York, PA 17401
Phone: (717) 846-8496
(800) 729-9227
Fax: (717) 771-9884

**Branch address:**
 130 Carlisle St., Hanover, PA 17331
 Phone: (717) 633-7706

 4 Barlo Cir., P.O. Box 338, Dillsburg, PA 17019
 Phone: (717) 432-3095

**Contact:** Connie Sturm, Adoption Coordinator.
**Description:** Public, county agency.
**Serves:** York County.
**Requirements:** Adults, 21 yrs. and older, who are financially stable, have sufficient bed space for a foster/adoptive child and who can provide personal references.
**Description of children:** Children from 0 to 18 yrs. of all races, some with a wide range of problems.
**Licensing procedure:**
 1) Attend orientation;
 2) participate in pre-service preparation classes;
 3) complete a first aid class;
 4) background checks and inspections;
 5) undergo home study.
**Average length of time for licensing:** Approx. 3 mos.
**Inspections:**
 1) Medical examinations of foster parents;
 2) childline clearance (abuse/neglect);
 3) state police clearances;
 4) fire and safety home checks.
After placement social worker visits monthly.
**Maximum number of children allowed in licensed foster care home:** 6.

**Interracial placement:** Permitted but not desirable.

**Type of foster care and description of procedures:** Emergency and long-term.

**Per diem stipend:** $11.43-$15.67 depending upon age.

**Additional funds available:**
Special medical rate: $9/day extra;
special behavioral rate: $6/day extra;
medical/dental and miscellaneous, if required.

# RHODE ISLAND

**★1142★**
**Casey Family Services - Rhode Island Division**
250 Centerville Rd.
Warwick, RI 02886
Phone: (401) 738-7141

**Contact:** James R. Gannaway, Division Director.

**Serves:** Residents of Rhode Island.

**Requirements:** Applicants must be at least 21 yrs. old who are not on public assistance and who can provide a separate bedroom for a foster child.

**Description of children:** Children with special needs, emotional problems or attachment disorders.

**Licensing procedure:** 1) Inquiry; 2) follow-up Interest Sheet; 3) screening; 4) home study; 5) licensure.

**Average length of time for licensing:** 6 mos. or less.

**Inspections:** 1) Fire; 2) Medical clearances for all household members; 3) personal references. After placement, child's caseworker visits between 30 and 52 times a year.

**Maximum number of children allowed in licensed foster care home:** Approx. 5.

**Interracial placement:** In exceptional instances.

**Type of foster care and description of procedures:** Long-term and therapeutic.

**Per diem stipend:** $20.

**Additional funds available:** Medicaid and clothing allowance.

**★1143★**
**Department for Children and Their Families**
610 Mt. Pleasant Ave.
Providence, RI 02908
Phone: (401) 457-5306
Fax: (401) 457-4541

**Contact:** Rick Barry, Supervisor, Adoption Unit or Sandra M. Poirier, Licensing Administrator.

**Serves:** State of Rhode Island.

**Requirements:** Adults, 21 yrs. and older, who meet the requirements of home size and financial eligibility.

**Description of children:** Children from 0 to 18 yrs. (some exceptions for youth to age 21 yrs.).

**Licensing procedure:**
1) Initial inquiry;
2) complete clearance and inspections;
3) undergo home study;
4) home study resolution;
5) participate in pre-service training.

**Average length of time for licensing:** 4-6 wks.

**Inspections:**
1) Fire;
2) sanitation;

3) law enforcement and child abuse/neglect checks;
4) physician's reference.
After placement direct service social worker visits monthly.

**Maximum number of children allowed in licensed foster care home:** 8.

**Interracial placement:** Permitted.

**Type of foster care and description of procedures:** Emergency, short and long-term, and pre-adoptive.

**Per diem stipend:** Ages:
0 - 11 yrs.: $55/wk.;
12 yrs. and up: $68/wk.

**Additional funds available:** Medical/dental, some clothing allowance and miscellaneous.

**★1144★**
**Family Service, Inc.**
55 Hope St.
Providence, RI 02906
Phone: (401) 331-1350

**Contact:** Ellen Schaeffer, Manager of Foster Care Support Services.

**Serves:** Residents of Rhode Island.

**Requirements:** Applicants must be at least 21 yrs. old, who are financially stable and who have a sufficient number of bedrooms.

**Description of children:** Adolescent girls between the ages of 12 and 15 yrs.

**Licensing procedure:** 1) Agency inquiry; 2) application; 3) 8-10 hrs. of home study interviews; 4) 12 hrs. of training.

**Average length of time for licensing:** 6 mos. or less.

**Inspections:** 1) Fire; 2) medical clearances for all household members; 3) personal references. After placement social worker visits weekly.

**Maximum number of children allowed in licensed foster care home:** Assessed on a case by case basis.

**Interracial placement:** Permitted.

**Type of foster care and description of procedures:** Emergency, long-term, therapeutic and specialized.

**Per diem stipend:** $125/wk.

**Additional funds available:** Medicaid and $450 annual clothing allowance.

**★1145★**
**North American Family Institute**
648 Main St.
Warren, RI 02885
Phone: (401) 245-1174

**Contact:** Patricia A. Carter, Director.

**Serves:** Residents of Rhode Island.

**Requirements:** Applicants must be at least 21 yrs. old who have sufficient space to accommodate a foster child.

**Description of children:** Children who are in the custody of the Department of Children, Youth and Families.

**Licensing procedure:** 1) Home study; 2) background checks; 3) pre-service training; 4) licensure.

**Average length of time for licensing:** 6 mos. or less.

**Inspections:** 1) Fire; 2) sanitation; 3) medical clearances for all household members; 4) personal references; 5) Background Criminal Investigation check. After licensure, social worker visits a minimum of weekly.

**Maximum number of children allowed in licensed foster care home:** 2 foster.

**Interracial placement:** Permitted.

**Type of foster care and description of procedures:** Emergency and long-term.

**Per diem stipend:** $50.

**Additional funds available:** Medical/dental.

---

# SOUTH CAROLINA

**★ 1146 ★**
**South Carolina Department of Social Services**
P.O. Box 1520
Columbia, SC 29202-1520
Phone: (803) 734-5670
Fax: (803) 734-6285

**Contact:** County office.

**Serves:** State of South Carolina.

**Requirements:** Adults 21 yrs. and older who are age appropriate to the child placed, who can provide adequate living space for a foster child, including a separate bed and storage space, who have sufficient financial resources to cover the needs of their own family and who can provide 3 personal references.

**Description of children:** Children from birth to 18 yrs.

**Licensing procedure:**
1) Attend Intake Meeting;
2) participate in Orientation;
3) submit application;
4) complete group or individual study depending upon county procedures;
5) attend 10 hrs. of training.

**Average length of time for licensing:** Within 90 days.

**Inspections:**
1) Fire;
2) sanitation;
3) medical examinations of all household members;
4) state law enforcement check (discretionary).
After placement social worker visits monthly.

**Maximum number of children allowed in licensed foster care home:** 6.

**Interracial placement:** Permitted but not preferred.

**Type of foster care and description of procedures:** Emergency, short and long-term, pre-adoptive and therapeutic.

**Per diem stipend:**
Ages 0-5 yrs.: $5.07;
6-12 yrs.: $5.80;
13-18 yrs.: $7.53.

**Additional funds available:** Medicaid, EPSDST, yearly clothing allowance and mileage.

---

# SOUTH DAKOTA

**★ 1147 ★**
**South Dakota Department of Social Services**
**Child Protection Services**
700 Governors Dr.
Pierre, SD 57501-2291
Phone: (605) 773-3227
Fax: (605) 773-4855

**Contact:** David R. Hanson, Program Specialist.

**Serves:** State of South Dakota.

**Requirements:** Applicants must meet requirements of age and financial eligibility and provide personal references.

**Description of children:** Abused and/or neglected children.

**Licensing procedure:**
1) Initial inquiry;
2) participate in orientation training;
3) file application;
4) central registry, reference, and criminal record checks;
5) home visits;
6) physical examination with TB test and immunization records;
7) licensure.

**Average length of time for licensing:** Up to 120 days.

**Inspections:** Medical examination of foster parents.
After placement, foster home is visited by placement worker monthly and licensing worker 2-4 times a year.

**Maximum number of children allowed in licensed foster care home:** 6.

**Interracial placement:** Permitted.

**Type of foster care and description of procedures:** Emergency, long-term, pre-adoptive and therapeutic.

**Per diem stipend:**
1)Ages:
0-6 yrs.: $8.34;
7-14 yrs.: $10.24;
15-18 yrs.: $12.31.
2)Specialized (requires different training):
Ages 0-6 yrs.: $16.77;
7-11 yrs.: $18.49;
12-14 yrs.: $20.31;
15-18 yrs.: $21.92.
3)Emergency care: $16.58.

**Additional funds available:** Above ratios include incidental and clothing allowances.

---

# TENNESSEE

**★ 1148 ★**
**Family and Educational Advisory Associates**
2921 Harlin Dr.
Nashville, TN 37211
Phone: (615) 831-0020

**Contact:** Phil Trevathan, Supervisor.

**Serves:** State of Tennessee.

**Requirements:** Adults, 25 yrs. and older who can provide personal references and who have sufficient financial resources and living space.

**Description of children:** Adolescents from 16 to 18 yrs. who are working toward independent living skills.

**Licensing procedure:**
1) Submit application;
2) complete home study;
3) participate in individual and group training.

**Average length of time for licensing:** 1-2 mos.

**Inspections:**
1) Fire;
2) sanitation;
3) medical examinations for all household members.
After placement social worker visits weekly.

**Maximum number of children allowed in licensed foster care home:** 1 foster child and 3 biological/adopted children.

**Interracial placement:** Permitted if all parties agree.

**Type of foster care and description of procedures:** Long-term and therapeutic.

**Per diem stipend:** $300/mo. training stipend and $283/mo. room and board.

**Additional funds available:** Medicaid, clothing allowance and funds for teen's personal allowance and education.

# TEXAS

★ 1149 ★
**The Bair Foundation**
8800 Business Park Dr.
Austin, TX 78759
Phone: (512) 346-3555

**Contact:** Mary Ann Miller, Foster Home Secretary.

**Serves:** Residents of Region 7.

**Requirements:** Applicants must be at least 21 yrs. old, have sufficient living space to care for a child and enough income to meet their own expenses.

**Description of children:** Children with emotional and behavioral problems.

**Licensing procedure:** 1) Orientation; 2) paperwork; 3) home study; 4) criminal history check; 5) approval by director.

**Average length of time for licensing:** Less than 6 mos.

**Inspections:** 1) Fire; 2) sanitation; 3) criminal history check; 4) personal references.

**Maximum number of children allowed in licensed foster care home:** 12.

**Interracial placement:** Permitted.

**Type of foster care and description of procedures:** Emergency, long-term and therapeutic.

**Per diem stipend:** $12.84 - $35.54 depending upon the level of care.

**Additional funds available:** Medicare.

★ 1150 ★
**Cherokee Home for Children**
P.O. Box 295
Cherokee, TX 76832
Phone: (915) 622-4201

**Contact:** Bob Sisk, Director of Child Placing.

**Serves:** Residents of Texas.

**Requirements:** Church of Christ married couples who are at least 21 yrs. old and who can fill the state requirements for home space. If younger children are placed, one parent must not be employed full-time outside the home.

**Description of children:** Children in need of care.

**Licensing procedure:** 1) Application; 2) home visit; 3) home inspections.

**Average length of time for licensing:** 6 mos. or less.

**Inspections:** 1) Fire Department inspection; 2) Sanitation Department inspection; 3) medical clearances for all household members; 4) personal references. After approval, foster home is visited at least quarterly.

**Maximum number of children allowed in licensed foster care home:** 5.

**Interracial placement:** Permitted.

**Type of foster care and description of procedures:** Emergency, long-term and pre-adoptive.

**Per diem stipend:** Varies with child and level of care.

**Additional funds available:** Medical/dental and clothing allowance.

★ 1151 ★
**Christian Services of East Texas**
807 W. Glenwood
Tyler, TX 75701
Phone: (903) 592-3850
Fax: (903) 592-1404

**Contact:** Sally Miller, Caseworker.

**Serves:** Residents of 36 counties in northeast Texas.

**Requirements:** Church of Christ applicants between the ages of 21 and 70 yrs. who have sufficient finances to meet their own needs apart from the foster stipend and who have sufficient living space to meet minimum standard. Married couples are preferred with one parent available to provide full-time childcare.

**Description of children:** Children of all races between the ages of birth and 17 yrs. with limited behavioral and/or medical problems.

**Licensing procedure:** 1) Orientation; 2) application; 3) reference checks; 4) inspections; 5) home study; 6) pre-service training.

**Average length of time for licensing:** 6 mos. or less.

**Inspections:** 1) Fire; 2) sanitation; 3) medical clearances for all household members including TB test; 4) personal references. After placement, social worker visits quarterly.

**Maximum number of children allowed in licensed foster care home:** 6.

**Interracial placement:** Permitted.

**Type of foster care and description of procedures:** Emergency, short-term and pre-adoptive.

**Per diem stipend:** $11.

**Additional funds available:** Medical/dental and clothing reimbursement.

★ 1152 ★
**Coastal Bend Youth City**
2547 U.S. Hwy 77
Driscoll, TX 78351
Phone: (512) 387-4513

**Mailing address:**
  P.O. Box 268, Driscoll, TX 78351

**Branch address:**
  P.O. Box 927, Corpus Christi, TX 78403
  Phone: (512) 882-2171

**Contact:** Brenda Cantu, Director of Foster Care; Pam Cox, Director of Public Relations; Michael Sparks, Director of Children's Services.

**Serves:** Residents within a 60 mi. radius of Driscoll.

**Requirements:** Emotionally mature married couples who can provide 40 sq. ft. of living space per foster child.

**Description of children:** Children between the ages of 10 and 17 yrs. who are in need of a healthy home environment.

**Licensing procedure:** 1) 30 hrs. of training; 2) application; 3) reference checks; 4) criminal background checks; 5) TB test; 6) CPR and First Aid certification; 7) home inspections; 8) home plan sketch; 9) home study; 10) placement agreement.

**Average length of time for licensing:** 6 mos. or less.

**Inspections:** 1) Fire; 2) sanitation; 3) TB test; 4) 3 personal references; 5) proof of pet vaccination; 6) criminal background check. After placement agreement is signed, social worker visits quarterly.

**Maximum number of children allowed in licensed foster care home:** 5.

**Interracial placement:** Unavailable.

**Type of foster care and description of procedures:** Long-term and therapeutic.

**Per diem stipend:** $600/mo.

**Additional funds available:** Medicaid and other allocations made on a case by case basis.

★ 1153 ★
**Deep East Texas Mental Health/Mental Retardation Center**
4101 S. Medford Dr.
Lufkin, TX 75901
Phone: (409) 639-1411
Fax: (409) 639-5837

**Contact:** Foster care coordinator.

**Serves:** 13 counties of East Texas.

**Requirements:** Applicants must provide personal references and meet the requirements for age, home size and financial eligibility. While a child is in placement one parent must be at home full-time.

**Description of children:** Children who are mentally retarded and/or developmentally delayed.

**Licensing procedure:**
1) Initial inquiry;
2) submit application;
3) complete home study and inspections;
4) attend training.

**Average length of time for licensing:** 1-2 mos.

**Inspections:**
1) Fire;
2) sanitation;
3) medical examinations of foster parents.
After approval, social worker visits at least quarterly.

**Maximum number of children allowed in licensed foster care home:** 3.

**Interracial placement:** Permitted.

**Type of foster care and description of procedures:** Long-term.

**Per diem stipend:** $600/mo.

**Additional funds available:** Medicare/Medicaid and occasionally clothing.

★ 1154 ★
**Harmony Family Services**
P.O. Box 329
Abilene, TX 79604
Phone: (915) 672-8820

**Contact:** Doug Worthington.

**Serves:** Abilene.

**Requirements:** Applicants must provide personal references, an extra bedroom and at least one parent must have a job flexible enough to provide adequate supervision.

**Description of children:** Runaways and truants.

**Licensing procedure:**
1) Initial inquiry;

2) submit application;
3) home inspections;
4) complete home study;
5) participate in training.

**Average length of time for licensing:** 4-6 wks.

**Inspections:**
1) Fire;
2) sanitation.
After approval social worker visits quarterly.

**Maximum number of children allowed in licensed foster care home:** 4 (2 is typical).

**Interracial placement:** Permitted.

**Type of foster care and description of procedures:** Emergency and long-term.

**Per diem stipend:** $10.

**Additional funds available:** Miscellaneous.

★ 1155 ★
**Hendrick Home for Children**
P.O. Box 5195
Abilene, TX 79608
Phone: (915) 692-0112
Fax: (915) 692-6813

**Contact:** David Miller, President.

**Serves:** Primarily 100 mi. radius of Abilene.

**Requirements:** Applicants must provide personal references and meet the requirements for home size and marital status.

**Description of children:** Dependent children and children who have been neglected.

**Licensing procedure:**
1) Submit application with references;
2) all family members present for home visit;
3) attend individual foster parent interviews;
4) home inspections.

**Average length of time for licensing:** Approx. 30 days.

**Inspections:**
1) Fire;
2) sanitation.
After approval social worker visits quarterly.

**Maximum number of children allowed in licensed foster care home:** 6.

**Interracial placement:** Permitted.

**Type of foster care and description of procedures:** Emergency and long-term.

**Per diem stipend:**
Ages 0-12 yrs.: $7;
13 yrs. or older: $8.

**Additional funds available:** Medical/dental and clothing allowance.

★ 1156 ★
**High Plains Children's Home & Family Services, Inc.**
1501 W. 58th
Amarillo, TX 79114
Phone: (806) 355-6588

**Mailing address:**
  P.O. Box 7448, Amarillo, TX 79114

**Contact:** Lola W. Brownlee, M.Ed.

**Serves:** Residents of Texas.

**Requirements:** Applicants must be at least 21 yrs. old, members of the Church of Christ, have at least 2 bedrooms and have sufficient income to provide for a child.

**Description of children:** Infants and children to 2 yrs.

**Licensing procedure:** 1) Application; 2) references and Criminal Background checks; 3) home study; 4) agency approval; 5) licensure by Texas Department of Protective and Regulatory Services.

**Average length of time for licensing:** Less than 6 mos.

**Inspections:** 1) Personal references; 2) fire; 3) sanitation. After placement child's caseworker visits at least monthly.

**Maximum number of children allowed in licensed foster care home:** Varies with child and family.

**Interracial placement:** Permitted.

**Type of foster care and description of procedures:** Long-term and pre-adoptive.

**Per diem stipend:** None.

**Additional funds available:** Medical/dental.

★1157★
**Joy Home for Boys**
**P.A.T.H.**
1303 B. S. Washington
Kaufman, TX 75142
Phone: (214) 932-1400
(800) 446-9555

**Branch address:**
P.O. Box 550, Greenwood, LA 71033
Phone: (318) 938-5365

**Contact:** R. Scudder, Executive Director.

**Serves:** Residents of Louisiana and Texas.

**Requirements:** Applicants must be at least 30 yrs. old, be financially self-sufficient and have at least 2 bedrooms.

**Description of children:** Children in need of care.

**Licensing procedure:** 1) Inquiry; 2) application; 2) 40 -50 hrs. training; 3) home study.

**Average length of time for licensing:** 6 mos. or less.

**Inspections:** 1) Fire; 2) sanitation; 3) medical clearances for all household members; 4) finger printing; 5) personal references. After placement, child's caseworker visits weekly.

**Maximum number of children allowed in licensed foster care home:** 4.

**Interracial placement:** Permitted under certain circumstances.

**Type of foster care and description of procedures:** Long-term and therapeutic.

**Per diem stipend:** Varies.

**Additional funds available:** Medical/dental; food and clothing allowances.

★1158★
**Therapeutic Family Life**
1106 Clayton Ln., Ste. 490E
Austin, TX 78723
Phone: (512) 451-7310

**Branch address:**
Dallas-Ft. Worth Office 1301 S. Bowen Rd., Arlington, TX 76013

**Contact:** Bill Booker.

**Serves:** Residents of Texas.

**Requirements:** Applicants must be at least 21 yrs. old.

**Description of children:** Children of all ages and races who have been removed from their homes.

**Licensing procedure:** 1) 15 hrs. initial training; 2) application process; 3) background checks and inspections; 4) home study.

**Average length of time for licensing:** 6 mos. or less.

**Inspections:** 1) Fire; 2) sanitation; 3) TB tests for all household members; 4) criminal background checks; 5) personal references. After approval, social worker visits foster home several times a year.

**Maximum number of children allowed in licensed foster care home:** 12.

**Interracial placement:** Permitted.

**Type of foster care and description of procedures:** Emergency, long-term and therapeutic.

**Per diem stipend:** Unavailable.

**Additional funds available:** Medicaid; clothing allowance; mileage.

# UTAH

★1159★
**Utah State Department of Human Services**
120 N. 200 West
Salt Lake City, UT 84103
Phone: (801) 538-4100
Fax: (801) 538-4334

**Contact:** S. Roland Oliver, Program Specialist.

**Serves:** State of Utah.

**Requirements:** Adults, 21 yrs. and older who can provide personal references.

**Description of children:** Special needs children who have been abused, neglected, and/or abandoned, and mentally and/or physically handicapped children.

**Licensing procedure:**
1) File application;
2) complete home study;
3) complete 30 hrs. of training.

**Average length of time for licensing:** 30-60 days.

**Inspections:** Medical examinations and background checks of adult household members are required.

**Maximum number of children allowed in licensed foster care home:** Total of 6 children with no more than 4 foster children.

**Interracial placement:** Permitted.

**Type of foster care and description of procedures:** Emergency, basic, specialized, structured long-term and pre-adoptive. All foster homes are required to go through the licensing and training process. Homes are licensed across the state within each local area. Adoptive homes go through the same process in order to be approved for adoptive placements.

**Per diem stipend:** $10 to $25.

**Additional funds available:** Medicaid, clothing allowance, transportation and special needs.

# VERMONT

★ 1160 ★
**Casey Family Services**
**Vermont Division**
7 Palmer Ct.
White River Junction, VT 05001
Phone: (802) 649-1400
Fax: (802) 649-2351

**Contact:** Sara L. Kobylenski, ACSW, Division Director; Judith Bush, ACSW, Post Adoption Services.

**Description:** Permanency planning agency which is part of a national network of private child welfare agencies funded by the Annie E. Casey Foundation. Planned long-term placement of children in foster families when this is the best possible plan and post adoption services are the key programs in Vermont.

**Serves:** Vermont and New Hampshire families may receive post adoption services. Families within a 1 hr. radius can become foster families.

**Requirements:** Adults, 21 yrs. and older, who can provide personal references and who can sustain themselves financially may become foster parents.

**Description of children:** Children between the ages of 5 and 13 yrs. who are dealing with serious emotional issues may be placed in foster care. Any adopted child may receive post adoptive services.

**Licensing procedure:**
1) Telephone inquiry;
2) attend screening meeting;
3) participate in orientation workshops;
4) complete home study;
5) child matching and licensure approval;
6) pre-placement process;
7) placement.

**Average length of time for licensing:** Minimum of 4 mos.

**Inspections:**
1) Fire;
2) sanitation;
3) medical examinations for all household members.
After placement social worker visits a minimum of 12 times a year and as often as daily, if necessary.

**Maximum number of children allowed in licensed foster care home:** Follows state guidelines of New Hampshire and Vermont.

**Interracial placement:** Permitted.

**Type of foster care and description of procedures:** Long-term.

**Per diem stipend:** Unavailable.

**Additional funds available:** Medical/dental, clothing allowance and other as needed.

★ 1161 ★
**Family Life Services of New England**
72 Main St.
Vergennes, VT 05491
Phone: (802) 877-3166
(800) 639-0133
Fax: (802) 877-3193

**Contact:** Stephen G. Berry, Executive Director.
**Serves:** State of Vermont.

**Requirements:** Christian adults, 18 yrs. and older, who are either single or married and who can provide personal references.

**Description of children:** Children from 0 - 18 yrs.

**Licensing procedure:**
1) Initial inquiry;
2) attend 32 hr. pre-service training program.

**Average length of time for licensing:** 2-3 mos.

**Inspections:** Fire inspection required.
After placement, social worker visits a minimum of once, usually twice per month.

**Maximum number of children allowed in licensed foster care home:** 6.

**Interracial placement:** Permitted.

**Type of foster care and description of procedures:** Emergency, long-term and therapeutic.

**Per diem stipend:** $403-$620/mo. plus $1/mo. per child respite fund.

**Additional funds available:** Medical/dental.

# VIRGINIA

★ 1162 ★
**Carpe Diem of Virginia, Inc.**
4016 Raintree Rd., Ste. 200-A
Chesapeake, VA 23321
Phone: (804) 465-7234

**Contact:** John C. Faircloth, ACSW, Executive Director.

**Serves:** Residents of Greater Hapton Roads, VA.

**Requirements:** Applicants must be at least 25 yrs. old, have sufficient income to meet their own needs and sufficient space for a foster child.

**Description of children:** Children with severe physical disabilities, emotional problems and acting-out behavior; or who are terminally ill.

**Licensing procedure:** 1) Application phase; 2) 6 wks. of training; 3) home study; 4) background checks; 5) home visits; 6) reference checks.

**Average length of time for licensing:** 6 mos. or less.

**Inspections:** 1) Fire; 2) sanitation; 3) medical clearances for all household members; 4) personal and employment references; 5) criminal background check. After placement, child's case-worker visits a minimum of weekly.

**Maximum number of children allowed in licensed foster care home:** 4, but usually no more than one foster placement.

**Interracial placement:** Permitted.

**Type of foster care and description of procedures:** Long-term and therapeutic.

**Per diem stipend:** $13; $17 for ill or disabled children plus $379/mo.

**Additional funds available:** $300 annual clothing allowance.

★ 1163 ★
**Northern Virginia Family Service**
100 N. Washington St., Ste. 400
Falls Church, VA 22046
Phone: (703) 533-9727
Fax: (703) 241-1310

**Branch address:**
3321 Duke St., Alexandria, VA 22314-4597

Phone: (703) 370-3223

5622 Columbia Pike, No. 207, Fall Church, VA 22041
Phone: (703) 845-9333

14377 Hereford Rd., Dale City, VA 22193-2107
Phone: (703) 680-9358

106 Elden St., Ste. 14, Herndon, VA 22070-4809
Phone: (703) 689-0208

South Lakes High School,
Phone: (703) 476-5270 x247

Herndon High School,
Phone: (703) 437-6800 x253

P.O. Box 2277, Leesburg, VA 22075-7611
Phone: (703) 771-2595

**Contact:** Sarah Eggleston, Program Manager, Intensive Family Services.

**Serves:** Residents of northern Virginia.

**Requirements:** Applicants must be at least 21 yrs. old, able to meet state space requirements and be self-supporting.

**Description of children:** Children between the ages of infancy and 16 yrs. who have emotional, social, mental or physical special needs.

**Licensing procedure:** 1) Training; 2) inspections and checks; 3) home study.

**Average length of time for licensing:** 6 mos. or less.

**Inspections:** 1) Home health and safety; 2) finger printing; 3) medical clearances for all household members; 4) personal references. After placement, child's caseworker visits at least monthly.

**Maximum number of children allowed in licensed foster care home:** 8.

**Interracial placement:** Permitted.

**Type of foster care and description of procedures:** Long-term and therapeutic.

**Per diem stipend:** $16.50 plus room and board ranging from $256 - $379.

**Additional funds available:** Medicaid and $300 annual clothing allowance.

★ 1164 ★
**People Places, Inc.**
1215 N. Augusta St.
Staunton, VA 24401
Phone: (703) 885-8841
Fax: (703) 886-6379

**Contact:** Pat Campbell.

**Serves:** Virginia.

**Requirements:** Prefer adults over the age of 25 yrs. who are either single, married or divorced, who can provide adequate living space, who meet the financial eligibility requirements and who can provide 6 personal references.

**Description of children:** Behaviorally disordered, emotionally disturbed youth who are sometimes victims of abuse.

**Licensing procedure:**
1) Complete Parenting Skills training;
2) file application;
3) participate in 2 interviews.

**Average length of time for licensing:** 6-8 wks.

**Inspections:**
1) Sanitation;
2) medical examinations for all household members;
3) criminal records check and child protective services check. After placement, caseworker visits twice monthly.

**Maximum number of children allowed in licensed foster care home:** 2 except for sibling groups.

**Interracial placement:** Permitted.

**Type of foster care and description of procedures:** Emergency, long-term and therapeutic.

**Per diem stipend:** $20.

**Additional funds available:** Medicaid, clothing allowance, child's personal allowance and behavior management expenses.

★ 1165 ★
**Virginia Department of Social Services**
730 E. Broad St.
Richmond, VA 23219-1849
Phone: (804) 692-1290
(800) DO-ADOPT
Fax: (804) 692-1284

**Contact:** Brenda Kerr.

**Description:** Public, state agency.

**Serves:** State of Virginia.

**Requirements:** Adults, 18 yrs. and older, who can provide personal references, and who are not dependent upon adoption assistance for their own financial needs.

**Description of children:** 50% of children placed are abused and/or neglected.

**Licensing procedure:**
1) Attend orientation meeting;
2) submit application;
3) participate in adoptive parent training;
4) complete home study.

**Average length of time for licensing:** Varies.

**Inspections:**
1) Working smoke alarms;
2) criminal background checks;
3) medical examinations;
4) no attic or basement bedrooms without outside access;
5) Child Protective Services records checks.
After placement social worker visits quarterly until adoption finalization.

**Maximum number of children allowed in licensed foster care home:** 4 per adult.

**Interracial placement:** Permitted but not encouraged.

**Type of foster care and description of procedures:** Emergency, short and long-term, pre-adoptive, therapeutic and Independent Living Program.

**Per diem stipend:**
Ages 0-4 yrs.: $228/mo.
Ages 5-12 yrs.: $267/mo.
Ages 13 yrs. or older: $337/mo.

**Additional funds available:** Medicaid, initial clothing allowance with annual replacement.

# WASHINGTON

**★ 1166 ★**
**NAK NU WE SHA**
P.O. Box 151
Toppenish, WA 98948
Phone: (509) 865-5121 x495

**Contact:** Elizabeth R. Red Bear, Program Manager.

**Serves:** Residents of south central Washington.

**Requirements:** Applicants must be at least 18 yrs. old and have sufficient living space to safely accommodate themselves and a foster child.

**Description of children:** Children between the ages of birth and 18 yrs.

**Licensing procedure:** 1) 12 hrs. of pre-service orientation; 2) inspections and background checks; 3) CPR and First Aid certification; 4) home study; 5) site check.

**Average length of time for licensing:** 6 mos. or less.

**Inspections:** 1) TB tests for all household members; 2) 3 personal references; 3) HIV/AIDS cards; 4) smoke detectors and fire extinguisher check; 5) Criminal History check; 6) current driver's license and automobile insurance.

**Maximum number of children allowed in licensed foster care home:** 6 for a married couple and 4 for a single parent.

**Interracial placement:** Permitted.

**Type of foster care and description of procedures:** Emergency, long-term and pre-adoptive.

**Per diem stipend:** Varies with level of care.

**Additional funds available:** Medical coupons and Tribal Insurance; $40/mo. clothing allowance; $12/mo. incidental allowance.

**★ 1167 ★**
**Rainbow Youth and Family Services**
1606 E. 31st St.
Tacoma, WA 98404-4911
Phone: (206) 572-7741
(800) 6 RED HEN
Fax: (206) 572-5621

**Branch address:**
    Seattle,
    Phone: (206) 838-2809

    Olympia,
    Phone: (206) 352-8955

    Bremerton,
    Phone: (206) 373-3032

**Contact:** Ramona Bennet, Director or Elaine Fiddler, Licensing Social Worker.

**Serves:** Residents of Washington State.

**Requirements:** Applicants must be at least 18 yrs. old and meet state Department of Children and Family Services requirements for home size.

**Description of children:** Children of African American and Native American ethnicity; sibling groups of three or more; older children and children with special needs.

**Licensing procedure:** 1) Application and forms; 2) CPR and First Aide certification; 3) background checks and TB test; 4) physical and social home study; 5) pre-service training.

**Average length of time for licensing:** 6 mos. or less.

**Inspections:** 1) Criminal History check; 2) medical clearances including TB test; 3) personal references. After approval, foster home is visited 4 or 5 times annually by social worker.

**Maximum number of children allowed in licensed foster care home:** 6.

**Interracial placement:** Not usually, except for special needs.

**Type of foster care and description of procedures:** Emergency, long-term, therapeutic and pre-adoptive.

**Per diem stipend:** Depends on child's age and level of care.

**Additional funds available:** Medical/dental.

**★ 1168 ★**
**Toutle River Boys Ranch**
2232 S. Silverlake Rd.
Castle Rock, WA 98611
Phone: (206) 274-6611
Fax: (206) 274-9171

**Contact:** Jocelyn Watters.

**Serves:** Southwest Washington State.

**Requirements:** Adults, 21 yrs. and older who can provide personal references.

**Description of children:** Adolescent boys from 14 to 17 yrs.

**Licensing procedure:**
1) Initial inquiry;
2) attend interview;
3) submit application;
4) complete home study;
5) reference check and background clearances.

**Average length of time for licensing:** Approx. 1 mo.

**Inspections:**
1) Fire;
2) sanitation;
3) medical examinations of all household members.
After placement, social worker either contacts or visits foster home weekly.

**Maximum number of children allowed in licensed foster care home:** 2.

**Interracial placement:** Permitted.

**Type of foster care and description of procedures:** Long-term, therapeutic and pre-adoptive.

**Per diem stipend:** $13 - $50.

**Additional funds available:** Medical/dental, clothing allowance, and funds for recreation, boy's allowance and counseling.

**★ 1169 ★**
**Youth Advocates**
2317 E. John St.
Seattle, WA 98115
Phone: (206) 322-7838

**Contact:** Intake worker.

**Serves:** King County.

**Requirements:** Applicants must provide 4 personal references.

**Description of children:** Adolescents at risk.

**Licensing procedure:**
1) Initial inquiry;
2) attend interviews;
3) forward references;
4) complete home study;
5) attend orientation;
6) complete training.

**Average length of time for licensing:** 1-2 mos.

**Inspections:** Medical examinations with TB tests are required for all members of foster home household.

**Maximum number of children allowed in licensed foster care home:** 6.

**Interracial placement:** Permitted.

**Type of foster care and description of procedures:** Emergency, long-term, and therapeutic.

**Per diem stipend:** $284/mo.

**Additional funds available:** Special rate stipend: $120/mo., medical/dental, clothing allowance to $200 and exceptional cost plans.

# WEST VIRGINIA

★1170★
**The Children's Home of Wheeling**
14 Orchard Rd.
Wheeling, WV 26003
Phone: (304) 233-2585

**Contact:** Melanee Sinclair.

**Description:** The Children's Home of Wheeling is also licensed to do pre-adoption home studies.

**Serves:** 4 northern panhandle counties of West Virginia.

**Requirements:** Adults between the ages of 25 and 65 yrs. who can provide personal references and who are financially self-sustaining.

**Description of children:** Boys and girls, 6-18 yrs. who are victims of severe abuse and/or neglect with moderate emotional problems.

**Licensing procedure:** Complete home study and certification process and complete pre-service training. The home study process is for those who have already identified a child and need a study for the adoption process to proceed. Home study is a fee-for-service program.

**Average length of time for licensing:** Approx. 2 mos.

**Inspections:**
1) Fire;
2) sanitation;
3) medical examinations of all household members;
4) finger printing of foster parents.
After placement staff visits at least twice monthly.

**Maximum number of children allowed in licensed foster care home:** 2 foster children.

**Interracial placement:** Permitted.

**Type of foster care and description of procedures:** Long-term and pre-adoptive.

**Per diem stipend:** $450/mo. for foster parents.

**Additional funds available:** Medical/dental covered under a state Medicaid Card.

★1171★
**Northern Tier Youth Services**
105 Pennsylvania Ave.
Charleston, WV 25302
Phone: (304) 345-6897
Fax: (304) 343-1696

**Contact:** Martha L. Minter, BS, Administrator.

**Serves:** Foster youth in West Virginia.

**Requirements:** Prospective foster parents must meet all agency and state approval requirements.

**Description of children:** Neglected, abused and delinquent children between the ages of birth and 18 yrs.

**Adoption procedure:**
1) Return complete application;
2) undergo home study;
3) law enforcement clearances;
4) complete 30 hrs. of training;
5) attend individual interview;
6) undergo physical exam and receive medical release to demonstrate medical fitness;
7) yearly recertification required.

**Average length of time for licensing:** 8-10 wks.

**Inspections:**
1) Fire;
2) sanitation;
3) finger printing of foster parents;
4) medical examinations for all household members.
After placement social worker visits at least weekly.

**Maximum number of children allowed in licensed foster care home:** Usually 1-2; occasionally up to 4.

**Interracial placement:** Permitted.

**Type of foster care and description of procedures:** Emergency, long-term, therapeutic and occasionally pre-adoptive.

**Per diem stipend:** $18.50.

**Additional funds available:** Medical/dental, plus $250-$300/yr. clothing allowance.

★1172★
**Potomac Center**
1 Blue St.
Romney, WV 26757
Phone: (304) 822-3861
Fax: (301) 822-4297

**Branch address:**
P.O. Box 187, Elkins, WV 26241
Phone: (304) 636-5992

P.O. Box 1240, Petersburg, WV 26847
Phone: (304) 257-1317

1314 Edwin Miller Blvd., Martinsburg, WV 25401
Phone: (304) 263-1267

**Contact:** Linda L. Ward, Community Services Director.

**Serves:** 12 counties in and around the eastern panhandle of West Virginia.

**Requirements:** Adults, 21 yrs. and older, who meet the financial eligibility requirements, and who have adequate living space for another individual and who can provide personal references.

**Description of children:** Children and adults with mental retardation or developmental disabilities.

**Licensing procedure:**
1) Submit application;
2) reference and criminal identification checks;
3) complete structure study of home;
4) participate in pre-service training;
5) home visits;
6) sign performance contract;
7) approval.

**Average length of time for licensing:** Approx. 4-5 mos.

**Inspections:**
1) Fire;
2) sanitation;
3) medical examinations for all household members;
4) finger printing of all persons in household ages 18 yrs. or older.

After placement, social worker visits monthly, provides ongoing training, and annual evaluations.

**Maximum number of children allowed in licensed foster care home:** 2 individuals with special needs.

**Interracial placement:** Permitted.

**Type of foster care and description of procedures:** Emergency, long-term, therapeutic and pre-adoptive.

**Per diem stipend:** Varies by program.

**Additional funds available:** Medical/dental, clothing allowance, special equipment and respite care.

# WISCONSIN

★ 1173 ★
**HELP of Door County**
P.O. Box 319
Sturgeon Bay, WI 54235
Phone: (414) 743-8818

**Contact:** Gay Pustaver.

**Serves:** Door and Kewaunee counties.

**Requirements:** Adults 21 yrs. and older who can provide 2 personal references.

**Description of children:** Runaways up to age 18 yrs.

**Licensing procedure:**
1) Submit application;
2) home visit and meet license requirements.

**Average length of time for licensing:** Up to 60 days.

**Inspections:** Medical examination required for foster parent applicants. After approval social worker visits semi-annually.

**Maximum number of children allowed in licensed foster care home:** 2.

**Interracial placement:** Permitted.

**Type of foster care and description of procedures:** Emergency and temporary from 1 to 60 days.

**Per diem stipend:** None.

**Additional funds available:** None.

★ 1174 ★
**Northwest Passage**
Rte. 1, Box 349
Webster, WI 54893
Phone: (715) 866-8301
Fax: (715) 866-4774

**Contact:** Scott Treichel.

**Serves:** Northwest Wisconsin.

**Requirements:** Applicants must meet eligibility requirements for age and home size and provide personal references.

**Description of children:** Male adolescents between the ages of 12 and 17 with emotional and behavioral problems who are successfully completing residential treatment.

**Licensing procedure:**
1) Complete interviews;
2) undergo reference checks;
3) home inspections;

4) submit questionnaire and social history inventories.

**Average length of time for licensing:** Approx. 1 mo.

**Inspections:**
1) Fire;
2) sanitation;
3) medical examinations of all persons in the household.

After placement, social worker visits home between 1 and 4 times per mo.

**Maximum number of children allowed in licensed foster care home:** Varies according to home size, needs of children and parent(s)' ability to meet those needs.

**Interracial placement:** Permitted.

**Type of foster care and description of procedures:** Long-term, pre-adoptive and therapeutic.

**Per diem stipend:** Not available.

**Additional funds available:** Medical assistance and initial clothing allowance.

★ 1175 ★
**Wisconsin Department of Health and Social Services**
**Division of Community Services**
485 S. Military Rd.
Fond du Lac, WI 54935
Phone: (414) 929-2985
Fax: (414) 929-2785

**Contact:** Janet Deschaine.

**Description:** Public agency.

**Serves:** 17 counties in eastern Wisconsin.

**Requirements:** Adults, 18 yrs. or older, who can provide 3 personal references and who have 35 sq. ft. of bedroom space per child.

**Description of children:** Varies.

**Licensing procedure:**
1) Screening form;
2) complete individual group study;
3) police check;
4) have home visit; and
5) submit autobiography.

**Average length of time for licensing:** 3-6 mos.

**Inspections:**
1) Medical examination(s) for foster parent(s);
2) fire, as required;
3) sanitation, as required.

**Maximum number of children allowed in licensed foster care home:** Not available.

**Interracial placement:** Permitted.

**Type of foster care and description of procedures:** Emergency, pre-adoptive, therapeutic and post-disruption.

**Per diem stipend:** Depends upon the age of child and the degree of difficulty of care.

**Additional funds available:** Medical and initial clothing allowance.

# ALBERTA

★ 1176 ★
**Alberta Family and Social Services**
Seventh St. Plaza, 9th Fl.
10030 - 107th St.
Edmonton, AB, Canada T5J 3E4
Phone: (403) 422-5432
(800) 667-2372

**Contact:** Laura Alcock, Foster Care Specialist.

**Serves:** Residents of the Province of Alberta.

**Requirements:** Applicants must be at least 18 yrs. old, be financially stable and have adequate living space to accommodate foster child(ren). Placement of pre-school children requires that at least one parent not be employed full-time outside the home.

**Description of children:** Children of a variety of races and ethnicities from infancy to 18 yrs. Some have mental or physical challenges.

**Licensing procedure:** 1) Attend an awareness session; 2) 18 hrs. of pre-service training; 3) complete an application form; 4) background and reference checks; 5) home study; 6) home approval by local office. All foster homes are classified according to the skills the foster parents have developed. There are four classifications based on the foster parents' training, experience and type of service they can provide. The four classification are *accepted/approved, qualified, advanced and specialized.*.

**Average length of time for licensing:** Less than 6 mos.

**Inspections:** Medical clearances for all household members; personal references.

**Maximum number of children allowed in licensed foster care home:** 2-3 foster children depending upon the level of care.

**Interracial placement:** Permitted, but same race placements are preferred.

**Type of foster care and description of procedures:** Emergency, short and long-term, pre-adoptive and therapeutic.

**Per diem stipend:** Age 0-1: $12.85; 2-5: $14.67; 6-8: $16.10; 9-11: $17.00; 12-15: $19.27; 16-17: $22.02.

**Additional funds available:** Medical/dental, foster parent skill fees, initial clothing, treatment, education and occasional costs.

# BRITISH COLUMBIA

★ 1177 ★
**Ministry of Social Services**
5th Fl., 614 Humboldt St.
Victoria, BC, Canada V8V 1X4
Phone: (604) 387-7091

**Contact:** Deputy Superintendent.

**Serves:** Residents of British Columbia.

**Requirements:** Open.

**Description of children:** Children between the ages of birth and 19 yrs.

**Licensing procedure:** 1) Inquiry; 2) referral to one of ten regional offices; 3) training: 4) foster home study; 5) background checks; 6) if approved, placement.

**Average length of time for licensing:** Wait depends on the range of ages and special needs foster applicants are willing to consider and the children in need of fostering.

**Inspections:** 1) Medical clearances for all household members; 2) 3 personal references; 3) violent crime and sexual assault clearances; 4) home inspection. After a child is in placement, social worker visits from weekly to quarterly as the child's needs dictate.

**Maximum number of children allowed in licensed foster care home:** Dependent on home size and skill level of foster parent(s).

**Interracial placement:** Permitted although same ethnicity/cultural placements are preferred.

**Type of foster care and description of procedures:** Emergency, short and long-term, therapeutic and permanent.

**Per diem stipend:** Based on child's age, level of care and special needs.

**Additional funds available:** Medical/dental, clothing and special.

# MANITOBA

★ 1178 ★
**Child and Family Services of Central Manitoba**
25 Third St. SE
Portage la Prairie, MB, Canada R1N 1N1
Phone: (204) 857-8751

**Contact:** Foster Care coordinator.

**Serves:** Residents of central Manitoba.

**Requirements:** Applicants must be legal adults who can provide for their own needs apart from the foster stipend and who can provide a private living area for a foster child. If both foster parents were employed outside the home, they would not be considered for fostering an infant.

**Description of children:** Primarily preschool-age children who have been abandoned, abused and/or neglected.

**Licensing procedure:** 1) Application package; 2) background checks; 3) personal interviews and home visit; 4) supervisor approval process. At some time during the licensing process prospective foster parents are required to attend a 4-session orientation program.

**Average length of time for licensing:** 2 - 6 mos.

**Inspections:** 1) Criminal Record check; 2) Child Abuse Registry check; 3) medical clearances for foster parents; 4) 4 personal references; 5) home health and safety.
  After licensing and a child is in placement the foster care coordinator and the child's caseworker arrange a regular visitation schedule.

**Maximum number of children allowed in licensed foster care home:** 4 foster children. Exceptions made for sibling groups.

**Interracial placement:** Permitted.

**Type of foster care and description of procedures:** Emergency, short and long-term.

**Per diem stipend:** Basic maintenance based on child's age plus special rate based on child's care plan which is formulated approximately 1 mo. after placement.

**Additional funds available:** Medical/dental, activity money and special fund.

**★ 1179 ★**
**Child and Family Services of Western Manitoba**
340 Ninth St., Rm. 100
Brandon, MB, Canada R7A 6C2
Phone: (204) 726-6030

**Contact:** Foster Care.

**Serves:** Residents from the Saskatchewan border to the 49th parallel to Riding Mountain Park to Carberry.

**Requirements:** Applicants must be of the age of majority and be able to provide adequate living space for a foster child.

**Description of children:** Children from infancy to 18 yrs.

**Licensing procedure:** 1) Inquiry; 2) application and information package; 3) home study; 4) 5 session orientation; 5) approval process.

**Average length of time for licensing:** Less than 6 mos.

**Inspections:** 1) Medical clearances; 2) 4 personal references; 3) Child Abuse Registry check; 4) Criminal Records check; 5) home health and safety.
  After approval child's case worker and foster home support worker set up regular visitation.

**Maximum number of children allowed in licensed foster care home:** 4 unrelated children.

**Interracial placement:** Permitted.

**Type of foster care and description of procedures:** Emergency, short and long-term and therapeutic.

**Per diem stipend:** Fees for basic maintenance follow two schedules: 1) Children from 0 - 12 yrs.; and 2) children 13 yrs. and older.

**Additional funds available:** Medical/dental, skill based/special needs, initial clothing and activity funds.

**★ 1180 ★**
**West Region Child and Family Services**
38 First Ave. N.W.
Dauphin, MB, Canada R7N 1G7
Phone: (204) 638-6941

**Contact:** Foster Care.

**Serves:** Residents of western Manitoba.

**Requirements:** Open.

**Description of children:** Aboriginal children.

**Licensing procedure:** 1) Application; 2) consent for release of information; 3) letter of acknowledgment of receipt of completed application; 4) background checks; 5) foster home assessment; 6) foster home orientation.

**Average length of time for licensing:** 90 days.

**Inspections:** 1) Criminal Records check; 2) Child Abuse Registry check; 3) medical clearances for prospective foster parents; 4) personal references, operational smoke detectors and structural soundness.

**Maximum number of children allowed in licensed foster care home:** 4 unrelated children.

**Interracial placement:** The protocol of the placement of aboriginal children is to first seek a suitable placement within the extended family; next within the home community; next in other reserve communities; and only last, off reserve if the child's special needs mandate such a placement.

**Type of foster care and description of procedures:** Emergency, short and long-term and therapeutic.

**Per diem stipend:** Basic maintenance is based on age and the fee for service is based on the level of care.

**Additional funds available:** Respite and other addition services.

**★ 1181 ★**
**Winnipeg Child and Family Services**
404 - 1 Wesley Ave.
Winnipeg, MB, Canada R3C 4C6
Phone: (204) 944-4438

**Branch address:**
  Winnipeg Child and Family Services - Southwest Area, 239A Ness Ave., Winnipeg, MB R3J 1A5
  Phone: (204) 944-4475

  Winnipeg Child and Family Services - East Area, 123B Marion St., Winnipeg, MB R2H 0T3
  Phone: (204) 233-8931

  Winnipeg Child and Family Services - Northwest Area, 1386 Main St., Winnipeg, MB R3G 0N6
  Phone: (204) 944-4200

  Winnipeg Child and Family Services - Central Area, 831 Portage Ave., 2nd Fl., Winnipeg, MB R3G 0N6
  Phone: (204) 944-4200

**Contact:** Foster Care.

**Serves:** Residents of metropolitan Winnipeg and surrounding areas.

**Requirements:** Applicants must be able to provide each foster child with his/her own bed and children older than pre-school may not share a bedroom with another child of the opposite sex. Prospective foster parents who wish to foster an infant or preschooler may not work full-time outside the home or babysit children on a regular basis.

**Description of children:** Children between the ages of birth and 18 yrs., 85% of whom have experienced some kind of abuse and who have behavior problems as a result.

**Licensing procedure:** 1) Inquiry; 2) referral to branch office; 3) telephone intake; 4) information packet and application; 5) 4 wks. of orientation; 6) home visit; 7) assessment worker evaluation and home visit; 8) report and approval process.

**Average length of time for licensing:** 3 - 6 mos.

**Inspections:** 1) Physician's statement(s) for primary care giver(s); 2) 4 personal references; 3) Child Abuse Registry checks for all household members older than 18 yrs.; 4) agency records check; 5) home health and safety; 6) police records check for all household members older than 18 yrs.

**Maximum number of children allowed in licensed foster care home:** 4 foster children.

**Interracial placement:** Permitted.

**Type of foster care and description of procedures:** Emergency, short and long-term.

**Per diem stipend:** Basic maintenance rates based on a child's age.

**Additional funds available:** Medical/dental, reassessment for additional funds for exceptional needs computed after 30 days of care; recreational and holiday.

# NEW BRUNSWICK

**★ 1182 ★**
**New Brunswick Department of Health and Community Service**
P.O. Box 5100
Fredericton, NB, Canada E3B 5G8
Phone: (506) 453-3830

**Contact:** Foster Care.

**Serves:** Residents of the Province of New Brunswick.

**Requirements:** Applicants must be at least 19 yrs. old, financially self-sufficient and not have been hospitalized within the previous 12 mos. for any psychiatric disorder. Their marital status should be unchanged within the previous 12 mos. and their health should not impair their parenting functions. If there has been a history of drug or alcohol abuse, prospective foster parents must have been clean and sober for the previous 3 yrs. The prospective foster mother should not have been pregnant or have an infant under 1 yr. within the previous 12 mos. and the family must not have experienced a death or traumatic event within the previous 12 mos.

**Description of children:** Children from birth to 19 yrs. (and in some cases older), most of whom have a history of abuse and/or neglect.

**Licensing procedure:** 1) Inquiry; 2) referral to one of 14 offices in 7 regions within the province; 3) attend public information session; 4) application; 5) background checks; 6) 9 - 18 hrs. of pre-service training and orientation; 7) home study; 8) approval process.

**Average length of time for licensing:** 2 - 4 mos.

**Inspections:** 1) Health statements; 2) 3 personal references; 3) home health and safety; 4) criminal records check; 5) computerized information check.

**Maximum number of children allowed in licensed foster care home:** Regular: 5 children. Therapeutic: 2 children. Maximum of all possible dependents regardless of age: 7.

**Interracial placement:** Permitted.

**Type of foster care and description of procedures:** Emergency, short and long-term and therapeutic.

**Per diem stipend:** Child's maintenance and foster parent stipend based on experience and level of care.

**Additional funds available:** Medical/dental, respite and special item fee.

# NEWFOUNDLAND

★ 1183 ★
**Newfoundland Department of Social Services**
3rd Fl., West Block
Confederation Bldg
St. Johns, NF, Canada A1B 4J6
Phone: (709) 729-2493

**Mailing address:**
P.O. Box 8700, St. Johns, NF, Canada A1B 4J6

**Contact:** Foster Care consultant.

**Serves:** Residents of Newfoundland and Labrador.

**Requirements:** Applicants must be at least 19 yrs. old.

**Description of children:** Primarily adolescents or younger children with special needs.

**Licensing procedure:** 1) Inquiry and referral to one of 52 district offices; 2) application; 3) orientation; 4) licensing and home study.

**Average length of time for licensing:** 2 mos.

**Inspections:** 1) Medical clearances for all household members; 2) 3 personal references; 3) certificate of conduct for each household member over the age of 18 yrs.; 4) home health and safety; 5) verification of income.

**Maximum number of children allowed in licensed foster care home:** 2 foster children.

**Interracial placement:** Permitted but preferably within same culture and jurisdiction.

**Type of foster care and description of procedures:** Emergency, short and long-term and therapeutic.

**Per diem stipend:** Basic rate is determined by child's age and falls into two ranges: 0 - 12 yrs. and 13 yrs. and older. Special Care Supplement is based on the level of care required.

**Additional funds available:** Medical/dental.

# NORTHWEST TERRITORIES

★ 1184 ★
**Family Support**
**Government of the Northwest Territories Department of Health and Social Services**
Precambrian Bldg. 500
492 - 52nd St.
Yellowknife, NT, Canada X1A 3T1
Phone: (403) 873-8290

**Contact:** Mary Beauchamp.

**Serves:** Residents of the Northwest Territories.

**Requirements:** Applicants must be at least 18 yrs., have a source of income apart from the foster stipend and meet community standards for living space.

**Description of children:** Children of variable cultures from infancy to 18 yrs., some of whom are handicapped and/or abused and/or neglected and/or homeless and/or behaviorally disturbed.

**Licensing procedure:** 1) Application; 2) background checks; 3) home study; 4) department approval process.

**Average length of time for licensing:** Average of 6 -12 mos.

**Inspections:** 1) Medical clearances for all household members; 2) personal references; 3) Criminal Record Check. After approval social worker visits as often as the needs of the child dictate.

**Maximum number of children allowed in licensed foster care home:** 4 but exceptions can be made for sibling groups.

**Interracial placement:** Culturally appropriate placements are preferred.

**Type of foster care and description of procedures:** Emergency, short and long-term, therapeutic and extended family.

**Per diem stipend:** Basic: $24 but can vary by community and region.

**Additional funds available:** Medical/dental, monthly and seasonal clothing allowance, educational, recreational and comforts.

# NOVA SCOTIA

★ 1185 ★
**Department of Community Services**
**Family and Children's Services**
P.O. Box 696
Halifax, NS, Canada B3J 2T7
Phone: (902) 424-5097

**Branch address:**
Family and Children's Services of Annapolis County, Municipal Bldg., St. George St., P.O. Box 39, Annapolis Royal, NS, Canada B0S 1A0

Phone: (902) 532-2337

Children's Aid Society of Cape Breton, Provincial Bldg., Ste. 7, 360 Prince St., Sydney, NS, Canada B1P 5L1
Phone: (902) 563-3400

Children's Aid Society and Family Svcs. of Colchester County, 58 Willow St., P.O. Box 950, Truro, NS, Canada B2N 5G7
Phone: (902) 893-5950

Family and Children's Services of Cumberland County, P.O. Box 399, Amherst, NS, Canada B4H 3Z15
Phone: (902) 667-3336

Children's Aid Society of Halifax, 5244 South St., Halifax, NS, Canada B3J 1A4
Phone: (902) 425-5420

Family and Children's Services of Hants County, 1469 King St., P.O. Box 99, Windsor, NS, Canada B0N 2TO
Phone: (902) 798-2289

Children's Aid Society of Inverness-Richmond, P.O. Box 359, Port Hawkesbury, NS, Canada B0E 2V0
Phone: (902) 625-0660

Family and Children's Services of Kings County, 76 River St., P.O. Box 188, Kentville, NS, Canada B4N 1G9
Phone: (902) 678-6176

Family and Children's Services of Lunenburg County, Provincial Bldg., 99 High St., Ste. 105, P.O. Box 170, Bridgewater, NS, Canada B4V 1V8
Phone: (902) 543-2411

Children's Aid Society of Pictou, 7 Cambell's La., P.O. Box 488, New Glasgow, NS, Canada B2H 5E5
Phone: (902) 755-5950

Family and Children's Services of Queens County, 43 Carken St., P.O. Box 1360, Liverpool, NS, Canada B0T 1K0
Phone: (902) 354-2711

Children's Aid Society of Shelburne County, P.O. Box 9, Barrington, NS, Canada B0W 1E0
Phone: (902) 637-2337

Family and Children's Services of Yarmouth County, 10 Starrs Rd., Yarmouth, NS, Canada B5A 2T1
Phone: (902) 742-0700

Mi'K maq Family and Children's Services of Nova Scotia, P.O. Box 179, Shubenacadie, NS, Canada B0N 2H0
Phone: (902) 758-3553

Antigonish District Office, Department of Community Services, Provincial Bldg., Ste. 101, 11 James St., Antigonish, NS, Canada B2G 1R6
Phone: (902) 863-3213

Dartmouth District Office, Department of Community Services, Dartmouth Professional Centre, Ste. 100, 277 Pleasant St., Dartmouth, NS, Canada B2Y 4B7
Phone: (902) 424-3298

Digby District Office, Department of Community Services, Warwick St., P.O. Box 399, Digby, NS, Canada B0V 1A0

Phone: (902) 245-5811

Guysborough District Office, Department of Community Services, Chedabucto Mall, P.O. Box 90, Guysborough, NS, Canada N0H 1N0
Phone: (902) 533-4007

Sackville District Office, Department of Community Services, Cobequid Multi-Service Centre, 70 Memory La., Lower Sackville, NS, Canada B4C 2J3
Phone: (902) 865-5750

**Contact:** Coordinator of Children in Care.
**Serves:** Residents of the Province of Nova Scotia.
**Requirements:** Applicants must be at least 19 yrs. old.
**Description of children:** Children from infancy to 21 yrs.
**Licensing procedure:** Contact local child protection agency.
**Average length of time for licensing:** Dependent upon the intake of each local child protection agency.
**Inspections:** 1) Medical clearances; 2) personal references; 3) child abuse register check. After approval, social worker visits a minimum of quarterly.
**Maximum number of children allowed in licensed foster care home:** 4.
**Interracial placement:** Permitted if appropriate same race placement is unavailable.
**Type of foster care and description of procedures:** Emergency, short and long-term, pre-adoptive, relative/non-relative and therapeutic.
**Per diem stipend:** Varies with child's age and level of care.
**Additional funds available:** Medical/dental, $471 - $1088 annual clothing allowance and special needs requests.

# ONTARIO

**Children's Aid Society of Metropolitan Toronto**
4211 Yonge St., Ste. 300
Toronto, ON, Canada M2P 2A9
Phone: (416) 924-4646

**Branch address:**
Locations of the Children's Aid Societies of Ontario: Algoma, 65 Willow Ave., Saulte Ste. Marie, ON, Canada P6B 5B1
Phone: (705) 949-0162

Brant, 70 Chatham St., Box 774, Brantford, ON, Canada N3T 5R7
Phone: (519) 753-8681

Bruce, 30 Park St., Box 279, Walkerton, ON, Canada N0G 2V0
Phone: (519) 881-1822

Dufferin, Court House, 299 Broadway, Orangeville, ON, Canada L9W 1L4
Phone: (519) 941-1530

Durham, Midtown Mall, 200 John St. W., Box 321, Oshawa, ON, Canada L1H 7L3
Phone: (416) 433-1551

St. Thomas and Elgin, 27 Southwick St., St. Thomas, ON, Canada N5R 3R7

Phone: (519) 631-1492

Essex, 690 Cataraqui St., Windsor, ON, Canada N9A 3P1
Phone: (519) 252-1171

Essex R.C., 1700 Assumption St., Box 2306, Walkerville
Postal Station, Windsor, ON, Canada N8Y 4S2
Phone: (519) 256-4521

Frontenac, 329 Johnson St., Kingston, ON, Canada K7L 1Y8

Grey, 715 Third Ave. E., Box 129, Owen Sound, ON, Canada
N4K 5P1
Phone: (519) 376-7893

Hadimand, 653 Broad St. W., Box 909, Dunnville, ON, Canada
N1A 1T8
Phone: (416) 774-7471

Halton, 467 Speers Rd., Oakville, ON 16K 3S4
Phone: (416) 844-8211

Hamilton-Wentworth, 143 Wentworth St. S., Ste. A, P.O. Box
1107, Hamilton, ON, Canada L8N 2Z1
Phone: (416) 522-1121

Hamilton-Wentworth R.C., 499 King St. E., 2nd Fl., Hamilton,
ON, Canada L8N 1E1
Phone: (416) 525-2012

Hastings, 363 Dundas St. W., P.O. Box 186, Belleville, ON,
Canada K8P 1B3
Phone: (613) 962-9291

Huron, 46 Gloucester Ter., Goderich, ON, Canada N7A 1W7
Phone: (519) 524-7356

Kapuskasing, 20 Stewart St., P.O. Box 188, Kapuskasing, ON,
Canada P5N 2Y3
Phone: (705) 335-2301

Kawartha-Haliburton, 721 Vinette St., Peterborough, ON,
Canada K9H 7E9

Kenora, R.R. 1 Ocena Ave., Kenora, ON, Canada P9N 3W7
Phone: (807) 468-5508

Kent, 435 Grant Ave. W., Box 157, Chatham, ON, Canada
N7L 3Z4
Phone: (519) 352-0440

Sarnia-Lambton, 171 Kendall St., Point Edward, ON, Canada
N7V RG8
Phone: (519) 336-0623

Lanark, Box 37, Perth, ON, Canada K7H 3E2
Phone: (613) 264-1500

Leeds & Grenville, Box 549, R.R. 1, Prescott Rd., Brockville,
ON, Canada K6V 5V7
Phone: (613) 354-9744

Lennox & Addington, 41 Dundas W., Nepanee, ON, Canada
K7R 1Z5

London & Middlesex, 164 Alvert St., Box 848, Station B,
London, ON, Canada N6A 4Z5
Phone: (519) 434-8461

Muskoka, Stormon-Dundas-Glengarry, Box 1200,
Bracebridge, ON, Canada P0B 1C0
Phone: (705) 645-4426

Niagara Region, 311 Geneva St., Box 516, St. Catherines,
ON, Canada L2R 6W5
Phone: (416) 937-7731

Nipissing, 433 McIntrye St. N., Ste. 300, Box 1035, North Bay,
ON, Canada P1B 2Z3
Phone: (705) 472-0910

Northumberland, 1005 Burnham St., P.O. Box 2015,
Bobourge, ON, Canada K9A 5E9
Phone: (616) 372-1821

Ottawa-Carleton, 1370 Bank St., Ottawa, ON, Canada K1H
7Y3
Phone: (613) 733-0670

Oxford, 92 Light St., Box 312, Woodstock, ON, Canada N4S
7X6
Phone: (516) 539-6176

Parry Sound, 76 Church St., Parry Sound, ON, Canada P2A
1Z1
Phone: (705) 746-9354

Peel, 10 Peel Centre Dr., Brampton, ON, Canada L6T 4B9
Phone: (416) 791-5151

Perth, 380 Hibernia St., Box 278, Stratford, ON, Canada N5A
6T1
Phone: (519) 271-5290

Porcupine & District, 12 Elm St. N., Timmins, ON, Canada
P4N 6A1
Phone: (705) 264-4257

Prescott & Russell, 173 Main St., Box 248, Plantagenet, ON,
Canada K0B 1L0
Phone: (613) 673-5148

Prince Edward, 6 Ross St., Box 1510, Picton, ON, Canada
K0K 2T0
Phone: (613) 476-2765

Rainy River, 450 Scott St., P.O. Box 751, Ft. Frances, ON,
Canada P9A 3N1

Renfrew, 77 Mary St., Pembroke, ON, Canada K8A 5V4
Phone: (613) 735-6866

Simcoe, County Administration Centre, Midhurst, ON, Canada
L0L 1X0
Phone: (705) 726-6587

Temiskaming, 64 Government Rd. W., Box 1150, Kirkland
Lake, ON, Canada P2N 3M7
Phone: (705) 567-9201

Thunder Bay, 309 South Ct., Box 2027, Station P, Thunder
Bay, ON, Canada P7B 5E7
Phone: (807) 343-6100

Norfolk, 23 Argyle St., Box 601, Simcoe, ON, Canada N3Y
4LB

Waterloo, 355 Charles St. E., Kitchener, ON, Canada N2G 2P8
Phone: (519) 576-0540

Wellington, 55 Delhi St., Box 1088, Guelph, ON, Canada N1H 6N3
Phone: (519) 824-2410

York, 85 Eagle St. W., P.O. Box 358, Newmarket, ON, Canada L3Y 4X7
Phone: (416) 895-2318

Toronto R.C., 26 Maitland St., Toronto, ON, Canada M4Y 1R9
Phone: (416) 925-6641

**Contact:** Foster Care.

**Serves:** Residents of Meropolitan Toronto and residents of Durham and York counties with the permission of the Children's Aid Societies in those counties.

**Requirements:** Applicants must be legal adults.

**Description of children:** Children between the ages of infancy and 18 yrs.

**Licensing procedure:** 1) Intake forms; 2) attend informational meeting; 3) application; 4) home finding process; 5) 7 wks. of training and orientation.

**Average length of time for licensing:** Less than 6 mos.

**Inspections:** 1) Medical clearances for all household members over the age of 18 yrs.; 2) 3 personal references; 3) home health and safety; 4) police clearances.
After approval a family resource worker visits the foster home every 6 wks. and foster parents attend cluster meetings monthly except during July and August.

**Maximum number of children allowed in licensed foster care home:** 4 unrelated children with no more than 2 children under the age of 2 yrs. and no more than 3 children under the age of 4 yrs.

**Interracial placement:** Permitted.

**Type of foster care and description of procedures:** Emergency, short and long-term and treatment.

**Per diem stipend:** Basic maintenance: $24.15.

**Additional funds available:** Medical/dental, additional program rates, clothing and holiday.

★ 1187 ★

**Children's Aid Society of Sudbury-Manitoulin**
1492 Paris St.
Sudbury, ON, Canada P3E 3B8
Phone: (705) 522-8600

**Contact:** Foster Care.

**Serves:** Residents of the Sudbury-Manitoulin area.

**Requirements:** Applicants must be at least 19 yrs. old.

**Description of children:** Children between the ages of birth and 16 yrs. most of whom have been physically or sexually abused or who are at risk.

**Licensing procedure:** 1) Inquiry; 2) telephone intake; 3) internal record check; 4) application; 5) criminal records check and medical examination; 6) 5 wk. training course; 7) home study.

**Average length of time for licensing:** 3 - 6 mos.

**Inspections:** 1) Medical clearances for all household members over the age of 18 yrs.; 2) 5 character references; 3) home health and safety.
After placement both the foster parents' support worker and the child's case worker visit on a regularly scheduled basis.

**Maximum number of children allowed in licensed foster care home:** 4 foster children.

**Interracial placement:** Permitted.

**Type of foster care and description of procedures:** Emergency, short and long-term and supplemental.

**Per diem stipend:** Ages 0 - 6 yrs.: $15.98; 7-12 yrs.: $17.14; 13 yrs. or older: $20.54.

**Additional funds available:** Medical/dental, supplemental, clothing, spending money, Christmas and birthday.

★ 1188 ★

**Ontario Ministry of Community and Social Services Adoption Unit**
2 Bloor St. W.
Toronto, ON, Canada M7A 1E9
Phone: (416) 327-4730

**Description:** Adoption Unit approves and monitors foster care for the *private* adoption system in Ontario.

**Serves:** Residents of Ontario.

**Requirements:** Open, but one caregiver must not be employed outside the home full time.

**Description of children:** Primarily infants awaiting adoptive placement.

**Licensing procedure:** 1) Inquiry; 2) background checks; 3) assessment by an approved social worker.

**Average length of time for licensing:** Less than 6 mos.

**Inspections:** 1) Medical clearances for all household members; 2) personal references; 3) law enforcement clearances. Foster home must be visited annually for re-approval.

**Maximum number of children allowed in licensed foster care home:** Unavailable.

**Interracial placement:** Permitted.

**Type of foster care and description of procedures:** Emergency and pre-adoptive.

**Per diem stipend:** Varies with individual licensee's contract.

**Additional funds available:** Clothing.

# PRINCE EDWARD ISLAND

★ 1189 ★

**Health and Community Services Agency**
4 Sydney St.
Charlottetown, PE, Canada C1A 7N8
Phone: (902) 368-6130

**Mailing address:**
P.O. Box 2000, Charlottetown, PE, Canada C1A 7N8

**Contact:** Foster Care.

**Serves:** Residents of Prince Edward Island.

**Requirements:** Applicants must be at least 21 yrs. old.

**Description of children:** Children between the ages of infancy and 12 yrs. with some behavioral problems.

**Licensing procedure:** 1) Inquiry; 2) attend foster parent information night; 3) send letter of continuing interest; 4) intake assignment; 5) family assessment; 6) complete foster parent preparation program; 7) probationary approval; 8) apprenticeship program through first placement or 6 mos.
   Therapeutic foster placements involve different training and have different supports.

**Average length of time for licensing:** 3 - 6 mos.

**Inspections:** 1) Criminal records check through the R.C.M.P. for each household member 12 yrs. and older; 2) medical clearances; 3) 3 personal references; 4) home health and safety.

**Maximum number of children allowed in licensed foster care home:** 4 foster children.

**Interracial placement:** Permitted.

**Type of foster care and description of procedures:** Emergency, short and long-term and therapeutic.

**Per diem stipend:** Room and board rates vary by age. Special Care supplements vary by each child's needs and range from $100-$500.

**Additional funds available:** Medical/dental, clothing respite care, recreational and retainer system.

# QUEBEC

★ 1190 ★
**Centre Jeunesse de Quebec (CPEJ)**
540 Boul. Charest Est
Quebec, PQ, Canada G1K 8L1
Phone: (418) 529-7351
Fax: (418) 525-5716

**Branch address:**
   Centres Jeunesse Bas St-Laurent, Direction Protection Jeunesse, 92, 2eme rue Ouest, 2e, Rimouski, PQ G5L 8V5
   Phone: (418) 723-1255

   Centres Jeunesse Saguenay-Lac-St-Jean, Direction Protection Jeunesse, 520 Boule. Jacques Cartier est, Chicoutimi, PQ G7H 5B7
   Phone: (418) 549-2571

   Centres Jeunesse Mauricie-Bois-Franc, Direction Protection Jeunesse, 2700 Boule. des Forges/C.P.1330, Trois Rivieres, PQ G9A 5L2
   Phone: (819) 378-5481

   Centre Jeunesse Estrie, Direction Protection Jeunesse, 340 Dufferin, Sherbrooke, PQ J1H 4M7
   Phone: (819) 822-2727

   Centre Jeunesse Montreal, Direction Protection Jeunesse, 1001 de Maisonneuve est, 5e etage, Montreal, PQ H2L 4R5
   Phone: (514) 527-7211

   Centre Jeunesse Famille Batshaw, Direction Protection Jeunesse, 2155 rue Guy-10e etage, Montreal, PQ H3H 2R9
   Phone: (514) 989-1885

   Centre Jeunesse Outaouais, Direction Protection Jeunesse, 15 Boule. Gamelin, Hull, PQ J8Y 6N5
   Phone: (819) 776-6060

   Centre Jeunesse Abitibi-Temiscamingue, Direction Protection Jeunesse, 341 rue Principale Nord, Amos, PQ J9T 2L8
   Phone: (819) 732-3244

   Centre Jeunesse Cote Nord, Direction Protection Jeunesse, 815 Boul. Joliet, Baie Comeau, PQ G5C 1P5
   Phone: (418) 589-9927

   CSS Inuit - Baie d'Hudson, Direction Protection Jeunesse, Services Sociaux, Povungnituk, PQ J0M 1P0
   Phone: (819) 988-2957

   CSS Inuit - Ungava, Direction Protection Jeunesse, C.P. 10, Kuujjuaq, PQ J0M 1C0
   Phone: (819) 964-2919

   CSS Cri, Direction Protection Jeunesse, Chissasibi, Baie James, PQ J0M 1E0
   Phone: (819) 855-2855

   Centre Jeunesse Gaspesie/Les Iles, Direction Protection Jeunesse, 205 Boul. York, C.P. 39, Gaspe, PQ G0C 1R0
   Phone: (418) 368-1803

   Centre Jeunesse Chaudiere-Appalaches, Direction Protection Jeunesse, 25 Vincent Chagnon, Levis, PQ G6V 4V6
   Phone: (418) 837-9331

   Centre Jeunesse Laurentides, Direction Protection Jeunesse, 617 Boul. Labelle, Blainville, PQ J7C 2J1
   Phone: (514) 430-9250

   Centre Jeunesse Lanaudiere, Direction Protection Jeunesse, 260 Lavaltrie sud, Joliette, PQ J6E 5X7
   Phone: (514) 756-4555

   Centre Jeunesse Monteregie, Direction Protection Jeunesse, 25 Boul. Lafayette, Longueuil, PQ J4K 5C8
   Phone: (514) 679-0140

   Centre Jeunesse de Laval, Direction Protection Jeunesse, 2 Place Laval, Laval, PQ H7N 5N6
   Phone: (514) 668-7820

**Contact:** Richard Cote.

**Serves:** Residents of Quebec Metro, Charlevoix and Portneuf.

**Requirements:** Applicants must be between the ages of 25 and 65 yrs. and have one caregiver remain at home if fostering an infant.

**Description of children:** Children who have been abandoned, neglected and/or abused or who have behavioral problems.

**Licensing procedure:** 1) Written application; 2) home study; 3) approval process.

**Average length of time for licensing:** Less than 6 mos.

**Inspections:** 1) Medical clearances for all household members; 2) personal references. After approval social worker visits bi-monthly.

**Maximum number of children allowed in licensed foster care home:** 9.

**Interracial placement:** Permitted.

**Type of foster care and description of procedures:** Emergency, short and long-term and pre-adoptive.

**Per diem stipend:** Range based on age: $13.80 - $21.51.

**Additional funds available:** Medical/dental, clothing, academic and recreational.

# SASKATCHEWAN

★1191★
**Saskatchewan Social Services**
1920 Broad St.
Regina, SK, Canada S4P 3V6
Phone: (306) 787-3653
Fax: (306) 787-0925

**Contact:** Foster Care.

**Serves:** Residents of Saskatchewan.

**Requirements:** Applicants must be at the age of majority and be able to provide adequate living space for foster child(ren).

**Description of children:** Children between the ages of birth and 16 yrs.

**Licensing procedure:** 1) Inquiry; 2) referral to one of 25 offices in 11 regions; 3) interview; 4) introductory training; 5) home study; 6) approval process; 7) training module completion.
  Training module takes two forms: the first, for standard foster homes, and the second, for therapeutic foster homes.

**Average length of time for licensing:** 2 - 4 mos.

**Inspections:** 1) Child Abuse Registry check; 2) medical clearances; 3) 4 personal references; 4) Criminal Records check. After approval a regular visitation schedule is instituted to best suit the needs of the foster child(ren).

**Maximum number of children allowed in licensed foster care home:** Standard: 4 unrelated children. Therapeutic: 1 - 2.

**Interracial placement:** Permitted but same-culture placements are made in all but extraordinary circumstances.

**Type of foster care and description of procedures:** Emergency, short and long-term and therapeutic.

**Per diem stipend:** Basic maintenance based on child's age; Fee for Service based on level of care; and, Skill Base.

**Additional funds available:** Medical/dental and funds for specialized needs.

# YUKON

★1192★
**Department of Health and Social Services**
**Government of the Yukon**
Box 2703, H-10
Whitehorse, YK, Canada Y1A 2C6
Phone: (403) 667-3002

**Contact:** Maxine Kehoe, Supervisor.

**Serves:** Residents of the Yukon.

**Requirements:** Applicants must be adults with sufficient income and home size to assure health and safety.

**Description of children:** Children between the ages of infancy and 18 yrs.

**Licensing procedure:** 1) Home study; 2) Royal Canadian Mounted Police clearances; 3) reference checks; 4) medical clearances; 5) orientation.

**Average length of time for licensing:** Less than 6 mos.

**Inspections:** Medical clearances for all household members; personal references.

**Maximum number of children allowed in licensed foster care home:** 4 foster children.

**Interracial placement:** Permitted if a same culture placement is unavailable.

**Type of foster care and description of procedures:** Emergency, temporary, long-term, therapeutic, relative foster home, pre-adoptive and respite care.

**Per diem stipend:** $23.25 -$70 based on level of care.

**Additional funds available:** Medical/dental, clothing allowance, day care, recreation, travel, child allowance, fire and safety equipment, special needs equipment.

# Independent Adoption Services

## ALABAMA

★ 1193 ★
**John W. Green, III**
**Attorney at Law**
107 North Side Sq.
Huntsville, AL 35801
Phone: (205) 534-5671
Fax: (205) 533-3488

**Description of services:**
1) Provides outreach services to birthparents considering adoptive placement;
2) represents adoptive parents in court;
3) interviews both parties in the adoption;
4) prepares and files all legal documents;
5) provides medical arrangements for birthmother, if required.

**Fees:** $110/hr. plus court costs and expenses.

**Number of independent adoptions handled last year:** 2.

**Description of process:**
1) Prospective adoptive parents may locate expectant birthmother through their own efforts or through outreach efforts of attorney;
2) after child's birth attorney obtains necessary relinquishments and files temporary custody order of Juvenile Court which allows adoptive parents to leave hospital with child;
3) attorney files petition for permanent adoption in Probate or Juvenile Court.

**Licensed to place children:** Birthmother places child directly.

**Residency requirements for prospective adoptive parents:** Child or adoptive parent must be a resident of Alabama.

## ALASKA

★ 1194 ★
**Kasmar and Slone, P.C.**
3003 Minnesota Dr.
Anchorage, AK 99503
Phone: (907) 272-4471

**Description of services:** 1) Handles mostly identified adoptions; 2) represents adoptive parents in all legal proceedings; 3) screens birth parents on behalf of prospective adoptive parents; 4) interviews prospective adoptive parents on behalf of birth parents; 5) can make referrals for medical arrangements for birth mother.

**Fees:** Variable.

**Number of independent adoptions handled last year:** 7.

**Description of process:** 1) Initial interview of prospective adoptive parents; 2) development of search plan including advertising for adoptable child; 3) birthparent interview; 4) birth and relinquishment; 5) file adoption petition; 6) adoption hearing and finalization.

**Residency requirements for prospective adoptive parents:** Not necessarily.

## ARIZONA

★ 1195 ★
**Udall, Shuman, Blackhurst, Allen and Lyons**
Denise Lowell-Britt
30 W. 1st St.
Mesa, AZ 85201
Phone: (604) 461-5300

**Description of services:** 1) Screens prospective adoptive parents and birth parents considering an adoptive placement for their child; 2) interviews birth parents on behalf of adoptive parents and/or adoptive parents on behalf of birth parents; 3) represents adoptive applicants in all legal proceedings; 4) represents birth parents in all legal proceedings; 5) handles both identified adoptions and is aware of birth parents considering adoptive placement for their children.

**Fees:** $150/hr.

**Number of independent adoptions handled last year:** 10.

**Description of process:** Complies with Arizona law.

**Residency requirements for prospective adoptive parents:** None.

## ARKANSAS

★ 1196 ★
**Ogles Law Firm, P.A.**
John Ogles
1500 W. Main
Jacksonville, AR 72078
Phone: (501) 982-3339

**Mailing address:**
P.O. Box 891, Jacksonville, AR 72078

**Description of services:** 1) Handles both identified adoptions and is aware of birth parents considering an adoptive placement for their child; 2) screens perspective adoptive parents on behalf of birth parents and birth parents on behalf of adoptive parents; 3) represents adoptive parents in all legal proceedings; 4) provides medical arrangements for birth mother.

**Fees:** $5000 plus expenses.

**Number of independent adoptions handled last year:** 5.

**Description of process:** 1) Interview; 2) file petition for adoption; 3) court appearance; 4) consultation with birth parents and adoptive parents. Most adoptions are complete in 10 mos.

**Residency requirements for prospective adoptive parents:** None.

# CALIFORNIA

**★ 1197 ★**
**Adoption Center of San Diego**
5850 Oberlin Dr., Ste. 310
San Diego, CA 92121
Phone: (619) 535-3033
Fax: (619) 535-3032

**Contact:** Sarah Jensen, Director.

**Description of services:**
1) Outreach services to prospective adoptive parents and birthparents considering adoption for their child;
2) interviews both parties in the adoption;
3) counseling services for birth and adoptive parents;
4) coordination of childbirth classes, medical and hospital care;
5) support groups;
6) resume preparation assistance for prospective adoptive parents.

**Fees:** Approx. 5% of gross income. No fee to birthparents.

**Number of independent adoptions handled last year:** 21.

**Description of process:**
1) Birthparents select adoptive parents from resumes;
2) Center arranges meeting;
3) Center coordinates on-going contact during pregnancy;
4) after birth, Center liaisons between County and adoptive parents for home study.

**Licensed to place children:** Birthparents place their own infants.

**Residency requirements for prospective adoptive parents:** None.

**★ 1198 ★**
**Allen & Hoctor Counseling Center**
2621 Denver St., Ste. A-4
San Diego, CA 92110
Phone: (619) 275-3160

**Description of services:** 1) Pre- and post-placement adoption counseling; 2) networks with health and legal professionals, public and private adoption agencies.

**Fees:** $80/hr.

**Residency requirements for prospective adoptive parents:** None.

**★ 1199 ★**
**Law Offices of David H. Baum**
16255 Ventura Blvd., Ste. 704
Encino, CA 91436
Phone: (818) 501-8355

**Description of services:** 1) Handles identified adoptions and is aware of birth parents considering adoptive placements for their children; 2) screens adoptive parents on behalf of birth parents and birth parents on behalf of adoptive parents; 3) represents adoptive parents in all legal proceedings; 4) arranges medical arrangements for birth mother; 5) works with prospective adoptive parents in search for a child in need of adoptive placement.

**Fees:** Ranges from $1500 - $4900.

**Number of independent adoptions handled last year:** 30 - 50.

**Description of process:** 1) Inquiry; 2) resume and search plan development; 3) requisite arrangements made and supervised; 4) termination of parental rights; 5) post-placement final court appearance.

**Residency requirements for prospective adoptive parents:** None.

**★ 1200 ★**
**Martin Brandfon**
**Attorney at Law**
620 Jefferson Ave.
Redwood City, CA 94063
Phone: (415) 366-6789

**Description of services:**
1) Networks between prospective adoptive parents and birthparents considering adoption for their child;
2) represents adoptive parents in court;
3) arranges meetings and interviews between adoptive and birthparents;
4) handles finances;
5) prepares and executes all legal documents.

**Fees:** $175/hr. Average: $2500-$3000 plus medical and living expenses for birthparents, as required.

**Number of independent adoptions handled last year:** Unavailable.

**Description of process:**
1) Birthparents review photos and letters of prospective adoptive parents;
2) after initial interview with both parties, attorney arranges subsequent interviews and meetings;
3) attorney handles finances and can arrange medical care and living arrangements for birthmother.

**Licensed to place children:** Birthparents and licensed agencies place children in the State of California.

**Residency requirements for prospective adoptive parents:** Adoptive parents in California must be residents for 6 or more mos.

**★ 1201 ★**
**Law Offices of Vanessa Zecher Cain**
95 S. Market St., Ste. 300
San Jose, CA 95113
Phone: (408) 995-3240
Fax: (408) 995-3243

**Description of services:**
1) Networks with prospective adoptive parents to find birthparents considering adoption;
2) represents adoptive parents in court;
3) interviews birthparents on behalf of adoptive parents;
4) interviews adoptive parents on behalf of birthparents;
5) makes all legal and practical arrangements;
6) represents adoptive parents in contested adoptions.

**Fees:** Varies on a case by case basis.

**Number of independent adoptions handled last year:** 60-80.

**Description of process:**
1) Prospective adoptive parents advertise to locate birthparent(s) considering adoption;
2) law firm takes interested calls and screens birthparents;
3) introduces birthparents to adoptive parents either face-to-face or in a prepared profile, if preferred by all parties;
4) concludes legal adoption and provides follow-up services, if needed.

**Licensed to place children:** Not applicable since in the State of California only birthparents may place their children for adoption; attorneys and others provide only ancillary services.

**Residency requirements for prospective adoptive parents:** None.

★ 1202 ★
**Alvin M. Coen**
**Attorney at Law**
16152 Beach Blvd., Ste. 101
Huntington Beach, CA 92647
Phone: (714) 841-3444
(800) 788-9594

**Description of services:**
1) Networks between birthparents considering adoption and prospective adoptive parents;
2) represents adoptive parents in court;
3) interviews birthparents on behalf of adoptive parents;
4) interviews adoptive parents on behalf of birthparents.

**Fees:**
1)Basic fee (where the rights of the birthparents are voluntarily terminated and the adoption is finalized in Los Angeles, Orange, Riverside, San Diego or San Bernardino counties): $3950.
2)Basic fee in all other counties of California: $3950 plus travel expenses.
3)Additional fees:
Petition for freedom from parental custody: $750.
Petition to terminate rights of unwed father: $500.
Court required search for unavailable parent: $375.
Interstate Compact Application (to enable child born in another state to be brought to California): $750.
Per diem rates (depending upon service rendered): $1000-$1500.
Hourly fee: $250.

**Number of independent adoptions handled last year:** 50.

**Description of process:** Petition filed after child is placed in adoptive home. State law requires a minimum of 6 mos. statutory period of investigation after placement. If investigation is successfully completed and rights of both parents are terminated within that time, the adoption worker files a report with the Court, thereby enabling attorney to request a hearing date. Court hearing will generally occur between 8-9 mos. after date on which child was taken into the adoptive home, which in independent adoptions is after release from hospital.

**Licensed to place children:** California.

**Residency requirements for prospective adoptive parents:** Adoptive parents must be residents of California by clearly established criteria, e.g. California Driver's License, Voter Registration, active bank accounts, etc.

★ 1203 ★
**Cook and Linden**
**A Professional Corporation**
8383 Wilshire Blvd., Ste. 1030
Beverly Hills, CA 90211-2401
Phone: (213) 655-2611
Fax: (213) 852-0871

**Description of services:** 1) Offers birth family outreach and matching services;
2) screens birth parents on behalf of prospective adoptive parents;
3) interviews prospective adoptive parents on behalf of birth parents;
4) represents adoptive parents in all legal proceedings;
5) provides medical arrangements for birth mother.

**Fees:** $1000 - $7500 depending upon adoptive parents' and birth parents' state of residence, number of hours of legal service and if birth mother outreach is required.

**Number of independent adoptions handled last year:** 100.

**Description of process:** 1) Meet with prospective adoptive parents;
2) birth parent intake;
3) introductory meeting between birth and prospective adoptive parents.

**Residency requirements for prospective adoptive parents:** None.

★ 1204 ★
**Douglas R. Donnelly**
**Attorney at Law**
926 Garden St.
Santa Barbara, CA 93101
Phone: (805) 962-0988
(800) 350-5683
Fax: (805) 966-2993

**Description of services:**
1) Assists birthmother as she selects adopting couple;
2) prepares resume of couple interested in adopting;
3) represents adoptive parents and the birthparent(s) in court (California has recognized that adoption proceedings are not necessarily adversarial but rather a cooperative effort by both the birth and adoptive parents to serve the best interests of the child);
4) interviews both parties involved;
5) provides medical arrangements for birthmother (which may include counseling);
6) prepares and executes all legal documents.

**Fees:** Hourly rate.

**Number of independent adoptions handled last year:** Approx. 100.

**Description of process:**
1) Prepare and file resume of couple interested in adopting;
2) birthparents review resumes for a suitable placement for their child;
3) if a particular couple is of interest, attorney advises birthparent(s) of her rights and options, the advantages and disadvantages of each;
4) arrange telephone contact;
5) if favorable, arrange meeting.

**Licensed to place children:** In California only birthparents and licensed child-placement agencies may place children for adoption.

**Residency requirements for prospective adoptive parents:** Complies with Interstate Compact on the Placement of Children.

**★ 1205 ★**
**Family Life Institute**
12625 High Bluff Dr., Ste. 202
San Diego, CA 92130
Phone: (619) 792-5774
Fax: (619) 792-5095

**Description of services:** 1) Screens adoptive applicants on behalf of birth parents and/or birth parents on behalf of adoptive applicants; 2) makes attorney referrals; 3) counseling program for prospective adoptive parents around open adoption issues, infertility and parenting an adopted child; 4) counseling program for birth parents around decision-making, issues of loss, and assessment and communication skills.

**Fees:** Unavailable.

**Number of independent adoptions handled last year:** 20.

**Description of process:** 1) Interview; 2) counseling; 3) birth parents/prospective adoptive parent(s) interview; 4) adoption education; 5) grief counseling.

**Residency requirements for prospective adoptive parents:** None.

**★ 1206 ★**
**Family Options Independent Adoption Services**
1756 Fillmore St.
San Francisco, CA 94115-3130
Phone: (415) 346-6998

**Description of services:**
1) Assists birthparents seeking an adoptive placement for their children;
2) interviews birthparents on behalf of prospective adoptive parents;
3) provides medical arrangements for birthmothers;
4) interviews adoptive parents on behalf of the birthparents;
5) pre-adoption counseling for adoptive and birthparents;
6) pre-adoption assessment for older children;
7) negotiation for post-adoption problems;
8) attachment disorder couseling.

**Fees:** $75/hr.

**Number of independent adoptions handled last year:** 10.

**Description of process:** Family Options provides pre-adoption education and planning for adoptive and birthparents and facilitates their plan once they are matched.

**Licensed to place children:** Birthparents directly place their children.

**Residency requirements for prospective adoptive parents:** None.

**★ 1207 ★**
**Farano & Kieviet**
Janice June Doezie
2100 S. State College Blvd.
Anaheim, CA 92806
Phone: (714) 935-2400

**Description of services:** 1) Screens birth parents on behalf of prospective adoptive parents, i.e. medical and personal history including HIV and drug testing; 2) screens prospective adoptive parents on behalf of birth parents, i.e. medical and personal history; 3) provides birth parents with medical referrals; 4) represents adoptive and/or birth parents in all legal proceedings; 5) legal document preparation and execution.

**Fees:** $3500 - $3900; additional costs: $250 - $500.

**Number of independent adoptions handled last year:** At least 10.

**Description of process:** 1) Match between birth parent(s) and prospective adoptive parent(s); 2) mutual participation in pregnancy and delivery; 3) 9 - 12 mos. after birth, adoption is finalized.

**Residency requirements for prospective adoptive parents:** None.

**★ 1208 ★**
**Harley A. Feinstein**
4370 La Jolla Village Dr., No. 600
San Diego, CA 92122
Phone: (619) 552-8080

**Description of services:** 1) Networks between birth parents making an adoptive decision for their child and prospective adoptive parents; 2) interviews birth parents on behalf of adoptive parents and/or adoptive parents on behalf of birth parents;; 3) represents adoptive parents in all court proceedings and/or birth parents in all court proceedings.

**Fees:** Varies with case.

**Number of independent adoptions handled last year:** 6.

**Description of process:** 1) Birth parent(s) select adoptive parents; 2) representative of county takes consents; 3) court approves adoption.

**Residency requirements for prospective adoptive parents:** None.

**★ 1209 ★**
**Steven C. Fishbein**
1621 Executive Ct.
Sacramento, CA 95864
Phone: (916) 489-9300
Fax: (916) 483-8656

**Description of services:**
1) Represents prospective adoptive or birthparents in court;
2) interviews both parties to the adoption;
3) provides assistance in making medical arrangements for birthmothers;
4) prepares and files all legal documents.

**Fees:** Retainer and hourly rate.

**Number of independent adoptions handled last year:** Unavailable.

**Description of process:** In accordance with adoption law.

**Licensed to place children:** N/A.

**Residency requirements for prospective adoptive parents:** Interstate adoption done in accordance with the Interstate Compact on the Placement of Children.

**★ 1210 ★**
**Gianelli & Fores**
Alison A. Sconyers
1014 Sixteenth St.
Modesto, CA 95354
Phone: (209) 521-6260

**Mailing address:**
P.O. Box 3212, Modesto, CA 95354

**Description of services:** 1) Handles both identified adoptions and networks between birth parents seeking an adoptive placement for their children and prospective adoptive parents; 2) screens birth parents on behalf of prospective adoptive parents and prospective parents on behalf of birth parents; 30 represents adoptive parents in all legal proceedings; 4) makes referrals for birth mother's medical arrangements.

**Fees:** Identified adoptions: $5000; adoptions with child matching: $10,000.

**Number of independent adoptions handled last year:** 0.

**Description of process:** After child's birth, a 6 mo. minimum is required to complete medicals, home study and background reports. Finalization requires another 30 to 60 days.

**Residency requirements for prospective adoptive parents:** 6 mos.

### ★ 1211 ★
**Jane A. Gorman**
**Attorney at Law**
930 W. 17th St., Ste. D
Santa Ana, CA 92706
Phone: (714) 558-1099
Fax: (714) 285-9895

**Description of services:**
1) Networks between birthmothers considering adoption and prospective adoptive couples;
2) represents adoptive parents in court;
3) represents birthparents in court;
4) interviews birthparents on behalf of adoptive parents;
5) interviews adoptive parents on behalf of birthparents;
6) assists birthmother in making medical arrangements.

**Fees:** $250/hr.

**Number of independent adoptions handled last year:** Approx. 35.

**Description of process:** Unavailable.

**Residency requirements for prospective adoptive parents:** Prospective adoptive parents must be residents of California.

### ★ 1212 ★
**Independent Adoption Center**
391 Taylor Blvd., Ste. 100
Pleasant Hill, CA 94523
Phone: (510) 827-BABY
(800) 877-6736
Fax: (510) 603-0820

**Branch address:**
Midwest Office, Indiana,
Phone: (800) 771-3721

Independent Adoption Center, 8616 La Tijera Blvd., Ste. 304, Los Angeles, CA 90045
Phone: (310) 215-3180

**Contact:** Jacqueline Dever Celenza, Community Relations Director.

**Description of services:**
1) Assistance with the formulation of resumes;
2) networking plans;
3) outreach to birthmothers in CA and across the U.S.;
4) counseling and support services for birthparents;
5) support groups, pre- and post-adoption educational workshops and social activities for adoptive parents;
6) attorney referrals;
7) interviews both parties to the adoption;
8) provides opportunities for birth and adoptive parents to meet and plan for a mutually satisfactory arrangement.

**Fees:** Sliding scale. No fee to birthparents.

**Number of independent adoptions handled last year:** 80-90.

**Description of process:**
1) Prospective adoptive parents prepare resume;
2) outreach services bring birthmothers to the center;

3) birthparents who contact the Center are counseled and assisted with adoption planning, if that is their choice;
4) prospective adoptive and birthparents meet and plan the placement of the expected child.

**Licensed to place children:** Center assists birthparents in placing their children.

**Residency requirements for prospective adoptive parents:** None.

### ★ 1213 ★
**Karen Lane**
**Attorney at Law**
100 Wilshire Blvd., Ste. 2075
Santa Monica, CA 90401
Phone: (310) 393-9802

**Description of services:**
1) Networks between birthparents considering adoption and prospective adoptive parents;
2) makes all pre-birth arrangements for birthmother, including medical care;
3) represents adoptive parents in court and prepares all legal documents;
4) interviews birthparents on behalf of adoptive applicants;
5) interviews adoptive applicants on behalf of birthparents;
6) post-birth services.

**Fees:** $4000.

**Number of independent adoptions handled last year:** 100.

**Description of process:**
1) Birthmother chooses and places infant with adoptive family;
2) Dept. of Social Services assigns caseworker to do home study and take birthmother's consent.

**Licensed to place children:** N/A.

**Residency requirements for prospective adoptive parents:** Adoptive parents must be residents of California to adopt in California, but attorney represents clients in other jurisdictions to facilitate adoptions.

### ★ 1214 ★
**David C. Laredo**
**Attorney at Law**
606 Forest Ave.
Pacific Grove, CA 93950
Phone: (408) 646-1502
Fax: (408) 646-0377

**Description of services:**
1) Placement counseling;
2) termination of parental rights;
3) represents adoptive or birth parents in court (not in the same case);
4) interviews both parties involved;
5) will make medical arrangements for birth mother;
6) referrals to private social worker for services.

**Fees:** Range $250 and up.

**Number of independent adoptions handled last year:** 30.

**Description of process:**
1) Interviews both birth and adoptive parents;
2) referral for private social worker counseling, as appropriate;
3) assists in obtaining consents, termination of rights (if necessary);
4) court appearance for finalization.

**Licensed to place children:** In California only birthparents or agencies may place children.

**Residency requirements for prospective adoptive parents:** 6 mos.

★ 1215 ★
**David Keene Leavitt**
**Attorney at Law**
9454 Wilshire Blvd., Penthouse
Beverly Hills, CA 90212
Phone: (310) 273-3151
(800) 249-0210

**Description of services:**
1) Outreach to prospective adoptive parents and birthparents considering adoptive placement for their children;
2) represents adoptive and birthparents in court in uncontested adoptions;
3) interviews both parties in the adoption;
4) provides medical and living arrangements for birthmother;
5) prepares and files all legal documents;
6) provides transfer services at hospital;
7) expert witness in contested adoptions and malpractice cases;
8) litigation attorney in contested adoptions.

**Fees:** Basic in California: $3500. Interstate: $4000.

**Number of independent adoptions handled last year:** 150 or more.

**Description of process:** Birthparents select identified adoptive couple. Infant is usually placed directly from the hospital.

**Licensed to place children:** N/A.

**Residency requirements for prospective adoptive parents:** Office handles independent adoptions in, to and from California.

★ 1216 ★
**Law Offices of Diane Michelsen**
3190 Old Tunnel Rd.
Lafayette, CA 94549
Phone: (510) 945-1880
(800) 877-1880
Fax: (510) 933-6807

**Contact:** Diane Michelsen, Owner.

**Description of services:**
1) Outreach planning, i.e. birthparent letters, mailing list development, flyers, ads and personal networking;
2) locating birthparents through office's extensive outreach programs;
3) coordination of adoption plan with hospital and physician;
4) gathering of birthparents background, ethnic, social and health history, including AIDS and drug-related information;
5) arrangements for pre and post-adoption meetings between adoptive or birthparents, if desired;
6) counselor referrals for adoptive and birthparents;
7) representation of adoptive and birthparents in court in uncontested adoptions;
8) interview of prospective adoptive parents on behalf of birthparents.

**Fees:** $285/hr.

**Number of independent adoptions handled last year:** Approx. 90.

**Description of process:**
1) Meets separately with birth and/or prospective adoptive parents;
2) assists birthparents in locating adoptive parents who they decide are right for their child;
3) assists prospective adoptive parents in locating a birthmother planning to relinquish her child through their own efforts or the Offices extensive outreach programs;
4) facilitates information exchange and meeting between birth and adoptive parents;
5) helps plan for delivery and child transfer;
6) coordinates social services;
7) secures relinquishments and files petition;
8) appears with adoptive parents at final hearing.

**Licensed to place children:** In private adoption in California only birthparents may place their children.

**Residency requirements for prospective adoptive parents:** None.

★ 1217 ★
**Murphy & Jacobs**
Timothy P. Murphy
555 Capitol Mall, Ste. 1540
Sacramento, CA 95814
Phone: (916) 447-1800

**Description of services:** 1) Networks with birth parents seeking adoptive placements for their children and prospective adoptive parents; 2) screens birth parents on behalf of adoptive parents and/or adoptive parents on behalf of birth parents; 3) represents adoptive parents in all legal proceedings; 4) makes referrals for medical arrangements for birth mother; 5) termination of birth parent(s)' parental rights.

**Fees:** $150 - $175/hr.

**Number of independent adoptions handled last year:** 15.

**Description of process:** Situation varies with each case. Firm provides services necessary to obtain adoption decree.

**Residency requirements for prospective adoptive parents:** Residency required.

★ 1218 ★
**Sanford & Harmssen**
Peter L. Sanford
4 N. Second St., No. 825
San Jose, CA 95113
Phone: (408) 286-9700

**Branch address:**
109 Limestone Ln., Santa Cruz, CA 95060
Phone: (408) 429-9337

**Description of services:** 1) Handles identified adoptions; 2) represents adoptive parents in all legal proceedings; 3) interviews birth parents on behalf of prospective adoptive parents and prospective adoptive parents on behalf of birth parents; 4) makes medical referrals for birth mother, if necessary.

**Fees:** $185/hr. Adoptions in which both birth parents are available to give their consent average $1000. Extra fees might include: Interstate Compact work, termination of alleged birth father's parental rights.

**Number of independent adoptions handled last year:** 10.

**Description of process:** 1) Meet with prospective adoptive parents and birth parents; 2) file adoption petition; 3) monitor adoption process; 4) home study by Dept. of Social Services; 5) liaison with social worker; 6) final court hearing.

**Residency requirements for prospective adoptive parents:** Statement of county residency required.

## ★ 1219 ★
**Lindsay Kohut Slatter, Esq.**
**Attorney at Law**
**Slatter, Slatter & Kiesel**
123 Jewel St.
Santa Cruz, CA 95060

**Description of services:**
1) Networks between birthparents considering adoptive placement and prospective adoptive parents;
2) represents adoptive parents in court;
3) represents birthparents in court;
4) interviews birthparents on behalf of adoptive parents;
5) interviews adoptive parents on behalf of birthparents;
6) provides medical arrangements for birthmother;
7) prepares and files all legal documents;
8) liaisons with social services;
9) provides liaison services for future contact between members of the triad, if desired.

**Fees:** $175/hr. or $3500 total fees.

**Number of independent adoptions handled last year:** 40 or more.

**Description of process:**
1) Assesses all parties before introduction of birthparent(s) to adoptive parents;
2) provides support services through pregnancy and coordinates legal and social services;
3) files necessary legal documents and provides representation in court (unless working interstate with other counsel);
4) provides follow-up services with all parties;
5) liaison for future contact if parties so desire.

**Licensed to place children:** N/A.

**Residency requirements for prospective adoptive parents:** None.

## ★ 1220 ★
**Jed Somit**
**Attorney at Law**
1440 Broadway, Ste. 910
Oakland, CA 94612
Phone: (510) 839-3215
Fax: (510) 839-7041

**Description of services:**
1) Represents adoptive or birthparents in court;
2) plans realistic budget agreeable to adoptive and birthparents;
3) provides genetic, medical and social history of birthmother;
4) facilitates meeting and on-going contact with birthparents, if desired;
5) interviews both adoptive and birthparents;
6) provides transfer services at hospital;
7) liaisons with social services;
8) prepares and files all legal documents;
9) handles contested adoptions.

**Fees:** $225/hr. Average total expense is usually less than $8500.

**Number of independent adoptions handled last year:** 12.

**Description of process:**
1) Office conference to establish client relationship with prospective adoptive parents;
2) plan outreach strategy to locate an adoptable child: compose an effective letter and devise strategy for maximum exposure; attorney discusses profile of adoptive parents with birthparents who contact office;

3) after birthmother selects adoptive parents, attorney follows up and arranges meeting;
4) attorney meets with both parties separately, advises both of their rights and the law, establishes a budget, and devises a plan of prenatal meetings and hospital procedures;
5) attorney coordinates with hospital and social services;
6) after infant's birth, attorney obtains necessary papers or orders terminating birthparents' rights;
7) once the infant is in the adoptive home, attorney files a Petition for Adoption;
8) Dept. of Social Services investigates adoptive home;
9) approximately 6 mos. after placement, the Decree of Adoption is granted and a replacement birth certificate is issued listing the adoptive parents as the child's parents.

**Licensed to place children:** Birthmothers select adoptive parents and place their children accordingly.

**Residency requirements for prospective adoptive parents:** None.

## ★ 1221 ★
**Van Deusen, Youmans & Walmsley, Inc.**
Ted R. Youmans
614 Civic Center Dr., W., Ste. 300
Santa Ana, CA 92701
Phone: (714) 547-6226
(800) 722-3678

**Description of services:** 1) Handles identified adoptions and networks between birth parents seeking an adoptive placement for their children and prospective adoptive parents; 2) screens birth parents on behalf of prospective adoptive parents and prospective adoptive parents on behalf of birth parents; 3) represents adoptive parents or birth parents in all legal proceedings; 4) makes medical referrals for birth mother.

**Fees:** Range of $3000.

**Number of independent adoptions handled last year:** 30 - 40.

**Description of process:** 1) Birth parent contact; 2) screening; 3) selection by birth parent(s) of prospective adoptive family; 4) financial and medical arrangements; 5) termination of birth parent(s) parental rights; 6) final court appearance.

**Licensed to place children:** Birthparents select adoptive parents.

**Residency requirements for prospective adoptive parents:** Statement of residency required.

## ★ 1222 ★
**Webster & Bayliss**
**Adoption Associates**
4525 Wilshire Blvd., Ste. 201
Los Angeles, CA 90010
Phone: (213) 664-5600
(800) 622-3678
Fax: (213) 664-4551

**Contact:** Felice A. Webster, Partner.

**Description of services:**
1) Assists and represents prospective adoptive parents throughout the entire adoption process;
2) handles step parent, adult, and agency adoptions.

**Fees:** $3600 for basic uncontested adoption. Additional for termination of parental rights and interstate placements.

**Number of independent adoptions handled last year:** Approx. 15.

**Description of process:**
1) Networks with adoptive parents to locate birthmother considering adoptive placement;
2) interviews birthmother;
3) presents prospective adoptive parents for birthmother's consideration;
4) provides pre- and post-birth services to adoptive applicants and birthparents; liaisons with adoption counselors;
5) represents adoptive parents during court proceedings.

**Licensed to place children:** Since attorneys in California do not place children, no licensing is necessary.

**Residency requirements for prospective adoptive parents:** None.

★ 1223 ★
**Beverly R. Williscroft**
**Attorney at Law**
3018 Willow Pass Rd., Ste. 201
Concord, CA 94519
Phone: (510) 676-3961
Fax: (510) 676-6215

**Description:** Chairperson of Adoptions Committee North of the California State Bar Association.

**Description of services:** Legal services include helping with match and preliminary paper work, Interstate Compact, if required, filing adoption petition; working on consent/termination/relinquishment procedures and clarifying birth parent(s)' rights; handling birth parent's expenses and acting as liaison with hospital; preparing final papers and court appearance for adoption decree.

**Fees:** $2500 for up to 15 hours of services; $200/hr. thereafter.

**Number of independent adoptions handled last year:** Approx. 75.

**Description of process:** 1) Determine match which will include a meeting of the birth parent(s) with the prospective adoptive family; 2) Meet with birth parent(s) for personal history information and to determine commitment to adoption decision; 3) Collect preliminary papers, e.g. information release, medical authorization, etc. 4) Adoption Service Provider meetings with both parties; 5) File adoption petition; 6) Liaison with social services for home study; 7) Termination of alleged birth father's parental rights, if necessary; 8) File report; 9) Finalization. Process is usually complete in 6 months.

**Residency requirements for prospective adoptive parents:** Prospective adoptive parents must show intent to reside in California.

# COLORADO

★ 1224 ★
**Pamela A. Gordon**
**Attorney at Law**
**Gordon & Marschhausen**
468 Corona St.
Denver, CO 80218
Phone: (303) 777-6051

**Description of services:**
1) Networks between prospective adoptive parents and birthparents considering an adoptive placement for their child;
2) prepares and executes all legal documents;

3) represents adoptive parents, birthparents, and others in court;
4) interviews adoptive parents on behalf of birthparents.

**Fees:** $75/hr. out of court; $100/hr. in court.

**Number of independent adoptions handled last year:** Colorado does not recognize "independent" adoptions, although independent custody actions are permitted.

**Description of process:**
1) Child is located by adoptive parents or agency or attorney is aware of birthparents wishing to place their child adoptively;
2) home study is prepared by licensed child placement agency or the Dept. of Social Services;
3) attorney files adoption petition;
4) adoption is finalized after one-year waiting period.

**Licensed to place children:** In Colorado attorneys to not place children. All adoptions are court authorized.

**Residency requirements for prospective adoptive parents:** None.

# CONNECTICUT

★ 1225 ★
**Jewish Family Service**
2370 Park Ave.
Bridgeport, CT 06604
Phone: (203) 366-5438

**Description of services:** Licensed by the State of Connecticut to conduct home studies.

**Fees:** $1200.

**Home study description:** Assessment which addresses such issues family and personal history, health, finances, marital relationship (if applicable), attitudes about adoption, motivation and preparation for adoption.

**Residency requirements for prospective adoptive parents:** Residents of Connecticut.

★ 1226 ★
**Professional Counseling Center**
1 Eliot Pl.
Fairfield, CT 06430
Phone: (203) 259-5350

**Description of services:** Prepares and writes home studies for prospective adoptive parents pursuing inter-country or identified adoptions; post-placement counseling and services.

**Fees:** Home study: $850 $75/hr.; travel expenses.

**Number of independent adoptions handled last year:** Unavailable.

**Description of process:** N/A.

**Licensed to place children:** Connecticut.

**Residency requirements for prospective adoptive parents:** Connecticut residents.

# DISTRICT OF COLUMBIA

**★ 1227 ★**
**Joseph, Gajarsa, McDermott & Reiner, P.C.**
Mark T. McDermott
1300 - 19th St., NW, No. 400
Washington, DC 20036
Phone: (202) 331-1955

**Description:** Mark T. McDermott is a member of the American Academy of Adoption Attorneys.

**Description of services:** 1) screens birth parents on behalf of prospective adoptive parents and prospective adoptive parents on behalf of birth parents; 2) represents adoptive parents or birth parents in all legal proceedings; 3) makes medical arrangements for birth mother.

**Fees:** $195/hr.

**Number of independent adoptions handled last year:** 80.

**Description of process:** 1) Meet with prospective adoptive parents; 2) remain available while they search for birth parents; 3) legal document preparation and execution; 4) court appearance.

**Residency requirements for prospective adoptive parents:** None.

# FLORIDA

**★ 1228 ★**
**Law Offices of Bennett S. Cohn, P.A.**
205 Sixth St.
West Palm Beach, FL 33401
Phone: (407) 833-8747

**Description of services:** 1) Networks between birth parents seeking an adoptive placement for their children and prospective adoptive parents; 2) represents adoptive parents in all legal proceedings; 3) screens birth parents on behalf of prospective adoptive parents and screens prospective adoptive parents on behalf of birth parents; 4) provides medical arrangement for birth mother.

**Fees:** $2500 - $5000.

**Number of independent adoptions handled last year:** 50.

**Description of process:** 1) Locate birth mother; 2) termination of birth parents' parental rights; 3) finalization.

**Residency requirements for prospective adoptive parents:** 6 mos.

**★ 1229 ★**
**Grass and Grass, Attorneys**
Mikal W. Grass, Esq.
505 E. New Haven Ave.
Melbourne, FL 32901
Phone: (407) 722-1360

**Description of services:** 1) Birth family outreach and matching;
2) represents prospective adoptive parents in all legal proceedings;
3) screens birth parents on behalf of prospective adoptive parents;
4) interviews prospective adoptive parents on behalf of birth parents;
5) provides medical and counseling arrangements for birth mother.

**Fees:** Consultation: $175. Home study: $1350.

**Number of independent adoptions handled last year:** 50.

**Description of process:** 1) Initial interview:
2) birth family search based on adoptive family profile;
3) upon birth family location and acceptance, liaison services for home study, medical, etc.;
4) placement.

**Residency requirements for prospective adoptive parents:** Residents of Florida.

**★ 1230 ★**
**Clay Henderson**
**Attorney at Law**
1005 N. Dixie Freeway
New Smyrna Beach, FL 32168
Phone: (904) 427-2211
Fax: (904) 423-5507

**Description of services:**
1) Provides intermediary services between birthparents considering adoption and prospective adoptive parents;
2) represents adoptive parents in court;
3) interviews birthparents on behalf of adoptive parents;
4) consults with birthparents;
5) makes medical arrangements for birthmother;
6) liaisons with social service providers for home study.

**Fees:** $750-$3000. Total costs to adoptive parents can range from $1000-$10,000 depending upon circumstances of the birthmother, i.e. living expenses during pregnancy, medical bills, etc. Florida law limits intermediary fee to $1000 and caps living expenses at $2500.

**Number of independent adoptions handled last year:** 15.

**Description of process:**
1) Birthparents contact attorney;
2) assist birthparents in choosing suitable adoptive parents;
3) contact a licensed professional to conduct preliminary background check and home study on adoptive applicants; also interviews birthparents to ascertain that their decision is free and voluntary;
4) if adoptive applicants are approved, consents to adoption and termination of parental rights papers are signed after the infant's birth;
5) attorney receives child at hospital and places child in adoptive home;
6) 90 day post-placement period wherein licensed professional again visits adoptive home;
7) if report is favorable, the final judgment of adoption is rendered in a court hearing attended by adoptive parents and child.

**Licensed to place children:** In the State of Florida attorneys may act as intermediaries in adoptions.

**Residency requirements for prospective adoptive parents:** Prospective adoptive parents must be residents of the State of Florida.

**★ 1231 ★**
**Donald F. Jacobs**
**Attorney at Law**
**Jacobs & Jacobs, Chartered**
1214 E. Concord St.
Orlando, FL 32803
Phone: (407) 896-9400

**Description of services:**
1) Provides intermediary services between prospective adoptive parents and birthmothers considering adoption for their children;
2) represents adoptive or birthparents in court;
3) provides medical arrangements for birthmother;
4) interviews birthparents on behalf of adoptive parents;
5) prepares and files all legal documents.

**Fees:** Hourly rate plus costs and expenses.

**Number of independent adoptions handled last year:** 25.

**Description of process:**
1) Attorney interviews prospective adoptive parents to establish client relationship;
2) liaisons with Dept. of Health and Rehabilitative Services to meet requirements for adoptive placement;
3) attorney secures consent from birthparents after birth;
4) 90 days after placement, attorney and adoptive parents appear in court to finalize adoption.

**Licensed to place children:** Intermediaries may place children in the State of Florida.

**Residency requirements for prospective adoptive parents:** Adoptive parents must reside and work in the State of Florida.

★ 1232 ★
**Anthony B. Marchese**
**Attorney at Law**
4010 Boy Scout Blvd., Ste. 590
Tampa, FL 33607
Phone: (813) 877-6643

**Description of services:**
1) Provides outreach to prospective adoptive parents and birthparents considering an adoptive placement for their children;
2) represents adoptive parents in court;
3) represents birthparents in court in a contested adoption;
4) interviews both parties in the adoption;
5) provides medical arrangements for birthmother;
6) coordinates services of Dept. of Health & Rehabilitative Services;
7) prepares and files all legal documents.

**Fees:** Approx. $2500 subject to Court approval.

**Number of independent adoptions handled last year:** 24.

**Description of process:**
1) Prospective adoptive parents identify an adoptable child through their own efforts or the networking of the Law Offices;
2) prospective adoptive parents provide medical assistance to birthmother during her pregnancy;
3) consents for adoption are secured after child's birth;
4) child is placed in adoptive home subject to the approval of the Dept. of Health & Rehabilitative Services;
5) after Dept. of Health & Rehabilitative Services conducts its investigation and approves the adoptive home, adoptive parents appear in court with attorney to finalize adoption.

**Licensed to place children:** Florida allows the services of intermediaries to place children in adoptive homes.

**Residency requirements for prospective adoptive parents:** Adoptive parents must be residents of the State of Florida.

# GEORGIA

★ 1233 ★
**Adoption Information Services**
Marcia S. Baker
558 Dovie Pl.
Lawrenceville, GA 30244
Phone: (404) 339-7236

**Description of services:** 1) Conducts *Adoption Readiness Assessments*;
2) consultation and in-depth educational instruction with adoptive parents throughout adoption process;
3) provides information regarding domestic and international adoption;
4) provides referrals to agency and independent placement sources;
5) INS and dossier preparation assistance;
6) conducts *Adoption Process* and *Adoption Preparation* seminars.

**Fees:** Placement Sources Matching Services: $150
Confidential consultation: $50/hr.

**Number of independent adoptions handled last year:** 100.

**Description of process:** 1) Prospective adoptive parents complete confidential questionnaire; 2) facilitator matches desires and personal situation to comprehensive database of agency and independent adoption placement sources; 3) facilitator provides detailed program information on sources for which the prospective adoptive parents qualify and which meet with their specifications.

**Residency requirements for prospective adoptive parents:** None.

★ 1234 ★
**L. Daniel Butler, Attorney at Law**
561 Greene St.
Augusta, GA 30901
Phone: (706) 724-0070
Fax: (706) 724-5886

**Mailing address:**
P.O. Box 1210, Augusta, GA 30901

**Description of services:** 1) Facilitates primarily identified adoptions;
2) screens birth parents on behalf of prospective adoptive parents;
3) represents adoptive parents in all legal proceedings;
4) interviews prospective adoptive parents on behalf of birth parents;
5) provides medical arrangements for birth mother.

**Fees:** $150/hr.
Minimum fee for independent adoption: $1500.

**Number of independent adoptions handled last year:** 11.

**Description of process:** Unavailable.

**Residency requirements for prospective adoptive parents:** 6 mos. residency.

★ 1235 ★
**Ruth F. Clairborne, P.C.**
The Hurt Bldg., Ste. 995
50 Hurt Plaza
Atlanta, GA 30303
Phone: (404) 521-3100

**Description of services:** 1) Provides intermediary services between prospective adoptive parents and birth parents seeking an adoptive placement for their child;
2) screens birth parents on behalf of prospective adoptive parents;
3) screens prospective adoptive parents on behalf of birth parents;
4)represents adoptive parents in all legal proceedings;
5) can provide medial arrangements for birth mother.

**Fees:** $165/hr. plus $45/hr legal assistant and expenses.

**Number of independent adoptions handled last year:** 25.

**Description of process:** 1) Prospective adoptive parent(s) are interviewed re: their wishes and needs; 2) identification of birth family; 3) interview birth parents and explain all necessary documentation; 4) birth; 5) surrender documents signed and infant placed; 6) petition with exhibits signed.

**Residency requirements for prospective adoptive parents:** Residency required for full service, but can facilitate interstate adoptions with birth parent contact.

★ 1236 ★
**Cowen & Cowen**
**Attorneys at Law**
148 S. Main St.
Jonesboro, GA 30236
Phone: (404) 471-1683

**Mailing address:**
  P.O. Box 1195, Jonesboro, GA 30236

**Description of services:** 1) Handles identified adoptions; 2) represents adoptive parents in all court proceedings; 3) preparation of Petition and Surrender documents.

**Fees:** $500 - $1000.

**Number of independent adoptions handled last year:** At least 10.

**Description of process:** 1) Prepare documents or publish notice, if no surrender required; 2) filing of case with court; 3) schedule and attending any court hearings; 4) arrangements to have infant released to adoptive parents from hospital, if applicable.

**Residency requirements for prospective adoptive parents:** 6 mos.

★ 1237 ★
**Family Counseling Center of the CSRA, Inc.**
630 Ellis St.
Augusta, GA 30901-1464
Phone: (706) 722-6512

**Date established:** 1980.

**Description:** Private, non-profit agency licensed by the Georgia Department of Human Resources.

**Description of services:** Home studies conducted to meet the requirements of placing agency.

**Fees:** Home Study: $700. Home Study Update: $300.

**Number of independent adoptions handled last year:** N/A.

**Average length of time to complete home study:** 10 wks.

**Number of interviews:** 4.

**Home study description:** Assessment which generally includes prospective adoptive parents' motivation and expectations of an adopted child, marital relationship, home and community, home safety, ability to support child and attitudes of extended family.

**Residency requirements for prospective adoptive parents:** Residents of the Augusta metropolitan area.

★ 1238 ★
**Rhonda L. Fishbein, Esq.**
17 Executive Park Dr., Ste. 480
Atlanta, GA 30329
Phone: (404) 248-9205

**Description of services:** 1) Handles identified adoption; 2) screens birth parents on behalf of prospective adoptive parents and prospective adoptive parents on behalf of birth parents; 3) represents adoptive parents in all court proceedings; 4) provides medical arrangements for birth mother; 5) preparation and execution of all legal documents.

**Fees:** $175/hr.

**Number of independent adoptions handled last year:** 25.

**Description of process:** Unavailable.

**Residency requirements for prospective adoptive parents:** None.

★ 1239 ★
**Fulcher, Hagler, Reed, Hanks & Harper**
Mark C. Wilby
520 Greene St.
Augusta, GA 30901
Phone: (706) 724-0171

**Description of services:** 1) Handles mostly identified adoptions; 2) screens birth parents on behalf of prospective adoptive parents and prospective adoptive parents on behalf of birth parents; 3) represents adoptive parents in all legal proceedings.

**Fees:** Unavailable.

**Number of independent adoptions handled last year:** 15.

**Description of process:** Unavailable.

**Residency requirements for prospective adoptive parents:** None.

★ 1240 ★
**Philip F. Woodward**
P.O. Box 1678
Dalton, GA 30722-1678
Phone: (706) 278-3535

**Description of services:** 1) Handles mostly identified adoptions; 2) represents adoptive parents in all legal proceedings; 3) preparation and execution of all legal documents.

**Fees:** $500 attorney's fee; $60 court filing fee; $100/hr. additional for contested court hearing.

**Number of independent adoptions handled last year:** 30.

**Description of process:** 1) Initial consultation with prospective adoptive parents; 2) interview with birth parents; 3) drafting and executing of parental rights' surrender; 4) drafting and filing of adoption petition; 5) court hearing and finalization.

**Residency requirements for prospective adoptive parents:** 6 mos. prior to filing in Georgia.

# ILLINOIS

**★ 1241 ★**
**Michael W. Heller**
**Attorney at Law**
Commerce Bank Bldg., Ste. 916
Peoria, IL 61602-1103
Phone: (309) 674-1007
Fax: (309) 674-1045

**Description of services:**
1) Represents adoptive parents in court;
2) prepares and executes all legal documents;
3) petition for new birth certificate.

**Fees:** $400 - $500.

**Number of independent adoptions handled last year:** 6.

**Description of process:**
1) Adoptive parents identify child or expectant birthmother;
2) attorney interviews adopting parents to garner information;
3) attorney secures consent from birthparent(s);
4) attorney prepares and files Petition for Adoption;
5) attorney prepares and files Interim Order;
6) attorney prepares and files Order for Investigation;
7) adopting parents and attorney attend hearing;
8) entry of Decree of Adoption and new birth certificate.

**Licensed to place children:** N/A.

**Residency requirements for prospective adoptive parents:** Adoptive parents must be residents of Illinois for 1 yr.

**★ 1242 ★**
**Jessica Sticklin**
**Attorney at Law**
412 S. Franklin
Decatur, IL 62523
Phone: (217) 422-2280
Fax: (217) 422-0622

**Description of services:**
1) Prepares and files all legal documents;
2) represents adoptive parents in court;
3) obtains legal consents and publishes notice of impending adoption.

**Fees:** $500-$750 plus costs, if uncontested.

**Number of independent adoptions handled last year:** 12.

**Description of process:**
1) File petition for adoption;
2) prepare related documents, i.e. consent forms;
3) interim hearing held;
4) publish notice if necessary, i.e. no consent from putative father;
5) final hearing.

**Licensed to place children:** Not applicable since attorney does not provide intermediary/placement services but acts only in identified adoptions.

**Residency requirements for prospective adoptive parents:** Prospective adoptive parents must be residents of the State of Illinois for 1 yr.

# INDIANA

**★ 1243 ★**
**Steven M. Kirsh**
**Attorney at Law**
401 Pennsylvania Pkwy., Ste. 370
Indianapolis, IN 46280-1390
Phone: (317) 575-5555
Fax: (317) 575-5631

**Description of services:**
1) Represents either birth or adoptive parents in court;
2) interviews birth parents on behalf of adoptive parents;
3) interviews adoptive parents on behalf of birthparents;
4) provides medical arrangements for birthmother;
5) prepares consent forms for birthparents after infant's delivery;
6) provides transfer services at hospital.

**Fees:** Attorney fees for uncontested adoption: $2500-$5000.

**Number of independent adoptions handled last year:** 140-150.

**Description of process:**
1) Meet with both birth and adoptive parents;
2) provide arrangements for medical care and delivery;
3) provide consent forms after infant's delivery;
4) appear in court with adoptive parents;
5) accompany adoptive parents to hospital to assume custody.

**Licensed to place children:** N/A.

**Residency requirements for prospective adoptive parents:** Prospective adoptive parents must be residents of Indiana to adopt in Indiana courts but can provide interstate adoption services with attorney licensed in adoptive parents' state of residence. No residency requirement for families who adopt "hard-to-place" children. "Hard-to-place" includes medical special needs and black or racially mixed children.

**★ 1244 ★**
**Franklin I. Miroff**
**Attorney at Law**
**Miroff, Cross, Ruppert and Klineman**
251 E. Ohio, Ste. 1000
Indianapolis, IN 46204-2133
Phone: (317) 264-1040
Fax: (317) 264-1039

**Description of services:**
1) Prepares and executes all petitions and court orders;
2) filing of documents with various state agencies;
3) provides medical arrangements for birthmother and disburses funds necessary for those services;
4) represents adoptive parents in court;
5) interviews birthparents on behalf of adoptive parents and procures medical history, educational background, lifestyles, activities and condition;
6) protects the identities of both parties;
7) facilitates interstate placements;
8) adoption litigation.

**Fees:** Usual range from $1500 - $3000.

**Number of independent adoptions handled last year:** 35.

**Description of process:**
1) Interviews prospective adoptive parents;

2) interviews birthmother and informs her that he is representing the prospective adoptive parents, refers her to another attorney, if she so wishes, obtains her medical and social history, clarifies her legal alternatives with her; reviews the entire adoption procedure as well as a sample consent form and its consequences; defines the financial responsibility of the adoptive parents regarding medical and hospitalization expenses; and learns her preferences as to what type of adoptive parents she wishes for her child;

3) correlates with investigating agency for home study of prospective adoptive home;

4) provides medical arrangements for birthmother;

5) files petition;

6) after birth, obtains necessary consent(s);

7) court appearances and final decree.

**Licensed to place children:** In the State of Indiana, intermediaries are permitted to place children for adoption.

**Residency requirements for prospective adoptive parents:** By law. Complies with the Interstate Compact on the Placement of Children for interstate placements.

# KANSAS

**★ 1245 ★**
**Hazlett Law Offices**
Allan A. Hazlett
1608 SW Mulvane
Topeka, KS 66604-2746
Phone: (913) 232-2011

**Description of services:** 1) Handles both identified adoptions and is aware of birth parents seeking an adoptive placement for their children; 2) formulates search plan for birth family with prospective adoptive parents; 3) screens birth parents on behalf of prospective adoptive parents; 4) represents adoptive parents and/or birth parents in all legal proceedings; 5) provides medical arrangement for birth mother.

**Fees:** $500 - $5000.

**Number of independent adoptions handled last year:** 17.

**Description of process:** 1) Design of search plan; 2) interview with birth parents; 3) review of medical and counseling process; 4) preparation of legal documents; 5) ICPC facilitation, if necessary.

**Residency requirements for prospective adoptive parents:** None.

**★ 1246 ★**
**Richard A. Macias**
**Attorney at Law**
622 N. St. Francis
Wichita, KS 67214-3810
Phone: (316) 265-5289
(800) 362-2909
Fax: (316) 265-3953

**Description of services:** 1) Emotional and legal counseling for birth parents; 2) provides medical arrangements for birth mother; 3) educational and career counseling for birth mothers; 4) legal counsel for prospective adoptive parents; 5) provides intermediary services between birth parents considering adoption and prospective adoptive parents.

**Fees:** $125/hr.

**Number of independent adoptions handled last year:** 23.

**Description of process:** 1) Formulation of child search plan; 2) home study completed; 3) birth parents select prospective adoptive parents; 4) birth and placement; 5) finalization after 30-60 days.

**Residency requirements for prospective adoptive parents:** None.

# KENTUCKY

**★ 1247 ★**
**James A. Crumlin**
**Attorney at Law**
608 W. Muhammad Ali Blvd., Ste. 503
Louisville, KY 40203
Phone: (502) 585-2374
Fax: (502) 585-2375

**Description of services:**
1) Represents adoptive parents and/or birthparents in court;
2) interviews both parties in the adoption;
3) prepares and files all legal documents.

**Fees:** $300 plus court costs.

**Number of independent adoptions handled last year:** 2.

**Description of process:** Prospective adoptive parents identify adoptable child or expectant birthmother seeking an adoptive placement for her child.

**Licensed to place children:** N/A.

**Residency requirements for prospective adoptive parents:** Adoptive parents must be residents of Kentucky for 180 days.

# LOUISIANA

**★ 1248 ★**
**JoAnn Gines**
509 Marshall St., Ste. 712
Shreveport, LA 71101
Phone: (318) 424-5033
Fax: (318) 227-9101

**Mailing address:**
  P.O. Box 143, Shreveport, LA 71101

**Description of services:**
1) Represents adoptive parents in court;
2) represents birthparents in court;
3) interviews adoptive parents on behalf of birthparents;
4) interviews birthparents on behalf of adoptive parents;
5) provides medical arrangements for birthmother;
6) prepares pleadings;
7) prepares Act of Surrender or comparable document divesting parental rights;
8) prepares administrative agency documents;
9) 2 court appearances.

**Fees:** Minimum $1500.

**Number of independent adoptions handled last year:** 3-5.

**Description of process:**
1) Interview birthparents and adoptive applicants;
2) terminate parental rights;
3) petition for Interlocutory Judgment;
4) adoptive applicants complete home study by state licensed agency;
5) comply with Interstate Compact, if child is born outside of Louisiana;

6) petition for final decree of adoption;
7) service of process and Curator.

**Licensed to place children:** N/A.

**Residency requirements for prospective adoptive parents:** Adoptive applicants must be residents of Louisiana for at least 6 mos.

# MAINE

★ 1249 ★
**...and baby makes three, inc.**
Dale L. McKibben, President
RR 1, Box 822
South Lebanon, ME 04027-9737
Phone: (207) 339-2121

**Description of services:** 1) Interviews birth parents on behalf of prospective adoptive parents and prospective adoptive parents on behalf of birth parents; 2) helps prospective adoptive parents formulate a search plan for an adoptable child; 3) makes referrals for medical arrangements for birth mother; 4) makes legal referrals.

**Fees:** $2500.

**Number of independent adoptions handled last year:** 7.

**Description of process:** Clients provide information about themselves and their families and the type of child they are hoping will be placed with them. Facilitator passes this information to birth parents seeking an adoptive placement for their child. If the prospective adoptive family is selected by the birth parents, facilitator coordinates the adoption.

**Residency requirements for prospective adoptive parents:** None.

★ 1250 ★
**Susan E. Bowie**
**Attorney at Law**
66 Pearl St., Ste. 321
Portland, ME 04101
Phone: (207) 774-5621

**Description of services:**
1) Represents adoptive and/or birthparents in court;
2) provides medical arrangements for birthmother, if requested;
3) prepares and files all legal documents.

**Fees:** $125/hr.

**Number of independent adoptions handled last year:** Approx. 20.

**Description of process:** Prospective adoptive parents identify an adoptable child or a birthmother seeking an adoptive placement for her unborn child. Attorney represents client in all phases.

**Licensed to place children:** N/A.

**Residency requirements for prospective adoptive parents:** None.

# MICHIGAN

★ 1251 ★
**Adoption Law Center, P.C.**
Janis Weaver, Director
3250 Coolidge Hwy.
Berkley, MI 48072
Phone: (810) 548-1430

**Description of services:** 1) Represents either adoptive or birth parents in all legal proceedings; 2) can make referrals for birth mother's medical arrangements; 3) liaisons between prospective adoptive and birth parents; 4) refers prospective adoptive parents to venues of available children.

**Fees:** Hourly rate and cost of medical services.

**Number of independent adoptions handled last year:** Michigan State Law changed only in January, 1994 to permit independent adoption.

**Description of process:** Birth parents select the adoptive placement for their child. After birth, the child is placed *temporarily* in the adoptive home. Within 48 hrs, of that placement the court must be petitioned for a hearing date. Until that hearing the placement is considered *at risk* since it is then that birth parents surrender their parental rights.

**Residency requirements for prospective adoptive parents:** If child is to be placed in adoptive home prior to finalization, adoptive parents must be Michigan residents.

# MISSOURI

★ 1252 ★
**Robert A. Cox**
**The Cox Law Firm, P.C.**
6822 Delmar
St. Louis, MO 63130
Fax: (314) 726-2148

**Description of services:**
1) Outreach services to birthmothers considering adoptive placement for their children;
2) represents adoptive parents in court;
3) interviews birthparents on behalf of the adoptive parents;
4) provides medical arrangements for birthmother, if requested;
5) prepares and files all legal documents;
6) liaisons with social services for adoptive studies.

**Fees:** $150/hr. Estimated cost $2500-$5000 plus medical, agency and miscellaneous expenses.

**Number of independent adoptions handled last year:** Approx. 9.

**Description of process:**
1) Attorney refers birthmother to licensed agency for social services after interview and match with prospective adoptive parents;
2) following delivery, child may go into foster care pending termination of parental rights;
3) after custody is transferred and 9 mos. after placement, adoption can be finalized. Alternately, at adoptive parents' request, child can be placed without terminating parental rights which is an at-risk placement. Court orders transfer of custody and adoptive parents wait 9 mos. during which time birthmother can reclaim her child.

**Licensed to place children:** Intermediary services are legal in Missouri.

**Residency requirements for prospective adoptive parents:** None.

★ 1253 ★
**Ralph Levy III**
**Attorney at Law**
225 S. Meramec, Ste. 1100
St. Louis, MO 63105
Phone: (314) 727-7200

**Description of services:**
1) Represents adoptive parents in court;
2) prepares and files all legal documents.

**Fees:** Hourly rate.

**Number of independent adoptions handled last year:** Unavailable.

**Description of process:** Prospective adoptive parents identify an adoptable child or an expectant birthmother seeking an adoptive placement for her child. Attorney will prepare and file legal documents and represent adoptive parents in court.

**Licensed to place children:** N/A.

**Residency requirements for prospective adoptive parents:** Adoptive parents must be residents of Missouri.

# NEVADA

★ 1254 ★
**Cliff J. Young**
**Attorney at Law**
600 S. Virginia St., Ste. B
Reno, NV 89501
Phone: (702) 786-3882

**Description of services:**
1) Represents adoptive parents in court;
2) interviews birthparents on behalf of adoptive parents, if requested;
3) prepares and files all legal documents;
4) coordinates medical/hospital services for birthmother.

**Fees:** $500 plus filing fees, medical/hospital expenses.

**Number of independent adoptions handled last year:** 3.

**Description of process:**
1) Prospective adoptive parents identify adoptable child or expectant birthmother seeking an adoptive placement for her child;
2) attorney meets with adoptive parents to establish client relationship;
3) after child's birth, attorney files petition with consent of birthparent(s);
4) attorney appears with adoptive parents to finalize adoption in court.

**Licensed to place children:** N/A.

**Residency requirements for prospective adoptive parents:** None.

# NEW JERSEY

★ 1255 ★
**Carol S. Perlmutter**
**Attorney at Law**
P.O. Box 1012
Flemington, NJ 08822
Phone: (908) 782-5500

**Description of services:** 1) Handles predominantly identified adoptions, 50% of which are international; 2) screens birth parents on behalf of prospective adoptive parents; 3) represents adoptive parents in all legal proceedings; 4) makes referrals for medical arrangements for birth mother; 5) assists prospective adoptive parents in development of search plan for an adoptable child; 6) Finalizes adoptions in U.S. courts which may or may not have been finalized in a foreign jurisdiction.

**Fees:** Attorney fees vary with country and process.

**Number of independent adoptions handled last year:** 30.

**Description of process:** 1) Telephone interview to review options; 2) complete paperwork and procure medical background of birth parent(s); 3) referral for home study and background check (in NJ if a placement occurs in state, the home study may be done after placement, otherwise a satisfactory home study must be concluded before a child is placed in an adoptive home); 4) placement and filing of complaint for termination of birth parents' parental rights; 5) petition adoption; 6) post-placement supervision (1 visit before first court appearance and 2-3 supervisory meetings before second court appearance; 6) finalization after a minimum of 8 mos.

**Residency requirements for prospective adoptive parents:** Statement of residency required.

★ 1256 ★
**Eileen Rhea Tulipan**
**Attorney at Law**
**Tulipan, Goldman & Conk, P.C.**
26 Journal Square, Ste. 602
Jersey City, NJ 07306
Phone: (201) 963-0444
Fax: (201) 963-1396

**Mailing address:**
P.O. Box 6826, Jersey City, NJ 07306
**Branch address:**
George W. Conk, Esq., 76 South Orange Ave., South Orange, NJ 07079
Phone: (201) 763-1993

**Description of services:**
1) Facilitates identified adoption;
2) prepares and executes all legal documents;
3) represents adoptive parents in court;
4) application for revised birth certificate.

**Fees:** $750 minimum for an uncontested adoption. Other fees vary.

**Number of independent adoptions handled last year:** 4.

**Description of process:**
1) Prepares complaint;
2) orders fixing date for preliminary hearing;
3) orders fixing date for final hearing and judgment;
4) applies for revised birth certificate.

**Licensed to place children:** N/A.

**Residency requirements for prospective adoptive parents:** Adoptive parents must be residents of the State of New Jersey.

# NEW MEXICO

★ 1257 ★
**Anne H. Assink**
**Attorney at Law**
501 Tijeras N.W., Ste. 107
Albuquerque, NM 87107
Phone: (505) 242-9982
Fax: (505) 242-8702

**Description of services:** 1) Handles mainly identified adoptions; 2) interviews birth parents on behalf of prospective adoptive parents and prospective adoptive parents on behalf of birth parents; 3) represents adoptive parents/or birth parents in all legal proceedings; 4) makes medical arrangements for birth mother.

**Fees:** $150/hr.

**Number of independent adoptions handled last year:** Several.

**Residency requirements for prospective adoptive parents:** Must be a bona fide resident of New Mexico.

★ 1258 ★
**David R. Preininger**
1905 Venus Ct., N.E.
Albuquerque, NM 87112
Phone: (505) 299-5591
Fax: (505) 299-5591

**Description of services:**
  1) Interviews either adoptive or birthparents on behalf of the other party;
  2) prepares and writes home study of adoptive home;
  3) counsels birthparents considering relinquishment.

**Fees:** $600-$800 for complete home study.

**Number of independent adoptions handled last year:** 8.

**Description of process:**
  1) Prospective adoptive parents identify adoptable child or birth mother considering adoption for her child;
  2) counselor interviews all members of adoptive family;
  3) interviews prospective adoptee if appropriate;
  4) visits prospective adoptive home;
  5) counselor verifies employment of adoptive applicants, does criminal background checks and receives physician's report.

**Licensed to place children:** Home studies only.

**Residency requirements for prospective adoptive parents:** Adoptive parents must be residents of New Mexico for 6 mos.

# NEW YORK

★ 1259 ★
**Aaron Britvan**
**Attorney at Law**
7600 Jericho Trnpk.
Woodbury, NY 11797
Phone: (516) 496-2222

**Description of services:**
  1) Represents adoptive parents in court;
  2) may interview birth or adoptive parents on behalf of the other party;
  3) prepares and files all legal documents.

**Fees:** Case by case basis.

**Number of independent adoptions handled last year:** Unavailable because of confidentiality.

**Description of process:** Unavailable.

**Licensed to place children:** N/A.

**Residency requirements for prospective adoptive parents:** None.

★ 1260 ★
**Gloria A. Copland, Esq.**
**Copland & Copland**
99 Pine St.
P.O. Box 34
Albany, NY 12201-0034
Phone: (518) 434-0878

**Description of services:**
  1) Represents adoptive parents in court;
  2) prepares and files all legal documents.

**Fees:** Vary by case.

**Number of independent adoptions handled last year:** Unavailable.

**Description of process:** Prospective adoptive parents identify adoptable child or expectant birthmother seeking adoptive placement for her child.

**Licensed to place children:** N/A.

**Residency requirements for prospective adoptive parents:** Adoptive parents must be residents of New York State for at least 6 mos.

★ 1261 ★
**Raymond J. Dague**
200 Empire Bldg.
472 S. Salina St.
Syracuse, NY 13202
Phone: (315) 422-2052
Fax: (315) 422-4424

**Description of services:**
  1) Represents adoptive and/or birthparents in court;
  2) prepares and files all legal documents;
  3) interviews both parties to the adoption;
  4) provides medical arrangements for birthmother;
  5) networks between prospective adoptive parents and birthparents considering adoptive placement for their child.

**Fees:** Hourly rate.

**Number of independent adoptions handled last year:** Unavailable.

**Description of process:** Procedures differ dramatically depending on kind of adoption.

**Licensed to place children:** In New York State private placements may be performed without a license.

**Residency requirements for prospective adoptive parents:** Child must reside with his/her adoptive parents for 6 mos. prior to finalization.

★ 1262 ★
**Christine Mesberg**
**Attorney at Law**
28 Hilltop Rd.
Waccabuc, NY 10597
Phone: (914) 669-5401

**Description:** Member of the New York State Bar Association Adoption Committee and the American Academy of Adoption Attorneys. Practice is entirely devoted to adoption law.

**Description of services:** Document preparation, consultation with prospective adoptive parent(s), birth parent(s) and attorney for birth parent(s), arrange pre-natal care, if necessary, referral to another attorney to represent birth parent(s); finalization.

**Fees:** $175/hr. with $3250 cap for adoptions.

**Number of independent adoptions handled last year:** 30-40.

**Description of process:** After birth mother has contacted prospective adoptive parent(s), facilitator interviews birth mother, takes background information and arranges for verification of her pregnancy. Prenatal care can be arranged at that time, if necessary as well as referral to an attorney to represent birth parent(s). During consult with prospective adoptive parent(s), home study is reviewed, as well as New York's laws pertaining to adoption. Documents are prepared and facilitator represents adoptive parent(s) in court.

**Residency requirements for prospective adoptive parents:** Residents of New York State.

### ★ 1263 ★
**Jeanette F. Snyder**
**Attorney at Law**
183 E. Main St., Ste. 1024
Rochester, NY 14604
Phone: (716) 546-7258

**Description of services:**
1) Interviews adoptive parents;
2) preparation, execution and filing of legal documents;
3) obtains docket number and court date;
4) attends finalization hearing.

**Fees:** $300-$500 plus disbursements, if any.

**Number of independent adoptions handled last year:** 14 (all agency adoptions).

**Description of process:** Governed by NYS Domestic Relations Law, Article VII, Sec. 112-114.

**Licensed to place children:** N/A.

**Residency requirements for prospective adoptive parents:** New York State Domestic Relation Law, Article VII, section 113 states "proceeding to be in county where adoptive parents reside; if adoptive parents are non-residents of state, in county where authorized agency has its principal office.".

### ★ 1264 ★
**Eli I. Taub**
**Attorney at Law**
705 Union St.
Schenectady, NY 12305
Phone: (518) 370-5515
Fax: (518) 370-1613

**Description of services:**
1) Represents adoptive parents and/or birthparents in court;
2) interviews birthparents on behalf of adoptive parents, if necessary;
3) prepares and executes all legal documents;
4) coordinates with physician and arranges transfer of infant to adoptive parents;
5) liaisons with social services for home study of adoptive home.

**Fees:** $1000 and up.

**Number of independent adoptions handled last year:** 2.

**Description of process:**
1) Prospective adoptive parents identify birthmother seeking an adoptive placement for her child;
2) initial interview to establish client relationship with prospective adoptive parents;
3) meet with birthmother, if necessary;
4) after child's birth, obtain necessary consents, file petition and transfer of infant to adoptive home;
5) court appearance with adoptive parents;
6) coordinate with Social Services for home study;
7) final court appearance with adoptive parents, if necessary.

**Licensed to place children:** N/A.

**Residency requirements for prospective adoptive parents:** Adoptive parents must be New York State residents for 1 yr.

### ★ 1265 ★
**Golda Zimmerman, Esq.**
117 S. State St.
Syracuse, NY 13202
Phone: (315) 475-3322
Fax: (315) 475-7727

**Description of services:**
1) Represents adoptive or birthparents in court;
2) represents private adoptions agency;
3) assists with medical and/or living arrangements for birthparents, if requested;
4) represents clients seeking foreign adoption, mainly in China and the former Soviet Union;
5) prepares and files all legal documents.

**Fees:** Hourly basis plus disbursements.

**Description of process:** Prospective adoptive parents identify adoptable child or birthparent seeking an adoptive placement for her unborn child and contact attorney to facilitate arrangements.

**Licensed to place children:** In New York State, only licensed agencies and blood relatives may place children for adoption.

**Residency requirements for prospective adoptive parents:** Prospective adoptive parents must be New York State residents to finalize a private adoption in New York. Nonresidents of New York may finalize a New York agency adoption in New York State.

# NORTH CAROLINA

### ★ 1266 ★
**F. Kevin Gorham**
**Attorney at Law**
220 N. Eugene St.
Greensboro, NC 27401
Phone: (919) 272-8149

**Description of services:**
1) Represents adoptive and birthparents in uncontested adoption cases;
2) prepares and files all legal documents.

**Fees:** $100/hr.

**Number of independent adoptions handled last year:** 5-10.

**Description of process:**
1) Prospective adoptive parents identify adoptable child or expectant birthmother;
2) after birth attorney secures necessary relinquishments;
3) attorney files petition;
4) attorney represents client at final hearing.

**Licensed to place children:** N/A.

**Residency requirements for prospective adoptive parents:** Adoptive parents must be residents of North Carolina for at least 6 mos.

# OHIO

**★ 1267 ★**
**Stephen R. Hext**
**Attorney at Law**
1077 Celestial, Ste. 10
Cincinnati, OH 45202
Phone: (513) 684-9700
Fax: (513) 684-9701

**Description of services:**
1) Prepares and files all legal documents;
2) represents adoptive and birthparents in court in an uncontested adoption;
3) interviews both parties in the adoption;
4) makes referrals to birthmothers for medical and hospital care.

**Fees:** $1500 - $2000.

**Number of independent adoptions handled last year:** 5.

**Description of process:**
1) Occasionally provides intermediary services between prospective adoptive parents and birthparents seeking an adoptive placement for their child; or adoptive parents may identify an adoptable child or expectant birthmother;
2) probate court assigns home study;
3) child is placed upon approval;
4) finalization occurs after 3 post-placement visits and 6 mos. after interlocutory hearing.

**Licensed to place children:** In Ohio intermediaries may place children for adoption.

**Residency requirements for prospective adoptive parents:** Adoptive parents must be residents of Ohio.

**★ 1268 ★**
**Regional Family Counseling, Inc.**
635 W. Spring St.
Lima, OH 45801
Phone: (419) 225-1040

**Description of services:** Non-profit, state licensed agency providing home study services.

**Fees:** $50 application fee; $35/hr. for all adoptive services.

**Number of independent adoptions handled last year:** N/A.

**Description of process:**
1) File application;
2) complete home study;
3) reference checks.

**Licensed to place children:** In Ohio, private placement is lawful.

**Residency requirements for prospective adoptive parents:** Serves residents of Allen county and others within a 40 mi. radius.

**★ 1269 ★**
**Helen D. Russell**
5800 Monroe St., Bldg. E
Sylvania, OH 43560
Phone: (419) 885-3666

**Description of services:**
1) Counseling;
2) prepares and writes home study;
3) supervision of placement;
4) prepares reports for final hearing.

**Fees:**
Home study: $750;
supervision of placement: $80/visit;
counseling session: $90.

**Number of independent adoptions handled last year:** 5.

**Description of process:**
1) Prospective adoptive parents identify adoptable child or expectant birthmother;
2) home study is completed and written;
3) child is placed upon approval of home study;
4) adoptive home is visited 3 times after placement;
5) finalization.

**Licensed to place children:** No placement services provided.

**Residency requirements for prospective adoptive parents:** Adoptive parents must be Ohio residents for 6 mos.

**★ 1270 ★**
**Worly Family Adoption Studies, Inc.**
Susan Laudick, Director
552 Linwood Ave.
Columbus, OH 43205
Phone: (614) 258-5247

**Branch address:**
P.O. Box 247, Galena, OH 43021
Phone: (614) 965-4747

**Description of services:** 1) Licensed by the Ohio Dept. of Human Services to conduct home studies; 2) licensed by the Ohio Dept. of Human Services to supervise placements prior to finalization.

**Fees:** Home study: $750. Post-placement supervision: $150. Mileage: $.26/mi. Background Criminal Investigation record check: $30/couple.

**Number of independent adoptions handled last year:** 12 home studies.

**Description of process:** World Family Adoption Studies, Inc. works with adoptive parents who have already identified adoptable children whether in the U.S. or internationally and those who wish to work with private facilitators, out-of-state or foreign agencies.

**Residency requirements for prospective adoptive parents:** 6 mos.

# OKLAHOMA

**★ 1271 ★**
**Maria Erbar**
**Attorney at Law**
**Erbar & Erbar, Attorneys, P.C.**
5900 Mosteller Dr.
1800 United Founders Tower
Oklahoma City, OK 73112
Phone: (405) 842-5015

**Branch address:**
300 N. Choctaw, El Reno, OK 73036
Phone: (415) 262-4477

**Description of services:**
1) Provides intermediary services between birthparents considering adoption and prospective adoptive parents;
2) interviews adoptive parent on behalf of birthparents;
3) provides medical arrangements for birthmother;
4) consults with caseworker;
5) drafts and files legal documents;
6) coordination with other attorneys;
7) court appearances.

**Fees:** Hourly plus cost retainer.

**Number of independent adoptions handled last year:** 10.

**Description of process:**
1) Interview birth and adoptive parents;
2) arrange medical care, i.e. doctor and hospital visits;
3) hospital visit;
4) draft and file legal petition;
5) consultation with social worker;
6) legal hearing.

**Licensed to place children:** Oklahoma.

**Residency requirements for prospective adoptive parents:** Adoptive parents must be residents of Oklahoma.

# OREGON

★ 1272 ★
**John W. Jensen**
**Attorney at Law**
180 Church St., S.E.
Salem, OR 97301
Phone: (503) 399-1678

**Description of services:**
1) Represents adoptive parents in court;
2) interviews both parties in the adoption;
3) prepares and files all legal documents;
4) occasionally provides intermediary services between prospective adoptive parents and birthparents considering adoptive placements for their children;
5) provides medical arrangements for birthmother, if necessary.

**Fees:** $125/hr.

**Number of independent adoptions handled last year:** 10-12.

**Description of process:** Unavailable.

**Licensed to place children:** Intermediaries may lawfully place children in the State of Oregon.

**Residency requirements for prospective adoptive parents:** Birthmother and child must be residents of Oregon.

★ 1273 ★
**Laurence H. Spiegel**
**Attorney at Law**
4040 S.W. Douglas Way
Lake Oswego, OR 97035
Phone: (503) 635-7773
Fax: (503) 635-1526

**Description of services:**
1) Networks with applicants to find child;
2) represents adoptive parents in court;
3) represents birthparents in court;
4) interviews birthparents on behalf of adoptive parents and advises them to retain their own counsel;
5) interviews adoptive parents on behalf of birthparents with birthparents present (if possible);

6) arranges medical care for birthmother;
7) prepares and files all legal documents.

**Fees:** $80/hr.

**Number of independent adoptions handled last year:** 20.

**Description of process:**
1) Locate birthparent(s) who are considering adoptive placement for their child;
2) complete home study which is not required but useful in getting irrevocable consent sooner;
3) after infant's birth, birthmother signs consent to Adoption Certificate of Irrevocability;
4) file petition immediately after infant's birth;
5) decree final in 3-5 mos. where biological father is married to birthmother, lived with/supported birthmother or attempted to support child; filed for paternity and signed with putative father registry.

**Licensed to place children:** In Oregon only birthparents and child placement agencies may make actual placements.

**Residency requirements for prospective adoptive parents:** None.

# PENNSYLVANIA

★ 1274 ★
**James B. Wiltse**
37 McMurray Rd., Bldg. 1, Ste. LL6
Pittsburgh, PA 15241
Phone: (412) 854-4811

**Description of services:** 1) Handles predominantly identified adoptions; 2) screens birth parents on behalf of prospective adoptive parents and prospective adoptive parents on behalf of birth parents; 3) represents adoptive parents and/or birth parents in all legal proceedings; 4) provides medical arrangements for birth mother.

**Fees:** $600.

**Number of independent adoptions handled last year:** 5.

**Description of process:** 1) Petition of Intention to Adopt; 2) petition to terminate parental rights; 3) Adoption Petition; 4) Report of Intermediary including costs and fees.

**Residency requirements for prospective adoptive parents:** None.

# SOUTH CAROLINA

★ 1275 ★
**Bonnie P. Horn**
**Attorney at Law**
1215 Elmwood Ave.
Columbia, SC 29201
Phone: (803) 799-4208
(800) 849-4676
Fax: (803) 252-2305

**Description of services:**
1) Will represent either adoptive or birthparents in court but not in the same adoption proceeding;
2) interviews birthparents on behalf of adoptive parents when representing the latter;
3) interviews adoptive parents on behalf of birthparents when representing the latter;
4) provides medical arrangements for birthmother;
5) prepares and files all legal documents;

6) occasionally provides intermediary services between birthparent(s) considering adoptive placement and prospective adoptive parents.

**Fees:** Attorney fees range from $3000-$5000 depending upon the complexity of the case.

**Number of independent adoptions handled last year:** 2.

**Description of process:**
1) Interview client extensively;
2) client completes questionnaire;
3) in cases where client is the birthparent, attorney arranges housing and medical care.

**Licensed to place children:** N/A.

**Residency requirements for prospective adoptive parents:** None but must comply with Interstate Compact on the Placement of Children.

# SOUTH DAKOTA

★ 1276 ★
**Terre Berkland, MSW, CSW/PIP**
1003 Burleigh St.
Yankton, SD 57078
Phone: (605) 665-2036
Fax: (605) 665-2036

**Branch address:**
  P.O. Box 798, Elk Point, SD 57025

**Description of services:**
1) Interviews both parties in the adoption, if requested;
2) counseling;
3) networks with prospective adoptive parents for sources of adoptable children both nationally and internationally;
4) studies adoptive families and prepares home studies;
5) provides supervision of placement;
6) makes attorney and physician referrals.

**Fees:**
Pre-screening services: $250;
home study: $750;
post-placement services: $500/child per 6 mos.;
remainder of fees would consist of medical/hospital, attorney, networking agency and foreign country where applicable.

**Number of independent adoptions handled last year:** 15.

**Description of process:**
1) Screen applicant families;
2) begin home study process;
3) meet with birthparents and refer to attorney or physician;
4) facilitate adoption process and meetings between parties;
5) complete home study;
6) after placement, provide follow-up services and supervision until finalization.

**Licensed to place children:** Licensed to perform home studies in South Dakota.

**Residency requirements for prospective adoptive parents:** Adoptive parents must be residents of Iowa, Nebraska or South Dakota.

# TEXAS

★ 1277 ★
**Vika Newsom**
3908 Manchaca
Austin, TX 78704
Phone: (512) 448-4605
Fax: (512) 448-1905

**Description of services:**
1) Represents adoptive and birthparents in court when matter is uncontested;
2) prepares and executes all legal documents.

**Fees:** $130/hr.

**Number of independent adoptions handled last year:** 35.

**Description of process:**
1) Voluntary or involuntary termination of parental rights;
2) prepares affidavits of relinquishment, Status of Child and Waiver of Interest in Child;
3) social study completed;
4) adoption decree issued.

**Licensed to place children:** Yes.

**Residency requirements for prospective adoptive parents:** Child must be a resident of Texas.

★ 1278 ★
**Stoker Adoption Agency**
1435 Sweetbriar
Odessa, TX 79761
Phone: (915) 362-2113
Fax: (915) 550-9944

**Description:** Non-profit source for independent adoptions.

**Description of services:**
1) Assists birthmothers in selecting adoptive placements for their children;
2) birthparent counseling;
3) provides home studies for adoptive applicants;
4) prepares and files all legal documents;
5) court representation.

**Fees:** Home studies range from $500 to $2000 depending on income.

**Number of independent adoptions handled last year:** 4.

**Description of process:**
1) Prospective adoptive parents file an application and undergo home study;
2) if approved, agency provides outreach services to find the right child for a particular couple;
3) agency counselor works with birthmothers;
4) placement.

**Licensed to place children:** Only birthparents and licensed child-placing agencies may place children in Texas.

**Residency requirements for prospective adoptive parents:** None. Agency works primarily with residents of Texas.

# UTAH

★1279★
**Marilyn Moody Brown**
**Attorney at Law**
2525 N. Canyon Rd.
Provo, UT 84604
Phone: (801) 373-2721

**Description of services:**
1) Provides intermediary services between birth parents considering adoptive placement and prospective adoptive parents;
2) represents either birth or adoptive parents in court;
3) interviews all parties involved;
4) provides medical arrangements for birthmother;
5) prepares and executes all legal documents.

**Fees:** $150/hr.

**Number of independent adoptions handled last year:** 14-16.

**Description of process:**
1) Initial intake for birth and adoptive parents;
2) oversees birthmother's needs during pregnancy;
3) after infant's birth, obtains legal consents in court;
4) if out of state, complies with Interstate Compact on the Placement of Children.

**Licensed to place children:** Intermediaries may place children in the State of Utah.

**Residency requirements for prospective adoptive parents:** Yes.

# VERMONT

★1280★
**Alfred J. Fenton**
196 Killington Ave.
Rutland, VT 05701
Phone: (802) 775-4065

**Description of services:**
1) Provides intermediary services between prospective adoptive parents and birthparents seeking to place their children adoptively;
2) interviews both parties in the adoption;
3) aids adoptive applicants in preparing biographies;
4) case summary for court.

**Fees:** $65/hr. plus prenatal and hospitization costs.

**Number of independent adoptions handled last year:** 3.

**Description of process:**
1) Interview adoptive applicants and compile histories;
2) Prospective adoptive parents write biographies which are kept on file;
3) birthparents are presented with several profiles from which to choose.

**Licensed to place children:** N/A.

**Residency requirements for prospective adoptive parents:** None.

★1281★
**Friends in Adoption, Inc.**
44 South St.
Middletown Springs, VT 05757
Phone: (802) 235-2373
(800) 982-3678
Fax: (802) 235-2311
**Mailing address:**
P.O. Box 1228, Middletown Springs, VT 05757
**Contact:** Dawn Smith-Pliner, Director; Pat Irwin, Program Director.
**Description of services:**
1) Provides intermediary services between birthparents considering adoption and prospective adoptive parents;
2) interviews birth parents on behalf of adoptive parents;
3) interviews adoptive parents on behalf of birthparents;
4) compiles resumes for adoptive applicants to use as a search tool for a child to adopt;
5) educates clients in advertising techniques as a search tool;
6) networks with the national community of people/organizations committed to the concept of independent adoption.
**Fees:** Sliding fees.

**Number of independent adoptions handled last year:** 75.

**Description of process:** "Get Acquainted" weekends are held monthly. Initial consultation is an intensive 2-3 hr. meeting which formulates step-by-step the individual adoption plan which may include national networking, advertising, and the creation of resumes. Friends in Adoption, Inc. works with the client until a child is placed.

**Licensed to place children:** Vermont, New York, Connecticut, and Rhode Island.

**Residency requirements for prospective adoptive parents:** None.

# VIRGINIA

★1282★
**Edward A. Kaplan**
**Attorney at Law**
1307 Texas Ave.
Alexandria, VA 71315
Phone: (318) 448-0831
(800) 246-1769
Fax: (318) 473-1980

**Mailing address:**
P.O. Box 12386, Alexandria, VA 71315
**Description of services:**
1) Prepares and files all legal documents;
2) represents adoptive parents in court;
3) makes medical arrangements for birthmother.
**Fees:** $300 legal fees plus costs involved.

**Number of independent adoptions handled last year:** 10.

**Description of process:**
1) Interview adoptive parents (under Louisiana law, separate attorney is required for birthparents);
2) file suit for adoption proceedings;
3) home visit by the Dept. of Human Resources;
4) obtain final decree of adoption.
**Licensed to place children:** N/A.

**Residency requirements for prospective adoptive parents:** None.

# WASHINGTON

★ 1283 ★
**Adoption Advocacy Attorneys of the Northwest**
J. Eric Gustafson Attorney at Law
222 N. 3rd St.
Yakima, WA 98901
Phone: (509) 248-7220
(800) 238-KIDS

**Mailing address:**
P.O. 1689, Yakima, WA 98901

**Description of services:** 1) Assists prospective adoptive parents in locating birth parents considering adoptive placement for their children; 2) interviews birth parents on behalf of prospective adoptive parents and prospective adoptive parents on behalf of birth parents; 3) represents prospective adoptive parents or birth parents in all legal proceedings; 4) makes medical arrangements for birth mother. 800 number is for birth parents only.

**Fees:** Attorney: $140/hr. Initial consult: $325. Search process: $500. Birth mother match: $2000. Adoption Case Manager: $60 plus costs and expenses, including those of birth mother. Total cost range: $2000 - $16,000.

**Number of independent adoptions handled last year:** 40-50.

**Description of process:** 1) Initial consult; 2) preparation of adoptive family profile including photo, biographical and other matching information; 3) networking - assisting with creative search efforts to find an adoptive match; 4) advertising - preparation, placement and response; 5) presentation to birth parents; 6) meeting facilitation; 7) legal, medical counseling and social services coordination and arrangements; 8) placement.

**Residency requirements for prospective adoptive parents:** None.

★ 1284 ★
**Adoption Facilitators, Inc.**
8624 NE Juanita Dr.
Kirkland, WA 98034
Phone: (206) 823-3060

**Description:** AFI is licensed in the State of Washington by the Department of Social and Health Services to provide assistance to people who wish to build their families by independent adoption.

**Description of services:** 1) Adoption Readiness Workshops - 6 week series of classes to prepare for the process of adoption; 2) preparation of introductory materials, e.g. letters of introduction, family album, networking letter; 3) plan a strategy which determines the amounts and locations of advertising and networking to locate a birth family; 4) assistance in effective ad writing for specifically targeted areas and/or manpower for networking campaign; 5) receipt and screening of telephone calls from prospective birth families; 6) match facilitation of possible birth families with prosecutive adoptive families based on heritage, social and medical histories; 7) assistance after matching including counseling, referrals, etc. 8) post-placement services.

**Fees:** Application fee: $125. Adoption Readiness Workshop: $175. 2 year contract of Facilitation and Consultation: $2200 (payment schedule may be arranged). Other expenses included are those incurred by any independent adoption.

**Number of independent adoptions handled last year:** January - July, 1994: 2.

**Residency requirements for prospective adoptive parents:** None.

★ 1285 ★
**Law Office of Beresford, Booth & Demaray, Inc., P.S.**
Mark M. Demaray
1420 Fifth Ave., Ste. 3650
Seattle, WA 98101-2387
Phone: (206) 682-4000
Fax: (206) 682-4004

**Description:** Mark M. Demaray is an Executive Board Member and Treasurer of the Washington State Adoption Council, facilitator of the Standards of Practice Subcommittee of the Senate Interim Adoption Study in 1989 and was appointed to the Washington State Adoption Commission. He is an Executive Member of the American Bar Association Adoption Committee and a member of the American Academy of Adoption Attorneys.

**Description of services:** 1) Assists prospective adoptive parents in locating available children; 2) handles both identified adoptions and is occasionally aware of birth parents seeking an adoptive placement for their children; 3) screens medical and social history of birth parents according to Washington State law; 4) facilitates medical services for birth mother; 5) represents adoptive parents and/or birth parents in all legal proceedings.

**Fees:** Medical: $500 - $8000. Financial assistance to Birth parent(s): $200 - $3200. Legal expenses: $2000 - $6000. All costs and fees are estimated and vary according to extent of work and time involved. Advertising costs, home study, and travel are not included.

**Number of independent adoptions handled last year:** 80 - 100.

**Description of process:** In private placement adoption, custody transfer and placement can occur no sooner than 48 hrs. after the child's birth or signature on a consent by the birth parent. In newborn cases, adoptive parents usually take the baby home from the hospital.

**Residency requirements for prospective adoptive parents:** None.

★ 1286 ★
**Case Study Services**
Sue Koentopp, M.S.W., Director
P.O. Box 14811
Spokane, WA 99214-0811
Phone: (509) 924-0624

**Description:** C.S.S. is a Washington state licensed child placing agency and one facet of a social work consulting business,

**Technical Assistance by Sue Koentopp** (T.A.S.K.).

**Description of services:** 1) Prepares pre-placement and post-placement reports; 2) conducts home studies and post-placement supervision; 3) Interstate Compact coordination.

**Fees:** Adoption pre-placement report: $500 Adoption post-placement report: $200 per child Post-placement supervision; $50/hr. Interstate Compact coordination: $50/hr.

**Number of independent adoptions handled last year:** 14.

**Residency requirements for prospective adoptive parents:** Washington State residents only.

★1287★
**Connolly, Holm, Tacon & Meserve**
Margaret Cunniff Holm
201 W. 5th, Ste. 301
Olympia, WA 98501
Phone: (206) 943-6747

**Description of services:** 1) Screens birth parents on behalf of prospective adoptive parents and prospective adoptive parents on behalf of birth parents; 2) represents adoptive parents and birth parents in all legal proceedings; 3) makes medical arrangements for birth mother; 4) coordinates legal, social services, counseling and hospital staffs.

**Fees:** $135/hr.

**Number of independent adoptions handled last year:** 50-75.

**Residency requirements for prospective adoptive parents:** None.

★1288★
**Dubar, Lirhus & Engel**
2200 Sixth Ave.
Seattle, WA 98121
Phone: (206) 728-5858

**Description of services:** 1) Assists prospective adoptive parents in locating birth parents considering adoptive placements for their children; 2) interviews birth parents on behalf of prospective adoptive parents; 3) represents adoptive parents in all legal proceedings; 4) can provide medical referrals for birth mothers.

**Fees:** Unavailable.

**Number of independent adoptions handled last year:** 40-50.

**Description of process:** 1) Helps prospective adoptive parents contact birth parents; 2) arranges legal termination of parents rights; 3) provides all legal services relating to open adoption agreements, counseling and financial assistance.

**Residency requirements for prospective adoptive parents:** None.

★1289★
**Phylliss Eberhardy, MS, CCDCI**
11126 SE 256th St., Ste. 0-204
Kent, WA 98031
Phone: (206) 852-1586

**Description of services:** Family therapist who provides grief counseling and open adoption mediation for identified adoptions only.

**Fees:** $50/hr.

**Number of independent adoptions handled last year:** 5.

**Description of process:** Using mediation and counseling services before, during and after birth, prospective adoptive parents and birth parents work out a mutually satisfactory open adoption.

**Residency requirements for prospective adoptive parents:** None.

★1290★
**Law Offices of Joseph A. Holeman**
3315 S. 23rd St., No. 215
Tacoma, WA 98405
Phone: (206) 627-7212

**Description of services:** Practice limited to identified and agency adoptions.

**Fees:** Adoption finalization: $300 Adoption finalization (step-parent): $400.

**Number of independent adoptions handled last year:** None.

**Description of process:** 1) Termination or relinquishment of birth parents' rights; 2) preparation of legal documents; 3) finalization.

**Residency requirements for prospective adoptive parents:** 6 mos.

★1291★
**Leach, Brown & Andersen**
David V. Andersen, Esq.
999 Third Ave., Ste. 4040
Seattle, WA 98104
Phone: (206) 583-2714
Fax: (206) 583-2766

**Description of services:** 1) Handles identified adoptions and is aware of birth families considering adoptive placement for their children; 2) works with adoption agencies for legal services; 3) represents adoptive parents in all legal proceedings; 4) interviews birth parents on behalf of prosepctive birth parents; 5) makes medical arrangements for birth mother; 6) Interstate Compact on the Placement of Children work.

**Fees:** $130/hr. plus costs.

**Number of independent adoptions handled last year:** 20.

**Description of process:** 1) Ensure qualifications of prospective adoptive parents; 2) gather legal/social/medical information; 3) prepare legal documents; 4) termination of birth parent(s)' parental rights; 5) finalization.

**Residency requirements for prospective adoptive parents:** None.

★1292★
**John H. Loeffler**
**Attorney at Law**
8414 N. Wall, Ste. A
Spokane, WA 99208
Phone: (509) 467-6767

**Description of services:**
1) Intermediary between birthparents considering adoption for their child and prospective adoptive parents;
2) Represents adoptive and birthparents in court;
3) interviews both parties to the adoption;
4) provides medical arrangements for birthmother;
5) prepares and executes all legal documents.

**Fees:**
$90/hr.
Complete adoption with relinquishment: approx. $1000.

**Number of independent adoptions handled last year:** Approx. 30.

**Description of process:**
1) Obtain consents from birthparents or set termination hearing;
2) appear at relinquishment hearing;
3) adoption finalized 60 days later at hearing.

**Licensed to place children:** Intermediaries may place children in the State of Washington.

**Residency requirements for prospective adoptive parents:** None if child is a resident of Washington State.

## ★ 1293 ★
**Precious Connections, Inc.**
9185 Spargur Loop Rd.
Bainbridge Island, WA 98110
Phone: (206) 842-6658
(206) 842-6673

**Branch address:**
6499 Eagle Harbor Dr. NE, Bainbridge Island, WA 98110

**Description of services:** 1) Searches for an adoptable child for waiting families; 2) mediates connection between prospective adoptive parents and birth parents; 3) screens birth parents for prospective adoptive parents; 4) interviews prospective adoptive parents for birth parents; 5) makes referrals for medical arrangements for birth mother; 6) 1 yr. post-adoption follow-up.

**Fees:** $3500. Home study, attorney fees and birth mother expenses are extra.

**Number of independent adoptions handled last year:** 11.

**Description of process:** 1) Education in independent and other adoption issues; 2) referrals to attorneys, social workers and support groups; 3) compilation of photo album and *Birth mother letters*; 4) personalizing and mailing *birth mother* letters; 5) screening birthmother calls; 6) hospital liaison; 7) post-placement services for adoptive and birth family.

**Residency requirements for prospective adoptive parents:** None.

## ★ 1294 ★
**Eileen S. Putter, M.S.**
14011 SE 49th Pl
Bellevue, WA 98006
Phone: (206) 562-6244

**Description of services:** 1) Counseling of birth parents before, during and after birth; 2) facilitates placement.

**Fees:** $60/hr.

**Number of independent adoptions handled last year:** 4.

**Residency requirements for prospective adoptive parents:** None.

## ★ 1295 ★
**Skellenger, Bender, Mathias & Bender**
Rita L. Bender
1301 Fifth Ave.
Seattle, WA 98101
Phone: (206) 623-6501

**Description of services:** 1) Handles both identified adoptions and acts as an intermediary between birth parents seeking an adoptive placement for their children and prospective adoptive parents; 2) interviews birth parents on behalf of adoptive parents and prospective adoptive parents on behalf of birth parents; 3) represents either adoptive parents or birth parents in all legal proceedings; 4) makes medical arrangements for birth mother.

**Fees:** $160/hr. and $65/hr. for paralegal time.

**Number of independent adoptions handled last year:** 55.

**Description of process:** State of Washington permits termination of parental rights either 48 hrs. after child's birth or 48 hrs. after the signing of consent forms, whichever is later.

**Residency requirements for prospective adoptive parents:** None.

## ★ 1296 ★
**Sound Counseling Service**
4238 SW 314 St.
Federal Way, WA 98023
Phone: (206) 815-0416
(206) 661-0181

**Description of services:** Provides counseling including medical referrals for birth mothers making an adoption plan for their children.

**Fees:** $50/hr.

**Number of independent adoptions handled last year:** None.

**Residency requirements for prospective adoptive parents:** None.

## ★ 1297 ★
**Laurel A. Terpening**
**Adoption Caseworker Services**
3616 120th Pl. SE
Everett, WA 98208
Phone: (206) 337-4068

**Description of services:** 1) Handles only identified adoptions; 2) screens prospective adoptive parents for birth parents; 3) interviews birth parents on behalf of prospective adoptive parents; 4) conducts home studies.

**Fees:** Unavailable.

**Number of independent adoptions handled last year:** 32.

**Residency requirements for prospective adoptive parents:** Prospective adoptive families must be domiciled in state.

## ★ 1298 ★
**Tolman & Kirk**
**Attorneys at Law**
Michael A. Kirk
P.O. Box 851
Poulsbo, WA 98370
Phone: (206) 779-5561

**Description of services:** 1) Handles mostly identified adoptions; 2) interviews birth parents on behalf of adoptive parents; 3) termination of birth parents' rights; 4) represents adoptive parents in all legal proceedings.

**Fees:** $1500 minimum.

**Number of independent adoptions handled last year:** 10.

**Description of process:** 1) Termination of birth parents' rights including location of birth father, if necessary; 2) adoption finalization; 3) issuance of birth certificate.

**Residency requirements for prospective adoptive parents:** None.

## ★ 1299 ★
**Cheryl Tonnes**
**Independent Adoption Social Worker**
10220 Larimer Rd.
Everett, WA 98208
Phone: (206) 337-2089

**Description of services:** 1) Guidance in searching for birth family; 2) screens prospective adoptive parents on behalf of birth parents; 3) conducts home study; 4) post-placement services; 5) guidance in parenting an adopted child.

**Fees:** Home study: $375. Home study update: $150. Post-placement: $100.

**Number of independent adoptions handled last year:** 24.

**Description of process:** 1) 1st interview and begin paper work; 2) 2nd interview and completion of paper work; 3) interviewing.

**Residency requirements for prospective adoptive parents:** Residents of Washington State only.

★ 1300 ★
**Eric B. Watness & Associates**
101 Yesler Way, Ste. 603
Seattle, WA 98104
Phone: (206) 628-0310

**Description of services:** 1) Handles mostly identified or agency adoptions; 2) Represents adoptive parents in all legal proceedings; 3) liaisons with social services; 4) prepares all legal documents.

**Fees:** $135/hr.

**Number of independent adoptions handled last year:** 5.

**Description of process:** 1) Initial interview; 2) process and file paperwork; 3) attend court hearings; 4) prepare and file adoption decree and order new birth certificate.

**Residency requirements for prospective adoptive parents:** None.

# WEST VIRGINIA

★ 1301 ★
**William T. Watson, Esq.**
The Frederick Bldg., Ste. 203
Huntington, WV 25715
Phone: (304) 522-6454
Fax: (304) 525-3754

**Mailing address:**
P.O. Box 1371, Huntington, WV 25715

**Description of services:**
1) Interviews parties involved;
2) preparation of petitions, consent and relinquishment forms;
3) will make medical arrangements with physicians and hospitals for birthmother;
4) represents adoptive parents in court;
5) keeps a waiting list of prospective adoptive parents for infants whose birthmothers are considering adoptive placement;
6) provides transfer services at the hospital between the birthparents and the adoptive parents;
7) correlates with social service agencies for home studies.

**Fees:** Case by case basis.

**Number of independent adoptions handled last year:** 2.

**Description of process:**
1) Interviews adoptive and birthparents;
2) obtains medical history of birthparents' bloodline;
3) reviews medical documents pertinent to the pregnancy and monitors birthmother's condition through her pregnancy with her and her physician;
4) prepares and executes consent and relinquishment forms;
5) prepares petition to the court for temporary custody;
6) represents adoptive parents in court;
7) transfers child to adoptive parents at hospital;
8) arranges for home study interview;
9) prepares for final adoption hearing and final order.

**Licensed to place children:** Licensed to practice law in Kentucky, North Carolina and West Virginia. In the former intermediaries may place children; in the latter two birthparents place their own children directly.

**Residency requirements for prospective adoptive parents:** If the adoptive parents are not residents of one of the states in which this attorney is licensed to practice law, then necessary affiliation with counsel of that particular state would be necessary.

# WISCONSIN

★ 1302 ★
**Susan M. De Groot**
**Attorney at Law**
**Stolper, Koritzinsky, Brewster & Neider, S.L.**
P.O. Box 5510
Madison, WI 53705-0510
Phone: (608) 833-7617
Fax: (608) 833-7954

**Description of services:**
1) Represents adoptive parents in court;
2) prepares and files all legal documents;
3) coordination of social service investigations and reports.

**Fees:** $125/hr.

**Number of independent adoptions handled last year:** 2.

**Description of process:**
1) Prospective adoptive parents identify adoptable child or birthmother seeking an adoptive placement for her child;
2) after child's birth, attorney files termination of parental rights petition and Petition for Adoptive Placement;
3) social service agency performs study and writes court report;
4) Guardian Ad Litem investigation and court hearing;
5) if approved, placement.

**Licensed to place children:** N/A.

**Residency requirements for prospective adoptive parents:** Adoptive parents must be residents of Wisconsin.

★ 1303 ★
**Edward J. Plagemann**
744 N. 4th St., Ste. 400
Milwaukee, WI 53203
Phone: (414) 271-3399
Fax: (414) 271-8882

**Branch address:**
610 Main St., Rm. 108, Racine, WI 53403
Phone: (414) 633-5155

**Description of services:**
1) Provides intermediary services between prospective adoptive parents and birthparents seeking an adoptive placement for their child;
2) interviews both parties in the adoption;
3) will represent adoptive parents and/or birthparents in court;
4) prepares and executes all legal documents.

**Fees:** $125/hr. Total fees are usually between $1700 and $2200.

**Number of independent adoptions handled last year:** 3.

**Description of process:** Unavailable.

**Licensed to place children:** N/A.

**Residency requirements for prospective adoptive parents:** None. Can place children out-of-state under the provisions of the Interstate Compact on the Placement of Children.

# WYOMING

**★ 1304 ★**
**Peter J. Feeney**
**Attorney at Law**
123 W. 1st St., Ste. 675
Casper, WY 82602
Phone: (307) 266-4422

**Mailing address:**
P.O. Box 437, Casper, WY 82602

**Description of services:**
1) Provides intermediary services between adoptive applicants and birthparents considering an adoptive placement for their child;
2) represents adoptive parents in court;
3) interviews birthparents on behalf of the adoptive parents;
4) interviews adoptive parents on behalf of the birthparents;
5) makes medical arrangements for birthmother;
6) prepares relinquishment papers and other legal documents;
7) provides coordination and transfer services at hospital;
8) applies for amended birth certificate.

**Fees:** $1500-$2500.

**Number of independent adoptions handled last year:** 5.

**Description of process:**
1) Interview birth and adoptive parents;
2) prepare relinquishments;
3) coordinate with physician and hospital;
4) transfer at hospital;
5) prepare and file pleadings;
6) represent adoptive family in court;
7) apply for amended birth certificate.

**Licensed to place children:** None required.

**Residency requirements for prospective adoptive parents:** Adoptive parents must be residents of the State of Wyoming for at least 60 days.

**★ 1305 ★**
**William D. Hjelmstad**
**Attorney at Law**
300 S. Wolcott, Ste. 240
Casper, WY 82601
Phone: (307) 577-0934

**Description of services:**
1) Provides intermediary services between prospective adoptive parents and birthparents considering adoption for their child;
2) represents adoptive parents in court;
3) interviews both parties in the adoption;
4) can provide medical arrangements for the birthmother;
5) prepares and executes all legal documents.

**Fees:** $300 and up.

**Number of independent adoptions handled last year:** 12.

**Description of process:**
1) Birthparents select adoptive couple for their child;
2) after infant's birth, biological parents relinquish parent rights;
3) file interlocutory decree;
4) final decree after 6 mos.

**Licensed to place children:** In the State of Wyoming intermediaries may place children.

**Residency requirements for prospective adoptive parents:** Adoptive parents must be state residents for 60 days prior to filing petition.

**★ 1306 ★**
**Carol A. Serelson**
**Attorney at Law**
400 Majestic Bldg.
Cheyenne, WY 82001
Phone: (307) 635-4365

**Description of services:**
1) Represents either adoptive or birthparents in court;
2) provides medical arrangements for birthmother, if necessary;
3) liaisons with social services;
4) prepares and files all legal documents.

**Fees:** Beginning at $1000.

**Number of independent adoptions handled last year:** Unavailable.

**Description of process:**
1) Prepare petition;
2) file verification and consents;
3) adoptive home studied and report written and submitted with medical report on child;
4) interlocutory decree;
5) final decree.

**Licensed to place children:** N/A.

**Residency requirements for prospective adoptive parents:** Adoptive parents must be residents of Wyoming for at least 60 days prior to filing.

# ALBERTA

**★ 1307 ★**
**Private Adoptions Society of Alberta**
10116 - 105th Ave., No. 203
Edmonton, AB, Canada T5H 0K2
Phone: (403) 441-3970

**Description of services:** 1) Acts as an intermediary between birth parents seeking an adoptive placement for their children and prospective adoptive parents; 2) screens prospective adoptive parents for birth parents; 3) provides medical arrangements for birth mother; 4) represents birth parents and/or adoptive parents in court; 5) takes medical and social history of birth parents; 6) provides counseling for birth parents.

**Fees:** None.

**Number of independent adoptions handled last year:** 40.

**Description of process:** 1) Interview with prospective adoptive parents; 2) meets with birth parents; 3) birth parents select adoptive family from files; 4) adoptive family meets birth family; 5) placement. Adoptive family usually stays in touch with birth family by means of photos and/or visits.

**Residency requirements for prospective adoptive parents:** 6 mos.

# ONTARIO

## ★ 1308 ★
**Acri, MacPherson, Fader & Baldock**
**Barristers & Solicitors**
Juliet C. Baldock
Ste. 101, 134 Queen St. E.
Brampton, ON, Canada L6V 1B2
Phone: (416) 459-6160
Fax: (416) 459-4606

**Description of services:** 1) Provides intermediary services between birth parents seeking an adoptive placement for their child(ren) and prospective adoptive parents;
2) facilitates identified adoptions;
3) represents adoptive parents in court provided there is no dispute;
4) interviews birth parents on behalf of prospective adoptive parents and prospective adoptive parents on behalf of birth parents;
5) prepares documents for submission to Ministry of Community Social Services;
6) referral to social worker for supervision of placement;
7) prepares consent documents;
8) counselling referrals;
9) prepares all court documents.

**Fees:** Hourly fee.

**Number of independent adoptions handled last year:** 6.

**Description of process:** 1) Licensee meets with both birth and prospective adoptive parents individually;
2) counsels with birth parents on selection of adoptive family;
3) arranges meeting of birth and adoptive parents, if required;
4) submit home study and social/medical histories to Ministry;
5) secures consents;
6) attends to placement;
7) arranges monitoring of placement by social worker;
8) refers birth parents to counselling, if necessary;
9) prepares court documents;
10) attends court hearing.

**Residency requirements for prospective adoptive parents:** Residents of Ontario.

## ★ 1309 ★
**Adoption Advisory and Counseling Service**
Roger A. Bowring, M.S.W., C.S.W., Proprietor
8 Trafalgar St.
St. Catharines, ON, Canada L2R 3L7
Phone: (905) 682-5166

**Description of services:** 1) Facilitates both identified and international adoptions;
2) screens birth parents as per provincial regulations;
3) provides medical arrangements for birth mother;
4) conducts home studies for prospective adoptive parents;
5) assists in preparation of court documents.

**Fees:** Unavailable.

**Number of independent adoptions handled last year:** 6.

**Description of process:** 1) Interview birth parents to obtain a social and medical history;
2) prepare adoption home study of adoptive applicants;
3) provide choice of homes to birth parents;
4) birth parents select adoptive family;
5) if mutually requested, birth parents meet with adoptive parents;

6) upon Ministry approval, licensee places child with adoptive family;
7) placement is supervised for 6 mos. by licensee;
8) represents adoptive parents at court for adoption order.

**Residency requirements for prospective adoptive parents:** Residents of Ontario.

## ★ 1310 ★
**Adoption Resource and Counseling Services**
162 Phillips St.
Kingston, ON, Canada K7M 2Z8
Phone: (613) 542-0275

**Description of services:** 1) Provides intermediary services between prospective adoptive parents and birth parents considering an adoptive placement for their child;
2) screens birth parents according to provincial regulations;
3) conducts home studies;
4) provides medical arrangements for birth mother;
5) represents birth and/or adoptive parents in court.

**Fees:** Birth parent counselling.

**Number of independent adoptions handled last year:** 20.

**Description of process:** Once the adoptive parents have completed their home study and explored issues related to adoption, they meet with the birth parents who have had their social history taken and completed counselling and education to prepare them for the meeting with the prospective adoptive family. Counselling continues through and after placement.

**Residency requirements for prospective adoptive parents:** Canadian citizens.

## ★ 1311 ★
**Baker & Janssen**
Samuel R. Baker
207 Queen's Quay West
Toronto, ON, Canada M5J 1A7
Phone: (416) 368-0881

**Mailing address:**
 P.O. Box 109, Toronto, ON, Canada M5J 1A7

**Description of services:** 1) Handles only identified adoptions; 2) represents adoptive parents and/or birth parents in all legal proceedings; 3) Liaisons between prospective adoptive and birth parents; 4) can make medical arrangements for birth mother.

**Fees:** Varies with service provided.

**Number of independent adoptions handled last year:** 2.

**Residency requirements for prospective adoptive parents:** Permanent residence or employment authorization.

## ★ 1312 ★
**Beechie, Madison, Sawchuk & Seabrook**
**Barristers and Solicitors**
Theodore Madison
439 Waterloo St.
London, ON, Canada N6B 2P1
Phone: (519) 673-1070
Fax: (519) 439-4363

**Description of services:** 1) Handles only identified adoptions;
2) interviews birth parents on behalf of prospective adoptive parents and prospective adoptive parents on behalf of birth parents;
3) makes medical referrals for birth mother;
4) prepares all legal documents;

5) represents birth and adoptive parents in court.

**Fees:** Vary.

**Number of independent adoptions handled last year:** Unavailable.

**Description of process:** Prospective adoptive parents have already identified the child they wish to adopt.
 1) Home study conducted by licensed social worker; 2) documents signed; 3) 21 day wait; 4) court order.

**Residency requirements for prospective adoptive parents:** Residents of Ontario.

---

### ★ 1313 ★
**Ellery & Cox, Solicitors**
Justin Ellery
202 - 85 Pine St. S.
Timmins, ON, Canada P4N 7W7
Phone: (705) 264-9591
Fax: (705) 264-1393

**Mailing address:**
 Box 1540, Timmins, ON, Canada P4N 7W7

**Description of services:** 1) Preparation of all legal documents;
 2) represents adoptive parents in court;
 3) occasionally provides intermediary services between prospective adoptive parents and birth parents seeking an adoptive placement for their child(ren).

**Fees:** Hourly fee plus expenses.

**Number of independent adoptions handled last year:** 2.

**Description of process:** 1) Request and receive authorization from Adoption Unit to place child with prospective adoptive parents;
 2) placement;
 3) 6 mos. probationary placement period;
 4) final adoption order.

**Residency requirements for prospective adoptive parents:** Residents of Ontario for at least 1 yr.

---

### ★ 1314 ★
**Giesbrecht, Griffin & Ritter**
**Barristers, Solicitors and Notaries Public**
Theodore Giesbrecht
60 College St.
Kitchener, ON, Canada N2G 3Y9
Phone: (519) 579-4300
Fax: (519) 579-8745

**Mailing address:**
 P.O. Box 425, Kitchener, ON, Canada N2G 3Y9

**Description of services:** 1) Facilitates both identified adoptions and can provide intermediary services for prospective adoptive parents and birth parents seeking an adoptive placements for their child(ren);
 2) represents birth and adoptive parents in court;
 3) interviews birth parents on behalf of prospective adoptive parents and prospective adoptive parents on behalf of birth parents;
 4) facilitates placement;
 5) applies for adoption order.

**Fees:** Fees based on an hourly rate.

**Number of independent adoptions handled last year:** 8.

**Description of process:** Unavailable.

**Residency requirements for prospective adoptive parents:** Ontario residents for adoption to be finalized in the province, but licensee does facilitate out-of-province adoptions.

### ★ 1315 ★
**Huckabone, Shaw, O'Brien, Radley-Walters & Reimer**
Richard A. Reimer
284 Pembroke St. E.
Pembroke, ON, Canada K8A 6X7
Phone: (613) 735-2341
Fax: (613) 735-0920

**Mailing address:**
 P.O. Box 487, Pembroke, ON, Canada K8A 6X7

**Branch address:**
 7 Hilda St., P.O. Box 148, Petawawa, ON, Canada K8H 2X2

**Description of services:** 1) Provides intermediary services between prospective adoptive parents and birth parents seeking an adoptive placement for their child(ren);
 2) represents adoptive parents in court;
 3) preparation of all legal documents.

**Fees:** $3200.

**Number of independent adoptions handled last year:** 1.

**Description of process:** After approval by government agency, child is placed by licensee in adoptive home. After 6 mos. probationary period and confirmation by follow-up study that child is adjusting well, adoption if finalized.

**Residency requirements for prospective adoptive parents:** Residents of Ontario.

---

### ★ 1316 ★
**Judith Holzman Law Offices**
218 Adelaide St. W., 3rd Fl.
Toronto, ON, Canada M5H 1W7
Phone: (416) 977-3050
Fax: (416) 977-6253

**Description of services:** 1) Screens birth parents on behalf of prospective adoptive parents; 2) screens prospective adoptive parents on behalf of birth parents; 3) represents adoptive parents in all legal proceedings; 4) makes medical referrals for birth mother.

**Fees:** Hourly fee based on time and complexity of case.

**Number of independent adoptions handled last year:** 1.

**Description of process:** Unavailable.

**Residency requirements for prospective adoptive parents:** Adoptive parents must be residents of Ontario and child must be born in Ontario.

---

### ★ 1317 ★
**Andres Koziar, Ph.D., L.L.B.**
72 Centre St. N.
Oshawa, ON, Canada L1G 4B6
Phone: (905) 571-3214
Fax: (905) 571-3832

**Description of services:** 1) Conducts mostly identified adoptions, but can provide intermediary services as well;
 2) helps prepare *family profile* for birth parents to review;
 3) represents both birth and adoptive families in court provided there is no conflict.

**Fees:** $4000 - $5000.

**Number of independent adoptions handled last year:** 5 - 15.

**Description of process:** Family *profiles* are reviewed by birth parents. Once a prospective adoptive home is selected and the Ministry approves the home study and placement, the child is placed. After a probationary period, finalization occurs in Family Court.

**Residency requirements for prospective adoptive parents:** Residents of Ontario for adoption to be finalized in the province, but licensee does facilitate out-of-province adoptions.

★ 1318 ★
**Paquette, Lalande and Keast, Barristers and Solicitors**
Randall W. Lalande
1188 St. Jerome St., No. 200
Sudbury, ON, Canada P3A 2V9
Phone: (705) 560-2121
Fax: (705) 560-8072

**Description of services:** 1) Handles mostly identified adoptions;
2) represents prospective adoptive parents in court;
3) prepares application for adoption order;
5) interviews birth parents on behalf of prospective adoptive parents;
6) interviews prospective adoptive parents on behalf of birth parents;
7) private placement work;
8) contracts with social worker for adoptive home study.
**Fees:** $1500 - $4000.
**Number of independent adoptions handled last year:** 5.
**Description of process:** 1) Interviews birth parents;
2) hires social worker for home study;
3) contracts with foster parents, if necessary;
4) liaisons with physician and hospital;
5) obtain final approval;
6) arrange placement;
7) monitor placement for 6 mos.;
8) apply to court for adoption order.
**Residency requirements for prospective adoptive parents:** None, but process is more involved if prospective adoptive parents live out of Ontario.

★ 1319 ★
**A. Maxine Smith, Adoption Licensee**
14 Letchworth Rd.
Ottawa, ON, Canada K1S 0J4
Phone: (613) 563-4092
Fax: (613) 563-4107

**Description of services:** 1) Provides intermediary services between prospective adoptive parents and birth parents seeking an adoptive placement for their child(ren);
2) conducts home study and provides adoptive parent preparation for adoptive applicants;
3) assists birth mother in obtaining health insurance, if necessary;
4) counsels birth parents and obtains social histories.
**Fees:** $5000 - $8000.
**Number of independent adoptions handled last year:** 11.
**Description of process:** 1) Home study or update along with birth parent histories proposed to Ministry;
2) approval granted by Ministry;
3) placement;
4) minimum 6 mos. supervised probationary period;
5) report on child;

6) Director's recommendation;
7) Adoption Order.
**Residency requirements for prospective adoptive parents:** Prospective adoptive parents must be residents of Ontario until the adoption order is obtained.

★ 1320 ★
**Anne Toth, M.S.W., C.S.W.**
546 N. Christina St., Ste. 503
Sarnia, ON, Canada N7T 5W6
Phone: (519) 344-3357

**Mailing address:**
P.O. Box 922, Sarnia, ON, Canada N7T 5W6

**Description of services:** 1) Provides intermediary services between prospective adoptive parents and birth parents considering an adoptive placement for their child;
2) screens birth parents according to provincial regulations;
3) conducts home studies for prospective adoptive parents;
4) provides medical arrangements for birth mother;
5) document preparation for lawyer;
6) post-placement supervision;.
**Fees:** $3000 - $5000.
**Number of independent adoptions handled last year:** 6.
**Description of process:** Prospective adoptive and birth parents mutually select one another based on the verbal description of the social worker and written non-identifying information. If desired, parties may meet face-to face. Social worker follows adoption from placement to finalization with both the adoptive and birth parents for approximately one year.
**Residency requirements for prospective adoptive parents:** Residents of Canada at least 50% of the time.

★ 1321 ★
**Valeriote and Valeriote, Barristers and Solicitors**
Francis M. Valeriote
373 Woolwich St.
Guelph, ON, Canada N1H 7A1
Phone: (519) 837-0300

**Mailing address:**
P.O. Box 1839, Guelph, ON, Canada N1H 7A1

**Description of services:** 1) Represents birth and/or adoptive parents at court;
2) prepares all legal documents;
3) interviews birth parents on behalf of prospective adoptive parents ;
4) interviews prospective adoptive parents on behalf of birth parents.
**Fees:** Hourly fee.
**Number of independent adoptions handled last year:** 1.
**Description of process:** Legal representation for identified adoptions.
**Residency requirements for prospective adoptive parents:** Residents of Ontario.

# Support Groups

## ALABAMA

★ 1322 ★
**Alabama Friends of Adoption**
4 Office Park Circle, Ste. 303
Birmingham, AL 35223
Phone: (205) 870-7093

**Founded:** 1979.

**Membership:** 500.

**Budget:** Unavailable.

**Staff:** All volunteer.

**Description:** An incorporated, non-profit, tax-exempt support group providing adoption information, support, education and aid.

**Description of services:** AFOA provides adoption support, educational opportunites for adoptive parents and social workers, sponsors cultural events and education for internationally adopted children, promotes special needs adoption, coordinates *Wednesday's Child Program* with the Alabama Department of Human Resources and an adoption "hotline," and provides aid to homeless children in Third World countries.

**Dues:** $15/yr.

**Publications:** *AFOA Newsletter* published quarterly.

**Meetings:** Three annual social events, quarterly board meetings, informational dinner meetings as scheduled.

## ALASKA

★ 1323 ★
**Anchorage Adoptive Parents Association**
P.O. Box 91685
Anchorage, AK 99509-1685
Phone: (907) 248-4506

**Founded:** 1979.

**Membership:** 60 families.

**Staff:** 10-15 volunteers.

**Description:** Non-profit parent support group.

**Description of services:** Sponsors public education on adoption issues; makes referrals for legal sources of adoption; provides support and social activities for adoptive families.

**Dues:** $10/yr.

**Publications:** Newsletter published bi-monthly.

**Meetings:** Monthly business meeting and meeting for parents of older adopted children. Annual public information meeting.

## ARIZONA

★ 1324 ★
**Advocates for Single Adoption Parenting (ASAP)**
1701 E. Linden
Tucson, AZ 88719
Phone: (602) 327-6478

**Founded:** 1980.

**Description:** Advisory group sharing 70 cumulative years of adoption efforts.

**Description of services:** ASAP provides peer counseling and referrals.

**Dues:** $12/yr. (optional).

**Meetings:** Monthly.

★ 1325 ★
**Extensions**
7835 E. Glenrosa, No. 4
Scottsdale, AZ 85251
Phone: (602) 946-6470

**Contact:** Randi Sweet, President.

**Date established:** 1990.

**Membership:** 75 families.

**Budget:** Unavailable.

**Staff:** All volunteer.

**Description:** Support group for families who have adopted internationally.

**Description of services:** Provides support, education and cultural activities.

**Dues:** $18.

**Publications:** *Extensions* published quarterly.

**Meetings:** Monthly.

★ 1326 ★
**Search Triad, Inc.**
P.O. Box 1432
Litchfield Park, AZ 85340
Phone: (602) 935-1405
(602) 935-4974

**Founded:** 1976.

**Membership:** 150. Members must be 18 to search.

**Budget:** Approx. $5000 annually.

**Staff:** Executive board (volunteer) and 10 volunteer search assistants.

**Description:** Non-profit organization dedicated to reuniting individuals separated by adoption, foster care or divorce. Member of the American Adoption Congress.

**Description of services:** Provides moral support, search assistance, use of library (over 100 books), networking with other groups, a speaker's bureau, and panel presentations for local adoption agencies.

**Dues:** $45/1st yr.; $25/yr. renewal. Free international registry.

**Publications:** Newsletter published bi-monthly.

**Meetings:** 2nd Thursday of every month in Phoenix.

★ 1327 ★
**Tracers, Ltd.**
P.O. Box 18511
Tucson, AZ 85731
Phone: (602) 886-8865
Fax: (602) 722-0025

**Contact:** Gari-Sue Greene, Owner.

**Founded:** 1983.

**Membership:** 582.

**Staff:** 1.

**Description:** For profit professional adoption search and support organization. Member of the American Adoption Congress.

**Description of services:** Provides full paid search and private search assistance; peer support and referrals to qualified counseling therapists; maintains a speakers bureau.

**Dues:** $50/yr.

# ARKANSAS

★ 1328 ★
**Adoptive Parents And Children Together**
**A.P.A.C.T.**
c/o Jim & Geri Ramsfield
20089 Center Rd.
Winslow, AR 72959
Phone: (501) 634-2722

**Founded:** 1983.

**Staff:** All volunteer.

**Description:** Non-profit support group for adoptive families, especially those who have adopted special needs children.

**Description of services:** Provides support, social events and participates in an annual statewide family retreat weekend.

**Dues:** None.

**Publications:** *AFACT* Newsletter published 4-5 times a year.

**Meetings:** 1-4 p.m. on the 1st Saturdays irregularly.

★ 1329 ★
**Arkansas Families and Adoptive Children Together**
**AFACT**
c/o Ray & Kathy Allen
16 Ridgewood
Russellville, AR 72801

**Founded:** 1981.

**Membership:** 20-25.

**Budget:** $450 annually.

**Staff:** 15-20.

**Description:** Non-profit corporation.

**Description of services:** AFACT provides member support, promotes public awareness of adoption, makes referrals, sponsors fundraisers and Adoption Week activities.

**Dues:** $10/yr.

**Publications:** *AFACT* Newsletter published quarterly.

**Meetings:** Quarterly in January, April, June and October. Adoption Family Weekend Retreat in August.

★ 1330 ★
**Parent Center**
192 E. Main
Batesville, AR 72501
Phone: (501) 793-4385

**Contact:** Carolyn Pollett.

**Date established:** 1985.

**Membership:** Unavailable.

**Budget:** $10,000.

**Staff:** 1 salaried and 2 volunteers.

**Description:** Non-profit parent support service.

**Description of services:** Provides support group for parents and offers parenting classes.

**Dues:** None.

**Publications:** None.

**Meetings:** Parent classes Monday from 9 - 11 A.M. and Tuesday from 7 - 9 P.M.

# CALIFORNIA

★ 1331 ★
**Adoptee Birth Family Registry**
P.O. Box 803
Sacramento, CA 95609
Phone: (916) 485-4119

**Contact:** Trudy Helmlinger.

**Date established:** 1991.

**Membership:** Non-membership.

**Description:** A reference book which lists the most requested non-identifying information about adoptees and birth family members. Adoptees describe their accomplishments, childhoods and lives as adults. Birth family members outline the circumstances surrounding the adoption, personal characteristics, family background and their current lives. Names and addresses are not printed. Information is indexed by birth date and birth place of the adoptee (who must be at least 21 yrs. old to register).

**Description of services:** Available in public libraries, adoption agencies, support groups throughout the U.S. and Canada.

**Dues:** No charge to be listed.

★ 1332 ★
**Adoption Assistance and Information Group**
16255 Ventura Blvd., Ste. 704
Encino, CA 91436-2302
Phone: (818) 501-6800
Fax: (818) 501-8465

**Contact:** David H. Baum, Chairman.

**Date established:** 1994.

**Membership:** 25-75.

**Budget:** N/A.

**Staff:** All volunteer.

**Description:** Non-profit support group and member of Adoptive Families of America for individuals or couples interested in adopting, in the process of adoption or who have successfully adopted.

**Description of services:** Provides support, advice, referrals and compassionate networking through the entirety of the adoption process.

**Dues:** $25/yr.

**Publications:** None.

**Meetings:** Last Wednesday of each month at 7:00 P.M. at the Conference Center of the Manufacturer's Bank Building, Ste. 210.

★ 1333 ★
**Down Syndrome Association of Los Angeles**
8949 Reseda Blvd., No. 109
Northridge, CA 91324-3943
Phone: (818) 718-6363
(800) 464-8995
Fax: (818) 718-6362

**Founded:** 1975.

**Membership:** 350.

**Budget:** $150,000 annually.

**Staff:** 2 salaried and many volunteer.

**Description:** Not-for-profit corporation for parents of children with Down Syndrome.

**Description of services:** Provides mutual support, peer counseling for new parents, information, referrals, a lending library of books, articles, videotapes, and cassette tapes. Offers sub-groups and conferences and hosts guest speakers on topics of interest to parents of children with Down's Syndrome. Toll free number for Southern California only.

**Dues:** $10/yr.

**Publications:** Newsletter published monthly.

**Meetings:** Call for schedule.

★ 1334 ★
**FACES**
**Families Adopting Children: Education & Support**
2510 Smith Grade Rd.
Santa Cruz, CA 95060
Phone: (408) 423-3870

**Contact:** June Davies, President.

**Date established:** 1985.

**Membership:** 100.

**Budget:** Based on annual dues.

**Staff:** All volunteer.

**Description:** Adoptive family support group.

**Description of services:** Provides support, referral and a means of networking for adoptive families involved with all methods of adoption; hosts social events.

**Dues:** $10/yr.

**Publications:** *FACES* published quarterly.

**Meetings:** Quarterly.

★ 1335 ★
**Friends of Holt-Korea**
c/o Mrs. Jinny Fruin
22365 Carta Blanca
Cupertino, CA 95014
Phone: (408) 739-4167

**Contact:** Jinny Fruin, President.

**Founded:** 1974.

**Staff:** All volunteer.

**Description:** Non-profit, tax exempt charitable corporation.

**Description of services:** Solicits donations and raises funds for Korean orphans.

**Publications:** *Friends of Holt Notes* published 2 - 6 times a year.

★ 1336 ★
**Hand In Hand of Greater Sacramento**
874 Phillip Ct.
El Dorado Hills, CA 95762
Phone: (916) 933-4562

**Contact:** Chris Winston, Coordinator.

**Date established:** 1970's.

**Membership:** 100 families.

**Budget:** $2200/yr.

**Staff:** All volunteer.

**Description:** Adoptive family support group and affiliate member of

**Adoptive Families of America** .

**Description of services:** Provides information, referrals and supports; hosts cultural and social activities; sponsors an adult-only meeting for adult inter-country adoptees and search direction for adult Korean adoptees.

**Dues:** $27/yr.

**Publications:** *Hand In Hand* Newsletter published quarterly.

**Meetings:** Monthly.

★ 1337 ★
**Independent Search Consultants**
P.O. Box 10192
Costa Mesa, CA 92627

**Founded:** 1980.

**Description:** Professional association of adoption search consultants which seeks to promote ethical standards and a means of certification for active search consultants.

**Description of services:** Offers search consultant certification on national, state, and specialized levels; sponsors panels, seminars and workshops on adoption search; makes referral to search organizations and a network of 75 search consultants in the U.S. and Canada; offers a speakers' bureau; and maintains a 100 volume library on adoption, heredity and state law.

**Publications:** *Consultant Newsletter* published monthly, Consultants Directory published semi-annually; a series of State Search Books; Class Manual and Consultant Training Manual.

★ 1338 ★
**Open Door Society of Los Angeles**
12235 Silva Pl.
Cerritos, CA 90701
Phone: (213) 402-3664

**Contact:** Donna L. Salisbury, Warmline Director.

**Founded:** 1969.

**Membership:** 152.

**Staff:** 20 volunteer.

**Description:** Non-profit corporation providing preparation, education and support to adoptive families.

**Description of services:** Provides Adoption Warm-Line, information, referrals, peer counseling, pre- and post-adoption support, and a speakers bureau. Special focus on older and special needs adoptions.

**Dues:** $20/yr.

**Publications:** *Open Door Society of Los Angeles* newsletter published bimonthly.

**Meetings:** Bi-monthly, parent and family activities as scheduled.

### ★ 1339 ★
### Orange County Adoptive Parents Association (OCAPA)
P.O. Box 11371
Santa Ana, CA 92711
Phone: (714) 770-6201

**Contact:** Carol-Ann Cada, Director; Alice Kelly, President.

**Founded:** 1968.

**Membership:** Approx. 100-150.

**Staff:** All volunteer.

**Description:** Non-profit, incorporated association for adoptive parents and children.

**Description of services:** Provides an open forum for adoptive parents and children to air their feeling about adoption; sponsors public awareness of adoption; hosts social events and provides a fund for the ''extra'' needs of foster children.

**Dues:** $15/yr. per person and $30/yr. per family.

**Publications:** *OCAPA ODES* published quarterly.

**Meetings:** Monthly.

### ★ 1340 ★
### Sierra Adoption Services
123 Nevada St.
Nevada City, CA 95959
Phone: (916) 265-6959
Fax: (916) 265-9223

**Mailing address:**
P.O. Box 361, Nevada City, CA 95959

**Branch address:**
8928 Volunteer Ln., Ste. 240, Sacramento, CA 95826
Phone: (916) 368-5114

**Date established:** 1983.

**Budget:** $645,000.

**Staff:** 13 salaried and 7 volunteers.

**Description:** Agency allied, non-profit child centered organization whose purpose is to recruit adoptive families for U.S. waiting children and offer post-adoptive support.

**Description of services:** Specialized adoption therapy available to adoptive families and children as well as adoptive family preparation.

**Dues:** Donations are welcome.

**Publications:** *Homecoming* published quarterly.

**Meetings:** ''Exploring Adoption'' classes offered monthly in Nevada City and Sacramento.

# COLORADO

### ★ 1341 ★
### Concerned United Birthparents, Inc.
10511 W. 104th Ave.
Broomfield, CO 80020
Phone: (303) 825-3430

**Founded:** 1976.

**Staff:** All volunteer.

**Description:** Non-profit support group for all triad members.

**Description of services:** Provides support, search workshops and makes referrals.

**Dues:** $50/first yr. and $35/renewal.

**Publications:** National newsletters.

**Meetings:** Last Sunday of each month with holiday exceptions.

### ★ 1342 ★
### International Concerns Committee for Children
911 Cypress Dr.
Boulder, CO 80303
Phone: (303) 494-8333

**Contact:** A. M. Merrill.

**Date established:** 1979.

**Membership:** Varies.

**Budget:** $40,000/yr.

**Staff:** 3 member Board of Directors and 37 member Advisory Board.

**Description:** A tax-exempt, not-for-profit corporation whose charitable and educational directives are: 1) *acquaint* the concerned public with various ways to provide assistance to homeless children; 2) *educate* those interested personally and professionally about procedures; 3) *inform* prospective parents of the availability of ''waiting children'' in foreign countries.

**Description of services:** ICCC provides personal counseling in adoption by experienced adoptive parents and maintains an *Adoption Photolisting* with monthly updates for children still in their birth countries for whom agencies are seeking adoptive homes. Some children are already in the U.S. but need new adoptive parents.

**Dues:** ICCC depends entirely on donations for its funding and requests donation in amounts from $2.50 to $25 for its various publications.

**Publications:** *Report on Foreign Adoption* published annually with ten monthly updates which includes approximate costs, waiting periods and types of children available from dozens of agencies and other organizations which follow the ethical guidelines for adoption developed by the Joint Council for International Children's Services of North America and who place children in North American homes. The publication includes requirements for parents, single-parent information, I-600 orphan visa procedure, medical issues, coping with children's adjustment and a bibliography of useful books. *Newsletter* published quarterly which contains information on refugees, sponsorships, legislation, medical issues, health care and adoption. Five issue papers which deal with different aspects of adoption.

**Meetings:** Annual.

**★ 1343 ★**
**Orphan Voyage**
2141 Road 2300
Cedaredge, CO 81413
Phone: (303) 856-3937

**Contact:** Jean M. Paton, Director.

**Founded:** 1953.

**Membership:** Indeterminate.

**Staff:** 1 volunteer.

**Description:** A communication, referral and educational center for people interested in reunion between adoptees and birth families.

**Description of services:** Offers guidance for search problems; makes referrals; and provides consultation and speakers bureau service on a fee basis.

**Dues:** Contributions only.

**Publications:** Annual report, newsletter.

**Meetings:** None.

**★ 1344 ★**
**RESOLVE of Colorado**
P.O. Box 61096
Denver, CO 80206
Phone: (303) 469-5261

**Founded:** 1974.

**Membership:** 250.

**Staff:** All volunteer.

**Description:** Local chapter of RESOLVE, Somerville, MA.

**Description of services:** Provides support and information for those experiencing infertility problems.

**Dues:** $35/yr. for Colorado and national memberships.

**Publications:** Newsletter published quarterly.

**Meetings:** Call or write for schedule.

# CONNECTICUT

**★ 1345 ★**
**Attachment Disorder Parents Network of Connecticut**
85 Westwood Ave.
Plainville, CT 06062
Phone: (203) 747-5294

**Contact:** Janet Bedell.

**Date established:** Unavailable.

**Membership:** 75.

**Budget:** Unavailable.

**Staff:** All volunteer.

**Description:** Non-profit parent support group.

**Description of services:** Provides support, information and referrals.

**Dues:** $10/yr.

**Publications:** Newsletter published quarterly.

**Meetings:** Last Friday of each month.

**★ 1346 ★**
**Latin American Parents Association**
P.O. Box 523
Unionville, CT 06085
Phone: (203) 270-1424

**Contact:** Christine Hamilton, President.

**Date established:** 1981.

**Membership:** 300 families.

**Budget:** $10,000 annually.

**Staff:** 10 member volunteer Board of Directors.

**Description:** Tax-exempt, not-for-profit support group for prospective adoptive parents and adoptive parents of Latin American children.

**Description of services:** The four goals of LAPA-CT are:
1) To distribute information on adoption and citizenship requirements to prospective adoptive parents for Latin American adoptions;
2) To keep updated sources and acquire new sources for adoptions in Latin America;
3) To offer aid to orphanages and other institutions in Latin America;
4) To help families who have adopted from Latin America remain in contact with one another, learn about Latin American culture and exchange ideas on rearing adopted children.
LAPA-CT implements these goals by advocacy, sponsoring workshops, hosting guest speakers, maintaining a lending library, fundraising and providing social and cultural events for parents and children.

**Dues:** $30/yr.

**Publications:** *Nuestros Ninos Bonitos* published bi-monthly.

**Meetings:** Call for schedule.

**★ 1347 ★**
**Stars of David**
c/o Jewish Family Services
740 N. Main St., Ste. A
West Hartford, CT 06117
Phone: (203) 232-6052

**Founded:** 1987.

**Membership:** 32 families.

**Description:** Non-profit support group for Jewish families.

**Description of services:** Support, Jewish holiday family activities and adult workshops.

**Dues:** $10/yr. per family.

**Publications:** *Hartford Stars* published twice a year.

**Meetings:** Quarterly.

# DELAWARE

**★ 1348 ★**
**Adoptive Families with Information and Support**
**AFIS**
P.O. Box 7268
Wilmington, DE 19810
Phone: (302) 475-8925

**Mailing address:**
2610 Northgate Rd., Wilmington, DE 19810

**Contact:** Mary Lou Edgar, President.

**Founded:** 1973.

**Membership:** 250.

**Staff:** 15 volunteer.

**Description:** Adoption support group of adoptive parents, prospective adoptive parents, adoption professionals and adoption advocates dedicated to meeting the needs of those touched by adoption.

**Description of services:** Provides parenting education, support, children's groups, and seminars.

**Dues:** $12/yr.

**Publications:** *AFIS* Newsletter published 4 times yearly.

**Meetings:** Regular meetings for specific groups within the membership.

---

# DISTRICT OF COLUMBIA

## ★ 1349 ★
**ASIA Family and Friends**
**Adoption Service Information Agency, Inc. (ASIA)**
7720 Alaska Ave., N.W.
Washington, DC 20012
Phone: (202) 726-7193

**Contact:** Theodore U.C. Kim.

**Date established:** 1981.

**Membership:** 250 affiliated members.

**Budget:** $700,000.

**Staff:** 8 salaried full time and 5 salaried part time.

**Description:** Non-profit, licensed child placing agency which offers post-legal services to adoptive families.

**Description of services:** Provides counseling, education and cultural activities for adoptees and their parents.

**Dues:** $18/yr.

**Publications:** *Asia Newsletter* published quarterly.

**Meetings:** At least quarterly activity events.

## ★ 1350 ★
**Families for Private Adoption**
P.O. Box 6375
Washington, DC 20015
Phone: (202) 722-0338

**Founded:** 1984.

**Membership:** 400.

**Budget:** Less than $25,000.

**Description of services:** Provides information on non-agency assisted adoption, its procedures and legal concerns; offers referrals to private adoption sources; organizes workshops and professional and peer support groups.

**Publications:** *FPA Bulletin* published quarterly and a handbook, *Successful Private Adoption.*

## ★ 1351 ★
**National Council for Adoption**
1930 17th St., N.W.
Washington, DC 20009
Phone: (202) 328-1200

**Founded:** 1980.

**Membership:** 1200 in 20 state groups.

**Budget:** Over $500,000.

**Staff:** Approx. 10 salaried.

**Description:** Committee of private agencies, adoptive parents, adoptees and birthparents which works to protect the institution of adoption, ensure the confidentiality of all involved and strives to eliminate non-agency-assisted adoptions.

**Description of services:** Provides an information clearinghouse; conducts research programs; maintains speakers' bureau, 2000 volume library, as well as files on adoption, maternity services and infertility; bestows Friend of Adoption Award.

**Dues:** Individual: $50/yr.; Supporter: $100/yr.; Sustainer; $200/yr.; Chairman's Club: $1000/yr. Organizational: Begin at $500 and $1000.

**Publications:** *Memo* published semi-monthly; *National Adoption Reports* published bi-monthly; *Directory of Resources* published annually; *Unmarried Parents Today* published periodically; and other related materials, pamphlets, handbook and *Adoption Factbook.*

**Meetings:** Annual convention.

---

# FLORIDA

## ★ 1352 ★
**ALARM**
**Advocating Legislation for Adoption Reform Movement**
P.O. Box 1860
Cape Coral, FL 33904
Phone: (813) 542-1342
Fax: (813) 549-9393

**Contact:** Sandy Musser, Director.

**Founded:** 1987.

**Membership:** 150.

**Budget:** $7500 annually.

**Staff:** All volunteer.

**Description:** Non-profit incorporated support group whose purpose is to open adoption records for all members of the triad.

**Description of services:** ALARM provides search and support; maintains files of pertinent literature; advocates for adoptees' rights; hosts workshops and seminars; and makes referrals.

**Dues:** $35/yr.

**Publications:** *Freedom Rider.*

**Meetings:** Call for schedule and location.

## ★ 1353 ★
**First Coast Jewish Family and Community Services, Inc.**
3601 Cardinal Point Rd.
Jacksonville, FL 32257
Phone: (904) 448-1933
Fax: (904) 448-0349

**Staff:** 17 salaried, 10 volunteer.

**Description:** Full service adoption agency under the auspices of a non-profit, incorporated Jewish social service agency, a United Way member.

**Description of services:** All forms of adoption, information and referrals, and adoptee search.

**Publications:** *Family Matters* published semi-annually.

**★ 1354 ★**
**Hope! Share And Care! Adoption Support Group**
4062 Greenwillow Ln. E.
Jacksonville, FL 32277
Phone: (904) 744-1549
(904) 743-9024

**Contact:** Jerry Woodbridge and Kimberly Hale, Group Leaders.

**Date established:** 1992.

**Membership:** 25 couples.

**Budget:** Unavailable.

**Staff:** 2 volunteer group leaders.

**Description:** Non-profit support group and member of
**Adoptive Families of America** for adoptive and birth parents,
adoptees and prospective adoptive parents.

**Description of services:** Provides information and support to
all members of the adoption triad as well as those considering
adoption.

**Dues:** Unavailable.

**Publications:** Newsletter published bi-monthly.

**Meetings:** 3rd Thursday of each month 7 P.M. at the Baptist
Medical Center, Suite 207 - Howard Building.

**★ 1355 ★**
**Oasis, Inc.**
P.O. Box 53-0761
Miami Shores, FL 33161
Phone: (305) 948-8933

**Contact:** Rachel S. Rivers.

**Date established:** 1980.

**Membership:** 2500.

**Budget:** Unavailable.

**Staff:** All volunteer.

**Description:** Non-profit, incorporated support group for persons
separated by adoption and seeking reunion.

**Description of services:** Provides support and search
assistance.

**Dues:** $70/yr.

**Publications:** Various papers on pertinent topics.

**Meetings:** None.

**★ 1356 ★**
**Organized Adoption Search Information Services**
P.O. Box 53-0761
Miami Shores, FL 33153
Phone: (305) 945-2758

**Contact:** Rachel S. Rivers, Director.

**Founded:** 1980.

**Staff:** All volunteer.

**Description:** Not for profit search and support group
incorporated in and chartered by the State of Florida. Member
of the American Adoption Congress.

**Description of services:** Maintains confidential files for each
searching member and a match-up registry of date of birth and
place of birth. Special search assistance provided to all
members on an individual basis. Offers on-going support for all
who are actively searching and who have been reunited with
their families. Works in unison with the International Soundex
Reunion Registry.

**Dues:** $70/yr.

**Meetings:** Vary.

**★ 1357 ★**
**Special Needs Adoptive Parents (S.N.A.P.)**
15913 Layton Ct.
Tampa, FL 33647
Phone: (813) 971-4752
(813) 689-3034

**Contact:** Nancy Ellison, Co-Leader.

**Date established:** 1989.

**Membership:** 35 families.

**Budget:** None.

**Staff:** All volunteer.

**Description:** Loosely-knit support group and affiliate of
**Adoptive Families of America** for families who have adopted
children who have been physically or sexually abused,
neglected or abandoned.

**Description of services:** Provides ongoing support, referrals
and a means of networking.

**Dues:** None.

**Publications:** Newsletter published sporadically.

**Meetings:** 2 - 3 times annually.

# GEORGIA

**★ 1358 ★**
**Adopted Kids and Parents Support Group (AKAPS)**
4137 Bellflower Ct.
Roswell, GA 30075
Phone: (404) 640-0031
(404) 978-7134

**Contact:** Midge Miller.

**Date established:** 1987.

**Membership:** 75.

**Budget:** $1500/yr.

**Staff:** 4 volunteers.

**Description:** Non-profit metro Atlanta support group and
affiliate of
**Adoptive Families of America** for adoptive and pre-adoptive
families.

**Description of services:** Provides information, resources, pre-
and post-adoption support, cultural education and social
activities.

**Dues:** $15/yr.

**Publications:** *AKAPS* Newsletter published 4 - 6 times a year.

**Meetings:** 6-8 times a year at various metro Atlanta locations.

**★ 1359 ★**
**Adoptive Parents Association**
911 Moss Dr.
Savannah, GA 31410
Phone: (912) 897-6840

**Contact:** Karon Turner, President.

**Date established:** 1980.

**Membership:** 30.

**Budget:** Variable.

**Staff:** 3-4 volunteers.

**Description:** Non-profit support group offering support to persons in all phases of the adoption process. APA maintains membership in OURS and Adoptive Families of America, two national adoption organizations.

**Description of services:** Provides educational programs, social activities and discussions on current adoption issues.

**Dues:** $15/yr.

**Publications:** Newsletter.

**Meetings:** Monthly from September to May.

★ 1360 ★
**American-Romanian Connection**
1343 Summit Chase Dr.
Snellville, GA 30278
Phone: (404) 978-0019

**Contact:** Mary Springer.

**Date established:** 1991.

**Membership:** 60 families.

**Staff:** All volunteer.

**Description:** Non-profit, adoptive family support group.

**Description of services:** Provides support, referrals and information to adoptive and prospective adoptive families.

**Dues:** $5./yr.

**Publications:** American-Romanian Connection published biannually.

**Meetings:** As needed as well as an annual picninc.

★ 1361 ★
**Augusta Adoption League**
P.O. Box 15354
Augustsa, GA 30919-1354
Phone: (706) 863-0583

**Contact:** Pam Brown.

**Membership:** 20 members.

**Budget:** Unavailable.

**Staff:** Volunteer.

**Description:** Support group for adoptive parents and those considering adoption.

**Description of services:** Provides support and advocacy particularly for the adoption of older children and/or children with special needs.

**Dues:** $20/yr.

**Publications:** None.

**Meetings:** Monthly from September to May.

★ 1362 ★
**Bartow/Paulding Adoptive Families**
c/o Sylvia Baldwin
69 Stoker Rd.
Cartersville, GA 30120
Phone: (404) 387-1008

**Date established:** 1992.

**Membership:** Informal.

**Budget:** Less than $500. annually.

**Staff:** All volunteer.

**Description:** Non-profit adoptive family support group.

**Description of services:** Provides support and referrals for adoptive families as well as social activites for parents and children. Makes My Turn Book and its monthly updates available.

**Dues:** None.

**Publications:** Families Forever published quarterly.

**Meetings:** Entire families are welcome on the 2nd Saturday of each month at 10 A.M.

★ 1363 ★
**Central Savannah River Area Council on Adoptable Children**
c/o Lamont and Tamarra Marsh
4046 Pinnacle Way
Hephzibah, GA 30815
Phone: (706) 790-5985

**Date established:** November, 1993.

**Membership:** 20-25 families.

**Budget:** Less than $500./yr.

**Staff:** All volunteer.

**Description:** Non-profit educational and support group.

**Description of services:** Provides support, education, advocacy and service training.

**Dues:** $5./mo.

**Publications:** CSRA COAC Dispatch published monthly.

**Meetings:** 2nd Thursday of each month.

★ 1364 ★
**Clarke County Adoption Resource Exchange**
**C.C.A.R.E.**
P.O. Box 6311
Athens, GA 30604
Phone: (404) 542-9800

**Contact:** Susan Jones, Coordinator.

**Founded:** 1986.

**Membership:** Approx. 20 families.

**Staff:** All volunteer.

**Description:** Non-profit support group for adoptive and prospective adoptive families, and interested others.

**Description of services:** C.C.A.R.E. provides education and resources relating to the adoption experience and provides support for prospective adoptive parents and adoptive families.

**Dues:** $12/yr.

**Publications:** C.C.A.R.E. Newsletter published quarterly.

**Meetings:** 4th Tuesday of each month.

★ 1365 ★
**Families Adopting Across Racial Lines**
910 River Rock Dr.
Woodstock, GA 30188
Phone: (404) 924-8645

**Contact:** Karen Slevert.

**Date established:** 1993.

**Membership:** 23 families.

**Budget:** None.

**Staff:** All volunteer.

**Description:** Adoptive family support group.

**Description of services:** Provides parent support and information as well as activities for children.

**Dues:** None.

**Meetings:** Quarterly.

★ 1366 ★

**Flint River Adoptive Parent Association**
c/o Spalding County Department of Children
P.O. Box 1610
Griffin, GA 30224
Phone: (404) 954-2354
(404) 228-1386

**Date established:** 1993.

**Membership:** 20 families.

**Budget:** Less than $500 annually.

**Staff:** All volunteer.

**Description:** Adoptive family support group.

**Description of services:** Provides information, referrals and support.

**Dues:** None.

**Meetings:** Second Monday of each month.

★ 1367 ★

**Home B.A.S.E. (Birthparents and Adoptees Supportive Environment)**
P.O. Box 624
Evans, GA 30809
Phone: (706) 650-2162

**Contact:** Mimi Hopson.

**Membership:** 12.

**Budget:** Unavailable.

**Staff:** All volunteer.

**Description:** Support group for individuals search for a missing family member, particularly those lost through adoption.

**Description of services:** Provides search assistance and strategies.

**Dues:** $10/yr.

**Publications:** None.

**Meetings:** 7 P.M. on 2nd Tuesday of each month from September to May.

★ 1368 ★

**Parent Support Group of Adoption Services, Inc.**
P.O. Box 155
Payvo, GA 31778
Phone: (912) 859-2654

**Contact:** Anne Losquist, Adoption Counselor.

**Date established:** 1992.

**Membership:** 50 couples.

**Budget:** None.

**Staff:** 1 salaried and volunteers.

**Description:** Adoptive parent support group.

**Description of services:** Provides information, education and parent support.

**Dues:** None.

**Meetings:** Monthly.

★ 1369 ★

**RESOLVE of Georgia**
Box 343
2480-4 Briarcliff Rd.
Atlanta, GA 30329
Phone: (404) 233-8443

**Contact:** Carol Jones, President.

**Founded:** 1980.

**Membership:** 200 couples.

**Budget:** Approx. $3000-$5000 annually.

**Staff:** All volunteer.

**Description:** Non-profit, tax-exempt, incorporated support group for couples and individual experiencing infertility; chapter of national RESOLVE.

**Description of services:** Provides seminars, symposia and workshops, peer support; makes referrals and maintains contact with an advisory board of infertility specialists, counselors, clergy and adoption specialists; and maintains a lending library.

**Dues:** $35/yr.

**Publications:** *RESOLVE of Georgia* Newsletter published quarterly.

**Meetings:** 3rd Tuesday of the month from September through June.

★ 1370 ★

**Single Women Adopting Children**
c/o Lauri Lanning
1538 Chantilly Dr., Apt. C102
Atlanta, GA 30324
Phone: (404) 730-4593

**Date established:** 1989.

**Membership:** 40 members.

**Budget:** None.

**Staff:** All volunteer.

**Description:** Non-profit adoptive family support group.

**Description of services:** Provides information, peer support, education and social interaction.

**Dues:** $10/yr.

**Meetings:** Monthly.

★ 1371 ★

**Warren, Glascock and McDuffie Support Group**
c/o Dwight and Jan Cumber
205 No. Gibson St.
Warrenton, GA 30828
Phone: (706) 465-9694

**Date established:** 1993.

**Membership:** 10 families.

**Budget:** Less than $500./yr.

**Staff:** All volunteer.

**Description:** Non-profit adoptive family support group.

**Description of services:** Provides education, referrral and peer support.

**Dues:** None.

**Publications:** Monthly newsletter.

**Meetings:** Monthly.

# HAWAII

## ★ 1372 ★
**Hawaii International Child Placement and Family Services, Inc.**
P.O. Box 240486
Honolulu, HI 96824-0486
Phone: (808) 377-0881
Fax: (808) 373-5095

**Founded:** 1975.

**Staff:** 5 salaried.

**Description:** Non-profit, adoptive family support group.

**Description of services:** Provides support, counseling and referrals for domestic and international adoption.

**Meetings:** Call or write for schedule.

## ★ 1373 ★
**RESOLVE of Hawaii**
3721 Omao
Koloa, HI 96756
Phone: (808) 742-8885

**Contact:** Bev Parker-Evans.

**Date established:** 1992.

**Membership:** 150.

**Budget:** $3000/yr.

**Staff:** 12 volunteer part-time officers and coordinators.

**Description:** Non-profit support group for those involved in issues surrounding infertility and member of

**Adoptive Families of America**.

**Description of services:** Provides support and peer counseling; maintain lending library and hosts seminars and symposiums.

**Dues:** Unavailable.

**Publications:** *RESOLVE of Hawaii* newsletter published quarterly.

**Meetings:** Groups meet on each of the 4 islands. Call for time and location.

# IDAHO

## ★ 1374 ★
**Adoptees' Liberty Movement Association (ALMA)**
P.O. Box 190655
Boise, ID 83719-0655
Phone: (208) 362-2364

**Founded:** 1971.

**Description:** Association of persons separated by adoption and seeking reunion.

**Description of services:** International Reunion Registry, support and search assistance.

**Publications:** *SEARCHLIGHT* published quarterly.

**Meetings:** 1st Tuesday of each month.

## ★ 1375 ★
**Idaho Voluntary Adoption Registry**
**Center for Vital Statistics and Health Policy**
450 W. State St., 1st Fl.
P.O. Box 83720
Boise, ID 83720-0036
Phone: (208) 334-5990

**Founded:** 1985.

**Staff:** .25 salaried employee.

**Description:** Confidential cross-referenced file of people who are or were the principal parties in an adoption established by the Idaho State Legislature.

**Description of services:** Provides reunion services for Idaho-born adopted persons, 18 yrs. or older, with similarly registered birthparents.

**Dues:** $10 application fee.

**Publications:** None.

**Meetings:** None.

# ILLINOIS

## ★ 1376 ★
**Adoptees Liberty Movement Association**
**Central Illinois Chapter**
P.O. Box 81
Bloomington, IL 61702
Phone: (309) 828-2217

**Contact:** Susan Lentz, Chapter Coordinator.

**Founded:** 1981.

**Staff:** All volunteer.

**Description:** Non-profit, search and support group for adult adoptees and their families.

**Description of services:** Sponsors public education on the injustice of sealed adoption records; provides search assistance and support.

**Dues:** $65.

## ★ 1377 ★
**Adoption Triangle**
1819 S. Neil St.
Champaign, IL 61820
Phone: (217) 359-8815

**Contact:** Karen Morgan, Supervisor; Neysa Buckle, Facilitator.

**Description:** Support group for all members of the adoption triangle.

**Description of services:** Provides a forum for discussion on adoption, related topics and concerns; support; and raises awareness of adoption-related issues.

**Meetings:** 6:30 - 8:30 p.m. on 1st Monday of each month.

## ★ 1378 ★
**Adoption Triangle**
P.O. Box 384
Park Forest, IL 60466
Phone: (708) 481-8916

**Founded:** 1982.

**Membership:** Approx. 100.

**Budget:** $600 annually.

**Staff:** 5 volunteer.

**Description:** Non-profit support group for members of the adoption triad.

**Description of services:** Provides search, support and referrals.

**Dues:** $5/meeting or $50/consultation fee.

**Meetings:** 1st Thursday of the month.

★ 1379 ★
**Adoption Triangle**
512 Oneida St.
Joliet, IL 60435
Phone: (815) 722-4999

**Contact:** Lydia Granda.

**Date established:** 1992.

**Membership:** Varies.

**Budget:** Unavailable.

**Staff:** All volunteer.

**Description:** Non-profit search and support group.

**Description of services:** Provides support and search assistance for those separated by adoption.

**Dues:** $3/meeting.

**Publications:** None.

**Meetings:** First Monday of each month (call first).

★ 1380 ★
**Adoptive Families Today**
P.O. Box 1726
Barrington, IL 60011
Phone: (708) 382-7607

**Date established:** 1989.

**Membership:** 100 couples.

**Budget:** $4500/yr.

**Staff:** All volunteer.

**Description:** Non-profit support group for adoptive and prospective adoptive families and member group of Adoptive Families of America.

**Description of services:** Provides support and referrals; maintains children's library; hosts educational meetings, annual conference, mom & tots groups and children's activities.

**Dues:** $25/yr. membership; $15/yr. newsletter only.

**Publications:** *AdoptNews* published monthly from August to May.

**Meetings:** 3rd Thursday of each month from September through May.

★ 1381 ★
**All-Adopt**
727 Ramona Pl.
Godfrey, IL 62035
Phone: (618) 466-8926

**Date established:** 1986.

**Membership:** 25 families.

**Budget:** Unavailable.

**Staff:** All volunteer.

**Description:** Adoptive family member support group of Adoptive Families of America.

**Description of services:** Provides information, education and support for adoptive families; hosts social and cultural activities.

**Dues:** $12.

**Publications:** Newsletter published monthly.

**Meetings:** Potluck dinner and activity on 2nd Saturday of each month at 6 P.M.

★ 1382 ★
**Central Illinois Adoptive Families**
2014 Lake Bluff
Bloomington, IL 61704
Phone: (309) 828-2353

**Contact:** Anne Bettendorf.

**Date established:** Unavailable.

**Membership:** Unavailable.

**Budget:** Unavailable.

**Staff:** 4 volunteer.

**Description:** Adoptive parent support group.

**Description of services:** Provides support to adoptive families.

**Dues:** $10/yr.

**Publications:** None.

**Meetings:** Third Sunday of the month.

★ 1383 ★
**Christian Adoption Ministries**
327 N. High St.
Carlinville, IL 62626
Phone: (217) 854-8871

**Contact:** Katrina Schmitz, President.

**Date established:** 1991.

**Membership:** Unavailable.

**Budget:** Unavailable.

**Staff:** All volunteer.

**Description:** Non-profit adoptive family support and advocacy group and affiliate of
**Adoptive Families of America** .

**Description of services:** Provides information, support and referrals; maintains speakers' bureau.

**Dues:** None.

**Publications:** Newsletter to be published quarterly.

**Meetings:** Call for time and location.

★ 1384 ★
**Hands Around the World, Inc.**
c/o Gail C. Walton
1417 E. Miner St.
Arlington Heights, IL 60004
Phone: (708) 255-8309

**Contact:** Gail C. Walton, President.

**Date established:** 1993.

**Membership:** 130 families.

**Budget:** Unavailable.

**Staff:** All volunteer.

**Description:** A member of
**Adoptive Families of America** and support group for families who have adopted interculturally which is directed by the following goals:
1) To enhance self-esteem as a member of one's birth culture, one's adoptive family and the community of the world;
2) To learn to balance a healthy pride in one's self and one's heritage with respect for other's feelings and appreciation for their heritage;

3) To embrace all cultures and invite diverse families, including families touched by adoption, to share their heritages with others;
4) To support all members of the organization in discovering their own identity while having fun;
5) To educate members as well as the general public about the value of diversity.

**Description of services:** Provides support, guidance and peer counseling; hosts hand-on educational activities, outings and multicultural day camp.

**Dues:** None.

**Publications:** *Hands Around the World* published 3 to 4 time a year.

**Meetings:** Call for time and location.

★ 1385 ★
**Healing Hearts, Inc.**
P.O. 606
Normal, IL 61761
Phone: (309) 379-5401
(309) 692-3028

**Date established:** 1991.
**Membership:** 36.
**Budget:** Based on dues and fundraising.
**Staff:** 4 Executive Officers and 4 Directors At Large.
**Description:** Not-for-profit search and support group.
**Description of services:** Provides education, referrals, search techniques and counseling as well as consciousness raising on effects of those touched by adoption.
**Dues:** $30/yr.
**Publications:** None.
**Meetings:** 4th Thursday of each month from January to October in Rm. 301, University High, at the Normal Campus of Illinois State University, Main & Gregory Sts.

★ 1386 ★
**Heritage Finders**
1102 Erie St.
Elgin, IL 60123
Phone: (708) 741-2189

**Contact:** Alice Lumbard.
**Membership:** Attendance at support group varies.
**Budget:** N/A.
**Staff:** Volunteer.
**Description:** Support group for members of the adoption triad in search.
**Description of services:** Provides support, referrals and search assistance for adoptees, birth and adoptive parents primarily in Illinois.
**Dues:** None.
**Publications:** None.
**Meetings:** Monthly.

★ 1387 ★
**Kishwaukee OURS**
303 N. 2nd St.
DeKalb, IL 60115
Phone: (815) 758-4307

**Contact:** Mary Kowalski.
**Founded:** 1985.

**Membership:** 15 families.
**Budget:** $200 annually.
**Staff:** 6 volunteer officers.
**Description:** Adoptive family support group.
**Description of services:** Provides support, educational services and social activities; makes referrals to appropriate social service agencies; Korean school for children born in South Korea.
**Dues:** $10/yr.
**Publications:** Newsletter published quarterly.
**Meetings:** Monthly meetings, dates vary.

★ 1388 ★
**The Lost Connection**
2210 N. Illinois St., No. 155
Belleville, IL 62221
Phone: (618) 235-9409
Fax: (618) 233-2715

**Contact:** Karen Saunders, Searcher.
**Date established:** 1992.
**Membership:** Unavailable.
**Budget:** Unavailable.
**Staff:** All volunteer.
**Description:** Support group for all members of the adoption triad.
**Description of services:** Provides search and support. Will also conduct private searches in response to mail inquiries.
**Dues:** None.
**Publications:** Unavailable.
**Meetings:** 2nd Wednesday of each month.

★ 1389 ★
**Missing Pieces**
P.O. Box 7541
Springfield, IL 62791-7541
Phone: (217) 787-8450

**Contact:** Maggie Ruby, Coordinator.
**Date established:** 1988.
**Membership:** 25.
**Budget:** Based on dues.
**Staff:** All volunteer.
**Description:** Search and support group for those touched by adoption.
**Description of services:** Provides support and referrals for those engaged in adoption search.
**Dues:** $35/1st yr. and $25 renewal.
**Publications:** None.
**Meetings:** 1st Monday of the month 7 P.M. in the Lincoln Room of St. John's Hospital, Springfield, IL.

★ 1390 ★
**OURS of Northern Illinois**
2619 Hampden Ct.
Rockford, IL 61107
Phone: (815) 397-2040

**Contact:** Pam Coughlin, President.
**Date established:** Unavailable.
**Membership:** Unavailable.

**Budget:** Unavailable.
**Staff:** All volunteer.
**Description:** Adoption support group and member of Adoptive Families of America.
**Description of services:** Provides information and support.
**Dues:** $15/yr.
**Publications:** *OURS of Northern Illinois* published quarterly.
**Meetings:** Varied schedule. Call for times.

★ 1391 ★
**Ours thru Adoption, Inc.**
2929 - 27th Ave. A
Moline, IL 61265
Phone: (309) 762-8061
**Contact:** Ann Vermeire.
**Founded:** 1977, incorporated 1986.
**Staff:** All volunteer.
**Description:** Non-profit, family-oriented, parent support group of those interested in the issues and aspects of adoption, foreign aid and orphan sponsorship, ethnic and cultural awareness and parent education.
**Description of services:** Hosts ethnic, cultural and social events; provides medical and financial aid to foreign agencies, orphan sponsorship and educational opportunities for parents and agencies; and lobbies for legislative change in the state of Illinois in the area of foreign adoption.
**Dues:** $15/yr. per family.
**Publications:** Newsletter published monthly.
**Meetings:** 2nd Monday of each month at the Edwards Congregational Church, Davenport, IA.

★ 1392 ★
**Quincy Adoption Support Group**
1405 S. 24th
Quincy, IL 62301
Phone: (217) 222-4813
**Contact:** Debbie Brink, President.
**Date established:** Unavailable.
**Membership:** 30 families.
**Budget:** Based on donations.
**Staff:** All volunteer.
**Description:** Support group for adoptive and foster families and those awaiting adoptive placements.
**Description of services:** Provides support, information and referrals; hosts guest speakers.
**Dues:** Donations accepted.
**Publications:** None.
**Meetings:** Bi-monthly.

★ 1393 ★
**Single Adoptive Parent Support Group**
c/o Susan Weiss
1132 N. Euclid Ave.
Oak Park, IL 60302-1219
Phone: (708) 524-8908
**Branch address:**
**Contact:** Susan Weiss.
**Founded:** 1986.
**Membership:** 45.

**Staff:** All volunteer.
**Description:** Support group for single adoptive parents, their children and prospective single adoptive parents.
**Description of services:** Sponsors social meetings, family activities and educational sessions; provides information.
**Dues:** $20.
**Meetings:** 2nd Saturday of each month.

★ 1394 ★
**Stars of David International, Inc.**
3175 Commercial Ave., Ste. 100
Northbrook, IL 60062-1915
Phone: (708) 205-1200 x 34
**Mailing address:**
P.O. Box 374, Northbrook, IL 60062-1915
**Branch address:**
East Bay Chapter

South Bay (Sunnyvale)

Denver

Hartford

Lauderhill

Atlanta

Chicago

Central Maryland

Eastern-Central Massachusetts

Detroit

St. Paul

St. Louis

Central New Jersey

Northern New Jersey

Erie County

Pittsburgh

Providence

Houston,
**Contact:** Susan M. Katz, National Chapter Coordinator.
**Date established:** 1984.
**Membership:** 500 members in 20 chapters in the US and Canada.
**Budget:** Unavailable.
**Staff:** All volunteer.
**Description:** Non-profit, incorporated information and support network for Jewish and partly-Jewish adoptive families.
**Description of services:** Provides support and social activities through its local chapters.
**Dues:** $8 national plus chapter dues.
**Publications:** *Star Tracks* published quarterly.
**Meetings:** Call or write for local chapter information.

## ★ 1395 ★
**Truth Seekers in Adoption**
P.O. Box 366
Prospect Heights, IL 60070-0366
Phone: (708) 342-TSIA

**Founded:** 1973.

**Membership:** C. 1000.

**Staff:** Volunteer.

**Description:** Non-profit organization aiding adoption-separated families; member of the American Adoption Congress.

**Description of services:** Provides individualized search plans; monthly meetings for support and reunion preparation; ongoing support during search and after reunion; telephone counseling; intermediary services; source referrals; sponsored group therapy; adoption library; reunion registry, and a speakers bureau.

**Dues:** $75/yr. for support group and registry only; $25 registry only (one-time fee for indefinite time); $175 for all of the above and search start. When search is completed, balance of $700 is due. Payment plans are available.

**Publications:** *AAC* (Adoption Congress newsletter) is provided to new members.

**Meetings:** 7-10 p.m. on the last Monday of the month at Lutheran General Hospital (Johnson Auditorium), 1775 Dempster, Park Ridge, IL.

# INDIANA

## ★ 1396 ★
**Adoptees' Identity Doorway**
P.O. Box 361
South Bend, IN 46624
Phone: (219) 272-3520

**Founded:** 1979.

**Membership:** 10-15.

**Staff:** Betty Heide, President.

**Description:** Search and support group for all members of the triad.

**Description of services:** Provides support, search assistance and registration in the Reunion Registry of Indiana.

**Dues:** None.

**Publications:** None.

**Meetings:** 2nd Wednesday of each month at the Valley American Bank, Town and Country Shopping Center, Mishawaka, IN.

## ★ 1397 ★
**Adoption/Birthmother Search for Tomorrow, Inc.**
P.O. Box 441
New Haven, IN 46774
Phone: (219) 749-4392

**Contact:** Martha Barrow, Executive Director.

**Founded:** 1977.

**Membership:** 3000 or more.

**Staff:** 5 volunteer.

**Description:** Non-profit search and support group.

**Description of services:** Provides access to the Indiana Reunion and Search Registry, individual search assistance, counseling and support; sponsors seminars and workshops; and advocates for change in adoption laws in Indiana.

**Dues:** $35 application fee.

**Publications:** Newsletter.

**Meetings:** 3rd Wednesday of the month from September to June.

## ★ 1398 ★
**Association for the Rights of Children**
**ARC**
P.O. Box 509
Notre Dame, IN 46556
Phone: (219) 234-7992

**Contact:** Mary Filbert, Vice President.

**Founded:** 1972.

**Membership:** 40 families.

**Budget:** Approx. $500 annually.

**Staff:** All volunteer.

**Description:** Non-profit support group of adoptive and pre-adoptive families.

**Description of services:** Sponsors family activities and discussion groups; recruits adoptive families through "Sunday's Child" feature in the *South Bend Tribune*; and awards post-secondary scholarships to adopted children through the Peg Donovan Scholarship Fund.

**Dues:** $12/yr.

**Publications:** Newsletter published quarterly.

**Meetings:** Monthly.

## ★ 1399 ★
**Illiana Adoptive Parents**
c/o Ann Grant
8240 Beech Ave.
Munster, IN 46321
Phone: (219) 972-0729

**Contact:** Ann Grant, President.

**Date established:** 1985.

**Membership:** 40 families.

**Budget:** Based on dues.

**Staff:** 9 volunteer board members.

**Description:** Non-profit adoptive family support group and affiliate of

**Adoptive Families of America** .

**Description of services:** Provides information and support; offers parenting and child esteem education; maintains a lending library; and hosts social events.

**Dues:** $18/yr.

**Publications:** Newsletter published quarterly.

**Meetings:** Bi-monthly board meeting.

## ★ 1400 ★
**Indiana RESOLVE, Inc.**
6103 Ashway Court
Indianapolis, IN 46224
Phone: (317) 329-9519

**Founded:** 1979.

**Membership:** 450.

**Staff:** 7 volunteer member board.

**Description:** State chapter of national, non-profit, charitable organization for individuals with impaired fertility and professionals involved with their care.

**Description of services:** Provides information, telephone counseling and referrals; offers peer support and education; maintains a lending library and bookstore; and advocates for medically infertile persons.

**Dues:** $35/yr. basic membership.

**Publications:** *Indiana Adoption Resource Guide* and newsletter published 4 times yearly.

**Meetings:** Monthly.

# IOWA

**★ 1401 ★**
**Concerned United Birthparents (CUB)**
2000 Walker St.
Des Moines, IA 50317
Phone: (515) 263-9558
(800) 822-2777

**Contact:** Kristi Carman, Office Manager.

**Founded:** 1976.

**Membership:** 2500 in 35 member groups.

**Budget:** Approx. $25,000 annually.

**Staff:** All volunteer, one part-time staff.

**Description:** Non-profit association of birthparents and others who support adoption reform.

**Description of services:** Provides support to members who are coping with problems of adoption separation, access to Reunion Registry; maintains a speakers' bureau and telephone support network; advocates for legislative change to open birth records for adoptees and their birthparents; makes referrals to search groups; and sponsors a bookstore.

**Dues:** $50/1st yr.; $35 renewal.

**Publications:** *Communicator* published monthly; research results, booklets, books and papers.

**Meetings:** Monthly and an annual conference.

**★ 1402 ★**
**Iowa Foster and Adoptive Parents Association**
c/o Larry Kruckenberg
218 E. Howard St.
Colfax, IA 50054
Phone: (515) 674-3600

**Founded:** 1970.

**Membership:** 400-500.

**Staff:** 4 member Executive Board.

**Description:** Non-profit, foster and adoptive parent and child welfare organization.

**Description of services:** Advocates for the needs of children, uniformity of adoption procedures, permanency planning for all children and for health, education and welfare of children in foster care; provides parent support.

**Dues:** $15 state and $25 national.

**Publications:** *Iowa News and Views* published quarterly.

**Meetings:** Last Sunday of January, April, July and October.

# KENTUCKY

**★ 1403 ★**
**Concerned United Birthparents**
P.O. Box 22795
Louisville, KY 40252-0795
Phone: (502) 423-1438
(502) 942-9579

**Contact:** Secretary.

**Date established:** 1984.

**Membership:** 10.

**Budget:** Based on dues.

**Staff:** All volunteer.

**Description:** Non-profit branch of national support group for adoptees, birth and adoptive parents and significant others.

**Description of services:** Provides support, referral and search assistance.

**Dues:** $50/1st yr. and $35/yr. renewal.

**Publications:** *The CUB Communicator* published monthly.

**Meetings:** 3rd Thursday of each month at 7 P.M. at the Highland Presbyterian Church, Louisville.

**★ 1404 ★**
**Families And Adoptive Children Together**
150 Ridgemont Rd.
Paducah, KY 42003
Phone: (502) 554-0203

**Contact:** Patty Klutts.

**Date established:** May 17, 1985.

**Membership:** 75.

**Budget:** Based on donations and fund raising.

**Staff:** 10 volunteer staff members.

**Description:** Non-profit adoptive family support group.

**Description of services:** Provides information and support for those who have already adopted as well as families considering adoption; maintains a lending library; hosts fundraisers and social activities, including an annual picnic.

**Dues:** $18/yr.

**Publications:** Newsletter published bi-monthly.

**Meetings:** 2nd weekend of every other month. Call for time and location.

**★ 1405 ★**
**Kentuckiana Alliance for Multiracial Families**

Phone: (502) 456-5821

**Contact:** Hope Dittmeier.

**Date established:** 1993.

**Membership:** Approx. 60.

**Budget:** Less than $500/yr.

**Staff:** All volunteer.

**Description:** Non-profit support/educational group for multiracial families. 60% of the families are multiracial due to adoption.

**Description of services:** Provides support, activities and a resource network.

**Publications:** *Blendings* published quarterly.

**Meetings:** 2nd Sunday of each month from 3-6 P.M. Children's playgroup meets each Saturday at 10 A.M.

★ 1406 ★
**Kentuckiana Families for Adoption**
601 Creebvalley
Louisville, KY 40243
Phone: (502) 244-0433

**Contact:** Sharon Zdunek, Co-President.

**Date established:** Unavailable.

**Membership:** 60 Families.

**Budget:** Unavailable.

**Staff:** All volunteer.

**Description:** Non-profit adoptive family support group and affiliate of

**Adoptive Families of America** .

**Description of services:** Provides support and information; sponsors social and cultural activities for families who have adopted domestically and internationally.

**Dues:** $15/yr.

**Publications:** Newsletter published bi-monthly.

**Meetings:** Call for time and location.

★ 1407 ★
**Parents And Adopted Children of Kentucky**
c/o Carolyn Brown
139 Highland Dr.
Madisonville, KY 42431
Phone: (502) 825-2158

**Founded:** 1985.

**Membership:** 100 or more families.

**Budget:** $400 - $500 annually.

**Staff:** All volunteer.

**Description:** Non-profit, incorporated support group for adoptive families.

**Description of services:** Provides support, education and fundraising for foreign orphanages; advocates for children.

**Dues:** $10/yr.; newsletter only: $6/yr.

**Publications:** *P.A.C.K. Newsletter* published semiannually.

**Meetings:** March, June, September and November.

★ 1408 ★
**RESOLVE Adoptive Parent Support Group**
1401 Elkin Station Rd.
Winchester, KY 40391
Phone: (606) 745-4319

**Contact:** Peggy Moody, Ph.D., Adoption Support Group Coordinator.

**Date established:** 1993.

**Membership:** 40 couples.

**Budget:** $5000.

**Staff:** All volunteer.

**Description:** Non-profit support group and affiliate of

**Adoptive Families of America** for adoptive families and those considering adoption.

**Description of services:** Provides education and support; maintains a lending library of adoption related materials; and co-sponsors an annual conference on infertility and adoption.

**Dues:** RESOLVE membership: $35. Adoption group: None at present.

**Publications:**
**RESOLVE** of Kentucky Newsletter published quarterly.

**Meetings:** 1st Monday evening of each month.

★ 1409 ★
**Shades**
c/o Brick by Brick Church
1018 New Circle Rd., NE, Ste. 105
Lexington, KY 40505

**Contact:** Susan Fister.

**Date established:** Unavailable.

**Membership:** Unavailable.

**Budget:** $500.

**Staff:** All volunteer.

**Description:** Non-profit, multi-racial adoptive family support group.

**Description of services:** Provides support, education and hosts social events.

**Dues:** None.

**Publications:** *Brick by Brick Church* Newsletter.

**Meetings:** 2nd Saturday of each month at 5:30PM.

# LOUISIANA

★ 1410 ★
**Adopt Older Kids, Inc. (A-OK)**
527 Claude St.
Breaux Bridge, LA 70517
Phone: (318) 332-4794

**Contact:** Glen Breaux, President.

**Founded:** 1988.

**Membership:** 55.

**Budget:** $6,000 annually.

**Staff:** All volunteer, including 8 member Board of Directors.

**Description:** A non-profit organization dedicated to placing older children in adoptive homes and out of foster care.

**Description of services:** A-OK provides mutual member support, social activities and fundraisers to supply some of the needs of the Lafayette Regional Adoption Unit, a state agency, which finds adoptive homes for older children, and helps in the training of adoptive parents.

**Dues:** $5/yr.

**Meetings:** Quarterly on the 1st Thursday of February, May, August and November.

★ 1411 ★
**Adoption Triad Network, Inc,**
P.O. Box 3932
Lafayette, LA 70503
Phone: (318) 984-3682
(318) 984-3682
Fax: (318) 269-9545

**Contact:** Johnnie Kocurek, Search Coordinator.

**Founded:** 1978.

**Staff:** All volunteer.

**Description:** Non-profit search and support group for members of the adoption triangle, social workers and interested others.

**Description of services:** Provides support, education, and search assistance and actively advocates for open adoption.

**Dues:** $30 initial year; $15 each year thereafter.

**Meetings:** 2 p.m. on the 3rd Saturday of each month except December.

# MAINE

★ 1412 ★
**Adoption Search Consultants of Maine**
P.O. Box 2793
South Portland, ME 04106
Phone: (207) 799-4760

**Contact:** Edward A. Bicknell, Treasurer.

**Founded:** 1979.

**Membership:** Approx. 500.

**Budget:** Less than $25,000 annually.

**Staff:** All volunteer.

**Description:** Affiliate of the American Adoption Congress.

**Description of services:** Provides search and support assistance, referrals, peer counseling, conferences, workshops and media presentations. Sponsors public education of adoption related issues and offers a Reunion Registry.

**Dues:** $30/yr. registration fee.

**Publications:** *ASCME* Newsletter published quarterly.

**Meetings:** Monthly from September to May.

# MARYLAND

★ 1413 ★
**Adoptees in Search, Inc.**
P.O. Box 41016
Bethesda, MD 20824
Phone: (301) 656-8555
Fax: (301) 652-2106

**Contact:** Joanne W. Small, MSW, Director.

**Founded:** 1974.

**Membership:** Hundreds.

**Staff:** Professional staff.

**Description:** Professional, non-profit, search and support organization offering a total search program concerned with adoptee/birth relative searches, etc. All AIS search assistance and support is a direct service and is confidential, individualized, and personal.

**Description of services:** AIS provides professional adoptee/birth relative search assistance, maintains the Mid-Atlantic States Search Registry, disseminates information regarding adoption procedures, laws and public policy which affect adoptees and provides a speakers' bureau.

**Dues:** $70 tax-deductible membership donation and $50 tax-deductible renewal.

**Publications:** *AIS News Notes* (newsletter), *AIS Search Notes* (guide to search), and others.

★ 1414 ★
**Adoptive Family Network**
P.O. Box 7
Columbia, MD 21045-0007
Phone: (410) 379-0891

**Contact:** Jennifer Geipe, President.

**Date established:** 1994.

**Membership:** 185 families.

**Budget:** Unavailable.

**Staff:** 14 volunteer board members.

**Description:** Non-profit organization of adoptive families, interested citizens and adoption professionals dedicated to support, education and advocacy. The Adoptive Family Network is a member of Adoptive Families of America (AFA) and The North American Council on Adoptable Children (NACAC).

**Description of services:** Adoptive Family Network conducts pre-adoption courses throughout the year; is engaged in community outreach in the areas of adoption awareness and legislation affecting adoption; sponsors educational seminars, panel discussions and speakers on a variety of adoption-related topics; maintains and updates books on waiting children at the Howard County Library; hosts multicultural events as well as regular social events for children and adults; and sponsors playgroups for preschoolers and discussions groups for school-age children.

**Dues:** $12/yr.

**Publications:** *Network News* published quarterly.

**Meetings:** Quarterly educational meeting and quarterly social activities.

★ 1415 ★
**Children in Common**
P.O. Box 21016
Catonsville, MD 21228
Phone: (410) 788-6490

**Contact:** Janice Pearse, President.

**Date established:** 1992.

**Membership:** 150.

**Budget:** Unavailable.

**Staff:** All volunteer.

**Description:** Adoptive parent support group for families who have adopted from Eastern Europe.

**Description of services:** Provides support and information; sponsors overseas relief efforts and social events.

**Dues:** $25/yr.

**Publications:** *Children In Common* Newsletter published quarterly.

**Meetings:** 2 - 3 times annually.

★ 1416 ★
**Committee for Single Adoptive Parents**
P.O. Box 15084
Chevy Chase, MD 20825

**Founded:** 1973.

**Membership:** Approx. 500.

**Budget:** $10,700 annually.

**Staff:** 1 salaried, 1 volunteer.

**Description:** Non-profit, incorporated information service for single men and women interested in adoption.

**Description of services:** Provides sources of adoptable children who will accept single applicants and other information of interest to prospective single adoptive parents.

**Dues:** $18 for 2 years (for Source List); *Handbook* is $15.

**Publications:** *Handbook for Single Adoptive Parents*; *Source List* (of sources of adoptable children that will accept single applicants).

### ★ 1417 ★
**Latin American Parent Association**
**National Capital Region**
P.O. Box 4403
Silver Spring, MD 20904
Phone: (301) 431-3407

**Contact:** Sheila Mooney, President.

**Staff:** All volunteer.

**Description:** Non-profit support group for adoptive families whose children are Latin American.

**Description of services:** Provides workshops, social activities and a Helpline.

**Dues:** $25/yr.

**Publications:** *Buenas Noticias* published 4 times a year.

**Meetings:** Monthly.

### ★ 1418 ★
**Mutual Consent Voluntary Adoption Registry**
311 W. Saratoga St.
Baltimore, MD 21201
Phone: (410) 767-7372
(800) 492-1978
Fax: (410) 333-0392

**Contact:** Lillian B. Lansberry, Coordinator.

**Description:** State-wide reunion registry for adoptees over 21 years old, birthparents andbirthsiblings when adoption occurred in Maryland or was facilitated by a Maryland licensed agency. Toll free number is for Maryland only.

# MASSACHUSETTS

### ★ 1419 ★
**The Adoption Connection**
11 Peabody Sq., Rm. 6
Peabody, MA 01960
Phone: (508) 532-1261
Fax: (508) 532-0427

**Contact:** Susan C. Darke, Director.

**Founded:** 1976.

**Staff:** All volunteer.

**Description:** Non-profit, tax-exempt organization of adoptees, birth parents and adoptive parents.

**Description of services:** Provides support, referrals, counseling and adoptee search.

**Dues:** Registration: $50; search fee: $400.

**Publications:** *HAPPENINGS* published quarterly.

**Meetings:** Monthly.

### ★ 1420 ★
**Latin American Adoptive Families**
**LAAF**
40 Upland Rd.
Duxbury, MA 02332
Phone: (617) 934-6756
Fax: (617) 934-5096

**Founded:** 1986.

**Membership:** Approx. 500 families and 30 agencies.

**Staff:** All volunteer.

**Description:** Non-profit, adoptive family support group.

**Description of services:** Provides support, information exchange and sponsors cultural events.

**Dues:** $24/4 issues of publication.

**Publications:** *LAAF Quarterly* published 4 times a yr. and *Member Directory*.

**Meetings:** 4-6 times per yr.

### ★ 1421 ★
**Open Door Society of Massachusetts, Inc.**
P.O. Box 1158
Westboro, MA 01581-6158
Phone: (617) 527-5660
(800) 93-ADOPT

**Contact:** Joan Clark, Executive Director.

**Founded:** 1967.

**Membership:** Approx. 1700 families.

**Budget:** $15,000 annually.

**Staff:** 15 volunteer Board of Directors.

**Description:** Non-profit, statewide, incorporated organization of adoptive families, prospective adopters, foster parents, and adoption professionals.

**Description of services:** Provides adoption information, both foreign and domestic, publicizes available children, sponsors educational meetings and family social events, advocates for better child welfare laws, provides peer support for adoptive families, promotes agency-adoptive parent communication, organizes the annual New England Adoption Conference, the largest of its kind in the U.S., and has a lending library of over 200 audio/video tapes available to members free via the mail.

**Dues:** $15/yr. per family.

**Publications:** Newsletter published bi-monthly.

**Meetings:** Each chapter sets its own local meeting schedule.

# MICHIGAN

### ★ 1422 ★
**A.D.O.P.T. (All Doing Our Part Together)**
6939 Shield Ct.
Saginaw, MI 48603
Phone: (517) 781-2089

**Contact:** Maxine Bergen.

**Founded:** 1980.

**Staff:** All volunteer.

**Description:** Non-profit support group.

**Description of services:** A.D.O.P.T. provides adoption information and support, activities, programs and social events as well as spearheading efforts to supply orphanages.

**Dues:** $10/yr. membership; $7/yr. newsletter only.

**Publications:** Newsletter published every other month.
**Meetings:** Monthly.

★ 1423 ★
**Adoption Identity Movement of Grand Rapids**
P.O. Box 9265
Grand Rapids, MI 49509
Phone: (616) 531-1380

**Contact:** Peg Richer, Director.
**Founded:** 1977.
**Staff:** All volunteer.
**Description:** Non-profit, support group for individuals who have been separated by adoption.
**Description of services:** Provides support, post-reunion counseling and search assistance for adoptees, birthparents and siblings and others who have been separated from their birth families for a variety of reasons.
**Dues:** $30 donation fee.
**Publications:** None.
**Meetings:** 1st and 3rd Wednesday of each month.

★ 1424 ★
**F.I.A.A.-OURS of Greater Ann Arbor**
c/o Shirley Wolfe
1213 Olivia Ave.
Ann Arbor, MI 48104
Phone: (313) 668-6835

**Contact:** Shirley Wolfe.
**Founded:** 1975.
**Membership:** 35 families.
**Budget:** $240 annually.
**Staff:** Volunteer officers.
**Description:** Non-profit support group for adoptive families and those interested in adoption particularly of Asian children.
**Description of services:** Provides support, information and cultural activities for children.
**Dues:** $12.50/yr.
**Publications:** Newsletter published monthly.
**Meetings:** 2nd Wednesday of the month.

★ 1425 ★
**Families for Children, Inc.**
7166 Balfour
Allen Park, MI 48101
Phone: (313) 389-1846

**Contact:** Jeff Galloway, Coordinator.
**Founded:** 1974.
**Membership:** 325 families.
**Budget:** $4000- $5000.
**Staff:** All volunteer.
**Description:** Non-profit, tax-exempt, support group for families who have adopted in the Metro-Detroit area. Most of the member families have adopted internationally.
**Description of services:** Provides support, social events and cultural activities which highlight the countries of the adoptees.
**Dues:** $15/yr.
**Publications:** Newlsetter published monthly.
**Meetings:** 3rd Friday of the month from September to June.

★ 1426 ★
**Families of Latin Kids (FOLK)**
P.O. Box 15537
Ann Arbor, MI 48106
Phone: (313) 429-4312

**Contact:** Kathi Nelson, Education Director.
**Date established:** 1988.
**Membership:** 80 families.
**Budget:** Based on dues.
**Staff:** 8 volunteer Board members.
**Description:** Adoptive family support group and affiliate of **Adoptive Families of America** for parents who have adopted or are in the process of adopting children from Latin America.
**Description of services:** Provides support and a means of networking; maintains a lending library; and sponsors social events.
**Dues:** $20/yr.
**Publications:** Newsletter published quarterly.
**Meetings:** Monthly.

★ 1427 ★
**The Family Tree**
27821 Santa Barbara
Lathrup Village, MI 48076
Phone: (810) 557-3501

**Contact:** Janis Weaver, Executive Director.
**Date established:** 1989.
**Membership:** 120 families.
**Budget:** Based on dues.
**Staff:** All volunteer.
**Description:** Adoptive family support group and affiliate member of **Adoptive Families of America** .
**Description of services:** Provides education and support for adoptive families and those considering adoption; hosts social events and activities.
**Dues:** $25/yr. per family.
**Publications:** *The Family Tree News* published three time a year.
**Meetings:** Call for time and location.

★ 1428 ★
**National Coalition to End Racism in America's Child Care System**
22075 Koths
Taylor, MI 48180
Phone: (313)295-0257

**Contact:** Carol Coccia, President.
**Founded:** 1984.
**Membership:** 1000.
**Budget:** Less than $25,000.
**Staff:** All volunteer.
**Description:** Non-profit and incorporated confederation of support groups, child care agencies, state offices of the U.S. Dept. of Social Services, etc. dedicated to assuring all children requiring placement in foster care or adoption outside their birth homes are placed in the earliest available home most qualified to meet the child's needs and, in the case of foster care placement, not be moved after initial placement to match race or culture.

**Description of services:** Encourages the recruitment of foster and adoptive homes of all races and cultures; conducts workshops; and maintains speakers' bureau.

**Dues:** $20/yr. subscription; $35/yr. organization.

**Publications:** *The Children's Voice* Newsletter published quarterly.

**Meetings:** None.


★ 1429 ★
**Truths In Adoption Triad**
2462 Kansas
Saginaw, MI 48601
Phone: (517) 777-6666

**Founded:** 1984.

**Membership:** 100.

**Staff:** All volunteer.

**Description:** Non-profit search and support group for all members of the triad in southeastern Michigan who are interested in "humanizing" adoption. Affiliated with the American Adoption Congress, Concerned United Birthparents and International Soundex Reunion Registry. Phone number is for 7 pm - 9:30 pm weeknights.

**Description of services:** Provides support and search assistance. Educates the public about adoption.

**Dues:** $30 one-time donation.

**Meetings:** Bi-monthly.


# MINNESOTA

★ 1430 ★
**Adoptive Families of America**
333 Highway 100 North
Minneapolis, MN 55422-2752
Phone: (612) 535-4829
(800) 372-3300

**Date established:** 1967.

**Membership:** 15,000.

**Budget:** $500,000.

**Staff:** 8 full-time and 3 part-time.

**Description:** National headquarters of a private non-profit membership organization of more than 250 adoptive and prostective adoptive parent support groups nationwide.

**Description of services:** Media and legislative advocacy, aid to waiting children, education, information and support including a 24 hour Helpline. AFA makes available more than 450 different books and tapes on adoption.

**Dues:** $24 /yr.

**Publications:** Adoptive Families, published monthly.

**Meetings:** Annual nation-wide conference.


★ 1431 ★
**Central Minnesota Korean Cultural Society, Inc.**
101 Norway Dr.
Baxter, MN 56401
Phone: (218) 828-4076

**Branch address:**
   Camp Moon Hwa, 3804 Second St. NW, Rochester, MN 55901

**Contact:** Kathi Hefti, Director; Pat Gallenburg for Rochester, MN camp.

**Date established:** 1982.

**Membership:** 106.

**Budget:** $5000.

**Staff:** 18 salaried and more than 100 volunteers.

**Description:** Non-profit, incorporated camp for Korean adoptees and their families.

**Description of services:** Sponsors Kamp Kimchee, a Korean cultural camp, whose purposes are:
   1) to foster positive self-esteem;
   2) to enkindle an appreciation for Korean culture;
   3) to establish relationships between teachers and students as well as among the students themselves;
   4) to build positive feelings about each family's international heritage; and
   5) to involve each family enrolled.

**Dues:** Camp fee: $45.

**Publications:** None.

**Meetings:** Camps are held in mid-July.


★ 1432 ★
**Concerned United Birthparents (CUB)**
**Twin City-Metro Area**
c/o Sandra Sperrazza
6429 Mendelssohn Ln.
Edina, MN 55343-8424
Phone: (612) 938-5866
(612) 930-9058

**Contact:** Sandra L. Sperrazza, Branch Coordinator.

**Founded:** 1976.

**Staff:** All volunteer.

**Description:** Non-profit support group working for openness in adoption by changing legal barriers.

**Description of services:** CUB provides support, search assistance, speakers bureau and resource information to researchers, and aid to those experiencing an unplanned pregnancy.

**Dues:** $50/1st yr.; $35/yr.- renewal.

**Publications:** *Communicator* published monthly.

**Meetings:** 7 p.m. second Wednesday of each month at 5005 W. 36th St., St. Louis Park, MN.


★ 1433 ★
**Families of Multi-Racial Adoptions**
**FOMRA**
**c/o Gary Zandstra**
2057 Roe Crest Dr.
North Mankato, MN 56003
Phone: (507) 345-4279

**Founded:** 1988.

**Membership:** Approx. 100.

**Staff:** All volunteer.

**Description:** Non-profit adoptive family support group and member of OURS, Inc. interested in sharing information and resources.

**Description of services:** Provides support, information, referrals and educational activities; maintains lending library; and hosts social activities.

**Dues:** $10/yr.

**Meetings:** Quarterly in October, January, April and July.

★ 1434 ★
**Liberal Education For Adoptive Families of Minnesota**
23247 Lofton Court North
Scandia, MN 55073
Phone: (612) 433-5211

**Contact:** Patty O'Gorman, Secretary.

**Founded:** 1975.

**Description:** Non-profit service organization addressing post-adoption issues.

**Description of services:** Lobbies for access to original birth records for adult adoptees, search assistance and counseling.

★ 1435 ★
**North American Council on Adoptable Children (NACAC)**
970 Raymond Ave., Ste. 106
St. Paul, MN 55114-1149
Phone: (612) 644-3036
Fax: (612) 644-9848

**Founded:** 1972.

**Staff:** 7.

**Description:** Non-profit, broad-based coalition of volunteer adoptive parent support and citizen advocacy groups, involved individuals and agencies committed to meeting the needs of waiting children in the U.S. and Canada.

**Description of services:** *NACAC* provides support group development and encouragement, recruits minority adoptive families, hosts training opportunities for adoptive parents and child welfare professionals, sponsors and is involved in advocacy and the development of a post-legal adoption support model.

**Dues:** $30/yr. - individual and parent groups; $150/yr. - organizations.

**Publications:** *ADOPTALK* published quarterly.

**Meetings:** Annual conference in August.

★ 1436 ★
**RESOLVE of the Twin Cities**
1313 5th St., S.E.
Minneapolis, MN 55414
Phone: (612) 533-8147

**Contact:** Lisa McKay, Executive Director.

**Founded:** 1974.

**Membership:** 700.

**Staff:** Part-time salaried staff director and approx. 100 volunteers.

**Description:** Non-profit organization for those experiencing impaired fertility.

**Description of services:** Provides support, information and referrals.

**Dues:** Graduated $30, $40 and $50 per year.

**Publications:** Newsletter published bi-monthly.

**Meetings:** Call or write for schedule.

★ 1437 ★
**Resources for Adoptive Parents (RAP)**
4049 Brookside Ave. S.
Minneapolis, MN 55416
Phone: (612) 926- 6959

**Contact:** Karen Harrison-Hatchell, Program Specialist.
**Date established:** 1988.

**Budget:** $259,000.

**Staff:** 4 full-time, 7 part-time and volunteer numbers vary.

**Description:** Non-profit, independent, parent-led grass-roots organization.

**Description of services:** Provides education, advocacy, support, peer counseling and respite care. Maintains a lending library and hosts Mom's Retreats.

**Dues:** Membership fees range from $20 -$250. Support group fees are dependent upon the course. Monthly meeting donations are $5.

**Publications:** *Adoption Post* published quarterly.

**Meetings:** Second Tuesday of each month. Call for time and location.

★ 1438 ★
**Rochester Area Adoptive Families Together**
729 Ninth St. SW
Rochester, MN 55902
Phone: (507) 288-8559

**Contact:** Nancy Johnson, Vice President.

**Date established:** 1987.

**Membership:** Unavailable.

**Budget:** Unavailable.

**Staff:** All volunteer.

**Description:** Non-profit support group and member of

**Adoptive Families of America** for adoptive families and those who are considering adoption or who are awaiting placement.

**Description of services:** Provides support, adult education and family activities.

**Dues:** $25/yr.

**Publications:** Newsletter published monthly.

**Meetings:** 3rd Monday of each month.

# MISSISSIPPI

★ 1439 ★
**Mississippi Advocates for Minority Adoptions, Inc.**
P.O. Box 22971
Jackson, MS 39222-2971
Phone: (601) 355-6713

**Contact:** Mr. E.J. Ivory, President.

**Founded:** 1984.

**Budget:** $2000 annually.

**Staff:** All volunteer.

**Description:** Non-profit, incorporated support group for those interested in special needs adoption. Currently inactive.

**Description of services:** Provides support, makes referrals, advocates and lobbies for special needs adoption and does some adoptee search.

**Dues:** $5/yr.

**Publications:** *The Advocate* still in the planning stage.

**Meetings:** 1st Wednesday quarterly.

# MISSOURI

★ 1440 ★
**International Families**
P.O. Box 1352
St. Charles, MO 63302
Phone: (314) 441-2589
(314) 838-0481

**Contact:** Nancy Sublette, President.

**Founded:** 1978.

**Membership:** 250 families.

**Budget:** $1500 annually.

**Staff:** 10 volunteer officers and board members.

**Description:** Non-profit, incorporated, tax-exempt for families who have adopted children from other countries.

**Description of services:** Provides support, friendship and direction to those interested in foreign adoption; promotes cultural awareness and ethnic pride, educates the public and community concerning international adoption; maintains library and sponsors informational workshops and social events.

**Dues:** $15/yr.

**Publications:** *International Families* newsletter published monthly.

**Meetings:** 7 p.m. on the 1st Tuesday of each month at South Minster Presbyterian Church, 10126 E. Watson Rd., Crestwood, MO (babysitting provided).

★ 1441 ★
**International Families of Mid-America**
11609 E. 78th St.
Raytown, MO 64138
Phone: (816) 358-5431

**Contact:** DeAnn Matthews, President.

**Date established:** Unavailable.

**Membership:** 60.

**Budget:** Based on yearly dues.

**Staff:** 4 volunteer officers and 12 volunteer board members.

**Description:** Non-profit adoptive family support group and member of Adoptive Families of America.

**Description of services:** Provides peer counseling, referral and a resource network; hosts a Culture Camp and social activities.

**Dues:** $12/yr.

**Publications:** Newsletter published quarterly.

**Meetings:** Annual general membership meeting and bi-monthly board meetings.

★ 1442 ★
**Kansas City Adult Adoptees Organization**
P.O. Box 11828
Kansas City, MO 64138
Phone: (816) 229-4075
(816) 356-5213

**Founded:** 1979.

**Membership:** 1063.

**Staff:** 5 volunteer.

**Description:** Not-for-profit organization dedicated to member support and education.

**Description of services:** Provides support, education, counseling and referrals. Hosts seminars.

**Dues:** $35 lifetime; $15 annual renewal of newsletter.

**Publications:** *Adoptologist.*

**Meetings:** 10 a.m. on the third Saturday of every month.

# MONTANA

★ 1443 ★
**Montana Post Adoption Center, Inc.**
P.O. Box 634
Helena, MT 59624
Phone: (406) 449-3266

**Contact:** Allyn Ann Bernau Cummins, ACSW, Director.

**Founded:** 1988.

**Description:** Private, non-profit corporation dedicated to raising the awareness of adoption as a lifetime issue, providing support and encouragement to members of the adoption triad and to providing training to the social service, mental health, and education professionals who work with them.

**Description of services:** Provides a clearinghouse for statewide post-adoption services, education/training on adoption issues by and for mental health providers, in-state library, information resource and referral center; enhances placement agency post-adoption services; and advocates for adoption triad members and the professionals serving them.

# NEBRASKA

★ 1444 ★
**Kearney Area Adoption Association**
P.O. Box 132
Kearney, NE 68848
Phone: (308) 583-2402
(308) 234-4715

**Founded:** 1985.

**Membership:** 22.

**Budget:** $165 annually.

**Staff:** All volunteer.

**Description:** Non-profit association of adoptive parents, birth parents and adoptees.

**Description of services:** Provides support, referrals and hosts speakers.

**Dues:** $15/yr.

**Meetings:** 3rd Monday of September, November, and April. January family get-together.

★ 1445 ★
**Open Hearts Adoption Support Group**
4023 S. 81st St.
Lincoln, NE 68506
Phone: (402) 483-7634

**Contact:** Kay Lytle.

**Date established:** Unavailable.

**Membership:** 40 families.

**Budget:** Based on dues.

**Staff:** All volunteer.

**Description:** Adoptive family support group.

**Description of services:** Provides support and host social events.

**Dues:** $10/yr.

**Publications:** Newsletter published several times a year.

**Meetings:** Monthly.

# NEVADA

**★ 1446 ★**
**Adoption and Family Search Consultants**
P.O. Box 61078
Boulder City, NV 89006
Phone: (702) 29-FOUND
(702) 293-3973
Fax: (702) 293-0844

**Founded:** 1987.

**Description:** An adoption and family disruption search service.

**Description of services:** Provides search and counseling services and makes referrals to other search groups; speakers bureau for general adoption education and adoptee search.

# NEW HAMPSHIRE

**★ 1447 ★**
**Open Door Society of New Hampshire, Inc.**
P.O. Box 792
Derry, NH 03038
Phone: (603) 434-9542

**Date established:** 1980.

**Membership:** 130 families.

**Budget:** Varies with dues and fundraisers.

**Staff:** All volunteer.

**Description:** Non-profit, statewide adoption information and support group for those in all phases of the adoption process as well as for existing adoptive families.

**Description of services:** The Open Door Society provides an agency and attorney referral lists; maintains a lending library which includes adoption exchange photolisting books; and hosts family events as well as an annual conference.

**Dues:** $15/yr. per family.

**Publications:** Newsletter and calendar of events.

**Meetings:** Second Saturday of each month.

# NEW JERSEY

**★ 1448 ★**
**Camp Sejong**
79 South St.
Demarest, NJ 07627
Phone: (201) 784-1081

**Contact:** Lindy Morris-Gelber.

**Date established:** 1991.

**Membership:** 100 campers.

**Budget:** Unavailable.

**Staff:** 50 volunteers.

**Description:** Non-profit 501(c)(3) public foundation and member of Adoptive Families of America dedicated to providing cultural activities for Korean-American children.

**Description of services:** Provides cultural exchanges, citizenship classes, *Big Sib/Little Sib* programs and counseling.

**Fees:** $375/wk.

**Publications:** None.

**Meetings:** Monthly staff meetings.

**★ 1449 ★**
**Concerned Persons For Adoption**
P.O. Box 179
Whippany, NJ 07981
Phone: (908) 273-5694

**Contact:** Pat Bennett, President.

**Founded:** 1972.

**Membership:** 350.

**Budget:** Less than $25,000 annually.

**Staff:** All volunteer.

**Description:** Non-profit support group dedicated to the belief that every child deserves a family. Member of NACAC.

**Description of services:** Provides support, educational and social assistance to adoptive parents; recruits prospective adoptive families; monitors related legislative activities; holds workshops on international adoption and provides a calendar of social events; has charity committee; provides adoption awareness program in high schools.

**Dues:** $25/first time; $20 renewal.

**Publications:** *Adoption Today Newsletter* published monthly from September to June; descriptive brochures and agency fact sheets.

**Meetings:** Bi-monthly workshops; monthly general programs; and an annual conference.

**★ 1450 ★**
**Latin America Parents Association, Inc.**
**LAPA, Inc.**
P.O. Box 2013
Brick, NJ 08724
Phone: (908) 249-5600
Fax: (609) 795-1820

**Contact:** Lehea Potter Kuphal, Co-President.

**Founded:** 1975.

**Membership:** 100 or more.

**Staff:** All volunteer.

**Description:** Non-profit, support group for families who have adopted children or who are in the process of adopting children from Latin America.

**Description of services:** Provides support and guidance; provides information about members' experiences with specific sources, orphanages, and attorneys in Latin America; hosts social and cultural activities for adopted children; and provides financial support and supplies through International Relief Program.

**Dues:** $30/yr.

**Publications:** *Que Pasa* published quarterly.

**Meetings:** Bimonthly.

★ 1451 ★
**Rainbow Families**
c/o Karthleen Becker
670 Oakley Pl.
Oradell, NJ 07649
Phone: (201) 261-1148

**Founded:** 1982.

**Membership:** 60 families.

**Staff:** 5 volunteer board members.

**Description:** Adoptive family support group for those who have adopted internationally, primarily Korean children.

**Description of services:** Provides support, adoptive parenting information and family social events; fosters cultural pride for international adoptees.

**Dues:** $15/yr.

**Publications:** *Rainbow Families* newsletter published 6 times a year.

**Meetings:** Call or write for schedule of parent meetings and social events.


★ 1452 ★
**Roots & Wings Adoption Magazine**
P.O. Box 638
Chester, NJ 07930
Phone: (908) 637-8828

**Contact:** Cynthia Peck, Editor/Publisher.

**Date established:** 1979.

**Budget:** $50,000.

**Staff:** 1.

**Description:** *Roots & Wings* is quarterly adoption magazine which offers readers views from all parts of the adoption circle as well as professional articles, book reviews and research.

**Dues:** $19.95/yr.


# NEW MEXICO

★ 1453 ★
**Parents of Inter-Cultural Adoption, Inc.**
P.O. Box 91175
Albuquerque, NM 87199

**Contact:** Susan Hayward or Jeanine Henderson.

**Founded:** 1987.

**Membership:** 200 families.

**Staff:** All volunteer.

**Description:** Non-profit, incorporated adoptive family support group.

**Description of services:** Provides education, support, referrals, social and cultural activities, maintains a lending library and hosts a summer day camp.

**Publications:** *PICA News* published quarterly.

**Meetings:** Varies.


# NEW YORK

★ 1454 ★
**Adopted Children of Romania Network (ACORN)**
299 Oak St.
Patchogue, NY 11772
Phone: (516) 289-9274
(516) 654-5379

**Contact:** Karen Lo Grippo or Carol Jansson, Co-editors.

**Date established:** 1991.

**Membership:** 150.

**Budget:** Unavailable.

**Staff:** 2 volunteers.

**Description:** Adoptive parent support group for those who have adopted children from Romania.

**Description of services:** Provides support and opportunities to network; hosts annual picnic and holiday parties; sponsors fundraising activities for Romanian relief.

**Dues:** $10/yr. subscription.

**Publications:** *ACORN* Newsletter published quarterly.

**Meetings:** Semi-annual.


★ 1455 ★
**Adoptees' Liberty Movement Association**
**ALMA**
P.O. Box 727, Radio City Sta.
New York, NY 10101-0727
Phone: (212) 581-1568

**Contact:** Jeanie Jackson, Secretary.

**Founded:** 1971.

**Membership:** 50,000.

**Description:** Non-profit, incorporated organization which offers support and assistance to its members who are searching for birth families and works for legislative change to open birth records to adult adoptees.

**Description of services:** International Reunion Registry, 56 pg. step-by-step searchers' guide, search workshops, volunteer search assistants, library of search sources, and support sessions.

**Dues:** $60 initial registration; $40 renewal per year.

**Publications:** *Searchlight* published quarterly and *ALMA Official Searchers' Guide.*

**Meetings:** Monthly.


★ 1456 ★
**Adoption Advisory Council**
2448 Stuart St.
Brooklyn, NY 11229
Phone: (718) 332-4163
Fax: (718) 332-4163

**Contact:** Irene Ganelli, Director.

**Founded:** 1985.

**Staff:** 6.

**Description of services:** Provides information and support on adoption counselling, information on active sources, conditions and laws within countries, and travel advice. Write for information.

## ★ 1457 ★
**Adoption Crossroads**
401 E. 74th St., Ste. 12D
New York, NY 10021
Phone: (212) 988-0110
Fax: (212) 988-0291

**Contact:** Joe Soll, CSW, Director.

**Founded:** 1986.

**Membership:** 300 plus.

**Budget:** $20,000.

**Staff:** 6 volunteer.

**Description:** Not-for-profit search and support group for all members of the triad.

**Description of services:** Provides eduational outreach and registration with the International Soundex Reunion Registry; maintains a speakers bureau; makes referrals to therapists, attorneys, counselors and search services; provides peer counseling and support groups.

**Dues:** Sliding scale from $0-$100.

**Publications:** *Access* published quarterly.

**Meetings:** Meetings scheduled monthly on Saturday afternoons and every Wednesday and Friday evening.

## ★ 1458 ★
**Adoption Resource Network, Inc.**
P.O. Box 178
Pittsford, NY 14534
Phone: (716) 586-9586
(716) 924-5295

**Date established:** November, 1992.

**Membership:** 300 or more.

**Budget:** Unavailable.

**Staff:** 25 volunteer member Board of Directors.

**Description:** Non-for-profit, incorporated support group composed of adoptees, adoptive parents, birth parents, social workers, mental health professional and other interested individuals.

**Description of services:** Provides support, referrals, educational programs including workshops, conferences, presentations to schools and some social activities.

**Dues:** $5/yr. individual or family; $15/yr. parent group; $25/yr. agency or professional corp.

**Publications:** *Perspective on Adoption* published three times a year; Calendar of Events published bi-monthly.

**Meetings:** Monthly Board of Directors' meeting.

## ★ 1459 ★
**Adoptive Families Association of Tompkins County, NY**
P.O. Box 219
Ithaca, NY 14851-0219

**Contact:** Jennifer C. Grecae, Treasurer.

**Founded:** 1970.

**Membership:** Approx. 100 families.

**Staff:** 12 volunteer board members.

**Description:** Non-profit, incorporated organization dedicated to the support of adoptive families of all kinds.

**Description of services:** Provides educational programs for families and adoption professionals, information on different types of adoption to prospective adoptive parents, hosts social activites, runs parents support group, and makes referrals to therapists, attorneys and other families.

**Dues:** $15/yr.- individual; $35/yr. - agency.

**Publications:** *AFA Newsletter* published 5 times a year and "Finalizing Your Adoption in Tompkins County without an Attorney".

**Meetings:** Board meetings monthly.

## ★ 1460 ★
**Adoptive Families of Long Island**
831 Montauk Ave
Islip Terrace, NY 11752
Phone: (516) 277-7149

**Contact:** Deborah Vola, President.

**Date established:** 1989.

**Membership:** Unavailable.

**Budget:** None set. Government grants when available.

**Staff:** 2 volunteer.

**Description:** Non-profit, incorporated adoptive and foster family support group.

**Description of services:** Provides support, counseling and referrals. Advocates for waiting children.

**Dues:** None.

**Publications:** None.

**Meetings:** Meetings and workshops as needed.

## ★ 1461 ★
**Adoptive Families of Older Children**
149-32A Union Tpk.
Flushing, NY 11367
Phone: (718) 380-7234

**Contact:** Roberta Bentz-Letts, Co-Founder.

**Date established:** 1993.

**Membership:** 6 - 8 families.

**Budget:** In development.

**Staff:** All volunteer.

**Description:** Adoptive parent support group for families who have adopted children 7 yrs. or older.

**Description of services:** Provides support and referral for post-adoption challenges of adopting older children.

**Dues:** In development.

**Publications:** Newsletter in development.

**Meetings:** Monthly.

## ★ 1462 ★
**Adoptive Parents Committee of New York State**
**Long Island Chapter**
P.O. Box 71
Bellmore, NY 11710
Phone: (516) 872-5830

**Contact:** Carol and Mike Hogan.

**Founded:** 1955.

**Membership:** 900 or more families.

**Staff:** All volunteer.

**Description:** Non-profit volunteer organization providing information and support for pre- and post-adoption issues.

**Description of services:** Sponsors pre- and post-adopt workshops; adoption bookstore; resource information; and hosts family activities.

**Dues:** $45 first year member; $25/yr. renewal.

**Publications:** *ADOPTALK* published 10 times per year; Journal published annually.

**Meetings:** 3rd Saturday of each month from September through May.

★ 1463 ★

**The Association of Black Social Workers' Child Adoption, Counseling and Referral Service**
1969 Madison Ave.
New York, NY 10035
Phone: (212) 831-5181

**Contact:** Jancie Shindler, Associate Director.

**Date established:** 1975.

**Membership:** Non-membership.

**Budget:** Unavailable.

**Staff:** 7 salaried and 40 consultants.

**Description:** Non-profit, incorporated community-based program providing services to the child welfare community in the metro New York City area.

**Description of services:** Recruitment, home studies, training, support groups, post-adoption counseling, advocacy, independent living skills and workshops.

★ 1464 ★

**Birthparents Support Network**
c/o Gail Davenport, CSW, ACSW
P.O. Box 120
North White Plains, NY 10603
Phone: (914) 682-2250

**Founded:** 1983.

**Staff:** All volunteer.

**Description:** Search and support group for birthparents.

**Description of services:** Provides search assistance and support for triad members; maintains a speakers bureau. Individual counseling by licensed social worker/birthmother available on a sliding fee scale.

**Dues:** $10.

**Meetings:** In North White Plains on the third Saturday of each month except August.

★ 1465 ★

**Central New York Friends of Love the Children, Inc.**
4324 Carrigan Cir.
Syracuse, NY 13215-1332
Phone: (315) 468-4170

**Contact:** Louis Girolamo, Treasurer.

**Date established:** 1980.

**Membership:** 120.

**Budget:** $3000/yr.

**Staff:** 9 member volunteer board.

**Description:** Non-profit, incorporated tax-exempt charitable and social organization; affiliate of
**Adoptive Families of America** .

**Description of services:** Sponsors fundraising for orphanages in South Korea; hosts social events.

**Dues:** $15/yr. per family.

**Publications:** Newsletter published quarterly.

**Meetings:** Annual general membership meeting and bi-monthly board meetings.

★ 1466 ★

**Children Awaiting Parents, Inc.**
700 Exchange St.
Rochester, NY 14608
Phone: (716) 232-5110

**Contact:** Peggy Soule.

**Date established:** 1972.

**Membership:** Unavailable.

**Budget:** $300,000.

**Staff:** 5 salaried and 30 volunteers.

**Description:** Non-profit, incorporated organization dedicated to uniting waiting children with permanent families.

**Description of services:** Publishes national photolisitng of waiting children in looseleaf form with bi-weekly updates; advocates for children who await permanent adoptive homes; recruits adoptive parents; and operates adoption information and referral services.

**Dues:** None.

**Publications:** *The Cap Book.*

**Meetings:** Office hours: 8:30-4:30.

★ 1467 ★

**Council for Equal Rights in Adoption**
401 E. 74 St.
New York, NY 10021
Phone: (212) 988-0110
Fax: (212) 988-0110

**Contact:** Joe Soll, CSW, Director.

**Founded:** 1991.

**Membership:** 900 individual/300 organizations.

**Budget:** $25,000 annually.

**Staff:** 1 salaried, 26 volunteer.

**Description:** Not-for-profit corporation promoting openness and honesty in adoption.

**Description of services:** Sponsors regional and national educational conferences and makes referrals to member groups for search, support and counseling.

**Dues:** $20/yr. - individual; $50/yr. - organization.

**Publications:** *Access* published quarterly.

**Meetings:** Vary by region.

★ 1468 ★

**The Council of Adoptive Parents**
P.O. Box 964
Penfield, NY 14526
Phone: (716) 383-0947

**Contact:** Terry Savini, Director.

**Date established:** Early 1970's.

**Membership:** Unavailable.

**Budget:** Based on dues, donations and grants.

**Staff:** All volunteer.

**Description:** Non-profit, incorporated adoptive and pre-adoptive family support group.

**Description of services:** Provides information and a means of networking for adoptive families and those considering adoption.

**Dues:** $15 - $40.

**Publications:** *Montage* published monthly and complimentary brochure available upon request.

**Meetings:** Call for time and location.

## ★ 1469 ★
**Families Through Adoption**
301 Middle Rd.
Oneida, NY 13421
Phone: (315) 363-4634

**Contact:** Cheryl Anderson, Coordinator.

**Date established:** 1983.

**Membership:** 50 families.

**Budget:** $400/yr.

**Staff:** All volunteer.

**Description:** Non-profit adoptive family support group and member group of the Adoptive Families of America (AFA).

**Description of services:** Provides adoptive family support and information and host fellowship activities for parents and children.

**Dues:** $10/yr.

**Publications:** Newsletter published monthly.

**Meetings:** Monthly as well as holiday parties.

## ★ 1470 ★
**Finger Lakes Adoption Group (F.L.A.G.)**
15 Ridge St.
Seneca Falls, NY 13148
Phone: (315) 568-2171

**Contact:** M. Joan Blanchard, Co-Chair.

**Date established:** 1989.

**Membership:** 30 families.

**Budget:** $300/yr.

**Staff:** All volunteer.

**Description:** Adoptive family support group.

**Description of services:** Provides current adoption information and hosts social events.

**Dues:** $8/yr.

**Publications:** Newsletter published five time a year.

**Meetings:** Annual business meeting and 5 to 7 social events.

## ★ 1471 ★
**International Adoptive Families**
P.O. Box 13903
Albany, NY 12212

**Date established:** 1984.

**Membership:** 100 families.

**Budget:** $4000/yr.

**Staff:** 8 volunteer board members.

**Description:** Non-profit, incorporated adoptive family support group and affiliate of

**Adoptive Families of America** .

**Description of services:** Provides support, referrals, opportunities to network; sponsors Korean language school and co-sponsors Korean culture camp; maintains lending library; hosts social and cultural activities and play groups.

**Dues:** $20/yr.

**Publications:** Newsletter published quarterly and an annual report.

**Meetings:** Bi-monthly board meetings and annual picnic.

## ★ 1472 ★
**KinQuest Inc.**
P.O. Box 873
Bowling Green Station
New York, NY 10274-0873
Phone: (516) 541-7383
(718) 356-3674
Fax: (718) 356-3674

**Contact:** Carol Komissaroff, Treasurer.

**Founded:** 1988.

**Membership:** Membership organization.

**Staff:** All volunteer.

**Description:** Incorporated adoption reform association of adoptees, adoptive parents and birthparents.

**Description of services:** Provides guidance and support for adoptive families, birthparents who have or who are considering surrendering a child for adoption and adoptees; maintains lending library; assists in adoptee search and makes referral to search groups; provides referrals to adoption agencies and other sources of adoptable children; and explores other issues in adoption.

**Dues:** Fees for service.

**Publications:** *Quest.*

**Meetings:** Call or write for discussion group schedule.

## ★ 1473 ★
**Latin American Families**
104 Cooper Rd.
Rochester, NY 14617
Phone: (716) 342-4247

**Contact:** Laura Garrison.

**Date established:** 1990.

**Membership:** 75 families.

**Budget:** Less than $100/yr.

**Staff:** 2 volunteer organizers.

**Description:** Support group for families who have adopted from Latin America.

**Description of services:** Provides information, support and hosts social events.

**Dues:** None.

**Publications:** *LAF Lines* published quarterly.

**Meetings:** Call for schedule.

## ★ 1474 ★
**Latin American Parents Association (LAPA)**
P.O. Box 339
Brooklyn, NY 11234-0339
Phone: (718) 236-8689

**Founded:** 1975.

**Membership:** 3000 in 7 regional groups.

**Description:** National, not-for-profit volunteer group of parents who have adopted children from Latin America.

**Description of services:** LAPA provides adoption information and support throughout the adoption process; keeps current records on procedures, expenses and new sources throughout Latin America; sponsors educational, cultural and social programs for the adoptive family; and sends clothing and medical supplies to Latin American orphanages.

**Dues:** $30 initial membership includes $25 packet of adoption information; $30/yr. renewal.

**Publications:** *Que Tal* Newsletter published periodically.

**Meetings:** Call for times and locations.

★ 1475 ★
**New York Council on Adoptable Children**
666 Broadway, Ste. 820
New York, NY 10012
Phone: (212) 475-0222
Fax: (212) 475-1972

**Contact:** Ernesto Loperena, Executive Director.

**Founded:** 1970.

**Budget:** $750,000 annually.

**Staff:** 10 salaried.

**Description:** Incorporated, non-profit organization whose purpose is to assure that every child has a permanent, loving and nurturing family.

**Description of services:** Provides information and referral for families interested in adoption, post-adoptive services; and recruits and prepares prospective adoptive families for children in foster care who are eligible for adoption.

**Dues:** $25/yr.

**Publications:** Newsletter published semi-annually.

**Meetings:** Monthly.

★ 1476 ★
**New York Singles Adopting Children**
**NYSAC**
2448 Stuart St.
Brooklyn, NY 11229
Phone: (718) 332-4163
Fax: (718) 332-4163

**Founded:** 1985.

**Membership:** 150.

**Staff:** 6 volunteers.

**Description:** Local adoptive parent support group.

**Description of services:** NYSAC provides information and support.

**Dues:** $15/yr.

**Publications:** *NYSAC* published monthly from September to June.

**Meetings:** Call or write for schedule.

★ 1477 ★
**New York State Citizens' Coalition for Children, Inc.**
614 W. State St.
Ithaca, NY 14850
Phone: (607) 272-0034
Fax: (607) 272-0035

**Contact:** Judith Ashton, Executive Director.

**Founded:** 1975.

**Membership:** 155 adoptive and foster parent organizations and concerned individuals and agencies throughout New York State.

**Description:** The purpose of the Coalition is to advocate for the right of every child to permanence and continuity of parental care.

**Description of services:** The activities of the Coalition include adoption and foster care reform, administrative and legislative advocacy, community education, parent group development, family support services, and the recruitment of families for waiting children.

★ 1478 ★
**Richmond Adoptive Parents Group**
P.O. Box 020665
Staten Island, NY 10302
Phone: (718) 876-0348

**Contact:** Joan Immitti, President.

**Date established:** 1987.

**Membership:** 400.

**Budget:** Unavailable.

**Staff:** All volunteer.

**Description:** Non-profit support group for adoptive and pre-adoptive families.

**Description of services:** Provides information and support for adoptive families and those considering adoption; host guest speakers and social activities.

**Dues:** $20/yr. per family.

**Publications:** Newsletter.

**Meetings:** Bi-monthly, holiday celebrations and annual dinner.

# NORTH CAROLINA

★ 1479 ★
**Adoption Search Consultants**
P.O. Box 1917
Matthews, NC 28106
Phone: (704) 537- 5919

**Contact:** Chris Lee.

**Date established:** Unavailable.

**Membership:** Unavailable.

**Budget:** Unavailable.

**Staff:** Salaried employees.

**Description:** For profit search and counseling service.

**Description of services:** Provides support and search assistance.

**Dues:** Fees charged.

**Publications:** None.

**Meetings:** 2nd Wednesday of each month.

★ 1480 ★
**Capital Area Families for Adoption (CAFA)**
c/o Pauline McNeill
4616 Thendare Way
Raleigh, NC 27612
Phone: (919) 571-8330

**Contact:** Pauline McNeill, President.

**Date established:** 1988.

**Membership:** 45 families and agencies.

**Budget:** $800/yr.

**Staff:** All volunteer.

**Description:** Non-profit adoptive family support group.

**Description of services:** Provides support, education and matching services; hosts guest speakers, children's activities and social events.

**Dues:** $20/yr.

**Publications:** *Adoption Primer* 1992, updated 1994.

**Meetings:** 3rd Sunday of each month from 3-5 P.M.

★ 1481 ★
**Carolina Adoption Triangle Support (CATS)**
404 Bank St.
Graham, NC 27253
Phone: (910) 226-4591

**Contact:** Bob Foote.
**Date established:** 1984.
**Membership:** Unavailable.
**Budget:** Varies.
**Staff:** 8 volunteers.
**Description:** Non-profit support group for adoptees, birth and adoptive parents.
**Description of services:** Provides support and some search assistance.
**Dues:** Unavailable.
**Publications:** Newsletter published monthly.
**Meetings:** 3rd Monday of each month.

★ 1482 ★
**North Carolina Adoption Connections**
P.O. Box 4153
Chapel Hill, NC 27515-4153
Phone: (919) 967-5010

**Date established:** 1991.
**Membership:** Unavailable.
**Budget:** Unavailable.
**Staff:** All volunteer.
**Description:** Non-profit adoptee support group.
**Description of services:** Provides support, education and search assistance.
**Dues:** $20/yr.
**Publications:** Newsletter published quarterly.

★ 1483 ★
**Southern Piedmont Adoptive Families of America**
P.O. Box 221946
Charlotte, NC 28222-1946
Phone: (704) 541-3614

**Contact:** Karen Kidwell.
**Date established:** Early 1980's.
**Membership:** 300.
**Budget:** Less than $5000 annually.
**Staff:** 13 volunteer member Board of Directors.
**Description:** Non-profit adoptive family support group and member of Adoptive Families of America.
**Description of services:** Provides support, referrals and information.
**Dues:** $35/yr.
**Publications:** *SPAFA Newsletter* published monthly.
**Meetings:** 3rd Tuesday of each month.

★ 1484 ★
**SPICE**
604 Rollingwood Dr.
Greensboro, NC 27410
Phone: (910) 854-9559

**Contact:** Lynn Beard.
**Date established:** 1984.

**Membership:** Approx. 50 families.
**Budget:** Based on returns from camp program.
**Staff:** All volunteer.
**Description:** Adoptive family support group dedicated to preserving children's Indian heritage.
**Description of services:** Provides adoptive family support and cultural enrichment activities including a yearly heritage camp for families; sponsors fundraising for organizations working with Indian adoptions.
**Dues:** $75 camp registration per family.
**Publications:** *Our Spice of Life* published semi-annually before and after annual camp.
**Meetings:** Annual camp and organizational committees.

★ 1485 ★
**Tri-Adopt**
Box 51331
Shannon Plaza
Durham, NC 27707
Phone: (919) 286-2891

**Contact:** Annie Nashold.
**Date established:** Early 1980's.
**Membership:** Unavailable.
**Budget:** Based on dues.
**Staff:** 4 volunteer officers.
**Description:** Adoptive parent support group and affiliate meber of
**Adoptive Families of America** .
**Description of services:** Provides support and referrals.
**Dues:** $15/yr.
**Publications:** Newsletter published bimonthly.
**Meetings:** Bimonthly.

# OHIO

★ 1486 ★
**Adoptive Families of Greater Cincinnati**
c/o Peggy Schramm
267 Hillcrest Dr.
Cincinnati, OH 45215
Phone: (513) 821-6342

**Founded:** 1981.
**Membership:** 100 families.
**Staff:** 8 volunteer board members.
**Description:** Non-profit adoptive parent support group of families formed by foreign or transracial adoption.
**Description of services:** Provides information on parenting the adopted child, referrals, and social events for adoptive families.
**Dues:** $15/yr.
**Publications:** *AF of GC* Newsletter published bimonthly.
**Meetings:** 8 adult meetings ard 2 family gatherings per year.

★ 1487 ★
**Adoptive Families Support Association, Inc.**
P.O. Box 91247
Cleveland, OH 44101-3247
Phone: (216) 491-4638

**Date established:** 1972.

**Membership:** 135 families.

**Budget:** Based in dues.

**Staff:** All volunteer.

**Description:** Non-profit, incorporated adoptive family support group and affiliate of

**Adoptive Families of America** .

**Description of services:** Sponsors pre-parenting classes, culture camp for internationally adopted children and fundraisers for children awaiting adoption and children's services; hosts guest speakers and special seminars; provides support and information.

**Dues:** Initial dues: $30/family; annual renewal: $25/family.

**Publications:** *Outreach* published monthly.

**Meetings:** 1st Saturday of each month except July and August. Children's class runs concurrently.

## ★ 1488 ★
**Concern for Children**
c/o Pat Burns
746 Grove Ave.
Kent, OH 44240
Phone: (216) 678-0090

**Founded:** 1978.

**Membership:** 150 families.

**Staff:** All volunteer.

**Description:** Non-profit volunteer organization that assists agencies, child care centers, or individuals who are actively involved in caring for or placing children for adoption. Currently committed to working in Colombia, Honduras, and Brazil.

**Description of services:** Supports programs for non-adoptable children; helps provide medical, financial and material support to orphanages and hospitals in the designated countries; disseminates adoption information; sponsors education and preparation for adoptive applicants; and provides post-placement assistance and an educational and cultural exchange with adoptive families throughout Ohio.

**Dues:** $24/yr.

**Publications:** Newsletter published quarterly.

**Meetings:** 1st Friday of each month.

## ★ 1489 ★
**European Adoption Consultants**
9800 Boston Rd.
North Royalton, OH 44133
Phone: (216) 582-3900

**Branch address:**
Chicago, IL
Phone: (708) 475-2254

Atlanta, GA

Newark, NJ

Cleveland, OH

Ft. Lauderdale, FL

Los Angeles, CA

**Date established:** 1994.

**Membership:** Excess of 100.

**Budget:** Unavailable.

**Staff:** All volunteer.

**Description:** Adoptive parent support group.

**Description of services:** Provides support before, during and after adoption; information for dealing with immigration requirements and opportunities for socializing with other adoptive families.

**Dues:** $30/yr. Newsletter subscription.

**Publications:** *European Adoption News.*

**Meetings:** Call for times and locations.

## ★ 1490 ★
**New Roots - Adoptive Family Support Group**
P.O. Box 14953
Columbus, OH 43214
Phone: (614) 267-3638

**Contact:** Catherine Gines, President.

**Date established:** 1983.

**Membership:** 100 families.

**Budget:** $3500.

**Staff:** All volunteer.

**Description:** Non-profit adoptive family support group and member of

**Adoptive Families of America**.

**Description of services:** Provides support and information for families in all stages of the adoption process.

**Dues:** $25/yr.

**Publications:** *Off Shoots* published eight times a year.

**Meetings:** 2nd Wednesday of each month.

## ★ 1491 ★
**RESOLVE of Ohio, Inc. (Cleveland)**
P.O. Box 361334
Cleveland, OH 44136
Phone: (216) 291-3500

**Contact:** Dawn Gerz, Coordinator.

**Founded:** 1974.

**Membership:** 260.

**Budget:** $10,000.

**Staff:** All volunteer.

**Description:** Non-profit branch of a national organization for those experiencing infertility.

**Description of services:** Sponsors programs on medical and emotional issues and preadoption classes; provides adoption information, physician referrals and resource library; hosts monthly coffees.

**Dues:** $35/yr.

**Publications:** *RESOLVE of Ohio* Newsletter published 10 times yearly and *The Ohio Guide to Adoption.*

**Meetings:** Monthly support groups throughout the state on various topics. In addition, RESOLVE of Ohio sponsors educational seminars intermittently throughout the state.

## ★ 1492 ★
**RESOLVE of Ohio, Inc. (Dayton)**
P.O. Box 31219
Dayton, OH 45437
Phone: (513) 433-1973

**Contact:** Shannon Duvall, Coordinator.

**Founded:** 1973.

**Membership:** 440.

**Staff:** All volunteer.

**Description:** Non-profit, charitable organization for persons experiencing infertility problems.

**Description of services:** Provides counseling, support, education and information to couples experiencing infertility and seeks to educate associated professionals.

**Dues:** $30/yr.

**Publications:** Newsletter published monthly.

**Meetings:** 2nd Thursday of each month. Inquire for meetings scheduled in Cincinnati, Cleveland, Dayton and Portsmouth.

★ 1493 ★
**Reunite, Inc.**
P.O. Box 694
Reynoldsburg, OH 43068
Phone: (614) 861-2584
Fax: (614) 861-2584

**Contact:** Kathy Singer, Search Coordinator.

**Founded:** 1980.

**Membership:** 500.

**Staff:** All volunteer.

**Description:** Non-profit, incorporated and tax-exempt adoption triad advocacy search and support group affiliated with the National Adoption Congress.

**Description of services:** Lobbies for legislative adoption reform; assists in adult adoptee/birthparent search; maintains library; provides counseling and makes referrals to appropriate organizations and researchers.

**Dues:** $35/yr. donation.

**Meetings:** 4th Wednesday of the month from September through July; annual picnic in August.

★ 1494 ★
**Southeast Ohio Adoptive Family Support Group**
P.O. Box 75
Athens, OH 45701
Phone: (614) 592-3061

**Contact:** Bonnie Carroll, President.

**Membership:** Unavailable.

**Budget:** Based on dues.

**Staff:** All volunteer.

**Description:** Non-profit adoptive parent support group and affiliate of

**Adoptive Families of America** .

**Description of services:** Provides education, information; support and an informal networking system of respite care; hosts social events.

**Dues:** $10/yr.

**Publications:** None.

**Meetings:** 1st Thursday of each month from 6:30 P.M. to 8:30 P.M. at 145 Stonybrook Dr.

# OKLAHOMA

★ 1495 ★
**Adopt a Special Kid - Oklahoma Chapter**
**AASK-Oklahoma Chapter**
5150 N. Harrah Rd.
Harrah, OK 73045
Phone: (405) 454-2913

**Contact:** Rita Laws, Ph.D., Director.

**Founded:** 1988.

**Staff:** 3 volunteers.

**Description:** Non-profit organization whose purpose is to facilitate special needs adoption, adoption support, and positive special needs adoption legislative change.

**Description of services:** Provides support, information, referrals, peer counseling, matching of adoptive families with waiting children, and post-legal support for special needs adoptive families by mail, phone, and computer modem.

**Dues:** None.

★ 1496 ★
**Adoptive Families Support Association (AFSA) - An Adoptive Families Network**
2009 W. Dena Dr.
Edmond, OK 73003
Phone: (405) 359-0812

**Contact:** Judy K. Smith, Founder.

**Date established:** 1992.

**Membership:** 40.

**Budget:** $400/yr.

**Staff:** 3 volunteer.

**Description:** Non-profit adoptive family support group and affiliate of

**Adoptive Families of America** .

**Description of services:** Provides support for adoptive families and a mentoring program for prospective adoptive families.

**Dues:** $20/yr.

**Publications:** *AFSA* Newsletter published monthly.

**Meetings:** Monthly.

★ 1497 ★
**Adoptive Parents of Central Oklahoma (APCO)**
1237 Mountain Brook Dr.
Norman, OK 73072
Phone: (405) 364-8488

**Contact:** Lonna Yeary, President.

**Date established:** 1987.

**Membership:** 25 families.

**Budget:** Based on dues and small grants.

**Staff:** All volunteer.

**Description:** Adoptive family support group and affiliate of

**Adoptive Families of America** .

**Description of services:** Provides support, referrals and pre-adoptive education; fosters adoption and cultural awareness in the schools and community.

**Dues:** $15/yr.

**Publications:** Newsletter published quarterly.

**Meetings:** Monthly.

★ 1498 ★
**Oklahoma Council on Adoptable Children**
2609 N.W. 38th St.
Oklahoma City, OK 73112
Phone: (405) 942-0810

**Contact:** Dale Williams, President.

**Founded:** 1980.

**Membership:** 40.

**Staff:** 1.

**Description:** Non-profit, incorporated support group.

**Description of services:** Provides support for adoptive families.

**Publications:** Newsletter irregularly published.

**Meetings:** Call for schedule.

# OREGON

★ 1499 ★
**Family Ties**
c/o Helen Gallagher
4537 Souza St.
Eugene, OR 97402
Phone: (503) 461-0752

**Founded:** 1982.

**Description:** Non-profit search and support group for members of the adoption triad, children of divorce, and/or any person seeking blood relatives.

**Description of services:** Provides peer and professional counseling, emotional support and search assistance; access to national networking and International Soundex Reunion Registry; and community education.

**Dues:** $25 one-time membership fee.

**Meetings:** 7 p.m. on 3rd Wednesdays of each month.

★ 1500 ★
**Northwest Adoptive Families Association, Inc.**
P.O. Box 25355
Portland, OR 97225-0355
Phone: (503) 243-1356

**Contact:** Kathy Johnson, President.

**Founded:** 1979.

**Membership:** 300 families.

**Budget:** $8000 annually.

**Staff:** All volunteer.

**Description:** Non-profit, incorporated organization of adoptive families.

**Description of services:** NAFA offers pre-adoptive classes, hosts parent and family social activities, provides a lending library, organizes a biannual conference, biannual culture camp, and support groups.

**Dues:** $15/yr.

**Publications:** *Northwest Adoptive Families Assoc., Inc.* newsletter published bi-monthly and "Adoption in Oregon" information booklet.

**Meetings:** Board meets once a month and monthly family socials or educational events.

★ 1501 ★
**Oregon Adoptive Rights Association**
**OARA**
P.O. Box 882
Portland, OR 97207
Phone: (503) 235-3669

**Founded:** 1978.

**Membership:** Approx. 250.

**Staff:** 7 volunteer.

**Description:** Non-profit, incorporated support group for members of the triad and all others touched by the emotional affects of adoption.

**Description of services:** Provides birthdate registry, support, search assistance, workshops; hosts guest speakers; and promotes public education on the ramifications of adoption.

**Dues:** $40/1st. yr. and $25 renewal.

**Publications:** Newsletter published quarterly.

**Meetings:** 3rd Wednesday of each month.

★ 1502 ★
**Southern Oregon Adoptive Families**
P.O. Box 322
Medford, OR 97501
Phone: (503) 779-6008

**Date established:** 1984.

**Membership:** 20 families.

**Budget:** $380/yr.

**Staff:** 8 volunteers.

**Description:** Non-profit adoptive family support group and affiliate of
**Adoptive Families of America** .

**Description of services:** Provides support and referral; hosts social activities.

**Dues:** $18/yr.

**Publications:** Newsletter published monthly.

**Meetings:** Monthly.

★ 1503 ★
**Southern Oregon Adoptive Rights**
1605 S.W. K St.
Grants Pass, OR 97526
Phone: (503) 479-3143

**Founded:** 1980.

**Staff:** 4 volunteer.

**Description:** Non-profit support group promoting openness in adoption.

**Description of services:** Provides search assistance and support; post-reunion support; and distributes adoption-related information.

# PENNSYLVANIA

★ 1504 ★
**Council on Adoptable Children**
P.O. Box 81044
Pittsburgh, PA 15217
Phone: (412) 363-5693
Fax: (412) 363-8553

**Contact:** John Strait, President.

**Founded:** 1978.

**Membership:** Approx. 100 families.

**Budget:** $540 annually.

**Description:** Non-profit, incorporated parent support group for adoptive families in all stages of the adoption process.

**Description of services:** Provides support, education, referrals, peer counseling and social activities.

**Dues:** $10/yr.

**Publications:** *COAC Newsletter* published monthly.

**Meetings:** 7:30-9:30 p.m. of the 2nd Wednesday of each month at the Sixth Presbyterian Church, Corner of Forbes and Murray Aves., Squirrel Hill (Pittsburgh), PA.

★ 1505 ★
**Families Together**
731 Apollo Ln.
Rochester, PA 15074
Phone: (412) 774-7260

**Contact:** Susan Pedaline.

**Date established:** 1991.

**Membership:** 50 families.

**Budget:** Based on dues collected.

**Staff:** All volunteer.

**Description:** Non-profit support group for adoptive families.

**Description of services:** Provides support and social events for adoptive parents and their children.

**Dues:** $10/yr. per family.

**Publications:** *Families Together* published bi-monthly.

**Meetings:** Bi-monthly.

★ 1506 ★
**International Adoptive Families**
402 Pebble Creek Dr.
Cranberry Township, PA 16066-5652
Phone: (412) 772-5787

**Date established:** Unavailable.

**Membership:** 60 families.

**Budget:** Unavailable.

**Staff:** All volunteer.

**Description:** Non-profit support group and member of Adoptive Families of America for families who are international by adoption.

**Description of services:** Provides support, cultural activities and social events for adoptive parents and their children.

**Dues:** $15/yr.

**Publications:** *Newsletter* published bi-monthly.

**Meetings:** Bi-monthly.

★ 1507 ★
**Parents of Adopted African American Children (PAAAC)**
544 W. 31 St.
Erie, PA 16508
Phone: (814) 455-2149

**Contact:** Barbara Ann Lewis, Coordinator.

**Date established:** 1991.

**Membership:** Unavailable.

**Budget:** Unavailable.

**Staff:** All volunteer.

**Description:** Non-profit support group and member of **Adoptive Families of America** for families who are interracial because of adoption.

**Description of services:** Provides support and education for adoptive interracial families and those considering interracial adoption; sponsors social and cultural activities to enhance adoptees' understanding of their black heritage and history; supports a local network of families who can mentor others considering interracial adoption.

**Dues:** $10/yr. for a single parent, $20/yr. for a couple.

**Publications:** *PAAAC* published quarterly.

**Meetings:** Monthly during the school year either from 7-9 PM on the 3rd Friday for adult informational meetings or from 2-4 PM on the 3rd Sunday for family socials.

★ 1508 ★
**Pittsburgh Adoption Lifeline**
P.O. Box 52
Gibsonia, PA 15044-0052
Phone: (412) 443-3370

**Founded:** 1976.

**Membership:** Approx. 700.

**Budget:** Approx. $1200 annually.

**Staff:** 1.

**Description:** Non-profit, search and support groups for all members of the adoption triangle.

**Description of services:** Provides support, referral, counseling and search assistance. 500 searches have been completed to date.

**Dues:** $15/1st yr.; $10/yr. - renewal.

**Publications:** *Lifeline* published 3 times per year.

**Meetings:** 2nd Sunday of every month except May.

# RHODE ISLAND

★ 1509 ★
**G.I.F.T. of R.I., Inc.**
**Getting International/Transcultural Families Together**
c/o Susan Round
9 Shippee Schoolhouse Rd.
Foster, RI 02825
Phone: (401) 647-2021

**Contact:** Susan Round, Board of Directors.

**Founded:** 1986.

**Membership:** 75-100 families.

**Budget:** $1500 annually.

**Staff:** 4 volunteer officers and 7 volunteer board members.

**Description:** Non-profit support group for pre-adoptive and adoptive families in Rhode Island and southeastern Massachusetts, most of whom have adopted interracially or internationally.

**Description of services:** Provides support, information and referrals; sponsors an Information Booth in the community during National Adoption Week; and hosts social events for parents-only, families and adolescents-only.

**Dues:** $15/yr. per family.

**Publications:** G.I.F.T. Newsletter published 6 times yearly.

**Meetings:** 3 adult meetings in the fall, winter and spring.

# SOUTH CAROLINA

★ 1510 ★
**Adoptees & Birth Parents in Search**
P.O. Box 5551
Cayce-West Columbia, SC 29171
Phone: (803) 791-1133
(803) 246-1968

**Founded:** 1980.

**Membership:** Approx. 400.

**Staff:** All volunteer.

**Description:** Support group.

**Description of services:** Provides support, search assistance and referrals to other groups with similar aims. Speakers available.

**Dues:** $25/yr.

**Publications:** Newsletter published quarterly.

**Meetings:** Monthly at 4 locations.

★ 1511 ★
**Family Counseling Center of Greenville, Inc.**
County Square, Ste. 5500
301 University Ridge
Greenville, SC 29601-3674
Phone: (803) 467-3434

**Contact:** Kathleen R. Howard, MSW, LISW, Executive Director.

**Description:** Non-profit, social service agency no longer providing adoptive placement but which will assist adoptees, adoptive parents, and birthparents who were onceserved by Family Counseling Center of Greenville, Inc.

# SOUTH DAKOTA

★ 1512 ★
**Families through Adoption**
P.O. Box 851
Sioux Falls, SD 57101
Phone: (605) 371-1404

**Contact:** Twila Baedke, President.

**Founded:** 1981.

**Membership:** 40 families.

**Budget:** $200 annually.

**Staff:** 10 volunteer.

**Description:** Non-profit, incorporated support group.

**Description of services:** Provides support, referrals, and adoption education; sponsors community awareness of adoption and updates a list of 80 adoption agencies.

**Dues:** $6/yr. per family.

**Publications:** *Families through Adoption* Newsletter published bi-monthly.

**Meetings:** Every other month. Call or write for schedule.

★ 1513 ★
**South Dakota Adoption Council**
P.O. Box 105
Philip, SD 57567
Phone: (605) 859-2039
(800) 244-3678

**Contact:** Carol Heltzel, Consultant.

**Founded:** 1982.

**Staff:** All volunteer.

**Description:** Non-profit adoptive family and adoption professionals organization.

**Description of services:** Provides support and legislative advocacy for child welfare and exemplary adoption practices in South Dakota, resource referrals, and annual training conference.

**Dues:** $10/yr.

**Publications:** Newsletter published semi-annually.

**Meetings:** Quarterly.

# TENNESSEE

★ 1514 ★
**Mid-South Families Through Adoption**
c/o Libby Bilderbeck
7781 Foster Ridge Rd.
Germantown, TN 38138
Phone: (901) 758-2271

**Branch address:**
c/o Jean Bedwell, 7185 Lamesa, Bartlett, TN 38133
Phone: (901) 372-6621

**Founded:** 1985.

**Membership:** 50 families and 11 agencies.

**Staff:** 20 volunteer.

**Description:** Non-profit adoptive parent and prospective adoptive parent support group, information exchange and member of Adoptive Families of America.

**Description of services:** MSFTA provides support, referrals, social activities and information to families, couples and singles in all phases of the adoption process; offers workshops and sponsors public awareness of adoption in the Mid-South area.

**Dues:** $15/yr.

**Publications:** *Mid-South Families Through Adoption* newsletter published bi-monthly.

**Meetings:** Bi-monthly on the 2nd Thursday beginning in February.

★ 1515 ★
**OURS of Middle Tennessee**
c/o 2102 Kidd Rd.
Nolensville, TN 37135
Phone: (615) 776-5082

**Founded:** 1983.

**Membership:** 50 families.

**Budget:** Approx. $500 annually.

**Staff:** All volunteer.

**Description:** Non-profit, incorporated support group for families who have adopted internationally.

**Description of services:** Provides support, current foreign adoption information and social activities.

**Dues:** $15/yr. per family.
**Publications:** *OURS* Newsletter published bi-monthly.
**Meetings:** 1st Saturday of February, April, June, August, October and December.

# TEXAS

### ★ 1516 ★
**Adopting Children Together**
P.O. Box 120966
Arlington, TX 76012
Phone: (817) 461-5022

**Contact:** Debbie Sanders, Administrative Assistant.

**Date established:** 1989.

**Membership:** 250.

**Budget:** Unavailable.

**Staff:** 1 salaried and 30-40 volunteers.

**Description:** Non-profit, incorporated 501(c)3 charity and member of

**Adoptive Families of America** advocating adoption.

**Description of services:** Provides support and encouragement for adoptive families as well as those considering adoption; sponsors *How To* workshops and adoptive parent training; maintains a lending library.

**Dues:** $10/yr.

**Publications:** Newsletter published monthly.

**Meetings:** 3rd Friday of each month - Dallas; 3rd Saturday of each month - Ft. Worth.

### ★ 1517 ★
**Adoption Advocates**
800 N.W. Loop 410, Ste. 355
San Antonio, TX 78216
Phone: (210) 344-4838

**Contact:** Cynda Reznicek, Office Administrator.

**Date established:** 1991.

**Membership:** Unavailable.

**Budget:** Unavailable.

**Staff:** 11 salaried employees and several volunteers.

**Description:** Non-profit 501(c)3 charity which offers support to members of the adoption triad.

**Description of services:** Provides counseling, referrals, support and adoption planning to birth and adoptive parents.
**Dues:** None.

**Publications:** *Legacy* Newsletter published quarterly.
**Meetings:** Wednesday from 5-6:30 PM for birth parents; 1st Saturday of each month for adoptive families.

### ★ 1518 ★
**Little People of America, Inc.**
**Adoption Committee**
c/o Nancy Rockwood
6504 Meadow Lakes Ct.
Fort Worth, TX 76180
Phone: (817) 656-1360

**Founded:** 1961.

**Membership:** Approx. 3000.

**Staff:** All volunteer.

**Description:** Non-profit organization of persons of small stature and their families.

**Description of services:** Provides support for small statured people and their families and maintains contact with approx. 2000 agencies in the U.S. and abroad as a home-finding service for dwarf children.

**Dues:** $15/yr. per family.

**Publications:** *LPA Today* published 5 times a year.

**Meetings:** Local chapters have monthly meetings, semi-annual district meeting and annual national meeting.

### ★ 1519 ★
**Parents Aiding and Lending Support (PALS)**
c/o Donna Thompson
3709 Canterbury
Baytown, TX 77521
Phone: (713) 427-7293

**Contact:** Donna Thompson, Membership Chairperson.

**Date established:** Early 1980's.

**Membership:** 175 families.

**Budget:** Based on annual fundraiser.

**Staff:** 8 member volunteer Executive Board.

**Description:** Non-profit support group for adoptive and pre-adoptive families.

**Description of services:** Provides education and support; hosts adoption seminars and an annual banquet; sponsors fundraisers and social activities.

**Dues:** None.

**Publications:** *PALS* published 5 times a year.

**Meetings:** 1st Thursday of each month except July, August and December.

### ★ 1520 ★
**The Post Adoption Center of the Southwest**
8600 Wurzbach Rd., Ste. 1110
San Antonio, TX 78240-4334
Phone: (210) 614-0299
Fax: (210) 614-0511

**Contact:** Dorothy H. Barkley, Executive Director.

**Date established:** 1988.

**Membership:** Non-membership.

**Description:** Non-profit, private social service agency licensed by the Texas Department of Human Services offering counseling, support and therapeutic groups, education, psychiatric services, workshops and a large lending library focusing on adoption issues.

**Description of services:** 1) Training for adoption and other mental health professionals; 2) training and consultation in Open Adoption by a Certified Open Adoption Practitioner; 3) certified Mediator specializing in re-negotiating open adoptions; 4) preparational counseling for adoptee and birth parent reunions; 5) post-counseling following reunions; 6) referrals made to support groups and agencies in other areas; 7) a few local adoptive placements.

**Fees:** Accepted by Champus, Medicaid and many insurance companies. Also accepts Visa and Master Card.

★ 1521 ★
**Right To Know**
P.O. Box 1409
Grand Prairie, TX 75050
Fax: (214) 264-7581

**Contact:** Tommie Smith, Director.
**Founded:** 1980.
**Staff:** 1.
**Description of services:** Receives and stores information volunteered by adopted children, adoptive parents and birthparents. Matches information for contributors while protecting their privacy. Persons contribute as much information as they wish, and designate whether or not it would be appropriate for contact to be arranged.

★ 1522 ★
**Searchline of Texas, Inc.**
1516 Old Orchard
Irving, TX 75061
Phone: (214) 445-7005

**Contact:** Pat Palmer, Co-Founder.
**Founded:** 1979.
**Membership:** Approx. 1000.
**Staff:** All volunteer.
**Description:** Non-profit incorporated search and support group.
**Description of services:** Provides support, referrals and adoptee/birthparent search.
**Dues:** $50/yr. plus $150 expenses for search.
**Meetings:** 2nd Saturday of each month.

## UTAH

★ 1523 ★
**Black Adoption Focus Group**
c/o Marsha Hodges
1363 VanBuren Ave.
Salt Lake City, UT 84104
Phone: (801) 972-0906

**Date established:** 1988.
**Membership:** 12 families.
**Budget:** Less than $100./yr.
**Staff:** All volunteer.
**Description:** Non-proft adoptive family support group.
**Description of services:** Provides support, referrals and peer counseling. Fosters same race adoptions and offers collateral support for transracial families. Maintains a speakers bureau.
**Dues:** None.
**Publications:** Focus on Black Adoption.
**Meetings:** Monthly.

★ 1524 ★
**L.A.M.B.**
672 East 2025 South
Bountiful, UT 84010
Phone: (801) 298-8520

**Contact:** Charlotte Slater, Director.
**Date established:** 1990.
**Membership:** Unavailable.

**Budget:** Based on donations.
**Staff:** All volunteer.
**Description:** Search and support group for all members of the adoption triad.
**Description of services:** Provides support and search assistance for those separated by adoption.
**Dues:** None, but contributions are welcomed and some fees are assessed as required for search.
**Publications:** None.
**Meetings:** 2nd Tuesday of each month at 261 South 900 East, Salt Lake City, UT.

## VERMONT

★ 1525 ★
**Adoption Alliance of Vermont**
**Rutland Office**
17 Hopkins St.
Rutland, VT 05701
Phone: (802) 773-7078

**Contact:** Maureen Vincent.
**Date established:** 1980.
**Membership:** 40.
**Budget:** Varies.
**Staff:** All volunteer.
**Description:** Non-profit search and support group for birth families, adoptees and adoptive families.
**Description of services:** Provides search and support for those seeking family members separated by adoption.
**Dues:** $10/yr.
**Publications:** None.
**Meetings:** Second Tuesday of each month from 7 P.M. to 9:30 P.M.

★ 1526 ★
**Adoption Alliance of Vermont**
**Shelburne Office**
P.O. Box 641
Shelburne, VT 05482-0641
Phone: (802) 985-2464

**Contact:** Enoch Tompkins.
**Date established:** 1981.
**Membership:** Unavailable.
**Budget:** Unavailable.
**Staff:** Six volunteers.
**Description:** Non-profit, incorporated search and support group for birth families, adoptees and adoptive families.
**Description of services:** Provides counseling, support and search assistance; advocates for legislative change of adoption laws, including opening sealed adoption records; maintains a speakers bureau and makes adoption-related literature and other educational materials available.
**Dues:** $10/yr.
**Publications:** None.
**Meetings:** First Thursday of each month from 6:30 P.M. to 9:30 P.M. at the Shelburne Methodist Church.

### ★ 1527 ★
**The Chosen Children from Romania**
P.O. Box 401
Barre, VT 05641
Phone: (802) 479-2848

**Contact:** K. Mark Treen, President.

**Date established:** 1991.

**Membership:** 525 families throughout North America.

**Budget:** Varies.

**Staff:** All volunteer.

**Description:** Non-profit, incorporated charitable organization and member of

**Adoptive Families of America.** .

**Description of services:** Provides humanitarian aid and training to three orphanages in Romania.

**Dues:** $20/yr.

**Publications:** *Our Chosen Children* published quarterly.

**Meetings:** Call for time and location.

### ★ 1528 ★
**Friends in Adoption, Inc.**
44 South St.
P.O. Box 1228
Middletown Springs, VT 05757
Phone: (802) 235-2373
(800) 982-3678
Fax: (802) 235-2311

**Contact:** Dawn Smith-Pliner, Director.

**Founded:** 1986.

**Membership:** 800 or more.

**Staff:** 10 salaried and numerous volunteer.

**Description:** Non-profit, tax-exempt corporation dedicated to meeting the needs of couples/singles considering adoption and pregnant women/couples contemplating making an adoption decision for their child.

**Description of services:** Provides education and support for prospective adoptive and birth parents and nationwide networking services for all parties.

**Dues:** Varies depending upon need.

**Publications:** *Friends in Adoption* Newsletter published quarterly.

**Meetings:** Call for schedule.

# VIRGINIA

### ★ 1529 ★
**Blue Ridge Adoption Group**
1453 Wolf Creek Dr.
Vinton, VA 24179
Phone: (703) 890-5813

**Contact:** Janet Scheid, President.

**Date established:** 1993.

**Membership:** 35 families.

**Budget:** $600-$800.

**Staff:** All volunteer.

**Description:** Non-profit adoptive family support group and member of *Adoptive Families of America*.

**Description of services:** Provides support, information and networking for families considering both international and domestic adoptions as well as those who have already adopted; promotes public awareness; and hosts social activities for parents and children.

**Dues:** $15/yr. per family.

**Publications:** Newsletter published bi-monthly.

**Meetings:** Monthly.

### ★ 1530 ★
**Concerned Adoption Triad Support ("CATS")**
508 Meadowfield Rd.
Yorktown, VA 23692
Phone: (804) 898-1182

**Contact:** Dixie Wilson (804) 898-1182; Sandra Shaw (804) 898-5432.

**Date established:** 1993.

**Membership:** Non-membership.

**Budget:** Unavailable.

**Staff:** 2 volunteers.

**Description:** Non-profit consulting service.

**Description of services:** Provides search support and assistance.

**Dues:** N/A.

**Publications:** None.

**Meetings:** None.

### ★ 1531 ★
**Parents And Adoptees In Search**
2500 Lauderdale Dr.
Richmond, VA 23233
Phone: (804) 741-1719

**Contact:** Eugene Pembleton, President.

**Date established:** 1987.

**Membership:** 85.

**Budget:** N/A.

**Staff:** 5 volunteers.

**Description:** Non-profit search and support group for all members of the adoption triad.

**Description of services:** Provides support, information and search assistance.

**Dues:** $10/membership yr.

**Publications:** Monthly newsletter.

**Meetings:** 1st and 3rd Wednesday of every month.

# WASHINGTON

### ★ 1532 ★
**Adoption Resource Center**
**Children's Home Society of Washington**
3300 N.E. 65th St.
Seattle, WA 98115
Phone: (206) 527-6068
(800) 398-1ARC in WA
Fax: (206) 527-1667

**Mailing address:**
P.O. Box 15190, Seattle, WA 98115

**Contact:** Debra Foreman, Administrative Assistant.

**Date established:** 1986.

**Membership:** N/A.

**Budget:** $500,000/yr.

**Staff:** 9.5 staff positions and 50 volunteers.

**Description:** Non-profit outreach center of the Children's Home Society of Washington whose focus is to provide information, education, support and therapy to members of the adoption triad.

**Description of services:** Maintains *Adoption Resource Room* which offers lending library privileges of books and articles on adoption as well as a collection of information from adoption organizations across the nation and offers for purchase hard to find adoption titles; offers therapeutic services to teens, birth and adoptive parents as well as those considering adoption for themselves or their child; hosts ongoing support groups.

**Dues:** $5/per household per session of support group attended with sliding scale.

**Publications:** *Washington Post Adoption Project Newsletter* published quarterly. Quarterly program offerings; articles and position papers on a variety of topics.

**Meetings:** *Adoptive Parent's Support Group*, 1st Sundays, 2:30-4 P.M.; *The Kid's Group*, 1st Sundays, 2:30-4 P.M.; *Multi-Racial Family Group*, 2nd Sundays, 2-4 P.M.; *Support Group for Families of Children Adopted from Orphanages*, 4th Sunday adults only; *Waiting Parents Group*, 3rd Mondays, 7 P.M. Additional groups meet at the Children's Resource Center and are listed separately under the group's name.

## ★ 1533 ★
**Adoption Workshops**
19533 - 34th, N.E.
Seattle, WA 98153
Phone: (206) 364-8270

**Date established:** 1992.

**Budget:** N/A.

**Staff:** 3.

**Description:** A six session course for parents considering building families by adoption.

**Description of services:** An intensive adoptive parent preparation workshop which meets weekly and emphasizes the adoption process and long-term issues. Topics include: adoption readiness, home study process, entitlement and infertility issues, agency assisted adoptions, independent adoptions, international adoptions, birth parent panel, and assessment of prospective birth families. Enrollment is limited to 3-6 families.

**Publications:** Brochure available on request.

**Meetings:** Call for schedule.

## ★ 1534 ★
**Adoptive Families Network**
P.O. Box 112188
Tacoma, WA 98411
Phone: (206) 759-0284

**Contact:** Josie Silver, Co-President.

**Founded:** 1979.

**Membership:** 50 families.

**Budget:** Approx. $1000 annually.

**Staff:** All volunteer.

**Description:** Non-profit, adoptive parents' group for south King, Pierce and Kitsap County residents.

**Description of services:** Provides information amd support before, during and after adoption and hosts children's and family social activities.

**Dues:** $15/yr.

**Publications:** Newsletter published bi-monthly.

**Meetings:** Once each month.

## ★ 1535 ★
**Birth Parent Support Group**
**Children's Home Society of Washington**
3300 N.E. 65th St.
Seattle, WA 98115
Phone: (206) 524-6020

**Contact:** May Boyden or Sheila Jones.

**Date established:** 1987.

**Membership:** Unavailable.

**Budget:** Unavailable.

**Staff:** Salaried and volunteer.

**Description:** Non-profit support group for birth parents who have been separated from their child by adoption.

**Description of services:** Provides support, referrals, information and a confidential forum in which to share feelings and experiences; hosts guest speakers and topics for discussion.

**Dues:** $5/meeting.

**Publications:** None.

**Meetings:** 1st and 3rd Tuesday of each month from 7 PM to 9 PM at the Adoption Resource Center, Downstairs, No. 43.

## ★ 1536 ★
**Children's Home Society of Washington**
201 S. 34th St.
Tacoma, WA 98408
Phone: (206) 472-3355

**Contact:** Sharon Hayden.

**Date established:** Unavailable.

**Membership:** Varies with class selected.

**Budget:** Regional budget $700,000.

**Staff:** 20 salaried and 17 volunteers.

**Description:** On-going support groups for adoptive parents, adopted teens and latency age adoptees.

**Description of services:** Provides therapy services for all members of the adoption triad and pre-service training for adoptive families; maintains Adoption Library and offers classes of particular interest to adoptees, adoptive parents and those considering adoption.

**Dues:** None.

**Publications:** *Washington Child* published quarterly.

**Meetings:** Adoptive Parent Group - 2nd Tuesday of each month 6:00-7:30 P.M. Call for times of other groups.

## ★ 1537 ★
**Forever Families**
c/o Shannon Wainscott
3215-177th Ave. N.E.
Redmond, WA 98052
Phone: (206) 885-3477

**Membership:** 20 families.

**Budget:** Less than $300 annually.

**Staff:** All vounteer.

**Description:** Adoption support group serving King County by providing information on domestic, intercountry and private adoption.

**Description of services:** Provides pre and post-adoption support; sponsors informational meetings and social events for adoptive families.

**Dues:** $10/yr.

**Publications:** *Forever Families.*

**Meetings:** Monthly.

### ★ 1538 ★
**Friends In Adoption (F.I.A.)**
P.O. Box 659
Auburn, WA 98071-0659
Phone: (206) 343-3153

**Contact:** Debbie Allman, President.

**Date established:** 1989.

**Membership:** 95 or more.

**Budget:** Based on fundraising and donations.

**Staff:** 7 volunteer Board of Directors.

**Description:** Non-profit support and friendship group made up of families who have adopted and families who want to adopt.

**Description of services:** Provides support, education and referrals; hosts family outings, adult gatherings and Waiting Parents Teas.

**Dues:** $12/yr.

**Publications:** Newsletter published monthly.

**Meetings:** 1st Thursday of each month for educational meeting with guest speaker. 3rd Tuesday of each month for waiting families.

### ★ 1539 ★
**Gay and Lesbian Adoptive Family Support Group**
**Adoption Resource Center**
3300 N.E. 65th St.
Seattle, WA 98115
Phone: (206) 523-2330 x168

**Contact:** Penny Vedgroff, Co-coordinator.

**Date established:** 1990.

**Membership:** 180.

**Budget:** Part of the Adoption Resource Center of the Children's Home Society of Washington's budget.

**Staff:** 3 volunteer coordinators.

**Description:** Support group that is sensitive to the unique issues of gay and lesbian parents.

**Description of services:** Provides support, referrals, media assistance, information, education and a means of networking.

**Dues:** $5 per session.

**Publications:** Individual articles of interest.

**Meetings:** 2nd Wednesday of each month at 7 P.M. information meeting; 4th Thursday of each month at 6:30 P.M. for potluck and social.

### ★ 1540 ★
**Interracial Family Association**
4421 S. Ferdinand
Seattle, WA 98118
Phone: (206) 685-1692

**Date established:** 1965.

**Membership:** 20.

**Budget:** None.

**Staff:** All volunteer.

**Description:** Non-profit, incorporated adoptive parent support group.

**Description of services:** Provides support network for parents in interracial families whose adopted children are facing adolescent issues.

**Dues:** None.

**Publications:** Information pamphlet.

**Meetings:** 1st and 3rd Mondays of each month.

### ★ 1541 ★
**Kitsap Adoption Group**
11869 Olympic Terrace Ave. N.E.
Bainbridge Island, WA 98110
Phone: (206) 697-2997

**Date established:** Unavailable.

**Membership:** Unavailable.

**Budget:** Unavailable.

**Staff:** All volunteer.

**Description:** Non-profit, incorporated parent support group and member of Adoptive Families of America.

**Description of services:** Provides information and support to adoptive parents and hosts social and topic-oriented meetings.

**Dues:** $15/yr.

**Publications:** Newsletter published monthly.

**Meetings:** Call for schedule.

### ★ 1542 ★
**Korean Identity Development Society**
**(KIDS)**
8315 Lake City Way N.E., Ste. 120
Seattle, WA 98115
Phone: (206) 340-0937

**Founded:** 1983.

**Staff:** All volunteer.

**Description:** A non-profit, incorporated, tax-exempt, volunteer organization whose goal is to teach Korean-American children and their families about their Korean heritage and instill in them a positive sense of identity and pride.

**Description of services:** KIDS sponsors a Korean Culture Camp, educational workshops, language classes and holiday events; maintains resource lists and bibliographies of books relating to Korea.

**Dues:** Donations gladly accepted.

**Publications:** None named.

**Meetings:** Call or write for schedule.

### ★ 1543 ★
**North Central Washington Adoption Support Network**
P.O. Box 3731
Wenatchee, WA 98807-3731
Phone: (509) 662-2180

**Contact:** Janelle Gray, Secretary.

**Date established:** 1993.

**Membership:** Unavailable.

**Budget:** $500/yr.

**Staff:** All volunteer.

**Description:** Non-profit adoptive family support group and affiliate of

**Adoptive Families of America** .

**Description of services:** Provides support, information, resources and opportunities to network to all touched by adoption.

**Dues:** $10/yr. Membership: $27.

**Publications:** *Newsletter of the NCW Adoption Support Network* published quarterly.

**Meetings:** 1st Thursday of each month.

★ 1544 ★
**Post-Search and Reunion Support Group**
**Children's Home Society of Washington**
3300 N.E. 65th St.
Seattle, WA 98115
Phone: (206) 524-6020

**Contact:** May Boyden.

**Date established:** 1987.

**Membership:** Unavailable.

**Budget:** Unavailable.

**Staff:** Salaried and volunteer.

**Description:** Non-profit support group for all members of the adoption triad or anyone touched by adoption search and reunion in their personal lives.

**Description of services:** Provides support and opportunity to share experience in a confidential setting; hosts speakers and topics for discussion.

**Dues:** $5/meeting.

**Publications:** None.

**Meetings:** 2nd and 4th Tuesday of each month at the Adoption Resource Center, Downstairs, No. 43.

★ 1545 ★
**RESOLVE of Washington State**
P.O. Box 31231
Seattle, WA 98103-1231
Phone: (206) 524-7257

**Founded:** 1985.

**Membership:** 350.

**Budget:** Less than $25,000 annually.

**Staff:** 11 volunteer Board of Directors.

**Description:** Non-profit organization for people experiencing impaired fertility.

**Description of services:** Provides small group support, information meetings and discussion groups, medical referrals, speakers bureau and HelpLine.

**Dues:** 4 categories: $35, $45, $55; $80 - professional member.

**Publications:** Newsletter published quarterly.

**Meetings:** 2nd Monday of every month in Seattle; 4th Tuesday of every month in Tacoma; last Tuesday of every month in Spokane; and 3rd Monday of every month in Bellingham.

★ 1546 ★
**Washington Adoptees Rights Movement**
**WARM**
5950 Sixth Ave. S. Ste. 107
Seattle, WA 98108
Phone: (206) 767-9510
Fax: (206) 767-4803

**Founded:** 1976.

**Staff:** 4 part-time and 40 or more volunteers.

**Description:** Non-profit search and support group for adult adoptees, birthparents and adoptive parents.

**Description of services:** Maintains library; offers search assistance, support, the services of volunteer search advisors and confidential intermediaries to make initial contact with "lost" relatives and/or conduct the search using the court records under an Oath of Confidentiality for Washington State adoptions and births only. $500 fee for court search services; $250 for non-court services.

**Dues:** $25/yr.

**Publications:** *Journey* published quarterly.

**Meetings:** General support group meetings: Bremerton: 4th Monday, 7 p.m., Miggs Fire Station, Arsenal & Kitsap Way; Everett: 4th Sunday, 7 p.m., Everett Housing Authority, 1401 Poplar; Mount Vernon: 3rd Thursday, 7:30 p.m., Emmanuel Baptist Church, 1515 E. College Way, Rm. 24; Olympia: 3rd Tuesday, 7:00 p.m., Capital Medical Center, 3900 Capital Mall Dr. S.W., classroom; Seattle: 1st and 3rd Wednesdays, 7:30 p.m., Seattle International Trade Center, 2601 Elliott Ave.; Spokane: 2nd and 4th Thursdays, 7:00 p.m., Sacred Heart Hospital, Mary Bede Rm.; Tacoma: 2nd Thursday, 7:00 p.m., Tacoma Community College (call 566-5152 for room number); Vancouver: 1st week of each month (call office for exact date), 7:00 p.m., 703 Broadway, Rm. 725.
Birthparent support group: Everett: 2nd Wednesday, 7:00 p.m. (call WARM office for location); Seattle (Southend-Eastside): Last Monday, 7:00 p.m., Highlands Community Church, 3031 N.E. 10th Renton.
Adoptees post-reunion support group: Seattle: 2nd and 4th Wednesdays, 7:30 p.m., Seattle International Trade Center, 2601 Elliott Ave.

# WEST VIRGINIA

★ 1547 ★
**Appalachian Families for Adoption**
**AFFA**
P.O. Box 2775
Charleston, WV 25330
Phone: (304) 562-7180
(304) 744-6078

**Contact:** Richard Watson, President.

**Founded:** 1983.

**Membership:** 250-300.

**Staff:** All volunteer.

**Description:** Non-profit adoptive family support group.

**Description of services:** Provides support, educational and social events including an annual workshop; sponsors community education, fundraising for adoption related groups, a preschool play group and support group for school-age adoptees.

**Dues:** $15/yr.

**Publications:** *AFFA Notes* published bimonthly.

**Meetings:** Monthly planning meetings.

# WISCONSIN

### ★ 1548 ★
**Adoption Information & Direction, Inc.**
P.O. Box 1343
Milwaukee, WI 53201-1343

**Founded:** 1980.

**Budget:** Variable.

**Staff:** 3 volunteer Executive Board Members and 10 volunteer Board of Directors.

**Description:** Non-profit search and support groups for adult adoptees, age 18 and older, and birth and adoptive parents.

**Description of services:** Provides support, referral network of over 200 search groups throughout the world and search consultants in almost every state; makes speakers available for workshops, seminars and community groups and offers a forum for the exchange of ideas and educational guidelines and materials on adoption-related topics.

**Dues:** $25/yr. - individual; $30/yr. - family.

**Publications:** *Adoption Information & Direction, Inc.* newsletter published quarterly.

**Meetings:** Call or write for meeting schedule and location.

### ★ 1549 ★
**Adoptive Families Network**
1939 Zimmerman St.
Wausau, WI 54403
Phone: (715) 845-9447

**Contact:** Jeanne Lewis, President.

**Date established:** 1992.

**Membership:** 25 families.

**Budget:** $250/yr.

**Staff:** All volunteer.

**Description:** Grass-roots support group and member of *Adoptive Families of America* for adoptive families in North Central Wisconsin.

**Description of services:** Provides support and referrals; hosts information fairs and social events for parents and children.

**Dues:** $10/yr.

**Publications:** Newsletter published quarterly.

**Meetings:** Call for schedule.

### ★ 1550 ★
**Adoptive Parents Group**
1408 Vilas Ave.
Madison, WI 53711
Phone: (608) 251-0736

**Founded:** 1984.

**Membership:** Approx. 200.

**Budget:** $200 annually.

**Staff:** 8 member steering committee.

**Description:** Non-profit educational support group.

**Description of services:** Provides education, support and referrals; conducts regional workshops to train therapists and adoptive parents; sponsors social events.

**Dues:** Voluntary contribution.

**Publications:** Adoptive Parent Group Newsletter published semi-annually.

**Meetings:** Monthly.

### ★ 1551 ★
**Celebrate Adoption**
2727 Bristol Ct.
Waukesha, WI 53188
Phone: (414) 544-6448

**Contact:** Jody Graves.

**Date established:** Unavailable.

**Membership:** 160.

**Budget:** $200/yr.

**Staff:** 2 co-coordinators.

**Description:** Adoptive parent support group.

**Description of services:** Provides support and information.

**Dues:** $60/yr.

**Publications:** None.

**Meetings:** Call for schedule.

### ★ 1552 ★
**Namaste/Children from India**
c/o Nancy Reinbold
546 Black Earth Ct.
Wales, WI 53183
Phone: (414) 968-4564

**Contact:** Nancy Reinbold.

**Founded:** 1975.

**Membership:** 100 families.

**Staff:** All volunteer.

**Description:** Non-profit support group for Wisconsin adoptive families of Indian children.

**Description of services:** Provides support and cultural activities.

**Dues:** $10/yr.

**Publications:** *Namaste* published quarterly.

**Meetings:** 4-6 times yearly at different locations in Wisconsin.

### ★ 1553 ★
**Ours Through Adoption of Southeastern Wisconsin**
4232 Garden Dr.
Racine, WI 53403
Phone: (414) 554-9351

**Contact:** Judy Joosse, President and Secretary.

**Founded:** 1975.

**Membership:** 20 families.

**Budget:** About $100 annually.

**Staff:** 1 volunteer.

**Description:** Non-profit adoptive family support group.

**Description of services:** Provides support, information and a copy of the *Wisconsin Adoption Exchange Photolisting Book* to share with interested families; hosts cultural and social activities.

**Dues:** $5/yr.

**Publications:** *Ours Through Adoption of Southeastern Wisconsin* published monthly.

**Meetings:** Bi-monthly.

★ 1554 ★
**RESOLVE of Southern Wisconsin, Inc.**
P.O. Box 23406
Milwaukee, WI 53223
Phone: (414) 521-4590

**Contact:** Marilyn Shovers, President.

**Founded:** 1977.

**Membership:** 200 couples.

**Staff:** 30 volunteers.

**Description:** Non-profit chapter of national support group for individuals dealing with infertility.

**Description of services:** Provides education, support, peer counseling and referrals.

**Dues:** $30/yr. includes national and local membership.

**Publications:** *RESOLVE of Southern Wisconsin, Inc.* Newsletter published 5 times a year.

**Meetings:** 2nd Tuesday of each month from September through May.

★ 1555 ★
**S.E.A.R.C.H.**
617 Grove St.
Neenah, WI 54956
Phone: (414) 788-4609

**Contact:** Charlotte Bletzinger.

**Date established:** 1979 as Adoption And Direction Information.

**Membership:** Unavailable.

**Budget:** Unavailable.

**Staff:** All volunteer.

**Description:** Support group for post-adoption triad.

**Description of services:** Provides support and search assistance.

**Dues:** None.

**Publications:** None.

**Meetings:** 1st Tuesday of each month at 7 P.M. at the United Methodist Church, Appleton, WI.

★ 1556 ★
**St. Croix Valley Korean American Cultural Society, Inc.**
671 Bradhurst Dr.
Hudson, WI 54016
Phone: (715) 386-2069

**Contact:** Kerry Geurkink, Board President.

**Date established:** 1994.

**Membership:** Approx. 100 families.

**Budget:** $15,000.

**Staff:** 70 volunteers.

**Description:** Non-profit organization and member of *Adoptive Families of America* whose purpose is to organize a cultural camp for Korean-American youth between the ages of 5 and 18 yrs.

**Description of services:** *Camp Choson* provides young adoptees to explore issues surrounding adoption and racial identity in a camp setting.

**Dues:** None.

**Publications:** Newsletters and camp information published as needed.

**Meetings:** Board meetings, as needed.

★ 1557 ★
**Special Needs Adoption Network**
P.O. Box 10176
Milwaukee, WI 53210
Phone: (414) 475-1246

**Date established:** 1982.

**Membership:** Unavailable.

**Budget:** $200,000.

**Staff:** 5 full-time salaried and 10 volunteers.

**Description:** Non-profit support group with a 501.c3 designation.

**Description of services:** Provides training and pre and post-adoptive information for families involved in or considering the adoption of children with special needs. Registers families looking for waiting children and matches families with children.

**Dues:** None.

**Publications:** *Adopt* published monthly; *Adoption News* published quarterly.

**Meetings:** Call for schedule of activities.

★ 1558 ★
**They Adopt Special Kids (T.A.S.K.)**
825 E. Washington St., No. 9
West Bend, WI 53095
Phone: (414) 338-2603

**Contact:** Mary H. Cassoko.

**Date established:** 1992.

**Membership:** Unavailable.

**Budget:** Unavailable.

**Staff:** All volunteer.

**Description:** Grass roots support group of single parents who have adopted children with special needs.

**Description of services:** Provides support, fellowship and social activities.

**Dues:** None.

**Publications:** None.

**Meetings:** Call for schedule.

★ 1559 ★
**US/Chilean Adoptive Families (USCAF)**
2041 N. 107th St.
Wauwatosa, WI 53226
Phone: (414) 257-0248

**Contact:** Jean Hohn Morack, Membership Coordinator.

**Date established:** 1991.

**Membership:** 90.

**Budget:** Based on annual dues.

**Staff:** All volunteer.

**Description:** Non-profit organization whose members have adopted in Chile and/or have a strong interest in the Chilean people and culture. USCAF has an affiliation with the YMCA of Metropolitan Milwaukee which has a partnership relationship with the Chilean Federation of YMCAs.

**Description of services:** Provides information and support for families raising children adopted from Chile as well as opportunities to learn about and appreciate Chile's people and culture.

**Dues:** $20/yr.

**Publications:** *COPIHUE* published 3 times per year and Annual Membership Directory.

**Meetings:** Summer picnic and Chilean Independence Day celebration in September. Other YMCA Chilean events as scheduled.

### ★ 1560 ★
**Wisconsin Association of Single Adoptive Parents**
4520 N. Bartlett Ave.
Milwaukee, WI 53211-1509
Phone: (414) 962-9342

**Contact:** Laurie Glass, Coordinator.

**Date established:** 1986.

**Membership:** 30-40.

**Budget:** $400.

**Staff:** All volunteer.

**Description:** Adoptive parent support group for southern Wisconsin.

**Description of services:** Provides support, parent-to-parent reference and resource; hosts group activities.

**Dues:** Unavailable.

**Publications:** Newsletter published quarterly.

**Meetings:** Bi-monthly.

### ★ 1561 ★
**Wisconsin Single Adoptive Parents**
c/o Diane Karrow
127 Saint Lo Dr.
Prairie du Chien, WI 53821
Phone: (608) 326-6657

**Founded:** 1984.

**Staff:** All volunteer.

**Description:** Non-profit, single adoptive family support group.

**Description of services:** Provides information, support and social activities for parents and children.

**Dues:** $10 new member; renewed as required by account.

**Publications:** Newsletter published quarterly.

**Meetings:** Scheduled on various weekends.

## WYOMING

### ★ 1562 ★
**Northern Wyoming Adoptive Parents, Inc.**
603 W. "A" St.
Basin, WY 82410
Phone: (307) 568-2729

**Mailing address:**
  P.O. Box 788, Basin, WY 82410

**Contact:** June K. Tate, President.

**Date established:** 1989.

**Membership:** 30 families.

**Budget:** Based on dues.

**Staff:** 9 volunteers.

**Description:** Non-profit, incorporated adoptive parent support group and member of Adoptive Families of America.

**Description of services:** Provides support, information and social activities and maintains a lending library at the following locations: 620 Cary, Powell, WY (307) 754-5355 or 603 W. "A" St., Basin, WY (307) 568-2729.

**Dues:** $10/yr.

**Publications:** Newsletter published semi-annually.

**Meetings:** 1st Saturday of November and 2nd or 3rd Saturday of June.

## ALBERTA

### ★ 1563 ★
**Adoption Association of Olds and Area**
Box 1256
Didsbury, AB, Canada T0M 0W0
Phone: (403) 235-8540

**Date established:** 1992.

**Membership:** 5 families.

**Budget:** None.

**Staff:** All volunteer.

**Description:** Non-profit adoptive parent support group.

**Description of services:** Provides support.

**Dues:** None.

**Publications:** None.

**Meetings:** 3rd Tuesday of each month.

### ★ 1564 ★
**Adoption 2000 Consulting, Inc.**
409 7th St., NE
Medicine Hat, AB, Canada T1A 5P8
Phone: (403) 529-1406

**Contact:** Alice McNeil, Proprietor.

**Date established:** 1992.

**Membership:** Non-membership.

**Budget:** Unavailable.

**Staff:** 2 salaried and 20 volunteers.

**Description:** Incorporated proprietorship.

**Description of services:** Provides mediation, search and reunion, special needs parent support; public relations training.

**Dues:** Fee for services.

**Publications:** None.

**Meetings:** By appointment.

### ★ 1565 ★
**Battle River Adoption Group Society**
Box 270
Lougheed, AB, Canada
Phone: (403) 888-2124

**Contact:** Darlene Albrecht, President.

**Date established:** 1991.

**Membership:** Unavailable.

**Budget:** None.

**Staff:** All volunteer.

**Description:** Adoptive family support and charitable group.

**Description of services:** Maintains lending library of resource material; sponsors workshops; liaison with other support groups; advocates for adoption and adoption awareness.

**Dues:** None.

**Publications:** None.

**Meetings:** 3rd Thursday of each month.

★ 1566 ★
**Calgary Adoption Resource Foundation**
156 Brabourne Rd., SW
Calgary, AB, Canada T2W 2W3
Phone: (403) 276-9907

**Date established:** 1986.

**Membership:** 110.

**Budget:** $6000.

**Staff:** 2 volunteers and 1 contract from different budget.

**Description:** Non-profit adoptive family support group.

**Description of services:** Provides support and education for families involved in special needs adoption.

**Dues:** None.

**Publications:** *CARF News* published bimonthly.

**Meetings:** 4th Monday of each month.


★ 1567 ★
**Edmonton Adopting Beyond Infancy Association**
145 - 52150 Range Road 221
Sherwood Park, AB, Canada T8E 1C8
Phone: (403) 922-5483

**Contact:** Judy Thom, Chairperson/Coordinator. Support line: (403) 479-5268.

**Date established:** 1983.

**Membership:** Unavailable.

**Budget:** Unavailable.

**Staff:** Salaried coordinator and 8 volunteers.

**Description:** Non-profit adoptive parent support group for families with older and/or special needs adopted children.

**Description of services:** Sponsors workshops with guest speakers; *Buddy Connections* and an annual Mini Conference; maintains a Resources Library and a *Warm Line* for information and support; provides parent preparation in coordination with Alberta Family and Social Services.

**Dues:** $15/yr. per family.

**Publications:** Quarterly newsletter and *Project CARE* newsletter.

**Meetings:** 8 P.M. on the 3rd Tuesday of each month at St. Andrews Centre, 12728 - 111 Ave., Edmonton.


★ 1568 ★
**Lethbridge & Area Adoptive Parents Support Group**
c/o Debby McIlhargey
1706 - 22nd St. "A"
Coaldale, AB, Canada T1M 1K4
Phone: (403) 345-5750

**Contact:** Debby McIlhargey, Chairperson.

**Date established:** 1982.

**Membership:** 200.

**Budget:** $3500/yr.

**Staff:** All volunteer.

**Description:** Adoptive and prospective adoptive parent support group.

**Description of services:** Provides public education on adoption issues; access to workshops, training and conferences focusing on adoption issues; referrals to existing community agencies; maintains a lending library and hosts guest speakers and social events.

**Dues:** None.

**Publications:** None.

**Meetings:** Last Thursday of each month.


★ 1569 ★
**North East Adoption Resources**
Box 285
Elk Point, AB, Canada T0A 1A0
Phone: (403) 724-2216

**Contact:** Darlene Kozicky, Executive Director.

**Date established:** 1989.

**Membership:** Unavailable.

**Budget:** $25,000/yr.

**Staff:** 4 salaried and 12 volunteer.

**Description:** Non-profit society which offers support to families who have adopted children with special needs.

**Description of services:** Provides education and support; makes referrals and maintains a lending library; actively recruits adoptive homes for children with special needs and provides a 24 hour crisis line.

**Dues:** None.

**Publications:** None.

**Meetings:** Bi-monthly.


★ 1570 ★
**Private Adoption Society of Alberta**
10116 - 105th Ave., No. 203
Edmonton, AB, Canada T5H 0K2
Phone: (403) 441-3970

**Contact:** Valerie Land, Director.

**Date established:** 1983.

**Membership:** 300.

**Budget:** Unavailable.

**Staff:** 3 salaried and 75 volunteer.

**Description:** Non-profit charity offering support to birth parents.

**Description of services:** Provides support, information and counseling; hosts peer group interaction and social activities.

**Dues:** None.

**Publications:** Birthparents Newsletter published quarterly; Adoptive Parents Newsletter published quarterly; Birth Grandparents Newsletter published semi-annually.

**Meetings:** Monthly.


★ 1571 ★
**South Eastern Post Adoption Support Society**
631 Prospect Dr. S.W.
Medicine Hat, AB, Canada T1A 4C2
Phone: (403) 529-8916

**Contact:** Bobbi Unwin, Coordinator.

**Date established:** 1990.

**Membership:** Unavailable.

**Budget:** $22,000 annually.

**Staff:** 1 salaried and 10 volunteer.

**Description:** Non-profit support group for all members of the adoption triad in all the phases of adoption.

**Description of services:** Provides workshops and a speaker's bureau; maintains a resource library and a voluntary registry for those seeking reunion; offers support to adoptive and pre-adoptive families as well as adoptees in search of birth families; advocates for adoptees and adoptive families.

**Dues:** None.

**Publications:** *SEPASS* Newsletter published quarterly.
**Meetings:** Call for time and location.

**★ 1572 ★**
**South Peace Adoptive Families Association**
Box 502
Grande Prairie, AB, Canada T8V 3A7
Phone: (403) 532-6326

**Date established:** 1990.
**Membership:** 10.
**Budget:** $2000/yr.
**Staff:** All volunteer.
**Description:** Non-profit adoptive family support group.
**Description of services:** Provides support.
**Dues:** $15/family and $10/individual.
**Publications:** None.
**Meetings:** 3rd Tuesday of each month.

**★ 1573 ★**
**Taber Adoptive Parents Support Group**
6217 - 48th St.
Taber, AB, Canada T0K 2G0
Phone: (403) 223-4279

**Contact:** Arlene Czerniak, Chairperson.
**Date established:** 1993.
**Membership:** Unavailable.
**Budget:** None.
**Staff:** 2 volunteer officers.
**Description:** Non-profit adoptive family support group.
**Description of services:** Provides support for all members of the adoption triad as well as prospective adoptive parents.
**Dues:** None.
**Publications:** None.
**Meetings:** 1st Tuesday of each month from September to June.

# BRITISH COLUMBIA

**★ 1574 ★**
**Adoptive Parents Association of British Columbia**
15463 - 104th Ave., Ste. 205
Surrey, BC, Canada V3R 1N9
Phone: (604) 588-7300
Fax: (604) 588-1388

**Contact:** Jennifer L. Hillman, Adoption Support Worker.
**Date established:** 1977.
**Membership:** Unavailable.
**Budget:** Based on memberships, donation and funding from the Ministry of Social Services.
**Staff:** 7.
**Description:** Volunteer based, non-profit society and registered charitable organization dedicated to all children of all ages in need of homes in Canada and internationally.
**Description of services:** Provides peer support of buddy parents; hosts and coordinates workshops; maintains an extensive library.
**Dues:** $30/yr.
**Publications:** *WINDOWS on Adoption* published 9 times a year.

**Meetings:** Chapters exist in over 25 communities. Call for times and locations.

**★ 1575 ★**
**Forget Me Not Society (Adoption Circle)**
10693 - 135A St.
Surrey, BC, Canada V3T 4E3
Phone: (604) 581-0550

**Contact:** Cecilia Reekie, Vice President.
**Date established:** 1991.
**Membership:** 200.
**Budget:** Based on dues.
**Staff:** All volunteer.
**Description:** Non-profit, volunteer organization encompassing all members of the adoption circle offering service to adoptees, birth families, adoptive families and professionals.
**Description of services:** Provides support groups, individual peer support including a *Lean on Me List* and referrals to professionals or other service groups; offers resource material for purchase; and hosts workshops.
**Dues:** $24/yr.
**Publications:** *Adoption Circle* published quarterly.
**Meetings:** Monthly. Call for time and location.

**★ 1576 ★**
**Missing Pieces Through Adoption**
BC, Canada
Phone: (604) 590-1156

**Branch address:**
**Contact:** Marg Beddington.
**Date established:** 1988.
**Membership:** Unavailable.
**Budget:** Based on dues.
**Staff:** All volunteer.
**Description:** Non-profit, volunteer-maintained support group for all members of the adoption triad.
**Description of services:** Provides support; maintains a lending library of adoption-related materials; and hosts guest speakers.
**Dues:** $10/yr.
**Publications:** None.
**Meetings:** Monthly. Call for times and locations.

**★ 1577 ★**
**Parent Finders of Canada**
3998 Bayridge Ave.
West Vancouver, BC, Canada V7V 3J5
Phone: (604) 980-6005

**Contact:** Joan E. Vanstone, National Director.
**Date established:** 1974.
**Membership:** 36,000 plus.
**Budget:** Unavailable.
**Staff:** All volunteer.
**Description:** Non-profit self-help search and reunion group.
**Description of services:** Provides support and referrals; maintains the Canadian Adoption Reunion Register; assists members in search and reunion.
**Dues:** $35/yr.
**Publications:** None.

**Meetings:** Call for location of local groups.

★ 1578 ★
**Peruvian Adoptive Families**
448 W. 18th Ave.
Vancouver, BC, Canada V5Y 2B1
Phone: (604) 876-4543

**Contact:** Elsa Weinstein.
**Date established:** 1987.
**Membership:** 75 families.
**Budget:** Based on contributions.
**Staff:** All volunteer.
**Description:** Support group for families who have adopted from Peru, are considering Peruvian adoption or who are Peruvian.
**Description of services:** Provides support, information and referrals; sponsors social and cultural activities.
**Dues:** $10 contribution requested for each social or cultural function.
**Publications:** Newsletter published irregularly.
**Meetings:** Semi-annually.

★ 1579 ★
**Society of Special Needs Adoptive Parents (SNAP)**
1150 - 409 Granville St.
Vancouver, BC, Canada V6C 1T2
Phone: (604) 687-3114
(800) 663-7627
Fax: (604) 687-3364

**Contact:** Verna Booth, Administrative Assistant.
**Date established:** 1987. Registered as a charity in 1988.
**Membership:** 700.
**Budget:** Based on membership fees, donations, fundraising, workshop fees, private and government grants.
**Staff:** 3 salaried and the remainder volunteers.
**Description:** Registered charitable organization committed to assisting special needs adoptive families.
**Description of services:** Provides peer support; maintains a resource library of books, video and audio tapes, periodicals related to special needs and adoption; sponsors with the cooperation of other community organizations workshops on adoption and special needs related issues.
**Dues:** Individual: $15; Family: $20; Group/Society: $35; Corporate: $100.
 Subscription only: $12.
**Publications:** *SNAP Newsletter* published quarterly.
**Meetings:** Call for time and location throughout the province.

## NORTHWEST TERRITORIES

★ 1580 ★
**South Slave Foster Families Association**
Box 1524
Hay River, NT, Canada X0E 0R0
Phone: (403) 874-6048

**Contact:** Karen Gelinas, President.
**Date established:** 1993.
**Membership:** 15 families.
**Budget:** Unavailable.

**Staff:** All volunteer.
**Description:** Non-profit foster family support group.
**Description of services:** Provides training, support and advocacy.
**Dues:** $5/yr.
**Publications:** None.
**Meetings:** Monthly.

## NOVA SCOTIA

★ 1581 ★
**Adoptive Parent Association of Nova Scotia**
P.O. Box 2511, Station M
Halifax, NS, Canada B3J 3N5
Phone: (902) 422-2087

**Contact:** William G. Fraser.
**Founded:** 1985.
**Membership:** Approx. 100 families and agencies.
**Budget:** Approx. $1500 annual.
**Staff:** None.
**Description:** Non-profit, charitable, voluntary agency.
**Description of services:** Advocacy.
**Dues:** $15.
**Publications:** 3-4/yr.
**Meetings:** 4-5/yr.

★ 1582 ★
**Parent Finders - Nova Scotia**
Box 2502 RR2
Tantallon, NS, Canada B0J 3J0

**Contact:** J. Rantala, Group Leader.
**Date established:** 1974.
**Membership:** Unavailable.
**Budget:** Unavailable.
**Staff:** 15 volunteers.
**Description:** Non-profit search and support group for those separated by adoption or foster care.
**Description of services:** Provides assistance in obtaining background information as well creating a search plan; lobbies for legislative change; maintains a local Reunion Register and liaisons with the National Register; makes referrals to intermediaries and professional counsellors.
**Dues:** $25/yr.
**Publications:** *Nexus* published quarterly.
**Meetings:** 2nd Sunday of each month.

## ONTARIO

★ 1583 ★
**Adoption Council of Canada/Le Conseil d'adoption du Canada**
Box 8442, Station T
Ottawa, ON, Canada K1G 3H8
Phone: (613) 235-1566
Fax: (613) 788-5075

**Contact:** Elspeth Ross, Information Coordinator.

**Date established:** 1982; incorporated in 1991.

**Membership:** Unavailable.

**Budget:** Unavailable.

**Staff:** All volunteer.

**Description:** Federally incorporated charitable and educational organization.

**Description of services:** Provides information and referrals in response to adoption inquiries; facilitates the planning and implementation of conferences and workshops on adoption issues; maintains a lending library and a clearinghouse of adoption information in Canada; sponsors education for families, professionals and the public; promotes the placement of waiting children in permanent families.

**Dues:** $25/yr.

**Publications:** *Newsletter of the Adoption Council of Canada* published quarterly.

**Meetings:** Annual meeting.

★ 1584 ★

**Adoption Council of Ontario**
3216 Yonge St., Stes. 3 - 4 - 5
Toronto, ON, Canada M4N 2L2
Phone: (416) 482-0021
Fax: (416) 484-7454

**Date established:** 1987.

**Membership:** 500.

**Budget:** Unavailable.

**Staff:** 1 salaried; remainder volunteer.

**Description:** Non-profit, federally incorporated charitable organization of adoptees, adoptive parents, birth parents and professionals.

**Description of services:** Provides information and education on all aspects of adoption for families, professionals and the public; facilitates and coordinates services among groups; advocates for needed services and for children in need of homes.

**Dues:** Individual and professional.

**Publications:** *Adoption Round Up* published 5 times a year.

**Meetings:** Annual meeting in September; spring and fall forums.

★ 1585 ★

**Adoption Council of Ontario**
134 Clifton Rd.
Toronto, ON, Canada M4T 2G6
Phone: (416) 482-0021
Fax: (416) 484-7454

**Date established:** 1987.

**Membership:** Over 300 agencies, groups and individuals.

**Budget:** Unavailable.

**Staff:** All volunteer.

**Description:** A registered, province-wide, voluntary, charitable organization for all parties in the adoption circle.

**Description of services:** Provides information on all aspects of adoption and redirects specific queries to the best resources. Assists in search and reunion. Advocates to improve legislation and practice; for children in need of permanent families; for families in need of permanent children; and for birthparents and adoptees in search.

**Dues:** $25 individual; $50 agency.

**Publications:** *Adoption Roundup* published quarterly.

**Meetings:** Bi-monthly board meetings and annual meeting. Semi-annual educational forums: *How to Adopt* information seminars.

★ 1586 ★

**Canadian Foster Family Association**
608 - 251 Bank St.
Ottawa, ON, Canada K2P 1X3
Phone: (613) 237-2032
Fax: (613) 237-2732

**Contact:** Marlene MacDonald, Administrative Director.

**Date established:** 1979.

**Membership:** 3000.

**Budget:** Unavailable.

**Staff:** 1 - 5 salaries and volunteer Board of Directors.

**Description:** Non-profit, incorporated organization of foster parents and foster care agencies.

**Description of services:** Provides support, education and awareness of foster parenting and promotes national guidelines for the use of foster care agencies.

**Dues:** $15/yr.

**Publications:** *The Bulletin* published quarterly and *Safeguarding Children and Foster Families*.

**Meetings:** Annual symposium held in May.

★ 1587 ★

**Child Welfare League of Canada**
180 Argyle Ave., Ste. 312
Ottawa, ON, Canada K2P 1B7
Phone: (613) 235-4412
Fax: (613) 788-5075

**Date established:** 1991.

**Membership:** 55.

**Budget:** Unavailable.

**Staff:** 3 salaried.

**Description:** Non-profit, incorporated organization whose mission is to protect and promote the well being of children, youth and their families with particular attention directed to those who are disadvantaged in the areas of physical, social, emotional and mental health.

**Description of services:** Provides training, maintains a lending library and sponsors conferences and seminars.

**Dues:** Based on a sliding scale.

**Publications:** *In Brief* published 5 times a year and *Canada's Children* published 3 times a year.

**Meetings:** Annual meeting.

★ 1588 ★

**Children's Aid Society**
**District of Nipissing**
433 McIntyre St. W.
North Bay, ON, Canada P1B 2Z3
Phone: (705) 472-0910
Fax: (705) 472-9743

**Contact:** Ted V. Myers, Social Worker.

**Date established:** 1905.

**Membership:** 40.

**Budget:** Unavailable.

**Staff:** 60 salaried.

**Description:** Provincially funded agency providing pre- and post adoptive services.
**Description of services:** Provides adoption training sessions, post-adoption disclosure counselling and private and step-parent adoption facilitation.
**Dues:** None.
**Publications:** None.
**Meetings:** Call for schedule.

★ 1589 ★
**Kawartha-Haliburton Children's Aid Society**
42 Victoria Ave. North
Lindsay, ON, Canada K9V 4G2
Phone: (705) 324-3594
(800) 567-9136
Fax: (705) 324-7607

**Contact:** Margaret Davies, B.A., B.S.W., Adoption Worker.
**Date established:** 1913.
**Membership:** Unavailable.
**Budget:** $8,000,000.
**Staff:** 65 salaried.
**Description:** Non-profit society offering support services for members of the Adoption Triangle.
**Description of services:** Provides, support, referrals and counseling.
**Dues:** $10.
**Publications:** None.
**Meetings:** Monthly.

★ 1590 ★
**Waterloo Adoptive Family Association**
714 Sherring St.
Cambridge, ON, Canada N3H 2X4
Phone: (519) 653-8917

**Contact:** Angela and Gary Shields.
**Date established:** 1980.
**Membership:** 30.
**Budget:** None.
**Staff:** All volunteer.
**Description:** Informal adoptive parent support group.
**Description of services:** Provides support, information; hosts guest speakers and social events.
**Dues:** None.

**Publications:** Schedule of Meetings.
**Meetings:** Monthly.

# PRINCE EDWARD ISLAND

★ 1591 ★
**West Prince Adoption Awareness and Support Group**
c/o Mrs. Rhonda Shaw
O'Leary R.R. No. 3
, PE, Canada C0B 1V0
Phone: (902) 859-3257

**Contact:** Rhonda Shaw, Chairperson.
**Date established:** 1989.
**Membership:** 12 couples.
**Budget:** Based on dues.
**Staff:** All volunteer.
**Description:** Non-profit support group.
**Description of services:** Provides support and referrals.
**Dues:** $25/yr.
**Publications:** None.
**Meetings:** Monthly.

# SASKATCHEWAN

★ 1592 ★
**Saskatchewan Adoptive Parents Association**
210 - 2002 Quebec Ave.
Saskatoon, SK, Canada S7K 1W4
Phone: (306) 665-7272
Fax: (306) 665-7274

**Contact:** Shaune Rorke, Executive Director.
**Founded:** 1985.
**Membership:** Approx. 150.
**Budget:** Government funded.
**Description:** Provincial adoptive parent support group.
**Dues:** $20/yr.
**Publications:** *S.A.P.A. News* (bimonthly newsletter).

# Adoption Exchanges

★ 1593 ★
**AASK Midwest**
1025 N. Reynolds Rd., Ste. 201
Toledo, OH 43615
Phone: (419) 534-3350

**Branch address:**

Vanessa McQueen, 2828 Vernon Pl., Cincinnati, OH 45219
Phone: (513) 569-8500

Elizabeth Franks, 1005 W. 18th Terrace, Russelville, AR 72801

Lori Johnson, 1314 N. Boston Ave., Russelville, AR 72801

Mabel Stunkel, R.R. Box 131, Hennepin, IL 61327

Bonnie Henson, P.O. Box 402, Cicero, IN 46034

Teresa Webb, 2508 E. Royerton Rd., Muncie, IN 47303

Candee Bobalek, 3051 Siebert Rd., Rt. 8, Midland, MI 48640

Becky Dornoff, 4784 Bartlett, Williamsburg, MI 49690

Barb Ellington, 9786 Sommerset Rd., Detroit, MI 48224

Dawn Roberson, 5362 Sturgeon, Midland, MI 48640

Rose McNairy, 11396 Granger Tr., Florissant, MO 63033

Dorothy LaFever, Box 27-B, CR No. 16, Beaver Dams, NY 14812

Gail Weisend, Liaison, 1205 Grove St. NE, North Canton, OH 45219

Mary Gayle Adams, 1020 Mainsville Rd., Shippensburg, PA 17257

Eleanor Brown, P.O. Box 236, Shinnston, WV 26431

Bridgette Pits, 113 E. Queens Dr., Slidell, LA 70458

**Contact:** Beverly Moore, Matching Coordinator.
**Date established:** 1983.
**Description of services:** Referral service which matches adoptive families with waiting special needs families; registers both waiting children and families seeking to adopt; makes available numerous other photo-listing books and computer-linkage to other adoption exchanges.
**Requirements:** None, but adoptive parent(s) must be homestudied.
**Fees:** None.

**Description of children:** All children, especially severe special needs children which includes sibling groups, older, minority, handicapped, etc.
**Description of process:** AASK-Midwest matches children with families by grassroots networking with other exchanges, adoptive families, field representatives, and agencies and their staffs.
**Procedures:** Prospective adoptive parents may apply directly, or through any agency, exchange or support group.

★ 1594 ★
**AASK/Texas**
1060 W. Pipeline Rd., Ste. 106
Hurst, TX 76053
Phone: (817) 595-0497

**Description of services:** 1) Recruit families for children with special needs;
  2) locates available children throughout the U.S.;
  3) maintains a registry of children referred by their agencies;
  4) conducts home studies.
**Requirements:** Flexible but some requirements may be dictated by child's referring agency.
**Fees:** None except a $2000 placement fee for children in the conservatorship of AASK.
**Description of children:** Children with special needs.
**Description of process:** AASK registers any child in the custody of a licensed agency who is referred by his/her caseworker. AASK refers appropriate children to a registered family's caseworker and also liaisons between agencies.
**Procedures:** 1) Initial inquiry;
  2) return completed registration form;
  3) if applicants have an approved home study, AASK will refer appropriate children to applicant(s)' caseworker immediately; or
  3) AASK will conduct the home study.

★ 1595 ★
**Adoption Information Center (AIC)**
1011 Craycroft Rd., Ste. 470
Tucson, AZ 85711
Phone: (602) 327-3324

**Mailing address:**
  P.O. Box 17951, Tucson, AZ 85711

**Contact:** Mary Kaye Kuehnast, Office manager.
**Date established:** 1983.
**Description:** The Arizona Information Center is a project of **Arizona Families for Children**, a charitable, non-profit organization.

**Description of services:** 1) Pictures and descriptions of specific children needing homes;
2) Use of lending library with materials on adoption and related material;
3) Medical information on handicapping conditions for special needs children;
4) Subsidy information;
5) Current information on foreign adoption procedures and children in need of homes;
6) Current information on adoption agencies' procedures;
7) creation and maintenance of the *Arizona Adoption Exchange Book*;
8) member of the National Adoption Network with computerized databases available for searches;
9) presents parenting classes and workshops for adoptive parents.

**Requirements:** None.

**Fees:** None.

**Description of children:** Children with special needs from many states and countries.

**Description of process:** 1) Inquiry; 2) discussion to ascertain what kind of child applicants are seeking; 3) location of home study; 4) child search and match; 5) referral to prospective adoptive parents' caseworker.

**Procedures:** In order to register with AIC prospective adoptive parents must have a recent home study. The staff at AIC can make referrals to those without home studies for agencies licensed to conduct home studies.

★ 1596 ★
**Adoption Information Center of Illinois (AICI)**
188 W. Randolph St., Ste. 600
Chicago, IL 60601
Phone: (312) 346-1516
(800) 572-2390 (IL)
Fax: (312) 346-0004

**Contact:** Marilyn Panichi, Director.

**Date established:** 1981.

**Description of services:** The Adoption Center of Illinois was established to create an awareness of children waiting for adoption, connect prospective adoptive parents to adoption agencies and waiting children and help support families created by adoption. It coordinates adoption parties and community meetings which allow prospective adoptive families and waiting children a chance to interact in a relaxed atmosphere. The *Buddy Program* was developed to help demystify the adoption process and to provide prospective parents with the opportunity to discuss the adoption process informally and openly with people outside the agency structure. *Buddy Families* are available at every stage of the process.

**Requirements:** Individual agencies set their own requirements if any.

**Fees:** None.

**Description of children:** African-American children of all ages, including infants; Caucasian and Latino children over the age of 11; children with mental, physical and/or emotional disabilities; brothers and sisters who need to be adopted together into the same family.

**Description of process:** Once an adoptive applicant has completed an adoption study with a licensed agency, s/he can access all waiting children by registering with the Adoption Information Center of Illinois:

1) The Center publishes the *Adoption Listing Book* which has photos and descriptions of Illinois' waiting children which is available through community organizations, doctors' and dentists' offices and by subscription;
2) The Center also operates a computer matching service to link waiting children with prospective parents;
3) The Center has access to the National Adoption Center's database of children and families waiting for adoption.

★ 1597 ★
**Adoption Resource Exchange of Virginia**
**Virginia Department of Social Services**
Theater Row Building
730 East Broad St.
Richmond, VA 23219-1849
Phone: (804) 692-1280
1-800-DO-ADOPT

**Contact:** Interested prospective adoptive parents may access the exchange through any one of the 124 local departments of social services.

**Description of services:** The Adoption Resource Exchange of Virginia provides information, a photo-listing of children awaiting adoption in Virginia, matching and referral for registered families,.

**Requirements:** Prospective adoptive parents must be residents of Virginia.

**Fees:** N/A.

**Description of children:** Children in the custody of local Virginia Departments of Social Services. The majority are children with special needs, e.g. sibling groups, minorities and/or handicapped. Some children are available for out-of-state placement.

**Description of process:** Agencies and individuals are encouraged to call for information on available children. Initial contact is made through social workers.

★ 1598 ★
**Children Awaiting Parents, Inc.**
700 Exchange St.
Rochester, NY 14608
Phone: (716) 232-5110
Fax: (716) 232-2634

**Contact:** Rosann Markese.

**Date established:** 1972.

**Description of services:** The CAP (Children Awaiting Parents) Book is a national service which registers children from any place in North America. It is for children who need extra help and exposure to find adoptive families. Agencies are urged to first try their own exchanges and listing services. After registering a child in The CAP Book, caseworkers must be willing to consider families from outside their own state.

**Requirements:** None but individual agencies may have some requirements.

**Fees:** Subscription fees are $75/yr. One child or a sibling group may be registered for one year at $100; a sibling group of three or more children may be registered for one year at $200. No fee to call for referral for a particular child.

**Description of children:** Physically, mentally and emotionally handicapped children from all over North America; also, older children of all races, sibling groups, and children who have been abused.

**Description of process:** Children are registered directly by their agencies. The child's caseworker composes a description of the child and sends in a picture. Inquiries regarding the children are received from both adoption social workers and from families themselves. The CAP Book staff acts as a clearing house for calls and letters of inquiry and directs them to the appropriate agency and caseworker. All casework decisions concerning the children and families, placement, etc. are entirely in the hands of the agencies involved.

**Procedures:** Subscriptions are available to agencies, parent groups, libraries, doctors' offices and individuals. The CAP office is open from 8:30 a.m. - 4:30 p.m. Monday through Friday.

★ 1599 ★
**Connecticut Adoption Resource Exchange**
White Hall, Bldg. 2
Undercliff Rd.
Meriden, CT 06451
Phone: (203) 238-6640
(800) 842-6347

**Contact:** Liaison worker.

**Date established:** 1977.

**Description of services:** 1) Photo-listing of waiting children;
2) registration of families looking for a particular kind of child with special needs.

**Requirements:** Adults, 21 yrs. and older who have an up-to-date home study from a licensed agency.

**Fees:** None.

**Description of children:** Children with special needs.

**Description of process:** Prospective adoptive families interested in a particular child are referred to the child's caseworker.

**Procedures:** Photo-listing book is available at public libraries, through support groups and by calling the office to arrange an appointment to review it.

★ 1600 ★
**Down Syndrome Association of Greater Cincinnati**
Adoption Awareness Committee
5741 Davey Ave.
Cincinnati, OH 45224
Phone: (513) 542-3286

**Branch address:**
Down Syndrome Center 1821 Summit Rd., Ste. 102, Cincinnati, OH 45237

**Contact:** Robin Steele.

**Date established:** 1981.

**Description of services:** Provides information and support to birth families considering adoptive placement and to families considering the adoption of a child with Down Syndrome; networks with birth families, agencies and adoptive families to find placements for children with Down Syndrome.

**Requirements:** Committee encourages all interested families to inquire. Individual agencies or birth families with children seeking placement may have specific requirements.

**Fees:** None.

**Description of children:** Infants and children born with Down Syndrome.

**Description of process:** Information is available on specific children with Down Syndrome who are available for adoption.

**Procedures:** Application forms are sent on request or adoptive applicants may work through their social worker or agency.

★ 1601 ★
**Indiana Adoption Resource Exchange (IARE)**
**Division of Family and Children**
402 W. Washington St., W364
Indianapolis, IN 46204-2739
Phone: (317) 232-5613
Fax: (317) 232-4436

**Contact:** Joanne Ratcliffe.

**Date established:** 1974.

**Description of services:** IARE publishes a photo-listing with narrative of children in Indiana who have been free for adoption for a six month period but who have not been placed adoptively. IARE does not place children but facilitates the placement. The published listing also consists of Indiana families desiring to adopt special needs children. Services are for Indiana families only.

**Requirements:** Completion of the IARE Family Registration form and a home study approved by a licensed child placing agency or county department of public welfare.

**Fees:** Only those specified by the agency conducting the home study and registering the family on the IARE.

**Description of children:** Special needs and black male infants.

**Description of process:** IARE's photo-listing book is available for viewing at the 92 county public welfare offices, private agencies and through parent support groups.

**Procedures:** IARE's photo-listing book provides the names, agencies and addresses of each child's caseworker who may be contacted directly for more information.

★ 1602 ★
**International Concerns Committee for Children**
911 Cypress Dr.
Boulder, CO 80303
Phone: (303) 494-8333

**Branch address:**
1835 Troxell St., Allentown, PA 18103

130 Temple St., West Newton, MA 02165
Phone: (617) 969-7025

**Contact:** Anna Marie Merrill (Colorado);
Pat Sexton (Pennsylvania);
Betty Laning (Massachusetts).

**Date established:** 1979.

**Description of services:** ICCC is a non-profit, educational and referrral organization which provides the following services:
1) acquaints the concerned public and prospective adoptive parents with various ways to provide assistance to homeless children: sponsorship, fostering, and adoption;
2) educating those interested on the personal and professional level about these procedures;
3) informing prospective parents on the availability of "waiting children" in foreign countries and the U.S.

**Requirements:** Since ICCC is not a child-placing agency, these vary by state, foreign country or agency.

**Fees:** No fees for services other than nominal charges for related expenses.

**Description of children:** Sibling groups, older, minority, and handicapped children both in the U.S. and abroad.

**Description of process:** ICCC's Listing Service is available through their offices in Colorado and through agencies in the U.S. and abroad. The Listing Service, which is updated monthly, provides information about the availability of domestic and foreign children; information about foreign-born children whose U.S. adoptions have been disrupted and children whose placing agencies, for reasons of age and/or physical condition and/or number, are desperately seeking adoptive homes. Non-identifying information is given for those who are looking for that "special child".

**Procedures:** To access the ICCC's Listing Service, contact the Boulder, CO office (a $25.00 annual donation is requested) or contact your local agency.

★ 1603 ★
**Jewish Children's Adoption Network**
P.O. Box 16544
Denver, CO 80216-0544
Phone: (303) 573-8113

**Contact:** Vicki or Steve Krausz.

**Date established:** 1990.

**Description of services:** The Jewish Children's Adoption Network provides information, counseling, matching of children to prospective adoptive homes and publishes a quarterly newsletter.

**Requirements:** Prospective adoptive parents must intend to raise their adopted child in the Jewish religion.

**Fees:** None, but donations are welcome and tax-exempt.

**Description of children:** All children are Jewish. About 85% have special needs, e.g. Down's Syndrome or other forms of retardation, biracial or older. 15% are healthy infants.

**Description of process:** Agencies, attorneys, rabbis, etc. contact the Network about Jewish children in need of placement. The Network then advises registered adoptive applicants. If they express interest in a particular child, the Network refers their agency or attorney to the child's agency or attorney.

**Procedures:** Interested registrants may call the Network to request a registration form.

★ 1604 ★
**A K.I.D.S. Exchange**
**Adoption, Knowledge & Information on Down Syndrome**
56 Midchester Dr.
White Plains, NY 10606
Phone: (914) 428-1236

**Contact:** Janet Marchese.

**Date established:** 1976.

**Description of services:** A K.I.D.S. Exchange maintains a national listing of parents who adopt children with handicaps and others who wish to do so. The Exchange also counsels and assists parents and adoption agencies with children with Down's Syndrome and refers those interested to appropriate support groups.

**Requirements:** Prospective registrants with A K.I.D.S. Exchange must have a completed and approved home study from their state of residence.

**Fees:** None, but donations are welcome and tax deductible.

**Description of children:** Children with Down's Syndrome of all ages and races.

**Description of process:** The Exchange provides a link between birth parents, agencies and prospective adoptive applicants.

**Procedures:** Interested prospective adoptive parents may apply directly.

★ 1605 ★
**Lafayette Regional Office of Community Services**
1353 Surrey St.
Lafayette, LA 70501
Phone: (318) 262-5970
(800) 256-8611
Fax: (318) 262-1092

**Contact:** Foster or homefinding worker.

**Description:** Public, state agency.

**Area served:** Residents of Acadia, Evangeline, Iberia, Lafayette, St. Landry, St. Martin, St. Mary and Vermilion parishes.

**Requirements:** Single applicants or couples married at least 2 yrs. who are between the ages of 21 and 65 yrs. and not more than 50 yrs. older than the child placed, who are in good physical and emotional health and whose income will support another family member.

**Fees:** None.

**Number of children placed last year:** 42.

**Description of children:** Older children and children with special needs.

**Adoption procedure:**
 1) Initial inquiry;
 2) attend 10 wks. of pre-service training;
 3) open application file;
 4) meet certification requirements;
 5) placement;
 6) 6 mos. post-placement supervision;
 7) finalization.

**Average length of time between application and start of home study:** 1 mo. or less.

**Average length of time to complete home study:** 90 days.

**Number of interviews:** Approx. 2.

**Home study description:** Process which includes evaluation and education.

**Average wait for a child after approval of a home study:** 1-6 mos.

**Foster care:** Temporary and long-term.

★ 1606 ★
**The Massachusetts Adoption Resource Exchange**
867 Boylston St., 6th Fl.
Boston, MA 02116
Phone: (617) 536-0362
1-800-882-1176

**Contact:** Carolyn Smith, Executive Director or Luanne E. Gundersen, Director of Communications.

**Date established:** 1957.

**Description of services:** MARE provides information and referral, matching and referral services, support groups, educational series, adoption parties, photo-listing and newspaper and television recruitment of adoptive families.

**Requirements:** None.

**Fees:** None.

**Description of children:** Older, special needs, handicapped, minority, and emotionally handicapped.

**Description of process:** MARE links agencies, refers prospective adoptive parents to specific childrens' social workers, and registers children who are waiting and families who are looking for a special child.

**Procedures:** Families can register with MARE directly 6 months after their home studies are completed; social workers can register families sooner; waiting children can be registered by their social workers at any point.

## ★ 1607 ★

**My Turn Now, Inc.**
P.O. Box 7727
Atlanta, GA 30357
Phone: (404) 657-3479
Fax: (404) 657-3478

**Contact:** Kathryn Karp.

**Date established:** 1980.

**Description of services:** My Turn Now, Inc. publishes Georgia's photo-listing book of information about waiting children which is updated monthly; provides information and referral services on all phases of adoption and can arrange contacts with individuals who have already adopted; refer children to other exchanges and often work with the media to increase awareness about specific children.

**Requirements:** None.

**Fees:** None. A one time subscription to the photo album of waiting children: $20.

**Description of children:** Physically and emotionally handicapped; sibling groups; older children, some teens; minority and mixed race.

**Description of process:** My Turn Now, Inc. responds to direct inquiries from the public as well as agencies all over the U.S.

**Procedures:** *My Turn Now* album can be viewed at libraries in 23 states, adoptive parent groups and agencies. Call or write to find out where or to make an appointment.

## ★ 1608 ★

**National Adoption Exchange**
1500 Walnut St., Ste. 701
Philadelphia, PA 19102
Phone: (215) 735-9988
(800) TO-ADOPT
Fax: (215) 735-9410

**Contact:** Adoption coordinator.

**Description of services:** The National Adoption Exchange has two components, an Adoption Service Bureau and an Adoption Exchange. The Exchange provides information, registration, family recruitment, matching and referral services for children and potential adoptive parents. The Service Bureau provides technical and management services to exchanges and agencies. A photo-list of children representative of those registered on the exchange is available through subscription.

**Requirements:** Applicants must usually be between the ages of 23 and 40 and have room for an additional child.

**Fees:** $150 for initial hook-up. $20 monthly membership fee. $18/hr. of connect time.

**Description of children:** The children are primarily between the ages of 7 and 17. Some are sibling groups of 3 or more who must be placed together. Most of the children have mental, emotional and/or physical disabilities. Many of the children belong to minority groups.

**Description of process:** The National Adoption Exchange helps to link families and children together between agencies and across state lines. It does not determine where children will be placed. It works with social service, community and media efforts to give national visibility to children who have limited adoptive resources. Recruitment of families is targeted toward black, Hispanic and American Indian families and toward families for special needs children and adolescents.

**Procedures:** Child and family registration forms may be obtained from the Exchange. Agencies may register children at any time. People who have completed a home study may register themselves or be registered by their agencies. Once the completed forms are received, adoption coordinators review the files for potential placements and notify the child's and family's agencies and/or family directly.

## ★ 1609 ★

**Northwest Adoption Exchange**
1809 7th Ave., Ste. 409
Seattle, WA 98101
Phone: (206) 292-0082
(800) 927-9411
Fax: (206) 292-0084

**Contact:** Barbara Tucker Pearson.

**Date established:** 1976.

**Description of services:** A nonprofit information and referral agency enhancing adoption opportunities for older U.S. children awaiting adoption in the foster care system; recruits prospective parents; advocacy group for adoptive families; provides consultation and training to adoption professionals.

**Requirements:** Adoptive family must be approved by an agency which will provide post-placement supervision and long-term support.

**Fees:** None. $50 donation for photo-listing books.

**Description of children:** Most are over 10, have special needs and come from Alaska, Washington, Oregon, Idaho, Utah and Nevada.

**Description of process:** Families and their agencies are encouraged to read the *Northwest Adoption Exchange Photolisting Book,* published monthly, and call about any child. The Exchange can answer questions and refer to the child's agency.

**Procedures:** Families may view the photo-listing books without an intermediary or through their agencies. Placement decisions are made by agency with child custody.

## ★ 1610 ★

**Ohio Adoption Photo Listing**
**OAPL**
65 E. State St., 5th Fl.
Columbus, OH 43215
Phone: (614) 466-9274
(800) 686-1581

**Contact:** Lisa Keller, Coordinator.

**Date established:** 1947.

**Description of services:** OAPL provides matching and referral services and makes the Photo Listing book available.

**Requirements:** None.

**Fees:** None.

**Description of children:** Special needs children who are older, of a minority race, a member of a sibling group, or have a mental/physical handicap.

**Description of process:** OAPL is a registration and referral service for public and private adoption agencies. Ohio children who are legally available for adoption, as well as adoptive families who have been home studied and approved, are registered with OAPL by their adoption agencies. The OAPL does not directly place children for adoption.

**Procedures:** OAPL's services can be accessed through a prospective adoptive family's local agency or call directly for more information.

★ 1611 ★
**Rocky Mountain Adoption Exchange**
925 S. Niagara, Ste. 100
Denver, CO 80224
Phone: (303) 333-0845
(800) 451-5246
Fax: (303) 320-5434

**Branch address:**
610 Gold S.W., Albuquerque, NM 87102
Phone: (505) 247-1769

610 E. South Temple, Salt Lake City, UT 84102
Phone: (801) 359-7700

**Contact:** Dr. Dixie Davis, Executive Director.

**Date established:** 1983.

**Description of services:** The Rocky Mountain Adoption Exchange is an information and referral service which locates families for special needs children. It provides referrals, matching and a photo-listing of waiting children and families; provides training throughout the region for adoption workers and families; sponsors parent orientation sessions and media recruitment (4 TV stations/print media).

**Requirements:** Prospective adoptive families must have current home studies.

**Fees:**
Registration of families: $35/yr.;
photobook subscription: $45/yr.;
state membership (public agency): vary according to services provided;
private agency membership: $100/yr. (if state is a member).

**Description of children:** Children with special needs: age 8 and older, sibling groups, multi-challenged/severely disabled, developmentally disabled, and minority children.

**Description of process:** The Exchange acts as a link between a family's agency and a waiting child's agency; between an individual child and adoptive family; and as an interstate placement tool.

**Procedures:** Prospective adoptive applicants may inquire directly about a specific child or work through an agency.

★ 1612 ★
**The Southeastern Exchange of the United States**
408 N. Church St., Ste. C
Greenville, SC 29601-2103
Phone: (803) 242-0460

**Contact:** Nancy W. Godhold, Director.

**Date established:** 1982.

**Description of services:** Photo-list, referral services, matching service and comprehensive information on adoption agencies in the area.

**Requirements:** Varies with state and agency.

**Fees:** $50/yr. subscription; $20/yr. for family registration.

**Description of children:** 25% white children over the age of 12, sibling groups or multi-handicapped; 75% black, half of which are sibling groups of 3 or more, handicapped or healthy sibling groups of 4 or more.

**Description of process:** The Exchange connects agencies with waiting children to agencies and/or adoptive parents interested in them.

**Procedures:** Apply directly or through a local agency. The Exchange encourages families to look through the photo-listing for their own child but will make referrals through caseworkers.

★ 1613 ★
**Special Needs Adoption Network**
P.O. Box 10176
Milwaukee, WI 53210-0990
Phone: (414) 475-1246

**Contact:** Colleen Ellingson.

**Date established:** 1982.

**Description of services:** Publishes *ADOPT!* photolisting book; recruits adoptive families through WI Waiting Child Column in 180 publications. Provides a link to the National Adoption Exchange and a computerized registry of waiting children and families seeking to adopt.

**Requirements:** None.

**Fees:** None.

**Description of children:** Older special needs children: some sibling groups, neglected/abused, emotionally handicapped. Younger children usually have severe or multiple physical and/or mental handicaps.

**Description of process:** Serves as a clearinghouse for all special needs adoptions; links families with waiting children through their caseworkers.

**Procedures:** Upon telephone inquiry the Network will provide additional information about specific children and refer an interested family to the child's agency and/or caseworker. The Adoption Network also serves as a clearinghouse for adoption information, referrals, and post adoption information.

★ 1614 ★
**Three Rivers Adoption Council**
307 4th Ave., Ste. 710
Pittsburgh, PA 15222
Phone: (412) 471-8722
Fax: (412) 471-4861

**Contact:** Staff.

**Date established:** 1979.

**Description of services:** TRAC provides information, referral and matching services, photolisting of waiting children; Black Adoption Services and Family Connections, which provides post-adoption services.

**Requirements:** Requirements are determined by agency doing adoptive study.

**Fees:** None.

**Description of children:** Sibling groups, black children of all ages, children 8 yrs. and older, and developmentally disabled children.

**Description of process:** TRAC serves as a link between agencies responsible for children, agencies who have completed studies on parents ready to adopt special needs children, and adoptive applicants who wish to be referred to a listed child's caseworker.

**Procedures:** Applicant families with approved home studies may register themselves or they may be registered by their agency. Applicant families may call to view the photolisting of waiting children or to get additional information on a listed child.

★ 1615 ★

**West Virginia Adoption Exchange**
P.O. Box 2942
Charleston, WV 25330
Phone: (304) 346-0795
Fax: (304) 346-1062

**Branch address:**
432 Oakland St., P.O. Box 5533, Morgantown, WV 26505
Phone: (304) 599-6505

100 Fourth Ave., Princeton, WV 26740
Phone: (304) 425-8438

**Contact:** Social worker.

**Date established:** 1896.

**Description:** The West Virginia Adoption Exchange was created by the Children's Home Society of West Virginia. As such it provides a full service adoption program as well as the state's adoption exchange program. WVAE also operates the state's adoption reunion registry.

**Description of services:** Information and referral as well as access to WVAE, the photo-listing of children awaiting adoptive placement.

**Requirements:** Prospective applicants must be residents of West Virginia and have an approved home study by a licensed adoption agency for children in special circumstances.

**Fees:** 5% of gross annual income for adoption services.

**Description of children:** Children in special circumstances waiting in foster care.

**Description of process:** WVAE is available through many adoptive parent support groups by subscription.

**Procedures:** Prospective adoptive applicants interested in a particular child may apply directly to the Children's Home Society of West Virginia or through their own local agency.

# Foreign Requirements & Agencies

## BOLIVIA

★ 1616 ★

**Requirements:** Parental age: Applicants must be at least 25 yrs. old. Length of marriage: Couples must be married no later than the birth date of the child to be adopted.

**Documents required:** 1) Completed application from the ONAMFA;
2) I-600A application;
3) certificate of marriage;
4) birth certificates for both spouses;
5) proof of medical examinations by a licensed physician which attests to the applicants' good physical and mental health;
6) detailed social history;
7) certification of adoptive parents' education/preparation;
8) current passports;
9) police clearances.
*All documents must be translated into Spanish and verified..*

**Procedures:** For 5 yrs. after placement, annual reports verifying the adopted child's change of nationality, psychological, cultural and social adaptation, and health status must be forwarded to the Organismo Nacional del Menor, Mujer y Familia (ONAMFA).

**Agency list:**

Organismo Nacional del Menor, Mujer y Familia (ONAMFA)
Edif. Loteria Nacional
Casilla 5960
La Paz, Bolivia
376-862
350-072
350-123.

## CHILE

★ 1617 ★

**Requirements:** Parental age: 30-55 yrs. with a minimum age difference of 18 yrs. between parents and child. Length of marriage: Married at least 3 yrs. Preference is shown to infertile and/or childless couples. Description of children: Infants. Families are often prematched with birth mothers. Wait: From the time the dossier is sent to Chile until a child is assigned is approximately 6 mos. Travel required: Yes. Length of stay: 2 wks.

**Documents required:** *It is recommended that the dossier be presented all at once.*
1) Recent photographs of the applicants (print the complete names and maiden name of applicants). In order to certify the pictures, applicants must appear in person. Fee: $5 U.S. Otherwise, pictures and signatures of the applicants must be notarized and certified by the County Clerk or Secretary of State to finally be authorized by the Consulate. Fee: $7 U.S.
2) Birth Certificates: Bearing raised or impressed seal of the issuing authority with number and date of the specific entry in the applicable registers and signature of the issuer which is to be legalized at the Consulate. Free of charge.
3) Marriage Certificate: As in num ber 2 above.
4) Divorce Decree: As in number 2 above. If a photocopy of a divorce decree is presented, it must be notarized and authenticated by the County Clerk or the Secretary of State to be legalized by the Consulate. Free of charge.
5) Adoptive Home Study: Issued by a State licensed adoption agency together with a copy of the current accredited social worker's license, notarized, certified by the County Clerk (or the Secretary of State) to be legalized by the Consulate. Free of charge.
5a) Physical and Psychological Report: A letter from a doctor and psychiatrist stating mental and physical capacity to adopt which must be notarized and certified by the County Clerk prior to legalization by the Consulate. Free of charge.
6) Certificates of Economic Status: Bank statements or 1040s notarized and certified by the County Clerk to be authorized by the Consulate of Chile. Fee: $7 U.S.
7) Three (3) letters of recommendation: From community, religious or governmental authorities, notarized, certified by the County Clerk and authorized by the Consulate. Fee: $7 U.S.
8) Approved Petition for Pre-Adoption: Original Immigration & Naturalization Service Form 171H (no photocopies) and a copy of the I-600. Legalization by the Consulate: free of charge.
9) License of the Agency for International Adoption: Current license, notarized and certified by County Clerk (or Secretary of State), legalized by Consulate. Fee: $12 U.S.
10) Court Certificate: Stating that applicants meet the requirements for definite adoption of a minor in accordance with the laws and regulations of the State of their residence. Legalization by Chilean Consulate: free of charge.
11) Powers of Attorney: Either a) prospective adopting parents to attorney in Chile to represent them before SENAME (Servicio Nacional de Menores); or b) agency to attorney in Chile to represent it before SENAME; and c) interspousal, when one spouse is unable to go to Chile to finalize guardianship. All must be notarized and verified by the County Clerk (or Secretary of State) to be legalized by the Chilean Consulate.

12) Covenant & Agreement: From adopting parents to Consulate, signed by both adoption parents, notarized and authenticated by the County Clerk. Free of charge.

13) Final Certificate of Compliance: Issued by the Consulate of Chile after verification of all pre-adoption procedures. Fee: $5 U.S.

14) Letter from Adopting Parents: Addressed to Servicio Nacional de Menores (SENAME), requesting the exit of a minor for adoption abroad, signed by the prospective adoptive parents only. No legalization required.

*Every document must be translated into Spanish, even though an official translation could be done in Chile. Translations must be done by an official translator..*

**Procedures:** 1) Adoptive parents should keep the Consul aware of their whereabouts (address and telephone numbers) until the Adoption Decree is granted in the U.S.

2) Forward to the Consulate:

A) Post-placement reports, translated into Spanish, bearing the signatures of a Notary Public and the County Clerk and legalized by the Consulate, must be forwarded to their attorney or representative in Chile to be presented to the corresponding court.

B) Final Decree of Adoption, issued by a U.S. court and bearing the signature and seal of the court's clerk, with a Spanish translation signed by a Notary Public and the County Clerk;

C) Photocopies of papers issued by the Chilean Court authorizing the child to leave Chile under prospective adoptive parents' tuition;

D) Copies of the child's Chilean birth certificate, first 5 pages of the child's Chilean passport and a copy of the child's American birth certificate which is issued after the final decree of adoption;

E) Photocopy of the child's Naturalization Certificate.

**Agency list:**

Chilean Governmental Agency
Servicio Nacional de Menores
Avenida Pedro de Valdivia 4070
Santiago, Chile
Telephone: (56-2) 239-2010
FAX: (56-2) 239-2427

Casa Nacional del Nino
Antonio Vargas No. 360
Santiago, Chile
Telephone: (56-2) 236-0482.

# COLOMBIA

**Requirements:** Preference is given to childless couples for infants. Couples with more than one biological child should not apply for children younger than 6 yrs. Single applicant status: Single parents are considered for children 5 yrs. and older. Wait: 12-18 mos. Travel required: Yes, by at least one parent. Length of stay: 2 trips or one stay of 4-6 wks.

**Documents required:** Letter from the agency conducting the adoption assessment indicating its commitment to:

a) continue supervision of the case by sending periodic reports to the Colombian Institute of Family Welfare until such time as the adoption is finalized in the country of the adopting parents;

b) send a notarized document, authenticated by the Colombian Consul showing that the adopted child was naturalized as a citizen of his/her new country.

Colombian Consulate

10 E. 46th St.
New York, NY 10017

The documents must be in their original form in the language of the country where they were issued and should be duly notarized and authenticated by the Colombian Consul. Photocopies of the documents should be attached. All documents must have been issued within 5 mos. preceding their remittance. If the documents have already been translated into Spanish, verification by an official Colombian translator is required. A bill for translation or verification will be sent to the applicants who must pay for such services immediately.

**Procedures:** Applicants must first address a letter expressing their desire to adopt one of Colombia's completely abandoned children to:

Chief
Adoptions Division
Colombian Institute of Family Welfare
Apartado Aereo 18116
Bogota
Colombia

The letter should provide personal and family information as well as the applicants' reasons for adoption.

After reviewing the information provided in the letter, the Adoption Division will determine if an application should be sent. The appliction must be returned in its original form completed in Spanish with recent photographs of the applicants. A home study prepared by an agency licensed to conduct adoptive assessments in the applicants' state of residence and translated into Spanish must accompany the application.

After review of these documents, the Adoption Committee will inform the applicants if they have been pre-selected.

Upon pre-selection and verification of the completed dossier, the file will be forwarded to one of Colombia's 26 regional offices where a child will be assigned and adoption proceedings will be initiated before the appropriate Court of Minors.

**Agency list:**

Casa de la Madre y el Nino
Calle 48 No. 28-30
Bogota, D.E.
Colombia
269-5845

Asociacion Amigos del Nino
(AYUDAME)
Calle 123 No. 7-33
Bogota, D.E.
Colombia
671-8591

Casa de Maria y el Nino
Calle 65 No. 73-272
San German
Medellin
Colombia
304-090 A.A. 062298

Centro de Rehabilitacion y Adopcion (CRAN)
Calle 27 No. 27-21
Bogota, D.E.
Colombia
245-9271
245-9844

Fundacion para la Adopcion de la Ninez Abandonada
(FANA)
Calle 71-A No. 5-51
Bogota, D.E.
Colombia

255-7995
249-6911
La Casita de Nicolas
Carrera 50 No. 65-23
Medellin
 Colombia
263-8086
Parental age: Between the ages of 30 and 50 yrs. Length of marriage: Only couples married at least 5 yrs. Number of children placed last year: 2. Decription of children: Children 4 yrs. and older. Fees: $7500 U.S. Requirements: Adoption must be finalized in Colombia.

Los Chiquitines
Avenida 9 Norte 7-67
Juanambu
Cali
Colombia
611 307 A.A. 4558.

# PARAGUAY

## ★ 1619 ★

**Requirements:** Parental age: Prospective adoptive parents must be at least 15 years older than the child to be adopted. Length of marriage: Adoptive applicants over the age of 60 yrs. will only be considered if they are childless and married a minimum of 5 yrs. Single applicant status: Widows or single persons cannot adopt any child of the opposite sex unless there is at least a 30 yr. age difference. Wait: Child match usually occurs within 6 mos. of dossier reaching Paraguay. After child assignment the process takes 3 - 5 mos. Travel required: Required. Length of stay: One trip of 3 - 4 wks. or two trips. Description of children: Infants and older children. Several minors without sex distinction may be adopted simultaneously.

**Documents required:** 1) Home Study signed by a certified social worker;
2) photocopies of adoptive applicant(s)' passports;
3) certified copies of adoptive applicant(s) birth certificate(s);
4) certified copy of adoptive parent(s) marriage certificate, if applicable;
5) certified copy of adoptive applicant(s)' divorce decree(s), if applicable;
6) 3 letters of recommendation;
7) adoptive applicant(s)' medical statement(s);
8) verification of employment;
9) adoptive applicant(s)' financial verification;
10) police clearances;
11) social worker's license and letter of guarantee;
12) family photograph;
13) power of attorney signed by adoptive applicant(s).
All documents (original and/or copies) must be certified by a Notary Public and the Secretary of State of the applicant(s) state of residence. In the case of New York State residents the Consulate will accept County Clerk certification instead of that of the Secretary of State.
Consular legalization is required for each one of the foregoing documents.

**Agency list:**

Daniele & Daniele
617 Swede St.
Norristown, PA 19401
(610) 275-6606
FAX: (610) 275-7366

Dawn Bonn & Associates
2206 Aeriel St.
North St. Paul, MN 55109
(612) 779-0273
FAX: (612) 779-7122.

# PHILIPPINES

## ★ 1620 ★

**Requirements:** Parental age: An age range of between 25 and 40 yrs. between the younger adoptive parent and the adopted child for an infant. Parents must be at least 15 yrs. older than the child requested. Length of marriage: Minimum of 3 yrs., 5 yrs. if previously divorced. Single applicant status: Single women are considered for children older than 11 yrs. Wait: Approximately 3-18 mos. for child assignment. Travel required: May be required for one parent to be interviewed by the social worker and attend court proceedings. Length of stay: 3 day minimum. Description of children: Children between the ages of infancy and 14 yrs. More boys than girls. Typical special needs: cerebral palsy, blindness, sibling groups, heart problems and delays in motor, physical or intellectual development.

**Note:** Priority for younger children in given to Filipino or Filipino-American applicants, those who have previously adopted a Filipino child, or childless, Christian, younger applicants.

**Documents required:** 1) Certified birth certificates;
2) certified marriage certificates;
3) certified death certificates, if either spouse has been widowed;
4) certified divorce decrees, if either spouse has been previously married.

**Agency list:**

Department of Social Welfare and Development
Philippine Inter-Country Adoption Unit
389 San Rafael St., cor. Legarda St.
Manila, Philippines.

Asilo de San Vincente de Paul
1148 United Nations Ave.
Manila, Philippines
59-47-45
Number of residents: 83.
Description of children: Female children and youth who are orphaned, neglected or delinquent.

White Cross, Inc.
278 Santolan Rd.
San Juan, Metro Manila
70-21-45
Number of residents: 70.
Description of children: Infants to age 8.

Hospicio de San Jose
Isla dela Convalescencia
Thru Ayala Bridge
Quiapo, Manila
47-24-24/47-79-80
Number of residents: 200.
Orphaned and abandoned children.

Sister Aida Violago, Administrator
Heart of Mary Villa
394 M.H. del Pilar St.
1477 Maysilo
Malabon, Metro Manila
23-38-88/22-37-26.
Number of residents: 393.

Parental age: Between 27 and 39 yrs. Length of marriage: Couples married at least 5 yrs.
Requirements: Preference shown to Christian applicants, particularly practicing Catholics.
Number of children placed last year: 25.
Description of children: Infants between birth and 5 mos. Travel requirements: Preferably by both spouses. Length of stay required: 7-10 days.

Eva Cruvido, Administrator
Asian Social Institute
Senden Home
2422 Pedro Gil St.
Sta. Ana, Manila
50-85-77
Number of residents: 105
Description of children: Street children and their families.

Ms. Angeles P. Fullerton, Executive Director
Chosen Children
No. 10 Apacible St.
Phil-Am Village, Las Pinas
Metro Manila
88-59-55/87-54-72
Number of residents: 30.
Description of children: Orphans and children with special needs.

# POLAND

★ 1621 ★

**Requirements:** Parental age: The maximum allowable age difference between adopting parents and an adopted child is 40 yrs. Length of marriage: Unspecified. Single applicant status: Single applicants will be considered. Description of children: Sibling groups, older children and children with health problems. Any child being offered for adoption to foreigners must have previously been offered for no less than 6 mos. to Polish families without being placed. Exceptions may be made in certain circumstances such as for a child with health problems who needs prompt medical attention. Note: Prospective adoptive parents need not be of Polish descent, but ties to Poland are a favorable factor. Travel required: The Central Adoption Commission may require that the adopting parents come to Poland to meet the child before tha adoption petition is submitted to the court.

**Documents required:**
1) Birth certificates of the adopting parent(s);
2) marriage certificate;
3) police clearance stating the prospective adoptive parent(s) have no criminal record;
4) documents detailing the prospective adoptive parent(s)' financial situation;
5) proof of citizenship;
6) statement from physician regarding the adopting parent(s)' health;
7) certified home study.
*All documents submitted to the Commission must be accompanied by Polish translations and be certifed by the Polish Embassy in Washington, DC or by the Polish Consulate in New York City, Chicago or Los Angeles..*

**Procedures:** The Central Adoption Commission will first review prospective adoptive parents' qualifications to adopt. If approved, the commission will then match them with a child or children. Once a prospective adoptive child is identified, a request for adoption must be submitted to the court having jurisdiction over the place where the child is located. The petition may be submitted by the applicants themselves, an attorney or other intermediary or by the orphanage where the child is living. If the adoption decree is approved, the adoption decree becomes final and irrevocable 21 days from the date of the hearing. An adopted child may be issued an immigrant visa only after the adoption is final and all applicable U.S. immigration law requirements have been met.

**Agency list:**

Central Adoption Commission
02-018 Warszawa
ul. Nowogrodzka 75
Warsaw
Poland.

# UKRAINE

★ 1622 ★

**Requirements:** Parental age: Adults of full legal age. Length of marriage: None specified. Single applicant status: Singles accepted. Wait: 2 - 6 mos. for child assignment. Travel required: One trip required. Length of stay: 8 - 14 days. Description of children: Boys and girls from infancy to 16 yrs. Some sibling groups.

**Documents required:** 1) A letter of intent including the names and addresses of the prospective parents, age and sex of the children they want to adopt, possible changes of data (such as name, surname, date of birth of the child).
2) If both spouses adopt a child, the application is joint; if only one of them, a written consent of the other is needed.
3) Home study performed by a legally licensed U.S. adoption agency or licensed social worker. The home study should include biographical data, family composition, information about children already in the home, etc.
4) License of the adoption agency, if home study is performed by a private agency.
5) Income declaration, i.e. a letter from the employer or financial declaration.
6) Medical certificates on both prospective adoptive parents.
7) Data regarding parents and siblings.
8) Copy of the marriage license.
9) Copies of the passports.
*All documents must be notarized and registered by the Consular division of the Embassy of the Ukraine and accompanied by a notarized professional translation into the Ukrainian or Russian languages..*

**Description of process:** 1) A request is submitted to the respective state authorities of the regions, cities of Kiev and Sevastopol or the Council of Ministers of the Republic of Crimea.
2) Foreign citizens intending to adopt a child are placed on a waiting list in the regional Board of Education.
3) If the adoption is judged to meet the child's interests, it is approved. In order to be approved, the signed consent of the biological parents is needed unless the parents have been deprived of their parental rights or if they have failed to show any interest in the care of the child for more than 1 yr. If the child is older than 10 yrs., his/her consent is also required.

4) The adoption is registered in the office of Vital Statistics ("ZAGS").

**Agency list:**

Administrative Offices, Kiev or Sevastopol
Council of Ministers
Crimea.

# Glossary

**AAP** A federal program, the Adoption Assistance Program, that provides financial assistance, including help with medical care and/or a monthly cash benefit, to families who adopt children with special needs.

**AAPI** Adult Adolescent Parenting Inventory - Assessment tool developed by the Family Development Association.

**ACBSW** Academy of Certified Baccalaureate of Social Workers

**ACSW** Academy of Certified Social Workers

**ACI** see Adoption Complaint Investigation

**Active Adoption Registry** Post-adoption registry wherein one party to the adoption may request a search and release of identifying information without the consent of the other parties involved.

**Adoption** The legal process by which permanent custody of a child is transferred from biological parents to adoptive parent(s).

**Adoption Complaint Investigation** In those states having a code of Civil Procedure the ACI is the first or initiatory pleading whose purpose is to present information garnered in a step-by-step observation on all the material parts on which the plaintiff relies to support his demand for finalization of the proposed adoption.

**Adoption disruption** Term used to describe the process whereby a child is removed from the adoptive home prior to the finalization of the adoption.

**Adoption exchange** Registry of children waiting for adoptive homes and sometimes of prospective adoptive parents seeking a particular type of child.

**Adoption finalization** The legal process of obtaining a decree of adoption from the court.

**Adoption subsidy** An adoption plan in which the Department of Health and Welfare continues financial involvement beyond the point of legal consummation of the adoption.

**Adoption triad** The members of the adoption triangle, i.e., adoptee, birth parents and adoptive parents.

**Agency Enhanced Identified Adoption** Similar to Identified Adoption with the addition of agency assistance in com-posing newspaper advertisements, networking advice and assistance in screening birth family responses. The prospective adoptive family would solicit birth families through ads, networking or a specific referral from a professional (e.g. physician, attorney, social worker, etc.) that would refer the birth parent directly to the agency. The agency would then work to facilitate a placement.

**Assignment** Also called "child offer." The papers describing the child selected for a particular prospective adoptive family or the assignment of that child.

**BCSW** Board Certified Social Worker

**Boarder Babies** Infants left in hospital nurseries after birth because of desertion or the inability of their parents to care for them. Babies may be boarded for periods of months or even years.

**CCSW** Certified Clinical Social Worker

**Child Welfare League of America (CWLA)** The largest privately supported, non-profit organization in North America devoted to helping deprived, neglected and abused children and their families. CWLA counts more than 500 member agencies and 1000 affiliates across the U.S. and Canada.

**CISW** Certified Independent Social Worker

**COA** see Council on Accreditation of Services for Families and Children, Inc.

**Cooperative adoption** Type of adoption wherein adoptive couples and birth parents are aware of one another through an intermediary. Identifying information may or may not be exchanged. Adoptive couples are evaluated as in a traditional, closed adoption. See also: Open Adoption.

**Council on Accreditation of Services for Families and Children, Inc.** Established by the Child Welfare League of America and Family Service America to provide an accreditation process for the mental health and social service fields. It provides a voluntary form of quality control which measures total agency operations against minimum requirements of state or provincial licensing. Any agency which provides one or more of the 40 services for which COA has accreditation standards may apply for accreditation.

**CPS** Child Protective Services

**Cradle Care** Very short-term foster care of a newborn before placement in an adoptive home.

**CSW** Certified Social Worker

**CSW-ACP** Certified Social Worker - Advanced Clinical Practice

**CWLA** see Child Welfare League of America

**Dependent child** One under the age of majority who is without a parent or other person responsible for his care or whose parent or custodian is unable to provide proper care and supervision.

**Designated adoption** An adoptive placement where the birth parent(s) have identified adoptive applicants with whom they wish to place their child for the purpose of legal adoption.

**Domestic child-placing agent** Usually a licensed social worker who is authorized by the state to provide adoptive services such as home study or post-placement supervision.

**Dossier** A collection of documents required by some foreign courts. Dossiers usually must be authenticated by the local consulate.

**Ex Parte** For the benefit of one party without a challenge from an opposing party.

**501(c)3** Designation attributed to an organization which indicates that it is not for profit and tax free

**Family Service America** A non-profit organization whose members are private, non-profit, voluntary organizations which offer services to support family life.

**Foreign child-placing entity** An agency or individual who is permitted within the particular country to place children for adoption. The placement may be either directly with an adoptive family or with the assistance of a U.S.-based international child-placing agency.

**Fost-Adopt** see Legal Risk Adoption

**Foster Care** Temporary service which places a child with a substitute family during a planned period while the birth parents are unable to care for the child.

*Emergency foster care* Type of foster care which results from a sudden problem wherein a child is placed in a foster home for no more than 30 days.

*Limited, short-term or temporary foster care* A type of foster care which is a temporary period of uncertain duration wherein the biological family is helped to prepare for the child's return.

*Pre-adoptive foster care* Type of foster placement wherein the child will be adopted by the foster parents as soon as the birth parents' rights are terminated. See also: Legal Risk Adoption.

*Permanent* Type of foster placement wherein special problems prevent adoption or reuniting with the birth family.

*Specialized* Also called therapeutic and treatment foster care. Foster care of disabled children, seriously ill and behaviorally disordered children, or unmarried minors with children of their own.

**FSA** see Family Service America

**Guardian ad litem** A court-appointed representative who seeks to determine a minor's best interests.

**Home study** The report prepared by a social worker which describes the family, home attitudes toward adoption and the type of child desired. Also the process of eliciting the information for such a report.

**Home study review** The process wherein home studies prepared by other agencies are reviewed by the placing agency.

**I-600 Petition** "Petition to Classify Orphan as an Immediate Relative." Petition which must be filed with Immigration and Naturalization Service to allow the immigration of an identified child into the U.S. for purposes of adoption.

**I-600A Petition** "Application for Advance Processing of Orphan Petition." Petition which may be filed with Immigration and Naturalization Service before an orphan is actually identified to speed the processing of the I-600 Petition once a child is assigned.

**ICWA** see Indian Child Welfare Act

**Identified Adoption** The adoption of a child already known to the adoptive parent(s) and not selected by an agency. Identified adoptions frequently occur in the case of stepparents and in the adoption of the child of a relative.

**Immigration and Naturalization Service** Frequently abbreviated INS. The service under the U.S. Department of Justice which has the responsibility of carrying out federal law concerning immigration and naturalization. Among other responsibilities the INS must process and approve the I-600 Petition.

**Indian Child Welfare Act of 1978** Federal law which gives Indian tribal organizations legal responsibility for all child welfare placement decisions concerning children who either are members of an Indian tribe or of Alaskan Native heritage. Each tribe or village has the power to determine eligibility and membership requirements. As federal law it takes precedence over any state law to the extent the two are inconsistent. Under the Indian Child Welfare Act termination of parental rights may not occur until a minimum of 10 days after birth and the child's tribe or village has the right to intervene as a party to any adoption proceeding and to have some input as to the proposed adoptive family. Preference must first be given to the child's extended family, then to the child's tribe or village, and then to another Indian family.

**INS** Abbreviation for the Immigration and Naturalization Service.

**Interlocutory decree** A decree or court order having only temporary force. There is usually a waiting period between the interlocutory and final decree.

**Interstate Compact on the Placement of Children** A reciprocal state law which has been enacted in all 50 states and in the Virgin Islands which establishes procedures for the interstate placement of children as well as defining the responsibilities for all involved persons. The provisions of the ICPC are interpreted differently in each state although it is generally interpreted such that it is a criminal offense to transfer a child between states in an adoption situation without having first received approval to make the transfer from the Interstate Compact Office in both states. In the event of a disrupted adoption the ICPC provides a solution by assigning responsibility to the child's birth state. It clarifies questions of guardianship and the rights of biological parents before placement and forbids non-agency assisted adoptions in agency-only states. ICPC is administered by the American Public Welfare Association, 1125 Fifteenth St., N.W., Washington, DC 20005.

**LCSW** Licensed Clinical Social Worker

**Legal Risk Adoption** The placement of children not legally free for adoption with families specifically prepared for the possible adoption of the child. Also called foster care adoption or fost-adopt.

**LMFT** Licensed Marriage and Family Therapist

**LMSW-ACP** Licensed Master of Social Work - Advanced Clinical Practice

**LPC** Licensed Professional Counselor

**LICSW** Licensed Independent Clinical Social Worker

**LISW** Licensed Independent Social Worker

**LSW** Licensed Social Worker

**MAPP** Abbreviation for "Model Approach to Partnership in Parenting." Educational series developed by the Child Welfare League of America and used in adoptive and foster parent preparation.

**Medicaid** Popular name of the Medical Assistance Program administered by the Health Care Financing Administration. A program of medical aid designed for those unable to afford regular medical service and financed jointly by the state and the federal government. Eligible costs include hospital in- and out-patient services, rural health clinic services, other laboratory and X-ray services, skilled nursing home services and others. Also called Title XIX.

**MMPI** Minnesota Multiphasic Personality Inventory.

**MSSA** Master of Science in Social Administration

**MSW** Master of Social Work

**MSSW** Master of Science in Social Work

**NASW** National Association of Social Workers

**Non-agency Assisted Adoption** An adoption which is conducted without an adoption agency. Also called private or independent adoption.

**NOVA** Training manual developed by the Behavior Sciences Center of Nova University, Ft. Lauderdale, FL, for foster parent pre-service preparedness training.

**Office of Visa Services of the U.S. Department of State** A division of the Bureau of Consular Affairs which has offices throughout the world, stationed in various U.S. Consulates and which is charged with the responsibility of investigating the circumstances of the orphaned child in the child's country or residence and of the approval and issuance of the child's visa.

**Open adoption** The placement process wherein the birth parent(s) choose a family for their child based on non-identifying information. It may include meeting the future parents of their child and on-going contact, either in-person or by the exchange of letters.

**Orphan Visa** The visa issued by the U.S. consular office located in the child's country of residence upon approval of the I-600 Petition.

**Parental placement** Placement in which no public or private child placing agency assumes custody of the child on an interim basis. The birth parent(s) select the adoptive parent(s) and place their child directly with them. A public or private agency may facilitate such a placement.

**Passive Adoption Registry** Post-adoption registry wherein no identifying information may be released unless both the birth parent(s) and the adoptee are registered and provide their consent.

**Placement** The time of arrival of the adopted child in the adoptive home.

**Post-placement** The period of time after the placement of the child and before finalization, usually a period wherein the placement is supervised by the placing agency.

**Respite Care** Short-term care in or out of the home which relieves the custodial family, either biological or foster, of the responsibility of care so that they may vacation, handle a family crisis or have time to relax. The goal of respite care is to support families to maintain their family members with special needs within the community.

**Special Needs** A child with special needs is one who is characterized by one or more of the following: a member of a sibling group which must be placed together; minority ethnic background, race, color or language; mental, physical, medical or emotional problem; over three yrs. of age; adverse parental background (e.g. drug addiction or mental illness).

**SSI** see Supplemental Security Income

**Supplemental Security Income** A program wherein the federal government makes monthly payments to the aged, blind and disabled who have little or no income or resources. SSI is administered through the Social Security Administration but is not the same. Blind or disabled individuals qualify for SSI regardless of age.

**Title XIX** see Medicaid

**United States-based International Child-placing Agency** An agency which may or may not be licensed within its home state, but has a connection with a child-placing entity in another country. If the agency is licensed, it can usually perform other adoptive functions, such as home studies and post-placement supervision. If it is not licensed in a given state, it may refer a child to a domestic child-placing agency for placement. It also functions in the capacity of making placements directly with families.

**Visa**  Document issued by the government of the child's country and required for travel to the U.S.

# New Titles in Adoption

Alexander-Roberts, Colleen, *The Essential Adoption Handbook,* Taylor Publishers, 1993.

Bolles, Edmund B., *The Penguin Adoption Handbook: A Guide to Creating Your New Family,* Penguin, 1993.

Bowen, John A., *A Canadian Guide to International Adoptions: How to Find, Adopt and Bring Home Your Child,* Self-Counsel Press, 1992.

Crain, Connie and Duff, Jan, *How to Adopt a Child: A Comprehensive Guide for Prospective Parents,* Nelson, 1994.

Gilman, Lois, *The Adoption Resource Book,* 3rd Ed., Harper Collins, 1992.

Humphrey, Michael and Humphrey, Heather, *Intercountry Adoption: Practical Experiences,* Routledge, 1993.

Jones, Katherine, ed., *Adoption Helper,* Hilborn, Robin, Publisher, 189 Springdale Blvd., Toronto, Ontario M4C 1Z6 Tel./FAX (416) 463-9412. Quarterly periodical. $28/yr. Sample copies and data files available on request.

Liviano, David, *The Official Guide to Adoptions in Eastern Europe 1993-94,* 3 Vol., Melador Publications, 1994.

Marindin, Hope, ed., *Handbook for Single Adoptive Parents,* Committee for Single Adoption, 1993.

McCoy, Theresa, *Getting Ready for Adoption,* Adoption World, 1993.

Melina, Lois R. and Roszia, Sharon K., *The Open Adoption Experience: A Complete Guide for Adoptive and Birth Families,* Harper Collins, 1993.

Murphy, Mary-Kate and Knoll, Jean, *International Adoption:* *Sensitive Advice for Prospective Parents,* Chicago Review, 1994.

Nelson-Eriksen, Jean and Nelson-Eriksen, Heino R., *How to Adopt from Asia, Europe and the South Pacific,* Los Ninos, 1991.

Nelson-Eriksen, Jean and Nelson-Eriksen, Heino R., *How to Adopt Internationally: A Guide for Agency-Directed and Independent Adoptions,* Los Ninos, 1993.

Reynolds, Nancy T., *Adopting Your Child: Options, Answers and Actions,* Self Counsel Press, 1993.

Schooler, Jane, *The Whole Life Adoption Book: Realistic Advice for Building a Healthy Adoptive Family,* Pinon Press, 1993.

Simon, Rita J., *The Case for Transracial Adoption,* American University Press, 1993.

Strassberger, Laurel, *Our Children from Latin America and Making Adoption Part of Your Life,* Tiresias Press, 1992.

Strauss, Jean A., *A Birthright: The Guide to Search and Reunion for Adoptees, Birthparents and Adoptive Parents,* Penguin Books, 1994.

Takas, Marianne and Warner, Edward, *To Love a Child: Adoption, Foster Parenting and Other Ways to Share Your Life with Children,* Addison Wesley, 1992.

Walsh, James and Walsh, Roberta, *Quality Care for Tough Kids: Studies of the Maintenance of Subsidized Foster Placements in the Casey Family Program,* Child Welfare League of America, 1990.

Wirth, Eileen M., *How to Adopt a Child from Another Country,* Abingdon, 1993.

# Appendix 1
# Where To Write For Vital Records

Alabama Department of Public Health
Vital Records Office
State Office Building
434 Monroe St., Rm. 215
Montgomery, AL 36130-1710
(205) 242-5039

Alaska Department of Health and Social
Services
Division of Public Health
Bureau of Vital Statistics
Alaska Office Bldg., Rm. 114
P.O. Box 110675
Juneau, AK 99811-0675
(907) 465-3392
FAX: (907) 586-1877

Arizona Department of Health Services
Division of Internal Affairs, Legal
Services and Operations
Office of Vital Records
2727 W. Glendale Ave.
Phoenix, AZ 85051
(602) 255-3260

Arkansas Department of Health
Division of Vital Records
4815 W. Markham St.
Little Rock, AR 72205
(501) 661-2370

California Health and Welfare Agency
Vital Statistics Branch
304 S St.
Sacramento, CA 95814
(916) 445-1719

Colorado Department of Health
Division of Health Statistics and Vital
Records
4210 E. 11th Ave.
Denver, CO 80220
(303) 692-2200

Connecticut Department of Health
Services
Division of Vital Statistics
150 Washington St.
Hartford, CT 06106
(203) 566-2334

Delaware Department of Health and
Social Services
Division of Public Health
Office of Vital Statistics
Jesse Cooper Bldg.
P.O. Box 637
Dover, DE 19903
(302) 739-4701

District of Columbia Department of
Human Services
Division of Research and Statistics
Vital Records Branch
425 I St., 3rd. Fl
Washington, DC 20001
(202) 727-5319

Florida Department of Health and
Rehabilitative Services
Office of Vital Statistics
1317 Winewood Blvd.
Tallahassee, FL 32399-0700
(904) 359-6970

Georgia Department of Human
Resources
Division of Public Health
47 Trinity Ave., SW
Atlanta, GA 30334-2102
(404) 656-4750

Hawaii Department of Health Research
and Statistics Office
Vital Records Section
1250 Punchbowl St.
Honolulu, HI 96813
(808) 586-4410

Idaho Department of Health and Welfare
Division of Health
Center for Health Statistics
450 W. State St., 1st Fl.
Boise, ID 83720
(208) 334-5976

Illinois Department of Public Health
Office of Administrative Services
Division of Vital Records
535 W. Jefferson St
Springfield, IL 62761
(217) 782-6553

Indiana Department of Health
Bureau of Public Health Policy
Division of Public Health Statistics
1330 W. Michigan St.
P.O. Box 1964
Indianapolis, IN 46206-1964
(317) 633-8512

Iowa Department of Public Health
Planning and Administration Division
Vital Records Bureau
Lucas State Office Bldg.
Des Moines, IA 50319
(515) 242-6332

Kansas Department of Health and
Environment
Division of Health
Bureau of Community Health
Vital Statistics Section
London State Office Bldg., Rm. 900
Topeka, KS 66612
(913) 296-1086

Kentucky Human Resources Cabinet
Department for Health Services
Division of Vital Resources and Health
Development
275 E. Main St.
Frankfort, KY 40621
(502) 564-8956
FAX: (502) 564-6533

Louisiana Department of Health and
Hospitals
Office of Public Health Services
Division of Vital Statistics
P.O. Box 60630
New Orleans, LA 70160
(504) 568-5172

Maine Department of Human Services
Office of Data, Research and Vital
Statistics
221 State St.
Augusta, ME 04333
(207) 624-5445
FAX: (207) 626-5555

Maryland Hall of Records
350 Rowe Bldg.
Annapolis, MD 21401
(410) 974-3914

Massachusetts Executive Office of
Health and Human Services
Department of Public Health
Division of Vital Statistics and Research
150 Tremont St.
Boston, MA 02111
(617) 727-0036

Michigan Department of Public Health
State Registrar and Center for Health
Statistics
3423 N. Logan St.
P.O. Box 30195
Lansing, MI 48909
(517) 335-8676

Minnesota Department of Health
Administration Bureau
Vital Records Section
717 Delaware St., S.E., Box 9441
Minneapolis, MN 55440
(612) 623-5121

Mississippi Department of Health
Bureau of Information Resources
Division of Vital Statistics
P.O. Box 1700
Jackson, MS 39215-1700
(601) 987-4983

Missouri Department of Health
Health Resources Division
Bureau of Vital Records
1730 E. Elm St.
P.O. Box 570
Jefferson City, MO 65102
(314) 751-6383

Montana Department of Health and
Environmental Sciences
Centralized Services Division
Bureau of Records and Statistics
Cogwell Bldg., Rm. C108
Helena, MT 59620
(406) 444-2614

Nebraska Department of Health
Division of Vital Statistics
301 Centennial Mall S., 3rd Fl.
P.O. Box 95007
Lincoln, NE 68509-5007
(402) 471-2871

Nevada Department of Human
Resources
Division of Health
Office of Vital Statistics
505 E. King St., Rm. 201
Carson City, NV 89710
(702) 687-4480

New Hampshire Department of Health
and Human Services
Division of Public Health Services
Bureau of Vital Records and Health
Statistics
6 Hazen St.
Concord, NH 03301
(603) 271-4651

New Jersey Department of Health
Bureau of Vital Statistics and
Registration
John Fitch Plaza, CN360
Trenton, NJ 08625-0360
(609) 292-6271

New Mexico Department of Health and
Environment
Bureau of Vital Statistics
Division of Public Health
Harold Runnels Bldg.
1190 St. Francis Dr.
P.O. Box 26110
Santa Fe, NM 87502-6110

New York Department of Health
Vital Statistics Section
Corning Tower, Empire State Plaza
Albany, NY 12237-0001
(518) 474-1094

*New York City birth certificates:*

Bureau of Vital Records
Dept. of Health of NYC
125 Worth St.
New York, NY 10013
(212) 566-8193 or 8194
(212) 566-6404 (credit card use)

*New York City marriage certificates:*

Marriage License Bureau
1780 Grand Concourse, 2nd Fl.
Bronx, NY 10457
(212) 731-2277

Marriage License Bureau
Municipal Bldg., Rm. 205
210 Joralemon St.
Brooklyn, NY 11201
(718) 802-3581

Marriage License Bureau
1 Centre St., Rm. 252
New York, NY 10007
(212) 669-8170

Marriage License Bureau
Queens Borough Hall
120-55 Queens Blvd.
Kew Gardens, NY 11424
(718) 520-3665

Marriage License Bureau
Staten Island Borough Hall
10 Richmond Ter., Rm. 311

Staten Island, NY 10301
(718) 390-5175 or 5176

North Carolina Department of
Environment, Health and Natural
Resources
Office of Health Director
Epidemiology Division
Vital Records Section
Cooper Bldg.
225 N. McDowell St.
P.O. Box 27687
Raleigh, NC 27611
(919) 733-3009

North Dakota Department of Health and
Consolidated Laboratories
Administrative Services Section
Vital Records Division
600 E. Boulevard Ave.
Bismarck, ND 58505-0200

Ohio Department of Health
Bureau of Supportive Services
Division of Vital Statistics
245 N. High St.
P.O. Box 118
Columbus, OH 43266-0588
(614) 466-2533

Oklahoma Department of Health
Division of Vital Records
1000 N.E. 10th St.
P.O. Box 53551
Oklahoma City, OK 73152
(405) 271-4040

Oregon Department of Human
Resources
Division of Health
Vital Statistics Section
1400 Fifth Ave. SW
P.O. Box 231
Portland, OR 97207
(503) 731-4000

Pennsylvania Department of Health
Division of Vital Records
P.O. Box 1528
New Castle, PA 16103
(412) 686-3111

Rhode Island Department of Health
Division of Vital Statistics
3 Capitol Hill
Providence, RI 02908-5097
(401) 277-2228

South Carolina Department of Health
and Environmental Control
Office of Vital Records and Public
Health Statistics
J. Marion Sims Bldg. & R.J. Aycock
Bldg.
2600 Bull St.
Columbia, SC 29201
(803) 734-4810

South Dakota Department of Health
Vital Records Program
445 E. Capitol
Pierre, SD 57501-3181
(605) 773-4961

Tennessee Department of Health
Administrative Services Bureau
Health Statistics Division
Vital Records Section
344 Cordell Hull Bldg.
Nashville, TN 37247-0101
(615) 741-1763

Texas Department of Health
Bureau of Vital Statistics
1100 W. 49th St.
Austin, TX 78756
(512) 458-7692

Utah Department of Health
Administrative Services Division
Bureau of Health Statistics and Vital
Records
P.O. Box 16700
Salt Lake City, UT 84116-0700
(801) 538-6360

Vermont Agency of Human Services
Department of Health
Division of Public Health Statistics
60 Main St.
P.O. Box 70
Burlington, VT 05402
(802) 863-7300

Virginia Department of Health and
Human Resources
Department of Health
Division of Vital Records
1500 E. Main St.
P.O. Box 2448
Richmond, VA 23219
(804) 786-6201

Washington Department of Social and
Health Services
Division of Vital Records
P.O. Box 45010
Olympia, WA 98504-5010
(206) 753-5936

West Virginia Department of Health and
Human Resources
Public Health Bureau
Office of Epidemiology and Health
Promotion
Health Statistics Division
State Capital Complex, Bldg. 3, Rm. 519
Charleston, WV 25301
(304) 558-9100

Wisconsin Department of Health and
Social Services
Division of Health
Office of Vital Statistics
1 W. Wilson St.
P.O. Box 7850
Madison, WI 53707
(608) 266-0330

Wyoming Department of Health
Division of Health and Medical Services
Vital Records Section
117 Hathaway Bldg.
Cheyenne, WY 82002-0710
(307) 777-7591

## Canada

Alberta Health
Director of Vital Statistics
10130 - 112th St.
Edmonton, AB T5K 2P2
(403) 427-2681 (certificate information)
(403) 427-8902 (marriage information)

Ministry of Health
Division of Vital Statistics
818 Fort St.
Victoria, BC V8W 1H8
(604) 387-4826

Manitoba Family Services
Vital Statistics
254 Portage Ave.
Winnipeg, MB R3C 0P6
(204) 945-3701

Department of Health and Community
Services
Registrar General of Vital Statistics
P.O. Box 6000
Fredericton, NB E3B 5H1 .
(506) 453-2385

Department of Health
Vital Statistics Division
Confederation Bldg.
P.O. Box 8700
St. Johns, NF A1B 4J6
(709) 729-3308

Department of Safety & Public Services
Registrar General, Vital Statistics
P.O. Box 1320
Yellowknife, NT X1A 2L9
(403) 873-7404

Department of Health
Vital Statistics
P.O. Box 157
Halifax, NS B3J 2M9
(902) 424-4380

Ministry of Consumer & Commercial
Relations
Registrar General
P.O. Box 4600
189 Red River Rd.
Thunder Bay, ON P7B 6L8
(800) 461-2156

Department of Health & Social Services
Vital Statistics
P.O. Box 2000
Charlottetown, PE C1A 7N8
(902) 368-4420

Ministere de la Justice
1200, rue de l'Eglise
Ste. Foy, PQ G1V 4M1
(418) 643-5140

Saskatchewan Health
Vital Statistics & Health Registration
1919 Rose St.
Regina, SK S4P 3V7
(306) 787-3092

Yukon Health & Social Services
Vital Statistics
P.O. Box 2703
Whitehorse, YT Y1A 2C6
(403) 667-5207

# Appendix 2
# Immigration and Naturalization Service Information

U.S. Citizens who plan to adopt an as-yet unidentified foreign orphan can have the Immigration paperwork done more quickly by using a procedure called *advanced processing.*

## The Orphan Petition Packet

1) I-600A Advanced Processing Application. In Block II on the reverse side of the petition, you may answer *unknown* to items 10 through 15. In item no. 16, *Where do you wish to file your orphan petition?,* you may check the first box and indicate the nearest office of INS in which case, when the child's country of origin is identified, you must notify that office in writing to which country you would like your approved application sent; or, if you are certain from which country your child will be coming, you may check the second box, "The American Consulate or Embassy at" and fill in the name of the city and country.
2) Filing fee.
3) Proof of US citizenship:
   A) Birth certificate or baptismal certificate under seal of the church or the affidavits of 2 U.S. citizens who have personal knowledge of the prospective petitioner's birth.
   B) Naturalization certificate or the naturalization certificate of a spouse or parent and associated birth or marriage certificate and a separate statement showing the date, port and means of his/her arrivals and departures into and out of the U.S.
   C) An unexpired U.S. passport valid for 5 yrs.
4) Proof of marriage of prospective petitioner and spouse, if applicable. Certificates must either be the original or official copies issued and bearing the seal of the official custodian of the records.
5) A home study which is not more than 6 mos. old with a statement or attachment recommending or approving of the proposed adoption signed by an official of the responsible state agency in the state of the child's proposed residence or of an agency authorized by the state, or, in the case of a child to be adopted abroad, of an appropriate public or private adoption agency which is licensed in the U.S. The home study must be submitted within 1 yr. of filing the I 600 A form and must contain:
   A) The financial ability of the prospective parent(s) to rear and educate the child;
   B) a detailed description of the living accommodations where the prospective parents now reside;
   C) a detailed description of the living accommodations where the child will reside;
   D) a factual evaluation of the physical, mental and moral capabilities of the prospective parent(s) in relation to rearing and educating the child;
   E) criminal history and abuse/violence registry clearances.
6) Fingerprints: 4 FD-258 cards, two for each spouse, if applicable. Fingerprints may be obtained at the local police station and are required for each member of the household, age 18 yrs. and older. Fingerprints are processed through the FBI and clearances are valid for 15 mos.
7) Orphan Petition: Once a child has been identified, a separate I-600 form must be filed on behalf of each child including the following documents and translations:
   A) Proof of age of orphan;
   B) death certificate of child's parent(s), if applicable;
   C) certified copy of adoption decree, if the orphan was lawfully adopted abroad;
   D) evidence of one of the following: the sole or surviving parent is incapable of providing for the child and has released the child for emigration and adoption; or that the child has been unconditionally abandoned;
   E) evidence that any pre-adoption requirements, if any, of the child's proposed state of residence have been met.

No additional fees are required for one I-600 Petition if filed prior to the expiration of an approved I-600A application.

## Immigration and Naturalization Service Offices

### Alaska

222 W. 7th Ave., No. 16, Rm. 233
Anchorage, AK 99513-7851

### Arizona

2035 N. Central
Phoenix, AZ 85004

### California

300 N. Los Angeles St.
Los Angeles, CA 90012

880 Front St.
San Diego, CA 92188

630 Sansome St.
Appraisers Bldg.
San Francisco, CA 94111

### Colorado

4730 Paris St.
Denver, CO 80209

### Connecticut

Ribicoff Federal Building
450 Main St., Rm. 410
Hartford, CT 06103-3060

### Florida

7880 Biscayne Blvd.
Miami, FL 33138

### Georgia

77 Forsyth St., S.W., Rm. G-85
Atlanta, GA 30303

### Hawaii

595 Ala Moana Blvd.
Honolulu, HI 96813

### Illinois

175 W. Jackson Blvd.
Chicago, IL 60604

### Louisiana

701 Loyola Ave., Rm. T-8005
New Orleans, LA 70113

### Maine

739 Warren Ave.
Portland, ME 04103

### Maryland

101 W. Lombard St.
Baltimore, MD 21201

### Massachusetts

JFK Federal Bldg.
Government Center, Rm. 700
Boston, MA 02203

### Michigan

333 Mt. Elliott St.
Federal Bldg.
Detroit, MI 48207

### Minnesota

2901 Metro Dr.
Bloomington, MN 55425

### Missouri

9747 N. Conant Ave.
Kansas City, MO 64153

### Montana

301 S. Park, Rm. 512
Drawer 10036
Helena, MT 59626

### Nebraska

3736 S. 132 St.
Omaha, NE 68144

### New Jersey

970 Broad St.
Federal Bldg.
Newark, NJ 07102

### New York

68 Court St.
Buffalo, NY 14202

26 Federal Plaza
New York, NY 10278

### Ohio

1240 E. 9th St., Rm. 1917
Cleveland, OH 44199

### Oregon

511 N.W. Broadway
Federal Bldg.
Portland, OR 97209

### Pennsylvania

1600 Callowhill Rd.
Philadelphia, PA 19130

### Texas

8101 N. Stemmons Fwy.
Dallas, TX 75247

700 E. San Antonio
P.O. Box 9398-79984
El Paso, TX 79901

2102 Teege Rd.
Harlingen, TX 78550

509 N. Belt
Houston, TX 77060

727 E. Durango, Ste. A301
San Antonio, TX 78206

### Virginia

4420 N. Fairfax Dr.
Arlington, VA 22203

### Washington

815 Airport Way, S.
Seattle, WA 98134

### Puerto Rico

Carlos Chardon St., 3rd Fl.
Hato Rey, Puerto Rico 00918

## REGIONAL OFFICES

### Northern

Fort Snelling, Federal Bldg., Rm. 480
Twin Cities, MN 55111

### Southern

7701 N. Stemmons Fwy.
Dallas, TX 75247

### Eastern

70 Kimball Ave.
Burlington, VT 05403-6813

### Western

24000 Avila Rd.
P.O. Box 30080
Laguna Niguel, CA 92677-8080

## SERVICE CENTERS

### Northern Service Center

100 Centennial Mall North, Rm. B-26
Lincoln, NE 68508

### Southern Service Center

P.O. Box 152122
Irving, TX 75015-2122

### Eastern Service Center

75 Lower Weldon St.
St. Albans, VT 05479-0001

### Western Service Center

P.O. Box 30040
Laguna Niguel, CA 92607-0040

# Subject Index

Subject categories, noted in bold, emphasize special interests. An entry number, not page number, follows each organization cited.

491

**American Indian** *see* **Native American**

**Attorneys**

**Subject Index**

Truth Seekers in Adoption **1395**
Truths In Adoption Triad **1429**
Washington Adoptees Rights Movement;
WARM **1546**

**Black adoption**
Adoption by Gentle Care **614**
Adoption Links Worldwide **441**
Adoption Resource Service, Inc. **800**
AGAPE of Central Alabama, Inc. **3**
Alamance County Department of Social
Services **543**
Americans for African Adoptions, Inc. (AFAA)
**203**
Anne Arundel County Department of Social
Services **287**
The Baby Fold **178**
The Barker Foundation **302**
Bethany Christian Services **464**
Bethany Christian Services of Asheville **560**
Bethany Christian Services of Chattanooga
**723**
Bethany Christian Services of Evergreen Park
**179**
Bethany Christian Services of Little Rock **27**
Bethany Christian Services of Maryland **303**
Bethany Christian Services of St. Louis **425**
Black Family And Child Services **18**
Black Homes for Black Children Program;
Child Saving Institute **442**
Bluegrass Christian Adoption Services, Inc.
**251**
Brookwood Child Care **1072**
Cambridge Family and Children's Service **317**
Caring Alternatives; Volunteers of America
**266**
Catholic Charities of Kansas City-St. Joseph,
Inc. **426**
Catholic Charities of Tennessee, Inc. **724**
Catholic Social and Community Services, Inc.;
Diocese of Biloxi **418**
Catholic Social Service of Columbus **618**
Catholic Social Services (of Lexington) **252**
Catholic Social Services; Archdiocese of
Philadelphia **687**
Catholic Social Services of Milwaukee **864**
Central Baptist Family Services **184**
Child and Family Services Division; Adoption
Resources Branch **118**
Children's Bureau of Indianapolis **211**
Children's Home of Cincinnati, Inc. **621**
The Children's Home Society of Florida **137**
Children's Home Society of New Jersey **470**
Christian Counseling Services **726**
Christian Family Services **712**
Cleveland County Department of Social
Services **544**
Coleman Adoption Services, Inc. **212**
Coordinators/2, Inc. **829**
Covenant Care Services **151**
Craven County Department of Social Services
**545**
Department of Social Services (of Baton
Rouge); Office of Community Services
**259**
Department of Social Services of Louisiana;
Division of Children, Youth & Family
Services **260**
Erie County Department of Human Services
**585**
Family And Child Services of Washington, DC
**123**
Family & Children's Services of Central
Maryland **306**
Family Service of Summit County **625**

Forsyth County Department of Social Services
**548**
Gail House **270**
Hampton Department of Social Services **810**
HARAMBEE: Services to Black Families **626**
Harlem-Dowling West Side Center for Children
and Family Services **531**
Indiana Adoption Resource Exchange (IARE);
Division of Family and Children **1601**
Isle of Wight Department of Social Services
**813**
Jefferson County Department of Social
Services **502**
Kansas Children's Service League **245**
Kansas Children's Service League; Black
Adoption Program **246**
Leap of Faith Adoption Services **851**
Love Basket, Inc. **433**
Lutheran Social Ministries of New Jersey **480**
Lutheran Social Service of the South, Inc.
(Dallas) **780**
Lutheran Social Services of the Miami Valley
**632**
Lutheran Social Services of Toledo **633**
The Maine Children's Home for Little
Wanderers **282**
Maternity and Adoption Services of Baptist
Children's Home **193**
New Horizons Adoption Agency, Inc. **412**
Oakland Family Services **393**
Orange County Department of Social Services
**554**
Orchards Children's Services **394**
Parent And Child Development Services **156**
Pitt County Department of Social Services **555**
PLAN International Adoption Service **663**
Porter-Leath Children's Center **730**
Prince George's County Department of Social
Services **295**
City of Richmond Department of Social
Services **821**
ROOTS, Planting Seeds to Secure Our Future,
Inc. **157**
Rowan County Department of Social Services
**557**
St. Joseph's Services for Children and
Families **538**
St. Peters Home for Children; Maternity and
Adoptive Services **731**
Santa Clara County Social Services Agency -
Adoptions **43**
Seegers Lutheran Center; Lutheran Child and
Family Services **196**
Texas Department of Protection and
Regulatory Services **741**
Three Rivers Adoption Council **1614**

**Boarder babies**
Brookwood Child Care **1072**
Harlem-Dowling West Side Center for Children
and Family Services **531**
Jewish Child Care Association **1079**
New Jersey Division of Youth and Family
Services **1068**

**Catholic**
Associated Catholic Charities **121**
Associated Catholic Charities of East
Tennessee **722**
Associated Catholic Charities of Oklahoma
City **642**
Boysville of Michigan **1020**
Caritas Family Services **403, 1047**
Catholic Charities (of Waukegan) **180**
Catholic Charities Adoption Agency of San
Diego **59**

Catholic Charities Adoption Services; Diocese
of Charleston, South Carolina **710**
Catholic Charities Bureau, Evansville **207**
Catholic Charities Bureau, Inc. **131**
Catholic Charities Counseling and Adoption
Services of Erie **682**
Catholic Charities: Counseling Services of
Collier County **132**
Catholic Charities, Diocese of Trenton **466**
Catholic Charities, Inc., Des Moines **225**
Catholic Charities, Inc.; Diocese of Crookston
**404**
Catholic Charities, Inc. of Jackson, MS **1054**
Catholic Charities, Metuchan Diocese;
Department of Maternity and Adoption
Services **467**
Catholic Charities of Ft. Wayne **208**
Catholic Charities of Greensburg **683**
Catholic Charities of Hartford; Catholic Family
Services **100**
Catholic Charities of Houston **760**
Catholic Charities of Kansas City-St. Joseph,
Inc. **426**
Catholic Charities of Norwich; Catholic Family
Services **101**
Catholic Charities of Ogdensburg **521**
Catholic Charities of Salina, Inc. **237**
Catholic Charities of Southwestern Virginia,
Inc. **826**
Catholic Charities of Tennessee, Inc. **724**
Catholic Charities of the Archdiocese of
Chicago **181**
Catholic Charities of the Archdiocese of
Dubuque **226**
Catholic Charities of the Archdiocese of St.
Paul/Minneapolis **405**
Catholic Charities of the Diocese of Arlington,
Inc. **827**
Catholic Charities of the Diocese of
Harrisburg, PA., Inc. **684**
Catholic Charities of the Diocese of
Pittsburgh, Inc. **685**
Catholic Charities of the Diocese of Sioux
City, Iowa, Inc. **227**
Catholic Charities of the Diocese of Winona
**406**
Catholic Charities of Tulsa **644**
Catholic Charities of Utica **522**
Catholic Charities of Wilmington, Delaware
**116**
Catholic Charities of Worcester **318**
Catholic Community Service of Seattle **846**
Catholic Community Services; Archdiocese of
Miami - Broward Region **134**
Catholic Community Services, Inc. of Trumbull
County **616**
Catholic Community Services of Baton Rouge;
Counseling, Maternity and Adoption
Department **267**
Catholic Community Services of Colorado
Springs **86**
Catholic Community Services of Nevada **1065**
Catholic Community Services of Nevada (Las
Vegas) **450**
Catholic Community Services of Nevada
(Reno) **451**
Catholic Community Services of South
Arizona, Inc. **19**
Catholic Community Services of Tacoma **847**
Catholic Community Services of the Newark
Archdiocese; Associated Catholic
Charities **468**
Catholic Community Services of Vancouver
**848**
Catholic Counseling Services of Dallas **761**

Subject Index

Bethany Adoption Service, Inc. of Oklahoma 643
Bethany Christian Services 464
Bethany Christian Services (of Baton Rouge) 265
Bethany Christian Services (of Burnt Hills) 520
Bethany Christian Services (of Des Moines) 223
Bethany Christian Services (of Eastern Michigan) 352
Bethany Christian Services (of Grand Rapids) 353
Bethany Christian Services (of Indiana) 205
Bethany Christian Services (of Van Buren County) 354
Bethany Christian Services, North Region 57
Bethany Christian Services of Asheville 560
Bethany Christian Services of Bellingham 845
Bethany Christian Services of Chattenooga 723
Bethany Christian Services of Colorado 85
Bethany Christian Services of Evergreen Park 179
Bethany Christian Services of Ft. Washington 679
Bethany Christian Services of Indianapolis 206
Bethany Christian Services of Little Rock 27
Bethany Christian Services of Maryland 303
Bethany Christian Services of Mississippi 417
Bethany Christian Services of Northwest Iowa 224
Bethany Christian Services of St. Louis 425
Bethany Christian Services, South Region 58
Bluegrass Christian Adoption Services, Inc. 251
Catholic Social Services of Lincoln 443
Catholic Social Services of Santa Fe, Inc. 484
Children's Choice 305
Christian Adoption and Family Services 62
Christian Adoption Ministries 1383
Christian Adoption Services 881
Christian Adoption Services, Inc. 565
Christian Care/Baptist Childrens Home and Family Ministry 374
Christian Counseling Services 726
Christian Cradle, Inc. 375
Christian Family Life Services, Inc. 571
Christian Family Services 376, 712
Christian Family Services of Colorado, Inc. 88
Christian Home and Bible School 139
Christian Homes for Children 471
Christian Homes of Abilene 766
Church of God Home for Children 727
Covenant Care Services 151
Cradle of Lawton, Inc. 645
Crisis Pregnancy Outreach 646
Dillon International, Inc. 648
Evangelical Child and Family Agency 187, 867
Families for Children; A Division of New Mexico Boys Ranch 488
Family Connections Adoption Agency 65
Family Life Services 241, 831
Family Life Services of New England 1161
Gateway Woods - Apostolic Christian Children's Home 991
Greater Love Adoption Decision (G.L.A.D.) 214
Highlands Child Placement Services 430
Hope's Promise 94
House of Samuel, Inc. 24
International Christian Adoptions 73
Jeremiah Agency, Inc. 215
Jewels for Jesus Adoption Agency 905
Kentucky One Church One Child Program; Louisville Urban League 255
Lifeline Children's Services, Inc. 6

LIGHT House Adoption Agency 432
Loving Alternative Adoption Agency 778
Lutheran Family and Children's Services of Missouri 434
Lutheran Social Service of the South, Inc. (Dallas) 780
Lutheran Social Services of North Dakota 572
MetroCenter for Family Ministries, Inc. 650
New Horizons Adoption Agency, Inc. 412
New Life Adoption Services 194
New Life Christian Services 783
New Life Family Services 413
Open Arms Christian Home 993
Paraclete Social Outreach, Inc. 1105
Protestant Social Service Bureau 328
St. Andre Home, Inc. 283
St. Elizabeth Foundation 274
St. Mary's Services 195
The Salvation Army; Children's Services 1137
Small World Ministries 732
Tender Mercy Ministries, Inc. 960
Touch of Hope Adoption Center 398
Wedgwood Christian Youth & Family Services 1045
Worldwide Love for Children, Inc. 436

**Church of Christ**
AGAPE of Central Alabama, Inc. 3
AGAPE of North Alabama, Inc. 4
Cherokee Home for Children 1150
Childplace 210
Christian Child Placement Service 487
Christian Family Services 138
Christian Family Services, Inc. 428
Christian Homes; A Program of Louisiana Child Care and Placement Services, Inc. 269
Christian Services of East Texas 1151
Christ's Haven for Children 767
Colorado Christian Services 90
High Plains Children's Home & Family Services, Inc. 773, 1156
Mid-Western Children's Home 634
Southeastern Children's Home 713

**Cradle care**
Adoption Access, Inc. 751
Andrel Adoptions, Inc. 758
Appletree Adoptions, Inc. 641
Bethany Christian Services (of Burnt Hills) 520
Bethany Christian Services (of Eastern Michigan) 352
Catholic Charities of Utica 522
Catholic Community Services of Nevada (Las Vegas) 450
Catholic Service League, Inc. 617
Children's Home Society of Minnesota 407
Christian Adoption Services, Inc. 565
Cradle of Life Adoption Agency, Inc. 769
Families First 958
The Family Tree Adoption Agency, Inc. 529
Growing Families, Inc. 474
High Plains Children's Home & Family Services, Inc. 773
Lutheran Counseling and Family Services, Wauwatosa 868
The Lutheran Home 410
New Horizons Adoption Agency, Inc. 412
St. Peters Home for Children; Maternity and Adoptive Services 731

**Emergency foster care**
Abbott House 1071
Alabama Department of Human Resources 2
Alabama State Department of Human Resources 921

Alberta Family and Social Services 1176
Aldersgate Youth Service Bureau 1125
Alternative Program Associates 1126
The Angel Guardian Home 519
Anne Arundel County Department of Social Services 287
Area Youth for Christ - Youth Guidance - Foster Care 1018
Arizona Department of Economic Security 14
Associated Youth Services 1005
Association of Village Council Presidents, Inc. 10, 922
The Baby Fold 178
The Bair Foundation 1149
Baltimore City Department of Human Resources 288
Baltimore County Department of Social Services 289
Bay County Department of Social Services 1019
Beech Brook 1093
Berea Children's home and Family Services 1094
Berks County Children and Youth Agency; County Services Center 666
Berrien County Department of Social Services 332
Best Nest, Inc. 1127
Bethany Christian Services (of Van Buren County) 354
Boysville of Michigan 1020
Branch County Department of Social Sciences 1021
Brookwood Child Care 1072
Bucks County Children and Youth Agency 667
Casa Central Foster Care Agency 966
Catholic Charities, Inc. of Jackson, MS 1054
Catholic Community Services of Nevada 1065
Catholic Social Agency of Allentown 1128
Catholic Social Service; St. Vincent Home 359
Central Baptist Family Services 184
Centre Jeunesse de Quebec (CPEJ) 1190
Chaffee County Department of Social Services 936
Cherokee Home for Children 1150
Chicago Commons 968
Child and Family Services Division; Adoption Resources Branch 118
Child and Family Services of Central Manitoba 1178
Child and Family Services of Western Manitoba 1179
Child Connect 998
The Child Placement Professionals, Inc. 1096
ChildKind, Inc. 955
Children and Youth Services of Delaware County 1129
Children, Youth and Families Dept. (New Mexico); Social Services Division 483
Children's Aid Society of Metropolitan Toronto 1186
Children's Aid Society of Sudbury-Manitoulin 1187
Children's Bureau of Southern California 929
Children's Home of Kingston (CHK) 1075
Children's Home Society of California 61
Children's Services Division of Oregon 1123
Chippewa County Department of Social Services 1023
Christian Heritage Children's Home 1063
Christian Services of East Texas 1151
Circle Family Care 970
The Community House 971
Concept 7 Foster Family Agency 930
Cuyohoga County Department of Children and Family Services 584

Roscommon County Department of Social Services **1039**

St. Augustine's Center; Child Welfare Services Department **1085**

St. Dominic's Family Service Center **1086**

St. Joseph County Office of Family and Social Service Administration; Division of Family and Children **994**

St. Joseph's Services for Children and Families **538**

St. Mary's Children & Family Services **1087**

The Salvation Army; Children's Services **1137**

San Francisco Department of Social Services; Adoption Services **40**

San Luis Obispo County Department of Social Services **41**

Sanilac County Department of Social Services **1040**

Saskatchewan Social Services **918, 1191**

Schenectady County Department of Social Services **511**

Schoharie County Department of Social Services **512**

Seguin Services Inc. **984**

Sertoma Foster Care **985**

Share Homes Foster Family Agency **933**

Shelby County Children Services Board **608**

Shelter, Inc. **986**

Sheriffs Youth Programs of Minnesota, Inc. **1051**

Jayne Shover Easter Seal Rehabilitative Center, Inc. **987**

Social and Rehabilitative Services of Vermont **798**

Society for Seamen's Children **1088**

South Carolina Department of Social Services **1146**

South Carolina Department of Social Services; Children, Family and Adult Services **709**

South Dakota Department of Social Services; Child Protection Services **1147**

Special Training for Exceptional People (STEP) **1060**

Specialized Alternatives For Families And Youth (S.A.F.Y.) **1110**

Spectrum Human Services **1041**

Stark County Department of Human Services **609**

State of Louisiana; Department of Social Services **264**

Suffolk County Department of Social Services **513**

Symbiont, Inc. **1111**

Tanager Place **1003**

Teaching-Family Homes of Upper Michigan **1042**

Tender Mercy Ministries, Inc. **960**

Texas Department of Protective and Regulatory Services; Region 11 **746**

Therapeutic Family Life **1158**

Toiyabe Indian Health Project; Family Services Department **934**

Tompkins County Department of Social Services **515**

Try Again Homes Inc. **1138**

Uhlich Children's Home **988**

United Homes for Children, Inc. **1017**

The United Methodist Children's Home **961**

Utah State Department of Human Services **1159**

Virginia Department of Social Services **1165**

Virginia Department of Social Services; Bureau of Child Welfare Services **823**

Volunteers of America; Family Treatment Program **1052**

Wabash County Office, Division of Family and Children **996**

Wake County Department of Social Services **559**

Walden Environment, Inc. **935**

Washington County Children and Youth Agency **675**

Washington County Children and Youth Services **1139**

Washington Department of Health and Social Services; Children, Youth & Family Services Administration **839**

Washtenaw County O'Brien Center Foster Care Program **1043**

Wedgwood Christian Youth & Family Services **1045**

Westchester County Department of Social Services **517, 1090**

Westmoreland County Children's Bureau **1140**

White's Family Services **997**

Winnipeg Child and Family Services **1181**

Wisconsin Department of Health and Social Services; Division of Community Services **1175**

York County Children and Youth Services **676, 1141**

Young House Family Services **1004**

Youth Advocates **1169**

Youth Engaged for Success, Inc. **1112**

Youth Focus, Inc. **1092**

Youth Services Network of S.W.O., Inc. **1113**

**Fost-adopt**

Adopt A Special Kid/Texas, Inc.; AASK/Texas, Inc. **750**

Adoption Agency & Counseling Service of Ontario **903**

Arizona Children's Home Association **17**

The Baby Fold **178**

Baltimore City Department of Human Resources **288**

Berks County Children and Youth Agency; County Services Center **666**

Chautauqua County Department of Social Services **494**

Children's Home Society of California **61**

Children's Services, Inc. **1130**

Cumberland County Department of Social Services **546**

Cuyohoga County Department of Children and Family Services **584**

Dauphin County Children and Youth Agency **668**

Department of Children's Services; Adoptions Division **30**

El Paso County Department of Social Services **939**

The Family Extension, Inc. **940**

The Family Foundation **849**

The Family Tree Adoption and Counseling Center **649**

Fresno County Department of Social Services **32**

Illinois Department of Children and Family Services; Peoria Office **174**

Lancaster County Children and Youth Social Service Agency **671**

Lucas County Children's Service Board **595**

Lutheran Community Services, Inc. **532**

Lutheran Social Services of Washington and Idaho **168**

Mission of the Immaculate Virgin - Mount Loretto **533**

Montgomery County Office of Children and Youth **672**

Orange County Department of Social Services **506**

Partners for Adoption **77**

Philadelphia County Children and Youth Agency **673**

Portsmouth Department of Social Services **818**

Project STAR **700**

Putnam County Department of Social Services **508**

San Francisco Department of Social Services; Adoption Services **40**

San Luis Obispo County Department of Social Services **41**

Santa Clara County Social Services Agency - Adoptions **43**

Santa Cruz County Department of Human Resources; Adoptions **44**

Sierra Adoption Services **78**

Talbot Perkins Children's Services **540**

Warren County Department of Social Services **516**

York County Children and Youth Services **676**

**Free Methodist Church of North America** *see* **Methodist**

**Hispanic adoption**

Abrazo Adoption Associates **749**

Adoption Services Associates **755**

Alternatives in Motion, Inc. **757**

Brookwood Child Care **1072**

Central Baptist Family Services **184**

The Children's Home Society of Florida **137**

Christian Family Services **712**

Harlem-Dowling West Side Center for Children and Family Services **531**

Infant of Prague Adoption Service **72**

Jewish Family Service of Greater Hartford **108**

Lutheran Social Service of the South, Inc. (Dallas) **780**

St. Joseph's Services for Children and Families **538**

Santa Clara County Social Services Agency - Adoptions **43**

Sharing In Adoption **284**

The Texas Cradle Society **786**

Texas Department of Protection and Regulatory Services **741**

Triad Adoption and Counseling Services, Inc. **491**

**Infant adoption**

A.M.O.R. Adoptions, Inc. **462**

ABC Counseling & Family Services **177**

Abrazo Adoption Associates **749**

An Act of Love; Alternative Options & Services for Children **791**

Adopt International **50**

Adoption Access, Inc. **751**

Adoption Advisory, Inc. **752**

Adoption Advocates **753**

Adoption Affiliates **639**

Adoption Affiliates, Inc. **754**

Adoption Agency & Counseling Service of Ontario **903**

Adoption Alliance **81**

Adoption Alliances; Jewish Family Services **299**

Adoption And Infertility Services, Inc. **463**

Adoption Associates, Inc. **349**

Adoption By Choice **128, 879**

Adoption by Gentle Care **614**

Adoption by Gentle Shepherd **424**

Adoption by Gentle Shepherd, Inc. **233**

Adoption Care Center, Inc. **15**

**Subject Index**

Baltimore County Department of Social Services **289**

Baptist Children's Home and Family Ministries **204**

Baptist Family Agency **843**

Bay County Department of Social Services **1019**

Beech Brook **1093**

Belmont County Children Services Board **577**

Berea Children's home and Family Services **1094**

Berks County Children and Youth Agency; County Services Center **666**

Berrien County Department of Social Services **332**

Best Nest, Inc. **1127**

Bethany Christian Services (of Grand Rapids) **353**

Bethany Christian Services (of Van Buren County) **354**

Black Family And Child Services **18**

D.A. Blodgett Services for Children and Families **355**

Bluegrass Residential and Support Services (B.R.A.S.S.) **1008**

Boysville of Michigan **1020**

Branch County Department of Social Sciences **1021**

Bristol Department of Social Services **805**

Brookwood Child Care **1072**

Brown County Department of Human Services **578**

Brunswick Department of Social Services **806**

Bucks County Children and Youth Agency **667**

Butler County Children's Services Board **579**

Cabrini-Green Youth and Family Services **965**

Calhoun County Department of Social Services **333**

Caroline Department of Social Services **807**

Carpe Diem of Virginia, Inc. **1162**

Carroll County Department of Human Services **580**

Carroll County Department of Social Services **291**

Casa Central Foster Care Agency **966**

The Casey Family Program **962, 963**

The Casey Family Services **945**

Casey Family Services - Rhode Island Division **1142**

Casey Family Services; Vermont Division **1160**

Catholic Charities Bureau, Evansville **207**

Catholic Charities of the Archdiocese of Chicago **181**

Catholic Charities of Wilmington, Delaware **116**

Catholic Community Services of Tacoma **847**

Catholic Family Center of the Diocese of Rochester **523, 1073**

Catholic Foster Services of Miami **954**

Catholic Social Agency (of Allentown) **686**

Catholic Social Agency of Allentown **1128**

Catholic Social Service of Belleville **182**

Catholic Social Service of Peoria **183**

Catholic Social Service; St. Vincent Home **359**

Catholic Social Services of Kent County **362**

Catholic Social Services of Lansing; St. Vincent Home for Children **363**

Central Baptist Family Services **184**

Centre Jeunesse de Quebec (CPEJ) **1190**

Chaffee County Department of Social Services **936**

Champaign County Department of Human Services **581**

Chautauqua County Department of Social Services **494**

Chemung County Department of Social Services **495**

Cherokee Home for Children **1150**

Chicago Child Care Society **967**

Chicago Commons **968**

Child and Family Services Division; Adoption Resources Branch **118**

Child and Family Services of Central Manitoba **1178**

Child and Family Services of Holland **369**

Child and Family Services of Southwestern Michigan, Inc. **372**

Child and Family Services of Western Manitoba **890, 1179**

Child Connect **998**

Child Development Support Corp. **1074**

CHILD, Inc. **949**

Child Placement Center of Texas **765**

The Child Placement Professionals, Inc. **1096**

Child Protective Services; Texas Department of Protective and Regulatory Services **737**

ChildKind, Inc. **955**

Children and Youth Services of Delaware County **1129**

Children's Aid Home and Society of Somerset County **689**

Children's Aid Society of Metropolitan Toronto **1186**

Children's Aid Society of Sudbury-Manitoulin **1187**

Children's Bureau of Indianapolis **211**

Children's Bureau of Southern California **929**

Children's Choice of Delaware **950**

Children's Home of Kingston (CHK) **1075**

The Children's Home of Wheeling **1170**

Children's Services Division of Oregon **1123**

Children's Services, Inc. **1130**

Chippewa County Department of Social Services **1023**

Christian Care/Baptist Childrens Home and Family Ministry **374**

Christian Heritage Children's Home **1063**

Christian Home and Bible School **139**

Christian Homes; A Program of Louisiana Child Care and Placement Services, Inc. **269**

Circle Family Care **970**

Clark County Department of Human Services **582**

Clarke County Department of Social Services **808**

Coastal Bend Youth City **1152**

Colorado State Department of Social Services **80**

Compassion, Inc. **1097**

Concept 7 Foster Family Agency **930**

Cree Nation Child & Family Caring Agency **891**

Cumberland County Department of Social Services **546**

Cuyohoga County Department of Children and Family Services **584**

Danville Division of Social Services **809**

Dauphin County Children and Youth Agency **668**

Deep East Texas Mental Health/Mental Retardation Services **1153**

Delaware County Children and Youth **669**

Delaware County Department of Social Services **496**

Delaware County Office of Family and Children Services **990**

Delta County Department of Social Services **1024**

Denver Alternative Youth Services; The Family Connection **937**

Denver Department of Social Services **938**

Department for Children and Their Families **1143**

Department for Social Services; State of Kentucky **250**

Department of Community Services (Nova Scotia); Family and Children's Services **900**

Department of Community Services; Family and Children's Services **1185**

Department of Family Services, Montana **1057**

Department of Family Services of Montana **438**

Department of Family Services of Wyoming **874**

Department of Health and Social Services, Alaska; Division of Family and Youth **923**

Department of Health and Social Services; Government of the Yukon **1192**

Department of Health and Welfare; Family and Community Services **964**

Department of Health and Welfare of Idaho; Division of Family and Community Services **163**

Department of Human Services; Commission on Social Services **952**

Department of Human Services; Division of Family and Human Services **26**

Department of Human Services; Family & Adult Services Division **159**

Department of Protective and Regulatory Services; Region 8 **738**

Department of Social Services **258**

Department of Social Services (of Baton Rouge); Office of Community Services **259**

Department of Social Services; Baton Rouge Region **1012**

Department of Social Services of Louisiana; Division of Children, Youth & Family Services **260**

Department of Social Services of Massachusetts **309**

DePelchin Children's Center **770**

Division for Children, Youth and Families, New Hampshire **455**

Division of Family and Children's Services (Georgia); State Adoption Unit **147**

Division of Family and Children's Services; Agency 2 - Georgia **956**

Division of Family and Youth Services of Alaska **9**

Division of Family Services (Delaware) **951**

Division of Family Services; Delaware Youth and Family Center **115**

Dutchess County Department of Social Services **497**

El Dorado County Dept. of Social Services; Adoption Services **31**

Erie County Children and Youth Agency **670**

Erie County Department of Human Services **585**

Essex County Department of Social Services **499**

Evangelical Child and Family Agency **187**

Evergreen Children's Services **378**

Extended Families **957**

Fairfield County Children's Services **586**

Families First **958**

Families for Children **64**

Families for Children; A Division of New Mexico Boys Ranch **488**

Families of Northeast Iowa **999**

Noble County Department of Human Services **602**

North American Family Institute **1145**

North Dakota Department of Human Services; Division of Children and Family Services **569**

Northeast Foster Care, Inc. **1135**

Northern Valley Catholic Social Service **932**

Northern Virginia Family Service **1163**

Northwest Passage **1174**

Nottoway Department of Social Services **817**

Oakland County Department of Social Services **344**

Office of Community Service (of Alexandria, LA) **262**

Office of Community Services; Lake Charles Region **263**

Ogemon County Department of Social Services **1035**

Ohel Children's Home and Family Services **1082**

Onondaga County Department of Social Services **505**

Open Arms Christian Home **993**

Options for Youth, Inc. **1104**

Orange County Department of Social Services **506, 554**

Orchards Children's Services **394**

Oregon Childrens Services Division **655**

Otsego County Department of Social Services **507**

Ottawa County Department of Human Services **603**

Paraclete Social Outreach, Inc. **1105**

Parenthesis Family Advocates **1106**

People Places, Inc. **1164**

Perry County Children's Services **604**

Philadelphia County Children and Youth Agency **673**

Pinebrook Services for Children and Youth **1136**

Pitt County Department of Social Services **555**

Pius XII Youth and Family Services **1083**

Porter-Leath Children's Center **730**

Potomac Center **1172**

Prince George's County Department of Social Services **295**

Professional Parenting/Adoption Plus **1091**

Project Impact **327**

Pulaski Department of Social Services **819**

Putnam County Department of Human Services **605**

Putnam County Department of Social Services **508**

Quakerdale Home **1002**

Radford Department of Welfare and Social Services **820**

Rainbow Youth and Family Services **1167**

Randolph County Department of Social Services **556**

Rensselaer County Department of Social Services **509**

Reverend Henry Rucker Memorial Services **983**

Richard Allen Center on Life **1084**

City of Richmond Department of Social Services **821**

Roscommon County Department of Social Services **1039**

Rosemont Center **1107**

Rowan County Department of Social Services **557**

Russell County Department of Social Services **822**

St. Anthony Villa **1108**

St. Augustine's Center; Child Welfare Services Department **1085**

St. Dominic's Family Service Center **1086**

St. Joseph Children's Treatment Center **1109**

St. Joseph County Office of Family and Social Service Administration; Division of Family and Children **994**

St. Joseph's Services for Children and Families **538**

St. Louis County Social Services; Adoption Unit-5th Floor **401**

St. Mary's Children & Family Services **1087**

St. Vincent and Sarah Fisher Center **395**

The Salvation Army; Children's Services **1137**

San Diego County Adoption **39**

San Luis Obispo County Department of Social Services **41**

Sanilac County Department of Social Services **1040**

Santa Cruz County Department of Human Resources; Adoptions **44**

Saskatchewan Social Services **1191**

Schenectady County Department of Social Services **511**

Schoharie County Department of Social Services **512**

Schuylkill County Children and Youth Agency **674**

Scioto County Children Services **606**

Seguin Services Inc. **984**

Sertoma Foster Care **985**

Share Homes Foster Family Agency **933**

Sheriffs Youth Programs of Minnesota, Inc. **1051**

Jayne Shover Easter Seal Rehabilitative Center, Inc. **987**

Social and Rehabilitative Services of Vermont **798**

Society for Seamen's Children **1088**

South Carolina Department of Social Services **1146**

South Carolina Department of Social Services; Children, Family and Adult Services **709**

South Dakota Department of Social Services; Child Protection Services **1147**

South Dakota Department of Social Services; Child Protective Services **715**

Southeastern Children's Home **713**

Special Training for Exceptional People (STEP) **1060**

Specialized Alternatives For Families And Youth (S.A.F.Y.) **1110**

Spectrum Human Services **1041**

Stark County Department of Human Services **609**

State of Louisiana; Department of Social Services **264**

State of Nevada; Division of Child and Family Services **449**

Suffolk County Department of Social Services **513**

Sunbeam Family Services **1119**

Symbiont, Inc. **1111**

Talbot Perkins Children's Services **540, 1089**

Tanager Place **1003**

Teaching-Family Homes of Upper Michigan **1042**

Teen Ranch, Inc. **397**

Tender Mercy Ministries, Inc. **960**

Tennessee Baptist Children's Home, Inc. **733**

Tennessee Department of Human Services **721**

Texas Department of Human Services; Region 1 **739**

Texas Department of Protective and Regulatory Services **742, 743, 745**

Texas Department of Protective and Regulatory Services; Region 11 **746**

Texas Department of Protective and Regulatory Services; Region 5 **747**

Therapeutic Family Life **1158**

Thompson Region; Health & Family Services, Manitoba **887**

Tioga County Department of Social Services **514**

Toiyabe Indian Health Project; Family Services Department **934**

Tompkins County Department of Social Services **515**

Toutle River Boys Ranch **1168**

Try Again Homes Inc. **1138**

Tulare County Adoptions **47**

Tulsa Boys' Home **1120**

Tuscarawas County Department of Human Services **611**

Tuscola County Department of Social Services **345**

Uhlich Children's Home **988**

Union County Department of Social Services **558**

United Homes for Children, Inc. **1017**

The United Methodist Children's Home **961**

United Methodist Family Services of Virginia **836**

Utah State Department of Human Services **1159**

Ventura County Public Social Services Agency **48**

Victor C. Neumann Association **989**

The Villages of Indiana, Inc. **220, 995**

Virginia Baptist Children's Home and Family Services **837**

Virginia Department of Social Services **1165**

Virginia Department of Social Services; Bureau of Child Welfare Services **823**

Volunteers of America; Family Treatment Program **1052**

Wabash County Office, Division of Family and Children **996**

Wake County Department of Social Services **559**

Walden Environment, Inc. **935**

Warren County Children Services **612**

Washington County Children and Youth Agency **675**

Washington County Children and Youth Services **1139**

Washington County Department of Social Services **297**

Washington County Social Services **402**

Washington Department of Health and Social Services; Children, Youth & Family Services Administration **839**

Washtenaw County O'Brien Center Foster Care Program **1043**

Wayne Community Living Services, Inc. **1044**

Wedgwood Christian Youth & Family Services **1045**

West Tennessee Baptist Children's Home **735**

West Virginia Department of Human Services **856**

Westchester County Department of Social Services **517**

Westmoreland County Children's Bureau **1140**

White's Family Services **997**

Wichita Child Guidance Center; Caring Connection **1007**

Winnipeg Child and Family Services **1181**

Winnipeg Child and Family Services (East Area) **888**

Wolverine Human Services **1046**

Subject Index

Four Tribes Social Services Program **242**
Indian Child And Family Services **71**
Sault Tribe Binogii Placement Agency **396**

**Native American foster care**
Cree Nation Child & Family Caring Agency **891**
Four Tribes Social Services Program **242**
In-Care Network, Inc. **1059**
Sault Tribe Binogii Placement Agency **396**
Toiyabe Indian Health Project; Family Services Department **934**

**Open adoption**
ABC Counseling & Family Services **177**
Adoption Advisory and Counseling Service **1309**
Adoption By Choice **879**
Adoption Care Center, Inc. **15**
Adoption Centre Inc. of Kansas **234**
Adoption Connection, Inc. **129**
The Adoption Cradle, Inc. **350**
The Adoption Option, Inc. **83**
Adoption Planning, Inc. **148**
Adoption Services; Crossroads Counselling Centre **880**
The Adoption Support Center, Inc. **201**
Adoptions From The Heart **677**
Bethany Christian Services of Bellingham **844, 845**
A Bond of Love Adoption Agency **130**
Martin Brandfon; Attorney at Law **1200**
Catholic Charities Adoption Agency of San Diego **59**
Catholic Charities: Counseling Services of Collier County **132**
Catholic Charities of Houston **760**
Catholic Charities of San Francisco **60**
Catholic Community Services of Baton Rouge; Counseling, Maternity and Adoption Department **267**
Catholic Community Services of Nevada (Las Vegas) **450**
Catholic Human Services, Inc. **357**
Catholic Social Service of Belleville **182**
Catholic Social Service of Great Bend **238**
Catholic Social Service of Peoria **183**
Catholic Social Services of Lake County **619**
Catholic Social Services of Lincoln **443**
A Child Among Us - The Center for Adoption, Inc. **102**
Child and Parent Services **373**
Children's Aid Society of Utah **792**
Christian Adoption and Family Services **62**
Christian Adoption Services **881**
Christian Counseling Services **165, 726**
Christian Cradle, Inc. **375**
Chrysalis House **63**
Community Adoption Center, Inc. **865**
Community Counseling and Adoption Services of Idaho, Inc. **166**
Community, Family and Children's Services **377**
Crisis Pregnancy Outreach **646**
Designated Adoption Services of Colorado, Inc. **91**
Phylliss Eberhardy, MS, CCDCI **1289**
Fairbanks Counseling and Adoption **12**
Family And Children's Aid of Mid-Fairfield, Inc. **103**
Family Counseling Clinic, Inc. **189**
Family Options Independent Adoption Services **1206**
Family Service Agency **23**
Family Services, Inc. **566**
The Family Tree Adoption Agency, Inc. **529**

The Family Tree Adoption and Counseling Center **649**
Friends in Adoption, Inc. **1281**
Gentle Shepherd Child Placement Services **243**
Greater Love Adoption Decision (G.L.A.D.) **214**
John W. Green, III; Attorney at Law **1193**
Holy Family Services, Counseling and Adoption **70**
Homes of St. Mark **774**
Idaho Youth Ranch Adoption Services **167**
Independent Adoption Center **1212**
Innovative Adoptions, Inc. **95**
Inserco **244**
John W. Jensen; Attorney at Law **1272**
Jewish Family Service of Greater Springfield, Inc. **323**
Karen Lane; Attorney at Law **1213**
Liberal Education For Adoptive Families of Minnesota **1434**
Lutheran Family Services **446**
Lutheran Social Service of the South, Inc. (Dallas) **780**
Lutheran Social Services of Washington and Idaho **168**
Lutheran Social Services of Washington & Idaho **852**
Anthony B. Marchese; Attorney at Law **1232**
Law Offices of Diane Michelsen **1216**
Mississippi Children's Home Society and Family Service Association **419**
Nebraska Children's Home Society **447**
New Hope Child and Family Agency **854**
Open Adoption and Family Services, Inc. **661**
Open Adoption & Family Services, Inc. **662**
Precious Connections, Inc. **1293**
Private Adoptions Society of Alberta **1307**
St. Gerard's Adoption Network, Inc. **275**
Shore Adoption Service **835**
Small Miracles Foundation of the Rockies **97**
Stoker Adoption Agency **1278**
Triad Adoption and Counseling Services, Inc. **491**
The Village Family Service Center **574**
Worldwide Love for Children, Inc. **436**
Wyoming Children's Society **875**

**Permanent foster care**
Adoption Alliance **81**
Adoption Alliances; Jewish Family Services **299**
Adventist Adoption and Family Services **656**
AGAPE of Central Alabama, Inc. **3**
Alabama Department of Human Resources **2**
Albermarle Department of Social Services **804**
Albertina Kerr Center for Children **657**
The Baby Fold **178**
Baltimore County Department of Social Services **289**
Baptist Family Agency **843**
D.A. Blodgett Services for Children and Families **355**
Bristol Department of Social Services **805**
Calhoun County Department of Social Services **333**
Caroline Department of Social Services **807**
Casey Family Services; New Hampshire Division **1066**
Catholic Social Service of Peoria **183**
Catholic Social Services of Kent County **362**
Catholic Social Services of Lansing; St. Vincent Home for Children **363**
Champaign County Department of Human Services **581**

Chautauqua County Department of Social Services **494**
Chemung County Department of Social Services **495**
Child and Family Services of Western Manitoba **889, 890**
Child Protective Services; Texas Department of Protective and Regulatory Services **737**
Christian Care/Baptist Childrens Home and Family Ministry **374**
Clark County Department of Human Services **582**
Clarke County Department of Social Services **808**
Colorado State Department of Social Services **80**
Danville Division of Social Services **809**
Dauphin County Children and Youth Agency **668**
Department for Social Services; State of Kentucky **250**
Department of Community Services (Nova Scotia); Family and Children's Services **900**
Department of Health and Social Services, Alaska; Division of Family and Youth **923**
Department of Health and Welfare of Idaho; Division of Family and Community Services **163**
Department of Human Services; Division of Family and Human Services **26**
Department of Human Services; Family & Adult Services Division **159**
Department of Protective and Regulatory Services; Region 8 **738**
Division of Family and Youth Services of Alaska **9**
Downey Side...Families for Youth **526**
Dutchess County Department of Social Services **497**
El Dorado County Dept. of Social Services; Adoption Services **31**
Fairfield County Children's Services **586**
Families for Children **64**
Family and Social Services Administration of Indiana; Division of Family and Children **199**
Florida Department of Health and Rehabilitative Services **127**
Four Tribes Social Services Program **242**
Genesee County Department of Social Services **334**
Guilford County Department of Social Services; Adoption Unit **549**
Hamilton County Department of Human Services **589**
Hampton Department of Social Services **810**
Hancock County Department of Human Services; Children's Protective Services **590**
Hand In Hand Foundation **68**
Henry County Department of Social Services **811**
Henry County Family Services **422**
Hillsdale County Department of Social Services **335**
Hopewell Department of Social Services **812**
House of Samuel, Inc. **24**
Huron Services for Youth, Inc. **383**
Illinois Department of Children and Family Services; Champaign Office **171**
Ingham County Dept. of Social Services **336**
Isle of Wight Department of Social Services **813**

Department of Health and Welfare; Family and Community Services **964**
Department of Human Services; Commission on Social Services **952**
Department of Protective and Regulatory Services; Region 8 **738**
Department of Social Services; Baton Rouge Region **1012**
Division of Family Services (Delaware) **951**
Door County Counseling Services, Inc. **866**
Families of Northeast Iowa **999**
Family Adoption Consultants **379**
Family and Children's Services **472**
The Family Extension, Inc. **940**
Family Partners Worldwide, Inc. **152**
Family Resources, Inc. **1000**
Family Service And Children's Aid **381**
Florida Department of Health and Rehabilitative Services **127**
Focus on Youth, Inc. **1099**
For Love of Children; FLOC **953**
Forestdale, Inc. **1076**
Fremont County Department of Social Services **941**
Give Us This Day, Inc. **1124**
Gladwin County Department of Social Services **1025**
Ray Graham Association for People with Disabilities **972**
Greene County Division of Family Services **421**
Gulf Coast Teaching Family Services **1013**
Gunnison/Hinsdale County Department of Social Services **942**
Heartshare Human Services of New York **1077**
High Plains Children's Home & Family Services, Inc. **1156**
Highlands Child Placement Services **430**
Holt International Children's Services **659**
HOPE Adoption and Family Services International, Inc. **409**
Hope Cottage **775**
Human Resource Training, Inc. **924**
Illinois Department of Children and Family Services; Aurora Office **170**
Illinois Department of Children and Family Services; Peoria Office **174**
Infant of Prague Adoption Service **72**
Jefferson County Department of Social Services **943**
Jewels for Jesus Adoption Agency **905**
Jewish Child Care Association **1079**
Jewish Family Service of Sylvania **627**
Jewish Family Service of Tidewater, Inc. **833**
Jewish Social Service Agency; Adoption Options **307**
Johnson County Mental Retardation Center **1006**
Journeys of the Heart Adoption Services **660**
Keane Center for Adoption **387**
Kemmerer Village **976**
Mary Kendall Home; Methodist Home of Kentucky, Inc. **1009**
Kids Are Really Essential, Inc. (KARE, Inc.) **1101**
Kinship Center **74**
La Hacienda Foster Care Resource Center, Inc. **925**
LDS Social Services **388**
Les Centres jeunesse de Quebec; Centre de protection de l'enfance de la jeunesse **912**
Little Flower Children's Services **1080**
Louisiana Department of Social Services; Office of Community Services **1014**

Lutheran Child and Family Service **1032**
Lutheran Social Services of Illinois **978**
Lutheran Social Services of New England, Inc. **948**
Lutheran Social Services of New England, Inc.; Connecticut **110**
Lutheran Social Services of New England, Inc., MA **325**
Lutheran Social Services of North Dakota **572**
Luzerne County Children and Youth Agency **1132**
Macomb County Department of Social Services **1033**
Maine Department of Human Services; Social Services **1015**
Maryville Academy **980**
Massachusetts Department of Social Services **1016**
Maternity and Adoption Services of Baptist Children's Home **981**
McMahon Services for Children **1081**
Mesa County Department of Social Services **944**
Monroe County Children and Youth Services **1133**
Montcalm County Department of Social Services **1034**
Montgomery County Office of Children and Youth **1134**
Morning Star Adoption Resource Services, Inc. **392**
NAK NU WE SHA **1166**
Nebraska Department of Social Services **1064**
New Hampshire Division for Children, Youth, and Families **1067**
New Jersey Division of Youth and Family Services **1068**
New Life Adoption Agency, Inc. **536**
New York City Department of Social Services; Division of Adoption/Foster Care Services/Home Assessment Services/Centralized Services **503**
Northeast Foster Care, Inc. **1135**
Northwest Passage **1174**
NSO-Project Adopt; Project Adopt Neighborhood Services Organization, Inc. **651**
Oakland County Department of Social Services **344**
Ogemon County Department of Social Services **1035**
Ohel Children's Home and Family Services **1082**
Ontario Ministry of Community and Social Services; Adoption Unit **1188**
Open Arms Christian Home **993**
The Open Door Adoption Agency, Inc. **155**
Options for Youth, Inc. **1104**
Paraclete Social Outreach, Inc. **1105**
Parent And Child Development Services **156**
Parenthesis Family Advocates **1106**
Pinebrook Services for Children and Youth **1136**
Pius XII Youth and Family Services **1083**
Potomac Center **1172**
Quakerdale Home **1002**
Rainbow Youth and Family Services **1167**
Randolph County Department of Social Services **556**
Reverend Henry Rucker Memorial Services **983**
Richard Allen Center on Life **1084**
The James A. Roberts Agency **248**
Roscommon County Department of Social Services **1039**

Sacramento County Department of Health and Human Services **37**
St. Augustine's Center; Child Welfare Services Department **1085**
St. Dominic's Family Service Center **1086**
St. Gerard's Adoption Network, Inc. **275**
St. Joseph County Office of Family and Social Service Administration; Division of Family and Children **994**
The Salvation Army; Children's Services **1137**
Seguin Services Inc. **984**
Share Homes Foster Family Agency **933**
Sheriffs Youth Programs of Minnesota, Inc. **1051**
Society for Seamen's Children **1088**
Somerset County Department of Social Services **296**
South Carolina Department of Social Services **1146**
South Carolina Department of Social Services; Children, Family and Adult Services **709**
South Dakota Department of Social Services; Child Protection Services **1147**
Spectrum Human Services **1041**
Sunny Ridge Family Centers **197**
Symbiont, Inc. **1111**
Talbot Perkins Children's Services **1089**
Tanager Place **1003**
Toiyabe Indian Health Project; Family Services Department **934**
Toutle River Boys Ranch **1168**
Treatment Homes, Inc. **928**
Trinity Adoption Services International, Inc. **788**
Try Again Homes Inc. **1138**
Uhlich Children's Home **988**
Union County Department of Social Services **558**
United Homes for Children, Inc. **1017**
The United Methodist Children's Home **961**
Utah State Department of Human Services **1159**
Van Buren County Department of Social Services **347**
Vermont Children's Aid Society, Inc. **802**
The Village for Families and Children **113**
The Villages of Indiana, Inc. **995**
Virginia Department of Social Services **1165**
Virginia Department of Social Services; Bureau of Child Welfare Services **823**
Volunteers of America; Family Treatment Program **1052**
Wabash County Office, Division of Family and Children **996**
Walden Environment, Inc. **935**
Washington County Children and Youth Services **1139**
Wayne Community Living Services, Inc. **1044**
Westchester County Department of Social Services **517, 1090**
White's Family Services **997**
Wisconsin Department of Health and Social Services; Division of Community Services **859, 1175**
Young House Family Services **1004**
Youth Engaged for Success, Inc. **1112**
Youth Focus, Inc. **1092**
Youth Services Network of S.W.O., Inc. **1113**

**Protective foster care**
Texas Department of Protection and Regulatory Services **741**

**Public agencies**
Alabama Department of Human Resources **2**

Kalamazoo County Department of Social Services **337**

Kent County Department of Social Services **338**

Knox County Children's Services/Department of Human Services **591**

Lafayette Regional Office of Community Services **261, 1605**

Lake County Department of Social Services **1029**

Lancaster County Children and Youth Social Service Agency **671**

Lawrence County Department Of Human Services **592**

Lenawee County Department of Social Services **339**

Lenoir County Department of Social Services **551**

Licking County Department of Human Services **593**

Logan County Children's Services Board **594**

Louisiana Department of Social Services; Office of Community Services **1014**

Lucas County Children's Service Board **595**

Luzerne County Children and Youth Agency **1132**

Macomb County Department of Social Services **340, 1033**

Madison County Department of Human Services **596**

Mahoning County Children Services **597**

Maine Department of Human Services; Child and Family Services **280**

Maine Department of Human Services; Social Services **1015**

Marin County Department of Health and Human Services; Adoptions **33**

Merced County Human Services Agency **34**

Mercer County Department of Human Services **599**

Mesa County Department of Social Services **944**

Michigan Department of Social Services **341**

Michigan Department of Social Services; Northern Michigan Adoption Program **342**

Mississippi Department of Human Services **416**

Missouri Department of Social Services **423**

Monroe County Department of Human Services **600**

Monroe County Department of Social Services **343**

Montcalm County Department of Social Services **1034**

Montgomery County Children Services **601**

Montgomery County Department of Social Services **294**

Montgomery County Office of Children and Youth **672, 1134**

Nash County Department of Social Services **552**

Nebraska Department of Social Services **440, 1064**

Nelson Department of Social Services **815**

New Hampshire Division for Children, Youth, and Families **1067**

New Hanover County Department of Social Services **553**

New Jersey Division of Youth and Family Services **1068**

New Jersey Division of Youth and Family Services; Adoption Unit **460**

New Jersey Division of Youth and Family Services; Adoption Unit (for mid-Jersey) **461**

New York City Department of Social Services; Division of Adoption/Foster Care Services/Home Assessment Services/Centralized Services **503**

Newport News Department of Social Services **816**

Niagara County Department of Social Services **504**

Noble County Department of Human Services **602**

North Dakota Department of Human Services; Division of Children and Family Services **569**

Nottoway Department of Social Services **817**

Oakland County Department of Social Services **344**

Office of Community Service (of Alexandria, LA) **262**

Office of Community Services; Lake Charles Region **263**

Ogemon County Department of Social Services **1035**

Oklahoma Department of Human Services **638**

Onondaga County Department of Social Services **505**

Orange County Department of Social Services **506, 554**

County of Orange Social Service Agency; Adoptions Program **35**

Oregon Childrens Services Division **655**

Otsego County Department of Social Services **507, 1036**

Ottawa County Department of Human Services **603**

Payne County Youth Services **1118**

Perry County Children's Services **604**

Philadelphia County Children and Youth Agency **673**

Pitt County Department of Social Services **555**

Portsmouth Department of Social Services **818**

Prince George's County Department of Social Services **295**

Pulaski Department of Social Services **819**

Putnam County Department of Human Services **605**

Putnam County Department of Social Services **508**

Radford Department of Welfare and Social Services **820**

Randolph County Department of Social Services **556**

Rensselaer County Department of Social Services **509**

Rhode Island Department for Children, Youth & Families **704**

City of Richmond Department of Social Services **821**

Riverside County Department of Social Services **36**

Roscommon County Department of Social Services **1039**

Rowan County Department of Social Services **557**

Russell County Department of Social Services **822**

Sacramento County Department of Health and Human Services **37**

St. Joseph County Office of Family and Social Service Administration; Division of Family and Children **994**

St. Lawrence County Department of Social Services **510**

St. Louis County Social Services; Adoption Unit-5th Floor **401**

San Bernardino Adoption Service **38**

San Diego County Adoption **39**

San Francisco Department of Social Services; Adoption Services **40**

San Luis Obispo County Department of Social Services **41**

Sanilac County Department of Social Services **1040**

Santa Barbara County Department of Social Services **42**

Santa Clara County Social Services Agency - Adoptions **43**

Santa Cruz County Department of Human Resources; Adoptions **44**

Saskatchewan Adoptive Parents Association **1592**

Schenectady County Department of Social Services **511**

Schoharie County Department of Social Services **512**

Schuylkill County Children and Youth Agency **674**

Scioto County Children Services **606**

Seneca County Department of Human Services **607**

Shasta County Adoptions **45**

Shelby County Children Services Board **608**

Social and Rehabilitative Services of Vermont **798**

Somerset County Department of Social Services **296**

South Carolina Department of Social Services **1146**

South Carolina Department of Social Services; Children, Family and Adult Services **709**

South Dakota Department of Social Services; Child Protection Services **1147**

South Dakota Department of Social Services; Child Protective Services **715**

Stark County Department of Human Services **609**

State Department of Social Services; Chico District Office **46**

State of Louisiana; Department of Social Services **264**

State of Nevada; Division of Child and Family Services **449**

Suffolk County Department of Social Services **513**

Summit County Children Services Board **610**

Tennessee Department of Human Services **721**

Texas Department of Human Services; Region 1 **739**

Texas Department of Human Services; Region 7 **740**

Texas Department of Protection and Regulatory Services **741**

Texas Department of Protective and Regulatory Services **742, 743, 744, 745**

Texas Department of Protective and Regulatory Services; Region 11 **746**

Texas Department of Protective and Regulatory Services; Region 5 **747**

Texas Department of Protective and Regulatory Services; Region 6 **748**

Tioga County Department of Social Services **514**

Tompkins County Department of Social Services **515**

Tulare County Adoptions **47**

Tuscarawas County Department of Human Services **611**

Tuscola County Department of Social Services **345**

Department of Human Services; Division of Family and Human Services **26**

Department of Human Services; Family & Adult Services Division **159**

Department of Protective and Regulatory Services; Region 8 **738**

Department of Social Services; Baton Rouge Region **1012**

Division of Family and Children's Services; Agency 2 - Georgia **956**

Division of Family Services (Delaware) **951**

Erie County Children and Youth Agency **670**

Erie County Department of Human Services **585**

Essex County Department of Social Services **499**

Families First **958**

Family Support; Government of the Northwest Territories Department of Health and Social Services **1184**

Florida Department of Health and Rehabilitative Services **127**

For Love of Children; FLOC **953**

Forsyth County Department of Social Services **548**

Franklin County Department of Children's Services **587**

Fulton County Department of Social Services **500**

Gunnison/Hinsdale County Department of Social Services **942**

Hamilton County Department of Social Services **501**

Healing the Children Northeast, Inc. **946**

Health and Community Services Agency **1189**

Henry County Family Services **422**

Hephzibah Children's Association **974**

Hillsdale County Department of Social Services **335**

Illinois Department of Children and Family Services; Aurora Office **170**

Illinois Department of Children and Family Services; Champaign Office **171**

Illinois Department of Children and Family Services; Marion Office **173**

Illinois Department of Children and Family Services; Rockford Office **175**

James City Department of Social Services **814**

Jewish Family Service of Greater Springfield, Inc. **323**

Juvenile Services, Inc. **1116**

Kansas Children's Service League **245**

LDS Social Services of Ogden **794**

Lifelink/Bensenville Home Society **191**

Lucas County Children's Service Board **595**

Lutheran Children & Family Service **698**

Lutheran Community Services, Inc. **532**

Lutheran Family Services in the Carolinas **567**

Lutheran Social Services of Fort Wayne **217**

Lutheran Social Services of New England, Inc., MA **325**

Lutheran Social Services of South Dakota **719**

Lydia Home Association **979**

Manitoba Department of Family Services; Child and Family Support Branch **886**

Massachusetts Department of Social Services **1016**

Merced County Human Services Agency **34**

Mesa County Department of Social Services **944**

Ministry of Social Services **1177**

Monroe County Department of Human Services **600**

Montgomery County Department of Social Services **294**

Montgomery County Office of Children and Youth **672**

Nebraska Department of Social Services **440, 1064**

New Brunswick Department of Health and Community Service **1182**

New Hampshire Catholic Charities, Inc. **458**

New Jersey Division of Youth and Family Services **1068**

New York City Department of Social Services; Division of Adoption/Foster Care Services/Home Assessment Services/ Centralized Services **503**

Newfoundland Department of Social Services **1183**

Noble County Department of Human Services **602**

Oakland County Department of Social Services **344**

Orange County Department of Social Services **506**

Philadelphia County Children and Youth Agency **673**

Portsmouth Department of Social Services **818**

Prince George's County Department of Social Services **295**

Putnam County Department of Social Services **508**

Rainbow Services for Youth and Families **1038**

Rensselaer County Department of Social Services **509**

City of Richmond Department of Social Services **821**

Russell County Department of Social Services **822**

St. Mary's Children & Family Services **1087**

St. Vincent and Sarah Fisher Center **395**

Saskatchewan Social Services **1191**

Schenectady County Department of Social Services **511**

Schoharie County Department of Social Services **512**

Shelby County Children Services Board **608**

Social and Rehabilitative Services of Vermont **798**

South Carolina Department of Social Services **1146**

South Carolina Department of Social Services; Children, Family and Adult Services **709**

State of Louisiana; Department of Social Services **264**

Suffolk County Department of Social Services **513**

Suncoast International Adoptions, Inc. **145**

Toiyabe Indian Health Project; Family Services Department **934**

Tompkins County Department of Social Services **515**

Virginia Department of Social Services **1165**

Virginia Department of Social Services; Bureau of Child Welfare Services **823**

Volunteers of America **278**

Wasatch Adoptions and Children's Services **795**

Washington County Children and Youth Agency **675**

Washington County Children and Youth Services **1139**

Washington Department of Health and Social Services; Children, Youth & Family Services Administration **839**

Westchester County Department of Social Services **517**

Westmoreland County Children's Bureau **1140**

Wicomico County Department of Social Services **298**

Winnipeg Child and Family Services **1181**

Wyoming Children's Society **875**

**Single parents**

ABC Counseling & Family Services **177**

Adoption Advocates **753**

Adoption Links Worldwide **441**

Advocates for Single Adoption Parenting (ASAP) **1324**

Associated Catholic Charities **121**

The Baby Fold **178**

Blessed Trinity Adoptions, Inc. **759**

Brown County Department of Human Services **578**

Calhoun County Department of Social Services **333**

Champaign County Department of Human Services **581**

Child Placement Center/Agape Social Services **764**

Child Protective Services; Texas Department of Protective and Regulatory Services **737**

Children, Youth and Families Dept. (New Mexico); Social Services Division **483**

Children's Aid Society of Mercer County **692**

Children's Home of Northern Kentucky **253**

Christian Adoption Services, Inc. **565**

Committee for Single Adoptive Parents **1416**

Coshocton County Children Services Board **583**

Department for Social Services; State of Kentucky **250**

Department of Human Services; Division of Family and Human Services **26**

Department of Social Services **258**

DePelchin Children's Center **770**

Erie County Children and Youth Agency **670**

Family Connections Adoption Agency **65**

The Family Tree Adoption Agency, Inc. **529**

Franklin County Department of Children's Services **587**

Greene County Division of Family Services **421**

Growing Families, Inc. **474**

HARAMBEE: Services to Black Families **626**

Hearts & Homes For Children **141**

HOPE Adoption and Family Services International, Inc. **409**

Hope's Promise **94**

Illinois Department of Children and Family Services; Marion Office **173**

Kansas Children's Service League **245**

Kansas Children's Service League; Black Adoption Program **246**

Lafayette Regional Office of Community Services **261, 1605**

Love Basket, Inc. **433**

Lutheran Social Services **124**

Lutheran Social Services of Illinois; Foster, Adoption and Maternity Services **192**

Madison County Department of Human Services **596**

Marion County Children Service Board **598**

Marywood Children and Family Services **781**

Methodist Home of Kentucky; Mary Kendall Adoptions **256**

Mission of the Immaculate Virgin - Mount Loretto **533**

New Hanover County Department of Social Services **553**

New Life Adoption Services **194**

Catholic Social Services of Lansing; St. Vincent Home for Children 363
Catholic Social Services of Milwaukee 864
Catholic Social Services of Monroe County 364
Catholic Social Services of South Bend 209
Catholic Social Services of Southwestern Ohio 620
Catholic Social Services of Vineland 469
Cecil County Department of Social Services 292
Central Baptist Family Services 184
Champaign County Department of Human Services 581
Chautauqua County Department of Social Services 494
Chemung County Department of Social Services 495
Child and Family Service of Holt 368
Child and Family Services 725
Child and Family Services Division; Adoption Resources Branch 118
Child and Family Services of Holland 369
Child and Family Services of Michigan, Inc. (Howell) 370
Child and Family Services of Saginaw County 371
Child and Family Services of Southwestern Michigan, Inc. 372
Child and Family Services of Western Manitoba 889, 890
Child Placement Center/Agape Social Services 764
Child Placement Center of Texas 765
Child Protective Services; Texas Department of Protective and Regulatory Services 737
Child-Rite, Inc. 486
Child Saving Institute 444
Children Awaiting Parents, Inc. 1598
Children Unlimited, Inc. 711
Children, Youth and Families Dept. (New Mexico); Social Services Division 483
Children's Aid Home and Society of Somerset County 689
The Children's Aid Society of Clearfield, PA 690
The Children's Aid Society of Franklin County 691
Children's Aid Society of New York 524
Children's Bureau of Indianapolis 211
Children's Choice 305
Children's Foundation - Adoption and Counseling 240
Children's Friend and Service 706
Children's Home and Aid Society of Illinois 185
The Children's Home Society of Florida 137
Children's Home Society of Minnesota 407
The Children's Home Society of Missouri 427
Children's Home Society of New Jersey 470
The Children's Home Society of North Carolina 564
Children's Home Society of Virginia 828
Children's Service Society of Utah 793
Christian Family Care Agency 20
Christian Family Services, Inc. 428
Christian Homes; A Program of Louisiana Child Care and Placement Services, Inc. 269
Christian Homes for Children 471
Christ's Haven for Children 767
Chrysalis House 63
Church of God Home for Children 727
Clark County Department of Human Services 582

Clarke County Department of Social Services 808
Cleveland County Department of Social Services 544
Coleman Adoption Services, Inc. 212
Colorado State Department of Social Services 80
Commonwealth Adoptions International, Inc. 21
Community Adoption Center, Inc. 865
Community Maternity Services 525
Concord Family Service 319
Coordinators/2, Inc. 829
Cradle of Hope Adoption Center, Inc. 122
The Cradle Society 186
Craven County Department of Social Services 545
Crossroads, Inc. 408
Cumberland County Department of Social Services 546
Cuyohoga County Department of Children and Family Services 584
Danville Division of Social Services 809
Dauphin County Children and Youth Agency 668
Davidson County Department of Social Services 547
Delaware County Children and Youth 669
Delaware County Department of Social Services 496
Department for Social Services; State of Kentucky 250
Department of Children and Youth Services, CT 99
Department of Children's Services; Adoptions Division 30
Department of Community Services (Nova Scotia); Family and Children's Services 900
Department of Family Services of Montana 438
Department of Family Services of Wyoming 874
Department of Health and Welfare of Idaho; Division of Family and Community Services 163
Department of Human Services; Division of Family and Human Services 26
Department of Human Services; Family & Adult Services Division 159
Department of Protective and Regulatory Services; Region 8 738
Department of Social and Rehabilitative Services; Youth & Adult Services 232
Department of Social Services 258
Department of Social Services (of Baton Rouge); Office of Community Services 259
Department of Social Services, Newfoundland 896
Department of Social Services of Louisiana; Division of Children, Youth & Family Services 260
Department of Social Services of Massachusetts 309
DePelchin Children's Center 770
Division for Children, Youth and Families, New Hampshire 455
Division of Family and Children's Services (Georgia); State Adoption Unit 147
Division of Family and Youth Services of Alaska 9
Division of Family Services; Delaware Youth and Family Center 115
Door County Counseling Services, Inc. 866

Down Syndrome Association of Los Angeles 1333
Downey Side...Families for Youth 526
Dutchess County Department of Social Services 497
Edmonton Adopting Beyond Infancy Association 1567
El Dorado County Dept. of Social Services; Adoption Services 31
Erie County Children and Youth Agency 670
Erie County Department of Social Services 498
Essex County Department of Social Services 499
Evangelical Child and Family Agency 187, 867
Evergreen Children's Services 378
Fairfield County Children's Services 586
Families for Children 64
Family Adoption Consultants 379
Family And Child Services of Washington, DC 123
Family and Children's Service 728
Family and Children's Services of Calhoun County 380
Family and Social Services Administration of Indiana; Division of Family and Children 199
Family Care Services 188
Family Connections Adoption Agency 65
Family Focus Adoption Services 527
The Family Foundation 849
The Family Network, Inc. 66
Family Partners Worldwide, Inc. 152
Family Service 694
Family Service And Children's Aid 381
Family Service and Children's Aid Society of Venango County 695
Family Service of Westchester 528
The Family Tree Adoption Agency, Inc. 529
The Family Tree Adoption and Counseling Center 649
Florida Department of Health and Rehabilitative Services 127
Forsyth County Department of Social Services 548
Franklin County Department of Children's Services 587
Frederick County Department of Social Services 293
Fresno County Department of Social Services 32
Friends of Children of Various Nations, Inc. 92
Fulton County Department of Social Services 500
Future Families, Inc. 67
Genesee County Department of Social Services 334
Gift of Life, Inc. Adoption Services 140
Golden Cradle Adoption Services, Inc. 473
Edwin Gould Services for Children 530
Greater Boston Catholic Charities 321
Greene County Division of Family Services 421
Guernsey County Childrens Services Board 588
Guilford County Department of Social Services; Adoption Unit 549
Hall Neighborhood House, Inc.; Adoption Services 105
Hamilton County Department of Human Services 589
Hampton Department of Social Services 810
Hancock County Department of Human Services; Children's Protective Services 590
Hand In Hand Foundation 68

Subject Index

Sacramento County Department of Health and Human Services **37**
St. Elizabeth's Home **219**
St. Joseph's Services for Children and Families **538**
St. Lawrence County Department of Social Services **510**
St. Louis County Social Services; Adoption Unit-5th Floor **401**
St. Vincent Adoption Services **144**
St. Vincent and Sarah Fisher Center **395**
San Bernardino Adoption Service **38**
San Diego County Adoption **39**
San Francisco Department of Social Services; Adoption Services **40**
San Luis Obispo County Department of Social Services **41**
Santa Barbara County Department of Social Services **42**
Santa Clara County Social Services Agency - Adoptions **43**
Santa Cruz County Department of Human Resources; Adoptions **44**
Saskatchewan Social Services **918**
Schenectady County Department of Social Services **511**
Schoharie County Department of Social Services **512**
Schuylkill County Children and Youth Agency **674**
Scioto County Children Services **606**
Seegers Lutheran Center; Lutheran Child and Family Services **196**
Seneca County Department of Human Services **607**
Shasta County Adoptions **45**
Shelby County Children Services Board **608**
Sierra Adoption Services **78**
Small Miracles International **652, 653**
Social and Rehabilitative Services of Vermont **798**
Societe D'Adoption Quebecoise Une Grande Famille **914**
Somerset County Department of Social Services **296**
South Carolina Department of Social Services; Children, Family and Adult Services **709**
South Dakota Department of Social Services; Child Protective Services **715**
Southeastern Children's Home **713**
The Southeastern Exchange of the United States **1612**
Spaulding for Children **481**
Special Children, Inc. **871**
Special Delivery Adoption Services, Inc. **277**
Special Needs Adoption Network **1613**
Stark County Department of Human Services **609**
State Department of Social Services; Chico District Office **46**
State of Louisiana; Department of Social Services **264**
State of Nevada; Division of Child and Family Services **449**
Suffolk County Department of Social Services **513**
Summit County Children Services Board **610**
Sunny Ridge Family Centers **197**
Talbot Perkins Children's Services **540**
Teen Ranch, Inc. **397**
Tennessee Conference Adoption Service **734**
Tennessee Department of Human Services **721**
Texas Department of Human Services; Region 1 **739**

Texas Department of Human Services; Region 7 **740**
Texas Department of Protection and Regulatory Services **741**
Texas Department of Protective and Regulatory Services **742, 743, 744, 745**
Texas Department of Protective and Regulatory Services; Region 11 **746**
Texas Department of Protective and Regulatory Services; Region 5 **747**
Texas Department of Protective and Regulatory Services; Region 6 **748**
Leslie Thacker Agency, Inc. **787**
Thompson Region; Health & Family Services, Manitoba **887**
Three Rivers Adoption Council **1614**
Tioga County Department of Social Services **514**
Tompkins County Department of Social Services **515**
Tressler Lutheran Services **702**
Tulare County Adoptions **47**
Tuscarawas County Department of Human Services **611**
Tuscola County Department of Social Services **345**
Union County Department of Social Services **558**
United Methodist Family Services of Virginia **836**
Upper Michigan Adoption Program **346**
Utah Department of Social Services **790**
Van Buren County Department of Social Services **347**
Ventura County Public Social Services Agency **48**
Vermont Catholic Charities, Inc. **801**
Vermont Children's Aid Society, Inc. **802**
Villa Hope **7**
The Village Family Service Center **574**
The Village for Families and Children **113**
The Villages of Indiana, Inc. **220**
Virginia Department of Social Services; Bureau of Child Welfare Services **823**
Volunteers of America **278**
Wake County Department of Social Services **559**
Warren County Children Services **612**
Warren County Department of Social Services **516**
Washington County Children and Youth Agency **675**
Washington County Department of Social Services **297**
Washington County Social Services **402**
Washington Department of Health and Social Services; Children, Youth & Family Services Administration **839**
Wayne County Child and Family Services **348**
West Tennessee Baptist Children's Home **735**
West Virginia Department of Human Services **856**
Westchester County Department of Social Services **517**
Wicomico County Department of Social Services **298**
Winnipeg Child and Family Services (East Area) **888**
Wisconsin Department of Health and Social Services; Division of Community Services **859**
Wood County Department of Human Services **613**
World Child, Inc. **125**
Wyoming Children's Society **875**

Wyoming County Department of Social Services **518**
Wyoming Parenting Society **876**
York County Children and Youth Services **676**

**Temporary foster care**
Adoption Advocates **753**
Adoption Affiliates **639**
Adoption Affiliates, Inc. **754**
Adoption Alliance **81**
Adoption Alliances; Jewish Family Services **299**
Adoption Associates, Inc. **349**
The Adoption Center **640**
Adoption Center, Inc. **310**
Adoption Choice Center **82**
Adoption Connection of Jewish Family and Children's Services **51**
The Adoption Cradle, Inc. **350**
Adoption Option **235**
The Adoption Option, Inc. **83**
Adoption Planning, Inc. **148**
Adoption Resource of Jewish Family and Children's Services, Boston **311**
Adoption Services Associates **755**
Adoptions: Advocacy and Alternatives **84**
Adoptions Forever, Inc. **301**
Adoptions Unlimited **54**
Adventist Adoption and Family Services **656**
AGAPE of Central Alabama, Inc. **3**
AGAPE of North Alabama, Inc. **4**
Alamance County Department of Social Services **543**
Albermarle Department of Social Services **804**
Allegany County Department of Social Services **286**
Alliance for Children, Inc. **312**
American Adoptions **236**
The Angel Guardian Home **519**
Arizona Children's Home Association **17**
Arizona Department of Economic Security **14**
Ashtabula County Children Services Board **576**
Associated Catholic Charities **121**
Associated Catholic Charities of East Tennessee **722**
Associated Catholic Charities of Oklahoma City **642**
Baltimore City Department of Human Resources **288**
Baptist Children's Home and Family Ministries **204**
Baptist Family Agency **843**
Belmont County Children Services Board **577**
Berkshire Center for Families and Children **314**
Bethanna **678**
Bethany Adoption Service, Inc. of Oklahoma **643**
Bethany Christian Services **464**
Bethany Christian Services (of Baton Rouge) **265**
Bethany Christian Services (of Des Moines) **223**
Bethany Christian Services (of Grand Rapids) **353**
Bethany Christian Services (of Indiana) **205**
Bethany Christian Services, North Region **57**
Bethany Christian Services of Asheville **560**
Bethany Christian Services of Bellingham **845**
Bethany Christian Services of Chattenooga **723**
Bethany Christian Services of Evergreen Park **179**
Bethany Christian Services of Ft. Washington **679**

Department of Community Services (Nova Scotia); Family and Children's Services **900**

Department of Family Services of Montana **438**

Department of Family Services of Wyoming **874**

Department of Health and Social Services; Government of the Yukon **1192**

Department of Social and Rehabilitative Services; Youth & Adult Services **232**

Department of Social Services **258**

Department of Social Services (of Baton Rouge); Office of Community Services **259**

Department of Social Services, Newfoundland **896**

Department of Social Services of Louisiana; Division of Children, Youth & Family Services **260**

Department of Social Services of Massachusetts **309**

DePelchin Children's Center **770**

Designated Adoption Services of Colorado, Inc. **91**

Dillon International, Inc. **648**

Dillon Southwest **22**

Division for Children, Youth and Families, New Hampshire **455**

Division of Family and Children's Services (Georgia); State Adoption Unit **147**

Division of Family and Youth Services of Alaska **9**

Division of Family Services; Delaware Youth and Family Center **115**

Dutchess County Department of Social Services **497**

El Dorado County Dept. of Social Services; Adoption Services **31**

Evangelical Child and Family Agency **187, 867**

Evergreen Children's Services **378**

Fairbanks Counseling and Adoption **12**

Families for Children; A Division of New Mexico Boys Ranch **488**

Family And Child Services of Washington, DC **123**

Family And Children's Aid of Mid-Fairfield, Inc. **103**

Family and Social Services Administration of Indiana; Division of Family and Children **199**

Family Care Services **188**

Family Life Services **241, 831**

The Family Network, Inc. **66**

Family Service **694**

Family Service Agency **23**

Family Service And Children's Aid **381**

Family Service and Children's Aid Society of Venango County **695**

Family Service of Summit County **625**

Family Service of Westchester **528**

Family Services, Inc. **566**

Forsyth County Department of Social Services **548**

Four Tribes Social Services Program **242**

Franciscan Family Care Center, Inc. **104**

Friends of Children of Various Nations, Inc. **92**

Future Families, Inc. **67**

Gail House **270**

Genesee County Department of Social Services **334**

Gift of Life, Inc. Adoption Services **140**

Gift of Love Adoption Agency **771**

The Gladney Center **772**

Golden Cradle Adoption Services, Inc. **473**

Good Samaritan Agency **281**

Edwin Gould Services for Children **530**

Greater Boston Catholic Charities **321**

Greater Love Adoption Decision (G.L.A.D.) **214**

Greene County Division of Family Services **421**

Guernsey County Childrens Services Board **588**

Guilford County Department of Social Services; Adoption Unit **549**

Hall Neighborhood House, Inc.; Adoption Services **105**

Hamilton County Department of Human Services **589**

Hampton Department of Social Services **810**

Hancock County Department of Human Services; Children's Protective Services **590**

Hand In Hand International Adoptions **93**

Harlem-Dowling West Side Center for Children and Family Services **531**

Harnett County Department of Social Services **550**

HELP of Door County **1173**

Henry County Department of Social Services **811**

Hillcrest Family Services **229**

Hillside Children's Center **1078**

Holy Family Services, Counseling and Adoption **70**

Hope Adoptions, Inc. **322**

HOPE for Children, Inc. **154**

Hope's Promise **94**

Hopewell Department of Social Services **812**

House of Samuel, Inc. **24**

Huron Services for Youth, Inc. **383**

Idaho Youth Ranch Adoption Services **167**

Illinois Department of Children and Family Services; Aurora Office **170**

Indian Child And Family Services **71**

Ingham County Dept. of Social Services **336**

Innovative Adoptions, Inc. **95**

Isle of Wight Department of Social Services **813**

Jefferson County Department of Social Services **502**

Jewish Child and Family Service **892**

Jewish Family and Children's Services **696**

Jewish Family and Community Services **142**

Jewish Family Service **729, 850**

Jewish Family Service of Southfield, Michigan **385**

Jewish Family Service of Tidewater, Inc. **832**

Jewish Family Services of Dayton **629**

Judson Center **386**

Kalamazoo County Department of Social Services **337**

Kansas Children's Service League; Black Adoption Program **246**

Knox County Children's Services/Department of Human Services **591**

Lafayette Regional Office of Community Services **261, 1605**

Lawrence County Department Of Human Services **592**

LDS Social Services **718**

Lenawee County Department of Social Services **339**

Lenoir County Department of Social Services **551**

Licking County Department of Human Services **593**

Lifeline Children's Services, Inc. **6**

LIGHT House Adoption Agency **432**

Logan County Children's Services Board **594**

Love Basket, Inc. **433**

Loving Alternative Adoption Agency **778**

Lutheran Child and Family Services **216**

Lutheran Family and Children's Services of Missouri **434**

Lutheran Family Services **446**

Lutheran Family Services of Colorado **96**

Lutheran Social Ministries of New Jersey **480**

Lutheran Social Service of Minnesota **411**

Lutheran Social Service of the South (Austin) **779**

Lutheran Social Service of the South, Inc. (Dallas) **780**

Lutheran Social Services **124, 390**

Lutheran Social Services of Central Ohio **631**

Lutheran Social Services of Illinois; Foster, Adoption and Maternity Services **192**

Lutheran Social Services of Indiana **218**

Lutheran Social Services of Iowa **230**

Lutheran Social Services of the Miami Valley **632**

Lutheran Social Services of Wisconsin and Upper Michigan **869**

Macomb County Department of Social Services **340**

Madison County Department of Human Services **596**

Mahoning County Children Services **597**

The Maine Children's Home for Little Wanderers **282**

Marin County Department of Health and Human Services; Adoptions **33**

Marion County Children Service Board **598**

Marywood Children and Family Services **781**

Maternity and Adoption Services of Baptist Children's Home **193**

Medina Children's Services **853**

Mercer County Department of Human Services **599**

MetroCenter for Family Ministries, Inc. **650**

Michigan Department of Social Services **341**

Michigan Department of Social Services; Northern Michigan Adoption Program **342**

Mid-Western Children's Home **634**

Mission of the Immaculate Virgin - Mount Loretto **533**

Mississippi Department of Human Services **416**

Missouri Department of Social Services **423**

Monroe County Department of Social Services **343**

Montgomery County Children Services **601**

Lee and Beulah Moor Children's Home **782**

Nash County Department of Social Services **552**

Nebraska Children's Home Society **447**

Nelson Department of Social Services **815**

New England Home for Little Wanderers **326**

New Hanover County Department of Social Services **553**

New Haven Family Alliance **111**

New Hope Family Services, Inc. **535**

New Horizons Adoptions **573**

New Jersey Division of Youth and Family Services; Adoption Unit **460**

New Jersey Division of Youth and Family Services; Adoption Unit (for mid-Jersey) **461**

New Life Christian Services **783**

New Life Family Services **413**

Newport News Department of Social Services **816**

Niagara County Department of Social Services **504**

Department of Community Services; Family and Children's Services **1185**

Department of Health and Social Services; Government of the Yukon **1192**

Department of Health and Welfare; Family and Community Services **964**

Department of Protective and Regulatory Services; Region 8 **738**

DePelchin Children's Center **770**

Division of Family Services; Delaware Youth and Family Center **115**

East Arkansas Regional Mental Health Center; Therapeutic Foster Care Program **927**

Erie County Children and Youth Agency **670**

Evangelical Child and Family Agency **187**

Families First **958**

Families for Children **64**

Families of Northeast Iowa **999**

Family and Educational Advisory Associates **1148**

The Family Extension, Inc. **940**

Family Life Services of New England **1161**

Family Service, Inc. **1144**

Family Support; Government of the Northwest Territories Department of Health and Social Services **1184**

Family Ties Therapeutic Foster Care; St. Joseph Orphanage **1098**

The Family Tree Adoption and Counseling Center **649**

Florida Department of Health and Rehabilitative Services **127**

For Love of Children; FLOC **953**

Forest Ridge Youth Services **1001**

Franklin County Department of Children's Services **587**

Fremont County Department of Social Services **941**

Future Families, Inc. **67**

Genesis Project **1114**

Gift of Life, Inc. Adoption Services **140**

Golden Triangle Community Mental Health Center **1058**

Ray Graham Association for People with Disabilities **972**

Gulf Coast Teaching Family Services **1013**

Gunnison/Hinsdale County Department of Social Services **942**

Habilitative Services, Inc. **1049**

Harborcreek Youth Services **1131**

Healing the Children - New Mexico Chapter **1069**

Health and Community Services Agency **1189**

Heartshare Human Services of New York **1077**

Hillcrest Health Center; Therapeutic Foster Care **1115**

Hogares, Inc. **1070**

Homes for Kids, Inc. **1100**

Human Resource Training, Inc. **924**

Huron Valley Child Guidance Clinic **1028**

Illinois Department of Children and Family Services; Aurora Office **170**

Illinois Department of Children and Family Services; Champaign Office **171**

Illinois Department of Children and Family Services; Rockford Office **175**

In-Care Network, Inc. **1059**

Indiana Youth Advocate Program, Inc. **992**

The Institute of Professional Practice (I.P.P.) **947**

Jackson County Community Mental Health Center **975**

Jefferson County Department of Social Services **943**

Jewish Child Care Association **1079**

Joy Home for Boys; P.A.T.H. **1157**

Kemmerer Village **976**

Kids Are Really Essential, Inc. (KARE, Inc.) **1101**

Kinship Center **74**

La Familia Placement Services, Inc. **489**

La Hacienda Foster Care Resource Center, Inc. **925**

Lafayette Regional Office of Community Services **261**

Lakeside Residence for Boys and Girls **1030**

Listening Ear Crisis Center, Inc. **1031**

Little Flower Children's Services **1080**

Louisiana Department of Social Services; Office of Community Services **1014**

Lutheran Child and Family Service **1032**

Lutheran Social Services of Illinois **978**

Lutheran Social Services of Iowa **230**

Lutheran Social Services of New England, Inc. **948**

Luzerne County Children and Youth Agency **1132**

Lydia Home Association **979**

Macomb County Department of Social Services **1033**

Maine Department of Human Services; Social Services **1015**

Manitoba Department of Family Services; Child and Family Support Branch **886**

Marion County Children Service Board **598**

The Marsh Foundation Teaching-Family Program **1102**

Maryville Academy **980**

Marywood Children and Family Services **781**

Ada S. McKinley Foster Care and Adoption Services **982**

Mentor Clinical Care **1103**

Mesa County Department of Social Services **944**

Ministry of Social Services **1177**

Monroe County Children and Youth Services **1133**

Montcalm County Department of Social Services **1034**

Montgomery County Office of Children and Youth **1134**

Mountain Circle Foster Family Agency **931**

Nebraska Department of Social Services **440, 1064**

New Brunswick Department of Health and Community Service **1182**

New Hampshire Division for Children, Youth, and Families **1067**

New Jersey Division of Youth and Family Services **1068**

New York City Department of Social Services; Division of Adoption/Foster Care Services/Home Assessment Services/ Centralized Services **503**

Newfoundland Department of Social Services **1183**

Northeast Ohio Adoption Services **635**

Northern Valley Catholic Social Service **932**

Northern Virginia Family Service **1163**

Northwest Passage **1174**

Ogemon County Department of Social Services **1035**

Oklahoma Department of Human Services **638**

Open Arms Christian Home **993**

Paraclete Social Outreach, Inc. **1105**

Parenthesis Family Advocates **1106**

Payne County Youth Services **1118**

People Places, Inc. **1164**

Perry County Children's Services **604**

Philadelphia County Children and Youth Agency **673**

The Phoenix Institute for Adolescents, Inc. **959**

Pinebrook Services for Children and Youth **1136**

Potomac Center **1172**

Professional Parenting/Adoption Plus **1091**

Putnam County Department of Social Services **508**

Quakerdale Home **1002**

Rainbow Services for Youth and Families **1038**

Rainbow Youth and Family Services **1167**

Rosemont Center **1107**

St. Anthony Villa **1108**

St. Augustine's Center; Child Welfare Services Department **1085**

St. Joseph Children's Treatment Center **1109**

St. Joseph County Office of Family and Social Service Administration; Division of Family and Children **994**

St. Joseph's Services for Children and Families **538**

The Salvation Army; Children's Services **1137**

San Francisco Department of Social Services; Adoption Services **40**

Saskatchewan Social Services **918, 1191**

Seven Counties Services, Inc.; Daybreak Family Treatment Homes **1010**

Share Homes Foster Family Agency **933**

Sheriffs Youth Programs of Minnesota, Inc. **1051**

South Carolina Department of Social Services **1146**

South Dakota Department of Social Services; Child Protection Services **1147**

Special Training for Exceptional People (STEP) **1060**

Specialized Alternatives For Families And Youth (S.A.F.Y.) **1110**

Suffolk County Department of Social Services **513**

Sunbeam Family Services **1119**

Symbiont, Inc. **1111**

Tanager Place **1003**

Texas Department of Protective and Regulatory Services; Region 11 **746**

Therapeutic Community Services; Presbyterian Foster Care Program **1011**

Therapeutic Family Life **1158**

Therapeutic Foster Care Program; Mental Health Center **1061**

Toiyabe Indian Health Project; Family Services Department **934**

Toutle River Boys Ranch **1168**

Treatment Homes, Inc. **928**

Try Again Homes Inc. **1138**

Tulsa Boys' Home **1120**

Tuscarawas County Department of Human Services **611**

Uhlich Children's Home **988**

United Homes for Children, Inc. **1017**

United Methodist Family Services of Virginia **836**

Victor C. Neumann Association **989**

The Villages of Indiana, Inc. **995**

Virginia Department of Social Services **1165**

Virginia Department of Social Services; Bureau of Child Welfare Services **823**

Volunteers of America; Family Treatment Program **1052**

Wake County Department of Social Services **559**

Walden Environment, Inc. **935**

# Geographic Index

This index provides access to all entries by geographic location. Organizations and their branches are listed alphabetically by city within each state. An entry number, not page number, follows each organization cited.

## ALABAMA

### Birmingham

AGAPE of Central Alabama, Inc. **3**
Alabama Friends of Adoption **1322**
Family Adoption Services, Inc. **5**
Lifeline Children's Services, Inc. **6**
Villa Hope **7**

### Enterprise

AGAPE of Central Alabama, Inc. **3**

### Florence

AGAPE of North Alabama, Inc. **4**

### Huntsville

AGAPE of North Alabama, Inc. **4**
John W. Green, III; Attorney at Law **1193**

### Montgomery

AGAPE of Central Alabama, Inc. **3**
Alabama Department of Human Resources **2**
Alabama State Department of Human
    Resources **921**

## ALASKA

### Anchorage

Anchorage Adoptive Parents Association **1323**
Catholic Social Services **11**
Kasmar and Slone, P.C. **1194**

### Bethel

Association of Village Council Presidents, Inc.
    **10**

### Fairbanks

Fairbanks Counseling and Adoption **12**

### Juneau

Department of Health and Social Services,
    Alaska; Division of Family and Youth **923**
Division of Family and Youth Services of
    Alaska **9**

## ARIZONA

### Apache Junction

Arizona Department of Economic Security **14**

### Benson

Arizona Department of Economic Security **14**

### Bisbee

Arizona Department of Economic Security **14**

### Casa Grande

Arizona Department of Economic Security **14**

### Clifton

Arizona Department of Economic Security **14**

### Coolidge

Arizona Department of Economic Security **14**

### Cottonwood

Arizona Department of Economic Security **14**

### Douglas

Arizona Department of Economic Security **14**

### Flagstaff

Arizona Department of Economic Security **14**

### Kingman

Arizona Department of Economic Security **14**

### Lake Havasu

Arizona Department of Economic Security **14**

### Lakeside

Arizona Department of Economic Security **14**

### Litchfield Park

Search Triad, Inc. **1326**

### Mesa

Adoption Care Center, Inc. **15**
Udall, Shuman, Blackhurst, Allen and Lyons
    **1195**

### Nogales

Arizona Department of Economic Security **14**

### Page

Arizona Department of Economic Security **14**

### Parker

Arizona Department of Economic Security **14**

### Payson

Arizona Department of Economic Security **14**

### Phoenix

Aid to Adoption of Special Kids - Arizona **16**
Arizona Children's Home Association **17**
Arizona Department of Economic Security **14**
Black Family And Child Services **18**
Christian Family Care Agency **20**
Family Service Agency **23**
Human Resource Training, Inc. **924**

### Prescott

Arizona Department of Economic Security **14**

### Riviera

Arizona Department of Economic Security **14**

### Safford

Arizona Department of Economic Security **14**

### St. Johns

Arizona Department of Economic Security **14**

### Scottsdale

Dillon Southwest **22**
Extensions **1325**

### Sierra Vista

Arizona Department of Economic Security **14**
Catholic Community Services of South
    Arizona, Inc. **19**

### Tempe

Human Resource Training, Inc. **924**

### Tucson

Adoption Information Center (AIC) **1595**
Advocates for Single Adoption Parenting
    (ASAP) **1324**
Arizona Children's Home Association **17**
Arizona Department of Economic Security **14**
Catholic Community Services of South
    Arizona, Inc. **19**
Commonwealth Adoptions International, Inc.
    **21**
Hand In Hand International Adoptions **93**

House of Samuel, Inc. **24**
La Hacienda Foster Care Resource Center, Inc. **925**
Tracers, Ltd. **1327**

**Wilcox**

Arizona Department of Economic Security **14**

**Winslow**

Arizona Department of Economic Security **14**

**Yuma**

Arizona Department of Economic Security **14**
Catholic Community Services of South Arizona, Inc. **19**

# ARKANSAS

**Batesville**

Parent Center **1330**

**Helena**

East Arkansas Regional Mental Health Center; Therapeutic Foster Care Program **927**

**Jacksonville**

Ogles Law Firm, P.A. **1196**

**Little Rock**

Bethany Christian Services of Little Rock **27**
Centers for Youth and Families **926**
Department of Human Services; Division of Family and Human Services **26**
Treatment Homes, Inc. **928**

**Russellville**

Arkansas Families and Adoptive Children Together; AFACT **1329**

**Russelville**

AASK Midwest **1593**

**Winslow**

Adoptive Parents And Children Together; A.P.A.C.T. **1328**

# CALIFORNIA

**Anaheim**

Farano & Kieviet **1207**

**Aptos**

Future Families, Inc. **67**

**Bellflower**

Bethany Christian Services, South Region **58**

**Belmont**

Adoption Connection of Jewish Family and Children's Services **51**

**Beverly Hills**

Cook and Linden; A Professional Corporation **1203**
David Keene Leavitt; Attorney at Law **1215**

**Bishop**

Toiyabe Indian Health Project; Family Services Department **934**

**Carmichael**

Walden Environment, Inc. **935**

**Cerritos**

Open Door Society of Los Angeles **1338**

**Chatsworth**

Bal Jagat; Children's World, Inc. **55**

**Chico**

State Department of Social Services; Chico District Office **46**

**Chino**

Adoptions Unlimited **54**

**Chula Vista**

San Diego County Adoption **39**

**Coleville**

Toiyabe Indian Health Project; Family Services Department **934**

**Concord**

Beverly R. Williscroft; Attorney at Law **1223**

**Costa Mesa**

Independent Search Consultants **1337**

**Covina**

Department of Children's Services; Adoptions Division **30**

**Cupertino**

Friends of Holt-Korea **1335**

**El Dorado Hills**

Hand In Hand of Greater Sacramento **1336**

**El Monte**

Children's Bureau of Southern California **929**

**Encino**

Adoption Assistance and Information Group **1332**
Law Offices of David H. Baum **1199**

**Eureka**

Adoption Horizons, Inc.; The Birth Parent Center **52**

**Fresno**

Chrysalis House **63**
Fresno County Department of Social Services **32**
Infant of Prague Adoption Service **72**

**Grand Terrace**

Concept 7 Foster Family Agency **930**

**Greenville**

Mountain Circle Foster Family Agency **931**

**Hemet**

Indian Child And Family Services **71**

**Huntington Beach**

Alvin M. Coen; Attorney at Law **1202**

**Lafayette**

Law Offices of Diane Michelsen **1216**

**Laguna Hills**

Concept 7 Foster Family Agency **930**

**Lakewood**

Department of Children's Services; Adoptions Division **30**

**Lancaster**

Department of Children's Services; Adoptions Division **30**

**Lodi**

Share Homes Foster Family Agency **933**

**Lone Pine**

Toiyabe Indian Health Project; Family Services Department **934**

**Los Angeles**

Children's Bureau of Southern California **929**
Children's Home Society of California **61**
Department of Children's Services; Adoptions Division **30**
Holy Family Services, Counseling and Adoption **70**
Independent Adoption Center **1212**
Webster & Bayliss; Adoption Associates **1222**

**Merced**

Merced County Human Services Agency **34**

**Mission Hills**

Walden Environment, Inc. **935**

**Modesto**

Bethany Christian Services, North Region **57**
Family Connections Adoption Agency **65**
Gianelli & Fores **1210**

**Monterey**

The Family Network, Inc. **66**
Kinship Center **74**

**Mountain View**

Bay Area Adoption Services **56**

**Nevada City**

Sierra Adoption Services **78**

**Northridge**

Down Syndrome Association of Los Angeles **1333**

## Oakland

AASK America; Aid to Adoption of Special Kids **49**
Alameda County Social Services Dept.; Adoption Services (I) **29**
Children's Home Society of California **61**
Jed Somit; Attorney at Law **1220**

## Oceanside

San Diego County Adoption **39**

## Pacific Grove

David C. Laredo; Attorney at Law **1214**

## Placerville

El Dorado County Dept. of Social Services; Adoption Services **31**

## Pleasant Hill

Independent Adoption Center **1212**

## Rancho Cucamonga

San Bernardino Adoption Service **38**

## Redding

Northern Valley Catholic Social Service **932**
Shasta County Adoptions **45**

## Redwood City

Adopt International **50**
Martin Brandfon; Attorney at Law **1200**

## Riverside

Riverside County Department of Social Services **36**

## Sacramento

Adoptee Birth Family Registry **1331**
Children's Home Society of California **61**
Families for Children **64**
Steven C. Fishbein **1209**
Holt International Children's Services **659**
Murphy & Jacobs **1217**
Sacramento County Department of Health and Human Services **37**
Sierra Adoption Services **78**

## San Bernardino

San Bernardino Adoption Service **38**

## San Diego

Adoption Center of San Diego **1197**
Allen & Hoctor Counseling Center **1198**
Catholic Charities Adoption Agency of San Diego **59**
Children's Home Society of California **61**
Family Life Institute **1205**
Harley A. Feinstein **1208**
San Diego County Adoption **39**
Walden Environment, Inc. **935**

## San Francisco

Adoption Connection of Jewish Family and Children's Services **51**
Catholic Charities of San Francisco **60**
Family Options Independent Adoption Services **1206**
San Francisco Department of Social Services; Adoption Services **40**

## San Jose

Law Offices of Vanessa Zecher Cain **1201**
Children's Home Society of California **61**
Future Families, Inc. **67**
Sanford & Harmssen **1218**
Santa Clara County Social Services Agency - Adoptions **43**

## San Luis Obispo

San Luis Obispo County Department of Social Services **41**

## San Rafael

Adoption Connection of Jewish Family and Children's Services **51**
Marin County Department of Health and Human Services; Adoptions **33**

## Santa Ana

Children's Home Society of California **61**
Jane A. Gorman; Attorney at Law **1211**
Holy Family Services, Counseling and Adoption **70**
Orange County Adoptive Parents Association (OCAPA) **1339**
County of Orange Social Service Agency; Adoptions Program **35**
Van Deusen, Youmans & Walmsley, Inc. **1221**

## Santa Barbara

Douglas R. Donnelly; Attorney at Law **1204**
Santa Barbara County Department of Social Services **42**

## Santa Cruz

FACES; Families Adopting Children: Education & Support **1334**
Hand In Hand Foundation **68**
Sanford & Harmssen **1218**
Santa Cruz County Department of Human Resources; Adoptions **44**
Lindsay Kohut Slatter, Esq.; Attorney at Law **1219**

## Santa Fe Springs

Concept 7 Foster Family Agency **930**

## Santa Maria

Santa Barbara County Department of Social Services **42**

## Santa Monica

Karen Lane; Attorney at Law **1213**

## Santa Rosa

Adoption Connection of Jewish Family and Children's Services **51**
Partners for Adoption **77**

## Stockton

Help The Children, Inc. **69**

## Temecula

Christian Adoption and Family Services **62**
International Christian Adoptions **73**

## Tustin

Life Adoption Services **75**

## Van Nuys

Children's Home Society of California **61**

## Ventura

Adoption Services International **53**
Ventura County Public Social Services Agency **48**

## Visalia

Tulare County Adoptions **47**

## Windsor

North Bay Adoptions **76**

# COLORADO

## Akron

Colorado State Department of Social Services **80**

## Alamosa

Colorado State Department of Social Services **80**

## Aspen

Colorado State Department of Social Services **80**

## Aurora

Adoption Alliance **81**
The Adoption Option, Inc. **83**
Christian Family Services of Colorado, Inc. **88**

## Black Hawk

Colorado State Department of Social Services **80**

## Boulder

Colorado State Department of Social Services **80**
International Concerns Committee for Children **1342**

## Breckenridge

Colorado State Department of Social Services **80**

## Broomfield

Concerned United Birthparents, Inc. **1341**

## Burlington

Colorado State Department of Social Services **80**

## Canon City

Colorado State Department of Social Services **80**
Fremont County Department of Social Services **941**

## Castle Rock

Colorado State Department of Social Services **80**
Hope's Promise **94**

## Cedaredge

Orphan Voyage **1343**

## Cheyenne Wells

Colorado State Department of Social Services **80**

## Colorado Springs

Adoption Choice Center **82**
Catholic Community Services of Colorado Springs **86**
Colorado State Department of Social Services **80**
El Paso County Department of Social Services **939**
Hand In Hand International Adoptions **93**
Lutheran Family Services of Colorado **96**

## Commerce City

Colorado State Department of Social Services **80**

## Conejo

Colorado State Department of Social Services **80**

## Cortez

Colorado State Department of Social Services **80**

## Craig

Colorado State Department of Social Services **80**

## Del Norte

Colorado State Department of Social Services **80**

## Delta

Colorado State Department of Social Services **80**

## Denver

Bethany Christian Services of Colorado **85**
Colorado State Department of Social Services **80**
Denver Alternative Youth Services; The Family Connection **937**
Denver Department of Social Services **938**
Friends of Children of Various Nations, Inc. **92**
Pamela A. Gordon; Attorney at Law **1224**
Innovative Adoptions, Inc. **95**
Jewish Children's Adoption Network **1603**
Lutheran Family Services of Colorado **96**
Rainbow House International **490**
RESOLVE of Colorado **1344**
Rocky Mountain Adoption Exchange **1611**

## Dove Creek

Colorado State Department of Social Services **80**

## Durango

Colorado State Department of Social Services **80**

## Eads

Colorado State Department of Social Services **80**

## Eagle

Colorado State Department of Social Services **80**

## Englewood

Colorado Christian Services **90**
Small Miracles Foundation of the Rockies **97**

## Fairplay

Colorado State Department of Social Services **80**

## Ft. Collins

Adoptions: Advocacy and Alternatives **84**
Colorado Adoption Center **89**
Colorado State Department of Social Services **80**
Lutheran Family Services of Colorado **96**

## Ft. Morgan

Colorado State Department of Social Services **80**

## Georgetown

Colorado State Department of Social Services **80**

## Glenwood Springs

Colorado State Department of Social Services **80**

## Golden

Colorado State Department of Social Services **80**

## Grand Junction

Colorado State Department of Social Services **80**
Mesa County Department of Social Services **944**

## Greeley

Adoptions: Advocacy and Alternatives **84**

## Greely

Colorado State Department of Social Services **80**

## Gunnison

Colorado State Department of Social Services **80**
Gunnison/Hinsdale County Department of Social Services **942**

## Holyoke

Colorado State Department of Social Services **80**

## Hot Sulphur Spring

Colorado State Department of Social Services **80**

## Hugo

Colorado State Department of Social Services **80**

## Juleburg

Colorado State Department of Social Services **80**

## La Junta

Colorado State Department of Social Services **80**

## Lakewood

The Adoption Option, Inc. **83**
Designated Adoption Services of Colorado, Inc. **91**
Jefferson County Department of Social Services **943**

## Lamar

Colorado State Department of Social Services **80**

## Las Animas

Colorado State Department of Social Services **80**

## Leadville

Colorado State Department of Social Services **80**

## Littleton

Chinese Children Adoption International **87**
Colorado State Department of Social Services **80**

## Longmont

The Family Extension, Inc. **940**

## Meeker

Colorado State Department of Social Services **80**

## Montrose

Colorado State Department of Social Services **80**

## Ordway

Colorado State Department of Social Services **80**

## Ouray

Colorado State Department of Social Services **80**

## Pagosa Springs

Colorado State Department of Social Services **80**

## Pueblo

Colorado State Department of Social Services **80**

## Saguache

Colorado State Department of Social Services **80**

## Salida

Chaffee County Department of Social Services **936**

National Council for Adoption **1351**
World Child, Inc. **125**

# FLORIDA

## Boca Raton

Adoption Connection, Inc. **129**

## Bradenton

Florida Department of Health and
Rehabilitative Services **127**

## Cape Coral

ALARM; Advocating Legislation for Adoption
Reform Movement **1352**

## Cocoa

Catholic Social Services (of Orlando) **135**
Florida Department of Health and
Rehabilitative Services **127**

## Dade City

Florida Department of Health and
Rehabilitative Services **127**

## Daytona Beach

The Children's Home Society of Florida **137**
Florida Department of Health and
Rehabilitative Services **127**

## Ft. Lauderdale

Catholic Community Services; Archdiocese of
Miami - Broward Region **134**
The Children's Home Society of Florida **137**
Jewish Family Service of Broward County **143**

## Ft. Meyers

Florida Department of Health and
Rehabilitative Services **127**

## Ft. Myers

The Children's Home Society of Florida **137**
Hearts & Homes For Children **141**

## Ft. Pierce

The Children's Home Society of Florida **137**
Florida Department of Health and
Rehabilitative Services **127**

## Gainesville

Christian Family Services **138**
Florida Department of Health and
Rehabilitative Services **127**

## Hollywood

Jewish Family Service of Broward County **143**

## Jacksonville

The Children's Home Society of Florida **137**
First Coast Jewish Family and Community
Services, Inc. **1353**
Florida Department of Health and
Rehabilitative Services **127**
Hope! Share And Care! Adoption Support
Group **1354**
Jewish Family and Community Services **142**

## Key West

Florida Department of Health and
Rehabilitative Services **127**

## Lakeland

The Children's Home Society of Florida **137**
Florida Department of Health and
Rehabilitative Services **127**

## Largo

Florida Department of Health and
Rehabilitative Services **127**
Suncoast International Adoptions, Inc. **145**

## Lauderhill

Florida Department of Health and
Rehabilitative Services **127**

## Madison

Florida Department of Health and
Rehabilitative Services **127**

## Melbourne

Grass and Grass, Attorneys **1229**

## Miami

Catholic Foster Services of Miami **954**
The Children's Home Society of Florida **137**
Florida Department of Health and
Rehabilitative Services **127**
St. Vincent Adoption Services **144**

## Miami Shores

Oasis, Inc. **1355**
Organized Adoption Search Information
Services **1356**

## Mt. Dora

Christian Home and Bible School **139**

## Naples

Catholic Charities: Counseling Services of
Collier County **132**

## New Port Richey

Florida Department of Health and
Rehabilitative Services **127**

## New Smyrna Beach

Clay Henderson; Attorney at Law **1230**

## Ocala

The Children's Home Society of Florida **137**
Florida Department of Health and
Rehabilitative Services **127**

## Orlando

Catholic Social Services (of Orlando) **135**
The Children's Home Society of Florida **137**
Florida Department of Health and
Rehabilitative Services **127**
Donald F. Jacobs; Attorney at Law **1231**

## Panama City

Florida Department of Health and
Rehabilitative Services **127**

## Pensacola

The Children's Home Society of Florida **137**
Florida Department of Health and
Rehabilitative Services **127**

## Quincy

Florida Department of Health and
Rehabilitative Services **127**

## Rockledge

The Children's Home Society of Florida **137**

## St. Augustine

Catholic Charities Bureau, Inc. **131**

## St. Petersburg

Catholic Charities, Diocese of St. Petersburg,
Inc. **133**
The Children's Home Society of Florida **137**
Gift of Life, Inc. Adoption Services **140**

## Sarasota

A Bond of Love Adoption Agency **130**
Florida Department of Health and
Rehabilitative Services **127**

## Sebring

Florida Department of Health and
Rehabilitative Services **127**

## Stuart

Florida Department of Health and
Rehabilitative Services **127**

## Tallahassee

Catholic Social Services (of Tallahassee) **136**
The Children's Home Society of Florida **137**
Florida Department of Health and
Rehabilitative Services **127**

## Tampa

Adoption By Choice **128**
Florida Department of Health and
Rehabilitative Services **127**
Anthony B. Marchese; Attorney at Law **1232**
Special Needs Adoptive Parents (S.N.A.P.)
**1357**

## Vero Beach

Florida Department of Health and
Rehabilitative Services **127**

## West Palm Beach

The Children's Home Society of Florida **137**
Law Offices of Bennett S. Cohn, P.A. **1228**
Florida Department of Health and
Rehabilitative Services **127**

# GEORGIA

## Athens

Clarke County Adoption Resource Exchange;
C.C.A.R.E. **1364**

## Atlanta

Adoption Planning, Inc. **148**
Catholic Social Services, Inc. of Atlanta **150**
ChildKind, Inc. **955**

Ruth F. Clairborne, P.C. **1235**
Division of Family and Children's Services
    (Georgia); State Adoption Unit **147**
Division of Family and Children's Services;
    Agency 2 - Georgia **956**
Extended Families **957**
Families First **958**
Family Partners Worldwide, Inc. **152**
Rhonda L. Fishbein, Esq. **1238**
Heart to Heart Adoption Service; Lutheran
    Ministries of Georgia, Inc. **153**
My Turn Now, Inc. **1607**
RESOLVE of Georgia **1369**
Single Women Adopting Children **1370**
Tender Mercy Ministries, Inc. **960**

### Augusta

L. Daniel Butler, Attorney at Law **1234**
Family Counseling Center of the CSRA, Inc.
    **1237**
Fulcher, Hagler, Reed, Hanks & Harper **1239**
The United Methodist Children's Home **961**

### Augustsa

Augusta Adoption League **1361**

### Cartersville

Bartow/Paulding Adoptive Families **1362**

### College Park

ROOTS, Planting Seeds to Secure Our Future,
    Inc. **157**

### Dalton

The United Methodist Children's Home **961**
Philip F. Woodward **1240**

### Decatur

The United Methodist Children's Home **961**

### Evans

Home B.A.S.E. (Birthparents and Adoptees
    Supportive Environment) **1367**

### Gainesville

Heart to Heart Adoption Service; Lutheran
    Ministries of Georgia, Inc. **153**

### Griffin

Flint River Adoptive Parent Association **1366**

### Hephzibah

Central Savannah River Area Council on
    Adoptable Children **1363**

### Jonesboro

Cowen & Cowen; Attorneys at Law **1236**

### Lawrenceville

Adoption Information Services **1233**

### Macon

Covenant Care Services **151**

### Marietta

HOPE for Children, Inc. **154**
The Phoenix Institute for Adolescents, Inc.
    **959**

### Pavo

Adoption Services, Inc. **149**

### Payvo

Parent Support Group of Adoption Services,
    Inc. **1368**

### Roswell

Adopted Kids and Parents Support Group
    (AKAPS) **1358**

### Savannah

Adoptive Parents Association **1359**
Parent And Child Development Services **156**

### Snellville

American-Romanian Connection **1360**

### Thomasville

The Open Door Adoption Agency, Inc. **155**

### Warrenton

Warren, Glascock and McDuffie Support
    Group **1371**

### Woodstock

Families Adopting Across Racial Lines **1365**

## HAWAII

### Captain Cook, Kona

Department of Human Services; Family &
    Adult Services Division **159**

### Hilo

The Casey Family Program **962**
Department of Human Services; Family &
    Adult Services Division **159**

### Honolulu

The Casey Family Program **962**
Catholic Services to Families **160**
Department of Human Services; Family &
    Adult Services Division **159**
Hawaii International Child **161**
Hawaii International Child Placement and
    Family Services, Inc. **1372**

### Koloa

RESOLVE of Hawaii **1373**

### Lihue

Department of Human Services; Family &
    Adult Services Division **159**

### Wailuku

Department of Human Services; Family &
    Adult Services Division **159**

## IDAHO

### Arimo

Children's Aid of Idaho **164**

### Boise

Adoptees' Liberty Movement Association
    (ALMA) **1374**
The Casey Family Program **963**
Children's Aid of Idaho **164**
Community Counseling and Adoption Services
    of Idaho, Inc. **166**
Department of Health and Welfare; Family and
    Community Services **964**
Department of Health and Welfare of Idaho;
    Division of Family and Community Services
    **163**
Idaho Voluntary Adoption Registry; Center for
    Vital Statistics and Health Policy **1375**
Idaho Youth Ranch Adoption Services **167**

### Caldwell

Department of Health and Welfare; Family and
    Community Services **964**
Department of Health and Welfare of Idaho;
    Division of Family and Community Services
    **163**

### Coeur d'Alene

Department of Health and Welfare; Family and
    Community Services **964**
Department of Health and Welfare of Idaho;
    Division of Family and Community Services
    **163**
Lutheran Social Services of Washington and
    Idaho **168**

### Idaho Falls

Children's Aid of Idaho **164**
Christian Counseling Services **165**
Department of Health and Welfare; Family and
    Community Services **964**
Department of Health and Welfare of Idaho;
    Division of Family and Community Services
    **163**

### Lewiston

Children's Aid of Idaho **164**
Department of Health and Welfare; Family and
    Community Services **964**
Department of Health and Welfare of Idaho;
    Division of Family and Community Services
    **163**

### Pocatello

Department of Health and Welfare; Family and
    Community Services **964**
Department of Health and Welfare of Idaho;
    Division of Family and Community Services
    **163**

### Twin Falls

Children's Aid of Idaho **164**
Department of Health and Welfare; Family and
    Community Services **964**
Department of Health and Welfare of Idaho;
    Division of Family and Community Services
    **163**

## ILLINOIS

### Addison

Seegers Lutheran Center; Lutheran Child and
    Family Services **196**

## Alsip

Sertoma Foster Care **985**

## Arlington Heights

Hands Around the World, Inc. **1384**
St. Mary's Services **195**
Shelter, Inc. **986**

## Assumption

Kemmerer Village **976**

## Aurora

Illinois Department of Children and Family
    Services; Aurora Office **170**

## Barrington

Adoptive Families Today **1380**

## Belleville

Catholic Social Service of Belleville **182**
The Lost Connection **1388**
Seegers Lutheran Center; Lutheran Child and
    Family Services **196**

## Bensenville

Lifelink/Bensenville Home Society **191**

## Bloomington

ABC Counseling & Family Services **177**
Adoptees Liberty Movement Association;
    Central Illinois Chapter **1376**
Catholic Social Service of Peoria **183**
Central Illinois Adoptive Families **1382**

## Breese

Catholic Social Service of Belleville **182**

## Burr Ridge

St. Mary's Services **195**

## Carbondale

Jackson County Community Mental Health
    Center **975**

## Carlinville

Christian Adoption Ministries **1383**

## Champaign

Adoption Triangle **1377**
Catholic Social Service of Peoria **183**
Illinois Department of Children and Family
    Services; Champaign Office **171**
Lifelink/Bensenville Home Society **191**

## Chicago

Adoption Information Center of Illinois (AICI)
    **1596**
Cabrini-Green Youth and Family Services **965**
Casa Central Foster Care Agency **966**
Catholic Charities of the Archdiocese of
    Chicago **181**
Central Baptist Family Services **184**
Chicago Child Care Society **967**
Chicago Commons **968**
Circle Family Care **970**
Evangelical Child and Family Agency **187**
Family Care Services **188**
Lutheran Social Services of Illinois **978**

Lutheran Social Services of Illinois; Foster,
    Adoption and Maternity Services **192**
Lydia Home Association **979**
Ada S. McKinley Foster Care and Adoption
    Services **982**
New Life Adoption Services **194**
Reverend Henry Rucker Memorial Services
    **983**
St. Mary's Services **195**
Uhlich Children's Home **988**
Victor C. Neumann Association **989**

## Cicero

Seguin Services Inc. **984**

## Crystal Lake

St. Mary's Services **195**

## Decatur

Jessica Sticklin; Attorney at Law **1242**

## DeKalb

Kishwaukee OURS **1387**

## Des Plaines

Lutheran Social Services of Illinois **978**
Maryville Academy **980**

## Edwardsville

Lifelink/Bensenville Home Society **191**

## Elgin

Heritage Finders **1386**
Jayne Shover Easter Seal Rehabilitative
    Center, Inc. **987**

## Elmhurst

Ray Graham Association for People with
    Disabilities **972**

## Evanston

The Cradle Society **186**

## Evergreen Park

Bethany Christian Services of Evergreen Park
    **179**

## Fairview Heights

Christian Family Services, Inc. **428**
Illinois Department of Children and Family
    Services; Fairview Heights Office **172**

## Galesburg

Catholic Social Service of Peoria **183**

## Godfrey

All-Adopt **1381**

## Grayslake

Family Counseling Clinic, Inc. **189**

## Hennepin

AASK Midwest **1593**

## Hinsdale

The Community House **971**

## Joliet

Adoption Triangle **1379**
Guardian Angel Home **973**

## Marion

Catholic Social Service of Belleville **182**
Illinois Department of Children and Family
    Services; Marion Office **173**

## Moline

Family Resources, Inc. **1000**
Lifelink/Bensenville Home Society **191**
Lutheran Social Services of Illinois **978**
Ours thru Adoption, Inc. **1391**

## Mt. Carmel

Catholic Social Service of Belleville **182**

## Mt. Vernon

Maternity and Adoption Services of Baptist
    Children's Home **193**

## Normal

The Baby Fold **178**
Healing Hearts, Inc. **1385**

## Northbrook

Stars of David International, Inc. **1394**

## Oak Park

Hephzibah Children's Association **974**
Lutheran Social Services of Illinois **978**
Single Adoptive Parent Support Group **1393**

## Park Forest

Adoption Triangle **1378**

## Peoria

Catholic Social Service of Peoria **183**
Michael W. Heller; Attorney at Law **1241**
Illinois Department of Children and Family
    Services; Peoria Office **174**
Lutheran Social Services of Illinois **978**

## Prospect Heights

Truth Seekers in Adoption **1395**

## Quincy

Family Service Agency of Adams County **190**
Quincy Adoption Support Group **1392**

## River Forest

Seegers Lutheran Center; Lutheran Child and
    Family Services **196**

## Rock Island

Catholic Social Service of Peoria **183**

## Rockford

Children's Development Center **969**
Children's Home and Aid Society of Illinois
    **185**
Illinois Department of Children and Family
    Services; Rockford Office **175**
Lifelink/Bensenville Home Society **191**
OURS of Northern Illinois **1390**

## Round Lake

Catholic Charities (of Waukegan) **180**

## Springfield

Illinois Department of Children and Family
Services; Springfield Office **176**
Missing Pieces **1389**

## Waukegan

Catholic Charities (of Waukegan) **180**
Catholic Charities of the Archdiocese of
Chicago **181**

## Wheaton

Evangelical Child and Family Agency **187**
Sunny Ridge Family Centers **197**

## Yorkville

Kendall County Human Services **977**

# INDIANA

## Albion

Family and Social Services Administration of
Indiana; Division of Family and Children
**199**

## Anderson

Family and Social Services Administration of
Indiana; Division of Family and Children
**199**

## Angola

Family and Social Services Administration of
Indiana; Division of Family and Children
**199**

## Auburn

Family and Social Services Administration of
Indiana; Division of Family and Children
**199**

## Bedford

Family and Social Services Administration of
Indiana; Division of Family and Children
**199**

## Bloomfield

Family and Social Services Administration of
Indiana; Division of Family and Children
**199**

## Bloomington

Family and Social Services Administration of
Indiana; Division of Family and Children
**199**
The Villages of Indiana, Inc. **220**

## Bluffton

Family and Social Services Administration of
Indiana; Division of Family and Children
**199**

## Boonville

Family and Social Services Administration of
Indiana; Division of Family and Children
**199**

## Brazil

Family and Social Services Administration of
Indiana; Division of Family and Children
**199**

## Brookville

Family and Social Services Administration of
Indiana; Division of Family and Children
**199**

## Brownstown

Family and Social Services Administration of
Indiana; Division of Family and Children
**199**

## Cicero

AASK Midwest **1593**

## Clarksville

Family and Social Services Administration of
Indiana; Division of Family and Children
**199**

## Columbia City

Family and Social Services Administration of
Indiana; Division of Family and Children
**199**

## Columbus

Family and Social Services Administration of
Indiana; Division of Family and Children
**199**

## Connersville

Family and Social Services Administration of
Indiana; Division of Family and Children
**199**

## Corydon

Family and Social Services Administration of
Indiana; Division of Family and Children
**199**

## Covington

Family and Social Services Administration of
Indiana; Division of Family and Children
**199**

## Crawfordsville

Family and Social Services Administration of
Indiana; Division of Family and Children
**199**

## Danville

Family and Social Services Administration of
Indiana; Division of Family and Children
**199**

## Decatur

Family and Social Services Administration of
Indiana; Division of Family and Children
**199**

## Delphi

Family and Social Services Administration of
Indiana; Division of Family and Children
**199**

## Elkhart

Adoption Resource Services, Inc. **200**
Family and Social Services Administration of
Indiana; Division of Family and Children
**199**

## English

Family and Social Services Administration of
Indiana; Division of Family and Children
**199**

## Evansville

Catholic Charities Bureau, Evansville **207**
Family and Social Services Administration of
Indiana; Division of Family and Children
**199**
Greater Love Adoption Decision (G.L.A.D.)
**214**

## Ft. Wayne

Adoption Resource Services, Inc. **200**
Catholic Charities of Ft. Wayne **208**
Family and Social Services Administration of
Indiana; Division of Family and Children
**199**
Lutheran Social Services of Fort Wayne **217**
Specialized Alternatives For Families And
Youth (S.A.F.Y.) **1110**

## Fowler

Family and Social Services Administration of
Indiana; Division of Family and Children
**199**

## Frankfort

Family and Social Services Administration of
Indiana; Division of Family and Children
**199**

## Franklin

Family and Social Services Administration of
Indiana; Division of Family and Children
**199**

## Gary

Family and Social Services Administration of
Indiana; Division of Family and Children
**199**

## Greencastle

Family and Social Services Administration of
Indiana; Division of Family and Children
**199**

## Greenfield

Family and Social Services Administration of
Indiana; Division of Family and Children
**199**

## Greensburg

Family and Social Services Administration of
Indiana; Division of Family and Children
**199**

## Greenwood

Jeremiah Agency, Inc. **215**

## Griffith

Lutheran Social Services of Indiana **218**

## Hartford City

Family and Social Services Administration of
   Indiana; Division of Family and Children
   **199**

## Highland

Sunny Ridge Family Centers **197**

## Huntington

Family and Social Services Administration of
   Indiana; Division of Family and Children
   **199**

## Indianapolis

The Adoption Support Center, Inc. **201**
Americans for African Adoptions, Inc. (AFAA)
   **203**
Bethany Christian Services of Indianapolis **206**
Children's Bureau of Indianapolis **211**
Coleman Adoption Services, Inc. **212**
Family and Social Services Administration of
   Indiana; Division of Family and Children
   **199**
Indiana Adoption Resource Exchange (IARE);
   Division of Family and Children **1601**
Indiana RESOLVE, Inc. **1400**
Indiana Youth Advocate Program, Inc. **992**
Steven M. Kirsh; Attorney at Law **1243**
Lutheran Child and Family Services **216**
Franklin I. Miroff; Attorney at Law **1244**
St. Elizabeth's Home **219**
White's Family Services **997**

## Jasper

Family and Social Services Administration of
   Indiana; Division of Family and Children
   **199**

## Jeffersonville

Childplace **210**

## Knox

Family and Social Services Administration of
   Indiana; Division of Family and Children
   **199**

## Kokomo

Family and Social Services Administration of
   Indiana; Division of Family and Children
   **199**

## Lafayette

Family and Social Services Administration of
   Indiana; Division of Family and Children
   **199**

## LaGrange

Family and Social Services Administration of
   Indiana; Division of Family and Children
   **199**

## LaPorte

Family and Social Services Administration of
   Indiana; Division of Family and Children
   **199**

## Lawrenceburg

Family and Social Services Administration of
   Indiana; Division of Family and Children
   **199**

## Lebanon

Family and Social Services Administration of
   Indiana; Division of Family and Children
   **199**

## Leo

Gateway Woods - Apostolic Christian
   Children's Home **991**

## Liberty

Family and Social Services Administration of
   Indiana; Division of Family and Children
   **199**

## Logansport

Family and Social Services Administration of
   Indiana; Division of Family and Children
   **199**

## Madison

Family and Social Services Administration of
   Indiana; Division of Family and Children
   **199**

## Marion

Family and Social Services Administration of
   Indiana; Division of Family and Children
   **199**

## Martinsville

Family and Social Services Administration of
   Indiana; Division of Family and Children
   **199**

## Monticello

Family and Social Services Administration of
   Indiana; Division of Family and Children
   **199**

## Morocco

Family and Social Services Administration of
   Indiana; Division of Family and Children
   **199**

## Mount Vernon

Family and Social Services Administration of
   Indiana; Division of Family and Children
   **199**

## Muncie

AASK Midwest **1593**
Delaware County Office of Family and
   Children Services **990**
Family and Social Services Administration of
   Indiana; Division of Family and Children
   **199**

## Munster

Illiana Adoptive Parents **1399**

## Nashville

Family and Social Services Administration of
   Indiana; Division of Family and Children
   **199**

## New Albany

Family and Social Services Administration of
   Indiana; Division of Family and Children
   **199**

## New Castle

Family and Social Services Administration of
   Indiana; Division of Family and Children
   **199**

## New Haven

Adoption/Birthmother Search for Tomorrow,
   Inc. **1397**

## Newport

Family and Social Services Administration of
   Indiana; Division of Family and Children
   **199**

## Noblesville

Family and Social Services Administration of
   Indiana; Division of Family and Children
   **199**

## Notre Dame

Association for the Rights of Children; ARC
   **1398**

## Oakland City

Compassionate Care **213**

## Paoli

Family and Social Services Administration of
   Indiana; Division of Family and Children
   **199**

## Peru

Family and Social Services Administration of
   Indiana; Division of Family and Children
   **199**

## Petersburg

Family and Social Services Administration of
   Indiana; Division of Family and Children
   **199**

## Pittsboro

Specialized Alternatives For Families And
   Youth (S.A.F.Y.) **1110**

## Plymouth

Family and Social Services Administration of
   Indiana; Division of Family and Children
   **199**

## Portland

Family and Social Services Administration of
   Indiana; Division of Family and Children
   **199**

**Princeton**

Family and Social Services Administration of
Indiana; Division of Family and Children
**199**

**Rensselaer**

Family and Social Services Administration of
Indiana; Division of Family and Children
**199**

**Richmond**

Family and Social Services Administration of
Indiana; Division of Family and Children
**199**

**Rising Sun**

Family and Social Services Administration of
Indiana; Division of Family and Children
**199**

**Rochester**

Family and Social Services Administration of
Indiana; Division of Family and Children
**199**

**Rockport**

Family and Social Services Administration of
Indiana; Division of Family and Children
**199**

**Rockville**

Family and Social Services Administration of
Indiana; Division of Family and Children
**199**

**Rushville**

Family and Social Services Administration of
Indiana; Division of Family and Children
**199**

**Salem**

Family and Social Services Administration of
Indiana; Division of Family and Children
**199**

**Schererville**

Bethany Christian Services (of Indiana) **205**

**Scottsburg**

Family and Social Services Administration of
Indiana; Division of Family and Children
**199**

**Shelbyville**

Family and Social Services Administration of
Indiana; Division of Family and Children
**199**

**Shoals**

Family and Social Services Administration of
Indiana; Division of Family and Children
**199**

**South Bend**

Adoptees' Identity Doorway **1396**
Adoptions Alternatives **202**
Catholic Social Services of South Bend **209**

Family and Social Services Administration of
Indiana; Division of Family and Children
**199**
St. Joseph County Office of Family and Social
Service Administration; Division of Family
and Children **994**

**Spencer**

Family and Social Services Administration of
Indiana; Division of Family and Children
**199**

**Sullivan**

Family and Social Services Administration of
Indiana; Division of Family and Children
**199**

**Switz City**

Open Arms Christian Home **993**

**Tell City**

Family and Social Services Administration of
Indiana; Division of Family and Children
**199**

**Terre Haute**

Family and Social Services Administration of
Indiana; Division of Family and Children
**199**

**Tipton**

Family and Social Services Administration of
Indiana; Division of Family and Children
**199**

**Valparaiso**

Baptist Children's Home and Family Ministries
**204**
Family and Social Services Administration of
Indiana; Division of Family and Children
**199**
White's Family Services **997**

**Vernon**

Family and Social Services Administration of
Indiana; Division of Family and Children
**199**

**Versailles**

Family and Social Services Administration of
Indiana; Division of Family and Children
**199**

**Vevay**

Family and Social Services Administration of
Indiana; Division of Family and Children
**199**

**Vincennes**

Family and Social Services Administration of
Indiana; Division of Family and Children
**199**

**Wabash**

Family and Social Services Administration of
Indiana; Division of Family and Children
**199**
Wabash County Office, Division of Family and
Children **996**
White's Family Services **997**

**Warsaw**

Family and Social Services Administration of
Indiana; Division of Family and Children
**199**

**Washington**

Family and Social Services Administration of
Indiana; Division of Family and Children
**199**

**Williamsport**

Family and Social Services Administration of
Indiana; Division of Family and Children
**199**

**Winamac**

Family and Social Services Administration of
Indiana; Division of Family and Children
**199**

**Winchester**

Family and Social Services Administration of
Indiana; Division of Family and Children
**199**

# IOWA

**Ames**

Catholic Charities of the Archdiocese of
Dubuque **226**
Lutheran Social Services of Iowa **230**

**Ankeny**

Baptist Children's Home and Family Ministries
**204**

**Bettendorf**

Family Resources, Inc. **1000**

**Burlington**

Young House Family Services **1004**

**Carroll**

Catholic Charities of the Diocese of Sioux
City, Iowa, Inc. **227**

**Carter Lake**

Holt International Children's Services **659**

**Cedar Rapids**

Catholic Charities of the Archdiocese of
Dubuque **226**
Hillcrest Family Services **229**
Iowa Department of Human Services **222**
Tanager Place **1003**

**Colfax**

Iowa Foster and Adoptive Parents Association
**1402**

**Council Bluffs**

Catholic Charities, Inc., Des Moines **225**
Child Connect **998**
Iowa Department of Human Services **222**

**Davenport**

Family Resources, Inc. **1000**

Iowa Department of Human Services **222**

**Des Moines**

Bethany Christian Services (of Des Moines) **223**
Catholic Charities, Inc., Des Moines **225**
Concerned United Birthparents (CUB) **1401**
Iowa Department of Human Services **222**
Lutheran Social Services of Iowa **230**

**Dubuque**

Catholic Charities of the Archdiocese of Dubuque **226**

**Estherville**

Forest Ridge Youth Services **1001**

**Ft. Dodge**

Catholic Charities of the Diocese of Sioux City, Iowa, Inc. **227**

**Iowa City**

Lutheran Social Services of Iowa **230**

**Maquoketa**

Families of Northeast Iowa **999**

**Marshalltown**

Quakerdale Home **1002**

**Mason City**

Catholic Charities of the Archdiocese of Dubuque **226**
Iowa Department of Human Services **222**
Lutheran Social Services of Iowa **230**

**New Providence**

Quakerdale Home **1002**

**Orange City**

Bethany Christian Services of Northwest Iowa **224**

**Ottumwa**

Iowa Department of Human Services **222**
Tanager Place **1003**

**Sioux City**

Catholic Charities of the Diocese of Sioux City, Iowa, Inc. **227**
The Crittenton Center **228**
Iowa Department of Human Services **222**
Lutheran Social Services of Iowa **230**

**Waterloo**

Catholic Charities of the Archdiocese of Dubuque **226**
Iowa Department of Human Services **222**
Lutheran Social Services of Iowa **230**
Quakerdale Home **1002**

## KANSAS

**Arkansas City**

Family Life Services **241**

**Dodge City**

Catholic Social Service of Great Bend **238**

**Garden City**

Catholic Social Service of Great Bend **238**

**Great Bend**

Catholic Social Service of Great Bend **238**

**Hays**

Catholic Charities of Salina, Inc. **237**

**Horton**

Four Tribes Social Services Program **242**

**Kansas City**

Associated Youth Services **1005**
Kansas Children's Service League **245**
Kansas Children's Service League; Black Adoption Program **246**

**Lenexa**

Johnson County Mental Retardation Center **1006**

**Louisburg**

Children's Foundation - Adoption and Counseling **240**

**Mayetta**

Four Tribes Social Services Program **242**

**Olathe**

Gentle Shepherd Child Placement Services **243**

**Overland Park**

Adoption by Gentle Shepherd, Inc. **233**
Adoption Option **235**
American Adoptions **236**
The James A. Roberts Agency **248**

**Salina**

Catholic Charities of Salina, Inc. **237**

**Topeka**

Department of Social and Rehabilitative Services; Youth & Adult Services **232**
Hazlett Law Offices **1245**

**Wichita**

Adoption Centre Inc. of Kansas **234**
Catholic Social Services, Inc. of Wichita **239**
Inserco **244**
Lutheran Social Service of Kansas and Oklahoma **247**
Richard A. Macias; Attorney at Law **1246**
Small Miracles International **652**
Wichita Child Guidance Center; Caring Connection **1007**

## KENTUCKY

**Buckhorn**

Therapeutic Community Services; Presbyterian Foster Care Program **1011**

**Covington**

Children's Home of Northern Kentucky **253**

**Frankfort**

Department for Social Services; State of Kentucky **250**

**Lexington**

Bluegrass Christian Adoption Services, Inc. **251**
Catholic Social Services (of Lexington) **252**
Shades **1409**

**Louisville**

Childplace **210**
Concerned United Birthparents **1403**
James A. Crumlin; Attorney at Law **1247**
Jewish Family and Vocational Service **254**
Kentuckiana Families for Adoption **1406**
Kentucky One Church One Child Program; Louisville Urban League **255**
Seven Counties Services, Inc.; Daybreak Family Treatment Homes **1010**

**Madisonville**

Parents And Adopted Children of Kentucky **1407**

**Owensboro**

Mary Kendall Home; Methodist Home of Kentucky, Inc. **1009**
Methodist Home of Kentucky; Mary Kendall Adoptions **256**

**Paducah**

Families And Adoptive Children Together **1404**

**Somerset**

Bluegrass Residential and Support Services (B.R.A.S.S.) **1008**

**Winchester**

RESOLVE Adoptive Parent Support Group **1408**

## LOUISIANA

**Alexandria**

Louisiana Department of Social Services; Office of Community Services **1014**
Office of Community Service (of Alexandria, LA) **262**
Volunteers of America **278**

**Baton Rouge**

Bethany Christian Services (of Baton Rouge) **265**
Catholic Community Services of Baton Rouge; Counseling, Maternity and Adoption Department **267**
Department of Social Services **258**
Department of Social Services (of Baton Rouge); Office of Community Services **259**
Department of Social Services; Baton Rouge Region **1012**
Gail House **270**
Gulf Coast Teaching Family Services **1013**

Louisiana Department of Social Services; Office of Community Services **1014**
St. Elizabeth Foundation **274**
Special Delivery Adoption Services, Inc. **277**

## Breaux Bridge

Adopt Older Kids, Inc. (A-OK) **1410**

## Covington

Department of Social Services (of Baton Rouge); Office of Community Services **259**
Department of Social Services; Baton Rouge Region **1012**

## Eunice

St. Gerard's Adoption Network, Inc. **275**

## Greenwood

Joy Home for Boys; P.A.T.H. **1157**

## Gretna

Gulf Coast Teaching Family Services **1013**

## Houma

Gulf Coast Teaching Family Services **1013**

## Lafayette

Adoption Triad Network, Inc, **1411**
Catholic Social Services of Lafayette **268**
Gulf Coast Teaching Family Services **1013**
Lafayette Regional Office of Community Services **261**
Louisiana Department of Social Services; Office of Community Services **1014**

## Lake Charles

Louisiana Department of Social Services; Office of Community Services **1014**
Office of Community Services; Lake Charles Region **263**

## Metairie

Caring Alternatives; Volunteers of America **266**

## Monroe

Department of Social Services of Louisiana; Division of Children, Youth & Family Services **260**
Louisiana Department of Social Services; Office of Community Services **1014**

## New Iberia

Gulf Coast Teaching Family Services **1013**

## New Orleans

Gulf Coast Teaching Family Services **1013**
The Jewish Children's Regional Service **272**
Jewish Family Service (of New Orleans) **273**
Louisiana Department of Social Services; Office of Community Services **1014**
St. Vincent's Infant and Maternity Program; Associated Catholic Charities **276**

## Shreveport

Christian Homes; A Program of Louisiana Child Care and Placement Services, Inc. **269**
JoAnn Gines **1248**

Holy Cross Child Placement Agency, Inc. **271**
Louisiana Department of Social Services; Office of Community Services **1014**
State of Louisiana; Department of Social Services **264**
Volunteers of America **278**

## Slidell

AASK Midwest **1593**

## Thibodaux

Louisiana Department of Social Services; Office of Community Services **1014**

# MAINE

## Augusta

The Maine Children's Home for Little Wanderers **282**
Maine Department of Human Services; Child and Family Services **280**
Maine Department of Human Services; Social Services **1015**

## Bangor

Good Samaritan Agency **281**
Maine Department of Human Services; Social Services **1015**

## Biddeford

Maine Department of Human Services; Social Services **1015**
St. Andre Home, Inc. **283**

## Caribou

Maine Department of Human Services; Social Services **1015**

## Dover-Foxcroft

Maine Department of Human Services; Social Services **1015**

## Ellsworth

Maine Department of Human Services; Social Services **1015**

## Ft. Kent

Maine Department of Human Services; Social Services **1015**

## Gorham

Sharing In Adoption **284**

## Houlton

Maine Department of Human Services; Social Services **1015**

## Lewiston

Maine Department of Human Services; Social Services **1015**

## Machias

Maine Department of Human Services; Social Services **1015**

## Portland

Susan E. Bowie; Attorney at Law **1250**

Maine Department of Human Services; Social Services **1015**

## Rockland

Maine Department of Human Services; Child and Family Services **280**
Maine Department of Human Services; Social Services **1015**

## Skowhegan

Maine Department of Human Services; Child and Family Services **280**
Maine Department of Human Services; Social Services **1015**

## South Lebanon

...and baby makes three, inc. **1249**

## South Portland

Adoption Search Consultants of Maine **1412**

## Waterville

The Maine Children's Home for Little Wanderers **282**

# MARYLAND

## Annapolis

Anne Arundel County Department of Social Services **287**

## Baltimore

Adoption Alliances; Jewish Family Services **299**
The Adoption Resource Center, Inc. **300**
Catholic Charities of Baltimore **304**
Family & Children's Services of Central Maryland **306**
Mutual Consent Voluntary Adoption Registry **1418**

## Bethesda

Adoptees in Search, Inc. **1413**

## Cabin John

The Barker Foundation **302**

## Catonsville

Children in Common **1415**

## Chevy Chase

Committee for Single Adoptive Parents **1416**

## Columbia

Adoptive Family Network **1414**

## Crofton

Bethany Christian Services of Maryland **303**

## Cumberland

Allegany County Department of Social Services **286**

## East Baltimore

Baltimore City Department of Human Resources **288**

**Elkton**

Cecil County Department of Social Services
292

**Frederick**

Frederick County Department of Social
Services 293

**Gaithersburg**

The Datz Foundation 830

**Hagerstown**

Washington County Department of Social
Services 297

**Hyattsville**

Prince George's County Department of Social
Services 295

**Prince Frederick**

Calvert County Department of Social Services
290

**Princess Anne**

Somerset County Department of Social
Services 296

**Rockville**

Adoptions Forever, Inc. 301
Jewish Social Service Agency; Adoption
Options 307
Montgomery County Department of Social
Services 294

**Salisbury**

Catholic Charities of Wilmington, Delaware
116
Children's Choice 305
Wicomico County Department of Social
Services 298

**Silver Spring**

Adoption Service Information Agency, Inc.
(ASIA) 120
Latin American Parent Association; National
Capital Region 1417
World Child, Inc. 125

**Silver Springs**

Associated Catholic Charities 121

**Takoma Park**

Lutheran Social Services 124

**Towson**

Baltimore County Department of Social
Services 289

**Westminster**

Carroll County Department of Social Services
291

# MASSACHUSETTS

**Agawam**

Wide Horizons For Children, Inc. 330

**Arlington**

Massachusetts Department of Social Services
1016

**Attleboro**

Department of Social Services of
Massachusetts 309

**Beverly**

Department of Social Services of
Massachusetts 309

**Boston**

Adoption Resource of Jewish Family and
Children's Services, Boston 311
Department of Social Services of
Massachusetts 309
The Massachusetts Adoption Resource
Exchange 1606
Massachusetts Department of Social Services
1016
New England Home for Little Wanderers 326
Project Impact 327
United Homes for Children, Inc. 1017

**Brockton**

Department of Social Services of
Massachusetts 309

**Brookline**

Adoption Resource of Jewish Family and
Children's Services, Boston 311

**Cambridge**

Adoption Center, Inc. 310
Cambridge Family and Children's Service 317
Department of Social Services of
Massachusetts 309
Love the Children 697
Massachusetts Department of Social Services
1016

**Canton**

Adoption Resource of Jewish Family and
Children's Services, Boston 311

**Chelsea**

Department of Social Services of
Massachusetts 309

**Concord**

Concord Family Service 319

**Dorchester**

Department of Social Services of
Massachusetts 309

**Duxbury**

Latin American Adoptive Families; LAAF 1420

**Fall River**

Department of Social Services of
Massachusetts 309

**Fitchburg**

Catholic Charities of Worcester 318
Department of Social Services of
Massachusetts 309

**Framingham**

Department of Social Services of
Massachusetts 309
Jewish Family Service of Metrowest 324

**Great Barrington**

Beacon Adoption Center, Inc. 313

**Greenfield**

Department of Social Services of
Massachusetts 309

**Haverhill**

Department of Social Services of
Massachusetts 309

**Holyoke**

Department of Social Services of
Massachusetts 309

**Jamaica Plain**

Department of Social Services of
Massachusetts 309

**Lawrence**

Department of Social Services of
Massachusetts 309

**Lowell**

Florence Crittenton League 320
Department of Social Services of
Massachusetts 309

**Lynn**

Department of Social Services of
Massachusetts 309

**Malden**

Adoption Resource of Jewish Family and
Children's Services, Boston 311
Department of Social Services of
Massachusetts 309

**Marion**

Southeastern Adoption Services, Inc. 329

**Merrimac**

United Homes for Children, Inc. 1017

**New Bedford**

Department of Social Services of
Massachusetts 309

**Northampton**

Department of Social Services of
Massachusetts 309

**Peabody**

The Adoption Connection 1419

**Pittsfield**

Berkshire Center for Families and Children
314
Department of Social Services of
Massachusetts 309

**Plymouth**

Department of Social Services of
  Massachusetts **309**

**Quincy**

Protestant Social Service Bureau **328**

**Roxbury**

Department of Social Services of
  Massachusetts **309**

**Somerville**

Greater Boston Catholic Charities **321**

**South Weymouth**

Department of Social Services of
  Massachusetts **309**

**South Yarmouth**

Department of Social Services of
  Massachusetts **309**

**Southbridge**

Catholic Charities of Worcester **318**

**Springfield**

Department of Social Services of
  Massachusetts **309**
Downey Side...Families for Youth **526**
Jewish Family Service of Greater Springfield,
  Inc. **323**
Massachusetts Department of Social Services
  **1016**

**Taunton**

Department of Social Services of
  Massachusetts **309**
Massachusetts Department of Social Services
  **1016**

**Tewksbury**

United Homes for Children, Inc. **1017**

**Townsend**

Hope Adoptions, Inc. **322**

**Waltham**

Department of Social Services of
  Massachusetts **309**
Wide Horizons For Children, Inc. **330**

**Watertown**

Cambridge Adoption and Counseling
  Associates, Inc. **316**

**Wellesley**

Alliance for Children, Inc. **312**

**West Newton**

International Concerns Committee for Children
  **1602**

**West Springfield**

The Brightside for Families and Children **315**

**Westboro**

Open Door Society of Massachusetts, Inc.
  **1421**

**Westfield**

Department of Social Services of
  Massachusetts **309**

**Whitinsville**

Department of Social Services of
  Massachusetts **309**

**Worcester**

Catholic Charities of Worcester **318**
Department of Social Services of
  Massachusetts **309**
Lutheran Social Services of New England, Inc.
  **948**
Lutheran Social Services of New England,
  Inc., MA **325**

# MICHIGAN

**Adrian**

Lenawee County Department of Social
  Services **339**

**Allen Park**

Families for Children, Inc. **1425**

**Alpena**

Catholic Human Services of Alpena **1022**
Community, Family and Children's Services
  **377**
Rainbow Services for Youth and Families
  **1038**

**Ann Arbor**

Catholic Social Services of Washtenaw
  County **367**
F.I.A.A.-OURS of Greater Ann Arbor **1424**
Families of Latin Kids (FOLK) **1426**
Huron Services for Youth, Inc. **383**
Ozone House **1037**
Washtenaw County O'Brien Center Foster
  Care Program **1043**

**Baldwin**

Lake County Department of Social Services
  **1029**

**Battle Creek**

The Adoption Cradle, Inc. **350**
Area Youth for Christ - Youth Guidance -
  Foster Care **1018**
Calhoun County Department of Social
  Services **333**
Family and Children's Services of Calhoun
  County **380**

**Bay City**

Bay County Department of Social Services
  **1019**
Lutheran Adoption Service **389**
Lutheran Child and Family Service **1032**

**Benton Harbor**

Berrien County Department of Social Services
  **332**

**Berkeley**

Oakland Family Services **393**

**Berkley**

Adoption Law Center, P.C. **1251**

**Berrien Springs**

Adventist Adoption and Family Services **656**

**Bingham Farms**

Child and Parent Services **373**

**Birmingham**

Americans for International Aid and Adoption
  **351**

**Caro**

Tuscola County Department of Social Services
  **345**

**Cheboygan**

Rainbow Services for Youth and Families
  **1038**

**Clinton**

Boysville of Michigan **1020**
St. Anthony Villa **1108**

**Coldwater**

Branch County Department of Social Sciences
  **1021**

**Dearborn**

Keane Center for Adoption **387**

**Detroit**

AASK Midwest **1593**
Boysville of Michigan **1020**
Lutheran Child and Family Service **1032**
Methodist Children's Home Society **391**
Wayne County Child and Family Services **348**
Wolverine Human Services **1046**

**Escanaba**

Catholic Social Services of the Upper
  Peninsula **366**
Delta County Department of Social Services
  **1024**
Upper Michigan Adoption Program **346**

**Farmington Hills**

Catholic Social Services/Oakland County **360**
LDS Social Services **388**
St. Vincent and Sarah Fisher Center **395**

**Flint**

Catholic Social Services of Flint **361**
Genesee County Department of Social
  Services **334**

**Fremont**

Bethany Christian Services (of Grand Rapids)
  **353**

**Garden City**

Huron Services for Youth, Inc. **383**

**Gaylord**

Catholic Human Services, Inc. 357
Otsego County Department of Social Services
1036
Rainbow Services for Youth and Families
1038

**Gladwin**

Gladwin County Department of Social
Services 1025

**Grand Haven**

Child and Family Services of Holland 369

**Grand Rapids**

Adoption Identity Movement of Grand Rapids
1423
Bethany Christian Services (of Grand Rapids)
353
D.A. Blodgett Services for Children and
Families 355
Catholic Social Services of Kent County 362
Kent County Department of Social Services
338
Wedgwood Christian Youth & Family Services
1045

**Hartford**

Touch of Hope Adoption Center 398
Van Buren County Department of Social
Services 347

**Hillsdale**

Hillsdale County Department of Social
Services 335

**Holland**

Bethany Christian Services (of Grand Rapids)
353
Child and Family Services of Holland 369

**Holt**

Child and Family Service of Holt 368

**Houghton**

Catholic Social Services of the Upper
Peninsula 366

**Howell**

Child and Family Services of Michigan, Inc.
(Howell) 370

**Iron Mountain**

Catholic Social Services of the Upper
Peninsula 366

**Ironwood**

Catholic Social Services of the Upper
Peninsula 366
Gogebic County Department of Social
Services 1026

**Ithaca**

Gratiot County Department of Social Services
1027

**Jackson**

Family Service And Children's Aid 381

**Jenison**

Adoption Associates, Inc. 349
Child and Family Services of Holland 369

**Kalamazoo**

Catholic Family Services of Kalamazoo 356
Family Adoption Consultants 379
Kalamazoo County Department of Social
Services 337
Lakeside Residence for Boys and Girls 1030

**Lansing**

Catholic Social Service; St. Vincent Home 359
Catholic Social Services of Lansing; St.
Vincent Home for Children 363
Christian Cradle, Inc. 375
Ingham County Dept. of Social Services 336
Lutheran Adoption Service 389
Michigan Department of Social Services 341

**Lathrup Village**

The Family Tree 1427

**Livonia**

Spectrum Human Services 1041

**Madison Heights**

Bethany Christian Services (of Eastern
Michigan) 352

**Manistique**

Sault Tribe Binogii Placement Agency 396

**Marlette**

Teen Ranch, Inc. 397

**Marquette**

Catholic Social Services of the Upper
Peninsula 366
Lutheran Social Services 390
Teaching-Family Homes of Upper Michigan
1042

**Midland**

AASK Midwest 1593

**Mio**

Rainbow Services for Youth and Families
1038

**Monroe**

Catholic Social Services of Monroe County
364
Monroe County Department of Social Services
343

**Mount Clemens**

Catholic Services of Macomb 358
Macomb County Department of Social
Services 340

**Mt. Pleasant**

Listening Ear Crisis Center, Inc. 1031

**Niles**

Adoptions Alternatives 202

**Oak Park**

Evergreen Children's Services 378

**Oscoda**

Rainbow Services for Youth and Families
1038

**Paw Paw**

Bethany Christian Services (of Van Buren
County) 354

**Pontiac**

Catholic Social Services/Oakland County 360
Oakland County Department of Social
Services 344
Oakland Family Services 393

**Port Huron**

Catholic Social Services of St. Clair County
365

**Rochester**

Family Adoption Consultants 379

**Rogers City**

Rainbow Services for Youth and Families
1038

**Roscommon**

Rainbow Services for Youth and Families
1038
Roscommon County Department of Social
Services 1039

**Royal Oak**

Judson Center 386
Morning Star Adoption Resource Services,
Inc. 392

**Saginaw**

A.D.O.P.T. (All Doing Our Part Together) 1422
Boysville of Michigan 1020
Child and Family Services of Saginaw County
371
Truths In Adoption Triad 1429

**St. Clair Shores**

Adoption Associates, Inc. 349

**St. Ignace**

Sault Tribe Binogii Placement Agency 396

**St. Joseph**

Child and Family Services of Southwestern
Michigan, Inc. 372

**St. Louis**

Christian Care/Baptist Childrens Home and
Family Ministry 374

**Sandusky**

Sanilac County Department of Social Services
1040

**Sault Ste. Marie**

Catholic Social Services of the Upper
Peninsula 366

Chippewa County Department of Social
Services **1023**
Sault Tribe Binogii Placement Agency **396**
Upper Michigan Adoption Program **346**

## Southfield

Christian Family Services **376**
Jewish Family Service of Southfield, Michigan
**385**
Judson Center **386**
Lutheran Adoption Service **389**
Lutheran Child and Family Service **1032**
Orchards Children's Services **394**
Spectrum Human Services **1041**
Teen Ranch, Inc. **397**
Wedgwood Christian Youth & Family Services
**1045**

## Stanton

Montcalm County Department of Social
Services **1034**

## Taylor

National Coalition to End Racism in America's
Child Care System **1428**

## Temperance

Catholic Social Services of Monroe County
**364**

## Traverse City

Community, Family and Children's Services
**377**
Michigan Department of Social Services;
Northern Michigan Adoption Program **342**
Wedgwood Christian Youth & Family Services
**1045**

## Utica

Catholic Services of Macomb **358**

## Walled Lake

Oakland Family Services **393**

## Warren

Catholic Services of Macomb **358**

## Waterford

Oakland Family Services **393**

## Wayne

Wayne Community Living Services, Inc. **1044**

## West Branch

Ogemon County Department of Social
Services **1035**

## Williamsburg

AASK Midwest **1593**

## Wyandotte

International Adoption Consultants **384**

## Ypsilanti

Catholic Social Services of Washtenaw
County **367**
Golden Cradle International **382**
Huron Valley Child Guidance Clinic **1028**

# MINNESOTA

## Austin

Sheriffs Youth Programs of Minnesota, Inc.
**1051**

## Baxter

Central Minnesota Korean Cultural Society,
Inc. **1431**

## Belle Plaine

The Lutheran Home **410**

## Bloomington

The Lutheran Home **410**

## Chaska

Carver County Community Social Services **400**

## Coon Rapids

New Life Family Services **413**

## Crookston

Catholic Charities, Inc.; Diocese of Crookston
**404**

## Duluth

St. Louis County Social Services; Adoption
Unit-5th Floor **401**

## Edina

Concerned United Birthparents (CUB); Twin
City-Metro Area **1432**

## Frost

New Horizons Adoption Agency, Inc. **412**

## Mankato

Catholic Charities of the Diocese of Winona
**406**

## Minneapolis

Adoptive Families of America **1430**
Crossroads, Inc. **408**
Lutheran Social Service of Minnesota **411**
New Life Family Services **413**
RESOLVE of the Twin Cities **1436**
Resources for Adoptive Parents (RAP) **1437**
Volunteers of America; Family Treatment
Program **1052**
Wellspring Adoption Agency, Inc. **414**

## North Mankato

Families of Multi-Racial Adoptions; FOMRA
**1433**

## Rochester

Catholic Charities of the Diocese of Winona
**406**
Central Minnesota Korean Cultural Society,
Inc. **1431**
New Life Family Services **413**
Rochester Area Adoptive Families Together
**1438**

## St. Cloud

Caritas Family Services **403**

## St. Paul

Catholic Charities of the Archdiocese of St.
Paul/Minneapolis **405**
Children's Home Society of Minnesota **407**
Crosstreets **1048**
The Lutheran Home **410**
Nekton Family Network **1050**
New Life Family Services **413**
North American Council on Adoptable
Children (NACAC) **1435**
Sheriffs Youth Programs of Minnesota, Inc.
**1051**

## Scandia

Liberal Education For Adoptive Families of
Minnesota **1434**

## Stillwater

HOPE Adoption and Family Services
International, Inc. **409**
Washington County Social Services **402**

## Windom

Habilitative Services, Inc. **1049**

## Winona

Catholic Charities of the Diocese of Winona
**406**

## Worthington

Catholic Charities of the Diocese of Winona
**406**

# MISSISSIPPI

## Biloxi

Catholic Social and Community Services, Inc.;
Diocese of Biloxi **418**

## Columbus

Bethany Christian Services of Mississippi **417**

## Hattiesburg

Bethany Christian Services of Mississippi **417**

## Jackson

Bethany Christian Services of Mississippi **417**
Catholic Charities, Inc. of Jackson, MS **1054**
Heart to Heart Adoption Service; Lutheran
Ministries of Georgia, Inc. **153**
Mississippi Advocates for Minority Adoptions,
Inc. **1439**
Mississippi Children's Home Society and
Family Service Association **419**
Mississippi Department of Human Services
**416**
Mississippi State Department of Human
Services **1055**

## Natchez

Catholic Charities, Inc. of Jackson, MS **1054**

## Tupelo

Alpha House **1053**

## MISSOURI

### Bridgeton
Missouri Baptist Children's Home 435

### Cape Girardeau
Lutheran Family and Children's Services of Missouri 434

### Clinton
Henry County Family Services 422

### Florissant
AASK Midwest 1593

### Hillsboro
Love Basket, Inc. 433

### Jefferson City
Missouri Department of Social Services 423

### Kansas City
Catholic Charities of Kansas City-St. Joseph, Inc. 426
Children's Foundation - Adoption and Counseling 240
Gentle Shepherd Child Placement Services 243
Highlands Child Placement Services 430
Kansas Children's Service League; Black Adoption Program 246
Kansas City Adult Adoptees Organization 1442
LIGHT House Adoption Agency 432
The James A. Roberts Agency 248

### Lee's Summit
Adoption Option 235

### Raytown
International Families of Mid-America 1441

### St. Charles
International Families 1440

### St. Joseph
Catholic Charities of Kansas City-St. Joseph, Inc. 426

### St. Louis
Adoption by Gentle Shepherd 424
Adoption by Gentle Shepherd, Inc. 233
Bethany Christian Services of St. Louis 425
The Children's Home Society of Missouri 427
Christian Family Services, Inc. 428
Robert A. Cox; The Cox Law Firm, P.C. 1252
The Family Network, Inc. 66
Jewish Family and Children's Services 431
Ralph Levy III; Attorney at Law 1253
Lutheran Family and Children's Services of Missouri 434

### Springfield
Family Therapy of the Ozarks 429
Greene County Division of Family Services 421
Worldwide Love for Children, Inc. 436

### Warrensburg
Catholic Charities of Kansas City-St. Joseph, Inc. 426

## MONTANA

### Billings
Department of Family Services of Montana 438
In-Care Network, Inc. 1059
Special Training for Exceptional People (STEP) 1060
Youth Dynamics, Inc. 1062

### Bozeman
Department of Family Services of Montana 438
Youth Dynamics, Inc. 1062

### Butte
Department of Family Services of Montana 438

### Cut Bank
Department of Family Services of Montana 438

### Glasgow
Department of Family Services of Montana 438

### Glendive
Youth Dynamics, Inc. 1062

### Great Falls
Department of Family Services of Montana 438
Golden Triangle Community Mental Health Center 1058

### Hamilton
Department of Family Services of Montana 438

### Hardin
In-Care Network, Inc. 1059

### Haure
Department of Family Services of Montana 438

### Helena
Department of Family Services, Montana 1057
Department of Family Services of Montana 438
Montana Post Adoption Center, Inc. 1443

### Kalispell
Department of Family Services of Montana 438
Therapeutic Foster Care Program; Mental Health Center 1061

### Lewistown
Department of Family Services of Montana 438
Special Training for Exceptional People (STEP) 1060

### Livingston
Youth Dynamics, Inc. 1062

### Miles City
Department of Family Services of Montana 438
Youth Dynamics, Inc. 1062

### Missoula
Department of Family Services of Montana 438
Innovative Adoptions, Inc. 95

### Red Lodge
Special Training for Exceptional People (STEP) 1060

### Sidney
Department of Family Services of Montana 438

## NEBRASKA

### Beatrice
Nebraska Department of Social Services 440

### Blair
Nebraska Department of Social Services 1064

### Broken Bow
Nebraska Department of Social Services 440

### Columbus
Nebraska Department of Social Services 1064

### Fremont
Nebraska Department of Social Services 1064

### Gering
Nebraska Department of Social Services 440

### Grand Island
Nebraska Department of Social Services 440

### Hastings
Catholic Social Services of Lincoln 443

### Hickman
Christian Heritage Children's Home 1063

### Kearney
Kearney Area Adoption Association 1444

### Lincoln
Catholic Social Services of Lincoln 443
Nebraska Department of Social Services 440
Open Hearts Adoption Support Group 1445

### Norfolk
Nebraska Department of Social Services 440

### North Platte
Nebraska Department of Social Services 440

## Omaha

Adoption Links Worldwide **441**
Black Homes for Black Children Program;
  Child Saving Institute **442**
Child Saving Institute **444**
Jewish Family Service of Omaha **445**
Lutheran Family Services **446**
Nebraska Children's Home Society **447**
Nebraska Department of Social Services **440**

## Pender

Nebraska Department of Social Services **1064**

## Pierce

Nebraska Department of Social Services **1064**

## NEVADA

### Boulder City

Adoption and Family Search Consultants **1446**

### Carson City

State of Nevada; Division of Child and Family
  Services **449**

### Elko

State of Nevada; Division of Child and Family
  Services **449**

### Ely

State of Nevada; Division of Child and Family
  Services **449**

### Fallon

State of Nevada; Division of Child and Family
  Services **449**

### Hawthorne

State of Nevada; Division of Child and Family
  Services **449**

### Las Vegas

Catholic Community Services of Nevada **1065**
Catholic Community Services of Nevada (Las
  Vegas) **450**
Catholic Community Services of Nevada
  (Reno) **451**
Jewish Family Service Agency **452**
Latter Day Saints Social Services; LDS Social
  Services **453**
Specialized Alternatives For Families And
  Youth (S.A.F.Y.) **1110**
State of Nevada; Division of Child and Family
  Services **449**

### Lovelock

State of Nevada; Division of Child and Family
  Services **449**

### Reno

Catholic Community Services of Nevada **1065**
Catholic Community Services of Nevada (Las
  Vegas) **450**
Catholic Community Services of Nevada
  (Reno) **451**
State of Nevada; Division of Child and Family
  Services **449**
Cliff J. Young; Attorney at Law **1254**

## Tonopah

State of Nevada; Division of Child and Family
  Services **449**

## Winnemucca

State of Nevada; Division of Child and Family
  Services **449**

## Yearington

State of Nevada; Division of Child and Family
  Services **449**

## NEW HAMPSHIRE

### Concord

Casey Family Services; New Hampshire
  Division **1066**
Division for Children, Youth and Families, New
  Hampshire **455**
Lutheran Social Services of New England, Inc.
  **457**
New Hampshire Division for Children, Youth,
  and Families **1067**
Wide Horizons For Children, Inc. **330**

### Derry

Open Door Society of New Hampshire, Inc.
  **1447**

### Manchester

Child and Family Services of New Hampshire
  **456**
New Hampshire Catholic Charities, Inc. **458**

## NEW JERSEY

### Asbury Park

Jewish Family And Children's Services; Jewish
  Family Services of Monmouth County **476**

### Bloomfield

New Jersey Division of Youth and Family
  Services; Adoption Unit **460**

### Brick

Latin America Parents Association, Inc.;
  LAPA, Inc. **1450**

### Camden

Spaulding for Children **481**

### Cherry Hill

Golden Cradle Adoption Services, Inc. **473**
Jewish Family And Children's Services of
  Southern New Jersey **477**

### Chester

Roots & Wings Adoption Magazine **1452**

### Clinton

Children's Home Society of New Jersey **470**

### Cranbury

Jewish Family Service; Adoption Resource
  Center **478**

## Demarest

Camp Sejong **1448**

## East Brunswick

Jewish Family Service; Adoption Resource
  Center **478**

## East Orange

Spaulding for Children **481**

## Edison

New Jersey Division of Youth and Family
  Services; Adoption Unit **460**
New Jersey Division of Youth and Family
  Services; Adoption Unit (for mid-Jersey)
  **461**

## Elizabeth

Family and Children's Services **472**
Jewish Family Service of Central New Jersey
  **479**

## Fanwood

Jewish Family Service of Central New Jersey
  **479**

## Flemington

Casa Del Mundo, Inc. **465**
Carol S. Perlmutter; Attorney at Law **1255**

## Freehold

Growing Families, Inc. **474**

## Hackensack

Christian Homes for Children **471**

## Haddonfield

Adoptions From The Heart **677**

## Hammonton

New Jersey Division of Youth and Family
  Services; Adoption Unit **460**

## Hawthorne

Bethany Christian Services **464**

## Holmdel

Adoption And Infertility Services, Inc. **463**

## Jersey City

Eileen Rhea Tulipan; Attorney at Law **1256**

## Kearny

Catholic Community Services of the Newark
  Archdiocese; Associated Catholic Charities
  **468**

## Lakewood

Children's Home Society of New Jersey **470**

## Lincroft

Adoption And Infertility Services, Inc. **463**

## Matawan

A.M.O.R. Adoptions, Inc. **462**

**Millington**

Catholic Charities, Metuchan Diocese;
  Department of Maternity and Adoption
  Services **467**

**Morganville**

Jewish Family And Children's Services; Jewish
  Family Services of Monmouth County **476**

**Oradell**

Rainbow Families **1451**

**Paterson**

New Jersey Division of Youth and Family
  Services; Adoption Unit **460**

**Red Bank**

Catholic Charities, Diocese of Trenton **466**

**South Orange**

Eileen Rhea Tulipan; Attorney at Law **1256**

**Sparta**

Christian Homes for Children **471**

**Teaneck**

Homestudies, Inc. **475**

**Trenton**

Catholic Charities, Diocese of Trenton **466**
Children's Home Society of New Jersey **470**
Holt International Children's Services **659**
New Jersey Division of Youth and Family
  Services **1068**
New Jersey Division of Youth and Family
  Services; Adoption Unit **460**

**Turnersville**

Children's Choice **305**

**Vineland**

Catholic Social Services of Vineland **469**

**Westfield**

Spaulding for Children **481**

**Whippany**

Concerned Persons For Adoption **1449**

**Yardville**

Lutheran Social Ministries of New Jersey **480**

# NEW MEXICO

**Albuqerque**

Healing the Children - New Mexico Chapter
  **1069**

**Albuquerque**

Anne H. Assink; Attorney at Law **1257**
Chaparral Maternity and Adoption Services
  **485**
Child-Rite, Inc. **486**
Families for Children; A Division of New
  Mexico Boys Ranch **488**
Hogares, Inc. **1070**

La Familia Placement Services, Inc. **489**
Parents of Inter-Cultural Adoption, Inc. **1453**
David R. Preininger **1258**
Rocky Mountain Adoption Exchange **1611**
Triad Adoption and Counseling Services, Inc.
  **491**

**Belen**

Rainbow House International **490**

**Las Cruces**

Christian Child Placement Service **487**

**Portales**

Christian Child Placement Service **487**

**Santa Fe**

Catholic Social Services of Santa Fe, Inc. **484**
Child-Rite, Inc. **486**
Children, Youth and Families Dept. (New
  Mexico); Social Services Division **483**

**Taos**

Child-Rite, Inc. **486**

# NEW YORK

**Albany**

Albany County Department of Social Services
  **493**
Community Maternity Services **525**
Gloria A. Copland, Esq. **1260**
International Adoptive Families **1471**

**Baldwinsville**

Americans for International Aid and Adoption
  **351**

**Beaver Dams**

AASK Midwest **1593**

**Bellmore**

Adoptive Parents Committee of New York
  State; Long Island Chapter **1462**

**Bronx**

Pius XII Youth and Family Services **1083**
St. Dominic's Family Service Center **1086**

**Brooklyn**

Adoption Advisory Council **1456**
The Angel Guardian Home **519**
Brookwood Child Care **1072**
Child Development Support Corp. **1074**
Heartshare Human Services of New York
  **1077**
Latin American Parents Association (LAPA)
  **1474**
Little Flower Children's Services **1080**
New York Singles Adopting Children; NYSAC
  **1476**
Ohel Children's Home and Family Services
  **1082**
St. Joseph's Services for Children and
  Families **538**
Society for Seamen's Children **1088**

**Buffalo**

Erie County Department of Social Services
  **498**
St. Augustine's Center; Child Welfare Services
  Department **1085**

**Burnt Hills**

Bethany Christian Services (of Burnt Hills) **520**

**Canton**

St. Lawrence County Department of Social
  Services **510**

**Carmel**

Putnam County Department of Social Services
  **508**

**Clifton Park**

The Family Tree Adoption Agency, Inc. **529**

**Cobleskill**

Community Maternity Services **525**

**Cooperstown**

Otsego County Department of Social Services
  **507**

**Delaware**

Delaware County Department of Social
  Services **496**

**Dunkirk**

Chautauqua County Department of Social
  Services **494**

**East Islip**

New Hope Family Services, Inc. **535**

**Elizabethtown**

Essex County Department of Social Services
  **499**

**Elmira**

Chemung County Department of Social
  Services **495**

**Flushing**

Adoptive Families of Older Children **1461**

**Forest Hills**

Forestdale, Inc. **1076**

**Gloversville**

Community Maternity Services **525**

**Goshen**

Orange County Department of Social Services
  **506**

**Granville**

Community Maternity Services **525**

**Hauppauge**

Suffolk County Department of Social Services
  **513**

## Hudson

V.I.D.A., Inc.; Voices for International Development and Adoption, Inc. **541**

## Ilion

Community Maternity Services **525**

## Indian Lake

Hamilton County Department of Social Services **501**

## Irvington

Abbott House **1071**

## Islip Terrace

Adoptive Families of Long Island **1460**

## Ithaca

Adoptive Families Association of Tompkins County, NY **1459**
New York State Citizens' Coalition for Children, Inc. **1477**
Tompkins County Department of Social Services **515**

## Jamestown

Chautauqua County Department of Social Services **494**

## Johnstown

Fulton County Department of Social Services **500**

## Kingston

Children's Home of Kingston (CHK) **1075**

## Lackawanna

Our Lady of Victory Infant Home **537**

## Lake George

Community Maternity Services **525**
Warren County Department of Social Services **516**

## Little Neck

Family Focus Adoption Services **527**

## Lockport

Niagara County Department of Social Services **504**

## Malone

Catholic Charities of Ogdensburg **521**

## Mayville

Chautauqua County Department of Social Services **494**

## Middletown

Pius XII Youth and Family Services **1083**

## Mineola

New Beginnings Family and Children's Services, Inc. **534**

## New York

Adoptees' Liberty Movement Association; ALMA **1455**
Adoption Crossroads **1457**
The Association of Black Social Workers' Child Adoption, Counseling and Referral Service **1463**
Children's Aid Society of New York **524**
Council for Equal Rights in Adoption **1467**
Downey Side...Families for Youth **526**
Edwin Gould Services for Children **530**
Harlem-Dowling West Side Center for Children and Family Services **531**
Jewish Child Care Association **1079**
KinQuest Inc. **1472**
Lutheran Community Services, Inc. **532**
McMahon Services for Children **1081**
New York City Department of Social Services; Division of Adoption/Foster Care Services/Home Assessment Services/Centralized Services **503**
New York Council on Adoptable Children **1475**
Richard Allen Center on Life **1084**
Spence-Chapin Services to Families and Children **539**
Talbot Perkins Children's Services **540**

## Newburgh

Pius XII Youth and Family Services **1083**

## Niagara Falls

Niagara County Department of Social Services **504**

## North White Plains

Birthparents Support Network **1464**

## Ogdensburg

Catholic Charities of Ogdensburg **521**

## Oneida

Catholic Charities of Utica **522**
Families Through Adoption **1469**

## Oneonta

Community Maternity Services **525**

## Owego

Tioga County Department of Social Services **514**

## Patchogue

Adopted Children of Romania Network (ACORN) **1454**

## Penfield

The Council of Adoptive Parents **1468**

## Pittsford

Adoption Resource Network, Inc. **1458**

## Plattsburgh

Catholic Charities of Ogdensburg **521**

## Poughkeepsie

Dutchess County Department of Social Services **497**

## Rochester

Catholic Family Center of the Diocese of Rochester **523**
Children Awaiting Parents, Inc. **1466**
Hillside Children's Center **1078**
Latin American Families **1473**
Jeanette F. Snyder; Attorney at Law **1263**

## Rome

Catholic Charities of Utica **522**

## Ronkonkoma

Wide Horizons For Children, Inc. **330**

## Schenectady

Schenectady County Department of Social Services **511**
Eli I. Taub; Attorney at Law **1264**

## Schoharie

Schoharie County Department of Social Services **512**

## Seneca Falls

Finger Lakes Adoption Group (F.L.A.G.) **1470**

## Staten Island

Mission of the Immaculate Virgin - Mount Loretto **533**
Richmond Adoptive Parents Group **1478**
Society for Seamen's Children **1088**

## Syosset

St. Mary's Children & Family Services **1087**

## Syracuse

Central New York Friends of Love the Children, Inc. **1465**
Raymond J. Dague **1261**
New Hope Family Services, Inc. **535**
New Life Adoption Agency, Inc. **536**
Onondaga County Department of Social Services **505**
Golda Zimmerman, Esq. **1265**

## Troy

Community Maternity Services **525**
Rensselaer County Department of Social Services **509**

## Utica

Catholic Charities of Utica **522**

## Waccabuc

Christine Mesberg; Attorney at Law **1262**

## Wading River

Little Flower Children's Services **1080**

## Warsaw

Wyoming County Department of Social Services **518**

## Watertown

Catholic Charities of Ogdensburg **521**
Jefferson County Department of Social Services **502**

*Geographic Index*

**White Plains**

Family Service of Westchester **528**
A K.I.D.S. Exchange; Adoption, Knowledge & Information on Down Syndrome **1604**
Westchester County Department of Social Services **517**

**Woodbury**

Aaron Britvan; Attorney at Law **1259**

# NORTH CAROLINA

**Asheboro**

Randolph County Department of Social Services **556**

**Asheville**

Bethany Christian Services of Asheville **560**
Catholic Social Services of Charlotte **563**
Professional Parenting/Adoption Plus **1091**

**Burlington**

Alamance County Department of Social Services **543**

**Cary**

The Datz Foundation **830**

**Chapel Hill**

North Carolina Adoption Connections **1482**

**Charlotte**

Bethany Christian Services of Asheville **560**
Catholic Social Services of Charlotte **563**
Southern Piedmont Adoptive Families of America **1483**

**Durham**

Tri-Adopt **1485**

**Fayetteville**

Catholic Social Ministries of the Diocese of Raleigh, Inc. **562**
Cumberland County Department of Social Services **546**

**Graham**

Carolina Adoption Triangle Support (CATS) **1481**

**Greensboro**

Carolina Adoption Services, Inc. **561**
The Children's Home Society of North Carolina **564**
F. Kevin Gorham; Attorney at Law **1266**
Guilford County Department of Social Services; Adoption Unit **549**
SPICE **1484**
Youth Focus, Inc. **1092**

**Greenville**

Catholic Social Ministries of the Diocese of Raleigh, Inc. **562**
The Children's Home Society of North Carolina **564**
Pitt County Department of Social Services **555**

**Hillsborough**

Orange County Department of Social Services **554**

**Kinston**

Lenoir County Department of Social Services **551**

**Lexington**

Davidson County Department of Social Services **547**

**Lillington**

Harnett County Department of Social Services **550**

**Matthews**

Adoption Search Consultants **1479**
Christian Adoption Services, Inc. **565**

**Monroe**

Union County Department of Social Services **558**

**Morganton**

Professional Parenting/Adoption Plus **1091**

**Nashville**

Nash County Department of Social Services **552**

**New Bern**

Craven County Department of Social Services **545**

**Raleigh**

Bethany Christian Services of Asheville **560**
Capital Area Families for Adoption (CAFA) **1480**
Catholic Social Ministries of the Diocese of Raleigh, Inc. **562**
The Children's Home Society of North Carolina **564**
Lutheran Family Services in the Carolinas **567**
Wake County Department of Social Services **559**

**Salisbury**

Rowan County Department of Social Services **557**

**Shelby**

Cleveland County Department of Social Services **544**

**Wilmington**

New Hanover County Department of Social Services **553**

**Winston-Salem**

Catholic Social Services of Charlotte **563**
Family Services, Inc. **566**
Forsyth County Department of Social Services **548**
Professional Parenting/Adoption Plus **1091**

# NORTH DAKOTA

**Bismarck**

Catholic Family Service (of Fargo) **570**
Lutheran Social Services of North Dakota **572**
New Horizons Adoptions **573**
North Dakota Department of Human Services; Division of Children and Family Services **569**
The Village Family Service Center **574**

**Fargo**

Catholic Family Service (of Fargo) **570**
Christian Family Life Services, Inc. **571**
Lutheran Social Services of North Dakota **572**
The Village Family Service Center **574**

**Grand Forks**

Catholic Family Service (of Fargo) **570**
The Village Family Service Center **574**

**Minot**

Lutheran Social Services of North Dakota **572**
The Village Family Service Center **574**

**Williston**

Lutheran Social Services of North Dakota **572**

# OHIO

**Ada**

The Child Placement Professionals, Inc. **1096**

**Akron**

Family Service of Summit County **625**
Jewish Family Services of Akron **628**
Mentor Clinical Care **1103**
Summit County Children Services Board **610**

**Ashtabula**

Ashtabula County Children Services Board **576**

**Athens**

Southeast Ohio Adoptive Family Support Group **1494**

**Barberton**

Family Service of Summit County **625**

**Bedford Heights**

Specialized Alternatives For Families And Youth (S.A.F.Y.) **1110**

**Bellafontaine**

Logan County Children's Services Board **594**

**Berea**

Berea Children's home and Family Services **1094**
Options for Youth, Inc. **1104**

**Bowling Green**

Wood County Department of Human Services **613**

## Bryan

Lutheran Social Services of Toledo **633**

## Bucyrus

Lutheran Social Services of Toledo **633**

## Caldwell

Noble County Department of Human Services **602**

## Cambridge

Guernsey County Childrens Services Board **588**

## Canton

Mentor Clinical Care **1103**
Specialized Alternatives For Families And Youth (S.A.F.Y.) **1110**
Stark County Department of Human Services **609**

## Carrollton

Carroll County Department of Human Services **580**

## Celina

Mercer County Department of Human Services **599**

## Cincinnati

AASK Midwest **1593**
Adoptive Families of Greater Cincinnati **1486**
Catholic Social Services of Southwestern Ohio **620**
Children's Home of Cincinnati, Inc. **621**
Down Syndrome Association of Greater Cincinnati **1600**
Family Ties Therapeutic Foster Care; St. Joseph Orphanage **1098**
Focus on Youth, Inc. **1099**
Hamilton County Department of Human Services **589**
Stephen R. Hext; Attorney at Law **1267**
Lutheran Social Services of the Miami Valley **632**
Specialized Alternatives For Families And Youth (S.A.F.Y.) **1110**

## Cleveland

Adoptive Families Support Association, Inc. **1487**
Beech Brook **1093**
Beech Brook; Spaulding Adoption Program **615**
Cuyohoga County Department of Children and Family Services **584**
HARAMBEE: Services to Black Families **626**
RESOLVE of Ohio, Inc. (Cleveland) **1491**

## Columbus

Adoption by Gentle Care **614**
Catholic Social Service of Columbus **618**
Crittendon Family Services **622**
Franklin County Department of Children's Services **587**
Lutheran Social Services of Central Ohio **631**
New Roots - Adoptive Family Support Group **1490**
Ohio Adoption Photo Listing; OAPL **1610**
Parenthesis Family Advocates **1106**

Rosemont Center **1107**
Specialized Alternatives For Families And Youth (S.A.F.Y.) **1110**
Worly Family Adoption Studies, Inc. **1270**

## Coshocton

Coshocton County Children Services Board **583**

## Dayton

Catholic Social Services of the Miami Valley **1095**
Jewish Family Services of Dayton **629**
Kids Are Really Essential, Inc. (KARE, Inc.) **1101**
Lutheran Social Services of the Miami Valley **632**
Montgomery County Children Services **601**
RESOLVE of Ohio, Inc. (Dayton) **1492**
St. Joseph Children's Treatment Center **1109**
Specialized Alternatives For Families And Youth (S.A.F.Y.) **1110**
Youth Engaged for Success, Inc. **1112**
Youth Services Network of S.W.O., Inc. **1113**

## Defiance

Lutheran Social Services of Toledo **633**

## Delphos

Specialized Alternatives For Families And Youth (S.A.F.Y.) **1110**

## Findlay

Hancock County Department of Human Services; Children's Protective Services **590**
Lutheran Social Services of Toledo **633**

## Fremont

Lutheran Social Services of Toledo **633**

## Galena

Worly Family Adoption Studies, Inc. **1270**

## Georgetown

Brown County Department of Human Services **578**

## Hamilton

Butler County Children's Services Board **579**
Catholic Social Services of Southwestern Ohio **620**

## Hayesville

Compassion, Inc. **1097**

## Hudson

LIMIAR: U.S.A., Inc. **630**

## Independence

Mentor Clinical Care **1103**
Options for Youth, Inc. **1104**

## Ironton

Lawrence County Department Of Human Services **592**

## Kent

Concern for Children **1488**

## Lancaster

Fairfield County Children's Services **586**

## Lebanon

Warren County Children Services **612**

## Lima

Regional Family Counseling, Inc. **1268**
Specialized Alternatives For Families And Youth (S.A.F.Y.) **1110**

## London

Madison County Department of Human Services **596**

## Macedonia

Family Adoption Consultants **379**

## Marion

Marion County Children Service Board **598**

## Maumee

Paraclete Social Outreach, Inc. **1105**

## Mt. Vernon

Knox County Children's Services/Department of Human Services **591**

## Napoleon

Lutheran Social Services of Toledo **633**

## New Boston

Scioto County Children Services **606**

## New Lexington

Perry County Children's Services **604**

## New Philadelphia

Tuscarawas County Department of Human Services **611**

## Newark

Catholic Social Service of Columbus **618**
Licking County Department of Human Services **593**
Symbiont, Inc. **1111**

## Niles

Homes for Kids, Inc. **1100**

## North Canton

AASK Midwest **1593**

## North Royalton

European Adoption Consultants **623**

## Norwalk

Mentor Clinical Care **1103**

## Oak Harbor

Ottawa County Department of Human Services **603**

**Ottawa**

Putnam County Department of Human
Services **605**

**Painesville**

Catholic Social Services of Lake County **619**

**Perrysburg**

Lutheran Social Services of Toledo **633**

**Pleasant Plain**

Mid-Western Children's Home **634**

**Portsmouth**

Catholic Social Service of Columbus **618**

**Reynoldsburg**

Reunite, Inc. **1493**

**St. Clairsville**

Belmont County Children Services Board **577**

**Sandusky**

Erie County Department of Human Services
**585**
Lutheran Social Services of Toledo **633**

**Sidney**

Catholic Social Services of the Miami Valley
**1095**
Shelby County Children Services Board **608**
Specialized Alternatives For Families And
Youth (S.A.F.Y.) **1110**

**Springfield**

Baptist Children's Home and Family Ministries
**204**
Clark County Department of Human Services
**582**

**Steubenville**

Family Service Association **624**

**Sylvania**

Jewish Family Service of Sylvania **627**
Helen D. Russell **1269**

**Tiffin**

Seneca County Department of Human
Services **607**

**Toledo**

AASK Midwest **1593**
Boysville of Michigan **1020**
Lucas County Children's Service Board **595**
Lutheran Social Services of Toledo **633**
St. Anthony Villa **1108**
Specialized Alternatives For Families And
Youth (S.A.F.Y.) **1110**

**Urbana**

Champaign County Department of Human
Services **581**

**Van Wert**

The Marsh Foundation Teaching-Family
Program **1102**

**Warren**

Catholic Community Services, Inc. of Trumbull
County **616**
Northeast Ohio Adoption Services **635**

**Wickliffe**

Catholic Social Services of Lake County **619**

**Woodsfield**

Monroe County Department of Human
Services **600**

**Worthington**

United Methodist Children's Home **636**

**Youngstown**

Catholic Service League, Inc. **617**
Mahoning County Children Services **597**
Mentor Clinical Care **1103**

**Zanesville**

Catholic Social Service of Columbus **618**

# OKLAHOMA

**Bartlesville**

Youth and Family Services of Washington
County **1122**

**Bethany**

Bethany Adoption Service, Inc. of Oklahoma
**643**

**Edmond**

Adoptive Families Support Association (AFSA)
- An Adoptive Families Network **1496**
MetroCenter for Family Ministries, Inc. **650**

**El Reno**

Maria Erbar; Attorney at Law **1271**

**Enid**

Youth and Family Services of North Central
Oklahoma **1121**

**Harrah**

Adopt a Special Kid - Oklahoma Chapter;
AASK-Oklahoma Chapter **1495**

**Jones**

Genesis Project **1114**

**Lawton**

Cradle of Lawton, Inc. **645**

**Midwest City**

Small Miracles International **652**

**Norman**

Adoptive Parents of Central Oklahoma
(APCO) **1497**
The Family Tree Adoption and Counseling
Center **649**
Juvenile Services, Inc. **1116**

**Oklahoma City**

Associated Catholic Charities of Oklahoma
City **642**
Colorado Christian Services **90**
Deaconess Home: Pregnancy and Adoption
Services **647**
Maria Erbar; Attorney at Law **1271**
Hillcrest Health Center; Therapeutic Foster
Care **1115**
Lutheran Social Service of Kansas and
Oklahoma **247**
NSO-Project Adopt; Project Adopt
Neighborhood Services Organization, Inc.
**651**
Oklahoma Council on Adoptable Children
**1498**
Oklahoma Department of Human Services
**638**
Sunbeam Family Services **1119**

**Ponca City**

Northern Oklahoma Youth Service Center and
Shelter, Inc. **1117**

**Stillwater**

Payne County Youth Services **1118**

**Tulsa**

Adoption Affiliates **639**
The Adoption Center **640**
Appletree Adoptions, Inc. **641**
Catholic Charities of Tulsa **644**
Crisis Pregnancy Outreach **646**
Dillon International, Inc. **648**
Tulsa Boys' Home **1120**

# OREGON

**Albany**

Children's Services Division of Oregon **1123**

**Astoria**

Children's Services Division of Oregon **1123**

**Baker**

Children's Services Division of Oregon **1123**

**Bend**

Children's Services Division of Oregon **1123**

**Boardman**

Children's Services Division of Oregon **1123**

**Burns**

Children's Services Division of Oregon **1123**

**Condon**

Children's Services Division of Oregon **1123**

**Coos Bay**

Children's Services Division of Oregon **1123**

**Corvallis**

Children's Services Division of Oregon **1123**

**The Dalles**

Children's Services Division of Oregon **1123**

**Dalls**

Children's Services Division of Oregon **1123**

**Enterprise**

Children's Services Division of Oregon **1123**

**Eugene**

Children's Services Division of Oregon **1123**
Family Ties **1499**
Holt International Children's Services **659**
Open Adoption and Family Services, Inc. **661**

**Gold Beach**

Children's Services Division of Oregon **1123**

**Grants Pass**

Children's Services Division of Oregon **1123**
Southern Oregon Adoptive Rights **1503**

**Hermiston**

Children's Services Division of Oregon **1123**

**Hillsboro**

Children's Services Division of Oregon **1123**
Journeys of the Heart Adoption Services **660**

**Hood River**

Children's Services Division of Oregon **1123**

**John Day**

Children's Services Division of Oregon **1123**

**Klamath Falls**

Children's Services Division of Oregon **1123**

**LaGrande**

Children's Services Division of Oregon **1123**

**Lake Oswego**

Laurence H. Spiegel; Attorney at Law **1273**

**Lakeview**

Children's Services Division of Oregon **1123**

**Madras**

Children's Services Division of Oregon **1123**

**Marylhurst**

Children's Services Division of Oregon **1123**

**McMinnville**

Children's Services Division of Oregon **1123**
PLAN International Adoption Service **663**

**Medford**

Children's Services Division of Oregon **1123**
Southern Oregon Adoptive Families **1502**

**Newport**

Children's Services Division of Oregon **1123**

**Ontario**

Children's Services Division of Oregon **1123**

**Pendleton**

Children's Services Division of Oregon **1123**

**Portland**

Adventist Adoption and Family Services **656**
Albertina Kerr Center for Children **657**
Children's Services Division of Oregon **1123**
Give Us This Day, Inc. **1124**
Heritage Adoption Services **658**
Northwest Adoptive Families Association, Inc. **1500**
Open Adoption and Family Services, Inc. **661**
Oregon Adoptive Rights Association; OARA **1501**

**Prineville**

Children's Services Division of Oregon **1123**

**Reedsport**

Children's Services Division of Oregon **1123**

**Roseburg**

Children's Services Division of Oregon **1123**

**St. Helens**

Children's Services Division of Oregon **1123**

**Salem**

Children's Services Division of Oregon **1123**
John W. Jensen; Attorney at Law **1272**
Oregon Childrens Services Division **655**

**Tillamook**

Children's Services Division of Oregon **1123**

**Woodburn**

Children's Services Division of Oregon **1123**

# PENNSYLVANIA

**Allentown**

Adoptions From The Heart **677**
Catholic Social Agency (of Allentown) **686**
Catholic Social Agency of Allentown **1128**
International Concerns Committee for Children **1602**

**Ardmore**

Adoptions From The Heart **677**

**Beaver**

Beaver County Children and Youth Agency **665**

**Chambersburg**

The Children's Aid Society of Franklin County **691**

**Chester**

Children and Youth Services of Delaware County **1129**
Delaware County Children and Youth **669**

**Clearfield**

The Children's Aid Society of Clearfield, PA **690**

**Cranberry Township**

International Adoptive Families **1506**

**Delmont**

Welcome House Special Services of the Pearl S. Buck Foundation **681**

**Dillsburg**

York County Children and Youth Services **1141**

**Doylestown**

Bucks County Children and Youth Agency **667**

**DuBois**

Catholic Charities Counseling and Adoption Services of Erie **682**

**Erie**

Catholic Charities Counseling and Adoption Services of Erie **682**
Erie County Children and Youth Agency **670**
Parents of Adopted African American Children (PAAAC) **1507**

**Ft. Washington**

Bethany Christian Services of Ft. Washington **679**

**Gibsonia**

Pittsburgh Adoption Lifeline **1508**

**Glenside**

Lutheran Children & Family Service **698**

**Greensburg**

Catholic Charities of Greensburg **683**
Lutheran Service Society of Western Pennsylvania **699**
Westmoreland County Children's Bureau **1140**

**Hanover**

York County Children and Youth Services **1141**

**Harborcreek**

Harborcreek Youth Services **1131**

**Harrisburg**

Catholic Charities of the Diocese of Harrisburg, PA., Inc. **684**
Dauphin County Children and Youth Agency **668**

**Hawley**

Today's Adoption Agency, Ltd. **701**

**Hazelton**

Luzerne County Children and Youth Agency **1132**

**Lancaster**

Adoptions From The Heart **677**
Bethany Christian Services of Lancaster **680**
Family Service **694**
Lancaster County Children and Youth Social Service Agency **671**

**Matamoras**

New Beginnings Family and Children's Services, Inc. **534**

**Media**

Children and Youth Services of Delaware County **1129**

**Mercer**

Children's Aid Society of Mercer County **692**

**Norristown**

Montgomery County Office of Children and Youth **672**

**Oil City**

Family Service and Children's Aid Society of Venango County **695**

**Parkersburg**

Try Again Homes Inc. **1138**

**Perkasie**

Welcome House Special Services of the Pearl S. Buck Foundation **681**

**Philadelphia**

Best Nest, Inc. **1127**
Bethanna **678**
Catholic Social Services; Archdiocese of Philadelphia **687**
Children's Choice **305**
Children's Choice of Delaware **950**
Children's Services, Inc. **1130**
Jewish Family and Children's Services **696**
National Adoption Exchange **1608**
Philadelphia County Children and Youth Agency **673**
The Salvation Army; Children's Services **1137**

**Pittsburgh**

Alternative Program Associates **1126**
Catholic Charities of the Diocese of Pittsburgh, Inc. **685**
Council on Adoptable Children **1504**
Family Adoption Center **693**
Project STAR **700**
Three Rivers Adoption Council **1614**
James B. Wiltse **1274**

**Pottsville**

Schuylkill County Children and Youth Agency **674**

**Quakertown**

Love the Children **697**

**Reading**

Berks County Children and Youth Agency; County Services Center **666**

**Rochester**

Families Together **1505**

**Scranton**

Catholic Social Services of Lackawanna County **688**

**Sharon**

Catholic Charities Counseling and Adoption Services of Erie **682**

**Shippensburg**

AASK Midwest **1593**
Welcome House Special Services of the Pearl S. Buck Foundation **681**

**Somerset**

Children's Aid Home and Society of Somerset County **689**

**Southampton**

Bethanna **678**

**Stroudsburg**

Monroe County Children and Youth Services **1133**

**Uniontown**

Try Again Homes Inc. **1138**

**Washington**

Try Again Homes Inc. **1138**
Washington County Children and Youth Agency **675**
Washington County Children and Youth Services **1139**

**Whitehall**

Pinebrook Services for Children and Youth **1136**

**Wilkes-Barre**

Luzerne County Children and Youth Agency **1132**
Northeast Foster Care, Inc. **1135**

**Williamsport**

Tressler Lutheran Services **702**

**Willow Grove**

Aldersgate Youth Service Bureau **1125**

**York**

Tressler Lutheran Services **702**
York County Children and Youth Services **676**

# RHODE ISLAND

**Foster**

G.I.F.T. of R.I., Inc.; Getting International/ Transcultural Families Together **1509**

**Pawtucket**

Alliance for Children, Inc. **312**

**Providence**

Catholic Social Services **705**
Children's Friend and Service **706**
Department for Children and Their Families **1143**
Family Service, Inc. **1144**
Gift of Life Adoption Services, Inc. **707**
Rhode Island Department for Children, Youth & Families **704**

**Wakefield**

Wide Horizons For Children, Inc. **330**

**Warren**

North American Family Institute **1145**

**Warwick**

Casey Family Services - Rhode Island Division **1142**

# SOUTH CAROLINA

**Cayce-West Columbia**

Adoptees & Birth Parents in Search **1510**

**Charleston**

Catholic Charities Adoption Services; Diocese of Charleston, South Carolina **710**

**Columbia**

Children Unlimited, Inc. **711**
Bonnie P. Horn; Attorney at Law **1275**
South Carolina Department of Social Services **1146**
South Carolina Department of Social Services; Children, Family and Adult Services **709**
Specialized Alternatives For Families And Youth (S.A.F.Y.) **1110**

**Duncan**

Southeastern Children's Home **713**

**Florence**

South Carolina Department of Social Services; Children, Family and Adult Services **709**

**Fort Mill**

Christian Family Services **712**

**Greenville**

Family Counseling Center of Greenville, Inc. **1511**
South Carolina Department of Social Services; Children, Family and Adult Services **709**
The Southeastern Exchange of the United States **1612**

**North Charleston**

South Carolina Department of Social Services; Children, Family and Adult Services **709**

**Rock Hill**

South Carolina Department of Social Services; Children, Family and Adult Services **709**

# SOUTH DAKOTA

**Aberdeen**

Catholic Family Services **716**

**Brookings**

South Dakota Department of Social Services; Child Protective Services **715**

**Elk Point**

Terre Berkland, MSW, CSW/PIP **1276**

## Hot Springs

South Dakota Department of Social Services; Child Protective Services **715**

## Philip

South Dakota Adoption Council **1513**

## Pierre

South Dakota Department of Social Services; Child Protection Services **1147**
South Dakota Department of Social Services; Child Protective Services **715**

## Rapid City

LDS Social Services **718**
South Dakota Department of Social Services; Child Protective Services **715**

## Sioux Falls

Catholic Family Services **716**
Christian Counseling Services **717**
Families through Adoption **1512**
Lutheran Social Services of South Dakota **719**
South Dakota Department of Social Services; Child Protective Services **715**

## Watertown

South Dakota Department of Social Services; Child Protective Services **715**

## Yankton

Terre Berkland, MSW, CSW/PIP **1276**

## TENNESSEE

## Bartlett

Mid-South Families Through Adoption **1514**

## Brentwood

Tennessee Baptist Children's Home, Inc. **733**

## Chattanooga

Associated Catholic Charities of East Tennessee **722**
Bethany Christian Services of Chattenooga **723**

## Germantown

Mid-South Families Through Adoption **1514**

## Hermitage

Small World Ministries **732**

## Jonesborough

Associated Catholic Charities of East Tennessee **722**

## Knoxville

Associated Catholic Charities of East Tennessee **722**
Child and Family Services **725**

## Memphis

Jewish Family Service **729**
Porter-Leath Children's Center **730**
St. Peters Home for Children; Maternity and Adoptive Services **731**

West Tennessee Baptist Children's Home **735**

## Nashville

Catholic Charities of Tennessee, Inc. **724**
Christian Counseling Services **726**
Family and Children's Service **728**
Family and Educational Advisory Associates **1148**
Tennessee Conference Adoption Service **734**
Tennessee Department of Human Services **721**

## Nolensville

OURS of Middle Tennessee **1515**

## Sevierville

Church of God Home for Children **727**

# TEXAS

## Abilene

Christian Homes of Abilene **766**
Harmony Family Services **1154**
Hendrick Home for Children **1155**
Texas Department of Protective and Regulatory Services **745**

## Amarillo

Catholic Family Services, Inc.; Diocese of Amarillo and Lubbock **763**
High Plains Children's Home & Family Services, Inc. **773**
Texas Department of Human Services; Region 1 **739**

## Arlington

Adopting Children Together **1516**
Specialized Alternatives For Families And Youth (S.A.F.Y.) **1110**
Texas Department of Protective and Regulatory Services **743**
Therapeutic Family Life **1158**

## Austin

Andrel Adoptions, Inc. **758**
The Bair Foundation **1149**
Lutheran Social Service of the South (Austin) **779**
Marywood Children and Family Services **781**
Vika Newsom **1277**
Texas Department of Human Services; Region 7 **740**
Texas Department of Protective and Regulatory Services **744**
Therapeutic Family Life **1158**

## Baytown

DePelchin Children's Center **770**
Parents Aiding and Lending Support (PALS) **1519**

## Beaumont

Cradle of Life Adoption Agency, Inc. **769**

## Belton

Texas Department of Human Services; Region 7 **740**

## Brookshire

DePelchin Children's Center **770**

## Bryan

Child Placement Center of Texas **765**
Texas Department of Human Services; Region 7 **740**

## Cherokee

Cherokee Home for Children **1150**

## Corpus Christi

Coastal Bend Youth City **1152**
Texas Department of Protective and Regulatory Services; Region 11 **746**

## Dallas

Adoption Access, Inc. **751**
Adoption Advisory, Inc. **752**
Catholic Counseling Services of Dallas **761**
Child Placement Center/Agape Social Services **764**
A Cradle of Hope; Adoption Counseling Center **768**
Gift of Love Adoption Agency **771**
Hope Cottage **775**
Lutheran Social Service of the South, Inc. (Dallas) **780**
Placement Services Agency **784**

## Driscoll

Coastal Bend Youth City **1152**

## El Paso

Child Protective Services; Texas Department of Protective and Regulatory Services **737**
Lee and Beulah Moor Children's Home **782**

## Ft. Worth

Adoption Access, Inc. **751**
Adoption Services, Inc. **756**
Catholic Counseling Services of Dallas **761**
The Gladney Center **772**
Little People of America, Inc.; Adoption Committee **1518**

## Galveston

Leslie Thacker Agency, Inc. **787**

## Grand Prairie

Right To Know **1521**

## Houston

Blessed Trinity Adoptions, Inc. **759**
Catholic Charities of Houston **760**
DePelchin Children's Center **770**
Homes of St. Mark **774**
New Life Christian Services **783**
Texas Department of Protection and Regulatory Services **741**
Texas Department of Protective and Regulatory Services; Region 6 **748**
Leslie Thacker Agency, Inc. **787**
Trinity Adoption Services International, Inc. **788**

## Humble

Alternatives in Motion, Inc. **757**

### Hurst

AASK/Texas **1594**
Adopt A Special Kid/Texas, Inc.; AASK/
Texas, Inc. **750**

### Irving

Searchline of Texas, Inc. **1522**

### Kaufman

Joy Home for Boys; P.A.T.H. **1157**

### Keller

Christ's Haven for Children **767**

### Killeen

Child Placement Center of Texas **765**

### Kingsville

Texas Department of Protective and
Regulatory Services; Region 11 **746**

### Longview

Catholic Counseling Services of Dallas **761**

### Lufkin

Deep East Texas Mental Health/Mental
Retardation Center **1153**

### McAllen

Texas Department of Protective and
Regulatory Services; Region 11 **746**

### Midland

Texas Department of Protective and
Regulatory Services **742**

### Nacogdoches

Texas Department of Protective and
Regulatory Services; Region 5 **747**

### Odessa

Stoker Adoption Agency **785**

### San Antonio

Abrazo Adoption Associates **749**
Adoption Advocates **753**
Adoption Affiliates **639**
Adoption Affiliates, Inc. **754**
Adoption Services Associates **755**
Catholic Family and Children's Services, Inc.;
Archdiocese of San Antonio **762**
Department of Protective and Regulatory
Services; Region 8 **738**
The Post Adoption Center of the Southwest
**1520**
The Texas Cradle Society **786**

### Stafford

DePelchin Children's Center **770**

### Tyler

Christian Services of East Texas **1151**
Loving Alternative Adoption Agency **778**

### Waco

Child Placement Center of Texas **765**

Texas Department of Human Services; Region
7 **740**

### Webster

Catholic Charities of Houston **760**

### Wichita Falls

Inheritance Adoptions **776**

### The Woodlands

DePelchin Children's Center **770**
Los Ninos (The Children's) International
Adoption Center **777**

## UTAH

### Blanding

Utah Department of Social Services **790**

### Bountiful

L.A.M.B. **1524**

### Brigham City

Utah Department of Social Services **790**

### Cedar City

Utah Department of Social Services **790**

### Clearfield

Utah Department of Social Services **790**

### Delta

Utah Department of Social Services **790**

### Kanab

Utah Department of Social Services **790**

### Kaysville

Wasatch Adoptions and Children's Services
**795**

### Logan

Utah Department of Social Services **790**

### Manti

Utah Department of Social Services **790**

### Moab

Utah Department of Social Services **790**

### Murray

An Act of Love; Alternative Options &
Services for Children **791**

### Nephi

Utah Department of Social Services **790**

### Ogden

Children's Aid Society of Utah **792**
LDS Social Services of Ogden **794**
Utah Department of Social Services **790**

### Panguitch

Utah Department of Social Services **790**

### Price

Utah Department of Social Services **790**

### Provo

Marilyn Moody Brown; Attorney at Law **1279**
Utah Department of Social Services **790**
West Sands Adoptions **796**

### Roosevelt

Utah Department of Social Services **790**

### St. George

Utah Department of Social Services **790**

### Salt Lake City

Black Adoption Focus Group **1523**
Children's Service Society of Utah **793**
Rocky Mountain Adoption Exchange **1611**
Utah Department of Social Services **790**
Utah State Department of Human Services
**1159**

### Sandy

An Act of Love; Alternative Options &
Services for Children **791**

### Syracuse

Wasatch Adoptions and Children's Services
**795**

### Tooele

Utah Department of Social Services **790**

### Vernal

Utah Department of Social Services **790**

## VERMONT

### Barre

The Chosen Children from Romania **1527**
Social and Rehabilitative Services of Vermont
**798**

### Burlington

The Adoption Centre **799**
Adoption Resource Service, Inc. **800**
Social and Rehabilitative Services of Vermont
**798**
Vermont Catholic Charities, Inc. **801**

### Middletown Springs

Friends in Adoption, Inc. **1281**

### Monkton

Wide Horizons For Children, Inc. **330**

### Morrisville

Social and Rehabilitative Services of Vermont
**798**

### Rutland

Adoption Alliance of Vermont; Rutland Office
**1525**
Alfred J. Fenton **1280**
Social and Rehabilitative Services of Vermont
**798**
Vermont Catholic Charities, Inc. **801**

Vermont Children's Aid Society, Inc. **802**

**St. Johnsbury**

Social and Rehabilitative Services of Vermont **798**

**Shelburne**

Adoption Alliance of Vermont; Shelburne Office **1526**

**Springfield**

Social and Rehabilitative Services of Vermont **798**

**Vergennes**

Family Life Services of New England **1161**

**Waterbury**

Social and Rehabilitative Services of Vermont **798**

**White River Junction**

Casey Family Services; Vermont Division **1160**

**Winooski**

Vermont Children's Aid Society, Inc. **802**

**Woodstock**

Vermont Children's Aid Society, Inc. **802**

# VIRGINIA

**Alexandria**

Catholic Charities of the Diocese of Arlington, Inc. **827**
Edward A. Kaplan; Attorney at Law **1282**
Northern Virginia Family Service **1163**
United Methodist Family Services of Virginia **836**

**Annandale**

Jewish Social Service Agency; Adoption Options **307**

**Arlington**

Catholic Charities of the Diocese of Arlington, Inc. **827**
Washington Department of Health and Social Services; Children, Youth & Family Services Administration **839**

**Berryville**

Clarke County Department of Social Services **808**

**Bowling Green**

Caroline Department of Social Services **807**

**Bristol**

Bristol Department of Social Services **805**

**Burke**

Catholic Charities of the Diocese of Arlington, Inc. **827**

**Charlottesville**

Albermarle Department of Social Services **804**

**Chesapeake**

Carpe Diem of Virginia, Inc. **1162**

**Christiansburg**

Welcome House Special Services of the Pearl S. Buck Foundation **681**

**Collinsville**

Henry County Department of Social Services **811**

**Dale City**

Northern Virginia Family Service **1163**

**Danville**

Danville Division of Social Services **809**

**Fall Church**

Northern Virginia Family Service **1163**

**Falls Church**

Adoption Service Information Agency, Inc. (ASIA) **120**
Lutheran Social Services **124**
Northern Virginia Family Service **1163**

**Fredericksburg**

Catholic Charities of the Diocese of Arlington, Inc. **827**

**Hampton**

Hampton Department of Social Services **810**

**Herndon**

Northern Virginia Family Service **1163**

**Hopewell**

Hopewell Department of Social Services **812**

**Isle of Wight**

Isle of Wight Department of Social Services **813**

**Lawrenceville**

Brunswick Department of Social Services **806**

**Lebanon**

Russell County Department of Social Services **822**

**Leesburg**

Northern Virginia Family Service **1163**

**Lovington**

Nelson Department of Social Services **815**

**Lynchburg**

Family Life Services **831**

**McLean**

The Barker Foundation **302**

**Newport News**

Jewish Family Service of Tidewater, Inc. **832**

Newport News Department of Social Services **816**

**Norfolk**

Jewish Family Service of Tidewater, Inc. **832**

**Nottoway**

Nottoway Department of Social Services **817**

**Portsmouth**

Portsmouth Department of Social Services **818**

**Pulaski**

Pulaski Department of Social Services **819**

**Radford**

Radford Department of Welfare and Social Services **820**

**Richmond**

Adoption Resource Exchange of Virginia; Virginia Department of Social Services **1597**
Welcome House Special Services of the Pearl S. Buck Foundation **681**
Catholic Charities of Richmond, Inc. **825**
Children's Home Society of Virginia **828**
Coordinators/2, Inc. **829**
Jewish Family Services, Inc. **834**
Parents And Adoptees In Search **1531**
City of Richmond Department of Social Services **821**
United Methodist Family Services of Virginia **836**
Virginia Department of Social Services **1165**
Virginia Department of Social Services; Bureau of Child Welfare Services **823**

**Roanoke**

Catholic Charities of Southwestern Virginia, Inc. **826**
Children's Home Society of Virginia **828**

**Salem**

Virginia Baptist Children's Home and Family Services **837**

**Staunton**

People Places, Inc. **1164**

**Vienna**

The Datz Foundation **830**

**Vinton**

Blue Ridge Adoption Group **1529**

**Virginia Beach**

Shore Adoption Service **835**
United Methodist Family Services of Virginia **836**

**Williamsburg**

James City Department of Social Services **814**

**Winchester**

Catholic Charities of the Diocese of Arlington, Inc. **827**

*Geographic Index*

## Yorktown

Concerned Adoption Triad Support ("CATS") **1530**
York/Poquoson Department of Social Service **824**

# WASHINGTON

## Aberdeen

Washington Department of Health and Social Services; Children, Youth & Family Services Administration **839**

## Auburn

Friends In Adoption (F.I.A.) **1538**

## Bainbridge Island

Kitsap Adoption Group **1541**
Precious Connections, Inc. **1293**

## Bellevue

Jewish Family Service **850**
Eileen S. Putter, M.S. **1294**
Washington Department of Health and Social Services; Children, Youth & Family Services Administration **839**

## Bellingham

Bethany Christian Services of Bellingham **844**
The Family Foundation **849**
Washington Department of Health and Social Services; Children, Youth & Family Services Administration **839**

## Bremerton

Washington Department of Health and Social Services; Children, Youth & Family Services Administration **839**

## Castle Rock

Toutle River Boys Ranch **1168**

## Clarkston

Washington Department of Health and Social Services; Children, Youth & Family Services Administration **839**

## Colfax

Washington Department of Health and Social Services; Children, Youth & Family Services Administration **839**

## Colville

Washington Department of Health and Social Services; Children, Youth & Family Services Administration **839**

## Ellensburg

Washington Department of Health and Social Services; Children, Youth & Family Services Administration **839**

## Everett

Laurel A. Terpening; Adoption Caseworker Services **1297**
Cheryl Tonnes; Independent Adoption Social Worker **1299**

Washington Department of Health and Social Services; Children, Youth & Family Services Administration **839**

## Federal Way

Sound Counseling Service **1296**

## Kelso

Washington Department of Health and Social Services; Children, Youth & Family Services Administration **839**

## Kennewick

Washington Department of Health and Social Services; Children, Youth & Family Services Administration **839**

## Kent

Phylliss Eberhardy, MS, CCDCI **1289**
Leap of Faith Adoption Services **851**
Washington Department of Health and Social Services; Children, Youth & Family Services Administration **839**

## Kirkland

Adoption Facilitators, Inc. **1284**

## Moses Lake

Washington Department of Health and Social Services; Children, Youth & Family Services Administration **839**

## Mount Vernon

Washington Department of Health and Social Services; Children, Youth & Family Services Administration **839**

## Mountlake Terrace

Lutheran Social Services of Washington & Idaho **852**

## Oak Harbor

Washington Department of Health and Social Services; Children, Youth & Family Services Administration **839**

## Olympia

Connolly, Holm, Tacon & Meserve **1287**
Washington Department of Health and Social Services; Children, Youth & Family Services Administration **839**

## Port Angeles

Adoption Advocates International **840**
Washington Department of Health and Social Services; Children, Youth & Family Services Administration **839**

## Port Townsend

Washington Department of Health and Social Services; Children, Youth & Family Services Administration **839**

## Poulsbo

Tolman & Kirk; Attorneys at Law **1298**

## Redmond

Forever Families **1537**

## Renton

Adoption Services of WACAP (Western Association of Concerned Adoptive Parents) **841**

## Seattle

Adoption Resource Center; Children's Home Society of Washington **1532**
Adoption Workshops **1533**
Baptist Family Agency **843**
Law Office of Beresford, Booth & Demaray, Inc., P.S. **1285**
Birth Parent Support Group; Children's Home Society of Washington **1535**
Catholic Community Service of Seattle **846**
Dubar, Lirhus & Engel **1288**
Gay and Lesbian Adoptive Family Support Group; Adoption Resource Center **1539**
Interracial Family Association **1540**
Jewish Family Service **850**
Korean Identity Development Society; (KIDS) **1542**
Leach, Brown & Andersen **1291**
Medina Children's Services **853**
New Hope Child and Family Agency **854**
Northwest Adoption Exchange **1609**
Open Adoption and Family Services, Inc. **661**
Post-Search and Reunion Support Group; Children's Home Society of Washington **1544**
RESOLVE of Washington State **1545**
Skellenger, Bender, Mathias & Bender **1295**
Washington Adoptees Rights Movement; WARM **1546**
Washington Department of Health and Social Services; Children, Youth & Family Services Administration **839**
Eric B. Watness & Associates **1300**
Youth Advocates **1169**

## Shelton

Washington Department of Health and Social Services; Children, Youth & Family Services Administration **839**

## South Bend

Washington Department of Health and Social Services; Children, Youth & Family Services Administration **839**

## Spokane

Americans for International Aid and Adoption **351**
Americans for International Aid and Adoption; Washington State Branch **842**
Case Study Services **1286**
John H. Loeffler; Attorney at Law **1292**
Washington Department of Health and Social Services; Children, Youth & Family Services Administration **839**

## Sunnyside

Washington Department of Health and Social Services; Children, Youth & Family Services Administration **839**

## Tacoma

Adoptive Families Network **1534**
Bethany Christian Services of Bellingham **844**
Catholic Community Services of Tacoma **847**
Children's Home Society of Washington **1536**
Law Offices of Joseph A. Holeman **1290**

Medina Children's Services **853**
Rainbow Youth and Family Services **1167**
Washington Department of Health and Social
 Services; Children, Youth & Family
 Services Administration **839**

## Toppenish

NAK NU WE SHA **1166**
Washington Department of Health and Social
 Services; Children, Youth & Family
 Services Administration **839**

## Vancouver

Adventist Adoption and Family Services **656**
Catholic Community Services of Vancouver
 **848**
Washington Department of Health and Social
 Services; Children, Youth & Family
 Services Administration **839**

## Walla Walla

Washington Department of Health and Social
 Services; Children, Youth & Family
 Services Administration **839**

## Wenatchee

North Central Washington Adoption Support
 Network **1543**
Washington Department of Health and Social
 Services; Children, Youth & Family
 Services Administration **839**

## White Salmon

Washington Department of Health and Social
 Services; Children, Youth & Family
 Services Administration **839**

## Yakima

Adoption Advocacy Attorneys of the
 Northwest **1283**
Washington Department of Health and Social
 Services; Children, Youth & Family
 Services Administration **839**

# WEST VIRGINIA

## Charleston

Appalachian Families for Adoption; AFFA
 **1547**
Northern Tier Youth Services **1171**
Try Again Homes Inc. **1138**
West Virginia Adoption Exchange **1615**
West Virginia Department of Human Services
 **856**

## Elkins

Potomac Center **1172**

## Fairmont

Try Again Homes Inc. **1138**

## Huntington

William T. Watson, Esq. **1301**

## Martinsburg

Potomac Center **1172**

## Morgantown

West Virginia Adoption Exchange **1615**

## Petersburg

Potomac Center **1172**

## Princeton

West Virginia Adoption Exchange **1615**

## Romney

Potomac Center **1172**

## Scott Depot

Burlington United Methodist Family Services,
 Inc. **857**

## Shinnston

AASK Midwest **1593**

## South Charleston

West Virginia Adoption Exchange **1615**

## Wheeling

The Children's Home of Wheeling **1170**

# WISCONSIN

## Ashland

Wisconsin Department of Health and Social
 Services; Division of Community Services
 **859**

## Beloit

Catholic Social Service of Madison **863**

## Eau Claire

Wisconsin Department of Health and Social
 Services; Division of Community Services
 **859**

## Elm Grove

Special Children, Inc. **871**

## Fond du Lac

Catholic Social Services of Milwaukee **864**
Wisconsin Department of Health and Social
 Services; Division of Community Services
 **859**

## Green Bay

Adoption Services of Green Bay and Fox
 Valley, Inc. **862**
Wisconsin Department of Health and Social
 Services; Division of Community Services
 **859**

## Hudson

St. Croix Valley Korean American Cultural
 Society, Inc. **1556**

## Janesville

Catholic Social Service of Madison **863**
Community Adoption Center, Inc. **865**

## Kenosha

Catholic Social Services of Milwaukee **864**

## La Crosse

Wisconsin Department of Health and Social
 Services; Division of Community Services
 **859**

## Madison

Adoptive Parents Group **1550**
Catholic Social Service of Madison **863**
Susan M. De Groot; Attorney at Law **1302**
Wisconsin Department of Health and Social
 Services; Division of Community Services
 **859**

## Manitowoc

Community Adoption Center, Inc. **865**

## Milwaukee

Adoption Choice, Inc. **860**
Adoption Information & Direction, Inc. **1548**
Catholic Social Services of Milwaukee **864**
Evangelical Child and Family Agency **187**
Edward J. Plagemann **1303**
RESOLVE of Southern Wisconsin, Inc. **1554**
Special Needs Adoption Network **1557**
Wisconsin Association of Single Adoptive
 Parents **1560**

## Neenah

S.E.A.R.C.H. **1555**

## Portage

Pauquette Children's Services **870**

## Prairie du Chien

Wisconsin Single Adoptive Parents **1561**

## Racine

Catholic Social Services of Milwaukee **864**
Ours Through Adoption of Southeastern
 Wisconsin **1553**
Edward J. Plagemann **1303**

## Rhinelander

Wisconsin Department of Health and Social
 Services; Division of Community Services
 **859**

## Sheboygan

Catholic Social Services of Milwaukee **864**
Lutheran Social Services of Wisconsin and
 Upper Michigan **869**
Van Dyke, Inc.; Romanian Adoption
 Assistance **872**

## Sturgeon Bay

Door County Counseling Services, Inc. **866**
HELP of Door County **1173**

## Wales

Namaste/Children from India **1552**

## Waukesha

The Adoption Option, Inc. **861**
Catholic Social Services of Milwaukee **864**
Celebrate Adoption **1551**
Wisconsin Department of Health and Social
 Services; Division of Community Services
 **859**

**Wausau**

Adoptive Families Network **1549**

**Wauwatosa**

Community Adoption Center, Inc. **865**
Lutheran Counseling and Family Services, Wauwatosa **868**
US/Chilean Adoptive Families (USCAF) **1559**

**Webster**

Northwest Passage **1174**

**West Bend**

Catholic Social Services of Milwaukee **864**
They Adopt Special Kids (T.A.S.K.) **1558**

**Wisconsin Rapids**

Wisconsin Department of Health and Social Services; Division of Community Services **859**

# WYOMING

**Basin**

Northern Wyoming Adoptive Parents, Inc. **1562**

**Buffalo**

Department of Family Services of Wyoming **874**

**Casper**

Department of Family Services of Wyoming **874**
Peter J. Feeney; Attorney at Law **1304**
William D. Hjelmstad; Attorney at Law **1305**

**Cheyenne**

Department of Family Services of Wyoming **874**
Carol A. Serelson; Attorney at Law **1306**
Wyoming Children's Society **875**

**Cody**

Department of Family Services of Wyoming **874**

**Douglas**

Department of Family Services of Wyoming **874**

**Evanston**

Department of Family Services of Wyoming **874**

**Gillette**

Department of Family Services of Wyoming **874**

**Glenrock**

Department of Family Services of Wyoming **874**

**Greybull**

Department of Family Services of Wyoming **874**

**Jackson**

Department of Family Services of Wyoming **874**
Wyoming Parenting Society **876**

**Kemmerer**

Department of Family Services of Wyoming **874**

**Lander**

Department of Family Services of Wyoming **874**

**Laramie**

Department of Family Services of Wyoming **874**

**Lovell**

Department of Family Services of Wyoming **874**

**Lusk**

Department of Family Services of Wyoming **874**

**Newcastle**

Department of Family Services of Wyoming **874**

**Pinedale**

Department of Family Services of Wyoming **874**

**Powell**

Department of Family Services of Wyoming **874**

**Rawlins**

Department of Family Services of Wyoming **874**

**Riverton**

Department of Family Services of Wyoming **874**

**Rock Springs**

Department of Family Services of Wyoming **874**

**Sheridan**

Department of Family Services of Wyoming **874**

**Sundance**

Department of Family Services of Wyoming **874**

**Thermopolis**

Department of Family Services of Wyoming **874**

**Torrington**

Department of Family Services of Wyoming **874**

**Wheatland**

Department of Family Services of Wyoming **874**

**Worland**

Department of Family Services of Wyoming **874**

# ALBERTA

**Calgary**

Adoption By Choice **879**
Calgary Adoption Resource Foundation **1566**
Christian Adoption Services **881**

**Coaldale**

Lethbridge & Area Adoptive Parents Support Group **1568**

**Didsbury**

Adoption Association of Olds and Area **1563**

**Edmonton**

Alberta Family and Social Services **878**
Private Adoption Society of Alberta **1570**
Private Adoptions Society of Alberta **1307**

**Elk Point**

North East Adoption Resources **1569**

**Grande Prairie**

South Peace Adoptive Families Association **1572**

**Lethbridge**

Adoption Services; Crossroads Counselling Centre **880**

**Lougheed**

Battle River Adoption Group Society **1565**

**Medicine Hat**

Adoption 2000 Consulting, Inc. **1564**
South Eastern Post Adoption Support Society **1571**

**Sherwood Park**

Edmonton Adopting Beyond Infancy Association **1567**

**Taber**

Taber Adoptive Parents Support Group **1573**

# BRITISH COLUMBIA

**Abbotsford**

Hope Pregnancy Counseling and Adoption **884**

**Surrey**

Adoptive Parents Association of British Columbia **1574**
Forget Me Not Society (Adoption Circle) **1575**

**Vancouver**

Peruvian Adoptive Families **1578**

Society of Special Needs Adoptive Parents (SNAP) **1579**

## Victoria

Ministry of Social Services **1177**
Ministry of Social Services; Family and Child Services, Adoption Services **883**

## West Vancouver

Parent Finders of Canada **1577**

# MANITOBA

## Bausejour

Manitoba Department of Family Services; Child and Family Support Branch **886**

## Brandon

Child and Family Services of Western Manitoba **889**
Manitoba Department of Family Services; Child and Family Support Branch **886**

## Churchill

Manitoba Department of Family Services; Child and Family Support Branch **886**

## Dauphin

Manitoba Department of Family Services; Child and Family Support Branch **886**
West Region Child and Family Services **1180**

## Fairford

Manitoba Department of Family Services; Child and Family Support Branch **886**

## Hodgson

Manitoba Department of Family Services; Child and Family Support Branch **886**

## The Pas

Cree Nation Child & Family Caring Agency **891**
Manitoba Department of Family Services; Child and Family Support Branch **886**

## Portage la Prairie

Child and Family Services of Central Manitoba **1178**
Manitoba Department of Family Services; Child and Family Support Branch **886**

## Selkirk

Manitoba Department of Family Services; Child and Family Support Branch **886**

## Thompson

Thompson Region; Health & Family Services, Manitoba **887**

## Winnipeg

Jewish Child and Family Service **892**
Manitoba Department of Family Services; Child and Family Support Branch **886**
Winnipeg Child and Family Services **1181**
Winnipeg Child and Family Services (East Area) **888**

# NEW BRUNSWICK

## Fredericton

Department of Health and Community Service **894**
New Brunswick Department of Health and Community Service **1182**

# NEWFOUNDLAND

## St. Johns

Department of Social Services, Newfoundland **896**
Newfoundland Department of Social Services **1183**

# NORTHWEST TERRITORIES

## Hay River

South Slave Foster Families Association **1580**

## Yellowknife

Department of Social Services; Government of the Northwest Territories **898**
Family Support; Government of the Northwest Territories Department of Health and Social Services **1184**

# NOVA SCOTIA

## Amherst

Department of Community Services (Nova Scotia); Family and Children's Services **900**
Department of Community Services; Family and Children's Services **1185**

## Annapolis Royal

Department of Community Services (Nova Scotia); Family and Children's Services **900**
Department of Community Services; Family and Children's Services **1185**

## Antigonish

Department of Community Services (Nova Scotia); Family and Children's Services **900**
Department of Community Services; Family and Children's Services **1185**

## Barrington

Department of Community Services (Nova Scotia); Family and Children's Services **900**
Department of Community Services; Family and Children's Services **1185**

## Bridgewater

Department of Community Services (Nova Scotia); Family and Children's Services **900**
Department of Community Services; Family and Children's Services **1185**

## Dartmouth

Department of Community Services (Nova Scotia); Family and Children's Services **900**
Department of Community Services; Family and Children's Services **1185**

## Digby

Department of Community Services (Nova Scotia); Family and Children's Services **900**
Department of Community Services; Family and Children's Services **1185**

## Guysborough

Department of Community Services (Nova Scotia); Family and Children's Services **900**
Department of Community Services; Family and Children's Services **1185**

## Halifax

Adoptive Parent Association of Nova Scotia **1581**
Department of Community Services (Nova Scotia); Family and Children's Services **900**
Department of Community Services; Family and Children's Services **1185**

## Kentville

Department of Community Services (Nova Scotia); Family and Children's Services **900**
Department of Community Services; Family and Children's Services **1185**

## Liverpool

Department of Community Services (Nova Scotia); Family and Children's Services **900**
Department of Community Services; Family and Children's Services **1185**

## Lower Sackville

Department of Community Services (Nova Scotia); Family and Children's Services **900**
Department of Community Services; Family and Children's Services **1185**

## New Glasgow

Department of Community Services (Nova Scotia); Family and Children's Services **900**
Department of Community Services; Family and Children's Services **1185**

## Port Hawkesbury

Department of Community Services (Nova Scotia); Family and Children's Services **900**
Department of Community Services; Family and Children's Services **1185**

## Shubenacadie

Department of Community Services (Nova Scotia); Family and Children's Services **900**

Department of Community Services; Family and Children's Services **1185**

### Sydney

Department of Community Services (Nova Scotia); Family and Children's Services **900**

Department of Community Services; Family and Children's Services **1185**

### Tantallon

Parent Finders - Nova Scotia **1582**

### Truro

Department of Community Services (Nova Scotia); Family and Children's Services **900**

Department of Community Services; Family and Children's Services **1185**

### Windsor

Department of Community Services (Nova Scotia); Family and Children's Services **900**

Department of Community Services; Family and Children's Services **1185**

### Yarmouth

Department of Community Services (Nova Scotia); Family and Children's Services **900**

Department of Community Services; Family and Children's Services **1185**

# ONTARIO

### Barrie

M. M. Kelly Counseling and Adoption Agency **907**

### Belleville

Children's Aid Society of Metropolitan Toronto **1186**

### Bobourge

Children's Aid Society of Metropolitan Toronto **1186**

### Bracebridge

Children's Aid Society of Metropolitan Toronto **1186**

### Brampton

Acri, MacPherson, Fader & Baldock; Barristers & Solicitors **1308**

Children's Aid Society of Metropolitan Toronto **1186**

### Brantford

Children's Aid Society of Metropolitan Toronto **1186**

### Brockville

Children's Aid Society of Metropolitan Toronto **1186**

### Burlington

Adoption Agency & Counseling Service of Ontario **903**

### Cambridge

Waterloo Adoptive Family Association **1590**

### Chatham

Children's Aid Society of Metropolitan Toronto **1186**

### Dunnville

Children's Aid Society of Metropolitan Toronto **1186**

### Ft. Frances

Children's Aid Society of Metropolitan Toronto **1186**

### Goderich

Children's Aid Society of Metropolitan Toronto **1186**

### Guelph

Children's Aid Society of Metropolitan Toronto **1186**

Valeriote and Valeriote, Barristers and Solicitors **1321**

### Hamilton

Beginnings Counseling and Adoption Services of Ontario Inc. **904**

Children's Aid Society of Metropolitan Toronto **1186**

### Kapuskasing

Children's Aid Society of Metropolitan Toronto **1186**

### Kenora

Children's Aid Society of Metropolitan Toronto **1186**

### Kingston

Adoption Resource and Counseling Services **1310**

Children's Aid Society of Metropolitan Toronto **1186**

### Kirkland Lake

Children's Aid Society of Metropolitan Toronto **1186**

### Kitchener

Children's Aid Society of Metropolitan Toronto **1186**

Giesbrecht, Griffin & Ritter; Barristers, Solicitors and Notaries Public **1314**

### Lindsay

Kawartha-Haliburton Children's Aid Society **1589**

### London

Beechie, Madison, Sawchuk & Seabrook; Barristers and Solicitors **1312**

Children's Aid Society of Metropolitan Toronto **1186**

### Midhurst

Children's Aid Society of Metropolitan Toronto **1186**

### Mississauga

Jewels for Jesus Adoption Agency **905**

### Nepanee

Children's Aid Society of Metropolitan Toronto **1186**

### Newmarket

Children's Aid Society of Metropolitan Toronto **1186**

### North Bay

Children's Aid Society; District of Nipissing **1588**

Children's Aid Society of Metropolitan Toronto **1186**

### Oakville

Children's Aid Society of Metropolitan Toronto **1186**

### Orangeville

Children's Aid Society of Metropolitan Toronto **1186**

### Oshawa

Children's Aid Society of Metropolitan Toronto **1186**

Andres Koziar, Ph.D., L.L.B. **1317**

### Ottawa

Adoption Council of Canada/Le Conseil d'adoption du Canada **1583**

Canadian Foster Family Association **1586**

Child Welfare League of Canada **1587**

Children's Aid Society of Metropolitan Toronto **1186**

A. Maxine Smith, Adoption Licensee **1319**

### Owen Sound

Children's Aid Society of Metropolitan Toronto **1186**

### Parry Sound

Children's Aid Society of Metropolitan Toronto **1186**

### Pembroke

Children's Aid Society of Metropolitan Toronto **1186**

Huckabone, Shaw, O'Brien, Radley-Walters & Reimer **1315**

### Perth

Children's Aid Society of Metropolitan Toronto **1186**

### Petawawa

Huckabone, Shaw, O'Brien, Radley-Walters & Reimer **1315**

### Peterborough

Children's Aid Society of Metropolitan Toronto **1186**

*The Adoption Directory, 2nd ed.*                                          **Yukon**

**Picton**

Children's Aid Society of Metropolitan Toronto
1186

**Plantagenet**

Children's Aid Society of Metropolitan Toronto
1186

**Point Edward**

Children's Aid Society of Metropolitan Toronto
1186

**St. Catharines**

Adoption Advisory and Counseling Service
1309

**St. Catherines**

Children's Aid Society of Metropolitan Toronto
1186

**St. Thomas**

Children's Aid Society of Metropolitan Toronto
1186

**Sarnia**

Anne Toth, M.S.W., C.S.W. 1320

**Saulte Ste. Marie**

Children's Aid Society of Metropolitan Toronto
1186

**Simcoe**

Children's Aid Society of Metropolitan Toronto
1186

**Stratford**

Children's Aid Society of Metropolitan Toronto
1186

**Sudbury**

Children's Aid Society of Sudbury-Manitoulin
1187
Paquette, Lalande and Keast, Barristers and
Solicitors 1318

**Thunder Bay**

Children's Aid Society of Metropolitan Toronto
1186

**Timmins**

Children's Aid Society of Metropolitan Toronto
1186
Ellery & Cox, Solicitors 1313

**Toronto**

Adoption Council of Ontario 1584
Baker & Janssen 1311
Children's Aid Society of Metropolitan Toronto
1186
Judith Holzman Law Offices 1316
Ministry of Community Social Services;
Management and Support Branch,
Adoption and Operational Services 902
Ontario Ministry of Community and Social
Services; Adoption Unit 1188

**Walkerton**

Children's Aid Society of Metropolitan Toronto
1186

**Willowdale**

Jewish Child and Family Services of Metro
Toronto 906

**Windsor**

Children's Aid Society of Metropolitan Toronto
1186

**Woodstock**

Children's Aid Society of Metropolitan Toronto
1186

# PRINCE EDWARD ISLAND

**Charlottetown**

Health and Community Services Agency 1189
Provincial Health and Community Services
Agency 909

# QUEBEC

**Amos**

Centre Jeunesse de Quebec (CPEJ) 1190

**Baie Comeau**

Centre Jeunesse de Quebec (CPEJ) 1190

**Blainville**

Centre Jeunesse de Quebec (CPEJ) 1190

**Boucherville**

Enfants d'Orient Adoption et Parrainage du
Quebec, Inc. 911

**Cecotomy**

Espoir Des Enfants En Adoption Inc. 913

**Chicoutimi**

Centre Jeunesse de Quebec (CPEJ) 1190

**Chissasibi, Baie Jam**

Centre Jeunesse de Quebec (CPEJ) 1190

**Gaspe**

Centre Jeunesse de Quebec (CPEJ) 1190

**Hull**

Centre Jeunesse de Quebec (CPEJ) 1190

**Joliette**

Centre Jeunesse de Quebec (CPEJ) 1190

**Kuujjuaq**

Centre Jeunesse de Quebec (CPEJ) 1190

**Laval**

Centre Jeunesse de Quebec (CPEJ) 1190

**Levis**

Centre Jeunesse de Quebec (CPEJ) 1190

**Longueuil**

Centre Jeunesse de Quebec (CPEJ) 1190

**Montreal**

Centre Jeunesse de Quebec (CPEJ) 1190
Enfants d'Orient Adoption et Parrainage du
Quebec, Inc. 911
Les Centres jeunesse de Quebec; Centre de
protection de l'enfance de la jeunesse 912
Societe D'Adoption Quebecoise Une Grande
Famille 914

**Povungnituk**

Centre Jeunesse de Quebec (CPEJ) 1190

**Quebec**

Centre Jeunesse de Quebec (CPEJ) 1190

**Rimouski**

Centre Jeunesse de Quebec (CPEJ) 1190

**Sherbrooke**

Centre Jeunesse de Quebec (CPEJ) 1190

**Sillery**

Societe Pour L'Adoption Internationale 915

**Trois Rivieres**

Centre Jeunesse de Quebec (CPEJ) 1190
Soleil des Nations 916

# SASKATCHEWAN

**Regina**

Saskatchewan Social Services 918

**Saskatoon**

Saskatchewan Adoptive Parents Association
1592

# YUKON

**Whitehorse**

Department of Health and Social Services;
Family and Children's Services H-10 920
Department of Health and Social Services;
Government of the Yukon 1192

**Geographic Index**

# Alphabetical Index

This index lists, in a single alphabetic sequence, all organizations included in *The Adoption Directory, 2nd ed.* An entry number, not page number, follows each organization cited.

## A

A.D.O.P.T. (All Doing Our Part Together) **1422**
A.M.O.R. Adoptions, Inc. **462**
A. Maxine Smith, Adoption Licensee **1319**
Aaron Britvan; Attorney at Law **1259**
AASK America; Aid to Adoption of Special Kids **49**
AASK Midwest **1593**
AASK/Texas **1594**
Abbott House **1071**
ABC Counseling & Family Services **177**
Abrazo Adoption Associates **749**
Acri, MacPherson, Fader & Baldock; Barristers & Solicitors **1308**
An Act of Love; Alternative Options & Services for Children **791**
Ada S. McKinley Foster Care and Adoption Services **982**
Adopt a Special Kid - Oklahoma Chapter; AASK-Oklahoma Chapter **1495**
Adopt A Special Kid/Texas, Inc.; AASK/Texas, Inc. **750**
Adopt International **50**
Adopt Older Kids, Inc. (A-OK) **1410**
Adopted Children of Romania Network (ACORN) **1454**
Adopted Kids and Parents Support Group (AKAPS) **1358**
Adoptee Birth Family Registry **1331**
Adoptees & Birth Parents in Search **1510**
Adoptees' Identity Doorway **1396**
Adoptees in Search, Inc. **1413**
Adoptees' Liberty Movement Association (ALMA) **1374**
Adoptees' Liberty Movement Association; ALMA **1455**
Adoptees Liberty Movement Association; Central Illinois Chapter **1376**
Adopting Children Together **1516**
Adoption Access, Inc. **751**
Adoption Advisory and Counseling Service **1309**
Adoption Advisory Council **1456**
Adoption Advisory, Inc. **752**
Adoption Advocacy Attorneys of the Northwest **1283**
Adoption Advocates **753, 1517**
Adoption Advocates International **840**
Adoption Affiliates **639**
Adoption Affiliates, Inc. **754**
Adoption Agency & Counseling Service of Ontario **903**
Adoption Alliance **81**
Adoption Alliance of Vermont; Rutland Office **1525**

Adoption Alliance of Vermont; Shelburne Office **1526**
Adoption Alliances; Jewish Family Services **299**
Adoption and Family Search Consultants **1446**
Adoption And Infertility Services, Inc. **463**
Adoption Assistance and Information Group **1332**
Adoption Associates, Inc. **349**
Adoption Association of Olds and Area **1563**
Adoption/Birthmother Search for Tomorrow, Inc. **1397**
Adoption By Choice **128, 879**
Adoption by Gentle Care **614**
Adoption by Gentle Shepherd **424**
Adoption by Gentle Shepherd, Inc. **233**
Adoption Care Center, Inc. **15**
The Adoption Center **640**
Adoption Center, Inc. **310**
Adoption Center of San Diego **1197**
Adoption Center of Washington **119**
The Adoption Centre **799**
Adoption Centre Inc. of Kansas **234**
Adoption Choice Center **82**
Adoption Choice, Inc. **860**
The Adoption Connection **1419**
Adoption Connection, Inc. **129**
Adoption Connection of Jewish Family and Children's Services **51**
Adoption Council of Canada/Le Conseil d'adoption du Canada **1583**
Adoption Council of Ontario **1584, 1585**
The Adoption Cradle, Inc. **350**
Adoption Crossroads **1457**
Adoption Facilitators, Inc. **1284**
Adoption Horizons, Inc.; The Birth Parent Center **52**
Adoption Identity Movement of Grand Rapids **1423**
Adoption Information & Direction, Inc. **1548**
Adoption Information Center (AIC) **1595**
Adoption Information Center of Illinois (AICI) **1596**
Adoption Information Services **1233**
Adoption Law Center, P.C. **1251**
Adoption Links Worldwide **441**
Adoption Option **235**
The Adoption Option, Inc. **83, 861**
Adoption Planning, Inc. **148**
Adoption Resource and Counseling Services **1310**
Adoption Resource Center; Children's Home Society of Washington **1532**
The Adoption Resource Center, Inc. **300**

Adoption Resource Exchange of Virginia; Virginia Department of Social Services **1597**
Adoption Resource Network, Inc. **1458**
Adoption Resource of Jewish Family and Children's Services, Boston **311**
Adoption Resource Service, Inc. **800**
Adoption Resource Services, Inc. **200**
Adoption Search Consultants **1479**
Adoption Search Consultants of Maine **1412**
Adoption Service Information Agency, Inc. (ASIA) **120**
Adoption Services Associates **755**
Adoption Services; Crossroads Counselling Centre **880**
Adoption Services, Inc. **149, 756**
Adoption Services International **53**
Adoption Services of Green Bay and Fox Valley, Inc. **862**
Adoption Services of WACAP (Western Association of Concerned Adoptive Parents) **841**
The Adoption Support Center, Inc. **201**
Adoption Triad Network, Inc, **1411**
Adoption Triangle **1377, 1378, 1379**
Adoption 2000 Consulting, Inc. **1564**
Adoption Workshops **1533**
Adoptions: Advocacy and Alternatives **84**
Adoptions Alternatives **202**
Adoptions Forever, Inc. **301**
Adoptions From The Heart **677**
Adoptions Unlimited **54**
Adoptive Families Association of Tompkins County, NY **1459**
Adoptive Families Network **1534, 1549**
Adoptive Families of America **1430**
Adoptive Families of Greater Cincinnati **1486**
Adoptive Families of Long Island **1460**
Adoptive Families of Older Children **1461**
Adoptive Families Support Association (AFSA) - An Adoptive Families Network **1496**
Adoptive Families Support Association, Inc. **1487**
Adoptive Families Today **1380**
Adoptive Families with Information and Support; AFIS **1348**
Adoptive Family Network **1414**
Adoptive Parent Association of Nova Scotia **1581**
Adoptive Parents And Children Together; A.P.A.C.T. **1328**
Adoptive Parents Association **1359**
Adoptive Parents Association of British Columbia **1574**
Adoptive Parents Committee of New York State; Long Island Chapter **1462**

Childplace 210
Children and Youth Services of Delaware County 1129
Children Awaiting Parents, Inc. 1466, 1598
Children in Common 1415
Children Unlimited, Inc. 711
Children, Youth and Families Dept. (New Mexico); Social Services Division 483
Children's Aid Home and Society of Somerset County 689
Children's Aid of Idaho 164
Children's Aid Society; District of Nipissing 1588
The Children's Aid Society of Clearfield, PA 690
The Children's Aid Society of Franklin County 691
Children's Aid Society of Mercer County 692
Children's Aid Society of Metropolitan Toronto 1186
Children's Aid Society of New York 524
Children's Aid Society of Sudbury-Manitoulin 1187
Children's Aid Society of Utah 792
Children's Bureau of Indianapolis 211
Children's Bureau of Southern California 929
Children's Choice 305
Children's Choice of Delaware 950
Children's Development Center 969
Children's Foundation - Adoption and Counseling 240
Children's Friend and Service 706
Children's Home and Aid Society of Illinois 185
Children's Home of Cincinnati, Inc. 621
Children's Home of Kingston (CHK) 1075
Children's Home of Northern Kentucky 253
The Children's Home of Wheeling 1170
Children's Home Society of California 61
The Children's Home Society of Florida 137
Children's Home Society of Minnesota 407
The Children's Home Society of Missouri 427
Children's Home Society of New Jersey 470
The Children's Home Society of North Carolina 564
Children's Home Society of Virginia 828
Children's Home Society of Washington 1536
Children's Service Society of Utah 793
Children's Services Division of Oregon 1123
Children's Services, Inc. 1130
Chinese Children Adoption International 87
Chippewa County Department of Social Services 1023
The Chosen Children from Romania 1527
Christian Adoption and Family Services 62
Christian Adoption Ministries 1383
Christian Adoption Services 881
Christian Adoption Services, Inc. 565
Christian Care/Baptist Childrens Home and Family Ministry 374
Christian Child Placement Service 487
Christian Counseling Services 165, 717, 726
Christian Cradle, Inc. 375
Christian Family Care Agency 20
Christian Family Life Services, Inc. 571
Christian Family Services 138, 376, 712
Christian Family Services, Inc. 428
Christian Family Services of Colorado, Inc. 88
Christian Heritage Children's Home 1063
Christian Home and Bible School 139
Christian Homes; A Program of Louisiana Child Care and Placement Services, Inc. 269
Christian Homes for Children 471
Christian Homes of Abilene 766
Christian Services of East Texas 1151

Christine Mesberg; Attorney at Law 1262
Christ's Haven for Children 767
Chrysalis House 63
Church of God Home for Children 727
Circle Family Care 970
City of Richmond Department of Social Services 821
Clairborne, P.C.; Ruth F. 1235
Clark County Department of Human Services 582
Clarke County Adoption Resource Exchange; C.C.A.R.E. 1364
Clarke County Department of Social Services 808
Clay Henderson; Attorney at Law 1230
Cleveland County Department of Social Services 544
Cliff J. Young; Attorney at Law 1254
Coastal Bend Youth City 1152
Coen; Attorney at Law; Alvin M. 1202
Cohn, P.A.; Law Offices of Bennett S. 1228
Coleman Adoption Services, Inc. 212
Colorado Adoption Center 89
Colorado Christian Services 90
Colorado State Department of Social Services 80
Committee for Single Adoptive Parents 1416
Commonwealth Adoptions International, Inc. 21
Community Adoption Center, Inc. 865
Community Counseling and Adoption Services of Idaho, Inc. 166
Community, Family and Children's Services 377
The Community House 971
Community Maternity Services 525
Compassion, Inc. 1097
Compassionate Care 213
Concept 7 Foster Family Agency 930
Concern for Children 1488
Concerned Adoption Triad Support ("CATS") 1530
Concerned Persons For Adoption 1449
Concerned United Birthparents 1403
Concerned United Birthparents (CUB) 1401
Concerned United Birthparents (CUB); Twin City-Metro Area 1432
Concerned United Birthparents, Inc. 1341
Concord Family Service 319
Connecticut Adoption Resource Exchange 1599
Connolly, Holm, Tacon & Meserve 1287
Cook and Linden; A Professional Corporation 1203
Coordinators/2, Inc. 829
Copland & Copland 1260
Copland, Esq.; Gloria A. 1260
Coshocton County Children Services Board 583
Council for Equal Rights in Adoption 1467
The Council of Adoptive Parents 1468
Council on Adoptable Children 1504
County of Orange Social Service Agency; Adoptions Program 35
Covenant Care Services 151
Cowen & Cowen; Attorneys at Law 1236
Cox; The Cox Law Firm, P.C.; Robert A. 1252
Cradle of Hope Adoption Center, Inc. 122
A Cradle of Hope; Adoption Counseling Center 768
Cradle of Lawton, Inc. 645
Cradle of Life Adoption Agency, Inc. 769
The Cradle Society 186
Craven County Department of Social Services 545

Cree Nation Child & Family Caring Agency 891
Crisis Pregnancy Outreach 646
Crittendon Family Services 622
The Crittenton Center 228
Crittenton League; Florence 320
Crossroads, Inc. 408
Crosstreets 1048
Crumlin; Attorney at Law; James A. 1247
Cumberland County Department of Social Services 546
Cuyohoga County Department of Children and Family Services 584

# D

D.A. Blodgett Services for Children and Families 355
Dague; Raymond J. 1261
Danville Division of Social Services 809
The Datz Foundation 830
Dauphin County Children and Youth Agency 668
David C. Laredo; Attorney at Law 1214
David Keene Leavitt; Attorney at Law 1215
David R. Preininger 1258
Davidson County Department of Social Services 547
De Groot; Attorney at Law; Susan M. 1302
Deaconess Home: Pregnancy and Adoption Services 647
Deep East Texas Mental Health/Mental Retardation Center 1153
Delaware County Children and Youth 669
Delaware County Department of Social Services 496
Delaware County Office of Family and Children Services 990
Delta County Department of Social Services 1024
Denver Alternative Youth Services; The Family Connection 937
Denver Department of Social Services 938
Department for Children and Their Families 1143
Department for Social Services; State of Kentucky 250
Department of Children and Youth Services, CT 99
Department of Children's Services; Adoptions Division 30
Department of Community Services (Nova Scotia); Family and Children's Services 900
Department of Community Services; Family and Children's Services 1185
Department of Family Services, Montana 1057
Department of Family Services of Montana 438
Department of Family Services of Wyoming 874
Department of Health and Community Service 894
Department of Health and Social Services, Alaska; Division of Family and Youth 923
Department of Health and Social Services; Family and Children's Services H-10 920
Department of Health and Social Services; Government of the Yukon 1192
Department of Health and Welfare; Family and Community Services 964
Department of Health and Welfare of Idaho; Division of Family and Community Services 163

Alphabetical Index

Gentle Shepherd Child Placement Services **243**

Gianelli & Fores **1210**

Giesbrecht, Griffin & Ritter; Barristers, Solicitors and Notaries Public **1314**

Gift of Life Adoption Services, Inc. **707**

Gift of Life, Inc. Adoption Services **140**

Gift of Love Adoption Agency **771**

Gines; JoAnn **1248**

Give Us This Day, Inc. **1124**

The Gladney Center **772**

Gladwin County Department of Social Services **1025**

Gloria A. Copland, Esq. **1260**

Gogebic County Department of Social Services **1026**

Golda Zimmerman, Esq. **1265**

Golden Cradle Adoption Services, Inc. **473**

Golden Cradle International **382**

Golden Triangle Community Mental Health Center **1058**

Good Samaritan Agency **281**

Gordon & Marschhausen **1224**

Gordon; Attorney at Law; Pamela A. **1224**

Gorham; Attorney at Law; F. Kevin **1266**

Gorman; Attorney at Law; Jane A. **1211**

Gould Services for Children; Edwin **530**

Graham Association for People with Disabilities; Ray **972**

Grass and Grass, Attorneys **1229**

Gratiot County Department of Social Services **1027**

Greater Boston Catholic Charities **321**

Greater Love Adoption Decision (G.L.A.D.) **214**

Green, III; Attorney at Law; John W. **1193**

Greene County Division of Family Services **421**

Growing Families, Inc. **474**

Guardian Angel Home **973**

Guernsey County Childrens Services Board **588**

Guilford County Department of Social Services; Adoption Unit **549**

Gulf Coast Teaching Family Services **1013**

Gunnison/Hinsdale County Department of Social Services **942**

### H

Habilitative Services, Inc. **1049**

Hall Neighborhood House, Inc.; Adoption Services **105**

Hamilton County Department of Human Services **589**

Hamilton County Department of Social Services **501**

Hampton Department of Social Services **810**

Hancock County Department of Human Services; Children's Protective Services **590**

Hand In Hand Foundation **68**

Hand In Hand International Adoptions **93**

Hand In Hand of Greater Sacramento **1336**

Hands Around the World, Inc. **1384**

HARAMBEE: Services to Black Families **626**

Harborcreek Youth Services **1131**

Harlem-Dowling West Side Center for Children and Family Services **531**

Harley A. Feinstein **1208**

Harmony Family Services **1154**

Harnett County Department of Social Services **550**

Hawaii International Child **161**

Hawaii International Child Placement and Family Services, Inc. **1372**

Hazlett Law Offices **1245**

Healing Hearts, Inc. **1385**

Healing the Children - New Mexico Chapter **1069**

Healing the Children Northeast, Inc. **946**

Health and Community Services Agency **1189**

Heart to Heart Adoption Service; Lutheran Ministries of Georgia, Inc. **153**

Hearts & Homes For Children **141**

Heartshare Human Services of New York **1077**

Helen D. Russell **1269**

Heller; Attorney at Law; Michael W. **1241**

HELP of Door County **1173**

Help The Children, Inc. **69**

Henderson; Attorney at Law; Clay **1230**

Hendrick Home for Children **1155**

Henry County Department of Social Services **811**

Henry County Family Services **422**

Hephzibah Children's Association **974**

Heritage Adoption Services **658**

Heritage Finders **1386**

Hext; Attorney at Law; Stephen R. **1267**

High Plains Children's Home & Family Services, Inc. **773, 1156**

Highlands Child Placement Services **430**

Hillcrest Family Services **229**

Hillcrest Health Center; Therapeutic Foster Care **1115**

Hillsdale County Department of Social Services **335**

Hillside Children's Center **1078**

Hjelmstad; Attorney at Law; William D. **1305**

Hogares, Inc. **1070**

Holeman; Law Offices of Joseph A. **1290**

Holt International Children's Services **659**

Holy Cross Child Placement Agency, Inc. **271**

Holy Family Services, Counseling and Adoption **70**

Home B.A.S.E. (Birthparents and Adoptees Supportive Environment) **1367**

Homes for Kids, Inc. **1100**

Homes of St. Mark **774**

Homestudies, Inc. **475**

HOPE Adoption and Family Services International, Inc. **409**

Hope Adoptions, Inc. **322**

Hope Cottage **775**

HOPE for Children, Inc. **154**

Hope Pregnancy Counseling and Adoption **884**

Hope! Share And Care! Adoption Support Group **1354**

Hope's Promise **94**

Hopewell Department of Social Services **812**

Horn; Attorney at Law; Bonnie P. **1275**

House of Samuel, Inc. **24**

Huckabone, Shaw, O'Brien, Radley-Walters & Reimer **1315**

Human Resource Training, Inc. **924**

Huron Services for Youth, Inc. **383**

Huron Valley Child Guidance Clinic **1028**

### I

Idaho Voluntary Adoption Registry; Center for Vital Statistics and Health Policy **1375**

Idaho Youth Ranch Adoption Services **167**

Illiana Adoptive Parents **1399**

Illinois Department of Children and Family Services; Aurora Office **170**

Illinois Department of Children and Family Services; Champaign Office **171**

Illinois Department of Children and Family Services; Fairview Heights Office **172**

Illinois Department of Children and Family Services; Marion Office **173**

Illinois Department of Children and Family Services; Peoria Office **174**

Illinois Department of Children and Family Services; Rockford Office **175**

Illinois Department of Children and Family Services; Springfield Office **176**

In-Care Network, Inc. **1059**

Independent Adoption Center **1212**

Independent Search Consultants **1337**

Indian Child And Family Services **71**

Indiana Adoption Resource Exchange (IARE); Division of Family and Children **1601**

Indiana RESOLVE, Inc. **1400**

Indiana Youth Advocate Program, Inc. **992**

Infant of Prague Adoption Service **72**

Ingham County Dept. of Social Services **336**

Inheritance Adoptions **776**

Innovative Adoptions, Inc. **95**

Inserco **244**

The Institute of Professional Practice (I.P.P.) **947**

International Adoption Consultants **384**

International Adoptive Families **1471, 1506**

International Alliance For Children, Inc. (IAC) **106**

International Christian Adoptions **73**

International Concerns Committee for Children **1342, 1602**

International Families **1440**

International Families of Mid-America **1441**

Interracial Family Association **1540**

Iowa Department of Human Services **222**

Iowa Foster and Adoptive Parents Association **1402**

Isle of Wight Department of Social Services **813**

### J

Jackson County Community Mental Health Center **975**

Jacobs & Jacobs, Chartered **1231**

Jacobs; Attorney at Law; Donald F. **1231**

James A. Crumlin; Attorney at Law **1247**

The James A. Roberts Agency **248**

James B. Wiltse **1274**

James City Department of Social Services **814**

Jane A. Gorman; Attorney at Law **1211**

Jayne Shover Easter Seal Rehabilitative Center, Inc. **987**

Jeanette F. Snyder; Attorney at Law **1263**

Jed Somit; Attorney at Law **1220**

Jefferson County Department of Social Services **502, 943**

Jensen; Attorney at Law; John W. **1272**

Jeremiah Agency, Inc. **215**

Jessica Sticklin; Attorney at Law **1242**

Jewels for Jesus Adoption Agency **905**

Jewish Child and Family Service **892**

Jewish Child and Family Services of Metro Toronto **906**

Jewish Child Care Association **1079**

Jewish Children's Adoption Network **1603**

The Jewish Children's Regional Service **272**

Jewish Family and Children's Services **431, 696**

Jewish Family And Children's Services; Jewish Family Services of Monmouth County **476**

Jewish Family And Children's Services of Southern New Jersey **477**

Jewish Family and Community Services **142**

Jewish Family and Vocational Service **254**

Jewish Family Service **729, 850, 1225**

Alphabetical Index

Maine Department of Human Services; Social Services **1015**

Manitoba Department of Family Services; Child and Family Support Branch **886**

Marchese; Attorney at Law; Anthony B. **1232**

Maria Erbar; Attorney at Law **1271**

Marilyn Moody Brown; Attorney at Law **1279**

Marin County Department of Health and Human Services; Adoptions **33**

Marion County Children Service Board **598**

The Marsh Foundation Teaching-Family Program **1102**

Martin Brandfon; Attorney at Law **1200**

Mary Kendall Home; Methodist Home of Kentucky, Inc. **1009**

Maryville Academy **980**

Marywood Children and Family Services **781**

The Massachusetts Adoption Resource Exchange **1606**

Massachusetts Department of Social Services **1016**

Maternity and Adoption Services of Baptist Children's Home **193, 981**

McKinley Foster Care and Adoption Services; Ada S. **982**

McMahon Services for Children **1081**

Medina Children's Services **853**

Mentor Clinical Care **1103**

Merced County Human Services Agency **34**

Mercer County Department of Human Services **599**

Mesa County Department of Social Services **944**

Mesberg; Attorney at Law; Christine **1262**

Methodist Children's Home Society **391**

Methodist Home of Kentucky; Mary Kendall Adoptions **256**

MetroCenter for Family Ministries, Inc. **650**

Michael W. Heller; Attorney at Law **1241**

Michelsen; Law Offices of Diane **1216**

Michigan Department of Social Services **341**

Michigan Department of Social Services; Northern Michigan Adoption Program **342**

Mid-South Families Through Adoption **1514**

Mid-Western Children's Home **634**

Ministry of Community Social Services; Management and Support Branch, Adoption and Operational Services **902**

Ministry of Social Services **1177**

Ministry of Social Services; Family and Child Services, Adoption Services **883**

Miroff; Attorney at Law; Franklin I. **1244**

Miroff, Cross, Ruppert and Klineman **1244**

Missing Pieces **1389**

Missing Pieces Through Adoption **1576**

Mission of the Immaculate Virgin - Mount Loretto **533**

Mississippi Advocates for Minority Adoptions, Inc. **1439**

Mississippi Children's Home Society and Family Service Association **419**

Mississippi Department of Human Services **416**

Mississippi State Department of Human Services **1055**

Missouri Baptist Children's Home **435**

Missouri Department of Social Services **423, 1056**

Monroe County Children and Youth Services **1133**

Monroe County Department of Human Services **600**

Monroe County Department of Social Services **343**

Montana Post Adoption Center, Inc. **1443**

Montcalm County Department of Social Services **1034**

Montgomery County Children Services **601**

Montgomery County Department of Social Services **294**

Montgomery County Office of Children and Youth **672, 1134**

Moor Children's Home; Lee and Beulah **782**

Morning Star Adoption Resource Services, Inc. **392**

Mountain Circle Foster Family Agency **931**

Murphy & Jacobs **1217**

Mutual Consent Voluntary Adoption Registry **1418**

My Turn Now, Inc. **1607**

# N

NAK NU WE SHA **1166**

Namaste/Children from India **1552**

Nash County Department of Social Services **552**

National Adoption Exchange **1608**

National Coalition to End Racism in America's Child Care System **1428**

National Council for Adoption **1351**

Nebraska Children's Home Society **447**

Nebraska Department of Social Services **440, 1064**

Nekton Family Network **1050**

Nelson Department of Social Services **815**

New Beginnings Family and Children's Services, Inc. **534**

New Brunswick Department of Health and Community Service **1182**

New England Home for Little Wanderers **326**

New Hampshire Catholic Charities, Inc. **458**

New Hampshire Division for Children, Youth, and Families **1067**

New Hanover County Department of Social Services **553**

New Haven Family Alliance **111**

New Hope Child and Family Agency **854**

New Hope Family Services, Inc. **535**

New Horizons Adoption Agency, Inc. **412**

New Horizons Adoptions **573**

New Jersey Division of Youth and Family Services **1068**

New Jersey Division of Youth and Family Services; Adoption Unit **460**

New Jersey Division of Youth and Family Services; Adoption Unit (for mid-Jersey) **461**

New Life Adoption Agency, Inc. **536**

New Life Adoption Services **194**

New Life Christian Services **783**

New Life Family Services **413**

New Roots - Adoptive Family Support Group **1490**

New York City Department of Social Services; Division of Adoption/Foster Care Services/Home Assessment Services/Centralized Services **503**

New York Council on Adoptable Children **1475**

New York Singles Adopting Children; NYSAC **1476**

New York State Citizens' Coalition for Children, Inc. **1477**

Newfoundland Department of Social Services **1183**

Newport News Department of Social Services **816**

Newsom; Vika **1277**

Niagara County Department of Social Services **504**

Noble County Department of Human Services **602**

North American Council on Adoptable Children (NACAC) **1435**

North American Family Institute **1145**

North Bay Adoptions **76**

North Carolina Adoption Connections **1482**

North Central Washington Adoption Support Network **1543**

North Dakota Department of Human Services; Division of Children and Family Services **569**

North East Adoption Resources **1569**

Northeast Foster Care, Inc. **1135**

Northeast Ohio Adoption Services **635**

Northern Oklahoma Youth Service Center and Shelter, Inc. **1117**

Northern Tier Youth Services **1171**

Northern Valley Catholic Social Service **932**

Northern Virginia Family Service **1163**

Northern Wyoming Adoptive Parents, Inc. **1562**

Northwest Adoption Exchange **1609**

Northwest Adoptive Families Association, Inc. **1500**

Northwest Passage **1174**

Nottoway Department of Social Services **817**

NSO-Project Adopt; Project Adopt Neighborhood Services Organization, Inc. **651**

# O

Oakland County Department of Social Services **344**

Oakland Family Services **393**

Oasis, Inc. **1355**

Office of Community Service (of Alexandria, LA) **262**

Office of Community Services **264**

Office of Community Services; Lake Charles Region **263**

Ogemon County Department of Social Services **1035**

Ogles Law Firm, P.A. **1196**

Ohel Children's Home and Family Services **1082**

Ohio Adoption Photo Listing; OAPL **1610**

Oklahoma Council on Adoptable Children **1498**

Oklahoma Department of Human Services **638**

Onondaga County Department of Social Services **505**

Ontario Ministry of Community and Social Services; Adoption Unit **1188**

Open Adoption and Family Services, Inc. **661**

Open Adoption & Family Services, Inc. **662**

Open Arms Christian Home **993**

The Open Door Adoption Agency, Inc. **155**

Open Door Society of Los Angeles **1338**

Open Door Society of Massachusetts, Inc. **1421**

Open Door Society of New Hampshire, Inc. **1447**

Open Hearts Adoption Support Group **1445**

Options for Youth, Inc. **1104**

Orange County Adoptive Parents Association (OCAPA) **1339**

Orange County Department of Social Services **506, 554**

Orange Social Service Agency; Adoptions Program; County of **35**

Orchards Children's Services **394**

Oregon Adoptive Rights Association; OARA **1501**

Oregon Childrens Services Division **655**
Organized Adoption Search Information
    Services **1356**
Orphan Voyage **1343**
Otsego County Department of Social Services
    **507, 1036**
Ottawa County Department of Human
    Services **603**
Our Lady of Victory Infant Home **537**
OURS of Middle Tennessee **1515**
OURS of Northern Illinois **1390**
Ours Through Adoption of Southeastern
    Wisconsin **1553**
Ours thru Adoption, Inc. **1391**
Ozone House **1037**

## P

Pamela A. Gordon; Attorney at Law **1224**
Paquette, Lalande and Keast, Barristers and
    Solicitors **1318**
Paraclete Social Outreach, Inc. **1105**
Parent And Child Development Services **156**
Parent Center **1330**
Parent Finders - Nova Scotia **1582**
Parent Finders of Canada **1577**
Parent Support Group of Adoption Services,
    Inc. **1368**
Parenthesis Family Advocates **1106**
Parents Aiding and Lending Support (PALS)
    **1519**
Parents And Adopted Children of Kentucky
    **1407**
Parents And Adoptees In Search **1531**
Parents of Adopted African American Children
    (PAAAC) **1507**
Parents of Inter-Cultural Adoption, Inc. **1453**
Partners for Adoption **77**
Pauquette Children's Services **870**
Payne County Youth Services **1118**
People Places, Inc. **1164**
Perlmutter; Attorney at Law; Carol S. **1255**
Perry County Children's Services **604**
Peruvian Adoptive Families **1578**
Peter J. Feeney; Attorney at Law **1304**
Philadelphia County Children and Youth
    Agency **673**
Philip F. Woodward **1240**
The Phoenix Institute for Adolescents, Inc.
    **959**
Phylliss Eberhardy, MS, CCDCI **1289**
Pinebrook Services for Children and Youth
    **1136**
Pitt County Department of Social Services **555**
Pittsburgh Adoption Lifeline **1508**
Pius XII Youth and Family Services **1083**
Placement Services Agency **784**
Plagemann; Edward J. **1303**
PLAN International Adoption Service **663**
Porter-Leath Children's Center **730**
Portsmouth Department of Social Services
    **818**
The Post Adoption Center of the Southwest
    **1520**
Post-Search and Reunion Support Group;
    Children's Home Society of Washington
    **1544**
Potomac Center **1172**
Precious Connections, Inc. **1293**
Preininger; David R. **1258**
Prince George's County Department of Social
    Services **295**
Private Adoption Society of Alberta **1570**
Private Adoptions Society of Alberta **1307**
Professional Counseling Center **1226**
Professional Parenting/Adoption Plus **1091**

Project Impact **327**
Project STAR **700**
Protestant Social Service Bureau **328**
Provincial Health and Community Services
    Agency **909**
Pulaski Department of Social Services **819**
Putnam County Department of Human
    Services **605**
Putnam County Department of Social Services
    **508**
Putter, M.S.; Eileen S. **1294**

## Q

Quakerdale Home **1002**
Quincy Adoption Support Group **1392**

## R

Radford Department of Welfare and Social
    Services **820**
Rainbow Families **1451**
Rainbow House International **490**
Rainbow Services for Youth and Families
    **1038**
Rainbow Youth and Family Services **1167**
Ralph Levy III; Attorney at Law **1253**
Randolph County Department of Social
    Services **556**
Ray Graham Association for People with
    Disabilities **972**
Raymond J. Dague **1261**
Regional Family Counseling, Inc. **1268**
Rensselaer County Department of Social
    Services **509**
RESOLVE Adoptive Parent Support Group
    **1408**
RESOLVE of Colorado **1344**
RESOLVE of Georgia **1369**
RESOLVE of Hawaii **1373**
RESOLVE of Ohio, Inc. (Cleveland) **1491**
RESOLVE of Ohio, Inc. (Dayton) **1492**
RESOLVE of Southern Wisconsin, Inc. **1554**
RESOLVE of the Twin Cities **1436**
RESOLVE of Washington State **1545**
Resources for Adoptive Parents (RAP) **1437**
Reunite, Inc. **1493**
Reverend Henry Rucker Memorial Services
    **983**
Rhode Island Department for Children, Youth
    & Families **704**
Rhonda L. Fishbein, Esq. **1238**
Richard A. Macias; Attorney at Law **1246**
Richard Allen Center on Life **1084**
Richmond Adoptive Parents Group **1478**
Richmond Department of Social Services; City
    of **821**
Right To Know **1521**
Riverside County Department of Social
    Services **36**
Robert A. Cox; The Cox Law Firm, P.C. **1252**
Roberts Agency; The James A. **248**
Rochester Area Adoptive Families Together
    **1438**
Rocky Mountain Adoption Exchange **1611**
Roots & Wings Adoption Magazine **1452**
ROOTS, Planting Seeds to Secure Our Future,
    Inc. **157**
Roscommon County Department of Social
    Services **1039**
Rosemont Center **1107**
Rowan County Department of Social Services
    **557**
Russell County Department of Social Services
    **822**

Russell; Helen D. **1269**
Ruth F. Clairborne, P.C. **1235**

## S

S.E.A.R.C.H. **1555**
Sacramento County Department of Health and
    Human Services **37**
St. Andre Home, Inc. **283**
St. Anthony Villa **1108**
St. Augustine's Center; Child Welfare Services
    Department **1085**
St. Croix Valley Korean American Cultural
    Society, Inc. **1556**
St. Dominic's Family Service Center **1086**
St. Elizabeth Foundation **274**
St. Elizabeth's Home **219**
St. Gerard's Adoption Network, Inc. **275**
St. Joseph Children's Treatment Center **1109**
St. Joseph County Office of Family and Social
    Service Administration; Division of
    Family and Children **994**
St. Joseph's Services for Children and
    Families **538**
St. Lawrence County Department of Social
    Services **510**
St. Louis County Social Services; Adoption
    Unit-5th Floor **401**
St. Mary's Children & Family Services **1087**
St. Mary's Services **195**
St. Peters Home for Children; Maternity and
    Adoptive Services **731**
St. Vincent Adoption Services **144**
St. Vincent and Sarah Fisher Center **395**
St. Vincent's Infant and Maternity Program;
    Associated Catholic Charities **276**
The Salvation Army; Children's Services **1137**
San Bernardino Adoption Service **38**
San Diego County Adoption **39**
San Francisco Department of Social Services;
    Adoption Services **40**
San Luis Obispo County Department of Social
    Services **41**
Sanford & Harmssen **1218**
Sanilac County Department of Social Services
    **1040**
Santa Barbara County Department of Social
    Services **42**
Santa Clara County Social Services Agency -
    Adoptions **43**
Santa Cruz County Department of Human
    Resources; Adoptions **44**
Saskatchewan Adoptive Parents Association
    **1592**
Saskatchewan Social Services **918, 1191**
Sault Tribe Binogii Placement Agency **396**
Schenectady County Department of Social
    Services **511**
Schoharie County Department of Social
    Services **512**
Schuylkill County Children and Youth Agency
    **674**
Scioto County Children Services **606**
Search Triad, Inc. **1326**
Searchline of Texas, Inc. **1522**
Seegers Lutheran Center; Lutheran Child and
    Family Services **196**
Seguin Services Inc. **984**
Seneca County Department of Human
    Services **607**
Serelson; Attorney at Law; Carol A. **1306**
Sertoma Foster Care **985**
Seven Counties Services, Inc.; Daybreak
    Family Treatment Homes **1010**
Shades **1409**
Share Homes Foster Family Agency **933**

Alphabetical Index